D1199025

Images of MAN

ROBERT W. BOYNTON

Principal, Senior High School
Germantown Friends School

MAYNARD MACK

Professor of English
Fellow of Davenport College
Yale University

READINGS

of *MAN*

IN ENGLISH LITERATURE

PRENTICE-HALL, INC.

Englewood Cliffs, N. J.

IMAGES OF MAN

READINGS IN ENGLISH LITERATURE

by Robert W. Boynton and Maynard Mack

Library of Congress Catalog Card No. 64-10256

Printed in the United States of America
45115-E

PREFACE

We have prepared this book of readings in English literature for teachers who believe in their subject matter, in their students, and in themselves; and for students who want the best their literary heritage can bring them as insight into what it means to be a responsible human being. Though in making our selections we have not sought difficulty for its own sake, we have not been afraid of it when it appeared inseparable from excellence; and consequently we have produced a volume that few will call easy. We offer no apology for this. What we have sought to achieve in our selections, our commentaries, our questions, our writing topics, and all aspects of our work, is a level of difficulty and maturity more suitable than that of existing texts for students in their final year of secondary education, who are either going on to college-level courses, or to the even more perplexing responsibilities, civic and personal, of being young adults in a challenging and anxious world.

We have included most of the best-known and most highly respected selections in English literature, those which have formed the backbone of courses at the upper high school level for many years. In arranging English literature for teaching at the upper high school level, we believe we have made a significant improvement by setting aside organization according to chronology in favor of organization by topics, or themes. The advantages of doing this are great. In the first place, arrangement by topics provides an intelligible and exciting way, as arrangement by chronology does not, of approaching the vicarious experiences and the intellectual and moral issues which literature brings before us. When, for example, we consider Shakespeare's *Hamlet,* Swift's *A Modest Proposal,* Blake's *London,* and D. H. Lawrence's *The Rocking-Horse Winner* as explorations of a common theme, we are led naturally and easily to insights and discussions which are forced, if not impossible, as long as works are treated as separate beads on the string of time. When literature is taught chronologically, the relationship which inevitably occupies the center of the stage is that of a work to its period; and this is not the relationship which matters most, or ought to matter most, to any reader prior to his attendance at graduate school. The relationship that *does* matter becomes central when literature is taught by topics. With this method the masterpieces of the past no longer seem immovably rooted to their time and place by chronological insistence, but rather live in the present as the student comes to realize that all literature is a continuing conversation about topics of eternal human concern in which he has a vested and consuming interest.

A second advantage of arrangement by topics is that it frees the teacher of the burden of presenting the large quantities of historical information which are required as each new author or period is reached in a chronologically oriented course. Such presentations usually fail, it seems to us. First, because there is insufficient time for them. Second, because years of specialization are needed to do justice to a single period, or a single major author. And third, because a pennyworth of chronology at this grade level is likely to be bought at an exorbitant price—the price of continuing to graduate young men and women from our secondary schools whom we have convinced that "literature" is chiefly a matter of "information" unrelated to experience, and who are therefore determined to have little further to do with it.

In our plan of arrangement for the selections in this volume we have chosen six topics, obvious landmarks of every human life, representing not only different areas of experience but different avenues of discovery and realization: the discovery and realization of *others, ourselves, love, evil, success,* and *faith.* Under these rubrics we have gathered what we believe is an exceptionally readable and diversified collection of stories, poems, plays, essays and other prose, which is predominantly from English literature, but which embraces some foundation stones of the Western world's moral and literary imagination, including Sophocles's *King Oedipus* and *Antigone* and Plato's account of the trial and death of Socrates from *The Apology* and *The Phaedo.* From English literature proper seventy authors are represented, ranging in time from Chaucer and the author of *Sir Gawain and the Green Knight* to William Butler Yeats, and in magnitude from Shakespeare and Milton to Sir John Suckling and Frank Swinnerton.

We believe that we have provided in this book a study apparatus of exceptional utility and scope. Each selection (or, occasionally, a group of selections) is prefaced with a headnote supplying historical and biographical information where this is indispensable for understanding, and also relating the selection to the topic of the unit in which it falls and to selections already studied. Each selection is fully annotated: its allusions are explained and its difficult words glossed. Each selection is followed by questions which, far from being merely perfunctory and informational, are keyed to stimulate class discussion and lead to further understanding of the work. The questions begin with references to syntax, allusions, images, and other such particulars involved in close reading, and proceed to relate to larger meanings and implications. A culmination point is reached in the topics for written work, which call on the student to take a considered view of the work in its entirety. Thus each set of questions will be found to function collectively as a step-by-step reader's guide, and where several questions are collected under a single numeral it may be assumed that the group as a whole frames a matter of some substance suited to fuller consideration in the classroom. For reasons of convenience, each set of questions is divided into two parts: those listed under Roman numeral II should be answered in essay form; those listed under Roman numeral I may be answered in essay form if the teacher or student chooses.

For further flexibility and ready reference, we have provided, in addition to a standard table of contents, a listing of the selections by literary types and also by chronology. Quite arbitrarily, we have arranged Unit I, which focuses on the variety of personalities with which the world abounds, in reverse chronological order (except for the final selection, a full-length play). Again, quite arbitrarily, we have arranged Unit II, which focuses on the theme of self-discovery, according to literary types. Our purpose has been to present the materials of each unit in the order best suited to arouse student interest, but we hope it makes clear also that an approach to literature by themes need not wholly exclude chronology and type. In the four units which follow the first two, the arrangement disregards chronology and type, however, in favor of relevance to common human concerns. At this level, for reasons already stated, considerations of specific historical period or treatment within a given genre are not of first importance.

Our book provides a glossary of critical terms; a biographical appendix which briefly summarizes the career of each author represented; suggestions for broad writing topics which reach beyond the contents of the book to the world in which we live; and an extensive bibliography of the long-playing recordings which are available for many of the selections.

For the most part, whole works are presented here, including the complete texts of five full-length plays. Sometimes, in the case of very long works, we have had to be satisfied with selecting excerpts. We have never used snippets, which serve only to fatten tables of contents, but have always included enough of a work to do justice to it as a whole. Our hope is that teachers and students will want to go to such selections as *The Canterbury Tales, Paradise Lost,* and *Don Juan* for more than we could include.

Finally, we repeat our initial statement. This is a book for those whose concern is primarily with direct and searching experience of good literature. It is a book for those who prefer or need to use anthologies and who yet are not satisfied with anthologies in which the main emphasis is on peripheral matters that overshadow and often negate the literary experience for both student and teacher. It is, quite simply, a book for those who know that the kind of teaching and learning we respect and come to love is the kind that makes us reach.

R. W. B.
M. M.

CONTENTS BY UNITS

UNIT TWO

OURSELVES   128–237

UNIT THREE

LOVE 238–363

UNIT FOUR

EVIL 364–547

UNIT FIVE

SUCCESS   548–723

UNIT SIX

FAITH 724–807

CONTENTS BY LITERARY FORMS

NON-FICTIONAL PROSE

ESSAYS

POETRY

CONTENTS BY CHRONOLOGICAL LISTING OF AUTHORS

"*O brave new world*

That has such people in it."

William Shakespeare, *The Tempest*

Unit One

OTHERS

Have you ever thought that you know—really know—very few people? Perhaps you know a few hundred, but think what a small percentage that is of the millions of fascinating individuals in existence. Although you may rub shoulders with a variety of persons, you cannot be truly understanding of any but those who share your daily concerns intimately.

When we are children most of us feel at ease only with our own kind. We may have been taught to be friendly and have good manners, but inside we are likely to think "what a relief" when strangers have gone. As long as we remain children, we seldom venture beyond our own small plot of ground: we are uncertain of our reception if we step outside it, and we don't like feeling ill at ease.

One of the rewards of growing up, therefore—one of the compensations for losing that delighted self-centeredness which marks childhood—is that in the process we are able to widen our humanity by stretching it to take into account the personalities of others. We become more aware of what a man is, and can be, as we puzzle over the paradox that human beings are at once so different, and yet so alike. We awaken to the joys, tensions, surprises, disappointments, and adjustments that living with others imposes on us. We realize that the world does not center in us, but that, in a sense, we are centered in a common humanity. We discover that while we may move with ease only in the circle of our daily life, we can gradually increase the circumference of that circle. To the extent that we resist the widening, we remain captive in the narrowness of childhood.

We can help the widening by turning our senses more fully on the people around us: by trying to see the world through our brother's eyes; by giving ear to the sound of our friend's breathing. We can also help that widening by placing ourselves at the very center of all the fears and failures, hopes and victories that men have known—through literature. By means of literature we can move beyond the restrictions of our particular time and place without carfare, without passport, without magic. We can travel through the courtesy of the novelist, poet, dramatist, essayist, and at his expense. All it takes is a tuning in of our own powers of perception. What the artist creates, the reader can re-create if he takes the time and trouble. And the re-creation brings with it a new attitude toward "strangers." We find that they are not so different from us after all; that they are refreshingly frank, especially about the kind of personal feelings we seldom admit to ourselves and never to our family or friends; that they make good company, perfectly willing to move in and out of our lives at our pleasure. Most of all, we find we owe them a lasting debt, for they give us a close look at ourselves when we take a close look at them.

You will find a fascinating assortment of human beings in the selections that follow. There are individuals here who stand out clear and alive, as real as the long-time friend next door: James Boswell on the high road to London; Chaucer's Pardoner or Prioress traveling to Canterbury; Samuel Johnson writing to Lord Chesterfield a masterful defense of his independence of mind. There are also character types, not altogether flesh and blood, but all too recognizable as vivid reminders of the human condition: the "busybody"; the University snob; Will Wimble, very busy doing nothing; Clarinda and her empty diary. Some of these people, like Henry Hastings, Chaucer's Knight, and the Duke of Ferrara, have passed with the society that fostered them; some, like Samuel Pickwick and Sir Roger de Coverley, have an element of caricature and loom larger than life; but all give evidence of the richness that lies in human personality.

The emphasis here is on individuals— real and fictional—reacting in a variety of ways to common human problems. Some of the individuals are products of our own century; most of them belong to the more distant past. You should look for differences, and delight in the freshness that comes through experiencing ways of behavior different from your own. But more important, you should look for the consistencies in human nature, for the feelings and reactions that tell us, for instance, that the people Chaucer met on the road to Canterbury in the 14th century would find, if they were to reappear in today's society, that personal needs, wants, and hopes have changed little in six hundred years.

QUALITY   *[1912]*

John Galsworthy

This short story lets us see what "quality" can mean to a man who has spent a lifetime devoted to the demands of craftsmanship. The theme concerns what happens when mass production methods and advertising put the individual artisan at a competitive disadvantage. The author lets us watch Gessler, the bootmaker, live his answer to what "quality" is. In doing so he asks the reader to test his own commitment to "quality," no matter what the consequences.

I knew him from the days of my extreme youth, because he made my father's boots;[1] inhabiting with his elder brother two little shops let into one, in a small by-street—now no more, but then most fashionably placed in the West End.[2]

That tenement had a certain quiet distinction; there was no sign upon its face that he made for any of the Royal Family[3]— merely his own German name of Gessler Brothers; and in the window a few pairs of boots. I remember that it always troubled me to account for those unvarying boots in the window, for he made only what was ordered, reaching nothing down, and it seemed so inconceivable that what he made could ever have failed to fit. Had he bought them to put there? That, too, seemed inconceivable. He would never have tolerated in his house leather on which he had not worked himself. Besides, they were too beautiful—the pair of pumps, so inexpressibly slim, the patent leathers with cloth tops,

making water come into one's mouth, the tall brown riding boots with marvelous sooty glow, as if, though new, they had been worn a hundred years. Those pairs could only have been made by one who saw before him the Soul of Boot—so truly were they prototypes incarnating the very spirit of all foot-gear. These thoughts, of course, came to me later, though even when I was promoted to him,[4] at the age of perhaps fourteen, some inkling haunted me of the dignity of himself and brother. For to make boots— such boots as he made—seemed to me then, and still seems to me, mysterious and wonderful.

I remember well my shy remark, one day, while stretching out to him my youthful foot:

"Isn't it awfully hard to do, Mr. Gessler?"

And his answer, given with a sudden smile from out of the sardonic redness of his beard: "Id is an Ardt!"

Himself, he was a little as if made from leather, with his yellow crinkly face, and crinkly reddish hair and beard, and neat folds slanting down his cheeks to the corners of his mouth, and his guttural and one-toned voice; for leather is a sardonic substance, and stiff and slow of purpose. And that was the character of his face, save that his eyes, which were gray-blue, had in them the

1. BOOTS: British for shoes.
2. WEST END: fashionable section of London, where the story takes place.
3. MADE . . . ROYAL FAMILY: Most British concerns, if patronized by members of the Royal Family, carry a boast of this in their windows. Gessler is too modest to boast.

4. PROMOTED TO HIM: i.e., from a child's shoemaker.

simple gravity of one secretly possessed by the Ideal. His elder brother was so very like him—though watery, paler in every way, with a great industry—that sometimes in early days I was not quite sure of him until the interview was over. Then I knew that it was he, if the words, "I will ask my brudder," had not been spoken; and that, if they had, it was his elder brother.

When one grew old and wild and ran up bills, one somehow never ran them up with Gessler Brothers. It would not have seemed becoming to go in there and stretch out one's foot to that blue iron-spectacled glance, owing him for more than—say—two pairs, just the comfortable reassurance that one was still his client.

For it was not possible to go to him very often—his boots lasted terribly, having something beyond the temporary—some, as it were, essence of boot stitched into them.

One went in, not as into most shops, in the mood of: "Please serve me, and let me go!" but restfully, as one enters a church; and, sitting on the single wooden chair, waited—for there was never anybody there. Soon, over the top edge of that sort of well—rather dark, and smelling soothingly of leather—which formed the shop, there would be seen his face, or that of his elder brother, peering down. A guttural sound, and the tip-tap of bast slippers beating the narrow wooden stairs, and he would stand before one without coat, a little bent, in leather apron, with sleeves turned back, blinking— as if awakened from some dream of boots, or like an owl surprised in daylight and annoyed at this interruption.

And I would say: "How do you do, Mr. Gessler? Could you make me a pair of Russia leather boots?"

Without a word he would leave me, re- tiring whence he came, or into the other portion of the shop, and I would continue to rest in the wooden chair, inhaling the incense of his trade. Soon he would come back, holding in his thin, veined hand a piece of gold-brown leather. With eyes

fixed on it, he would remark: "What a beau- tiful biece!" When I, too, had admired it, he would speak again. "When do you wand dem?" And I would answer: "Oh! As soon as you conveniently can." And he would say: "Tomorrow fordnighd?" Or if he were his elder brother: "I will ask my brudder!"

Then I would murmur: "Thank you! Good morning, Mr. Gessler." "Goot-morn- ing!" he would reply, still looking at the leather in his hand. And as I moved to the door, I would hear the tip-tap of his bast slippers restoring him, up the stairs, to his dream of boots. But if it were some new kind of foot-gear that he had not yet made me, then indeed he would observe ceremony —divesting me of my boot and holding it long in his hand, looking at it with eyes at once critical and loving, as if recalling the glow with which he had created it, and re- buking the way in which one had disorgan- ized this masterpiece. Then, placing my foot on a piece of paper, he would two or three times tickle the outer edges with a pencil and pass his nervous fingers over my toes, feeling himself into the heart of my require- ments.

I cannot forget that day when I had oc- casion to say to him: "Mr. Gessler, that last pair of town walking-boots creaked, you know."

He looked at me for a time without reply- ing, as if expecting me to withdraw or qualify the statement, then said:

"Id shouldn'd'ave greaked."

"It did, I'm afraid."

"You goddem wed before dey found demselves?"

"I don't think so."

At that he lowered his eyes, as if hunting for memory of those boots, and I felt sorry I had mentioned this grave thing.

"Zend dem back!" he said; "I will look at dem."

A feeling of compassion for my creaking boots surged up in me, so well could I imagine the sorrowful long curiosity of re- gard which he would bend on them.

"Zome boods," he said slowly, "are bad from birdt. If I can do noding wid dem, I dake dem off your bill."

Once (once only) I went absent-mindedly into his shop in a pair of boots bought in an emergency at some large firm's. He took my order without showing me any leather, and I could feel his eyes penetrating the inferior integument of my foot. At last he said:

"Dose are nod my boods."

The tone was not one of anger, nor of sorrow, not even of contempt, but there was in it something quiet that froze my blood. He put his hand down and pressed a finger on the place where the left boot, endeavoring to be fashionable, was not quite comfortable.

"Id 'urds you dere," he said. "Dose big virms 'ave no self-respect. Drash!" And then, as something had given way within him, he spoke long and bitterly. It was the only time I ever heard him discuss the conditions and hardships of his trade.

"Dey get id all," he said, "dey get id by advertisement, nod by work. Dey dake it away from us, who lofe our boods. Id gomes to this—bresently I haf no work. Every year id gets less—you will see." And looking at his lined face I saw things I had never noticed before, bitter things and bitter struggle—and what a lot of gray hairs there seemed suddenly in his red beard!

As best I could, I explained the circumstances of the purchase of those ill-omened boots. But his face and voice made a so deep impression that during the next few minutes I ordered many pairs. Nemesis fell! They lasted more terribly than ever. And I was not able conscientiously to go to him for nearly two years.

When at last I went I was surprised to find that outside one of the two little windows of his shop another name was painted, also that of a bootmaker—making, of course, for the Royal Family. The old familiar boots, no longer in dignified isolation, were huddled in the single window. Inside, the now contracted well of the one little shop was more scented and darker than ever. And it was longer than usual, too, before a face peered down, and the tip-tap of the bast slippers began. At last he stood before me, and, gazing through those rusty iron spectacles, said:

"Mr. —, isn'd it?"

"Ah, Mr. Gessler," I stammered, "but your boots are really too good, you know! See, these are quite decent still!" And I stretched out to him my foot. He looked at it.

"Yes," he said, "beople do nod wand good boods, id seems."

To get away from his reproachful eyes and voice, I hastily remarked: "What have you done to your shop?"

He answered quietly: "Id was too exbensif. Do you wand some boods?"

I ordered three pairs, though I had only wanted two, and quickly left. I had, I do not know quite what feeling of being part, in his mind, of a conspiracy against him; or not perhaps so much against him as against his idea of boot. One does not, I suppose, care to feel like that; for it was again many months before my next visit to his shop, paid, I remember, with the feeling: "Oh! well, I can't leave the old boy—so here goes! Perhaps it'll be his elder brother!"

For his elder brother, I knew, had not character enough to reproach me, even dumbly.

And, to my relief, in the shop there did appear to be his elder brother, handling a piece of leather.

"Well, Mr. Gessler," I said, "how are you?"

He came close, and peered at me.

"I am breddy well," he said slowly; "but my elder brudder is dead."

And I saw that it was indeed himself—but how aged and wan! And never before had I heard him mention his brother. Much shocked, I murmured: "Oh! I am sorry!"

"Yes," he answered, "he was a good man, he made a good bood; but he is dead." And he touched the top of his head, where the hair had suddenly gone as thin as it had been on that of his poor brother, to indicate, I suppose, the cause of death. "He could nod ged over losing de oder shop. Do you wand any boods?" And he held up the leather in his hand: "Id's a beaudiful biece."

I ordered several pairs. It was very long before they came—but they were better than ever. One simply could not wear them out. And soon after that I went abroad.

It was over a year before I was again in London. And the first shop I went to was my old friend's. I had left a man of sixty, I came back to one of seventy-five, pinched and worn and tremulous, who genuinely, this time, did not at first know me.

"Oh! Mr. Gessler," I said, sick at heart; "how splendid your boots are! See, I've been wearing this pair nearly all the time I've been abroad; and they're not half worn out, are they?"

He looked long at my boots—a pair of Russia leather, and his face seemed to regain steadiness. Putting his hand on my instep, he said:

"Do dey vid you here? I 'ad drouble wid dat bair, I remember."

I assured him that they had fitted beautifully.

"Do you wand any boods?" he said. "I can make dem quickly; id is a slack dime."

I answered: "Please, please! I want boots all round—every kind!"

"I will make a fresh model. Your food must be bigger." And with utter slowness, he traced round my foot, and felt my toes, only once looking up to say:

"Did I dell you my brudder was dead?"

To watch him was painful, so feeble had he grown; I was glad to get away. I had given those boots up, when one evening they came. Opening up the parcel, I set the four pairs out in a row. Then one by one I tried them on. There was no doubt about it. In shape and fit, in finish and quality of leather, they were the best he had ever made me. And in the mouth of one of the town walking-boots I found his bill. The amount was the same as usual, but it gave me quite a shock. He

had never before sent it in till quarter day.[5] I flew downstairs and wrote a check, and posted it at once with my own hand.

A week later, passing the little street, I thought I would go in and tell him how splendidly the new boots fitted. But when I came to where his shop had been, his name was gone. Still there, in the window, were the slim pumps, the patent leathers with cloth tops, the sooty riding boots.

I went in, very much disturbed. In the two little shops—again made into one—was a young man with an English face.

"Mr. Gessler in?" I said.

He gave me a strange, ingratiating look.

"No, sir," he said, "no. But we can attend to anything with pleasure. We've taken the shop over. You've seen our name, no doubt, next door. We make for some very good people."

"Yes, yes," I said; "but Mr. Gessler?"

"Oh!" he answered; "dead."

"Dead! But I only received these boots from him last Wednesday week."

"Ah!" he said; "a shockin' go. Poor old man starved 'imself."

"Good God!"

"Slow starvation, the doctor called it! You see he went to work in such a way! Would keep the shop on; wouldn't have a soul touch his boots except himself. When he got an order, it took him such a time. People won't wait. He lost everybody. And there he'd sit, goin' on and on—I will say that for him—not a man in London made a better boot! But look at the competition! He never advertised! Would 'ave the best leather, too, and do it all 'imself. Well, there it is. What could you expect with his ideas?"

"But starvation—!"

"That may be a bit flowery, as the sayin' is—but I know myself he was sittin' over his boots day and night, to the very last. You see I used to watch him. Never gave 'imself time to eat; never had a penny in the house. All went in rent and leather. How he lived

---

5. QUARTER DAY: i.e., the day that begins a new quarter of the year, as April 1st, July 1st, etc.

so long I don't know. He regular let his fire go out. He was a character. But he made good boots."

"Yes," I said, "he made good boots."

And I turned and went out quickly, for I did not want that youth to know that I could hardly see.

I

1. What details does Galsworthy bring out to convince you that the Gessler brothers are good bootmakers who take pride in their work? Don't be satisfied with pointing out only the most obvious ones. Try to see how a good writer constantly tries to involve the reader in making judgments from evidence given.

2. How do Galsworthy's descriptions of the physical appearance of Gessler help reveal his character?

3. At one point the narrator says that one went into Gessler's shop as *one enters a church.* Find other expressions that support this giving to the Gesslers' craftsmanship a partly religious meaning. Is Galsworthy justified in using such a connection? Why or why not?

4. Point out some of the obvious contrasts between the younger Gessler and the new proprietor; between the narrator and the new proprietor. What does the phrase *good boots* mean to each of the three?

5. What do the *boots in the window* stand for? Why does the narrator say they are "too beautiful"? What is significant about the fact that the new proprietor keeps them in the window?

II

1. Discuss the following questions in a short essay: If Galsworthy is saying that there is no place for the artisan in a society dominated by mass production, is he right? Is craftsmanship a matter of manual skill or of an attitude towards one's work? Is Gessler foolish to stick to old ways in a new situation?

FIRST CONFESSION [1]   [*1952*]

Frank O'Connor

Much as we have to respect, perhaps even admire, Gessler's single-minded devotion to high standards, there is not much about the man that would make anyone *like* him. Galsworthy is so obviously incensed about the triumph of salesmanship over craftsmanship that he robs his hero of any warmth, and our sympathy is for the man's attitude, not for the man.

In the following story it is also obvious that the author is annoyed by false standards, this time parading in the guise of self-satisfied piety. But his humorous treatment of the theme is far different from Galsworthy's sober moralizing. A small boy, victimized by his sister's misguided attitude, is filled with doubts and fears over his "first confession," but his moment of terror becomes a moment of triumph, mainly because a parish priest happens to understand small boys.

The humor in the story comes from O'Connor's enabling us to stand back from the event and watch the boy react to a situation new and terrifying to him but not at all so to us. He takes himself and his plight very seriously. The priest, too, takes the affair seriously, but in a very different sense. In our detachment as readers we see the two attitudes blend delightfully, and we respond with sympathetic amusement to sanctimoniousness squelched.

---

1. FIRST CONFESSION: In the Catholic Church confession is the act of acknowledging one's sins to a priest and asking God's forgiveness.

It was a Saturday afternoon in early spring. A small boy whose face looked as though it had been but newly scrubbed was being led by the hand by his sister through a crowded street. The little boy showed a marked reluctance to proceed; he affected to be very interested in the shop-windows. Equally, his sister seemed to pay no attention to them. She tried to hurry him; he resisted. When she dragged him he began to bawl. The hatred with which she viewed him was almost diabolical, but when she spoke, her words and tone were full of passionate sympathy.

"Ah, sha,[2] God help us!" she intoned into his ear in a whine of commiseration.

"Leave me go!" he said, digging his heels into the pavement. "I don't want to go. I want to go home."

"But, sure, you can't go home, Jackie. You'll have to go. The parish priest will be up to the house with a stick."

"I don't care. I won't go."

"Oh, Sacred Heart,[3] isn't it a terrible pity you weren't a good boy? Oh, Jackie, me heart bleeds for you! I don't know what they'll do to you at all, Jackie, me poor child. And all the trouble you caused your poor old nanny,[4] and the way you wouldn't eat in the same room with her, and the time you kicked her on the shins, and the time you went for me with the bread knife under the table. I don't know will he ever listen to you at all, Jackie. I think meself he might sind you to the bishop. Oh, Jackie, how will you think of all your sins?"

Half stupefied with terror, Jackie allowed himself to be led through the sunny streets to the very gates of the church. It was an old one with two grim iron gates and a long, low, shapeless stone front. At the gates he stuck, but it was already too late. She dragged him behind her across the yard, and the commiserating whine with which she had tried to madden him gave place to a yelp of triumph.

"Now you're caught! Now, you're caught. And I hope he'll give you the pinitintial[5] psalms! That'll cure you, you suppurating little caffler!"[6]

Jackie gave himself up for lost. Within the old church there was no stained glass; it was cold and dark and desolate, and in the silence, the trees in the yard knocked hollowly at the tall windows. He allowed himself to be led through the vaulted silence, the intense and magical silence which seemed to have frozen within the ancient walls, buttressing them and shouldering the high wooden roof. In the street outside, yet seeming a million miles away, a ballad singer was drawling a ballad.

Nora sat in front of him beside the confession box. There were a few old women before her, and later a thin, sad-looking man with long hair came and sat beside Jackie. In the intense silence of the church that seemed to grow deeper from the plaintive moaning of the ballad singer, he could hear the buzz-buzz-buzz of a woman's voice in the box, and then the husky ba-ba-ba of the priest's. Lastly the soft thud of something that signalled the end of the confession, and out came the woman, head lowered, hands joined, looking neither to right nor left, and tip-toed up to the altar to say her penance.

It seemed only a matter of seconds till Nora rose and with a whispered injunction disappeared from his sight. He was all alone. Alone and next to be heard and the fear of damnation in his soul. He looked at the sad-faced man. He was gazing at the roof, his hands joined in prayer. A woman in a

---

2. SHA: pshaw, an exclamation of disgust.
3. SACRED HEART: the heart of Jesus and His love for men; here, a mild oath.
4. NANNY: grandmother.

5. PINITINTIAL: penitential; in the Douay Bible, the English translation used by Roman Catholics, the penitential psalms are 6, 31, 37, 50, 101, 129 and 142. Nora hopes the priest will make Jackie say those psalms as penance.
6. CAFFLER: from "caffle" (cavil), to argue, wrangle.

red blouse and black shawl had taken her place below him. She uncovered her head, fluffed her hair out roughly with her hand, brushed it sharply back, then, bowing, caught it in a knot and pinned it on her neck. Nora emerged. Jackie rose and looked at her with a hatred which was inappropriate to the occasion and the place. Her hands were joined on her stomach, her eyes modestly lowered, and her face had an expression of the most rapt and tender recollection. With death in his heart he crept into the compartment she left open and drew the door shut behind him.

He was in pitch darkness. He could see no priest nor anything else. And anything he had heard of confession got all muddled up in his mind. He knelt to the right-hand wall and said: "Bless me, father, for I have sinned. This is my first confession." Nothing happened. He repeated it louder. Still it gave no answer. He turned to the opposite wall, genuflected first, then again went on his knees and repeated the charm. This time he was certain he would receive a reply, but none came. He repeated the process with the remaining wall without effect. He had the feeling of someone with an unfamiliar machine, of pressing buttons at random. And finally the thought struck him that God knew. God knew about the bad confession he intended to make and had made him deaf and blind so that he could neither hear nor see the priest.

Then as his eyes grew accustomed to the blackness, he perceived something he had not noticed previously: a sort of shelf at about the height of his head. The purpose of this eluded him for a moment. Then he understood. It was for kneeling on.

He had always prided himself upon his powers of climbing, but this took it out of him. There was no foothold. He slipped twice before he succeeded in getting his knee on it, and the strain of drawing the rest of his body up was almost more than he was capable of. However, he did at last get his two knees on it, there was just room for those, but his legs hung down uncomfortably and the edge of the shelf bruised his shins. He joined his hands and pressed the last remaining button. "Bless me, father, for I have sinned. This is my first confession."

At the same moment the slide was pushed back and a dim light streamed into the little box. There was an uncomfortable silence, and then an alarmed voice asked, "Who's there?" Jackie found it almost impossible to speak into the grille which was on a level with his knees, but he got a firm grip of the molding above it, bent his head down and sideways, and as though he were hanging by his feet like a monkey found himself looking almost upside down at the priest. But the priest was looking sideways at him, and Jackie, whose knees were being tortured by this new position, felt it was a queer way to hear confessions.

" 'Tis me, father," he piped, and then, running all his words together in excitement, he rattled off, "Bless me, father, for I have sinned. This is my first confession."

"What?" exclaimed a deep and angry voice, and the somber soutaned figure stood bolt upright, disappearing almost entirely from Jackie's view. "What does this mean? What are you doing there? Who are you?"

And with the shock Jackie felt his hands lose their grip and his legs their balance. He discovered himself tumbling into space, and, falling, he knocked his head against the door, which shot open and permitted him to thump right into the center of the aisle. Straight on this came a small, dark-haired priest with a biretta well forward on his head. At the same time Nora came skeltering madly down the church.

"Lord God!" she cried. "The snivelling little caffler! I knew he'd do it! I knew he'd disgrace me!"

Jackie received a clout over the ear which reminded him that for some strange reason he had not yet begun to cry and that people might possibly think he wasn't hurt at all. Nora slapped him again.

"What's this? What's this?" cried the

priest. "Don't attempt to beat the child, you little vixen!"

"I can't do me pinance with him," cried Nora shrilly, cocking a shocked eye on the priest. "He have me driven mad. Stop your crying, you dirty scut! Stop it now or I'll make you cry at the other side of your ugly puss!"

"Run away out of this, you little jade!" growled the priest. He suddenly began to laugh, took out a pocket handkerchief, and wiped Jackie's nose. "You're not hurt, sure you're not. Show us the ould head. . . . Ah, 'tis nothing. 'Twill be better before you're twice married. . . . So you were coming to confession?"

"I was, father."

"A big fellow like you should have terrible sins. Is it your first?"

"'Tis, father."

"Oh, my, worse and worse! Here, sit down there and wait till I get rid of these ould ones and we'll have a long chat. Never mind that sister of yours."

With a feeling of importance that glowed through his tears Jackie waited. Nora stuck out her tongue at him, but he didn't even bother to reply. A great feeling of relief was welling up in him. The sense of oppression that had been weighing him down for a week, the knowledge that he was about to make a bad confession, disappeared. Bad confession, indeed! He had made friends, made friends with the priest, and the priest expected, even demanded terrible sins. Oh, women! Women! It was all women and girls and their silly talk. They had no real knowledge of the world!

And when the time came for him to make his confession he did not beat about the bush. He may have clenched his hands and lowered his eyes, but wouldn't anyone?

"Father," he said huskily, "I made it up to kill me grandmother."

There was a moment's pause. Jackie did not dare to look up, but he could feel the priest's eyes on him. The priest's voice also seemed a trifle husky.

"Your grandmother?" he asked, but he didn't after all sound very angry.

"Yes, father."

"Does she live with you?"

"She do, father."

"And why did you want to kill her?"

"Oh, God, father, she's a horrible woman!"

"Is she now?"

"She is, father."

"What way is she horrible?"

Jackie paused to think. It was hard to explain.

"She takes snuff, father."

"Oh, my!"

"And she goes round in her bare feet, father."

"Tut-tut-tut!"

"She's a horrible woman, father," said Jackie with sudden earnestness. "She takes porter. And she ates the potatoes off the table with her hands. And me mother do be out working most days, and since that one came 'tis she gives us our dinner and I can't ate the dinner." He found himself sniffling. "And she gives pinnies to Nora and she doesn't give no pinnies to me because she knows I can't stand her. And me father sides with her, father, and he bates me, and me heart is broken and wan night in bed I made it up the way I'd kill her."

Jackie began to sob again, rubbing his nose with his sleeve, as he remembered his wrongs.

"And what way were you going to kill her?" asked the priest smoothly.

"With a hatchet, father."

"When she was in bed?"

"No, father."

"How, so?"

"When she ates the potatoes and drinks the porter she falls asleep, father."

"And you'd hit her then?"

"Yes, father."

"Wouldn't a knife be better?"

"'Twould, father, only I'd be afraid of the blood."

"Oh, of course, I never thought of the blood."

"I'd be afraid of that, father. I was near

hitting Nora with the bread knife one time she came after me under the table, only I was afraid."

"You're a terrible child," said the priest with awe.

"I am, father," said Jackie noncommittally, sniffling back his tears.

"And what would you do with the body?"

"How, father?"

"Wouldn't someone see her and tell?"

"I was going to cut her up with a knife and take away the pieces and bury them. I could get an orange box for threepence and make a cart to take them away."

"My, my," said the priest. "You had it all well planned."

"Ah, I tried that," said Jackie with mounting confidence. "I borrowed a cart and practiced it by myself one night after dark."

"And weren't you afraid?"

"Ah, no," said Jackie half-heartedly. "Only a bit."

"You have terrible courage," said the priest. "There's a lot of people I want to get rid of, but I'm not like you. I'd never have the courage. And hanging is an awful death."

"Is it?" asked Jackie, responding to the brightness of a new theme.

"Oh, an awful blooming death!"

"Did you ever see a fellow hanged?"

"Dozens of them, and they all died roaring."

"Jay!" said Jackie.

"They do be swinging out of them for hours and the poor fellows lepping and roaring, like bells in a belfry, and then they put lime on them to burn them up. Of course, they pretend they're dead but sure, they don't be dead at all."

"Jay!" said Jackie again.

"So if I were you I'd take my time and think about it. In my opinion 'tisn't worth it, not even to get rid of a grandmother. I asked dozens of fellows like you that killed their grandmothers about it, and they all said, no, 'twasn't worth it. . . ."

Nora was waiting in the yard. The sunlight struck down on her across the high wall and its brightness made his eyes dazzle. "Well?" she asked. "What did he give you?"

"Three Hail Marys."[7]

"You mustn't have told him anything."

"I told him everything," said Jackie confidently.

"What did you tell him?"

"Things you don't know."

"Bah! He gave you three Hail Marys because you were a cry baby!"

Jackie didn't mind. He felt the world was very good. He began to whistle as well as the hindrance in his jaw permitted.

"What are you sucking?"

"Bull's eyes."[8]

"Was it he gave them to you?"

"'Twas."

"Almighty God!" said Nora. "Some people have all the luck. I might as well be a sinner like you. There's no use in being good."

---

7. HAIL MARYS: prayers to the Virgin Mary; here, to be said as penance.
8. BULL'S EYES: round hard candies.

I

1. Part of the humor in the story depends upon Jackie's lack of familiarity with the confessional. You can probably imagine what this one looks like even if you have never seen one. In the small, dark compartment anyone making confession kneels in front of a narrow shelf upon which he folds his hands. There is a sliding door behind a grille at shelf level which the priest opens so that he may hear confession. Try to visualize exactly what Jackie does. How do phrases like "pressing buttons at random" and "he had always prided himself on his powers of climbing" add to the humor of his actions?

2. What is Nora's attitude toward confession? Note her *yelp* of triumph as she drags Jackie across the churchyard and the brief description of her leaving the confessional. What other details in the story round out what confession means to her? What does it mean to the *sad-faced man* and the woman in the *red blouse and black shawl*?

3. Notice that the situation is seen through Jackie's eyes. What details show that the church is being seen through the emotions of a small, frightened boy? What details reveal the intense expectation with which he waits for his turn?

4. The priest sizes up the situation almost immediately. What is his attitude toward Nora? How does he quickly win the boy's confidence? Jackie had determined to make a *bad confession*. Why does he become so eager to tell all? How do the priest's responses show that he understands children?

5. Confession is a very serious and fundamental part of Catholicism, yet O'Connor treats lightheartedly a small boy's first confession. Why does his handling of the story convey no disrespect for Catholicism? Through whose understanding of confession is the humor shown?

II

1. We all have our moments of doubt and fear when we are faced with the necessity of doing some important thing for the first time, and we can usually look back on our experience with detachment and find humor in what was, at the time it happened, a serious matter. Recreate one such experience in the same vein of sympathetic amusement that O'Connor has used in "First Confession." The experience might be a tryout of some kind, a first date, an interview for college or a job—there are dozens of possibilities.

HOLIDAY MEMORY   [*1954*]

Dylan Thomas

The focus in the first two selections was on Gessler and Jackie, and both stand out as sharply drawn individuals. In this essay there is no central character, but rather a single consciousness—again that of a small boy—holding in suspension a townful of people rushing through a summer holiday of pleasure as though the next minute would be gone before they got to it.

Writing out of a memory crammed with the sights, sounds, and smells of a glorious Welsh boyhood holiday, Thomas re-creates a world that remained alive to him and comes alive to us.

August Bank Holiday[1]—a tune on an ice-cream cornet. A slap of sea and a tickle of sand. A fanfare of sunshades opening. A wince and whinny of bathers dancing into deceptive water. A tuck of dresses. A rolling of trousers. A compromise of paddlers.[2]

A sunburn of girls and a lark of boys. A silent hullabaloo of balloons.

I remember the sea telling lies in a shell held to my ear for a whole harmonious, hollow minute by a small, wet girl in an enormous bathing suit marked Corporation Property.

I remember sharing the last of my moist buns with a boy and a lion. Tawny and savage, with cruel nails and capacious mouth, the little boy tore and devoured. Wild as seedcake, ferocious as a hearthrug, the depressed and verminous lion nibbled like a mouse at his half a bun and hiccuped in the sad dusk of his cage.

---

1. AUGUST BANK HOLIDAY: What we call "legal holidays" the British call "bank holidays." In England the bank holidays are Good Friday, Easter Monday, Whitmonday, first Monday in August, Christmas Day, and Boxing Day.
2. PADDLERS: waders.

I remember a man like an alderman or a bailiff, bowlered and collarless, with a bag of monkeynuts[3] in his hand, crying "Ride 'em, cowboy!" time and again as he whirled in his chairaplane[4] giddily above the upturned laughing faces of the town girls bold as brass and the boys with padded shoulders and shoes sharp as knives; and the monkeynuts flew through the air like salty hail.

Children all day capered or squealed by the glazed or bashing sea, and the steam-organ wheezed its waltzes in the threadbare playground and the waste lot, where the dodgems[5] dodged, behind the pickle factory.

And mothers loudly warned their proud pink daughters or sons to put that jellyfish down; and fathers spread newspapers over their faces; and sandfleas hopped on the picnic lettuce; and someone had forgotten the salt.

In those always radiant, rainless, lazily rowdy and sky-blue summers departed, I remember August Monday from the rising of the sun over the stained and royal town to the husky hushing of the roundabout[6] music and the dowsing of the naphtha jets[7] in the seaside fair: from bubble-and-squeak[8] to the last of the sandy sandwiches.

There was no need, that holiday morning, for the sluggardly boys to be shouted down to breakfast; out of their jumbled beds they tumbled, and scrambled into their rumpled clothes; quickly at the bathroom basin they catlicked their hands and faces, but never forgot to run the water loud and long as though they washed like colliers; in front of the cracked looking-glass, bordered with

cigarette cards, in their treasure-trove bedrooms, they whisked a gap-tooth comb through their surly hair; and with shining cheeks and noses and tide-marked necks, they took the stairs three at a time.

But for all their scramble and scamper, clamor on the landing, catlick and toothbrush flick, hair-whisk and stair-jump, their sisters were always there before them. Up with the lady lark, they had prinked and frizzed and hot-ironed; and smug in their blossoming dresses, ribboned for the sun, in gymshoes white as the blanco'd[9] snow, neat and silly with doilies and tomatoes they helped in the higgledy[10] kitchen. They were calm; they were virtuous; they had washed their necks; they did not romp, or fidget; and only the smallest sister put out her tongue at the noisy boys.

And the woman who lived next door came into the kitchen and said that her mother, an ancient uncertain body who wore a hat with cherries, was having one of her days and had insisted, that very holiday morning, in carrying, all the way to the tramstop,[11] a photograph album and the cut-glass fruitbowl from the front room.

This was the morning when father, mending one hole in the thermos-flask, made three; when the sun declared war on the butter, and the butter ran; when dogs, with all the sweet-binned[12] backyards to wag and sniff and bicker in, chased their tails in the jostling kitchen, worried sandshoes, snapped at flies, writhed between legs, scratched among towels, sat smiling on hampers.

And if you could have listened at some of the open doors of some of the houses in the street you might have heard:—

"Uncle Owen says he can't find the bottle-opener—"

"Has he looked under the hallstand?"

"Willy's cut his finger—"

"Got your spade?"

---

3. MONKEYNUTS: peanuts.
4. CHAIRAPLANE: a fairground ride in which small chairs spin around above the heads of the crowd.
5. DODGEMS: small mechanical cars in an enclosure that drivers ram into each other with no intent to "dodge."
6. ROUNDABOUT: merry-go-round.
7. NAPHTHA JETS: gas flares that light the fairgrounds.
8. BUBBLE-AND-SQUEAK: cabbage fried with meat, served up for breakfast.

9. BLANCO'D: Blanco is white leather polish.
10. HIGGLEDY: topsy-turvy.
11. TRAMSTOP: streetcar stop.
12. SWEET-BINNED: i.e., with bins full of edibles.

"If somebody doesn't kill that dog—"

"Uncle Owen says why should the bottle-opener be under the hallstand?"

"Never again, never again—"

"I know I put the pepper somewhere—"

"Willy's bleeding—"

"Look, there's a bootlace in my bucket—"

"Oh come *on,* come *on*—"

"Let's have a look at the bootlace in your bucket—"

"If I lay my hands on that dog—"

"Uncle Owen's found the bottle-opener—"

"Willy's bleeding over the cheese—"

And the trams that hissed like ganders took us all to the beautiful beach.

There was cricket on the sand, and sand in the spongecake, sandflies in the watercress, and foolish, mulish, religious donkeys on the unwilling trot. Girls undressed in slipping[13] tents of propriety; under invisible umbrellas, stout ladies dressed for the male and immoral sea. Little naked navvies dug canals; children with spades and no ambition built fleeting castles; wispy young men, outside the bathing-huts, whistled at substantial young women and dogs who desired thrown stones more than the bones of elephants. Recalcitrant uncles huddled, over luke[14] ale, in the tiger-striped marquees. Mothers in black, like wobbling mountains, gasped under the discarded dresses of daughters who shrilly braved the gobbling waves. And fathers, in the once-a-year sun, took fifty winks. Oh, think of all the fifty winks along the paper-bagged sand.

Licorice allsorts,[15] and Welsh hearts,[16] were melting. And the sticks of rock, that we all sucked, were like barbers' poles made of rhubarb.

In the distance, surrounded by disappointed theoreticians and an ironmonger with a drum, a cross man on an orange-box shouted that holidays were wrong. And the waves rolled in, with rubber ducks and clerks upon them.

I remember the patient, laborious, and enamoring hobby, or profession, of burying relatives in sand.

I remember the princely pastime of pouring sand, from cupped hands or bucket, down collars of tops of dresses; the shriek, the shake, the slap.

I can remember the boy by himself, the beach-combing lone-wolf, hungrily waiting at the edge of family cricket; the friendless fielder, the boy uninvited to bat or to tea.

I remember the smell of sea and seaweed, wet flesh, wet hair, wet bathing-dresses, the warm smell as of a rabbity field after rain, the smell of pop and splashed sunshades and toffee, the stable-and-straw smell of hot, tossed, tumbled, dug and trodden sand, the swill-and-gaslamp smell of Saturday night, though the sun shone strong, from the bellying beer-tents, the smell of the vinegar on shelled cockles, winkle-smell, shrimp-smell, the dripping-oily back-street winter-smell of chips[17] in newspapers, the smell of ships from the sundazed docks round the corner of the sandhills, the smell of the known and paddled-in sea moving, full of the drowned and herrings, out and away and beyond and further still towards the antipodes that hung their koala-bears and Maoris, kangaroos and boomerangs, upside down over the backs of the stars.

And the noise of pummeling Punch and Judy falling, and a clock tolling or telling no time in the tenantless town; now and again a bell from a lost tower or a train on the lines behind us clearing its throat, and always the hopeless, ravenous swearing and pleading of the gulls, donkey-bray and hawker-cry, harmonicas and toy trumpets, shouting and laughing and singing, hooting of tugs and tramps, the clip of the chair-attendant's puncher,[18] the motorboat coughing in the

---

13. SLIPPING: i.e., undressing.
14. LUKE: luke-warm.
15. ALLSORTS: mixed candies.
16. WELSH HEARTS: rock candy.

---

17. CHIPS: French fried potatoes.
18. CLIP . . . PUNCHER: as he punches the ticket recording the rental of the chair.

bay, and the same hymn and washing of the sea that was heard in the Bible.

"If it could only just, if it could only just," your lips said again and again as you scooped, in the hob-hot[19] sand, dungeons, garages, torture-chambers, train tunnels, arsenals, hangars for zeppelins, witches' kitchens, vampires' parlors, smugglers' cellars, trolls' grog-shops, sewers, under the ponderous and cracking castle, "If it could only just be like this for ever and ever amen." August Monday all over the earth, from Mumbles[20] where the aunties grew like ladies on a seaside tree to brown, bear-hugging Henty-land and the turtled Ballantyne Islands.[21]

"Could donkeys go on the ice?"

"Only if they got snowshoes."

We snowshoed a meek, complaining donkey and galloped him off in the wake of the ten-foot-tall and Atlas-muscled Mounties,[22] rifled and pemmicanned, who always, in the white Gold Rush wastes, got their black-oathed-and-bearded Man.

"Are there donkeys on desert islands?"

"Only sort-of donkeys."

"What d'you mean, sort-of donkeys?"

"Native donkeys. They hunt things on them!"

"Sort-of walruses and seals and things?"

"Donkeys can't swim!"

"These donkeys can. They swim like whales, they swim like anything, they swim like—"

"Liar."

"Liar yourself."

And two small boys fought fiercely and silently in the sand, rolling together in a ball of legs and bottoms. Then they went and saw the pierrots,[23] or bought vanilla ices.

Lolling or larriking[24] that unsoiled, boiling beauty of a common day, great gods with their braces over their vests sang, spat pips, puffed smoke at wasps, gulped and ogled, forgot the rent, embraced, posed for the dicky-bird,[25] were coarse, had rainbow-colored armpits, winked, belched, blamed the radishes, looked at Ilfracombe,[26] played hymns on paper and comb, peeled bananas, scratched, found seaweed in their panamas, blew up paper-bags and banged them, wished for nothing. But over all the beautiful beach I remember most the children playing, boys and girls tumbling, moving jewels, who might never be happy again. And "happy as a sandboy" is true as the heat of the sun.

Dusk came down; or grew up out of the sands and the sea; or curled around us from the calling docks and the bloodily smoking sun. The day was done, the sands brushed and ruffled suddenly with a sea-broom of cold wind. And we gathered together all the spades and buckets and towels, empty hampers and bottles, umbrellas and fish-frails,[27] bats and balls and knitting, and went—oh, listen, Dad!—to the Fair in the dusk on the bald seaside field.

Fairs were no good in the day; then they were shoddy and tired; the voices of hoopla[28] girls were crimped as elocutionists; no cannonball could shake the roosting coconuts;[29] the gondolas[30] mechanically repeated their sober lurch; the Wall of Death[31] was safe as

19. HOB-HOT: hot as the "hob," or warming-ledge, in a fireplace.
20. MUMBLES: seaside town in Wales.
21. HENTY-LAND . . . BALLANTYNE ISLANDS: G. A. Henty and R. M. Ballantyne were well-known authors of stories for boys, full of adventure in strange lands.
22. MOUNTIES: members of the Northwest Mounted Police (now called the Royal Canadian Mounted Police).
23. PIERROTS: puppets.
24. LARRIKING: larking, having a rowdy time.
25. DICKY-BIRD: i.e., the "birdie" one is usually asked to look at while being photographed.
26. ILFRACOMBE: resort town across Bristol Channel from Wales.
27. FISHFRAILS: fish baskets.
28. HOOPLA: a ring-tossing game.
29. ROOSTING COCONUTS: i.e., waiting to be knocked off their perch by a skillful throw.
30. GONDOLAS: the cars of the roller coaster.
31. WALL OF DEATH: cylindrical enclosure around which motorcyclists ride at high speed.

a governess-cart; the wooden animals[32] were waiting for the night.

But in the night, the hoopla girls, like operatic crows, croaked at the coming moon; whizz, whirl, and ten for a tanner,[33] the coconuts rained from their sawdust like grouse from the Highland sky; tipsy the griffon-prowed gondolas weaved on dizzy rails, and the Wall of Death was a spinning rim of ruin, and the neighing wooden horses took, to a haunting hunting tune, a thousand Beecher's Brooks[34] as easily and breezily as hooved swallows.

Approaching, at dusk, the Fair-field from the beach, we scorched and gritty boys heard above the belaboring or the batherless sea the siren voices of the raucous, horsy barkers.

"Roll up, roll up!"

In her tent and her rolls of flesh the Fattest Woman in the World sat sewing her winter frock, another tent, and fixed her little eyes, blackcurrants in blancmange, on the skeletons who filed and sniggered by.

"Roll up, roll up, roll up to see the Largest Rat on the Earth, the Rover or Bonzo of vermin."

Here scampered the smallest pony, like a Shetland shrew. And here the Most Intelligent Fleas, trained, reined, bridled, and bitted, minutely cavorted in their glass corral.

Round galleries and shies[35] and stalls, pennies were burning holes in a hundred pockets. Pale young men with larded hair and Valentino-black sidewhiskers,[36] fags stuck to their lower lips, squinted along their swivel-sighted rifles and aimed at ping-pong balls dancing on fountains. In knife-creased, silver-grey, skirt-like Oxford bags,[37] and a

sleeveless, scarlet, zip-fastened shirt with yellow horizontal stripes, a collier at the strength-machine spat on his hands, raised the hammer, and brought it Thor-ing[38] down. The bell rang for Blaina.[39]

Outside his booth stood a bitten-eared and barn-door-chested pug with a nose like a twisted swede[40] and hair that startled from his eyebrows and three teeth yellow as a camel's, inviting any sportsman to a sudden and sickening basting in the sandy ring or a quid[41] if he lasted a round; and wiry, cocky, bow-legged, coal-scarred, boozed sportsmen by the dozen strutted in and reeled out; and still those three teeth remained, chipped and camel-yellow in the bored, teak face.

Draggled and stout[42]-wanting mothers, with haphazard hats, hostile hatpins, buns awry, bursting bags, and children at their skirts like pop-filled and jam-smeared limpets, screamed, before distorting mirrors, at their suddenly tapering or tubular bodies and huge ballooning heads, and the children gaily bellowed at their own reflected bogies withering and bulging in the glass.

Old men, smelling of Milford Haven[43] in the rain, shuffled, badgering and cadging, round the edges of the swaggering crowd, their only wares a handful of damp confetti. A daring dash of schoolboys, safely, shoulder to shoulder, with their fathers' trilbies[44] cocked at a desperate angle over one eye, winked at and whistled after the procession past the swings of two girls arm-in-arm: always one pert and pretty, and always one with glasses. Girls in skulled and crossboned tunnels shrieked, and were comforted. Young men, heroic after pints, stood up on the flying chairaplanes, tousled, crimson, and

---

32. WOODEN ANIMALS: of the merry-go-round.
33. TANNER: sixpence.
34. BEECHER'S BROOK: a famous water jump at the Aintree Race Course where the Grand National Steeplechase is held.
35. SHIES: booths where players try to knock objects off perches.
36. VALENTINO-BLACK SIDEWHISKERS: reference to Rudolph Valentino, a famous American movie idol in silent films.
37. BAGS: loose trousers.

38. THOR-ING: i.e., like Thor, the Norse god of thunder, whose great hammer kept the world in awe.
39. BLAINA: coal-mining district in Monmouthshire, England.
40. SWEDE: yellow turnip.
41. QUID: pound (British money).
42. STOUT: strong ale.
43. MILFORD HAVEN: Welsh port.
44. TRILBIES: Homburg hats.

against the rules. Jaunty girls gave sailors sauce.

All the Fun of the Fair in the hot, bubbling night. The Man in the sand-yellow Moon over the hurdy of gurdies.[45] The swingboats[46] swimming to and fro like slices of the moon. Dragons and hippogriffs at the prows of the gondolas breathing fire and Sousa.[47] Midnight roundabout riders tanti-fying[48] under the fairy-lights, huntsmen on billygoats and zebras hallooing under a circle of glow-worms.

And as we climbed home, up the gas-lit hill, to the still house over the mumbling bay, we heard the music die and the voices drift like sand. And we saw the lights of the Fair fade. And, at the far end of seaside field, they lit their lamps, one by one, in the caravans.[49]

---

45. THE HURDY OF GURDIES: i.e., the hurdy-gurdy of all hurdy-gurdies.
46. SWINGBOATS: boat-shaped swings.
47. SOUSA: i.e., band tunes by John Philip Sousa, American bandmaster and composer.

48. TANTIFYING: galloping.
49. CARAVANS: i.e., the wagons in which the fair people lived.

I

1. The charm of this entire essay lies in the word combinations that startle the reader into fresh sense impressions. A close look at the richness of the first paragraph will serve as an introduction to the rest. Try to indicate as precisely as possible what multiple meanings each sentence carries. For instance, how can there be a tune on *an ice-cream cornet?* What is a *wince and whinny of bathers?* How can there be a *silent hullabaloo?* Examples of such word play throughout the essay are too numerous to deal with individually. Indicate why the following are effective, and then pick out others that seem particularly striking to you:

a. "they catlicked their hands and faces."
b. "tide-marked necks."
c. "ribboned for the sun."
d. "stout ladies dressed for the male and immoral sea."
e. "towards the antipodes that hung their koala-bears and Maoris, kangaroos and boomerangs, upside down over the backs of the stars."
f. "We snowshoed a meek, complaining donkey and galloped him off in the wake of the ten-foot-tall and Atlas-muscled Mounties, rifled and pemmicanned, who always, in the white Gold Rush wastes, got their black-oathed-and-bearded Man."
g. "the voices of hoopla girls were crimped as elocutionists."
h. "hair that startled from his eyebrows."

2. Several specific characters are mentioned. Show how Thomas achieves a remarkably vivid sketch by the choice of a few specific details. You might start with the "barn-door-chested pug."

II

1. Describe a colorful holiday experience of your own in imitation of Thomas's emphasis on vivid sense impressions. Be willing to try unusual word combinations and daring associations of ideas.

ON UNIVERSITY SNOBS [*1847*]

William Makepeace Thackeray

As your holiday experiences and memories differ from those of Dylan Thomas, so may your typical day differ from one you might have spent a hundred years ago; fashions change, customs change, ways of living change. But there is underneath all human activities a disturbing—and also a reassuring—consistency which is little affected by change in time or place. You will find that the individuals mentioned in "On University Snobs," written over a century ago, bear a strong resemblance to people you know.

By "snobs" Thackeray means social climbers, persons seeking social distinction. You will not be familiar with some of the activities he mentions in his catalogue of University Snobs, and much of his vocabulary will be strange—"highlows," "fuddle," "Berlin glove," "Gyp," "blind-hookey"; but you will readily take note that the ways of the snob are in all periods painfully alike.

I should like to fill several volumes with accounts of various University Snobs, so fond are my reminiscences of them, and so numerous are they. I should like to speak, above all, of the wives and daughters of some of the Professor-Snobs—their amusements, habits, jealousies; their innocent artifices to entrap young men; their picnics, concerts, and evening parties. I wonder what has become of Emily Blades, daughter of Blades, the Professor of the Mandingo[1] language? I remember her shoulders to this day, as she sat in the midst of a crowd of about seventy young gentlemen, from Corpus and Catherine Hall,[2] entertaining them with ogles and French songs on the guitar. Are you married, fair Emily of the shoulders? What beautiful ringlets those were that used to dribble over them!—what a waist!—what a killing sea-green shot-silk[3] gown!—what a cameo, the size of a muffin! There were thirty-six young men of the University in love at one time with Emily Blades; and no words are sufficient to describe the pity, the sorrow, the deep, deep commiseration—the rage, fury, and uncharitableness, in other words—with which the Miss Trumps (daughter of Trumps, the Professor of Phlebotomy) regarded her, because she *didn't* squint, and because she *wasn't* marked with the smallpox.

As for the young University Snobs, I am getting too old, now, to speak of such very familiarly. My recollections of them lie in the far, far past—almost as far back as Pelham's[4] time.

We *then* used to consider Snobs rawlooking lads, who never missed chapel; who wore highlows[5] and no straps;[6] who walked two hours on the Trumpington[7] road every day of their lives; who carried off the college scholarships, and who overrated themselves in hall.[8] We were premature in pronouncing our verdict of youthful Snobbishness. The man without straps fulfilled his destiny and duty. He eased his old

---

1. MANDINGO: a language of the western Sudan.
2. CORPUS AND CATHERINE HALL: Cambridge residential colleges.
3. SHOT-SILK: silk woven so as to be changeable in tint.
4. PELHAM: hero of a novel by Edward Bulwer-Lytton entitled *Pelham, or the Adventures of a Gentleman* (1828).
5. HIGHLOWS: unfashionable ankle-high laced boots.
6. STRAPS: straps passing under the foot and fastened at each side of the trouser bottom to hold it down; fashionable at the time.
7. TRUMPINGTON: village near Cambridge.
8. HALL: i.e., dining hall.

governor,[9] the curate of Westmoreland, or helped his sister to set up the Ladies' School. He wrote a "Dictionary," or a "Treatise on Conic Sections," as his nature and genius prompted. He got a fellowship, and then took to himself a wife and a living.[10] He presides over a parish now, and thinks it rather a dashing thing to belong to the "Oxford and Cambridge Club"; and his parishoners love him, and snore under his sermons. No, no; *he* is not a Snob. It is not straps that make the gentleman, or high-lows that unmake him, be they ever so thick. My son, it is you who are the Snob if you lightly despise a man for doing his duty, and refuse to shake an honest man's hand because it wears a Berlin glove.[11]

We then used to consider it not the least vulgar for a parcel of lads who had been whipped three months previous, and were not allowed more than three glasses of port at home, to sit down to pine-apples and ices at each other's rooms, and fuddle themselves with champagne and claret.

One looks back to what was called "a wine party" with a sort of wonder. Thirty lads round a table covered with bad sweet-meats, drinking bad wines, telling bad stories, singing bad songs over and over again. Milk punch—smoking—ghastly headache—frightful spectacle of dessert-table next morning, and smell of tobacco; your guardian, the clergyman, dropping in, in the midst of this, expecting to find you deep in Algebra, and discovering the Gyp[12] administering soda-water.

There were young men who despised the lads who indulged in the coarse hospitalities of wine parties, who prided themselves in giving *récherché*[13] little French dinners. Both wine-party-givers and dinner-givers were Snobs.

There were what used to be called "dressy" Snobs:—Jimmy, who might be seen at five o'clock elaborately rigged out, with a camellia in his button-hole, glazed boots, and fresh kid-gloves twice a day; Jessamy, who was conspicuous for his "jewelry"—a young donkey, glittering all over with chains, rings, and shirt-studs; Jacky, who rode every day solemnly on the Blenheim Road, in pumps and white silk stockings, with his hair curled; —all three of whom flattered themselves they gave laws to the University about dress —all three most odious varieties of Snobs.

Sporting Snobs of course there were, and are always—those happy beings in whom Nature has implanted a love of slang; who loitered about the horsekeeper's stables, and drove the London coaches—a stage in and out[14]—and might be seen swaggering through the courts in pink[15] of early mornings, and indulged in dice and blind-hookey[16] at nights, and never missed a race or a boxing-match, and rode flat-races,[17] and kept bull-terriers. Worse Snobs even than these were poor miserable wretches who did not like hunting at all, and could not afford it, and were in mortal fear at a two-foot ditch, but who hunted because Glenlivat and Cinqbars[18] hunted. The Billiard Snob and the Boating Snob were varieties of these, and are to be found elsewhere than in Universities.

Then there were Philosophical Snobs, who used to ape statesmen at the spouting-clubs,[19] and who believed as a fact that Government always had an eye on the University for the selection of orators for the House of Commons. There were audacious young freethinkers, who adored nobody or nothing, except perhaps Robespierre[20] and the Koran, and panted for the day when the

---

9. OLD GOVERNOR: i.e., his father.
10. LIVING: salaried appointment to a church post.
11. BERLIN GLOVE: i.e., a knitted (not a leather) glove.
12. GYP: college servant.
13. RÉCHERCHÉ: excessively refined and exclusive.
14. A STAGE IN AND OUT: i.e., to and from the next "stop" on the Cambridge-London road.
15. PINK: i.e., in the scarlet coats fox hunters wear.
16. BLIND-HOOKEY: a card game.
17. FLAT-RACES: horse racing along level ground (not over obstacles).
18. GLENLIVAT AND CINQBARS: i.e., the aristocrats.
19. SPOUTING-CLUBS: debating societies.
20. ROBESPIERRE: leader of the French Revolution at the time when the revolutionists abolished Christianity in favor of the goddess "Reason."

pale name of priest should shrink and dwindle away before the indignation of an enlightened world.

But the worst of all University Snobs are those unfortunates who go to rack and ruin from their desire to ape their betters. Smith becomes acquainted with great people at college, and is ashamed of his father the tradesman. Jones has fine acquaintances, and lives after their fashion like a gay free-hearted fellow as he is, and ruins his father, and robs his sister's portion, and cripples his younger brother's outset in life, for the pleasure of entertaining my lord, and riding by the side of Sir John. And though it may be very good fun for Robinson to fuddle himself at home as he does at College, and to be brought home by the policeman he has just been trying to knock down—think what fun it is for the poor old soul his mother!—the half-pay captain's widow, who has been pinching herself all her life long, in order that that jolly young fellow might have a University education.

I

1. In paragraph one what is the speaker's attitude toward Emily Blades? How do such phrases as "fair Emily of the shoulders" and "ringlets . . . that used to dribble over them" help define his attitude? What is his attitude toward Miss Trumps?

2. What was the speaker's attitude toward the *raw-looking lads* when he was at the University? How has his attitude toward them changed? Why has it changed?

3. What does he mean by "a parcel of lads who had been whipped three months previous"? How does their status then help to account for their behavior now, at the University?

4. Point out how the speaker's choice of words vividly conveys his attitude toward the *Philosophical Snobs*.

5. For what kind of snob does he save his most tart comments? What contrast is there between these observations and the ones on the *raw-looking lads?*

6. What is the tone of the essay: smugly superior? caustic? mildly amused and detached? bitter? Support your answer with references to specific words and phrases in the essay.

II

1. Thackeray's *snob,* the person who tries to pretend he's something he isn't for the purpose of impressing others, is certainly still among us; in fact, each of us has a little of the snob in his make-up. Using present-day examples, particularly around school, write your own essay on snobs. Be sure to use the term in the same sense in which Thackeray is using it.

MY LAST DUCHESS   [*1842*]

Robert Browning

Every time we say or do anything we reveal more of what we really are than we realize. In an obvious way, Thackeray's Snobs gave to others an impression far different from that which they intended to give.

In this poem the Duke of Ferrara, a sixteenth century Italian nobleman, speaks about his "last Duchess" to an emissary who has come to arrange the details for his next marriage. His monologue creates an impression of himself far different from what he intends.

That's my last Duchess painted on the wall,
Looking as if she were alive. I call
That piece a wonder, now: Frà Pandolf's hands
Worked busily a day, and there she stands.
Will 't please you sit and look at her? I said   5
"Frà Pandolf" by design, for never read
Strangers like you that pictured countenance,
The depth and passion of its earnest glance,
But to myself they turned (since none puts by
The curtain I have drawn for you, but I)   10
And seemed as they would ask me, if they durst,
How such a glance came there; so, not the first
Are you to turn and ask thus. Sir, 'twas not
Her husband's presence only, called that spot
Of joy into the Duchess' cheek: perhaps   15
Frà Pandolf chanced to say, "Her mantle laps
Over my lady's wrist too much," or "Paint
Must never hope to reproduce the faint
Half-flush that dies along her throat:" such stuff
Was courtesy, she thought, and cause enough   20
For calling up that spot of joy. She had
A heart—how shall I say?—too soon made glad,
Too easily impressed; she liked whate'er
She looked on, and her looks went everywhere.
Sir, 'twas all one! My favor at her breast,   25
The dropping of the daylight in the West,
The bough of cherries some officious fool
Broke in the orchard for her, the white mule
She rode with round the terrace—all and each
Would draw from her alike the approving speech,   30
Or blush, at least. She thanked men,—good! but thanked

3. FRÀ PANDOLF: name of the (imaginary) Renaissance· artist who painted the portrait.
11. DURST: dared.

16. HER: the artist uses the third person form as a mark of deference to nobility.
25. FAVOR: i.e., gift.

Somehow—I know not how—as if she ranked
My gift of a nine-hundred-years-old name
With anybody's gift. Who'd stoop to blame
This sort of trifling? Even had you skill   35
In speech—(which I have not)—to make your will
Quite clear to such an one, and say, "Just this
Or that in you disgusts me; here you miss,
Or there exceed the mark"—and if she let
Herself be lessoned so, nor plainly set   40
Her wits to yours, forsooth, and made excuse,
—E'en then would be some stooping; and I choose
Never to stoop. Oh sir, she smiled, no doubt,
Whene'er I passed her; but who passed without
Much the same smile? This grew; I gave commands;   45
Then all smiles stopped together. There she stands
As if alive. Will 't please you rise? We'll meet
The company below, then. I repeat,
The Count your master's known munificence
Is ample warrant that no just pretense   50
Of mine for dowry will be disallowed;
Though his fair daughter's self, as I avowed
At starting, is my object. Nay, we'll go
Together down, sir. Notice Neptune, though,
Taming a sea-horse, thought a rarity,   55
Which Claus of Innsbruck cast in bronze for me!

54. NEPTUNE: the sea-god.
56. CLAUS OF INNSBRUCK: another imaginary Renaissance artist.

I

1. This is a dramatic monologue, a one-sided conversation. We know the actions and reactions of the person addressed only by the indications the speaker gives us. We must expect sudden shifts in action without benefit of transitional words or phrases. Point out which of the Duke's comments indicate action or reaction in the emissary he is addressing. Read the poem aloud several times, letting your voice indicate its conversational structure.

2. What kind of person was the Duke's *last Duchess?* The Duke refers to her actions as "this sort of trifling" and says that she *disgusts* him. Just exactly what did she do that displeased him? How does the reader's response to her actions differ from the Duke's? From the evidence in the poem what would you say happened to her?

3. What kind of person is the Duke? Refer to specific lines that reveal his attitude toward himself. How does he justify himself according to his own standards of conduct? Why does the reader see him differently?

4. How does the Duke's obsession with owning "things" (his art work, for instance) help explain how he could do what he did? Why is the title of the poem particularly appropriate in this connection?

from THE PICKWICK PAPERS [*1836*]

Charles Dickens

Charles Dickens's imagination has filled English literature with an intriguing assortment of very real people. Perhaps you have already met Wilkins Micawber in *David Copperfield,* Sydney Carton in *A Tale of Two Cities,* or Pip in *Great Expectations,* to mention a few. Once met, they are never forgotten. In the *Posthumous Papers of the Pickwick Club,* one of Dickens's first efforts, we find some of his most enduring characters, particularly the mild-mannered, good-natured, eternally gullible Samuel Pickwick, and his faithful servant, guide, and protector, Sam Weller, the essence of common sense and uncommon good humor.

Only in the loosest sense a novel, the *Pickwick Papers* chronicles the fortunes of the Pickwick Club, a group of thoroughly innocent yet eager gentlemen. Dickens has harsh things to say at times about puffed-up magistrates, scheming lawyers, religious quacks, and cheats and frauds of all kinds, but essentially the *Pickwick Papers* strikes a blow for warm friendship, honest dealing, good manners, and simple human decency. What you will read here is only an appetizer; open the book itself anywhere, and get to know better some of the most delightful people in English literature—or anywhere else.

Chapter XXII

Mr. Pickwick journeys to Ipswich, and meets with a romantic adventure with a middle-aged lady in yellow curl papers.

"That 'ere your governor's[1] luggage, Sammy?" inquired Mr. Weller of his affectionate son, as he entered the yard of the Bull Inn, Whitechapel,[2] with a traveling bag and a small portmanteau.

"You might ha' made a worser guess than that, old feller," replied Mr. Weller the younger, setting down his burden in the yard, and sitting himself down upon it afterwards. "The Governor hisself'll be down here presently."

"He's a cabbin' it,[3] I suppose?" said the father.

"Yes, he's havin' two mile o' danger at eight-pence," responded the son. "How's mother-in-law this mornin'?"

"Queer, Sammy, queer," replied the elder Mr. Weller, with impressive gravity. "She's been gettin' rayther in the Methodistical[4] order lately, Sammy; and she is uncommon pious, to be sure. She's too good a creetur for me, Sammy. I feel I don't deserve her."

"Ah," said Mr. Samuel, "that's wery self-denyin' o' you."

"Wery," replied his parent, with a sigh. "She's got hold o' some inwention for grown-up people being born again.[5] Wouldn't I put her out to nurse!"

"What do you think them women does t'other day," continued Mr. Weller, after a short pause, during which he had significantly struck the side of his nose with his forefinger some half-dozen times. "What do

---

1. YOUR GOVERNOR'S: i.e., your employer's.
2. WHITECHAPEL: a section in East London.
3. A CABBIN' IT: i.e., coming by horsedrawn cab.

---

4. METHODISTICAL: Eighteenth and Nineteenth-century Methodism preached a straightforward doctrine of repentance and salvation, which captured especially the women of the working classes.
5. INWENTION . . . BORN AGAIN: referring to the doctrine of regeneration, i.e., being born again spiritually. Mr. Weller takes it in the physical sense.

you think they does, t'other day, Sammy?"

"Don't know," replied Sammy, "what?"

"Goes and gets up a grand tea drinkin' for a feller they calls their shepherd," said Mr. Weller. "I was a standing starin' in at the pictur shop down at our place, when I sees a little bill[6] about it; 'tickets half-a-crown. All applications to be made to the committee. Secretary, Mrs Weller'; and when I got home there was the committee a sittin' in our back parlor. Fourteen women; I wish you could ha' heard 'em, Sammy. There they was, a passin' resolutions, and wotin' supplies, and all sorts o' games. Well, what with your mother-in-law a worrying me to go, and what with my looking for'ard to seein' some queer starts if I did, I put my name down for a ticket; at six o'clock on the Friday evenin' I dresses myself out wery smart, and off I goes with the old 'ooman, and up we walks into a fust floor where there was tea things for thirty, and a whole lot o' women as begins whisperin' at one another, and lookin' at me, as if they'd never seen a rayther stout gen'l'm'n of eight-and-fifty afore. By-and-bye, there comes a great bustle downstairs, and a lanky chap with a red nose and a white neckcloth rushes up, and sings out, 'Here's the shepherd a coming to wisit his faithful flock'; and in comes a fat chap in black, with a great white face, a smilin' avay like clockwork. Such goin's on, Sammy! 'The kiss of peace,' says the shepherd; and then he kissed the women all round, and ven he'd done, the man vith the red nose began. I was just a thinkin' whether I hadn't better begin too—'specially as there was a wery nice lady a sittin' next me—ven in comes the tea, and your mother-in-law, as had been makin' the kettle bile downstairs. At it they went, tooth and nail. Such a precious loud hymn, eatin' and drinkin'! I wish you could ha' seen the shepherd walkin' into the ham and muffins. I never see such a chap to eat and drink; never. The red-nosed man warn't by no means the sort of person you'd like to grub by contract, but he was nothin' to the shepherd. Well; arter the tea was over, they sang another hymn, and then the shepherd began to preach: and wery well he did it, considerin' how heavy them muffins must have lied on his chest. Presently he pulls up, all of a sudden, and hollers out 'Where is the sinner; where is the mis'rable sinner?' Upon which, all the women looked at me, and began to groan as if they was a dying. I thought it was rather sing'ler, but hows'ever, I says nothing. Presently he pulls up again, and lookin' wery hard at me, says, 'Where is the sinner; where is the mis'rable sinner?' and all the women groans again, ten times louder than afore. I got rather wild at this, so I takes a step or two for'ard and says, 'My friend,' says I, 'did you apply that 'ere observation to me?' 'Stead of begging my pardon as any gen'l'm'n would ha' done, he got more abusive than ever: called me a wessel, Sammy—a wessel of wrath—and all sorts o' names. So my blood being reg'larly up, I first give him two or three for himself, and then two or three more to hand over to the man with the red nose, and walked off. I wish you could ha' heard how the women screamed, Sammy, ven they picked up the shepherd from under the table——Hallo! here's the governor, the size of life."

As Mr. Weller spoke, Mr. Pickwick dismounted from a cab, and entered the yard.

"Fine mornin', sir," said Mr. Weller senior.

"Beautiful indeed," replied Mr. Pickwick.

"Beautiful indeed," echoed a red-haired man with an inquisitive nose and spectacles, who had unpacked himself from a cab at the same moment as Mr. Pickwick. "Going to Ipswich,[7] sir?"

"I am," replied Mr. Pickwick.

"Extraordinary coincidence. So am I."

Mr. Pickwick bowed.

"Going outside?"[8] said the red-haired man.

Mr. Pickwick bowed again.

---

6. BILL: poster.

7. IPSWICH: town in Suffolk, northeast of London.
8. OUTSIDE: i.e., riding outside on the stagecoach that would take them from London to Ipswich.

"Bless my soul, how remarkable—I am going outside, too," said the red-haired man: "we are positively going together." And the red-haired man, who was an important-looking, sharp-nosed, mysterious-spoken personage, with a bird-like habit of giving his head a jerk every time he said anything, smiled as if he had made one of the strangest discoveries that ever fell to the lot of human wisdom.

"I am happy in the prospect of your company, sir," said Mr. Pickwick.

"Ah," said the new-comer, "it's a good thing for both of us, isn't it? Company, you see—company is—is—it's a very different thing from solitude—ain't it?"

"There's no denying that 'ere," said Mr. Weller, joining in the conversation, with an affable smile. "That's what I call a self-evident proposition, as the dog's-meat man said, when the housemaid told him he warn't a gentleman."

"Ah," said the red-haired man, surveying Mr. Weller from head to foot with a supercilious look. "Friend of yours, sir?"

"Not exactly a friend," replied Mr. Pickwick in a low tone. "The fact is, he is my servant, but I allow him to take a good many liberties; for, between ourselves, I flatter myself he is an original,[9] and I am rather proud of him."

"Ah," said the red-haired man, "that, you see, is a matter of taste. I am not fond of anything original; I don't like it; don't see the necessity for it. What's your name, sir?"

"Here is my card, sir," replied Mr. Pickwick, much amused by the abruptness of the question, and the singular manner of the stranger.

"Ah," said the red-haired man, placing the card in his pocket-book, "Pickwick; very good. I like to know a man's name, it saves so much trouble. That's my card, sir, Magnus, you will perceive, sir—Magnus is my name. It's rather a good name, I think, sir?"

"A very good name, indeed," said Mr.

Pickwick, wholly unable to repress a smile.

"Yes, I think it is," resumed Mr. Magnus. "There's a good name before it, too, you will observe. Permit me, sir—if you hold the card a little slanting, this way, you catch the light upon the up-stroke. There—Peter Magnus—sounds well, I think, sir."

"Very," said Mr. Pickwick.

"Curious circumstance about those initials, sir," said Mr. Magnus. "You will observe—P.M.—post meridian. In hasty notes to intimate acquaintance, I sometimes sign myself 'Afternoon.' It amuses my friends very much, Mr. Pickwick."

"It is calculated to afford them the highest gratification, I should conceive," said Mr. Pickwick, rather envying the ease with which Mr. Magnus's friends were entertained.

"Now, gen'l'm'n," said the hostler, "coach is ready, if you please."

"Is all my luggage in?" inquired Mr. Magnus.

"All right, sir."

"Is the red bag in?"

"All right, sir."

"And the striped bag?"

"Fore boot,[10] sir."

"And the brown-paper parcel?"

"Under the seat, sir."

"And the leather hat-box?"

"They're all in, sir."

"Now, will you get up?" said Mr. Pickwick.

"Excuse me," replied Magnus, standing on the wheel. "Excuse me, Mr. Pickwick. I cannot consent to get up, in this state of uncertainty. I am quite satisfied from that man's manner, that that leather hat-box is not in."

The solemn protestations of the hostler being wholly unavailing, the leather hat-box was obliged to be raked up from the lowest depth of the boot, to satisfy him that it had been safely packed; and after he had been assured on this head,[11] he felt a solemn presentiment, first, that the red bag was

---

9. AN ORIGINAL: a "character" we would say.

10. FORE BOOT: forward baggage compartment.
11. HEAD: i.e., point.

mislaid, and next that the striped bag had been stolen, and then that the brown-paper parcel "had come untied."

At length when he had received ocular demonstration of the groundless nature of each and every of these suspicions, he consented to climb up to the roof of the coach, observing that now he had taken everything off his mind, he felt quite comfortable and happy.

"You're given to nervousness, an't you, sir?" inquired Mr. Weller senior, eyeing the stranger askance, as he mounted to his place.

"Yes; I always am rather, about these little matters," said the stranger, "but I am all right now—quite right."

"Well, that's a blessin'," said Mr. Weller. "Sammy, help your master up to the box: t'other leg, sir, that's it; give us your hand, sir. Up with you. You was a lighter weight when you was a boy, sir."

"True enough, that, Mr. Weller," said the breathless Mr. Pickwick, good humoredly, as he took his seat on the box beside him.

"Jump up in front, Sammy," said Mr. Weller. "Now Villam, run 'em out. Take care o' the archvay, gen'lm'n. 'Heads,' as the pieman says. That'll do, Villam. Let 'em alone." And away went the coach up Whitechapel, to the admiration of the whole population of that pretty-densely populated quarter.

"Not a wery nice neighborhood this, sir," said Sam, with a touch of the hat, which always preceded his entering into conversation with his master.

"It is not indeed, Sam," replied Mr. Pickwick, surveying the crowded and filthy street through which they were passing.

"It's a wery remarkable circumstance, sir," said Sam, "that poverty and oysters always seems to go together."

"I don't understand you, Sam," said Mr. Pickwick.

"What I mean, sir," said Sam, "is, that the poorer a place is, the greater call there seems to be for oysters. Look here, sir; here's a oyster stall to every half-dozen

houses. The street's lined with 'em. Blessed if I don't think that ven a man's wery poor, he rushes out of his lodgings, and eats oysters in reg'lar desperation."

"To be sure he does," said Mr. Weller senior; "and it's just the same vith pickled salmon!"

"Those are two very remarkable facts, which never occurred to me before," said Mr. Pickwick. "The very first place we stop at, I'll make a note of them."

By this time they had reached the turnpike at Mile End; a profound silence prevailed until they had got two or three miles further on, when Mr. Weller senior, turning suddenly to Mr. Pickwick, said:

"Wery queer life is a pike-keeper's, sir."

"A what?" said Mr. Pickwick.

"A pike-keeper."

"What do you mean by a pike-keeper?" inquired Mr. Peter Magnus.

"The old 'un means a turnpike keeper, gen'l'm'n," observed Mr. Samuel Weller, in explanation.

"Oh," said Mr. Pickwick, "I see. Yes; very curious life. Very uncomfortable."

"They're all on 'em men as has met vith some disappointment in life," said Mr. Weller senior.

"Ay, ay?" said Mr. Pickwick.

"Yes. Consequence of vich, they retires from the world, and shuts themselves up in pikes; partly with the view of being solitary, and partly to revenge themselves on mankind, by takin' tolls."

"Dear me," said Mr. Pickwick, "I never knew that before."

"Fact, sir," said Mr. Weller; "if they was gen'l'm'n you'd call 'em misanthropes, but as it is, they only takes to pike-keepin'."

With such conversation, possessing the inestimable charm of blending amusement with instruction, did Mr. Weller beguile the tediousness of the journey, during the greater part of the day. Topics of conversation were never wanting for even when any pause occurred in Mr. Weller's loquacity, it was abundantly supplied by the desire evinced by Mr. Magnus to make himself acquainted with the whole of the personal history of his fellow-travelers, and his loudly expressed anxiety at every stage, respecting the safety and well-being of the two bags, the leather hat-box, and the brown-paper parcel.

In the main street of Ipswich, on the left-hand side of the way, a short distance after you have passed through the open space fronting the Town Hall, stands an inn known far and wide by the appellation of The Great White Horse, rendered the more conspicuous by a stone statue of some rampacious[12] animal with flowing mane and tail, distantly resembling an insane cart-horse, which is elevated above the principal door. The Great White Horse is famous in the neighborhood, in the same degree as a prize ox, or county paper-chronicled turnip,[13] or unwieldy pig—for its enormous size. Never were such labyrinths of uncarpeted passages, such clusters of mouldy, ill-lighted rooms, such huge numbers of small dens for eating or sleeping in, beneath any one roof, as are collected together between the four walls of the Great White Horse at Ipswich.

It was at the door of this overgrown tavern that the London coach stopped, at the same hour every evening; and it was from this same London coach, that Mr. Pickwick, Sam Weller, and Mr. Peter Magnus dismounted, on the particular evening to which this chapter of our history bears reference.

*　　*　　*　　*　　*

"Very well," replied Mr. Pickwick, looking round him. It was a tolerably large double-bedded room, with a fire; upon the whole, a more comfortable-looking apartment than Mr. Pickwick's short experience of the accommodations of the Great White Horse had led him to expect.

"Nobody sleeps in the other bed, of course," said Mr. Pickwick.

"Oh, no, sir."

---

12. RAMPACIOUS: rampageous, unruly.
13. COUNTY PAPER-CHRONICLED TURNIP: i.e., a turnip so unusual that an account of it appears in the county papers.

"Very good. Tell my servant to bring me up some hot water at half-past eight in the morning, and that I shall not want him any more tonight."

"Yes, sir." And bidding Mr. Pickwick good night, the chamber-maid retired, and left him alone.

Mr. Pickwick sat himself down in a chair before the fire, and fell into a train of rambling meditations . . . which came back to the Great White Horse at Ipswich, with sufficient clearness to convince Mr. Pickwick that he was falling asleep. So he roused himself, and began to undress, when he recollected he had left his watch on the table downstairs.

Now, this watch was a special favorite with Mr. Pickwick, having been carried about, beneath the shadow of his waistcoat, for a greater number of years than we feel called upon to state at present. The possibility of going to sleep, unless it were ticking gently beneath his pillow, or in the watch-pocket over his head, had never entered Mr. Pickwick's brain. So as it was pretty late now, and he was unwilling to ring his bell at that hour of the night, he slipped on his coat, of which he had just divested himself, and taking the japanned candlestick in his hand, walked quietly downstairs.

The more stairs Mr. Pickwick went down, the more stairs there seemed to be to descend, and again and again, when Mr. Pickwick got into some narrow passage, and began to congratulate himself on having gained the ground-floor, did another flight of stairs appear before his astonished eyes. At last he reached a stone hall, which he remembered to have seen when he entered the house. Passage after passage did he explore; room after room did he peep into; at length, as he was on the point of giving up the search in despair, he opened the door of the identical room in which he had spent the evening, and beheld his missing property on the table.

Mr. Pickwick seized the watch in triumph, and proceeded to re-trace his steps to his bed-chamber. If his progress downward had been attended with difficulties and uncertainty, his journey back was infinitely more perplexing. Rows of doors, garnished with boots[14] of every shape, make, and size, branched off in every possible direction. A dozen times did he softly turn the handle of some bedroom door which resembled his own, when a gruff cry from within of "Who the devil's that?" or "What do you want here?" caused him to steal away, on tiptoe, with a perfectly marvelous celerity. He was reduced to the verge of despair, when an open door attracted his attention. He peeped in. Right at last! There were the two beds, whose situation he perfectly remembered, and the fire still burning. His candle, not a long one when he first received it, had flickered away in the drafts of air through which he had passed, and sank into the socket as he closed the door after him. "No matter," said Mr. Pickwick, "I can undress myself just as well by the light of the fire."

The bedsteads stood one on each side of the door; and on the inner side of each was a little path, terminating in a rush-bottomed chair, just wide enough to admit of a person's getting into, or out of bed, on that side, if he or she thought proper. Having carefully drawn the curtains of his bed on the outside, Mr. Pickwick sat down on the rush-bottomed chair, and leisurely divested himself of his shoes and gaiters. He then took off and folded up his coat, waistcoat, and neckcloth, and slowly drawing on his tasseled nightcap secured it firmly on his head, by tying beneath his chin the strings which he always had attached to that article of dress. It was at this moment that the absurdity of his recent bewilderment struck upon his mind. Throwing himself back in the rush-bottomed chair, Mr. Pickwick laughed to himself so heartily, that it would have been quite delightful to any man of well-constituted mind to have watched the smiles that expanded

___
14. GARNISHED WITH BOOTS: In English inns shoes were placed outside the door for polishing by the bootblack.

his amiable features as they shone forth from beneath the nightcap.

"It is the best idea," said Mr. Pickwick to himself, smiling till he almost cracked the night-cap strings: "It is the best idea, my losing myself in this place, and wandering about those staircases, that I ever heard of. Droll, droll, very droll." Here Mr. Pickwick smiled again, a broader smile than before, and was about to continue the process of undressing, in the best possible humor, when he was suddenly stopped by a most unexpected interruption; to wit, the entrance into the room of some person with a candle, who, after locking the door, advanced to the dressing table, and set down the light upon it.

The smile that played on Mr. Pickwick's features was instantaneously lost in a look of the most unbounded and wonder-stricken surprise. The person, whoever it was, had come in so suddenly and with so little noise, that Mr. Pickwick had had no time to call out, or oppose their entrance. Who could it be? A robber? Some evil-minded person who had seen him come upstairs with a handsome watch in his hand, perhaps. What was he to do!

The only way in which Mr. Pickwick could catch a glimpse of his mysterious visitor with the least danger of being seen himself, was by creeping on to the bed, and peeping out from between the curtains on the opposite side. To this maneuver he accordingly resorted. Keeping the curtains carefully closed with his hand, so that nothing more of him could be seen than his face and nightcap, and putting on his spectacles, he mustered up courage, and looked out.

Mr. Pickwick almost fainted with horror and dismay. Standing before the dressing-glass was a middle-aged lady, in yellow curl-papers, busily engaged in brushing what ladies call their "back-hair." However the unconscious middle-aged lady came into that room, it was quite clear that she contemplated remaining there for the night; for she had brought a rushlight and shade with her, which, with praiseworthy precaution against fire, she had stationed in a basin on the floor, where it was glimmering away, like a gigantic lighthouse in a particularly small piece of water.

"Bless my soul," thought Mr. Pickwick, "what a dreadful thing!"

"Hem!" said the lady; and in went Mr. Pickwick's head with automaton-like rapidity.

"I never met with anything so awful as this," thought poor Mr. Pickwick, the cold perspiration starting in drops upon his nightcap. "Never. This is fearful."

It was quite impossible to resist the urgent desire to see what was going forward. So out went Mr. Pickwick's head again. The prospect was worse than before. The middle-aged lady had finished arranging her hair; had carefully enveloped it in a muslin nightcap with a small plaited border; and was gazing pensively on the fire.

"This matter is growing alarming," reasoned Mr. Pickwick with himself. "I can't allow things to go on in this way. By the self-possession of that lady it is clear to me that I must have come into the wrong room. If I call out she'll alarm the house; but if I remain here the consequences will be still more frightful."

Mr. Pickwick, it is quite unnecessary to say, was one of the most modest and delicate-minded of mortals. The very idea of exhibiting his nightcap to a lady overpowered him, but he had tied those confounded strings in a knot, and, do what he would, he couldn't get it off. The disclosure must be made. There was only one other way of doing it. He shrunk behind the curtains, and called out very loudly:

"Ha——hum!"

That the lady started at this unexpected sound was evident, by her falling up against the rushlight shade; that she persuaded herself it must have been the effect of imagination was equally clear, for when Mr. Pickwick, under the impression that she had fainted away stone-dead from fright, ventured to peep out again, she was gazing pensively on the fire as before.

"Most extraordinary female this," thought Mr. Pickwick, popping in again. "Ha——hum!"

These last sounds, so like those in which, as legends inform us, the ferocious giant Blunderbore[15] was in the habit of expressing his opinion that it was time to lay the cloth,[16] were too distinctly audible to be again mistaken for the workings of fancy.

"Gracious Heaven!" said the middle-aged lady, "what's that?"

"It's—it's—only a gentleman, Ma'am," said Mr. Pickwick from behind the curtains.

"A gentleman!" said the lady with a terrific scream.

"It's all over!" thought Mr. Pickwick.

"A strange man!" shrieked the lady. Another instant and the house would be alarmed. Her garments rustled as she rushed towards the door.

"Ma'am," said Mr. Pickwick, thrusting out his head, in the extremity of his desperation, "Ma'am!"

Now, although Mr. Pickwick was not actuated by any definite object in putting out his head, it was instantaneously productive of a good effect. The lady, as we have already stated, was near the door. She must pass it, to reach the staircase, and she would most undoubtedly have done so by this time, had not the sudden apparition of Mr. Pickwick's nightcap driven her back into the remotest corner of the apartment, where she stood staring wildly at Mr. Pickwick, while Mr. Pickwick in his turn stared wildly at her.

"Wretch," said the lady, covering her eyes with her hands, "what do you want here?"

"Nothing, Ma'am; nothing, whatever, Ma'am," said Mr. Pickwick earnestly.

"Nothing!" said the lady, looking up.

"Nothing, Ma'am, upon my honor," said Mr. Pickwick, nodding his head so energetically that the tassel of his nightcap danced again. "I am almost ready to sink,

---

15. BLUNDERBORE: a giant in "Jack the Giant Killer."

16. LAY THE CLOTH: i.e., set the table for a meal.

Ma'am, beneath the confusion of addressing a lady in my nightcap (here the lady hastily snatched off hers), but I can't get it off, Ma'am (here Mr. Pickwick gave it a tremendous tug, in proof of the statement). It is evident to me, Ma'am, now, that I have mistaken this bedroom for my own. I had not been here five minutes, Ma'am, when you suddenly entered it."

"If this improbable story be really true, sir," said the lady, sobbing violently, "you will leave it instantly."

"I will, Ma'am, with the greatest pleasure," replied Mr. Pickwick.

"Instantly, sir," said the lady.

"Certainly, Ma'am," interposed Mr. Pickwick very quickly. "Certainly, Ma'am. I—I—am very sorry, Ma'am," said Mr. Pickwick, making his appearance at the bottom of the bed, "to have been the innocent occasion of this alarm and emotion; deeply sorry, Ma'am."

The lady pointed to the door. One excellent quality of Mr. Pickwick's character was beautifully displayed at this moment, under the most trying circumstances. Although he had hastily put on his hat over his nightcap, after the manner of the old patrol; although he carried his shoes and gaiters in his hand, and his coat and waistcoat over his arm; nothing could subdue his native politeness.

"I am exceedingly sorry, Ma'am," said Mr. Pickwick, bowing very low.

"If you are, sir, you will at once leave the room," said the lady.

"Immediately, Ma'am; this instant, Ma'am," said Mr. Pickwick, opening the door, and dropping both his shoes with a crash in so doing.

"I trust, Ma'am," resumed Mr. Pickwick, gathering up his shoes, and turning round to bow again: "I trust, Ma'am, that my unblemished character, and the devoted respect I entertain for your sex, will plead as some slight excuse for this"—But before Mr. Pickwick could conclude the sentence the lady had thrust him into the passage, and locked and bolted the door behind him.

Whatever grounds of self-congratulation Mr. Pickwick might have for having escaped so quietly from his late awkward situation, his present position was by no means enviable. He was alone, in an open passage, in a strange house, in the middle of the night, half dressed; it was not to be supposed that he could find his way in perfect darkness to a room which he had been wholly unable to discover with a light, and if he made the slightest noise in his fruitless attempts to do so, he stood every chance of being shot at, and perhaps killed, by some wakeful traveler. He had no resource but to remain where he was until daylight appeared. So after groping his way a few paces down the passage, and, to his infinite alarm, stumbling over several pairs of boots in so doing, Mr. Pickwick crouched into a little recess in the wall, to wait for morning as philosophically as he might.

He was not destined, however, to undergo this additional trial of patience: for he had not been long ensconced in his present concealment when, to his unspeakable horror, a man, bearing a light, appeared at the end of the passage. His horror was suddenly converted into joy, however, when he recognized the form of his faithful attendant. It was indeed Mr. Samuel Weller, who after sitting up thus late, in conversation with the Boots,[17] who was sitting up for the mail, was now about to retire to rest.

"Sam," said Mr. Pickwick, suddenly appearing before him, "where's my bedroom?"

Mr. Weller stared at his master with the most emphatic surprise; and it was not until the question had been repeated three several times, that he turned round, and led the way to the long-sought apartment.

"Sam," said Mr. Pickwick as he got into bed, "I have made one of the most extraordinary mistakes tonight, that ever were heard of."

"Wery likely, sir," replied Mr. Weller drily.

"But of this I am determined, Sam," said

17. THE BOOTS: i.e., the bootblack.

Mr. Pickwick; "that if I were to stop in this house for six months, I would never trust myself about it, alone, again."

"That's the wery prudentest resolution as you could come to, sir," replied Mr. Weller. "You rayther want somebody to look arter you, sir, wen your judgment goes out a wisitin'."

"What do you mean by that, Sam?" said Mr. Pickwick. He raised himself in bed, and extended his hand, as if he were about to say something more; but suddenly checking himself, turned round, and bade his valet "Good night."

"Good night, sir," replied Mr. Weller. He paused when he got outside the door—shook his head—walked on—stopped—snuffed the candle—shook his head again—and finally proceeded slowly to his chamber, apparently buried in the profoundest meditation.

I

1. Characterize the older Weller. What details bring out the humor of his account of the meeting with the "shepherd a coming to wisit his faithful flock"?

2. What makes Peter Magnus a humorous character? What does his comment on his name show about him? What other details help?

3. What attitude does Dickens want the reader to take toward Mr. Pickwick? He shows him doing some rather foolish things, and we laugh at his reactions, but what saves him from being like Peter Magnus? In this connection notice how Dickens has Pickwick respond to Magnus.

4. Picture clearly Mr. Pickwick's predicament in the lady's room. Describe the layout of the room to make clear why he cannot escape unperceived. How is the humor in the situation heightened by close attention to such detail as the problem of the nightcaps?

5. Why does Sam Weller respond the way he does to Mr. Pickwick's sudden appearance in the hallway and his subsequent comments? What must be our attitude toward Mr. Pickwick to find humor in Sam's attitude?

II

1. Compare the humor inherent in Mr. Pickwick's predicament with that inherent in Jackie's predicament in "First Confession." What do the two situations have in common? Consider the lack of information each has about his predicament and the amount the reader has. Consider, also, the question of sympathetic response to the person involved; in other words, how have we been prepared to be favorably disposed toward his confusion and his response to it? Lastly, consider the upshot of the affair: how serious are the consequences of the predicament? A general consideration might be the question of how detached the reader is from what befalls the small, frightened boy or the modest Mr. Pickwick. One way of handling this essay might be to consider what conditions would make either predicament anything but humorous.

from LIFE OF JOHNSON [1791]

James Boswell

Samuel Pickwick, like Gessler and the Duke of Ferrara, is wholly a creation of the author's imagination, though undeniably based on a composite of individuals known in real life. The next three selections have to do with actual people, Samuel Johnson and James Boswell, two of the great personalities of eighteenth-century London.

Boswell is perhaps the best-known English diarist, mainly because he did such a remarkable job of recording in great detail the personal life of the chief literary figure of the middle and late eighteenth century, Samuel Johnson. But Boswell was more than just a human recording machine; his lately discovered journals prove him to have been a man of infinite capacity for doing things and meeting people—and for keeping a full record of what he did and whom he met. He did not have Johnson's learning or his critical powers or even his common sense, but he did have a capacity for friendship and a delight in every detail of daily life that endeared him to the older man. He also had a keen sense of drama, which enabled him again and again to transform into memorable scenes the sometimes mundane happenings he set down.

Despite the difference in their ages—Boswell was 22, Johnson 55 when they met—they formed an almost perfect friendship: Boswell sought improvement and guidance from the wisest mind and heart of the age and was never disappointed; Johnson found a willing ear, a steady flow of thoughtful questions, a generous respect, and an uncomplaining willingness to take friendship on whatever basis it was offered. Johnson was undoubtedly the greater man, and Boswell has sometimes been referred to as merely his "shadow," with the implication that the finest biography in the English language somehow wrote itself while Boswell held the pen. Johnson's own letters and Boswell's other works easily give the lie to that idea.

The first selection of the three is from Boswell's *Life of Johnson*. The *Life* was published in 1791, seven years after Johnson's death and some twenty-eight years after Boswell had first met him. The faithfulness with which Boswell kept notes can be seen from the detail in the selection we have here. Notice that there is little *obvious* organization. Boswell wants to show as much as possible of Johnson in action; to do so he sets the stage and lets his characters do the talking. Occasionally he interjects a comment, but for the most part he lets the drama unfold itself.

This[1] is to me a memorable year; for in it I had the happiness to obtain the acquaintance of that extraordinary man whose memoirs I am now writing; an acquaintance which I shall ever esteem as one of the most fortunate circumstances in my life. Though then but two-and-twenty, I had for several years read his works with delight and instruction, and had the highest reverence for their author, which had grown up in my fancy into a kind of mysterious veneration, by figuring to myself a state of solemn elevated abstraction, in which I supposed him to live in the immense metropolis of London.

*   *   *   *   *

Mr. Thomas Davies the actor, who then kept a bookseller's shop in Russell Street, Covent Garden,[2] told me that Johnson was very much his friend, and came frequently to his house, where he more than once invited me to meet him: but by some unlucky accident or other he was prevented from coming to us.

*   *   *   *   *

At last, on Monday the 16th of May, when I was sitting in Mr. Davies's back-parlor, after having drunk tea with him and Mrs. Davies, Johnson unexpectedly came into the shop; and Mr. Davies having perceived him through the glass-door in the room in which we were sitting, advancing towards us,—he announced his awful[3] approach to me, somewhat in the manner of an actor in the part of Horatio, when he addresses Hamlet on the appearance of his father's ghost, "Look, my Lord, it comes." I found that I had a very perfect idea of Johnson's figure, from the portrait of him

1. THIS: 1763.
2. COVENT GARDEN: section of London; main flower, fruit and vegetable market in the city.
3. AWFUL: i.e., awe-inspiring.

painted by Sir Joshua Reynolds[4] soon after he had published his Dictionary,[5] in the attitude of sitting in his easy chair in deep meditation: which was the first picture his friend did for him, which Sir Joshua very kindly presented to me, and from which an engraving has been made for this work. Mr. Davies mentioned my name, and respectfully introduced me to him. I was much agitated; and recollecting his prejudice against the Scotch, of which I had heard much, I said to Davies, "Don't tell where I come from."—"From Scotland," cried Davies, roguishly. "Mr. Johnson, (said I) I do indeed come from Scotland, but I cannot help it." I am willing to flatter myself that I meant this as light pleasantry to soothe and conciliate him, and not as an humiliating abasement at the expense of my country. But however that might be, this speech was somewhat unlucky; for with that quickness of wit for which he was so remarkable, he seized the expression "come from Scotland," which I used in the sense of being of that country; and, as if I had said that I had come away from it, or left it, retorted, "That, Sir, I find is what a very great many of your countrymen cannot help." This stroke stunned me a good deal; and when we had sat down, I felt myself not a little embarrassed, and apprehensive of what might come next. He then addressed himself to Davies: "What do you think of Garrick?[6] He has refused me an order[7] for the play for Miss Williams,[8] because he knows the house will be full, and that an order would be worth three shillings." Eager to take any opening to get into conversation with him, I ventured to say, "O, Sir, I cannot think Mr. Garrick would grudge such a trifle to you." "Sir, (said he, with a stern look,) I have known David Garrick longer than you have done: and I know no right you have to talk to me on the subject." Perhaps I deserved this check; for it was rather presumptuous in me, an entire stranger, to express any doubt of the justice of his animadversion upon his old acquaintance and pupil. I now felt myself much mortified, and began to think, that the hope which I had long indulged of obtaining his acquaintance was blasted. And, in truth, had not my ardor been uncommonly strong, and my resolution uncommonly perservering, so rough a reception might have deterred me forever from making any further attempts. Fortunately, however, I remained upon the field not wholly discomfited, and was soon rewarded by hearing some of his conversation, of which I preserved the following short minute,[9] without marking the questions and observations by which it was produced.

"People (he remarked) may be taken in once, who imagine that an author is greater in private life than other men. Uncommon parts[10] require uncommon opportunities for their exertion.

"In barbarous society, superiority of parts is of real consequence. Great strength or great wisdom is of much value to an individual. But in more polished times there are people to do everything for money; and then there are a number of other superiorities, such as those of birth and fortune, and rank, that dissipate men's attention, and leave no extraordinary share of respect for personal and intellectual superiority. This is wisely ordered by Providence, to preserve some equality among mankind.

* * * * *

"The notion of liberty amuses the people of England, and helps to keep off the *tedium*

---

4. SIR JOSHUA REYNOLDS: famous English portrait painter and friend of Johnson's.
5. DICTIONARY: Johnson's Dictionary (1755), the first English dictionary to illustrate the meanings of words by quoting passages from well-known authors in which they were used.
6. GARRICK: David Garrick, boyhood friend of Johnson's, at this time manager and chief actor at the Drury Lane Theater.
7. ORDER: i.e., ticket.
8. MISS WILLIAMS: a blind lady who lived with Johnson.

---

9. MINUTE: i.e., note.
10. PARTS: talents.

vitae.[11] When a butcher tells you that *his heart bleeds for his country,* he has, in fact, no uneasy feeling."

*   *   *   *   *

I was highly pleased with the extraordinary vigor of his conversation, and regretted that I was drawn away from it by an engagement at another place. I had, for a part of the evening, been left alone with him, and had ventured to make an observation now and then, which he received very civilly; so that I was satisfied that though there was a roughness in his manner, there was no ill-nature in his disposition. Davies followed me to the door, and when I complained to him a little of the hard blows which the great man had given me, he kindly took upon him to console me by saying, "Don't be uneasy. I can see he likes you very well."

A few days afterwards I called on Davies, and asked him if I thought I might take the liberty of waiting on Mr. Johnson at his chambers in the Temple.[12] He said I certainly might, and that Mr. Johnson would take it as a compliment. So on Tuesday the 24th of May, after having been enlivened by the witty sallies of Messieurs Thornton, Wilkes, Churchill, and Lloyd, with whom I had passed the morning, I boldly repaired to Johnson. His chambers were on the first floor of No. 1, Inner Temple Lane, and I entered them with an impression given me by the Reverend Dr. Blair,[13] of Edinburgh, who had been introduced to him not long before, and described his having "found the Giant in his den", an expression which, when I came to be pretty well acquainted with Johnson, I repeated to him, and he was diverted at this picturesque account of himself. Dr. Blair had been presented to him by Dr. James Fordyce. At this time the controversy concerning the pieces published by Mr. James Macpherson, as translations of

11. TEDIUM VITAE: boredom.
12. TEMPLE: district of London.
13. REVEREND DR. BLAIR: Hugh Blair, a professor at the University of Edinburgh, famous as a lecturer and preacher.

Ossian, was at its height. Johnson had all along denied their authenticity; and, what was still more provoking to their admirers, maintained that they had no merit. The subject having been introduced by Dr. Fordyce, Dr. Blair, relying on the internal evidence of their antiquity, asked Dr. Johnson whether he thought any man of a modern age could have written such poems? Johnson replied, "Yes, Sir, many men, many women, and many children." Johnson at this time, did not know that Dr. Blair had just published a Dissertation, not only defending their authenticity, but seriously ranking them with the poems of Homer and Virgil; and when he was afterwards informed of this circumstance, he expressed some displeasure at Dr. Fordyce's having suggested the topic, and said, "I am not sorry that they got thus much for their pains. Sir, it was like leading one to talk of a book, when the author is concealed behind the door."

He received me very courteously: but, it must be confessed, that his apartment, and furniture, and morning dress, were sufficiently uncouth. His brown suit of clothes looked very rusty: he had on a little old shriveled unpowdered wig which was too small for his head; his shirt-neck and knees of his breeches were loose, his black worsted stockings ill drawn up; and he had a pair of unbuckled shoes by way of slippers. But all these slovenly particularities were forgotten the moment that he began to talk. Some gentlemen, whom I do not recollect, were sitting with him; and when they went away, I also rose; but he said to me, "Nay, don't go."—"Sir, (said I) I am afraid that I intrude upon you. It is benevolent to allow me to sit and hear you." He seemed pleased with this compliment, which I sincerely paid him, and answered, "Sir, I am obliged to any man who visits me."—I have preserved the following short minute of what passed this day.

"Madness frequently discovers itself merely by unnecessary deviation from the usual modes of the world. My poor friend

Smart[14] showed the disturbance of his mind, by falling upon his knees, and saying his prayers in the street, or in any other unusual place. Now although, rationally speaking, it is greater madness not to pray at all, than to pray as Smart did, I am afraid there are so many who do not pray, that their understanding is not called in question."

Concerning this unfortunate poet, Christopher Smart, who was confined in a madhouse, he had, at another time, the following conversation with Dr. Burney.[15]—BURNEY. "How does poor Smart do, Sir; is he likely to recover?" JOHNSON. "It seems as if his mind had ceased to struggle with the disease; for he grows fat upon it." BURNEY. "Perhaps, Sir, that may be from want of exercise." JOHNSON. "No, Sir; he has partly as much exercise as he used to have, for he digs in the garden. Indeed, before his confinement, he used for exercise to walk to the alehouse; but he was *carried* back again. I did not think he ought to be shut up. His infirmities were not noxious to society. He insisted on people praying with him; and I'd as lief pray with Kit Smart as anyone else. Another charge was, that he did not love clean linen;[16] and I have no passion for it."

Johnson continued. "Mankind have a great aversion to intellectual labor; but even supposing knowledge to be easily attainable,

14. SMART: Christopher Smart, English satiric and religious poet.
15. DR. BURNEY: Charles Burney, musician and writer.
16. LINEN: i.e., shirts.

more people would be content to be ignorant than would take even a little trouble to acquire it.

"The morality of an action depends on the motive from which we act. If I fling half a crown to a beggar with intention to break his head, and he picks it up and buys victuals with it, the physical effect is good; but, with respect to me, the action is very wrong. So, religious exercises, if not performed with an intention to please God, avail us nothing. As our Savior says of those who perform them from other motives, 'Verily they have their reward.' "

*   *   *   *   *

When I rose a second time, he again pressed me to stay, which I did.

He told me, that he generally went abroad at four in the afternoon and seldom came home till two in the morning. I took the liberty to ask if he did not think it wrong to live thus, and not make more use of his great talents. He owned it was a bad habit. On reviewing, at the distance of many years, my journal of this period, I wonder how, at my first visit, I ventured to talk to him so freely, and that he bore it with so much indulgence.

Before we parted, he was so good as to promise to favor me with his company one evening at my lodgings: and, as I took my leave, shook me cordially by the hand. It is almost needless to add, that I felt no little elation at having now so happily established an acquaintance of which I had been so long ambitious.

I

1. Boswell says there was a *roughness* in Johnson's manner but no *ill-nature*. How is that borne out here? How does he show that there is humor and kindness in the man? What does Johnson's attitude toward Christopher Smart show about him? What difference do his personal habits make in your attitude toward him?

2. Point out instances in which Boswell seems to be judging and interpreting rather than merely reporting. Point out other instances in which he leaves the interpreting up to the reader. Boswell obviously admired Johnson. How well does he let the reader see him in action so that he can make up his own mind about the man?

3. Boswell reproves Johnson for keeping late hours and for not making wiser use of his talents. And yet Boswell constantly sought out Johnson for advice and guidance. What evidence is there here of the kind of common sense and worldly wisdom in Johnson that Boswell looked for and found?

from LONDON JOURNAL   [*1763*]

James Boswell

The Dr. Johnson we saw briefly in the selection from the *Life of Johnson* is clearly the product of Boswell's memory, his painstaking care in recording conversations, and, above all, his imaginative ordering of details. In other words, the Dr. Johnson of the biography is *Boswell's* Johnson, and although there is certainly historical accuracy in the picture given, we have to remember that we are seeing Johnson as Boswell wants us to see him.

For many readers Boswell himself has proved as fascinating a figure as his more illustrious subject. The journals or diaries he kept have only recently been published. They reveal a man who was uncommonly frank about his own strengths and weaknesses and about his likes and dislikes. They also show him to have been seriously dedicated to the business of journal-keeping as a means of self-expression and self-improvement.

In these excerpts we find revealing comments on why he chose to keep a record of all that happened to him, and we get the original notes made on his first meeting with Johnson and subsequent visit to the latter's lodgings. The difference between the journal entry and the account in the *Life* written twenty-eight years later throws light on Boswell's literary skill in presenting Johnson.

Journal from the Time of My Leaving Scotland

15 November 1762

INTRODUCTION. The ancient philosopher certainly gave a wise counsel when he said, "Know thyself."[1] For surely this knowledge is of all the most important. I might enlarge upon this. But grave and serious declamation is not what I intend at present. A man cannot know himself better than by attending to the feelings of his heart and to his external actions, from which he may with tolerable certainty judge "what manner of person he is." I have therefore determined to keep a daily journal[2] in which I shall set down my various sentiments and my various conduct, which will be not only useful but very agreeable. It will give me a habit of application and improve me in expression; and knowing that I am to record my transactions will make me more careful to do well. Or if I should go wrong, it will assist me in resolutions of doing better. I shall here put down my thoughts on different subjects at different times, the whims that may seize me and the sallies of my luxuriant imagination. I shall mark the anecdotes and the stories that I hear, the instructive or amusing conversations that I am present at, and the various adventures that I may have.

I was observing to my friend Erskine that a plan of this kind was dangerous, as a man might in the openness of his heart say many things and discover[3] many facts that might do him great harm if the journal should fall into the hands of my[4] enemies. Against which there is no perfect security. "Indeed," said he, "I hope there is no danger at all; for I fancy you will not set down your robberies

1. PHILOSOPHER . . . "KNOW THYSELF": Socrates, among others; this is what the oracle of Apollo at Delphi admonished man to do.
2. JOURNAL: we would use the word *diary.*

3. DISCOVER: reveal.
4. MY: i.e., his.

From *Boswell's London Journal, 1762–1763,* edited by Frederick A. Pottle. Copyright 1950, by Yale University. Quoted with permission of Yale University and the McGraw-Hill Book Company, Inc.

on the highway, or the murders that you commit. As to other things there can be no harm." I laughed heartily at my friend's observation, which was so far true. I shall be upon my guard to mention nothing that can do harm. Truth shall ever be observed, and these things (if there should be any such) that require the gloss of falsehood shall be passed by in silence. At the same time I may relate things under borrowed names with safety that would do much mischief if particularly known.

In this way I shall preserve many things that would otherwise be lost in oblivion. I shall find daily employment for myself, which will save me from indolence and help to keep off the spleen, and I shall lay up a store of entertainment for my after[5] life. Very often we have more pleasure in reflecting on agreeable scenes that we have been in than we had from the scenes themselves. I shall not study much correctness, lest the labor of it should make me lay it aside altogether. I hope it will be of use to my worthy friend Johnston,[6] and that while he laments my personal absence, this journal may in some measure supply that defect and make him happy.

MONDAY 15 NOVEMBER. Elated with the thoughts of my journey to London, I got up. I called upon my friend Johnston, but found he was not come from the country, which vexed me a little, as I wished to bid him cordially adieu. However, I excused him to myself, and as Cairnie told me that people never took leave in France, I made the thing sit pretty easy. I had a long serious conversation with my father and mother. They were very kind to me. I felt parental affection was very strong towards me; and I felt a very warm filial regard for them. The scene of being a son setting out from home for the wide world and the idea of being my own master, pleased me much. I parted with my brother Davy, leaving him my best advices to be diligent at his business as a banker and to make rich and be happy.

At ten I got into my chaise, and away I went. As I passed the Cross,[7] the cadies[8] and the chairmen[9] bowed and seemed to say, "God prosper long our noble Boswell." I rattled down the High Street in high elevation of spirits, bowed and smiled to acquaintances, and took up my partner at Boyd's Close.[10] He was a Mr. Stewart, eldest son to Ardsheal, who was forfeited[11] in the year 1746. He had made four voyages to the East Indies, and was now going out first mate. I made the chaise stop at the foot of the Canongate; asked pardon of Mr. Stewart for a minute; walked to the Abbey of Holyroodhouse, went round the Piazzas, bowed thrice: once to the Palace itself, once to the crown of Scotland above the gate in front, and once to the venerable old Chapel. I next stood in the court before the Palace, and bowed thrice to Arthur Seat, that lofty romantic mountain on which I have so often strayed in my days of youth, indulged meditation and felt the raptures of a soul filled with ideas of the magnificence of God and his creation. Having thus gratified my agreeable whim and superstitious humor, I felt a warm glow of satisfaction. Indeed, I have a strong turn to what the cool[12] part of mankind have named superstition. But this proceeds from my genius for poetry[13] which ascribes many fanciful properties to everything. This I have great pleasure from; as

---

5. AFTER: later.
6. JOHNSTON: an Edinburgh friend of Boswell's, not the writer Johnson, whom Boswell has not yet met. The journal was sent to Johnston weekly.
7. CROSS: Edinburgh monument, formerly the site of its public market.
8. CADIES: porters.
9. CHAIRMEN: sedan chair carriers.
10. CLOSE: A close is a passage from a main street to an inner courtyard.
11. FORFEITED: i.e., forfeited his estates to the government for having supported the rebellion of 1745, when "Bonnie Prince Charlie" unsuccessfully asserted his claim to the English throne. Bonnie Prince Charlie was grandson to James II, who had been ousted from the throne in 1688.
12. COOL: unimaginative.
13. GENIUS FOR POETRY: inclination toward imaginative thinking.

I have now by experience and reflection gained the command of it so far that I can keep it within just bounds by the power of reason, without losing the agreeable feeling and play to the imagination which it bestows. I am surely much happier in this way than if I just considered Holyroodhouse as so much stone and lime which has been put together in a certain way, and Arthur Seat as so much earth and rock raised above the neighboring plain.

We then pursued our journey. I found my companion a jolly honest[14] plain fellow. I set out with a determined resolution against *shaving,*[15] that is to say, playing upon people; and therefore I talked sensibly and roughly. We did very well till we passed Old Camus, when one of the wheels of our chaise was so much broke that it was of no use. The driver proposed that we should mount the horses and ride to Berwick. But this I would by no means agree to; and as my partner let me be the principal man and take the direction of our journey, I made the chaise be dragged on to Ayton, where we waited till the driver rode to Berwick and brought us a chaise. Never did I pass three hours more unhappily. We were set down in a cold alehouse in a little dirty village. We had a beefsteak ill-dressed[16] and had nothing to drink but thick muddy beer. We were both out of humor so that we could not speak. We tried to sleep but in vain. We only got a drowsy headache. We were scorched by the fire on the one hand and shivering with frost on the other. At last our chaise came, and we got to Berwick about twelve at night. We had a slice of hard dry toast, a bowl of warm negus, and went comfortable to bed.

TUESDAY 16 NOVEMBER. We set off at six; breakfasted at Alnwick, where we had with us a Captain Elliot of the East Indies, and were hearty. Stewart and I began now to be acquainted and to talk about the Peace[17] and voyages and ways of living. We had a safe day, and got at night to Durham.

WEDNESDAY 17 NOVEMBER. We had a very good day of it, and got at night to Doncaster.

THURSDAY 18 NOVEMBER. We chatted a good deal. Stewart told me that some blacks in India were attacking their boat in order to plunder it, and that he shot two with his own hand. In the afternoon between Stamford and Stilton there was a young unruly horse in the chaise which run away with the driver, and jumping to one side of the road, we were overturned. We got a pretty severe rap. Stewart's head and my arm were somewhat hurt. However, we got up and pursued our way. During our two last stages this night, which we traveled in the dark, I was a good deal afraid of robbers. A great many horrid ideas filled my mind. There is no passion so distressing as fear, which gives us great pain and makes us appear contemptible in our own eyes to the last degree. However, I affected resolution, and as each of us carried a loaded pistol in his hand, we were pretty secure. We got at night to Biggleswade.

FRIDAY 19 NOVEMBER. It was very cold. Stewart was as effeminate[18] as I. I asked him how he, who shivered if a pane of glass was broke in a post-chaise, could bear the severe hardship of a sea life. He gave me to understand that necessity made anything be endured. Indeed this is very true. For when the mind knows that it cannot help itself by struggling, it quietly and patiently submits to whatever load is laid upon it. When we came upon Highgate hill and had a view of London, I was all life and joy. I repeated Cato's soliloquy on the immortality of the soul,[19] and my soul bounded forth to a certain prospect of happy futurity. I sung all manner of songs, and began to make one about an amorous meeting with a pretty girl,

14. HONEST: frank.
15. SHAVING: making fun of; talking foolishly.
16. ILL-DRESSED: poorly prepared.
17. PEACE: i.e., the peace terms that were soon to end the Seven Years War (1756-63) of Austria, France and Russia against Prussia and England.
18. EFFEMINATE: i.e., neither liked to be physically uncomfortable.
19. CATO'S . . . SOUL: from Addison's tragedy, *Cato* (1713), about the staunch defender of the Roman republic who took his own life rather than yield to Julius Caesar, who he rightly saw would destroy the republic.

the burthen of which was as follows:

> She gave me *this,* I gave her *that;*
> And tell me, had she not tit for tat?

I gave three huzzas, and we went briskly in.

I got from Digges[20] a list of the best houses[21] on the road, and also a direction to a good inn at London. I therefore made the boy drive me to Mr. Hayward's, at the Black Lion, Water Lane, Fleet Street. The noise, the crowd, the glare of shops and signs agreeably confused me. I was rather more wildly struck than when I first came to London.[22] My companion could not understand my feelings. He considered London just as a place where he was to receive orders from the East India Company.[23] We now parted, with saying that we had agreed well and been happy, and that we should keep up the acquaintance. I then had a bit of dinner, got myself shaved and cleaned, and had my landlord, a civil jolly man, to take a glass of wine with me. I was all in a flutter at having at last got to the place which I was so madly fond of, and being restrained, had formed so many wild schemes to get back to. I had recourse to philosophy,[24] and so rendered myself calm.

I immediately went to my friend Douglas's,[25] surgeon in Pall Mall,[26] a kind-hearted, plain, sensible man, where I was cordially received. His wife is a good-humored woman, and is that sort of character which is often met with in England: very lively without much wit. Her fault is speaking too much, which often tires people. He was my great adviser as to everything; and in the meantime insisted that I should have a bed in his house till I got a lodging to my mind. I agreed to come there next day. I went to Covent Garden[27]—*Every Man in His Humor.*[28] Woodward played Bobadil[29] finely. He entertained me much. It was fine after the fatigues of my journey to find myself snug in a theatre, my body warm and my mind elegantly amused. I went to my inn, had some negus, and went comfortably to bed.

MONDAY 16 MAY . . . I drank tea at Davies's in Russell Street, and about seven came in the great Mr. Samuel Johnson, whom I have so long wished to see. Mr. Davies introduced me to him. As I knew his mortal antipathy at the Scotch, I cried to Davies, "Don't tell where I come from." However, he said, "From Scotland." "Mr. Johnson," said I, "indeed I come from Scotland, but I cannot help it." "Sir," replied he, "that, I find, is what a very great many of your countrymen cannot help." Mr. Johnson is a man of a most dreadful appearance. He is a very big man, is troubled with sore eyes, the palsy,[30] and the king's evil.[31] He is very slovenly in his dress and speaks with a most uncouth voice. Yet his great knowledge and strength of expression command vast respect and render him very excellent company. He has great humor and is a worthy man. But his dogmatical roughness of manners is disagreeable. I shall mark what I remember of his conversation.

He said that people might be taken in once in imagining that an author is greater than other people in private life. "Uncommon parts require uncommon opportunities for their exertion.

"In barbarous society superiority of parts is of real consequence. Great strength or wisdom is of value to an individual. But in more polished times you have people to do everything for money. And then there are a number of other superiorities, such as those of birth and fortune and rank, that

20. DIGGES: an actor whom Boswell had met in Edinburgh.
21. HOUSES: inns.
22. WHEN . . . LONDON: in 1760.
23. EAST INDIA COMPANY: Stewart's employer, one of the chief trading companies of the time.
24. PHILOSOPHY: i.e., sobering thoughts.
25. DOUGLAS: Boswell had met him in 1760.
26. PALL MALL: a street in West London.
27. COVENT GARDEN: London theater.

28. EVERY MAN IN HIS HUMOR: a comedy by Ben Jonson.
29. BOBADIL: a boastful soldier, actually a coward.
30. PALSY: in this context, "occasional facial twitches."
31. KING'S EVIL: scrofula; Boswell is referring to the scars from the disease.

dissipate men's attention and leave superiority of parts no extraordinary share of respect. And this is wisely ordered by Providence, to preserve a mediocrity."

*   *   *   *   *

"The notion of liberty amuses the people of England and helps to keep off the *tedium vitae*. When a butcher says that he is in distress for his country, he has no uneasy feeling."

*   *   *   *   *

I was sorry to leave him there at ten, when I had engaged to be at Dr. Pringle's,[32] with whom I had a serious conversation much to my mind."

*   *   *   *   *

TUESDAY 24 MAY. . . . I went and waited upon Mr. Samuel Johnson, who received me very courteously. He has chambers in the Inner Temple, where he lives in literary state, very solemn and very slovenly. He had some people with him, and when they left him, I rose too. But he cried, "No, don't go away." "Sir," said I, "I am afraid that I intrude upon you. It is benevolent to allow me to sit and hear you." He was

_____
32. DR. PRINGLE: well-known London scientist.

pleased with this compliment, which I sincerely paid him, and he said he was obliged to any man who visited him. I was proud to sit in such company.

He said that mankind had a great aversion at intellectual employment. But even supposing knowledge easily attained, most people were equally content to be ignorant.

"Moral good depends on the motive from which we act. If I fling half a crown at a begger with intention to break his head, and he picks it up and buys victuals with it, the physical effect is good; but with respect to me, the action is very wrong. In the same way, religious services, if not performed with an intention to please God, avail us nothing. As our Savior saith of people who perform them from other motives, 'Verily they have their reward.' "

*   *   *   *   *

I begged that he would favor me with his company at my lodgings some evening. He promised he would. I then left him, and he shook me cordially by the hand. Upon my word, I am very fortunate. I shall cultivate this acquaintance.

*   *   *   *   *

I

1. The appeal of a diary to a reader lies in the feeling that he is getting the truth, not a fanciful cover-up for what really happened. Point out some details that give convincing evidence that Boswell is an honest reporter, and a good one. What do his reasons for keeping a diary show about him?

2. Compare Boswell with his traveling companion. What do his reactions to Stewart reveal about his own character? What does Stewart probably do when Boswell excuses himself just as the journey starts? What is Stewart's reaction to being in London?

3. This is only a small part of the *Journal*, but we get a surprisingly full introduction to the kind of person Boswell is. What do the following comments show?

a. "I shall be on my guard to mention nothing that can do harm."

b. "I parted with my brother Davy, leaving him my best advices to be diligent at his business as a banker and to make rich and be happy."

c. "As I passed the Cross, the cadies and the chairmen bowed and seemed to say, 'God prosper long our noble Boswell.' "

d. "I was all in a flutter at having at last got to the place which I was so madly fond of, and being restrained, had formed so many wild schemes to get back to. I had recourse to philosophy, and so rendered myself calm."

4. English grammar and English usage were far more fluid and unsettled in Boswell's time than they became later. Find several usages that do not conform to our present standards of good usage.

II

1. The entries for May 16 and May 24, 1763, of the *London Journal* and the selections reproduced here from the *Life of Johnson* both deal with the same period in Boswell's life.

In the latter he has taken the raw material of the *Journal* and has fashioned it, much later, into a biography. How has he added to his comments in the *Journal*? What has he deleted and why? What differences do you see between the Boswell in the *Life* and the young man in the *London Journal* excerpts?

TO THE RIGHT HONORABLE THE EARL OF CHESTERFIELD   *[1755]*

Samuel Johnson

In the selection from the *Life of Johnson* we saw some sides of Johnson's character as Boswell chose to present them: the outspokenness, the forcefulness, the high spirits, the somewhat gruff friendliness. In the following letter of Johnson's to Lord Chesterfield we see the man directly, not through Boswell's eyes. We get a clear idea of the power of mind and pen that made Johnson the most respected literary man of his time; we also get a reinforcing of some of the impressions Boswell has given us.

In 1747 Johnson had published a *Plan* for a dictionary of the English language, a very ambitious undertaking, since there was little prior work of the kind to build on. He indicated that he intended to dedicate the work to Lord Chesterfield, a wealthy and influential nobleman, in what he later admitted to Boswell was a not very sincere attempt to get Chesterfield's support as a patron. Chesterfield paid little attention to the offhand appeal, but when the *Dictionary* finally was ready for publication seven years later, he made two references to it in a literary periodical, indicating in the course of them that he expected the *Dictionary* to be dedicated to him. Johnson's response shows what he thought of Chesterfield's belated recognition of his seven years of hard and unrewarded work.

February 7, 1755

MY LORD,

I have been lately informed by the proprietor of *The World*[1] that two papers, in which my dictionary is recommended to the public, were written by your lordship. To be so distinguished is an honor which, being very little accustomed to favors from the great, I know not well how to receive, or in what terms to acknowledge.

When, upon some slight encouragement, I first visited your lordship, I was overpowered, like the rest of mankind, by the enchantment of your address, and could not forbear to wish that I might boast myself *Le vainqueur du vainqueur de la terre*[2]— that I might obtain that regard for which I saw the world contending—but I found my attendance so little encouraged that neither pride nor modesty would suffer[3] me to continue it. When I had once addressed your lordship in public, I had exhausted all the

---

1. THE WORLD: a literary periodical (1753-56).

2. LE VAINQUEUR . . . TERRE: "The conqueror of the conqueror of the earth" (Boileau).

3. SUFFER: permit.

art of pleasing which a retired[4] and un-courtly scholar can possess. I had done all that I could; and no man is well pleased to have his all neglected, be it ever so little.

Seven years, my lord, have now passed since I waited in your outward rooms or was repulsed from your door, during which time I have been pushing on my work through difficulties of which it is useless to complain, and have brought it at last to the verge of publication, without one act of assistance, one word of encouragement, or one smile of favor. Such treatment I did not expect, for I had never had a patron before.

The shepherd in Virgil grew at last acquainted with love, and found him a native of the rocks.[5]

Is not a patron, my lord, one who looks with unconcern upon a man struggling for life in the water and when he has reached

———
4. RETIRED: secluded.
5. THE SHEPHERD . . . ROCKS: Johnson alludes to the grieving shepherd in Virgil's *Eclogue* VIII, 43ff, who, because his loved one is indifferent to him, refers to Love as hard-hearted.

ground encumbers him with help? The notice which you have been pleased to take of my labors, had it been early, had been kind; but it has been delayed till I am indifferent and cannot enjoy it; till I am solitary[6] and cannot impart it; till I am known[7] and do not want it. I hope it is no very cynical asperity not to confess obligations where no benefit has been received, or to be unwilling that the public should consider me as owing that to a patron which Providence has enabled me to do for myself.

Having carried on my work thus far with so little obligation to any favorer of learning, I shall not be disappointed though I should conclude it, if less be possible, with less; for I have been long wakened from that dream of hope in which I once boasted myself with so much exaltation,

My lord,
Your lordship's most humble,
Most obedient servant,
SAM: JOHNSON.

———
6. SOLITARY: Johnson's wife had died in 1752.
7. KNOWN: His reputation was well-established by the time the *Dictionary* was published.

I

1. Whether Johnson should rightly have expected more than he received is not important for us. He sincerely felt that the Chesterfield articles implied an obligation he had no reason to feel, and he says so in unmistakable terms. The fierce pride of the man comes through sharply. What is the effect of saying at the outset, "To be so distinguished is an honor . . . I know not well how to receive, or in what terms to acknowledge"? How well does he know how to receive and acknowledge such an *honor?*

2. He puts on a humbleness he doesn't have by using such words as "overpowered," "retired and uncourtly scholar," "be it ever so little," and "repulsed." How can the reader be sure that Johnson means just the opposite of what these words seem to mean? Point out other ironic comments.

II

1. Suppose yourself Lord Chesterfield and reply to Johnson's letter. Remember that Chesterfield was an important literary person in his own right—and a nobleman; remember also that the unpleasantness about the dedication wasn't necessarily his fault. Actually, Chesterfield had high praise for the skill with which the letter was written, although there is no record of any written acknowledgment.

PORTRAIT OF ATTICUS

from Epistle to Dr. Arbuthnot [*1734*]

Alexander Pope

This portrait is from Pope's "Epistle to Dr. Arbuthnot," a public letter in verse written by Pope to defend himself against the attacks of some of his contemporaries. Atticus is Pope's name in the poem for Joseph Addison, one of the major writers of the early eighteenth century and author of the *Spectator* papers, which appear next in this book.

As a skillful dissection of a talented but spineless fence-straddler this acid sketch has few equals in English literature. How much the portrait is fair to Addison matters little; much more important for us is the character that takes on life quite outside the Addison-Pope quarrel. We all have something of Atticus in us and something of the spirit that despises him.

> Peace to all such! but were there One whose fires
> True Genius kindles, and fair Fame inspires;
> Blest with each talent and art to please,
> And born to write, converse, and live with ease:
> Should such a man, too fond to rule alone, 5
> Bear, like the Turk, no brother near the throne,
> View him with scornful, yet with jealous eyes,
> And hate for arts that caused himself to rise;
> Damn with faint praise, assent with civil leer,
> And without sneering, teach the rest to sneer; 10
> Willing to wound, and yet afraid to strike,
> Just hint a fault, and hesitate dislike;
> Alike reserved to blame, or to commend,
> A timorous foe, and a suspicious friend;
> Dreading even fools, by Flatterers besieged, 15
> And so obliging, that he ne'er obliged;
> Like Cato, give his little Senate laws,
> And sit attentive to his own applause;
> While Wits and Templars every sentence raise,
> And wonder with a foolish face of praise:— 20
> Who but must laugh, if such a man there be?
> Who would not weep, if Atticus were he?

1. PEACE . . . SUCH: refers to a number of minor writers Pope has been attacking in the poem before he gets to Atticus.
6. NO . . . THRONE: Sultans were reputed to have kinsmen murdered so that they might not try to usurp the throne.
17. CATO: reference to Addison's play by that name; in it the hero leaves Rome in protest over Caesar's tyranny and goes to the little republic of Utica in Africa.
19. TEMPLARS: law students, who often dabbled in literature; so-called because they had chambers in the Inner or Middle Temple in London. RAISE: exalt.
22. ATTICUS: a famous Roman scholar of the first century B.C.

I

1. This excerpt is not easy to read, but the final pleasure of insight makes it worth the effort to understand.

    a. Notice that the piece is all one sentence; it starts with two "if" (or "suppose") ideas that carry through to the last two lines. What are they?

    b. With the overall pattern in mind, try to get the rest of the grammar straight. What words (some verbs, some adjectives) modify "such a man"(5)? What does "him" in line 1 refer to? What does "himself" in line 8 refer to? Who are "the rest"(10)? Who are "his little Senate"(17)? What does it mean to say that he sits "attentive to his own applause"(18)?

With these considerations clear, read the selection over several times out loud, trying to fit your reading to your grasp of the structure.

2. The speaker in the first four lines admits the virtues of Atticus in glowing terms: "One whose fires/True Genius kindles" and "Blest with each talent and each art to please." Why does he admit the man's virtues if he is going to attack him? What is the effect of the double question at the end? Why does he wait until the end to identify the person he is referring to? Why *laugh* in one line and *weep* in the next? In what sense is *weep* meant?

3. The condemnation is built on a series of seeming contradictions: for instance, Atticus *damns* with *praise,* and as a *friend* he is *suspicious.* Point out others. Try to indicate how each of these contradictions makes sense; i.e., how can one *damn* with *praise?* Try to indicate also how these contradictions taken collectively embody the character of the man they describe.

SUNDAY WITH SIR ROGER

The Spectator, No. 112: Monday, July 9, 1711

Joseph Addison

Like Samuel Pickwick, Sir Roger de Coverley, a kind-hearted, harmlessly eccentric country squire, is one of the most engaging characters in English literature. While Sir Roger's England has long since disappeared, happily the old·squire's candor and good will find their counterparts in today's world.

The Spectator, from which this sketch of Sir Roger is taken, was a periodical published daily for a short year-and-a-half in 1711-1712. Remarkably, it has not suffered the quiet slip into oblivion that is the lot of most periodicals. It remains a landmark in English literature for several reasons. Together with its predecessor, *The Tatler,* it marked the beginnings of the periodical essay, the purpose of which was to amuse and instruct. Each issue (a single sheet printed on both sides in double columns) dealt with a single subject in a serious, yet essentially light-hearted way. The authors of most of the numbers were Joseph Addison and Richard Steele, who were concerned with pointing out the shortcomings in the manners and morals of the day for the express purpose of bringing about improvement. Their principal target was the growing middle class—merchants, tradesmen, small landowners, and the like—with whom they were in complete sympathy, and for whom they wished to provide guidance toward refinement of manners and taste. Their technique was to prod but not offend, to use kid gloves but avoid brass knuckles. They also made it a point to stay away from controversial topics such as politics.

They proposed at the outset to build their essays around imaginary members of the Spectator Club, made up of individuals from the various social groups they were eager to improve. Although they paid little attention to this original plan, one of the Club members, Sir Roger de Coverley, appears in some thirty of the essays. Most of these depict the life of the English countryside as the English countryman liked to imagine it was, but as it was only rarely in fact.

In the following essay we meet Sir Roger on a Sunday at church among his tenants. Through the deliberate fairytale relationship between the squire and his flock Addison has his fun at the squire's expense, but there is no suggestion of severe ridicule.

Ἀθανάτους μὲν πρῶτα θεούς, νόμῳ ὡς διάκειται,
Τίμα—
    —PYTHAGORAS, ["*Golden Verses,*" 1-2].

First, in obedience to thy country's rites,
Worship the immortal gods.
    —Pythagoras ("Golden Verses," 1-2)

I am always very well pleased with a country Sunday, and think, if keeping holy the seventh day were only a human institution, it would be the best method that could have been thought of for the polishing and civilizing of mankind. It is certain the country people would soon degenerate into a kind of savages and barbarians were there not such frequent returns of a stated time in which the whole village meet together with their best faces, and in their cleanliest habits, to converse with one another upon indifferent[1] subjects, hear their duties explained to them, and join together in adoration of the Supreme Being. Sunday clears away the rust of the whole week, not only as it refreshes in their minds the notions of religion, but as it puts both the sexes upon appearing in their most agreeable forms, and exerting all such qualities as are apt to give them a figure in the eye of the village. A country fellow distinguishes himself as much in the churchyard as a citizen does upon the 'Change,[2] the whole parish politics being generally discussed in that place either after sermon or before the bell rings.

My friend Sir Roger, being a good churchman, has beautified the inside of his church with several texts[3] of his own choosing; he had likewise given a handsome pulpit-cloth, and railed in the communion-table at his own expense. He has often told me that, at his coming to his estate,[4] he found his parishioners very irregular; and that, in order to make them kneel and join in the responses, he gave every one of them a hassock and a common-prayer book, and at the same time employed an itinerant singing-master, who goes about the country for that purpose, to instruct them rightly in the tunes of the Psalms; upon which they now very much value themselves, and indeed outdo most of the country churches that I have ever heard.

As Sir Roger is landlord to the whole congregation, he keeps them in very good order, and will suffer nobody to sleep in it besides himself; for, if by chance he has been surprised[5] into a short nap at sermon, upon recovering out of it he stands up and looks about him, and, if he sees anybody else nodding, either wakes them himself, or sends his servant to them. Several other of the old knight's particularities[6] break out upon these occasions; sometimes he will be lengthening out a verse in the Singing-Psalms half a minute after the rest of the congregation have done with it; sometimes, when he is pleased with the matter of his devotion, he pronounces "Amen" three or four times to the same prayer; and sometimes stands up when everybody else is upon their knees, to count the congregation, or see if any of the tenants are missing.

I was yesterday very much surprised to

---

1. INDIFFERENT: unimportant to either party.
2. 'CHANGE: i.e., the London Exchange, center of commerce in Addison's day.
3. TEXTS: verses of Scripture.

4. COMING . . . ESTATE: i.e., when he first inherited his landed property.
5. SURPRISED: driven.
6. PARTICULARITIES: peculiarities.

hear my old friend, in the midst of the service, calling out to one John Matthews to mind what he was about, and not disturb the congregation. This John Matthews, it seems, is remarkable for being an idle fellow, and at that time was kicking his heels for his diversion. This authority of the knight, though exerted in that odd manner which accompanies him in all circumstances of life, has a very good effect upon the parish, who are not polite[7] enough to see anything ridiculous in his behavior; besides that[8] the general good sense and worthiness of his character makes his friends observe these little singularities as foils that rather set off than blemish his good qualities.

As soon as the sermon is finished, nobody presumes to stir till Sir Roger is gone out of the church. The knight walks down from his seat in the chancel between a double row of his tenants, that stand bowing to him on each side, and every now and then inquires how such an one's wife, or mother, or son, or father do, whom he does not see at church—which is understood as a secret reprimand to the person that is absent.

The chaplain has often told me that, upon a catechizing day, when Sir Roger has been pleased with a boy that answers well, he has ordered a Bible to be given him next day for his encouragement, and sometimes accompanies it with a flitch of bacon to his mother. Sir Roger has likewise added five pounds a year to the clerk's place;[9] and, that he may encourage the young fellows to make themselves perfect in the church service, has promised, upon the death of the present incumbent, who is very old, to bestow it according to merit.

The fair understanding between Sir Roger and his chaplain, and their mutual concurrence in doing good, is the most remarkable because the very next village is famous for the differences and contentions that rise between the parson and the squire, who live in a perpetual state of war. The parson is always preaching at the squire, and the squire, to be revenged on the parson, never comes to church. The squire has made all his tenants atheists and tithe-stealers,[10] while the parson instructs them every Sunday in the dignity of his order, and insinuates to them in almost every sermon that he is a better man than his patron. In short, matters are come to such an extremity that the squire has not said his prayers either in public or in private this half year; and that the parson threatens him, if he does not mend his manners, to pray for him in the face of the whole congregation.

Feuds of this nature, though too frequent in the country, are very fatal to the ordinary people, who are so used to be dazzled with riches that they pay as much deference to the understanding of a man of an estate as of a man of learning; and are very hardly brought to regard any truth, how important soever it may be, that is preached to them, when they know there are several men of five hundred a year[11] who do not believe it.

---

7. POLITE: i.e., polished, refined.
8. BESIDES THAT: i.e., besides the fact that.
9. CLERK'S PLACE: i.e., the position of clerk of the parish.

10. TITHE-STEALERS: those who fail to pay their tithes.
11. FIVE HUNDRED A YEAR: £500—in Addison's day a very comfortable income.

I

1. Why does the Spectator think that church-going on Sunday is a good thing in a country village? What is his attitude toward the *ordinary people?* Why does he think that squires and parsons ought to get along the way Sir Roger and his parson get along?

2. Explain what the Spectator means in saying that Sir Roger's friends look on his "little singularities as foils that rather set off than blemish his good qualities." What are his *good qualities?* What are his *singularities?* Show that the speaker is in agreement with this attitude, and that there is no malice in such humorous comments as "and will suffer nobody to sleep in it besides himself."

3. Explain the relationship of the last paragraph to the rest of the essay. How has the moralizing at the end been prepared for?

II

1. People who are eccentric can either be annoying or rather pleasant to live with. Try to determine what it is that makes the difference. In this connection compare Sir Roger with the younger Gessler brother in "Quality" or Peter Magnus in *Pickwick Papers*. Also consider people you know personally.

WILL WIMBLE

The Spectator, No. 108: Wednesday, July 4, 1711

Joseph Addison

Sir Roger's friend, Will Wimble, visits the squire in this issue of *The Spectator,* and Addison uses him for further instruction on what is wrong with the social situation of the day.

Will is a "younger brother" in a titled family, which meant in those days that he had few of the rights and privileges that went with being the first son and heir. To go into some useful business was, for such men, just "not done." Instead, a career in the church or in the armed services, or else a kind of enforced leisure, was all that was open to them.

Will is an amiable soul, a kind of jack-of-all-skills, whose talents, nevertheless, are of necessity wasted on trivial pursuits. We are not encumbered these days by the kind of social conventions that determined Will Wimble's way of life, but we do have our routine jobs and our excessive leisure that make some men lead lives almost as useless as his.

Gratis anhelans, multa agendo nihil agens.
Out of breath to no purpose, and very busy about nothing.

—Phaedrus

As I was yesterday morning walking with Sir Roger before his house, a country fellow brought him a huge fish which, he told him, Mr. William Wimble had caught that very morning; and that he presented it, with his service,[1] to him, and intended to come and dine with him. At the same time he delivered a letter, which my friend read to me as soon as the messenger left him.

Sir Roger,

I desire you to accept of a jack,[2] which is the best I have caught this season. I intend to come and stay with you a week, and see how the perch bite in the Black River. I observed, with some concern, the last time I saw you upon the bowling-green, that your whip wanted a lash to it: I will bring half a dozen with me that I twisted last week, which I hope will serve you all the time you are in the country. I have not been out of the saddle for six days last past,[3] having been at Eton[4] with Sir John's eldest son. He takes to his learning hugely.

I am,
Sir,
Your humble servant,
Will Wimble.

This extraordinary letter, and message that accompanied it, made me very curious to know the character and quality of the

---

1. SERVICE: profession of respect.
2. JACK: pike.

3. SIX DAYS LAST PAST: the last six days.
4. ETON: famous boys' school in Eton, Buckinghamshire.

gentlemen who sent them; which I found to be as follows: Will Wimble is younger brother to a baronet, and descended of the ancient family of the Wimbles. He is now between forty and fifty; but being bred to no business and born to no estate, he generally lives with his elder brother as superintendent of his game. He hunts a pack of dogs better than any man in the country, and is very famous for finding out a hare. He is extremely well versed in all the little handicrafts of an idle man: he makes a May-fly[5] to a miracle; and furnishes the whole country with angle-rods. As he is a good-natured officious[6] fellow, and very much esteemed upon account of his family, he is a welcome guest at every house, and keeps up a good correspondence among all the gentlemen about him. He carries a tulip-root[7] in his pocket from one to another, or exchanges a puppy between a couple of friends that live perhaps in the opposite sides of the county. Will is a particular favorite of all the young heirs, whom he frequently obliges with a net that he has weaved, or a setting-dog[8] that he has *made*[9] himself: he now and then presents a pair of garters of his own knitting to their mothers or sisters; and raises a great deal of mirth among them, by inquiring as often as he meets them *how they wear?* These gentlemanlike manufactures and obliging little humors, make Will the darling of the country.

Sir Roger was proceeding in the character of him, when we saw him make up to[10] us, with two or three hazel-twigs in his hand that he had cut in Sir Roger's woods, as he came through them, in his way to the house. I was very much pleased to observe on one side the hearty and sincere welcome with which Sir Roger received him, and on the other the secret joy which his guest discovered at

sight of the good old knight. After the first salutes were over, Will desired Sir Roger to lend him one of his servants to carry a set of shuttlecocks he had with him in a little box to a lady that lived about a mile off, to whom it seems he had promised such a present for above this half year. Sir Roger's back was no sooner turned, but honest Will began to tell me of a large cock pheasant that he had sprung in one of the neighboring woods, with two or three other adventures of the same nature. Odd and uncommon characters are the game that I look for, and most delight in; for which reason I was as much pleased with the novelty of the person that talked to me, as he could be for his life with the springing of a pheasant, and therefore listened to him with more than ordinary attention.

In the midst of his discourse the bell rung to dinner, where the gentleman I have been speaking of had the pleasure of seeing the huge jack, he had caught, served up for the first dish in a most sumptuous manner. Upon our sitting down to it he gave us a long account how he had hooked it, played with it, foiled it, and at length drew it out upon the bank, with several other particulars that lasted all the first course. A dish of wild-fowl that came afterwards furnished conversation for the rest of the dinner, which concluded with a late invention of Will's for improving the quail-pipe.[11]

Upon withdrawing into my room after dinner, I was secretly touched with compassion towards the honest gentleman that had dined with us; and could not but consider with a great deal of concern, how so good an heart and such busy hands were wholly employed in trifles; that so much humanity should be so little beneficial to others, and so much industry so little advantageous to himself. The same temper of mind and application to affairs might have recommended him to the public esteem, and have raised his fortune in another station of

5. MAY-FLY: fishing lure imitating the May fly.
6. OFFICIOUS: kind.
7. TULIP-ROOT: i.e., tulip bulb (the tulip being at this time a new and much coveted flower).
8. SETTING-DOG: setter.
9. MADE: trained.
10. MAKE UP TO: i.e., come toward.

11. QUAIL-PIPE: hunting lure imitating the quail's note.

life. What good to his country or himself might not a trader or merchant have done with such useful though ordinary qualifications?

Will Wimble's is the case of many a younger brother of a great family, who had rather see their children starve like gentlemen, than thrive in a trade or profession that is beneath their quality. This humor fills several parts of Europe with pride and beggary. It is the happiness[12] of a trading nation, like ours, that the younger sons, though uncapable of any liberal art or profession, may be placed in such a way of life, as may perhaps enable them to vie with the best of their family: accordingly we find several citizens that were launched into the world with narrow fortunes, rising by an honest industry to greater estates than those of their elder brothers. It is not improbable but Will was formerly tried at divinity, law, or physic;[13] and that finding his genius did not lie that way, his parents gave him up at length to his own inventions: but certainly, however improper he might have been for studies of a higher nature, he was perfectly

---

12. HAPPINESS: good fortune.
13. PHYSIC: medicine.

well turned for the occupations of trade and commerce. As I think this is a point which cannot be too much inculcated, I shall desire my reader to compare what I have here written with what I have said in my twenty-first speculation.[14]

---

14. TWENTY-FIRST SPECULATION: In *The Spectator*, No. 21, Addison complains that "the three great professions of divinity, law, and physic . . . are . . . over-burdened with practitioners, and filled with multitudes of ingenious gentlemen that starve one another." He suggests that many of them ought to go into trade.

I

1. What talents does Will Wimble have? Why does the Spectator call him an "idle man" when he seems so busy? What is the Spectator's definition of "idle"?

2. How does the Spectator reveal his sympathy for Will Wimble even though he has little respect for his accomplishments and activities?

II

1. Write a character sketch of someone you know with whose way of life you may not be in sympathy but whose personal qualities you admire or respect.

A LADY'S DIARY

The Spectator No. 323: Tuesday, March 11, 1712

Joseph Addison

Will Wimble's pursuits may have been trivial, but at least they had the virtue of a certain usefulness to his friends. The lady in *The Spectator,* No. 323, is so devoted to futility that she is incapable of making obvious judgments. She kept a five-day diary of her aimless and silly pursuits and then commented: "I find that I am at a loss to know whether I pass my time well or ill."

Will Wimble's was one kind of enforced idleness; Clarinda's is another. With the increase in general wealth through trading and manufacturing in the eighteenth century came a new leisure class: women in families of reasonable means who literally had nothing to do with their time. As much as we may be prompted to smile at Clarinda's inanity, the smile should be tempered by the thought that hers was not an isolated case in Addison's time and that the world still has its share of Clarindas.

Modo vir, modo femina.
Sometimes a man, sometimes a woman.
—Virgil, (*Aeneid,* vi 448, misquoted)

The Journal with which I presented my reader on Tuesday last,[1] has brought me in several letters with accounts of many private lives cast into that form. I have the *Rake's Journal,* the *Sot's Journal,* the *Whoremaster's Journal,* and among several others a very curious piece, entitled, *The Journal of a Mohock.*[2] By these instances I find that the intention of my last Tuesday's paper has been mistaken by many of my readers. I did not design so much to expose vice as idleness, and aimed at those persons who pass away their time rather in trifles and impertinence,[3] than in crimes and immoralities. Offenses of this later kind are not to be dallied with, or treated in so ludicrous a manner. In short, my journal only holds up folly to the light, and shows the disagreeableness of such actions as are indifferent in themselves, and blameable only as they proceed from creatures endowed with reason.

My following correspondent, who calls herself Clarinda, is such a journalist as I require: she seems by her letter to be placed in a modish state of indifference between vice and virtue, and to be susceptible of either, were there proper pains taken with her. Had her journal been filled with gallantries, or such occurrences as had shown her wholly divested of her natural innocence, notwithstanding it might have been more pleasing to the generality of readers, I should not have published it; but as it is only the picture of a life filled with a fashionable kind of gaiety and laziness, I shall set down five days of it, as I have received it from the hand of my correspondent.

---

1. JOURNAL . . . TUESDAY LAST: He had suggested that his readers keep diaries.
2. MOHOCK: one of a band of young hoodlums who roamed the streets of London in the early eighteenth century.
3. IMPERTINENCE: irrelevance.

Dear Mr. Spectator,

You having set your readers an exercise in one of your last week's papers, I have performed mine according to your orders, and herewith send it you enclosed. You must know, Mr. Spectator, that I am a maiden lady of a good fortune, who have had several matches offered me for these ten years last past, and have at present warm applications made to me by a very pretty[4] fellow. As I am at my own disposal,[5] I come up to town every winter, and pass my time in it after the manner you will find in the following journal, which I began to write upon the very day after your *Spectator* upon that subject.

TUESDAY *night.* Could not go to sleep till one in the morning for thinking of my journal.

WEDNESDAY. *From Eight till Ten.* Drank two dishes of chocolate in bed, and fell asleep after them.

From Ten to Eleven. Eat[6] a slice of bread and butter, drank a dish of bohea,[7] read the *Spectator.*

From Eleven to One. At my toilette, tried a new head.[8] Gave orders for Veny[9] to be combed and washed. Mem. I look best in blue.

From One till half an hour after Two. Drove to the 'Change. Cheapened[10] a couple of fans.

Till Four. At dinner. Mem. Mr. Froth passed by in his new liveries.

From Four to Six. Dressed, paid a visit to old Lady Blithe and her sister, having before heard they were gone out of town that day.

From Six to Eleven. At basset.[11] Mem. Never set again upon the ace of diamonds.

---

4. PRETTY: appealing.
5. AT . . . DISPOSAL: i.e., not in the care of any guardian.
6. EAT: pronounced *et;* past tense.
7. BOHEA: tea.
8. HEAD: hair-dress.
9. VENY: her dog.
10. CHEAPENED: bargained for.
11. BASSET: card game.

THURSDAY. *From Eleven at night to Eight in the morning.* Dreamed that I punted[12] to Mr. Froth.

From Eight to Ten. Chocolate. Read two acts in *Aurengzebe*[13] a-bed.

From Ten to Eleven. Tea-table. Sent to borrow Lady Faddle's Cupid for Veny. Read the play-bills. Received a letter from Mr. Froth. Mem. Locked it up in my strong box.

Rest of the morning. Fontagne, the tire-woman,[14] her account of my Lady Blithe's wash.[15] Broke a tooth in my little tortoise-shell comb. Sent Frank to know how my Lady Hectic rested after her monkey's leaping out a window. Looked pale. Fontagne tells me my glass is not true. Dressed by Three.

From Three to Four. Dinner cold before I sat down.

From Four to Eleven. Saw company. Mr. Froth's opinion of Milton. His account of the Mohocks. His fancy for a pin-cushion. Picture in the lid of his snuffbox. Old Lady Faddle promises me her woman to cut my hair. Lost five guineas at crimp.[16]

Twelve o'clock at night. Went to bed.

FRIDAY. *Eight in the morning.* A-bed. Read over all Mr. Froth's letters. Cupid and Veny.

Ten o'clock. Stayed within all day, not at home.

From Ten to Twelve. In conference with my mantua-maker.[17] Sorted[81] a suit of ribands. Broke my blue china cup.

From Twelve to One. Shut myself up in my chamber, practiced Lady Betty Modely's skuttle.[19]

One in the afternoon. Called for my flowered handkerchief. Worked half a violet leaf in it. Eyes ached and head out of order. Threw by my work, and read over the remaining part of *Aurengzebe*.

From Three to Four. Dined.

From Four to Twelve. Changed my mind, dressed, went abroad, and played at crimp till midnight. Found Mrs. Spitely at home. Conversation: Mrs. Brilliant's necklace false stones. Old Lady Loveday going to be married to a young fellow that is not worth a groat.[20] Miss Prue gone into the country. Tom Townley has red hair. Mem. Mrs. Spitely whispered in my ear that she had something to tell me about Mr. Froth. I am sure it is not true.

Between Twelve and One. Dreamed that Mr. Froth lay at my feet, and called me Indamora.[21]

SATURDAY. Rose at eight o'clock in the morning. Sat down to my toilette.

From Eight to Nine. Shifted a patch[22] for half an hour before I could determine it. Fixed it above my left eyebrow.

From Nine to Twelve. Drank my tea, and dressed.

From Twelve to Two. At chapel. A great deal of good company. Mem. The third air in the new opera. Lady Blithe dressed frightfully.

From Three to Four. Dined. Miss Kitty called upon me to go to the opera, before I was risen from table.

From Dinner to Six. Drank tea. Turned off[23] a footman for being rude to Veny.

Six o'clock. Went to the opera. I did not see Mr. Froth till the beginning of the second act. Mr. Froth talked to a gentleman in a black wig. Bowed to a lady in the front box. Mr. Froth and his friend clapped Nicolini[24] in the third act. Mr. Froth cried out "Ancora,"[25] Mr. Froth led me to my chair. I think he squeezed my hand.

12. PUNTED TO: wagered against at basset.
13. AURENGZEBE: highly romantic tragedy by Dryden.
14. TIRE-WOMAN: lady's-maid.
15. WASH: lotion.
16. CRIMP: card game.
17. MANTUA-MAKER: dress-maker.
18. SORTED: chose.
19. SKUTTLE: short, hasty steps.
20. GROAT: coin worth fourpence.
21. INDAMORA: heroine of *Aurengzebe*.
22. PATCH: beauty patch.
23. TURNED OFF: fired.
24. NICOLINI: famous operatic tenor in Addison's time.
25. "ANCORA": Italian for "Encore."

Eleven at night. Went to bed. Melancholy dreams. Methought Nicolini said he was Mr. Froth.

SUNDAY. Indisposed.

MONDAY. *Eight o'clock.* Waked by Miss Kitty. *Aurengzebe* lay upon the chair by me. Kitty repeated without book the eight best lines in the play. Went in our mobs[26] to the dumb man[27] according to appointment. Told me that my lover's name began with a G. Mem. The conjurer was within a letter of Mr. Froth's name, etc.

Upon looking back into this my journal, I find that I am at a loss to know whether I pass my time well or ill; and indeed never thought of considering how I did it before I perused your speculation upon that subject. I scarce find a single action in these five days that I can thoroughly approve of, except the working upon the violet-leaf, which I am resolved to finish the first day I am at leisure. As for Mr. Froth and Veny, I did not think they took up so much of my time and thoughts as I find they do upon my journal. The latter of them I will turn off, if you insist upon it; and if Mr. Froth does not bring matters to a conclusion very

---

26. MOBS: mob-caps, large, full caps fitting down over the ears.
27. DUMB MAN: a deaf-and-dumb fortune teller.

suddenly, I will not let my life run away in a dream. Your humble servant,

CLARINDA.

To resume one of the morals of my first paper, and to confirm Clarinda in her good inclinations, I would have her consider what a pretty figure she would make among posterity, were the history of her whole life published like these five days of it. I shall conclude my paper with an epitaph written by an uncertain author[28] on Sir Philip Sidney's sister, a lady who seems to have been of a temper very much different from that of Clarinda. The last thought of it is so very noble, that I dare say my reader will pardon me the quotation.

ON THE COUNTESS DOWAGER OF PEMBROKE

Underneath this marble hearse[29]
Lies the subject of all verse,
Sidney's sister, Pembroke's mother:
Death, ere thou hast killed another,
Fair and learned and good as she,
Time shall throw a dart at thee.[30]

---

28. UNCERTAIN AUTHOR: now known to have been William Browne (1591-1643).
29. HEARSE: a framework over a tomb to which epitaphs are attached.
30. TIME . . . THEE: i.e., Time shall kill thee.

I

1. What kind of *offenses* is the Spectator concerned about in this issue? What kind are not fit for the sort of essays he writes?

2. Point out the details that most effectively show how shallow and insensitive Clarinda is. Does the Spectator intend to reveal her as merely silly or as almost incapable of moral judgment? Explain.

3. What do the last three lines of the epitaph on the Countess Dowager of Pembroke

mean? Why does Addison end the essay with the epitaph?

II

1. Fortunately, Clarinda is an amusing exaggeration, and not an individual at all, but we would be foolish to laugh and let it go at that. Try keeping a diary of what you do over a five-day period (including a weekend) and compare it with Clarinda's record, or, better, with that of any of your friends.

from THE DIARY   *[July 14, 1667]*

Samuel Pepys

Johnson we know as a person largely through Boswell's *Life* and the journals on which it was based. Samuel Pepys is a man whom we know through his own diary, kept through most of the decade of the 1660's. Next to Boswell, Pepys is easily the most widely read of English diarists. The two men have much in common as recorders of daily life: a frankness that spared neither their friends nor themselves, a thoroughness that saw great events and insignificant acts with the same eye for detail, and a sensibleness that makes us feel, no matter where we open and read, that we are in the company of men who respect their strengths and weaknesses.

Pepys was a successful and highly regarded public official, eventually Secretary to the Admiralty, a post roughly equivalent to that held by our Secretary of the Navy. His diary is full of references to important people and events in the London of his time. But for most readers the diary is fascinating as an intimate account of one man's tempestuous married life, his sentimentality, his worries about money and his reputation, and his love of the sights and sounds of a busy, brawling city. You won't discover all sides of Pepys in the one day recorded here, but you will get a taste of his quality. For more, just open the diary at any date and start reading.

(14TH) (LORD'S DAY). Up, and my wife, a little before four, and to make us ready; and by and by Mrs. Turner come to us, by agreement, and she and I stayed talking below, while my wife dressed herself, which vexed me that she was so long about it keeping us till past five o'clock before she was ready. She ready; and, taking some bottles of wine, and beer, and some cold fowl with us into the coach, we took coach and four horses, which I had provided last night, and so away. A very fine day, and so towards Epsom,[1] talking all the way pleasantly. . . . The country very fine, only the way very dusty. We got to Epsom by eight o'clock, to the well; where much company, and there we 'light, and I drank the water: they did not, but do go about and walk a little among the women, but I did drink four pints. . . . Here I met with divers of our town, among others with several of the tradesmen of our office, but did talk but little with them, it growing hot in the sun, and so we took coach again and to the town, to the King's Head,[2] where our coachman carried us, and there had an ill room for us to go into, but the best in the house that was not taken up. Here we called for drink, and bespoke dinner; and hear that my Lord Buckhurst and Nelly[3] are lodged at the next house, and Sir Charles Sedley with them: and keep a merry house. Poor girl! I pity her; but more the loss of her at the King's house. Here I saw Gilsthrop, Sir W. Batten's clerk that hath been long sick, he looks like a dying man, with a consumption got, as is believed, by the pox, but God knows that the man is in a sad condition, though he finds himself much better since his coming thither, he says. W. Hewer rode with us, and I left him and the women, and myself walked to church,

1. EPSOM: in Surrey, famous for its horse-racing, and also for its waters, from which Epsom salts were made.

2. KING'S HEAD: i.e., an inn with the King's Head for a sign.
3. NELLY: Nell Gwynn, actress, and later mistress to Charles II.

where few people, contrary to what I expected, and none I knew, but all the Houblons, brothers, and them after sermon I did salute,[4] and walk with towards my inn, which was in[5] their way to their lodgings. They come last night to see their elder brother, who stays here at the waters, and away tomorrow. James did tell me that I was the only happy man of the Navy, of whom, he says, during all this freedom the people have taken of speaking treason, he hath not heard one bad word of me, which is a great joy to me; for I hear the same of others, but do know that I have deserved as well as most. We parted to meet anon,[6] and I to my women into a better room, which the people of the house borrowed for us, and there to dinner, a good dinner, and were merry, and Pendleton come to us, who happened to be in the house, and there talked and were merry.

After dinner, he gone, we all lay down after dinner (the day being wonderful[7] hot) to sleep, and each of us took a good nap, and then rose. . . . and we took coach and to take the air, there being a fine breeze abroad; and I went and carried them to the well, and there filled some bottles of water to carry home with me; and there talked with the two women that farm the well, at £12 per annum,[8] of the lord of the manor. . . . Here W. Hewer's horse broke loose, and we had the sport to see him taken again. Then I carried them to see my cousin Pepys's house, and 'light, and walked round about it, and they like it, as indeed it deserves, very well, and is a pretty place; and then I walked them to the wood hard by,[9] and there got them in the thickets till they had lost themselves, and I could not find the way into any of the walks in the wood, which indeed are very

pleasant, if I could have found them. At last got out of the wood again; and I, by leaping down the little bank, coming out of the wood, did sprain my right foot, which brought me great present pain, but presently, with walking, it went away for the present, and so the women and W. Hewer and I walked upon the Downs,[10] where a flock of sheep was; and the most pleasant and innocent sight that ever I saw in my life—we find a shepherd and his little boy reading, far from any houses or sight of people, the Bible to him; so I made the boy read to me, which he did, with the forced tone that children do usually read, that was mighty pretty, and then I did give him something, and went to the father, and talked with him; and I find he had been a servant in my cousin Pepys's house, and told me what was become of their old servants. He did content himself mightily in my liking his boy's reading, and did bless God for him, the most like one of the old patriarchs that ever I saw in my life, and it brought those thoughts of the old age of the world in my mind for two or three days after. We took notice of his woolen knit stockings of two colors mixed, and of his shoes shod with iron shoes, both at the toe and heels, and with great nails in the soles of his feet, which was mighty pretty: and, taking notice of them, "Why," says the poor man, "the Downs, you see, are full of stones, and we are fain to shoe ourselves thus; and these," says he, "will make the stones fly till they sing before me." I did give the poor man something, for which he was mighty thankful, and I tried to cast stones with his horn crook. He values his dog mightily, that would turn a sheep any way which he would have him, when he goes to fold them: told me there was about eighteen score sheep in his flock, and that he hath four shillings a week the year round for keeping of them: so we posted thence with mighty pleasure in the discourse we had with this poor man, and

---

4. SALUTE: greet.
5. IN: on.
6. ANON: soon.
7. WONDERFUL: exceedingly.
8. FARM . . . ANNUM: i.e., operate it as concessionaires for a rent of £12 annually.
9. HARD BY: near by.

---

10. THE DOWNS: treeless chalk uplands along the southeast coast of England; the North Downs run through Surrey.

Mrs. Turner, in the common fields here, did gather one of the prettiest nosegays that ever I saw in my life.

So to our coach, and through Mr. Minnes's wood, and looked upon Mr. Evelyn's house; and so over the common, and through Epsom town to our inn, in the way stopping a poor woman with her milk-pail, and in one of my gilt tumblers did drink our bellyfuls of milk, better than any cream; and so to our inn, and there had a dish of cream, but it was sour, and so had no pleasure in it; and so paid our reckoning, and took coach, it being about seven at night, and passed and saw the people walking with their wives and children to take the air, and we set out for home, the sun by and by going down, and we in the cool of the evening all the way with much pleasure home, talking and pleasing ourselves with the pleasure of this day's work, Mrs. Turner mightily pleased with my resolution, which, I tell her, is never to keep a country-house, but to keep a coach, and with my wife on the Saturday to go sometimes for a day to this place, and then quit to another place; and there is more variety and as little charge, and no trouble, as there is in a country-house. Anon it grew dark, and as it grew dark we had the pleasure to see several glow-worms, which was mighty pretty, but my foot begins more and more to pain me, which Mrs. Turner, by keeping her warm hand upon it, did much ease; but so that when we come home, which was just at eleven at night, I was not able to walk from the lane's end to my house without being helped, which did trouble me, and therefore to bed presently, but, thanks be to God, found that I had not been missed, nor any business happened in my absence. So to bed, and there had a cerecloth laid to my foot and leg along, but in great pain all night long.

I

1. What kind of a man is Pepys as you see him in this excerpt from his diary? What kinds of things interest him? What is his attitude toward other people? Toward himself? Refer to specific examples to support any generalizations you make.

2. Pepys kept his diary in a private shorthand which wasn't deciphered until 1825. Obviously, he was not writing for others but for himself. Show how his "frankness" and "eye for detail" are revealed in this excerpt.

II

1. Write up a day of your own in the manner of Pepys. Consider the kinds of things he thinks worth recording and the way in which he keeps his personal feelings in the forefront.

HENRY HASTINGS   [1753]

Anthony Ashley Cooper, First Earl of Shaftesbury[1]

Henry Hastings was, like Will Wimble, a "younger brother" in a titled family with no particular responsibilities beyond finding something to do with himself all day long. Unlike Will Wimble, who was a product of Addison's imagination, Henry Hastings was real, a seventeenth century "copy of our nobility in ancient days," as Shaftesbury calls him.

There may be some things in his rough-and-ready way of life that do not appeal to your ideas about manners and morals, but you will find yourself more than a little fascinated by the vitality of the man. He lived for almost one hundred years, and the impression Shaftesbury gives is that every day was crowded with the feverish activity of a busy idle man.

Mr. Hastings, by his quality, being the son, brother and uncle to the Earls of Huntingdon, and his way of living, had the first place amongst us. He was peradventure an original in our age, or rather the copy of our nobility in ancient days in hunting and not warlike times: he was low,[2] very strong and very active, of a reddish flaxen hair, his clothes always green cloth, and never all worth when new five pounds. His house was perfectly of the old fashion, in the midst of a large park well stocked with deer, and near the house rabbits to serve his kitchen, many fish ponds, and great store of wood and timber; a bowling-green in it, long but narrow, full of high ridges, it being never leveled since it was plowed; they used round sand bowls, and it had a banqueting house like a stand,[3] a large one built in a tree. He kept all manner of sport hounds that ran buck, fox, hare, otter, and badger, and hawks long and short winged; he had all sorts of nets for fishing; he had a walk[4] in the New Forest and the manor of Christ Church. This last supplied him with red deer, sea and river fish; and indeed all his neighbors' grounds and royalties[5] were free to him, who bestowed all his time in such sports, but what he borrowed to caress his neighbors' wives and daughters, there being not a woman in all his walks of the degree[6] of a yeoman's wife or under, and under the age of forty, but it was extremely her fault if he were not intimately acquainted with her. This made him very popular, always speaking kindly to the husband, brother, or

father, who was to boot[7] very welcome to his house whenever he came; there he found beef pudding and small[8] beer in great plenty, a house not so neatly kept as to shame him or his dirty shoes, the great hall strewed with marrow bones, full of hawks' perches, hounds, spaniels, and terriers, the upper sides of the hall hung with the fox skins of this and the last year's skinning, here and there a polecat intermixed, guns and keepers' and huntsmen's poles in abundance. The parlor was a large long room, as properly furnished; in a great hearth paved with brick lay some terriers and the choicest hounds and spaniels; seldom but two of the great chairs had litters of young cats in them, which were not to be disturbed, he having always three or four attending him at dinner, and a little white round stick of fourteen inches long lying by his trencher that he might defend such meat as he had no mind to part with to them. The windows, which were very large, served for places to lay his arrows, crossbows, stonebows, and other such like accouterments; the corners of the room full of the best chose[9] hunting and hawking poles; an oyster table at the lower end, which was of constant use twice a day all the year round, for he never failed to eat oysters before dinner and supper through all seasons: the neighboring town of Poole supplied him with them. The upper part of this room had two small tables and a desk, on the one side of which was a church Bible, on the other the Book of Martyrs;[10] on the tables were hawks' hoods, bells, and such like, two or three old green hats with the crowns thrust in so as to hold ten or a dozen eggs, which were of a pheasant kind of poultry he took much care of and fed himself; tables, dice, cards, and boxes were not wanting. In the hole of the desk were store of tobacco pipes that had

---

1. Shaftesbury lived from 1621 to 1683. This extract from his "Fragment of an Autobiography" was first published in *A Collection of Letters from the Original Manuscripts* (compiled by one Leonard Howard) in 1753.
2. LOW: i.e., short.
3. BANQUETING . . . STAND: "banqueting" here refers to small repasts between meals; a "stand" is a raised platform for watching sporting events.
4. WALK: i.e., hunting rights.
5. ROYALTIES: privileges derived originally from a royal grant.
6. DEGREE: rank.

---

7. TO BOOT: besides.
8. SMALL: i.e., weak.
9. CHOSE: i.e., chosen.
10. BOOK OF MARTYRS: John Foxe's account of the persecution of the Protestant reformers (1563).

been used. On one side of this end of the room was the door of a closet, wherein stood the strong beer and the wine, which never came thence but in single glasses, that being the rule of the house exactly observed, for he never exceeded in drink or permitted it. On the other side was a door into an old chapel not used for devotion; the pulpit, as the safest place, was never wanting of a cold chine of beef, pasty of venison, gammon of bacon, or great apple pie with thick crust extremely baked. His table cost him not much, though it was very good to eat at, his sports supplying all but beef and mutton, except Friday, when he had the best sea fish he could get, and was the day that his neighbors of best quality most visited him. He never wanted a London pudding, and always sung it in with "my part lies there-in-a." He drank a glass of wine or two at meals, very often syrup of gilliflower in his sack, and had always a tun glass without feet stood by him holding a pint of small beer, which he often stirred with a great sprig of rosemary. He was well natured, but soon angry, calling his servants bastard and cuckoldy knaves, in one of which he often spoke truth to his own knowledge, and

sometimes in both, though of the same man. He lived to a hundred, never lost his eyesight, but always writ and read without spectacles, and got to horse without help. Until past fourscore he rode to the death of a stag as well as any.

I

1. What does Shaftesbury mean by his opening sentence? In what sense do you suppose Hastings's house was *perfectly of the old fashion?*

2. What details most effectively reveal what manner of man Hastings is?

3. What kind of relationship did he have with his neighbors? Why was he *very popular* with them?

4. What habits did he have that might strike us today as rather crude? How has Shaftesbury made him an appealing person in spite of his manners and morals?

II

1. How does the Spectator's attitude toward Will Wimble differ from Shaftesbury's attitude toward Henry Hastings? Which of the two men do you feel you know better and why? Write a paper comparing them, and try to decide what each writer's purpose was in describing his man.

PORTRAIT OF ZIMRI
from **Absalom and Achitophel**   [*1681*]

John Dryden

Pope's sharply sketched verse portrait of Atticus was one of many such character studies abounding in seventeenth and eighteenth century poems that dealt frankly with the personalities and issues of the day. Another is Dryden's portrait of Zimri from his poem "Absalom and Achitophel," which satirizes the attempt of certain political groups to get the Protestant Duke of Monmouth named as heir to the throne in place of Charles II's Catholic brother, the Duke of York (later James II). Zimri is Dryden's name for George Villiers, Duke of Buckingham, an important political figure favoring Monmouth.

As Atticus has stood as the epitome of the uncommitted fence-straddler, Zimri has come down to us as the perfect embodiment of the inconstant muddler, the man who sticks to nothing for long and lives in perpetual confusion.

In the first rank of these did Zimri stand:
A man so various, that he seemed to be
Not one, but all mankind's epitome:
Stiff in opinions, always in the wrong;
Was everything by starts, and nothing long;
But, in the course of one revolving moon,
Was chemist, fiddler, statesman, and buffoon:
Then all for women, painting, rhyming, drinking,
Besides ten thousand freaks that died in thinking.
Blest madman, who could every hour employ,   10
With something new to wish or to enjoy!
Railing and praising were his usual themes;
And both (to show his judgment) in extremes:
So over-violent, or over-civil,
That every man, with him, was God or Devil.   15
In squandering wealth was his peculiar art:
Nothing went unrewarded, but desert.
Beggared by fools, whom still he found too late:
He had his jest, and they had his estate.
He laughed himself from court; then sought relief   20
By forming parties, but could ne'er be chief:
For, spite of him, the weight of business fell
On Absalom and wise Achitophel:
Thus wicked but in will, of means bereft,
He left not faction, but of that was left.

---

1. THESE: refers to other supporters of Monmouth. ZIMRI: In I Kings 16:8-20, Zimri is the traitor who murdered his master, Elah, King of Israel, and reigned briefly (seven days); he took his own life when the people made Omri king.
18. STILL: always. FOUND: found out.
23. ABSALOM: the Duke of Monmouth, Charles II's illegitimate son. In the Bible Absalom is King David's illegitimate son who conspired against his father. ACHITOPHEL: the Earl of Shaftesbury, chief architect of the plan to put Monmouth on the throne. This is the same Earl of Shaftesbury who wrote the portrait of Henry Hastings. In the Bible Achitophel is counselor to Absalom in his conspiracy.

I

1. What do the following mean:
a. "he seemed to be/Not one, but all mankind's epitome" (2-3)?
b. "Was everything by starts and nothing long" (5)?
c. "Besides ten thousand freaks that died in thinking" (9)?
a. "he seemed to be/Not one, but all man- (17)?
e. "wicked but in will" (24)?
f. "He left not faction, but of that was left." (25)?

2. What impressions is Dryden trying to give in the following phrases: "Stiff in opinions" (4)? the reference to the "revolving moon" (6)? the four activities listed in line 7? What extreme contrasts does he use to describe Zimri? To what extent do Dryden's contrasts do the same kind of job as the contradictions in Pope's "Atticus"?

II

1. In speaking of the art of satirizing people through such character studies Dryden said: "How easy it is to call rogue and villain, and that wittily! But how hard to make a man appear a fool, a blockhead, or a knave, without using any of these opprobrious terms! . . .

there is still a vast difference betwixt the slovenly butchering of a man, and the fineness of a stroke that separates the head from the body, and leaves it standing in its place." What is the distinction he is making here between crude ridicule and art? Show that the "fineness of a stroke" he speaks of is apparent here and in Pope's portrait of Atticus.

THE BUSYBODY [*1608*]

Joseph Hall

About a half century before Dryden so skillfully "beheaded" Zimri, a number of English writers had established a fashion for drawing character sketches, or portraits, which they called "characters." The aim of these portraits was to dramatize in brief descriptions some human qualities the author wished to praise or censure. The emphasis was on types, rather than on distinct individuals: The Wise Man, The Hypocrite, A Pretender to Learning, A Vulgar-spirited Man.

We have seen what the character sketch became in the hands of Shaftesbury, Dryden, Pope, and Addison. They applied the techniques of the "character" writers to the delineation of specific individuals and lifted the art of character sketching to a high level of subtlety and reader interest. The sketch that follows, Joseph Hall's "The Busybody," may not have the direct personal appeal of those dealing with Henry Hastings or Sir Roger de Coverley, but it easily persuades us that it speaks the truth about human nature.

In the Busybody we see a type as familiar in our own day as in Hall's. None of his annoying habits has altered much in the last three hundred and fifty years. Notice how carefully Hall shows him in action, how he uses specific details and appropriate analogies to make the reader *see* the kind of man he is picturing.

His estate is too narrow for his mind and therefore he is fain to make himself room in others' affairs, yet ever in pretense of love. No news can stir but by his door; neither can he know that which he must not tell. What every man ventures in Guiana voyage,[1] and what they gained, he knows to a hair. Whether Holland will have peace,[2] he knows; and what conditions, and with what success, is familiar to him, ere it be concluded. No post[3] can pass him without a question; and rather than he will lose the news, he rides back with him to appose[4] him of tidings: and then to the next man he meets he supplies the wants of his hasty intelligence,[5] and makes up a perfect tale; wherewith he so haunteth the patient auditor, that, after many excuses, he is fain to endure rather the censure of his manners in running away, than the tediousness of an impertinent discourse. His speech is oft broken off with a succession of long parentheses, which he ever vows to

1. VENTURES . . . VOYAGE: i.e., invests in trade with the newly discovered South America lands.
2. WHETHER . . . PEACE: Holland and England spent much of the seventeenth century in uneasy trade rivalries, which at times turned into warfare.

3. POST: i.e., a messenger with news.
4. APPOSE: question about.
5. SUPPLIES . . . INTELLIGENCE: fabricates whatever is necessary to make a good story.

fill up ere the conclusion; and perhaps would effect it, if the other's ear were as unweariable as his tongue. If he sees but two men talk, and read a letter in the street, he runs to them, and asks if he may not be partner of that secret relation; and if they deny it, he offers to tell, since he may not hear, wonders; and then falls upon the report of the Scottish mine, or of the great fish taken up at Lynn, or of the freezing of the Thames;[6] and, after many thanks and dismissions, is hardly entreated silence. He undertakes as much as he performs little. This man will thrust himself forward, to be the guide of the way he knows not; and calls at his neighbor's window, and asks why his servants are not at work. The market hath no commodity which he prizeth not, and which the next table shall not hear recited. His tongue, like the tail of Samson's foxes,[7] carries firebrands, and is enough to set the whole field of the world on a flame. Himself begins table talk of his neighbor at another's board; to whom he bears the first news, and adjures him to conceal the reporter; whose choleric answer he returns to his first host, enlarged with a second edition; so, as it uses to be

done in the fight of unwilling mastiffs, he claps each on the side apart, and provokes them to an eager conflict. There can no act pass without his comment, which is ever far-fetched, rash, suspicious, dilatory.[8] His ears are long, and his eyes quick, but most of all to imperfections, which as he easily sees, so he increases with intermeddling. He harbors another man's servant; and, amidst his entertainment, asks what fare is usual at home, what hours are kept, what talk passeth their meals, what his master's disposition is, what his government,[9] what his guests; and when he hath by curious inquiries extracted all the juice and spirit of hoped intelligence, turns him off whence he came, and works on a new. He hates constancy,[10] as an earthen dullness, unfit for men of spirit; and loves to change his work and his place; neither yet can he be so soon weary of any place as every place is weary of him; for as he sets himself on[11] work, so others pay him with hatred. And look, how many masters he hath, so many enemies; neither is it possible that any should not hate him but who know him not. So then he labors without thanks, talks without credit, lives without love, dies without tears, without pity; save that some say, "It was pity he died no sooner."

---

6. REPORT . . . THAMES: typical "wonders," i.e., tall tales that the busybody circulates.
7. SAMSON'S FOXES: See Judges 15:4-5, where Samson burns up the grain of his enemies by tying torches to the tails of foxes and turning them loose in the fields.

8. DILATORY: expansive.
9. GOVERNMENT: behavior.
10. CONSTANCY: i.e., steadfastness.
11. ON: to.

I

1. Be sure you get the pronoun references straight throughout the piece. For instance, whom does "he" refer to in line 18? and "his" in line 25?

2. What habit does the example of the *fight of unwilling mastiffs* illustrate?

3. What do the following mean:

a. "No news can stir but by his door; neither can he know that which he must not tell."

b. "the patient auditor . . . is fain to endure rather the censure of his manners in running away, than the tediousness of an impertinent discourse."

c. "He undertakes as much as he performs little."

d. "The market hath no commodity which he prizeth not, and which the next table shall not hear recited."

e. "His ears are long, and his eyes quick, but most of all to imperfections, which as he easily sees, so he increases with intermeddling."

f. "neither is it possible that any should not hate him but who know him not."

4. Toward the end the speaker moves away from describing the Busybody in action. To what does he turn instead?

5. What is the speaker's attitude toward the Busybody: tolerant amusement? disgust? indifference? or none of these? Support your choice by specific reference to the language of the sketch.

II

1. Supply your own particulars in showing a mid-twentieth century busybody in operation, either in school or around the neighborhood.

ON A CERTAIN LORD
from King Henry the Fourth, Part One   [*1598*]

William Shakespeare

A widespread interest in character delineation may have been characteristic of the seventeenth century, but a moment's reflection will reveal that no age has been without writers whose concern has been largely with the varieties and subtleties of human personality. The short story in our own time has been dominated by attention to character portrayal, and the greatest work in Middle English, Chaucer's *Canterbury Tales,* owes its continuing popularity largely to Chaucer's genius for creating unforgettable people.

Shakespeare is no exception. Perhaps no writer has so successfully probed the complexities of human nature. The individuals who crowd his works have long since become touchstones by which we measure and understand humanity. Falstaff, Brutus, Hamlet, Iago, Cleopatra—these and many another are no longer simply characters in a fiction but, as it were, the horizons of our own species, extending far and wide around the little span and space of time we call our neighbors and ourselves.

From *King Henry the Fourth, Part One,* we have extracted a brief passage spoken by young Henry Percy, nicknamed Hotspur, to illustrate the impetuousness, belligerence, and simple-mindedness that are his besetting sins. This speech comes in Act I, Scene 3, lines 29-69. Hotspur, an exuberant and valiant soldier, has won a notable victory for his King, Henry IV. The King has demanded that he turn over the titled prisoners taken, and Hotspur has so far refused. Part of his reason is Henry's unwillingness to ransom his brother-in-law, captured elsewhere. The rest of the reason he gives in the lines that follow. His description of the "certain lord" who came from Henry with the demand for the prisoners is a trenchant portrait of a pantywaist in action; it is also suggestive in its vigor, pungency, and downrightness of the great virtues which are the other face of Hotspur's weaknesses.

HOTSPUR: My liege, I did deny no prisoners.
But I remember, when the fight was done,
When I was dry with rage and extreme toil,
Breathless and faint, leaning upon my sword,
Came there a certain lord, neat, and trimly dressed,   5
Fresh as a bridegroom; and his chin new reaped
Showed like a stubble-land at harvest-home.
He was perfumed like a milliner;
And 'twixt his finger and his thumb he held
A pouncet-box, which ever and anon   10

He gave his nose and took't away again;
Who therewith angry, when it next came there,
Took it in snuff; and still he smiled and talked,
And as the soldiers bore dead bodies by,
He called them untaught knaves, unmannerly,   15
To bring a slovenly unhandsome corse
Betwixt the wind and his nobility.
With many holiday and lady terms
He questioned me; amongst the rest, demanded
My prisoners in your Majesty's behalf.   20
I then, all smarting with my wounds being cold,
To be so pestered with a popinjay,
Out of my grief, and my impatience
Answered neglectingly—I know not what,
He should, or he should not; for he made me mad   25
To see him shine so brisk and smell so sweet
And talk so like a waiting-gentlewoman
Of guns and drums and wounds,—God save the mark!—
And telling me the sovereign'st thing on earth
Was parmaceti for an inward bruise;   30
And that it was great pity, so it was,
This villainous salt-peter should be digged
Out of the bowels of the harmless earth,
Which many a good tall fellow had destroyed
So cowardly; and but for these vile guns,   35
He would himself have been a soldier.
This bald unjointed chat of his, my lord,
I answered indirectly, as I said;
And I beseech you, let not his report
Come current for an accusation   40
Betwixt my love and your high Majesty.

---

6. CHIN NEW REAPED: shaved (becoming a custom of courtiers but disapproved of by Hotspur).
7. HARVEST-HOME: harvest time.
10. POUNCET-BOX: perfume box. EVER AND ANON: from time to time.
13. TOOK . . . SNUFF: play on the word *snuff:* to "smell" and to "resent." STILL: continually.
16. CORSE: corpse.
18. HOLIDAY: affected.

22. POPINJAY: parrot.
23. GRIEF: pain.
27. WAITING-GENTLEWOMAN: maid-in-waiting.
28. GOD . . . MARK!: an exclamation of impatience.
29. SOVEREIGN'ST: very best.
30. PARMACETI: spermaceti, ointment made from sperm whale oil.
34. TALL: brave.
38. INDIRECTLY: thoughtlessly (see line 24).
40. COME CURRENT: be taken at face value.

I

1. What details show us the kind of person the *certain lord* is? How is he dressed? What does his chin look like? How does the reference to the reaction of his nose to the snuff (line 9-13) prepare for the comment in lines 15-17? Why does Hotspur call him a "popinjay" (22)? Why would his comments on war anger Hotspur at this moment?

2. What picture do we get of Hotspur? What phrases reveal his bluntness? his disgust with unmanly behavior? his impetuousness? What traces of humor do you find in him? Consider lines 9-13, 16-17, 29-30.

THE GENERAL PROLOGUE TO THE CANTERBURY TALES   [*c. 1385*]

Geoffrey Chaucer

Geoffrey Chaucer's band of pilgrims, bound for the shrine of Thomas à Becket in Canterbury, gathered at the Tabard Inn in Southwark, a small suburb outside of London, almost six hundred years ago. They made their pilgrimage and went their several ways, but not to oblivion, for each one is as alive today in the mind of the reader, new or old, as he was in the mind of his creator and fellow pilgrim. The fourteenth century lives in the particulars of their callings, their dress, their speech, their customs; their humanity, however, belongs as much to the twentieth century as to the fourteenth.

Pilgrimages were a popular pastime in Chaucer's day, much as cruises and trips abroad are today. Not everyone could afford to go, but a surprising number managed it. The journeys had their inconveniences and perils, but they were minor compared to the possibilities for pleasure. The religious purpose behind the pilgrimage—to prove the strength of one's faith and seek atonement for one's sins—was supposedly the primary reason for going, and for some pilgrims it was the only reason; but for many the religious purpose was only a good excuse for a pleasant trip. Indeed, many religious reformers of Chaucer's day denounced pilgrimages as a mockery of true religion.

The most famous shrine in England at that time was that of the martyred Thomas à Becket at Canterbury, a cathedral town some sixty miles southeast of London. Becket had been a trusted adviser to King Henry II and had been made Archbishop of Canterbury in a move to secure Henry's dominance over the Church in England. But once in office he took his position seriously and defended the Church against Henry's interference. He was murdered in 1170 by some of Henry's supporters and was canonized as a saint two years later. It is to the shrine of this "holy, blisful martyr" that Chaucer's twenty-nine pilgrims set out on an ordinary April day some six hundred years ago.

The framework of a group of pilgrims traveling on horseback on a two- or three-day trip to Canterbury and then back is perfect for Chaucer's purposes. He can include people from almost all segments of society, from the noble Knight down to the lowly Plowman; and he can show all kinds of human strength and weakness, from the poor Parson, who lived the Christ-like life he preached, to the depraved Pardoner, who gloried in his depravity. The whole structure of fourteenth century society moves in miniature along the road to Canterbury in the persons of his pilgrims: the still strong feudal organization, the growing, town-centered merchant and tradesman class existing outside the feudal structure, and the all-pervading, powerful Catholic Church.

This brief background is necessary to set the stage, but we are concerned, as Chaucer was, with the personalities who move upon the stage. In order to make the journey more pleasant, the host of the Tabard Inn, Harry Bailly, had suggested that each pilgrim tell two tales on the way to Canterbury and two on the return, with the one who told the best tale receiving a dinner at his inn, at the expense

of the others. Chaucer had set himself a large order. He never finished more than
about a fifth of the proposed plan, and we don't know who won the free meal,
but this has never bothered the generations of readers who have been introduced
to the pilgrims at the Tabard. The personalities themselves have proved more
fascinating than the stories they tell, even though a number of the tales make
wonderful reading.

The most engaging and best-known characters from the "Prologue" are met
here. For two of the portraits—the Prioress and the Parson—there are specific
discussions of what Chaucer was trying to accomplish, and a few analytical questions on how he went about it.

Immediately following the "Prologue" is a brief analysis of the ways in which
Chaucer's English differed from our own, plus several sections in Middle English
to give you the chance to see the original and try your hand at reading it aloud.

> As soon as April pierces to the root
> The drought of March, and bathes each bud and shoot
> Through every vein of sap with gentle showers
> From whose engendering liquor spring the flowers;
> When zephyrs have breathed softly all about   5
> Inspiring every wood and field to sprout,
> And in the zodiac the youthful sun
> His journey halfway through the Ram has run;
> When little birds are busy with their song
> Who sleep with open eyes the whole night long   10
> Life stirs their hearts and tingles in them so,
> On pilgrimages people long to go
> And palmers to set out for distant strands
> And foreign shrines renowned in many lands.
> And specially in England people ride   15
> To Canterbury from every countryside
> To visit there the blessed martyred saint
> Who gave them strength when they were sick and faint.
>
> In Southwark at the Tabard one spring day
> It happened, as I stopped there on my way,   20
> Myself a pilgrim with a heart devout
> Ready for Canterbury to set out,
> At night came all of twenty-nine assorted
> Travelers, and to that same inn resorted,
> Who by a turn of fortune chanced to fall   25
> In fellowship together, and they were all

8. RAM: first sign of the zodiac (Aries).

13. PALMERS: pilgrims, who often carried palm branches. DISTANT STRANDS: foreign lands.

16. CANTERBURY: about sixty miles southeast of London.

"The General Prologue to the Canterbury Tales"
from *The Portable Chaucer* selected and translated
by Theodore Morrison. Copyright 1949 by Theodore Morrison. Reprinted by permission of The
Viking Press, Inc.

17. MARTYRED SAINT: Thomas à Becket, murdered in Canterbury cathedral in 1170.

19. SOUTHWARK: suburb south of London. TABARD: an inn.

Pilgrims who had it in their minds to ride
Toward Canterbury. The stable doors were wide,
The rooms were large, and we enjoyed the best,
And shortly, when the sun had gone to rest,   30
I had so talked with each that presently
I was a member of their company
And promised to rise early the next day
To start, as I shall show, upon our way.

But none the less, while I have time and space,   35
Before this tale has gone a further pace,
I should in reason tell you the condition
Of each of them, his rank and his position,
And also what array they all were in;
And so then, with a knight I will begin.   40

A Knight was with us, and an excellent man,
Who from the earliest moment he began
To follow his career loved chivalry,
Truth, openhandedness, and courtesy.
He was a stout man in the king's campaigns   45
And in that cause had gripped his horse's reins
In Christian lands and pagan through the earth,
None farther, and always honored for his worth.
He was on hand at Alexandria's fall.
He had often sat in precedence to all   50
The nations at the banquet board in Prussia.
He had fought in Lithuania and in Russia,
No Christian knight more often; he had been
In Moorish Africa at Benmarin,
At the siege of Algeciras in Granada,   55
And sailed in many a glorious armada
In the Mediterranean, and fought as well
At Ayas and Attalia when they fell
In Armenia and on Asia Minor's coast.
Of fifteen deadly battles he could boast,   60
And in Algeria, at Tremessen,
Fought for the faith and killed three separate men
In single combat. He had done good work
Joining against another pagan Turk
With the king of Palathia. And he was wise,   65
Despite his prowess, honored in men's eyes,

---

38. POSITION: i.e., social position.
48. NONE: no man.
49. ALEXANDRIA'S FALL: captured in 1365.
54. BENMARIN: in Morocco.
55. ALGECIRAS: captured in 1343. GRANADA: in
southern Spain.
58. AYAS: in Armenia—1367. ATTALIA: in Asia
Minor—1361.
61. ALGERIA, AT TREMESSEN: northwest Africa.
65. PALATHIA: in Turkey.

Meek as a girl and gentle in his ways.
He had never spoken ignobly all his days
To any man by even a rude inflection.
He was a knight in all things to perfection.   70
He rode a good horse, but his gear was plain,
For he had lately served on a campaign.
His tunic was still spattered by the rust
Left by his coat of mail, for he had just
Returned and set out on his pilgrimage.   75

His son was with him, a young Squire, in age
Some twenty years as near as I could guess.
His hair curled as if taken from a press.
He was a lover and would become a knight.
In stature he was of a moderate height   80
But powerful and wonderfully quick.
He had been in Flanders, riding in the thick
Of forays in Artois and Picardy,
And bore up well for one so young as he,
Still hoping by his exploits in such places   85
To stand the better in his lady's graces.
He wore embroidered flowers, red and white,
And blazed like a spring meadow to the sight.
He sang or played his flute the livelong day.
He was as lusty as the month of May.   90
His coat was short, its sleeves were long and wide.
He sat his horse well, and knew how to ride,
And how to make a song and use his lance,
And he could write and draw well, too, and dance.
So hot his love that when the moon rose pale   95
He got no more sleep than a nightingale.
He was modest, and helped whomever he was able,
And carved as his father's squire at the table.

But one more servant had the Knight beside,
Choosing thus simply for the time to ride: 100
A Yeoman, in a coat and hood of green.
His peacock-feathered arrows, bright and keen,
He carried under his belt in tidy fashion.
For well-kept gear he had a yeoman's passion.
No draggled feather might his arrows show,   105
And in his hand he held a mighty bow.
He kept his hair close-cropped, his face was brown.
He knew the lore of woodcraft up and down.
His arm was guarded from the bowstring's whip

78. PRESS: curling iron.
82-83. FLANDERS . . . PICARDY: all regions in northern France.
98. AND . . . TABLE: one of a squire's duties.
99. BUT: only.

By a bracer, gaily trimmed. He had at hip   110
A sword and buckler, and at his other side
A dagger whose fine mounting was his pride,
Sharp-pointed as a spear. His horn he bore
In a sling of green, and on his chest he wore
A silver image of St. Christopher,   115
His patron, since he was a forester.

    There was also a Nun, a Prioress,
Whose smile was gentle and full of guilelessness.
"By St. Loy!" was the worst oath she would say.
She sang mass well, in a becoming way,   120
Intoning through her nose the words divine,
And she was known as Madame Eglantine.
She spoke good French, as taught at Stratford-Bow,
For the Parisian French she did not know.
She was schooled to eat so primly and so well   125
That from her lips no morsel ever fell.
She wet her fingers lightly in the dish
Of sauce, for courtesy was her first wish.
With every bite she did her skillful best
To see that no drop fell upon her breast.   130
She always wiped her upper lip so clean
That in her cup was never to be seen
A hint of grease when she had drunk her share.
She reached out for her meat with comely air.
She was a great delight, and always tried   135
To imitate court ways, and had her pride,
Both amiable and gracious in her dealings.
As for her charity and tender feelings,
She melted at whatever was piteous.
She would weep if she but came upon a mouse   140
Caught in a trap, if it were dead or bleeding.
Some little dogs that she took pleasure feeding
On roasted meat or milk or good wheat bread
She had, but how she wept to find one dead
Or yelping from a blow that made it smart,   145
And all was sympathy and loving heart.
Neat was her wimple in its every plait,
Her nose well formed, her eyes as gray as slate.
Her mouth was very small and soft and red.
She had so wide a brow I think her head   150
Was nearly a span broad, for certainly
She was not undergrown, as all could see.

---

110. BRACER: wrist-guard.
111. BUCKLER: small shield.
115. SILVER . . . ST. CHRISTOPHER: medal of St. Christopher, patron saint of Foresters.
119. "BY ST. LOY!": a gentle oath.
123. STRATFORD-BOW: the Prioress's nunnery; the French taught there would not sound like Parisian French.

She wore her cloak with dignity and charm,
And had her rosary about her arm,
The small beads coral and the larger green,   155
And from them hung a brooch of golden sheen,
On it a large A and a crown above;
Beneath, "All things are subject unto love."

A priest accompanied her toward Canterbury,
And an attendant Nun, her secretary.   160

There was a Monk, and nowhere was his peer,
A hunter, and a roving overseer.
He was a manly man, and fully able
To be an abbot. He kept a hunting stable,
And when he rode the neighborhood could hear   165
His bridle jingling in the wind as clear
And loud as if it were a chapel bell.
Wherever he was master of a cell
The principles of good St. Benedict,
For being a little old and somewhat strict,   170
Were honored in the breach, as past their prime.
He lived by the fashion of a newer time.
He would have swapped that text for a plucked hen
Which says that hunters are not holy men,
Or a monk outside his discipline and rule   175
Is too much like a fish outside his pool;
That is to say, a monk outside his cloister.
But such a text he deemed not worth an oyster.
I told him his opinion made me glad.
Why should he study always and go mad,   180
Mewed in his cell with only a book for neighbor?
Or why, as Augustine commanded, labor
And sweat his hands? How shall the world be served?
To Augustine be all such toil reserved!
And so he hunted, as was only right.   185
He had greyhounds as swift as birds in flight.
His taste was all for tracking down the hare,
And what his sport might cost he did not care.
His sleeves I noticed, where they met his hand,
Trimmed with gray fur, the finest in the land.   190
His hood was fastened with a curious pin
Made of wrought gold and clasped beneath his chin,
A love knot at the tip. His head might pass,
Bald as it was, for a lump of shining glass,

---

162. ROVING OVERSEER: manager of property outside the monastery.
168. CELL: subordinate monastery.
169. ST. BENEDICT: founder of the Benedictine order of monks.

181. MEWED: caged.
182. AUGUSTINE: St. Augustine, one of the four great Fathers of the Church.

And his face was glistening as if anointed.   195
Fat as a lord he was, and well appointed.
His eyes were large, and rolled inside his head
As if they gleamed from a furnace of hot lead.
His boots were supple, his horse superbly kept.
He was a prelate to dream of while you slept.   200
He was not pale nor peaked like a ghost.
He relished a plump swan as his favorite roast.
He rode a palfrey brown as a ripe berry.

    A Friar was with us, a gay dog and a merry.
Who begged his district with a jolly air.   205
No friar in all four orders could compare
With him for gallantry; his tongue was wooing.
Many a girl was married by his doing.
And at his own cost it was often done.
He was a pillar, and a noble one,   210
To his whole order. In his neighborhood
Rich franklins knew him well, who served good food,
And worthy women welcomed him to town;
For the license that his order handed down,
He said himself, conferred on him possession   215
Of more than a curate's power of confession.
Sweetly the list of frailties he heard,
Assigning penance with a pleasant word.
He was an easy man for absolution
Where he looked forward to a contribution,   220
For if to a poor order a man has given
It signifies that he has been well shriven,
And if a sinner let his purse be dented
The Friar would stake his oath he had repented.
For many men become so hard of heart   225
They cannot weep, though conscience makes them smart.
Instead of tears and prayers, then, let the sinner
Supply the poor friars with the price of dinner.
For pretty women he had more than shrift.
His cape was stuffed with many a little gift,   230
As knives and pins and suchlike. He could sing
A merry note, and pluck a tender string,
And had no rival at all in balladry.
His neck was whiter than a fleur-de-lis,
And yet he could have knocked a strong man down.   235
He knew the taverns well in every town.

204. FRIAR: Unlike monks, who were supposed to
stick to the monastery, friars went out into the
world, preaching the gospel, ministering to the
sick and needy, and begging alms.
206. FOUR ORDERS: i.e., Dominicans, Franciscans,
Carmelites, and Augustinians.

209. AT . . . COST: i.e., he provided the dowries.
212. FRANKLINS: country squires.
214. LICENSE: license to beg and preach.
216. CURATE'S: parish priest's.
222. SHRIVEN: confessed and pardoned.
226. SMART: grieve.

The barmaids and innkeepers pleased his mind
Better than beggars and lepers and their kind.
In his position it was unbecoming
Among the wretched lepers to go slumming.   240
It mocks all decency, it seems no stitch
To deal with such riffraff; but with the rich,
With sellers of victuals, that's another thing.
Wherever he saw some hope of profiting,
None so polite, so humble. He was good,   245
The champion beggar of his brotherhood.
Should a woman have no shoes against the snow,
So pleasant was his *"In principio"*
He would have her widow's mite before he went.
He took in far more than he paid in rent   250
For his right of begging within certain bounds.
None of his brethren trespassed on his grounds!
He loved as freely as a half-grown whelp.
On arbitration-days he gave great help,
For his cloak was never shiny nor threadbare   255
Like a poor cloistered scholar's. He had an air
As if he were a doctor or a pope.
It took stout wool to make his semicope
That plumped out like a bell for portliness.
He lisped a little in his rakishness   260
To make his English sweeter on his tongue,
And twanging his harp to end some song he'd sung
His eyes would twinkle in his head as bright
As the stars twinkle on a frosty night.
Hubert this gallant Friar was by name.   265

    Among the rest a Merchant also came.
He wore a forked beard and a beaver hat
From Flanders. High up in the saddle he sat,
In figured cloth, his boots clasped handsomely,
Delivering his opinions pompously,   270
Always on how his gains might be increased.
At all costs he desired the sea policed
From Middleburg in Holland to Orwell.
He knew the exchange rates, and the time to sell
French currency, and there was never yet   275
A man who could have told he was in debt
So grave he seemed and hid so well his feelings
With all his shrewd engagements and close dealings.
You'd find no better man at any turn;
But what his name was I could never learn.   280

248. "IN PRINCIPIO": John I:1—"In the beginning was the word"; a form of greeting.
254. ARBITRATION-DAYS: days on which disputes were settled.
258. SEMICOPE: short cape.
273. MIDDLEBURG . . . ORWELL: ports in Holland and England.

There was an Oxford Student too, it chanced,
Already in his logic well advanced.
He rode a mount as skinny as a rake,
And he was hardly fat. For learning's sake
He let himself look hollow and sober enough.   285
He wore an outer coat of threadbare stuff,
For he had no benefice for his enjoyment
And was too unworldly for some lay employment.
He much preferred to have beside his bed
His twenty volumes bound in black or red   290
All packed with Aristotle from end to middle
Than a sumptuous wardrobe or a merry fiddle.
For though he knew what learning had to offer
There was little coin to jingle in his coffer.
Whatever he got by touching up a friend   295
On books and learning he would promptly spend
And busily pray for the soul of anybody
Who furnished him the wherewithal for study.
His scholarship was what he truly heeded.
He never spoke a word more than was needed,   300
And that was said with dignity and force,
And quick and brief. He was of grave discourse,
Giving new weight to virtue by his speech,
And gladly would he learn and gladly teach.

    *   *   *   *   *

A worthy woman there was from near the city   305
Of Bath, but somewhat deaf, and more's the pity.
For weaving she possessed so great a bent
She outdid the people of Ypres and of Ghent.
No other woman dreamed of such a thing
As to precede her at the offering,   310
Or if any did, she fell in such a wrath
She dried up all the charity in Bath.
She wore fine kerchiefs of old-fashioned air,
And on a Sunday morning, I could swear,
She had ten pounds of linen on her head.   315
Her stockings were of finest scarlet-red,
Laced tightly, and her shoes were soft and new.
Bold was her face, and fair, and red in hue.
She had been an excellent woman all her life.
Five men in turn had taken her to wife,   320
Omitting other youthful company—
But let that pass for now! Over the sea
She had traveled freely; many a distant stream

287-88. FOR . . . EMPLOYMENT: i.e., he had no ecclesiastical position and couldn't get a secular job.
295. TOUCHING UP: borrowing from.
306. BATH: in southwest England.

308. YPRES . . . GHENT: weaving centers in Flanders.
310. AT THE OFFERING: in church.
312. CHARITY: Christian love.

She crossed, and visited Jerusalem
Three times. She had been at Rome and at Boulogne,　　325
At the shrine of Compostella, and at Cologne.
She had wandered by the way through many a scene.
Her teeth were set with little gaps between.
Easily on her ambling horse she sat.
She was well wimpled, and she wore a hat　　330
As wide in circuit as a shield or targe.
A skirt swathed up her hips, and they were large.
Upon her feet she wore sharp-roweled spurs,
She was a good fellow; a ready tongue was hers.
All remedies of love she knew by name,　　335
For she had all the tricks of that old game.

　　There was a good man of the priest's vocation,
A poor town Parson of true consecration,
But he was rich in holy thought and work.
Learned he was, in the truest sense a clerk　　340
Who meant Christ's gospel faithfully to preach
And truly his parishioners to teach.
He was a kind man, full of industry,
Many times tested by adversity
And always patient. If tithes were in arrears,　　345
He was loth to threaten any man with fears
Of excommunication; past a doubt
He would rather spread his offering about
To his poor flock, or spend his property.
To him a little meant sufficiency.　　350
Wide was his parish, with houses far asunder,
But he would not be kept by rain or thunder,
If any had suffered a sickness or a blow,
From visiting the farthest, high or low,
Plodding his way on foot, his staff in hand.　　355
He was a model his flock could understand,
For first he did and afterward he taught.
That precept from the Gospel he had caught,
And he added as a metaphor thereto,
"If the gold rusts, what will the iron do?"　　360
For if a priest is foul, in whom we trust,
No wonder a layman shows a little rust.
A priest should take to heart the shameful scene
Of shepherds filthy while the sheep are clean.
By his own purity a priest should give　　365
The example to his sheep, how they should live.
He did not rent his benefice for hire,

325-26. ROME . . . COLOGNE: famous shrines, the　　331. TARGE: shield.
last three being in France, Spain, and Germany.　　358. GOSPEL: Matthew 5:19.

Leaving his flock to flounder in the mire,
And run to London, happiest of goals,
To sing paid masses in St. Paul's for souls,   370
Or as chaplain from some rich guild take his keep,
But dwelt at home and guarded well his sheep
So that no wolf should make his flock miscarry.
He was a shepherd, and not a mercenary.
And though himself a man of strict vocation
He was not harsh to weak souls in temptation,
Not overbearing nor haughty in his speech,
But wise and kind in all he tried to teach.
By good example and just words to turn
Sinners to heaven was his whole concern.   380
But should a man in truth prove obstinate,
Whoever he was, of rich or mean estate,
The Parson would give him a snub to meet the case.
I doubt there was a priest in any place
His better. He did not stand on dignity   385
Nor affect in conscience too much nicety,
But Christ's and his disciples' word he sought
To teach, and first he followed what he taught.

There was a Plowman with him on the road,
His brother, who had forked up many a load   390
Of good manure. A hearty worker he,
Living in peace and perfect charity.
Whether his fortune made him smart or smile,
He loved God with his whole heart all the while
And his neighbor as himself. He would undertake,   395
For every luckless poor man, for the sake
Of Christ to thresh and ditch and dig by the hour
And with no wage, if it was in his power.
His tithes on goods and earnings he paid fair.
He wore a coarse, rough coat and rode a mare.   400

*   *   *   *   *

As tough a yokel as you care to meet
The Miller was. His big-beefed arms and thighs
Took many a ram put up as wrestling prize.
He was a thick, squat-shouldered lump of sins.
No door but he could heave it off its pins   405
Or break it running at it with his head.
His beard was broader than a shovel, and red
As a fat sow or fox. A wart stood clear
Atop his nose, and red as a pig's ear
A tuft of bristles on it. Black and wide   410

---

370. ST. PAUL'S: St. Paul's Cathedral in London.   393. SMART OR SMILE: i.e., feel pain or joy.
383. SNUB: rebuke.   397. DITCH: make ditches.

His nostrils were. He carried at his side
A sword and buckler. His mouth would open out
Like a great furnace, and he would sing and shout
His ballads and jokes of harlotries and crimes.
He could steal corn and charge for it three times,   415
And yet was honest enough, as millers come,
For a miller, as they say, has a golden thumb.
In white coat and blue hood this lusty clown,
Blowing his bagpipes, brought us out of town.

                *   *   *   *   *

        There was a Pardoner of Rouncivalle   420
With him, of the blessed Mary's hospital,
But now come straight from Rome (or so said he).
Loudly he sang, "Come hither, love, to me,"
While the Summoner's counterbass trolled out profound—
No trumpet blew with half so vast a sound.   425
This Pardoner had hair as yellow as wax,
But it hung as smoothly as a hank of flax.
His locks trailed down in bunches from his head,
And he let the ends about his shoulders spread,
But in thin clusters, lying one by one.   430
Of hood, for rakishness, he would have none,
For in his wallet he kept it safely stowed.
He traveled, as he thought, in the latest mode,
Disheveled. Save for his cap, his head was bare,
And in his eyes he glittered like a hare.   435
A Veronica was stitched upon his cap,
His wallet lay before him in his lap
Brimful of pardons from the very seat
In Rome. He had a voice like a goat's bleat.
He was beardless and would never have a beard.   440
His cheek was always smooth as if just sheared.
I think he was a gelding or a mare;
But in his trade, from Berwick down to Ware,
No pardoner could beat him in the race,
For in his wallet he had a pillow case   445
Which he represented as Our Lady's veil;
He said he had a piece of the very sail
St. Peter, when he fished in Galilee
Before Christ caught him, used upon the sea.

---

417. FOR . . . THUMB: The proverb goes: "An
honest miller has a golden thumb"—an impossibility.

420. ROUNCIVALLE: Hospital of the Blessed Mary
of Rouncivalle in London.

424. SUMMONER: another of the pilgrims.

436. VERONICA: the image of Christ's face on a
cloth; the legend is that Veronica, one of the
women who followed Christ to Calvary, wiped
the blood from his face and found his image on
the handkerchief she used.

442. GELDING . . . MARE: sexually abnormal.

443. BERWICK . . . WARE: from one end of England
to the other (north to south).

446. OUR LADY'S: i.e., Mary's.

He had a latten cross embossed with stones   450
And in a glass he carried some pig's bones,
And with these holy relics, when he found
Some village parson grubbing his poor ground,
He would get more money in a single day
Than in two months would come the parson's way.   455
Thus with his flattery and his trumped-up stock
He made dupes of the parson and his flock.
But though his conscience was a little plastic
He was in church a noble ecclesiastic.
Well could he read the Scripture of saint's story,   460
But best of all he sang the offertory,
For he understood that when this song was sung,
Then he must preach, and sharpen up his tongue
To rake in cash, as well he knew the art,
And so he sang out gaily, with full heart.   465

   Now I have set down briefly, as it was,
Our rank, our dress, our number, and the cause
That made our sundry fellowship begin
In Southwark, at this hospitable inn
Known as the Tabard, not far from the Bell.   470
But what we did that night I ought to tell,
And after that our journey, stage by stage,
And the whole story of our pilgrimage.
But first, in justice, do not look askance
I plead, nor lay it to my ignorance   475
If in this matter I should use plain speech
And tell you just the words and style of each,
Reporting all their language faithfully.
For it must be known to you as well as me
That whoever tells a story after a man   480
Must follow him as closely as he can.
If he takes the tale in charge, he must be true
To every word, unless he would find new
Or else invent a thing or falsify.
Better some breadth of language than a lie!   485
He may not spare the truth to save his brother.
He might as well use one word as another.
In Holy Writ Christ spoke in a broad sense,
And surely his word is without offense.
Plato, if his are pages you can read,   490
Says let the word be cousin to the deed.
So I petition your indulgence for it

---

461. OFFERTORY: that part of the church service
   in which the bread and wine are offered to
   God; not the "collection of money," which is
   the meaning current today.

470. BELL: another inn.
480. WHOEVER . . . MAN: i.e., whoever repeats
   someone else's story.
485. BREADTH: bluntness.

If I have cut the cloth just as men wore it,
Here in this tale, and shown its very weave.
My wits are none too sharp, you must believe.   495

Our Host gave each of us a cheerful greeting
And promptly of our supper had us eating.
The victuals that he served us were his best.
The wine was potent, and we drank with zest.
Our Host cut such a figure, all in all,   500
He might have been a marshall in a hall.
He was a big man, and his eyes bulged wide.
No sturdier citizen lived in all Cheapside,
Lacking no trace of manhood, bold in speech,
Prudent, and well versed in what life can teach,   505
And with all this he was a jovial man.
And so when supper ended he began
To jolly us, when all our debts were clear.
"Welcome," he said. "I have not seen this year
So merry a company in this tavern as now,   510
And I would give you pleasure if I knew how.
And just this very minute a plan has crossed
My mind that might amuse you at no cost.

"You go to Canterbury—may the Lord
Speed you, and may the martyred saint reward   515
Your journey! And to while the time away
You mean to talk and pass the time of day,
For you would be as cheerful all alone
As riding on your journey dumb as stone.
Therefore, if you'll abide by what I say,   520
Tomorrow, when you ride off on your way,
Now, by my father's soul, and he is dead,
If you don't enjoy yourselves, cut off my head!
Hold up your hands, if you accept my speech."

Our counsel did not take us long to reach.   525
We bade him give his orders at his will.
"Well, sirs," he said, "then do not take it ill,
But hear me in good part, and for your sport.
Each one of you, to make our journey short,
Shall tell two stories, as we ride, I mean,   530
Toward Canterbury; and coming home again
Shall tell two other tales he may have heard
Of happenings that some time have occurred.
And the one of you whose stories please us most,
Here in this tavern, sitting by this post   535
Shall sup at our expense while we make merry

---

503. CHEAPSIDE: London's old market area.

When we come riding home from Canterbury.
And to cheer you still the more, I too will ride
With you at my own cost, and be your guide.
And if anyone my judgment shall gainsay   540
He must pay for all we spend along the way.
If you agree, no need to stand and reason.
Tell me, and I'll be stirring in good season."

    This thing was granted, and we swore our pledge
To take his judgment on our pilgrimage,   545
His verdict on our tales, and his advice.
He was to plan a supper at a price
Agreed upon; and so we all assented
To his command, and we were well contented.
The wine was fetched; we drank, and went to rest.   550

    Next morning, when the dawn was in the east,
Up sprang our Host, who acted as our cock,
And gathered us together in a flock,
And off we rode, till presently our pace
Had brought us to St. Thomas' watering place.   555
And there our Host began to check his horse.
"Good sirs," he said, "you know your promise, of course.
Shall I remind you what it was about?
If evensong and matins don't fall out,
We'll soon find who shall tell us the first tale.   560
But as I hope to drink my wine and ale,
Whoever won't accept what I decide
Pays everything we spend along the ride.
Draw lots, before we're farther from the Inn.
Whoever draws the shortest shall begin.   565
Sir Knight," said he, "my master, choose your straw.
Come here, my lady Prioress, and draw,
And you, Sir Scholar, don't look thoughtful, man!
Pitch in now, everyone!" So all began
To draw the lots, and as the luck would fall   570
The draw went to the Knight, which pleased us all.
And when this excellent man saw how it stood,
Ready to keep his promise, he said, "Good!
Since it appears that I must start the game,   575
Why then, the draw is welcome, in God's name.
Now let's ride on, and listen, what I say."
And with that word we rode forth on our way,
And he, with his courteous manner and good cheer,
Began to tell his tale, as you shall hear.

---

555. ST. THOMAS' WATERING PLACE: a brook near
   the Tabard.
559. IF . . . OUT: i.e., if you feel the same this
morning ("matins") as you felt last night
("evensong").

CHAUCER'S ENGLISH

Chaucer's English is not difficult to read if you get used to the spelling and if you are willing to note the meanings of words that have passed out of English or have undergone a change in meaning over the years. The word order is not far different from present-day English. Even reading aloud can be done reasonably well with a little attention to some details of how his Midland dialect probably sounded. We have printed here the well-known opening lines in the original, plus the portraits of the Wife of Bath and the Pardoner. The translation we have used by Theodore Morrison, excellent as it is, is not Chaucer, and Morrison would be the first to admit it. In fact, in discussing the difficulties of translation, he bemoans the fact that in trying to catch the flavor of the original as it might have sounded to one of Chaucer's listeners, he feels too often that "the light-wine sparkle of Chaucer has been turned into beer if not outright dishwater."

You might get some idea of the music of the original poetry if you read the selections reprinted here in Chaucer's English with some approximation of his pronunciation. Follow this brief and very simplified analysis:

A. Certain syllables which are no longer pronounced were pronounced:
  1. For our purposes, pronounce as separate syllables *es* and *ed* at the ends of words ("shour*es*" and "bath*ed*").
  2. The ending *ion* or *ioun* is pronounced as two syllables ("con-di-ci-*oun*").
  3. Final *e* is normally pronounced (like the *a* in sof*a*), and always when the word is at the end of a line ("end*e*" or "corag*e*"). There are two exceptions:

a) when the next word begins with a vowel or an *h*.
b) when the meter of the line doesn't need it.

B. Certain consonants which are silent in today's speech were pronounced in Chaucer's English: *k* as in *"k*now" or *"k*night"; *gh* as in "kni*gh*t" (pronounced like the *ch* in modern German: the sound made by saying the word "he" while exhaling heavily), or in "thou*gh*te" (pronounced like the *ch* in scottish "loch"); *l* in such words as "halve."

C. The vowels were quite different:
  1. Single vowels:
     a: the sound in "father."
     e: long, the sound in "mate"; short, the sound in "bet."
     i or y: the sound in "feet"; short, the sound in "hit."
     o: long, the sound in "tone"; short, the sound in "folly."
     u: long, the sound in "tune"; short, the sound in "full."

(There is a third Chaucerian e that sounds like the e in "where," and a third Chaucerian o that sounds like the o in "cloth," but these occur infrequently and for present purposes have been ignored)
  2. Diphthongs:
     ei (or *ey* or *ay*): the sound in "*say*."
     au (or *aw*): the sound in *"house."*
     oi (or *oy*): the sound in *"boy."*
     ou (or *ow,* or *o* before *gh*): the sound in *"you."*

With these guides in mind, simply use the same stress pattern that you use with present-day English, and you should get something approximating Chaucer's speech.

The General Prologue

Whan that Aprill with his shoures soote
The droughte of March hath perced to the roote,
And bathed every veine in swich licour,
Of which vertu engendred is the flour;
When Zephyrus eek with his sweete breeth   5
Inspired hath in every holt and heeth
The tendre croppes, and the yonge sonne
Hath in the Ram his halve cours yronne,
And smale foweles maken melodye
That sleepen al the night with open yë—   10
So priketh hem Nature in hir corages—
Thanne longen folk to goon on pilgrimages,
And palmeres for to seeken straunge strondes
To ferne halwes, couthe in sondry londes;
And specially from every shires ende   15
Of Engelond to Caunterbury they wende,
The holy blisful martyr for to seeke
That hem hath holpen whan that they were seke.

    Bifel that in that seson on a day,
In Southwerk at the Tabard as I lay,   20
Redy to wenden on my pilgrimage
To Caunterbury with ful devout corage,
At night was come into that hostelrye
Wel nine and twenty in a compaignye
Of sondry folk, by aventure yfalle   25
In felaweshipe, and pilgrimes were they alle
That toward Caunterbury wolden ride.
The chambres and the stables weren wide,
And wel we weren esed atte beste.
And shortly, whan the sonne was to reste,   30
So hadde I spoken with hem everichon
That I was of hir felaweshipe anon,
And made forward erly for to rise,
To take oure way ther as I you devise.

---

1. SHOURES: showers. SOOTE: sweet.
3. SWICH LICOUR: such moisture.
4. VERTU: power. FLOUR: flower.
5. ZEPHYRUS: the west wind. EEK: also.
6. HOLT AND HEETH: wood and field.
7. CROPPES: sprouts.
8. YRONNE: run.
9. FOWELES: birds.
10. YË: eyes.
11. PRIKETH HEM: goads them. HIR CORAGES: their feelings.
13. STRONDES: shores.
14. FERNE HALWES: distant shrines. COUTHE: known.
16. WENDE: go.
17. BLISFUL: blessed. SEEKE: visit.
18. SEKE: sick.
19. BIFEL: (it) befell.
25. BY AVENTURE YFALLE: met by chance.
29. ESED ATTE BESTE: well taken care of.
33. FORWARD: agreement.

The Wif of Bathe

A good Wif was ther of biside Bathe,
But she was somdeel deef, and that was scathe.
Of cloth-making she hadde swich an haunt,
She passed hem of Ypres and of Gaunt.
In al the parissh wif ne was ther noon   5
That to the offring bifore hire sholde goon,
And if ther dide, certain so wroth was she
That she was out of alle charitee.
Hir coverchiefs ful fine were of ground—
I dorste swere they weyeden ten pound   10
That on a Sonday weren upon hir heed.
Hir hosen weren of fin scarlet reed,
Ful straite yteyd, and shoes ful moiste and newe.
Bold was hir face and fair and reed of hewe.
She was a worthy womman al hir live: 15
Housbondes at chirche dore she hadde five,
Withouten other compaignye in youthe—
But therof needeth nat to speke as nouthe.
And thries hadde she been at Jerusalem;
She hadde passed many a straunge streem;   20
At Rome she hadde been, and at Boloigne,
In Galice at Saint Jame, and at Coloigne:
She coude muchel of wandring by the waye.
Gat-tothed was she, soothly for to saye.
Upon an amblere esily she sat,   25
Ywimpled wel, and on hir heed an hat
As brood as is a bokeler or a targe,
A foot-mantel aboute hir hipes large,
And on hir feet a paire of spores sharpe.
In felaweshipe wel coude she laughe and carpe: 30
Of remedies of love she knew parchaunce,
For she coude of that art the olde daunce.

---

1. OF BISIDE: from near.
2. SOMDEEL: somewhat. SCATHE: too bad.
3. HAUNT: skill.
4. GAUNT: Ghent.
9. COVERCHIEFS: kerchiefs. GROUND: texture.
13. FUL STRAITE YTEYD: tightly tied. MOISTE: soft.
17. WITHOUTEN: besides.
18. NOUTHE: for the moment.
22. GALICE: Spain.
23. COUDE MUCHEL: knew much.
24. GAT-TOTHED: gap-toothed. SOOTHLY: truth-

fully.
25. AMBLERE: ambling horse.
26. YWIMPLED: with a wimple on.
27. BOKELER: buckler.
28. FOOT-MANTEL: outer skirt.
29. SPORES: spurs.
30. CARPE: talk.
31. PARCHAUNCE: without doubt.
32. SHE . . . DAUNCE: i.e., she knew all there was
to know about love.

The Pardoner

This Pardoner hadde heer as yelow as wex,
But smoothe it heeng as dooth a strike of flex;
By ounces heenge his lokkes that he hadde,
And therwith he his shuldres overspradde,
But thinne it lay, by colpons, oon by oon;   5
But hood for jolitee wered he noon,
For it was trussed up in his walet:
Him thoughte he rood al of the newe jet.
Dischevelee save his cappe he rood al bare.
Swiche glaring yën hadde he as an hare.   10
A vernicle hadde he sowed upon his cappe,
His walet lay biforn him in his lappe,
Bretful of pardon, comen from Rome al hoot.
A vois he hadde as smal as hath a goot;
No beerd hadde he, ne nevere sholde have;   15
As smoothe it was as it were late yshave:
I trowe he were a gelding or a mare.
But of his craft, fro Berwik into Ware,
Ne was there swich another pardoner;
For in his male he hadde a pilwe-beer   20
Which that he seyde was Oure Lady veil;
He seyde he hadde a gobet of the sail
That Sainte Peter hadde whan that he wente
Upon the see, til Jesu Crist him hente.
He hadde a crois of laton, ful of stones,   25
And in a glas he hadde pigges bones,
But with thise relikes whan that he foond
A poore person dwelling upon lond,
Upon a day he gat him more moneye
Than that the person gat in monthes twaye;   30
And thus with feined flaterye and japes
He made the person and the peple his apes.

But trewely to tellen atte laste,
He was in chirche a noble ecclesiaste;
Well coude he rede a lesson or a storye,   35

2. STRIKE: hank.
3. BY OUNCES: in strands.
5. COLPONS: clumps.
6. WERED: wore.
7. WALET: sack.
8. JET: style.
9. DISCHEVELEE: with hair hanging loose. BARE: i.e., bareheaded.
10. YËN: eyes.
11. VERNICLE: Veronica.
13. BRETFUL: brimful.

14. GOOT: goat.
17. TROWE: think.
20. MALE: bag. PILWE-BEER: pillow case.
22. GOBET: small piece.
24. HENTE: summoned.
25. CROIS OF LATON: cross of brass.
28. PERSON: parson. UPON LOND: in the country.
30. TWAYE: two.
31. JAPES: tricks.
32. APES: dupes.

But alderbest he soong an offertorye,
For wel he wiste whan that song was songe,
He moste preche and wel affile his tonge
To winne silver, as he ful well coude—
Therefore he soong the merierly and loude.   40

---

36. ALDERBEST: best of all.   38. AFFILE: make smooth.
37. WISTE: knew.   39. COUDE: knew how.

The Prioress

To understand Chaucer's gentle satire on the Prioress, it is necessary to understand a few things that are not obvious to the modern reader. For one, Madame Eglantine had no business on the pilgrimage at all. Her place was in the Priory, not on the road to Canterbury; the Church authorities at the time had expressly forbidden such pilgrimages for those who had taken monastic vows. For another, her dainty eating habits, her fine clothes, and the expensive rosary were part of the feminine lures of courtly ladies, certainly not of nuns. Nuns, moreover, were expressly forbidden to keep pets; how doubly wrong she was in feeding roast meat and wheat bread, luxuries then for the human animal, to her "little dogs." Lastly, the description of her apparent physical charms makes her more appropriate for the heroine's role in a fourteenth century romance than for the religious role she is supposed to fill.

All this would have been immediately apparent to Chaucer's contemporaries, if not so today. But there is more to the portrait which does not depend on a knowledge of fourteenth century manners and morals.

1. The speaker says that she had *tender feelings* and that she *melted at whatever was piteous.* True, but just what kinds of things brought forth her *sympathy and loving heart?* What should she have given her *charity* to?
2. Why does the speaker go to such lengths to show her consciously elegant and *dainty* table manners? Is he impressed by them? Is the reader? Explain.
3. The motto on her brooch was, "All things are subject unto love." What different meanings does the word *love* have, and what is the irony of her wearing such a brooch?

The Parson

There are several idealized characters in the *Canterbury Tales,* one of whom is the "poor town Parson." In contrast to the Prioress, and more obviously to such scoundrels as the Pardoner, the Parson is a thoroughly admirable churchman, and Chaucer almost eagerly lists the qualities that make him such. There is very little of the reformer in Chaucer, but quite obviously he presents in the Knight, the Parson, and the Plowman his convictions of what all men might be if they lived the kind of life they professed to live, or should live. There is no satire here, but rather straightforward, unabashed respect.

1. In what respects was the Parson a good priest? What made him *a model his flock could understand?*
2. Point out the series of contrasts Chaucer uses between the way the Parson acts and the way some other priests act.
3. What do the following lines tell about him?

    a.   "If tithes were in arrears,

He was loth to threaten any man
  with fears
Of excommunication."
b. "To him a little meant sufficiency."

c. "For first he did and afterward he
  taught."
d. "He was a shepherd, and not a
  mercenary."

I

1. Characterize Chaucer the pilgrim. Notice that in describing the other pilgrims he repeats at face value what they tell him of themselves, and he professes admiration for most of them, even those whom we cannot possibly find admirable: the Friar is described as "a pillar, and a noble one, To his whole order"; of the Merchant he comments, "You'd find no better man at any turn"; and of the Monk he says simply, "Nowhere was his peer." Find other examples of the uncritical acceptance of any kind of unsavory behavior on the part of Chaucer the pilgrim. Certainly, Chaucer the poet is not so naive. What does he gain by making himself one of the pilgrims, and by adopting an assumed personality so different from what he really is?

2. The portrait of the Parson is an idealized one: he is the perfect parish priest. The Knight, the Plowman, and to a certain extent the Student, the Squire, and the Yeoman, are also ideal examples of their kind. Each represents one of the major groups in fourteenth century society: the Church, the nobility, and the peasantry. There are few hints of satiric comment in these portraits, and we can be sure that Chaucer the poet agrees with Chaucer the pilgrim that these are admirable people. Specifically, what qualities do they possess? How do these qualities provide the standard against which we are to judge the other pilgrims? Show specifically how less desirable character traits contrast with ones presented as admirable.

3. We looked closely at the Prioress and saw that Chaucer selected details that give us a penetrating picture of the woman. Disregarding the problem of historical background, comment on the sharpness and effectiveness of two other characterizations.

4. Take some pains to read aloud the sections in Chaucer's English. Use the brief guide to pronunciation to get the sounds reasonably straight, but don't worry too much about being letter-perfect. Try to *hear* what Morrison meant in the quoted comment about the inadequacies of translation.

II

1. By reference to as many different characters as possible, show that the comment about similarities in individual behavior in the fourteenth and twentieth centuries is valid. For comparison bring in your own experiences, and your reading of contemporary magazines and newspapers.

SHE STOOPS TO CONQUER
or The Mistakes of a Night   [*1773*]

Oliver Goldsmith

The various kinds of people we have met in this section have certainly suggested the unlimited range of human behavior. Some of the personalities in the foregoing selections have probably seemed plausible enough even if quite different from any actual people you may have met. What you make of the characters in the comedy that follows—removed as they are from the world we know—depends on your willingness to recognize in yourself the universal qualities of conclusion-jumping, play-acting, people-manipulating, and self-justifying that operate every hour of every day.

She Stoops to Conquer is pure comedy, but there would be nothing to laugh at—or along with—if the antics of the principals in this compounding-of-confusion were not a mixture of exaggeration and truth. The play is partly a good-natured protest against the overly sentimental and painfully dull dramas that made up the bulk of eighteenth century theatrical fare, but more important, it presents a stageful of characters who are not lifeless abstractions or faceless caricatures, but memorable people spotlighted for the moment in an implausible but delightful mix-up.

CHARACTERS
in the order of their appearance

MRS. HARDCASTLE

MR. HARDCASTLE—*her husband*

TONY LUMPKIN—*Mrs. Hardcastle's son by her first husband*

KATE HARDCASTLE—*their daughter*

CONSTANCE NEVILLE—*Mrs. Hardcastle's niece*

LANDLORD—*proprietor of the* Three Pigeons

CHARLES MARLOW—*Miss Hardcastle's would-be suitor*

GEORGE HASTINGS—*Miss Neville's suitor*

DIGGORY—*Mr. Hardcastle's servant*

JEREMY—*Charles Marlow's servant*

SIR CHARLES MARLOW—*young Charles's father*

Tony's companions at the Three Pigeons, *various servants, and Miss Hardcastle's maid*

To Samuel Johnson, L.L.D.

Dear Sir,

By inscribing this slight performance to you, I do not mean so much to compliment you as myself. It may do me some honor to inform the public that I have lived many years in intimacy with you. It may serve the interests of mankind also to inform them that the greatest wit may be found in a character, without impairing the most unaffected piety.

I have, particularly, reason to thank you for your partiality to this performance. The undertaking a comedy not merely sentimental was very dangerous; and Mr. Colman,[1] who saw this piece in its various stages, always thought it so. However I ventured to trust it to the public; and, though it was necessarily delayed till late in the season, I have every reason to be grateful.

    I am, Dear Sir,

      Your most sincere friend,

      And admirer,

        Oliver Goldsmith

---

1. MR. COLMAN: the manager of the Covent Garden Theater.

PROLOGUE
By David Garrick, Esq.[2]

Enter MR. WOODWARD,[3] *dressed in black, and holding a handkerchief to his eyes.*

Excuse me, Sirs, I pray—I can't yet speak—
I'm crying now—and have been all the week!
'Tis not alone this morning suit, good masters;
I've that within[4]—for which there are no plasters!
Pray would you know the reason why I'm crying?
The comic muse, long sick, is now a dying!
And if she goes, my tears will never stop;
For as a player, I can't squeeze out one drop:
I am undone, that's all—shall lose my bread—
I'd rather, but that's nothing—lose my head.
When the sweet maid is laid upon the bier,
Shuter[5] and I shall be chief mourners here.
To *her* a mawkish drab of spurious breed,

---

2. DAVID GARRICK, ESQ.: the most celebrated actor of the day.
3. MR. WOODWARD: a well-known comic actor.
4. 'TIS . . . WITHIN: See *Hamlet,* I, ii, 77-78.
5. SHUTER: another comic actor (the "Poor Ned" the third line after this one).

Who deals in *sentimentals* will succeed!
Poor Ned and I are dead to all intents,
We can as soon speak *Greek* as *sentiments!*
Both nervous grown, to keep our spirits up,
We now and then take down a hearty cup.
What shall we do?—If Comedy forsake us!
They'll turn us out, and no one else will take us,
But why can't I be moral?—Let me try—
My heart thus pressing—fixed my face and
    eye—
With a sententious look that nothing means
(Faces are blocks in sentimental scenes)
Thus I begin—*All is not gold that glitters,*
Pleasure seems sweet, but proves a glass of
    bitters.
When ignorance enters, folly is at hand;
Learning is better far than house and land.
Let not your virtue trip, who trips may stumble,
And virtue is not virtue if she tumble.
    I give it up—morals won't do for me;
To make you laugh I must play tragedy.
One hope remains—hearing the maid was ill,
A *doctor*[6] comes this night to show his skill.
To cheer her heart, and give your muscles
    motion,
He in *five draughts*[7] prepared, presents a potion:
A kind of magic charm—for be assured,
If you will *swallow it,* the maid is cured:
But desperate the Doctor, and her case is,
If you reject the dose and make wry faces!
This truth he boasts, will boast it while he lives,
No *poisonous drugs* are mixed in what he gives;
Should he succeed, you'll give him his degree;
If not, within he will receive no fee![8]
The college *you,* must his pretentions back,
Pronounce him *regular,* or dub him *quack.*

ACT ONE

Scene, *A chamber in an old-fashioned house*

Enter MRS. HARDCASTLE *and* MR. HARD-
CASTLE.

MRS. HARDCASTLE. I vow, Mr. Hardcastle,
you're very particular. Is there a creature
in the whole country but ourselves that does
not take a trip to town now and then, to rub
off the rust a little? There's the two Miss
Hoggs, and our neighbor, Mrs. Grigsby, go
to take a month's polishing every winter.

HARDCASTLE. Ay, and bring back vanity
and affectation to last them the whole year.
I wonder why London cannot keep its own
fools at home. In my time the follies of the
town crept slowly among us, but now they
travel faster than a stagecoach. Its fopperies
come down, not only as inside passengers,
but in the very basket.[1]

MRS. HARDCASTLE. Ay, *your* times were
fine times, indeed; you have been telling us
of *them* for many a long year. Here we live
in an old rumbling mansion, that looks for
all the world like an inn, but that we never
see company. Our best visitors are old Mrs.
Oddfish, the curate's wife, and little Cripple-
gate, the lame dancing-master: And all our
entertainment your old stories of Prince
Eugene and the Duke of Marlborough.[2] I
hate such old-fashioned trumpery.

HARDCASTLE. And I love it. I love every
thing that's old: old friends, old times, old
manners, old books, old wine; and, I believe,
Dorothy (*taking her hand*) you'll own I have
been pretty fond of an old wife.

MRS. HARDCASTLE. Lord, Mr. Hardcastle,
you're forever at your Dorothy's and your
old wife's. You may be a Darby, but I'll be
no Joan,[3] I promise you. I'm not so old as
you'd make me, by more than one good year.
Add twenty to twenty, and make money of
that.

HARDCASTLE. Let me see; twenty added to
twenty, makes just fifty and seven.

MRS. HARDCASTLE. It's false, Mr. Hardcastle: I was but twenty when I was brought
to bed of Tony, that I had by Mr. Lumpkin,
my first husband; and he's not come to years
of discretion[4] yet.

---

6. A DOCTOR: i.e., Dr. Oliver Goldsmith.
7. FIVE DRAUGHTS: five acts.
8. WITHIN . . . FEE: i.e., no one will buy tickets.

1. BASKET: luggage compartment.
2. PRINCE EUGENE . . . DUKE OF MARLBOROUGH:
Austrian and English generals victorious at
Blenheim (1704), Oudenarde (1708), and Mal-
plaquet (1709).
3. DARBY . . . JOAN: in a ballad called "The Happy
Old Couple" Darby and Joan are the sweet and
loving couple.
4. COME . . . DISCRETION: i.e., come of age;
reached 21.

HARDCASTLE. Nor ever will, I dare answer for him. Ay, you have taught *him* finely.

MRS. HARDCASTLE. No matter, Tony Lumpkin has a good fortune. My son is not to live by his learning. I don't think a boy wants much learning to spend fifteen hundred a year.[5]

HARDCASTLE. Learning, quotha![6] A mere composition of tricks and mischief.

MRS. HARDCASTLE. Humor, my dear: nothing but humor. Come, Mr. Hardcastle, you must allow the boy a little humor.

HARDCASTLE. I'd sooner allow him an horse-pond.[7] If burning the footmen's shoes, frighting the maids, and worrying the kittens, be humor, he has it. It was but yesterday he fastened my wig to the back of my chair, and when I went to make a bow, I popped my bald head in Mrs. Frizzle's face.

MRS. HARDCASTLE. And am I to blame? The poor boy was always too sickly to do any good. A school would be his death. When he comes to be a little stronger, who knows what a year or two's Latin may do for him?

HARDCASTLE. Latin for him! A cat and fiddle. No, no, the alehouse and the stable are the only schools he'll ever go to.

MRS. HARDCASTLE. Well, we must not snub[8] the poor boy now, for I believe we shan't have him long among us. Anybody that looks in his face may see he's consumptive.

HARDCASTLE. Ay, if growing too fat be one of the symptoms.

MRS. HARDCASTLE. He coughs sometimes.

HARDCASTLE. Yes, when his liquor goes the wrong way.

MRS. HARDCASTLE. I'm actually afraid of his lungs.

HARDCASTLE. And truly so am I; for he sometimes whoops like a speaking trumpet[9]

—(TONY *hallooing behind the scenes*)—O there he goes—A very consumptive figure, truly.

Enter TONY, *crossing the stage.*

MRS. HARDCASTLE. Tony, where are you going, my charmer? Won't you give papa and I a little of your company, lovee?

TONY. I'm in haste, mother. I cannot stay.

MRS. HARDCASTLE. You shan't venture out this raw evening, my dear. You look most shockingly.

TONY. I can't stay, I tell you. The Three Pigeons[10] expects me down every moment. There's some fun going forward.

HARDCASTLE. Ay; the alehouse, the old place. I thought so.

MRS. HARDCASTLE. A low, paltry set of fellows.

TONY. Not so low neither. There's Dick Muggins the excise-man, Jack Slang the horse doctor, Little Aminadab that grinds the music box, and Tom Twist that spins the pewter platter.

MRS. HARDCASTLE. Pray, my dear, disappoint them for one night at least.

TONY. As for disappointing *them,* I should not much mind; but I can't abide to disappoint *myself.*

MRS. HARDCASTLE (*detaining him*). You shan't go.

TONY. I will, I tell you.

MRS. HARDCASTLE. I say you shan't.

TONY. We'll see which is strongest, you or I. (*Exit, hauling her out.*)

HARDCASTLE *solus.*[11]

HARDCASTLE. Ay, there goes a pair that only spoil each other. But is not the whole age in a combination to drive sense and discretion out of doors? There's my pretty darling Kate; the fashions of the times have almost infected her too. By living a year or two in town, she is as fond of gauze and French frippery, as the best of them.

---

5. FIFTEEN HUNDRED A YEAR: fifteen hundred pounds a year income, a very handsome sum.
6. QUOTHA!: indeed!
7. HORSE-POND: i.e., to duck him in.
8. SNUB: restrain.
9. SPEAKING TRUMPET: megaphone.

---

10. THE THREE PIGEONS: a tavern nearby.
11. SOLUS: alone.

Enter MISS HARDCASTLE.

HARDCASTLE. Blessings on my pretty innocence! Dressed out as usual, my Kate. Goodness! What a quantity of superfluous silk hast thou got about thee, girl! I could never teach the fools of this age that the indigent world could be clothed out of the trimmings of the vain.

MISS HARDCASTLE. You know our agreement, Sir. You allow me the morning to receive and pay visits, and to dress in my own manner; and in the evening I put on my housewife's dress to please you.

HARDCASTLE. Well, remember I insist on the terms of our agreement; and, by the bye, I believe I shall have occasion to try your obedience this very evening.

MISS HARDCASTLE. I protest, Sir, I don't comprehend your meaning.

HARDCASTLE. Then to be plain with you, Kate, I expect the young gentleman I have chosen to be your husband from town this very day. I have his father's letter, in which he informs me his son is set out, and that he intends to follow himself shortly after.

MISS HARDCASTLE. Indeed! I wish I had known something of this before. Bless me, how shall I behave? It's a thousand to one I shan't like him; our meeting will be so formal, and so like a thing of business, that I shall find no room for friendship or esteem.

HARDCASTLE. Depend upon it, child, I'll never control your choice; but Mr. Marlow, whom I have pitched upon[12] is the son of my old friend, Sir Charles Marlow, of whom you have heard me talk so often. The young gentleman has been bred a scholar, and is designed for an employment in the service of his country. I am told he's a man of an excellent understanding.

MISS HARDCASTLE. Is he?

HARDCASTLE. Very generous.

MISS HARDCASTLE. I believe I shall like him.

HARDCASTLE. Young and brave.

MISS HARDCASTLE. I'm sure I shall like him.

HARDCASTLE. And very handsome.

MISS HARDCASTLE. My dear papa, say no more (*kissing his hand*) he's mine, I'll have him.

HARDCASTLE. And to crown all, Kate, he's one of the most bashful and reserved young fellows in all the world.

MISS HARDCASTLE. Eh! you have frozen me to death again. That word reserved has undone all the rest of his accomplishments. A reserved lover, it is said, always makes a suspicious husband.

HARDCASTLE. On the contrary, modesty seldom resides in a breast that is not enriched with nobler virtues. It was the very feature in his character that first struck me.

MISS HARDCASTLE. He must have more striking features to catch me, I promise you. However, if he be so young, so handsome, and so everything, as you mention, I believe he'll do still. I think I'll have him.

HARDCASTLE. Ay, Kate, but there is still an obstacle. It's more than an even wager, he may not have *you*.

MISS HARDCASTLE. My dear papa, why will you mortify one so?—Well, if he refuses, instead of breaking my heart at his indifference, I'll only break my glass[13] for its flattery. Set my cap to some newer fashion,[14] and look out for some less difficult admirer.

HARDCASTLE. Bravely resolved! In the mean time I'll go prepare the servants for his reception; as we seldom see company they want as much training as a company of recruits, the first day's muster. (*Exit.*)

MISS HARDCASTLE *sola.*

MISS HARDCASTLE. Lud,[15] this news of Papa's puts me all in a flutter. Young, handsome; these he put last; but I put them foremost. Sensible, good-natured; I like all that. But then reserved, and sheepish, that's much against him. Yet can't he be cured of his timidity, by being taught to be proud of his

12. PITCHED UPON: chosen.

13. GLASS: mirror.
14. SET . . . FASHION: arrange my hat to look most beguiling (to attract a man).
15. LUD: Lord, a mild oath.

wife? Yes, and can't I—But I vow I'm disposing of the husband, before I have secured the lover.

Enter MISS NEVILLE.

MISS HARDCASTLE. I'm glad you're come, Neville, my dear. Tell me, Constance, how do I look this evening? Is there anything whimsical[16] about me? Is it one of my well looking days, child? Am I in face today?

MISS NEVILLE. Perfectly, my dear. Yet now I look again—bless me!—sure no accident has happened among the canary birds or the gold fishes. Has your brother or the cat been meddling? Or has the last novel been too moving?

MISS HARDCASTLE. No; nothing of all this. I have been threatened—I can scarce get it out—I have been threatened with a lover.

MISS NEVILLE. And his name——

MISS HARDCASTLE. Is Marlow.

MISS NEVILLE. Indeed!

MISS HARDCASTLE. The son of Sir Charles Marlow.

MISS NEVILLE. As I live, the most intimate friend of Mr. Hastings, *my* admirer. They are never asunder. I believe you must have seen him when we lived in town.

MISS HARDCASTLE. Never.

MISS NEVILLE. He's a very singular character, I assure you. Among women of reputation and virtue, he is the modestest man alive; but his acquaintance give him a very different character among creatures of another stamp: you understand me.

MISS HARDCASTLE. An odd character, indeed. I shall never be able to manage him. What shall I do? Pshaw, think no more of him, but trust to occurrences for success. But how goes on your own affair my dear, has my mother been courting you for my brother Tony, as usual?

MISS NEVILLE. I have just come from one of our agreeable tête-à-têtes. She has been saying a hundred tender things, and setting off her pretty monster as the very pink of perfection.

MISS HARDCASTLE. And her partiality is such that she actually thinks him so. A fortune like yours is no small temptation. Besides, as she has the sole management of it, I'm not surprised to see her unwilling to let it go out of the family.

MISS NEVILLE. A fortune like mine, which chiefly consists in jewels, is no such mighty temptation. But at any rate if my dear Hastings be but constant, I make no doubt to be too hard for her at last. However, I let her suppose that I am in love with her son, and she never once dreams that my affections are fixed upon another.

MISS HARDCASTLE. My good brother holds out stoutly. I could almost love him for hating you so.

MISS NEVILLE. It is a good natured creature at bottom, and I'm sure would wish to see me married to anybody but himself. But my aunt's bell rings for our afternoon's walk round the improvements.[17] Allons.[18] Courage is necessary, as our affairs are critical.

MISS HARDCASTLE. Would it were bed time and all were well.[19]

(*Exeunt.*)

Scene, *An alehouse room. Several shabby fellows with punch and tobacco.* TONY *at the head of the table, a little higher than the rest: A mallet in his hand.*

OMNES.[20] Hurrah, hurrah, hurrah, bravo.

FIRST FELLOW. Now, gentlemen, silence for a song. The Squire is going to knock himself down for a song.[21]

OMNES. Ay, a song, a song.

TONY. Then I'll sing you, gentlemen, a song I made upon this alehouse, the Three Pigeons.

16. WHIMSICAL: odd; queer.

17. IMPROVEMENTS: in the ground of the Hardcastle estate.
18. ALLONS: let's go.
19. WOULD . . . WELL: In *Henry IV, Part I,* V, i, 126, Falstaff says on the eve of battle, "I would't were bed-time, Hal, and all well."
20. OMNES: all.
21. KNOCK . . . SONG: the reference is to auctioneering; the blow of the mallet ("knock down") signals that a bid is accepted.

SONG

Let school-masters puzzle their brain,
  With grammar, and nonsense, and
    learning;
Good liquor, I stoutly maintain,
  Gives genus[22] a better discerning.
Let them brag of their Heathenish Gods,
  Their Lethes, their Styxes, and
    Stygians;[23]
Their Quis, *and their* Quæs, *and their*
    Quods,[24]
  They're all but a parcel of Pigeons.[25]
    Toroddle, toroddle, toroll.

When Methodist preachers come down,
  A preaching that drinking is sinful,
I'll wager the rascals a crown,
  They always preach best with a skinful.
But when you come down with your
    pence,
  For a slice of their scurvy religion,
I'll leave it to all men of sense,
  But you, my good friend, are the
    pigeon.
    Toroddle, toroddle, toroll.

Then come, put the jorum[26] about,
  And let us be merry and clever,
Our hearts and our liquors are stout,
  Here's the Three Jolly Pigeons for ever.
Let some cry up[27] woodcock or hare,
  Your bustards, your ducks, and your
    widgeons;
But of all the birds in the air,
  Here's a health to the Three Jolly
    Pigeons.
    Toroddle, toroddle, toroll.

OMNES. Bravo, bravo.

FIRST FELLOW. The Squire has got spunk in him.

SECOND FELLOW. I loves to hear him sing, bekeays[28] he never gives us nothing that's *low.*[29]

THIRD FELLOW. O damn anything that's *low,* I cannot bear it.

FOURTH FELLOW. The genteel thing is the genteel thing at any time. If so be that a gentleman bees in a concatenation accordingly.

THIRD FELLOW. I like the maxum of it, Master Muggins. What, tho' I am obligated to dance a bear,[30] a man may be a gentleman for all that. May this be my poison if my bear ever dances but to the very genteelest of tunes. Water Parted,[31] or the minuet in Ariadne.[32]

SECOND FELLOW. What a pity it is the Squire is not come to his own.[33] It would be well for all the publicans within ten miles round of him.

TONY. Ecod and so it would, Master Slang. I'd then show what it was to keep choice of company.

SECOND FELLOW. O, he takes after his own father for that. To be sure old Squire Lumpkin was the finest gentleman I ever set my eyes on. For winding the straight horn,[34] or beating a thicket for a hare or a wench, he never had his fellow. It was a saying in the place that he kept the best horses, dogs, and girls in the whole county.

TONY. Ecod, and when I'm of age I'll be no bastard I promise you. I have been thinking of Bet Bouncer and the miller's grey mare to begin with. But come, my boys, drink about and be merry, for you pay no

---

22. GENUS: genius.
23. LETHES . . . STYGIANS: Lethe and Styx are rivers of the lower world; Stygian refers to Styx.
24. QUIS . . . QUODS: Latin for who, which, what.
25. PIGEONS: dupes.
26. JORUM: a large drinking vessel.
27. CRY UP: praise loudly in public.

28. BEKEAYS: because.
29. LOW: vulgar; Goldsmith is here making fun of the extremely delicate tastes of his contemporaries through the mockery of these "shabby fellows."
30. DANCE A BEAR: Muzzled bears were often led through the streets and made to perform to get money for the owner.
31. WATER PARTED: a song from a contemporary play.
32. ARIADNE: an opera.
33. TO HIS OWN: to his inheritance.
34. WINDING . . . HORN: blowing the hunter's horn.

reckoning.[35] Well Stingo, what's the matter?

Enter LANDLORD.

LANDLORD. There be two gentlemen in a post-chaise at the door. They have lost their way upo' the forest; and they are talking something about Mr. Hardcastle.

TONY. As sure as can be one of them must be the gentleman that's coming down to court my sister. Do they seem to be Londoners?

LANDLORD. I believe they may. They look woundily[36] like Frenchmen.

TONY. Then desire[37] them to step this way, and I'll set them right in a twinkling. (*Exit* LANDLORD.) Gentlemen, as they mayn't be good enough company for you, step down for a moment, and I'll be with you in the squeezing of a lemon.

(*Exeunt* MOB.)

TONY *solus.*

TONY. Father-in-law[38] has been calling me whelp, and hound, this half year. Now if I pleased, I could be so revenged upon the old grumbletonian.[39] But then I'm afraid—afraid of what! I shall soon be worth fifteen hundred a year, and let him frighten me out of *that* if he can.

Enter LANDLORD, *conducting* MARLOW *and* HASTINGS.

MARLOW. What a tedious uncomfortable day have we had of it! We were told it was but forty miles across the country, and we have come above threescore.

HASTINGS. And all Marlow, from that unaccountable reserve of yours, that would not let us inquire more frequently on the way.

MARLOW. I own, Hastings, I am unwilling to lay myself under an obligation to every one I meet, and often stand the chance of an unmannerly answer.

HASTINGS. At present, however, we are not likely to receive any answer.

TONY. No offense, gentlemen. But I'm told you have been inquiring for one Mr. Hardcastle, in these parts. Do you know what part of the country you are in?

HASTINGS. Not in the least Sir, but should thank you for information.

TONY. Nor the way you came?

HASTINGS. No, Sir; but if you can inform us——

TONY. Why, gentlemen, if you know neither the road you are going, nor where you are, nor the road you came, the first thing I have to inform you is, that—You have lost your way.

MARLOW. We wanted no ghost to tell us that.[40]

TONY. Pray, gentlemen, may I be so bold as to ask the place from whence you came?

MARLOW. That's not necessary towards directing us where we are to go.

TONY. No offense; but question for question is all fair, you know. Pray, gentlemen, is not this same Hardcastle a cross-grained, old-fashioned, whimsical fellow with an ugly face, a daughter, and a pretty son?

HASTINGS. We have not seen the gentleman, but he has the family you mention.

TONY. The daughter, a tall, traipsing, trolloping, talkative maypole——The son, a pretty, well-bred, agreeable youth, that everybody is fond of.

MARLOW. Our information differs in this. The daughter is said to be well-bred and beautiful; the son, an awkward booby, reared up, and spoiled at his mother's apron-string.

TONY. He-he-hem—Then, gentlemen, all I have to tell you is, that you won't reach Mr. Hardcastle's house this night, I believe.

HASTINGS. Unfortunate!

TONY. It's a damned long, dark, boggy, dirty, dangerous way. Stingo, tell the gentlemen the way to Mr. Hardcastle's; (*winking upon the* LANDLORD) Mr. Hardcastle's, of Quagmire Marsh, you understand me.

---

35. YOU . . . RECKONING: this costs you nothing.
36. WOUNDILY. very much.
37. DESIRE: ask.
38. FATHER-IN-LAW: i.e., step-father.
39. GRUMBLETONIAN: name applied by their opponents to a certain seventeenth century political party; from "grumble."

---

40. WE . . . THAT: See *Hamlet,* I, v, 125.

LANDLORD. Master Hardcastle's! Lock-a-daisy,[41] my masters, you're come a deadly deal wrong! When you came to the bottom of the hill, you should have crossed down Squash Lane.

MARLOW. Cross down Squash Lane!

LANDLORD. Then you were to keep straight forward, till you came to four roads.

MARLOW. Come to where four roads meet!

TONY. Ay; but you must be sure to take only one of them.

MARLOW. O Sir, you're facetious.

TONY. Then keeping to the right, you are to go sideways till you come upon Crackskull common: there you must look sharp for the track of the wheel, and go forward, till you come to farmer Murrain's barn. Coming to the farmer's barn, you are to turn to the right, and then to the left, and then to the right about again, till you find out the old mill——

MARLOW. Zounds, man! we could as soon find out the longitude!

HASTINGS. What's to be done, Marlow?

MARLOW. This house promises but a poor reception; though perhaps the Landlord can accommodate us.

LANDLORD. Alack, master, we have but one spare bed in the whole house.

TONY. And to my knowledge, that's taken up by three lodgers already. (*after a pause, in which the rest seem disconcerted*) I have hit it. Don't you think, Stingo, our landlady could accommodate the gentlemen by the fireside, with——three chairs and a bolster?

HASTINGS. I hate sleeping by the fireside.

MARLOW. And I detest your three chairs and a bolster.

TONY. You do, do you?——then let me see——what—if you go on a mile further, to the Buck's Head; the old Buck's Head on the hill, one of the best inns in the whole county?

HASTINGS. O ho! so we have escaped an adventure for this night, however.[42]

LANDLORD. (*apart to* TONY) Sure, you

ben't[43] sending them to your father's as an inn, be you?

TONY. Mum, you fool you. Let *them* find that out. (*to them*) You have only to keep on straight forward, till you come to a large old house by the road side. You'll see a pair of large horns over the door. That's the sign. Drive up the yard, and call stoutly[44] about you.

HASTINGS. Sir, we are obliged to you. The servants can't miss the way?

TONY. No, no. But I tell you though, the landlord is rich, and going to leave off business; so he wants to be thought a gentleman, saving your presence, he! he! he! He'll be for giving you his company, and ecod if you mind him, he'll persuade you that his mother was an alderman, and his aunt a justice of the peace.

LANDLORD. A troublesome old blade[45] to be sure; but a[46] keeps as good wines and beds as any in the whole country.

MARLOW. Well, if he supplies us with these, we shall want no further connection. We are to turn to the right, did you say?

TONY. No, no; straight forward. I'll just step myself, and show you a piece of the way. (*to the* LANDLORD) Mum.

LANDLORD. Ah, bless your heart, for a sweet, pleasant——damned mischievous son of a whore.

(*Exeunt.*)

ACT TWO

Scene, *An old-fashioned house*

Enter HARDCASTLE, *followed by three or four awkward* SERVANTS.

HARDCASTLE. Well, I hope you're perfect in the table exercise[1] I have been teaching you these three days. You all know your posts and your places, and can show that you

---

41. LOCK-A-DAISY: alackaday (or alack), an exclamation of regret.
42. HOWEVER: in any case.

43. BEN'T: be not.
44. STOUTLY: loudly.
45. BLADE: a sharp-witted fellow.
46. A: he.
1. TABLE EXERCISE: waiting on table.

have been used to good company, without ever stirring from home.

OMNES. Ay, ay.

HARDCASTLE. When company comes, you are not to pop out and stare, and then run in again, like frighted rabbits in a warren.

OMNES. No, no.

HARDCASTLE. You, Diggory, whom I have taken from the barn, are to make a show at the side-table; and you, Roger, whom I have advanced from the plough, are to place yourself behind *my* chair. But you're not to stand so, with your hands in your pockets. Take your hands from your pockets, Roger; and from your head, you blockhead you. See how Diggory carries his hands. They're a little too stiff, indeed, but that's no great matter.

DIGGORY. Ay, mind how I hold them. I learned to hold my hands this way, when I was upon drill for the militia. And so being upon drill——

HARDCASTLE. You must not be so talkative, Diggory. You must be all attention to the guests. You must hear us talk, and not think of talking; you must see us drink, and not think of drinking; you must see us eat, and not think of eating.

DIGGORY. By the laws, your worship, that's perfectly unpossible. Whenever Diggory sees yeating going forward, ecod he's always wishing for a mouthful himself.

HARDCASTLE. Blockhead! Is not a bellyful in the kitchen as good as a bellyful in the parlor? Stay your stomach with that reflection.

DIGGORY. Ecod I thank your worship, I'll make a shift to stay my stomach with a slice of cold beef in the pantry.

HARDCASTLE. Diggory, you are too talkative. Then if I happen to say a good thing, or tell a good story at table, you must not all burst out a-laughing, as if you made part of the company.

DIGGORY. Then ecod your worship must not tell the story of Ould Grouse in the gunroom: I can't help laughing at that—he! he! he!—for the soul of me. We have

laughed at that these twenty years—ha! ha! ha!

HARDCASTLE. Ha! ha! ha! The story is a good one. Well, honest Diggory, you may laugh at that—but still remember to be attentive. Suppose one of the company should call for a glass of wine, how will you behave? A glass of wine, Sir, if you please (*to* DIGGORY)—Eh, why don't you move?

DIGGORY. Ecod, your worship, I never have courage till I see the eatables and drinkables brought upo' the table, and then I'm as bauld[2] as a lion.

HARDCASTLE. What, will nobody move?

FIRST SERVANT. I'm not to leave this place.

SECOND SERVANT. I'm sure it's no place of mine.

THIRD SERVANT. Nor mine, for sartain.

DIGGORY. Wauns,[3] and I'm sure it canna be mine.

HARDCASTLE. You numbskulls! and so while, like your betters, you are quarreling for places, the guests must be starved. O you dunces! I find I must begin all over again.—But don't I hear a coach drive into the yard? To your posts you blockheads. I'll go in the meantime and give my old friend's son a hearty reception at the gate.

(*Exit* HARDCASTLE.)

DIGGORY. By the elevens,[4] my place is gone quite out of my head.

ROGER. I know that my place is to be everywhere.

FIRST SERVANT. Where the devil is mine?

SECOND SERVANT. My place is to be nowhere at all; and so I'ze[5] go about my business. (*Exeunt* SERVANTS, *running about as if frighted, different ways.*)

Enter SERVANT *with candles, showing in* MARLOW *and* HASTINGS.

SERVANT. Welcome, gentlemen, very welcome. This way.

HASTINGS. After the disappointments of

2. BAULD: bold.
3. WAUNS: zounds.
4. BY THE ELEVENS: origin unknown; probably a euphemistic rhyme for "by heavens."
5. I'ZE: I'll.

the day, welcome once more, Charles, to the comforts of a clean room and a good fire. Upon my word, a very well-looking house; antique but creditable.

MARLOW. The usual fate of a large mansion. Having first ruined the master by good housekeeping, it at last comes to levy contributions as an inn.

HASTINGS. As you say, we passengers are to be taxed to pay all these fineries. I have often seen a good sideboard, or a marble chimney-piece, tho' not actually put in the bill, enflame a reckoning[6] confoundedly.

MARLOW. Travelers, George, must pay in all places. The only difference is, that in good inns you pay dearly for luxuries; in bad inns you are fleeced and starved.

HASTINGS. You have lived pretty much among them. In truth, I have been often surprised that you who have seen so much of the world, with your natural good sense, and your many opportunities, could never yet acquire a requisite share of assurance.

MARLOW. The Englishman's malady. But tell me, George, where could I have learned that assurance you talk of? My life has been chiefly spent in a college or an inn,[7] in seclusion from that lovely part of the creation that chiefly teach men confidence. I don't know that I was ever familiarly acquainted with a single modest woman—except my mother—But among females of another class you know—

HASTINGS. Ay, among them you are impudent enough of all conscience.

MARLOW. They are of *us,* you know.

HASTINGS. But in the company of women of reputation I never saw such an idiot, such a trembler; you look for all the world as if you wanted an opportunity of stealing out of the room.

MARLOW. Why man that's because I *do* want to steal out of the room. Faith, I have often formed a resolution to break the ice, and rattle away at any rate. But I don't know how, a single glance from a pair of fine eyes has totally overset my resolution. An impudent fellow may counterfeit modesty, but I'll be hanged if a modest man can ever counterfeit impudence.

HASTINGS. If you could but say half the fine things to them that I have heard you lavish upon the barmaid of an inn, or even a college bedmaker—

MARLOW. Why, George, I can't say fine things to them. They freeze, they petrify me. They may talk of a comet, or a burning mountain, or some such bagatelle. But to me, a modest woman, dressed out in all her finery, is the most tremendous object of the whole creation.

HASTINGS. Ha! ha! ha! At this rate, man, how can you ever expect to marry!

MARLOW. Never, unless as among kings and princes, my bride were to be courted by proxy. If, indeed, like an Eastern bridegroom, one were to be introduced to a wife he never saw before, it might be endured. But to go through all the terrors of a formal courtship, together with the episode of aunts, grandmothers and cousins, and at last to blurt out the broad staring question of *madam will you marry me?* No, no, that's a strain much above me I assure you.

HASTINGS. I pity you. But how do you intend behaving to the lady you are come down to visit at the request of your father?

MARLOW. As I behave to all other ladies. Bow very low. Answer yes, or no, to all her demands—But for the rest, I don't think I shall venture to look in her face, till I see my father's again.

HASTINGS. I'm surprised that one who is so warm a friend can be so cool a lover.

MARLOW. To be explicit, my dear Hastings, my chief inducement down was to be instrumental in forwarding your happiness, not my own. Miss Neville loves you, the family don't know you, as my friend you are sure of a reception, and let honor do the rest.

HASTINGS. My dear Marlow! But I'll suppress the emotion. Were I a wretch, meanly seeking to carry off a fortune, you should be

---

6. ENFLAME A RECKONING: enlarge a bill.
7. INN: students' lodging.

the last man in the world I would apply to for assistance. But Miss Neville's person is all I ask, and that is mine, both from her deceased father's consent, and her own inclination.

MARLOW. Happy man! You have talents and art to captivate any woman. I'm doomed to adore the sex, and yet to converse with the only part of it I despise. This stammer in my address, and this awkward prepossessing visage of mine, can never permit me to soar above the reach of a milliner's 'prentice, or one of the duchesses of Drury Lane.[8] Pshaw! this fellow here to interrupt us.

Enter HARDCASTLE.

HARDCASTLE. Gentlemen, once more you are heartily welcome. Which is Mr. Marlow? Sir, you're heartily welcome. It's not my way, you see, to receive my friends with my back to the fire. I like to give them a hearty reception in the old style at my gate. I like to see their horses and trunks taken care of.

MARLOW (*aside*). He has got our names from the servants already. (*to him*) We approve your caution and hospitality, Sir. (*to* HASTINGS) I have been thinking, George, of changing our traveling dresses in the morning. I am grown confoundedly ashamed of mine.

HARDCASTLE. I beg, Mr. Marlow, you'll use no ceremony in this house.

HASTINGS. I fancy, Charles, you're right: the first blow is half the battle. I intend opening the campaign with the white and gold.

HARDCASTLE. Mr. Marlow—Mr. Hastings —gentlemen—pray be under no constraint in this house. This is Liberty Hall, gentlemen. You may do just as you please here.

MARLOW. Yet, George, if we open the campaign too fiercely at first, we may want ammunition before it is over. I think to reserve the embroidery to secure a retreat.

HARDCASTLE. Your talking of a retreat, Mr. Marlow, puts me in mind of the Duke of Marlborough, when we went to besiege Denain.[9] He first summoned the garrison.

MARLOW. Don't you think the *ventre d'or*[10] waistcoat will do with the plain brown?

HARDCASTLE. He first summoned the garrison, which might consist of about five thousand men——

HASTINGS. I think not. Brown and yellow mix but very poorly.

HARDCASTLE. I say, gentlemen, as I was telling you, he summoned the garrison, which might consist of about five thousand men——

MARLOW. The girls like finery.

HARDCASTLE. Which might consist of about five thousand men, well appointed with stores, ammunition, and other implements of war. Now, says the Duke of Marlborough to George Brooks, that stood next to him— You must have heard of George Brooks; I'll pawn my Dukedom, says he, but I take that garrison without spilling a drop of blood. So——

MARLOW. What, my good friend, if you gave us a glass of punch in the meantime, it would help us to carry on the siege with vigor.

HARDCASTLE. Punch, Sir! (*aside*) This is the most unaccountable kind of modesty I ever met with.

MARLOW. Yes, Sir, punch. A glass of warm punch, after our journey, will be comfortable. This is Liberty Hall, you know.

HARDCASTLE. Here's cup, Sir.

MARLOW (*aside*). So this fellow, in his Liberty Hall, will only let us have just what he pleases.

HARDCASTLE (*taking the cup*). I hope you'll find it to your mind. I have prepared it with my own hands, and I believe you'll own the ingredients are tolerable. Will you be so good as to pledge me, Sir? Here, Mr. Marlow, here is to our better acquaintance. (*drinks*)

---

8. DUCHESSES OF DRURY LANE: women of the streets.

9. DENAIN: English defeat in 1712.
10. VENTRE D'OR: gold-fronted.

MARLOW (*aside*). A very impudent fellow this! but he's a character, and I'll humor him a little. Sir, my service to you. (*drinks*)

HASTINGS (*aside*). I see this fellow wants to give us his company, and forgets that he's an innkeeper, before he has learned to be a gentleman.

MARLOW. From the excellence of your cup, my old friend, I suppose you have a good deal of business in this part of the country. Warm work, now and then, at elections, I suppose.

HARDCASTLE. No, Sir, I have long given that work over. Since our betters have hit upon the expedient of electing each other, there's no business *for us that sell ale*.[11]

HASTINGS. So, then you have no turn for politics, I find.

HARDCASTLE. Not in the least. There was a time, indeed, I fretted myself about the mistakes of government, like other people; but finding myself every day grow more angry, and the government growing no better, I left it to mend itself. Since that, I no more trouble my head about *Heyder Ally,*[12] or *Ally Cawn,*[13] than about *Ally Croaker.*[14] Sir, my service to you.

HASTINGS. So that with eating above stairs, and drinking below, with receiving your friends within, and amusing them without, you lead a good pleasant bustling life of it.

HARDCASTLE. I do stir about a great deal, it's certain. Half the differences of the parish are adjusted in this very parlor.

MARLOW (*after drinking*). And you have an argument in your cup, old gentleman, better than any in Westminster Hall.

HARDCASTLE. Ay, young gentleman, that, and a little philosophy.

MARLOW (*aside*). Well, this is the first time I ever heard of an innkeeper's philosophy.

HASTINGS. So then, like an experienced general, you attack them on every quarter. If you find their reason manageable, you attack it with your philosophy; if you find they have no reason, you attack them with this. Here's your health, my philosopher. (*drinks*)

HARDCASTLE. Good, very good, thank you; ha, ha. Your Generalship puts me in mind of Prince Eugene, when he fought the Turks at the battle of Belgrade.[15] You shall hear.

MARLOW. Instead of the battle of Belgrade, I believe it's almost time to talk about supper. What has your philosophy got in the house for supper?

HARDCASTLE. For supper, Sir! (*aside*) Was ever such a request to a man in his own house!

MARLOW. Yes, Sir, supper, Sir; I begin to feel an appetite. I shall make devilish work tonight in the larder, I promise you.

HARDCASTLE (*aside*). Such a brazen dog sure never my eyes beheld. (*to him*) Why really, Sir, as for supper I can't well tell. My Dorothy, and the cook maid, settle these things between them. I leave these kind of things entirely to them.

MARLOW. You do, do you?

HARDCASTLE. Entirely. By-the-bye, I believe they are in actual consultation upon what's for supper this moment in the kitchen.

MARLOW. Then I beg they'll admit *me* as one of their privy council. It's a way I have got. When I travel, I always choose to regulate my own supper. Let the cook be called. No offense I hope, Sir.

HARDCASTLE. O no, Sir, none in the least; yet, I don't know how: our Bridget, the cook maid, is not very communicative upon these occasions. Should we send for her, she might scold us all out of the house.

HASTINGS. Let's see your list of the larder then. I ask it as a favor. I always match my appetite to my bill of fare.

MARLOW. (*to* HARDCASTLE, *who looks at*

---

11. FOR . . . ALE: for common people.
12. HEYDER ALLY: Haider Ali (1722-1782), Sultan of Mysore.
13. ALLY CAWN: Ali Kahn: Sultan of Bengal.
14. ALLY CROAKER: hero of a well-known Irish ballad.

---

15. BELGRADE: defeat of the Turks, 1717.

them with surprise) Sir, he's very right, and it's my way too.

HARDCASTLE. Sir, you have a right to command here. Here, Roger, bring us the bill of fare for tonight's supper. I believe it's drawn out. Your manner, Mr. Hastings, puts me in mind of my uncle, Colonel Wallop. It was a saying of his, that no man was sure of his supper till he had eaten it.

HASTINGS (*aside*). All upon the high ropes![16] His uncle a colonel! We shall soon hear of his mother being a justice of peace. But let's hear the bill of fare.

MARLOW (*perusing*). What's here? For the first course; for the second course; for the dessert. The devil, Sir, do you think we have brought down the whole Joiners' Company,[17] or the Corporation of Bedford,[18] to eat up such a supper? Two or three little things, clean and comfortable, will do.

HASTINGS. But, let's hear it.

MARLOW (*reading*). For the first course at the top, a pig, and prune sauce.

HASTINGS. Damn your pig, I say.

MARLOW. And damn your prune sauce, say I.

HARDCASTLE. And yet, gentlemen, to men that are hungry, pig, with prune sauce is very good eating.

MARLOW. At the bottom, a calf's tongue and brains.

HASTINGS. Let your brains be knocked out, my good Sir; I don't like them.

MARLOW. Or you may clap them on a plate by themselves. I do.

HARDCASTLE (*aside*). Their impudence confounds me. (*to them*) Gentlemen, you are my guests, make what alterations you please. Is there anything else you wish to retrench[19] or alter, gentlemen?

MARLOW. Item. A pork pie, a boiled rabbit and sausages, a florentine,[20] a shaking

pudding,[21] and a dish of tiff—taff—taffety cream![22]

HASTINGS. Confound your made dishes, I shall be as much at a loss in this house as at a green and yellow dinner[23] at the French ambassador's table. I'm for plain eating.

HARDCASTLE. I'm sorry, gentlemen, that I have nothing you like, but if there be any thing you have a particular fancy to——

MARLOW. Why, really, Sir, your bill of fare is so exquisite, that any one part of it is full as good as another. Send us what you please. So much for supper. And now to see that our beds are aired, and properly taken care of.

HARDCASTLE. I entreat you'll leave all that to me. You shall not stir a step.

MARLOW. Leave that to you! I protest, Sir, you must excuse me, I always look to these things myself.

HARDCASTLE. I must insist, Sir, you'll make yourself easy on that head.

MARLOW. You see I'm resolved on it. (*aside*) A very troublesome fellow this, as ever I met with.

HARDCASTLE. Well, Sir, I'm resolved at least to attend you. (*aside*) This may be modern modesty, but I never saw anything look so like old-fashioned impudence.

(*Exeunt* MARLOW *and* HARDCASTLE.)

HASTINGS *solus*.

HASTINGS. So I find this fellow's civilities begin to grow troublesome. But who can be angry at those assiduities which are meant to please him? Ha! what do I see? Miss Neville, by all that's happy!

Enter MISS NEVILLE.

MISS NEVILLE. My dear Hastings! To what unexpected good fortune? to what accident am I to ascribe this happy meeting?

HASTINGS. Rather let me ask the same question, as I could never have hoped to meet my dearest Constance at an inn.

MISS NEVILLE. An inn! sure you mistake!

16. ALL UPON THE HIGH ROPES!: i.e., nothing but big talk! (image from rope-dancing).
17. JOINERS' COMPANY: Woodworkers' Union.
18. CORPORATION OF BEDFORD: the municipal authorities of the town of Bedford.
19. RETRENCH: remove.
20. FLORENTINE: meat pie.

21. SHAKING PUDDING: blanc-mange.
22. TAFFETY CREAM: a very fancy dessert.
23. GREEN . . . DINNER: just frills, no substantial foods.

my aunt, my guardian, lives here. What could induce you to think this house an inn?

HASTINGS. My friend Mr. Marlow, with whom I came down, and I, have been sent here as to an inn, I assure you. A young fellow whom we accidentally met at a house[24] hard by directed us hither.

MISS NEVILLE. Certainly it must be one of my hopeful cousin's tricks, of whom you have heard me talk so often, ha! ha! ha! ha!

HASTINGS. He whom your aunt intends for you? He of whom I have such just apprehensions?

MISS NEVILLE. You have nothing to fear from him, I assure you. You'd adore him if you knew how heartily he despises me. My aunt knows it too, and has undertaken to court me for him, and actually begins to think she has made a conquest.

HASTINGS. Thou dear dissembler! You must know, my Constance, I have just seized this happy opportunity of my friend's visit here to get admittance into the family. The horses that carried us down are now fatigued with their journey, but they'll soon be refreshed; and then if my dearest girl will trust in her faithful Hastings, we shall soon be landed in France, where even among slaves the laws of marriage are respected.

MISS NEVILLE. I have often told you, that though ready to obey you, I yet should leave my little fortune behind with reluctance. The greatest part of it was left me by my uncle, the India Director,[25] and chiefly consists in jewels. I have been for some time persuading my aunt to let me wear them. I fancy I'm very near succeeding. The instant they are put into my possession you shall find me ready to make them and myself yours.

HASTINGS. Perish the baubles! Your person is all I desire. In the meantime, my friend Marlow must not be let into his mistake. I know the strange reserve of his temper is such, that if abruptly informed of it, he would instantly quit the house before our plan was ripe for execution.

MISS NEVILLE. But how shall we keep him in the deception? Miss Hardcastle is just returned from walking; what if we still continue to deceive him?—This, this way ——(*They confer.*)

Enter MARLOW.

MARLOW. The assiduities of these good people tease[26] me beyond bearing. My host seems to think it ill manners to leave me alone, and so he claps not only himself but his old-fashioned wife on my back. They talk of coming to sup with us too; and then, I suppose, we are to run the gantlet through all the rest of the family.—What have we got here!—

HASTINGS. My dear Charles! Let me congratulate you!—The most fortunate accident!—Who do you think is just alighted?

MARLOW. Cannot guess.

HASTINGS. Our mistresses, boy, Miss Hardcastle and Miss Neville. Give me leave to introduce Miss Constance Neville to your acquaintance. Happening to dine in the neighborhood, they called, on their return to take fresh horses, here. Miss Hardcastle has just stepped into the next room, and will be back in an instant. Wasn't it lucky? eh!

MARLOW (*aside*). I have just been mortified enough of all conscience, and here comes something to complete my embarrassment.

HASTINGS. Well! but wasn't it the most fortunate thing in the world?

MARLOW. Oh! yes. Very fortunate—a most joyful encounter——But our dresses, George, you know, are in disorder——What if we should postpone the happiness till tomorrow?——Tomorrow at her own house ——It will be every bit as convenient—— And rather more respectful——Tomorrow let it be. (*offering to go*)

MISS NEVILLE. By no means, Sir. Your ceremony will displease her. The disorder of

---

24. HOUSE: tavern.
25. INDIA DIRECTOR: an officer in the influential and prosperous East India Company.

26. TEASE: annoy.

your dress will show the ardor of your impatience. Besides, she knows you are in the house, and will permit you to see her.

MARLOW. O! the devil! how shall I support it? Hem! hem! Hastings, you must not go. You are to assist me, you know. I shall be confoundedly ridiculous. Yet, hang it! I'll take courage. Hem!

HASTINGS. Pshaw man! it's but the first plunge, and all's over. She's but a woman, you know.

MARLOW. And of all women, she that I dread most to encounter!

Enter MISS HARDCASTLE *as returned from walking, a bonnet, &c.*

HASTINGS (*introducing them*). Miss Hardcastle, Mr. Marlow, I'm proud of bringing two persons of such merit together, that only want to know, to esteem each other.

MISS HARDCASTLE (*aside*). Now, for meeting my modest gentleman with a demure face, and quite in his own manner. (*after a pause, in which he appears very uneasy and disconcerted*) I'm glad of your safe arrival, Sir——I'm told you had some accidents by the way.

MARLOW. Only a few, madam. Yes, we had some. Yes, madam, a good many accidents, but should be sorry—madam—or rather glad of any accidents—that are so agreeably concluded. Hem!

HASTINGS (*to him*). You never spoke better in your whole life. Keep it up, and I'll insure you the victory.

MISS HARDCASTLE. I'm afraid you flatter, Sir. You that have seen so much of the finest company can find little entertainment in an obscure corner of the country.

MARLOW (*gathering courage*). I have lived, indeed, in the world, madam; but I have kept very little company. I have been but an observer upon life, madam, while others were enjoying it.

MISS NEVILLE. But that, I am told, is the way to enjoy it at last.

HASTINGS (*to him*). Cicero[27] never spoke

better. Once more, and you are confirmed in assurance forever.

MARLOW (*to him*). Hem! Stand by me then, and when I'm down, throw in a word or two to set me up again.

MISS HARDCASTLE. An observer, like you, upon life, were, I fear, disagreeably employed, since you must have had much more to censure than to approve.

MARLOW. Pardon me, madam. I was always willing to be amused. The folly of most people is rather an object of mirth than uneasiness.

HASTINGS (*to him*). Bravo, bravo. Never spoke so well in your whole life. Well, Miss Hardcastle, I see that you and Mr. Marlow are going to be very good company. I believe our being here will but embarrass the interview.

MARLOW. Not in the least, Mr. Hastings. We like your company of all things. (*to him*) Zounds! George, sure you won't go? How can you leave us?

HASTINGS. Our presence will but spoil conversation, so we'll retire to the next room. (*to him*) You don't consider, man, that we are to manage a little tête-à-tête of our own. (*Exeunt.*)

MISS HARDCASTLE (*after a pause*). But you have not been wholly an observer, I presume, Sir. The ladies I should hope have employed some part of your addresses.

MARLOW (*relapsing into timidity*). Pardon me, madam, I—I—I—as yet have studied—only—to—deserve them.

MISS HARDCASTLE. And that some say is the very worst way to obtain them.

MARLOW. Perhaps so, madam. But I love to converse only with the more grave and sensible part of the sex.——But I'm afraid I grow tiresome.

MISS HARDCASTLE. Not at all, Sir; there is nothing I like so much as grave conversation myself; I could hear it forever. Indeed I have often been surprised how a man of *sentiment*[28] could ever admire those light

27. CICERO: famous Roman orator.

28. SENTIMENT: refined feeling.

airy pleasures, where nothing reaches the heart.

MARLOW. It's—a disease—of the mind, madam. In the variety of tastes there must be some who, wanting a relish—for—um—a—um.

MISS HARDCASTLE. I understand you, Sir. There must be some, who wanting a relish for refined pleasures, pretend to despise what they are incapable of tasting.

MARLOW. My meaning, madam, but infinitely better expressed. And I can't help observing—a——

MISS HARDCASTLE (*aside*). Who could ever suppose this fellow impudent upon some occasions. (*to him*) You were going to observe, Sir——

MARLOW. I was observing, madam——I protest, madam, I forget what I was going to observe.

MISS HARDCASTLE (*aside*). I vow and so do I. (*to him*) You were observing, Sir, that in this age of hypocrisy—something about hypocrisy, Sir.

MARLOW. Yes, madam. In this age of hypocrisy there are few who upon strict inquiry do not—a—a—a——

MISS HARDCASTLE. I understand you perfectly, Sir.

MARLOW (*aside*). Egad! and that's more than I do myself.

MISS HARDCASTLE. You mean that in this hypocritical age there are few that do not condemn in public what they practice in private, and think they pay every debt to virtue when they praise it.

MARLOW. True, madam; those who have most virtue in their mouths, have least of it in their bosoms. But I'm sure I tire you, madam.

MISS HARDCASTLE. Not in the least, Sir; there's something so agreeable and spirited in your manner, such life and force—pray, Sir, go on.

MARLOW. Yes, madam. I was saying——that there are some occasions——when a total want of courage, madam, destroys all

the——and puts us——upon a——a——a——

MISS HARDCASTLE. I agree with you entirely, a want of courage upon some occasions assumes the appearance of ignorance, and betrays us when we most want to excel. I beg you'll proceed.

MARLOW. Yes, madam. Morally speaking, madam——But I see Miss Neville expecting us in the next room. I would not intrude for the world.

MISS HARDCASTLE. I protest, Sir, I never was more agreeably entertained in all my life. Pray go on.

MARLOW. Yes, madam. I was——But she beckons us to join her. Madam, shall I do myself the honor to attend you?

MISS HARDCASTLE. Well then, I'll follow.

MARLOW (*aside*). This pretty smooth dialogue has done for me. (*Exit.*)

MISS HARDCASTLE *sola.*

MISS HARDCASTLE. Ha! ha! ha! Was there ever such a sober sentimental interview? I'm certain he scarce looked in my face the whole time. Yet the fellow, but for his unaccountable bashfulness, is pretty well too. He has good sense, but then so buried in his fears, that it fatigues one more than ignorance. If I could teach him a little confidence, it would be doing somebody that I know of a piece of service. But who is that somebody?—that, faith, is a question I can scarce answer. (*Exit.*)

Enter TONY *and* MISS NEVILLE, *followed by* MRS. HARDCASTLE *and* HASTINGS.

TONY. What do you follow me for, cousin Con? I wonder you're not ashamed to be so very engaging.[29]

MISS NEVILLE. I hope, cousin, one may speak to one's own relations, and not be to blame.

TONY. Ay, but I know what sort of a relation you want to make me though; but it won't do. I tell you, cousin Con, it won't do, so I beg you'll keep your distance, I

29. ENGAGING: seductive.

want no nearer relationship. (*She follows coquetting him to the back scene.*)

MRS. HARDCASTLE. Well! I vow, Mr. Hastings, you are very entertaining. There's nothing in the world I love to talk of so much as London, and the fashions, though I was never there myself.

HASTINGS. Never there! You amaze me! From your air and manner, I concluded you had been bred all your life either at Ranelagh,[30] St. James's,[31] or Tower Wharf.[32]

MRS. HARDCASTLE. O! Sir, you're only pleased to say so. We country persons can have no manner at all. I'm in love with the town, and that serves to raise me above some of our neighboring rustics; but who can have a manner, that has never seen the Pantheon,[33] the Grotto Gardens,[34] the Borough,[35] and such places where the nobility chiefly resort? All I can do, is to enjoy London at second-hand. I take care to know every tête-à-tête from the Scandalous Magazine, and have all the fashions as they come out, in a letter from the two Miss Rickets of Crooked Lane. Pray how do you like this head,[36] Mr. Hastings?

HASTINGS. Extremely elegant and dégagée,[37] upon my word, madam. Your friseur[38] is a Frenchman, I suppose?

MRS. HARDCASTLE. I protest I dressed it myself from a print in the Ladies Memorandum-book for the last year.

HASTINGS. Indeed. Such a head in a side-box, at the Playhouse, would draw as many gazers as my Lady Mayoress at a City Ball.

MRS. HARDCASTLE. I vow, since inoculation[39] began, there is no such thing to be seen as a plain woman; so one must dress a little particular or one may escape[40] in the crowd.

HASTINGS. But that can never be your case, madam, in any dress. (*bowing*)

MRS. HARDCASTLE. Yet, what signifies *my* dressing when I have such a piece of antiquity by my side as Mr. Hardcastle; all I can say will never argue down a single button from his clothes. I have often wanted him to throw off his great flaxen wig, and where he was bald, to plaster it over like my Lord Pately, with powder.

HASTINGS. You are right, madam; for, as among the ladies there are none ugly, so among the men there are none old.

MRS. HARDCASTLE. But what do you think his answer was? Why, with his usual Gothic[41] vivacity, he said I only wanted him to throw off his wig to convert it into a tête[42] for my own wearing.

HASTINGS. Intolerable! At your age you may wear what you please, and it must become you.

MRS. HARDCASTLE. Pray, Mr. Hastings, what do you take to be the most fashionable age about town?

HASTINGS. Some time ago, forty was all the mode; but I'm told the ladies intend to bring up fifty for the ensuing winter.

MRS. HARDCASTLE. Seriously? Then I shall be too young for the fashion.

HASTINGS. No lady begins now to put on jewels till she's past forty. For instance, Miss there, in a polite circle, would be considered as a child, as a mere maker of samplers.

---

30. RANELAGH: Ranelagh Gardens, a fashionable place of public entertainment in London.
31. ST. JAMES'S: the London residence of the royal family.
32. TOWER WHARF: a resort frequented by the worst kind of people; in the East End, London.
33. PANTHEON: very fancy bazaar on Oxford Street, a work of James Wyatt (distinguished architect); opened January, 1772, or about fourteen months before this play.
34. GROTTO GARDENS: in the Clerkenwell section of London, very famous; Clerkenwell was a fashionable residential section at the time.
35. THE BOROUGH: short for the Borough of Southwark, across the Thames.
36. HEAD: i.e., her hair style.
37. DÉGAGÉE: unconstrained.
38. FRISEUR: hairdresser.

---

39. INOCULATION: Small-pox inoculation was introduced into England in 1718 by Lady Mary Wortley Montagu; hence, no women were now disfigured as so many used to be.
40. ESCAPE: i.e., escape notice; be overlooked.
41. GOTHIC: barbarous.
42. TÊTE: wig.

MRS. HARDCASTLE. And yet Mrs. Niece[43] thinks herself as much a woman and is as fond of jewels as the oldest of us all.

HASTINGS. Your niece, is she? And that young gentleman, a brother of yours, I should presume?

MRS. HARDCASTLE. My son, Sir. They are contracted to each other. Observe their little sports. They fall in and out ten times a day, as if they were man and wife already. (*to them*) Well Tony, child, what soft things are you saying to your cousin Constance this evening?

TONY. I have been saying no soft things; but that it's very hard to be followed about so. Ecod! I've not a place in the house now that's left to myself but the stable.

MRS. HARDCASTLE. Never mind him, Con, my dear. He's in another story[44] behind your back.

MISS NEVILLE. There's something generous in my cousin's manner. He falls out before faces[45] to be forgiven in private.

TONY. That's a damned confounded——crack.[46]

MRS. HARDCASTLE. Ah! he's a sly one. Don't you think they're like each other about the mouth, Mr. Hastings? The Blenkinsop mouth to a T. They're of a size too. Back to back, my pretties, that Mr. Hastings may see you. Come Tony.

TONY. You had as good not make me, I tell you. (*measuring*)

MISS NEVILLE. O lud! he has almost cracked my head.

MRS. HARDCASTLE. O the monster! For shame, Tony. You a man, and behave so!

TONY. If I'm a man, let me have my fortin.[47] Ecod! I'll not be made a fool of no longer.

MRS. HARDCASTLE. Is this, ungrateful boy, all that I'm to get for the pains I have taken in your education? I that have rocked you in your cradle, and fed that pretty mouth with a spoon! Did not I work[48] that waistcoat to make you genteel? Did not I prescribe for you every day, and weep while the receipt was operating?

TONY. Ecod! you had reason to weep, for you have been dosing me ever since I was born. I have gone through every receipt in the complete huswife ten times over; and you have thoughts of coursing me through *Quincy*[49] next spring. But, Ecod! I tell you, I'll not be made a fool of no longer.

MRS. HARDCASTLE. Wasn't it all for your good, viper? Wasn't it all for your good?

TONY. I wish you'd let me and my good alone then. Snubbing[50] this way when I'm in spirits. If I'm to have any good, let it come of itself; not to keep dinging[51] it, dinging it into one so.

MRS. HARDCASTLE. That's false; I never see you when you're in spirits. No, Tony, you then go to the alehouse or kennel. I'm never to be delighted with your agreeable, wild notes, unfeeling monster!

TONY. Ecod! Mama, your own notes are the wildest of the two.

MRS. HARDCASTLE. Was ever the like? But I see he wants to break my heart, I see he does.

HASTINGS. Dear madam, permit me to lecture the young gentleman a little. I'm certain I can persuade him to his duty.

MRS. HARDCASTLE. Well! I must retire. Come, Constance, my love. You see, Mr. Hastings, the wretchedness of my situation: Was ever poor woman so plagued with a dear, sweet, pretty, provoking, undutiful boy.

Exeunt MRS. HARDCASTLE *and* MISS NEVILLE.

HASTINGS, TONY.

TONY (*singing*). *There was a young man riding by, and fain would have his will.*

---

43. MRS. NIECE: i.e., my niece.
44. IN ANOTHER STORY: i.e., tells another story.
45. FALLS . . . FACES: i.e., denies his love in public.
46. CRACK: lie.
47. FORTIN: fortune.
48. WORK: embroider.
49. COMPLETE . . . QUINCY: *The Complete Housewife* and John Quincy's *The Complete English Dispensatory* were popular home medical guides.
50. SNUBBING: chiding.
51. DINGING: talking incessantly and complainingly.

Rang do didlo dee. Don't mind her. Let her cry. It's the comfort of her heart. I have seen her and sister cry over a book for an hour together, and they said they liked the book the better the more it made them cry.

HASTINGS. Then you're no friend to the ladies, I find, my pretty young gentleman?

TONY. That's as I find 'um.

HASTINGS. Not to her of your mother's choosing, I dare answer? And yet she appears to me a pretty well-tempered girl.

TONY. That's because you don't know her as well as I. Ecod! I know every inch about her; and there's not a more bitter cantankerous toad in all Christendom.

HASTINGS (*aside*). Pretty encouragement this for a lover!

TONY. I have seen her since the height of that.[52] She has as many tricks as a hare in a thicket, or a colt the first day's breaking.

HASTINGS. To me she appears sensible and silent!

TONY. Ay, before company. But when she's with her playmates she's as loud as a hog in a gate.

HASTINGS. But there is a meek modesty about her that charms me.

TONY. Yes, but curb her never so little, she kicks up, and you're flung in a ditch.

HASTINGS. Well, but you must allow her a little beauty.—Yes, you must allow her some beauty.

TONY. Bandbox![53] She's all a made up thing, mun.[54] Ah! could you but see Bet Bouncer of these parts, you might then talk of beauty. Ecod, she has two eyes as black as sloes, and cheeks as broad and red as a pulpit cushion. She'd make two of she.

HASTINGS. Well, what say you to a friend that would take this bitter bargain off your hands?

TONY. Anon?[55]

---

52. SINCE . . . THAT: i.e., since she was *that* high (indicating the height of a small girl).
53. BANDBOX: flimsy, unsubstantial.
54. MUN: man.
55. ANON?: How's that?

HASTINGS. Would you thank him that would take Miss Neville and leave you to happiness and your dear Betsy?

TONY. Ay; but where is there such a friend, for who would take *her?*

HASTINGS. I am he. If you but assist me, I'll engage to whip her off to France, and you shall never hear more of her.

TONY. Assist you! Ecod I will, to the last drop of my blood. I'll clap a pair of horses to your chaise that shall trundle you off in a twinkling, and maybe get you a part of her fortin beside, in jewels, that you little dream of.

HASTINGS. My dear squire, this looks like a lad of spirit.

TONY. Come along then, and you shall see more of my spirit before you have done with me. (*singing*) *We are the boys that fears no noise where the thundering cannons roar.*

(*Exeunt.*)

ACT THREE

Enter HARDCASTLE *solus.*

HARDCASTLE. What could my old friend Sir Charles mean by recommending his son as the modestest young man in town? To me he appears the most impudent piece of brass that ever spoke with a tongue. He has taken possession of the easy chair by the fireside already. He took off his boots in the parlor, and desired me to see them taken care of. I'm desirous to know how his impudence affects my daughter.—She will certainly be shocked at it.

Enter MISS HARDCASTLE, *plainly dressed.*

HARDCASTLE. Well, my Kate, I see you have changed your dress as I bid you; and yet, I believe, there was no great occasion.

MISS HARDCASTLE. I find such a pleasure, Sir, in obeying your commands, that I take care to observe them without ever debating their propriety.

HARDCASTLE. And yet, Kate, I sometimes

give you some cause, particularly when I recommended my *modest* gentleman to you as a lover today.

MISS HARDCASTLE. You taught me to expect something extraordinary, and I find the original exceeds the description.

HARDCASTLE. I was never so surprised in my life! He has quite confounded all my faculties!

MISS HARDCASTLE. I never saw anything like it: And a man of the world, too!

HARDCASTLE. Ay, he learned it all abroad, —what a fool was I, to think a young man could learn modesty by traveling. He might as soon learn wit at a masquerade.

MISS HARDCASTLE. It seems all natural to him.

HARDCASTLE. A good deal assisted by bad company and a French dancing-master.

MISS HARDCASTLE. Sure you mistake, papa! a French dancing-master could never have taught him that timid look,—that awkward address,—that bashful manner——

HARDCASTLE. Whose look? whose manner? child!

MISS HARDCASTLE. Mr. Marlow's: his mauvaise honte,[1] his timidity struck me at the first sight.

HARDCASTLE. Then your first sight deceived you; for I think him one of the most brazen first sights that ever astonished my senses.

MISS HARDCASTLE. Sure, Sir, you rally![2] I never saw any one so modest.

HARDCASTLE. And can you be serious! I never saw such a bouncing swaggering puppy since I was born. Bully Dawson[3] was but a fool to him.

MISS HARDCASTLE. Surprising! He met me with a respectful bow, a stammering voice, and a look fixed on the ground.

HARDCASTLE. He met me with a loud voice, a lordly air, and a familiarity that made my blood freeze again.

---

1. MAUVAISE HONTE: false shame.
2. RALLY: banter.
3. BULLY DAWSON: a well-known rake and bully in London during the Restoration.

MISS HARDCASTLE. He treated me with diffidence and respect; censured the manners of the age; admired the prudence of girls that never laughed; tired me with apologies for being tiresome; then left the room with a bow, and, "Madam, I would not for the world detain you."

HARDCASTLE. He spoke to me as if he knew me all his life before. Asked twenty questions, and never waited for an answer. Interrupted my best remarks with some silly pun, and when I was in my best story of the Duke of Marlborough and Prince Eugene, he asked if I had not a good hand at making punch. Yes, Kate, he asked your father if he was a maker of punch!

MISS HARDCASTLE. One of us must certainly be mistaken.

HARDCASTLE. If he be what he has shown himself, I'm determined he shall never have my consent.

MISS HARDCASTLE. And if he be the sullen thing I take him, he shall never have mine.

HARDCASTLE. In one thing then we are agreed—to reject him.

MISS HARDCASTLE. Yes. But upon conditions. For if you should find him less impudent, and I more presuming; if you find him more respectful, and I more importunate—I don't know—the fellow is well enough for a man—Certainly we don't meet many such at a horse race in the country.

HARDCASTLE. If we should find him so ——But that's impossible. The first appearance has done my business. I'm seldom deceived in that.

MISS HARDCASTLE. And yet there may be many good qualities under that first appearance.

HARDCASTLE. Ay, when a girl finds a fellow's outside to her taste, she then sets about guessing the rest of his furniture. With her, a smooth face stands for good sense, and a genteel figure for every virtue.

MISS HARDCASTLE. I hope, Sir, a conversation begun with a compliment to my good sense won't end with a sneer at my understanding?

HARDCASTLE. Pardon me, Kate. But if young Mr. Brazen can find the art of reconciling contradictions, he may please us both, perhaps.

MISS HARDCASTLE. And as one of us must be mistaken, what if we go to make further discoveries?

HARDCASTLE. Agreed. But depend on't I'm in the right.

MISS HARDCASTLE. And depend on't I'm not much in the wrong.   (*Exeunt.*)

Enter TONY *running in with a casket.*

TONY. Ecod! I have got them. Here they are. My cousin Con's necklaces, bobs[4] and all. My mother shan't cheat the poor souls out of their fortune neither. O! my genus,[5] is that you?

Enter HASTINGS.

HASTINGS. My dear friend, how have you managed with your mother? I hope you have amused her with pretending love for your cousin, and that you are willing to be reconciled at last? Our horses will be refreshed in a short time, and we shall soon be ready to set off.

TONY. And here's something to bear your charges by the way. (*giving the casket*) Your sweetheart's jewels. Keep them, and hang those, I say, that would rob you of one of them.

HASTINGS. But how have you procured them from your mother?

TONY. Ask me no questions, and I'll tell you no fibs. I procured them by the rule of thumb. If I had not a key to every drawer in mother's bureau, how could I go to the alehouses so often as I do? An honest man may rob himself of his own at any time.

HASTINGS. Thousands do it every day. But to be plain with you; Miss Neville is endeavoring to procure them from her aunt this very instant. If she succeeds, it will be the most delicate way at least of obtaining them.

TONY. Well, keep them, till you know how

it will be. But I know how it will be well enough, she'd as soon part with the only sound tooth in her head.

HASTINGS. But I dread the effects of her resentment, when she finds she has lost them.

TONY. Never you mind her resentment, leave *me* to manage that. I don't value her resentment the bounce[6] of a cracker.[7] Zounds! here they are! Morrice,[8] Prance.[9]

(*Exit* HASTINGS.)

TONY, MRS. HARDCASTLE, MISS NEVILLE.

MRS. HARDCASTLE. Indeed, Constance, you amaze me. Such a girl as you want jewels? It will be time enough for jewels, my dear, twenty years hence, when your beauty begins to want repairs.

MISS NEVILLE. But what will repair beauty at forty, will certainly improve it at twenty, Madam.

MRS. HARDCASTLE. Yours, my dear, can admit of none. That natural blush is beyond a thousand ornaments. Besides, child, jewels are quite out at present. Don't you see half the ladies of our acquaintance, my lady Killdaylight, and Mrs. Crump, and the rest of them, carry their jewels to town, and bring nothing but Paste and Marcasites[10] back?

MISS NEVILLE. But who knows, Madam, but somebody that shall be nameless would like me best with all my little finery about me?

MRS. HARDCASTLE. Consult your glass, my dear, and then see, if with such a pair of eyes, you want any better sparklers. What do you think, Tony, my dear, does your cousin Con want any jewels, in your eyes, to set off her beauty?

TONY. That's as thereafter may be.

MISS NEVILLE. My dear aunt, if you knew how it would oblige me.

---

4. BOBS: earrings.
5. GENUS: Tony's malapropism for "genius"—applied to Hastings.

6. BOUNCE: loud noise, bang.
7. CRACKER: firecracker.
8. MORRICE: i.e., get going, vamoose; dialect word still in use; also spelled "Morris."
9. PRANCE: same general meaning here as "Morrice."
10. PASTE AND MARCASITES: inexpensive imitation jewels.

MRS. HARDCASTLE. A parcel of old-fashioned rose and table-cut things.[11] They would make you look like the court of king Solomon at a puppet-show. Besides, I believe I can't readily come at them. They may be missing, for aught I know to the contrary.

TONY (*apart to* MRS. HARDCASTLE). Then why don't you tell her so at once, as she's so longing for them. Tell her they're lost. It's the only way to quiet her. Say they're lost, and call me to bear witness.

MRS. HARDCASTLE (*apart to* TONY). You know, my dear, I'm only keeping them for you. So if I say they're gone, you'll bear me witness, will you? He! he! he!

TONY. Never fear me. Ecod! I'll say I saw them taken out with my own eyes.

MISS NEVILLE. I desire them but for a day, madam. Just to be permitted to show them as relics, and then they may be locked up again.

MRS. HARDCASTLE. To be plain with you, my dear Constance, if I could find them, you should have them. They're missing, I assure you. Lost, for aught I know; but we must have patience wherever they are.

MISS NEVILLE. I'll not believe it; this is but a shallow pretense to deny me. I know they're too valuable to be so slightly kept, and as you are to answer for the loss.

MRS. HARDCASTLE. Don't be alarmed, Constance. If they be lost, I must restore an equivalent. But my son knows they are missing, and not to be found.

TONY. That I can bear witness to. They are missing, and not to be found, I'll take my oath on't.

MRS. HARDCASTLE. You must learn resignation, my dear; for though we lose our fortune, yet we should not lose our patience. See me, how calm I am.

MISS NEVILLE. Ay, people are generally calm at the misfortunes of others.

MRS. HARDCASTLE. Now, I wonder a girl of your good sense should waste a thought upon such trumpery. We shall soon find them; and, in the meantime, you shall make use of my garnets till your jewels be found.

MISS NEVILLE. I detest garnets.

MRS. HARDCASTLE. The most becoming things in the world to set off a clear complexion. You have often seen how well they look upon me. You *shall* have them. (*Exit.*)

MISS NEVILLE. I dislike them of all things. You shan't stir.—Was ever anything so provoking to mislay my own jewels, and force me to wear her trumpery.

TONY. Don't be a fool. If she gives you the garnets, take what you can get. The jewels are your own already. I have stolen them out of her bureau, and she does not know it. Fly to your spark,[12] he'll tell you more of the matter. Leave me to manage *her*.

MISS NEVILLE. My dear cousin.

TONY. Vanish. She's here, and has missed them already. Zounds! how she fidgets and spits about like a Catharine wheel.[13]

Enter MRS. HARDCASTLE.

MRS. HARDCASTLE. Confusion! thieves! robbers! We are cheated, plundered, broke open, undone.

TONY. What's the matter, what's the matter, mama? I hope nothing has happened to any of the good family!

MRS. HARDCASTLE. We are robbed. My bureau has been broke open, the jewels taken out, and I'm undone.

TONY. Oh! is that all? Ha, ha, ha. By the laws, I never saw it better acted in my life. Ecod, I thought you was ruined in earnest, ha, ha, ha.

MRS. HARDCASTLE. Why, boy, I *am* ruined in earnest. My bureau has been broke open, and all taken away.

TONY. Stick to that; ha, ha, ha; stick to that. I'll bear witness, you know, call me to bear witness.

MRS. HARDCASTLE. I tell you, Tony, by all that's precious, the jewels are gone, and I shall be ruined forever.

TONY. Sure I know they're gone, and I am to say so.

---

11. PARCEL . . . THINGS: "Rose" and "table-cut" refer to cuts of precious stones.

12. SPARK: lover.

13. CATHARINE WHEEL: revolving wheel of fireworks.

MRS. HARDCASTLE. My dearest Tony, but hear me. They're gone, I say.

TONY. By the laws, mama, you make me for to laugh, ha, ha. I know who took them well enough, ha, ha, ha.

MRS. HARDCASTLE. Was there ever such a blockhead, that can't tell the difference between jest and earnest. I tell you I'm not in jest, booby.

TONY. That's right, that's right: You must be in a bitter passion, and then nobody will suspect either of us. I'll bear witness that they are gone.

MRS. HARDCASTLE. Was there ever such a cross-grained brute, that won't hear me! Can you bear witness that you're no better than a fool? Was ever poor woman so beset with fools on one hand, and thieves on the other!

TONY. I can bear witness to that.

MRS. HARDCASTLE. Bear witness again, you blockhead you, and I'll turn you out of the room directly. My poor niece, what will become of *her!* Do you laugh, you unfeeling brute, as if you enjoyed my distress?

TONY. I can bear witness to that.

MRS. HARDCASTLE. Do you insult me, monster? I'll teach you to vex your mother, I will.

TONY. I can bear witness to that. (*He runs off, she follows him.*)

Enter MISS HARDCASTLE *and* MAID.

MISS HARDCASTLE. What an unaccountable creature is that brother of mine, to send them to the house as an inn, ha, ha. I don't wonder at his impudence.

MAID. But what is more, madam, the young gentleman as you passed by in your present dress, asked me if you were the barmaid? He mistook you for the barmaid, madam.

MISS HARDCASTLE. Did he? Then as I live I'm resolved to keep up the delusion. Tell me, Pimple, how do you like my present dress? Don't you think I look something like Cherry in the *Beaux' Stratagem?*[14]

MAID. It's the dress, madam, that every lady wears in the country, but when she visits or receives company.

MISS HARDCASTLE. And are you sure he does not remember my face or person?

MAID. Certain of it.

MISS HARDCASTLE. I vow I thought so; for though we spoke for some time together, yet his fears were such, that he never once looked up during the interview. Indeed, if he had, my bonnet would have kept him from seeing me.

MAID. But what do you hope from keeping him in his mistake?

MISS HARDCASTLE. In the first place, I shall be *seen,* and that is no small advantage to a girl who brings her face to market. Then I shall perhaps make an acquaintance, and that's no small victory gained over one who never addresses any but the wildest of her sex. But my chief aim is to take my gentleman off his guard, and like an invisible champion of romance examine the giant's force before I offer to combat.

MAID. But you are sure you can act your part, and disguise your voice, so that he may mistake that, as he has already mistaken your person?

MISS HARDCASTLE. Never fear me. I think I have got the true bar cant.—Did your honor call?——Attend the Lion there.—— Pipes and tobacco for the Angel.—The Lamb has been outrageous this half hour.[15]

MAID. It will do, madam. But he's here. (*Exit* MAID.)

Enter MARLOW.

MARLOW. What a bawling in every part of the house; I have scarce a moment's repose. If I go to the best room, there I find my host and his story. If I fly to the gallery, there we have my hostess with her curtsey down to the ground. I have at last got a moment to myself, and now for recollection. (*walks and muses*)

14. CHERRY . . . BEAUX' STRATAGEM: Cherry is the daughter of the innkeeper in George Farquhar's comedy, *The Beaux' Stratagem* (1707).

15. ATTEND . . . HALF HOUR: The rooms in an inn were often named instead of numbered.

MISS HARDCASTLE. Did you call, Sir? did your honor call?

MARLOW (*musing*). As for Miss Hardcastle, she's too grave and sentimental for me.

MISS HARDCASTLE. Did your honor call? (*She still places herself before him, he turning away.*)

MARLOW. No, child. (*musing*) Besides from the glimpse I had of her, I think she squints.

MISS HARDCASTLE. I'm sure, Sir, I heard the bell ring.

MARLOW. No, no. (*musing*) I have pleased my father, however, by coming down, and I'll tomorrow please myself by returning. (*taking out his tablets,*[16] *and perusing*)

MISS HARDCASTLE. Perhaps the other gentleman called, Sir?

MARLOW. I tell you, no.

MISS HARDCASTLE. I should be glad to know, Sir. We have such a parcel of servants.

MARLOW. No, no, I tell you. (*looks full in her face*) Yes, child, I think I did call. I wanted——I wanted——I vow, child, you are vastly handsome!

MISS HARDCASTLE. O la, Sir, you'll make one ashamed.

MARLOW. Never saw a more sprightly malicious eye. Yes, yes, my dear, I did call. Have you got any of your—a—what d'ye call it in the house?

MISS HARDCASTLE. No, Sir, we have been out of that these ten days.

MARLOW. One may call in this house, I find, to very little purpose. Suppose I should call for a taste, just by way of trial, of the nectar of your lips; perhaps I might be disappointed in that too.

MISS HARDCASTLE. Nectar! nectar! that's a liquor there's no call for in these parts. French, I suppose. We keep no French wines here, Sir.

MARLOW. Of true English growth, I assure you.

MISS HARDCASTLE. Then it's odd I should not know it. We brew all sorts of wines in this house, and I have lived here these eighteen years.

MARLOW. Eighteen years! Why one would think, child, you kept the bar before you were born. How old are you?

MISS HARDCASTLE. O! Sir, I must not tell my age. They say women and music should never be dated.

MARLOW. To guess at this distance, you can't be much above forty. (*approaching*) Yet nearer I don't think so much. (*approaching*) By coming close to some women they look younger still; but when we come very close indeed. (*attempting to kiss her*)

MISS HARDCASTLE. Pray, Sir, keep your distance. One would think you wanted to know one's age as they do horses, by mark of mouth.

MARLOW. I protest, child, you use me extremely ill. If you keep me at this distance, how is it possible you and I can be ever acquainted?

MISS HARDCASTLE. And who wants to be acquainted with you? I want no such acquaintance, not I. I'm sure you did not treat Miss Hardcastle that was here awhile ago in this obstropalous[17] manner. I'll warrant me, before her you looked dashed, and kept bowing to the ground, and talked, for all the world, as if you was before a justice of peace.

MARLOW (*aside*). Egad! she has hit it, sure enough. (*to her*) In awe of her, child? Ha! ha! ha! A mere, awkward, squinting thing, no, no. I find you don't know me. I laughed, and rallied her a little; but I was unwilling to be too severe. No, I could not be too severe, *curse me!*

MISS HARDCASTLE. O! then, Sir, you are a favorite, I find, among the ladies?

MARLOW. Yes, my dear, a great favorite. And yet, hang me, I don't see what they find in me to follow. At the Ladies Club in town I'm called their agreeable Rattle. Rattle,

---

16. TABLETS: memorandum book.

17. OBSTROPALOUS: obstreperous.

child, is not my real name, but one I'm known by. My name is Solomons. Mr. Solomons, my dear, at your service. (*offering to salute her*)

MISS HARDCASTLE. Hold, Sir; you were introducing me to your club, not to yourself. And you're so great a favorite there you say?

MARLOW. Yes, my dear. There's Mrs. Mantrap, Lady Betty Blackleg, the Countess of Sligo, Mrs. Langhorns, old Miss Biddy Buckskin, and your humble servant, keep up the spirit of the place.

MISS HARDCASTLE. Then it's a very merry place, I suppose.

MARLOW. Yes, as merry as cards, suppers, wine, and old women can make us.

MISS HARDCASTLE. And their agreeable Rattle, ha! ha! ha!

MARLOW (*aside*). Egad! I don't quite like this chit. She looks knowing, methinks. You laugh, child!

MISS HARDCASTLE. I can't but laugh to think what time they all have for minding their work or their family.

MARLOW (*aside*). All's well, she don't laugh at me. (*to her*) Do *you* ever work, child?

MISS HARDCASTLE. Ay, sure. There's not a screen or a quilt in the whole house but what can bear witness to that.

MARLOW. Odso! Then you must show me your embroidery. I embroider and draw patterns myself a little. If you want a judge of your work you must apply to me. (*seizing her hand*)

MISS HARDCASTLE. Ay, but the colors don't look well by candlelight. You shall see all in the morning. (*struggling*)

MARLOW. And why not now, my angel? Such beauty fires beyond the power of resistance.——Pshaw! the father here! My old luck: I never nicked seven[18] that I did not throw ames ace[19] three times following. (*Exit* MARLOW.)

18. NICKED SEVEN: winning throw in the game of hazard, an old dice game.
19. AMES ACE: two aces, lowest possible throw.

Enter HARDCASTLE, *who stands in surprise.*

HARDCASTLE. So, madam! So I find *this* is your *modest* lover. This is your humble admirer that kept his eyes fixed on the ground, and only adored at humble distance. Kate, Kate, art thou not ashamed to deceive your father so?

MISS HARDCASTLE. Never trust me, dear papa, but he's still the modest man I first took him for, you'll be convinced of it as well as I.

HARDCASTLE. By the hand of my body, I believe his impudence is infectious! Didn't I see him seize your hand? Didn't I see him haul you about like a milkmaid? and now you talk of his respect and his modesty, forsooth!

MISS HARDCASTLE. But if I shortly convince you of his modesty, that he has only the faults that will pass off with time, and the virtues that will improve with age, I hope you'll forgive him.

HARDCASTLE. The girl would actually make one run mad! I tell you I'll not be convinced. I am convinced. He has scarcely been three hours in the house, and he has already encroached on all my prerogatives. You may like his impudence, and call it modesty. But my son-in-law, madam, must have very different qualifications.

MISS HARDCASTLE. Sir, I ask but this night to convince you.

HARDCASTLE. You shall not have half the time, for I have thoughts of turning him out this very hour.

MISS HARDCASTLE. Give me that hour then, and I hope to satisfy you.

HARDCASTLE. Well, an hour let it be then. But I'll have no trifling with your father. All fair and open, do you mind me?

MISS HARDCASTLE. I hope, Sir, you have ever found that I considered your commands as my pride; for your kindness is such that my duty as yet has been inclination.

(*Exeunt.*)

ACT FOUR

Enter HASTINGS *and* MISS NEVILLE.

HASTINGS. You surprise me! Sir Charles Marlow expected here this night? Where have you had your information?

MISS NEVILLE. You may depend upon it. I just saw his letter to Mr. Hardcastle, in which he tells him he intends setting out a few hours after his son.

HASTINGS. Then, my Constance, all must be completed before he arrives. He knows me; and should he find me here, would discover my name, and perhaps my designs, to the rest of the family.

MISS NEVILLE. The jewels, I hope, are safe.

HASTINGS. Yes, yes. I have sent them to Marlow, who keeps the keys of our baggage. In the meantime, I'll go to prepare matters for our elopement. I have had the Squire's promise of a fresh pair of horses; and, if I should not see him again, will write him further directions. (*Exit.*)

MISS NEVILLE. Well! success attend you. In the meantime, I'll go amuse my aunt with the old pretense of a violent passion for my cousin. (*Exit.*)

Enter MARLOW, *followed by a* SERVANT.

MARLOW. I wonder what Hastings could mean by sending me so valuable a thing as a casket to keep for him, when he knows the only place I have is the seat of a post-coach at an inn-door. Have you deposited the casket with the landlady, as I ordered you? Have you put it into her own hands?

SERVANT. Yes, your honor.

MARLOW. She said she'd keep it safe, did she?

SERVANT. Yes, she said she'd keep it safe enough; she asked me how I came by it? and she said she had a great mind to make me give an account of myself. (*Exit* SERVANT.)

MARLOW. Ha! ha! ha! They're safe however. What an unaccountable set of beings have we got amongst! This little barmaid though runs in my head most strangely and

drives out the absurdities of all the rest of the family. She's mine; she must be mine, or I'm greatly mistaken.

Enter HASTINGS.

HASTINGS. Bless me! I quite forgot to tell her that I intended to prepare at the bottom of the garden. Marlow here, and in spirits too!

MARLOW. Give me joy, George! Crown me, shadow me with laurels! Well, George, after all, we modest fellows don't want for success among the women.

HASTINGS. Some women you mean. But what success has your honor's modesty been crowned with now, that it grows so insolent upon us?

MARLOW. Didn't you see the tempting, brisk, lovely little thing that runs about the house with a bunch of keys to its girdle?

HASTINGS. Well! and what then?

MARLOW. She's mine, you rogue you. Such fire, such motion, such eyes, such lips—— but egad! she would not let me kiss them though.

HASTINGS. But are you sure, so very sure of her?

MARLOW. Why man, she talked of showing me her work above-stairs, and I am to improve the pattern.

HASTINGS. But how can *you*, Charles, go about to rob a woman of her honor?

MARLOW. Pshaw! pshaw! we all know the honor of the barmaid of an inn. I don't intend to *rob* her, take my word for it, there's nothing in this house, I shan't honestly *pay* for.

HASTINGS. I believe the girl has virtue.

MARLOW. And if she has, I should be the last man in the world that would attempt to corrupt it.

HASTINGS. You have taken care, I hope, of the casket I sent you to lock up? It's in safety?

MARLOW. Yes, yes. It's safe enough. I have taken care of it. But how could you think the seat of a post-coach at an inn-door a place of safety? Ah! numbskull! I have taken better precautions for you than you did for yourself.——I have——

HASTINGS. What!

MARLOW. I have sent it to the landlady to keep for you.

HASTINGS. To the landlady!

MARLOW. The landlady.

HASTINGS. You did.

MARLOW. I did. She's to be answerable for its forth-coming, you know.

HASTINGS. Yes, she'll bring it forth, with a witness.

MARLOW. Wasn't I right? I believe you'll allow that I acted prudently upon this occasion?

HASTINGS (*aside*). He must not see my uneasiness.

MARLOW. You seem a little disconcerted though, methinks. Sure nothing has happened?

HASTINGS. No, nothing. Never was in better spirits in all my life. And so you left it with the landlady, who, no doubt, very readily undertook the charge?

MARLOW. Rather too readily. For she not only kept the casket; but, through her great precaution, was going to keep the messenger too. Ha! ha! ha!

HASTINGS. He! he! he! They're safe however.

MARLOW. As a guinea in a miser's purse.

HASTINGS (*aside*). So now all hopes of fortune are at an end, and we must set off without it. (*to him*) Well, Charles, I'll leave you to your meditations on the pretty barmaid, and, he! he! he! may you be as successful for yourself as you have been for me.

(*Exit.*)

MARLOW. Thank ye, George! I ask no more. Ha! ha! ha!

Enter HARDCASTLE.

HARDCASTLE. I no longer know my own house. It's turned all topsy-turvy. His servants have got drunk already. I'll bear it no longer, and yet, from my respect for his father, I'll be calm. (*to him*) Mr. Marlow,

your servant. I'm your very humble servant (*bowing low*)

MARLOW. Sir, your humble servant. (*aside*) What's to be the wonder now?

HARDCASTLE. I believe, Sir, you must be sensible, Sir, that no man alive ought to be more welcome than your father's son, Sir. I hope you think so?

MARLOW. I do from my soul, Sir. I don't want much entreaty. I generally make my father's son welcome wherever he goes.

HARDCASTLE. I believe you do, from my soul, Sir. But though I say nothing to your own conduct, that of your servants is insufferable. Their manner of drinking is setting a very bad example in this house, I assure you.

MARLOW. I protest, my very good Sir, that's no fault of mine. If they don't drink as they ought *they* are to blame. I ordered them not to spare the cellar. I did, I assure you. (*to the side scene*[1]) Here, let one of my servants come up. (*to him*) My positive directions were, that as I did not drink myself, they should make up for my deficiencies below.

HARDCASTLE. Then they had your orders for what they do! I'm satisfied!

MARLOW. They had, I assure you. You shall hear from one of themselves.

Enter SERVANT, *drunk.*

MARLOW. You, Jeremy! Come forward, sirrah[2]! What were my orders? Were you not told to drink freely, and call for what you thought fit, for the good of the house?

HARDCASTLE (*aside*). I begin to lose my patience.

JEREMY. Please your honor, liberty and Fleet Street[3] forever! Though I'm but a

---

1. SIDE SCENE: the stage wings.
2. SIRRAH: term of address to an inferior.
3. LIBERTY AND FLEET STREET: This is a reference to the protests of the business elements (the shopkeepers of Fleet Street, the old Cits of Restoration days) against the Tory conservatism of George III's government, which was being effectively attacked by John Wilkes, the hero of the business classes.

servant, I'm as good as another man. I'll drink for no man before supper, Sir, dammy! Good liquor will sit upon a good supper, but a good supper will not sit upon——hiccup ——upon my conscience, Sir.

MARLOW. You see, my old friend, the fellow is as drunk as he can possibly be. I don't know what you'd have more, unless you'd have the poor devil soused in a beer-barrel.

HARDCASTLE. Zounds! He'll drive me distracted if I contain myself any longer. Mr. Marlow, Sir; I have submitted to your insolence for more than four hours, and I see no likelihood of its coming to an end. I'm now resolved to be master here, Sir, and I desire that you and your drunken pack may leave my house directly.

MARLOW. Leave your house!—Sure, you jest, my good friend? What, when I'm doing what I can to please you.

HARDCASTLE. I tell you, Sir, you don't please me; so I desire you'll leave my house.

MARLOW. Sure you cannot be serious! At this time o'night, and such a night. You only mean to banter me?

HARDCASTLE. I tell you, Sir, I'm serious; and, now that my passions are roused, I say this house is mine, Sir; this house is mine, and I command you to leave it directly.

MARLOW. Ha! ha! ha! A puddle in a storm. I shan't stir a step, I assure you. (*in a serious tone*) This your house, fellow! It's my house. This is my house. Mine, while I choose to stay. What right have you to bid me leave this house, Sir? I never met with such impudence, curse me, never in my whole life before.

HARDCASTLE. Nor I, confound me if ever I did. To come to my house, to call for what he likes, to turn me out of my own chair, to insult the family, to order his servants to get drunk, and then to tell me *This house is mine, Sir*. By all that's impudent it makes me laugh. Ha! ha! ha! Pray, Sir, (*bantering*) as you take the house, what think you of taking the rest of the furniture? There's a pair of silver candlesticks, and there's a fire-screen, and here's a pair of brazen nosed bellows, perhaps you may take a fancy to them?

MARLOW. Bring me your bill, Sir, bring me your bill, and let's make no more words about it.

HARDCASTLE. There are a set of prints too. What think you of the Rake's Progress[4] for your own apartment?

MARLOW. Bring me your bill, I say; and I'll leave you and your infernal house directly.

HARDCASTLE. Then there's a mahogany table, that you may see your own face in.

MARLOW. My bill, I say.

HARDCASTLE. I had forgot the great chair, for your own particular slumbers, after a hearty meal.

MARLOW. Zounds! bring me my bill, I say, and let's hear no more on't.

HARDCASTLE. Young man, young man, from your father's letter to me I was taught to expect a well-bred modest man as a visitor here, but now I find him no better than a coxcomb and a bully; but he will be down here presently and shall hear more of it. (*Exit.*)

MARLOW. How's this! Sure, I have not mistaken the house! Everything looks like an inn. The servants cry, coming. The attendance is awkward; the barmaid too to attend us. But she's here and will further inform me. Whither so fast, child. A word with you.

Enter MISS HARDCASTLE.

MISS HARDCASTLE. Let it be short then. I'm in a hurry. (*aside*) I believe he begins to find out his mistake, but it's too soon quite to undeceive him.

MARLOW. Pray, child, answer me one question. What are you, and what may your business in this house be?

MISS HARDCASTLE. A relation of the family, Sir.

MARLOW. What. A poor relation?

---

4. THE RAKE'S PROGRESS: a series of engravings by William Hogarth, published in 1735, depicting the "progress" downhill of a dissolute young man.

MISS HARDCASTLE. Yes, Sir. A poor relation appointed to keep the keys, and to see that the guests want nothing in my power to give them.

MARLOW. That is, you act as the barmaid of this inn.

MISS HARDCASTLE. Inn. O law—What brought that in your head. One of the best families in the county keep an inn. Ha! ha! ha! old Mr. Hardcastle's house an inn.

MARLOW. Mr. Hardcastle's house! Is this house Mr. Hardcastle's house, child!

MISS HARDCASTLE. Ay, sure. Whose else should it be.

MARLOW. So then all's out, and I have been damnably imposed on. O, confound my stupid head, I shall be laughed at over the whole town. I shall be stuck up in caricatura in all the print-shops. The Dullissimo Maccaroni.[5] To mistake this house of all others for an inn, and my father's old friend for an innkeeper. What a swaggering puppy must he take me for. What a silly puppy do I find myself. There again, may I be hanged, my dear, but I mistook you for the barmaid.

MISS HARDCASTLE. Dear me! dear me! I'm sure there's nothing in my behavior to put me upon a level with one of that stamp.

MARLOW. Nothing, my dear, nothing. But I was in for a list of blunders, and could not help making you a subscriber. My stupidity saw everything the wrong way. I mistook your assiduity for assurance, and your simplicity for allurement. But it's over—this house I no more show *my* face in!

MISS HARDCASTLE. I hope, Sir, I have done nothing to disoblige you. I'm sure I should be sorry to affront any gentleman who has been so polite, and said so many civil things to me. I'm sure I should be sorry (*pretending to cry*) if he left the family upon my account. I'm sure I should be sorry, people said anything amiss, since I have no fortune but my character.

MARLOW (*aside*). By heaven, she weeps.

5. CARICATURA . . . MACCARONI: i.e., caricatures of him as a stupid fop would be sold in all the print-shops.

This is the first mark of tenderness I ever had from a modest woman, and it touches me. (*to her*) Excuse me, my lovely girl, you are the only part of the family I leave with reluctance. But to be plain with you, the difference of our birth, fortune and education, make an honorable connection impossible; and I can never harbor a thought of seducing simplicity that trusted in my honor, or bringing ruin upon one whose only fault was being too lovely.

MISS HARDCASTLE (*aside*). Generous man! I now begin to admire him. (*to him*) But I'm sure my family is as good as Miss Hardcastle's, and though I'm poor, that's no great misfortune to a contented mind, and, until this moment, I never thought that it was bad to want fortune.

MARLOW. And why now, my pretty simplicity?

MISS HARDCASTLE. Because it puts me at a distance from one that if I had a thousand pound I would give it all to.

MARLOW (*aside*). This simplicity bewitches me, so that if I stay I'm undone. I must make one bold effort, and leave her. (*to her*) Your partiality in my favor, my dear, touches me most sensibly, and were I to live for myself alone, I could easily fix my choice. But I owe too much to the opinion of the world, too much to the authority of a father, so that—I can scarcely speak it—it affects me. Farewell. (*Exit.*)

MISS HARDCASTLE. I never knew half his merit till now. He shall not go, if I have power or art to detain him. I'll still preserve the character in which I stooped to conquer, but will undeceive my papa, who, perhaps, may laugh him out of his resolution.

(*Exit.*)

Enter TONY, MISS NEVILLE.

TONY. Ay, you may steal for yourselves the next time. I have done my duty. She has got the jewels again, that's a sure thing; but she believes it was all a mistake of the servants.

MISS NEVILLE. But, my dear cousin, sure you won't forsake us in this distress. If she in the least suspects that I am going off, I shall certainly be locked up, or sent to my aunt Pedigree's, which is ten times worse.

TONY. To be sure, aunts of all kinds are damned bad things. But what can I do? I have got you a pair of horses that will fly like Whistlejacket,[6] and I'm sure you can't say but I have courted you nicely before her face. Here she comes; we must court a bit or two more, for fear she should suspect us. (*They retire, and seem to fondle.*)

Enter MRS. HARDCASTLE.

MRS. HARDCASTLE. Well, I was greatly fluttered, to be sure. But my son tells me it was all a mistake of the servants. I shan't be easy, however, till they are fairly married, and then let her keep her own fortune. But what do I see! Fondling together, as I'm alive. I never saw Tony so sprightly before. Ah! have I caught you, my pretty doves! What, billing, exchanging stolen glances, and broken murmurs. Ah!

TONY. As for murmurs, mother, we grumble a little now and then, to be sure. But there's no love lost between us.

MRS. HARDCASTLE. A mere sprinkling, Tony, upon the flame, only to make it burn brighter.

MISS NEVILLE. Cousin Tony promises to give us more of his company at home. Indeed, he shan't leave us anymore. It won't leave us cousin Tony, will it?

TONY. O! it's a pretty creature. No, I'd sooner leave my horse in a pound than leave you when you smile upon one so. Your laugh makes you so becoming.

MISS NEVILLE. Agreeable cousin! Who can help admiring that natural humor, that pleasant, broad, red, thoughtless, (*patting his cheek*) ah! it's a bold face.

MRS. HARDCASTLE. Pretty innocence.

TONY. I'm sure I always loved cousin Con's hazel eyes, and her pretty long fingers that she twists this way and that over the haspicholls,[7] like a parcel of bobbins.

MRS. HARDCASTLE. Ah, he would charm

the bird from the tree. I was never so happy before. My boy takes after his father, poor Mr. Lumpkin, exactly. The jewels, my dear Con, shall be yours incontinently. You shall have them. Isn't he a sweet boy, my dear? You shall be married tomorrow, and we'll put off the rest of his education, like Dr. Drowsy's sermons, to a fitter opportunity.

Enter DIGGORY.

DIGGORY. Where the Squire? I have got a letter for your worship.

TONY. Give it to my mama. She reads all my letters first.

DIGGORY. I had orders to deliver it into your own hands.

TONY. Who does it come from?

DIGGORY. Your worship mun ask that o' the letter itself.

TONY. I could wish to know, though. (*turn-the letter, and gazing on it*)

MISS NEVILLE (*aside*). Undone, undone. A letter to him from Hastings. I know the hand. If my aunt sees it, we are ruined forever. I'll keep her employed a little if I can. (*to* MRS. HARDCASTLE) But I have not told you, Madam, of my cousin's smart answer just now to Mr. Marlow. We so laughed—You must know, madam—this way a little, for he must not hear us. (*They confer.*)

TONY (*still gazing*). A damned cramp piece of penmanship as ever I saw in my life. I can read your print-hand very well. But here there are such handles, and shanks, and dashes, that one can scarce tell the head from the tail. *To Anthony Lumpkin, Esquire.* It's very odd, I can read the outside of my letters, where my own name is, well enough. But when I come to open it, it's all—buzz. That's hard, very hard; for the inside of the letter is always the cream of the correspondence.

MRS. HARDCASTLE. Ha, ha, ha. Very well, very well. And so my son was too hard for the philosopher.

MISS NEVILLE. Yes, madam; but you must hear the rest, madam. A little more this way,

6. WHISTLEJACKET: a famous racehorse.
7. HASPICHOLLS: harpsichord.

or he may hear us. You'll hear how he puzzled him again.

MRS. HARDCASTLE. He seems strangely puzzled now himself, methinks.

TONY (*still gazing*). A damned up and down hand, as if it was disguised in liquor. (*reading*) *Dear Sir.* Ay, that's that. Then there's an *M,* and a *T,* and an *S,* but whether the next be an *izzard*[8] or an *R,* confound me, I cannot tell.

MRS. HARDCASTLE. What's that, my dear. Can I give you any assistance?

MISS NEVILLE. Pray, aunt, let me read it. Nobody reads a cramp hand better than I. (*twitching the letter from her*) Do you know who it is from?

TONY. Can't tell, except from Dick Ginger the feeder.

MISS NEVILLE. Ay, so it is, (*pretending to read*) *Dear Squire, Hoping that you're in health, as I am at this present. The gentleman of the Shake bag club has cut the gentlemen of goose-green quite out of feather. The odds*—um—*odd battle*—um *long fighting*—um here, here, it's all about cocks, and fighting; it's of no consequence, here, put it up, put it up. (*thrusting the crumpled letter upon him*)

TONY. But I tell you, Miss, it's of all the consequence in the world. I would not lose the rest of it for a guinea. Here, mother, do you make it out. Of no consequence! (*giving* MRS. HARDCASTLE *the letter*)

MRS. HARDCASTLE. How's this! (*reads*) *Dear Squire, I'm now waiting for Miss Neville, with a post-chaise and pair, at the bottom of the garden, but I find my horses yet unable to perform the journey. I expect you'll assist us with a pair of fresh horses, as you promised. Dispatch is necessary, as the* hag (ay the hag) *your mother will otherwise suspect us. Yours, Hastings.* Grant me patience. I shall run distracted. My rage chokes me.

MISS NEVILLE. I hope, Madam, you'll suspend your resentment for a few moments,

and not impute to me any impertinence or sinister design that belongs to another.

MRS. HARDCASTLE (*curtseying very low*). Fine spoken, madam, you are most miraculously polite and engaging, and quite the very pink of courtesy and circumspection, madam. (*changing her tone*) And you, you great ill-fashioned oaf, with scarce sense enough to keep your mouth shut. Were you too joined against me? But I'll defeat all your plots in a moment. As for you, madam, since you have got a pair of fresh horses ready, it would be cruel to disappoint them. So, if you please, instead of running away with your spark, prepare, this very moment, to run off with *me.* Your old aunt Pedigree will keep you secure, I'll warrant me. You too, Sir, may mount your horse, and guard us upon the way. Here, Thomas, Roger, Diggory, I'll show you, that I wish you better than you do yourselves. (*Exit.*)

MISS NEVILLE. So now I'm completely ruined.

TONY. Ay, that's a sure thing.

MISS NEVILLE. What better could be expected from being connected with such a stupid fool, and after all the nods and signs I made him.

TONY. By the laws, Miss, it was your own cleverness, and not my stupidity, that did your business. You were so nice and so busy with your Shake-bags and Goose-greens, that I thought you could never be making believe.

Enter HASTINGS.

HASTINGS. So, Sir, I find by my servant, that you have shown my letter and betrayed us. Was this well done, young gentleman?

TONY. Here's another. Ask Miss there who betrayed you. Ecod, it was her doing, not mine.

Enter MARLOW.

MARLOW. So I have been finely used here among you. Rendered contemptible, driven into ill manners, despised, insulted, laughed at.

_____
8. IZZARD: the letter "z."

TONY. Here's another. We shall have old Bedlam[9] broke loose presently.

MISS NEVILLE. And there, Sir, is the gentleman to whom we all owe every obligation.

MARLOW. What can I say to him, a mere boy, an idiot, whose ignorance and age are a protection.

HASTINGS. A poor contemptible booby, that would but disgrace correction.

MISS NEVILLE. Yet with cunning and malice enough to make himself merry with all our embarrassments.

HASTINGS. An insensible cub.

MARLOW. Replete with tricks and mischief.

TONY. Baw! damme, but I'll fight you both one after the other,——with baskets.[10]

MARLOW. As for him, he's below resentment. But your conduct, Mr. Hastings, requires an explanation. You knew of my mistakes, yet would not undeceive me.

HASTINGS. Tortured as I am with my own disappointments, is this a time for explanations? It is not friendly, Mr. Marlow.

MARLOW. But, Sir—

MISS NEVILLE. Mr. Marlow, we never kept on your mistake till it was too late to undeceive you. Be pacified.

Enter SERVANT.

SERVANT. My mistress desires you'll get ready immediately, madam. The horses are putting to. Your hat and things are in the next room. We are to go thirty miles before morning. (*Exit* SERVANT.)

MISS NEVILLE. Well, well; I'll come presently.

MARLOW (*to* HASTINGS). Was it well done, Sir, to assist in rendering me ridiculous? To hang me out for the scorn of all my acquaintance. Depend upon it, Sir, I shall expect an explanation.

HASTINGS. Was it well done, Sir, if you're upon that subject, to deliver what I en-

trusted to yourself, to the care of another, Sir?

MISS NEVILLE. Mr. Hastings. Mr. Marlow. Why will you increase my distress by this groundless dispute? I implore, I entreat you——

Enter SERVANT.

SERVANT. Your cloak, madam. My mistress is impatient.

MISS NEVILLE. I come. Pray be pacified. If I leave you thus, I shall die with apprehension.

Enter SERVANT.

SERVANT. Your fan, muff, and gloves, madam. The horses are waiting.

MISS NEVILLE. O, Mr. Marlow! if you knew what a scene of constraint and ill-nature lies before me, I'm sure it would convert your resentment into pity.

MARLOW. I'm so distracted with a variety of passions, that I don't know what I do. Forgive me, madam. George, forgive me. You know my hasty temper, and should not exasperate it.

HASTINGS. The torture of my situation is my only excuse.

MISS NEVILLE. Well, my dear Hastings, if you have that esteem for me that I think, that I am sure you have, your constancy for three years will but increase the happiness of our future connection. If—

MRS. HARDCASTLE (*within*). Miss Neville. Constance, why Constance, I say.

MISS NEVILLE. I'm coming. Well, constancy. Remember, constancy is the word.
(*Exit.*)

HASTINGS. My heart! How can I support this. To be so near happiness, and such happiness.

MARLOW (*to* TONY). You see now, young gentleman, the effects of your folly. What might be amusement to you is here disappointment, and even distress.

TONY (*from a reverie*). Ecod, I have hit it. It's here. Your hands. Yours and yours, my poor Sulky. My boots there, ho. Meet

---

9. BEDLAM: any madhouse; contraction for Beth-lehem, a lunatic asylum in London.
10. BASKETS: swords with basket-like protecting shields for the hands.

me two hours hence at the bottom of the garden; and if you don't find Tony Lumpkin a more good-natured fellow than you thought for, I'll give you leave to take my best horse, and Bet Bouncer into the bargain. Come along. My boots, ho!

(Exeunt.)

ACT FIVE

Scene continues

Enter HASTINGS *and* SERVANT.

HASTINGS. You saw the Old Lady and Miss Neville drive off, you say.

SERVANT. Yes, your honor. They went off in a post coach, and the young Squire went on horseback. They're thirty miles off by this time.

HASTINGS. Then all my hopes are over.

SERVANT. Yes, Sir. Old Sir Charles is arrived. He and the Old Gentleman of the house have been laughing at Mr. Marlow's mistake this half hour. They are coming this way.

HASTINGS. Then I must not be seen. So now to my fruitless appointment at the bottom of the garden. This is about the time.

(Exit.)

Enter SIR CHARLES *and* HARDCASTLE.

HARDCASTLE. Ha, ha, ha. The peremptory tone in which he sent forth his sublime commands.

SIR CHARLES. And the reserve with which I suppose he treated all your advances.

HARDCASTLE. And yet he might have seen something in me above a common inn-keeper, too.

SIR CHARLES. Yes, Dick, but he mistook you for an uncommon innkeeper, ha, ha, ha.

HARDCASTLE. Well, I'm in too good spirits to think of anything but joy. Yes, my dear friend, this union of our families will make our personal friendships hereditary; and though my daughter's fortune is but small——

SIR CHARLES. Why, Dick, will you talk of fortune to *me*. My son is possessed of more than a competence already, and can want nothing but a good and virtuous girl to share his happiness and increase it. If they like each other, as you say they do——

HARDCASTLE. *If,* man. I tell you they *do* like each other. My daughter as good as told me so.

SIR CHARLES. But girls are apt to flatter themselves, you know.

HARDCASTLE. I saw him grasp her hand in the warmest manner, myself; and here he comes to put you out of your *ifs,* I warrant him.

Enter MARLOW.

MARLOW. I come, Sir, once more, to ask pardon for my strange conduct. I can scarce reflect on my insolence without confusion.

HARDCASTLE. Tut, boy, a trifle. You take it too gravely. An hour or two's laughing with my daughter will set all to rights again. She'll never like you the worse for it.

MARLOW. Sir, I shall be always proud of her approbation.

HARDCASTLE. Approbation is but a cold word, Mr. Marlow; if I am not deceived, you have something more than approbation thereabouts. You take me?

MARLOW. Really, Sir, I have not that happiness.

HARDCASTLE. Come, boy, I'm an old fellow, and know what's what, as well as you that are younger. I know what has past between you; but mum.

MARLOW. Sure, Sir, nothing has past between us but the most profound respect on my side, and the most distant reserve on hers. You don't think, Sir, that my impudence has been passed upon all the rest of the family.

HARDCASTLE. Impudence! No, I don't say that—not quite impudence——though girls like to be played with, and rumpled a little too, sometimes. But she has told no tales, I assure you.

MARLOW. I never gave her the slightest cause.

HARDCASTLE. Well, well, I like modesty in its place well enough. But this is over-acting, young gentleman. You *may* be open. Your father and I will like you the better for it.

MARLOW. May I die, Sir, if I ever——

HARDCASTLE. I tell you, she don't dislike you; and as I'm sure you like her——

MARLOW. Dear Sir—I protest, Sir——

HARDCASTLE. I see no reason why you should not be joined as fast as the parson can tie you.

MARLOW. But hear me, Sir——

HARDCASTLE. Your father approves the match, I admire it, every moment's delay will be doing mischief, so——

MARLOW. But why won't you hear me? By all that's just and true, I never gave Miss Hardcastle the slightest mark of my attachment, or even the most distant hint to suspect me of affection. We had but one interview, and that was formal, modest and uninteresting.

HARDCASTLE (*aside*). This fellow's formal modest impudence is beyond bearing.

SIR CHARLES. And you never grasped her hand, or made any protestations!

MARLOW. As heaven is my witness, I came down in obedience to your commands. I saw the lady without emotion, and parted without reluctance. I hope you'll exact no further proofs of my duty, nor prevent me from leaving a house in which I suffer so many mortifications. (*Exit.*)

SIR CHARLES. I'm astonished at the air of sincerity with which he parted.

HARDCASTLE. And I'm astonished at the deliberate intrepidity of his assurance.

SIR CHARLES. I dare pledge my life and honor upon his truth.

HARDCASTLE. Here comes my daughter, and I would stake my happiness upon her veracity.

Enter MISS HARDCASTLE.

HARDCASTLE. Kate, come hither, child. Answer us sincerely, and without reserve; has Mr. Marlow made you any professions of love and affection?

MISS HARDCASTLE. The question is very abrupt, Sir! But since you require unreserved sincerity, I think he has.

HARDCASTLE (*to* SIR CHARLES). You see.

SIR CHARLES. And pray, madam, have you and my son had more than one interview?

MISS HARDCASTLE. Yes, Sir, several.

HARDCASTLE (*to* SIR CHARLES). You see.

SIR CHARLES. But did he profess any attachment?

MISS HARDCASTLE. A lasting one.

SIR CHARLES. Did he talk of love?

MISS HARDCASTLE. Much, Sir.

SIR CHARLES. Amazing! And all this formally?

MISS HARDCASTLE. Formally.

HARDCASTLE. Now, my friend, I hope you are satisfied.

SIR CHARLES. And how did he behave, madam?

MISS HARDCASTLE. As most professed admirers do. Said some civil things of my face, talked much of his want of merit, and the greatness of mine; mentioned his heart, gave a short tragedy speech, and ended with pretended rapture.

SIR CHARLES. Now I'm perfectly convinced, indeed. I know his conversation among women to be modest and submissive. This forward canting ranting manner by no means describes him, and I am confident, he never sat for the picture.

MISS HARDCASTLE. Then what, Sir, if I should convince you to your face of my sincerity? If you and my papa, in about half an hour, will place yourselves behind that screen, you shall hear him declare his passion to me in person.

SIR CHARLES. Agreed. And if I find him what you describe, all my happiness in him must have an end. (*Exit.*)

MISS HARDCASTLE. And if you don't find him what I describe—I fear my happiness must never have a beginning.

(*Exeunt.*)

Scene changes to the back of the garden.

Enter HASTINGS.

HASTINGS. What an idiot am I to wait here for a fellow who probably takes a delight in mortifying me. He never intended to be punctual, and I'll wait no longer. What do I see. It is he, and perhaps with news of my Constance.

Enter TONY, *booted and spattered.*

HASTINGS. My honest Squire! I now find you a man of your word. This looks like friendship.

TONY. Ay, I'm your friend, and the best friend you have in the world, if you knew but all. This riding by night, by the bye, is cursedly tiresome. It has shook me worse than the basket of a stage-coach.

HASTINGS. But how? Where did you leave your fellow travelers? Are they in safety? Are they housed?

TONY. Five and twenty miles in two hours and a half is no such bad driving. The poor beasts have smoked for it. Rabbet me,[1] but I'd rather ride forty miles after a fox, then ten with such *varment.*

HASTINGS. Well, but where have you left the ladies? I die with impatience.

TONY. Left them? Why, where should I leave them, but where I found them?

HASTINGS. This a riddle.

TONY. Riddle me this, then. What's that goes round the house, and round the house, and never touches the house?

HASTINGS. I'm still astray.

TONY. Why that's it, mon. I have led them astray. By jingo, there's not a pond or slough within five miles of the place but they can tell the taste of.

HASTINGS. Ha, ha, ha, I understand; you took them in a round, while they supposed themselves going forward. And so you have at last brought them home again.

TONY. You shall hear. I first took them down Feather-bed Lane, where we stuck fast in the mud. I then rattled them crack over the stones of Up-and-down Hill—I then introduced them to the gibbet on Heavy-tree Heath, and from that, with a circumbendibus,[2] I fairly lodged them in the horsepond at the bottom of the garden.

HASTINGS. But no accident, I hope.

TONY. No, no. Only mother is confoundedly frightened. She thinks herself forty miles off. She's sick of the journey, and the cattle can scarce crawl. So if your own horses be ready, you may whip off with cousin, and I'll be bound that no soul here can budge a foot to follow you.

HASTINGS. My dear friend, how can I be grateful?

TONY. Ay, now it's dear friend, noble Squire. Just now, it was all idiot, cub, and run me through the guts. Damn *your* way of fighting, I say. After we take a knock in this part of the country, we kiss and be friends. But if you had run me through the guts, then I should be dead, and you might go kiss the hangman.

HASTINGS. The rebuke is just. But I must hasten to relieve Miss Neville; if you keep the old lady employed, I promise to take care of the young one. (*Exit* HASTINGS.)

TONY. Never fear me. Here she comes. Vanish. She's got from the pond, and draggled up to the waist like a mermaid.

Enter MRS. HARDCASTLE.

MRS. HARDCASTLE. Oh, Tony, I'm killed. Shook. Battered to death. I shall never survive it. That last jolt that laid us against the quickset hedge[3] has done my business.

TONY. Alack, mama, it was all your own fault. You would be for running away by night, without knowing one inch of the way.

MRS. HARDCASTLE. I wish we were at home again. I never met so many accidents in so short a journey. Drenched in the mud, overturned in a ditch, stuck fast in a slough, jolted to a jelly, and at last to lose our way. Whereabouts do you think we are, Tony?

TONY. By my guess we should be upon

---

1. RABBET ME: drat me; dialect expletive.
2. CIRCUMBENDIBUS: a roundabout way or process.
3. QUICKSET HEDGE: hawthorn hedge.

Crackskull common, about forty miles from home.

MRS. HARDCASTLE. O lud! O lud! the most notorious spot in all the country. We only want a robbery to make a complete night on't.

TONY. Don't be afraid, mama, don't be afraid. Two of the five that kept here are hanged, and the other three may not find us. Don't be afraid. Is that a man that's galloping behind us? No; it's only a tree. Don't be afraid.

MRS. HARDCASTLE. The fright will certainly kill me.

TONY. Do you see anything like a black hat moving behind the thicket?

MRS. HARDCASTLE. O death!

TONY. No, it's only a cow. Don't be afraid, mama; don't be afraid.

MRS. HARDCASTLE. As I'm alive, Tony, I see a man coming towards us. Ah! I'm sure on't. If he perceives us, we are undone.

TONY (*aside*). Father-in-law,[4] by all that's unlucky, come to take one of his night walks. (*to her*) Ah, it's a highwayman, with pistols as long as my arm. A damned ill-looking fellow.

MRS. HARDCASTLE. Good heaven defend us! He approaches.

TONY. Do you hide yourself in that thicket, and leave me to manage him. If there be any danger I'll cough and cry hem. When I cough be sure to keep close. (MRS. HARDCASTLE *hides behind a tree in the back scene.*)

Enter HARDCASTLE.

HARDCASTLE. I'm mistaken, or I heard voices of people in want of help. Oh, Tony, is that you? I did not expect you so soon back. Are your mother and her charge in safety?

TONY. Very safe, Sir, at my aunt Pedigree's. Hem.

MRS. HARDCASTLE (*from behind*). Ah death! I find there's danger.

HARDCASTLE. Forty miles in three hours; sure, that's too much, my youngster.

TONY. Stout horses and willing minds make short journeys as they say. Hem.

MRS. HARDCASTLE (*from behind*). Sure he'll do the dear boy no harm.

HARDCASTLE. But I heard a voice here; I should be glad to know from whence it came?

TONY. It was I, Sir, talking to myself, Sir. I was saying that forty miles in four hours was very good going. Hem. As to be sure it was. Hem. I have got a sort of cold by being out in the air. We'll go in, if you please. Hem.

HARDCASTLE. But if you talked to yourself, you did not answer yourself. I am certain I heard two voices, and am resolved (*raising his voice*) to find the other out.

MRS. HARDCASTLE (*from behind*). Oh! he's coming to find me out. Oh!

TONY. What need you go, Sir, if I tell you? Hem. I'll lay down my life for the truth—hem—I'll tell you all, Sir. (*detaining him*)

HARDCASTLE. I tell you I will not be detained. I insist on seeing. It's in vain to expect I'll believe you.

MRS. HARDCASTLE (*running forward from behind*). O lud, he'll murder my poor boy, my darling. Here, good gentleman, whet your rage upon me. Take my money, my life, but spare that young gentleman, spare my child, if you have any mercy.

HARDCASTLE. My wife! as I'm a Christian. From whence can she come, or what does she mean!

MRS. HARDCASTLE (*kneeling*). Take compassion on us, good Mr. Highwayman. Take our money, our watches, all we have, but spare our lives. We will never bring you to justice, indeed we won't, good Mr. Highwayman.

HARDCASTLE. I believe the woman's out of her senses. What, Dorothy, don't you know *me*?

MRS. HARDCASTLE. Mr. Hardcastle, as I'm alive! My fears blinded me. But who, my

---

4. FATHER-IN-LAW: i.e., step-father.

dear, could have expected to meet you here, in this frightful place, so far from home. What has brought you to follow us?

HARDCASTLE. Sure, Dorothy, you have not lost your wits! So far from home, when you are within forty yards of your own door! (*to him*) This is one of your old tricks, you graceless rogue you. (*to her*) Don't you know the gate, and the mulberry-tree; and don't you remember the horsepond, my dear?

MRS. HARDCASTLE. Yes, I shall remember the horsepond as long as I live; I have caught my death in it. (*to* TONY) And is it to you, you graceless varlet, I owe all this? I'll teach you to abuse your mother, I will.

TONY. Ecod, mother, all the parish says you have spoiled me, and so you may take the fruits on't.

MRS. HARDCASTLE. I'll spoil you, I will. (*Follows him off the stage. Exit.*)

HARDCASTLE. There's morality, however, in his reply. (*Exit.*)

Enter HASTINGS *and* MISS NEVILLE.

HASTINGS. My dear Constance, why will you deliberate thus? If we delay a moment, all is lost for ever. Pluck up a little resolution, and we shall soon be out of the reach of her malignity.

MISS NEVILLE. I find it impossible. My spirits are so sunk with the agitations I have suffered that I am unable to face any new danger. Two or three years patience will at last crown us with happiness.

HASTINGS. Such a tedious delay is worse than inconstancy. Let us fly, my charmer. Let us date our happiness from this very moment. Perish fortune. Love and content will increase what we possess beyond a monarch's revenue. Let me prevail.

MISS NEVILLE. No, Mr. Hastings; no. Prudence once more comes to my relief, and I will obey its dictates. In the moment of passion, fortune may be despised, but it ever produces a lasting repentance. I'm resolved to apply to Mr. Hardcastle's compassion and justice for redress.

HASTINGS. But though he had the will, he has not the power to relieve you.

MISS NEVILLE. But he has influence, and upon that I am resolved to rely.

HASTINGS. I have no hopes. But since you persist, I must reluctantly obey you. (*Exeunt.*)

Scene changes [to the parlor].

Enter SIR CHARLES *and* MISS HARDCASTLE.

SIR CHARLES. What a situation am I in! If what you say appears, I shall then find a guilty son. If what he says be true, I shall then lose one that of all others I most wished for a daughter.

MISS HARDCASTLE. I am proud of your approbation, and to show I merit it, if you place yourselves as I directed, you shall hear his explicit declaration. But he comes.

SIR CHARLES. I'll to your father, and keep him to the appointment. (*Exit* SIR CHARLES.)

Enter MARLOW.

MARLOW. Though prepared for setting out, I come once more to take leave, nor did I, till this moment, know the pain I feel in the separation.

MISS HARDCASTLE (*in her own natural manner*). I believe these sufferings cannot be very great, Sir, which you can so easily remove. A day or two longer, perhaps, might lessen your uneasiness, by showing the little value of what you now think proper to regret.

MARLOW (*aside*). This girl every moment improves upon me. (*to her*) It must not be, madam. I have already trifled too long with my heart. My very pride begins to submit to my passion. The disparity of education and fortune, the anger of a parent, and the contempt of my equals, begin to lose their weight; and nothing can restore me to myself, but this painful effort of resolution.

MISS HARDCASTLE. Then go, Sir. I'll urge nothing more to detain you. Though my family be as good as hers you came down to visit, and my education, I hope, not inferior, what are these advantages without equal affluence? I must remain contented with the slight approbation of imputed merit. I must have only the mockery of your addresses, while all your serious aims are fixed on fortune.

Enter HARDCASTLE *and* SIR CHARLES *from behind.*

SIR CHARLES. Here, behind this screen.

HARDCASTLE. Ay, ay, make no noise. I'll engage my Kate covers him with confusion at last.

MARLOW. By heavens, madam, fortune was ever my smallest consideration. Your beauty at first caught my eye; for who could see that without emotion? But every moment that I converse with you, steals in some new grace, heightens the picture, and gives it stronger expression. What at first seemed rustic plainness now appears refined simplicity. What seemed forward assurance now strikes me as the result of courageous innocence and conscious virtue.

SIR CHARLES. What can it mean! He amazes me!

HARDCASTLE. I told you how it would be. Hush!

MARLOW. I am now determined to stay, madam, and I have too good an opinion of my father's discernment, when he sees you, to doubt his approbation.

MISS HARDCASTLE. No, Mr. Marlow, I will not, cannot detain you. Do you think I could suffer a connection, in which there is the smallest room for repentance? Do you think I would take the mean advantage of a transient passion, to load you with confusion? Do you think I could ever relish that happiness which was acquired by lessening yours?

MARLOW. By all that's good, I can have no happiness but what's in your power to grant me. Nor shall I ever feel repentance but in not having seen your merits before. I will stay, even contrary to your wishes; and though you should persist to shun me, I will make my respectful assiduities atone for the levity of my past conduct.

MISS HARDCASTLE. Sir, I must entreat you'll desist. As our acquaintance began, so let it end, in indifference. I might have given an hour or two to levity; but seriously, Mr. Marlow, do you think I could ever submit to a connection where *I* must appear mercenary, and *you* imprudent? Do you think I could ever catch at the confident addresses of a secure admirer?

MARLOW (*kneeling*). Does this look like security? Does this look like confidence? No, madam, every moment that shows me your merit, only serves to increase my diffidence and confusion. Here let me continue——

SIR CHARLES. I can hold it no longer. Charles, Charles, how hast thou deceived me! Is this your indifference, your uninteresting conversation!

HARDCASTLE. Your cold contempt; your formal interview. What have you to say now?

MARLOW. That I'm all amazement! What can it mean!

HARDCASTLE. It means that you can say and unsay things at pleasure. That you can address a lady in private, and deny it in public; that you have one story for us, and another for my daughter.

MARLOW. Daughter!—this lady your daughter!

HARDCASTLE. Yes, Sir, my only daughter. My Kate, whose else should she be?

MARLOW. Oh, the devil.

MISS HARDCASTLE. Yes, Sir, that very identical tall squinting lady you were pleased to take me for. (*curtseying*) She that you addressed as the mild, modest, sentimental man of gravity, and the bold forward agreeable Rattle of the ladies club; ha, ha, ha.

MARLOW. Zounds, there's no bearing this; it's worse than death.

MISS HARDCASTLE. In which of your characters, Sir, will you give us leave to address you? As the faltering gentleman, with looks on the ground, that speaks just to be heard, and hates hypocrisy; or the loud confident creature, that keeps it up with Mrs. Mantrap, and old Miss Biddy Buckskin, till three in the morning; ha, ha, ha.

MARLOW. Oh, curse on my noisy[5] head. I never attempted to be impudent yet that I was not taken down. I must be gone.

HARDCASTLE. By the hand of my body, but you shall not. I see it was all a mistake. and I am rejoiced to find it. You shall not, Sir, I tell you. I know she'll forgive you. Won't you forgive him, Kate? We'll all forgive you. Take courage, man. (*They retire, she tormenting him to the back scene.*)

Enter MRS. HARDCASTLE, TONY.

MRS. HARDCASTLE. So, so, they're gone off. Let them go, I care not.

HARDCASTLE. Who gone?

MRS. HARDCASTLE. My dutiful niece and her gentleman, Mr. Hastings, from town. He who came down with our modest visitor here.

SIR CHARLES. Who, my honest George Hastings? As worthy a fellow as lives, and the girl could not have made a more prudent choice.

HARDCASTLE. Then, by the hand of my body, I'm proud of the connection.

MRS. HARDCASTLE. Well, if he has taken away the lady, he has not taken her fortune; that remains in this family to console us for her loss.

HARDCASTLE. Sure, Dorothy, you would not be so mercenary?

MRS. HARDCASTLE. Ay, that's my affair, not yours.

HARDCASTLE. But you know if your son, when of age, refuses to marry his cousin, her whole fortune is then at her own disposal.

MRS. HARDCASTLE. Ay, but he's not of age, and she has not thought proper to wait for his refusal.

Enter HASTINGS *and* MISS NEVILLE.

MRS. HARDCASTLE (*aside*). What, returned so soon. I begin not to like it.

HASTINGS (*to* HARDCASTLE). For my late

---

5. NOISY: garrulous.

attempt to fly off with your niece, let my present confusion be my punishment. We are now come back, to appeal from your justice to your humanity. By her father's consent I first paid her my addresses, and our passions were first founded in duty.

MISS NEVILLE. Since his death I have been obliged to stoop to dissimulation to avoid oppression. In an hour of levity I was ready even to give up my fortune to secure my choice. But I'm now recovered from the delusion, and hope from your tenderness what is denied me from a nearer connection.

MRS. HARDCASTLE. Pshaw, pshaw, this is all but the whining end of a modern novel.

HARDCASTLE. Be it what it will, I'm glad they're come back to reclaim their due. Come hither, Tony boy. Do you refuse this lady's hand whom I now offer you?

TONY. What signifies my refusing? You know I can't refuse her till I'm of age, father.

HARDCASTLE. While I thought concealing your age boy was likely to conduce to your improvement, I concurred with your mother's desire to keep it secret. But since I find she turns it to a wrong use, I must now declare you have been of age these three months.

TONY. Of age! Am I of age, father?

HARDCASTLE. Above three months.

TONY. Then you'll see the first use I'll make of my liberty. (*taking* MISS NEVILLE'S *hand*) Witness all men by these presents, that I, Anthony Lumpkin, Esquire, of BLANK place, refuse you, Constantia Neville, spinster, of no place at all, for my true and lawful wife. So Constance Neville may marry whom she pleases, and Tony Lumpkin is his own man again.

SIR CHARLES. O brave Squire.

HASTINGS. My worthy friend.

MRS. HARDCASTLE. My undutiful offspring.

MARLOW. Joy, my dear George, I give you joy sincerely. And could I prevail upon my little tyrant here to be less arbitrary, I should be the happiest man alive, if you would return me the favor.

HASTINGS (*to* MISS HARDCASTLE). Come,

madam, you are now driven to the very last scene of all your contrivances. I know you like him, I'm sure he loves you, and you must and shall have him.

HARDCASTLE (*joining their hands*). And I say so too. And Mr. Marlow, if she makes as good a wife as she has a daughter, I don't believe you'll ever repent your bargain. So now to supper, tomorrow we shall gather all the poor of the parish about us, and the Mistakes of the Night shall be crowned with a merry morning; so boy take her; and as you have been mistaken in the mistress, my wish is, that you may never be mistaken in the wife.

EPILOGUE

Well, having stooped to conquer with success,
And gained a husband without aid from dress,
Still as a barmaid, I could wish it too,
As I have conquered him to conquer you:
And let me say, for all your resolution,
That pretty barmaids have done execution.
Our life is all a play, composed to please,
"We have our exits and our entrances." [1]
The first act shows the simple country maid,
Harmless and young, of everything afraid;
Blushes when hired, and with unmeaning action,
I hopes as how to give you satisfaction.

---

1. OUR LIFE . . . ENTRANCES: See Shakespeare's *As You Like It,* II, vii, 139, beginning: "All the world's a stage,/And all the men and women merely players./They have their exits and their entrances." The rest of the Epilogue follows out this passage.

Her second act displays a livelier scene,—
The unblushing barmaid of a country inn,
Who whisks about the house, at market caters,[2]
Talks loud, coquets the guests, and scolds the waiters.
Next the scene shifts to town, and there she soars,
The chop-house toast of ogling connoisseurs.
On Squires and cits[3] she there displays her arts,
And on the gridiron broils her lovers' hearts—
And as she smiles, her triumphs to complete,
Even Common Councilmen forget to eat.
The fourth act shows her wedded to the Squire,
And Madam now begins to hold it higher;
Pretends to taste, at operas cries *caro,*[4]
And quits her Nancy Dawson,[5] for *Che Faro.*[6]
Dotes upon dancing, and in all her pride,
Swims round the room, the *Heinel*[7] of Cheapside:[8]
Ogles and leers with artificial skill,
Till having lost in age the power to kill,
She sits all night at cards, and ogles at spadille.[9]
Such, through our lives, the eventful history—
The fifth and last act still remains for me.
The barmaid now for your protection prays,
Turns female barrister, and pleads for Bayes.[10]

---

2. CATERS: procures food.
3. CITS: townsmen (citizens).
4. CARO: wonderful.
5. NANCY DAWSON: popular song.
6. CHE FARO: song from *Orfeo ed Euridice* (1762), an opera by Christoph Willibald Gluck.
7. HEINEL: Madame Heinel was a well-known German dancer.
8. CHEAPSIDE: London street, noted for its shops.
9. SPADILLE: the ace of spades.
10. BAYES: a character in Buckingham's *The Rehearsal* (1671); a satire upon John Dryden. Here it means Goldsmith.

I

Act One

1. What is revealed in the first scene between Mr. and Mrs. Hardcastle: about their attitude toward each other, toward "society" and their manner of living, and toward Mrs. Hardcastle's son, Tony Lumpkin? Characterize the Hardcastles.

2. Why is Tony introduced briefly in this opening scene? What is he like? Answer the same two questions about Kate and Constance. What further pieces of information do we get

in the dialogue between Kate and Constance that are essential to the plot?

3. What purpose is served by the first part of the scene at the Three Pigeons? What are Marlow and Hastings like? How has Tony's inspired bit of waggery been prepared for? Why are Hardcastle and Marlow and Hastings perfect butts for such a practical joke?

Act Two

1. What is amusing about the give-and-take between Hardcastle and his servants? In what sense is he something like them and they like

him? What does he mean when he says, "You numbskulls! and so, while, like your betters, you are quarreling for places, the guests must be starved."?

2. If you were directing the play, how would you handle the scene in which Hardcastle first encounters Marlow and Hastings and the two continue their conversation while Hardcastle tries in vain to be a part of it? In particular, how would you handle the asides? Answer the same questions in connection with the misunderstood requests and compliments of the rest of the scene.

3. Why must Marlow be uninformed about the duplicity? Hastings gives one reason; what are some others?

4. Characterize Hasting's dialogue with Mrs. Hardcastle. Is there any ill will in his flattery or banter? Why or why not? Why does he go to such pains to flatter her?

Act Three

1. How is the opening dialogue between Hardcastle and Kate built, first, on a series of ambiguous statements and then on a series of carefully balanced opposites? How consistent is the attitude of each with what we have learned of them previously?

2. How does Mrs. Hardcastle's maneuvering about the jewels backfire on her? If you were playing Tony's part, how would you handle this particular scene? Should he be portrayed as brash and flippant, something of a brat who has never grown up, or should he be the artful manipulator who uses his wits to get his way and make fun of stodgy people? Or something else? How appealing a character should he be?

3. How has Kate's assuming the role of barmaid been carefully prepared for? What is amusing about the maid's comment on Kate's dress: "It's the dress, madam, that every lady wears in the country, but when she visits, or receives company."? Why does Kate take advantage of Marlow's mistake and play the part of barmaid?

4. As director, how would you handle the first part of the scene between Marlow and Kate-as-barmaid when he pays no attention to her for the moment? How would you handle the by-play of the rest of the scene? In other words, how is Kate to lure him on and yet fend

him off, laugh at him and yet not insult him?

5. After Marlow leaves in disgust when Hardcastle shows up, why doesn't Kate explain to him that Marlow has mistaken her for a barmaid?

Act Four

1. What further examples of misunderstanding are there in the first part of Act IV, and why are they funny? Why doesn't Hastings want Marlow to know what a mistake he has made about the jewels? Why has Marlow encouraged his personal servants to drink as much as they like? What first convinces Marlow to prepare to depart at once? What soon convinces him even more?

2. What in Marlow's behavior convinces Kate that he is the man for her? What in her behavior (in her role as *poor relation*) convinces him that she is the girl for him?

3. As director, how would you handle the scene where Constance, Tony, Marlow, and Hastings all berate each other for the mix-ups that have seemingly spoiled everyone's hopes?

4. How has Goldsmith carefully arranged his complicated plot so that everything is left in the air to be resolved in the final act? How has he closed Act IV on a note of expectancy?

Act Five

1. Hardcastle's assurance that all is well does not last long as Act V opens. Why does Kate persist in not revealing the cause of Hardcastle's and Sir Charles's confusion?

2. Why has Tony gone to such pains to lead Constance and Mrs. Hardcastle astray? After the mix-up about the highwayman and Mrs. Hardcastle's chagrin over Tony's practical joke, why does Hardcastle say, "There's morality, however, in his reply"?

3. If you were staging the play, how would you handle the scene in the back of the garden when Tony heaps the final indignities on his mother? What dangers are involved in both overplaying and underplaying the scene?

4. How does Kate successfully manipulate Marlow into professing love for her for her own sake, not simply as Hardcastle's daughter?

5. Why do Hastings and Constance return instead of running off while they had the chance? When they enter, why does Mrs. Hardcastle say, "What! returned so soon! I begin not to like it"? How are all the confusions of the plot finally resolved to the happiness of all concerned (except Mrs. Hardcastle)?

II

1. *"She Stoops to Conquer* has many of the characteristics of farce: ludicrous situations, impossible coincidences, undeveloped motivations, but it does not have one essential ingredient—one-sided, faceless characters." Write an essay on the accuracy of the quoted comment, concentrating particularly on the question of completeness of characterization.

2. In the Prologue there is reference to "a mawkish drab of spurious breed,/ Who deals in *sentimentals."* Define what is meant by *sentimentals,* and show how Goldsmith handles his light and romantic plot without "deal[ing] in *sentimentals"* and yet without resorting to outright slapstick.

3. Goldsmith is obviously having his fun at the expense of writers of highly complicated and ridiculous plots and of audiences who attend the theater to have a good, untroubled cry. What other foibles of the time does Goldsmith poke fun at during the course of the play? Consider particularly Mrs. Hardcastle's dealings with all the principal characters. Consider also the purpose served by the Prologue and the Epilogue.

*"If you wish to know yourself, observe
how others act; if you wish to understand
others, look into your own heart."*
Johann Christoph Friedrich von Schiller, *Votive Tablets*

Unit Two

OURSELVES

You probably hear much advice about "being yourself," especially from your elders, who surround the advice with not so subtle suggestions that "being yourself" involves self-improvement—on their terms. On the other hand, little good is accomplished when, in response, you convince yourself that you *are* "being yourself" and that adult advice springs from a misguided tendency to meddle.

There is truth on both sides. The adult world often contributes advice that it seldom takes itself. And few of us, older or younger, are moved much beyond an easy acceptance of "the way we are" as being good enough. The fact is that few of us know "the way we are"; all of us could spend fruitful days discovering ourselves by applying to "us" the standards, expectations, and prejudices that we usually apply only to "them."

The selections in this unit are not very different in kind from those in Unit I. What is different is the point of view with which we approach them. We are concerned here with self-discovery. In each selection we see a character going through the process of discovering what kind of person he really is, or we share with an author some conviction about what kinds of experience most clearly reveal to us what we are.

Illustrated particularly are some of the ways in which self-discovery comes. It may come in the sudden flash of insight when a person's carefully nurtured delusions about himself run headlong into truth: the young boy in "Araby" discovers how easy it is to play the fool over a girl; Oedipus, seeking all the facts, gets them suddenly and discovers that his wisdom is ignorance. Or it may come in looking back in retrospect at scenes past, where vanished joys and heartaches are reviewed in the sober half-light of maturer judgment: such is the effect of George Orwell's bitter memories of his early school days in "Such, Such Were the Joys . . . ," or of Dylan Thomas's "Fern Hill." Or it may come as the pathetic self-revelation that changes nothing: J. Alfred Prufrock sees himself as the trapped, spineless creature he is and accepts what he sees; the lovers in "The Dill Pickle" never understand very clearly how their self-centered ways rob them of any chance at happiness. Finally, it may come in the recognition of what one's deepest self finds fulfillment in: with Wordsworth the healing force of nature operating through memory, as revealed in "I Wandered Lonely as a Cloud" or "Tintern Abbey"; with John Donne, in "Meditation XVII," the power of suffering to bring one into closer relation with God.

The search for self-knowledge can never end, but it can have many beginnings. To the reader who is awake, who lets himself learn easily through the insights of others who have learned painfully, the world of literature provides many opportunities for making beginnings.

"SUCH, SUCH WERE THE JOYS . . ." [*1952*]

George Orwell

It is very difficult to look at oneself objectively. Few people, for instance, ever feel that a photograph of themselves does them justice. Still fewer are willing to admit that others might understand them better than they understand themselves. There is nothing unusual about this; it is simply the way our egos work.

Sometimes the passage of time allows us to become more frank in assessing what kind of person we are—or were. If our memory serves us well, we can evaluate the meaning of particular experiences in the light of calmer and maturer judgment. The following essay by George Orwell, an account of his early school days, is an excellent example of how forthrightness and memory can combine to produce self-discovery.

Orwell wrote the essay relatively late in his career. The title alludes to a poem by William Blake called "The Echoing Green," one of a group published as *Songs of Innocence,* poems expressive of the wonder and joy of childhood:

> "Such, such were the joys
> When we all, girls and boys,
> In our youth time were seen
> On the Echoing Green."

You will understand the significance of the allusion when you compare this scene with what Orwell has to say about his own "youth time" at "Crossgates," a boarding school for boys between the ages of about six or seven and thirteen. In England, such schools prepare students for the large private boarding-schools, which the English call "public" schools to distinguish that type of collective education from "private" education by a tutor.

However much your own schooling may differ from Orwell's, you will recognize the application of many of his insights to the school experiences of each of us.

. . . Very early it was impressed upon me that I had no chance of a decent future unless I won a scholarship at a public school. Either I won my scholarship, or I must leave school at fourteen and become, in Sim's[1] favorite phrase, "a little office boy at forty pounds a year." In my circumstances it was natural that I should believe this. Indeed, it was universally taken for granted at Crossgates that unless you went to a "good" public school (and only about fifteen schools came under this heading) you were ruined for life. It is not easy to convey to a grown-up person the sense of strain, of nerving oneself for some terrible, all-deciding combat, as the date of the examination crept nearer—eleven years old, twelve years old, then thirteen, the fatal year itself![2] Over a period of about two years, I do not think there was ever a day when "the exam," as I called it,

---

1. SIM: students' nickname for the headmaster of "Crossgates."

---

2. FATAL YEAR ITSELF: An English boy's admission to a *good public school* depends on his competitive performance on national examinations, given at age thirteen to thousands of boys all over the country.

was quite out of my waking thoughts. In my prayers it figured invariably: and whenever I got the bigger portion of a wishbone, or picked up a horseshoe, or bowed seven times to the new moon, or succeeded in passing through a wishing-gate without touching the sides, then the wish I earned by doing so went on "the exam" as a matter of course. And yet curiously enough I was also tormented by an almost irresistible impulse *not* to work. There were days when my heart sickened at the labors ahead of me, and I stood stupid as an animal before the most elementary difficulties. In the holidays, also, I could not work. Some of the scholarship boys received extra tuition from a certain Mr. Batchelor, a likeable, very hairy man who wore shaggy suits and lived in a typical bachelor's "den"—booklined walls, overwhelming stench of tobacco—somewhere in the town. During the holidays Mr. Batchelor used to send us extracts from Latin authors to translate, and we were supposed to send back a wad of work once a week. Somehow I could not do it. The empty paper and the black Latin dictionary lying on the table, the consciousness of a plain duty shirked, poisoned my leisure, but somehow I could not start, and by the end of the holidays I would only have sent Mr. Batchelor fifty or a hundred lines. Undoubtedly part of the reason was that Sim and his cane[3] were far away. But in term time, also, I would go through periods of idleness and stupidity when I would sink deeper and deeper into disgrace and even achieve a sort of feeble defiance, fully conscious of my guilt and yet unable or unwilling—I could not be sure which—to do any better. Then Bingo[4] or Sim would send for me, and this time it would not even be a caning.

Bingo would search me with her baleful eyes. (What color were those eyes, I wonder? I remember them as green, but actually

no human being has green eyes. Perhaps they were hazel.) She would start off in her peculiar, wheedling, bullying style, which never failed to get right through one's guard and score a hit on one's better nature.

"I don't think it's awfully decent of you to behave like this, is it? Do you think it's quite playing the game by your mother and father to go on idling your time away, week after week, month after month? Do you *want* to throw all your chances away? You know your people aren't rich, don't you? You know they can't afford the same things as other boys' parents. How are they to send you to a public school if you don't win a scholarship? I know how proud your mother is of you. Do you *want* to let her down?"

"I don't think he wants to go to a public school any longer," Sim would say, addressing himself to Bingo with a pretense that I was not there. "I think he's given up that idea. He wants to be a little office boy at forty pounds a year."

The horrible sensation of tears—a swelling in the breasts, a tickling behind the nose—would already have assailed me. Bingo would bring out her ace of trumps:

"And do you think it's quite fair to *us*, the way you're behaving? After all we've done for you? You *do* know what we've done for you, don't you?" Her eyes would pierce deep into me, and though she never said it straight out, I did know. "We've had you here all these years—we even had you here for a week in the holidays so that Mr. Batchelor could coach you. We don't *want* to have to send you away, you know, but we can't keep a boy here just to eat up our food, term after term. *I* don't think it's very straight, the way you're behaving. Do you?"

I never had any answer except a miserable "No, Mum," or "Yes, Mum" as the case might be. Evidently it was *not* straight, the way I was behaving. And at some point or other the unwanted tear would always force its way out of the corner of my eye, roll down my nose, and splash.

Bingo never said in plain words that I was a non-paying pupil, no doubt because

3. CANE: Beating with a cane for poor performance, academic or behavioral, was long an established feature of English schooling and persists in some schools today.
4. BINGO: Sim's wife.

vague phrases like "all we've done for you" had a deeper emotional appeal. Sim, who did not aspire to be loved by his pupils, put it more brutally, though, as was usual with him, in pompous language. "You are living on my bounty" was his favorite phrase in this context. At least once I listened to these words between blows of the cane. I must say that these scenes were not frequent, and except on one occasion they did not take place in the presence of other boys. In public I was reminded that I was poor and that my parents "wouldn't be able to afford" this or that, but I was not actually reminded of my dependent position. It was a final unanswerable argument, to be brought forth like an instrument of torture when my work became exceptionally bad.

To grasp the effect of this kind of thing on a child of ten or twelve, one has to remember that the child has little sense of proportion or probability. A child may be a mass of egoism and rebelliousness, but it has not accumulated experience to give it confidence in its own judgments. On the whole it will accept what it is told, and it will believe in the most fantastic way in the knowledge and power of the adults surrounding it. Here is an example.

I have said that at Crossgates we were not allowed to keep our own money. However, it was possible to hold back a shilling or two, and sometimes I used furtively to buy sweets which I kept hidden in the loose ivy on the playing-field wall. One day when I had been sent on an errand I went into a sweetshop a mile or more from the school and bought some chocolates. As I came out of the shop I saw on the opposite pavement a small sharp-faced man who seemed to be staring very hard at my school cap. Instantly a horrible fear went through me. There could be no doubt as to who the man was. He was a spy placed there by Sim! I turned away unconcernedly, and then, as though my legs were doing it of their own accord, broke into a clumsy run. But when I got round the next corner, I forced myself to walk again, for to run was a sign of guilt,

and obviously there would be other spies posted here and there about the town. All that day and the next I waited for the summons to the study, and was surprised when it did not come. It did not seem to me strange that the headmaster of a private school should dispose of[5] an army of informers, and I did not even imagine that he would have to pay them. I assumed that any adult, inside the school or outside, would collaborate voluntarily in preventing us from breaking the rules. Sim was all-powerful, and it was natural that his agents should be everywhere. When this episode happened I do not think I can have been less than twelve years old.

I hated Bingo and Sim, with a sort of shamefaced, remorseful hatred, but it did not occur to me to doubt their judgment. When they told me that I must either win a public school scholarship or become an office boy at fourteen, I believed that those were the unavoidable alternatives before me. And above all, I believed Bingo and Sim when they told me they were my benefactors. I see now, of course, that from Sim's point of view I was a good speculation. He sank money in me, and he looked to get it back in the form of prestige. If I had "gone off,"[6] as promising boys sometimes do, I imagine that he would have got rid of me swiftly. As it was I won him two scholarships when the time came, and no doubt he made full use of them in his prospectuses. But it is difficult for a child to realize that a school is primarily a commercial venture.[7] A child believes that the school exists to educate and that the schoolmaster disciplines him either for his own good, or from a love of bullying. Sim and Bingo had chosen to befriend me, and their friendship included canings, reproaches, and humiliations, which were good for me and saved me from an office stool. That was their version, and I believed in it. It was therefore clear that

---

5. DISPOSE OF: i.e., employ.
6. "GONE OFF": i.e., failed.
7. COMMERCIAL VENTURE: In England, a majority of schools are privately owned.

I owed them a vast debt of gratitude. But I was *not* grateful, as I very well knew. On the contrary, I hated both of them. I could not control my subjective feelings, and I could not conceal them from myself. But it is wicked, is it not, to hate your benefactors? So I was taught, and so I believed. A child accepts the codes of behavior that are presented to it, even when it breaks them. From the age of eight, or even earlier, the consciousness of sin was never far away from me. If I contrived to seem callous and defiant, it was only a thin cover over a mass of shame and dismay. All through my boyhood I had a profound conviction that I was no good, that I was wasting my time, wrecking my talents, behaving with monstrous folly and wickedness and ingratitude—and all this, it seemed, was inescapable, because I lived among laws which were absolute, like the law of gravity, but which it was not possible for me to keep.

*   *   *   *   *

The various codes which were presented to you at Crossgates—religious, moral, social and intellectual—contradicted one another if you worked out their implications. The essential conflict was between the tradition of nineteenth-century asceticism and the actually existing luxury and snobbery of the pre-1914 age. On the one side were low-church Bible Christianity, sex puritanism, insistence on hard work, respect for academic distinction, disapproval of self-indulgence: on the other, contempt for "braininess" and worship of games, contempt for foreigners and the working class, an almost neurotic dread of poverty, and, above all, the assumption not only that money and privilege are the things that matter, but that it is better to inherit them than to have to work for them. Broadly, you were bidden to be at once a Christian and a social success, which is impossible. At the time I did not perceive that the various ideals which were set before us cancelled out. I merely saw that they were all, or nearly all, unattainable, so far as I was

concerned, since they all depended not only on what you did but on what you *were*.

Very early, at the age of only ten or eleven, I reached the conclusion—no one told me this, but on the other hand I did not simply make it up out of my own head: somehow it was in the air I breathed—that you were no good unless you had £100,000. I had perhaps fixed on this particular sum as a result of reading Thackeray. The interest on £100,000 a year (I was in favor of a safe 4 per cent) would be £4,000 and this seemed to me the minimum income that you must possess if you were to belong to the real top crust, the people in the country houses. But it was clear that I could never find my way into that paradise, to which you did not really belong unless you were born into it. You could only *make* money, if at all, by a mysterious operation called "going into the City,"[8] and when you came out of the City, having won your £100,000, you were fat and old. But the truly enviable thing about the top-notchers was that they were rich while young. For people like me, the ambitious middle class, the examination passers, only a bleak, laborious kind of success was possible. You clambered upward on a ladder of scholarships into the Home Civil Service or the Indian Civil Service,[9] or possibly you became a barrister. And if at any point you "slacked" or "went off" and missed one of the rungs in the ladder, you became "a little office boy at forty pounds a year." But even if you climbed to the highest niche that was open to you, you could still only be an underling, a hanger-on of the people who really counted.

*   *   *   *   *

By the social standards that prevailed about me, I was no good, and could not be

---

8. "GOING . . . CITY": The "City" refers to the commercial center of London (like "Wall Street" in New York City).
9. HOME . . . SERVICE: career jobs in the British government.

any good. But all the different kinds of virtue seemed to be mysteriously interconnected and to belong to much the same people. It was not only money that mattered: there were also strength, beauty, charm, athleticism, and something called "guts" or "character," which in reality meant the power to impose your will on others. I did not possess any of these qualities. At games, for instance, I was hopeless. I was a fairly good swimmer and not altogether contemptible at cricket, but these had no prestige value, because boys only attach importance to a game if it requires strength and courage. What counted was football, at which I was a funk. I loathed the game, and since I could see no pleasure or usefulness in it, it was very difficult for me to show courage at it. Football, it seemed to me, is not really played for the pleasure of kicking a ball about, but is a species of fighting. The lovers of football are large, boisterous, nobbly[10] boys who are good at knocking down and trampling on slightly smaller boys. That was the pattern of school life—a continuous triumph of the strong over the weak. Virtue consisted in winning: it consisted in being bigger, stronger, handsomer, richer, more popular, more elegant, more unscrupulous than other people—in dominating them, bullying them, making them suffer pain, making them look foolish, getting the better of them in every way. Life was hierarchical and whatever happened was right. There were the strong, who deserved to win and always did win, and there were the weak, who deserved to lose and always did lose, everlastingly.

I did not question the prevailing standards, because so far as I could see there were no others. How could the rich, the strong, the elegant, the fashionable, the powerful, be in the wrong? It was their world, and the rules they made for it must be the right ones. And yet from a very early age I was aware of the impossibility of any *subjective* conformity. Always at the center of my heart

the inner self seemed to be awake, pointing out the difference between the moral obligation and the psychological *fact*. It was the same in all matters, worldly or other-worldly. Take religion, for instance. You were supposed to love God, and I did not question this. Till the age of about fourteen I believed in God, and believed that the accounts given of him were true. But I was well aware that I did not love him. On the contrary, I hated him, just as I hated Jesus and the Hebrew patriarchs. If I had sympathetic feelings toward any character in the Old Testament, it was towards such people as Cain, Jezebel, Haman, Agag, Sisera: in the New Testament my friends, if any, were Ananias, Caiaphas, Judas, and Pontius Pilate.[11] But the whole business of religion seemed to be strewn with psychological impossibilities. The Prayer Book told you, for example, to love God and fear him: but how could you love someone whom you feared? With your private affections it was the same. What you *ought* to feel was usually clear enough, but the appropriate emotion could not be commanded. Obviously it was my duty to feel grateful toward Bingo and Sim; but I was not grateful. It was equally clear that one ought to love one's father, but I knew very well that I merely disliked my own father, whom I had barely seen before I was eight and who appeared to me simply as a gruff-voiced elderly man forever saying "Don't." It was not that one did not want to possess the right qualities or feel the correct emotions, but that one could not. The good and the possible never seemed to coincide.

There was a line of verse that I came across, not actually while I was at Crossgates, but a year or two later, and which seemed to strike a sort of leaden echo in my heart. It was: "The armies of unalterable law."[12] I understood to perfection what it

---

10. NOBBLY: rough.

11. CAIN . . . PONTIUS PILATE: all evil characters in the Old and New Testaments.
12. "THE . . . LAW": See George Meredith's sonnet on pp. 200-201.

meant to be Lucifer, defeated and justly defeated, with no possibility of revenge. The schoolmasters with their canes, the millionaires with their Scottish castles, the athletes with their curly hair—these were the armies of the unalterable law. It was not easy, at that date, to realize that in fact it *was* alterable. And according to that law I was damned. I had no money, I was weak, I was ugly, I was unpopular, I had a chronic cough, I was cowardly, I smelt. This picture, I should add, was not altogether fanciful. I was an unattractive boy. Crossgates soon made me so, even if I had not been so before. But a child's belief of its own shortcomings is not much influenced by facts. I believed, for example, that I "smelt," but this was based simply on general probability. It was notorious that disagreeable people smelt, and therefore presumably I did so too. Again, until after I had left school for good I continued to believe that I was preternaturally ugly. It was what my schoolfellows had told me, and I had no other authority to refer to. The conviction that it was *not possible* for me to be a success went deep enough to influence my actions till far into adult life. Until I was about thirty I always planned my life on the assumption not only that any major undertaking was bound to fail, but that I could only expect to live a few years longer.

But this sense of guilt and inevitable failure was balanced by something else; that is, the instinct to survive. Even a creature that is weak, ugly, cowardly, smelly, and in no way justifiable still wants to stay alive and be happy after its own fashion. I could not invert the existing scale of values, or turn myself into a success, but I could accept my failure and make the best of it. I could resign myself to being what I was, and then endeavor to survive on those terms.

*   *   *   *   *

Only by resurrecting our own memories can we realize how incredibly distorted is the child's vision of the world. Consider this, for example. How would Crossgates appear to me now, if I could go back, at my present age, and see it as it was in 1915? What should I think of Bingo and Sim, those terrible, all-powerful monsters? I should see them as a couple of silly, shallow, ineffectual people, eagerly clambering up a social ladder which any thinking person could see to be on the point of collapse. I would be no more frightened of them than I would be frightened of a dormouse. Moreover, in those days they seemed to me fantastically old, whereas—though of this I am not certain—I imagine they must have been somewhat younger than I am now. And how would Johnny Hall appear, with his blacksmith's arms and his red, jeering face? Merely a scruffy little boy, barely distinguishable from hundreds of other scruffy little boys. The two sets of facts can lie side by side in my mind, because these happen to be my own memories. But it would be very difficult for me to see with the eyes of any other child, except by an effort of the imagination which might lead me completely astray. The child and the adult live in different worlds. If that is so, we cannot be certain that school, at any rate boarding school, is not still for many children as dreadful an experience as it used to be. Take away God, Latin, the cane, class distinctions, and sexual taboos, and the fear, the hatred, the snobbery and the misunderstanding might still all be there. It will have been seen that my own main trouble was an utter lack of any sense of proportion or probability. This led me to accept outrages and believe absurdities, and to suffer torments over things which were in fact of no importance. It is not enough to say that I was "silly" and "ought to have known better." Look back into your own childhood and think of the nonsense you used to believe and the trivialities which could make you suffer. Of course my own case had its individual variations, but essentially it was that of countless other boys. The weakness of the child is that it starts with a blank sheet. It neither understands nor questions the society in which it lives, and because of its credulity other people can work upon it, infecting it with the sense of inferiority and the dread of offending against mysterious, terrible laws. It may be that everything that happened to me at Crossgates could happen in the most "enlightened" school, though perhaps in subtler forms. Of one thing, however, I do feel fairly sure, and that is that boarding schools are worse than day schools. A child has a better chance with the sanctuary of its home near at hand. And I think the characteristic faults of the English upper and middle classes may be partly due to the practice, general until recently, of sending children away from home as young as nine, eight or even seven.

I have never been back to Crossgates. In a way it is only within the last decade that I have really thought over my schooldays, vividly though their memory has haunted me. Nowadays, I believe, it would make very little impression on me to see the place again, if it still exists. And if I went inside and smelt again the inky, dusty smell of the big schoolroom, the rosiny smell of the chapel, the stagnant smell of the swimming bath and the cold reek of the lavatories, I think I should only feel what one invariably feels in revisiting any scene of childhood: How small everything has grown, and how terrible is the deterioration in myself!

I

1. In what sense does Orwell mean that "a school is primarily a commercial venture"? What part did he, a scholarship boy, play in the venture?

2. Judging by the way Sim and Bingo treated him, why does Orwell say that his hatred of them was *a shamefaced, remorseful hatred?* If they were using him, and didn't mind bullying and beating him, why did he feel guilty about his hatred of them?

3. What was his instinctive attitude toward adults in school? Consider such statements as "a child accepts the codes of behavior that are presented to it, even when it breaks them," and "the child has little sense of proportion or probability." Illustrate these observations from your own experience if you can.

4. Put in your own words what he means by "the instinct to survive."

5. Orwell says, "Broadly you were bidden to be at once a Christian and a social success, which is impossible." Why *impossible?* What does he mean by being a *Christian,* and how would he define *social success?* Do you agree with him? Why or why not?

6. He says that from a very early age he was "aware of the impossibility of any subjective conformity." What does he mean by the phrase *subjective conformity* and with what kind of conformity does it contrast?

II

1. Why does he feel that no matter what changes occur in schools, there will still be essentially the same adult-child relationship he remembers? In discussing this question, try to determine what self-knowledge Orwell got from his experiences and his remembrance of them.

2. What points of similarity do you find between Orwell's analysis of his feelings and responses and your own reactions to past or present schooling? Do you think the very nature of the school-student relationship brings about conflict between what adults want for you, or think you need, and what you want for yourself, or think you need? Why or why not?

from GULLIVER'S TRAVELS   *[1726]*

Jonathan Swift

Orwell's experiences at Crossgates provide him and us with unforgettable reminders of what human beings are capable of doing in the name of "education." In the excerpts that follow from Swift's *Gulliver's Travels* we get a scathing indictment of what human beings are capable of believing in the name of "civilization."

In a much-cut, expurgated version, *Gulliver's Travels* has long been a favorite book for children. This fact attests to the fulfillment of one of Swift's intentions: to write a book of imaginary travels and adventures with so much precise descriptive detail that it would be hard to distinguish from the many other books describing *real* voyages which were popular in Swift's day.

But Swift had other intentions, which he also fulfilled. Most of the voyage-books spoke glowingly of the unspoiled dignity and natural goodness of primitive man uncontaminated by civilization. Swift showed what sentimental nonsense such faulty observation or wishful thinking was. The human beings Gulliver met with in *his* voyages, always grotesque and in some cases despicable, represented a tough-minded, skeptical comment on the notion of there being such a thing as a "noble savage." Furthermore, Swift built into his *Travels* one of the bitterest attacks in all literature on man's pride and inhumanity to man. Sending Gulliver to country after country whose inhabitants look strange to him, but profoundly human to us, Swift forces us to see that all the vices and follies he has shown us are our own. We have sailed to the ends of the earth, but what we have each time uncovered is another dimension of human nature.

The voyages are autobiographical, told faithfully by one Lemuel Gulliver, ship's surgeon, sometimes captain. His first voyage is to the land of the Lilliputians, creatures in human form and with human qualities, but only six inches tall. Gulliver acts toward them with almost excessive kindness and understanding, though we see on close attention that his understanding remains pretty shallow; they in turn show only pettiness, jealousy, and a silly pride, and make him a shabby return indeed for all that he does for them. Swift misses no opportunities in Voyage I to make the pretenses of civilized man look ridiculous as man-in-miniature puffs himself up in a six-inch world.

In Voyage II Gulliver goes ashore on a strange coast with some companions to look for water and "make . . . discoveries." His shipmates abandon him in their haste to escape from one of the natives—the Brobdingnagians—who are creatures in human form as many times larger than Gulliver as the Lilliputians were smaller. To Gulliver the huge people seem as gross and coarse as he did to the Lilliputians, while to them he seems as petty and proud as the Lilliputians did to him. In the end it is the Brobdingnagians, crude to Gulliver's senses but full of kindness and understanding toward him, who become admirable because of their common sense and humane wisdom. Gulliver is upset, even shocked, by the King's inability to see anything noble about European civilization; but he finds this attitude a defect in the King, ignoring the fact that the defect lies in the European vices he has so boastfully described to the King without realizing they are vices. His complacency is a little shaken but not really changed.

The awakening comes in Voyage IV. "Set . . . on shore in an unknown land" after a mutiny of his sailors, Gulliver enters a topsy-turvy world in which horses (the noble Houyhnhnms) are masters, and creatures in human form (the vicious Yahoos) are despised beasts. At first he does not recognize the human-Yahoo relationship, but the Houyhnhnms do, and soon he, too, is compelled to acknowledge it.

Swift's satire has a double edge in this last voyage. Gulliver's simple-minded insensitivity to the evils of European civilization and his hollow pride in his beloved country are brought home to him by the Houyhnhnms, who, he finds, do not even have words to express the vile ways of the European world. Accordingly, he at last views himself as a deluded and despicable being, worse even than the Yahoos, who at least make no pretense to being rational and intelligent. Yet in heaping derision on himself, Gulliver makes as fatal a mistake as he had made in the earlier voyages in not recognizing his complacency and pride. Whatever he actually is, he is not altogether a Yahoo, as he ought to be able to see for himself. Moreover, he ought to be able to see that his admired horses are not as ideal as he thinks them. They represent a static, sterile, wholly "rational" society which is just as inhuman in its own way as Gulliver's Europe.

Gulliver remains deluded, and his voyages of discovery come to an end, but they have provided ever since Swift's time a guide to self-discovery for any man who retraces them in print. If we are thoughtful readers we shall hardly fail to find elements of ourselves in Gulliver and also in the several peoples whom he visits. If we are honest readers we shall have to acknowledge that vanity, pride, ignorance, insensitivity, and self-delusion do lurk, as Swift maintains, beneath a great deal that purports to be courtesy, reasonableness, and compassion. Yet if we are constructive readers, we shall recognize both in the smug optimism with which Gulliver first views himself and his European world, and in the paralyzing pessimism and despair which later overtakes him, the extremes between which true self-knowledge must steer.

Part I

A Voyage to Lilliput

Chapter Three

The Author diverts the emperor and his nobility of both sexes, in a very uncommon manner. The diversions of the court of Lilliput described. The Author hath his liberty granted him upon certain conditions.

My gentleness and good behavior had gained so far on the emperor and his court, and indeed upon the army and people in general, that I began to conceive hopes of getting my liberty in a short time. I took all possible methods to cultivate this favorable disposition. The natives came by degrees to be less apprehensive of any danger from me. I would sometimes lie down, and let five to six of them dance on my hand. And at last the boys and girls would venture to come and play at hide and seek in my hair. I had now made a good progress in understanding and speaking their language. The emperor had a mind one day to entertain me with several of the country shows; wherein they exceed all nations I have known, both for dexterity and magnificence. I was diverted with none so much as that of the rope dancers, performed upon a slender white thread, extended about two foot, and twelve inches from the ground. Upon which, I shall desire liberty, with the reader's patience, to enlarge a little.

This diversion is only practiced by those persons, who are candidates for great employments, and high favor, at court. They are trained in this art from their youth, and are not always of noble birth, or liberal education. When a great office is vacant, either by death or disgrace (which often happens), five or six of those candidates petition the emperor to entertain his Majesty and the court with a dance on the rope; and whoever jumps the highest without falling, succeeds in the office. Very often the chief ministers themselves are commanded to show their skill, and to convince the emperor that they have not lost their faculty. Flimnap, the Treasurer, is allowed[1] to cut a caper on the strait rope,[2] at least an inch higher than any other lord in the whole empire. I have seen him do the somersault several times together, upon a trencher[3] fixed on the rope, which is no thicker than a common packthread in England. My friend Reldresal, principal Secretary for Private Affairs, is, in my opinion, if I am not partial, the second after the Treasurer; the rest of the great officers are much upon a par.

These diversions[4] are often attended with fatal accidents, whereof great numbers are on record. I myself have seen two or three candidates break a limb. But the danger is much greater, when the ministers themselves are commanded to show their dexterity: for, by contending to excel themselves and their

fellows, they strain so far, that there is hardly one of them who hath not received a fall; and some of them two or three. I was assured, that a year or two before my arrival, Flimnap would have infallibly broke his neck, if one of the king's cushions, that accidentally lay on the ground, had not weakened the force of his fall.

There is likewise another diversion, which is only shown before the emperor and empress, and first minister, upon particular occasions. The emperor lays on a table three fine silken threads, of six inches long. One is blue, the other red, and the third green. These threads are proposed as prizes, for those persons whom the emperor hath a mind to distinguish by a peculiar mark of his favor. The ceremony is performed in his Majesty's great chamber of State; where the candidates are to undergo a trial of dexterity very different from the former, and such as I have not observed the least resemblance of in any other country of the Old or the New World. The emperor holds a stick in his hands, both ends parallel to the horizon, while the candidates advancing one by one, sometimes leap over the stick, sometimes creep under it backwards and forwards several times, according as the stick is advanced or depressed. Sometimes the emperor holds one end of the stick, and his first minister the other; sometimes the minister hath it entirely to himself. Whoever performs his part with most agility, and holds out the longest in leaping and creeping, is rewarded with the blue-colored silk; the red is given to the next, and the green to the third, which they all wear girt twice round about the middle; and you see few great persons about this court, who are not adorned with one of these girdles.

The horses of the army, and those of the royal stables, having been daily led before me, were no longer shy, but would come up to my very feet, without starting.[5] The riders would leap them over my hand as I held it on the ground; and one of the emperor's

---

1. ALLOWED: reported as being able to.
2. STRAIT ROPE: tight rope.
3. TRENCHER: platter.
4. DIVERSIONS: These paragraphs are Swift's comments on the antics of courtiers and politicians. (Specifically, Flimnap is probably Walpole, first minister to George I and George II; the King's "cushion" is probably the Duchess of Kendal, a royal mistress who helped restore Walpole to power after he had lost favor between 1717 and 1721; the blue, red, and green threads are the orders of the Garter, Bath, and Thistle, which Walpole used to buy subservience to his policies.)

---

5. STARTING: darting, jumping (in fright).

huntsmen, upon a large courser, took[6] my foot, shoe and all; which was indeed a prodigious leap. I had the good fortune to divert the emperor one day, after a very extraordinary manner. I desired he would[7] order several sticks of two foot high, and the thickness of an ordinary cane, to be brought me; whereupon his Majesty commanded the master of his woods to give directions accordingly; and the next morning, six wood men arrived with as many carriages, drawn by eight horses to each. I took nine of these sticks, and fixing them firmly in the ground in a quadrangular figure, two foot and a half square; I took four other sticks, and tied them parallel at each corner, about two foot from the ground; then I fastened my handkerchief to the nine sticks that stood erected; and extended it on all sides, until it was as tight as the top of a drum; and the four parallel sticks rising about five inches higher than the handkerchief, served as ledges on each side. When I had finished my work, I desired the emperor to let a troop of his best horse, twenty four in number, come and exercise upon this plain. His Majesty approved of the proposal, and I took them up one by one in my hands, ready mounted and armed, with the proper officers to exercise them. As soon as they got into order, they divided into two parties, performed mock skirmishes, discharged blunt arrows, drew their swords, fled and pursued, attacked and retired; and in short discovered the best military discipline I ever beheld. The parallel sticks secured them and their horses from falling over the stage; and the emperor was so much delighted, that he ordered this entertainment to be repeated several days; and once was pleased to be lifted up, and give the word of command; and, with great difficulty, persuaded even the empress herself to let me hold her in her close chair,[8] within two yards of the stage, from whence she was able to take a full view of the whole performance. It was my good fortune that no ill accident happened in these entertainments; only once a fiery horse that belonged to one of the captains, pawing with his hoof struck a hole in my handkerchief, and his foot slipping, he overthrew his rider and himself; but I immediately relieved[9] them both: for, covering the hole with one hand, I set down the troop with the other, in the same manner as I took them up. The horse that fell was strained in the left shoulder, but the rider got no hurt; and I repaired my handkerchief as well as I could: however, I would not trust to the strength of it anymore in such dangerous enterprises.

About two or three days before I was set at liberty, as I was entertaining the court with these kinds of feats, there arrived an express[10] to inform his Majesty, that some of his subjects riding near the place where I was first taken up, had seen a great black substance lying on the ground, very oddly shaped, extending its edges round as wide as his Majesty's bed-chamber, and rising up in the middle as high as a man: that it was no living creature, as they at first apprehended; for it lay on the grass without motion, and some of them had walked round it several times: that by mounting upon each other's shoulders, they had got to the top, which was flat and even; and, stamping upon it, they found it was hollow within: that they humbly conceived it might be something belonging to the Man Mountain; and if his Majesty pleased, they would undertake to bring it with only five horses. I presently knew what they meant; and was glad at heart to receive this intelligence. It seems, upon my first reaching the shore, after our shipwreck, I was in such confusion, that before I came to the place where I went to sleep, my hat, which I had fastened with a string to my head while I was rowing, and had stuck on all the time I was swimming, fell off after I came to land; the string, as I conjecture, breaking by some accident which

---

6. TOOK: jumped over.
7. DESIRED HE WOULD: asked him to.
8. CLOSE CHAIR: sedan chair.

9. RELIEVED: picked up.
10. EXPRESS: messenger.

I never observed, but thought my hat had been lost at sea. I entreated his Imperial Majesty to give orders it might be brought to me as soon as possible, describing to him the use and the nature of it: and the next day the wagoners arrived with it, but not in a very good condition; they had bored two holes in the brim, within an inch and a half of the edge, and fastened two hooks in the holes; these hooks were tied by a long cord to the harness, and thus my hat was dragged along for above half an English mile: but the ground in that country being extremely smooth and level, it received less damage than I expected.

Two days after this adventure, the emperor having ordered that part of his army, which quarters in and about his metropolis, to be in a readiness, took a fancy of diverting himself in a very singular manner. He desired I would stand like a Colossus,[11] with my legs as far asunder as I conveniently could. He then commanded his general (who was an old experienced leader, and a great patron of mine) to draw up the troops in close order, and march them under me; the foot[12] by twenty-four in a breast, and the horse[13] by sixteen, with drums beating, colors flying, and pikes advanced. This body consisted of three thousand foot, and a thousand horse. His Majesty gave orders, upon pain of death, that every soldier in his march should observe the strictest decency, with regard to my person; which, however, could not prevent some of the younger officers from turning up their eyes as they passed under me. And, to confess the truth, my breeches were at that time in so ill a condition, that they afforded some opportunities for laughter and admiration.

I had sent so many memorials and petitions for my liberty, that his Majesty at length mentioned the matter first in the Cabinet, and then in a full council; where it was opposed by none, except Skyresh Bolgo-lam,[14] who was pleased, without any provocation, to be my mortal enemy. But it was carried against him by the whole board, and confirmed by the emperor. That minister was Galbet, or Admiral of the Realm; very much in his master's confidence, and a person well versed in affairs, but of a morose and sour complexion. However, he was at length persuaded to comply; but prevailed that the articles and conditions upon which I should be set free, and to which I must swear, should be drawn up by himself. These articles were brought to me by Skyresh Bolgolam in person, attended by two under secretaries, and several persons of distinction. After they were read, I was demanded to swear to the performance of them; first in the manner of my own country, and afterwards in the method prescribed by their laws; which was to hold my right foot in my left hand, to place the middle finger of my right hand on the crown of my head, and my thumb on the tip of my right ear. But, because the reader may perhaps be curious to have some idea of the style and manner of expression peculiar to that people, as well as to know the articles upon which I recovered my liberty; I have made a translation of the whole instrument, word for word, as near as I was able; which I here offer to the public.

'Golbasto Momaren Evlame Gurdilo Shefin Mully Ully Gue, most mighty emperor of Lilliput, delight and terror of the universe, whose dominions extend five thousand *blust-rugs,* (about twelve miles in circumference) to the extremities of the globe: monarch of all monarchs: taller than the sons of men; whose feet press down to the center, and whose head strikes against the sun: at whose

---

11. COLOSSUS: a gigantic statue, legs astride.
12. FOOT: i.e., the soldiers on foot.
13. HORSE: i.e., those on horses.

14. SKYRESH BOLGOLAM: For Swift's first readers there was an additional dimension of satire in the fact that some of his names referred to known people, places, or situations—Skyresh Bolgolam to the Earl of Nottingham, for instance, an important figure in English government circles.

nod the princes of the earth shake their knees; pleasant as the spring, comfortable as the summer, fruitful as autumn, dreadful as winter. His most sublime Majesty proposeth to the Man Mountain, lately arrived at our celestial dominions, the following articles, which by a solemn oath he shall be obliged to perform.

'First, the Man Mountain shall not depart from our dominions, without our license under our great seal.

'Secondly, he shall not presume to come into our metropolis, without our express order; at which time, the inhabitants shall have two hours' warning to keep within their doors.

'Thirdly, the said Man Mountain shall confine his walks to our principal high roads; and not offer to walk or lie down in a meadow, or field of corn.

'Fourthly, as he walks the said roads, he shall take the utmost care not to trample upon the bodies of any of our loving subjects, their horses, or carriages; nor take any of our said subjects into his hands, without their own consent.

'Fifthly, if an express require extraordinary dispatch; the Man Mountain shall be obliged to carry in his pocket the messenger and horse, a six days' journey once in every moon, and return the said messenger back (if so required) safe to our imperial presence.

'Sixthly, he shall be our ally against our enemies in the island of Blefuscu,[15] and do his utmost to destroy their fleet, which is now preparing to invade us.

'Seventhly, that the said Man Mountain shall, at his times of leisure, be aiding and assisting to our workmen, in helping to raise certain great stones, towards covering the wall of the principal park, and other our royal buildings.

'Eighthly, that the said Man Mountain shall, in two moons' time, deliver in an exact survey the circumference of our dominions, by a computation of his own paces round the coast.

'Lastly, that upon his solemn oath to observe all the above articles, the said Man Mountain shall have a daily allowance of meat and drink, sufficient for the support of 1724 of our subjects; with free access to our royal person, and other marks of our favor. Given at our palace at Belfaborac the twelfth day of the ninety-first moon of our reign.'

I swore and subscribed to these articles with great cheerfulness and content, although some of them were not so honorable as I could have wished; which proceeded wholly from the malice of Skyresh Bolgolam the High Admiral: whereupon my chains were immediately unlocked, and I was at full liberty: the emperor himself, in person, did me the honor to be by at the whole ceremony. I made my acknowledgments, by prostrating myself at his Majesty's feet: but he commanded me to rise; and after many gracious expressions, which, to avoid the censure of vanity, I shall not repeat; he added, that he hoped I should prove a useful servant, and well deserve all the favors he had already conferred upon me, or might do for the future.

The reader may please to observe, that in the last article for the recovery of my liberty, the emperor stipulates to allow me a quantity of meat and drink, sufficient for the support of 1724 Lilliputians. Some time after, asking a friend at court how they came to fix on that determinate number; he told me, that his Majesty's mathematicians, having taken the height of my body by the help of a quadrant, and finding it to exceed theirs in the proportion of twelve to one, they concluded from the similarity of their bodies, that mine must contain at least 1724 of theirs, and consequently would require as much food as was necessary to support that number of Lilliputians. By which, the reader may conceive an idea of the ingenuity of that people, as well as the prudent and exact economy of so great a prince.

15. BLEFUSCU: France, whose power England had momentarily broken in the War of the Spanish Succession, 1701-1713.

Chapter Four

Mildendo, the metropolis of Lilliput described, together with the emperor's palace. A conversation between the Author and a principal secretary, concerning the affairs of that empire: the Author's offers to serve the emperor in his wars.

The first request I made after I had obtained my liberty, was, that I might have license to see Mildendo,[16] the metropolis; which the emperor easily granted me, but with a special charge to do no hurt, either to the inhabitants, or their houses. The people had notice by proclamation of my design to visit the town. The wall which encompassed it, is two feet and a half high, and at least eleven inches broad, so that a coach and horses may be driven very safely round it; and it is flanked with strong towers at ten feet distance. I stepped over the great western gate, and passed very gently and sideling through the two principal streets, only in my short waistcoat, for fear of damaging the roofs and eaves of the houses with the skirts of my coat. I walked with the utmost circumspection, to avoid treading on any stragglers, who might remain in the streets, although the orders were very strict, that all people should keep in their houses, at their own peril. The garret windows, and tops of houses were so crowded with spectators, that I thought in all my travels I had not seen a more populous place. The city is an exact square, each side of the wall being five hundred foot long. The two great streets which run cross and divided it into four quarters, are five foot wide. The lanes and alleys which I could not enter, but only viewed them as I passed, are from twelve to eighteen inches. The town is capable of holding five hundred thousand souls. The houses are from three to five stories. The shops and markets well provided.

The emperor's palace is in the center of the city, where the two great streets meet. It is enclosed by a wall of two foot high, and twenty foot distant from the buildings. I had his Majesty's permission to step over this wall; and the space being so wide between that and the palace, I could easily view it on every side. The outward court is a square of forty foot, and includes two other courts: in the inmost are the royal apartments, which I was very desirous to see, but found it extremely difficult; for the great gates, from one square into another, were but eighteen inches high, and seven inches wide. Now the buildings of the outer court were at least five foot high; and it was impossible for me to stride over them, without infinite damage to the pile, although the walls were strongly built of hewn stone, and four inches thick. At the same time, the emperor had a great desire that I should see the magnificence of his palace: but this I was not able to do until three days after, which I spent in cutting down with my knife some of the largest trees in the royal park, about an hundred yards distant from the city. Of these trees I made two stools, each about three foot high, and strong enough to bear my weight. The people having received notice a second time, I went again through the city to the palace, with my two stools in my hands. When I came to the side of the outer court, I stood upon one stool, and took the other in my hand: this I lifted over the roof, and gently set it down on the space between the first and second court, which was eight foot wide. I then stepped over the buildings very conveniently from one stool to the other, and drew up the first after me with a hooked stick. By this contrivance I got into the inmost court; and lying down upon my side, I applied my face to the windows of the middle stories, which were left open on purpose, and discovered the most splendid apartments that can be imagined. There I saw the empress, and the young princes in their several lodgings, with their chief attendants about them. Her Imperial Majesty was pleased to smile very graciously upon me, and gave me out of the window her hand to kiss.

But I shall not anticipate the reader with further descriptions of this kind, because I

---

16. MILDENDO: London.

reserve them for a greater work, which is now almost ready for the press; containing a general description of this empire, from its first erection, through a long series of princes, with a particular account of their wars and politics, laws, learning, and religion; their plants and animals, their peculiar manners and customs, with other matters very curious and useful; my chief design at present being only to relate such events and transactions as happened to the public, or, to myself, during a residence of about nine months in that empire.

One morning, about a fortnight after I had obtained my liberty, Reldresal, Principal Secretary (as they style him) of Private Affairs, came to my house, attended only by one servant. He ordered his coach to wait at a distance, and desired I would give him an hour's audience; which I readily consented to, on account of his quality, and personal merits, as well as of the many good offices he had done me during my solicitations at court. I offered to lie down, that he might the more conveniently reach my ear; but he chose rather to let me hold him in my hand during our conversation. He began with compliments on my liberty; said, he might pretend to some merit in it; but, however, added, that if it had not been for the present situation of things at court, perhaps I might not have obtained it so soon. "For," said he, "as flourishing a condition as we appear to be in to foreigners, we labor under two mighty evils; a violent faction at home, and the danger of an invasion by a most potent enemy from abroad. As to the first, you are to understand, that for above seventy moons past, there have been two struggling parties in this empire, under the names of Tramecksan and Slamecksan,[17] from the high and low heels on their shoes, by which they distinguish themselves.

"It is alleged indeed, that the high-heels are most agreeable to our ancient constitution: but however this be, his Majesty hath determined to make use of only low-heels in the administration of the Government, and all offices in the gift of the Crown; as you cannot but observe; and particularly, that his Majesty's imperial heels are lower at least by a *drurr* than any of his court; (*drurr* is a measure about the fourteenth part of an inch.) The animosities between these two parties run so high, that they will neither eat nor drink, nor talk with each other. We compute the Tramecksan, or high-heels, to exceed us in number; but the power is wholly on our side. We apprehend his Imperial Highness, the heir to the crown, to have some tendency towards the high-heels; at least we can plainly discover one of his heels higher than the other; which gives him a hobble in his gait. Now, in the midst of these intestine[18] disquiets, we are threatened with an invasion from the island of Blefuscu, which is the other great empire of the universe, almost as large and powerful as this of his Majesty. For as to what we have heard you affirm, that there are other kingdoms and states in the world, inhabited by human creatures as large as yourself, our philosophers are in much doubt; and would rather conjecture, that you dropped from the moon, or one of the stars; because it is certain, that an hundred mortals of your bulk, would, in a short time, destroy all the fruits and cattle of his Majesty's dominions. Besides, our histories of six thousand moons make no mention of any other regions, than the two great empires of Lilliput and Blefuscu. Which two mighty powers have, as I was going to tell you, been engaged in a most obstinate war for six and thirty moons past. It began upon the following occasion.[19] It is allowed on all hands, that the primitive way of breaking eggs before we eat them, was upon the larger end: but his present Majesty's

---

17. TRAMECKSAN AND SLAMECKSAN: The High-Heels are the Tory and high-church party; the Low-Heels are the Whig and low-church party. George I favored the latter; his son (while Prince of Wales) favored both.

18. INTESTINE: internal.

19. OCCASION: Swift refers in the passage that follows to the hostility of the English Roman Catholics (Big-Endians) and Protestants (Little-Endians), and to the recent wars between Catholic France and Protestant England.

grandfather, while he was a boy, going to eat an egg, and breaking it according to the ancient practice, happened to cut one of his fingers. Whereupon the emperor his father, published an edict, commanding[20] all his subjects, upon great penalties, to break the smaller end of their eggs. The people so highly resented this law, that our histories tell us, there have been six rebellions raised on that account; wherein one[21] emperor lost his life, and another[22] his crown. These civil commotions were constantly fomented by the monarchs of Blefuscu; and when they were quelled, the exiles always fled for refuge to that empire. It is computed, that eleven thousand persons have, at several times, suffered death, rather than submit to break their eggs at the smaller end. Many hundred large volumes have been published upon this controversy: but the books of the Big-Endians have been long forbidden,[23] and the whole party rendered incapable by law of holding employments.[24] During the course of these troubles, the emperors of Blefuscu did frequently expostulate by their ambassadors, accusing us of making a schism in religion, by offending against a fundamental doctrine of our great prophet Lustrog, in the fifty-fourth chapter of the *Brundrecal,* (which is their *Alcoran*[25]). This, however, is thought to be a mere strain upon the text: for the words are these; 'That all true believers shall break their eggs at the convenient end': and which is the convenient end, seems in my humble opinion, to be left to every man's conscience, or at least in the power of the chief magistrate to determine. Now the Big-Endian exiles have found so much credit in the Emperor of Blefuscu's

court; and so much private assistance and encouragement from their party here at home, that a bloody war hath been carried on between the two empires for six and thirty moons with various success; during which time we have lost forty capital ships, and a much greater number of smaller vessels, together with thirty thousand of our best seamen and soldiers; and the damage received by the enemy is reckoned to be somewhat greater than ours. However, they have now equipped a numerous fleet, and are just preparing to make a descent upon us: and his Imperial Majesty, placing great confidence in your valor and strength, hath commanded me to lay this account of his affairs before you."

I desired the secretary to present my humble duty to the emperor, and to let him know, that I thought it would not become me, who was a foreigner, to interfere with parties; but I was ready, with the hazard of my life, to defend his person and state against all invaders.

Chapter Five

The Author by an extraordinary stratagem prevents an invasion. A high title of honor is conferred upon him. Ambassadors arrive from the Emperor of Blefuscu, and sue for peace.

The empire of Blefuscu, is an island situated to the north northeast side of Lilliput, from whence it is parted only by a channel of eight hundred yards wide. I had not yet seen it, and upon this notice of an intended invasion, I avoided appearing on that side of the coast, for fear of being discovered by some of the enemy's ships, who had received no intelligence of me; all intercourse between the two empires having been strictly forbidden during the war, upon pain of death; and an embargo laid by our emperor upon all vessels whatsoever. I communicated to his Majesty a project I had formed of seizing the enemy's whole fleet; which, as our scouts assured us, lay at anchor in the harbor ready to sail with the first fair wind. I consulted the most

---

20. COMMANDING: a reference to Henry VIII's establishment of the English church.
21. ONE: Charles I, beheaded in 1649.
22. ANOTHER: James II, deposed in 1688.
23. LONG FORBIDDEN: since the reign of Edward VI.
24. INCAPABLE . . . EMPLOYMENTS: by the Test Acts, 1673 and later, which made it impossible for Catholics and Nonconformists to hold public office.
25. ALCORAN: Koran.

experienced seamen, upon the depth of the channel, which they had often plumbed; who told me, that in the middle at high water it was seventy *glumgluffs* deep, which is about six foot of European measure; and the rest of it fifty *glumgluffs* at most. I walked to the northeast coast over against Blefuscu; where, lying down behind a hillock, I took out my small pocket perspective glass,[26] and viewed the enemy's fleet at anchor, consisting of about fifty men of war, and a great number of transports: I then came back to my house, and gave order (for which I had a warrant) for a great quantity of the strongest cable and bars of iron. The cable was about as thick as packthread, and the bars of the length and size of a knitting-needle. I trebled the cable to make it stronger; and for the same reason I twisted three of the iron bars together, binding the extremities into a hook. Having thus fixed fifty hooks to as many cables, I went back to the northeast coast, and putting off my coat, shoes, and stockings, walked into the sea in my leathern jerken, about half an hour before high water. I waded with what haste I could, and swam in the middle about thirty yards until I felt the ground; I arrived to the fleet in less than half an hour. The enemy was so frighted when they saw me, that they leaped out of their ships, and swam to shore; where there could not be fewer than thirty thousand souls. I then took my tackling, and fastening a hook to the hole at the prow of each, I tied all the cords together at the end. While I was thus employed, the enemy discharged several thousand arrows, many of which stuck in my hands and face; and besides the excessive smart, gave me much disturbance in my work. My greatest apprehension was for mine eyes, which I should have infallibly lost, if I had not suddenly thought of an expedient. I kept, among other little necessaries, a pair of spectacles in a private pocket, which, as I observed before, had escaped the emperor's searchers. These I took out, and fastened as strongly as I

could upon my nose; and thus armed went on boldly with my work in spite of the enemy's arrows; many of which struck against the glasses of my spectacles, but without any other effect, further than a little to discompose[27] them. I had now fastened all the hooks, and taking the knot in my hand, began to pull; but not a ship would stir, for they were all too fast held by their anchors; so that the boldest part of my enterprise remained. I therefore let go the cord, and leaving the hooks fixed to the ships, I resolutely cut with my knife the cables that fastened the anchors; receiving about two hundred shots in my face and hands: then I took up the knotted end of the cables to which my hooks were tied; and with great ease drew fifty of the enemy's largest men of war after me.

The Blefuscudians, who had not the least imagination of what I intended, were at first confounded with astonishment. They had seen me cut the cables, and thought my design was only to let the ships run adrift, or fall foul on each other: but when they perceived the whole fleet moving in order, and saw me pulling at the end; they set up such a scream of grief and despair, that it is almost impossible to describe or conceive. When I had got out of danger, I stopped a while to pick out the arrows that stuck in my hands and face, and rubbed on some of the same ointment that was given me at my first arrival, as I have formerly mentioned. I then took off my spectacles, and waiting about an hour until the tide was a little fallen, I waded through the middle with my cargo, and arrived safe at the royal port of Lilliput.[28]

The emperor and his whole court stood on the shore, expecting the issue[29] of this great adventure. They saw the ships move forward in a large half moon, but could not discern me, who was up to my breast in water. When

26. PERSPECTIVE GLASS: telescope.

27. DISCOMPOSE: knock askew.
28. ARRIVED . . . LILLIPUT: reference in this incident is to the English successes in the War of the Spanish Succession.
29. EXPECTING THE ISSUE: awaiting the outcome.

I advanced to the middle of the channel, they were yet more in pain because I was under water to my neck. The emperor concluded me to be drowned, and that the enemy's fleet was approaching in a hostile manner: but he was soon eased of his fear; for the channel growing shallower every step I made, I came in a short time within hearing; and holding up the end of the cable by which the fleet was fastened, I cried in a loud voice, "Long live the most puissant Emperor of Lilliput!" This great prince received me at my landing with all possible encomiums, and created me a Nardac upon the spot, which is the highest title of honor among them.

His Majesty desired I would take some other opportunity of bringing all the rest[30] of his enemy's ships into his ports. And so unmeasurable is the ambition of princes, that he seemed to think of nothing less than reducing the whole empire of Blefuscu into a province, and governing it by a viceroy; of destroying the Big-Endian exiles, and compelling that people to break the smaller end of their eggs; by which he would remain sole monarch of the whole world. But I endeavored to divert him from this design, by many arguments drawn from the topics of policy as well as justice: and I plainly protested, that I would never be an instrument of bringing a free and brave people into slavery: and when the matter was debated in council, the wisest part of the ministry were of my opinion.

This open bold declaration of mine, was so opposite to the schemes and politics of his Imperial Majesty, that he could never forgive me: he mentioned it in a very artful manner at council, where, I was told, that some of the wisest appeared, at least by their silence, to be of my opinion; but others, who were my secret enemies, could not forbear some expressions, which by a side-wind[31] reflected on me. And from this time began an intrigue between his Majesty, and a junta of ministers maliciously bent against me, which broke out in less than two months, and had like to have ended in my utter destruction. Of so little weight are the greatest services to princes, when put into the balance with a refusal to gratify their passions.

About three weeks after this exploit, there arrived a solemn embassy from Blefuscu, with humble offers of a peace;[32] which was soon concluded upon conditions very advantageous to our emperor; wherewith I shall not trouble the reader. There were six ambassadors, with a train of about five hundred persons; and their entry was very magnificent, suitable to the grandeur of their master, and the importance of their business. When their treaty was finished, wherein I did them several good offices by the credit I now had, or at least appeared to have at court; their excellencies, who were privately told how much I had been their friend, made me a visit in form.[33] They began with many compliments upon my valor and generosity; invited me to that kingdom in the emperor their master's name; and desired me to show them some proofs of my prodigious strength, of which they had heard so many wonders; wherein I readily obliged them, but shall not interrupt the reader with the particulars.

When I had for some time entertained their excellencies to their infinite satisfaction and surprise, I desired they would do me the honor to present my most humble respects to the emperor their master, the renown of whose virtues had so justly filled the whole world with admiration, and whose royal person I resolved to attend before I returned to my own country. Accordingly, the next time I had the honor to see our emperor, I desired his general license to wait on the Blefuscudian monarch, which he was pleased to grant me, as I could plainly perceive, in a very cold manner; but could not guess the reason, until I had a whisper from a certain person, that

---

30. ALL THE REST: alluding to the Whig desire in 1710 to destroy France utterly, a policy the Tories opposed.
31. BY A SIDE-WIND: indirectly.

32. PEACE: reference is to the Treaty of Utrecht (1713).
33. VISIT IN FORM: i.e., a formal visit.

Flimnap and Bolgolam had represented my intercourse with those ambassadors, as a mark of disaffection, from which I am sure my heart was wholly free. And this was the first time I began to conceive some imperfect idea of courts and ministers.

It is to be observed, that these ambassadors spoke to me by an interpreter; the languages of both empires differing as much from each other as any two in Europe, and each nation priding itself upon the antiquity, beauty, and energy of their own tongues, with an avowed contempt for that of their neighbor: yet our emperor standing upon the advantage he had got by the seizure of their fleet, obliged them to deliver their credentials, and make their speech in the Lilliputian tongue. And it must be confessed, that from the great intercourse of trade and commerce between both realms; from the continual reception of exiles, which is mutual among them; and from the custom in each empire to send their young nobility and richer gentry to the other, in order to polish themselves by seeing the world, and understanding men and manners; there are few persons of distinction, or merchants, or seamen, who dwell in the maritime parts, but what can hold conversation in both tongues; as I found some weeks after, when I went to pay my respects to the Emperor of Blefuscu, which in the midst of great misfortunes, through the malice of my enemies, proved a very happy adventure to me, as I shall relate in its proper place. . . .

Part II
A Voyage to Brobdingnag

Chapter Three

The Author sent for to court. The queen buys him of his master the farmer, and presents him to the king. An apartment at court provided for the Author. He is in high favor with the queen. He stands up for the honor of his own country.

. . . The queen became so fond of my company, that she could not dine without me. I had a table placed upon the same at which her Majesty eat, just at her left elbow; and a chair to sit on. Glumdalclitch[34] stood upon a stool on the floor, near my table, to assist and take care of me. I had an entire set of silver dishes and plates, and other necessaries, which in proportion to those of the queen, were not much bigger than what I have seen in a London toyshop, for the furniture of a baby-house: these, my little nurse kept in her pocket, in a silver box, and gave me at meals as I wanted them; always cleaning them herself. No person dined with the queen but the two princesses royal; the elder sixteen years old, and the younger at that time thirteen and a month. Her Majesty used to put a bit of meat upon one of my dishes, out of which I carved for myself; and her diversion was to see me eat in miniature. For the queen (who had indeed but a weak stomach) took up at one mouthful, as much as a dozen English farmers could eat at a meal, which to me was for some time a very nauseous sight. She would craunch[35] the wing of a lark, bones and all, between her teeth, although it were nine times as large as that of a full grown turkey; and put a bit of bread in her mouth, as big as two twelve-penny loaves. She drank out of a golden cup, above a hogshead at a draught. Her knives were twice as long as a scythe set straight upon the handle. The spoons, forks, and other instruments, were all in the same proportion. I remember when Glumdalclitch carried me out of curiosity to see some of the tables at court, where ten or a dozen of these enormous knives and forks were lifted up together; I thought I had never until then beheld so terrible a sight.

It is the custom, that every Wednesday, (which as I have before observed, was their

---

34. GLUMDALCLITCH: The nine-year-old daughter of the farmer whose servant found Gulliver; she has become his nurse.
35. CRAUNCH: crunch.

sabbath) the king and queen, with the royal issue of both sexes, dine together in the apartment of his Majesty; to whom I was now become a favorite; and, at these times my little chair and table were placed at his left hand before one of the salt-sellers. This prince took a pleasure in conversing with me; enquiring into the manners, religion, laws, government, and learning of Europe, wherein I gave him the best account I was able. His apprehension[36] was so clear, and his judgment so exact, that he made very wise reflections and observations upon all I said. But, I confess, that after I had been a little too copious in talking of my own beloved country; of our trade, and wars by sea and land, of our schisms in religion, and parties in the State; the prejudices of his education prevailed so far, that he could not forbear taking me up in his right hand, and stroking me gently with the other, after an hearty fit of laughing, asked me whether I were a Whig or a Tory. Then turning to his first minister, who waited behind him with a white staff, near as tall as the mainmast of the *Royal Sovereign*;[37] he observed, how contemptible a thing was human grandeur, which could be mimicked[38] by such diminutive insects as I: "And yet," said he, "I dare engage,[39] those creatures have their titles and distinctions of honor; they contrive[40] little nests and burrows, that they call houses and cities; they make a figure in dress and equipage;[41] they love, they fight, they dispute, they cheat, they betray." And thus he continued on, while my color came and went several times, with indignation, to hear our noble country, the mistress of arts and arms, the scourge of France, the arbitress of Europe, the seat of virtue, piety, honor, and

truth, the pride and envy of the world, so contemptuously treated.

But, as I was not in a condition to resent injuries, so, upon mature thoughts, I began to doubt whether I were injured or no. For after having been accustomed several months to the sight and converse of this people, and observed every object upon which I cast mine eyes to be of proportionable magnitude, the horror I had first conceived from their bulk and aspect was so far worn off, that if I had then beheld a company of English lords and ladies in their finery and birthday [42] clothes, acting their several parts in the most courtly manner of strutting, and bowing, and prating; to say the truth, I should have been strongly tempted to laugh as much at them, as this king and his grandees did at me. Neither indeed could I forbear smiling at myself, when the queen used to place me upon her hand towards a looking-glass, by which both our persons appeared before me in full view together; and there could nothing be more ridiculous than the comparison: so that I really began to imagine myself dwindled many degrees below my usual size. . . .

Chapter Six

The king inquires into the state of Europe, which the Author relates to him. The king's observations thereon.

. . . He was perfectly astonished with the historical account I gave him of our affairs during the last century; protesting it was only a heap of conspiracies, rebellions, murders, massacres, revolutions, banishments; the very worst effects that avarice, faction, hypocrisy, perfidiousness, cruelty, rage, madness, hatred, envy, lust, malice, and ambition could produce.

His Majesty in another audience, was at the pains to recapitulate the sum of all I had spoken; compared the questions he made with the answers I had given; then taking me

---

36. APPREHENSION: understanding.
37. ROYAL SOVEREIGN: one of the largest British naval vessels.
38. MIMICKED: ridiculed by imitation.
39. I DARE ENGAGE: I dare say.
40. CONTRIVE: plan and build.
41. MAKE . . . EQUIPAGE: have fancy clothes and carriages to make an impression.

---

42. BIRTHDAY: Royal Birthday festivities.

into his hands, and stroking me gently, delivered himself in these words, which I shall never forget, nor the manner he spoke them in. "My little friend Grildrig;[43] you have made a most admirable panegyric upon your country. You have clearly proved that ignorance, idleness, and vice, are the proper ingredients for qualifying a legislator. That laws are best explained, interpreted, and applied by those whose interest and abilities lie in perverting, confounding, and eluding them. I observe among you, some lines of an institution, which in its original might have been tolerable; but these half erased, and the rest wholly blurred and blotted by corruptions. It doth not appear, from all you have said, how any one perfection is required towards the procurement of any one station among you; much less that men are ennobled on account of their virtue, that priests are advanced for their piety or learning, soldiers for their conduct or valor, judges for their integrity, senators for the love of their country, or counselors for their wisdom. As for yourself," continued the king, "who have spent the greatest part of your life in traveling, I am well disposed to hope you may hitherto have escaped many vices of your country. But by what I have gathered from your own relation, and the answers I have with much pains wringed and extorted from you, I cannot but conclude the bulk of your natives to be the most pernicious race of little odious vermin that nature ever suffered to crawl upon the surface of the earth."

Chapter Seven

The Author's love of his country. He makes a proposal of much advantage to the king, which is rejected. The king's great ignorance in politics. The learning of that country very imperfect and confined.

Nothing but an extreme love of truth could have hindered me from concealing this part of my story. It was in vain to discover my resentments, which were always turned into ridicule: and I was forced to rest with patience, while my noble and most beloved country was so injuriously treated. I am heartily sorry as any of my readers can possibly be, that such an occasion was given: but this prince happened to be so curious and inquisitive into every particular, that it could not consist[44] either with gratitude or good manners to refuse giving him what satisfaction I was able. Yet thus much I may be allowed to say in my own vindication; that I artfully eluded many of his questions; and gave to every point a more favorable turn by many degrees than the strictness of truth would allow. For I have always borne that laudable partiality to my own country, which Dionysius Halicarnassensis with so much justice recommends[45] to an historian. I would hide the frailties and deformities of my political mother, and place her virtues and beauties in the most advantageous light. This was my sincere endeavor in those many discourses I had with that monarch, although it unfortunately failed of success.

But great allowances should be given to a king who lives wholly secluded from the rest of the world, and must therefore be altogether unacquainted with the manners and customs that most prevail in other nations: the want of which knowledge, will ever produce many *prejudices,* and a certain *narrowness of thinking;* from which we and the politer countries of Europe are wholly exempted. And, it would be hard indeed, if so remote a prince's notions of virtue and vice were to be offered as a standard for all mankind.

To confirm what I have now said, and further to show the miserable effects of a

---

43. GRILDRIG: the king's name for Gulliver.

44. CONSIST: be consistent with.

45. RECOMMENDS: The historian Dionysius of Halicarnassus confesses in his *Archaeologia* a desire to illustrate the greatness of Rome. Swift satirically makes Gulliver misapply the precedent, since Dionysius, who was not a Roman, is an instance of admiration for greatness wherever found, not an instance of complacent patriotism.

confined education, I shall here insert a passage which will hardly obtain belief.[46] In hopes to ingratiate myself farther into his Majesty's favor, I told him of an invention discovered between three and four hundred years ago, to make a certain powder; into an heap of which the smallest spark of fire falling would kindle the whole in a moment, although it were as big as a mountain; and make it all fly up in the air together, with a noise and agitation greater than thunder. That a proper quantity of this powder rammed into an hollow tube of brass or iron, according to its bigness, would drive a ball of iron or lead with such violence and speed, as nothing was able to sustain its force. That the largest balls thus discharged would not only destroy whole ranks of an army at once; but batter the strongest walls to the ground; sink down ships with a thousand men in each, to the bottom of the sea; and when linked together by a chain, would cut through masts and rigging; divide hundreds of bodies in the middle, and lay all waste before them. That we often put this powder into large hollow balls of iron, and discharged them by an engine into some city we were besieging; which would rip up the pavement, tear the houses to pieces, burst and throw splinters on every side, dashing out the brains of all who came near. That I knew the ingredients very well, which were cheap, and common; I understood the manner of compounding them, and could direct his workmen how to make those tubes of a size proportionable to all other things in his Majesty's kingdom; and the largest need not be above two hundred foot long; twenty or thirty of which tubes, charged with the proper quantity of powder and balls, would batter down the walls of the strongest town in his dominions in a few hours; or destroy the whole metropolis, if ever it should pretend[47] to dispute his absolute commands. This I humbly offered to his Majesty, as a small tribute of acknowledgment, in return of so many marks that I had received of his royal favor and protection.

The king was struck with horror at the description I had given of those terrible engines, and the proposal I had made. He was amazed how so impotent and groveling an insect as I (these were his expressions) could entertain such inhuman ideas, and in so familiar a manner as to appear wholly unmoved at all the scenes of blood and desolation, which I had painted as the common effects of those destructive machines; whereof he said, some evil genius, enemy to mankind, must have been the first contriver. As for himself, he protested that although few things delighted him so much as new discoveries in art or in nature, yet he would rather lose half his kingdom, than be privy to such a secret; which he commanded me, as I valued my life, never to mention any more.

A strange effect of *narrow principles* and *short views!* that a prince possessed of every quality which procures veneration, love and esteem; of strong parts, great wisdom and profound learning; endued with admirable talents for government, and almost adored by his subjects; should from a *nice*[48] *unnecessary scruple,* whereof in Europe we can have no conception, let slip an opportunity put into his hands, that would have made him absolute master of the lives, the liberties, and the fortunes of his people. Neither do I say this with the least intention to detract from the many virtues of that excellent king; whose character I am sensible[49] will on this account be very much lessened in the opinion of an English reader: but I take this defect among them to have risen from their ignorance; by not having hitherto reduced *politics* into a *science,* as the more acute wits of Europe have done. For I remember very well, in a discourse one day with the king, when I happened to say, there were several thousand books among us, written upon the *art of government,* it gave him (directly contrary

46. OBTAIN BELIEF: be believed.
47. PRETEND: attempt.

48. NICE: unduly refined.
49. SENSIBLE: aware.

to my intention) a very mean[50] opinion of our understandings. He professed both to abominate and despise all *mystery, refinement,* and *intrigue,* either in a prince or a minister. He could not tell what I meant by *secrets of State,* where an enemy or some rival nation were not in the case. He confined the knowledge of governing within very *narrow bounds;* to common sense and reason, to justice and lenity, to the speedy determination of civil and criminal causes;[51] with some other obvious topics which are not worth considering. And he gave it for his opinion, that whoever could make two ears of corn or two blades of grass to grow upon a spot of ground where only one grew before, would deserve better of mankind, and do more essential service to his country, than the whole race of politicians put together.

The learning of this people is very defective, consisting only in morality, history, poetry and mathematics; wherein they must be allowed to excel. But the last of these is wholly applied to what may be useful in life; to the improvement of agriculture and all mechanical arts; so that among us it would be little esteemed. . . .

Part IV

A Voyage to the Country of the Houyhnhnms[52]

Chapter Two

The Author conducted by a Houyhnhnm to his house. The Author's reception. The food of the Houyhnhnms. The Author in distress for want of meat, is at last relieved.

". . . we entered, and I saw three of those detestable creatures, whom I first met after my landing, feeding upon roots, and the flesh of some animals, which I afterwards found to be that of asses and dogs, and now and then a cow dead by accident or disease. They were all tied by the neck with strong withes,[53] fastened to a beam; they held their food between the claws of their fore-feet, and tore it with their teeth.

The master horse ordered a sorrel nag, one of his servants, to untie the largest of these animals, and take him into the yard. The beast and I were brought close together, and our countenances diligently compared, both by master and servant, who thereupon repeated several times the word *Yahoo.* My horror and astonishment are not to be described, when I observed in this abominable animal a perfect human figure; the face of it indeed was flat and broad, the nose depressed, the lips large, and the mouth wide. But these differences are common to all savage nations, where the lineaments of the countenance are distorted by the natives suffering their infants to lie groveling on the earth, or by carrying them on their backs, nuzzling with their face against the mother's shoulders. The fore-feet of the Yahoo differed from my hands in nothing else but the length of the nails, the coarseness and brownness of the palms, and the hairiness on the backs. There was the same resemblance between our feet, with the same differences, which I knew very well, though the horses did not, because of my shoes and stockings; the same in every part of our bodies, except as to hairiness and color, which I have already described.

The great difficulty that seemed to stick with the two horses, was to see the rest of my body so very different from that of a Yahoo, for which I was obliged to my clothes, whereof they had no conception. The sorrel nag offered me a root, which he held (after their manner, as we shall describe in its proper place) between his hoof and pastern; I took it in my hand, and having smelt it, returned it to him again as civilly as I could. He brought out of the Yahoo's kennel a piece

---

50. MEAN: low.
51. CAUSES: cases.
52. HOUYHNHNM: pronounced "Whinnim"—in imitation of the whinny of horses.

53. WITHES: halters made of flexible twigs.

of ass's flesh, but it smelt so offensively that I turned from it with loathing; he then threw it to the Yahoo, by whom it was greedily devoured. He afterwards showed me a wisp of hay, and a fetlock full of oats; but I shook my head, to signify that neither of these were food for me. And indeed, I now apprehended that I must absolutely starve, if I did not get to some of my own species; for as to those filthy Yahoos, although there were few greater lovers of mankind, at the time, than myself, yet I confess I never saw any sensitive being so detestable on all accounts; and the more I came near them, the more hateful they grew, while I stayed in that country. This the master horse observed in my behavior, and therefore sent the Yahoo back to his kennel. He then put his fore-hoof to his mouth, at which I was much surprised, although he did it with ease, and with a motion that appeared perfectly natural, and made other signs to know what I would eat; but I could not return him such an answer as he was able to apprehend; and if he had understood me, I did not see how it was possible to contrive any way for finding myself nourishment. While we were thus engaged, I observed a cow passing by; whereupon I pointed to her, and expressed a desire to let me go and milk her. This had its effect; for he led me back into the house, and ordered a mare-servant to open a room, where a good store of milk lay in earthen and wooden vessels, after a very orderly and cleanly manner. She gave me a large bowl full, of which I drank very heartily, and found myself well refreshed. . . .

Chapter Eight

The Author relates several particulars of the Yahoos. The great virtues of the Houyhnhnms. The education and exercise of their youth. Their general assembly.

As I ought to have understood human nature much better than I supposed it possible for my master to do, so it was easy to apply the character he gave of the Yahoos to myself and my countrymen; and I believed I could yet make farther discoveries from my own observation. I therefore often begged his favor to let me go among the herds of Yahoos in the neighborhood, to which he always very graciously consented, being perfectly convinced that the hatred I bore those brutes would never suffer me to be corrupted by them; and his Honor ordered one of his servants, a strong sorrel nag, very honest and good-natured, to be my guard, without whose protection I durst[54] not undertake such adventures. For I have already told the reader how much I was pestered by those odious animals upon my first arrival. I afterwards failed very narrowly three or four times of falling into their clutches, when I happened to stray at any distance without my hanger.[55] And I have reason to believe they had some imagination that I was their own species, which I often assisted myself, by stripping up my sleeves, and showing my naked arms and breast in their sight, when my protector was with me: at which times they would approach as near as they durst, and imitate my actions after the manner of monkeys, but ever with great signs of hatred; as a tame jack-daw with cap and stockings is always persecuted by the wild ones, when he happens to be got among them. . . .

Having already lived three years in this country, the reader I suppose will expect that I should, like all other travelers, give him some account of the manners and customs of its inhabitants, which it was indeed my principal study to learn.

As these noble Houyhnhnms are endowed by nature with a general disposition to all virtues, and have no conceptions or ideas of what is evil in a rational creature; so their grand maxim is, to cultivate *reason,* and to be wholly governed by it. Neither is *reason* among them a point problematical as with us, where men can argue with plausibility on both sides of the question; but strikes you

54. DURST: dared.
55. HANGER: short sword.

with immediate conviction; as it must needs do where it is not mingled, obscured, or discolored by passion and interest. I remember it was with extreme difficulty that I could bring my master to understand the meaning of the word *opinion,* or how a point could be disputable; because *reason* taught us to affirm or deny, only where we are certain; and beyond our knowledge, we cannot do either. So that controversies, wranglings, disputes, and positiveness in false or dubious propositions, are evils unknown among the Houyhnhnms. . . .

Friendship and *benevolence* are the two principal virtues among the Houyhnhnms; and these not confined to particular objects, but universal to the whole race: for a stranger from the remotest part is equally treated with the nearest neighbor, and wherever he goes, looks upon himself as at home. They preserve *decency* and *civility* in the highest degrees, but are altogether ignorant of *ceremony.* They have no fondness for their colts or foals; but the care they take in educating them proceedeth entirely from the dictates of *reason.* And I observed my master to show the same affection to his neighbor's issue,[56] that he had for his own. They will have it that[57] *nature* teaches them to love the whole species, and it is *reason* only that maketh a distinction of persons, where there is a superior degree of virtue.

When the matron Houyhnhnms have produced one of each sex, they no longer accompany with their consorts,[58] except[59] they lose one of their issue by some casualty, which very seldom happens: but in such a case they meet again; or when the like accident befalls a person whose wife is past bearing, some other couple bestows on him one of their own colts, and then go together a second time, until the mother be pregnant. This caution is necessary to prevent the country from being overburthened with num-

bers. But the race of inferior Houyhnhnms bred up to be servants is not so strictly limited upon this article; these are allowed to produce three of each sex, to be domestics in the noble families.

In their marriages, they are exactly careful to choose such colors as will not make any disagreeable mixture in the breed. *Strength* is chiefly valued in the male, and *comeliness* in the female; not upon the account of *love,* but to preserve the race from degenerating: for, where a female happens to excel in *strength,* a consort is chosen with regard to *comeliness.* Courtship, love, presents, jointures, settlements, have no place in their thoughts; or terms whereby to express them in their language. The young couple meet and are joined, merely because it is the determination of their parents and friends: it is what they see done every day; and they look upon it as one of the necessary actions in a reasonable being. But the violation of marriage, or any other unchastity, was never heard of: and the married pair pass their lives with the same friendship, and mutual benevolence, that they bear to all others of the same species who come into their way; without jealousy, fondness, quarreling, or discontent.

In educating the youth of both sexes, their method is admirable, and highly deserveth our imitation. These are not suffered to taste a grain of *oats,* except upon certain days, until eighteen years old; nor *milk,* but very rarely; and in summer, they graze two hours in the morning, and as many in the evening, which their parents likewise observe; but the servants are not allowed above half that time; and a great part of the grass is brought home, which they eat at the most convenient hours, when they can be best spared from work.

Temperance, industry, exercise, and *cleanliness,* are the lessons equally enjoined to the young ones of both sexes: and my master thought it monstrous in us to give the females a different kind of education from the males, except in some articles of domestic management; whereby, as he truly observed,

---

56. ISSUE: children.
57. WILL . . . THAT: believe.
58. CONSORTS: mates.
59. EXCEPT: unless.

one half of our natives were good for nothing but bringing children into the world: and to trust the care of their children to such useless animals, he said was yet a greater instance of brutality.

But the Houyhnhnms train up their youth to strength, speed, and hardiness, by exercising them in running races up and down steep hills, or over hard stony grounds; and when they are all in a sweat, they are ordered to leap over head and ears into a pond or river. Four times a year the youth of certain districts meet to show their proficiency in running, and leaping, and other feats of strength or agility; where the victor is rewarded with a song, made in his or her praise. On this festival, the servants drive a herd of Yahoos into the field, laden with hay, and oats, and milk for a repast to the Houyhnhnms; after which, these brutes are immediately driven back again, for fear of being noisome to the assembly.

Every fourth year, at the *vernal equinox,* there is a representative council of the whole nation, which meets in a plain about twenty miles from our house, and continueth about five or six days. Here they inquire into the state and condition of the several districts; whether they abound, or be deficient in hay, or oats, or cows, or Yahoos? And wherever there is any want (which is but seldom) it is immediately supplied by unanimous consent and contribution. Here likewise the regulation of children is settled: as for instance, if a Houyhnhnm hath two males, he changeth one of them with another who hath two females: and when a child hath been lost by any casualty, where the mother is past breeding, it is determined what family shall breed another to supply the loss.

Chapter Nine

The learning of the Houyhnhnms. . . . Their manner of burials.

The Houyhnhnms have no letters,[60] and consequently their knowledge is all tradi-

tional. But, there happening few events of any moment among a people so well united, naturally disposed to every virtue, wholly governed by reason, and cut off from all commerce with other nations; the historical part is easily preserved without burthening their memories. I have already observed, that they are subject to no diseases, and therefore can have no need of physicians. However, they have excellent medicines composed of herbs to cure accidental bruises and cuts in the pastern or frog[61] of the foot by sharp stones, as well as other maims and hurts in the several parts of the body.

They calculate the year by the revolution of the sun and the moon, but use no subdivisions into weeks. They are well enough acquainted with the motions of those two luminaries, and understand the nature of *eclipses;* and this is the utmost progress of their *astronomy.*

If they can avoid casualties, they die only of old age, and are buried in the obscurest places that can be found, their friends and relations expressing neither joy nor grief at their departure; nor does the dying person discover the least regret that he is leaving the world, any more than if he were upon returning home from a visit to one of his neighbors. I remember, my master having once made an appointment with a friend and his family to come to his house upon some affair of importance; on the day fixed, the mistress and her two children came very late; she made two excuses, first for her husband, who, as she said, happened that very morning to *lhduwhn.* The word is strongly expressed in their language, but not easily rendered into English; it signifies, *to retire to his first mother.* Her excuse for not coming sooner, was, that her husband dying late in the morning, she was a good while consulting her servants about a convenient place where his body should be laid; and I observed, she behaved herself at our house as cheerfully as the rest: she died about three months after. . . .

---

60. LETTERS: literature.

61. FROG: triangular horny pad on the sole of the foot.

Chapter Ten

The Author's economy, and happy life among the Houyhnhnms. His great improvement in virtue, by conversing with them. Their conversations. The Author has notice given him by his master that he must depart from the country. He falls into a swoon for grief, but submits. He contrives and finishes a canoe, by the help of a fellow-servant, and puts to sea at a venture.[62]

I had settled my little economy to my own heart's content. My master had ordered a room to be made for me after their manner, about six yards from the house; the sides and floors of which I plastered with clay, and covered with rush-mats of my own contriving: I had beaten hemp, which there grows wild, and made of it a sort of ticking; this I filled with the feathers of several birds I had taken with springes made of Yahoos' hairs, and were excellent food. I had worked[63] two chairs with my knife, the sorrel nag helping me in the grosser and more laborious part. When my clothes were worn to rags, I made myself others with the skins of rabbits, and of a certain beautiful animal about the same size, called *muhnoh*, the skin of which is covered with a fine down. Of these I likewise made very tolerable stockings. I soled my shoes with wood which I cut from a tree and fitted to the upper leather, and when this was worn out, I supplied it with the skins of Yahoos dried in the sun. I often got honey out of hollow trees, which I mingled with water, or ate with my bread. No man could more verify the truth of these two maxims, *That nature is very easily satisfied;* and *That necessity is the mother of invention.* I enjoyed perfect health of body, and tranquillity of mind; I did not feel the treachery or inconstancy of a friend, nor the injuries of a secret or open enemy. I had no occasion of bribing, flattering, or pimping to procure the favor of any great man or of his opinion. I wanted no fence against fraud or oppression: here was neither physician to destroy my body, nor lawyer to ruin my fortune; no informer to watch my words and actions, or forge accusations against me for hire; here were no gibers, censurers, backbiters, pickpockets, highwaymen, housebreakers, attorneys, bawds, buffoons, gamesters, politicians, wits, splenetics, tedious talkers, controvertists, ravishers, murderers, robbers, virtuosos; no leaders or followers of party and faction; no encouragers to vice, by seducement or examples; no dungeon, axes, gibbets, whipping-posts, or pillories; no cheating shopkeepers or mechanics; no pride, vanity, or affectation; no fops, bullies, drunkards, strolling whores, or poxes; no ranting, lewd, expensive wives; no stupid, proud pedants; no importunate, overbearing, quarrelsome, noisy, roaring, empty, conceited, swearing companions; no scoundrels raised from the dust for the sake of their vices; or nobility thrown into it on account of their virtues; no lords, fiddlers, judges, or dancing-masters.

I had the favor of being admitted to several Houyhnhnms, who came to visit or dine with my master; where his Honor graciously suffered me to wait in the room, and listen to their discourse. Both he and his company would often descend to ask me questions, and receive my answers. I had also sometimes the honor of attending my master in his visits to others. I never presumed to speak, except in answer to a question; and then I did it with inward regret, because it was a loss of so much time for improving myself; but I was infinitely delighted with the station of an humble auditor in such conversations, where nothing passed but what was useful, expressed in the fewest and most significant words; where (as I have already said) the greatest decency was observed, without the least degree of ceremony; where no person spoke without being pleased himself, and pleasing his companions; where there was no interruption, tediousness, heat, or difference of sentiments. They have a notion that when

---

62. AT A VENTURE: i.e., taking his chances.
63. WORKED: made.

people are met together, a short silence doth much improve conversation: this I found to be true; for during those little intermissions of talk, new ideas would arise in their minds, which very much enlivened the discourse. Their subjects are generally on friendship and benevolence; on order and economy; sometimes upon the visible operations of nature, or ancient traditions; upon the bounds and limits of virtue; upon the un-erring rules of reason, or upon some deter-minations to be taken at the next great assembly; and often upon the various ex-cellencies of poetry. I may add without vanity that my presence often gave them sufficient matter for discourse, because it afforded my master an occasion of letting his friends into the history of me and my country, upon which they were all pleased to descant in a manner not very advanta-geous to human kind; and for that reason I shall not repeat what they said: only I may be allowed to observe that his Honor, to my great admiration, appeared to understand the nature of Yahoos much better than my-self. He went through all our vices and fol-lies, and discovered many which I had never mentioned to him, by only supposing what qualities a Yahoo of their country, with a small proportion of reason, might be capable of exerting; and concluded, with too much probability, how vile as well as miserable such a creature must be.

I freely confess that all the little knowl-edge I have of any value was acquired by the lectures I received from my master, and from hearing the discourses of him and his friends; to which I should be prouder to listen than to dictate to the greatest and wisest assembly in Europe. I admired the strength, comeli-ness, and speed of the inhabitants; and such a constellation of virtues in such amiable per-sons produced in me the highest veneration. At first, indeed, I did not feel that natural awe which the Yahoos and all other animals bear towards them; but it grew upon me by degrees, much sooner than I imagined, and was mingled with a respectful love and grati-tude, that they would condescend to dis-tinguish me from the rest of my species.

When I thought of my family, my friends, my countrymen, or human race in general, I considered them as they really were, Yahoos in shape and disposition, perhaps a little more civilized, and qualified with the gift of speech, but making no other use of reason than to improve and multiply those vices whereof their brethren in this country had only the share that nature allotted them. When I happened to behold the reflection of my own form in a lake or fountain, I turned away my face in horror and detestation of myself, and could better endure the sight of a common Yahoo than of my own person. By conversing with the Houyhnhnms, and looking upon them with delight, I fell to imitate their gait and gesture, which is now grown into an habit; and my friends often tell me in a blunt way, that *I trot like a horse:* which, however, I take for a great compli-ment. Neither shall I disown that in speaking I am apt to fall into the voice and manner of the Houyhnhnms, and hear myself ridi-culed on that account without the least mortification.

In the midst of all this happiness, and when I looked upon myself to be fully settled for life, my master sent for me one morning a little earlier than his usual hour. I observed by his countenance that he was in some perplexity, and at a loss how to begin what he had to speak. After a short silence he told me he did not know how I would take what he was going to say: that in the last general assembly, when the affair of the Yahoos was entered upon, the representa-tives had taken offense at his keeping a Yahoo (meaning myself) in his family more like a Houyhnhnm than a brute animal. That he was known frequently to converse with me, as if he could receive some ad-vantage or pleasure in my company; that such a practice was not agreeable to reason or nature, nor a thing ever heard of before among them. The assembly did therefore *exhort* him, either to employ me like the rest of my species, or command me to swim back to the place from whence I came: that the first of these expedients was utterly rejected by all the Houyhnhnms, who had ever seen me at his house or their own: for they alleged that because I had some rudiments of reason, added to the natural pravity[64] of those animals, it was to be feared, I might be able to seduce them into the woody and mountainous parts of the country, and bring them in troops by night to destroy the Houyhnhnms' cattle, as being naturally of the ravenous kind, and averse from labor.

My master added, that he was daily pressed by the Houyhnhnms of the neighborhood to have the assembly's *exhortation* executed, which he could not put off much longer. He doubted it would be impossible for me to swim to another country; and therefore wished I would contrive some sort of vehicle resembling those I had described to him, that might carry me on the sea; in which work I should have the assistance of his own servants, as well as those of his neighbors. He concluded that for his own part he could have been content to keep me in his service as long as I lived; because he found I had cured myself of some bad habits and dispositions, by endeavoring, as far as my inferior nature was capable, to imitate the Houyhnhnms. . . .

I shall not trouble the reader with a particular description of my own mechanics: let it suffice to say that in six weeks' time, with the help of the sorrel nag, who performed the parts that required most labor, I finished a sort of Indian canoe, but much larger, covering it with the skins of Yahoos well stitched together, with hempen threads of my own making. My sail was likewise composed of the skins of the same animal; but I made use of the youngest I could get, the older being too tough and thick; and I likewise provided myself with four paddles. I laid in a stock of boiled flesh, of rabbits and fowls; and took with me two vessels, one filled with milk, and the other with water.

I tried my canoe in a large pond near my master's house, and then corrected in it what was amiss; stopping all the chinks with Yahoos' tallow, until I found it stanch, and able to bear me, and my freight. And when it was as complete as I could possibly make it, I had it drawn on a carriage very gently by Yahoos, to the seaside, under the conduct of the sorrel nag, and another servant.

When all was ready, and the day came for my departure, I took leave of my master and lady, and the whole family, mine eyes flowing with tears, and my heart quite sunk with grief. But his Honor, out of curiosity, and perhaps (if I may speak it without vanity) partly out of kindness, was determined to see me in my canoe; and got several of his neighboring friends to accompany him. I was forced to wait above an hour for the tide, and then observing the wind very fortunately bearing towards the island, to which I intended to steer my course, I took a second leave of my master: but, as I was going to prostrate myself to kiss his hoof, he did me the honor to raise it gently to my mouth. I am not ignorant how much I have been censured for mentioning this last particular. Detractors are pleased to think it improbable, that so illustrious a person should descend to give so great a mark of distinction to a creature so inferior as I. Neither have I forgot, how apt some travelers are to boast of extraordinary favors they have received. But, if these censurers were better acquainted with the noble and courteous disposition of the Houyhnhnms, they would soon change their opinion.

I paid my respects to the rest of the Houyhnhnms in his Honor's company; then getting into my canoe, I pushed off from shore.

Chapter Eleven

The Author's dangerous voyage. He arrives at New Holland,[65] hoping to settle there. Is wounded with an arrow by one of the natives.

---

64. PRAVITY: depravity.

65. NEW HOLLAND: early name for Australia.

*Is seized and carried by force into a Portu-
guese ship. The great civilities of the Captain,
Pedro de Mendez. The Author arrives at
England.*

. . . Our voyage passed without any considerable accident. In gratitude to the Captain I sometimes sat with him at his earnest
request, and strove to conceal my antipathy
to human kind, although it often broke out;
which he suffered to pass without observation. But the greatest part of the day I
confined myself to my cabin, to avoid seeing
any of the crew. The Captain had often
entreated me to strip myself of my savage
dress, and offered to lend me the best suit
of clothes he had. This I would not be prevailed on to accept, abhorring to cover myself with any thing that had been on the back
of a Yahoo. I only desired he would lend
me two clean shirts, which having been
washed since he wore them, I believed would
not so much defile me. These I changed
every second day, and washed them myself. . . .

My wife and family received me with great
surprise and joy, because they concluded me
certainly dead; but I must freely confess the
sight of them filled me only with hatred, disgust, and contempt; and the more by reflecting on the near alliance I had to them.
For although since my unfortunate exile from
the Houyhnhnm country, I had compelled
myself to tolerate the sight of Yahoos, and
to converse with Don Pedro de Mendez, yet
my memory and imagination were perpetually filled with the virtues and ideas of
those exalted Houyhnhnms. And when I
began to consider that by copulating with
one of the Yahoo species I had become a
parent of more, it struck me with the utmost
shame, confusion, and horror.

As soon as I entered the house, my wife
took me in her arms and kissed me; at
which, having not been used to the touch
of that odious animal for so many years, I
fell in a swoon for almost an hour. At the
time I am writing, it is five years since my

last return to England: during the first year
I could not endure my wife or children in
my presence, the very smell of them was
intolerable; much less could I suffer them
to eat in the same room. To this hour they
dare not presume to touch my bread, or
drink out of the same cup; neither was I
ever able to let one of them take me by the
hand. The first money I laid out was to buy
two young stone-horses, which I keep in a
good stable, and next to them the groom
is my greatest favorite; for I feel my spirits
revived by the smell he contracts in the
stable. My horses understand me tolerably
well; I converse with them at least four hours
every day. They are strangers to bridle or
saddle; they live in great amity with me, and
friendship to each other.

Chapter Twelve

*The Author's veracity. His design in pub-
lishing this work. His censure of those travelers who swerve from the truth. The Author
clears himself from any sinister ends in writing. An objection answered. The method
of planting colonies. His native country
commended. The right of the Crown to
those countries described by the Author, is
justified. The difficulty of conquering them.
The Author takes his last leave of the reader;
proposeth his manner of living for the future;
gives good advice, and concludeth.*

. . . I began last week to permit my wife
to sit at dinner with me, at the farthest end
of a long table; and to answer (but with the
utmost brevity) the few questions I asked
her. Yet the smell of a Yahoo continuing
very offensive, I always keep my nose well
stopped with rue, lavender, or tobacco-
leaves. And although it be hard for a man
late in life to remove old habits; I am not
altogether out of hopes in some time to suffer
a neighbor Yahoo in my company, without
the apprehensions I am yet under of his teeth
or his claws.

My reconcilement to the Yahoo-kind in

general might not be so difficult, if they would be content with those vices and follies only which nature hath entitled them to. I am not in the least provoked at the sight of a lawyer, a pickpocket, a colonel, a fool, a lord, a gamester, a politician, a whore-monger, a physician, an evidence,[66] a sub-orner, an attorney, a traitor, or the like: this is all according to the due course of things: but, when I behold a lump of deformity, and diseases both in body and mind, smitten with *pride,* it immediately breaks all the measures of my patience; neither shall I be ever able to comprehend how such an animal and such a vice could tally together. The wise and virtuous Houyhnhnms, who abound in all excellencies that can adorn a rational creature, have no name for this vice in their language, which hath no terms to express any thing that is evil, except those whereby they describe the detestable qualities of their Yahoos; among which they were not able to distinguish this of pride, for want of thor-oughly understanding human nature, as it showeth itself in other countries, where that animal presides. But I, who had more ex-perience, could plainly observe some rudi-ments of it among the wild Yahoos.

But the Houyhnhnms, who live under the government of reason, are no more proud of the good qualities they possess, than I should be for not wanting[67] a leg or an arm, which no man in his wits would boast of, although he must be miserable without them. I dwell the longer upon this subject from the desire I have to make the society of an English Yahoo by any means not insupport-able; and therefore, I here entreat those who have any tincture of this absurd vice, that they will not presume to appear in my sight.

66. EVIDENCE: informer.

67. WANTING: lacking.

Part One

I

1. Characterize the Lilliputians as you see them in these chapters. What concerns them most? Consider his Imperial Majesty's desire to have his army march through Gulliver's legs; the elaborate articles and conditions which Gul-liver must meet to get his liberty; the Big-Endian—Little-Endian controversy; the desire of some officials and the king to make Blefuscu a province. What other details throw light on Lilliputian society?

2. Explain the satire involved in the way Lilliputians decide fitness for public office by agility on the tight rope. What is being satirized in the elaborate ritual Gulliver must go through in swearing *to the performance* of the *articles and conditions?* What is being sati-rized in Reldresal's comments about "other kingdoms and states"? Point out other ex-amples of satire in Part I.

3. What criticism of kings and government officials is made in Chapter Five? How does the king treat Gulliver when the latter opposes some of the proposals about Blefuscu? What examples of jealousy and injured merit are shown?

4. What is Gulliver like in these excerpts? Consider his anxiousness to please, the admira-tion with which he tells of the diversion of the silken threads, and his delight in staging a mili-tary review. What is revealed in such comments as "I swore and subscribed to these articles with great cheerfulness and content, although some of them were not so honorable as I could have wished"; "Her Imperial Majesty was pleased to smile very graciously upon me"; and "About three weeks after this exploit, there arrived a solemn embassy from Blefuscu, with humble offers of a peace"? How is the satire strength-ened by having things seen through the eyes of such a man as Gulliver?

Part Two

I

1. In various parts of the second voyage Gulliver goes to great length to describe the coarseness and ugliness of the Brobdingnagians, whose bodies would appear that way because magnified some twelve times human size. How does his straightforward account of the queen's eating habits automatically make the very process of eating seem brutal and disgusting?

He thinks the queen a superior person, and she is; how does that fact add to the satire?

2. Gulliver means literally what he says about the wisdom of the king. There is also no suggestion of a tongue-in-cheek attitude in his loud praise of his own country. How does the reduction in size of normal man in relation to the Brobdingnagians put all of man's activities in a completely different light? To further appreciate the contrast, you might consider how the plans and activities of yourself and your friends (or of your parents and their friends) would look if presented seriously and straightforwardly as the plans and activities of a group of five-year-olds.

3. What is the irony in Gulliver's recognition of the king's wisdom and good sense, and in his conviction that the king doesn't really understand a superior civilization, that he is the victim of a *confined education* and is therefore very naive? How do Gulliver's very words about the king's *narrow principles, short views,* and *nice unnecessary scruples* throw the light of truth on Gulliver himself? Why is Gulliver, as an innocent admirer of fraud and deception and the arts of war, more vicious than a cold-blooded advocate of such acts would be? Or isn't he "more vicious"? Who are our present-day Gullivers?

Part Four

I

1. It doesn't take Gulliver long to be thoroughly awed by the wisdom and virtue of the Houyhnhnms. What attributes do the Houyhnhnms have that you would call wise and virtuous? Does Gulliver find some that seem to you to be doubtful virtues, or not virtues at all? Explain. Consider carefully all the implications of their "virtues."

2. Gulliver says that he could not make his master understand the word *opinion,* that reason taught the Houyhnhnms to "affirm or deny only where we are certain." Are there things about which there cannot be certainty? If not, as evidently with the Houyhnhnms, what conclusions can you draw about the nature of their society in this respect?

3. In speaking of Houyhnhnm marriages Gulliver comments that they are "without jealousy, fondness, quarreling, or discontent." Note the word *fondness.* It could mean "foolish

affection or tenderness," in which case it would go well with the other three words, but judging by the use of the word just before this point— ("They have no fondness for their colts or foals. . . . I observed my master to show the same affection to his neighbor's issue that he had for his own"), and by the denial of love to marriage, the word means "affection or tenderness" without the "foolish." If so, for the reader it is certainly in strange company with "jealousy," "quarreling," and "discontent."

a. How does this fact indicate that Gulliver's worship of the Houyhnhnms is blinding him to the kind of value judgments that should be the essence of his humanity?

b. Apply the same reasoning to his comments on the four-year meeting: what different kinds of things are divided up in like manner?

c. Note carefully his listing of *vices and follies* at the end. How is the same kind of inability to make distinctions in operation here?

4. What purpose is served by:

a. Gulliver's pride in being able to *trot like a horse* and use the *voice and manners of the Houyhnhnms*?

b. the matter-of-factness with which he talks of using the *skins of Yahoos* ("the youngest I could get") and *Yahoos' tallow?*

c. the manner in which he tells how his master gave him *so great a mark of distinction* on parting? What would be the normal objection to his action in kissing the horse's foot? What does he say the objection is? How is this treatment of the incident ironic?

d. the civility and human understanding of Don Pedro, and Gulliver's reaction to him.

II

1. It would be a mistake to conclude that Gulliver's final judgments are those of Jonathan Swift also. Lemuel Gulliver is not Jonathan Swift. If Gulliver remains deluded and hopelessly wrong, where does Swift stand? Certainly the savagery of the attack on man's inhumanity comes from Swift's disgust with what he saw around him, but does that mean that his final comment is as bleak as Gulliver's is? He has satirized Gulliver all along, and in seeming

to allow him a measure of self-discovery in Part Four, he only concludes by making a fool of him in the end. What is he saying about a blind and inhuman defeatism as well as about a thoughtless and simple-minded optimism? In answering, comment on Swift's view of human nature and on what definitions he might give to the words *virtue* and *vice*.

2. Plan an imaginary voyage of your own—perhaps out of this world—during which you run into situations similar to ones you are familiar with either personally or through the newspapers. In Swift's ironic manner of praising human attitudes and actions that should not be praised and condemning others that should be praised, write an account of the voyage.

THE CAVE OF DESPAIR
from The Faerie Queene, Book I, Canto IX [*1590*]

Edmund Spenser

Gulliver's voyages leave him thoroughly confused about himself and his relations with other human beings. The reader may see human behavior in clearer terms but Gulliver remains miserable and helpless.

Quite different are the responses of two other literary travelers to the experiences which they encounter in the two greatest allegories in English literature: Edmund Spenser's *The Faerie Queene* and John Bunyan's *The Pilgrim's Progress*. In broad terms both works deal with the trials and pitfalls that lie in the path of all men seeking deliverance from the operations and consequences of their own sinful natures. In imaginative narratives full of enchantment, mystery, narrow escapes from destruction, and terrifying physical and mental ordeals, these two very different accounts of spiritual high adventure—one in magnificent verse, the other in simple but powerful Biblical prose—have retained their hold on the imaginations of generations of readers, young and old, for three centuries.

What follows is only a brief section of each, but the power of the whole is nonetheless fully evident. In both episodes the hero's antagonist is Despair, or the death-wish, and in both episodes the formidable vice of Despair is underscored by the dreadful appearance of the physical embodiment of this human sin as it attempts to draw its victim to destruction.

The Faerie Queene, unfinished at Spenser's death, was originally planned as a twelve-part allegory, each part to deal with the nature of a single virtue, such as Temperance, Fidelity, Justice, Chastity, and the like. Each year at the court of Gloriana, the Faerie Queene, a twelve-day feast was held, from which, on separate days, a knight embodying one of the virtues would set forth to fulfill a quest in upholding the particular virtue against the workings of the vices that endanger it. Only six (and part of the seventh) of the proposed twelve books were finished, each of these books containing political and philosophical implications that we will not deal with here.

Book I, from which the following selection is taken, deals with the virtue of Holiness in its struggles against the vices that negate it, among which are Error, Heresy, Pride, Hypocrisy, Despair. The hero of the book is the Red Cross Knight (or St. George) whose quest is to save the parents of Princess Una from the

Dragon that threatens their destruction. Before he meets Despair, he has had many adventures, the most terrifying of which has been his long imprisonment in the castle of the giant Orgoglio (Pride). Through the help of Una, the Red Cross Knight, though greatly tempted by the seductive arguments of Despair, overcomes the temptation and is thereby one step further along the road to the House of Holiness.

As with all of the other selections in the book, we have modernized the spelling in the stanzas that follow, except where the archaic spellings are necessary, as for rhyme. To give an idea of what Spenserian spelling looks like, we have reproduced below the first two stanzas of this selection as they appear in the original editions. The variant spellings have been italicized.

So as they *traueild,* lo they gan espy
An armed knight towards them gallop fast,
That seemed from some feared foe to fly,
Or other *griesly* thing, that him *agast.*
Still as he fled, his eye was backward cast,
As if his *feare* still followed him behind;
Als flew his steed, as he his bands had brast,
And with his winged *heeles* did tread the wind,
As he had *beene* a *fole* of Pegasus, his kind.

Nigh as he drew, they might *perceiue* his head
To be *vnarmd,* and *curld vncombed heares*
Vpstaring stiffe, dismayd with *vncouth* dread;
Nor drop of *bloud* in all his face *appeares*
Nor life in *limbe:* and to increase his *feares,*
In *fowle reproch* of knighthoods *faire* degree,
About his neck an hempen rope he *weares,*
That with his *glistring armes* does ill agree;
But he of rope or *armes* has now no *memoree.*

21

So as they traveled, lo! they gan espy
An armèd knight towàrds them gallop fast,
That seemèd from some fearèd foe to fly,
Or other grisly thing that him aghast.
Still as he fled his eye was backward cast,   5
As if his fear still followed him behind:
Als flew his steed as he his bands had brast,
And with his wingèd heels did tread the wind,
As he had been a foal of Pegasus his kind.

---

1. GAN: began.
4. AGHAST: terrified; the verb is transitive.
7. ALS: likewise. BANDS: (1) bands by which he was tethered? (2) bands by which he was harnessed and controlled? BRAST: burst.
9. AS: as if. FOAL . . . KIND: a foal of the same breed as Pegasus (Bellerophon's winged horse).

22

Nigh as he drew, they might perceive his head 10
To be unarmed, and curled uncombèd hairs
Upstaring stiff, dismayed with uncouth dread:
Nor drop of blood in all his face appears,
Nor life in limb; and, to increase his fears,
In foul reproach of knighthood's fair degree, 15
About his neck an hempen rope he wears,
That with his glistering arms does ill agree;
But he of rope or arms has now no memory.

23

The Red Cross Knight towàrd him crossèd fast,
To weet what mister wight was so dismayed. 20
There him he finds all senseless and aghast,
That of himself he seemed to be afraid;
Whom hardly he from flying forward stayed,
Till he these words to him deliver might:
"Sir knight aread who hath ye thus arrayed, 25
And eke from whom make ye this hasty flight?
For never knight I saw in such misseeming plight."

24

He answered nought at all; but adding new
Fear to his first amazement, staring wide
With stony eyes and heartless hollow hue, 30
Astonished stood, as one that had espied
Infernal furies with their chains untied.
Him yet again, and yet again, bespake
The gentle knight; who nought to him replied;
But, trembling every joint, did inly quake, 35
And faltering tongue, at last, these words seemed forth to shake;

25

"For God's dear love, Sir knight, do me not stay;
For lo! he comes, he comes fast after me."
Eft looking back would fain have run away;
But he him forced to stay and tellen free 40

12. UPSTARING: standing on end.
15. REPROACH: i.e., because death by hanging was shameful for a knight, being reserved for common criminals.
20. WEET: know. MISTER WIGHT: kind of creature.
25. AREAD: explain. ARRAYED: i.e., with a rope.
26. EKE: also.
30. HEARTLESS: i.e., bloodless. HUE: appearance.
35. INLY: inwardly.
37. STAY: delay.
39. EFT: again. WOULD: i.e., he would.
40. TELLEN: tell.

The secret cause of his perplexity:
Yet nathemore by his bold hearty speech
Could his blood-frozen heart emboldened be,
But through his boldness rather fear did reach;
Yet, forced, at last he made through silence sudden breach.   45

26

"And am I now in safety sure," quoth he,
"From him that would have forcèd me to die?
And is the point of death now turned from me,
That I may tell this hapless history?"
"Fear nought," quoth he, "no danger now is nigh."   50
"Then shall I you recount a rueful case,"
Said he, "the which with this unlucky eye
I late beheld; and, had not greater grace
Me reft from it, had been partaker of the place.

27

"I lately chanced (Would I had never chanced!)   55
With a fair knight to keepen company,
Sir Terwin hight, that well himself advanced
In all affairs, and was both bold and free;
But not so happy as mote happy be:
He loved, as was his lot, a Lady gent   60
That him again loved in the least degree;
For she was proud, and of too high intent,
And joyed to see her lover languish and lament:

28

"From whom returning sad and comfortless,
As on the way together we did fare,   65
We met that villain, (God from him me bless!)
That cursèd wight, from whom I scaped whyleare,
A man of hell that calls himself Despair:
Who first us greets, and after fair areads
Of tidings strange, and of adventures rare: 70
So creeping close, as Snake in hidden weeds,
Inquireth of our states, and of our knightly deeds.

---

42. NATHEMORE: none the more.
50. HE: the Red Cross Knight.
52. HE: the stranger, later identified as Sir Trevi-
    san.
54. REFT: torn away.
57. HIGHT: called.

58. FREE: well-bred.
59. MOTE: may.
60. GENT: of gentle birth; noble.
66. BLESS: protect.
67. WHYLEARE: just now.
69. AREADS: talks.

29

"Which when he knew, and felt our feeble hearts
Embossed with bale, and bitter biting grief,
Which love had launchèd with his deadly darts,   75
With wounding words, and terms of foul reprief,
He plucked from us all hope of due relief,
That erst us held in love of lingering life;
Then hopeless, heartless, gan the cunning thief
Persuade us die, to stint all further strife: 80
To me he lent this rope, to him a rusty knife.

30

"With which sad instrument of hasty death,
That woeful lover, loathing lenger light,
A wide way made to let forth living breath:
But I, more fearful or more lucky wight,   85
Dismayed with that deformèd dismal sight,
Fled fast away, half dead with dying fear;
Ne yet assured of life by you, Sir knight,
Whose like infirmity like chance may bear;
But God you never let his charmèd speeches hear!"   90

31

"How may a man," said he, "with idle speech
Be won to spoil the Castle of his health?"
"I wot," quoth he, "whom trial late did teach,
That like would not for all this worldes wealth.
His subtle tongue like dropping honey melt'h   95
Into the heart, and searcheth every vein;
That, ere one be aware, by secret stealth
His power is reft, and weakness doth remain.
O! never, Sir, desire to try his guileful train."

32

"Certès," said he, "hence shall I never rest,   100
Till I that treacherous art have heard and tried;

---

74. EMBOSSED: exhausted (like a hunted animal).
    BALE: woe.
75. LAUNCHED: lanced.
76. REPRIEF: disgrace.
78. ERST: previously.
80. STINT: end.
83. LENGER: longer.
88. NE: nor.

91. HE: the Red Cross Knight.
92. BE . . . HEALTH: i.e., be talked into harming his body (literally killing himself).
93. WOT: know. HE: Sir Trevisan.
94. WORLDES: world's.
95. MELT'H: melteth.
99. TRY: test. TRAIN: trickery.
100. CERTÈS: certainly. HE: the Red Cross Knight.

And you, Sir knight, whose name mote I request,
Of grace do me unto his cabin guide."
"I, that hight Trevisan," quoth he, "will ride
Against my liking back to do you grace: 105
But nor for gold nor glee will I abide
By you, when ye arrive in that same place;
For lever had I die than see his deadly face."

33

Ere long they come where that same wicked wight
His dwelling has, low in an hollow cave,   110
Far underneath a craggy cliff ypight,
Dark, doleful, dreary, like a greedy grave,
That still for carrion carcasses doth crave:
On top whereof aye dwelt the ghastly Owl,
Shrieking his baleful note, which ever drave   115
Far from that haunt all other cheerful fowl;
And all about it wandering ghosts did wail and howl.

34

And all about old stocks and stubs of trees,
Whereon nor fruit nor leaf was ever seen,
Did hang upon the ragged rocky knees;   120
On which had many wretches hangèd been,
Whose carcasses were scattered on the green,
And thrown about the cliffs. Arrivèd there,
That bare-head knight, for dread and doleful teen,
Would fain have fled, ne durst approachen near;   125
But th'other forced him stay, and comforted in fear.

35

That darksome cave they enter, where they find
That cursèd man, low sitting on the ground,
Musing full sadly in his sullen mind:
His greasy locks, long growèn and unbound,   130
Disordered hung about his shoulders round,
And hid his face, through which his hollow eyne
Looked deadly dull, and starèd as astound;

---

102. MOTE: may.
103. GRACE: kindness. CABIN: cave.
104. HIGHT: am called.
105. DO YOU GRACE: oblige you.
106. GLEE: brightness; "gold or glee" is a doublet
     like "time and tide," both words meaning much
     the same.
108. LEVER: liefer; rather.

111. YPIGHT: placed.
114. AYE: always.
115. DRAVE: drove.
116. FOWL: birds.
120. KNEES: crags, knee-like in shape.
124. TEEN: anguish.
132. EYNE: eyes.
133. ASTOUND: astonished.

His raw-bone cheeks, through penury and pine,
Were shrunk into his jaws, as he did never dine.   135

36

His garment, nought but many raggèd clouts,
With thorns together pinned and patchèd was,
The which his naked sides he wrapped abouts;
And him beside there lay upon the grass
A dreary corse, whose life away did pass,   140
All wallowed in his own yet luke-warm blood,
That from his wound yet wellèd fresh, alas!
In which a rusty knife fast fixèd stood,
And made an open passage for the gushing flood.

37

Which piteous spectacle, approving true   145
The woeful tale that Trevisan had told,
Whenas the gentle Red Cross Knight did view,
With fiery zeal he burnt in courage bold
Him to avenge before his blood were cold,
And to the villain said; "Thou damnèd wight,   150
The author of this fact we here behold,
What justice can but judge against thee right,
With thine own blood to price his blood, here shed in sight?"

38

"What frantic fit," quoth he, "hath thus distraught
Thee, foolish man, so rash a doom to give?   155
What justice ever other judgment taught,
But he should die who merits not to live?
None else to death this man despairing drive
But his own guilty mind, deserving death.
Is then unjust to each his due to give?   160
Or let him die, that loatheth living breath,
Or let him die at ease, that liveth here uneath?

39

"Who travels by the weary wandering way,
To come unto his wishèd home in haste,

---

134. PINE: suffering.
135. AS: as if.
140. DREARY: gory.
147. WHENAS: when.
151. FACT: crime.
153. PRICE: pay for.

154. HE: Despair.
157. BUT: than that.
160. IS THEN: is it then.
161. OR: either.
162. UNEATH: uneasily.

And meets a flood that doth his passage stay,   165
Is not great grace to help him over past,
Or free his feet that in the mire stick fast?
Most envious man, that grieves at neighbor's good;
And fond, that joyest in the woe thou hast!
Why wilt not let him pass, that long hath stood   170
Upon the bank, yet wilt thyself not pass the flood?

40

"He there does now enjoy eternal rest
And happy ease, which thou dost want and crave,
And further from it daily wanderest:
What if some little pain the passage have,   175
That makes frail flesh to fear the bitter wave,
Is not short pain well borne, that brings long ease,
And lays the soul to sleep in quiet grave?
Sleep after toil, port after stormy seas,
Ease after war, death after life, does greatly please.   180

41

The knight much wondered at his sudden wit,
And said; "The term of life is limited,
Ne may a man prolong, nor shorten, it:
The soldier may not move from watchful stead,
Nor leave his stand until his Captain bed."   185
"Who life did limit by almighty doom,"
Quoth he, "knows best the terms established;
And he, that points the sentinel his room,
Doth license him depart at sound of morning droom.

42

"Is not his deed, whatever thing is done   190
In heaven and earth? Did not he all create
To die again? All ends that was begun:
Their times in his eternal book of fate
Are written sure, and have their certain date.
Who then can strive with strong necessity,   195
That holds the world in his still changing state,
Or shun the death ordained by destiny?
When hour of death is come, let none ask whence, nor why.

---

166. IS NOT: is it not.
169. FOND: foolish.
181. THE KNIGHT: the Red Cross Knight. WIT:
    wisdom.
184. STEAD: place.
185. BED: bid; command.

186. DOOM: judgment.
187. HE: Despair.
188. POINTS: appoints.
189. LICENSE HIM: permit him to. DROOM: drum.
190. IS NOT: is it not.
196. HIS: its.

43

"The longer life, I wot, the greater sin;
The greater sin, the greater punishment: 200
All those great battles, which thou boasts to win
Through strife, and bloodshed, and avengement,
Now praised, hereafter dear thou shalt repent;
For life must life, and blood must blood, repay.
Is not enough thy evil life forespent?   205
For he that once hath missèd the right way,
The further he doth go, the further he doth stray.

44

"Then do no further go, no further stray,
But here lie down, and to thy rest betake,
Th' ill to prevent, that life ensewen may;   210
For what hath life that may it lovèd make,
And gives not rather cause it to forsake?
Fear, sickness, age, loss, labor, sorrow, strife,
Pain, hunger, cold that makes the heart to quake,
And ever fickle fortune rageth rife;   215
All which, and thousands mo, do make a loathsome life.

45

"Thou, wretched man, of death hast greatest need,
If in true balance thou wilt weigh thy state;
For never knight, that darèd warlike deed,
More luckless disadventures did amate: 220
Witness the dungeon deep, wherein of late
Thy life shut up for death so oft did call;
And though good luck prolongèd hath thy date,
Yet death then would the like mishaps forestall,
Into the which hereafter thou mayst happen fall.   225

46

"Why then dost thou, O man of sin! desire
To draw thy days forth to their last degree?
Is not the measure of thy sinful hire
High heapèd up with huge iniquity,
Against the day of wrath to burden thee?   230
Is not enough, that to this Lady mild

---

199. WOT: know.
203. DEAR: dearly; at a high price.
205. FORESPENT: gone by.
210. ENSEWEN: ensuing.
215. RIFE: abundantly.

216. MO: more.
220. AMATE: dismay.
223. DATE: i.e., life.
230. DAY OF WRATH: Last Judgment.

Thou falsèd hast thy faith with perjury,
And sold thyself to serve Duessa vild,
With whom in all abuse thou hast thyself defiled?

47

"Is not he just, that all this doth behold   235
From highest heaven, and bears an equal eye?
Shall he thy sins up in his knowledge fold,
And guilty be of thine impiety?
Is not his law, Let every sinner die;
Die shall all flesh? What then must needs be done,   240
Is it not better to do willingly,
Than linger till the glass be all outrun?
Death is the end of woes: die soon, O faerie's son!"

48

The knight was much enmovèd with his speech,
That as a sword's point through his heart did perse,   245
And in his conscience made a secret breach,
Well knowing true all that he did rehearse,
And to his fresh remembrance did reverse
The ugly view of his deformèd crimes;
That all his manly powers it did disperse,   250
As he were charmèd with enchanted rimes;
That oftentimes he quaked, and fainted oftentimes.

49

In which amazement when the Miscreaunt
Perceivèd him to waver, weak and frail,
Whiles trembling horror did his conscience daunt,   255
And hellish anguish did his soul assail;
To drive him to despair, and quite to quail,
He showed him, painted in a table plain,
The damnèd ghosts that do in torments wail,
And thousand fiends that do them endless pain   260
With fire and brimstone, which forever shall remain.

231-234. LADY . . . DEFILED: The Red Cross Knight
had started out in Book I with the Princess Una
to save her parents from a dragon. Along the
way he gets parted from Una and is duped into
accompanying Duessa (whose name means
"two-faced"), a witch who is bent on preventing him from achieving his quest.

233. VILD: vile.

236. BEARS . . . EYE: judges all things equally.

237. SHALL . . . FOLD: Shall he simply know thy
sins and not judge them and punish you for
them?

243. O FAERIE'S SON: The Red Cross Knight has
come from the court of Queen Gloriana, *That
greatest Glorious Queene of Faerie land.*

245. PERSE: pierce.

246. BREACH: wound.

248. REVERSE: return.

251. AS: as if.

253. MISCREAUNT: miscreant; villain.

257. QUAIL: quell; i.e., overcome (him).

258. TABLE: picture.

260. DO: cause.

50

The sight whereof so throughly him dismayed,
That nought but death before his eyes he saw,
And ever burning wrath before him laid,
By righteous sentence of th' Almighty's law.   265
Then gan the villain him to overcraw,
And brought unto him swords, ropes, poison, fire,
And all that might him to perdition draw;
And bade him choose what death he would desire;
For death was due to him that had provoked God's ire.   270

51

But, whenas none of them he saw him take,
He to him raught a dagger sharp and keen,
And gave it him in hand: his hand did quake
And tremble like a leaf of Aspin green,
And troubled blood through his pale face was seen   275
To come and go with tidings from the heart,
As it a running messenger had been.
At last, resolved to work his final smart,
He lifted up his hand, that back again did start.

52

Which whenas Una saw, through every vein   280
The crudled cold ran to her well of life,
As in a swown: but, soon relived again,
Out of his hand she snatched the cursèd knife,
And threw it to the ground, enragèd rife,
And to him said; "Fie, fie, faint hearted knight!   285
What meanest thou by this reproachful strife?
Is this the battle which thou vauntst to fight
With that fire-mouthèd Dragon, horrible and bright?

53

"Come, come away, frail, feeble, fleshly wight,
Ne let vain words bewitch thy manly heart,   290
Ne divelish thoughts dismay thy constant spright:

---

262. THROUGHLY: thoroughly.
266. OVERCRAW: crow over (because he thought
he had won).
268. PERDITION: damnation.
272. RAUGHT: handed.
281. CRUDLED: curdled.
282. SWOWN: swoon. RELIVED: revived.

284. RIFE: abundantly.
287–288. BATTLE . . . DRAGON: See note, lines 231–
234.
289. FLESHLY: tender; weak-willed, but with special reference to the general human state of sin
(see Romans 8:1).
291. DIVELISH: devilish. SPRIGHT: spirit.

In heavenly mercies hast thou not a part?
Why shouldst thou then despair, that chosen art?
Where justice grows, there grows eke greater grace,
The which doth quench the brond of hellish smart,   295
And that accurst hand-writing doth deface.
Arise, Sir knight; arise, and leave this cursed place."

54

So up he rose, and thence amounted straight.
Which when the carle beheld, and saw his guest
Would safe depart, for all his subtle sleight,   300
He chose an halter from among the rest,
And with it hung himself, unbid, unblest.
But death he could not work himself thereby;
For thousand times he so himself had drest,
Yet nathèless it could not do him die,   305
Till he should die his last, that is, eternally.

293. CHOSEN: i.e., by God's mercy chosen for salvation.
295. BROND: brand.
296. AND . . . DEFACE: See Colossians 2:8-15.
298. AMOUNTED: mounted (his horse).

299. CARLE: churl.
300. SLEIGHT: trickery.
304. DREST: treated.
305. DO: cause.

I

1. Explain the following lines: 15-18, 93-94, 125-126, 156-157, 168-171, 222-225, 294-296.

2. What details in stanzas 21-24 convince the reader of the intensity of the strange knight's terror?

3. Why was Sir Terwin an easy victim of Despair? What shows that he was an easy victim? Why is the Red Cross Knight so eager to seek out Despair?

4. Outline specifically Despair's line of reasoning with the Red Cross Knight. What makes him a formidable foe to those seeking Holiness? Why is the Red Cross Knight susceptible to Despair's *guileful train?* With what arguments does he try to answer Despair? Why do they seem so feeble in comparison to Despair's arguments?

5. What is the gist of Una's saving reminder to the Red Cross Knight? Why hadn't the Red Cross Knight been able to give his own effective answer to Despair?

DOUBTING CASTLE

from The Pilgrim's Progress   [*1678*]

John Bunyan

John Bunyan's *The Pilgrim's Progress* is an allegorical account of the pilgrimage of Christian, as the chief character is significantly called, from the human sinfulness of the City of Destruction to the heavenly perfection of the Celestial City. From it we have taken the episode in which Christian and his traveling companion, Hopeful, are imprisoned by a Giant, Despair, in the dungeons of Doubting Castle, and are tempted to end it all.

The episode is but one of many trials which face Christian in his pilgrimage. For Bunyan the allegory represents the temptations which any committed Christian must undergo in facing the evils of a sinful world and earning the final reward of God's grace and acceptance into His heavenly kingdom. His main characters, Christian and Faithful, and later Hopeful, travel through the temptations of such places as the Slough of Despond, the Valley of the Shadow of Death, and Vanity Fair on their way to final salvation, learning along the way what it means to rely on God's strength and guidance.

Unlike Gulliver, who never understands what his true nature is, but like the Red Cross Knight, Christian finally remembers what he should have known all along about God's promises, and secures deliverance from the despair of Doubting Castle.

Neither could they, with all the skill they had, get again to the stile that night. Wherefore, at last, lighting under a little shelter, they sat down there until the daybreak; but, being weary, they fell asleep. Now there was, not far from the place where they lay, a castle called Doubting Castle, the owner whereof was Giant Despair; and it was in his grounds they now were sleeping: wherefore he, getting up in the morning early, and walking up and down in his fields, caught Christian and Hopeful asleep in his grounds. Then, with a grim and surly voice, he bid them awake; and asked them whence they were, and what they did in his grounds. They told him they were pilgrims, and that they had lost their way. Then said the Giant, You have this night trespassed on me, by trampling in and lying on my grounds, therefore you must go along with me. So they were forced to go, because he was stronger than they. They also had but little to say, for they knew themselves in a fault. The Giant, therefore, drove them before him, and put them into his castle, into a very dark dungeon, nasty and stinking to the spirits of these two men (Psalms, 88:18). Here, then, they lay from Wednesday morning till Saturday night, without one bit of bread, or drop of drink, or light, or any to ask how they did; they were, therefore, here in evil case, and were far from friends and acquaintance. Now in this place Christian had double sorrow, because 'twas through his unadvised haste that they were brought into this distress.

Now, Giant Despair had a wife, and her name was Diffidence. So when he was gone to bed, he told his wife what he had done; to wit, that he had taken a couple of prisoners and cast them into his dungeon, for trespassing on his grounds. Then he asked her also what he had best to do further to them. So she asked him what they were, whence they came, and whither they were bound; and he told her. Then she counseled him that when he arose in the morning he should beat them without any mercy. So, when he arose in the morning he getteth him a grievous crab-tree cudgel,[1] and goes down into the dungeon to them, and there first falls to rating[2] of them as if they were dogs, although they never gave him a word of distaste. Then he falls upon them, and beats them fearfully, in such sort, that they were not able to help themselves, or to turn them upon the floor. This done, he withdraws and leaves them, there to condole their misery, and to mourn under their distress. So all that day they spent the time in nothing but sighs and bitter lamentations. The next night, she, talking with her husband about them further, and understanding they were yet alive, did advise him to counsel them to make away themselves. So when morning was come, he goes to them in a surly manner as before, and perceiving them to be very sore with the stripes that he had given them the day before, he told them, that since they were never like to come out of that place, their only way would be forthwith to make an end of themselves, either with knife, halter, or poison, for why, said he, should you choose life, seeing it is attended with so much bitterness? But they desired him to let them go. With that he looked ugly upon them, and, rushing to them, had doubtless made an end of them himself, but that he fell into one of his fits (for he sometimes, in sunshine weather, fell into fits), and lost for a time the use of his hand; wherefore he withdrew, and left them as before, to consider what to do. Then did the prisoners consult between themselves, whether it was best to take his counsel or no; and thus they began to discourse:—

---

1. GETTETH . . . CUDGEL: got himself a heavy club made from a crab-apple tree.
2. RATING: chiding abusively.

Christian. Brother, said Christian, what shall we do? The life that we now live is miserable. For my part I know not whether it is best, to live thus, or to die out of hand. "My soul chooseth strangling rather than life," and the grave is more easy for me than this dungeon (Job, 7:15). Shall we be ruled by the Giant?

Hopeful. Indeed, our present condition is dreadful, and death would be far more welcome to me than thus forever to abide; but yet, let us consider, the Lord of the country to which we are going hath said, Thou shalt do no murder: no, not to another man's person; much more, then, are we forbidden to take his counsel to kill ourselves. Besides, he that kills another can but commit murder upon his body; but for one to kill himself is to kill body and soul at once. And, moreover, my brother, thou talkest of ease in the grave; but hast thou forgotten the hell, whither for certain the murderers go? For "no murderer hath eternal life" (John, 3:15), etc. And let us consider, again, that all the law is not in the hand of Giant Despair. Others, so far as I can understand, have been taken by him, as well as we; and yet have escaped out of his hand. Who knows, but that God that made the world may cause that Giant Despair may die? or that, at some time or other, he may forget to lock us in? or but he may, in a short time, have another of his fits before us, and may lose the use of his limbs? and if ever that should come to pass again, for my part, I am resolved to pluck up the heart of a man, and to try my utmost to get from under his hand. I was a fool that I did not try to do it before; but, however, let's be patient, and endure a while. The time may come that may give us a happy release; but let us not be our own murderers. With these words, Hopeful at present did moderate the mind of his brother; so they continued together (in the dark) that day, in their sad and doleful condition.

Well, towards evening, the Giant goes down into the dungeon again, to see if his prisoners had taken his counsel; but when he came there he found them alive; and truly, alive was all; for now, what for want of bread and water, and by reason of the wounds they received when he beat them, they could do little but breathe. But, I say, he found them alive; at which he fell into a grievous rage, and told them that, seeing they had disobeyed his counsel, it should be worse with them than if they had never been born.

At this they trembled greatly, and I think that Christian fell into a swoon; but, coming a little to himself again, they renewed their discourse about the Giant's counsel; and whether yet they had best to take it or no. Now Christian again seemed to be for doing it, but Hopeful made his second reply as followeth:—

Hopeful. My brother, said he, rememberest thou not how valiant thou hast been heretofore? Apollyon[3] could not crush thee, nor could all that thou didst hear, or see, or feel, in the Valley of the Shadow of Death. What hardship, terror, and amazement hast thou already gone through! And art thou now nothing but fear! Thou seest that I am in the dungeon with thee, a far weaker man by nature than thou art; also, this Giant has wounded me as well as thee, and hath also cut off the bread and water from my mouth; and with thee I mourn without the light. But let us exercise a little more patience; remember how thou playedst the man at Vanity Fair,[4] and wast neither afraid of the chain, nor cage, nor yet of bloody death. Wherefore let us (at least to avoid the shame, that becomes not a Christian to be found in) bear up with patience as well as we can.

Now, night being come again, and the Giant and his wife being in bed, she asked him concerning the prisoners, and if they had taken his counsel. To which he replied, they are sturdy rogues, they choose rather to bear all hardship, than to make away themselves. Then said she, take them into the castle-yard tomorrow, and show them the bones and skulls of those that thou hast already dispatched, and make them believe, ere a week comes to an end, thou also wilt tear them in pieces, as thou hast done their fellows before them.

So when the morning was come, the Giant goes to them again, and takes them into the castle-yard, and shows them, as his wife had bidden him. These, said he, were pilgrims as you are, once, and they trespassed in my grounds, as you have done; and when I thought fit, I tore them in pieces, and so, within ten days, I will do you. Go, get you down to your den again; and with that he beat them all the way thither. They lay, therefore, all day on Saturday in a lamentable case, as before. Now, when night was come, and when Mrs. Diffidence and her husband, the Giant, were got to bed, they began to renew their discourse of their prisoners; and withal the old Giant wondered, that he could neither by his blows nor his counsel bring them to an end. And with that his wife replied, I fear, said she, that they live in hope that some will come to relieve them, or that they have picklocks about them, by the means of which they hope to escape. And sayest thou so, my dear? said the Giant; I will, therefore, search them in the morning.

Well, on Saturday, about midnight, they began to pray, and continued in prayer till almost break of day.

Now, a little before it was day, good Christian, as one half amazed, brake out in this passionate speech: What a fool, quoth he, am I, thus to lie in a stinking dungeon, when I may as well walk at liberty! I have a key in my bosom, called Promise, that will (I am persuaded), open any lock in Doubting Castle. Then said Hopeful, That is good news, good brother; pluck it out of thy bosom, and try.

Then Christian pulled it out of his bosom, and began to try at the dungeon door, whose

3. APOLLYON: a devil whom Christian had fought successfully in the Valley of Humiliation.
4. VANITY FAIR: where Christian and Hopeful were beaten and caged.

bolt (as he turned the key) gave back, and the door flew open with ease, and Christian and Hopeful both came out. Then he went to the outward door that leads into the castle-yard, and, with his key, opened that door also. After, he went to the iron gate, for that must be opened too; but the lock went *damnable* hard, yet the key did open it. Then they thrust open the gate to make their escape with speed, but that gate, as it opened, made such a creaking, that it waked Giant Despair, who, hastily rising to pursue his prisoners, felt his limbs to fail, for his fits took him again, so that he could by no means go after them. Then they went on, and came to the King's highway, and so were safe, because they were out of his jurisdiction.

Now, when they were gone over the stile, they began to contrive with themselves what they should do at that stile, to prevent those that should come after, from falling into the hands of Giant Despair. So they consented to erect there a pillar, and to engrave upon the side thereof this sentence—"Over this stile is the way to Doubting Castle, which is kept by Giant Despair, who despiseth the King of the Celestial Country, and seeks to destroy his holy pilgrims." Many, therefore, that followed after, read what was written, and escaped the danger. . . .

I

1. How did Giant Despair manage to ensnare Christian and Hopeful?

2. Why did the Giant have fits just as he was about to administer another beating to Christian and Hopeful and when he rose to prevent them from escaping?

3. What do the following mean in context:

a. "Now in this place Christian had double sorrow, because 'twas through his unadvised haste that they were brought into this distress."

b. "he that kills another can but commit murder upon his body; but for one to kill himself is to kill body and soul at once."

c. "I am resolved to pluck up the heart of a man."

4. What is the "key . . . called Promise"? What brought on Christian's remembrance that he had it with him? Why had he forgotten that he had it?

5. Indicate what it is that Christian learns in this episode, and show how the allegory underscores this insight in each detail.

II

1. Why should *Despair* be an obstacle to salvation? Compare and contrast the reactions of the Red Cross Knight and Christian to it, and the way Spenser and Bunyan imaginatively present the encounter in each case.

MEDITATION XVII   [*1624*]

John Donne

Bunyan's fervent conviction that this earthly existence is one vast City of Destruction led him to the companion conviction that one could find oneself only in total commitment to God. *The Pilgrim's Progress* is a direct and uncomplicated dramatization of this belief. Christian will reach the Celestial City if he remembers God's words and resists the tempters who plague his pilgrimage.

With a similar intensity of conviction but with a vastly different turn of mind, John Donne reveals the nature of religious self-discovery in the Meditation reproduced here, one of a series of Meditations on life and death that grew out of a serious illness Donne went through in 1623. It reflects the spiritual insight he came to out of suffering and pain. The focus is not on the suffering itself but on the power of suffering to bring men closer to an understanding of their true relation to others and to God.

Nunc lento sonitu dicunt, morieris.
(Now this bell tolling softly for another, says to me, Thou must die.)

Perchance he for whom this bell tolls[1] may be so ill as that he know not it tolls for him; and perchance I may think myself so much better than I am, as that they who are about me and see my state may have caused it to toll for me, and I know not that. The church is catholic, universal, so are all her actions; all that she does belongs to all. When she baptizes a child, that action concerns me; for that child is thereby connected to that head which is my head too, and engrafted into that body whereof I am a member.[2] And when she buries a man, that action concerns me: all mankind is of one author and is one volume; when one man dies, one chapter is not torn out of the book, but translated into a better language;[3] and every chapter must be so translated. God employs several translators; some pieces are translated by age, some by sickness, some by war, some by justice; but God's hand is in every translation, and his hand shall bind up all our scattered leaves again for that library where every book shall lie open to one another.[4] As therefore the bell that rings to a sermon calls not upon the preacher only, but upon the congregation to come, so this bell calls us all; but how much more me, who am brought so near the door by this sickness. There was a contention as far as a suit (in which piety and dignity, religion and estimation,[5] were mingled) which of the religious orders[6] should ring to prayers first in the morning; and it was determined that they should ring first that rose earliest. If we understand aright the dignity of this bell that tolls for our evening prayer, we would be glad to make it ours by rising early, in that application,[7] that it might be ours as well as his whose indeed it is. The bell doth toll for him that thinks it doth; and though it intermit again, yet from that minute that that occasion wrought upon him, he is united to God. Who casts not up his eye to the sun when it rises? but who takes off his eye from a comet when that breaks out? Who bends not his ear to any bell which upon any occasion rings? but who can remove it from that bell which is passing a piece of himself out of this world? No man is an island, entire[8] of itself; every man is a piece of the continent, a part of the main.[9] If a clod be washed away by the sea, Europe is the less, as well as if a promontory were, as well as if a manor of thy friend's or of thine own were. Any man's death diminishes me because I am involved in mankind, and therefore never send to know for whom the bell tolls; it tolls for thee. Neither can we call this a begging of misery or a borrowing of misery, as though we were not miserable enough of ourselves but must fetch in more from the

1. PERCHANCE . . . TOLL: In his illness, Donne meditates on the tolling of the church bell for the dying.
2. WHEREOF . . . MEMBER: referring to the Christian doctrine that all those who are baptized are members of "the Body of Christ."
3. TRANSLATED . . . LANGUAGE: i.e., translated to heaven. Donne puns on two meanings of translate: (1) render into another language, and (2) carry away.
4. LIBRARY . . . ANOTHER: Donne refers to St. Paul's statement (I Corinthians 13:12) that on earth we "see through a glass, darkly . . . but then in heaven shall I know even as also I am known."
5. ESTIMATION: self-esteem.
6. ORDERS: monastic groups.
7. IN THAT APPLICATION: i.e., drawing from it the moral.
8. ENTIRE: perfect and complete.
9. MAIN: mainland.

next house, in taking upon us the misery of our neighbors. Truly it were an excusable covetousness if we did; for affliction is a treasure, and scarce any man hath enough of it. No man hath affliction enough that is not matured and ripened by it and made fit for God by that affliction. If a man carry treasure in bullion, or in a wedge of gold, and have none coined into current money, his treasure will not defray him as he travels. Tribulation is treasure in the nature of it, but it is not current money in the use of it, except we get nearer and nearer our home, heaven, by it. Another man may be sick too, and sick to death, and this affliction may lie in his bowels as gold in a mine and be of no use to him; but this bell that tells me of his affliction digs out and applies that gold to me, if by this consideration of another's danger I take mine own into contemplation and so secure myself by making my recourse to my God, who is our only security.

I

1. Donne's chief metaphors in this passage are those of the book, the island, and the treasure. List the words and phrases in which each of these metaphors recurs.

2. What does the speaker mean by, ". . . so this bell calls us all; but how much more me, who am brought so near the door by this sickness"?

3. By what reasonings does he reach the idea that the bell that tolls for one man's approaching death tolls for us all?

4. Explain his argument that accepting the fact that the bell "tolls for thee" is not "a begging . . . or borrowing of misery."

ELEGY WRITTEN IN A COUNTRY CHURCHYARD   [1751]

Thomas Gray

In Thomas Gray's "Elegy Written in a Country Churchyard," the speaker, in a sense, is also saying that the bell tolls for *him,* that we are all "a piece of the continent." There is here the same recognition of kinship with the fate of all men, growing out of meditations on the speaker's own situation called forth by the death of a young man like himself.

The title is instructive, but it can also mislead. Though an "elegy" is a lament, usually for the dead, and Gray began the poem soon after the untimely death of his friend, Richard West, it took him eight years to finish. It can, therefore, hardly be regarded as an elegy primarily about West. Similarly, the indication in the title of a churchyard setting might kindle suggestions of the macabre or the morbid which would be quite foreign to what Gray actually says in the poem. Obviously, he is concerned with death and the vanity of human hopes and achievements, but he is much more concerned with one's attitude toward these facts of existence than he is with lamenting them.

> The Curfew tolls the knell of parting day,
> The lowing herd winds slowly o'er the lea,
> The plowman homeward plods his weary way,
> And leaves the world to darkness and to me.

Now fades the glimmering landscape on the sight,   5
And all the air a solemn stillness holds,
Save where the beetle wheels his droning flight,
And drowsy tinklings lull the distant folds;

Save that from yonder ivy-mantled tower
The moping owl does to the moon complain   10
Of such, as wandering near her secret bower,
Molest her ancient solitary reign.

Beneath those rugged elms, that yew-tree's shade,
Where heaves the turf in many a moldering heap,
Each in his narrow cell forever laid,   15
The rude forefathers of the hamlet sleep.

The breezy call of incense-breathing Morn,
The swallow twittering from the straw-built shed,
The cock's shrill clarion, or the echoing horn,
No more shall rouse them from their lowly bed.   20

For them no more the blazing hearth shall burn,
Or busy housewife ply her evening care:
No children run to lisp their sire's return,
Or climb his knees the envied kiss to share.

Oft did the harvest to their sickle yield,   25
Their furrow oft the stubborn glebe has broke;
How jocund did they drive their team afield!
How bowed the woods beneath their sturdy stroke!

Let not Ambition mock their useful toil,
Their homely joys, and destiny obscure;   30
Nor Grandeur hear with a disdainful smile,
The short and simple annals of the poor.

The boast of heraldry, the pomp of power,
And all that beauty, all that wealth e'er gave,
Awaits alike the inevitable hour.   35
The paths of glory lead but to the grave.

Nor you, ye proud, impute to these the fault,
If Memory o'er their tomb no trophies raise,
Where through the long-drawn aisle and fretted vault
The pealing anthem swells the note of praise.   40

---

16. RUDE: unlearned.
19. HORN: hunting horn.
33. BOAST . . . POWER: i.e., even the men of highest birth or position.

35. HOUR: "hour" is the subject of "awaits."
39-40. i.e., these humble people are not buried *in*
  the church, as the gentry would be.

Can storied urn or animated bust
Back to its mansion call the fleeting breath?
Can Honor's voice provoke the silent dust,
Or Flattery soothe the dull cold ear of Death?

Perhaps in this neglected spot is laid   45
Some heart once pregnant with celestial fire,
Hands, that the rod of empire might have swayed,
Or waked to ecstasy the living lyre.

But Knowledge to their eyes her ample page
Rich with the spoils of time did ne'er unroll;   50
Chill Penury repressed their noble rage,
And froze the genial current of the soul.

Full many a gem of purest ray serene,
The dark unfathomed caves of ocean bear:
Full many a flower is born to blush unseen,   55
And waste its sweetness on the desert air.

Some village-Hampden, that with dauntless breast
The little Tyrant of his fields withstood;
Some mute inglorious Milton here may rest,
Some Cromwell guiltless of his country's blood.   60

The applause of listening senates to command,
The threats of pain and ruin to despise,
To scatter plenty o'er a smiling land,
And read their History in a nation's eyes

Their lot forbade: nor circumscribed alone   65
Their growing virtues, but their crimes confined;
Forbade to wade through slaughter to a throne,
And shut the gates of mercy on mankind,

The struggling pangs of conscious truth to hide,
To quench the blushes of ingenuous shame,   70
Or heap the shrine of Luxury and Pride
With incense kindled at the Muse's flame.

---

41. STORIED URN: i.e., engraved with the history (*story*) of the dead. ANIMATED: life-like.
43. HONOR'S VOICE: e.g., the description of the dead man's honors on his tomb. PROVOKE: summon.
44. FLATTERY: i.e., false compliments paid a man on his tombstone.
46. CELESTIAL FIRE: Both the statesman's ambition (47) and the poet's genius (48) are thought of as sharing in the *celestial* creativeness of the gods.

51. RAGE: passion.
52. GENIAL: creative.
57. VILLAGE-HAMPDEN: John Hampden, who defied Charles I's attempts to enforce certain unjust taxes prior to the Civil Wars.
60. CROMWELL: Oliver Cromwell, chief figure of the Commonwealth after Charles I was beheaded (1649).
65. THEIR LOT FORBADE: refers to lines 61-64.
72. INCENSE . . . FLAME: i.e., flattery in verse.

Far from the madding crowd's ignoble strife,
Their sober wishes never learned to stray;
Along the cool sequestered vale of life   75
They kept the noiseless tenor of their way.

Yet even these bones from insult to protect
Some frail memorial still erected nigh,
With uncouth rhymes and shapeless sculpture decked,
Implores the passing tribute of a sigh.   80

Their names, their years, spelt by the unlettered Muse,
The place of fame and elegy supply:
And many a holy text around she strews,
That teach the rustic moralist to die.

For who to dumb forgetfulness a prey,   85
This pleasing anxious being e'er resigned,
Left the warm precincts of the cheerful day,
Nor cast one longing lingering look behind?

On some fond breast the parting soul relies,
Some pious drops the closing eye requires;   90
Even from the tomb the voice of Nature cries,
Even in our ashes live their wonted fires.

For thee, who mindful of the unhonored dead
Dost in these lines their artless tale relate;
If chance, by lonely contemplation led,   95
Some kindred spirit shall inquire thy fate,

Haply some hoary-headed swain may say,
"Oft have we seen him at the peep of dawn
Brushing with hasty steps the dews away
To meet the sun upon the upland lawn.   100

"There, at the foot of yonder nodding beech
That wreathes its old fantastic roots so high,
His listless length at noontide would he stretch,
And pore upon the brook that babbles by.

"Hard by yon wood, now smiling as in scorn,   105
Muttering his wayward fancies he would rove,

---

74. THEIR . . . STRAY: i.e., as the *wishes* described
in 65-72 *did* stray.
78. STILL: always.
81. UNLETTERED MUSE: i.e., some uneducated
versifier.
86. BEING: i.e., oneself.

91. VOICE OF NATURE: i.e., the "natural" desire to
be loved and remembered.
93. THEE: i.e., the speaker, who now addresses
himself in the second person and imagines himself being thought about after his death, as he
has thought about these villagers after theirs.

remembered

Now drooping, woeful wan, like one forlorn,
Or crazed with care, or crossed in hopeless love.

"One morn I missed him on the customed hill,
Along the heath and near his favorite tree;   110
Another came; nor yet beside the rill,
Nor up the lawn, nor at the wood was he;

"The next with dirges due in sad array
Slow through the church-way path we saw him borne.
Approach and read (for thou canst read) the lay,   115
Graved on the stone beneath yon aged thorn."

The Epitaph

Here rests his head upon the lap of Earth
A youth to Fortune and to Fame unknown:
Fair Science frowned not on his humble birth,
And Melancholy marked him for her own.   120

Large was his bounty, and his soul sincere,
Heaven did a recompense as largely send:
He gave to Misery all he had, a tear,
He gained from Heaven ('twas all he wished) a friend.

No farther seek his merits to disclose,   125
Or draw his frailties from their dread abode,
(There they alike in trembling hope repose)
The bosom of his Father and his God.

116. GRAVED: engraved.   119. SCIENCE: knowledge learned systematically.

I

1. Where is the speaker standing in the opening stanzas? What does he see from where he stands? How specific are his observations; is this a specific night at a specific graveyard, or any night at any graveyard? How concerned is the speaker with a description of the graveyard itself? What kinds of details does he give about village life (17-28)? What are these details meant to convey?

2. With what other burial place is the country churchyard compared (29-44)? Who are buried there? What kind of memorials do *they* receive? What kind of memorials do the humble folk receive? Why, according to the speaker, are memorials necessary (85-92)?

3. If the *paths of glory lead but to the grave,* where do the paths of non-glory lead? And if they both lead to the same place, what difference is there between the life of the lowly and the life of the great? What are the lowly denied? What are they spared? What do the lowly and the great have in common?

4. Is the speaker one of the lowly? How do you know? In the thoughts of his own death, does he associate himself with the lowly or the great? How do you know?

5. What is the tone of the opening stanzas and how is it achieved? What are the dominant vowel sounds? Compare the meter with that of Milton's "On the Late Massacre in Piedmont" which begins:

Avenge, O Lord, thy slaughtered saints,
  whose bones
Lie scattered on the Alpine mountains cold;

Like Milton's poem, the "Elegy" is basically

in iambic pentameter. Yet there is a vast difference in tone between the two. What causes the difference? How is Gray's tone suited to what he has to say?

II

1. A common comment on the "Elegy" goes something like this: "Gray bemoans the lot of the villagers who might have been great if society had ever given them a chance, but he realizes in the end that perhaps the simple, unspoiled life is best in this evil world." Why is this inadequate as a response to the poem even at an elementary level? Consider what is said in the Epitaph in the light of the whole poem. What are the speaker's reasons for choosing the graveyard and not the church for his own burial? Note that the *hoary-headed swain* cannot read the epitaph (115) and that it will take *some kindred spirit*—perhaps a sensitive reader—to understand the position of the speaker. How do these factors modify what the poem "says"? How would you characterize the speaker's self-discovery?

THREE POEMS

William Wordsworth

From one point of view, the four selections we have just examined stress the discovery of inner personal resources that give shape and meaning to life. Spenser, Bunyan, and Donne focus on the summoning of spiritual strengths; Gray meditates on the common fate of all men and forswears the ways of vanity.

The following three poems by William Wordsworth also stress the discovery of inner resources. For Wordsworth the discovery is embodied in experiences with nature, both direct and "recollected in tranquillity," through memory. Nature is a source of wisdom and strength, the outward body of an indwelling "presence," a living proof of the divine plan for harmony, stability, and peace in the world.

"I Wandered Lonely as a Cloud" is a poem about nature and the importance of memory, and about achieving the paradox of companionship in solitude. We may be *alone* in the physical sense, but a well-stocked memory or imagination can put us immediately in the most delightful company; with the "inward eye" we recreate all that we have been or known and thus perpetuate what otherwise would be transient moments.

"The Solitary Reaper" is much the same kind of poem. The "solitary Highland lass" who "sings a melancholy strain" provides immediate pleasure to Wordsworth as onlooker, and the process of memory will bring back her song "long after" it is heard no more.

In the last poem in the group, "Lines Composed a Few Miles Above Tintern Abbey," we have one of Wordsworth's most eloquent statements of our human capacity to liberate understanding from desire, so that we may value people and things for their own sakes and not for the sake of any design upon them. This is, in part, what Wordsworth means by:

> . . . that blessed mood,
> In which the burthen of the mystery,
> In which the heavy and the weary weight
> Of all this unintelligible world,
> Is lightened . . .
> Until . . .
> we are laid asleep
> In body, and become a living soul:
> While with an eye made quiet by the power
> Of harmony, and the deep power of joy,
> We see into the life of things.

That Nature is the power which best evokes such a state in us many today will doubt; Wordsworth's notion of the means to the end was peculiar partly to his times and partly to himself. But he was right about the end, and no poem of his presents it more beautifully than "Tintern Abbey."

I WANDERED LONELY AS A CLOUD [*1804*]

I wandered lonely as a cloud
That floats on high o'er vales and hills,
When all at once I saw a crowd,
A host of golden daffodils;
Beside the lake, beneath the trees,   5
Fluttering and dancing in the breeze.

Continuous as the stars that shine
And twinkle on the milky way,
They stretched in never-ending line
Along the margin of a bay: 10
Ten thousand saw I at a glance,
Tossing their heads in sprightly dance.

The waves beside them danced, but they
Outdid the sparkling waves in glee:—
A poet could not but be gay   15
In such a jocund company:
I gazed—and gazed—but little thought
What wealth the show to me had brought.

For oft when on my couch I lie
In vacant or in pensive mood,   20
They flash upon that inward eye
Which is the bliss of solitude,
And then my heart with pleasure fills,
And dances with the daffodils.

I

1. How does the first line delineate the speaker's frame of mind, the mood he was in, when he came upon the daffodils? Why "lonely as a *cloud*"? What is his frame of mind in the last stanza when he recalls the experience? What relationship is there between the two?

2. The speaker describes the daffodils and the waves in human terms: *crowd, host, dancing, glee,* and speaks of being in their *jocund company* as if they were his companions. They not only bring pleasure; they share it too. Obviously, daffodils and waves do not do any of these things. What does the speaker gain by speaking of them as if they do?

3. The poem is a re-creation of an actual experience. In the first stanza how does the speaker communicate the sense of sudden discovery he experienced when he chanced upon the daffodils? Consider the order of events in the stanza. Also show how and why the pace quickens as the stanza proceeds.

4. What is the poem saying about the way pleasurable experiences come, either for the first time or, as Wordsworth wrote elsewhere, *"recollected in tranquillity"*?

THE SOLITARY REAPER [*1807*]

Behold her, single in the field,
Yon solitary Highland lass!
Reaping and singing by herself;
Stop here, or gently pass!
Alone she cuts and binds the grain,   5
And sings a melancholy strain;
O listen! for the Vale profound
Is overflowing with the sound.

No nightingale did ever chaunt
More welcome notes to weary bands   10
Of travelers in some shady haunt,
Among Arabian sands:
A voice so thrilling ne'er was heard
In springtime from the cuckoo-bird,
Breaking the silence of the seas   15
Among the farthest Hebrides.

Will no one tell me what she sings?—
Perhaps the plaintive numbers flow
For old, unhappy, far-off things,
And battles long ago: 20
Or is it some more humble lay,
Familiar matter of today?
Some natural sorrow, loss, or pain,
That has been, and may be again?

Whate'er the theme, the maiden sang
As if her song could have no ending;
I saw her singing at her work,
And o'er the sickle bending:—
I listened, motionless and still;
And, as I mounted up the hill,   30
The music in my heart I bore,
Long after it was heard no more.

---

2. HIGHLAND: i.e., from the mountain regions in
   the north of Scotland called "The Highlands."
9. CHAUNT: chant.
16. HEBRIDES: islands off the northwest coast of
   Scotland.
18. NUMBERS: verses.

I

1. What fact about the Highland Lass and
her song is emphasized in stanza 1?

2. In stanza 2, what two comparisons does
the speaker use to describe the effect the song
has on him? What is suggested about the song's
qualities by the first of these? by the second?
What contrasts are there between the two comparisons? What likenesses?

3. In stanza 3, the speaker does not use
comparisons but hypotheses to describe the
effect of the song. What is the hypothesis of
17-20? of 21-24? What contrasts are there between them? What likenesses? What does each
suggest about the qualities of the song?

4. The situation described in 9-12 has at least
one element in common with that described in
17-20. What is it? The situations described in
13-16 and 21-24 also have an element in
common. What is it? You may find a clue to
these questions by pausing to consider the location of the Hebrides with relation to the
speaker, who is on a journey through Scotland.

5. Why does stanza 4 shift from the present
to the past tense? What is said in stanza 4 that
underscores this shift?

6. At the close of stanza 1 the song is said
to be *overflowing* the whole valley. How might
stanza 2 be said to extend this suggested overflow of the girl's song? How might stanza 3
be said to extend it still further? How might
stanza 4 be said to extend it even further and
in another dimension altogether?

LINES

*Composed a Few Miles Above Tintern Abbey
on Revisiting the Banks of the Wye
During a Tour, July 13, 1798*

Five years have past; five summers, with the length
Of five long winters! and again I hear
These waters, rolling from their mountain-springs
With a soft inland murmur.—Once again
Do I behold these steep and lofty cliffs,   5
That on a wild secluded scene impress
Thoughts of more deep seclusion; and connect
The landscape with the quiet of the sky.

The day is come when I again repose
Here, under this dark sycamore, and view   10
These plots of cottage-ground, these orchard-tufts,
Which at this season, with their unripe fruits,
Are clad in one green hue, and lose themselves
'Mid groves and copses. Once again I see
These hedge-rows, hardly hedge-rows, little lines   15
Of sportive wood run wild: these pastoral farms,
Green to the very door; and wreaths of smoke
Sent up, in silence, from among the trees!
With some uncertain notice, as might seem
Of vagrant dwellers in the houseless woods,   20
Or of some Hermit's cave, where by his fire
The Hermit sits alone.

              These beauteous forms,
Through a long absence, have not been to me
As is a landscape to a blind man's eye:
But oft, in lonely rooms, and 'mid the din
Of towns and cities, I have owed to them,   25
In hours of weariness, sensations sweet,
Felt in the blood, and felt along the heart;
And passing even into my purer mind,
With tranquil restoration:—feelings too
Of unremembered pleasure: such, perhaps,   30
As have no slight or trivial influence
On that best portion of a good man's life,
His little, nameless, unremembered acts
Of kindness and of love. Nor less, I trust,
To them I may have owed another gift,   35
Of aspect more sublime; that blessed mood,
In which the burthen of the mystery,
In which the heavy and the weary weight
Of all this unintelligible world,
Is lightened:—that serene and blessed mood,   40
In which the affections gently lead us on,—
Until, the breath of this corporeal frame
And even the motion of our human blood
Almost suspended, we are laid asleep
In body, and become a living soul: 45
While with an eye made quiet by the power
Of harmony, and the deep power of joy,
We see into the life of things.

                  If this
Be but a vain belief, yet, oh! how oft—
In darkness and amid the many shapes   50
Of joyless daylight; when the fretful stir

Unprofitable, and the fever of the world,
Have hung upon the beatings of my heart—
How oft, in spirit, have I turned to thee,   55
O sylvan Wye! thou wanderer thro' the woods,
How often has my spirit turned to thee!

And now, with gleams of half-extinguished thought
With many recognitions dim and faint,
And somewhat of a sad perplexity,   60
The picture of the mind revives again:
While here I stand, not only with the sense
Of present pleasure, but with pleasing thoughts
That in this moment there is life and food
For future years. And so I dare to hope,   65
Though changed, no doubt, from what I was when first
I came among these hills; when like a roe
I bounded o'er the mountains, by the sides
Of the deep rivers, and the lonely streams,
Wherever nature led: more like a man   70
Flying from something that he dreads than one
Who sought the thing he loved. For nature then
(The coarser pleasures of my boyish days,
And their glad animal movements all gone by)
To me was all in all.—I cannot paint   75
What then I was. The sounding cataract
Haunted me like a passion: the tall rock,
The mountain, and the deep and gloomy wood,
Their colors and their forms, were then to me
An appetite; a feeling and a love,   80
That had no need for a remoter charm,
By thought supplied, nor any interest
Unborrowed from the eye.—That time is past,
And all its aching joys are now no more,
And all its dizzy raptures. Not for this   85
Faint I, nor mourn nor murmur; other gifts
Have followed; for such loss, I would believe,
Abundant recompense. For I have learned
To look on nature, not as in the hour
Of thoughtless youth; but hearing oftentimes   90
The still, sad music of humanity,
Nor harsh nor grating, though of ample power
To chasten and subdue. And I have felt
A presence that disturbs me with the joy
Of elevated thoughts; a sense sublime   95
Of something far more deeply interfused,
Whose dwelling is the light of setting suns,
And the round ocean and the living air,

---

86. FAINT: lose heart.

And the blue sky, and in the mind of man:
A motion and a spirit, that impels   100
All thinking things, all objects of all thought,
And rolls through all things. Therefore am I still
A lover of the meadows and the woods,
And mountains; and of all that we behold
From this green earth; of all the mighty world   105
Of eye, and ear,—both what they half create,
And what perceive; well pleased to recognize
In nature and the language of the sense
The anchor of my purest thoughts, the nurse,
The guide, the guardian of my heart, and soul   110
Of all my moral being.

         Nor perchance,
If I were not thus taught, should I the more
Suffer my genial spirits to decay:
For thou art with me here upon the banks
Of this fair river; thou my dearest Friend,   115
My dear, dear Friend; and in thy voice I catch
The language of my former heart, and read
My former pleasures in the shooting lights
Of thy wild eyes. Oh! yet a little while
May I behold in thee what I was once,   120
My dear, dear Sister! and this prayer I make,
Knowing that Nature never did betray
The heart that loved her; 'tis her privilege
Through all the years of this our life, to lead
From joy to joy: for she can so inform   125
The mind that is within us, so impress
With quietness and beauty, and so feed
With lofty thoughts, that neither evil tongues,
Rash judgments, nor the sneers of selfish men,
Nor greetings where no kindness is, nor all   130
The dreary intercourse of daily life,
Shall e'er prevail against us, or disturb
Our cheerful faith, that all which we behold
Is full of blessings. Therefore let the moon
Shine on thee in thy solitary walk;   135
And let the misty mountain-winds be free
To blow against thee: and, in after years,
When these wild ecstasies shall be matured
Into a sober pleasure; when thy mind
Shall be a mansion for all lovely forms,   140
Thy memory be as a dwelling-place

---

112. TAUGHT: trained, guided.
113. GENIAL: cheerful.
115. FRIEND: Wordsworth's sister, Dorothy.

For all sweet sounds and harmonies; oh! then,
If solitude, or fear, or pain, or grief
Should be thy portion, with what healing thoughts
Of tender joy wilt thou remember me,   145
And these my exhortations! Nor, perchance—
If I should be where I no more can hear
Thy voice, nor catch from thy wild eyes these gleams
Of past existence—wilt thou then forget
That on the banks of this delightful stream   150
We stood together; and that I, so long
A worshipper of Nature, hither came
Unwearied in that service: rather say
With warmer love—oh! with far deeper zeal
Of holier love. Nor wilt thou then forget   155
That after many wanderings, many years
Of absence, these steep woods and lofty cliffs,
And this green pastoral landscape, were to me
More dear, both for themselves and for thy sake!

I

1. The poem is divided into four sections: lines 1-22, 23-57, 58-111, and 111-159. The first section is a description of a landscape near Tintern Abbey that the speaker had visited five years before. What kind of landscape does he see? What details show that it is seen at a distance? Why is this fact significant in supporting the point of view of lines 6-7? What does the speaker suggest is the relationship between nature here and those who live on *these pastoral farms?*

2. In the second section what world is he contrasting with the one in the first section? What three *gifts* does he say he has *owed* to the *beauteous forms* of lines 1-22 in the five years he has been absent from them? Note lines 25-30, 30-35, and 37-49. How does the third *gift* differ in kind from the first two?

3. What doubt do lines 49-50 express and how is it resolved? What is the effect of the repetition of "how oft" (50 and 55) and "How often" (57)? What repeated word in lines 1-22 do these repetitions echo?

4. What double gain does the speaker get from this second visit to the *sylvan Wye* (58-65)? What three stages of his response to Nature are recalled in lines 67-102? what in 73-74? what in 67-85 (not including 73-74)? what in 88-102? What changed attitude toward Nature does maturity bring? Why does the speaker think that the *gifts* of the stage of mature reflection are *abundant recompense* for the loss of childhood's *thoughtless* joy? Is the gift of lines 88-102 the same as the gift of lines 37-49? Why or why not?

5. Lines 88-102 have been particularly remembered by countless readers of English poetry. What relation do they have with all that has gone before in the poem? How do they sum up what the speaker feels toward Nature in his maturity? What is the "still, sad music of humanity"? If "presence," "sense sublime," "motion," and "spirit" all refer to the same "something" (96), why does he use all the terms? Is the vagueness justified?

6. In section four, what *stage* has his sister reached in communion with Nature? Note lines 116-119. What is his *prayer* for her? What does he say Nature will bring to *the heart that love[s] her?* How does the last section indicate that human nature is to Wordsworth part of the world of Nature that sustains him? Consider lines 121-134 and refer to lines 30-35.

II

1. One critic has said that Wordsworth was trying to express the inexpressible in his poems dealing with his convictions about Nature as

the embodiment of the divine spirit in the world. While this may be true, few readers can remain indifferent to his convictions about what is at the same time most human and most nearly divine about our situation. Try to express in your own words the insights into man and Nature that Wordsworth reveals in the three poems included here. In addition, discuss whether his ideas coincide with your own experiences or convictions in any way.

ON FIRST LOOKING INTO
CHAPMAN'S HOMER   *[1816]*

John Keats

The tolling bell spoke to John Donne of spiritual health in physical sickness; the song of the solitary "Highland lass" remained in Wordsworth's memory as a source of renewable pleasure "long after it was heard no more." Each simple incident carried a meaning far beyond the normal one. In the following sonnet by John Keats a similar experience of unexpected self-discovery is described.

The poem was the direct result of Keats's first encounter with the translation of Homer's *Odyssey* by the Elizabethan poet and playwright, George Chapman. Keats and a close friend had spent a good part of the night reading to each other from Chapman's book, and in the excitement of discovery, he wrote the poem and sent it to his friend early the following morning. The sonnet is focused on the finding of a great poem—a great Homeric "world" of imagination—through Chapman; but the experience itself and the sonnet's expression of it stand for all moments when some deep responsive chord within us is struck.

> Much have I traveled in the realms of gold,
>   And many goodly states and kingdoms seen;
>   Round many western islands have I been
> Which bards in fealty to Apollo hold.
> Oft of one wide expanse had I been told   5
>   That deep-browed Homer ruled as his demesne;
>   Yet did I never breathe its pure serene
> Till I heard Chapman speak out loud and bold:
> Then felt I like some watcher of the skies
>   When a new planet swims into his ken;   10
> Or like stout Cortez when with eagle eyes
>   He stared at the Pacific—and all his men
> Looked at each other with a wild surmise—
>   Silent, upon a peak in Darien.

1. REALMS OF GOLD: i.e., literature.
3. WESTERN ISLANDS: great works of Western, i.e., English and European, literature.
4. APOLLO: god of poetry.

11. CORTEZ: Spanish adventurer of the early sixteenth century; actually, the discoverer of the Pacific was Balboa.
14. DARIEN: Isthmus of Panama.

I

1. Keats's reference to *realms of gold* is a way of comparing the riches of literature to the lands full of gold that the early explorers sought in North and South America. What, in literary terms, must the *many goodly states and king-doms* be, which he says he has already visited? What would you gather about the nature of Homer's poems from the fact that he is referred to as *deep-browed*, that the region under his rule is *wide,* and that the translation of his work is said to speak out *loud and bold?*

2. Keats throws light on the feelings and attitudes accompanying his discovery of Homer's poem by alluding to two other instances of discovery in the final six lines. What are they? How are they like the metaphor in the first eight? How do they differ from it? What does each contribute to our understanding of the feelings involved in Keats's discovery of Homer through Chapman?

FERN HILL [*1943*]

Dylan Thomas

Another poem stemming from a deep awareness of the powers of nature and a recognition of the operation of memory in bringing self-knowledge is Dylan Thomas's "Fern Hill."

The subject of Thomas's "Holiday Memory" was a long day at the seashore, which in the mind of the child experiencing it seemed to go luxuriously on and on—*almost* as if there were no such thing as time. In "Fern Hill" he deals again with the child's sense of living in a timeless world, setting the exuberance of the child's imaginary freedom against the adult's larger awareness that we are inevitably subject to time. Neither point of view is allowed to triumph over the other. We are born dying, the poem tells us, yet we are also born capable of the happiness the poem so vividly commemorates. We cannot escape our mortal prison, yet we may "sing in our chains like the sea."

Now as I was young and easy under the apple boughs
About the lilting house and happy as the grass was green,
   The night above the dingle starry,
     Time let me hail and climb
   Golden in the heydays of his eyes, 5
And honored among wagons I was prince of the apple towns
And once below a time I lordly had the trees and leaves
     Trail with daisies and barley
   Down the rivers of the windfall light.

And as I was green and carefree, famous among the barns 10
About the happy yard and singing as the farm was home,

In the sun that is young once only,
    Time let me play and be
  Golden in the mercy of his means,
And green and golden I was huntsman and herdsman, the calves   15
Sang to my horn, the foxes on the hills barked clear and cold,
    And the sabbath rang slowly
  In the pebbles of the holy streams.

All the sun long it was running, it was lovely, the hay-
Fields high as the house, the tunes from the chimneys, it was air   20
    And playing, lovely and watery
      And fire green as grass.
    And nightly under the simple stars
As I rode to sleep the owls were bearing the farm away,
All the moon long I heard, blessed among stables, the nightjars   25
    Flying with the ricks, and the horses
    Flashing into the dark.

And then to awake, and the farm, like a wanderer white
With the dew, come back, the cock on his shoulder: it was all
    Shining, it was Adam and maiden,   30
    The sky gathered again
    And the sun grew round that very day.
So it must have been after the birth of the simple light
In the first, spinning place, the spellbound horses walking warm
    Out of the whinnying green stable   35
    On to the fields of praise.

And honored among foxes and pheasants by the gay house
Under the new made clouds and happy as the heart was long,
    In the sun born over and over,
      I ran my heedless ways,   40
    My wishes raced through the house-high hay
And nothing I cared, at my sky blue trades, that time allows
In all his tuneful turning so few and such morning songs
    Before the children green and golden
    Follow him out of grace.   45

Nothing I cared, in the lamb white days, that time would take me
Up to the swallow thronged loft by the shadow of my hand,
    In the moon that is always rising,
      Nor that riding to sleep
    I should hear him fly with the high fields   50
And wake to the farm forever fled from the childless land.
Oh as I was young and easy in the mercy of his means,
    Time held me green and dying
    Though I sang in my chains like the sea.

I

1. Part of this poem's appeal comes from its verbal music. Consider the use of the following devices and find other examples of the same:

a. internal rhyme: *"Time* let me hail and *climb"* (4); "And the sabbath rang *slowly*/In the pebbles of the *holy* streams" (17-18).
b. alliteration: "About the lilting *house* and *happy* as the *grass* was *green*" (2); *"house-high hay"* (41).
c. assonance: "And once bel*ow* a time I lordly had the tr*ees* and l*ea*ves" (7).
d. consonance: the "z" sound alone (ea*sy*, bou*ghs*, wa*s*, heyda*ys*, e*yes*, etc.) occurs forty-four times in the first twenty-seven lines.
e. matching of rhythm to sense: the breathlessness of "All the sun long it was running, it was lovely" (19); the stateliness of "I lordly had the trees and leaves" (7).
f. the use of the boy's-eye-view: "the sun born over and over" (39); "house-high hay" (41).
g. childlike delight in fresh and unusual word combinations: "lilting house" (2); "whinnying green stable" (35).
h. the plays on words and sounds: "In the sun that is young once only" (12); "Adam and maiden" (30).

2. All these factors combine to produce a vivid impression in our minds of the intoxicating ease and abandon of the child's world, conveyed by the intoxicating ease and abandon with which the child moves among words and sounds. But always the picture of the child's experience has for its frame the adult's wider knowledge. Show how such phrases as "Time *let* me hail and climb," "Time *let* me play and be," and "I ran my *heedless* ways" put the adult stamp on the child's world. Find other words and phrases which also act as counterthrusts to the child's ease and abandon. Show how the last stanza in particular emphasizes the contrast between the worlds of child and adult. Consider especially the paradoxes of the last two lines.

II

1. While there are obviously great differences in treatment between "Fern Hill" and "Tintern Abbey," the two poems can be compared in several respects. Both deal in part with the response to Nature of *thoughtless* or *heedless* youth; both are concerned with the contrast between the worlds of the child and the adult; both center around the operations of memory. What similarities do you find between the two poems? What differences? Consider both the ideas expressed and the treatment of those ideas.

THE WILD SWANS AT COOLE [*1919*]

William Butler Yeats

The sense of nature's permanence that resounds so strongly in Wordsworth's poems and in "Fern Hill" recurs in the following poem, "The Wild Swans at Coole," but the kind of self-discovery that comes to Yeats has none of Wordsworth's conviction that "Nature never did betray the heart that loved her," nor even any of Thomas's vision of the co-existence of change and timelessness.

What the yearly presence of the wild swans symbolizes to Yeats is the imperishability of nature in contrast to the transience of man. He knows, of course, that change is common to all things, but the scene that he views for the "nineteenth autumn" *seems* to him no different from the one he saw the first autumn at Coole. At the same time he is deeply aware of how different *he* is, and the sight of the swans brings that fact sharply into focus.

The trees are in their autumn beauty,
The woodland paths are dry,
Under the October twilight the water
Mirrors a still sky;
Upon the brimming water among
   the stones   5
Are nine-and-fifty swans.

The nineteenth autumn has come upon me
Since I first made my count;
I saw, before I had well finished,
All suddenly mount   10
And scatter wheeling in great broken rings
Upon their clamorous wings.

I have looked upon those brilliant creatures,
And now my heart is sore.

All's changed since I, hearing at twilight, 15
The first time on this shore,
The bell-beat of their wings above my head,
Trod with a lighter tread.

Unwearied still, lover by lover,
They paddle in the cold   20
Companionable streams or climb the air;
Their hearts have not grown old;
Passion or conquest, wander where they will,
Attend upon them still.

But now they drift on the still water   25
Mysterious, beautiful;
Among what rushes will they build,
By what lake's edge or pool
Delight men's eyes when I awake some day
To find they have flown away?   30

Title. COOLE: the home of Lady Gregory in Galway, Ireland; Yeats spent most of his summers there after he reached his thirties.

I

1. How is the effect of a still-life painting achieved in stanza 1? In line 4, is it the sky that is *still* or the water? Explain. What is suggested by the word *brimming*? Why does the speaker want to effect an impression of motionlessness?

2. Why does he give the exact figure of "nine-and-fifty swans"? Why does he count them? How is the stillness of stanza 1 broken in stanza 2? How does he achieve an effect of confusion and noise in lines 11-12?

3. What shift occurs in stanza 3? What does he mean by "my heart is sore" (14), "All's changed" (15), and "Trod with a lighter tread" (18)?

4. In stanza 4, what does he mean by "Unwearied still" (19), and why does he say "lover by lover" (19)? How does the phrase *cold companionable streams* convey his attitude toward nature? How can the streams be both *cold* and *companionable*? What do "Passion" and "conquest" suggest, and why does he say that these two things *attend upon* the swans?

5. How is stanza 5 connected to stanza 1? Why does he ask the question contained in the last four lines? Why does he say, "when I awake some day/To find they have flown away" when he has indicated previously that they are permanent and he is not? Awake from what? Awake into what?

THE BURIED LIFE [*1852*]

Matthew Arnold

The specific experience of seeing the wild swans at Coole brought to Yeats's mind a sense of isolation and impermanence. It is usually the case that some seemingly insignificant experience can reveal most clearly to us what kind of person we are: perhaps a flush of pleasure when we are warmly thanked or a flash of jealousy over someone else's success.

But often our self-discovery comes through a carefully worked-out conviction about being human that applies not just to ourselves but to everyone. We saw just such conviction simply and compellingly dramatized in the "Doubting Castle" episode from *The Pilgrim's Progress.* And we see it again in the poem that follows, "The Buried Life." For Arnold the everyday surface life is dominated by "blind uncertainty," but underneath lies the "buried life" which we see only rarely, if at all, and then only when some human touch brings it out. It is in these rare moments when

> The eye sinks inward, and the heart lies plain,
> And what we mean, we say, and what we would, we know...

that we comprehend what sort of person we really are.

> Light flows our war of mocking words, and yet,
> Behold, with tears mine eyes are wet!
> I feel a nameless sadness o'er me roll.
> Yes, yes, we know that we can jest,
> We know, we know that we can smile!   5
> But there's a something in this breast,
> To which thy light words bring no rest,
> And thy gay smiles no anodyne.
> Give me thy hand, and hush awhile,
> And turn those limpid eyes on mine,   10
> And let me read there, love! thy inmost soul.
> Alas! is even love too weak
> To unlock the heart, and let it speak?
> Are even lovers powerless to reveal
> To one another what indeed they feel?   15
> I knew the mass of men concealed
> Their thoughts, for fear that if revealed
> They would by other men be met
> With blank indifference, or with blame reproved;
> I knew they lived and moved   20
> Tricked in disguises, alien to the rest
> Of men, and alien to themselves—and yet
> The same heart beats in every human breast!

But we, my love!—doth a like spell benumb
Our hearts, our voices?—must we too be dumb?   25
Ah! well for us, if even we,
Even for a moment, can get free
Our heart, and have our lips unchained;
For that which seals them hath been deep-ordained!

Fate, which foresaw   30
How frivolous a baby man would be—
By what distractions he would be possessed,
How he would pour himself in every strife,
And well-nigh change his own identity—
That it might keep from his capricious play   35
His genuine self, and force him to obey
Even in his own despite his being's law,
Bade through the deep recesses of our breast
The unregarded river of our life
Pursue with indiscernible flow its way;   40
And that we should not see
The buried stream, and seem to be
Eddying at large in blind uncertainty,
Though driving on with it eternally.

But often, in the world's most crowded streets,   45
But often, in the din of strife,
There rises an unspeakable desire
After the knowledge of our buried life;
A thirst to spend our fire and restless force
In tracking out our true, original course;   50
A longing to inquire
Into the mystery of this heart which beats
So wild, so deep in us—to know
Whence our lives come and where they go.
And many a man in his own breast then delves,   55
But deep enough, alas! none ever mines.
And we have been on many thousand lines,
And we have shown, on each, spirit and power;
But hardly have we, for one little hour,
Been on our own line, have we been ourselves—   60
Hardly had skill to utter one of all
The nameless feelings that course through our breast,
But they course on forever unexpressed.
And long we try in vain to speak and act
Our hidden self, and what we say and do   65
Is eloquent, is well—but 'tis not true!
And then we will no more be racked
With inward striving, and demand
Of all the thousand nothings of the hour

Their stupefying power;   70
Ah yes, and they benumb us at our call!
Yet still, from time to time, vague and forlorn,
From the soul's subterranean depth upborne
As from an infinitely distant land,
Come airs, and floating echoes, and convey   75
A melancholy into all our day.

Only—but this is rare—
When a belovèd hand is laid in ours,
When, jaded with the rush and glare
Of the interminable hours,   80
Our eyes can in another's eyes read clear,
When our world-deafened ear
Is by the tones of a loved voice caressed—
A bolt is shot back somewhere in our breast,
And a lost pulse of feeling stirs again;   85
The eye sinks inward, and the heart lies plain,
And what we mean, we say, and what we would, we know.
A man becomes aware of his life's flow,
And hears its winding murmur; and he sees
The meadows where it glides, the sun, the breeze.   90

And there arrives a lull in the hot race
Wherein he doth forever chase
That flying and elusive shadow, rest.
An air of coolness plays upon his face,
And an unwonted calm pervades his breast.   95
And then he thinks he knows
The hills where his life rose,
And the sea where it goes.

I

1. Whom is the speaker talking to? What is "our war of mocking words" (1)? What is the "something in this breast" (6) that gets "no rest"? Discuss whether the illusion of conversation is sustained throughout the poem.

2. Why, according to the speaker, do the *mass of men* conceal their thoughts (16-23)?

3. Lines 30-44 might be difficult to unravel grammatically. "It" (35) refers to "Fate," and "Fate" is the subject of "Bade." What are the objects of "Bade"? How is the metaphor of the river developed in lines 39-44? How is it expanded upon throughout the rest of the poem? What keeps the river "unregarded" and "buried"?

4. What are the "many thousand lines" of line 57? Why does the "inner striving" last so short a time? What does "demand/Of all the thousand nothings of the hour/Their stupefying power" (68-70) mean? Why should the "airs" and "floating echoes" that occasionally arise in us "convey/A melancholy into all our day" (75-76)?

5. What does "world-deafened ear" (82) mean? Explain the metaphor in "A bolt is shot back somewhere in our breast" (84). What does line 86 mean? What brings the *buried life* to the surface?

6. Put in your own words what Arnold means by the "buried life."

7. Most of the poem consists of plain statement in very abstract terms. It would be hard to define, except in other abstract terms, such phrases as: "His genuine self" (36), "his being's law" (37), "the deep recesses of our breast" (38), "our fire and restless force" (49), "our true, original course" (50). Point out other examples of the same sort of indefinable phrasing. How has Arnold kept the poem from being simply a series of such generalizations? "Tintern Abbey" is full of the same kind of generalizing (see, for instance, lines 93-102 of that poem). Compare the two poems in this respect. Which gives the reader a stronger impression that the generalizations have their roots in deeply felt personal experience? Why?

II

1. Relate what "The Buried Life" shows Arnold to be distressed by to what "A Lady's Diary" shows Addison to be distressed by. Compare and contrast the tones adopted by the two men toward their materials. Do you feel that one of the two tones is better adapted than the other to this kind of material? Why?

LUCIFER IN STARLIGHT   [*1883*]

George Meredith

"The Buried Life" expresses Arnold's belief that the best part of us lies deeply hidden inside and can be brought to the surface only by the workings of human love. Few of us would deny the existence of that "better self" which possesses us at inexplicable moments, however difficult it is to account for in theory.

The following poem, "Lucifer in Starlight," focuses on essentially the same kind of discovery: that there is more to life than our senses or our reason can fathom. This time, however, the discovery comes not from the inside, the "buried life," but from the outside, the daily proof that there is an order in the universe that unexplainably persists. The poem dramatizes this fact by showing that even total Evil in the person of Lucifer is subject to "unalterable law."

On a starred night Prince Lucifer uprose.
Tired of his dark dominion swung the fiend
Above the rolling ball in cloud part screened,
Where sinners hugged their specter of repose.
Poor prey to his hot fit of pride were those.   5
And now upon his western wing he leaned,
Now his huge bulk o'er Afric's sands careened,
Now the black planet shadowed Arctic snows.
Soaring through wider zones that pricked his scars

Title. LUCIFER: the popular name for the archangel who led the revolt against God and was cast into Hell to rule over that *dark* dominion.

3. THE ROLLING BALL: the earth.
8. BLACK PLANET: i.e., Lucifer.
9. SCARS: received in the rebellion against God.

With memory of the old revolt from Awe,   10
He reached the middle height, and at the stars,
Which are the brain of heaven, he looked, and sank.
Around the ancient track marched, rank on rank,
The army of unalterable law.

I

1. What is Lucifer intent on doing? Why does he pass by *the rolling ball* when his chief function as ruler of Hell is usually to corrupt mankind?

2. How does Meredith make Lucifer seem a powerful and awe-inspiring force? Put lines 6-8 into your own words.

3. What is meant by "wider zones" (9) and "the middle height" (11)? Why does Meredith call the stars "the brain of heaven" (12)? What do the stars stand for? Why is Lucifer's return reported in the single word *sank* after such elaborate detail has described his rising from Hell? What are some of the meanings that *sank* can have here?

4. What is meant by "The army of unalterable law" (14)? What does Lucifer learn in this short-lived second attempt at revolt? Ob-

viously, Meredith is not simply concerned with writing a sequel to the original Lucifer myth. What is he saying to us about man and his relation to *unalterable law,* and why does he choose to say it in terms of a second rebellion attempt by Lucifer?

5. What is the force of "swung" (2), "careened" (7), "shadowed" (8), and "Soaring" (9)? How do the verbs of lines 11-12 contrast with them and why is the contrast effective?

6. There are only two run-on lines and no internal pauses in the first ten lines. What is the effect thus achieved? Why, by contrast, are there several pauses in lines 11, 12, and 13? What kind of vowel sounds predominate throughout the poem and what effect do they produce? Why is the last line particularly effective in this respect, and how is the key word *unalterable* made to stand out?

THE LOVE SONG OF J. ALFRED PRUFROCK [*1917*]

T. S. Eliot

To Meredith, Lucifer's discovery that even the thought of rebellion against God's control is doomed to failure points out to man how insignificant his own feelings of self-importance and pride are. Yet, despite the fact that Lucifer sinks back to Hell when faced with "The army of unalterable law," there is in his renewed revolt, as Meredith presents it, a majestic defiance, requiring for its defeat the overwhelming power of a controlled and ordered universe.

In striking contrast is another poem of unsuccessful revolt, "The Love Song of J. Alfred Prufrock." Here there is no defiance, no majesty, nothing worth rebelling against. Middle-aged, "grown slightly bald," trapped by the sterility of his tea-in-the-drawing-room world, Prufrock recites his love song to himself and finds it only a song of frustration and regret. He has the insight to see himself for what he is, but he is too timid, too afraid of what the world might say, to do anything about it.

This poem is a dramatic monologue, similar in form to Browning's "My Last Duchess." In the latter you had to supply transitions to understand the logical development of the poem. Here the problem is to forget about the logical development of ideas and concentrate on the association of images and the suggestiveness of historical and literary allusions.

Particularly important is the quotation at the beginning of the poem. It comes from Dante's "Inferno," Canto XXVII, lines 61-66. The "Inferno" is an account of Dante's guided tour through Hell, during which he meets all kinds of evil-doers, who are suffering various forms of eternal punishment for their deeds. In Canto XXVII Dante describes his meeting with Count Guido da Montefeltro, a man who on earth had been an Evil Counselor and whose punishment is to be wrapped in a great tongue-like flame symbolic of his evil counseling. When Dante asks Guido why he is being punished, the Count begins his reply with the quoted lines:

> "If I believed that my reply were made
> to one who could ever climb to the world again,
> this flame would shake no more. But since no shade
>
> ever returned—if what I am told is true—
> from this blind world into the living light,
> without fear of dishonor I answer you.*

The connection between Montefeltro's words and Prufrock's will become clearer as you read.

> *S'io credesse che mia riposta fosse*
> *A persona che mai tornasse al mondo,*
> *Questa fiamma staria senza piu scosse.*
> *Ma perciocche giammai di questo fondo*
> *Non torno vivo alcun, s'i'odo il vero,*
> *Senza tema d'infamia ti rispondo.*

> Let us go then, you and I,
> When the evening is spread out against the sky
> Like a patient etherized upon a table;
> Let us go, through certain half-deserted streets,
> The muttering retreats   5
> Of restless nights in one-night cheap hotels
> And sawdust restaurants with oyster-shells:
> Streets that follow like a tedious argument
> Of insidious intent
> To lead you to an overwhelming question . . .   10
> Oh, do not ask, "What is it?"
> Let us go and make our visit.

In the room the women come and go
Talking of Michelangelo.

The yellow fog that rubs its back upon the window-panes,   15
The yellow smoke that rubs its muzzle on the window-panes
Licked its tongue into the corners of the evening,
Lingered upon the pools that stand in drains,
Let fall upon its back the soot that falls from chimneys,
Slipped by the terrace, made a sudden leap,   20
And seeing that it was a soft October night,
Curled once about the house, and fell asleep.

And indeed there will be time
For the yellow smoke that slides along the street,
Rubbing its back upon the window-panes;   25
There will be time, there will be time
To prepare a face to meet the faces that you meet;
There will be time to murder and create,
And time for all the works and days of hands
That lift and drop a question on your plate;   30
Time for you and time for me,
And time yet for a hundred indecisions,
And for a hundred visions and revisions,
Before the taking of a toast and tea.

In the room the women come and go   35
Talking of Michelangelo.

And indeed there will be time
To wonder, "Do I dare?" and, "Do I dare?"
Time to turn back and descend the stair,
With a bald spot in the middle of my hair—   40
(They will say: "How his hair is growing thin!")
My morning coat, my collar mounting firmly to the chin,
My necktie rich and modest, but asserted by a simple pin—
(They will say: "But how his arms and legs are thin!")
Do I dare   45
Disturb the universe?
In a minute there is time
For decisions and revisions which a minute will reverse.

For I have known them all already, known them all:
Have known the evenings, mornings, afternoons,   50

---

14. MICHELANGELO: Italian Renaissance artist, whose genius in painting, sculpture, and architecture is ironically set over against the inane chatter of the women who talk about him and in no way comprehend his creative powers.

29. WORKS AND DAYS: recalls a poem by Hesiod, a Greek poet of the eighth century B.C., extolling the virtues of tilling the soil; the contrast with Prufrock's world is obvious.

I have measured out my life with coffee spoons;
I know the voice dying with a dying fall
Beneath the music from a farther room.
    So how should I presume?
And I have known the eyes already, known them all—   55
The eyes that fix you in a formulated phrase,
And when I am formulated, sprawling on a pin,
When I am pinned and wriggling on the wall,
Then how should I begin
To spit out all the butt-ends of my days and ways?   60
    And how should I presume?

And I have known the arms already, known them all—
Arms that are braceleted and white and bare
(But in the lamplight, downed with light brown hair!)
Is it perfume from a dress   65
That makes me so digress?
Arms that lie along a table, or wrap about a shawl.
    And should I then presume?
    And how should I begin?
                                        .   .   .   .   .

Shall I say, I have gone at dusk through narrow streets   70
And watched the smoke that rises from the pipes
Of lonely men in shirt-sleeves, leaning out of windows? . . .

I should have been a pair of ragged claws
Scuttling across the floors of silent seas.
                                        .   .   .   .   .

And the afternoon, the evening, sleeps so peacefully!   75
Smoothed by long fingers,
Asleep . . . tired . . . or it malingers,
Stretched on the floor, here beside you and me.
Should I, after tea and cakes and ices,
Have the strength to force the moment to its crisis?   80
But though I have wept and fasted, wept and prayed,
Though I have seen my head (grown slightly bald) brought in
    upon a platter,
I am no prophet—and here's no great matter;
I have seen the moment of my greatness flicker,
And I have seen the eternal Footman hold my coat, and snicker,   85
And in short, I was afraid.

And would it have been worth it, after all,
After the cups, the marmalade, the tea,
Among the porcelain, among some talk of you and me,

---

83. NO PROPHET: i.e., no John the Baptist; see
    Matthew 14:1-11.

Would it have been worth while, 90
To have bitten off the matter with a smile,
To have squeezed the universe into a ball
To roll it toward some overwhelming question,
To say: "I am Lazarus, come from the dead,
Come back to tell you all, I shall tell you all"— 95
If one, settling a pillow by her head,
    Should say: "That is not what I meant at all;
    That is not it, at all."

And would it have been worth it, after all,
Would it have been worth while, 100
After the sunsets and the dooryards and the sprinkled streets,
After the novels, after the teacups, after the skirts that
    trail along the floor—
And this, and so much more?—
It is impossible to say just what I mean!
But as if a magic lantern threw the nerves in patterns on a 105
    screen:
Would it have been worth while
If one, settling a pillow or throwing off a shawl,
And turning toward the window, should say:
    "That is not it at all,
    That is not what I meant, at all." 110

       . . . . .

No! I am not Prince Hamlet, nor was meant to be;
Am an attendant lord, one that will do
To swell a progress, start a scene or two,
Advise the prince; no doubt, an easy tool,
Deferential, glad to be of use, 115
Politic, cautious, and meticulous;
Full of high sentence, but a bit obtuse;
At times, indeed, almost ridiculous—
Almost, at times, the Fool.

I grow old . . . I grow old . . . 120
I shall wear the bottoms of my trousers rolled.

---

94. LAZARUS: see John 11:1-44, and Luke 16:19-31.

105. MAGIC LANTERN: an optical instrument for projecting enlarged pictures on a screen.

111. HAMLET: Hamlet was full of doubts and hesitations, but he was aware of the necessity to act and does so finally.

112. AN ATTENDANT LORD: a minor character (with the implication of a subservient attitude).

113. SWELL A PROGRESS: i.e., fill out the crowd scenes.

117. FULL . . . SENTENCE: i.e., full of trite advice (like Polonius in *Hamlet*).

121. I . . . ROLLED: i.e., try to appear younger by wearing cuffed trousers (just coming into fashion at the time the poem was written); lines 122-124 carry on this idea.

Shall I part my hair behind? Do I dare to eat a peach?
I shall wear white flannel trousers, and walk upon the beach.
I have heard the mermaids singing, each to each.

I do not think that they will sing to me.   125

I have seen them riding seaward on the waves
Combing the white hair of the waves blown back
When the wind blows the water white and black.

We have lingered in the chambers of the sea
By sea-girls wreathed with seaweed red and brown   130
Till human voices wake us, and we drown.

---

124. MERMAIDS SINGING: recalls the sirens singing
to Ulysses.

I

1. Prufrock tells his own story, and we see the world through his eyes and his consciousness. For instance, the fact that he sees the evening "spread out against the sky/Like a patient etherized upon a table" tells us something about his frame of mind. So does the fact that the streets seem to him to be *following* him— both *like a tedious argument* and like something with *insidious intent*. So does the fact that he no sooner mentions the *overwhelming question* than he evades it, leaves it unformulated. From these clues, and other evidence in the first twelve lines, how would you define his state of mind?

2. How does the extended metaphor describing "the yellow fog" (15-22) relate to the *etherized* one?

3. What kind of a group does Prufrock live among? To judge from lines 35-68 what do they do? What do they talk about? Why is Prufrock afraid of them? What evidence is there in the poem that Prufrock has wider sympathies than do those of his own group? What evidence is there that he has more self-knowledge than they?

4. Why do you gather that the "you and I" are going to the room where "the women come and go/Talking of Michelangelo"? What do you take the "overwhelming question" to be? What may we infer about the question from the way he visualizes the room in lines 62-69? from the scene his mind turns to in lines 70-72? from the words he utters in 73-74?

5. Who do you suppose the "eternal Footman" (85) is, and why does he *snicker* behind Prufrock's back?

6. The "one" mentioned in line 96 must be the lady of the "love song." If this is so, she is not the "you" of "you and I." Who, then, might the "you" be?

7. Why does Prufrock return to sea imagery at the end of the poem (recall 73-74)? Why does he say that he does not think the mermaids "will sing to me" (125)?

8. Why does he shift to "we" in the last three lines? What does the last line of the poem mean? How can one *drown* on being wakened?

II

1. Discuss what part the allusions in the poem contribute to the total meaning. Consider particularly the quotation from the "Inferno," Michelangelo, John the Baptist, Lazarus, Hamlet, "an attendant lord," and Ulysses.

2. Whether Prufrock is the embodiment of modern man—aware of the tawdriness, the superficiality, the cowardice of his existence, but unable or unwilling to change—is open to question; but that there is something of Prufrock in each of us is indisputable. He is not particularly admirable; neither is he despicable. He simply cannot get off the dead center of a rather fruitless life. Looking at yourself frankly, in what ways do you find yourself brother or sister to Prufrock at times?

THE DILL PICKLE   [*1920*]

Katherine Mansfield

Prufrock sees himself clearly, much as he does not like what he sees and helpless as he is to do anything about it. In the following story by Katherine Mansfield, two sharply drawn people are revealed fully to the reader but remain ignorant of themselves. Whatever we may think of the couple whose lives we see for a brief moment in "The Dill Pickle," we cannot dismiss their imprisonment in self as a unique set of circumstances. We, too, are subject to that blind giant, Ego; and no matter how honest we may be with ourselves, we remain in some part unaware of our own foibles, follies, and vices, and of the impressions other people form of us.

As in all of her stories, Katherine Mansfield is concerned here not with fanciful exploits or heroic deeds but rather with quiet moments of self-revelation. There is little story in the usual sense of the word; the external action is slight. What we must do as readers is to follow her into the minds of her characters and be willing to pay close attention to every detail.

And then, after six years, she saw him again. He was seated at one of those little bamboo tables decorated with a Japanese vase of paper daffodils. There was a tall plate of fruit in front of him, and very carefully, in a way she recognized immediately as his "special" way, he was peeling an orange.

He must have felt that shock of recognition in her for he looked up and met her eyes. Incredible! He didn't know her! She smiled; he frowned. She came toward him. He closed his eyes an instant, but opening them his face lit up as though he had struck a match in a dark room. He laid down the orange and pushed back his chair, and she took her little warm hand out of her muff and gave it to him.

"Vera!" he exclaimed. "How strange. Really, for a moment I didn't know you. Won't you sit down? You've had lunch? Won't you have some coffee?"

She hesitated, but of course she meant to.

"Yes, I'd like some coffee." And she sat down opposite him.

"You've changed. You've changed very much," he said, staring at her with that eager, lighted look. "You look so well. I've never seen you look so well before."

"Really?" She raised her veil and unbuttoned her high fur collar. "I don't feel very well. I can't bear this weather, you know."

"Ah, no. You hate the cold—"

"Loathe it." She shuddered. "And the worst of it is that the older one grows—"

He interrupted her. "Excuse me," and tapped on the table for the waitress. "Please bring some coffee and cream." To her: "You are sure you won't eat anything? Some fruit, perhaps. The fruit here is very good."

"No, thanks. Nothing."

"Then that's settled." And smiling just a hint too broadly he took up the orange again. "You were saying—the older one grows—"

"The colder," she laughed. But she was thinking how well she remembered that trick of his—the trick of interrupting her—

and of how it used to exasperate her six years ago. She used to feel then as though he, quite suddenly, in the middle of what she was saying, put his hand over her lips, turned from her, attended to something different, and then took his hand away, and with just the same slightly too broad smile, gave her his attention again—Now we are ready. That is settled.

"The colder!" He echoed her words, laughing too. "Ah, ah. You still say the same things. And there is another thing about you that is not changed at all—your beautiful voice—your beautiful way of speaking." Now he was very grave; he leaned toward her, and she smelled the warm, stinging scent of the orange peel. "You have only to say one word and I would know your voice among all other voices. I don't know what it is—I've often wondered—that makes your voice such a— haunting memory. . . . Do you remember that first afternoon we spent together at Kew Gardens?[1] You were so surprised because I did not know the names of any flowers. I am still just as ignorant for all your telling me. But whenever it is very fine and warm, and I see some bright colors— It's awfully strange—I hear your voice saying: 'Geranium, marigold and verbena.' And I feel those three words are all I recall of some forgotten, heavenly language—You remember that afternoon?"

"Oh, yes, very well." She drew a long, soft breath, as though the paper daffodils between them were almost too sweet to bear. Yet, what had remained in her mind of that particular afternoon was an absurd scene over the tea table. A great many people taking tea in a Chinese pagoda, and he behaving like a maniac about the wasps— waving them away, flapping at them with his straw hat, serious and infuriated out of all proportions to the occasion. How delighted the sniggering tea drinkers had been. And how she had suffered.

---

1. KEW GARDENS: the Royal Botanic Gardens in Surrey.

But now, as he spoke, that memory faded. His was the truer. Yes, it had been a wonderful afternoon, full of geranium and marigold and verbena—and warm sunshine. Her thoughts lingered over the last two words as though she sang them.

In the warmth, as it were, another memory unfolded. She saw herself sitting on a lawn. He lay beside her, and suddenly, after a long silence, he rolled over and put his head in her lap.

"I wish," he said, in a low, troubled voice, "I wish that I had taken poison and were about to die—here now!"

At that moment, a little girl in a white dress, holding a long, dripping water lily, dodged from behind a bush, stared at them, and dodged back again. But he did not see. She leaned over him.

"Ah, why do you say that? I could not say that."

But he gave a kind of soft moan, and taking her hand he held it to his cheek.

"Because I know I am going to love you too much—far too much. And I shall suffer so terribly, Vera, because you never, never will love me."

He was certainly far better looking now than he had been then. He had lost that dreamy vagueness and indecision. Now he had the air of a man who has found his place in life and fills it with a confidence and an assurance which was, to say the least, impressive. He must have made money, too. His clothes were admirable, and at that moment he pulled a Russian cigarette case out of his pocket.

"Won't you smoke?"

"Yes, I will." She hovered over them. "They look very good."

"I think they are. I get them made for me by a little man in St. James's Street. I don't smoke very much. I'm not like you— but when I do, they must be delicious, very fresh cigarettes. Smoking isn't a habit with me; it's a luxury—like perfume. Are you still so fond of perfumes? Ah, when I was in Russia—"

She broke in: "You've really been to Russia?"

"Oh, yes. I was there for over a year. Have you forgotten how we used to talk of going there?"

"No, I've not forgotten."

He gave a strange half laugh and leaned back in his chair. "Isn't it curious? I have really carried out all those journeys that we planned. Yes, I have been to all those places that we talked of, and stayed in them long enough to—as you used to say, 'air oneself' in them. In fact I have spent the last three years of my life traveling all the time. Spain, Corsica, Siberia, Russia, Egypt. The only country left is China, and I mean to go there, too, when the war is over."

As he spoke, so lightly, tapping the end of his cigarette against the ash tray, she felt the strange beast that had slumbered so long within her bosom stir, stretch itself, yawn, prick up its ears, and suddenly bound to its feet, and fix its longing, hungry stare upon those faraway places. But all she said was, smiling gently: "How I envy you."

He accepted that. "It has been," he said, "very wonderful—especially Russia. Russia was all that we had imagined, and far, far more. I even spent some days on a river boat on the Volga. Do you remember that boatman's song you used to play?"

"Yes." It began to play in her mind as she spoke.

"Do you ever play it now?"

"No, I've no piano."

He was amazed at that. "But what has become of your beautiful piano?"

She made a little grimace. "Sold. Ages ago."

"But you were so fond of music," he wondered.

"I've no time for it now," said she.

He let it go at that. "That river life," he went on, "is something quite special. After a day or two you cannot realize that you have ever known another. And it is not necessary to know the language—the life of the boat creates a bond between you and the people that's more than sufficient. You eat with them, pass the day with them, and in the evening there is that endless singing."

She shivered, hearing the boatman's song break out again loud and tragic, and seeing the boat floating on the darkening river with melancholy trees on either side—"Yes, I should like that," she said, stroking her muff.

"You'd like almost everything about Russian life," he said warmly. "It's so informal, so impulsive, so free without question. And then the peasants are so splendid. They are such human beings—yes, that is it. Even the man who drives your carriage has—has some real part in what is happening. I remember the evening a party of us, two friends of mine and the wife of one of them, went for a picnic by the Black Sea. We took supper and champagne and ate and drank on the grass. And while we were eating the coachman came up. 'Have a dill pickle,' he said. He wanted to share with us. That seemed to me so right, so—you know what I mean?"

And she seemed at that moment to be sitting on the grass beside the mysteriously Black Sea, black as velvet, and rippling against the banks in silent, velvet waves. She saw the carriage drawn up to one side of the road, and the little group on the grass, their faces and hands white in the moonlight. She saw the pale dress of the woman outspread and her folded parasol, lying on the grass like a huge pearl crochet hook. Apart from them, with his supper in a cloth on his knees, sat the coachman. "Have a dill pickle," said he, and although she was not certain what a dill pickle was, she saw the greenish glass jar with a red chili like a parrot's beak glimmering through. She sucked in her cheeks; the dill pickle was terribly sour—

"Yes, I know perfectly what you mean," she said.

In the pause that followed they looked at each other. In the past when they had looked at each other like that they had felt such a boundless understanding between them that their souls had, as it were, put their arms around each other and dropped into the same sea, content to be drowned, like mournful lovers. But now, the surprising thing was that it was he who held back. He who said:

"What a marvelous listener you are. When you look at me with those wild eyes I feel that I could tell you things that I would never breathe to another human being."

Was there just a hint of mockery in his voice or was it her fancy? She could not be sure.

"Before I met you," he said, "I had never spoken of myself to anybody. How well I remember one night, the night that I brought you the little Christmas tree, telling you all about my childhood. And of how I was so miserable that I ran away and lived under a cart in our yard for two days without being discovered. And you listened, and your eyes shone, and I felt that you had even made the little Christmas tree listen too, as in a fairy story."

But of that evening she had remembered a little pot of caviar. It had cost seven and sixpence. He could not get over it. Think of it—a tiny jar like that costing seven and sixpence. While she ate it he watched her, delighted and shocked.

"No, really, that is eating money. You could not get seven shillings into a little pot that size. Only think of the profit they must make—" And he had begun some immensely complicated calculations—But now good-by to the caviar. The Christmas tree was on the table, and the little boy lay under the cart with his head pillowed on the yard dog.

"The dog was called Bosun," she cried delightedly.

But he did not follow. "Which dog? Had you a dog? I don't remember a dog at all."

"No, no. I mean the yard dog when you were a little boy." He laughed and snapped the cigarette case to.

"Was he? Do you know I had forgotten that. It seems such ages ago. I cannot believe that it is only six years. After I had

recognized you today—I had to take such a leap—I had to take a leap over my whole life to get back to that time. I was such a kid then." He drummed on the table. "I've often thought how I must have bored you. And now I understand so perfectly why you wrote to me as you did—although at the time that letter nearly finished my life. I found it again the other day, and I couldn't help laughing as I read it. It was so clever—such a true picture of me." He glanced up. "You're not going?"

She had buttoned her collar again and drawn down her veil.

"Yes, I am afraid I must," she said, and managed a smile. Now she knew that he had been mocking.

"Ah, no, please," he pleaded. "Don't go just for a moment," and he caught up one of her gloves from the table and clutched at it as if that would hold her. "I see so few people to talk to nowadays, that I have turned into a sort of barbarian," he said. "Have I said something to hurt you?"

"Not a bit," she lied. But as she watched him draw her glove through his fingers, gently, gently, her anger really did die down, and besides, at the moment he looked more like himself of six years ago—

"What I really wanted then," he said softly, "was to be a sort of carpet—to make myself into a sort of carpet for you to walk on so that you need not be hurt by the sharp stones and the mud that you hated so. It was nothing more positive than that—nothing more selfish. Only I did desire, eventually, to turn into a magic carpet and carry you away to all those lands you longed to see."

As he spoke she lifted her head as though she drank something; the strange beast in her bosom began to purr—

"I felt that you were more lonely than anybody else in the world," he went on, "and yet, perhaps, that you were the only person in the world who was really, truly alive. Born out of your time," he murmured, stroking the glove, "fated."

Ah, God! What had she done! How had

she dared to throw away her happiness like this. This was the only man who had ever understood her. Was it too late? Could it be too late? *She* was that glove that he held in his fingers—

"And then the fact that you had no friends and never had made friends with people. How I understood that, for neither had I. Is it just the same now?"

"Yes," she breathed. "Just the same. I am as alone as ever."

"So am I," he laughed gently, "just the same."

Suddenly with a quick gesture he handed her back the glove and scraped his chair on the floor. "But what seemed to me so mysterious then is perfectly plain to me now. And to you, too, of course—It simply was that we were such egoists, so self-engrossed, so wrapped up in ourselves that we hadn't a corner in our hearts for anybody else. Do you know," he cried, naïve and hearty, and dreadfully like another side of that old self again, "I began studying a Mind System when I was in Russia, and I found that we were not peculiar at all. It's quite a well-known form of—"

She had gone. He sat there, thunderstruck, astounded beyond words—And then he asked the waitress for his bill.

"But the cream has not been touched," he said. "Please do not charge me for it."

I

1. What indications are there of the man's stinginess toward others but not toward himself? How serious is he when he speaks to Vera of what she means to him? Why does he interrupt her? What other annoying habits does he have?

2. What details show us what kind of person Vera is? How does her attitude toward the foreign places differ from his? Why does she leave abruptly? What is meant by "the strange beast in her bosom"?

3. What is the significance of the title?

4. What is revealing about the fact that he says quite bluntly toward the end, ". . . we were such egoists, so self-engrossed, so wrapped up in ourselves that we hadn't a corner in our hearts for anybody else"? How well do they understand each other or themselves?

5. We do not see anything of their previous relationship, but what do you suppose it was like? The man comments that he has changed during the six years. What indications are there that this is or is not so? What indications are there that Vera has or has not changed?

II

1. Try your hand at a character sketch—or even a short story—of a person in a situation in which he shows himself totally unaware (at least at the moment) of the impression he is making on somebody else, or in which he does not care what impression he is making. If you can recreate a personal experience, so much the better.

ARABY

James Joyce

As all of us have our moments of self-centeredness, so have all of us taken turns at playing the fool. Perhaps one of the sure signs of maturity is a recognition that there is a gulf between what we are and what we might hope to be. Often we fancy ourselves isolated from a world that does not understand how special we are; and yet, if we are at all objective about ourselves, just as often are we deflated by the realization that our vanity has mocked us. On the surface, the following short story is about a young boy's disillusionment and humiliation, but it has implications that go to the heart of man's awareness of what he is.

"Araby" is one of a number of short stories in a collection by Joyce entitled *Dubliners*. Each deals with some aspect of Dublin life as Joyce knew it in the early years of this century. As with the stories of Katherine Mansfield the emphasis is on the revelation of character through a series of seemingly insignificant happenings. The revelations about Dublin men—and all men—that Joyce laid bare are not necessarily pleasant, but they are hauntingly accurate.

North Richmond Street, being blind,[1] was a quiet street except at the hour when the Christian Brothers' School set the boys free. An uninhabited house of two stories stood at the blind end, detached from its neighbors in a square ground. The other houses of the street, conscious of decent lives within them, gazed at one another with brown imperturbable faces.

The former tenant of our house, a priest, had died in the back drawing-room. Air, musty from having been long enclosed, hung in all the rooms, and the waste room behind the kitchen was littered with old useless papers. Among these I found a few paper-covered books, the pages of which were curled and damp: *The Abbot,*[2] by Walter Scott, *The Devout Communicant,* and *The Memoirs of Vidocq.*[3] I liked the last best, because its leaves were yellow. The wild garden behind the house contained a central apple tree and a few straggling bushes, under one of which I found the late tenant's rusty bicycle-pump. He had been a very charitable priest; in his will he had left all his money to institutions and the furniture of his house to his sister.

When the short days of winter came, dusk fell before we had well eaten our dinners. When we met in the street, the houses had grown somber. The space of sky above us was the color of ever-changing violet, and towards it the lamps of the street lifted their feeble lanterns. The cold air stung us and we played till our bodies glowed. Our shouts echoed in the silent street. The career of our play brought us through the dark muddy lanes behind the houses where we ran the gantlet of the rough tribes from the cottages, to the back doors of the dark dripping gardens where odors arose from the ashpits, to the dark odorous stables where a coachman smoothed and combed the horse or shook music from the buckled harness. When we returned to the street, if uncle was seen turning the corner, we hid in the shadow until we had seen him safely housed. Or if

1. BLIND: i.e., a dead end street.
2. THE ABBOT: one of Sir Walter Scott's historical novels (1820).
3. THE MEMOIRS OF VIDOCQ: François Eugène Vidocq was a famous Chief of Detectives in Paris (1809-27).

Mangan's sister came out on the doorstep to call her brother in to his tea, we watched her from our shadow peer up and down the street. We waited to see whether she would remain or go in, and, if she remained, we left our shadow and walked up to Mangan's steps resignedly. She was waiting for us, her figure defined by the light from the half-opened door. Her brother always teased her before he obeyed, and I stood by the railings looking at her. Her dress swung as she moved her body, and the soft rope of her hair tossed from side to side.

Every morning I lay on the floor in the front parlor watching her door. The blind was pulled down to within an inch of the sash, so that I could not be seen. When she came out on the doorstep my heart leaped. I ran to the hall, seized my books, and followed her. I kept her brown figure always in my eye, and, when we came near the point at which our ways diverged, I quickened my pace and passed her. This happened morning after morning. I had never spoken to her, except for a few casual words, and yet her name was like a summons to all my foolish blood.

Her image accompanied me even in places the most hostile to romance. On Saturday evenings, when my aunt went marketing, I had to go to carry some of the parcels. We walked through the flaring streets, jostled by drunken men and bargaining women, amid the curses of laborers, the shrill litanies of shop-boys, who stood on guard by the barrels of pigs' cheeks, the nasal chanting of street-singers, who sang a *come-all-you*[4] about O'Donovan Rossa,[5] or a ballad about the troubles in our native land. These noises converged in a single sensation of life for me: I imagined that I bore my chalice safely through a throng of foes. Her name sprang to my lips at moments in strange prayers and praises which I myself did not understand. My eyes were often full of tears (I could not tell why) and at times a flood from my heart seemed to pour itself out into my bosom. I thought little of the future. I did not know whether I would ever speak to her or not, or, if I spoke to her, how I could tell her of my confused adoration. But my body was like a harp, and her words and gestures were like fingers running upon the wires.

One evening I went into the back drawing-room, in which the priest had died. It was a dark rainy evening, and there was no sound in the house. Through one of the broken panes I heard the rain impinge upon the earth, the fine incessant needles of water playing in the sodden beds. Some distant lamp or lighted window gleamed below me. I was thankful that I could see so little. All my senses seemed to desire to veil themselves, and, feeling that I was about to slip from them, I pressed the palms of my hands together until they trembled, murmuring: *"O love! O love!"* many times.

At last she spoke to me. When she addressed the first words to me, I was so confused that I did not know what to answer. She asked me was I going to *Araby*. I forget whether I answered yes or no. It would be a splendid bazaar; she said she would love to go.

"And why can't you?" I asked.

While she spoke, she turned a silver bracelet round and round her wrist. She could not go, she said, because there would be a retreat that week in her convent.[6] Her brother and two other boys were fighting for their caps, and I was alone at the railings. She held one of the spikes, bowing her head towards me. The light from the lamp opposite our door caught the white curve of her neck, lit up her hair that rested there, and, falling, lit up the hand upon the railing. It fell over one side of her dress and caught the white border of a petticoat, just visible as she stood at ease.

---

4. COME-ALL-YOU: any popular English or Irish ballad, so called because many of the first lines began with these words.
5. O'DONOVAN ROSSA: nineteenth century Irish rebel.

---

6. CONVENT: school run by an order of nuns.

"It's well for you," she said.

"If I go," I said, "I will bring you something."

What innumerable follies laid waste my waking and sleeping thoughts after that evening! I wished to annihilate the tedious intervening days. I chafed against the work of school. At night in my bedroom and by day in the classroom her image came between me and the page I strove to read. The syllables of the word *Araby* were called to me through the silence in which my soul luxuriated and cast an Eastern enchantment over me. I asked for leave to go to the bazaar on Saturday night. My aunt was surprised and hoped it was not some Freemason[7] affair. I answered few questions in class. I watched my master's face pass from amiability to sternness; he hoped I was not beginning to idle. I could not call my wandering thoughts together. I had hardly any patience with the serious work of life, which, now that it stood between me and my desire, seemed to me child's play, ugly monotonous child's play.

On Saturday morning I reminded my uncle that I wished to go to the bazaar in the evening. He was fussing at the hallstand looking for the hat-brush, and answered me curtly:

"Yes, boy, I know."

As he was in the hall, I could not go into the front parlor and lie at the window. I left the house in bad humor and walked slowly towards the school. The air was pitilessly raw, and already my heart misgave me.

When I came home to dinner, my uncle had not yet been home. Still, it was early. I sat staring at the clock for some time, and, when its ticking began to irritate me, I left the room. I mounted the staircase and gained the upper part of the house. The high cold empty gloomy rooms liberated me and I went from room to room singing. From the front window I saw my companions playing below in the street. Their cries reached me weakened and indistinct, and, leaning my forehead

against the cool glass, I looked over at the dark house where she lived. I may have stood there for an hour, seeing nothing but the brown-clad figure cast by my imagination, touched discreetly by the lamplight at the curved neck, at the hand upon the railings, and at the border below the dress.

When I came downstairs again, I found Mrs. Mercer sitting at the fire. She was an old garrulous woman, a pawnbroker's widow, who collected used stamps for some pious purpose. I had to endure the gossip of the tea-table. The meal was prolonged beyond an hour, and still my uncle did not come. Mrs. Mercer stood up to go: she was sorry she couldn't wait any longer, but it was after eight o'clock and she did not like to be out late, as the night air was bad for her. When she had gone, I began to walk up and down the room, clenching my fists. My aunt said:

"I'm afraid you may put off your bazaar for this night of Our Lord."

At nine o'clock I heard my uncle's latch-key in the halldoor. I heard him talking to himself and heard the hallstand rocking when it had received the weight of his overcoat. I could interpret these signs. When he was midway through his dinner, I asked him to give me the money to go to the bazaar. He had forgotten.

"The people are in bed and after their first sleep now," he said.

I did not smile. My aunt said to him energetically:

"Can't you give him the money and let him go? You've kept him late enough as it is."

My uncle said he was very sorry he had forgotten. He said he believed in the old saying: "All work and no play makes Jack a dull boy." He asked me where I was going, and, when I had told him a second time, he asked me did I know "The Arab's Farewell to His Steed."[8] When I left the kitchen, he was about to recite the opening lines of the piece to my aunt.

---

7. FREEMASON: European freemasonry had a reputation of being hostile to Christian doctrines.

8. THE ARAB'S FAREWELL TO HIS STEED: a poem by Caroline E. S. Norton; the exact title is, "The Arab to His Favorite Steed."

I held a florin tightly in my hand as I strode down Buckingham Street towards the station. The sight of the streets thronged with buyers and glaring with gas recalled to me the purpose of my journey. I took my seat in a third-class carriage[9] of a deserted train. After an intolerable delay the train moved out of the station slowly. It crept onward among ruinous houses and over the twinkling river. At Westland Row Station a crowd of people pressed to the carriage doors; but the porters moved them back, saying that it was a special train for the bazaar. I remained alone in the bare carriage. In a few minutes the train drew up beside an improvised wooden platform. I passed out onto the road and saw by the lighted dial of a clock that it was ten minutes to ten. In front of me was a large building which displayed the magical name.

I could not find any sixpenny entrance, and, fearing that the bazaar would be closed, I passed in quickly through a turnstile, handing a shilling to a weary-looking man. I found myself in a big hall girdled at half its height by a gallery. Nearly all the stalls were closed and the greater part of the hall was in darkness. I recognized a silence like that which pervades a church after a service. I walked into the center of the bazaar timidly. A few people were gathered about the stalls which were still open. Before a curtain, over which the words *Café Chantant* were written in colored lamps, two men were counting money on a salver. I listened to the fall of the coins.

9. THIRD-CLASS CARRIAGE: English and Irish trains have first, second, and third class accommodations, third class being the least expensive.

Remembering with difficulty why I had come, I went over to one of the stalls and examined porcelain vases and flowered tea-sets. At the door of the stall a young lady was talking and laughing with two young gentlemen. I remarked their English accents and listened vaguely to their conversation.

"O, I never said such a thing!"

"O, but you did!"

"O, but I didn't!"

"Didn't she say that?"

"Yes. I heard her."

"O, there's a . . . fib!"

Observing me, the young lady came over and asked me did I wish to buy anything. The tone of her voice was not encouraging; she seemed to have spoken to me out of a sense of duty. I looked humbly at the great jars that stood like eastern guards at either side of the dark entrance to the stall and murmured:

"No, thank you."

The young lady changed the position of one of the vases and went back to the two young men. They began to talk of the same subject. Once or twice the young lady glanced at me over her shoulder.

I lingered before her stall, though I knew my stay was useless, to make my interest in her wares seem the more real. Then I turned away slowly and walked down the middle of the bazaar. I allowed the two pennies to fall against the sixpence in my pocket. I heard a voice call from one end of the gallery that the light was out. The upper part of the hall was now completely dark.

Gazing up into the darkness, I saw myself as a creature driven and derided by vanity; and my eyes burned with anguish and anger.

I

1. What kind of mood or atmosphere is set in the opening paragraphs? Consider the words used to describe North Richmond Street in paragraph 1; the comments about the dead priest who once lived in the boy's house; and that fact that in paragraph 3 the street is described in wintertime at dusk. What has all this to do with the boy's growing feeling of estrangement from the everyday world in his secret worship of Mangan's sister?

2. Not much happens in the story, but there is a lot of carefully chosen detail, which plays an important part in the total impression the story gives. What details (things the boy does,

his relations with others) communicate the sense of isolation he feels from the normal world around him? What details suggest that he looks on his infatuation as almost a religious observance? How is this religious "ritual" idea carried throughout the story, from the very first paragraphs to the final description of the bazaar? What does it add to the ultimate self-discovery of the boy?

3. The word *Araby* is a poetic term for Arabia and it carries with it, for the boy, all the mysterious enchantment of the East. How does it reinforce the way in which he looks upon his infatuation with Mangan's sister? How are the word and its connotations ironically contrasted with the physical realities of the bazaar? How is his infatuation mocked by the idle chatter of the girl and the two young men at the stall before which "the great jars . . . stood like eastern guards"?

4. The story is told in the first person, but quite obviously not by the boy at the time of the particular experience, because this is certainly not the language of a young boy. What is significant about the fact that a grown man is recalling a boyhood experience that he can look on now as being rather foolish? Is there any indication that he sees it all in a humorous light, or does he seem to regard the affair quite seriously even though he knows that the shame must have been only momentary to the boy? What does your answer to the preceding question tell you about the significance of the experience to the grown man?

II

1. The boy's experience in playing the fool was probably neither his first nor his last. The game is universal. Recreate an experience you have had in which you acted the part of *the creature driven and derided by vanity*. Show how it, upon reflection, represents a significant insight into yourself.

KING OEDIPUS [*430* B.C.]

Sophocles

Perhaps the most enlightening and engrossing example of self-discovery in all literature is a play written almost twenty-four centuries ago, Sophocles's *King Oedipus*.

Most of you are probably familiar with the name *Oedipus* and some of you might have read the play or seen performances of it on the stage or in the movies. The myth of Oedipus is one of the great stories of the world, and the play based on it remains one of the most searching answers ever given to the question "What is man?"—or to put it in terms of Oedipus's dilemma—"Who am I?" The play is as modern and timeless as that question. And it speaks with a simplicity and directness that make background information useful but not necessary. For our purposes we will provide some details about the Athens of the fifth century B.C., a few notes about the Greek theater, and a brief account of the myth. But our main concern is with the play itself—how it is put together, and what it has to say about man's place in this world.

First, about Athens. In the early years of the fifth century, the small Greek city-states, led by Athens and Sparta, temporarily united in common defense and turned back the invasion attempt of the mighty Persian Empire, which dominated most of what is now known as the Middle East. In Athens (though not in Sparta) military success proved a spur to achievements of all kinds: the perfecting of the first genuine democracy the world had known (or would know for a long time to come); contributions of unprecedented quality in the sciences, mathematics, philosophy, history; masterpieces in literature and the arts of sculpture and architecture that may never be surpassed. With these achievements came the growing conviction that the Athenian intellect could do just about anything it set its mind to. The pride in man's achievement even cast doubt on such fundamental beliefs as the existence of the gods, the operation of any moral standard beyond personal advantage, the necessity of citizen responsibility in government. It is on this idolatry of man—self-made, self-sufficient—that Sophocles turns his spotlight. The modern reader will find all-too-uncomfortable parallels in the world today.

As for the theater, the fifth century Athenian writers evolved it out of religious dance and song performed as part of the worship of Dionysus, the wine-god, early in the spring. To the Chorus, or dance group, of some twelve to fifteen masked dancers were added individual actors, also masked, and the spoken drama as we know it was born. Although the Chorus declined in importance in the drama, its continued presence pointed up the fact that the plays produced during the festival of Dionysus were religious in intention and execution.

Huge crowds of Athenians (estimates indicate that the outdoor theaters could hold upwards of 15,000 people) came to spend a good part of the day on three successive days watching the plays. Each day a different author would present three tragedies and a short farce. It was a theater for everybody, not just the "better people," and the dramatist could count on a knowledgeable audience, eager to be moved to tears or laughter, and perfectly willing to let the writer know out loud what they thought of his efforts. Obviously, this was not the intimate theater we know. To appreciate the difference you have to imagine watching a performance on a stage placed in front of the goal posts of a vast college football stadium while you sit somewhere in the horseshoe. You might hear all right, but you could see only broad movements and would welcome the elaborate costumes and the slightly more than life-sized masks that would indicate broad types (young man, old man, old woman, and the like).

There were no programs and no announcements, but neither was necessary. The plays were based on legends the audience knew well, and the first few lines would suffice to indicate what particular story the dramatist was dealing with and where in the story he was beginning. Whatever background was needed the audience filled in for itself from its knowledge of the particular myth or legend involved. What the dramatist did with the story was another matter, and therein lay the interest for the audience.

The legend of Oedipus is as follows: the king and queen of Thebes, Laius and Jocasta, were told by the god Apollo that their son would one day kill his father and marry his mother. At the time of the prophecy they had no children, but when a son was born to them, they tried to prevent the prediction from coming true by killing the child. They pierced and bound its ankles and gave it to a servant, a shepherd, to abandon on Mt. Cithaeron, near Thebes. The shepherd, through pity, disobeyed and gave the child to another shepherd, from Corinth, far from Thebes. This shepherd gave the child to the childless king and queen of Corinth, Polybus and Merope, who named him Oedipus (meaning "swollen foot") and brought him up as their own son. Oedipus was never told as he grew to manhood that he was not the legitimate son of Polybus and Merope; and his real parents lived on, convinced that they had circumvented Apollo's prophecy.

How wrong they were! At a banquet, a man who had had too much to drink told Oedipus he was not the real son of Polybus and Merope. They insisted he was, but Oedipus, true to his nature, wanted to be sure, so he went to Delphi, to the oracle of Apollo, to find the truth. He received only the prophecy that he would kill his father and marry his mother. As Laius and Jocasta had done in the first place, he tried to prevent the prophecy from coming true by fleeing from Corinth and from those who he supposed were his true parents. On the road he met a traveler, obviously a man of importance, accompanied by several servants. They ordered Oedipus out of the way so that they could pass. Angered by their insolence, he slew the entire party, save one servant who escaped. Unknown to him, the traveler had been Laius.

Eventually Oedipus came to Thebes and found the city at the mercy of a terrible monster, the Sphinx, a combination bird-lion-woman, who would not leave until someone answered her riddle. She devoured those who tried and failed. The city was so desperate that they offered as a reward to the one who answered her riddle the throne of Thebes and the hand of the widowed Jocasta in marriage. News of Laius's death had reached them, but they were so terrorized by the Sphinx that they had made little effort to solve the killing.

The Sphinx's riddle was: "What is it that goes on four feet, then two feet, then three feet, has one voice, and is weakest when it goes on most feet?" Oedipus gave the answer, "Man"—who crawls as a child, walks upright as an adult, and needs the help of a stick as an old man. The Sphinx killed herself, and Oedipus fulfilled Apollo's prophecy by marrying Jocasta, who bore him two sons and two daughters during his long and apparently prosperous reign as king of Thebes. Sophocles begins his play as Theban prosperity is coming to an end. A plague has broken out, killing crops, animals, and citizens, and the Theban citizens come to Oedipus once more to save them from disaster. And Oedipus acts.

CHARACTERS

OEDIPUS, *King of Thebes*

JOCASTA, *wife of Oedipus*

ANTIGONE, *daughter of Oedipus*

ISMENE, *daughter of Oedipus*

CREON, *brother-in-law of Oedipus*

TIRESIAS, *a seer*

PRIEST

MESSENGERS

HERDSMAN

CHORUS

King Oedipus. Reprinted with permission of the publisher from *Collected Plays* by William Butler Yeats. Copyright 1934, 1952 by The Macmillan Company.

OEDIPUS. Children, descendants of old Cadmus,[1] why do you come before me, why do you carry branches of suppliants,[2] while the city smokes with incense and murmurs with prayer and lamentation? I would not learn from any mouth but yours, old man, therefore I question you myself. Do you know of anything that I can do and have not done? How can I, being the man I am, being King Oedipus, do other than all I

---

1. CADMUS: founder of Thebes.
2. BRANCHES OF SUPPLIANTS: Each suppliant placed a branch on the altar, signifying a request. If the request was acted upon, the branch was removed.

know? I were indeed hard of heart did I not pity such suppliants.

PRIEST. Oedipus, King of my country, we who stand before your door are of all ages, some too young to have walked so many miles, some—priests of Zeus such as I—too old. Among us stand the pick of the young men, and behind in the marketplaces the people throng, carrying suppliant branches. We all stand here because the city stumbles towards death, hardly able to raise up its head. A blight has fallen upon the fruitful blossoms of the land, a blight upon flock and field and upon the bed of marriage— plague ravages the city. Oedipus, King, not God but foremost of living men, seeing that when you first came to this town of Thebes you freed us from that harsh singer, the riddling Sphinx,[3] we beseech you, all we suppliants, to find some help; whether you find it by your power as a man, or because, being near the Gods, a God has whispered you. Uplift our State; think upon your fame; your coming brought us luck, be lucky to us still; remember that it is better to rule over men than over a waste place, since neither walled town nor ship is anything if it be empty and no man within it.

OEDIPUS. My unhappy children! I know well what need has brought you, what suffering you endure; yet, sufferers though you be, there is not a single one whose suffering is as mine—each mourns himself, but my soul mourns the city, myself, and you. It is not therefore as if you came to arouse a sleeping man. No! Be certain that I have wept many tears and searched hither and thither for some remedy. I have already done the thing that came into my head for all my search. I have sent the son of Menoeceus, Creon, my own wife's brother, to the Pythian House of Phoebus,[4] to hear if deed or word of mine may yet deliver this town. I am

troubled, for he is a long time away—a longer time than should be—but when he comes I shall not be an honest man unless I do whatever the God commands.

PRIEST. You have spoken at the right time. They have just signaled to us that Creon has arrived.

OEDIPUS. O King Apollo, may he bring brighter fortune, for his face is shining!

PRIEST. He brings good news, for he is crowned with bay.[5]

OEDIPUS. We shall know soon. Brother-in-law, Menoeceus's son, what news from the God?

CREON. Good news; for pain turns to pleasure when we have set the crooked straight.

OEDIPUS. But what is the oracle?—so far the news is neither good nor bad.

CREON. If you would hear it with all these about you, I am ready to speak. Or do we go within?

OEDIPUS. Speak before all. The sorrow I endure is less for my own life than these.

CREON. Then, with your leave, I speak. Our lord Phoebus bids us drive out a defiling thing that has been cherished in this land.

OEDIPUS. By what purification?

CREON. King Laius was our King before you came to pilot us.

OEDIPUS. I know—but not of my own knowledge, for I never saw him.

CREON. He was killed; and the God now bids us revenge it on his murderers, whoever they be.

OEDIPUS. Where shall we come upon their track after all these years? Did he meet his death in house or field, at home or in some foreign land?

CREON. In a foreign land: he was journeying to Delphi.

OEDIPUS. Did no fellow-traveler see the deed? Was there none there who could be questioned?

CREON. All perished but one man who

3. FREED . . . SPHINX: see the last two paragraphs of the Introduction to the play.
4. PYTHIAN HOUSE OF PHOEBUS: the oracle of Apollo (Phoebus) at Delphi; Apollo was the god of music, poetry, and the healing arts.
5. CROWNED WITH BAY: the bay, or laurel, wreath is traditionally the sign of victory or success.

fled in terror and could tell for certain but one thing of all he had seen.

OEDIPUS. One thing might be a clue to many things.

CREON. He said that they were fallen upon by a great troop of robbers.

OEDIPUS. What robbers would be so daring unless bribed from here?

CREON. Such things were indeed guessed at, but Laius once dead no avenger arose. We were amid our troubles.

OEDIPUS. But when royalty had fallen what troubles could have hindered search?

CREON. The riddling Sphinx put those dark things out of our thoughts—we thought of what had come to our own doors.

OEDIPUS. But I will start afresh and make the dark things plain. In doing right by Laius I protect myself, for whoever slew Laius might turn a hand against me. Come, my children, rise up from the altar steps; lift up these suppliant boughs and let all the children of Cadmus be called thither that I may search out everything and find for all happiness or misery as God wills.

PRIEST. May Phoebus, sender of the oracle, come with it and be our savior and deliverer!

The CHORUS *enters.*

CHORUS. What message comes to famous Thebes from the Golden House?[6]
What message of disaster from that sweet-throated Zeus?[7]
What monstrous thing our fathers saw do the seasons bring?
Or what that no man ever saw, what new monstrous thing?
Trembling in every limb I raise my loud importunate cry,
And in a sacred terror wait the Delian[8] God's reply.

Apollo chase the God of Death that leads no shouting men,
Bears no rattling shield and yet consumes this form with pain.
Famine takes what the plague spares, and all the crops are lost;
No new life fills the empty place—ghost flits after ghost
To that God-trodden western shore, as flit benighted birds.
Sorrow speaks to sorrow, but no comfort finds in words.

Hurry him from the land of Thebes with a fair wind behind
Out onto that formless deep where not a man can find
Hold for an anchor-fluke,[9] for all is world-enfolding sea;
Master of the thunder-cloud,[10] set the lightning free,
And add the thunder-stone to that and fling them on his head,
For death is all the fashion now, till even Death be dead.

We call against the pallid face of this God-hated God
The springing heel of Artemis[11] in the hunting sandal shod,
The tousel-headed Maenads,[12] blown torch and drunken sound,
The stately Lycian king[13] himself with golden fillet crowned,
And in his hands the golden bow and the stretched golden string,
And Bacchus' wine-ensanguined face that all the Maenads sing.

6. GOLDEN HOUSE: the oracle at Delphi.
7. ZEUS: father of Apollo, who spoke through his son.
8. DELIAN: Apollo was born on the island of Delos.
9. ANCHOR-FLUKE: the part of an anchor which fastens in the ground.
10. MASTER OF THE THUNDER-CLOUD: Zeus.
11. ARTEMIS: goddess of the hunt.
12. MAENADS: wild nymphs or women who attended Bacchus, god of wine.
13. LYCIAN KING: Apollo.

OEDIPUS. You are praying, and it may be that your prayer will be answered; that if you hear my words and do my bidding you may find help out of all your trouble. This is my proclamation, children of Cadmus. Whoever among you knows by what man Laius, son of Labdacus, was killed, must tell all he knows. If he fear for himself and being guilty denounce himself, he shall be in the less danger, suffering no worse thing than banishment. If on the other hand there be one that knows that a foreigner did the deed, let him speak, and I shall give him a reward and my thanks: but if any man keep silent from fear or to screen a friend, hear all what I will do to that man. No one in this land shall speak to him, nor offer sacrifice beside him; but he shall be driven from their homes as if he himself had done the deed. And in this I am the ally of the Pythian God and of the murdered man, and I pray that the murderer's life may, should he be so hidden and screened, drop from him and perish away, whoever he may be, whether he did the deed with others or by himself alone: and on you I lay it to make—so far as man may—these words good, for my sake, and for the God's sake, and for the sake of this land. And even if the God had not spurred us to it, it were a wrong to leave the guilt unpurged, when one so noble, and he your King, had perished; and all have sinned that could have searched it out and did not: and now since it is I who hold the power which he held once, and have his wife for wife—she who would have borne him heirs had he but lived—I take up this cause even as I would were it that of my own father. And if there be any who do not obey me in it, I pray that the Gods send them neither harvest of the earth nor fruit of the womb; but let them be wasted by this plague, or by one more dreadful still. But may all be blessed forever who hear my words and do my will!

CHORUS. We do not know the murderer, and it were indeed more fitting that Phoebus, who laid the task upon us, should name the man.

OEDIPUS. No man can make the Gods speak against their will.

CHORUS. Then I will say what seems the next best thing.

OEDIPUS. If there is a third course, show it.

CHORUS. I know that our lord Tiresias is the seer most like to our lord Phoebus, and through him we may unravel all.

OEDIPUS. So I was advised by Creon, and twice already have I sent to bring him.

CHORUS. If we lack his help we have nothing but vague and ancient rumors.

OEDIPUS. What rumors are they? I would examine every story.

CHORUS. Certain wayfarers were said to have killed the King.

OEDIPUS. I know, I know. But who was there that saw it?

CHORUS. If there is such a man, and terror can move him, he will not keep silence when they have told him of your curses.

OEDIPUS. He that such a deed did not terrify will not be terrified because of a word.

CHORUS. But there is one who shall convict him. For the blind prophet comes at last—in whom alone of all men the truth lives.

Enter TIRESIAS, *led by a boy.*

OEDIPUS. Tiresias, master of all knowledge, whatever may be spoken, whatever is unspeakable, whatever omens of earth and sky reveal, the plague is among us, and from that plague, Great Prophet, protect us and save us. Phoebus in answer to our question says that it will not leave us till we have found the murderers of Laius, and driven them into exile or put them to death. Do you therefore neglect neither the voice of birds,[14] nor any other sort of wisdom, but rescue yourself, rescue the State, rescue me, rescue all that are defiled by the deed. For

---

14. VOICE OF BIRDS: Some of the foreknowledge seers had was commonly thought to come from the voices of birds. Oedipus shows his scorn of such belief several times.

we are in your hands, and what greater task falls to a man than to help other men with all he knows and has?

TIRESIAS. Aye, and what worse task than to be wise and suffer for it? I know this well; it slipped out of mind, or I would never have come.

OEDIPUS. What now?

TIRESIAS. Let me go home. You will bear your burden to the end more easily, and I bear mine—if you but give me leave for that.

OEDIPUS. Your words are strange and unkind to the State that bred you.

TIRESIAS. I see that you, on your part, keep your lips tight shut, and therefore I have shut mine that I may come to no misfortune.

OEDIPUS. For God's love do not turn away—if you have knowledge. We suppliants implore you on our knees.

TIRESIAS. You are fools—I will bring misfortune neither upon you nor upon myself.

OEDIPUS. What is this? You know all and will say nothing? You are minded to betray me and Thebes?

TIRESIAS. Why do you ask these things? You will not learn them from me.

OEDIPUS. What! Basest of the base! You would enrage the very stones. Will you never speak out? Cannot anything touch you?

TIRESIAS. The future will come of itself though I keep silent.

OEDIPUS. Then seeing that come it must, you had best speak out.

TIRESIAS. I will speak no further. Rage if you have a mind to; bring out all the fierceness that is in your heart.

OEDIPUS. That will I. I will not spare to speak my thoughts. Listen to what I have to say. It seems to me that you have helped to plot the deed; and, short of doing it with your own hands, have done the deed yourself. Had you eyesight I would declare that you alone had done it.

TIRESIAS. So that is what you say? I charge you to obey the decree that you yourself have made, and from this day out

to speak neither to these nor to me. You are the defiler of this land.

OEDIPUS. So brazen in your impudence? How do you hope to escape punishment?

TIRESIAS. I have escaped; my strength is in my truth.

OEDIPUS. Who taught you this? You never got it by your art.

TIRESIAS. You, because you have spurred me to speech against my will.

OEDIPUS. What speech? Speak it again that I may learn it better.

TIRESIAS. You are but tempting me—you understood me well enough.

OEDIPUS. No; not so that I can say I know it; speak it again.

TIRESIAS. I say that you are yourself the murderer that you seek.

OEDIPUS. You shall rue it for having spoken twice such outrageous words.

TIRESIAS. Would you that I say more that you may be still angrier?

OEDIPUS. Say what you will. I will not let it move me.

TIRESIAS. I say that you are living with your next of kin in unimagined shame.

OEDIPUS. Do you think you can say such things and never smart for it?

TIRESIAS. Yes, if there be strength in truth.

OEDIPUS. There is; yes—for everyone but you. But not for you that are maimed in ear and in eye and in wit.

TIRESIAS. You are but a poor wretch flinging taunts that in a little while everyone shall fling at you.

OEDIPUS. Night, endless night has covered you up so that you can neither hurt me nor any man that looks upon the sun.

TIRESIAS. Your doom is not to fall by me. Apollo is enough: it is his business to work out your doom.

OEDIPUS. Was it Creon that planned this or you yourself?

TIRESIAS. Creon is not your enemy; you are your own enemy.

OEDIPUS. Power, ability, position, you bear all burdens, and yet what envy you create! Great must that envy be if envy of my power in this town—a power put into my hands unsought—has made trusty Creon, my old friend Creon, secretly long to take that power from me; if he has suborned this scheming juggler, this quack and trickster, this man with eyes for his gains and blindness in his art. Come, come, where did you prove yourself a seer? Why did you say nothing to set the townsmen free when the riddling Sphinx was here? Yet that riddle was not for the first-comer to read; it needed the skill of a seer. And none such had you! Neither found by help of birds, nor straight from any god. No, I came; I silenced her, I the ignorant Oedipus, it was I that found the answer in my mother-wit, untaught by any birds. And it is I that you would pluck out of my place, thinking to stand close to Creon's throne. But you and the plotter of all this shall mourn despite your zeal to purge the land. Were you not an old man, you had already learnt how bold you are and learnt it to your cost.

CHORUS. Both this man's words and yours, Oedipus, have been said in anger. Such words cannot help us here, nor any but those that teach us to obey the oracle.

TIRESIAS. King though you are, the right to answer when attacked belongs to both alike. I am not subject to you, but to Loxias;[15] and therefore I shall never be Creon's subject. And I tell you, since you have taunted me with blindness, that though you have your sight, you cannot see in what misery you stand, nor where you are living, nor with whom, unknowing what you do— for you do not know the stock you come of —you have been your own kin's enemy be they living or be they dead. And one day a mother's curse and father's curse alike shall drive you from this land in dreadful haste with darkness upon those eyes. Therefore, heap your scorn on Creon and on my message if you have a mind to; for no one of living men shall be crushed as you shall be crushed.

OEDIPUS. Begone this instant! Away, away! Get you from these doors!

TIRESIAS. I had never come but that you sent for me.

OEDIPUS. I did not know you were mad.

TIRESIAS. I may seem mad to you, but your parents thought me sane.

OEDIPUS. My parents! Stop! Who was my father?

TIRESIAS. This day shall you know your birth; and it will ruin you.

OEDIPUS. What dark words you always speak!

TIRESIAS. But you are not most skillful in the unraveling of dark words?

OEDIPUS. You mock me for that which made me great?

TIRESIAS. It was that fortune that undid you.

OEDIPUS. What do I care? For I delivered all this town.

TIRESIAS. Then I will go: boy, lead me out of this.

OEDIPUS. Yes, let him lead you. You take vexation with you.

TIRESIAS. I will go: but first I will do my errand. For frown though you may you cannot destroy me. The man for whom you look, the man you have been threatening in all the proclamations about the death of Laius, that man is here. He seems, so far as looks go, an alien; yet he shall be found a native Theban and shall nowise be glad of that fortune. A blind man, though now he has his sight; a beggar, though now he is most rich; he shall go forth feeling the ground before him with his stick; so you go in and think on that, and if you find I am in fault say that I have no skill in prophecy. (TIRESIAS *is led out by the boy.* OEDIPUS *enters the palace.*)

CHORUS. The Delphian rock has spoken out, now must a wicked mind,
　　Planner of things I dare not speak and of this bloody wrack,

---

15. LOXIAS: another name for Apollo.

Pray for feet that are as fast as the four hoofs of the wind:
Cloudy Parnassus[16] and the Fates[17] thunder at his back.

That sacred crossing-place of lines upon Parnassus' head,
Lines that have run through North and South, and run through
      West and East,
That navel of the world[18] bids all men search the mountain wood,
The solitary cavern, till they have found that infamous beast.

CREON *enters from the house.*

CREON. Fellow-citizens, having heard that King Oedipus accuses me of dreadful things, I come in my indignation. Does he think that he has suffered wrong from me in these present troubles, or anything that could lead to wrong, whether in word or deed? How can I live under blame like that? What life would be worth having if by you here, and by my nearest friends, called a traitor through the town?

CHORUS. He said it in anger, and not from his heart out.

CREON. He said it was I put up the seer to speak those falsehoods.

CHORUS. Such things were said.

CREON. And had he his right mind saying it?

CHORUS. I do not know—I do not know what my masters do.

OEDIPUS *enters.*

OEDIPUS. What brought you here? Have you a face so brazen that you come to my house—you, the proved assassin of its master—the certain robber of my crown? Come, tell me in the face of the gods what cowardice, or folly, did you discover in me that you plotted this? Did you think that I would not see what you were at till you had crept upon me, or seeing it would not ward it off? What madness to seek a throne, having neither friends nor followers!

16. PARNASSUS: mountain overlooking Delphi, sacred to Apollo.
17. FATES: the three avenging spirits who punished evildoers.
18. NAVEL OF THE WORLD: a stone at Delphi, thought of as the center of the world.

CREON. Now, listen, hear my answer, and then you may with knowledge judge between us.

OEDIPUS. You are plausible, but waste words now that I know you.

CREON. Hear what I have to say. I can explain it all.

OEDIPUS. One thing you will not explain away—that you are my enemy.

CREON. You are a fool to imagine that senseless stubbornness sits well upon you.

OEDIPUS. And you to imagine that you can wrong a kinsman and escape the penalty.

CREON. That is justly said, I grant you; but what is this wrong that you complain of?

OEDIPUS. Did you advise, or not, that I should send for that notorious prophet?

CREON. And I am of the same mind still.

OEDIPUS. How long is it, then, since Laius—

CREON. What, what about him?

OEDIPUS. Since Laius was killed by an unknown hand?

CREON. That was many years ago.

OEDIPUS. Was this prophet at his trade in those days?

CREON. Yes; skilled as now and in equal honor.

OEDIPUS. Did he ever speak of me?

CREON. Never certainly when I was within earshot.

OEDIPUS. And did you inquire into the murder?

CREON. We did inquire but learnt nothing.

OEDIPUS. And why did he not tell out his story then?

CREON. I do not know. When I know nothing I say nothing.

OEDIPUS. This much at least you know and can say out.

CREON. What is that? If I know it I will say it.

OEDIPUS. That if he had not consulted you he would never have said that it was I who killed Laius.

CREON. You know best what he said; but now, question for question.

OEDIPUS. Question your fill—I cannot be proved guilty of that blood.

CREON. Answer me then. Are you not married to my sister?

OEDIPUS. That cannot be denied.

CREON. And do you not rule as she does? And with a like power?

OEDIPUS. I give her all she asks for.

CREON. And am not I the equal of you both?

OEDIPUS. Yes: and that is why you are so false a friend.

CREON. Not so; reason this out as I reason it, and first weigh this: who would prefer to lie awake amid terrors rather than to sleep in peace, granting that his power is equal in both cases? Neither I nor any sober-minded man. You give me what I ask and let me do what I want, but were I King I would have to do things I did not want to do. Is not influence and no trouble with it better than any throne, am I such a fool as to hunger after unprofitable honors? Now all are glad to see me, everyone wishes me well, all that want a favor from you ask speech of me—finding in that their hope. Why should I give up these things and take those? No wise mind is treacherous. I am no contriver of plots, and if another took to them he would not come to me for help. And in proof of this go to the Pythian Oracle, and ask if I have truly told what the gods said: and after that, if you have found that I have plotted with the Soothsayer, take me and kill me; not by the sentence of one mouth only—but of two mouths, yours and my own. But do not condemn me in a corner, upon some fancy and without proof. What right have you to declare a good man bad or a bad

good? It is as bad a thing to cast off a true friend as it is for a man to cast away his own life—but you will learn these things with certainty when the time comes; for time alone shows a just man; though a day can show a knave.

CHORUS. King! He has spoken well, he gives himself time to think; a headlong talker does not know what he is saying.

OEDIPUS. The plotter is at his work, and I must counterplot headlong, or he will get his ends and I miss mine.

CREON. What will you do then? Drive me from the land?

OEDIPUS. Not so; I do not desire your banishment—but your death.

CREON. You are not sane.

OEDIPUS. I am sane at least in my own interest.

CREON. You should be in mine also.

OEDIPUS. No, for you are false.

CREON. But if you understand nothing?

OEDIPUS. Yet I must rule.

CREON. Not if you rule badly.

OEDIPUS. Hear him, O Thebes!

CREON. Thebes is for me also, not for you alone.

CHORUS. Cease, princes: I see Jocasta coming out of the house; she comes just in time to quench the quarrel.

JOCASTA *enters.*

JOCASTA. Unhappy men! Why have you made this crazy uproar? Are you not ashamed to quarrel about your own affairs when the whole country is in trouble? Go back into the palace, Oedipus, and you, Creon, to your own house. Stop making all this noise about some petty thing.

CREON. Your husband is about to kill me —or to drive me from the land of my fathers.

OEDIPUS. Yes: for I have convicted him of treachery against me.

CREON. Now may I perish accursed if I have done such a thing!

JOCASTA. For God's love believe it, Oedipus. First, for the sake of his oath, and then for my sake, and for the sake of these people here.

CHORUS. (*All*) King, do what she asks.

OEDIPUS. What would you have me do?

CHORUS. Not to make a dishonorable charge, with no more evidence than rumor, against a friend who has bound himself with an oath.

OEDIPUS. Do you desire my exile or my death?

CHORUS. No, by Helios,[19] by the first of all the gods, may I die abandoned by Heaven and earth if I have that thought! What breaks my heart is that our public griefs should be increased by your quarrels.

OEDIPUS. Then let him go, though I am doomed thereby to death or to be thrust dishonored from the land; it is your lips, not his, that move me to compassion; wherever he goes my hatred follows him.

CREON. You are as sullen in yielding as you were vehement in anger, but such natures are their own heaviest burden.

OEDIPUS. Why will you not leave me in peace and be gone?

CREON. I will go away; what is your hatred to me? In the eyes of all here I am a just man. (*He goes.*)

CHORUS. Lady, why do you not take your man in to the house?

JOCASTA. I will do so when I have learnt what has happened.

CHORUS. The half of it was blind suspicion bred of talk; the rest the wounds left by injustice.

JOCASTA. It was on both sides?

CHORUS. Yes.

JOCASTA. What was it?

CHORUS. Our land is vexed enough. Let the thing alone now that it is over. (*Exit* LEADER *of* CHORUS.)

JOCASTA. In the name of the gods, King, what put you in this anger?

OEDIPUS. I will tell you; for I honor you more than these men do. The cause is Creon and his plots against me.

JOCASTA. Speak on, if you can tell clearly how this quarrel arose.

OEDIPUS. He says that I am guilty of the blood of Laius.

JOCASTA. On his own knowledge, or on hearsay?

OEDIPUS. He has made a rascal of a seer his mouthpiece.

JOCASTA. Do not fear that there is truth in what he says. Listen to me, and learn to your comfort that nothing born of woman can know what is to come. I will give you proof of that. An oracle came to Laius once, I will not say from Phoebus, but from his ministers, that he was doomed to die by the hand of his own child sprung from him and me. When his child was but three days old, Laius bound its feet together and had it thrown by sure hands upon a trackless mountain; and when Laius was murdered at the place where three highways meet, it was, or so at least the rumor says, by foreign robbers. So Apollo did not bring it about that the child should kill its father, nor did Laius die in the dreadful way he feared by his child's hand. Yet that was how the message of the seers mapped out the future. Pay no attention to such things. What the God would show he will need no help to show it, but bring it to light himself.

OEDIPUS. What restlessness of soul, lady, has come upon me since I heard you speak, what a tumult of the mind!

JOCASTA. What is this new anxiety? What has startled you?

OEDIPUS. You said that Laius was killed where three highways meet.

JOCASTA. Yes: that was the story.

OEDIPUS. And where is the place?

JOCASTA. In Phocis where the road divides branching off to Delphi and to Daulis.

OEDIPUS. And when did it happen? How many years ago?

JOCASTA. News was published in this town just before you came into power.

OEDIPUS. O Zeus! What have you planned to do unto me?[20]

---

19. HELIOS: the sun; Apollo was the sun god.

20. DO UNTO ME: After this line Yeats has omitted the following two speeches:
Jocas. What is it that weighs on your soul?
Oedip. Don't ask me now; but tell me, what did Laius look like, and how old was he?

JOCASTA. He was tall; the silver had just come into his hair; and in shape not greatly unlike to you.

OEDIPUS. Unhappy that I am! It seems that I have laid a dreadful curse upon myself, and did not know it.

JOCASTA. What do you say? I tremble when I look on you, my King.

OEDIPUS. And I have a misgiving that the seer can see indeed. But I will know it all more clearly, if you tell me one thing more.

JOCASTA. Indeed, though I tremble I will answer whatever you ask.

OEDIPUS. Had he but a small troop with him; or did he travel like a great man with many followers?

JOCASTA. There were but five in all—one of them a herald; and there was one carriage with Laius in it.

OEDIPUS. Alas! It is now clear indeed. Who was it brought the news, lady?

JOCASTA. A servant—the one survivor.

OEDIPUS. Is he by chance in the house now?

JOCASTA. No; for when he found you reigning instead of Laius he besought me, his hand clasped in mine, to send him to the fields among the cattle that he might be far from the sight of this town; and I sent him. He was a worthy man for a slave and might have asked a bigger thing.

OEDIPUS. I would have him return to us without delay.

JOCASTA. Oedipus, it is easy. But why do you ask this?

OEDIPUS. I fear that I have said too much, and therefore I would question him.

JOCASTA. He shall come, but I too have a right to know what lies so heavy upon your heart, my King.

OEDIPUS. Yes: and it shall not be kept from you now that my fear has grown so heavy. Nobody is more to me than you, nobody has the same right to learn my good or evil luck. My father was Polybus of Corinth, my mother the Dorian Merope,[21]

21. POLYBUS . . . MEROPE: Oedipus thought that his father was Polybus, King of Corinth, and that his mother was the Queen, Merope.

and I was held the foremost man in all that town until a thing happened—a thing to startle a man, though not to make him angry as it made me. We were sitting at the table, and a man who had drunk too much cried out that I was not my father's son—and I, though angry, restrained my anger for that day; but the next day went to my father and my mother and questioned them. They were indignant at the taunt and that comforted me —and yet the man's words rankled, for they had spread a rumor through the town. Without consulting my father or my mother I went to Delphi, but Phoebus told me nothing of the thing for which I came, but much of other things—things of sorrow and of terror: that I should live in incest with my mother, and beget a brood that men would shudder to look upon; that I should be my father's murderer. Hearing those words I fled out of Corinth, and from that day have but known where it lies when I have found its direction by the stars. I sought where I might escape those infamous things—the doom that was laid upon me. I came in my flight to that very spot where you tell me this king perished. Now, lady, I will tell you the truth. When I had come close up to those three roads, I came upon a herald, and a man like him you have described seated in a carriage. The man who held the reins and the old man himself would not give me room, but thought to force me from the path, and I struck the driver in my anger. The old man, seeing what I had done, waited till I was passing him and then struck me upon the head. I paid him back in full, for I knocked him out of the carriage with a blow of my stick. He rolled on his back, and after that I killed them all. If this stranger were indeed Laius, is there a more miserable man in the world than the man before you? Is there a man more hated of Heaven? No stranger, no citizen, may receive him into his house, not a soul may speak to him, and no mouth but my own mouth has laid this curse upon me. Am I not wretched? May I be swept from this world before I have endured this doom!

CHORUS. These things, O King, fill us with terror; yet hope till you speak with him that saw the deed, and have learnt all.

OEDIPUS. Till I have learnt all, I may hope. I await the man that is coming from the pastures.

JOCASTA. What is it that you hope to learn?

OEDIPUS. I will tell you. If his tale agrees with yours, then I am clear.

JOCASTA. What tale of mine?

OEDIPUS. He told you that Laius met his death from robbers; if he keeps to that tale now and speaks of several slayers, I am not the slayer. But if he says one lonely way-farer, then beyond a doubt the scale dips to me.

JOCASTA. Be certain of this much at least, his first tale was of robbers. He cannot re-voke that tale—the city heard it and not I alone. Yet, if he should somewhat change his story, King, at least he cannot make the murder of Laius square with prophecy; for Loxias plainly said of Laius that he would die by the hand of my child. That poor innocent did not kill him, for it died before him. Therefore from this out I would not, for all divination can do, so much as look to my right hand or to my left hand, or fear at all.

OEDIPUS. You have judged well; and yet for all that, send and bring this peasant to me.

JOCASTA. I will send without delay. I will do all that you would have of me—but let us come into the house. (*They go into the house.*)

CHORUS.   For this one thing above all I would be praised as a man,
That in my words and my deeds I have kept those laws in mind
Olympian Zeus, and that high clear Empyrean,[22]
Fashioned, and not some man or people of mankind,
Even those sacred laws nor age nor sleep can blind.

A man becomes a tyrant out of insolence,
He climbs and climbs, until all people call him great,
He seems upon the summit, and God flings him thence;
Yet an ambitious man may lift up a whole State,
And in his death be blessed, in his life fortunate.

And all men honor such; but should a man forget
The holy images, the Delphian Sibyl's trance,[23]
And the world's navel-stone, and not be punished for it
And seem most fortunate, or even blessed perchance,
Why should we honor the gods, or join the sacred dance?

JOCASTA *enters from the palace.*

JOCASTA. It has come into my head, citi-zens of Thebes, to visit every altar of the Gods, a wreath in my hand and a dish of in-cense. For all manner of alarms trouble the soul of Oedipus, who instead of weighing new oracles by old, like a man of sense, is at the mercy of every mouth that speaks terror. Seeing that my words are nothing to him, I cry to you, Lycian Apollo, whose altar is the first I meet: I come, a suppliant, bearing symbols of prayer; O, make us clean, for now we are all afraid, seeing him afraid, even as they who see the helmsman afraid.

22. EMPYREAN: the heavens, dwelling place of the gods.
23. DELPHIAN SIBYL'S TRANCE: The priestess (Sibyl) at Delphi was supposed to speak her oracle out of a trance.

Enter MESSENGER.

MESSENGER. May I learn from you, strangers, where is the home of King Oedipus? Or better still, tell me where he himself is, if you know.

CHORUS. This is his house, and he himself, stranger, is within it, and this lady is the mother of his children.

MESSENGER. Then I call a blessing upon her, seeing what man she has married.

JOCASTA. May God reward those words with a like blessing, stranger! But what have you come to seek or to tell?

MESSENGER. Good news for your house, Lady, and for your husband.

JOCASTA. What news? From whence have you come?

MESSENGER. From Corinth, and you will rejoice at the message I am about to give you; yet, maybe, it will grieve you.

JOCASTA. What is it? How can it have this double power?

MESSENGER. The people of Corinth, they say, will take him for king.

JOCASTA. How then? Is old Polybus no longer on the throne?

MESSENGER. No. He is in his tomb.

JOCASTA. What do you say? Is Polybus dead, old man?

MESSENGER. May I drop dead if it is not the truth.

JOCASTA. Away! Hurry to your master with this news. O oracle of the Gods, where are you now? This is the man whom Oedipus feared and shunned lest he should murder him, and now this man has died a natural death, and not by the hand of Oedipus.

Enter OEDIPUS.

OEDIPUS. Jocasta, dearest wife, why have you called me from the house?

JOCASTA. Listen to this man, and judge to what the oracles of the Gods have come.

OEDIPUS. And he—who may he be? And what news has he?

JOCASTA. He has come from Corinth to tell you that your father, Polybus, is dead.

OEDIPUS. How, stranger? Let me have it from your own mouth.

MESSENGER. If I am to tell the story, the first thing is that he is dead and gone.

OEDIPUS. By some sickness or by treachery?

MESSENGER. A little thing can bring the aged to their rest.

OEDIPUS. Ah! He died, it seems, from sickness?

MESSENGER. Yes; and of old age.

OEDIPUS. Alas! Alas! Why, indeed, my wife, should one look to that Pythian seer, or to the birds that scream above our heads? For they would have it that I was doomed to kill my father. And now he is dead—hid already beneath the earth. And here am I—who had no part in it, unless indeed he died from longing for me. If that were so, I may have caused his death; but Polybus has carried the oracles with him into Hades[24]—the oracles as men have understood them—and they are worth nothing.

JOCASTA. Did I not tell you so, long since?

OEDIPUS. You did, but fear misled me.

JOCASTA. Put this trouble from you.[25]

OEDIPUS. Those bold words would sound better, were not my mother living. But as it is—I have some grounds for fear; yet you have said well.

JOCASTA. Yet your father's death is a sign that all is well.

OEDIPUS. I know that: but I fear because of her who lives.

MESSENGER. Who is this woman who makes you afraid?

24. HADES: home of departed spirits.
25. PUT . . . FROM YOU: Several more lines are missing following this one:
Oedip. But how can I not fear marrying my mother?
Jocas. What should any man fear, since Chance rules the world, and no one can know the future. It is wise to live at random, and make the best of what comes. Don't fear marrying your mother. Many a man before you has dreamed of sleeping with his mother. You cannot concern yourself with such things and live an easy life.

OEDIPUS. Merope, old man, the wife of Polybus.

MESSENGER. What is there in her to make you afraid?

OEDIPUS. A dreadful oracle sent from Heaven, stranger.

MESSENGER. Is it a secret, or can you speak it out?

OEDIPUS. Loxias said that I was doomed to marry my own mother, and to shed my father's blood. For that reason I fled from my house in Corinth; and I did right, though there is great comfort in familiar faces.

MESSENGER. Was it indeed for that reason that you went into exile?

OEDIPUS. I did not wish, old man, to shed my father's blood.

MESSENGER. King, have I not freed you from that fear?

OEDIPUS. You shall be fittingly rewarded.

MESSENGER. Indeed, to tell the truth, it was for that I came; to bring you home and be the better for it—

OEDIPUS. *No!* I will never go to my parents' home.

MESSENGER. Ah, my son, it is plain enough, you do not know what you do.

OEDIPUS. How, old man? For God's love, tell me.

MESSENGER. If for these reasons you shrink from going home.

OEDIPUS. I am afraid lest Phoebus has spoken true.

MESSENGER. You are afraid of being made guilty through Merope?

OEDIPUS. That is my constant fear.

MESSENGER. A vain fear.

OEDIPUS. How so, if I was born of that father and mother?

MESSENGER. Because they were nothing to you in blood.

OEDIPUS. What do you say? Was Polybus not my father?

MESSENGER. No more nor less than myself.

OEDIPUS. How can my father be no more to me than you who are nothing to me?

MESSENGER. He did not beget you any more than I.

OEDIPUS. No? Then why did he call me his son?

MESSENGER. He took you as a gift from these hands of mine.

OEDIPUS. How could he love so dearly what came from another's hands?

MESSENGER. He had been childless.

OEDIPUS. If I am not your son, where did you get me?

MESSENGER. In a wooded valley of Cithaeron.[26]

OEDIPUS. What brought you wandering there?

MESSENGER. I was in charge of mountain sheep.

OEDIPUS. A shepherd—a wandering, hired man.

MESSENGER. A hired man who came just in time.

OEDIPUS. Just in time—had it come to that?

MESSENGER. Have not the cords left their marks upon your ankles?

OEDIPUS. Yes, that is an old trouble.

MESSENGER. I took your feet out of the spancel.[27]

OEDIPUS. I have had those marks from the cradle.

MESSENGER. They have given you the name you bear.[28]

OEDIPUS. Tell me, for God's sake, was that deed my mother's or my father's?

MESSENGER. I do not know—he who gave you to me knows more of that than I.

OEDIPUS. What? You had me from another? You did not chance on me yourself?

MESSENGER. No. Another shepherd gave you to me.

OEDIPUS. Who was he? Can you tell me who he was?

MESSENGER. I think that he was said to be of Laius's household.

---

26. CITHAERON: a mountain near Corinth on which Oedipus was to be abandoned.
27. SPANCEL: a fetter used on the feet of animals.
28. NAME YOU BEAR: "Oedipus" means "swollen-foot."

OEDIPUS. The king who ruled this country long ago?

MESSENGER. The same—the man was herdsman in his service.

OEDIPUS. Is he alive, that I might speak with him?

MESSENGER. You people of this country should know that.

OEDIPUS. Is there anyone here present who knows the herd[29] he speaks of? Anyone who has seen him in the town pastures? The hour has come when all must be made clear.

CHORUS. I think he is the very herd you sent for but now; Jocasta can tell you better than I.

JOCASTA. Why ask about that man? Why think about him? Why waste a thought on what this man has said? What he has said is of no account.

OEDIPUS. What, with a clue like that in my hands and fail to find out my birth?

JOCASTA. For God's sake, if you set any value upon your life, give up this search— my misery is enough.

OEDIPUS. Though I be proved the son of a slave, yes, even of three generations of slaves, you cannot be made base-born.

JOCASTA. Yet, hear me, I implore you. Give up this search.

OEDIPUS. I will not hear of anything but searching the whole thing out.

JOCASTA. I am only thinking of your good —I have advised you for the best.

OEDIPUS. Your advice makes me impatient.

JOCASTA. May you never come to know who you are, unhappy man!

OEDIPUS. Go, someone, bring the herdsman here—and let that woman glory in her noble blood.

JOCASTA. Alas, alas, miserable man! Miserable! That is all that I can call you now or forever. (*She goes out.*)

CHORUS. Why has the lady gone, Oedipus, in such a transport of despair? Out of this silence will burst a storm of sorrows.

OEDIPUS. Let come what will. However lowly my origin I will discover it. That woman, with all a woman's pride, grows red with shame at my base birth. I think myself the child of Good Luck, and that the years are my foster-brothers. Sometimes they have set me up, and sometimes thrown me down, but he that has Good Luck for mother can suffer no dishonor. That is my origin, nothing can change it, so why should I renounce this search into my birth?

CHORUS.   Oedipus's nurse, mountain of many a hidden glen,
Be honored among men;
A famous man, deep-thoughted, and his body strong;
Be honored in dance and song.
Who met in the hidden glen? Who let his fancy run
Upon nymph of Helicon?[30]
Lord Pan[31] or Lord Apollo or the mountain lord
By the Bacchantes[32] adored?

OEDIPUS. If I, who have never met the man, may venture to say so, I think that the herdsman we await approaches; his venerable age matches with this stranger's, and I recognize as servants of mine those who bring him. But you, if you have seen the man before, will know the man better than I.

CHORUS. Yes, I know the man who is coming; he was indeed in Laius's service, and is still the most trusted of the herdsmen.

---

29. HERD: i.e., herdsman.
30. NYMPH OF HELICON: Helicon refers to a mountain near Thebes. In contrast to Oedipus's comments about a possible "lowly" origin, the Chorus speculates on the possibility that he is the son of a nymph and a god.
31. PAN: god of pastures, forests, flocks, and herds.
32. BACCHANTES: worshippers of Bacchus.

OEDIPUS. I ask you first, Corinthian stranger, is this the man you mean?

MESSENGER. He is the very man.

OEDIPUS. Look at me, old man! Answer my questions. Were you once in Laius's service?

HERDSMAN. I was: not a bought slave, but reared up in the house.

OEDIPUS. What was your work—your manner of life?

HERDSMAN. For the best part of my life I have tended flocks.

OEDIPUS. Where, mainly?

HERDSMAN. Cithaeron or its neighborhood.

OEDIPUS. Do you remember meeting with this man there?

HERDSMAN. What man do you mean?

OEDIPUS. This man. Did you ever meet him?

HERDSMAN. I cannot recall him to mind.

MESSENGER. No wonder in that, master; but I will bring back his memory. He and I lived side by side upon Cithaeron. I had but one flock and he had two. Three full half-years we lived there, from spring to autumn, and every winter I drove my flock to my own fold, while he drove his to the fold of Laius. Is that right? Was it not so?

HERDSMAN. True enough; though it was long ago.

MESSENGER. Come, tell me now—do you remember giving me a boy to rear as my own foster-son?

HERDSMAN. What are you saying? Why do you ask me that?

MESSENGER. Look at that man, my friend, he is the child you gave me.

HERDSMAN. A plague upon you! Cannot you hold your tongue?

OEDIPUS. Do not blame him, old man; your own words are more blamable.

HERDSMAN. And how have I offended, master?

OEDIPUS. In not telling of that boy he asks of.

HERDSMAN. He speaks from ignorance, and does not know what he is saying.

OEDIPUS. If you will not speak with a good grace you shall be made to speak.

HERDSMAN. Do not hurt me for the love of God, I am an old man.

OEDIPUS. Someone there, tie his hands behind his back.

HERDSMAN. Alas! Wherefore! What more would you learn?

OEDIPUS. Did you give this man the child he speaks of?

HERDSMAN. I did: would I had died that day!

OEDIPUS. Well, you may come to that unless you speak the truth.

HERDSMAN. Much more am I lost if I speak it.

OEDIPUS. What! Would the fellow make more delay?

HERDSMAN. No, no. I said before that I gave it to him.

OEDIPUS. Where did you come by it? Your own child, or another?

HERDSMAN. It was not my own child—I had it from another.

OEDIPUS. From any of those here? From what house?

HERDSMAN. Do not ask any more, master, for the love of God do not ask.

OEDIPUS. You are lost if I have to question you again.

HERDSMAN. It was a child from the house of Laius.

OEDIPUS. A slave? Or one of his own race?

HERDSMAN. Alas! I am on the edge of dreadful words.

OEDIPUS. And I of hearing: yet hear I must.

HERDSMAN. It was said to have been his own child. But your lady within can tell you of these things best.

OEDIPUS. How? It was she who gave it to you?

HERDSMAN. Yes, King.

OEDIPUS. To what end?

HERDSMAN. That I should make away with it.

OEDIPUS. Her own child?

HERDSMAN. Yes: from fear of evil prophecies.

OEDIPUS. What prophecies?

HERDSMAN. That he should kill his father.

OEDIPUS. Why, then, did you give him up to this old man?

HERDSMAN. Through pity, master, believing that he would carry him to whatever land he had himself come from—but he saved him for dreadful misery; for if you are what this man says, you are the most miserable of all men.

OEDIPUS. O! O! All brought to pass! All truth! Now O light, may I look my last upon you, having been found accursed in bloodshed, accursed in marriage, and in my coming into the world accursed! (*He rushes into the palace.*)

CHORUS. What can the shadow-like generations of man attain
But build up a dazzling mockery of delight that under their
    touch dissolves again?
Oedipus seemed blessed, but there is no man blessed amongst men.

Oedipus overcame the woman-breasted Fate;[33]
He seemed like a strong tower against Death and first among
    the fortunate;
He sat upon the ancient throne of Thebes, and all men called him great.

But, looking for a marriage-bed, he found the bed of his birth,
Tilled the field his father had tilled, cast seed into the same
    abounding earth;
Entered through the door that had sent him wailing forth.

Begetter and begot as one! How could that be hid?
What darkness cover up that marriage-bed? Time watches, he is
    eagle-eyed,
And all the works of man are known and every soul is tried.

Would you had never come to Thebes, nor to this house,
Nor riddled with the woman-breasted Fate, beaten off Death and
    succored us,
That I had never raised this song, heartbroken Oedipus!

SECOND MESSENGER *coming from the house.*

SECOND MESSENGER. Friends and kinsmen of this house! What deeds must you look upon, what burden of sorrow bear, if true to race you still love the House of Labdacus. For not Ister nor Phasis[34] could wash this house clean, so many misfortunes have been brought upon it, so many has it brought upon itself, and those misfortunes are always the worst that a man brings upon himself.

CHORUS. Great already are the misfortunes of this house, and you bring us a new tale.

SECOND MESSENGER. A short tale in the telling: Jocasta, our Queen, is dead.

CHORUS. Alas, miserable woman, how did she die?

SECOND MESSENGER. By her own hand. It cannot be as terrible to you as to one that saw it with his eyes, yet so far as words can serve, you shall see it. When she had come into the vestibule, she ran half crazed towards her marriage-bed, clutching at her hair with the fingers of both hands, and once

---

33. WOMAN-BREASTED FATE: the Sphinx.
34. ISTER NOR PHASIS: ancient names for the Danube and Rion Rivers.

within the chamber dashed the doors together behind her. Then called upon the name of Laius, long since dead, remembering that son who killed the father and upon the mother begot an accursed race. And wailed because of that marriage wherein she had borne a twofold race—husband by husband, children by her child. Then Oedipus with a shriek burst in and running here and there asked for a sword, asked where he would find the wife that was no wife but a mother who had borne his children and himself. Nobody answered him, we all stood dumb; but supernatural power helped him, for, with a dreadful shriek, as though beckoned, he sprang at the double doors, drove them in, burst the bolts out of their sockets, and ran into the room. There we saw the woman hanging in a swinging halter, and with a terrible cry he loosened the halter from her neck. When that unhappiest woman lay stretched upon the ground, we saw another dreadful sight. He dragged the golden brooches from her dress and lifting them struck them upon his eyeballs, crying out, "You have looked enough upon those you ought never to have looked upon, failed long enough to know those that you should have known; henceforth you shall be dark." He struck his eyes, not once, but many times, lifting his hands and speaking such or like words. The blood poured down and not with a few slow drops, but all at once over his beard in a dark shower as it were hail. (*The* CHORUS *wails and he steps further on to the stage.*) Such evils have come forth from the deeds of those two and fallen not on one alone but upon husband and wife. They inherited much happiness, much good fortune; but today, ruin, shame, death, and loud crying, all evils that can be counted up, all, all are theirs.

CHORUS. Is he any quieter?

SECOND MESSENGER. He cries for someone to unbar the gates and to show to all the men of Thebes his father's murderer, his mother's—the unholy word must not be spoken. It is his purpose to cast himself out of the land that he may not bring all this house under his curse. But he has not the strength to do it. He must be supported and led away. The curtain is parting; you are going to look upon a sight which even those who shudder must pity.

Enter OEDIPUS.

OEDIPUS. Woe, woe, is me! Miserable, miserable that I am! Where am I? Where am I going? Where am I cast away? Who hears my words?

CHORUS. Cast away indeed, dreadful to the sight of the eye, dreadful to the ear.

OEDIPUS. Ah, friend, the only friend left to me, friend still faithful to the blind man! I know that you are there; blind though I am, I recognize your voice.

CHORUS. Where did you get the courage to put out your eyes? What unearthly power drove you to that?

OEDIPUS. Apollo, friends, Apollo, but it was my own hand alone, wretched that I am, that quenched these eyes.

CHORUS. You were better dead than blind.

OEDIPUS. No, it is better to be blind. What sight is there that could give me joy? How could I have looked into the face of my father when I came among the dead, aye, or on my miserable mother, since against them both I sinned such things that no halter can punish? And what to me this spectacle, town, statue, wall, and what to me this people, since I, thrice wretched, I, noblest of Theban men, have doomed myself to banishment, doomed myself when I commanded all to thrust out the unclean thing?

CHORUS. It had indeed been better if that herdsman had never taken your feet out of the spancel or brought you back to life.

OEDIPUS. O three roads, O secret glen; O coppice and narrow way where three roads met; you that drank up the blood I spilt, the blood that was my own, my father's blood: remember what deeds I wrought for you to look upon, and then, when I had come hither, the new deeds that I wrought. O marriage bed that gave me birth and after that gave children to your child, creating an incestuous kindred of fathers, brothers, sons, wives, and mothers. Yes, all the shame and the uncleanness that I have wrought among men.

CHORUS. For all my pity I shudder and turn away.

OEDIPUS. Come near, condescend to lay your hands upon a wretched man; listen, do not fear. My plague can touch no man but me. Hide me somewhere out of this land for God's sake, or kill me, or throw me into the sea where you shall never look upon me more.

Enter CREON *and attendants.*

CHORUS. Here Creon comes at a fit moment; you can ask of him what you will, help or counsel, for he is now in your place. He is King.

OEDIPUS. What can I say to him? What can I claim, having been altogether unjust to him?

CREON. I have not come in mockery, Oedipus, nor to reproach you. Lead him into the house as quickly as you can. Do not let him display his misery before strangers.

OEDIPUS. I must obey, but first, since you have come in so noble a spirit, you will hear me.

CREON. Say what you will.

OEDIPUS. I know that you will give her that lies within such a tomb as befits your own blood, but there is something more, Creon. My sons are men and can take care of themselves, but my daughters, my two unhappy daughters, that have ever eaten at my own table and shared my food, watch over my daughters, Creon. If it is lawful, let me touch them with my hands. Grant it, Prince, grant it, noble heart. I would believe, could I touch them, that I still saw them. (ISMENE *and* ANTIGONE *are led in by attendants.*) But do I hear them sobbing? Has Creon pitied me and sent my children, my darlings? Has he done this?

CREON. Yes, I ordered it, for I know how greatly you have always loved them.

OEDIPUS. Then may you be blessed, and may Heaven be kinder to you than it has been to me! My children, where are you? Come hither—hither—come to the hands of him whose mother was your mother; the hands that put out your father's eyes, eyes once as bright as your own; his who, understanding nothing, seeing nothing, became your father by her that bore him. I weep when I think of the bitter life that men will make you live, and the days that are to come. Into what company dare you go, to what festival, but that you shall return home from it not sharing in the joys, but bathed in tears? When you are old enough to be married, what man dare face the reproach that must cling to you and to your children? What misery is there lacking? Your father killed his father, he begat you at the spring of his own being, offspring of her that bore him. That is the taunt that would be cast upon you and on the man that you should marry. That man is not alive; my children, you must wither away in barrenness. Ah, son of Menoeceus, listen. Seeing that you are the only father now left to them, for we their parents are lost, both of us lost, do not let them wander in beggary—are they not your own kindred?—do not let them sink down into my misery. No, pity them, seeing them utterly wretched in helpless childhood if you do not protect them. Show me that you promise, generous man, by touching me with your hand. (CREON *touches him.*) My children, there is much advice that I would give you were you but old enough to understand, but all I can do now is bid you pray that you may live wherever you are let live, and that your life be happier than your father's.

CREON. Enough of tears. Pass into the house.

OEDIPUS. I will obey, though upon conditions.

CREON. Conditions?

OEDIPUS. Banish me from this country. I know that nothing can destroy me, for I wait some incredible fate; yet cast me upon Cithaeron, chosen by my father and my mother for my tomb.

CREON. Only the gods can say yes or no to that.

OEDIPUS. No, for I am hateful to the gods.

CREON. If that be so you will get your wish the quicker. They will banish that which they hate.

OEDIPUS. Are you certain of that?

CREON. I would not say it if I did not mean it.

OEDIPUS. Then it is time to lead me within.

CREON. Come, but let your children go.

OEDIPUS. No, do not take them from me.

CREON. Do not seek to be master; you won the mastery but could not keep it to the end. (*He leads* OEDIPUS *into the palace, followed by* ISMENE, ANTIGONE, *and attendants.*)

CHORUS. Make way for Oedipus. All people said,
"That is a fortunate man";
And now what storms are beating on his head!
Call no man fortunate that is not dead.
The dead are free from pain.

I

1. Outline briefly the movement of the play. How is each piece of information almost forced into the open by unintended revelations: Tiresias determined to remain silent, but goaded into speaking; Jocasta making a casual reference to a place "where three highways meet"? Show that it's a poor observation to insist that "if Oedipus were as smart as he's supposed to be, he would have jumped to the right conclusion long before he stumbled on it."

2. What sort of man is Oedipus? How is the audience convinced that he is a man of great ability? What might be called faults in his character? Consider his treatment of Tiresias and Creon. How does he change during the course of the play?

3. Characterize Tiresias, Creon, and Jocasta. Why doesn't Tiresias want to reveal what he knows? Why does he do so? What are Creon's strengths and weaknesses? In what ways is Jocasta like Oedipus? How is she unlike him?

4. Indicate specifically what comment on the action of the play each choral ode brings out. If the Chorus is representative of the attitude of the citizens of Thebes, characterize them. What would be lost if the choral odes were omitted? In other words, how do the comments of the Chorus provide a background of normal behavior and belief against which the actions of Oedipus are viewed?

5. There is no secret in the play, to audience or reader, about what has happened or what will happen, although the characters themselves act in ignorance until the full truth is known. This fact sets up what is known as *dramatic irony:* almost everything said has more meaning to the audience than to those in the play, and the extra meaning has ironic overtones. For instance, early in the play Oedipus says to the citizens, "sufferers though you be, there is not a single one whose suffering is as mine—." He simply means that as a good ruler he naturally takes on the burdens of all his subjects. The audience gets this meaning, plus the ironic one that no man could be more wretched than Oedipus is, and will soon know himself to be. To see fully how important a part dramatic irony plays in *King Oedipus*, point out as many examples of it as you can.

6. There is another form of irony operating in *King Oedipus*. A number of things happen as the plot unfolds that are complete reversals of what is or might be expected: from being *foremost of living men* Oedipus becomes *accursed* beyond all other men; when he has his eyesight, he is truly *blind*, but when he puts out his eyes, it is because he at last *sees* clearly. There are many other examples of this ironic reversal; indicate as many as you can.

7. Point out the number of references to light-darkness and sight-blindness. How does the use of such imagery support the theme of the play?

II

1. Is Oedipus simply the innocent victim of some malign Fate, a puppet acting out the plans of the gods? What is the difference between something's being preordained and simply predicted? Show that the characters themselves, particularly Oedipus, feel that they are acting with free will. For instance, does he ever complain of divine injustice? What is the self-knowledge Oedipus comes to?

2. How does *King Oedipus* illustrate the characteristics of tragedy that Aristotle described (see "Tragedy" in the Glossary of Literary Terms at the end of the book). Aristotle based his discussion chiefly on this play by Sophocles.

3. We said in the introduction to the play that in *King Oedipus* Sophocles was obviously commenting on the "idolatry of man—self-made, self-sufficient" that was infecting Athenian society. There is little doubt that he was doing so, but if this were all that he was doing, the play would not have retained the impact on the imagination that is as vital today as it must have been twenty-four centuries ago. What is there in the man Oedipus and in the terror that he inherits and creates that makes *King Oedipus* more than simply a parable on pride of achievement?

"*Love is ever the beginning of
knowledge, as fire is of light.*"

Thomas Carlyle, *The Death of Goethe*

Unit Three

LOVE

Love, though a single word, may refer to many states of mind and feeling inspired by many kinds of objects. We speak of "love" for God, for our fellow man, for the members of our family. We single out a particular member of the opposite sex and fall in "love." We learn to "love" justice and liberty and our native land. We often "love" books or music. We may even "love" peanuts. Of course, there are words other than "love" available, synonyms that narrow the area of meaning to "devotion," "friendship," "affection," "adoration," "passion," "liking," and many more. But most of us continue to use "love" in preference to its synonyms unless we have a particular reason for being more precise.

Perhaps we are being wiser than we realize. Perhaps there is in the variety of attitudes and feelings covered by the single word "love" an essential unity that the single word underscores. Is the love of God for man and man for God a thing apart from earthly expressions of affection, desire, friendship, or service? Or is there common to all these relationships the idea that man finds fulfillment in going beyond himself to others? Perhaps the words of St. Paul to the Corinthians sum up best what love is:

Though I speak with the tongues of men
    and of angels,
And have not charity [love],
I am become as sounding brass,
Or a tinkling cymbal.
And though I have the gift of prophecy,
And understand all mysteries, and all
    knowledge;
And though I have all faith,
So that I could remove mountains,
And have not charity,
I am nothing.

We may well agree that if we "have not love," either to give or receive, we are "nothing," but agreement will not necessarily bring the desired state. The search for love demands, first of all, a rejection of the fakeries that too easily pass for it: the burning flame of a pulp magazine romance; the tired love ballad, without freshness or sincerity, coasting along on the rhyme of moon and June; the maudlin sentiments we often express but seldom feel. The second step in the search for love is to realize under how many outward forms it may be concealed. Expressions of delight, pain, despair, banter, scorn, frustration may all issue from a genuinely loving heart, as the selections which follow show.

You will find a majority of these selections concerned with love between man and woman, and that is as it should be if we want to reflect in this book the balance found in literature as a whole. But even so, the scope here is necessarily far broader than the notion of romantic love, broader even than the total pattern of relations between the sexes. For love, as we said at the beginning, has varying objects, and kindles varying moods. If these moods are sometimes dark ones, this fact is all the more a tribute to love's power. The demands love makes on the giving of oneself to another or others are too great to admit of easy satisfaction. We grow into love through growing out of self-centeredness, and we do it with pain as well as joy.

In Praise of Love

The nine poems that open this section are some of the best known "love poems" in English. You will find differences between them, but essentially they sing quite unashamedly the praises of fair and beautiful women in terms that have been common to English literature since the Middle Ages.

Even though the love poem has been in the forefront of our literature and our thought for seven or eight centuries, the idea of idealized, romantic love is, as C. S. Lewis points out in his illuminating book, *The Allegory of Love,* European in origin and relatively recent. Far from being either natural or common to mankind, he maintains, "there can be no mistake about the novelty of romantic love; our difficulty is to imagine in all its bareness the mental world that existed before its coming—to wipe out of our minds . . . nearly all that makes the food both of modern sentimentality and modern cynicism. We must conceive a world emptied of that ideal of 'happiness'—a happiness grounded on successful romantic love—which still supplies the motive of our popular fiction. In ancient literature [and in that of the Dark Ages and of such societies as Japan and India] love seldom rises above the levels of merry sensuality or domestic comfort, except to be treated as tragic madness."*

The modern Western world may be almost alone in its commitment to romantic love, but it has pursued that commitment with an intensity that convinces most of us that it speaks the truth about the relationship between men and women.

TO CELIA   [*1616*]

Ben Jonson

Drink to me only with thine eyes,
  And I will pledge with mine;
Or leave a kiss but in the cup
  And I'll not look for wine.
The thirst that from the soul doth rise   5
  Doth ask a drink divine;
But might I of Jove's nectar sup,
  I would not change for thine.

I sent thee late a rosy wreath,
  Not so much honoring thee   10
As giving it a hope that there
  It could not withered be;
But thou thereon didst only breathe
  And sent'st it back to me;
Since when it grows, and smells, I swear   15
  Not of itself but thee!

---

* C. S. Lewis, *The Allegory of Love* (New York: Oxford University Press).

I

1. To what is the loved lady compared throughout the first stanza? State why the lady will feel more and more complimented as she comes to each couplet in the stanza. (In doing this it will be helpful to imagine first that the stanza ends with line 2, then with line 4, then with line 6, finally with line 8.)

2. What exactly is the compliment that is paid the lady in stanza 2? In what way can it be said to be greater than any paid her in stanza 1?

3. How would you characterize the relationship between the two lovers? Judging from the behavior described in lines 13-14, should the lover give up hope? Can this behavior be interpreted as meaning the opposite of what it might seem to mean? What indication is there that the lover is choosing so to interpret it?

4. Describe the tone of the lover's address to the lady. Is it formal and polite? prim and proper? coy and artful? none of these? How would the tone of lines 1-4 alter if "with mine" (2) were replaced by "from here," and "wine" in line 4 by "beer"? Why?

MY LUVE IS LIKE A RED, RED ROSE [*1796*]

Robert Burns

O my luve is like a red, red rose,
  That's newly sprung in June:
O my luve is like the melodie,
  That's sweetly played in tune.

As fair art thou, my bonie lass,   5
  So deep in luve am I;
And I will luve thee still, my dear,
  Till a' the seas gang dry.

Till a' the seas gang dry, my dear,
  And the rocks melt wi' the sun;   10
And I will luve thee still, my dear,
  While the sands o' life shall run.

And fare thee weel, my only luve!
  And fare thee weel a while!
And I will come again, my luve,   15
  Tho' it were ten thousand mile.

8. A': all. GANG: go.

13. WEEL: well.

I

1. Does the comparison of the lady to a *red, red rose* depend on actual likenesses that can be imagined between a beautiful girl and a red rose in June? or on the fact that he feels about his loved one as one may feel about a beautiful rose? or on both? Ask yourself the same questions with respect to the *melodie*.

2. If the "sands o' life" in line 12 refer to his life, in what way would lines 11-12 be an anticlimax, coming after lines 7-10? How can "sands o' life" be understood so as to avoid this anticlimax?

3. Compare the following four lines with Burns's first stanza. Roughly speaking, they say the same thing. What makes Burns's lines superior?

O my luve is like a flower fair
  That blossoms late in May;
O my luve is like a sprightly song
  That's whistled all the day.

4. How do the exaggerations of the poem help communicate to us the lover's feeling? Are there exaggerations also in the preceding poem? How would you differentiate these from those?

II

1. Compare the tone of this lover's address with that of the lover in the preceding poem. Which seems to have more energy and impetuousness? Which seems to have more sophistication and restraint? How does the rhythm in each poem support and emphasize the tone?

SHE WAS A PHANTOM OF DELIGHT [*1804*]

William Wordsworth

She was a phantom of delight
When first she gleamed upon my sight;
A lovely apparition, sent
To be a moment's ornament;
Her eyes as stars of twilight fair;   5
Like twilight's, too, her dusky hair;
But all things else about her drawn
From Maytime and the cheerful dawn;   10
A dancing shape, an image gay,
To haunt, to startle, and waylay.

I saw her upon nearer view,
A spirit, yet a woman too!
Her household motions light and free,
And steps of virgin-liberty;

A countenance in which did meet   15
Sweet records, promises as sweet;
A creature not too bright or good
For human nature's daily food;
For transient sorrows, simple wiles,
Praise, blame, love, kisses, tears, and
    smiles.   20

And now I see with eye serene
The very pulse of the machine;
A being breathing thoughtful breath,
A traveler between life and death;
The reason firm, the temperate will,   25
Endurance, foresight, strength, and skill;
A perfect woman, nobly planned,
To warn, to comfort, and command;
And yet a spirit still, and bright
With something of angelic light.   30

---

1. SHE: refers to Mary Hutchinson, whom Wordsworth knew from childhood and married in 1802.

I

1. What does "phantom" mean in line 1 and "apparition" in line 3? How is the idea contained in these two words further stressed in the rest of the stanza?

2. How does the poet's point of view shift in stanza 2? What word in line 12 sums up the conception of the girl put forth in stanza 1? What word sums up the new conception put forth in this stanza? What other elements in the stanza confirm this new and changed conception of the young lady? How do lines 17-20 especially modify the old conception?

3. When is the "now" of line 21? How is stanza 3 a summation, or bringing together, of the conceptions in stanzas 1 and 2?

4. What indications are there that the three stanzas describe the lady at three different ages, and in three different kinds of relationship to the speaker? What are the ages? and the kinds of relationship?

SHE WALKS IN BEAUTY   [*1815*]

George Gordon, Lord Byron

She walks in beauty, like the night
  Of cloudless climes and starry skies;
And all that's best of dark and bright
  Meet in her aspect and her eyes:
Thus mellowed to that tender light   5
  Which heaven to gaudy day denies.

One shade the more, one ray the less,
  Had half impaired the nameless grace,
Which waves in every raven tress,

Or softly lightens o'er her face;   10
Where thoughts serenely sweet express
  How pure, how dear their dwelling-place.

And on that cheek, and o'er that brow,
  So soft, so calm, yet eloquent,
The smiles that win, the tints that glow,   15
  But tell of days in goodness spent,
A mind at peace with all below,
  A heart whose love is innocent!

---

1. SHE: Lady Wilmot Horton, Byron's cousin. He saw her at a ball, dressed in mourning, with silver spangles on her dress.

I

1. The speaker in lines 1-2 compares his lady's beauty to that of a particular kind of night—a night of "cloudless climes and starry skies." What phrases in later lines of the poem pick up and repeat the idea that her beauty is to be associated with the night? What later phrases pick up and repeat the idea that her beauty is to be associated with "cloudless climes"? with "starry skies"?

2. What do lines 17-18 mean?

II

1. Compare the praise bestowed on the lady who *walks in beauty* with that bestowed on the one who is a *phantom of delight*. What kind of beauty is each speaker most concerned about? Which lady is more attractive to you and why?

UPON JULIA'S CLOTHES   [*1648*]

Robert Herrick

Whenas in silks my Julia goes,
Then, then, methinks, how sweetly flows
That liquefaction of her clothes.

Next, when I cast mine eyes and see
That brave vibration each way free,
Oh, how that glittering taketh me!   5

---

1. WHENAS: when.

5. BRAVE: bright and splendid.

I

1. What quality in the silk of Julia's clothes is the speaker concerned with in the first stanza? How does the word *liquefaction* sum up this quality?

2. What causes the *brave vibration* of line 5? What does "each way free" mean? What quality is the speaker concerned with in stanza 2? What word sums it up?

3. How is the sense of "flowing" produced in the rhythm? Note particularly how line 2 moves into line 3, and line 4 into line 5. What is the effect of the rush of "Then, then, me-thinks . . ." (2) and "Oh, how that glittering taketh me" (6)?

4. Why isn't the title "Julia" instead of "Upon Julia's Clothes"?

STELLA'S BIRTHDAY   *[1719]*

Jonathan Swift

Stella this day is thirty-four
(We shan't dispute a year or more)—
However, Stella, be not troubled,
Although thy size and years are doubled,
Since first I saw thee at sixteen,   5
The brightest virgin on the green,
So little is thy form declined;
Made up so largely in thy mind.
   Oh, would it please the gods, to split
Thy beauty, size, and years, and wit;   10
No age could furnish out a pair
Of nymphs so graceful, wise, and fair:
With half the luster of your eyes,
With half your wit, your years, and size.
And then, before it grew too late,   15
How should I beg of gentle Fate
(That either nymph might have her swain)
To split my worship too in twain.

1. STELLA: Esther Johnson, whom Swift first knew as a pupil and had a deep affection for all his life.

6. VIRGIN: young girl. GREEN: town common.

7. FORM: essential character.

I

1. Indicate specifically how the speaker makes varied and flattering use of the processes of doubling and halving.

2. What is the effect of bringing up the lady's age in the very first line? Is the speaker being ungallant in referring to Stella's size as well as to her beauty and wit? What does "size" mean in the poem?

3. Why does the speaker ask Fate "to split my worship too in twain"?

II

1. Compare the tone taken toward the lady by the speaker of the poem with that taken in any or all of the preceding poems in this section.

LOVING IN TRUTH   [*1591*]

Sir Philip Sidney

Loving in truth, and fain in verse my love to show,
   That she, dear she, might take some pleasure of my pain,
   Pleasure might cause her read, reading might make her know,
   Knowledge might pity win, and pity grace obtain,—
I sought fit words to paint the blackest face of woe;   5
   Studying inventions fine, her wits to entertain,
   Oft turning others' leaves to see if thence would flow
   Some fresh and fruitful showers upon my sun-burned brain.
But words came halting forth, wanting invention's stay;
   Invention, nature's child, fled step-dame Study's blows,   10
   And others' feet still seemed but strangers in my way.
Thus, great with child to speak, and helpless in my throes,
   Biting my truant pen, beating myself for spite,
   Fool, said my muse to me, look in thy heart and write.

Title: This is the first of a long sonnet-sequence
   (108 sonnets) called "Astrophel and Stella"
   ("star-lover and star") that Sidney addressed
   to Penelope Devereaux.

9. STAY: support.

I

1. What do the following mean:
a. "my sun-burned brain" (8).
b. "Invention, nature's child, fled step-dame
   Study's blows" (10).
c. "great with child to speak" (12).
2. What line in lines 9-14 comes closest to
meaning: "You can lead a horse to water but
you can't make him drink"?
3. What word in line 11 shows that the *others*
whose *leaves* he was turning were writers of
verse?
4. In lines 1-4 the speaker pictures himself
trying to write a poem expressing his love so
that his lady might "take some pleasure of my
pain." State exactly in your own words the
lady's action as imagined by the speaker. What
pain does he refer to in line 2: the pain of
his love for her? or the pain required to write
in verse? Which of the two reasons might
reasonably anger the lady?
5. What words in lines 5-8 suggest that he is
at this stage more interested in "laying it on
thick" than in expressing what he actually
feels? What is the inevitable result of the effort
to *entertain?*

LOVE AMONG THE RUINS [*1855*]

Robert Browning

Where the quiet-colored end of evening smiles
   Miles and miles
On the solitary pastures where our sheep
   Half-asleep
Tinkle homeward through the twilight, stray or stop   5
   As they crop—
Was the site once of a city great and gay,
   (So they say)
Of our country's very capital, its prince
   Ages since   10
Held his court in, gathered councils, wielding far
   Peace or war.

Now,—the country does not even boast a tree,
   As you see,
To distinguish slopes of verdure, certain rills   15
   From the hills
Intersect and give a name to, (else they run
   Into one)
Where the domed and daring palace shot its spires
   Up like fires   20
O'er the hundred-gated circuit of a wall
   Bounding all,
Made of marble, men might march on nor be pressed,
   Twelve abreast.

And such plenty and perfection, see, of grass   25
   Never was!
Such a carpet as, this summer-time, o'erspreads
   And imbeds
Every vestige of the city, guessed alone,
   Stock or stone—   30
Where a multitude of men breathed joy and woe
   Long ago:
Lust of glory pricked their hearts up, dread of shame
   Struck them tame;
And that glory and that shame alike, the gold   35
   Bought and sold.

Now,—the single little turret that remains
   On the plains,
By the caper overrooted, by the gourd
   Overscored,   40
While the patching houseleek's head of blossom winks
   Through the chinks—
Marks the basement whence a tower in ancient time
   Sprang sublime,
And a burning ring, all round, the chariots traced   45
   As they raced,
And the monarch and his minions and his dames
   Viewed the games.

And I know, while thus the quiet-colored eve
   Smiles to leave   50
To their folding, all our many-tinkling fleece
   In such peace.
And the slopes and rills in undistinguished grey
   Melt away—
That a girl with eager eyes and yellow hair   55
   Waits me there
In the turret whence the charioteers caught soul
   For the goal,
When the king looked, where she looks now, breathless, dumb
   Till I come.   60

But he looked upon the city, every side,
   Far and wide,
All the mountains topped with temples, all the glades'
   Colonnades,
All the causeys, bridges, aqueducts,—and then,   65
   All the men!
When I do come, she will speak not, she will stand,
   Either hand
On my shoulder, give her eyes the first embrace
   Of my face,   70
Ere we rush, ere we extinguish sight and speech
   Each on each.

In one year they sent a million fighters forth
   South and North,
And they built their gods a brazen pillar high   75
   As the sky,
Yet reserved a thousand chariots in full force—
   Gold, of course.

Oh, heart! oh, blood that freezes, blood that burns!
   Earth's returns   80
For whole centuries of folly, noise and sin!
   Shut them in,
With their triumphs and their glories and the rest!
   Love is best.

I

1. What contrast is emphasized in the first four stanzas? By what specific details is the contrast developed?

2. What new contrast is introduced in stanza 5? What change in emphasis, insofar as the contrasts are concerned, occurs in stanzas 6 and 7? What change in the order of presentation occurs in stanza 6 and why? How does the change in order grow naturally out of stanza 5?

3. How is the presentation of the contrast in the last stanza quite different from that in the other six? Consider the word choices in lines 75-81. How does Browning force the reader to focus unusual attention on the last line, "Love is best"?

4. The verse form is unusual. Try to characterize the rhythm achieved through the contrast of long and short lines and the echoing effect of rhymes coming so close upon one another. How does the rhythmic structure of the poem support Browning's position that the soothing power of human love and gentle nature is enduring and that the pomp and glory of *whole centuries of folly, noise and sin* is not?

A VALEDICTION:

FORBIDDING MOURNING   *[1633]*

John Donne

As virtuous men pass mildly away,
   And whisper to their souls to go,
Whilst some of their sad friends do say,
   "The breath goes now," and some say,
      "No,"

So let us melt and make no noise,   5
   No tear-floods nor sigh-tempests move;
'Twere profanation of our joys
   To tell the laity our love.

Moving of th' earth brings harms and fears;
   Men reckon what it did and meant;   10
But trepidation of the spheres,
   Though greater far, is innocent.

---

9. MOVING . . . EARTH: earthquakes.
11. TREPIDATION . . . SPHERES: refers to the far greater but unnoticeable movement which was believed to occur in the concentric spheres that in Donne's time were thought to hold the earth, sun, planets and "fixed stars" in their places.
12. INNOCENT: harmless.

Title. VALEDICTION: A valediction is a farewell or leave-taking. Donne wrote this poem on the occasion of a necessary absence from his wife.

Dull sublunary lovers' love,
  Whose soul is sense, cannot admit
Absence, because it doth remove   15
  Those things which elemented it.

But we by a love so much refined
  That ourselves know not what it is,
Interassurèd of the mind,
  Care less eyes, lips, and hands to miss.   20

Our two souls, therefore, which are one,
  Though I must go, endure not yet
A breach, but an expansion,
  Like gold to airy thinness beat.

If they be two, they are two so   25
  As stiff twin compasses are two;
Thy soul, the fixed foot, makes no show
  To move, but doth if th' other do.

And though it in the center sit,
  Yet when the other far doth roam,   30
It leans and hearkens after it,
  And grows erect as that comes home.

Such wilt thou be to me, who must,
  Like th' other foot, obliquely run;
Thy firmness makes my circle just,   35
  And makes me end where I begun.

---

14. WHOSE . . . SENSE: i.e., the essential part of which is physical feeling or sensation.
16. ELEMENTED IT: i.e., made up its elements.

26. STIFF TWIN COMPASSES: dividers, used in mechanical drawing, etc., for making circles and arcs.
35. JUST: perfect.

I

1. In stanzas 1 and 2 what is there about the death of *virtuous men* that the speaker commends to his beloved as a model for their leave-taking? Who, from the lovers' point of view, are *the laity?* What does the use of that word—and of *profanation* in the preceding line—suggest about the character of the lovers' love?

2. How is stanza 3 related to stanzas 1 and 2? In other words, what is the speaker saying further about the differences between their love and the kind of love *the laity* knows?

3. In stanzas 4 and 5 what further distinction is the speaker making between "the laity" and the "we" of the poem?

4. Explain the image in line 24. How does it further develop the distinction made in stanzas 4, 5, and 6?

5. The "stiff twin compasses" of line 26 are not two compasses but the two legs of a single compass. Show clearly how the analogy is carefully developed, and how it is related to the central idea of the poem. Is the image appropriate in a poem on love? Why or why not?

II

1. Each of the last three poems centers on the relationship between man and woman from widely different points of view. The first, "Loving in Truth," is a consciously playful complimentary piece designed to flatter and, if accepted at all, to be accepted as elaborate flattery. "Love among the Ruins" pits love against the worship of power and glory and asserts quietly the ascendancy of love. "A Valediction: Forbidding Mourning" is an ingenious and daring intellectual argument that "proves" the indissolubility of a perfect love. Despite the great differences of treatment, each is an expression of romantic feeling about a woman. Which seems to you most successful as an expression of love, and why?

THE EVE OF ST. AGNES [*1820*]

John Keats

Each of the preceding poems celebrates in varying moods the beauty of body and mind that poets have found in women. Each is, moreover, a song of praise to romantic love, whether in the manner of Jonson's elaborate compliments, Wordsworth's delight in domestic virtues, Byron's adoration of pure beauty that bespeaks a pure heart, or Donne's subtle proofs that true lovers can never be separated.

Many of the attitudes seen thus far are present in John Keats's "The Eve of St. Agnes," a poem that, like Shakespeare's *Romeo and Juliet* (on which it is partly based), celebrates enchantingly the mystery and glory of romantic love. Here are all the ingredients necessary to high romance: a massive medieval castle, cold and dreary; a bitter blood-feud involving the families of two young lovers; the violence of harsh winter weather; the pervading presence of death and brutalized human behavior; and—in sharp contrast to this background—a pair of young lovers of surpassing innocence and physical charm whose love outshines, and is presumed to outlast, all the harshness of the world.

The story is built around a legend concerning St. Agnes, the patron saint of virgins. If a girl will follow certain rites (described in stanza 6) on the Eve of St. Agnes's Day (January 21), she will see her future husband in a dream.

St. Agnes' Eve—Ah, bitter chill it was!
The owl, for all his feathers, was a-cold;
The hare limped trembling through the frozen grass,
And silent was the flock in woolly fold:
Numb were the Beadsman's fingers, while he told   5
His rosary, and while his frosted breath,
Like pious incense from a censer old,
Seemed taking flight for heaven, without a death,
Past the sweet Virgin's picture, while his prayer he saith.

His prayer he saith, this patient, holy man;   10
Then takes his lamp, and riseth from his knees,
And back returneth, meager, barefoot, wan,
Along the chapel aisle by slow degrees:
The sculptured dead, on each side, seem to freeze,
Emprisoned in black, purgatorial rails: 15
Knights, ladies, praying in dumb orat'ries,
He passeth by; and his weak spirit fails
To think how they may ache in icy hoods and mails.

---

5. BEADSMAN'S: A beadsman was a poor man who said prayers in return for charity.

15. RAILS: robes.

16. ORAT'RIES: Oratories are small prayer chapels.

Northward he turneth through a little door,
And scarce three steps, ere Music's golden tongue   20
Flattered to tears this agèd man and poor;
But no—already had his deathbell rung:
The joys of all his life were said and sung:
His was harsh penance on St. Agnes' Eve:
Another way he went, and soon among   25
Rough ashes sat he for his soul's reprieve,
And all night kept awake, for sinners' sake to grieve.

That ancient Beadsman heard the prelude soft;
And so it chanced, for many a door was wide,
From hurry to and fro. Soon, up aloft,   30
The silver, snarling trumpets 'gan to chide:
The level chambers, ready with their pride,
Were glowing to receive a thousand guests:
The carvèd angels, ever eager-eyed,
Stared, where upon their heads the cornice rests,   35
With hair blown back, and wings put cross-wise on their breasts.

At length burst in the argent revelry,
With plume, tiara, and all rich array,
Numerous as shadows haunting faerily
The brain, new stuffed, in youth, with triumphs gay   40
Of old romance. These let us wish away,
And turn, sole-thoughted, to one Lady there,
Whose heart had brooded, all that wintry day,
On love, and winged St. Agnes' saintly care,
As she had heard old dames full many times declare.   45

They told her how, upon St. Agnes' Eve,
Young virgins might have visions of delight,
And soft adorings from their loves receive
Upon the honeyed middle of the night,
If ceremonies due they did aright;   50
As, supperless to bed they must retire,
And couch supine their beauties, lily white;
Nor look behind, nor sideways, but require
Of Heaven with upward eyes for all that they desire.

Full of this whim was thoughtful Madeline: 55
The music, yearning like a God in pain,
She scarcely heard: her maiden eyes divine,
Fixed on the floor, saw many a sweeping train

---

37. ARGENT REVELRY: revelers in shining dress.
53. REQUIRE: ask.

Pass by—she heeded not at all: in vain
Came many a tiptoe, amorous cavalier,   60
And back retired; not cooled by high disdain,
But she saw not: her heart was otherwhere:
She sighed for Agnes' dreams, the sweetest of the year.

She danced along with vague, regardless eyes,
Anxious her lips, her breathing quick and short: 65
The hallowed hour was near at hand: she sighs
Amid the timbrels, and the thronged resort
Of whisperers in anger, or in sport;
'Mid looks of love, defiance, hate, and scorn,
Hoodwinked with faery fancy; all amort,   70
Save to St. Agnes and her lambs unshorn,
And all the bliss to be before tomorrow morn.

So, purposing each moment to retire,
She lingered still. Meantime, across the moors,
Had come young Porphyro, with heart on fire   75
For Madeline. Beside the portal doors,
Buttressed from moonlight, stands he, and implores
All saints to give him sight of Madeline,
But for one moment in the tedious hours,
That he might gaze and worship all unseen;   80
Perchance speak, kneel, touch, kiss—in sooth such things have been.

He ventures in: let no buzzed whisper tell:
All eyes be muffled, or a hundred swords
Will storm his heart, Love's fev'rous citadel:
For him, those chambers held barbarian hordes,   85
Hyena foemen, and hot-blooded lords,
Whose very dogs would execrations howl
Against his lineage: not one breast affords
Him any mercy, in that mansion foul,
Save one old beldame, weak in body and in soul.   90

Ah, happy chance! the agèd creature came,
Shuffling along with ivory-headed wand,
To where he stood, hid from the torch's flame,
Behind a broad hall-pillar, far beyond
The sound of merriment and chorus bland: 95
He startled her; but soon she knew his face,

---

67. RESORT: gathering.
70. AMORT: listless, benumbed.

71. LAMBS UNSHORN: On St. Agnes's Day two lambs were sacrificed and the nuns wove the wool into cloth.
86. HYENA: hyena-like.

And grasped his fingers in her palsied hand,
Saying, "Mercy, Porphyro! hie thee from this place:
"They are all here tonight, the whole blood-thirsty race!

"Get hence! get hence! there's dwarfish Hildebrand;   100
"He had a fever late, and in the fit
"He cursèd thee and thine, both house and land:
"Then there's that old Lord Maurice, not a whit
"More tame for his gray hairs— Alas me! flit!
"Flit like a ghost away."— "Ah, Gossip dear,   105
"We're safe enough; here in this arm-chair sit,
"And tell me how"— "Good Saints! not here, not here;
"Follow me, child, or else these stones will be thy bier."

He followed through a lowly archèd way,
Brushing the cobwebs with his lofty plume,   110
And as she muttered "Well-a-well-a-day!"
He found him in a little moonlight room,
Pale, latticed, chill, and silent as a tomb.
"Now tell me where is Madeline," said he,
"O tell me, Angela, by the Holy loom   115
"Which none but secret sisterhood may see,
"When they St. Agnes' wool are weaving piously."

"St. Agnes! Ah! it is St. Agnes' Eve—
"Yet men will murder upon holy days:
"Thou must hold water in a witch's sieve,   120
"And be liege-lord of all the Elves and Fays,
"To venture so: it fills me with amaze
"To see thee, Porphyro!—St. Agnes' Eve!
"God's help! my lady fair the conjuror plays
"This very night: good angels her deceive!   125
"But let me laugh awhile, I've mickle time to grieve."

Feebly she laugheth in the languid moon,
While Porphyro upon her face doth look,
Like puzzled urchin on an agèd crone
Who keepeth closed a wond'rous riddle-book,   130
As spectacled she sits in chimney nook.
But soon his eyes grew brilliant, when she told
His lady's purpose; and he scarce could brook
Tears, at the thought of those enchantments cold,
And Madeline asleep in lap of legends old.   135

---

105. GOSSIP: godmother; here meaning "friend."   126. MICKLE: much.
117. "WHEN . . . PIOUSLY": see note, line 71.   133. BROOK: restrain, hold back.
120. WITCH'S SIEVE: i.e., a sieve that can hold
    water.

Sudden a thought came like a full-blown rose,
Flushing his brow, and in his painèd heart
Made purple riot: then doth he propose
A stratagem, that makes the beldame start:
"A cruel man and impious thou art: 140
"Sweet lady, let her pray, and sleep, and dream
"Alone with her good angels, far apart
"From wicked men like thee. Go, go!—I deem
"Thou canst not surely be the same that thou didst seem."

"I will not harm her, by all saints I swear,"   145
Quoth Porphyro: "O may I ne'er find grace
"When my weak voice shall whisper its last prayer,
"If one of her soft ringlets I displace,
"Or look with ruffian passion in her face:
"Good Angela, believe me by these tears;   150
"Or I will, even in a moment's space,
"Awake, with horrid shout, my foemen's ears,
"And beard them, though they be more fanged than wolves and bears."

"Ah! why wilt thou affright a feeble soul?
"A poor, weak, palsy-stricken, churchyard thing,   155
"Whose passing-bell may ere the midnight toll;
"Whose prayers for thee, each morn and evening,
"Were never missed."—Thus plaining, doth she bring
A gentler speech from burning Porphyro;
So woeful, and of such deep sorrowing,   160
That Angela gives a promise she will do
Whatever he shall wish, betide her weal or woe.

Which was, to lead him, in close secrecy,
Even to Madeline's chamber, and there hide
Him in a closet, of such privacy   165
That he might see her beauty unespied.
And win perhaps that night a peerless bride,
While legioned faeries paced the coverlet,
And pale enchantment held her sleepy-eyed.
Never on such a night have lovers met,   170
Since Merlin paid his Demon all the monstrous debt.

"It shall be as thou wishest," said the Dame:
"All cates and dainties shall be storèd there
"Quickly on this feast-night: by the tambour frame

---

155. CHURCHYARD: i.e., ready to die.
156. PASSING-BELL: bell that announces death.
158. PLAINING: complaining, murmuring.

171. SINCE . . . DEBT: i.e., died; Merlin was a wizard begotten by demons.

"Her own lute thou wilt see: no time to spare,   175
"For I am slow and feeble, and scarce dare
"On such a catering trust my dizzy head.
"Wait here, my child, with patience; kneel in prayer
"The while: Ah! thou must needs the lady wed,
"Or may I never leave my grave among the dead."   180

So saying, she hobbled off with busy fear.
The lover's endless minutes slowly passed;
The dame returned, and whispered in his ear
To follow her; with agèd eyes aghast
From fright of dim espial. Safe at last,   185
Through many a dusky gallery, they gain
The maiden's chamber, silken, hushed, and chaste;
Where Porphyro took covert, pleased amain.
His poor guide hurried back with agues in her brain.

Her faltering hand upon the balustrade,   190
Old Angela was feeling for the stair,
When Madeline, St. Agnes' charmèd maid,
Rose, like a missioned spirit, unaware:
With silver taper's light, and pious care,
She turned, and down the agèd gossip led   195
To a safe level matting. Now prepare,
Young Porphyro, for gazing on that bed;
She comes, she comes again, like ring-dove frayed and fled.

Out went the taper as she hurried in;
Its little smoke, in pallid moonshine, died: 200
She closed the door, she panted, all akin
To spirits of the air, and visions wide:
No uttered syllable, or, woe betide!
But to her heart, her heart was voluble,
Paining with eloquence her balmy side;   205
As though a tongueless nightingale should swell
Her throat in vain, and die, heart-stifled, in her dell.

A casement high and triple-arched there was,
All garlanded with carven imag'ries
Of fruits, and flowers, and bunches of knot-grass,   210
And diamonded with panes of quaint device,
Innumerable of stains and splendid dyes,
As are the tiger-moth's deep-damasked wings;

173-75: "ALL . . . SEE": According to the legend   198. FRAYED: frightened.
the loved one would bring fancy foods for his
future bride and would play soft music.

And in the midst, 'mong thousand heraldries,
And twilight saints, and dim emblazonings,   215
A shielded scutcheon blushed with blood of queens and kings.

Full on this casement shone the wintry moon,
And threw warm gules on Madeline's fair breast,
As down she knelt for heaven's grace and boon;
Rose-bloom fell on her hands, together prest,   220
And on her silver cross soft amethyst,
And on her hair a glory, like a saint:
She seemed a splendid angel, newly drest,
Save wings, for heaven:—Porphyro grew faint:
She knelt, so pure a thing, so free from mortal taint.   225

Anon his heart revives: her vespers done,
Of all its wreathèd pearls her hair she frees;
Unclasps her warmèd jewels one by one;
Loosens her fragrant bodice; by degrees
Her rich attire creeps rustling to her knees: 230
Half-hidden, like a mermaid in sea-weed,
Pensive awhile she dreams awake, and sees,
In fancy, fair St. Agnes in her bed,
But dares not look behind, or all the charm is fled.

Soon, trembling in her soft and chilly nest,   235
In sort of wakeful swoon, perplexed she lay,
Until the poppied warmth of sleep oppressed
Her soothèd limbs, and soul fatigued away;
Flown, like a thought, until the morrow-day;
Blissfully havened both from joy and pain;   240
Clasped like a missal where swart Paynims pray;
Blinded alike from sunshine and from rain,
As though a rose should shut, and be a bud again.

Stolen to this paradise, and so entranced,
Porphyro gazed upon her empty dress,   245
And listened to her breathing, if it chanced
To wake into a slumberous tenderness;
Which when he heard, that minute did he bless,
And breathed himself: then from the closet crept,
Noiseless as fear in a wide wilderness,   250
And over the hushed carpet, silent, stept,
And 'tween the curtains peeped, where, lo!—how fast she slept.

---

218. GULES: vertical red lines.
237. POPPIED: like poppy; opium.

241. SWART: swarthy. CLASPED . . . PRAY: i.e.,
unopened; Paynims (Pagans) would not open
missals (Christian prayer books).

Then by the bed-side, where the faded moon
Made a dim, silver twilight, soft he set
A table, and, half anguished, threw thereon   255
A cloth of woven crimson, gold, and jet:—
O for some drowsy Morphean amulet!
The boisterous, midnight, festive clarion,
The kettle-drum, and far-heard clarinet,
Affray his ears, though but in dying tone:—   260
The hall door shuts again, and all the noise is gone.

And still she slept an azure-lidded sleep,
In blanchèd linen, smooth, and lavendered,
While he from forth the closet brought a heap
Of candied apple, quince, and plum, and gourd;   265
With jellies soother than the creamy curd,
And lucent syrups, tinct with cinnamon;
Manna and dates, in argosy transferred
From Fez and spicèd dainties, every one,
From silken Samarcand to cedared Lebanon.   270

These delicates he heaped with glowing hand
On golden dishes and in baskets bright
Of wreathèd silver: sumptuous they stand
In the retired quiet of the night,
Filling the chilly room with perfume light.—   275
"And now, my love, my seraph fair, awake!
"Thou art my heaven, and I thine eremite:
"Open thine eyes, for meek St. Agnes' sake,
"Or I shall drowse beside thee, so my soul doth ache."

Thus whispering, his warm, unnervèd arm   280
Sank in her pillow. Shaded was her dream
By the dusk curtains:—'twas a midnight charm
Impossible to melt as icèd stream:
The lustrous salvers in the moonlight gleam;
Broad golden fringe upon the carpet lies: 285
It seemed he never, never could redeem
From such a steadfast spell his lady's eyes;
So mused awhile, entoiled in woofèd phantasies.

Awakening up, he took her hollow lute,—
Tumultuous,—and, in chords that tenderest be,   290

257. DROWSY MORPHEAN AMULET: a charm (amulet) that would bring on sleep (Morpheus was the god of sleep).
266. SOOTHER: smoother.
269. FEZ: Moroccan city.
270. SAMARCAND: Central Asian city. LEBANON: country at eastern end of the Mediterranean, north of Palestine.
271. DELICATES: delicacies.
277. EREMITE: religious hermit.
288. WOOFÈD: closely woven.

He played an ancient ditty, long since mute,
In Provence called, "La belle dame sans mercy":
Close to her ear touching the melody;—
Wherewith disturbed, she uttered a soft moan:
He ceased—she panted quick—and suddenly   295
Her blue affrayèd eyes wide open shone:
Upon his knees he sank, pale as smooth-sculptured stone.

Her eyes were open, but she still beheld,
Now wide awake, the vision of her sleep:
There was a painful change, that nigh expelled   300
The blisses of her dream so pure and deep
At which fair Madeline began to weep,
And moan forth witless words with many a sigh;
While still her gaze on Porphyro would keep;
Who knelt, with joinèd hands and piteous eye,   305
Fearing to move or speak, she looked so dreamingly.

"Ah, Porphyro!" said she, "but even now
"Thy voice was at sweet tremble in mine ear,
"Made tunable with every sweetest vow;
"And those sad eyes were spiritual and clear: 310
"How changed thou art! how pallid, chill, and drear!
"Give me that voice again, my Porphyro,
"Those looks immortal, those complainings dear!
"Oh, leave me not in this eternal woe,
"For if thou diest, my Love, I know not where to go."   315

Beyond a mortal man impassioned far
At these voluptuous accents, he arose,
Ethereal, flushed, and like a throbbing star
Seen mid the sapphire heaven's deep repose;
Into her dream he melted, as the rose   320
Blendeth its odor with the violet,—
Solution sweet: meantime the frost wind blows
Like Love's alarum pattering the sharp sleet
Against the window panes; St. Agnes' moon hath set.

'Tis dark: quick pattereth the flaw-blown sleet: 325
"This is no dream, my bride, my Madeline!"
'Tis dark: the icèd gusts still rave and beat:
"No dream! alas! alas! and woe is mine!
"Porphyro will leave me here to fade and pine.—

292. PROVENCE: region in Southern France. "LA   317. VOLUPTUOUS: pleasurable.
BELLE DAME SANS MERCY": "The beautiful lady   325. FLAW-BLOWN: blown by a gusty wind.
without mercy."

"Cruel! what traitor could thee hither bring?   330
"I curse not, for my heart is lost in thine,
"Though thou forsakest a deceivèd thing;—
"A dove forlorn and lost with sick unprunèd wing."

"My Madeline! sweet dreamer! lovely bride!
"Say, may I be for aye thy vassal blest?   335
"Thy beauty's shield, heart-shaped and vermeil-dyed?
"Ah, silver shrine, here will I take my rest
"After so many hours of toil and quest,
"A famished pilgrim,—saved by miracle.
"Though I have found, I will not rob thy nest   340
"Saving of thy sweet self; if thou think'st well
"To trust, fair Madeline, to no rude infidel.

"Hark! 'tis an elfin storm from faery land,
"Of haggard seeming, but a boon indeed:
"Arise! arise! the morning is at hand;—   345
"The bloated wassailers will never heed:—
"Let us away, my love, with happy speed;
"There are no ears to hear, or eyes to see,—
"Drowned all in Rhenish and the sleepy mead:
"Awake! arise! my love, and fearless be,   350
"For o'er the southern moors I have a home for thee."

She hurried at his words, beset with fears,
For there were sleeping dragons all around,
At glaring watch, perhaps, with ready spears—
Down the wide stairs a darkling way they found.—   355
In all the house was heard no human sound.
A chain-drooped lamp was flickering by each door;
The arras, rich with horseman, hawk, and hound,
Fluttered in the besieging wind's uproar;
And the long carpets rose along the gusty floor.   360

They glide, like phantoms, into the wide hall;
Like phantoms, to the iron porch, they glide;
Where lay the Porter, in uneasy sprawl,
With a huge empty flagon by his side:
The wakeful bloodhound rose, and shook his hide,   365
But his sagacious eye an inmate owns:
By one, and one, the bolts full easy slide;—
The chains lie silent on the footworn stones;—
The key turns, and the door upon its hinges groans.

335. AYE: ever.   349. RHENISH: a kind of wine.
336. VERMEIL-DYED: vermilion-dyed.   353. DRAGONS: i.e., enemies.
344. SEEMING: appearance.   363. PORTER: the gatekeeper.
346. WASSAILERS: drinkers.   366. OWNS: recognizes.

And they are gone: aye, ages long ago   370
These lovers fled away into the storm.
That night the Baron dreamt of many a woe,
And all his warrior-guests, with shade and form
Of witch, and demon, and large coffin-worm,
Were long be-nightmared. Angela   375
Died palsy-twitched, with meager face deform;
The Beadsman, after thousand aves told,
For aye unsought-for slept among his ashes cold.

377. AVES: prayers.

I

1. What is the purpose of the first three stanzas in setting the stage for the story? Consider what a beadsman is, the number of religious terms, the physical conditions in the chapel. What purpose is served by the contrast offered in stanzas 4 and 5? What connection is there between the Beadsman, the Lady, and the revelers?

2. How are we convinced of the purity of Porphyro's intention *to gaze and worship all unseen?* How is he contrasted with his enemies? What are they like? What is he like? How is his suggestion to Angela that he hide in Madeline's room kept from being crude? In other words, how does Keats surround the meeting of the lovers with a sense of purity, even of holiness?

3. How is Madeline's room described? How does it compare or contrast with the chapel, the "level chambers" of stanza 4, and Angela's room? Pay particular attention to the kind of details used and the choice of words.

4. What is Keats's purpose in giving the story a medieval setting? How does the word choice throughout the poem support the assertion in the last stanza that all this took place *ages long ago?*

5. The plot of the story could be given in a few sentences, yet Keats takes forty-two stanzas to tell it. Part of the effect of the poem lies in this leisurely telling, as if it were something to be savored—for it is. Reread the poem, paying attention to the richness of its language and imagery. Consider, for instance: the cooperation of details of the first two stanzas in creating an atmosphere of coldness and death; the description of Madeline in her chamber in stanzas 23-26; the lovers' banquet in stanzas 30-31.

II

1. What relation have the last four stanzas to the opening four? What details are focused on in each grouping? What kind of framework is thus provided for the love story? How have the deaths of Angela and the Beadsman been prepared for? What purpose do the two serve in the poem?

2. Why is it significant at the end when the lovers flee that the storm is still raging and the revelers are momentarily stilled ("drunken wassailers")? Into what kind of world do they flee? From what kind of world do they flee? In what sense is the poem about idealized romantic love? What is Keats saying about such love in this world?

AFTER THE THEATER   [*1917*]

Frank Swinnerton

The idealization of romantic love in literature can embrace the refinements of "The Eve of St. Agnes," the cheapness of the mass-produced "true romance," or something in between. In each kind of treatment the underlying assumption is that the highest human happiness can be found in "two hearts beating each to each" in perfect harmony. Whether the relationship built on that assumption is exalted or tawdry—or a little of both—depends on the kind of people involved, the motives on which they act, and the writer's attitude toward the romantic situation he creates.

Keats's idealized lovers never existed and never will exist, but like Romeo and Juliet they haunt our imaginations with the promise of what might be if the world were still the Garden of Eden. Unfortunately, it is not, and in the unweeded garden of the real world romantic love is likely to have more in common with the tender crudities of Emmy and Alf in the selection that follows than with the glory of Madeline and Porphyro.

"After the Theater" is a chapter from Frank Swinnerton's novel, *Nocturne,* which recounts a few hours in the lives of Jenny and Emmy Blanchard, their paralytic old father, and Alf, suitor to both sisters. In an introduction to the novel, H. G. Wells comments about this chapter: "If there exists a better writing of vulgar lovemaking, so base, so honest, so touchingly mean, so touchingly full of craving for happiness . . . I do not know of it. . . . A false note, one fatal line, would have ruined all. On the one hand lay brutality; a hundred imitative louts could have written a similar chapter brutally, with the soul left out. . . . On the other side was the still more dreadful fall into sentimentality, the tear of conscious tenderness, the redeeming glimpse of better things in Alf and Emmy that would at one stroke have converted their reality into a genteel masquerade."

Wells is using "vulgar," "base," and "mean" without their usual connotations of depravity or viciousness. He simply means common, unrefined, not guided by the niceties of cultured behavior. Emmy and Alf bear the stamp of the London slums, but they carry with them a vision, however dimly seen, of the happiness romantic love is said by poets to bring.

As will be obvious from things said in this chapter from *Nocturne,* there has been an unpleasant argument in the Blanchard household just prior to the events described here. For the solution to the mystery with which the chapter closes simply find the novel and read it.

I

After leaving the house Emmy and Alf pressed along in the darkness, Alf's arm still surrounding and supporting Emmy, Emmy still half jubilantly and half sorrowfully continuing to recognize her happiness and the smothered chagrin of her emotions. She was not able to feel either happy or miserable; but happiness was uppermost. Dislike of Jenny had its place, also; for she could account for every weakness of Alf's by reference to Jenny's baseness. But indeed Emmy

---

"After the Theater" from *Nocturne* by Frank Swinnerton. Reprinted by permission of the author.

could not think, and could only passively and excitedly endure the conflicting emotions of the moment. And Alf did not speak, but hurried her along as fast as his strong arm could secure her compliance with his own pace; and they walked through the night-ridden streets and full into the blaze of the theater entrance without any words at all. Then, when the staring vehemence of the electric lights whitened and shadowed her face, Emmy drew away, casting down her eyes, alarmed at the disclosures which the brilliance might devastatingly make. She slipped from his arm, and stood rather forlornly while Alf fished in his pockets for the tickets. With docility she followed him, thrilled when he stepped aside in passing the commissionaire[1] and took her arm. Together they went up the stairs, the heavy carpets with their drugget covers silencing every step, the gilded mirrors throwing their reflections backwards and forwards until the stairs seemed peopled with hosts of Emmys and Alfs. As they drew near the closed doors of the circle[2] the hush filling the staircases and vestibules of the theater was intensified. An aproned attendant seemed to Emmy's sensitiveness to look them up and down and superciliously to disapprove them. She moved with indignation. A dull murmur, as of single voices, disturbed the air somewhere behind the rustling attendant: and when the doors were quickly opened Emmy saw beyond the darkness and the intrusive flash of light caused by the opening doors a square of brilliance and a dashing figure upon the stage talking staccato. Those of the audience who were sitting near the doors turned angrily and with curiosity to view the newcomers; and the voice that Emmy had distinguished went more stridently on, with a strong American accent. In a flurry she found and crept into her seat, trying to understand the play, to touch Alf, to remove her hat, to discipline her excitements. And the staccato voice went on and on, detailing a plan of some sort which she could not

understand because they had missed the first five minutes of the play. Emmy could not tell that the actor was only pretending to be an American; she could not understand why, having spoken twenty words, he must take six paces farther from the footlights until he had spoken thirteen more; but she could and did feel most overwhelmingly exuberant at being as it were alone in that half-silent multitude, sitting beside Alf, their arms touching, her head whirling, her heart beating, and a wholly exquisite warmth flushing her cheeks.

II

The first interval[3] found the play well advanced. A robbery had been planned—for it was a "crook" play—and the heroine had already received wild-eyed the advances of a fur-coated millionaire. When the lights of the theater popped up, and members of the orchestra began once more unmercifully to tune their instruments, it was possible to look round at the not especially large audience. But in whichever direction Emmy looked she was always brought back as by a magnet to Alf, who sat ruminantly beside her. To Alf's side-eye Emmy was looking surprisingly lovely. The tired air and the slightly peevish mouth to which he was accustomed had given place to the flush and sparkle of an excited girl. Alf was aware of surprise. He blinked. He saw the lines smoothed away from round her mouth—the lines of weariness and dissatisfaction,—and was tempted by the softness of her cheek. As he looked quickly off again he thought how full Jenny would have been of comment upon the play, how he would have sat grinning with precious enjoyment at her merciless gibes during the whole of the interval. He had the sense of Jenny as all movement, as flashing and drawing him into quagmires of sensation, like a will-o'-the-wisp. Emmy was not like that. She sat tremulously smiling, humble before him, diffident, flattering. She was intelligent; that

---

1. COMMISSIONAIRE: ticket-taker.
2. CIRCLE: gallery or balcony.

---

3. INTERVAL: intermission.

was it. Intelligent was the word. Not lively, but restful. Critically he regarded her. Rather a nice girl, Emmy. . . .

Alf roused himself, and looked around.

"Here, miss!" he called; and "S-s-s-s" when she did not hear him. It was his way of summoning an attendant or a waitress. "S-s-s-s." The attendant brought chocolates, which Alf handed rather magnificently to his companion. He plunged into his pockets—in his rough-and-ready, muscular way—for the money, leaning far over the next seat, which was unoccupied. "Like some lemon?" he said to Emmy. Together they inspected the box of chocolates, which contained much imitation-lace paper and a few sweets. "Not half a sell,"[4] grumbled Alf to himself, thinking of the shilling he had paid; but he looked with gratification at Emmy's face as she enjoyingly ate the chocolates. As her excitement a little strained her nervous endurance Emmy began to pale under the eyes; her eyes seemed to grow larger; she lost the first air of sparkle, but she became more pathetic. "Poor little thing," thought Alf, feeling masculine. "Poor little thing: she's tired. Poor little thing."

III

In the middle of this hot, excitedly-talking audience they seemed to bask as in a warm pool of brilliant light. The brilliants[5] in the dome of the theater intensified all the shadows, heightened all the smiles, illumined all the silken blouses and silver bangles, the flashing eyes, the general air of fête.

"All right?" Alf inquired protectively. Emmy looked in gratitude towards him.

"Lovely," she said. "Have another?"

"I meant *you*," he persisted. "Yourself, I mean." Emmy smiled, so happily that nobody could have been unmoved at the knowledge of having given such pleasure.

"Oh, grand!" Emmy said. Then her eyes contracted. Memory came to her. The angry

scene that had passed earlier returned to her mind, hurting her, and injuring her happiness. Alf hurried to engage her attention, to distract her from the thoughts that had in them such discomfort as she so quickly showed.

"Like the play? I didn't quite follow what it was this old general had done to him. Did you?"

"Hadn't he kept him from marrying . . ." Emmy looked conscious for a moment. "Marrying the right girl? I didn't understand it either. It's only a play."

"Of course," Alf agreed. "See how that girl's eyes shone when old fur-coat went after her? Fair shone, they did. Like lamps. They'd got the limes[6] on her. . . . You couldn't see them. My—er—my friend's the electrician here. He says it drives him nearly crazy, the way he has to follow her about in the third act. She . . . she's got some pluck, he says; the way she fights three of them single-handed. They've all got revolvers. She's got one; but it's not loaded. Lights a cigarette, too, with them all watching her, ready to rush at her."

"There!" said Emmy, admiringly. She was thinking: "It's only a play."

"She gets hold of his fur coat, and puts it on. . . . Imitates his voice. . . . You can see it's her all the time, you know. So could they, if they looked a bit nearer. However, they don't. . . . I suppose there wouldn't be any play if they did. . . ."

Emmy was not listening to him: she was dreaming. She was as gauche and simple in his company as a young girl would have been; but her mind was different. It was practical in its dreams, and they had their disturbing unhappiness, as well, from the greater poignancy of her desire. She was not a young girl, to be agreeably fluttered and to pass on to the next admirer without a qualm. She loved him, blindly but painfully; without the ease of young love, but with all the sickness of first love. And she had jealousy, the feeling that she was not his

---

4. "NOT HALF A SELL": i.e., not worth half the price.

5. BRILLIANTS: the many-sided cut glass pieces in the ceiling lights.

6. LIMES: limelights, spotlights.

first object, to poison her feelings. She could not think of Jenny without tremors of anger. And still, for pain, her thoughts went throbbing on about Jenny whenever, in happiness, she had seen a home and Alf and a baby and the other plain clear consequences of earning his love—of taking him from Jenny.

And then the curtain rose, the darkness fell, and the orchestra's tune slithered into nothing. The play went on, about the crook and the general and the millionaire and the heroine and all their curiously simple-minded friends. And every moment something happened upon the stage, from fights to thefts, from kisses (which those in the gallery, not wholly absorbed by the play, generously augmented) to telephone calls, plots, speeches (many speeches, of irreproachable moral tone), shoutings, and sudden wild appeals to the delighted occupants of the gallery. And Emmy sat through it hardly heeding the uncommon events, aware of them as she would have been aware of distant shouting. Her attention was preoccupied with other matters. She had her own thoughts, serious enough in themselves. Above all, she was enjoying the thought that she was with Alf, and that their arms were touching; and she was wondering if he knew that.

IV

Through another interval they sat with silent embarrassment, the irreplaceable chocolates, which had earlier been consumed, having served their turn as a means of devouring attention. Alf was tempted to fly to the bar for a drink and composure, but he did not like to leave Emmy; and he could not think of anything which could safely be said to her in the middle of this gathering of hot and radiant persons. "To speak" in such uproar meant "to shout." He felt that every word he uttered would go echoing in rolls and rolls of sound out among the multitude. They were not familiar enough to make that a matter of indifference to him. He was in the stage of secretiveness. And Emmy, after

trying once or twice to open various small topics, had fallen back upon her own thoughts, and could invent nothing to talk about until the difficulties that lay between them had been removed. Her brow contracted. She moved her shoulders, or sat pressed reservedly against the back of her seat. Her voice, whenever she did not immediately hear some word fall from Alf, became sharp and self-conscious—almost "managing."

It was a relief to both of them, and in both the tension of sincere feeling had perceptibly slackened, when the ignored orchestra gave way before the rising curtain. Again the two drew together in the darkness, as all other couples were doing, comforted by proximity, and even by the unacknowledged mutual pleasure of it; again they watched the extraordinary happenings upon the stage. The fur coat was much used, cigarettes were lighted and flung away with prodigal recklessness, pistols were revealed—one of them was even fired into the air;—and jumping, trickling music heightened the effects of a number of strong speeches about love, and incorruptibility, and womanhood. . . . The climax was reached. In the middle of the climax, while yet the lover wooed and the villain died, the audience began to rustle, preparatory to going home. Even Emmy was influenced to the extent of discovering and beginning to adjust her hat. It was while she was pinning it, with her elbows raised, that the curtain fell. Both Emmy and Alf rose in the immediately successive re-illumination of the theater; and Emmy looked so pretty with her arms up, and with the new hat so coquettishly askew upon her head, and with a long hatpin between her teeth, that Alf could not resist the impulse to put his arm affectionately round her in leading the way out.

V

And then, once in the street, he made no scruple about taking Emmy's arm within the crook of his as they moved from the staring whiteness of the theater lamps out into the calmer moonshine. It was eleven o'clock. The night was fine, and the moon rode high above amid the twinkling stars. When Alf looked at Emmy's face it was transfigured in this beautiful light, and he drew her gently from the direct way back to the little house.

"Don't let's go straight back," he said. "Stroll ull do us good."

Very readily Emmy obeyed his guidance. Her heart was throbbing; but her brain was clear. He wanted to be with her; and the knowledge of that made Emmy happier than she had been since early childhood.

"It's been lovely," she said, with real warmth of gratitude, looking away from him with shyness.

"Em," growled Alf, in a voice of some confusion. "Er . . . you don't go much to the theater, do you?"

"Not much," Emmy agreed. "See, there's Pa. He always looks to me. . . ."

"Yes." Alf could not add anything to that for a long time. "Fine night," he presently recorded. "D'you like a walk? I mean . . . I'm very fond of it, a night like this. Mr. Blanchard's all right, I suppose?"

"Oh, yes. *She's* there." Emmy could not bring herself to name Jenny to him. Yet her mind was busy thinking of the earlier jar, recomposing the details, recalling the words that had passed. Memory brought tears into her eyes; but she would not allow Alf to see them, and soon she recovered her self-control. It had to be spoken of: the evening could not pass without reference to it; or it would spoil everything. Alf would think of her—he was bound to think of her—as a crying, petulant, jealous woman, to whom he had been merely kind. Patronizing, even! Perhaps, even, the remembrance of it would prevent him from coming again to the house. Men like Alf were so funny in that respect. It took so little to displease them, to drive them away altogether. At last she ventured: "It was nice of you to take me."

Alf fidgeted, jerking his head, and looking recklessly about him.

"Not at all," he grumbled. "Not tired, are you?" Emmy reassured him. "What I mean, I'm very glad. . . . Now, look here, Em. May as well have it out. . . ." Emmy's heart gave a bound: she walked mechanically beside him, her head as stiffly held as though the muscles of her neck had been paralyzed. "May as well, er . . . have it out," repeated Alf. "That's how I am—I like to be all shipshape from the start. When I came along this evening I *did* mean to ask young Jen to go with me. That was quite as you thought. I never thought you'd, you know, *care* to come with me. I don't know why; but there it is. I never meant to put it like I did . . . in that way . . . to have a fuss and upset anybody. I've . . . I mean, she's been out with me half-a-dozen times; and so I sort of naturally thought of her."

"Of course," agreed Emmy. "Of course."

"But I'm glad you came," Alf said. Something in his honesty, and the brusqueness of his rejoicing, touched Emmy, and healed her first wound—the thought that she might have been unwelcome to him. They went on a little way, more at ease; both ready for the next step in intimacy which was bound to be taken by one of them.

"I thought she might have said something to you—about me not *wanting* to come," Emmy proceeded, tentatively. "Made you think I never wanted to go out."

Alf shook his head. Emmy had there no opening for her resentment.

"No," he said, with stubborn loyalty. "She's always talked very nice about you."

"What does she say?" swiftly demanded Emmy.

"I forget. . . . Saying you had a rough time at home. Saying it was rough on you. That you're one of the best . . ."

"*She* said that?" gasped Emmy. "It's not like her to say that. Did she really? She's so touchy about me, generally. Sometimes, the way she goes on, anybody'd think I was the miserablest creature in the world, and always on at her about something. I'm not, you know; only she thinks it. Well, I can't help it, can I? If you knew how I have to work in that house, you'd be . . . surprised.

I'm always at it. The way the dirt comes in —you'd wonder where it all came from! And see, there's Pa and all. She doesn't take that into account. She gets on all right with him; but she isn't there all day, like I am. That makes a difference, you know. He's used to me. She's more of a change for him."

Alf was cordial in agreement. He was seeing all the difference between the sisters. In his heart there still lingered a sort of cherished enjoyment of Jenny's greater spirit. Secretly it delighted him, like a forbidden joke. He felt that Jenny—for all that he must not, at this moment, mention her name —kept him on the alert all the time, so that he was ever in hazardous pursuit. There was something fascinating in such excitement as she caused him. He never knew what she would do or say next; and while that disturbed and distressed him it also lacerated his vanity and provoked his admiration. He admired Jenny more than he could ever admire Emmy. But he also saw Emmy as different from his old idea of her. He had seen her trembling defiance early in the evening, and that had moved him and made him a little afraid of her; he had also seen her flushed cheeks at the theater, and Emmy had grown in his eyes suddenly younger. He could not have imagined her so cordial, so youthful, so interested in everything that met her gaze. Finally, he found her quieter, more amenable, more truly wifely than her sister. It was an important point in Alf's eyes. You had to take into account—if you were a man of common sense—relative circumstances. Devil was all very well in courtship; but mischief in a girl became contrariness in a domestic termagant. That was an idea that was very much in Alf's thoughts during this walk, and it lingered there like acquired wisdom.

"Say she's going with a sailor?" he suddenly demanded.

"So she told me. I've never seen him. She doesn't tell lies, though."

"I thought you said she did!"

Emmy flinched: she had forgotten the words spoken in her wild anger, and would have been ashamed to account for them in a moment of greater coolness.

"I mean, if she says he's a sailor, that's true. She told me he was on a ship. I suppose she met him when she was away that time. She's been very funny ever since. Not funny—restless. Anything I've done for her she's made a fuss. I give her a thorough good meal; and oh! there's such a fuss about it. 'Why don't we have ice creams, and merangs, and wine, and grouse, and sturgeon—' "

"Ph! silly talk!" said Alf, in contemptuous wonder. "I mean to say . . ."

"Oh, well: you know what flighty girls are. He's probably a swank-pot.[7] A stewart,[8] or something of that sort. I expect he has what's left over, and talks big about it. But she's got ideas like that in her head, and she thinks she's too good for the likes of us. It's too much trouble to her to be pelite[9] these days. I've got the fair sick of it, I can tell you. And then she's always out. . . . *Somebody's* got to be at home, just to look after Pa and keep the fire in. But Jenny— oh dear no! She's no sooner home than she's out again. Can't rest. Says it's stuffy indoors, and off she goes. I don't see her for hours. Well, I don't know . . . but if she doesn't quiet down a bit she'll only be making trouble for herself later on. She can't keep house, you know! She can scrub; but she can't cook so very well, or keep the place nice. She hasn't got the patience. You think she's doing the dusting; and you find her groaning about what she'd do if she was rich. 'Yes,' I tell her; 'it's all very well to do that; but you'd far better be doing something *useful*,' I say. 'Instead of wasting your time on idle fancies.' "

"Very sensible," agreed Alf, completely absorbed in such a discourse.

"She's trying,[10] you know. You can't leave her for a minute. She says I'm stodgy; but

---

7. SWANK-POT: show-off.
8. STEWART: Emmy's London Cockney pronunciation of "steward."
9. PELITE: polite.
10. TRYING: difficult to put up with.

I say it's better to be practical than flighty. Don't you think so, Alf?"

"Exackly!" said Alf, in a tone of the gravest assent. "Exackly."

VI

"I mean," pursued Emmy, "you must have a *little* common sense. But she's been spoilt—she's the youngest. I'm a little older than she is . . . *wiser,* I say; but she won't have it. . . . And Pa's always made a fuss of her. Really, sometimes, you'd have thought she was a boy. Racing about! My word, such a commotion! And then going out to the millinery,[11] and getting among a lot of other girls. You don't know *who* they are—if they're ladies or not. It's not a good influence for her. . . ."

"She ought to get out of it," Alf said. To Emmy it was a ghastly moment.

"She'll never give it up," she hurriedly said. "You know, it's in her blood. Off she goes! And they make a fuss of her. She mimics everybody, and they laugh at it—they think it's funny to mimic people who can't help themselves—if they *are* a bit comic. So she goes; and when she does come home Pa's so glad to see a fresh face that he makes a fuss of her, too. And she stuffs him up with all sorts of tales—things that never happened—to keep him quiet. She says it gives him something to think about. . . . Well, I suppose it does. I expect you think I'm very unkind to say such things about my own sister; but really I can't help seeing what's under my nose; and I sometimes get so—you know, worked up, that I don't know how to hold myself. She doesn't understand what it is to be cooped up indoors all day long, like I am; and it never occurs to her to say 'Go along, Em; you run out for a bit.' I have to say to her: 'You be in for a bit, Jen?' and then she p'tends[12] she's always in. And then there's a rumpus. . . ."

Alf was altogether subdued by this account: it had that degree of intimacy which, when one is in a sentimental mood, will always be absorbing. He felt that he really was getting to the bottom of the mystery known to him as Jenny Blanchard. The picture had verisimilitude. He could see Jenny as he listened. He was seeing her with the close and searching eye of a sister, as nearly true, he thought, as any vision could be. Once the thought "I expect there's another story" came sidling into his head; but it was quickly drowned in further reminiscence from Emmy, so that it was clearly a dying desire that he felt for Jenny. Had Jenny been there, to fling her gage into the field, Alf might gapingly have followed her, lost again in admiration of her more sparkling tongue and equipments.[13] But in such circumstances the arraigned party is never present. If Jenny had been there the tale could not have been told. Emmy's virtuous and destructive monologue would not merely have been interrupted: it would have been impossible. Jenny would have done all the talking. The others, all amaze, would have listened with feelings appropriate to each, though with feelings in common unpleasant to be borne.

"I bet there's a rumpus," Alf agreed. "Old Jen's not one to take a blow. She ups and gets in the first one." He couldn't help admiring Jenny, even yet. So he hastened to pretend that he did not admire her; out of a kind of tact. "But of course . . . that's all very well for a bit of sport, but it gets a bit wearisome after a time. I know what you mean. . . ."

"Don't think I've been complaining about her," Emmy said. "I wouldn't. Really, I wouldn't. Only I do think sometimes it's not quite fair that she should have all the fun, and me none of it. I don't want a lot. My tastes are very simple. But when it comes to none at all—well, Alf, what do *you* think?"

---

11. MILLINERY: i.e., millinery shop, where Jenny works.
12. P'TENDS: pretends.

---

13. EQUIPMENTS: character traits.

"It's a bit thick," admitted Alf. "And that's a fact."

"See, she's always having her own way. Does just what she likes. There's no holding her."

"Wants[14] a man to do that," ruminated Alf, with a half chuckle. "Eh?"

"Well," said Emmy, a little brusquely. "I pity the man who tries it on."[15]

VII

Emmy was not deliberately trying to secure from Alf a proposal of marriage. She was trying to show him the contrast between Jenny and herself, and to readjust the balances as he appeared to have been holding them. She wanted to impress him. She was as innocent of any other intention as any girl could have been. It was jealousy that spoke; not scheme. And she was perfectly sincere in her depreciation of Jenny. She could not understand what it was that made the admiring look come into the faces of those who spoke to Jenny, nor why the unwilling admiration that started into her own heart should ever find a place there. She was baffled by character, and she was engaged in the common task of rearranging life to suit her own temperament.

They had been walking for some little distance now along deserted streets, the moon shining upon them, their steps softly echoing, and Emmy's arm as warm as toast. It was like a real lovers' walk, she could not help thinking, half in the shadow and wholly in the stillness of the quiet streets. She felt very contented; and with her long account of Jenny already uttered, and her tough body already reanimated by the walk, Emmy was at leisure to let her mind wander among sweeter things. There was love, for example, to think about; and when she glanced sideways Alf's shoulder seemed such a little distance from her cheek. And his hand was lightly clasping her wrist. A strong hand, was

Alf's, with a broad thumb and big capable fingers. She could see it in the moonlight, and she had suddenly an extraordinary longing to press her cheek against the back of Alf's hand. She did not want any silly nonsense, she told herself; and the tears came into her eyes, and her nose seemed pinched and tickling with the cold at the mere idea of any nonsense; but she could not help longing with the most intense longing to press her cheek against the back of Alf's hand. That was all. She felt that if it might be granted she would be content, altogether happy. She wanted so little!

And as if Alf too had been thinking of somebody nearer to him than Jenny, he began:

"I don't know if you've ever thought at all about me, Em. But your saying what you've done . . . about yourself . . . it's made me think a bit. I'm all on my own now—have been for years; but the way I live isn't good for anyone. It's a fact it's not. I mean to say, my rooms that I've got . . . they're not big enough to swing a cat in; and the way the old girl at my place serves up the meals is a fair knock-out, if you notice things like I do. If I think of her, and then about the way you do things, it gives me the hump. Everything you do's so nice. But with her— the plates have still got bits of yesterday's mustard on them, and all fluffy from the dishcloth. . . ."

"Not washed prop'ly," Emmy interestedly remarked; "that's what it is."

"Exackly. And the meat's raw inside. Cooks it too quickly. And when I have a bloater[16] for my breakfast—I'm partial to a bloater—it's black outside, as if it was done in the cinders; and then inside—well, I like them done all through, like any other man. Then I can't get her to get me gammon[17] rashers.[18] She will get these little tiddy[19] rashers, with little white bones in them. Why,

---

14. WANTS: takes.
15. WHO . . . ON: i.e., who tries to hold her.

16. BLOATER: kippered herring.
17. GAMMON: the lower end of a side of bacon.
18. RASHERS: bacon slices.
19. TIDDY: tiny.

while you're cutting them out the bacon gets cold. You may think I'm fussy . . . fiddly with my food. I'm not, really; only I like it. . . ."

"Of course you do," Emmy said. "She's not interested, that's what it is. She thinks anything's food; and some people don't mind at all what they eat. They don't notice."

"No. I *do*. If you go to a restaurant you get it different. You get more of it, too. Well, what with one thing and another I've got very fed up with Madame Bucks. It's all dirty and half baked. There's great holes in the carpet of my sitting-room—holes you could put your foot through. And I've done that, as a matter of fact. Put my foot through and nearly gone over. *Should* have done that, only for the table. Well, I mean to say . . . you can't help being fed up with it. But she knows where I work, and I know she's hard up; so I don't like to go anywhere else, because if anybody asked me if he should go there, I couldn't honestly recommend him to; and yet, you see how it is, I shouldn't like to leave her in the lurch, if she knew I was just gone somewhere else down the street."

"No," sympathetically agreed Emmy. "I quite see. It's very awkward for you. Though it's no use being too kind-hearted with these people; because they *don't* appreciate it; and if you don't say anything they just go on in the same way, never troubling themselves about you. They think, as long as you don't say anything you're all right; and it's not their place to make any alteration. They're quite satisfied. Look at Jenny and me."

"Is she satisfied?" asked Alf.

"With herself, she is. She's never satisfied with me. She never tries to see it from my point of view."

"No," Alf nodded his head wisely. "That's what it is. They don't." He nodded again.

"Isn't it a lovely night," ventured Emmy. "See the moon over there."

They looked up at the moon and the stars and the unfathomable sky. It took them at once away from the streets and the subject of their talk. Both sighed as they stared

upwards, lost in the beauty before them. And when at last their eyes dropped, the street lamps had become so yellow and tawdry that they were like stupid spangles in contrast with the stars. Alf still held Emmy's arm so snugly within his own, and her wrist was within the clasp of his fingers. It was so little a thing to slide his fingers into a firm clasp of her hand, and they drew closer.

"Lovely, eh!" Alf ejaculated, with a further upward lift of his eyes. Emmy sighed again.

"Not like down here," she soberly said.

"No, it's different. Down here's all right, though," Alf assured her. "Don't you think it is?" He gave a rather nervous little laugh. "Don't you think it is?"

"Grand!" Emmy agreed, with the slightest hint of dryness.

"I say, it was awfully good of you to come tonight," said Alf. "I've . . . you've enjoyed it, haven't you?" He was looking sharply at her, and Emmy's face was illumined. He saw her soft cheeks, her thin soft little neck; he felt her warm gloved hand within his own. "D'you mind?" he asked, and bent abruptly so that their faces were close together. For a moment, feeling so daring that his breath caught, Alf could not carry out his threat. Then, roughly, he pushed his face against hers, kissing her. Quickly he released Emmy's arm, so that his own might be more protectingly employed; and they stood embraced in the moonlight.

VIII

It was only for a minute, for Emmy, with instinctive secrecy, drew away into the shadow. At first Alf did not understand, and thought himself repelled; but Emmy's hands were invitingly raised. The first delight was broken. One more sensitive might have found it hard to recapture; but Alf stepped quickly to her side in the shadow, and they kissed again. He was surprised at her passion. He had not expected it, and the flattery was welcome. He grinned a little in the safe darkness, consciously and even sheepishly, but with eagerness. They were both clumsy and a little trembling, not very practiced lovers, but curious and excited. Emmy felt her hat knocked a little sideways upon her head.

It was Emmy who moved first, drawing herself away from him, she knew not why.

"Where you going?" asked Alf, detaining her. "What is it? Too rough, am I?" He could not see Emmy's shaken head, and was for a moment puzzled at the ways of woman —so far from his grasp.

"No," Emmy said. "It's wonderful."

Peering closely, Alf could see her eyes shining.

"D'you think you're fond enough of me, Emmy?" She demurred.

"That's a nice thing to say! As if it was for me to tell you!" she whispered archly back.

"What ought I to say? I'm not . . . mean to say, I don't know how to say things, Emmy. You'll have to put up with my rough ways. Give us a kiss, old sport."

"How many more! You *are* a one!" Emmy was not pliant enough. In her voice there was the faintest touch of—something that was not self-consciousness, that was perhaps a sense of failure. Perhaps she was back again suddenly into her maturity, finding it somehow ridiculous to be kissed and to kiss with such abandon. Alf was not baffled, however. As she withdrew he advanced, so that his knuckle rubbed against the brick wall to which Emmy had retreated.

"I say," he cried sharply. "Here's the wall."

"Hurt yourself?" Emmy quickly caught his hand and raised it, examining the knuckle. The skin might have been roughened; but no blood was drawn. Painfully, exultingly, her dream realized, she pressed her cheek against the back of his hand.

IX

"What's that for?" demanded Alf.

"Nothing. Never you mind. I wanted to do it." Emmy's cheeks were hot as she spoke; but Alf marveled at the action, and at her confession of such an impulse.

"How long had you . . . wanted to do it?"

"Mind your own business. The idea! Don't you know better than that?" Emmy asked. It made him chuckle delightedly to have such a retort from her. And it stimulated his curiosity.

"I believe you're a bit fond of me," he said. "I don't see why. There's nothing about me to write home about, I shouldn't think. But there it is: love's a wonderful thing."

"Is it?" asked Emmy, distantly. Why couldn't he say he loved her? Too proud, was he? Or was he shy? He had only used the word "love" once, and that was in this general sense—as though there *was* such a thing. Emmy was shy of the word, too; but not as shy as that. She was for a moment anxious, because she wanted him to say the word, or some equivalent. If it was not said, she was dependent upon his charity later, and would cry sleeplessly at night for want of sureness of him.

"D'you love me?" she suddenly said. Alf whistled. He seemed for that instant to be quite taken aback by her inquiry. "There's no harm in me asking, I suppose." Into Emmy's voice there came a thread of roughness.

"No harm at all," Alf politely said. "Not at all." He continued to hesitate.

"Well?" Emmy waited, still in his arms, her ears alert.

"We're engaged, aren't we?" Alf muttered shamefacedly. "Erum . . . what sort of ring would you like? I don't say you'll get it . . . and it's too late to go and choose one to-night." Emmy flushed again; he felt her tremble.

"You *are* in a hurry," she said, too much moved for her archness to take effect.

"Yes, I am." Alf's quick answer was reassuring enough. Emmy's heart was eased. She drew him nearer with her arms about his neck, and they kissed again.

"I wish you'd say you love me," she whispered. "Mean such a lot to me."

"No!" cried Alf incredulously. "Really?"

"Do you?"

"I'll think about it. Do you—me?"

"Yes. I don't mind saying it if you will."

Alf gave a little whistle to himself, half under his breath. He looked carefully to right and left, and up at the house-wall against which they were standing. Nobody seemed to be in danger of making him feel an abject fool by overhearing such a confession as he was invited to make; and yet it was such a terrible matter. He was confronted with a difficulty of difficulties. He looked at Emmy, and knew that she was waiting, entreating him with her shining eyes.

"Er," said Alf, reluctantly and with misgiving. "Er . . . well, I suppose I . . . a . . . suppose I do. . . ."

Emmy gave a little cry, that was half a smothered laugh of happiness at her triumph. It was not bad! She had made him admit it on the first evening. Later, when she was more at ease, he should be more explicit.

X

"Well," said Alf, instantly regretting his admission, and inclined to bluster. "Now, I suppose you're satisfied."

"Awfully!" breathed Emmy. "You're a dear good soul. You're splendid, Alf!"

For a few minutes more they remained in that benign, unforgettable shadow; and then, very slowly, with Alf's arm about Emmy's waist, and Emmy's shoulder so confidingly against his breast, they began to return homewards. Both spoke very subduedly, and tried to keep their shoes from too loudly striking the pavement as they walked; and the wandering wind came upon them in glee round every corner and rustled like a busybody among all the consumptive bushes in the front gardens they passed. Sounds carried far. A long way away they heard the tramcars grinding along the main road. But here all was hush, and the beating of two hearts in unison; and to both of them happiness lay ahead. Their aims were similar, in no point jarring or divergent. Both wanted a home, and loving labor, and quiet evenings of pleasant occupation. To both the daily work came with regularity, not as an intru-

sion or a wrong to manhood and womanhood; it was inevitable, and was regarded as inevitable. Neither Emmy nor Alf ever wondered why they should be working hard when the sun shone and the day was fine. Neither compared the lot accorded by station[20] with an ideal fortune of blessed ease. They were not temperamentally restless. They both thought, with a practical sense that is as convenient as it is generally accepted, "somebody must do the work: may as well be me." No discontent would be theirs. And Alf was a good worker at the bench, a sober and honest man; and Emmy could make a pound go as far as any other woman in Kennington Park.[21] They had before them a faithful future of work in common, of ideals (workaday ideals) in common; and at this instant they were both marvelously content with the immediate outlook. Not for them to change the order of the world.

"I feel it's so suitable," Emmy startlingly said, in a hushed tone, as they walked. "Your . . . you know . . . 'supposing you do' . . . me; and me . . . doing the same for you."

Alf looked solemnly round at her. His Emmy skittish? It was not what he had thought. Still, it diverted him; and he ambled in pursuit.

"Yes," he darkly said. "What do you 'suppose you do' for me?"

"Why, love you," Emmy hurried to explain, trapping herself by speed into the use of the tabooed word. "Didn't you know? Though it seems funny to say it like that. It's so new. I've never dared to . . . you know . . . say it. I mean we're both of us quiet, and reliable . . . we're not either of us flighty, I mean. That's why I think we suit each other—better than if we'd been different. Not like we are."

"I'm sure we do," Alf said.

"Not like some people. You can't help wondering to yourself however they came to

20. STATION: position in life one is born to.
21. KENNINGTON PARK: district in the south of London within Lambeth Borough.

get married. They seem so unlike. Don't they! It's funny. Ah, well, love's a wonderful thing—as you say!" She turned archly to him, encouragingly.

"You seem happy," remarked Alf, in a critical tone. But he was not offended; only tingled into desire for her by the strange gleam of merriment crossing her natural seriousness, the jubilant note of happy consciousness that the evening's love-making had bred. Alf drew her more closely to his side, increasingly sure that he had done well. She was beginning to intrigue him. With an emotion that startled himself as much as it delighted Emmy, he said thickly in her ear, "D'you love me . . . like this?"

XI

They neared the road in which the Blanchards lived: Emmy began to press forward as Alf seemed inclined to loiter. In the neighborhood the church that had struck eight as they left the house began once more to record an hour.

"By George!" cried Alf. "Twelve . . . Midnight!" They could feel the day pass.

They were at the corner, beside the little chandler's shop[22] which advertised to the moon its varieties of tea; and Alf paused once again.

"Half a tick," he said. "No hurry, is there?"

"You'll come in for a bit of supper," Emmy urged. Then, plumbing his hesitation, she went on, in a voice that had steel somewhere in its depths. "They'll both be gone to bed. She won't be there."

"Oh, I wasn't thinking of that," Alf declared, with unconvincing nonchalance.

"I'll give you a drop of Pa's beer," Emmy said drily.

She took out a key, and held it up for his inspection.

"I say!" Alf pretended to be surprised at the sight of a key.

"Quite a big girl, aren't I! Well, you see: there are two, and Pa never goes out. So we have one each. Saves a lot of bother." As she spoke Emmy was unlocking the door and entering the house. "See, you can have supper with me, and then it won't seem so far to walk home. And you can throw Madame Bucks's rinds[23] at the back of the fire. You'll like that; and so will she."

Alf, now perfectly docile, and even thrilled with pleasure at the idea of being with her for a little while longer, followed Emmy into the passage, where the flickering gas showed too feeble a light to be of any service to them. Between the two walls they felt their way into the house, and Alf softly closed the door.

"Hang your hat and coat on the stand," whispered Emmy, and went tiptoeing forward to the kitchen. It was in darkness. "Oo, she is a monkey! She's let the fire out," Emmy continued, in the same whisper. "Have you got a match? The gas is out." She opened the kitchen door wide, and stood there taking off her hat, while Alf fumbled his way along the passage. "Be quick," she said.

Alf pretended not to be able to find the matches, so that he might give her a hearty kiss in the darkness. He was laughing to himself because he had only succeeded, in his random venture, in kissing her chin; and then, when she broke away with a smothered protest and a half laugh, he put his hand in his pocket again for the match-box. The first match fizzed along the box as it was struck, and immediately went out.

"Oh, *do* hurry up!" cried Emmy in a whisper, thinking he was still sporting with her. "Don't keep on larking about, Alf!"

"I'm not!" indignantly answered the delinquent. "It wouldn't strike. Half a tick!"

He moved forward in the darkness, to be nearer the gas; and as he took the step his foot caught against something on the floor. He exclaimed.

"Now what is it?" demanded Emmy. For answer Alf struck his match, and they both

22. CHANDLER'S SHOP: grocer's.

23. RINDS: bacon rinds.

looked at the floor by Alf's feet. Emmy gave a startled cry and dropped to her knees.

"Hul-lo!" said Alf; and with his lighted match raised he moved to the gas, stepping, as he did so, over the body of Pa Blanchard, which was lying at full length across the kitchen floor.

I

1. What is the purpose of showing Emmy and Alf together at the theater? Why didn't the author simply say they had been there and then concentrate on the walk home? What kind of play do they see? What connection is there between the kind of play being seen and their reaction to it and the drama being enacted between Emmy and Alf?

2. What is Emmy like? How does she respond to events at the theater? What accounts for her sudden outburst about Jenny, and how is it prepared for? Why does she keep coming back to "Jenny and me"? Why does she instinctively seek the shadow both in the lobby of the theater and later when Alf kisses her?

3. What kind of person is Alf? Consider, among other things, his thoughts about Jenny, his manner of buying the candy in the theater, his reactions to the play, his reasons for deciding that Emmy would make a good wife.

4. How do we know from this chapter what kind of person Jenny is? What appeal does she have for Alf? Why does Emmy *admire* her? Why does Alf? Why doesn't Emmy like her? Does Alf like her? Why or why not? What do their mixed reactions toward her show about Emmy and Alf?

5. How are Emmy and Alf alike? Are they both self-centered? Why or why not? In what ways are they different?

6. What details prove that "they were both clumsy and a little trembling, not very practiced lovers, but curious and excited"?

7. What contrast is there between the way they entered the theater and the way they entered Emmy's house? What change in their relationship has the *engagement* brought about and what details of behavior underscore that change?

II

1. How accurate do you think H. G. Wells's observation is that this presentation of *vulgar lovemaking* is kept from being either *brutal* or *sentimental*? Be sure to indicate clearly what you think Wells means by the italicized terms. Is this episode, in its own way, a celebration of romantic love, or is it, by its very nature, a denial of romantic love? Discuss.

The Dispassionate Lover

"Celebration" of romantic love and the loved one forms the chief business of the preceding pieces. But celebration is, of course, only one of several kinds of expression that love begets.

A lover may, at times, disentangle himself from his emotions long enough to view his loved one—and his feelings for her—in a more detached light. His praise may then take on a bantering tone, teasing her about her shortcomings, or asserting his delight at having broken free of his bondage to her. If he looks deeply, he may recognize that love—particularly romantic love—cannot last, or that the world makes demands on us which cannot be met simply by the love of man and woman, however happy.

Some of the finest love poems in English are those in which a great tenderness for the loved one, combining with one or more of these other considerations, convinces us that here is a love as durable and tough-minded as it is tender-hearted.

TO A YOUNG LADY
ON HER LEAVING THE TOWN
AFTER THE CORONATION   [*1717*]

Alexander Pope

As some fond virgin, whom her mother's care
Drags from the town to wholesome country air,
Just when she learns to roll a melting eye,
And hear a spark, yet think no danger nigh;
From the dear man unwilling she must sever,   5
Yet takes one kiss before she parts forever:
Thus from the world fair Zephalinda flew,
Saw others happy, and with sighs withdrew;
Not that their pleasures caused her discontent,
She sighed not that they stayed, but that she went.   10
   She went to plain work, and to purling brooks,
Old-fashioned halls, dull aunts, and croaking rooks;
She went from opera, park, assembly, play,
To morning walks, and prayers three hours a day;
To part her time 'twixt reading and bohea,   15
To muse, and spill her solitary tea,
Or o'er cold coffee trifle with the spoon,
Count the slow clock, and dine exact at noon;
Divert her eyes with pictures in the fire,
Hum half a tune, tell stories to the squire;   20
Up to her godly garret after seven,
There starve and pray, for that's the way to Heaven.
   Some squire, perhaps, you take delight to rack,
Whose game is whisk, whose treat a toast in sack;
Who visits with a gun, presents you birds,   25
Then gives a smacking buss, and cries—No words!
Or with his hounds comes hallowing from the stable,
Makes love with nods and knees beneath a table:
Whose laughs are hearty, tho' his jests are coarse,
And loves you best of all things—but his horse.   30
   In some fair evening, on your elbow laid,
You dream of triumphs in the rural shade;

Title. CORONATION: of George I, October 20, 1714.
7. ZEPHALINDA: Teresa Blount (Parthenia, line 46, is her sister, Martha); the use of fanciful assumed names in gallantries was common in Pope's time.
11. PLAIN WORK: i.e., not embroidery or fanci-work.

15. BOHEA: tea.
23. RACK: tease, torment.
24. WHISK: whist, a card game similar to bridge, not fashionable at the time. SACK: strong white wine.

In pensive thought recall the fancied scene,
See coronations rise on every green;
Before you pass the imaginary sights   35
Of lords, and earls, and dukes, and gartered knights,
While the spread fan o'ershades your closing eyes;
Then give one flirt, and all the vision flies.
Thus vanish scepters, coronets, and balls,
And leave you in lone woods or empty walls.   40
      So when your slave, at some dear idle time,
(Not plagued with headaches, or the want of rhyme)
Stands in the streets, abstracted from the crew,
And while he seems to study, thinks of you;
Just when his fancy points your sprightly eyes,   45
Or sees the blush of soft Parthenia rise,
Gay pats my shoulder, and you vanish quite;
Streets, chairs, and coxcombs rush upon my sight;
Vexed to be still in town, I knit my brow,
Look sour, and hum a tune—as you may now.   50

---

38. ONE FLIRT: i.e., of the fan.
41. SLAVE: i.e., the speaker.
42. HEADACHES: Pope suffered from violent headaches.

47. GAY: Pope's friend and fellow poet, John Gay.
48. CHAIRS: sedan chairs.

I

1. How are lines 9-10 important for our understanding of the young lady's discontent on leaving town?

2. What are the two main deficiencies of living in the country as described in lines 11-30?

3. How does the idea in lines 41-50 turn the tables on that in lines 31-40? What characteristics of the speaker, either stated or implied in the poem, differentiate him sharply from the country lover described in lines 23-30?

4. There is little or no attention paid to what charms the lady may possess, but still the impression is given that the poem deals with more than just a casual friendship. How is this impression achieved?

5. A critic has said that the tone of the poem is one of "teasing tenderness." How is this tone achieved? What does he mean by "teasing" and by "tenderness"?

CONSTANCY [1659]

Sir John Suckling

Out upon it! I have loved
   Three whole days together;
And am like to love three more,
   If it prove fair weather.

Time shall molt away his wings,   5
   Ere he shall discover

In the whole wide world again
   Such a constant lover.

But the spite on 't is, no praise
   Is due at all to me;   10
Love with me had made no stays,
   Had it any been but she.

Had it any been but she,
   And that very face,
There had been at least ere this   15
   A dozen dozen in her place.

I

1. What is the purpose of opening the poem with a startling statement? What does "Out upon it!" mean? Is line 4 in keeping with the speaker's assertions in lines 2 and 3?

2. What kind of person is the speaker? Does he admit his constancy reluctantly? eagerly? begrudgingly? boastfully? facetiously? a combination or none of these? Explain.

3. Should the lady be complimented by his constancy? by his expression of it? Why does he say "she" and not "you" in line 12 (ignoring the rhyme factor)?

SHALL I WASTING
IN DESPAIR [*1622*]

George Wither

Shall I wasting in despair
Die because a woman's fair?
Or make pale my cheeks with care
'Cause another's rosy are?
Be she fairer than the day,   5
Or the flow'ry meads in May,
  If she be not so to me,
  What care I how fair she be?

Shall my heart be grieved or pined
'Cause I see a woman kind?   10
Or a well-disposèd nature
Joinèd with a lovely feature?
Be she meeker, kinder, than
Turtle-dove or pelican,
  If she be not so to me,   15
  What care I how kind she be?

Shall a woman's virtues move
Me to perish for her love?
Or her well-deserving known
Make me quite forget mine own?   20
Be she with that goodness blest

Which may gain her name of best,
  If she be not such to me,
  What care I how good she be?

'Cause her fortune seems too high,   25
Shall I play the fool and die?
Those that bear a noble mind,
Where they want of riches find,
Think what with them they would do
That without them dare to woo;   30
  And unless that mind I see,
  What care I how great she be?

Great, or good, or kind, or fair,
I will ne'er the more despair;
If she love me, this believe,   35
I will die ere she shall grieve;
If she slight me when I woo,
I can scorn and let her go;
  For if she be not for me,
  What care I for whom she be?   40

I

1. There are some grammatical difficulties here. What punctuation would there usually be in line 1? What does line 19 mean? In lines 27-30 "where" does not refer to "mind," and "want" means "lack"; therefore, lines 27-28 mean something like, "Those of noble mind who find a lack of riches in someone else. . . ." Thus "think" is the verb in the sentence. What do the two "them's" refer to, and what does "they" in line 29 refer to?

2. What is the effect of the slightly changed repetition of the last two lines in each stanza?

3. What are the two attitudes expressed in lines 35-36 and 37-38?

4. How does the neatness of the organization of the poem (four stanzas, each on a different womanly asset, all carefully listed in the first line of stanza 5) suggest the attitude of the speaker? Is there something mechanical (and therefore revealing) about his protestation?

5. Discuss the validity of the following comments on the poem:

a. "It's an exercise in sour grapes; the speaker must have been jilted."
b. "It's obvious that the speaker is self-centered and smug."
c. "The whole thing is a lighthearted spoof of poetry which idolizes women."

---

14. PELICAN: often used to symbolize self-sacrificing love, based on the old belief that the mother pelican fed her young on her own blood.

GO, LOVELY ROSE
[*1645, 1664*]

Edmund Waller

Go, lovely rose!
Tell her that wastes her time and me
That now she knows,
When I resemble her to thee,
How sweet and fair she seems to be.   5

Tell her that's young
And shuns to have her graces spied,
That hadst thou sprung
In deserts where no men abide,
Thou must have uncommended died.   10

Small is the worth
Of beauty from the light retired;
Bid her come forth,
Suffer herself to be desired,
And not blush so to be admired.   15

Then die, that she
The common fate of all things rare
May read in thee;
How small a part of time they share
That are so wondrous sweet and fair!   20

I

1. What overtones or multiple meanings are
there in: "wastes" (2), "spied" (7), "retired"
(12), "Suffer" (14), "blush" (15), and "rare"
(17)? What would be lost if a comma were
put between "wondrous" and "sweet" (20)?
2. In each stanza, the lady and her behavior
are compared or contrasted with certain facts
about the rose that the lover sends to her. State
each contrast or comparison in your own words.
3. Apart from the compliment to her beauty,
what is gained by admonishing the young lady
through the example of the rose?
4. What is the tone of the poem? The
speaker is certainly objecting to the lady's
choice of seclusion, but how would you characterize the tone of his objection: cajoling? insistent? matter-of-fact? tender? not any of these?

WHEN I WAS
ONE-AND-TWENTY [*1896*]

A. E. Housman

When I was one-and-twenty
I heard a wise man say,
"Give crowns and pounds and guineas
But not your heart away;
Give pearls away and rubies   5
But keep your fancy free."
But I was one-and-twenty,
No use to talk to me.

When I was one-and-twenty
I heard him say again,   10
"The heart out of the bosom
Was never given in vain;
'Tis paid with sighs a-plenty
And sold for endless rue."
And I am two-and-twenty,   15
And oh, 'tis true, 'tis true.

I

1. What is the situation of the poem? What
kind of person is the speaker?
2. How does the advice of stanza 2 elaborate
on the advice of stanza 1? If the basic metaphor is built around the idea of a gift, what is
ironic about lines 13-14, with the verbs "paid"
and "sold"?
3. What has the speaker learned? How seriously are we to take the insight reached? How
endless is the rue of line 14 considering the
speaker's age?
4. The short, three-stress iambic line usually
gives a lightness of rhythm that can easily get
sing-songy. How does Housman keep the lightness and yet not fall into the sing-song pattern?
Consider, for example, the vowel pattern in

line 3 and the variation in rhythm in lines 11-12. What relation is there between rhythm and sense?

5. Would the poem be more, or less, effective had the speaker shifted his point of view at five-and-twenty? ten-and-twenty? Why?

TWO POEMS BY ROBERT BROWNING [*1845*]

Meeting at Night

The gray sea and the long black land;
And the yellow half-moon large and low;
And the startled little waves that leap
In fiery ringlets from their sleep,
As I gain the cove with pushing prow,   5
And quench its speed i' the slushy sand.

Then a mile of warm sea-scented beach;
Three fields to cross till a farm appears;
A tap at the pane, the quick sharp scratch
And blue spurt of a lighted match,   10
And a voice less loud, through its joys and fears,
Than the two hearts beating each to each!

Parting at Morning

Round the cape of a sudden came the sea,
And the sun looked over the mountain's rim:
And straight was a path of gold for him,
And the need of a world of men for me.

---

3. HIM: i.e., the sun.

I

1. The two poems quite obviously are meant to go together. What is the story that is suggested rather than told: in "Meeting at Night"? in "Parting at Morning"?

2. Does the speaker's concentrating on the details of the trip indicate that he doesn't really care about the girl? Or does this instead tell us how keenly he loves her? Explain.

3. What do the last two lines of "Parting at Morning" mean? What is the meaning of the "world of men"?

4. Both poems offer excellent examples of the intimate blending of sound, rhythm, and syntax with the sense:

a. How does the sound of lines 5-6 help support what is being said in them? Point out a similar effect in lines 9-10.

b. How does the absence of verbs in lines 1-4 and 7-12 (and of *main* verbs everywhere) help convey the emotion of the lover? What is the effect of the three "And's" which begin each of the last three lines?

c. There is a flat, lifeless rhythm in the lines of "Parting at Morning." How is it obtained? Why is it appropriate?

AFTER LONG SILENCE
[*1933*]

William Butler Yeats

Speech after long silence; it is right,
All other lovers being estranged or dead,
Unfriendly lamplight hid under its shade,
The curtains drawn upon unfriendly night,
That we descant and yet again descant   5
Upon the supreme theme of Art and Song:
Bodily decrepitude is wisdom; young
We loved each other and were ignorant.

I

1. What is the situation of the poem? Where are the two who loved each other sitting? In what time of life are they? Why does the speaker call the lamplight "Unfriendly"? Why is the night "unfriendly"? Consider why neither would have been thought of as unfriendly when the lovers were young.

2. How has their love changed? What do they now talk about? What do they mean by "Art and Song"? Why should *Art and Song* be the *supreme theme* to lovers who have grown old? What comment is being made about wisdom and ignorance in the last two lines? When does wisdom come, and what is lost along with ignorance when youth is lost?

3. Lines 4-5 give the basic iambic pentameter meter of the poem. The many variations on this pattern in other lines serve to give a conversational effect to the poem. Why is this effect desirable? How does Yeats get emphasis on the words "Speech" (1), "it" (1), "supreme theme" (6), and "young" (7), and why does he want to emphasize these words?

TO LUCASTA, GOING TO THE WARS
[*1649*]

Richard Lovelace

Tell me not, Sweet, I am unkind
　　That from the nunnery
Of thy chaste breast and quiet mind,
　　To war and arms I fly.

True, a new mistress now I chase,   5
　　The first foe in the field;
And with a stronger faith embrace
　　A sword, a horse, a shield.

Yet this inconstancy is such
　　As you too shall adore;   10
I could not love thee, dear, so much,
　　Loved I not honor more.

I

1. What real or imagined comment by his loved one is the speaker replying to?

2. What double meaning is there in the poet's use of the words *arms, chase,* and *embrace?* What is the effect of his describing his *going to the war* in terms of turning to a *new mistress?* Who specifically is to be the *new mistress?*

3. What is the central paradox of the poem? What is the "inconstancy" he refers to in line 9 and why should his loved one *adore* it? State in your own words the meaning of the last two lines.

II

1. Using any, or all, of the poems in this section, show how successfully or unsuccessfully for you they combine a tender feeling for —even a celebration of—the loved one with a tough-minded detachment that recognizes love's necessary co-existence with other demands on man's needs and desires.

THE RAPE OF THE LOCK   [*1714*]

Alexander Pope

For the combination of attitudes which places celebration of woman side by side with firm recognition of her frailties, which looks on the mating process as of greatest importance yet hilarious in its iron-clad conventions, there is no poem in English more satisfying than Pope's "The Rape of the Lock." Here is a delightful picture of the "war of the sexes" with its elaborate rites of flirtation and pursuit; and here, at the same time, a sober recognition of the fact that the battle is often viewed by contestants (and onlookers) whose vision has been blurred by ill-mannered insult, injured honor, and misplaced values. Pope makes fun of the courting game by exhibiting all its inanities, but beneath the fun is a sharp criticism of the ethical blindness that allows such a distortion of personal and social values to flourish.

The poem was prompted by an actual occurrence among people Pope knew. Lord Petre (the Baron in the poem) had clipped a few locks of hair from the head of a young lady he was fond of, Arabella Fermor (Belinda in the poem); she in turn had raised such a cry of injured merit at his bad manners that a serious breach began to develop between the two families involved. One of Pope's friends (the Caryll referred to in Canto I, line 3) asked him to write a light-hearted poem on the subject, hoping that a little satire would put the whole foolish incident in the proper perspective.

Pope's genius lifted the incident forever out of the specific context for which it was written and put it into the timeless world of great literature where old truths are forever new. Through the poem life becomes "art" and thereby available for our enjoyment even though all the participants and the poet who immortalized them are long since dead. The last two lines of the poem cap the mock-heroic treatment of the theme and provide a fitting commentary on Pope's achievement:

> This lock the muse shall consecrate to fame,
> And midst the stars inscribe Belinda's name.

Canto I

> What dire offense from amorous causes springs,
> What mighty contests rise from trivial things,
> I sing—This verse to Caryll, Muse! is due;
> This, even Belinda may vouchsafe to view:
> Slight is the subject, but not so the praise,   5
> If She inspire, and He approve my lays.
>   Say what strange motive, Goddess! could compel
> A well-bred Lord t' assault a gentle Belle?
> O say what stranger cause, yet unexplored,

1-3. The opening lines are a parody of the epic invocation.

Could make a gentle Belle reject a Lord?   10
In tasks so bold, can little men engage,
And in soft bosoms dwells such mighty Rage?
      Sol thro' white curtains shot a timorous ray,
And oped those eyes that must eclipse the day:
Now lap-dogs give themselves the rousing shake,   15
And sleepless lovers, just at twelve, awake:
Thrice rung the bell, the slipper knocked the ground,
And the pressed watch returned a silver sound.
Belinda still her downy pillow prest
Her guardian Sylph prolonged the balmy rest: 20
'Twas He had summoned to her silent bed
The morning-dream that hovered o'er her head;
A Youth more glittering than a Birth-night Beau,
(That even in slumber caused her cheek to glow)
Seemed to her ear his winning lips to lay,   25
And thus in whispers said, or seemed to say.
      "Fairest of mortals, thou distinguished care
Of thousand bright Inhabitants of Air!
If e'er one vision touched thy infant thought,
Of all the Nurse and all the Priest have taught: 30
Of airy Elves by moonlight shadows seen,
The silver token, and the circled green,
Or virgins visited by Angel-powers,
With golden crowns and wreaths of heavenly flowers;
Hear and believe! thy own importance know,   35
Nor bound thy narrow views to things below.
Some secret truths, from learnèd pride concealed,
To Maids alone and Children are revealed:
What tho' no credit doubting Wits may give?
The Fair and Innocent shall still believe.   40
Know, then, unnumbered Spirits round thee fly,
The light Militia of the lower sky:
These, tho' unseen, are ever on the wing,
Hang o'er the Box, and hover round the Ring.
Think what an equipage thou hast in Air,   45
And view with scorn two Pages and a Chair.
As now your own, our beings were of old,
And once enclosed in Woman's beauteous mold;

---

13. SOL: the sun.
14. OPED: opened.
17. THRICE . . . GROUND: Belinda summons her maid.
18. PRESSED WATCH: a watch for night use, which, when pressed, sounded the hour and quarter hour just passed.
19. BELINDA . . . PREST: She has fallen asleep again.
20. HER GUARDIAN SYLPH: see Canto I, 105–106.

23. BIRTH-NIGHT: i.e., dressed in finery for a royal birthday.
27–114. This speech parodies the epic message from Zeus delivered to a mortal by Mercury.
32. SILVER TOKEN: the sixpence that fairies leave in the shoe of maids they approve.
44. BOX: theater box. RING: a drive in Hyde Park, London, where ladies of fashion showed themselves off in their coaches.
46. CHAIR: sedan chair.

Thence, by a soft transition, we repair
From earthly Vehicles to these of air.   50
Think not, when Woman's transient breath is fled
That all her vanities at once are dead;
Succeeding vanities she still regards,
And tho' she plays no more, o'erlooks the cards.
Her joy in gilded Chariots, when alive,   55
And love of Ombre, after death survive.
For when the Fair in all their pride expire,
To their first Elements their Souls retire:
The Sprites of fiery Termagants in Flame
Mount up, and take a Salamander's name.   60
Soft yielding minds to Water glide away,
And sip, with Nymphs, their elemental Tea.
The graver Prude sinks downward to a Gnome,
In search of mischief still on Earth to roam.
The light Coquettes in Sylphs aloft repair,   65
And sport and flutter in the fields of Air.
    "Know further yet; whoever fair and chaste
Rejects mankind, is by some Sylph embraced:
For Spirits, freed from mortal laws, with ease
Assume what sexes and what shapes they please.   70
What guards the purity of melting Maids,
In courtly balls, and midnight masquerades,
Safe from the treacherous friend, the daring spark,
The glance by day, the whisper in the dark,
When kind occasion prompts their warm desires,   75
When music softens, and when dancing fires?
'Tis but their Sylph, the wise Celestials know,
Tho' Honor is the word with Men below.
    "Some nymphs there are, too conscious of their face
For life predestined to the Gnomes' embrace.   80
These swell their prospects and exalt their pride,
When offers are disdained, and love denied:
Then gay Ideas crowd the vacant brain,
While Peers, and Dukes, and all their sweeping train,
And Garters, Stars, and Coronets appear,   85
And in soft sounds, Your Grace salutes their ear.
'Tis these that early taint the female soul,
Instruct the eyes of young Coquettes to roll,

---

50. VEHICLES: i.e., bodies (note the punning reference to *equipage* and *Chair*).
55. CHARIOTS: carriages.
56. OMBRE: a card game, similar to bridge (see III, 27ff.).
60. SALAMANDER'S NAME: Salamanders were supposed to live in fire.
62. NYMPHS: here, minor sea goddesses.

63. GNOME: underground deity.
57-66. The "Fair" are being classified in four categories based on the theory of the four elements (earth, water, air, fire) and the supposed dominance of one of these in every temperament.
73. SPARK: beau.
83. IDEAS: images.

Teach Infant-cheeks a bidden blush to know,
And little hearts to flutter at a Beau.   90
    "Oft, when the world imagine women stray,
The Sylphs thro' mystic mazes guide their way,
Thro' all the giddy circle they pursue,
And old impertinence expel by new.
What tender maid but must a victim fall   95
To one man's treat, but for another's ball?
When Florio speaks, what virgin could withstand,
If gentle Damon did not squeeze her hand?
With varying vanities, from every part,
They shift the moving Toyshop of their heart;   100
Where wigs with wigs, with sword-knots sword-knots strive,
Beaux banish beaux, and coaches coaches drive.
This erring mortals Levity may call;
Oh blind to truth! the Sylphs contrive it all.
    "Of these am I, who thy protection claim,   105
A watchful sprite, and Ariel is my name.
Late, as I ranged the crystal wilds of air,
In the clear mirror of thy ruling Star
I saw, alas! some dread event impend,
Ere to the main this morning sun descend,   110
But heaven reveals not what, or how, or where:
Warned by the Sylph, oh pious maid, beware!
This to disclose is all thy guardian can:
Beware of all, but most beware of Man!"
    He said; when Shock, who thought she slept too long,   115
Leaped up, and waked his mistress with his tongue.
'Twas then, Belinda, if report say true,
Thy eyes first opened on a Billet-doux;
Wounds, Charms, and Ardors were no sooner read,
But all the Vision vanished from thy head.   120
    And now, unveiled, the Toilet stands displayed,
Each silver Vase in mystic order laid.
First, robed in white, the Nymph intent adores,
With head uncovered, the Cosmetic powers.
A heavenly image in the glass appears,   125
To that she bends, to that her eyes she rears;
Th' inferior Priestess, at her altar's side,
Trembling begins the sacred rites of Pride.
Unnumbered treasures ope at once, and here

---

89. BLUSH: i.e., by rouge.
94. IMPERTINENCE: folly.
97-98. FLORIO . . . DAMON: specific names used solely for the purpose of illustrating the general statements made in lines 93-96.
101. SWORD-KNOTS: ribbons on sword hilts.
115. SHOCK: Belinda's dog.

119. WOUNDS . . . ARDORS: the exaggerated language of the billet-doux.
121-148. The scene here is a parody of the arming of the epic hero for combat and of the celebration of religious rites before a god or goddess; Belinda is the chief priestess, her maid, the inferior one; Belinda's "image in the glass" is the goddess being prepared.

The various offerings of the world appear;   130
From each she nicely culls with curious toil,
And decks the Goddess with the glittering spoil.
This casket India's glowing gems unlocks,
And all Arabia breathes from yonder box.
The Tortoise here and Elephant unite,   135
Transformed to combs, the speckled, and the white.
Here files of pins extend their shining rows,
Puffs, Powders, Patches, Bibles, Billet-doux
Now awful Beauty puts on all its arms;
The fair each moment rises in her charms,   140
Repairs her smiles, awakens every grace,
And calls forth all the wonders of her face;
Sees by degrees a purer blush arise,
And keener lightnings quicken in her eyes.
The busy Sylphs surround their darling care,   145
These set the head, and those divide the hair,
Some fold the sleeve, whilst others plait the gown;
And Betty's praised for labors not her own.

Canto II

Not with more glories, in th' ethereal plain,
The Sun first rises o'er the purpled main,
Than, issuing forth, the rival of his beams
Launched on the bosom of the silver Thames.
Fair Nymphs, and well-drest Youths around her shone,   5
But every eye was fixed on her alone.
On her white breast a sparkling Cross she wore,
Which Jews might kiss, and Infidels adore.
Her lively looks a sprightly mind disclose,
Quick as her eyes, and as unfixed as those: 10
Favors to none, to all she smiles extends;
Oft she rejects, but never once offends.
Bright as the sun, her eyes the gazers strike,
And, like the sun, they shine on all alike.
Yet graceful ease, and sweetness void of pride,   15
Might hide her faults, if Belles had faults to hide:
If to her share some female errors fall,
Look on her face, and you'll forget 'em all.
  This Nymph, to the destruction of mankind,
Nourished two Locks, which graceful hung behind   20
In equal curls, and well conspired to deck
With shining ringlets the smooth ivory neck.
Love in these labyrinths his slaves detains,

---

138. PATCHES: beauty patches.
148. BETTY: Belinda's maid.
1-18. These lines parody the elaborate epic simile.

14. So God "maketh his sun to rise on the evil and on the good" (Matthew 5:45).

And mighty hearts are held in slender chains.
With hairy springes we the birds betray,   25
Slight lines of hair surprise the finny prey,
Fair tresses man's imperial race ensnare,
And beauty draws us with a single hair.
　　Th' adventurous Baron the bright locks admired;
He saw, he wished, and to the prize aspired.   30
Resolved to win, he meditates the way,
By force to ravish, or by fraud betray;
For when success a Lover's toil attends,
Few ask, if fraud or force attained his ends.
　　For this, ere Phœbus rose, he had implored   35
Propitious heaven, and every power adored,
But chiefly Love—to Love an Altar built,
Of twelve vast French Romances, neatly gilt.
There lay three garters, half a pair of gloves;
And all the trophies of his former loves;   40
With tender Billet-doux he lights the pyre,
And breathes three amorous sighs to raise the fire.
Then prostrate falls, and begs with ardent eyes
Soon to obtain, and long possess the prize:
The powers gave ear, and granted half his prayer,   45
The rest, the winds dispersed in empty air.
　　But now secure the painted vessel glides,
The sunbeams trembling on the floating tides:
While melting music steals upon the sky,
And softened sounds along the waters die;   50
Smooth flow the waves, the Zephyrs gently play,
Belinda smiled, and all the world was gay.
All but the Sylph—with careful thoughts opprest,
Th' impending woe sat heavy on his breast.
He summons straight his Denizens of air;   55
The lucid squadrons round the sails repair:
Soft o'er the shrouds aërial whispers breathe,
That seemed but Zephyrs to the train beneath.
Some to the sun their insect-wings unfold,
Waft on the breeze, or sink in clouds of gold;   60
Transparent forms, too fine for mortal sight,
Their fluid bodies half dissolved in light.
Loose to the wind their airy garments flew,
Thin glittering textures of the filmy dew,
Dipt in the richest tincture of the skies,   65

---

35. PHŒBUS: the sun.
35-46. These lines are a parody of the epic sacrifice and prayer (note what is being sacrificed
and the indication that only half the prayer will
be answered).

47. VESSEL: the boat on the Thames which is
carrying Belinda and her party to Hampton
Court.
53-72. A parody of the contravention of heavenly
powers in human affairs, which is characteristic
of epic.

Where light disports in ever-mingling dyes,
While every beam new transient colors flings,
Colors that change whene'er they wave their wings.
Amid the circle, on the gilded mast,
Superior by the head, was Ariel placed;   70
His purple pinions opening to the sun,
He raised his azure wand, and thus begun.
   "Ye Sylphs and Sylphids, to your chief give ear!
Fays, Fairies, Genii, Elves, and Dæmons, hear!
Ye know the spheres and various tasks assigned   75
By laws eternal to th' aërial kind.
Some in the fields of purest ether play,
And bask and whiten in the blaze of day.
Some guide the course of wandering orbs on high,
Or roll the planets thro' the boundless sky.   80
Some less refined, beneath the moon's pale light
Pursue the stars that shoot athwart the night,
Or suck the mists in grosser air below,
Or dip their pinions in the painted bow,
Or brew fierce tempests on the wintry main,   85
Or o'er the glebe distill the kindly rain.
Others on earth o'er human race preside,
Watch all their ways, and all their actions guide:
Of these the chief the care of Nations own,
And guard with Arms divine the British Throne.   90
   "Our humbler province is to tend the Fair,
Not a less pleasing, tho' less glorious care;
To save the powder from too rude a gale,
Nor let th' imprisoned essences exhale;
To draw fresh colors from the vernal flowers;   95
To steal from rainbows ere they drop in showers
A brighter wash; to curl their waving hairs,
Assist their blushes, and inspire their airs;
Nay oft, in dreams, invention we bestow,
To change a Flounce, or add a Furbelow.   100
   "This day, black Omens threat the brightest Fair
That e'er deserved a watchful spirit's care;
Some dire disaster, or by force, or slight;
But what, or where, the fates have wrapt in night:
Whether the nymph shall break Diana's law,   105
Or some frail China jar receive a flaw;
Or stain her honor or her new brocade;
Forget her prayers, or miss a masquerade;

---

70. SUPERIOR . . . HEAD: i.e., taller than the others (as the epic hero always is).
73-136. Parody of the formal epic address by a chieftain to his troops.

97. WASH: lotion.
101. THREAT: threaten.
103. SLIGHT: cunning.
105. DIANA'S LAW: vow of chastity.

Or lose her heart, or necklace, at a ball;
Or whether Heaven has doomed that Shock must fall.   110
Haste, then, ye spirits! to your charge repair:
The fluttering fan be Zephyretta's care;
The drops to thee, Brillante, we consign;
And, Momentilla, let the watch be thine;
Do thou, Crispissa, tend her favorite Lock;   115
Ariel himself shall be the guard of Shock.
   "To fifty chosen Sylphs, of special note,
We trust th' important charge, the Petticoat:
Oft have we known that seven-fold fence to fail,
Tho' stiff with hoops, and armed with ribs of whale;   120
Form a strong line about the silver bound,
And guard the wide circumference around.
   "Whatever spirit, careless of his charge,
His post neglects, or leaves the Fair at large,
Shall feel sharp vengeance soon o'ertake his sins,   125
Be stopped in vials, or transfixed with pins;
Or plunged in lakes of bitter washes lie,
Or wedged whole ages in a bodkin's eye:
Gums and Pomatums shall his flight restrain,
While clogged he beats his silken wings in vain;   130
Or Alum styptics with contracting power
Shrink his thin essence like a riveled flower:
Or, as Ixion fixed, the wretch shall feel
The giddy motion of the whirling Mill,
In fumes of burning Chocolate shall glow,   135
And tremble at the sea that froths below!"
   He spoke; the spirits from the sails descend;
Some, orb in orb, around the nymph extend;
Some thrid the mazy ringlets of her hair;
Some hang upon the pendants of her ear: 140
With beating hearts the dire event they wait,
Anxious, and trembling for the birth of Fate.

Canto III

Close by those meads, forever crowned with flowers,
Where Thames with pride surveys his rising towers,
There stands a structure of majestic frame,
Which from the neighboring Hampton takes its name.

112-115. The sylphs' names (roughly equivalent to "Fluttering," "Sparkling," "Timing," and "Curling") imply their functions.
113. DROPS: diamond earrings.
128. BODKIN'S: needle's.
129. POMATUMS: pomades.
132. RIVELED: shriveled.

133. IXION: In Greek mythology, Ixion was bound to a turning wheel for boastful behavior.
134. MILL: beater (for the hot chocolate).
139. THRID: thread.
3. STRUCTURE: Hampton Court, one of the royal residences.

Here Britain's statesmen oft the fall foredoom 5
Of foreign Tyrants and of Nymphs at home;
Here thou, great Anna! whom three realms obey,
Dost sometimes counsel take—and sometimes Tea.
    Hither the heroes and the nymphs resort,
To taste awhile the pleasures of a Court; 10
In various talk th' instructive hours they past,
Who gave the ball, or paid the visit last;
One speaks the glory of the British Queen,
And one describes a charming Indian screen;
A third interprets motions, looks, and eyes; 15
At every word a reputation dies.
Snuff, or the fan, supply each pause of chat,
With singing, laughing, ogling, *and all that.*
    Meanwhile, declining from the noon of day,
The sun obliquely shoots his burning ray; 20
The hungry Judges soon the sentence sign,
And wretches hang that jurymen may dine;
The merchant from th' Exchange returns in peace,
And the long labors of the Toilet cease.
Belinda now, whom thirst of fame invites, 25
Burns to encounter two adventurous knights,
At Ombre singly to decide their doom;
And swells her breast with conquests yet to come.
Straight the three bands prepare in arms to join,
Each band the number of the sacred Nine, 30
Soon as she spreads her hand, th' aërial guard
Descend, and sit on each important card:
First Ariel perched upon a Matadore,
Then each, according to the rank they bore;
For Sylphs, yet mindful of their ancient race, 35
Are, as when women, wondrous fond of place.
    Behold, four Kings in majesty revered,
With hoary whiskers and a forky beard;
And four fair Queens whose hands sustain a flower,
Th' expressive emblem of their softer power; 40
Four Knaves in garbs succinct, a trusty band,
Caps on their heads, and halberds in their hand;

---

7. ANNA . . . OBEY: Anne, Queen of England, Scotland, and Wales.
8. TEA: rhymes with obey.
25ff. The game as a whole parodies the single combats between knights in epic poetry.
27. In Ombre there are three players, each with nine cards. The high bidder is called the ombre and names the trumps. He must win more tricks than his opponents combined.

29. BANDS: i.e., the hands of cards.
30. NINE: the Muses.
33. MATADORE: The Matadores are the three highest trumps: ace of spades (Spadillio), lowest card of the trump suit (Manillio), and ace of clubs (Basto).
37ff. In the following lines Pope describes what the face cards look like.
41. SUCCINCT: tucked up.

And particolored troops, a shining train,
Draw forth to combat on the velvet plain.
   The skillful Nymph reviews her force with care: 45
Let Spades be trumps! she said, and trumps they were.
   Now move to war her sable Matadores,
In show like leaders of the swarthy Moors.
Spadillio first, unconquerable Lord!
Led off two captive trumps, and swept the board.   50
As many more Manillio forced to yield,
And marched a victor from the verdant field.
Him Basto followed, but his fate more hard
Gained but one trump and one Plebian card.
With his broad saber next, a chief in years,   55
The hoary Majesty of Spades appears,
Puts forth one manly leg, to sight revealed,
The rest, his many-colored robe concealed.
The rebel Knave, who dares his prince engage,
Proves the just victim of his royal rage.   60
Even mighty Pam, that Kings and Queens o'erthrew
And mowed down armies in the fights of Lu,
Sad chance of war! now destitute of aid,
Falls undistinguished by the victor spade!
   Thus far both armies to Belinda yield;   65
Now to the Baron fate inclines the field.
His warlike Amazon her host invades,
Th' imperial consort of the crown of Spades.
The Club's black Tyrant first her victim died,
Spite of his haughty mien, and barbarous pride: 70
What boots the regal circle on his head,
His giant limbs, in state unwieldy spread;
That long behind he trails his pompous robe,
And of all monarchs only grasps the globe?
   The Baron now his Diamonds pours apace;   75
Th' embroidered King who shows but half his face,
And his refulgent Queen, with powers combined,
Of broken troops an easy conquest find.
Clubs, Diamonds, Hearts, in wild disorder seen,
With throngs promiscuous strow the level green.   80
Thus when dispersed a routed army runs,
Of Asia's troops, and Afric's sable sons,
With like confusion different nations fly,
Of various habit, and of various dye,
The pierced battalions dis-united fall,   85

---

44. VELVET PLAIN: surface of the card table.
46. LET . . . WERE: Cf. Genesis 1:3—"And God
    said, 'Let there be light,' and there was light."
49-64. Belinda takes four successive tricks (of the
    nine possible) and thus needs one more to win.

61. PAM: knave of clubs, high card in game of loo
    (lu).
67-88. The Baron takes four successive tricks.

In heaps on heaps; one fate o'erwhelms them all.
   The Knave of Diamonds tries his wily arts,
And wins (oh shameful chance!) the Queen of Hearts.
At this, the blood the virgin's cheek forsook,
A livid paleness spreads o'er all her look;   90
She sees, and trembles at th' approaching ill,
Just in the jaws of ruin, and Codille.
And now (as oft in some distempered State)
On one nice Trick depends the general fate.
An Ace of Hearts steps forth: The King unseen   95
Lurked in her hand, and mourned his captive Queen:
He springs to Vengeance with an eager pace,
And falls like thunder on the prostrate Ace.
The nymph exulting fills with shouts the sky;
The walls, the woods, the long canals reply.   100
   Oh thoughtless mortals! ever blind to fate,
Too soon dejected, and too soon elate.
Sudden, these honors shall be snatched away,
And cursed forever this victorious day.
   For lo! the board with cups and spoons is crowned,   105
The berries crackle, and the mill turns round;
On shining Altars of Japan they raise
The silver lamp; the fiery spirits blaze:
From silver spouts the grateful liquors glide,
While China's earth receives the smoking tide: 110
At once they gratify their scent and taste,
And frequent cups prolong the rich repast.
Straight hover round the Fair her airy band;
Some, as she sipped, the fuming liquor fanned,
Some o'er her lap their careful plumes displayed,   115
Trembling, and conscious of the rich brocade.
Coffee (which makes the politician wise,
And see thro' all things with his half-shut eyes)
Sent up in vapors to the Baron's brain
New Stratagems, the radiant Lock to gain.   120
Ah cease, rash youth! desist ere 'tis too late,
Fear the just Gods, and think of Scylla's Fate!
Changed to a bird, and sent to flit in air,
She dearly pays for Nisus' injured hair!

---

92. CODILLE: failure to get the five tricks needed to win.
95. KING: In the red suits, the King is high.
99-100. Parody of epic "pride," which will lead to a fall.
105ff. Parody of the epic feast.
106. BERRIES: coffee beans. MILL: coffee mill.
107. ALTARS OF JAPAN: japanned, i.e., lacquered, tables.

110. WHILE . . . TIDE: The double reference is to the China cups and to the epic tradition of pouring libations to the gods on the ground.
122. SCYLLA'S FATE: Scylla, daughter of Nisus, was in love with Minos, her father's enemy. Thinking to please him, she cut from her father's head a purple hair on which the kingdom's prosperity depended. Minos drowned her for the treacherous act, and she was changed into a small sea bird.

But when to mischief mortals bend their will,   125
How soon they find fit instruments of ill!
Just then, Clarissa drew with tempting grace
A two-edged weapon from her shining case:
So Ladies in Romance assist their Knight,
Present the spear, and arm him for the fight.   130
He takes the gift with reverence, and extends
The little engine on his fingers' ends;
This just behind Belinda's neck he spread,
As o'er the fragrant steams she bends her head.
Swift to the Lock a thousand Sprites repair,   135
A thousand wings, by turns, blow back the hair;
And thrice they twitched the diamond in her ear;
Thrice she looked back, and thrice the foe drew near.
Just in that instant, anxious Ariel sought
The close recesses of the Virgin's thought;   140
As on the nosegay in her breast reclined,
He watched th' Ideas rising in her mind,
Sudden he viewed, in spite of all her art,
An earthly Lover lurking at her heart.
Amazed, confused, he found his power expired,   145
Resigned to fate, and with a sigh retired.
    The Peer now spreads the glittering Forfex wide,
T' inclose the Lock; now joins it, to divide.
Even then, before the fatal engine closed,
A wretched Sylph too fondly interposed;   150
Fate urged the shears, and cut the Sylph in twain,
(But airy substance soon unites again)
The meeting points the sacred hair dissever
From the fair head, forever, and forever!
    Then flashed the living lightning from her eyes,   155
And screams of horror rend th' affrighted skies.
Not louder shrieks to pitying heaven are cast,
When husbands, or when lap-dogs breathe their last;
Or when rich China vessels fallen from high,
In glittering dust and painted fragments lie!   160
    "Let wreaths of triumph now my temples twine
(The victor cried) the glorious Prize is mine!
While fish in streams, or birds delight in air,
Or in a coach and six the British Fair,
As long as Atalantis shall be read,   165
Or the small pillow grace a Lady's bed,

---

127. CLARISSA: another lady present.
128. TWO-EDGED WEAPON: scissors.
146. RESIGNED . . . RETIRED: See I: 67-68; the
    Sylph no longer can associate herself with
    Belinda.

147. FORFEX: Latin for scissors.
161-170. The Baron's turn for a display of epic
    "pride."
165. ATALANTIS: a "novel" of the day, full of scan-
    dal.

While visits shall be paid on solemn days,
When numerous wax-lights in bright order blaze,
While nymphs take treats, or assignations give,
So long my honor, name, and praise shall live!"   170
    What Time would spare, from Steel receives its date,
And monuments, like men, submit to fate!
Steel could the labor of the Gods destroy,
And strike to dust th' imperial towers of Troy;
Steel could the works of mortal pride confound,   175
And hew triumphal arches to the ground.
What wonder then, fair nymph! thy hairs should feel,
The conquering force of unresisted steel?

Canto IV

But anxious cares the pensive nymph oppressed,
And secret passions labored in her breast.
Not youthful kings in battle seized alive,
Not scornful virgins who their charms survive,
Not ardent lovers robbed of all their bliss,   5
Not ancient ladies when refused a kiss,
Not tyrants fierce that unrepenting die,
Not Cynthia when her manteau's pinned awry,
E'er felt such rage, resentment, and despair,
As thou, sad Virgin! for thy ravished Hair.   10
    For, that sad moment, when the Sylphs withdrew
And Ariel weeping from Belinda flew,
Umbriel, a dusky, melancholy sprite,
As ever sullied the fair face of light,
Down to the central earth, his proper scene,   15
Repaired to search the gloomy Cave of Spleen.
    Swift on his sooty pinions flits the Gnome,
And in a vapor reached the dismal dome.
No cheerful breeze this sullen region knows,
The dreaded East is all the wind that blows.   20
Here in a grotto, sheltered close from air,
And screened in shades from day's detested glare,
She sighs forever on her pensive bed,
Pain at her side, and Megrim at her head.

171-178. Parody of the weighty moral reflections in which epic abounds.

15ff. Parody of the epic visit to the underworld.

16. SPLEEN: The reference is to neurotic behavior here, not simply bad temper.

17. GNOME: The Gnome, Umbriel, has taken over from the Sylph, Ariel (cf. I, 63-64). Prudery and not coquetry is now in control of Belinda, and her behavior changes accordingly.

18. VAPOR: used in both its senses of "mist" and "peevishness."

20. EAST: The East wind was supposed to cause the spleen.

24. MEGRIM: i.e., "migraine," a severe headache.

Two handmaids wait the throne: alike in place,   25
But differing far in figure and in face.
Here stood Ill-nature like an ancient maid,
Her wrinkled form in black and white arrayed;
With store of prayers, for mornings, nights, and noons,
Her hand is filled; her bosom with lampoons.   30
  There Affectation, with a sickly mien,
Shows in her cheek the roses of eighteen,
Practiced to lisp, and hang the head aside,
Faints into airs, and languishes with pride;
On the rich quilt sinks with becoming woe,   35
Wrapt in a gown, for sickness, and for show.
The fair ones feel such maladies as these,
When each new night-dress gives a new disease.
  A constant Vapor o'er the palace flies;
Strange phantoms rising as the mists arise;   40
Dreadful, as hermit's dreams in haunted shades,
Or bright, as visions of expiring maids.
Now glaring fiends, and snakes on rolling spires,
Pale specters, gaping tombs, and purple fires:
Now lakes of liquid gold, Elysian scenes,   45
And crystal domes, and angels in machines.
  Unnumbered throngs on every side are seen,
Of bodies changed to various forms by Spleen.
Here living Tea-pots stand, one arm held out,
One bent; the handle this, and that the spout: 50
A Pipkin there, like Homer's Tripod walks;
Here sighs a Jar, and there a Goose-pie talks;
Men prove with child, as powerful fancy works,
And maids, turned bottles, call aloud for corks.
  Safe passed the Gnome thro' this fantastic band,   55
A branch of healing Spleenwort in his hand.
Then thus addressed the power: "Hail, wayward Queen!
Who rule the sex to fifty from fifteen:
Parent of vapors and of female wit,
Who give th' hysteric, or poetic fit,   60
On various tempers act by various ways,
Make some take physic, others scribble plays;
Who cause the proud their visits to delay,
And send the godly in a pet to pray.
A nymph there is, that all thy power disdains,   65
And thousands more in equal mirth maintains.
But oh! if e'er thy Gnome could spoil a grace,

39-54. Vapor refers to melancholia or "the blues";   51. PIPKIN: a small earthen pot.
  lines 40-54 describe the kind of strange de-   57. POWER: spleen.
  lusions experienced by those under the influence   64. PET: a fit of ill-humor.
  of the spleen.

Or raise a pimple on a beauteous face,
Like Citron waters matrons' cheeks inflame,
Or change complexions at a losing game;   70
If e'er with airy horns I planted heads,
Or rumpled petticoats, or tumbled beds,
Or caused suspicion when no soul was rude,
Or discomposed the head-dress of a Prude,
Or e'er to costive lap-dog gave disease,   75
Which not the tears of brightest eyes could ease:
Hear me, and touch Belinda with chagrin,
That single act gives half the world the spleen."
    The Goddess with a discontented air
Seems to reject him, tho' she grants his prayer.   80
A wondrous Bag with both her hands she binds,
Like that where once Ulysses held the winds;
There she collects the force of female lungs,
Sighs, sobs, and passions, and the war of tongues.
A Vial next she fills with fainting fears,   85
Soft sorrows, melting griefs, and flowing tears.
The Gnome rejoicing bears her gifts away,
Spreads his black wings, and slowly mounts to day.
    Sunk in Thalestris' arms the nymph he found,
Her eyes dejected and her hair unbound.   90
Full o'er their heads the swelling bag he rent,
And all the Furies issued at the vent.
Belinda burns with more than mortal ire,
And fierce Thalestris fans the rising fire.
"O wretched maid!" she spread her hands, and cried,   95
(While Hampton's echoes, "Wretched maid!" replied)
"Was it for this you took such constant care
The bodkin, comb, and essence to prepare?
For this your locks in paper durance bound,
For this with torturing irons wreathed around?   100
For this with fillets strained your tender head,
And bravely bore the double loads of lead?
Gods! shall the ravisher display your hair,
While the Fops envy, and the Ladies stare!
Honor forbid! at whose unrivaled shrine   105
Ease, pleasure, virtue, all, our sex resign.
Methinks already I your tears survey,

---

69. CITRON WATERS: brandy flavored with lemon peel.
81-82. In Book X of the *Odyssey*, Aeolus, the wind god, gives Ulysses a bag containing all the winds except the West Wind, which was to take him home quickly. Through the crew's folly the bag was opened when home was in sight, and the mad rush of wind drove them far away.

89. THALESTRIS: Belinda's friend (Mrs. Morley, sister of Sir George Brown, the "Sir Plume" of line 121).
98. BODKIN: The term is used here (and in V, 95) to mean a hairpin.
99. DURANCE: i.e., curlers.
101. FILLETS: headbands.

Already hear the horrid things they say,
Already see you a degraded toast,
And all your honor in a whisper lost!   110
How shall I, then, your helpless fame defend?
'Twill then be infamy to seem your friend!
And shall this prize, th' inestimable prize,
Exposed thro' crystal to the gazing eyes,
And heightened by the diamond's circling rays,   115
On that rapacious hand for ever blaze?
Sooner shall grass in Hyde Park Circus grow,
And wits take lodgings in the sound of Bow;
Sooner let earth, air, sea, to Chaos fall,
Men, monkeys, lap-dogs, parrots, perish all!"   120
    She said: then raging to Sir Plume repairs,
And bids her Beau demand the precious hairs:
(Sir Plume of amber snuff-box justly vain,
And the nice conduct of a clouded cane)
With earnest eyes, and round unthinking face,   125
He first the snuff-box opened, then the case,
And thus broke out—"My Lord, why, what the devil?
Z _ _ _ ds! damn the lock! 'fore God you must be civil!
Plague on 't! 'tis past a jest—nay prithee, pox!
Give her the hair"—he spoke, and rapped his box.   130
    "It grieves me much" (replied the Peer again)
"Who speaks so well should ever speak in vain.
But by this Lock, this sacred Lock, I swear,
(Which never more shall join its parted hair;
Which never more its honors shall renew,   135
Clipped from the lovely head where late it grew)
That while my nostrils draw the vital air,
This hand, which won it, shall forever wear."
He spoke, and speaking, in proud triumph spread
The long-contended honors of her head.   140
    But Umbriel, hateful Gnome! forbears not so;
He breaks the Vial whence the sorrows flow.
Then see! the nymph in beauteous grief appears,
Her eyes half-languishing, half-drowned in tears;
On her heaved bosom hung her drooping head,   145
Which, with a sigh, she raised; and thus she said.
    "Forever cursed be this detested day,
Which snatched my best, my favorite curl away!

114-115: i.e., the lock will be made up in a ring.
117. HYDE PARK CIRCUS: see note I, 44.
118. IN . . . BOW: i.e., fashionable people
    ("wits") will take lodgings within earshot of
    St. Mary-le-Bow, a Church in the unfashionable
    part of London.

124. CLOUDED: mottled.
131-138. Parody of the epic chieftain's oath to
    keep for ever some trophy he has won.
140. HONORS: hairs.
147ff. Parody of the epic lament.

Happy! ah ten times happy had I been,
If Hampton Court these eyes had never seen!   150
Yet am not I the first mistaken maid,
By love of Courts to numerous ills betrayed.
Oh had I rather unadmired remained
In some lone isle; or distant Northern land;
Where the gilt Chariot never marks the way,   155
Where none learn Ombre, none e'er taste Bohea!
There kept my charms concealed from mortal eye,
Like roses, that in deserts bloom and die.
What moved my mind with youthful Lords to roam?
Oh had I stayed, and said my prayers at home!   160
'Twas this, the morning omens seemed to tell,
Thrice from my trembling hand the patch-box fell;
The tottering China shook without a wind,
Nay, Poll sat mute, and Shock was most unkind!
A Sylph too warned me of the threats of fate,   165
In mystic visions, now believed too late!
See the poor remnants of these slighted hairs!
My hands shall rend what even thy rapine spares:
These in two sable ringlets taught to break,
Once gave new beauties to the snowy neck;   170
The sister-lock now sits uncouth, alone,
And in its fellow's fate foresees its own;
Uncurled it hangs, the fatal shears demands,
And tempts once more thy sacrilegious hands.
Oh hadst thou, cruel! been content to seize   175
Hairs less in sight, or any hairs but these!"

Canto V

She said: the pitying audience melt in tears.
But Fate and Jove had stopped the Baron's ears.
In vain Thalestris with reproach assails,
For who can move when fair Belinda fails?
Not half so fixed the Trojan could remain,   5
While Anna begged and Dido raged in vain.
Then grave Clarissa graceful waved her fan;
Silence ensued, and thus the nymph began.
    "Say why are Beauties praised and honored most,
The wise man's passion, and the vain man's toast?   10
Why decked with all that land and sea afford,

---

156. BOHEA: a kind of tea.
161ff. Parody of epic omens.
5. TROJAN: Aeneas. In *Aeneid* IV, Dido and her
sister Anna plead with Aeneas to stay in
Carthage.

9-34. Clarissa's speech is based on Sarpedon's
address to Glaucus in *Iliad* XII, the most
stirring speech in ancient epic.

Why Angels called, and Angel-like adored?
Why round our coaches crowd the white-gloved Beaux,
Why bows the side-box from its inmost rows;
How vain are all these glories, all our pains,   15
Unless good sense preserve what beauty gains:
That men may say, when we the front-box grace:
'Behold the first in virtue as in face!'
Oh! if to dance all night, and dress all day,
Charmed the small-pox, or chased old-age away;   20
Who would not scorn what housewife's cares produce,
Or who would learn one earthly thing of use?
To patch, nay ogle, might become a Saint,
Nor could it sure be such a sin to paint.
But since, alas! frail beauty must decay,   25
Curled or uncurled, since Locks will turn to grey;
Since painted, or not painted, all shall fade,
And she who scorns a man, must die a maid;
What then remains but well our power to use,
And keep good-humor still whate'er we lose?   30
And trust me, dear! good-humor can prevail,
When airs, and flights, and screams, and scolding fail.
Beauties in vain their pretty eyes may roll;
Charms strike the sight, but merit wins the soul."
So spoke the Dame, but no applause ensued;   35
Belinda frowned, Thalestris called her Prude.
"To arms, to arms!" the fierce Virago cries,
And swift as lightning to the combat flies.
All side in parties, and begin th' attack;
Fans clap, silks rustle, and tough whalebones crack;   40
Heroes' and Heroines' shouts confusedly rise,
And bass, and treble voices strike the skies.
No common weapons in their hands are found,
Like Gods they fight, nor dread a mortal wound.
So when bold Homer makes the Gods engage,   45
And heavenly breasts with human passions rage;
'Gainst Pallas, Mars; Latona, Hermes arms;
And all Olympus rings with loud alarms:
Jove's thunder roars, heaven trembles all around,
Blue Neptune storms, the bellowing deeps resound: 50
Earth shakes her nodding towers, the ground gives way,
And the pale ghosts start at the flash of day!
Triumphant Umbriel on a sconce's height
Clapped his glad wings, and sate to view the fight:

---

37. VIRAGO: manlike woman.
37ff. Parody of the "general battle" in epic (as
    contrasted with the encounter of single warriors
    parodied in the card game).
53. SCONCE: wall-bracket (for candles).

Propped on their bodkin spears, the Sprites survey   55
The growing combat, or assist the fray.
   While thro' the press enraged Thalestris flies,
And scatters death around from both her eyes,
A Beau and Witling perished in the throng,
One died in metaphor, and one in song.   60
"O cruel nymph! a living death I bear,"
Cried Dapperwit, and sunk beside his chair.
A mournful glance Sir Fopling upwards cast,
"Those eyes are made so killing"—was his last.
Thus on Maeander's flowery margin lies   65
Th' expiring Swan, and as he sings he dies.
   When bold Sir Plume had drawn Clarissa down,
Chloë stepped in, and killed him with a frown;
She smiled to see the doughty hero slain,
But, at her smile, the Beau revived again.   70
   Now Jove suspends his golden scales in air,
Weighs the Men's wits against the Lady's hair;
The doubtful beam long nods from side to side;
At length the wits mount up, the hairs subside.
   See, fierce Belinda on the Baron flies,   75
With more than usual lightning in her eyes:
Nor feared the Chief th' unequal fight to try,
Who sought no more than on his foe to die.
But this bold Lord with manly strength endued,
She with one finger and a thumb subdued: 80
Just where the breath of life his nostrils drew,
A charge of Snuff the wily virgin threw;
The Gnomes direct, to every atom just,
The pungent grains of titillating dust.
Sudden, with starting tears each eye o'erflows,   85
And the high dome re-echoes to his nose.
   "Now meet thy fate," incensed Belinda cried,
And drew a deadly bodkin from her side.
(The same, his ancient personage to deck,
Her great great grandsire wore about his neck,   90
In three seal-rings; which after, melted down,
Formed a vast buckle for his widow's gown:
Her infant grandame's whistle next it grew,
The bells she jingled, and the whistle blew;
Then in a bodkin graced her mother's hairs,   95
Which long she wore, and now Belinda wears.)

---

59. WITLING: a person of little wit, a fop.

62-63. DAPPERWIT . . . FOPLING: names suggestive of the kind of people so named.

65-66. THUS . . . SWAN: Homer is known as the Swan of Maeander (a river in Asia Minor).

68. CHLOË: another participating lady.

71-74. Parody of the way epic battles are decided by Zeus's scales.

89ff. Parody of the habit in epic of tracing the history of a favorite weapon.

"Boast not my fall" (he cried) "insulting foe!
Thou by some other shalt be laid as low,
Nor think, to die dejects my lofty mind:
All that I dread is leaving you behind!   100
Rather than so, ah let me still survive,
And burn in Cupid's flames—but burn alive."
        "Restore the Lock!" she cries; and all around
"Restore the Lock!" the vaulted roofs rebound.
Not fierce Othello in so loud a strain   105
Roared for the handkerchief that caused his pain.
But see how oft ambitious aims are crossed,
And chiefs contend 'till all the prize is lost!
The Lock, obtained with guilt, and kept with pain,
In every place is sought, but sought in vain: 110
With such a prize no mortal must be blest,
So heaven decrees! with heaven who can contest?
        Some thought it mounted to the Lunar sphere,
Since all things lost on earth are treasured there.
There Heroes' wits are kept in ponderous vases,   115
And beaux', in snuff-boxes and tweezer-cases.
There broken vows and death-bed alms are found,
And lovers' hearts with ends of riband bound,
The courtier's promises, and sick man's prayers,
The smiles of harlots, and tears of heirs,   120
Cages for gnats, and chains to yoke a flea,
Dried butterflies, and tomes of casuistry.
        But trust the Muse—she saw it upward rise,
Tho' marked by none but quick, poetic eyes:
(So Rome's great founder to the heavens withdrew,   125
To Proculus alone confessed in view)
A sudden Star, it shot thro' liquid air,
And drew behind a radiant trail of hair.
Not Berenice's Locks first rose so bright,
The heavens bespangling with disheveled light.   130
The Sylphs behold it kindling as it flies,
And pleased pursue its progress thro' the skies.
        This the Beau monde shall from the Mall survey,
And hail with music its propitious ray.
This the blest Lover shall for Venus take,   135
And send up vows from Rosamonda's lake.
This Partridge soon shall view in cloudless skies,

125. ROME'S GREAT FOUNDER: Romulus; his passage to heaven was reported by Proculus, a Roman senator.
129. BERENICE: wife of Ptolemy III, who pledged her hair for his safe return from battle; it became the constellation *Coma Berenices*.
133. BEAU MONDE: the fashionable world. MALL: a promenade in St. James's Park, London.
135. VENUS: the planet.
136. ROSAMONDA'S LAKE: a lake in St. James's Park identified with unhappy love.
137. PARTRIDGE: a contemporary maker of almanacs, which were full of unfounded predictions.

When next he looks thro' Galileo's eyes;
And hence th' egregious wizard shall foredoom
The fate of Louis, and the fall of Rome.   140
    Then cease, bright Nymph! to mourn thy ravished hair,
Which adds new glory to the shining sphere!
Not all the tresses that fair head can boast,
Shall draw such envy as the Lock you lost.
For, after all the murders of your eye,   145
When after millions slain, yourself shall die:
When those fair suns shall set, as set they must,
And all those tresses shall be laid in dust,
This Lock, the Muse shall consecrate to fame,
And 'midst the stars inscribe Belinda's name.   150

138. GALILEO'S EYES: Galileo built the first com-   140. LOUIS: Louis XIV of France.
plete telescope.

I

1. What is the situation in Canto I? What is the "morning-dream that hovered o'er" Belinda's bed (22-113)? Why is the information in the dream revealed "to Maids alone and Children" (38)? What do the "light Militia of the lower sky" (42) guard chaste women against and how do they do it? What is there in women's nature that makes the job difficult (67-104)? What is Ariel particularly concerned about at this time (105-114)? What two extended metaphors describe Belinda at her dressing table (121-148)? Indicate how each is specifically developed.

2. Where is Belinda at the opening of Canto II? How does the description of her in lines 1-28 relate to the goddess metaphor of the preceding canto? What actions in lines 1-18 are those of the kind of woman Ariel has advised her to be in Canto I? In what sense are her locks nourished *to the destruction of mankind* (19-28)? Why does the Baron want the locks? What is being satirized in lines 35-46? What do lines 44-45 mean? Why is Ariel troubled and what measures does he take to forestall "the birth of Fate" (53-142)?

3. Where are Belinda and her admirers in Canto III? What is being satirized in lines 4-18? Trace the fortunes in the card game. Who is the challenger (25-28; 139-146)? How does Belinda react to victory in the game (99-100)? What takes place in lines 105-116? Why does the Baron decide to clip the lock? Who helps

him and why (127-130)? Why can't Ariel warn Belinda (139-146)? How does the Baron react to victory?

4. Why does Umbriel take over from Ariel in Canto IV and go *to search the gloomy Cave of Spleen?* Who inhabits the Cave and what does it represent (24-54)? How are its inhabitants like Belinda after the loss of the lock? How will touching Belinda "with chagrin" give "half the world the spleen" (78)? What is it that bothers Thalestris most about the clipping of the lock (102-116)? What is the Baron's reply to Sir Plume's pleas that he return it? How is Sir Plume shown by the language to be a prime fool? The canto ends with Belinda's "chagrin" (147-176). What does she wish had been her fate? What is she most disturbed about? Would the Baron's returning the lock help matters any? Why or why not?

5. Put Clarissa's advice (Canto V, 9-34) into your own words. How does it set the values by which the actions of the rest are judged? Why does Thalestris call her "Prude" (36)? Describe the progress of the general battle that ensues. How does Belinda subdue the Baron? Who wins the fight? Why is it a hollow victory? What happens to the lock?

6. Who are the Sylphs and what do they represent symbolically (I, 65, 78)? Line 78 says that they represent "Honor," but what kind of honor are Belinda and Thalestris concerned about? Under what conditions are the Sylphs able to watch over womankind (I, 67-68)? Why does Ariel desert Belinda (III, 140-146)? Who

are the Gnomes and what is their symbolic significance (I, 63; IV, 13ff)?

7. How is Belinda described in Canto I, 121-148? How seriously are we to take her priestess-goddess role? Are we to believe that simply because her beauty is "put on" that it is not a beauty worthy of man's attention and adoration? Why or why not? What light do lines 1-18 of Canto II throw on these questions? There is obvious vanity in her, but what good reasons does she have for being vain?

8. What comments is Pope making on the confusion between a reputation for virtue and true virtue? What really disturbs Belinda and Thalestris about the Baron's act? Why is Clarissa's advice ignored?

9. Much of the delight of the poem lies in Pope's brilliant use of all the devices of epic convention (noted in the footnotes) and in his handling of the couplet form for all kinds of effects, from grandiose excess to the sharpest rapier thrusts at hypocrisy and inanity. Consider the description of a simple act of pouring tea from a pot into a cup:

From silver spouts the grateful liquors glide
While China's earth receives the smoking tide.

Or such lines as the following where the form Itself underscores the confusion of values:

Or stain her honor or her new brocade;
Forget her prayers or miss a masquerade.

The hungry Judges soon the sentence sign,
And wretches hang that jury-men may dine.

Point out other examples of either technique.

II

1. Discuss the following comment by Cleanth Brooks from his essay, "The Case of Miss Arabella Fermor," in *The Well Wrought Urn*: ". . . Pope is able to reduce the 'rape' to its true insignificance because he recognizes, as his characters do not, its real significance. Pope knows that the rape has more in it of compliment than of insult, though he hardly expects Belinda to interpret it thus."* What is the *real significance* of the war between the sexes and why is the Baron's act more of a *compliment* than an *insult*?

2. Mountains are made out of molehills daily, and we all spend a lot of valuable time getting upset and indignant over trifles. Take some trivial incident that has occurred recently around school or in your neighborhood that has brought on unreasonable behavior from the "injured" or "insulted" parties, and treat it in an essay with the kind of mock-seriousness Pope has used in "The Rape of the Lock."

* Cleanth Brooks, *The Well Wrought Urn* (New York: Harcourt, Brace & World, Inc.).

from DON JUAN   [1819]

George Gordon, Lord Byron

The mixture of romantic involvement and detached commentary on that involvement that we see in the preceding poems is perhaps nowhere more delightfully dramatized than in the following selection from Byron's *Don Juan*. All the ingredients of innocent and undefiled love are here: an enchanted setting on an isolated Aegean island; a young and handsome ship's passenger, sole survivor of a tragic shipwreck, lying close to death on a sandy beach; a beautiful maiden, innocent of the intrigues and deceptions of the outside world, who finds him and nurses him back to health. The idyllic love story unfolds poignantly and unashamedly, but all the while, as will be seen, Byron keeps it at arm's length both for himself and for the reader, not in mockery of romance but in recognition that any idyllic relationship is of necessity qualified by the realities of the human condition.

Title. The pronunciation is anglicized: Don Joó an.

Don Juan is a long, rambling poem built around the adventures of the young hero whose name gives the poem its title. As the following excerpt from Canto II will partly show, the poem serves as a vehicle for Byron's witty, often cynical, often deliberately distorted observations on the sentimentality, the self-seeking, the self-deception, the meanness, and even at times the dignity and decency, he saw in the world around him. His hero, victim of the misguided education of a foolish mother, wanders across Europe and finally to England, and his strange adventures give his creator a chance to take unerring aim at every kind of human folly. Although the episode with Haidée,* only the beginning of which is reproduced here, is one of the few in which human goodness seems to hold its own against baseness, Byron's intent was not simply to expose and ridicule. In Canto XII he says:

> I mean to show things really as they are,
> Not as they ought to be: for I avow,
>   That till we see what's what in fact, we're far
> From much improvement.

The first part of Canto II deals with Don Juan's expulsion from his native Spain, the subsequent series of storms at sea that wreck his ship, the trials suffered by a handful of survivors in a small lifeboat, and the death of all but Juan, who reaches shore, barely alive, on Haidée's island.

112

His eyes he opened, shut, again unclosed,
    For all was doubt and dizziness; he thought
He still was in the boat, and had but dozed,
    And felt again with his despair o'erwrought,
And wished it death in which he had reposed,   5
    And then once more his feelings back were brought,
And slowly by his swimming eyes was seen
A lovely female face of seventeen.

113

'Twas bending close o'er his, and the small mouth
    Seemed almost prying into his for breath;   10
And chafing him, the soft warm hand of youth
    Recalled his answering spirits back from death;
And, bathing his chill temples, tried to soothe
    Each pulse to animation, till beneath
Its gentle touch and trembling care, a sigh   15
To these kind efforts made a low reply.

---

* HAIDÉE: pronounced Hi'dee.

1ff. The scene which follows recalls Book VI of Homer's *Odyssey* where Odysseus receives similar treatment from Nausicaä, daughter of the Phaeacian king, Alcinous.

114

Then was the cordial poured, and mantle flung
    Around his scarce-clad limbs; and the fair arm
Raised higher the faint head which o'er it hung;
    And her transparent cheek, all pure and warm,   20
Pillowed his death-like forehead; then she wrung
    His dewy curls, long drenched by every storm;
And watched with eagerness each throb that drew
A sigh from his heaved bosom—and hers, too.

115

And lifting him with care into the cave,   25
    The gentle girl, and her attendant,—one
Young, yet her elder, and of brow less grave,
    And more robust of figure—then begun
To kindle fire, and as the new flames gave
    Light to the rocks that roofed them, which the sun   30
Had never seen, the maid, or whatso'er
She was, appeared distinct, and tall, and fair.

116

Her brow was overhung with coins of gold,
    That sparkled o'er the auburn of her hair,
Her clustering hair, whose longer locks were rolled   35
    In braids behind; and though her stature were
Even of the highest for a female mold,
    They nearly reached her heel; and in her air
There was a something which bespoke command,
As one who was a lady in the land.   40

117

Her hair, I said, was auburn; but her eyes
    Were black as death, their lashes the same hue,
Of downcast length, in whose silk shadow lies
    Deepest attraction; for when to the view
Forth from its raven fringe the full glance flies,   45
    Ne'er with such force the swiftest arrow flew;
'Tis as the snake late coiled, who pours his length,
And hurls at once his venom and his strength.

118

Her brow was white and low, her cheek's pure dye
    Like twilight rosy still with the set sun;   50
Short upper lip—sweet lips! that make us sigh
    Ever to have seen such; for she was one

Fit for the model of a statuary
    (A race of mere impostors, when all's done—
I've seen much finer women, ripe and real,   55
Than all the nonsense of their stone ideal).

119

I'll tell you why I say so, for 'tis just
    One should not rail without a decent cause:
There was an Irish lady, to whose bust
    I ne'er saw justice done, and yet she was   60
A frequent model; and if e'er she must
    Yield to stern Time and Nature's wrinkling laws,
They will destroy a face which mortal thought
Ne'er compassed, nor less mortal chisel wrought.

120

And such was she, the lady of the cave: 65
    Her dress was very different from the Spanish,
Simpler, and yet of colors not so grave;
    For, as you know, the Spanish women banish
Bright hues when out of doors, and yet, while wave
    Around them (what I hope will never vanish)   70
The basquina and the mantilla, they
Seem at the same time mystical and gay.

121

But with our damsel this was not the case:
    Her dress was many-colored, finely spun;
Her locks curled negligently round her face,   75
    But through them gold and gems profusely shone:
Her girdle sparkled, and the richest lace
    Flowed in her veil, and many a precious stone
Flashed on her little hand; but, what was shocking,
Her small snow feet had slippers, but no stocking.   80

122

The other female's dress was not unlike,
    But of inferior materials: she
Had not so many ornaments to strike,
    Her hair had silver only, bound to be
Her dowry; and her veil, in form alike,   85
    Was coarser; and her air, though firm, less free;
Her hair was thicker, but less long; her eyes
As black, but quicker, and of smaller size.

---

71. BASQUINA: a decorated petticoat. MANTILLA:
    a lace veil.

123

And these two tended him, and cheered him both
   With food and raiment, and those soft attentions,   90
Which are—(as I must own)—of female growth,
   And have ten thousand delicate inventions:
They made a most superior mess of broth,
   A thing which poesy but seldom mentions,
But the best dish that e'er was cooked since Homer's   95
Achilles ordered dinner for new comers.

124

I'll tell you who they were, this female pair,
   Lest they should seem princesses in disguise,
Besides, I hate all mystery, and that air
   Of clap-trap, which your recent poets prize;   100
And so, in short, the girls they really were
   They shall appear before your curious eyes,
Mistress and maid; the first was only daughter
Of an old man, who lived upon the water.

125

A fisherman he had been in his youth,   105
   And still a sort of fisherman was he,
But other speculations were, in sooth,
   Added to his connection with the sea,
Perhaps not so respectable, in truth:
   A little smuggling, and some piracy,   110
Left him, at last, the sole of many masters
Of an ill-gotten million of piasters.

126

A fisher, therefore, was he,—though of men,
   Like Peter the Apostle,—and he fished
For wandering merchant vessels, now and then,   115
   And sometimes caught as many as he wished;
The cargoes he confiscated, and gain
   He sought in the slave-market, too, and dished
Full many a morsel for that Turkish trade,
By which, no doubt, a good deal may be made.   120

95-96. BEST . . . COMERS: Cf. *Iliad,* Book IX, in which Achilles "ordered dinner" for Odysseus, Ajax, and Phoenix, who came to try to induce him to return to battle.

112. PIASTERS: name for coins of various countries, probably Turkish here.

113-114. FISHER . . . APOSTLE: Cf. Matthew 4:18-19 and Mark 1:16-17.

127

He was a Greek, and on his isle had built
  (One of the wild and smaller Cyclades)
A very handsome house from out his guilt,
  And there he lived exceedingly at ease;
Heaven knows what cash he got, or blood he spilt,   125
  A sad old fellow was he, if you please;
But this I know, it was a spacious building,
Full of barbaric carving, paint, and gilding.

128

He had an only daughter, called Haidée,
  The greatest heiress of the Eastern Isles;   130
Besides, so very beautiful was she,
  Her dowry was as nothing to her smiles:
Still in her teens, and like a lovely tree
  She grew to womanhood, and between whiles
Rejected several suitors, just to learn   135
How to accept a better in his turn.

129

And walking out upon the beach, below
  The cliff,—towards sunset, on that day she found,
Insensible,—not dead, but nearly so,—
  Don Juan, almost famished, and half drowned;   140
But being naked, she was shocked, you know,
  Yet deemed herself in common pity bound,
As far as in her lay, "to take him in,
A stranger" dying, with so white a skin.

130

But taking him into her father's house   145
  Was not exactly the best way to save,
But like conveying to the cat the mouse,
  Or people in a trance into their grave;
Because the good old man had so much "νους,"
  Unlike the honest Arab thieves so brave,   150
He would have hospitably cured the stranger
And sold him instantly when out of danger.

122. CYCLADES: Greek islands in the Aegean Sea.
149. νους: Greek for "spirit."

131

And therefore, with her maid, she thought it best
   (A virgin always on her maid relies)
To place him in the cave for present rest: 155
   And when, at last, he opened his black eyes,
Their charity increased about their guest;
   And their compassion grew to such a size,
It opened half the turnpike gates to heaven—
(St. Paul says, 'tis the toll which must be given).   160

132

They made a fire,—but such a fire as they
   Upon the moment could contrive with such
Materials as were cast up round the bay,—
   Some broken planks, and oars, that to the touch
Were nearly tinder, since so long they lay   165
   A mast was almost crumbled to a crutch;
But, by God's grace, here wrecks were in such plenty,
That there was fuel to have furnished twenty.

133

He had a bed of furs, and a pelisse,
   For Haidée stripped her sables off to make   170
His couch; and, that he might be more at ease,
   And warm, in case by chance he should awake,
They also gave a petticoat apiece,
   She and her maid,—and promised by daybreak
To pay him a fresh visit, with a dish   175
For breakfast, of eggs, coffee, bread, and fish.

134

And thus they left him to his lone repose:
   Juan slept like a top, or like the dead,
Who sleep at last, perhaps (God only knows),
   Just for the present; and in his lulled head   180
Not even a vision of his former woes
   Throbbed in accursèd dreams, which sometimes spread
Unwelcome visions of our former years,
Till the eye, cheated, opens thick with tears.

---

160. ST. PAUL: Cf. I Corinthians 13:1-13.
169. PELISSE: a long coat, usually made of fur or
   lined with fur.

135

Young Juan slept all dreamless:—but the maid,   185
    Who smoothed his pillow, as she left the den
Looked back upon him, and a moment stayed,
    And turned, believing that he called again.
He slumbered; yet she thought, at least she said
    (The heart will slip, even as the tongue and pen),   190
He had pronounced her name—but she forgot
That at this moment Juan knew it not.

136

And pensive to her father's house she went,
    Enjoining silence strict to Zoe, who
Better than her knew what, in fact, she meant,   195
    She being wiser by a year or two:
A year or two's an age when rightly spent,
    And Zoe spent hers, as most women do,
In gaining all that useful sort of knowledge
Which is acquired in Nature's good old college.   200

137

The morn broke, and found Juan slumbering still
    Fast in his cave, and nothing clashed upon
His rest: the rushing of the neighboring rill,
    And the young beams of the excluded sun,
Troubled him not, and he might sleep his fill;   205
    And need he had of slumber yet, for none
Had suffered more—his hardships were comparative
To those related in my grand-dad's "Narrative."

138

Not so Haidée: she sadly tossed and tumbled,
    And started from her sleep, and turning o'er,   210
Dreamed of a thousand wrecks, o'er which she stumbled,
    And handsome corpses strewed upon the shore;
And woke her maid so early that she grumbled,
    And called her father's old slaves up, who swore
In several oaths—Armenian, Turk, and Greek—   215
They knew not what to think of such a freak.

---

208. MY GRAND-DAD'S "NARRATIVE": Byron's grandfather, John Byron, had sailed around the
world. His "Narrative" (1768) contained an
account of a shipwreck off the coast of Chile.

139

But up she got, and up she made them get,
  With some pretense about the sun, that makes
Sweet skies just when he rises, or is set;
  And 'tis, no doubt, a sight to see when breaks   220
Bright Phœbus, while the mountains still are wet
  With mist, and every bird with him awakes,
And night is flung off like a mourning suit
Worn for a husband,—or some other brute.

140

I say, the sun is a most glorious sight: 225
  I've seen him rise full oft, indeed of late
I have sat up on purpose all the night,
  Which hastens, as physicians say, one's fate;
And so all ye, who would be in the right
  In health and purse, begin your day to date   230
From daybreak, and when coffined at four-score
Engrave upon the plate, you rose at four.

141

And Haidée met the morning face to face;
  Her own was freshest, though a feverish flush
Had dyed it with the headlong blood, whose race   235
  From heart to cheek is curbed into a blush,
Like to a torrent which a mountain's base,
  That overpowers some Alpine river's rush,
Checks to a lake, whose waves in circles spread;
Or the Red Sea—but the sea is not red.   240

142

And down the cliff the island virgin came,
  And near the cave her quick light footsteps drew,
While the sun smiled on her with his first flame,
  And young Aurora kissed her lips with dew,
Taking her for a sister; just the same   245
  Mistake you would have made on seeing the two,
Although the mortal, quite as fresh and fair,
Had all the advantage, too, of not being air.

---

221. PHŒBUS: the sun.
244. AURORA: goddess of the dawn.

143

And when into the cavern Haidée stepped
  All timidly, yet rapidly, she saw   250
That like an infant Juan sweetly slept;
  And then she stopped, and stood as if in awe
(For sleep is awful), and on tiptoe crept
  And wrapt him closer, lest the air, too raw,
Should reach his blood, then o'er him still as death   255
Bent, with hushed lips, that drank his scarce-drawn breath.

144

And thus like to an angel o'er the dying
  Who die in righteousness, she leaned; and there
All tranquilly the shipwrecked boy was lying,
  As o'er him lay the calm and stirless air: 260
But Zoe the meantime some eggs was frying,
  Since, after all, no doubt the youthful pair
Must breakfast, and betimes—lest they should ask it,
She drew out her provision from the basket.

145

She knew that the best feelings must have victual,   265
  And that a shipwrecked youth would hungry be;
Besides, being less in love, she yawned a little,
  And felt her veins chilled by the neighboring sea;
And so, she cooked their breakfast to a tittle;
  I can't say that she gave them any tea,   270
But there were eggs, fruit, coffee, bread, fish, honey,
With Scio wine,—and all for love, not money.

146

And Zoe, when the eggs were ready, and
  The coffee made, would fain have wakened Juan;
But Haidée stopped her with her quick small hand,   275
  And without a word, a sign her finger drew on
Her lip, which Zoe needs must understand;
  And, the first breakfast spoilt, prepared a new one,
Because her mistress would not let her break
That sleep which seemed as it would ne'er awake.   280

---

263. BETIMES: in a short time.
265. VICTUAL: food, pronounced "vittle."
272. SCIO: an island near Athens in the Aegean
    Sea.

147

For still he lay, and on his thin worn cheek
   A purple hectic played like dying day
On the snow-tops of distant hills; the streak
   Of sufferance yet upon his forehead lay,
Where the blue veins looked shadowy, shrunk, and weak;   285
   And his black curls were dewy with the spray,
Which weighed upon them yet, all damp and salt,
Mixed with the stony vapors of the vault.

148

And she bent o'er him, and he lay beneath,
   Hushed as the babe upon its mother's breast,   290
Drooped as the willow when no winds can breathe,
   Lulled like the depth of ocean when at rest,
Fair as the crowning rose of the whole wreath,
   Soft as the callow cygnet in its nest;
In short, he was a very pretty fellow,   295
Although his woes had turned him rather yellow.

149

He woke and gazed, and would have slept again,
   But the fair face which met his eyes forbade
Those eyes to close, though weariness and pain
   Had further sleep a further pleasure made;   300
For woman's face was never formed in vain
   For Juan, so that even when he prayed
He turned from grisly saints, and martyrs hairy,
To the sweet portraits of the Virgin Mary.

150

And thus upon his elbow he arose,   305
   And looked upon the lady, in whose cheek
The pale contended with the purple rose,
   As with an effort she began to speak;
Her eyes were eloquent, her words would pose,
   Although she told him, in good modern Greek,   310
With an Ionian accent, low and sweet,
That he was faint, and must not talk, but eat.

---

288. VAULT: cave.
294. CALLOW: lacking feathers. CYGNET: a young
   swan.

151

Now Juan could not understand a word,
   Being no Grecian; but he had an ear,
And her voice was the warble of a bird,   315
   So soft, so sweet, so delicately clear,
That finer, simpler, music ne'er was heard;
   The sort of sound we echo with a tear,
Without knowing why—an overpowering tone,
Whence melody descends as from a throne.   320

152

And Juan gazed as one who is awoke
   By a distant organ, doubting if he be
Not yet a dreamer, till the spell is broke
   By the watchman, or some such reality,
Or by one's early valet's cursèd knock;   325
   At least it is a heavy sound to me,
Who like a morning slumber—for the night
Shows stars and women in a better light.

153

And Juan, too, was helped out from his dream,
   Or sleep, or whatsoe'er it was, by feeling   330
A most prodigious appetite; the steam
   Of Zoe's cookery no doubt was stealing
Upon his senses, and the kindling beam
   Of the new fire, which Zoe kept up, kneeling,
To stir her viands, made him quite awake   335
And long for food, but chiefly a beef-steak.

154

But beef is rare within these oxless isles;
   Goat's flesh there is, no doubt, and kid, and mutton,
And, when a holiday upon them smiles,
   A joint upon their barbarous spits they put on: 340
But this occurs but seldom, between whiles,
   For some of these are rocks with scarce a hut on;
Others are fair and fertile, among which
This, though not large, was one of the most rich.

155

I say that beef is rare, and can't help thinking   345
    That the old fable of the Minotaur—
From which our modern rivals, rightly shrinking,
    Condemn the royal lady's taste who wore
A cow's shape for a mask—was only (sinking
    The allegory) a mere type, no more,   350
That Pasiphae promoted breeding cattle,
To make the Cretans bloodier in battle.

156

For we all know that English people are
    Fed upon beef—I won't say much of beer,
Because 'tis liquor only, and being far   355
    From this my subject, has no business here;
We know, too, they are very fond of war,
    A pleasure—like all pleasures—rather dear;
So were the Cretans—from which I infer
That beef and battles both were owing to her.   360

157

But to resume. The languid Juan raised
    His head upon his elbow, and he saw
A sight on which he had not lately gazed,
    As all his latter meals had been quite raw,
Three or four things, for which the Lord be praised,   365
    And, feeling still the famished vulture gnaw,
He fell upon whate'er was offered, like
A priest, a shark, an alderman, or pike.

158

He ate, and he was well supplied; and she
    Who watched him like a mother, would have fed   370
Him past all bounds, because she smiled to see
    Such appetite in one she had deemed dead:
But Zoe, being older than Haidée,
    Knew (by tradition, for she ne'er had read)
That famished people must be slowly nursed   375
And fed by spoonfuls, else they always burst.

346-351. MINOTAUR . . . PASIPHAE: The Minotaur was a mythical monster, offspring of Pasiphae, with a man's body and a bull's head. Minos, King of Crete, kept it in his labyrinth and fed it seven youths and seven maidens sent every year in tribute from Athens. The Athenian hero, Theseus, finally killed it.

159

And so she took the liberty to state,
  Rather by deeds than words, because the case
Was urgent, that the gentleman, whose fate
  Had made her mistress quit her bed to trace   380
The sea-shore at this hour, must leave his plate,
  Unless he wished to die upon the place—
She snatched it, and refused another morsel,
Saying, he had gorged enough to make a horse ill.

160

Next they—he being naked, save a tattered   385
  Pair of scarce decent trousers—went to work,
And in the fire his recent rags they scattered,
  And dressed him, for the present, like a Turk,
Or Greek—that is, although it not much mattered,
  Omitting turban, slippers, pistols, dirk,—   390
They furnished him, entire, except some stitches,
With a clean shirt, and very spacious britches.

161

And then fair Haidée tried her tongue at speaking,
  But not a word could Juan comprehend,
Although he listened so that the young Greek in   395
  Her earnestness would ne'er have made an end;
And, as he interrupted not, went eking
  Her speech out to her protégé and friend,
Till pausing at the last her breath to take,
She saw he did not understand Romaic.   400

162

And then she had recourse to nods, and signs,
  And smiles, and sparkles of the speaking eye,
And read (the only book she could) the lines
  Of his fair face, and found, by sympathy,
The answer eloquent, where the soul shines   405
  And darts in one quick glance a long reply;
And thus in every look she saw expressed
A world of words, and things at which she guessed.

---

400. ROMAIC: modern Greek.

163

And now, by dint of fingers and of eyes,
  And words repeated after her, he took   410
A lesson in her tongue; but by surmise,
  No doubt, less of her language than her look:
As he who studies fervently the skies
  Turns oftener to the stars than to his book,
Thus Juan learned his alpha beta better   415
From Haidée's glance than any graven letter.

164

'Tis pleasing to be schooled in a strange tongue
  By female lips and eyes—that is, I mean,
When both the teacher and the taught are young,
  As was the case, at least, where I have been;   420
They smile so when one's right, and when one's wrong
  They smile still more and then there intervene
Pressure of hands, perhaps even a chaste kiss;—
I learned the little that I know by this:

165

That is, some words of Spanish, Turk, and Greek,   425
  Italian not at all, having no teachers;
Much English I cannot pretend to speak,
  Learning that language chiefly from its preachers,
Barrow, South, Tillotson, whom every week
  I study, also Blair, the highest reachers   430
Of eloquence in piety and prose—
I hate your poets, so read none of those.

166

As for the ladies, I have nought to say,
  A wanderer from the British world of fashion,
Where I, like other "dogs, have had my day,"   435
  Like other men, too, may have had my passion—
But that, like other things, has passed away,
  And all her fools whom I *could* lay the lash on:
Foes, friends, men, women, now are nought to me
But dreams of what has been, no more to be.   440

429-430. BARROW . . . BLAIR: all famous preachers
  of the seventeenth and eighteenth centuries.

167

Return we to Don Juan. He begun
    To hear new words, and to repeat them; but
Some feelings, universal as the sun,
    Were such as could not in his breast be shut
More than within the bosom of a nun: 445
    He was in love,—as you would be, no doubt,
With a young benefactress,—so was she,
Just in the way we very often see.

168

And every day by daybreak—rather early
    For Juan, who was somewhat fond of rest,—   450
She came into the cave, but it was merely
    To see her bird reposing in his nest;
And she would softly stir his locks so curly,
    Without disturbing her yet slumbering guest,
Breathing all gently o'er his cheek and mouth,   455
As o'er a bed of roses the sweet south.

169

And every morn his color freshlier came,
    And every day helped on his convalescence;
'Twas well, because health in the human frame
    Is pleasant, besides being true love's essence,   460
For health and idleness to passion's flame
    Are oil and gunpowder; and some good lessons
Are also learnt from Ceres and from Bacchus,
Without whom Venus will not long attack us.

170

While Venus fills the heart (without heart really   465
    Love, though good always, is not quite so good),
Ceres presents a plate of vermicelli,—
    For love must be sustained like flesh and blood,
While Bacchus pours out wine, or hands a jelly:
    Eggs, oysters, too, are amatory food;   470
But who is their purveyor from above
Heaven knows—it may be Neptune, Pan, or Jove.

---

463. CERES: goddess of agriculture. BACCHUS: god   464. VENUS: goddess of love.
    of wine.   467. VERMICELLI: a thin spaghetti.

171

When Juan woke he found some good things ready,
  A bath, a breakfast, and the finest eyes
That ever made a youthful heart less steady,   475
  Besides her maid's, as pretty for their size;
But I have spoken of all this already—
  And repetition's tiresome and unwise,—
Well—Juan, after bathing in the sea,
Came always back to coffee and Haidée.   480

I

1. What physical details, word choices, and rhythmic patterns set the tone of tenderness that pervades stanzas 112-118? Do the images used to describe Haidée's eyes in stanza 117 clash with the established tone? Why or why not? If they do, what might be the purpose of such a contrast?

2. *Don Juan* is full of digressions—some short, some long—in which Byron makes purely personal comments on some point that comes up in the narrative. What is the first digression that occurs in this selection, what brings it on, what is the gist of it, and what purpose do you think it serves? What other less obvious indications are there in stanzas 112-118 that Byron as narrator is very much in evidence? Consider, for instance, lines 24 and 41, plus others.

3. Contrast the description of Zoe in stanza 122 with that of Haidée. How does the rhythmic structure and word choice of the stanza support the contrast Byron makes? In other words, how do they differ from those used to describe Haidée?

4. What attitude toward "this female pair" (line 97) is revealed in stanzas 123-124? Indicate specifically how you decided what the attitude is. Is this same attitude continued in stanzas 128-135? Why or why not? In what sense is Haidée "innocent"? In what sense is she not?

5. Indicate clearly what kind of man Haidée's father is (stanzas 125-127, 130). What is ironic about the reference to Peter the Apostle (stanza 126)? What is ironic about the reference to St. Paul in stanza 131?

6. What commentary on human nature is Byron making in the digression in stanza 140? How does it qualify the obvious eagerness and anticipation with which Haidée faces her new day (stanzas 138-139)? and the description of her hastening to the cave where Juan sleeps (stanzas 141-142)? How is the digression alluded to in later stanzas? Consider stanzas 152 and 168.

7. How is the mother-child imagery developed in stanzas 143, 148, and 158? What purpose does it serve?

8. What is Zoe's part in the narrative? Consider how she is described, what she does, and when she does it. Discuss whether her presence and attitude add to the seriousness with which we are to take the love story or detract from it.

9. Just what is being said in stanzas 154-156 and what connection does it have with the narrative?

10. Outline specifically Byron's comments on languages as revealed both in the Juan-Haidée "conversations" (stanzas 161-163, 167) and in his comments on them and on language-as-communication in general (stanzas 164-165).

11. What is the gist of stanzas 169-171? What connection is there between these comments and the other qualifications Byron makes about the operations of romantic love?

II

1. Write a short essay discussing Byron's use of deliberately distorted contrasts and/or anti-climax for satiric effect in this selection. (Anti-climax refers to a sudden shift in emphasis in

which a sober, serious line of thought is followed abruptly by something trivial or irrelevant or mock-serious.)

2. Write a short essay on the attitude toward romantic love revealed here. Consider how seriously the involvement between Juan and Haidée is meant to be taken in the light of the many irreverent digressions and the occasional bantering treatment of Haidée. Consider also the straightforward tenderness of most of stanzas 112-116, 138-139, 142-144, 150-151, and 162-163.

The Disenchanted Lover

As often as writers have found reason to sing love's praises, or to qualify those praises with lighthearted protests or sober recognition that the days and hours are not love's servants, they have just as often been moved to speak out in sharp and sometimes bitter comment on love's deceptions and corrosive possibilities.

The voice of protest usually sounds like the voice of experience. It may be the tongue-in-cheek cynicism of Donne's "Go and Catch a Falling Star"; it may be a bloodless dismissal of love as "this weak passion," as in Bacon's "Of Love"; it may be a conviction that the promises of enduring bliss are mocked by the realities of the marriage state, as in MacNeice's "Les Sylphides"; or it may be "keen lessons that love deceives/And wrings with wrong," as in Hardy's "Neutral Tones." Whatever its expression, the attitude toward romantic love revealed here shows the disruptive effect it can sometimes have on human relations.

SONG   [*1633*]

John Donne

Go and catch a falling star,
  Get with child a mandrake root,
Tell me where all past years are,
  Or who cleft the devil's foot;
Teach me to hear mermaids singing,   5
Or to keep off envy's stinging,
    And find
    What wind
Serves to advance an honest mind.

If thou be'st born to strange sights,   10
  Things invisible to see,
Ride ten thousand days and nights
  Till Age snow white hairs on thee;
Thou, when thou return'st, wilt tell me
All strange wonders that befell thee,   15
    And swear
    No where
Lives a woman true and fair.

If thou find'st one, let me know;
  Such a pilgrimage were sweet.   20
Yet do not; I would not go,
  Though at next door we might meet.
Though she were true when you met her,
And last, till you write your letter,
    Yet she   25
    Will be
False, ere I come, to two or three.

---

2. MANDRAKE ROOT: The mandrake plant has a large forked root, which makes it resemble the human body.
4. CLEFT . . . FOOT: Traditionally the devil is represented with a cloven foot.
5. MERMAIDS: the sirens.
8. WIND: rhymes with "find."
9. HONEST: chaste.

I

1. What is the nature of the tasks set in stanza 1? What do they have in common? Why are they put in the form of demands? What is the effect of putting last in the stanza the task to "find/ What wind/ Serves to advance an honest mind"?

2. How does stanza 2 build on stanza 1? What does the speaker gain by waiting until lines 16-18 to declare specifically what he is driving at? How has the reader's mind been conditioned before coming to the flat comment that women are faithless? What is it that not even supernatural powers can do?

3. What compliment does the term *pilgrimage* in line 20 make to the one honest woman who might conceivably be found? How do the last three lines use the compliment to intensify enormously the falseness of all women?

4. What is the effect of the two short rhymed lines in each stanza? How does Donne achieve a conversational tone and why does he use it?

5. How seriously does the speaker expect us to take his conclusion? What is the tone of the poem? flippant? wryly amused? bitter? fanciful? none of these? what?

THE CLOD AND THE PEBBLE   [*1794*]

William Blake

"Love seeketh not itself to please,
  Nor for itself hath any care,
But for another gives its ease,
  And builds a heaven in hell's despair."

So sung a little clod of clay,   5
  Trodden with the cattle's feet,
But a pebble of the brook
  Warbled out these meters meet:

"Love seeketh only self to please,
  To bind another to its delight,   10
Joys in another's loss of ease,
  And builds a hell in heaven's despite."

I

1. What is the view of love in stanza 1? What is the "ease" which it gives? What is the view in stanza 3? How does Love *please* itself by binding *another to its delight?* Is there yet a third view of love suggested that has relevance to the other two? Explain.

2. Would it make any difference if the second stanza went something like this:

Just so a pebble of the brook
Warbled out these meters meet;
But sung a little clod of clay,
Trodden with the cattle's feet:
Why or why not?

3. Compare line 4 to line 12. Building a *heaven in hell's despair* seems reasonable; by the same token, is it reasonable to expect "despite" after "heaven's"? Why or why not? Why is "despite" used?

OF LOVE

Francis Bacon

The stage is more beholding to[1] love than the life of man. For as to the stage, love is ever matter of comedies, and now and then of tragedies; but in life it doth much mischief, sometimes like a siren, sometimes like a fury. You may observe that amongst all the great and worthy persons whereof the memory remaineth, either ancient or recent, there is not one that hath been transported to the mad degree of love; which shows that great spirits and great business do keep out this weak passion. You must except, nevertheless, Marcus Antonius,[2] the half partner of the empire of Rome, and Appius Claudius,[3] the decemvir and lawgiver; whereof the former was indeed a voluptuous man, and inordinate; but the latter was an austere and wise man: and therefore it seems (though rarely) that love can find entrance not only into an open heart, but also into a heart well fortified, if watch be not well kept. It is a poor saying of Epicurus;[4] *Satis magnum alter alteri theatrum sumus:*[5] as if man, made for the contemplation of heaven and all noble objects, should do nothing but kneel before a little idol, and make himself subject, though not of the mouth, as beasts are, yet of the eye, which was given him for higher purposes. It is a strange thing to note the excess of this passion, and how it braves[6] the nature and value of things, by this, that the speaking in a perpetual hyperbole is comely in nothing but in love. Neither is it merely in the phrase; for whereas it hath been well said that the arch-flatterer, with whom all the petty flatterers have intelligence, is a man's self, certainly the lover is more. For there was never proud man thought so absurdly well of himself as the lover doth of the person loved; and therefore it was well said: "That it is impossible to love and to be wise." Neither doth this weakness appear to others only, and not to the party loved, but to the loved most of all, except the love be reciprocal. For it is a true rule, that love is ever rewarded either with the reciprocal or with an inward and secret contempt. By how much the more men ought to beware of this passion, which loseth not only other things, but itself. As for the other losses, the poet's relation doth well figure them: That he that preferred Helena quitted the gifts of Juno and Pallas. For whosoever esteemeth too much of amorous affection quitteth both riches and wisdom. This passion hath his floods in the very times of weakness; which are great prosperity and great adversity, though this latter hath been less observed: both which times kindle love, and make it more fervent, and therefore show it to be the child of folly. They do best who, if they cannot but admit love, yet make it keep quarter,[7] and sever it wholly from their serious affairs and actions of life; for if it check[8] once with business, it troubleth men's fortunes, and maketh men that they can no ways be true to their own ends. I know not how, but martial men are given to love: I think it is but as they are given to wine; for perils commonly ask to be paid in pleasures. There is in man's nature a secret inclination and motion towards love

---

1. BEHOLDING TO: attached to.
2. MARCUS ANTONIUS: Mark Antony, Cleopatra's lover.
3. APPIUS CLAUDIUS: a Roman ruler, who coveted Virginia, daughter of a plebian; when he made her his slave through a mock trial, her father killed her.
4. EPICURUS: Greek philosopher.
5. SATIS . . . SUMUS: "We are to each other spectacle enough."
6. BRAVES: insults.
7. KEEP QUARTER: keep within limits.
8. CHECK: interfere.

of others, which, if it be not spent upon some one or a few, doth naturally spread itself towards many, and maketh men become humane and charitable; as it is seen sometime in friars. Nuptial love maketh mankind; friendly love perfecteth it; but wanton love corrupteth and embaseth it.

I

1. Define "love" as Bacon is using the term throughout most of the essay. In what sense can you argue that the last sentence might better have been the first one? Or that it is better where it is? Consider what the subject of the essay is and how best the reader might understand in what sense the word *love* is being used.

2. This is obviously a direct piece of advice on how to act about love. By what kinds of argument does the speaker seek to persuade the reader that he would be wise to adopt the stated position? There is the appeal to authority in the opening sentences when he says that "great spirits and great business do keep out this weak passion"? What other arguments are used?

3. What does Bacon suggest might be the gains in not letting oneself get involved in *this weak passion?*

4. Direct advice of this sort is often the kind of thing one closes his mind to almost automatically. What is there in the essay that makes the reader respond, if only to argue or object? Consider the use of allusions, barbed phrases, and the appeal to authority.

5. You have probably had all kinds of practice in writing well-organized essays and have been given lots of perfectly good advice on how to do so:

   a. make an effective opening paragraph that clearly states in general terms your intentions.

   b. support your generalizations in a number of following paragraphs, each devoted to a single main idea and full of specific supporting evidence, with a topic sentence somewhere in each paragraph;

   c. close with a summation of some kind that reminds the reader that you had a plan in mind and followed it.

Obviously, Bacon's essay does few of these things. He used the term *essays* to designate a collection of "do it yourself" papers he wrote for young, inexperienced men on how to get along in the world of social relationships and practical affairs. Each is a series of loosely connected bits of advice held together by virtue of being on a common topic. Indicate places in "Of Love" where sentences build carefully on each other, and other places where there is little or no direct connection between one sentence and the next.

II

1. Try your hand at the kind of essay we have here. You might take the same subject from a different point of view, or you might take any general subject on which advice can be given, such as, "Of Friendship," "Of Athletics," or "On Being Popular."

LES SYLPHIDES   [*1939-1940*]

Louis MacNeice

Life in a day: he took his girl to the ballet;
Being shortsighted himself could hardly see it—
    The white skirts in the grey
    Glade and the swell of the music
    Lifting the white sails.   5

"Les Sylphides" from *Collected Poems, 1925-1948,* by Louis MacNeice. Reprinted with the permission of Faber and Faber, Ltd.

Title. Ballet; music by Frederic Chopin; first performed in St. Petersburg in 1908.

Calyx upon calyx, canterbury bells in the breeze
The flowers on the left mirror to the flowers on the right
   And the naked arms above
   The powdered faces moving
   Like seaweed in a pool.   10

Now, he thought, we are floating—ageless, oarless—
Now there is no separation, from now on
   You will be wearing white
   Satin and a red sash
   Under the waltzing trees.   15

But the music stopped, the dancers took their curtain,
The river had come to a lock—a shuffle of programs—
   And we cannot continue down
   Stream unless we are ready
   To enter the lock and drop.   20

So they were married—to be the more together—
And found they were never again so much together,
   Divided by the morning tea,
   By the evening paper,
   By children and tradesmen's bills.   25

Waking at times in the night she found assurance
In his regular breathing but wondered whether
   It was really worth it and where
   The river had flowed away
   And where were the white flowers.   30

6. CALYX: the leafy part of a flower.

I

1. What is being described in the first two stanzas? By what specific details is this description developed? What are the *white sails?* How can the *swell of the music* lift the *white sails?* What are the *flowers* on the left and right?

2. The *he* of the poem is said to be *short-sighted.* Is the scene pictured through his short-sightedness? Why or why not? How does the sentence structure in the first two stanzas support the description? What is significant about the fact that neither stanza is syntactically complete?

3. How does the "floating" in line 11 recall the scene of stanzas 1 and 2? What other words in stanza 3 relate to the scene? How does the scene symbolize the attitude the two lovers have toward each other at the ballet? What part does the syntax and the use of the three "now's" in stanza 3 play in communicating the lovers' attitudes?

4. How does the structure of lines 16 and 17 abruptly change the breathless movement of stanza 3? What is the effect of the use of assonance at the end of line 20? What does line 20 mean?

5. What is the contrast between the idyllic world of the first three stanzas and the marriage state in stanzas 5 and 6? Why is reference made to the idyllic world in lines 29-30? Is it significant that *he* does the projecting in stanza 3 but that *she* does the recalling in stanza 6? Why or why not?

NEUTRAL TONES   [*1925*]

Thomas Hardy

We stood by a pond that winter day,
And the sun was white, as though chidden of God,
And a few leaves lay on the starving sod;
—They had fallen from an ash, and were gray.

Your eyes on me were as eyes that rove   5
Over tedious riddles solved years ago;
And some words played between us to and fro
    On which lost the more by our love.

The smile on your mouth was the deadest thing
Alive enough to have strength to die;   10
And a grin of bitterness swept thereby
    Like an ominous bird a-wing. . . .

Since then, keen lessons that love deceives,
And wrings with wrong, have shaped to me
Your face, and the God-curst sun, and a tree,   15
    And a pond edged with grayish leaves.

I

1. What is the situation of the poem? Is the speaker addressing someone directly? If not, why does he use "your" in the last three stanzas?

2. Explain the meaning of the images of stanzas 2 and 3. What are the implications of "tedious" (6), "played" (7), and "grin of bitterness" (11)?

3. In lines 13-14 the speaker says that "keen lessons . . . have *shaped* to me/ Your face. . . ." Why "shaped"? What double meaning is there in "wrings"? How do lines 15-16 echo lines 1-4? What is gained by this echoing?

4. In what ways are the implications of the title carried out? Consider word choice, particularly in stanza 1. How do the images of stanzas 2 and 3 emphasize "neutralness"? What is an appropriate synonym for "neutral" in this context: uninvolved? uncommitted? indifferent? lifeless? In what sense is there nothing at all *neutral* about the tone of the poem?

5. How does Hardy, through the extensive use of "and's" in stanzas 1 and 4, reinforce the idea that the dead love affair can be, and constantly is, dredged up from memory?

6. What are the *keen lessons* to which the speaker refers in stanza 4? In other words, what has the dead love affair come to symbolize in his life?

TO MARGUERITE   [*1854*]

Matthew Arnold

Yes: in the sea of life enisled,
   With echoing straits between us thrown.
Dotting the shoreless watery wild,
   We mortal millions live *alone*.
The islands feel the enclasping flow,   5
And then their endless bounds they know.

But when the moon their hollows lights,
   And they are swept by balms of spring,
And in their glens, on starry nights,
   The nightingales divinely sing;   10
And lovely notes, from shore to shore,
Across the sounds and channels pour;

O then a longing like despair
   Is to their farthest caverns sent!
For surely once, they feel, we were   15
   Parts of a single continent.
Now round us spreads the watery plain—
O might our marges meet again!

Who ordered that their longing's fire
   Should be, as soon as kindled, cooled?   20
Who renders vain their deep desire?—

1. ENISLED: separated, as on an island.

A god, a god their severance ruled;
And bade betwixt their shores to be
The unplumbed, salt, estranging sea.

I

1. The speaker in the poem describes islands but is actually talking about human beings. State in your own words what he is using islands to say about human beings in stanza 1. In stanzas 2 and 3. In stanza 4.

2. What words in stanza 1 help to communicate the aloneness of islands—and human beings? How does a phrase like "We mortal millions" contribute to the sense of aloneness?

3. What changes in the described situation come about in stanzas 2 and 3? What does not change? If individuals are the islands of stanza 1, what do the "hollows" (7), "glens" (9), and "caverns" (14) stand for? Why does the speaker say in line 15, "For surely once, they feel, *we* were" instead of the expected, "For surely once, they feel, *they* were"?

4. The title "To Marguerite" suggests a more personal reference than the opening stanza might indicate. How does stanza 4 focus the comments of the poem on the personal estrangement and also keep it from being only personal? What do you suppose the speaker means by "A god, a god their severance ruled"? Note that the line is not "God, God their severance ruled."

THE LAGOON   [*1898*]

Joseph Conrad

   In the introduction to this unit on Love we indicated that most of the selections would deal with love between man and woman; so far, that has been the focus even though there have certainly been overtones in many of the selections that have taken us far beyond the usual connotations of romantic love.

   The rest of this section will probe other areas of man's relationships with his fellow man and with his God that are best understood in the light of St. Paul's

---

"The Lagoon" from *Tales of Unrest* by Joseph Conrad. Reprinted by permission of J. M. Dent & Sons, Ltd.

words quoted earlier. The following selection, Conrad's "The Lagoon," is a story of a man who had to make a choice between his love for a woman and his loyalty to his brother. You might ask yourself as you read whether Conrad is passing judgment on the decision made or whether he is simply saying that such decisions must be made and the consequences must be lived with. The clash of loyalties has always fascinated the literary artist, as it does any sensitive person who does not see the world in either-or terms. When the conflicting loyalties involve the deepest claims of love, as they do here, the result is inescapable spiritual torment.

The white man, leaning with both arms over the roof of the little house in the stern of the boat, said to the steersman:

"We will pass the night in Arsat's clearing. It is late."

The Malay only grunted, and went on looking fixedly at the river. The white man rested his chin on his crossed arms and gazed at the wake of the boat. At the end of the straight avenue of forests cut by the intense glitter of the river, the sun appeared unclouded and dazzling, poised low over the water that shone smoothly like a band of metal. The forests, somber and dull, stood motionless and silent on each side of the broad stream. At the foot of big, towering trees, trunkless nipa palms rose from the mud of the bank, in bunches of leaves enormous and heavy, that hung unstirring over the brown swirl of eddies. In the stillness of the air every tree, every leaf, every bough, every tendril of creeper and every petal of minute blossoms seemed to have been bewitched into an immobility perfect and final. Nothing moved on the river but the eight paddles that rose flashing regularly, dipped together with a single splash; while the steersman swept right and left with a periodic and sudden flourish of his blade describing a glinting semicircle above his head. The churned-up water frothed alongside with a confused murmur. And the white man's canoe, advancing upstream in the short-lived disturbance of its own making, seemed to enter the portals of a land from which the very memory of motion had forever departed.

The white man, turning his back upon the setting sun, looked along the empty and broad expanse of the sea-reach.[1] For the last three miles of its course the wandering, hesitating river, as if enticed irresistibly by the freedom of an open horizon, flows straight into the sea, flows straight to the east—to the east that harbors both light and darkness. Astern of the boat the repeated call of some bird, a cry discordant and feeble, skipped along over the smooth water and lost itself, before it could reach the other shore, in the breathless silence of the world.

The steersman dug his paddle into the stream, and held hard with stiffened arms, his body thrown forward. The water gurgled aloud; and suddenly the long straight reach seemed to pivot on its center, the forests swung in a semicircle, and the slanting beams of sunset touched the broadside of the canoe with a fiery glow, throwing the slender and distorted shadows of its crew upon the streaked glitter of the river. The white man turned to look ahead. The course of the boat had been altered at right angles to the stream, and the carved dragon head of its prow was pointing now at a gap in the fringing bushes of the bank. It glided through, brushing the overhanging twigs, and disappeared from the river like some slim and amphibious creature leaving the water for its lair in the forests.

The narrow creek was like a ditch: tortuous, fabulously deep; filled with gloom under the thin strip of pure and shining blue of the heaven. Immense trees soared up, invisible behind the festooned draperies of creepers. Here and there, near the glistening blackness of the water, a twisted root

---

1. SEA-REACH: the straight course of a river when it approaches the sea.

of some tall tree showed amongst the tracery of small ferns, black and dull, writhing and motionless, like an arrested snake. The short words of the paddlers reverberated loudly between the thick and somber walls of vegetation. Darkness oozed out from between the trees, through the tangled maze of the creepers, from behind the great fantastic and unstirring leaves; the darkness, mysterious and invincible; the darkness scented and poisonous of impenetrable forests.

The men poled in the shoaling water. The creek broadened, opening out into a wide sweep of a stagnant lagoon. The forests receded from the marshy bank, leaving a level strip of bright green, reedy grass to frame the reflected blueness of the sky. A fleecy pink cloud drifted high above, trailing the delicate coloring of its image under the floating leaves and the silvery blossoms of the lotus. A little house, perched on high piles, appeared black in the distance. Near it, two tall nibong palms, that seemed to have come out of the forests in the background, leaned slightly over the ragged roof, with a suggestion of sad tenderness and care in the droop of their leafy and soaring heads.

The steersman, pointing with his paddle, said, "Arsat is there. I see his canoe fast between the piles."

The polers ran along the sides of the boat glancing over their shoulders at the end of the day's journey. They would have preferred to spend the night somewhere else than on this lagoon of weird aspect and ghostly reputation. Moreover, they disliked Arsat, first as a stranger, and also because he who repairs a ruined house, and dwells in it, proclaims that he is not afraid to live amongst the spirits that haunt the places abandoned by mankind. Such a man can disturb the course of fate by glances or words; while his familiar ghosts are not easy to propitiate by casual wayfarers upon whom they long to wreak the malice of their human master. White men care not for such

things, being unbelievers and in league with the Father of Evil, who leads them unharmed through the invisible dangers of this world. To the warnings of the righteous they oppose an offensive pretense of disbelief. What is there to be done?

So they thought, throwing their weight on the end of their long poles. The big canoe glided on swiftly, noiselessly, and smoothly, towards Arsat's clearing, till, in a great rattling of poles thrown down, and the loud murmurs of "Allah be praised!" it came with a gentle knock against the crooked piles below the house.

The boatmen with uplifted faces shouted discordantly, "Arsat! O Arsat!" Nobody came. The white man began to climb the rude ladder giving access to the bamboo platform before the house. The juragan[2] of the boat said sulkily, "We will cook in the sampan, and sleep on the water."

"Pass my blankets and the basket," said the white man, curtly.

He knelt on the edge of the platform to receive the bundle. Then the boat shoved off, and the white man, standing up, confronted Arsat, who had come out through the low door of his hut. He was a man young, powerful, with broad chest and muscular arms. He had nothing on but his sarong. His head was bare. His big, soft eyes stared eagerly at the white man, but his voice and demeanor were composed as he asked, without any words of greeting:

"Have you medicine, Tuan?"[3]

"No," said the visitor in a startled tone. "No. Why? Is there sickness in the house?"

"Enter and see," replied Arsat, in the same calm manner, and turning short round, passed again through the small doorway. The white man, dropping his bundles, followed.

In the dim light of the dwelling he made out on a couch of bamboos a woman stretched on her back under a broad sheet of red cotton cloth. She lay still, as if

---

2. JURAGAN: master of the sampan.
3. TUAN: Sir; usually applied to Europeans.

dead; but her big eyes, wide open, glittered in the gloom, staring upwards at the slender rafters, motionless and unseeing. She was in a high fever, and evidently unconscious. Her cheeks were sunk slightly, her lips were partly open, and on the young face there was the ominous and fixed expression—the absorbed, contemplating expression of the unconscious who are going to die. The two men stood looking down at her in silence.

"Has she been long ill?" asked the traveler.

"I have not slept for five nights," answered the Malay, in a deliberate tone. "At first she heard voices calling her from the water and struggled against me who held her. But since the sun of today rose she hears nothing—she hears not me. She sees nothing. She sees not me—ME!"

He remained silent for a minute, then asked softly:

"Tuan, will she die?"

"I fear so," said the white man, sorrowfully. He had known Arsat years ago, in a far country in times of trouble and danger, when no friendship is to be despised. And since his Malay friend had come unexpectedly to dwell in the hut on the lagoon with a strange woman, he had slept many times there, in his journeys up and down the river. He liked the man who knew how to keep faith in council and how to fight without fear by the side of his white friend. He liked him—not so much perhaps as a man likes his favorite dog—but still he liked him well enough to help and ask no questions, to think sometimes vaguely and hazily in the midst of his own pursuits, about the lonely man and the long-haired woman with audacious face and triumphant eyes, who lived together hidden by the forests—alone and feared.

The white man came out of the hut in time to see the enormous conflagration of sunset put out by the swift and stealthy shadows that, rising like a black and impalpable vapor above the treetops, spread over the heaven, extinguishing the crimson glow of floating clouds and the red brilliance of departing daylight. In a few moments all the stars came out above the intense blackness of the earth and the great lagoon gleaming suddenly with reflected lights resembled an oval patch of night sky flung down into the hopeless and abysmal night of the wilderness. The white man had some supper out of the basket, then collecting a few sticks that lay about the platform, made up a small fire, not for warmth, but for the sake of the smoke, which would keep off the mosquitoes. He wrapped himself in the blankets and sat with his back against the reed wall of the house, smoking thoughtfully.

Arsat came through the doorway with noiseless steps and squatted down by the fire. The white man moved his outstretched legs a little.

"She breaths," said Arsat in a low voice, anticipating the expected question. "She breathes and burns as if with a great fire. She speaks not; she hears not—and burns!"

He paused for a moment, then asked in a quiet, incurious tone:

"Tuan . . . will she die?"

The white man moved his shoulders uneasily and muttered in a hesitating manner:

"If such is her fate."

"No, Tuan," said Arsat, calmly. "If such is my fate. I hear, I see, I wait. I remember. . . . Tuan, do you remember the old days? Do you remember my brother?"

"Yes," said the white man. The Malay rose suddenly and went in. The other, sitting still outside, could hear the voice in the hut. Arsat said: "Hear me! Speak!" His words were succeeded by a complete silence. "O Diamelen!" he cried, suddenly. After that cry there was a deep sigh. Arsat came out and sank down again in his old place.

They sat in silence before the fire. There was no sound within the house, there was no sound near them; but far away on the lagoon they could hear the voices of the boatmen ringing fitful and distinct on the calm water. The fire in the bows of the sampan shone faintly in the distance with a hazy red glow.

Then it died out. The voices ceased. The land and the water slept invisible, unstirring and mute. It was as though there had been nothing left in the world but the glitter of stars streaming, ceaseless and vain, through the black stillness of the night.

The white man gazed straight before him into the darkness with wide-open eyes. The fear and fascination, the inspiration and the wonder of death—of death near, unavoidable, and unseen, soothed the unrest of his race and stirred the most indistinct, the most intimate of his thoughts. The ever-ready suspicion of evil, the gnawing suspicion that lurks in our hearts, flowed out into the stillness round him—into the stillness profound and dumb, and made it appear untrustworthy and infamous, like the placid and impenetrable mask of an unjustifiable violence. In that fleeting and powerful disturbance of his being the earth enfolded in the starlight peace became a shadowy country of inhuman strife, a battlefield of phantoms terrible and charming, august or ignoble, struggling ardently for the possession of our helpless hearts. An unquiet and mysterious country of inextinguishable desires and fears.

A plaintive murmur rose in the night; a murmur saddening and startling, as if the great solitudes of surrounding woods had tried to whisper into his ear the wisdom of their immense and lofty indifference. Sounds hesitating and vague floated in the air round him, shaped themselves slowly into words; and at last flowed on gently in a murmuring stream of soft and monotonous sentences. He stirred like a man waking up and changed his position slightly. Arsat, motionless and shadowy, sitting with bowed head under the stars, was speaking in a low and dreamy tone:

". . . for where can we lay down the heaviness of our trouble but in a friend's heart? A man must speak of war and of love. You, Tuan, know what war is, and you have seen me in time of danger seek death as other men seek life! A writing may be lost; a lie may be written; but what

the eye has seen is truth and remains in the mind!"

"I remember," said the white man, quietly. Arsat went on with mournful composure:

"Therefore I shall speak to you of love. Speak in the night. Speak before both night and love are gone—and the eye of day looks upon my sorrow and my shame; upon my blackened face; upon my burnt-up heart."

A sigh, short and faint, marked an almost imperceptible pause, and then his words flowed on, without a stir, without a gesture.

"After the time of trouble and war was over and you went away from my country in the pursuit of your desires, which we, men of the islands, cannot understand, I and my brother became again, as we had been before, the sword bearers of the Ruler. You know we were men of family, belonging to a ruling race, and more fit than any to carry on our right shoulder the emblem of power. And in the time of prosperity Si Dendring showed us favor, as we, in time of sorrow, had showed to him the faithfulness of our courage. It was a time of peace. A time of deer hunts and cock fights; of idle talks and foolish squabbles between men whose bellies are full and weapons are rusty. But the sower watched the young rice shoots grow up without fear, and the traders came and went, departed lean and returned fat into the river of peace. They brought news, too. Brought lies and truth mixed together, so that no man knew when to rejoice and when to be sorry. We heard from them about you also. They had seen you here and had seen you there. And I was glad to hear, for I remembered the stirring times, and I always remembered you, Tuan, till the time came when my eyes could see nothing in the past, because they had looked upon the one who is dying there—in the house."

He stopped to exclaim in an intense whisper, "O Mara bahia! O Calamity!" then went on speaking a little louder:

"There's no worse enemy and no better friend than a brother, Tuan, for one brother knows another, and in perfect knowledge is strength for good or evil. I loved my brother. I went to him and told him that I could see nothing but one face, hear nothing but one voice. He told me: 'Open your heart so that she can see what is in it—and wait. Patience is wisdom. Inchi Midah may die or our Ruler may throw off his fear of woman!' . . . I waited! . . . You remember the lady with the veiled face, Tuan, and the fear of our Ruler before her cunning and temper. And if she wanted her servant, what could I do? But I fed the hunger of my heart on short glances and stealthy words. I loitered on the path to the bath-houses in the daytime, and when the sun had fallen behind the forest I crept along the jasmine hedges of the women's court-yard. Unseeing, we spoke to one another through the scent of flowers, through the veil of leaves, through the blades of long grass that stood still before our lips; so great was our prudence, so faint was the murmur of our great longing. The time passed swiftly . . . and there were whispers amongst women—and our enemies watched —my brother was gloomy, and I began to think of killing and of a fierce death. . . . We are of a people who take what they want—like you whites. There is a time when a man should forget loyalty and re-spect. Might and authority are given to rulers, but to all men is given love and strength and courage. My brother said, 'You shall take her from their midst. We are two who are like one.' And I answered, 'Let it be soon, for I find no warmth in sunlight that does not shine upon her.' Our time came when the Ruler and all the great peo-ple went to the mouth of the river to fish by torchlight. There were hundreds of boats, and on the white sand, between the water and the forests, dwellings of leaves were built for the households of the Rajahs. The smoke of cooking fires was like a blue mist of the evening, and many voices rang in it

joyfully. While they were making the boats ready to beat up the fish, my brother came to me and said, 'Tonight!' I looked to my weapons, and when the time came our canoe took its place in the circle of boats carrying the torches. The lights blazed on the water, but behind the boats there was darkness. When the shouting began and the excitement made them like mad we dropped out. The water swallowed our fire, and we floated back to the shore that was dark with only here and there the glimmer of embers. We could hear the talk of slave girls amongst the sheds. Then we found a place deserted and silent. We waited there. She came. She came running along the shore, rapid and leaving no trace, like a leaf driven by the wind into the sea. My brother said gloomily, 'Go and take her; carry her into our boat.' I lifted her in my arms. She panted. Her heart was beating against my breast. I said, 'I take you from those people. You came to the cry of my heart, but my arms take you into my boat against the will of the great!' 'It is right,' said my brother. 'We are men who take what we want and can hold it against many. We should have taken her in daylight.' I said, 'Let us be off'; for since she was in my boat I began to think of our Ruler's many men. 'Yes. Let us be off,' said my brother. 'We are cast out and this boat is our country now—and the sea is our refuge.' He lingered with his foot on the shore, and I entreated him to hasten, for I remembered the strokes of her heart against my breast and thought that two men cannot withstand a hundred. We left, paddling downstream close to the bank; and as we passed by the creek where they were fishing, the great shouting had ceased, but the murmur of voices was loud like the humming of insects flying at noon-day. The boats floated, clustered together, in the red light of torches, under a black roof of smoke; and men talked of their sport. Men that boasted, and praised, and jeered—men that would have been our friends in the morning, but on that night were already our enemies. We paddled swiftly past. We had no more friends in the country of our birth. She sat in the middle of the canoe with covered face; silent as she is now; unseeing as she is now—and I had no regret at what I was leaving because I could hear her breathing close to me—as I can hear her now."

He paused, listened with his ear turned to the doorway, then shook his head and went on:

"My brother wanted to shout the cry of challenge—one cry only—to let the people know we were freeborn robbers who trusted our arms and the great sea. And again I begged him in the name of our love to be silent. Could I not hear her breathing close to me? I knew the pursuit would come quick enough. My brother loved me. He dipped his paddle without a splash. He only said, 'There is half a man in you now—the other half is in that woman. I can wait. When you are a whole man again, you will come back with me here to shout defiance. We are sons of the same mother.' I made no answer. All my strength and all my spirit were in my hands that held the paddle—for I longed to be with her in a safe place beyond the reach of men's anger and of women's spite. My love was so great, that I thought it could guide me to a country where death was unknown, if I could only escape from Inchi Midah's fury and from our Ruler's sword. We paddled with haste, breathing through our teeth. The blades bit deep into the smooth water. We passed out of the river; we flew in clear channels amongst the shallows. We skirted the black coast; we skirted the sand beaches where the sea speaks in whispers to the land; and the gleam of white sand flashed back past our boat, so swiftly she ran upon the water. We spoke not. Only once I said, 'Sleep, Diamelen, for soon you may want all your strength.' I heard the sweetness of her voice, but I never turned my head. The sun rose and still we went on. Water fell from my face like rain from a cloud. We flew in the

light and heat. I never looked back, but I knew that my brother's eyes, behind me, were looking steadily ahead, for the boat went as straight as a bushman's dart, when it leaves the end of the sumpitan.[4] There was no better paddler, no better steersman than my brother. Many times, together, we had won races in that canoe. But we never had put out our strength as we did then—then, when for the last time we paddled together! There was no braver or stronger man in our country than my brother. I could not spare the strength to turn my head and look at him, but every moment I heard the hiss of his breath getting louder behind me. Still he did not speak. The sun was high. The heat clung to my back like a flame of fire. My ribs were ready to burst, but I could no longer get enough air into my chest. And then I felt I must cry out with my last breath, 'Let us rest!' . . . 'Good!' he answered; and his voice was firm. He was strong. He was brave. He knew not fear and no fatigue . . . My brother!"

A murmur powerful and gentle, a murmur vast and faint; the murmur of trembling leaves, of stirring boughs, ran through the tangled depths of the forests, ran over the starry smoothness of the lagoon, and the water between the piles lapped the slimy timber once with a sudden splash. A breath of warm air touched the two men's faces and passed on with a mournful sound—a breath loud and short like an uneasy sigh of the dreaming earth.

Arsat went on in an even, low voice.

"We ran our canoe on the white beach of a little bay close to a long tongue of land that seemed to bar our road; a long wooded cape going far into the sea. My brother knew that place. Beyond the cape a river has its entrance, and through the jungle of that land there is a narrow path. We made a fire and cooked rice. Then we lay down to sleep on the soft sand in the shade of our

---

4. SUMPITAN: a blowgun for discharging darts, usually poisoned.

canoe, while she watched. No sooner had I closed my eyes than I heard her cry of alarm. We leaped up. The sun was halfway down the sky already, and coming in sight in the opening of the bay we saw a prau manned by many paddlers. We knew it at once; it was one of our Rajah's praus. They were watching the shore, and saw us. They beat the gong, and turned the head of the prau into the bay. I felt my heart become weak within my breast. Diamelen sat on the sand and covered her face. There was no escape by sea. My brother laughed. He had the gun you had given him, Tuan, before you went away, but there was only a handful of powder. He spoke to me quickly: 'Run with her along the path. I shall keep them back, for they have no firearms, and landing in the face of a man with a gun is certain death for some. Run with her. On the other side of that wood there is a fisherman's house—and a canoe. When I have fired all the shots I will follow. I am a great runner, and before they can come up we shall be gone. I will hold out as long as I can, for she is but a woman—that can neither run nor fight, but she has your heart in her weak hands.' He dropped behind the canoe. The prau was coming. She and I ran, and as we rushed along the path I heard shots. My brother fired—once—twice—and the booming of the gong ceased. There was silence behind us. That neck of land is narrow. Before I heard my brother fire the third shot I saw the shelving shore, and I saw the water again; the mouth of a broad river. We crossed a grassy glade. We ran down to the water. I saw a low hut above the black mud, and a small canoe hauled up. I heard another shot behind me. I thought, 'That is his last charge.' We rushed down to the canoe; a man came running from the hut, but I leaped on him, and we rolled together in the mud. Then I got up, and he lay still at my feet. I don't know whether I had killed him or not. I and Diamelen pushed the canoe afloat. I heard yells behind me, and I saw my brother run across

the glade. Many men were bounding after him. I took her in my arms and threw her into the boat, then leaped in myself. When I looked back I saw that my brother had fallen. He fell and was up again, but the men were closing round him. He shouted, 'I am coming!' The men were close to him. I looked. Many men. Then I looked at her. Tuan, I pushed the canoe! I pushed it into deep water. She was kneeling forward looking at me, and I said, 'Take your paddle,' while I struck the water with mine. Tuan, I heard him cry. I heard him cry my name twice; and I heard voices shouting, 'Kill! Strike!' I never turned back. I heard him calling my name again with a great shriek, as when life is going out together with the voice—and I never turned my head. My own name! . . . My brother! Three times he called—but I was not afraid of life. Was she not there in that canoe? And could I not with her find a country where death is forgotten—where death is unknown!'"

The white man sat up. Arsat rose and stood, an indistinct and silent figure above the dying embers of the fire. Over the lagoon a mist drifting and low had crept, erasing slowly the glittering images of the stars. And now a great expanse of white vapor covered the land: it flowed cold and gray in the darkness, eddied in noiseless whirls round the tree trunks and about the platform of the house, which seemed to float upon a restless and impalpable illusion of a sea. Only far away the tops of the trees stood outlined on the twinkle of heaven, like a somber and forbidding shore—a coast deceptive, pitiless and black.

Arsat's voice vibrated loudly in the profound peace.

"I had her there! I had her! To get her I would have faced all mankind. But I had her—and—"

His words went out ringing into the empty distances. He paused, and seemed to listen to them dying away very far—beyond help and beyond recall. Then he said quietly:

"Tuan, I loved my brother."

A breath of wind made him shiver. High above his head, high above the silent sea of mist the drooping leaves of the palms rattled together with a mournful and expiring sound. The white man stretched his legs. His chin rested on his chest, and he murmured sadly without lifting his head:

"We all love our brothers."

Arsat burst out with an intense whispering violence:

"What did I care who died? I wanted peace in my own heart."

He seemed to hear a stir in the house—listened—then stepped in noiselessly. The white man stood up. A breeze was coming in fitful puffs. The stars shone paler as if they had retreated into the frozen depths of immense space. After a chill gust of wind there were a few seconds of perfect calm and absolute silence. Then from behind the black and wavy line of the forests a column of golden light shot up into the heavens and spread over the semicircle of the eastern horizon. The sun had risen. The mist lifted, broke into drifting patches, vanished into thin flying wreaths; and the unveiled lagoon lay, polished and black, in the heavy shadows at the foot of the wall of trees. A white eagle rose over it with a slanting and ponderous flight, reached the clear sunshine and appeared dazzlingly brilliant for a moment, then soaring higher, became a dark and motionless speck before it vanished into the blue as if it had left the earth forever. The white man, standing gazing upwards before the doorway, heard in the hut a confused and broken murmur of distracted words ending with a loud groan. Suddenly Arsat stumbled out with outstretched hands, shivered, and stood still for some time with fixed eyes. Then he said:

"She burns no more."

Before his face the sun showed its edge above the treetops rising steadily. The breeze freshened; a great brilliance burst upon the lagoon, came out of the clear shadows of the morning, became distinct, as if they had rushed nearer—to stop short in a great stir of leaves, of nodding boughs, of swaying branches. In the merciless sunshine the whisper of unconscious life grew louder, speaking in an incomprehensible voice round the dumb darkness of that human sorrow. Arsat's eyes wandered slowly, then stared at the rising sun.

"I can see nothing," he said half aloud to himself.

"There is nothing," said the white man, moving to the edge of the platform and waving his hand to his boat. A shout came faintly over the lagoon and the sampan began to glide towards the abode of the friend of ghosts.

"If you want to come with me, I will wait all the morning," said the white man, looking away upon the water.

"No, Tuan," said Arsat, softly. "I shall not eat or sleep in this house, but I must first see my road. Now I can see nothing—see nothing! There is no light and no peace in the world; but there is death—death for many. We are sons of the same mother—and I left him in the midst of enemies; but I am going back now."

He drew a long breath and went on in a dreamy tone:

"In a little while I shall see clear enough to strike—to strike. But she has died, and . . . now . . . darkness."

He flung his arms wide open, let them fall along his body, then stood still with unmoved face and stony eyes, staring at the sun. The white man got down into his canoe. The polers ran smartly along the sides of the boat, looking over their shoulders at the beginning of a weary journey. High in the stern, his head muffled up in white rags, the juragan sat moody, letting his paddle trail in the water. The white man, leaning with both arms over the grass roof of the little cabin, looked back at the shining ripple of the boat's wake. Before the sampan passed out of the lagoon into the creek he lifted his eyes. Arsat had not moved. He stood lonely in the searching sunshine; and he looked beyond the great light of a cloudless day into the darkness of a world of illusions.

I

1. The story has little plot, and we do not know much about any of the characters, including Arsat, who is the most fully developed. Also, Arsat's story is told by him, not dramatized for us, and it is told to the white man, who probably already knows most of the details since he has stayed with Arsat a number of times and knew him in his native country. Why might Conrad want to keep characterization vague, and why does he choose to have Arsat tell his own story at the moment of Diamelen's death? Consider how eager Arsat is to talk and how little his listener says.

2. Why is the white man nameless? What kind of person is he? Look carefully at what he says, and comment on whether he is simply indifferent or even heartless, or whether he fails to understand what is going on inside Arsat, or whether he realizes that no comment is the best comment under the circumstances. Does the comment that he "liked him—not so much perhaps as a man likes his favorite dog—but still he liked him well enough to help and ask no questions" sum up the relationship between the two men? Why or why not? What is his function in the story?

3. Reread the opening paragraphs carefully. What purpose does the detailed description of the river, the forest, the lagoon, and the entrance of the canoe serve? Why is the title of the story "The Lagoon"? Consider all this in relation to Arsat's words about Diamelen on her death bed: "She speaks not; she hears not—she burns!" and his statement just before she dies: "What did I care who died? I wanted peace in my own heart." How is the lagoon described in the morning, after her death? In general, how is the light-darkness idea carried out throughout the story? And how is the spiritual isolation of Arsat underscored?

4. Notice how in the last paragraph a number of phrases from the beginning of the story are repeated almost word for word in the description of the polers and the white man. What purposes does this serve?

5. What do you suppose the "world of illusions" is that Arsat is said to look into at the end? Are his love for Diamelen and his sense of loyalty to his brother illusions? If they are, how do they contrast with the *reality* of the forest, which *whisper[s] into the ear* of the white man *the wisdom of [its] immense and lofty indifference?*

II

1. How would you answer the question posed in the introduction on whether Conrad is passing judgment on Arsat's decision? Consider in this connection the fact that it was the brother who suggested running off with the girl, that the brother deplores having to do it at night and wishes to cry out at least one challenge, that Diamelen is a completely shadowy figure, and that at the very end of his story Arsat says: "I never turned back. I heard him calling my name again with a great shriek, as when life is going out together with the voice—and I never turned my head. My own name! . . . My brother! Three times he called—but I was not afraid of life. Was she not there in the canoe? And could I not with her find a country where death is forgotten—where death is unknown!" What kind of country had he found? And on what is his attention focused at the time of Diamelen's death?

A PRAYER FOR MY DAUGHTER   [*1921*]

William Butler Yeats

Arsat's anguish reflects his inability to escape the demands of brotherly love and find "peace in my own heart." Like his love for Diamelen, his love for his brother may well center in the "world of illusions," but if so, illusions are then what give deepest meaning to human experience. "The Lagoon" dramatizes man's need to live by the values he has accepted for himself and knows are right.

In the poem which follows, Yeats expresses his concern for his infant daughter's future happiness in a world of violence and prays that she may be guided by the values which he knows are right: "natural kindness," "courtesy," "intellectual humility," "custom," and "ceremony."

> Once more the storm is howling, and half hid
> Under this cradle-hood and coverlid
> My child sleeps on. There is no obstacle
> But Gregory's wood and one bare hill
> Whereby the haystack- and roof-leveling wind,   5
> Bred on the Atlantic, can be stayed;
> And for an hour I have walked and prayed
> Because of the great gloom that is in my mind.
>
> I have walked and prayed for this young child an hour
> And heard the sea-wind scream upon the tower,   10
> And under the arches of the bridge, and scream
> In the elms above the flooded stream;
> Imagining in excited reverie
> That the future years had come,
> Dancing to a frenzied drum,   15
> Out of the murderous innocence of the sea.
>
> May she be granted beauty and yet not
> Beauty to make a stranger's eye distraught,
> Or hers before a looking-glass, for such,
> Being made beautiful overmuch,   20
> Consider beauty a sufficient end,
> Lose natural kindness and maybe
> The heart-revealing intimacy
> That chooses right, and never find a friend.

Title. DAUGHTER: Anne Butler Yeats, born February 24, 1919.

4. GREGORY'S WOOD: In 1917 Yeats had bought a piece of Lady Gregory's estate in Galway; in an old Norman tower he had built himself a study.

Helen being chosen found life flat and dull   25
And later had much trouble from a fool,
While that great Queen, that rose out of the spray,
Being fatherless could have her way
Yet chose a bandy-leggèd smith for man.
It's certain that fine women eat   30
A crazy salad with their meat
Whereby the Horn of Plenty is undone.

In courtesy I'd have her chiefly learned;
Hearts are not had as a gift but hearts are earned
By those that are not entirely beautiful;   35
Yet many, that have played the fool
For beauty's very self, has charm made wise,
And many a poor man that has roved,
Loved and thought himself beloved,
From a glad kindness cannot take his eyes.   40

May she become a flourishing hidden tree
That all her thoughts may like the linnet be,
And have no business but dispensing round
Their magnanimities of sound,
Nor but in merriment begin a chase,   45
Nor but in merriment a quarrel.
O may she live like some green laurel
Rooted in one dear perpetual place.

My mind, because the minds that I have loved,
The sort of beauty that I have approved,   50
Prosper but little, has dried up of late,
Yet knows that to be choked with hate
May well be of all evil chances chief.
If there's no hatred in a mind
Assault and battery of the wind   55
Can never tear the linnet from the leaf.

An intellectual hatred is the worst,
So let her think opinions are accursed.
Have I not seen the loveliest woman born
Out of the mouth of Plenty's horn,   60
Because of her opinionated mind

25-26. HELEN . . . FOOL: Helen, wife of Menelaus, King of Sparta, ran off to Troy with Paris ("a fool").
27. QUEEN: Aphrodite (or Venus), born of the foam of the sea.
29. BANDY-LEGGÈD SMITH: Hephaestus (or Vulcan), Aphrodite's husband.
32. HORN OF PLENTY: horn given by Zeus to Amalthea, his nurse; it was always filled with whatever the possessor wanted.
42. LINNET: a small finch, known for its sweet song.
59. WOMAN: Maud Gonne, a beautiful Irish revolutionary whom Yeats had once loved; lines 59-64 refer to her activities in the struggle for Irish independence.

Barter that horn and every good
By quiet natures understood
For an old bellows full of angry wind?

Considering that, all hatred driven hence,   65
The soul recovers radical innocence
And learns at last that it is self-delighting,
Self-appeasing, self-affrighting,
And that its own sweet will is Heaven's will;
She can, though every face should scowl   70
And every windy quarter howl
Or every bellows burst, be happy still.

And may her bridegroom bring her to a house
Where all's accustomed, ceremonious;
For arrogance and hatred are the wares   75
Peddled in the thoroughfares.
How but in custom and in ceremony
Are innocence and beauty born?
Ceremony's a name for the rich horn,
And custom for the spreading laurel tree.   80

66. RADICAL: rooted; also fundamental.

I

1. What is the situation of the poem? What connection does the storm that "Once more . . . is howling" have with the great gloom that is in the speaker's mind? What is the "great gloom"? In other words, why is he concerned about the future that lies before his sleeping child? Why does he refer to the storm as coming "Out of the murderous innocence of the sea"? Why "murderous" and why "innocence"?

2. In stanzas 3 and 4 what kind of *beauty* does he pray that she may have? What are the dangers of "Being made beautiful overmuch"? What purpose do the allusions to Helen and Aphrodite serve? What do lines 30-31 mean? What does the Horn of Plenty symbolize if it is said to be "undone" by the kind of women Helen and Aphrodite were?

3. What is the speaker referring to by "courtesy" (33)? Is it the same as "charm" (37)? the same as "glad kindness" (40)? Why or why not?

4. In line 42 what does he mean in asking "That all her thoughts may like the linnet be"? What relationship is there between the linnet and the green laurel? In what sense does he

pray that she may be like both the linnet and the laurel?

5. How does the allusion to Maud Gonne and her faults in stanza 8 relate to the substance of stanzas 6 and 7? How is the allusion further related to stanza 9? What in stanza 9 does the speaker say her soul will learn that will allow his daughter to *be happy still?* How have the references to the wind in stanzas 1 and 2 been extended in stanzas 7, 8, and 9? Consider the relationship between the "murderous innocence" of line 16 and the "radical innocence" of line 66.

II

1. What is meant by "custom" and "ceremony" in stanza 10? The speaker sees these as the undergirding of a stable society. In what sense are innocence and beauty *born* out of them? In what sense is "Ceremony . . . a name for the rich horn" and "custom for the spreading laurel tree"? How does this relating of what the speaker wants for his daughter to *ceremony* and *custom* give substance to the seemingly simple virtues he prays for? In discussing these questions try to give particulars from your own society that would come under the headings "custom" and "ceremony."

ON CERTAIN MODERN WRITERS AND THE INSTITUTION OF THE FAMILY   [*1905*]

G. K. Chesterton

Our attitudes toward the Institution of the Family—and particularly our own family—are often difficult to pin down, primarily because so much depends on what happened at the dinner table the night before. No matter that at times we find family living as comfortable and reassuring as our favorite easy chair, we find it at other times a source of irritation and frustration. Those we love most live under the family roof; but here, if anywhere, we learn that love wears many moods and issues many demands.

In the following essay Chesterton extols the institution of the family, maintaining that its supposed shortcomings are its virtues. He says that the family is "not peaceful and not pleasant and not at one," and that for those very reasons we ought to be thankful for "the sublime and special romance" it brings.

The family may fairly be considered, one would think, an ultimate human institution. Everyone would admit that it has been the main cell and central unit of almost all societies hitherto, except, indeed, such societies as that of Lacedaemon,[1] which went in for "efficiency," and has, therefore, perished, and left not a trace behind. Christianity, even enormous as was its revolution, did not alter this ancient and savage sanctity; it merely reversed it. It did not deny the trinity of father, mother, and child. It merely read it backwards, making it run child, mother, father. This it called, not the family, but the Holy Family, for many things are made holy by being turned upside down. But some sages of our own decadence have made a serious attack on the family. They have impugned it, as I think wrongly; and its defenders have defended it, and defended it wrongly. The common defense of the family is that, amid the stress and fickleness of life, it is peaceful, pleasant, and at one.

But there is another defense of the family which is possible, and to me evident; this defense is that the family is not peaceful and not pleasant and not at one.

It is not fashionable to say much nowadays of the advantages of the small community. We are told that we must go in for large empires and large ideas. There is one advantage, however, in the small state, the city, or the village, which only the willfully blind can overlook. The man who lives in a small community lives in a much larger world. He knows much more of the fierce varieties and uncompromising divergences of men. The reason is obvious. In a large community we can choose our companions. In a small community our companions are chosen for us. Thus in all extensive and highly civilized societies groups come into existence founded upon what is called sympathy, and shut out the real world more sharply than the gates of a monastery. There is nothing really narrow about the clan; the thing which is really narrow is the clique. The men of the clan live together because they all wear the same tartan or are all descended from the same sacred cow; but in their souls, by the divine luck of things, there will always be more colors than in any tartan. But the men of the

---

1. LACEDAEMON: Sparta.

"On Certain Modern Writers and the Institution of the Family" from *Heretics* by G. K. Chesterton. Reprinted by permission of The Bodley Head, Ltd.

clique live together because they have the same kind of soul, and their narrowness is a narrowness of spiritual coherence and contentment, like that which exists in hell. A big society exists in order to form cliques. A big society is a society for the promotion of narrowness. It is a machinery for the purpose of guarding the solitary and sensitive individual from all experience of the bitter and bracing human compromises. It is, in the most literal sense of the words, a society for the prevention of Christian knowledge.

We can see this change, for instance, in the modern transformation of the thing called a club. When London was smaller, and the parts of London more self-contained and parochial, the club was what it still is in villages, the opposite of what it is now in great cities. Then the club was valued as a place where a man could be sociable. Now the club is valued as a place where a man can be unsociable. The more the enlargement and elaboration of our civilization goes on the more the club ceases to be a place where a man can have a noisy argument, and becomes more and more a place where a man can have what is somewhat fantastically called a quiet chop.[2] Its aim is to make a man comfortable, and to make a man comfortable is to make him the opposite of sociable. Sociability, like all good things, is full of discomforts, dangers, and renunciations. The club tends to produce the most degraded of all combinations—the luxurious anchorite, the man who combines the self-indulgence of Lucullus[3] with the insane loneliness of St. Simeon Stylites.[4]

If we were tomorrow morning snowed up in the street in which we live, we should step suddenly into a much larger and much wilder world than we have ever known. And it is the whole effort of the typically modern person to escape from the street in which he lives. First he invents modern hygiene and goes to Margate.[5] Then he invents modern culture and goes to Florence.[6] Then he invents modern imperialism and goes to Timbuctoo.[7] He goes to the fantastic borders of the earth. He pretends to shoot tigers. He almost rides on a camel. And in all this he is still essentially fleeing from the street in which he was born; and of this flight he is always ready with his own explanation. He says he is fleeing from his street because it is dull; he is lying. He is really fleeing from his street because it is a great deal too exciting. It is exciting because it is exacting; it is exacting because it is alive. He can visit Venice because to him the Venetians are only Venetians; the people in his own street are men. He can stare at the Chinese because for him the Chinese are a passive thing to be stared at; if he stares at the old lady in the next garden, she becomes active. He is forced to flee, in short, from the too stimulating society of his equals—of free men, perverse, personal, deliberately different from himself. The street in Brixton is too glowing and overpowering. He has to soothe and quiet himself among tigers and vultures, camels and crocodiles. These creatures are indeed very different from himself. But they do not put their shape or color or custom into a decisive intellectual competition with his own. They do not seek to destroy his principles and assert their own; the stranger monsters of the suburban street do seek to do this. The camel does not contort his features into a fine sneer because Mr. Robinson has not got a hump; the cultured gentleman at No. 5 does exhibit a sneer because Robinson has not got a dado.[8] The

2. A QUIET CHOP: lamb chop; i.e., lunch or dinner.
3. LUCULLUS: Roman general and provincial governor, notorious for his luxurious living.
4. ST. SIMEON STYLITES: Syrian Christian ascetic of the sixth century who spent sixty-eight years of his life exposed upon the top of pillars, with only such food as was hoisted to him by the passers-by below.

5. MARGATE: popular seaside resort in Kent, southeast England.
6. FLORENCE: an Italian city, famous for its art treasures.
7. TIMBUCTOO: town in northwest Africa.
8. DADO: decorative wainscot or wall paneling.

vulture will not roar with laughter because a man does not fly; but the major at No. 9 will roar with laughter because a man does not smoke. The complaint we commonly have to make of our neighbors is that they will not, as we express it, mind their own business. We do not really mean that they will not mind their own business. If our neighbors did not mind their own business they would be asked abruptly for their rent, and would rapidly cease to be our neighbors. What we really mean when we say that they cannot mind their own business is something much deeper. We do not dislike them because they have so little force and fire that they cannot be interested in themselves. We dislike them because they have so much force and fire that they can be interested in us as well. What we dread about our neighbors, in short, is not the narrowness of their horizon, but their superb tendency to broaden it. And all aversions to ordinary humanity have this general character. They are not aversions to its feebleness (as is pretended), but to its energy. The misanthropes pretend that they despise humanity for its weakness. As a matter of fact, they hate it for its strength.

Of course, this shrinking from the brutal vivacity and brutal variety of common men is a perfectly reasonable and excusable thing as long as it does not pretend to any point of superiority. It is when it calls itself aristocracy or aestheticism or a superiority to the bourgeoisie that its inherent weakness has in justice to be pointed out. Fastidiousness is the most pardonable of vices; but it is the most unpardonable of virtues. Nietzsche,[9] who represents most prominently this pretentious claim of the fastidious, has a description somewhere—a very powerful description in the purely literary sense—of the disgust and disdain which consume him at the sight of the common people with their common faces, their common voices, and their common minds. As I have said, this attitude is almost beautiful if we may regard it as pathetic. Nietzsche's aristocracy has about it all the sacredness that belongs to the weak. When he makes us feel that he cannot endure the innumerable faces, the incessant voices, the overpowering omnipresence which belongs to the mob, he will have the sympathy of anybody who has ever been sick on a steamer or tired in a crowded omnibus. Every man has hated mankind when he was less than a man. Every man has had humanity in his eyes like a blinding fog, humanity in his nostrils like a suffocating smell. But when Nietzsche has the incredible lack of humor and lack of imagination to ask us to believe that his aristocracy is an aristocracy of strong muscles or an aristocracy of strong wills, it is necessary to point out the truth. It is an aristocracy of weak nerves.

We make our friends; we make our enemies; but God makes our next-door neighbor. Hence he comes to us clad in all the careless terrors of nature; he is as strange as the stars, as reckless and indifferent as the rain. He is Man, the most terrible of the beasts. That is why the old religions and the old scriptural language showed so sharp a wisdom when they spoke, not of one's duty towards humanity, but one's duty towards one's neighbor. The duty towards humanity may often take the form of some choice which is personal or even pleasurable. That duty may be a hobby; it may even be a dissipation. We may work in the East End[10] because we are peculiarly fitted to work in the East End, or because we think we are; we may fight for the cause of international peace because we are very fond of fighting. The most monstrous martyrdom, the most repulsive experience, may be the result of choice or a kind of taste. We may be so made as to be particularly fond of lunatics or specially interested in leprosy. We may love Negroes because they are black or German Socialists because they are pedantic. But we have to love our neighbor because he is *there*—a much more alarming reason for

---

9. NIETZSCHE: German philosopher who had no use for the "common man" and called for the training of a race of "supermen."

10. EAST END: poor section of London.

a much more serious operation. He is the sample of humanity which is actually given us. Precisely because he may be anybody he is everybody. He is a symbol because he is an accident.

Doubtless men flee from small environments into lands that are very deadly. But this is natural enough; for they are not fleeing from death. They are fleeing from life. And this principle applies to ring within ring of the social system of humanity. It is perfectly reasonable that men should seek for some particular variety of the human type, so long as they are seeking for that variety of the human type, and not for mere human variety. It is quite proper that a British diplomatist should seek the society of Japanese generals, if what he wants is Japanese generals. But if what he wants is people different from himself, he had much better stop at home and discuss religion with the housemaid. It is quite reasonable that the village genius should come up to conquer London if what he wants is to conquer London. But if he wants to conquer something fundamentally and symbolically hostile and also very strong, he had much better remain where he is and have a row with the rector. The man in the suburban street is quite right if he goes to Ramsgate[11] for the sake of Ramsgate—a difficult thing to imagine. But if, as he expresses it, he goes to Ramsgate "for a change," then he would have a much more romantic and even melodramatic change if he jumped over the wall into his neighbor's garden. The consequences would be bracing in a sense far beyond the possibilities of Ramsgate hygiene.

Now, exactly as this principle applies to the empire, to the nation within the empire, to the city within the nation, to the street within the city, so it applies to the home within the street. The institution of the family is to be commended for precisely the same reasons that the institution of the nation, or the institution of the city, are in this

matter to be commended. It is a good thing for a man to live in a family for the same reason that it is a good thing for a man to be besieged in a city. It is a good thing for a man to live in a family in the same sense that it is a beautiful and delightful thing for a man to be snowed up in a street. They all force him to realize that life is not a thing from outside, but a thing from inside. Above all, they all insist upon the fact that life, if it be a truly stimulating and fascinating life, is a thing which, of its nature, exists in spite of ourselves. The modern writers who have suggested, in a more or less open manner, that the family is a bad institution, have generally confined themselves to suggesting, with much sharpness, bitterness, or pathos, that perhaps the family is not always very congenial. Of course the family is a good institution because it is uncongenial. It is wholesome precisely because it contains so many divergencies and varieties. It is, as the sentimentalists say, like a little kingdom, and, like most other little kingdoms, is generally in a state of something resembling anarchy. It is exactly because our brother George is not interested in our religious difficulties, but is interested in the Trocadero Restaurant, that the family has some of the bracing qualities of the commonwealth. It is precisely because our uncle Henry does not approve of the theatrical ambitions of our sister Sarah that the family is like humanity. The men and women who, for good reasons and bad, revolt against the family, are, for good reasons and bad, simply revolting against mankind. Aunt Elizabeth is unreasonable, like mankind. Papa is excitable, like mankind. Our youngest brother is mischievous, like mankind. Grandpapa is stupid, like the world; he is old, like the world.

Those who wish, rightly or wrongly, to step out of all this, do definitely wish to step into a narrower world. They are dismayed and terrified by the largeness and variety of the family. Sarah wishes to find a world wholly consisting of private theatricals; George wishes to think the Trocadero a

---

11. RAMSGATE: seaside resort in Kent, north of Dover.

cosmos. I do not say, for a moment, that the flight to this narrower life may not be the right thing for the individual, any more than I say the same thing about flight into a monastery. But I do say that anything is bad and artificial which tends to make these people succumb to the strange delusion that they are stepping into a world which is actually larger and more varied than their own. The best way that a man could test his readiness to encounter the common variety of mankind would be to climb down a chimney into any house at random, and get on as well as possible with the people inside. And that is essentially what each one of us did on the day that he was born.

This is, indeed, the sublime and special romance of the family. It is romantic because it is a toss-up. It is romantic because it is everything that its enemies call it. It is romantic because it is arbitrary. It is romantic because it is there. So long as you have groups of men chosen rationally, you have some special or sectarian atmosphere. It is when you have groups of men chosen irrationally that you have men. The element of adventure begins to exist; for an adventure is, by its nature, a thing that comes to us. It is a thing that chooses us, not a thing that we choose. Falling in love has been often regarded as the supreme adventure, the supreme romantic accident. In so much as there is in it something outside ourselves, something of a sort of merry fatalism, this is very true. Love does take us and transfigure and torture us. It does break our hearts with an unbearable beauty, like the unbearable beauty of music. But in so far as we have certainly something to do with the matter; in so far as we are in some sense prepared to fall in love and in some sense jump into it; in so far as we do to some extent choose and to some extent even judge—in all this falling in love is not truly romantic, is not truly adventurous at all. In this degree the supreme adventure is not falling in love. The supreme adventure is being born. There we do walk suddenly into a splendid and startling trap. There we do see something of

which we have not dreamed before. Our father and mother do lie in wait for us and leap out on us, like brigands from a bush. Our uncle is a surprise. Our aunt is, in the beautiful common expression, a bolt from the blue. When we step into the family, by the act of being born, we do step into a world which is incalculable, into a world which has its own strange laws, into a world which could do without us, into a world that we have not made. In other words, when we step into the family we step into a fairy-tale.

This color as of a fantastic narrative ought to cling to the family and to our relations with it throughout life. Romance is the deepest thing in life; romance is deeper even than reality. For even if reality could be proved to be misleading, it still could not be proved to be unimportant or unimpressive. Even if the facts are false, they are still very strange. And this strangeness of life, this unexpected and even perverse element of things as they fall out, remains incurably interesting. The circumstances we can regulate may become tame or pessimistic; but the "circumstances over which we have no control" remain god-like to those who, like Mr. Micawber,[12] can call on them and renew their strength. People wonder why the novel is the most popular form of literature; people wonder why it is read more than books of science or books of metaphysics. The reason is very simple; it is merely that the novel is more true than they are. Life may sometimes legitimately appear as a book of science. Life may sometimes appear, and with a much greater legitimacy, as a book of metaphysics. But life is always a novel. Our existence may cease to be a song; it may cease even to be a beautiful lament. Our existence may not be an intelligible justice, or even a recognizable wrong. But our existence is still a story. In the fiery alphabet of every sunset is written, "to be continued in our next."

---

12. MR. MICAWBER: a character in Dickens's *David Copperfield*, whose favorite sentiment was that something—some way *out* of his difficulties—would turn up.

If we have sufficient intellect, we can finish a philosophical and exact deduction, and be certain that we are finishing it right. With the adequate brain-power we could finish any scientific discovery, and be certain that we were finishing it right. But not with the most gigantic intellect could we finish the simplest or silliest story, and be certain that we were finishing it right. That is because a story has behind it, not merely intellect which is partly mechanical, but will, which is in its essence divine. The narrative writer can send his hero to the gallows if he likes in the last chapter but one. He can do it by the same divine caprice whereby he, the author, can go to the gallows himself, and to hell afterwards if he chooses. And the same civilization, the chivalric European civilization which asserted freewill in the thirteenth century, produced the thing called "fiction" in the eighteenth. When Thomas Aquinas[13] asserted the spiritual liberty of man, he created all the bad novels in the circulating libraries.

But in order that life should be a story or romance to us, it is necessary that a great part of it, at any rate, should be settled for us without our permission. If we wish life to be a system, this may be a nuisance; but if we wish it to be a drama, it is an essential. It may often happen, no doubt, that a drama may be written by somebody else which we like very little. But we should like it still less if the author came before the curtain every hour or so, and forced on us the whole

trouble of inventing the next act. A man has control over many things in his life; he has control over enough things to be the hero of a novel. But if he had control over everything, there would be so much hero that there would be no novel. And the reason why the lives of the rich are at bottom so tame and uneventful is simply that they can choose the events. They are dull because they are omnipotent. They fail to feel adventures because they can make the adventures. The thing which keeps life romantic and full of fiery possibilities is the existence of these great plain limitations which force all of us to meet the things we do not like or do not expect. It is vain for the supercilious moderns to talk of being in uncongenial surroundings. To be in a romance is to be in uncongenial surroundings. To be born into this earth is to be born into uncongenial surroundings, hence to be born into a romance. Of all these great limitations and frameworks which fashion and create the poetry and variety of life, the family is the most definite and important. Hence it is misunderstood by the moderns, who imagine that romance would exist most perfectly in a complete state of what they call liberty. They think that if a man makes a gesture it would be a startling and romantic matter that the sun should fall from the sky. They are seeking under every shape and form a world where there are no limitations—that is, a world where there are no outlines; that is, a world where there are no shapes. There is nothing baser than that infinity. They say they wish to be as strong as the universe, but they really wish the whole universe as weak as themselves.

13. THOMAS AQUINAS: medieval theologian, who consolidated the intellectual structure of Christianity.

I

1. What is the tone of the opening paragraph: irreverent? superior? amused? sarcastic? a combination of these, or none of these? Consider such comments as: "which went in for 'efficiency,' and has, therefore, perished," "this ancient and savage sanctity," "for many things are made holy by being turned upside down." What does the established tone suggest about the attitude with which the reader should approach the rest of the essay?

2. What distinctions does the speaker make between a small community and a large one? How do a clan and a clique differ? What changes does he say have taken place in the make-up of clubs?

3. Why does the *typically modern person* want *to escape from the street in which he lives*?

4. Why does the speaker call Nietzsche's aristocracy an "aristocracy of weak nerves"? What does he mean by, "Every man has hated mankind when he was less than a man"? by, "We make our friends; we make our enemies; but God makes our next-door neighbors"?

5. The title of the essay is "On Certain Modern Writers and the Institution of the Family." Why, then, does the speaker wait until half way through the essay before getting around to discussing the family?

6. What are the conditions of family living that give it its *sublime and special romance*? Be as specific as possible.

II

1. Chesterton's approach is to take a position in direct opposition to the one most commonly held. His defense of the family is to deny that it is *peaceful, pleasant, or at one,* and then to assert that its strength lies in the fact that it doesn't have these *virtues.* His style supports this contradictory approach: "A big society is a society for the promotion of narrowness"; "The misanthropes pretend that they despise humanity for its weakness. As a matter of fact, they hate it for its strength." Point out other examples of this technique. Using Chesterton's manner of supporting the opposite position from the one commonly held, write an essay on the family, on advertising, on going steady, on the values of formal education, or on a topic of your own choice.

from **AFFECTION**   [*1960*]

C. S. Lewis

As much as we use the word, it is seldom that we attempt to analyze the elements that go into the makeup of love. Indeed, we adopt the word as it comes to us, easily fitting it to the many emotions which pass for love in the daily give-and-take of our lives. If love is a controlling factor in much of human behavior, however, we should give serious thought to our own definition of the term, and in so doing, give deeper meaning to its applications.

In his book *The Four Loves,* C. S. Lewis discusses the natures of Affection, Friendship, Eros, and Charity. He says of the four that Affection is the "humblest and most widely diffused," providing "nine-tenths of whatever solid and durable happiness there is in our natural lives." The danger begins when we attempt to fit it to the other tenth. Lewis analyzes with biting wit those perversions of Affection which bring pain instead of happiness.

I begin with the humblest and most widely diffused of loves, the love in which our experience seems to differ least from that of the animals. Let me add at once that I do not on that account give it a lower value. Nothing in Man is either worse or better for being shared with the beasts. When we blame a man for being "a mere animal," we mean not that he displays animal characteristics (we all do) but that he displays these, and only these, on occasions where the specifically human was demanded. (When we call him "brutal" we usually mean that he commits cruelties impossible to most real brutes; they're not clever enough.)

The Greeks called this love *storge* (two syllables and the g is "hard"). I shall here call it simply Affection. My Greek Lexicon defines *storge* as "affection, especially of parents to offspring"; but also of offspring to parents. And that, I have no doubt, is the original form of the thing as well as the central meaning of the word. The image we must start with is that of a mother nursing a baby, a bitch or a cat with a basketful of puppies or kittens; all in a squeaking, nuzzling heap together; purrings, lickings, baby-talk, milk, warmth, the smell of young life. . . .

But even in animal life, and still more in our own, Affection extends far beyond the relation of mother and young. This warm comfortableness, this satisfaction in being together, takes in all sorts of objects. It is indeed the least discriminating of loves. There are women for whom we can predict few wooers and men who are likely to have few friends. They have nothing to offer. But almost anyone can become an object of Affection; the ugly, the stupid, even the exasperating. There need be no apparent fitness between those whom it unites. I have seen it felt for an imbecile not only by his parents but by his brothers. It ignores the barriers of age, sex, class and education. It can exist between a clever young man from the university and an old nurse, though their minds inhabit different worlds. It ignores even the barriers of species. We see it not only between dog and man but, more surprisingly, between dog and cat. Gilbert White[1] claims to have discovered it between a horse and a hen. . . .

"Dogs and cats should always be brought up together," said someone, "it broadens their minds so." Affection broadens ours; of all natural loves it is the most catholic, the least finical, the broadest. The people with whom you are thrown together in the family, the college, the mess, the ship, the religious house, are from this point of view a wider circle than the friends, however numerous, whom you have made for yourself in the outer world. By having a great many friends I do not prove that I have a wide appreciation of human excellence. You might as well say I prove the width of my literary taste by being able to enjoy all the books in my own study. The answer is the same in both cases—"You chose those books. You chose those friends. Of course they suit you." The truly wide taste in reading is that which enables a man to find something for his needs on the sixpenny tray outside any secondhand bookshop. The truly wide taste in humanity will similarly find something to appreciate in the cross-section of humanity whom one has to meet every day. In my experience it is Affection that creates this taste, teaching us first to notice, then to endure, then to smile at, then to enjoy, and finally to appreciate, the people who "happen to be there." Made for us? Thank God, no. They are themselves, odder than you could have believed and worth far more than we guessed.

And now we are drawing near the point of danger. Affection, I have said, gives itself no airs; charity, said St. Paul, is not puffed up. Affection can love the unattractive: God and His saints love the unlovable. Affection "does not expect too much," turns a blind eye to faults, revives easily after quarrels; just so charity suffers long and is kind and forgives. Affection opens our eyes to goodness we could not have seen, or should not have appreciated without it. So does humble sanctity. If we dwelled exclusively on these resemblances we might be led on to believe that this Affection is not simply one of the natural loves but is Love Himself working in our human hearts and fulfilling the law.[2] Were the Victorian novelists right after all? Is love (of this sort) really enough? Are the "domestic affections," when in their best and fullest development, the same thing as the Christian life? The

---

1. GILBERT WHITE: English naturalist (1720-1793).

2. LOVE . . . LAW: see Matthew 5:17-18.

answer to all these questions, I submit, is certainly No. . . .

How many of these "happy homes" really exist? Worse still; are all the unhappy ones unhappy because Affection is absent? I believe not. It can be present, causing the unhappiness. Nearly all the characteristics of this love are ambivalent. They may work for ill as well as for good. By itself, left simply to follow its own bent, it can darken and degrade human life. The debunkers and antisentimentalists have not said all the truth about it, but all they have said is true.

Symptomatic of this, perhaps, is the odiousness of nearly all those treacly tunes and saccharine poems in which popular art expresses Affection. They are odious because of their falsity. They represent as a ready-made recipe for bliss (and even for goodness) what is in fact only an opportunity. There is no hint that we shall have to do anything: only let Affection pour over us like a warm shower-bath and all, it is implied, will be well.

Affection, we have seen, includes both Need-love and Gift-love. I begin with the Need—our craving for the Affection of others.

Now there is a clear reason why this craving, of all love-cravings, easily becomes the most unreasonable. I have said that almost anyone may be the object of Affection. Yes; and almost everyone expects to be. The egregious Mr. Pontifex in *The Way of All Flesh*[3] is outraged to discover that his son does not love him; it is "unnatural" for a boy not to love his own father. It never occurs to him to ask whether, since the first day the boy can remember, he has ever done or said anything that could excite love. Similarly, at the beginning of *King Lear*[4]

the hero is shown as a very unlovable old man devoured with a ravenous appetite for Affection. I am driven to literary examples because you, the reader, and I do not live in the same neighborhood; if we did, there would unfortunately be no difficulty about replacing them with examples from real life. The thing happens every day. And we can see why. We all know that we must do something, if not to merit, at least to attract, erotic love or friendship. But Affection is often assumed to be provided, ready made, by nature; "built-in," "laid-on,"[5] "on the house."[6] We have a right to expect it. If the others do not give it, they are "unnatural."

This assumption is no doubt the distortion of a truth. Much has been "built-in." Because we are a mammalian species, instinct will provide at least some degree, often a high one, of maternal love. Because we are a social species familiar association provides a *milieu* in which, if all goes well, Affection will arise and grow strong without demanding any very shining qualities in its objects. If it is given us it will not necessarily be given us on our merits; we may get it with very little trouble. From a dim perception of the truth (many are loved with Affection far beyond their deserts) Mr. Pontifex draws the ludicrous conclusion, "Therefore I, without desert, have a right to it." It is as if, on a far higher plane, we argued that because no man by merit has a right to the Grace of God, I, having no merit, am entitled to it. There is no question of rights in either case. What we have is not "a right to expect" but a "reasonable expectation" of being loved by our intimates if we, and they, are more or less ordinary people. But we may not be. We may be intolerable. If we are, "nature" will work against us. For the very same conditions of intimacy which make Affection possible also—and no less naturally—make

---

3. THE WAY OF ALL FLESH: novel by Samuel Butler (1903). Mr. Pontifex, father of the hero, is a sanctimonious clergyman who bullies his family.
4. KING LEAR: one of Shakespeare's greatest tragedies. King Lear wants to divide his kingdom among his three daughters and demands verbal proof of their love as the play opens.

---

5. LAID-ON: gratuitous, included at no extra fee.
6. ON THE HOUSE: free; at the expense of "the house," usually referring to a public house or tavern.

possible a peculiarly incurable distaste; a hatred as immemorial, constant, unemphatic, almost at times unconscious, as the corresponding form of love. . . .

It would be absurd to say that Lear is lacking in Affection. In so far as Affection is Need-love he is half-crazy with it. Unless, in his own way, he loved his daughters he would not so desperately desire their love. The most unlovable parent (or child) may be full of such ravenous love. But it works to their own misery and everyone else's. The situation becomes suffocating. If people are already unlovable a continual demand on their part (as of right) to be loved —their manifest sense of injury, their reproaches, whether loud and clamorous or merely implicit in every look and gesture of resentful self-pity—produce in us a sense of guilt (they are intended to do so) for a fault we could not have avoided and cannot cease to commit. They seal up the very fountain for which they are thirsty. If ever, at some favored moment, any germ of Affection for them stirs in us, their demand for more and still more petrifies us again. And of course such people always desire the same proof of our love; we are to join their side, to hear and share their grievance against someone else. . . .

And all the while they remain unaware of the real road. "If you would be loved, be lovable," said Ovid.[7] That cheery old reprobate only meant, "If you want to attract the girls you must be attractive," but his maxim has a wider application. The amorist was wiser in his generation than Mr. Pontifex and King Lear.

The really surprising thing is not that these insatiable demands made by the unlovable are sometimes made in vain, but that they are so often met. Sometimes one sees a woman's girlhood, youth and long years of her maturity up to the verge of old age all spent in tending, obeying, caressing, and perhaps supporting, a maternal vampire

who can never be caressed and obeyed enough. The sacrifice—but there are two opinions about that—may be beautiful; the old woman who exacts it is not.

The "built-in" or unmerited character of Affection thus invites a hideous misinterpretation. So does its ease and informality.

We hear a great deal about the rudeness of the rising generation. I am an oldster myself and might be expected to take the oldster's side, but in fact I have been far more impressed by the bad manners of parents to children than by those of children to parents. Who has not been the embarrassed guest at family meals where the father or mother treated their grown-up offspring with an incivility which, offered to any other young people, would simply have terminated the acquaintance? Dogmatic assertions on matters which the children understand and their elders don't, ruthless interruptions, flat contradictions, ridicule of things the young take seriously—sometimes of their religion— insulting references to their friends, all provide an easy answer to the question "Why are they always out? Why do they like every house better than their home?" Who does not prefer civility to barbarism?

If you asked any of these insufferable people—they are not all parents of course— why they behaved that way at home, they would reply, "Oh, hang it all, one comes home to relax. A chap can't be always on his best behavior. If a man can't be himself in his own house, where can he? Of course we don't want Company Manners at home. We're a happy family. We can say *anything* to one another here. No one minds. We all understand."

Once again it is so nearly true yet so fatally wrong. Affection is an affair of old clothes, and ease, of the unguarded moment, of liberties which would be ill-bred if we took them with strangers. But old clothes are one thing; to wear the same shirt till it stank would be another. There are proper clothes for a garden party; but the clothes for home must be proper too, in their own different

---

7. OVID: Roman poet (43 B.C.-? 17 A.D.).

way. Similarly there is a distinction between public and domestic courtesy. The root principle of both is the same: "that no one give any kind of preference to himself." But the more public the occasion, the more our obedience to this principle has been "taped" or formalized. There are "rules" of good manners. The more intimate the occasion, the less the formalization; but not therefore the less need of courtesy. On the contrary, Affection at its best practices a courtesy which is incomparably more subtle, sensitive, and deep than the public kind. In public a ritual would do. At home you must have the reality which that ritual represented, or else the deafening triumphs of the greatest egoist present. You must really give no kind of preference to yourself; at a party it is enough to conceal the preference. Hence the old proverb "come live with me and you'll know me." Hence a man's familiar manners first reveal the true value of his (significantly odious phrase!) "Company" or "Party" manners. Those who leave their manners behind them when they come home from the dance or the sherry party have no real courtesy even there. They were merely aping those who had.

"We can say *anything* to one another." The truth behind this is that Affection at its best can say whatever Affection at its best wishes to say, regardless of the rules that govern public courtesy; for Affection at its best wishes neither to wound nor to humiliate nor to domineer. You may address the wife of your bosom as "Pig!" when she has inadvertently drunk your cocktail as well as her own. You may roar down the story which your father is telling once too often. You may tease and hoax and banter. You can say "Shut up. I want to read." You can do anything in the right tone and at the right moment—the tone and moment which are not intended to, and will not, hurt. The better the Affection the more unerringly it knows which these are (every love has its *art of love*). But the domestic Rudesby[8]

means something quite different when he claims liberty to say "anything." Having a very imperfect sort of Affection himself, or perhaps at that moment none, he arrogates to himself the beautiful liberties which only the fullest Affection has a right to or knows how to manage. He then uses them spitefully in obedience to his resentments; or ruthlessly in obedience to his egoism; or at best stupidly, lacking the art. And all the time he may have a clear conscience. He knows that Affection takes liberties. He is taking liberties. Therefore (he concludes) he is being affectionate. Resent anything and he will say that the defect of love is on your side. He is hurt. He has been misunderstood.

He then sometimes avenges himself by getting on his high horse and becoming elaborately "polite." The implication is of course, "Oh! So we are not to be intimate? We are to behave like mere acquaintances? I had hoped—but no matter. Have it your own way." This illustrates prettily the difference between intimate and formal courtesy. Precisely what suits the one may be a breach of the other. To be free and easy when you are presented to some eminent stranger is bad manners; to practice formal and ceremonial courtesies at home ("public faces in private places") is—and is always intended to be—bad manners. . . .

But we have not yet touched on jealousy. I suppose no one now believes that jealousy is especially connected with erotic love. If anyone does, the behavior of children, employees, and domestic animals ought soon to undeceive him. Every kind of love, almost every kind of association, is liable to it. The jealousy of Affection is closely connected with its reliance on what is old and familiar. So also with the total, or relative, unimportance for Affection of what I call Appreciative love. We don't want the "old, familiar faces" to become brighter or more beautiful, the old ways to be changed even for the better, the old jokes and interests to be replaced by exciting novelties. Change is a threat to Affection.

---

8. RUDESBY: an uncivil fellow.

A brother and sister, or two brothers—for sex here is not at work—grow to a certain age sharing everything. They have read the same comics, climbed the same trees, been pirates or spacemen together, taken up and abandoned stamp-collecting at the same moment. Then a dreadful thing happens. One of them flashes ahead—discovers poetry or science or serious music or perhaps undergoes a religious conversion. His life is flooded with the new interest. The other cannot share it; he is left behind. I doubt whether even the infidelity of a wife or husband raises a more miserable sense of desertion or a fiercer jealousy than this can sometimes do. It is not yet jealousy of the new friends whom the deserter will soon be making. That will come; at first it is jealousy of the thing itself—of this science, this music, of God (always called "religion" or "all this religion" in such contexts). The jealousy will probably be expressed by ridicule. The new interest is "all silly nonsense," contemptibly childish (or contemptibly grown-up); or else the deserter is not really interested in it at all—he's showing off, swanking; it's all affectation. Presently the books will be hidden, the scientific specimens destroyed, the radio forcibly switched off the classical programs. For Affection is the most instinctive, in that sense the most animal, of the loves; its jealousy is proportionately fierce. It snarls and bares its teeth like a dog whose food has been snatched away. And why would it not? Something or someone has snatched away from the child I am picturing his lifelong food, his second self. His world is in ruins.

But it is not only children who react thus. Few things in the ordinary peacetime life of a civilized country are more nearly fiendish than the rancor with which a whole unbelieving family will turn on the one member of it who has become a Christian, or a whole lowbrow family on the one who shows signs of becoming an intellectual. This is not, as I once thought, simply the innate and, as it were, disinterested hatred of darkness for light. A church-going family in which one has gone atheist will not always behave any better. It is the reaction to a desertion, even to robbery. Someone or something has stolen "our" boy (or girl). He who was one of Us has become one of Them. What right had anybody to do it? He is *ours*. But once change has thus begun, who knows where it will end? (And we all so happy and comfortable before and doing no harm to no one!)

Sometimes a curious double jealousy is felt, or rather two inconsistent jealousies which chase each other round in the sufferer's mind. On the one hand "This" is "All nonsense, all bloody high-brow nonsense, all canting humbug." But on the other, "Supposing—it can't be, it mustn't be, but just supposing—there were something in it?" Supposing there really were anything in literature, or in Christianity? How if the deserter has really entered a new world which the rest of us never suspected? But, if so, how unfair! Why him? Why was it never opened to us? "A chit of a girl—a whipper-snapper of a boy—being shown things that are hidden from their elders?" And since that is clearly incredible and unendurable, jealousy returns to the hypothesis "All nonsense."

Parents in this state are much more comfortably placed than brothers and sisters. Their past is unknown to their children. Whatever the deserter's new world is, they can always claim that they have been through it themselves and come out the other end. "It's a phase," they say. "It'll blow over." Nothing could be more satisfactory. It cannot be there and then refuted, for it is a statement about the future. It stings, yet— so indulgently said—is hard to resent. Better still, the elders may really believe it. Best of all, it may finally turn out to have been true. It won't be their fault if it doesn't.

. . . The conservative tenacity of Affection works both ways. It can be a domestic counterpart to that nationally suicidal type of education which keeps back the promising child because the idlers and dunces might be "hurt" if it were undemocratically moved into a higher class than themselves.

All these perversions of Affection are mainly connected with Affection as a Need-love. But Affection as a Gift-love has its perversions too.

I am thinking of Mrs. Fidget, who died a few months ago. It is really astonishing how her family have brightened up. The drawn look has gone from her husband's face; he begins to be able to laugh. The younger boy, whom I had always thought an embittered, peevish little creature, turns out to be quite human. The elder, who was hardly ever at home except when he was in bed, is nearly always there now and has begun to re-organize the garden. The girl, who was al-ways supposed to be "delicate" (though I never found out what exactly the trouble was), now has the riding lessons which were once out of the question, dances all night, and plays any amount of tennis. Even the dog who was never allowed out except on a lead is now a well-known member of the Lamp-post Club in their road.

Mrs. Fidget very often said that she lived for her family. And it was not untrue. Everyone in the neighborhood knew it. "She lives for her family," they said; "what a wife and mother!" She did all the washing; true, she did it badly, and they could have afforded to send it out to a laundry, and they fre-quently begged her not to do it. But she did. There was always a hot lunch for anyone who was at home and always a hot meal at night (even in midsummer). They implored her not to provide this. They protested almost with tears in their eyes (and with truth) that they liked cold meals. It made no difference. She was living for her family. She always sat up to "welcome" you home if you were out late at night; two or three in the morning, it made no odds; you would always find the frail, pale, weary face await-ing you, like a silent accusation. Which meant of course that you couldn't with any decency go out very often. She was always making things too; being in her own estima-

tion (I'm no judge myself) an excellent amateur dressmaker and a great knitter. And of course, unless you were a heart-less brute, you had to wear the things. (The Vicar tells me that, since her death, the contributions of that family alone to "sales of work" outweigh those of all his other parishioners put together.) And then her care for their health! She bore the whole burden of that daughter's "delicacy" alone. The Doctor—an old friend, and it was not being done on National Health[9]—was never allowed to discuss matters with his patient. After the briefest examination of her, he was taken into another room by the mother. The girl was to have no worries, no re-sponsibility for her own health. Only loving care; caresses, special foods, horrible tonic wines, and breakfast in bed: For Mrs. Fidget, as she so often said, would "work her fingers to the bone" for her family. They couldn't stop her. Nor could they—being decent people—quite sit still and watch her do it. They had to help. That is, they did things for her to help her to do things for them which they didn't want done. As for the dear dog, it was to her, she said, "Just like one of the children." It was in fact, as like one of them as she could make it. But since it had no scruples it got on rather better than they, and though vetted,[10] dieted and guarded within an inch of its life, contrived sometimes to reach the dust-bin or the dog next door.

The Vicar says Mrs. Fidget is now at rest. Let us hope she is. What's quite certain is that her family are.

It is easy to see how liability to this state is, so to speak, congenital in the maternal instinct. This, as we saw, is a Gift-love, but one that needs to give; therefore needs to be needed. But the proper aim of giving is to put the recipient in a state where he no longer needs our gift. We feed children

---

9. NATIONAL HEALTH: refers to the British system of free medical care.

10. VETTED: treated regularly by a veterinarian.

in order that they soon may be able to feed themselves; we teach them in order that they may soon not need our teaching. Thus a heavy task is laid upon this Gift-love. It must work towards its own abdication. We must aim at making ourselves superfluous. The hour when we can say "They need me no longer" should be our reward. But the instinct, simply in its own nature, has no power to fulfill this law. The instinct desires the good of its object, but not simply; only the good it can itself give. A much higher love—a love which desires the good of the object as such, from whatever source that good comes—must step in and help or tame the instinct before it can make the abdication. And of course it often does. But where it does not, the ravenous need to be needed will gratify itself either by keeping its objects needy or by inventing for them imaginary needs. It will do this all the more ruthlessly because it thinks (in one sense truly) that it is a Gift-love and therefore regards itself as "unselfish."

It is not only mothers who can do this. . . . My own profession—that of a university teacher—is in this way dangerous. If we are any good we must always be working towards the moment at which our pupils are fit to become our critics and rivals. We should be delighted when it arrives, as the fencing master is delighted when his pupil can pink and disarm him. And many are.

But not all. I am old enough to remember the sad case of Dr. Quartz. No university boasted a more effective or devoted teacher. He spent the whole of himself on his pupils. He made an indelible impression on nearly all of them. He was the object of much well merited hero-worship. Naturally, and delightfully, they continued to visit him after the tutorial relation had ended—went round to his house of an evening and had famous[11] discussions. But the curious thing is that this never lasted. Sooner or later—it might be within a few months or even a few weeks

---

11. FAMOUS: first rate.

—came the fatal evening when they knocked on his door and were told that the Doctor was engaged. After that he would always be engaged. They were banished from him forever. This was because, at their last meeting, they had rebelled. They had asserted their independence—differed from the master and supported their own view, perhaps not without success. Faced with that very independence which he had labored to produce and which it was his duty to produce if he could, Dr. Quartz could not bear it. . . .

I hope I am not being misunderstood. If this chapter leads anyone to doubt that the lack of "natural affection" is an extreme depravity I shall have failed. Nor do I question for a moment that Affection is responsible for nine-tenths of whatever solid and durable happiness there is in our natural lives. I shall therefore have some sympathy with those whose comment on the last few pages takes the form "Of course. Of course. These things do happen. Selfish or neurotic people can twist anything, even love, into some sort of misery or exploitation. But why stress these marginal cases? A little common sense, a little give and take, prevents their occurrence among decent people." But I think this comment itself needs a commentary.

. . . the comment in its own language admits the very thing I am trying to say. Affection produces happiness if—and only if—there is common sense and give and take and "decency." In other words, only if something more, and other, than Affection is added. The mere feeling is not enough. You need "common sense," that is, reason. You need "give and take"; that is, you need justice, continually stimulating mere Affection when it fades and restraining it when it forgets or would defy the *art* of love. You need "decency." There is no disguising the fact that this means goodness, patience, self-denial, humility, and the continual intervention of a far higher sort of love than Affection, in itself, can ever be. That is the whole point. If we try to live by Affection alone, Affection will "go bad on us."

How bad, I believe we seldom recognize. Can Mrs. Fidget really have been quite unaware of the countless frustrations and miseries she inflicted on her family? It passes belief. She knew—of course she knew—that it spoiled your whole evening to know that when you came home you would find her uselessly, accusingly, "sitting up for you." She continued all these practices because if she had dropped them she would have been faced with the fact she was determined not to see; would have known that she was not necessary. That is the first motive. Then too, the very laboriousness of her life silenced her secret doubts as to the quality of her love. The more her feet burned and her back ached, the better, for this pain whispered in her ear "How much I must love them if I do all this!" That is

the second motive. But I think there is a lower depth. The unappreciativeness of the others, those terrible, wounding words—anything will "wound" a Mrs. Fidget—in which they begged her to send the washing out, enabled her to feel ill-used, therefore, to have a continual grievance, to enjoy the pleasures of resentment. If anyone says he does not know those pleasures, he is a liar or a saint. It is true that they are pleasures only to those who hate. But then a love like Mrs. Fidget's contains a good deal of hatred. It was of erotic love that the Roman Poet[12] said, "I love and hate," but other kinds of love admit the same mixture. They carry in them the seeds of hatred. If Affection is made the absolute sovereign of a human life the seeds will germinate. Love, having become a god, becomes a demon.

12. ROMAN POET: (Catullus 84?-54 B.C.); *odi et amo, Carmen* LXXXV.

I

1. Put into your own words what Lewis means by "Affection." In what ways is it "the love in which our experience seems to differ least from that of the animals"?

2. How are Lewis's observations in the fourth paragraph similar to Chesterton's about one's neighbors and one's family?

3. What do the examples of Mr. Pontifex and King Lear illustrate about the dangers of a "craving for . . . Affection"? What further illustration is there of this same danger? Why is it difficult to resist the demands of this distortion of affection?

4. How can the necessary *ease and informality* of affection be distorted? Why must there be in private relations *a courtesy which is incomparably more subtle, sensitive, and deep than the public kind*? What are the conditions of "intimate . . . courtesy" that make it possible for one to say *anything* and not offend?

5. Why is affection particularly susceptible to the operations of jealousy? Does the experience that we all have had at times of feeling silent elation when someone close to us "comes

a cropper" illustrate the point Lewis makes about jealousy? Why or why not?

6. After outlining Mrs. Fidget's unfortunate habits, Lewis comments, "It is easy to see how liability to this state is, so to speak, congenital in the maternal instinct." What does he mean by the comment? What counteraction has to occur to keep the Mrs. Fidgets of this world under control? How is Dr. Quartz like Mrs. Fidget?

7. Why does Lewis say, "If we try to live by Affection alone, Affection will 'go bad on us' "? How, specifically, will it *go bad on us*? What else is needed besides affection to make affection do its work of bringing "nine-tenths of whatever solid and durable happiness there is in our natural lives"?

II

1. From your own experience show how Lewis's comments on Affection have relevance to your relations with others. Deal with at least one instance in which the positive values of Affection have been at work, and at least one in which some distortion of Affection has been obvious.

SONNETS 29, 73, and 116   [*1609*]

William Shakespeare

The three sonnets that follow are from a group of one hundred fifty-four that Shakespeare wrote relatively early in his career. Most of them, including those below, have reference to Shakespeare's friendship with a young man whose identity has never been established; the rest deal directly with a so-called "dark lady," also unknown to biographers. It matters little how closely personal or autobiographical the sonnets are. They afford incisive insights into human problems of friendship and love and give a foretaste of the kind of probing of the human heart that made Shakespeare the most remarkable dramatist and poet of his time, and possibly of all time.

To choose three sonnets from a total of one hundred fifty-four can do no more than suggest the variety of the whole. The ones we have here are concerned with the nature of love—or friendship, which is what is meant by love in these poems—as a sustaining or nourishing force. To avoid misunderstanding, we must bear in mind that the words "love" and "lover" were in Elizabethan speech as appropriate to the relation of friends as to the romantic relation of man and woman. As Edward Hubler puts it in his *The Sense of Shakespeare's Sonnets:*

> . . . when Brutus addresses the crowd as 'Romans, countrymen, lovers' he means by 'lovers' precisely what Mr. Roosevelt in his radio addresses meant by 'my friends.' There was also the Renaissance concept of the superiority of the friendship of man to man over the affection of man for woman. . . . The superiority of friendship was part of the age, and people heard it with no sense of strangeness.*

Sonnet 29

When in disgrace with fortune and men's eyes
I all alone beweep my outcast state,
And trouble deaf Heaven with my bootless cries,
And look upon myself and curse my fate,
Wishing me like to one more rich in hope,   5
Featured like him, like him with friends possessed,
Desiring this man's art and that man's scope,
With what I most enjoy contented least—
Yet in these thoughts myself almost despising,
Haply I think on thee, and then my state,   10

---

1. WHEN . . . EYES: i.e., when things are not going well for me.

* Edward Hubler, *The Sense of Shakespeare's Sonnets* (Princeton: Princeton University Press, 1952), p. 153.

3. BOOTLESS: fruitless.
5-6. Three different men are referred to in these lines.
7. ART: skill. SCOPE: range of ability and accomplishment.
10. HAPLY: by chance.

Like to the lark at break of day arising
From sullen earth, sings hymns at Heaven's gate.
  For thy sweet love remembered such wealth brings
  That then I scorn to change my state with kings.

I

1. Notice that the sonnet has two major divisions: the first eight lines form one long subordinate clause from "When" (1) to "contented least" (8); the last six lines play off against the first eight. What is the central idea of the first eight lines and by what specific details is it developed? What idea is played against this one in lines 9-12? What in line 13 summarizes lines 9-12? What in line 14 summarizes lines 1-8?

2. In lines 1-8 how does Shakespeare achieve the sense of unrelieved dejection—of a series of woes piled one on another with no letup? Why is heaven called "deaf"? Explain lines 3 and 8.

3. Are the last two lines necessary to the sense of the sonnet? Do they add or detract? Explain.

4. How is the rhythm of the lines quickened after line 8? How are the imagery and word choice different? In what sense does the speaker compare himself to the lark in lines 9-12?

5. Put into your own words what the speaker is saying about friendship. How important is the word *haply* to what is being said?

Sonnet 73

That time of year thou mayst in me behold
When yellow leaves, or none, or few, do hang
Upon those boughs which shake against the cold,
Bare ruined choirs where late the sweet birds sang.
In me thou see'st the twilight of such day   5
As after sunset fadeth in the west,
Which by and by black night doth take away,
Death's second self, that seals up all in rest.
In me thou see'st the glowing of such fire,
That on the ashes of his youth doth lie   10
As the deathbed whereon it must expire,
Consumed with that which it was nourished by.
  This thou perceivest, which makes thy love more strong,
  To love that well which thou must leave ere long.

---

4. CHOIR: where the singers in a church sit.
10. HIS: its.

12. CONSUMED . . . BY: i.e., choked by the ashes of the wood which fed it.

I

1. This poem is divided into three quatrains and a concluding couplet. What is the central image of the first quatrain: what time of year is it and how do you know? in what sense are the boughs *bare ruined choirs*? why *ruined*? why the reference to the *sweet birds*? What connection is there between the image and the speaker's condition?

2. What is the central image in the second quatrain and how is it developed: why *twilight* of a day that has a *sunset*? why "Death's second self"? How is this image related to the speaker's condition?

3. What is the central image of the third quatrain and how is it developed?

4. Put into your own words lines 13 and 14. How do the lines contrast with the carefully wrought images of the three quatrains? Is the speaker concerned about the friend's response to his condition or about the nature of friendship in a world controlled by inevitable decay and death? Consider why he uses "that" and "which" in line 14 and not "him" and "whom."

5. Now consider the relationship between the quatrains. What do the images have in common? In other words, if all deal with the question of time and death, what is the change in references to time span and to dying in each one that determines the order? How does line 12 act as a focal point for all that Shakespeare is saying in the sonnet? Put into your own words what he is saying.

Sonnet 116

Let me not to the marriage of true minds
Admit impediments. Love is not love
Which alters when it alteration finds,
Or bends with the remover to remove.
Oh no! It is an ever-fixèd mark   5
That looks on tempests and is never shaken.
It is the star to every wandering bark,
Whose worth's unknown, although his height be taken.
Love's not Time's fool, though rosy lips and cheeks
Within his bending sickle's compass come.   10
Love alters not with his brief hours and weeks,
But bears it out even to the edge of doom.
    If this be error and upon me proved,
    I never writ, nor no man ever loved.

1-2. LET . . . IMPEDIMENTS: recalls the marriage service in the Book of Common Prayer of the Anglican Church: "If any of you know cause or just impediment. . . ."
4. REMOVER: the one who is inconstant.
5. MARK: a sea-mark.

8. WHOSE WORTH'S UNKNOWN: i.e., the make-up of a star is unknown. ALTHOUGH . . . TAKEN: i.e., the star's altitude can be reckoned.
9. FOOL: dupe.
10. WITHIN . . . COMPASS: i.e., within the range the sickle can cut.
14. WRIT: wrote.

I

1. What does "his" (11) refer to? What does "it" (12) refer to? What is "the edge of doom"?

2. The sonnet celebrates *the marriage of true minds* through a series of comparisons built on the idea of something fixed and permanent. Some indicate what love is not, and some indicate what love is. Explain each comparison.

3. In what sense is it true that "Love's not Time's fool" (9) even though "rosy lips and cheeks" (9) come "Within his bending sickle's compass" (10)?

4. Line 14 obviously answers line 13 since the sonnet itself proves that the speaker has *writ.* Is the concluding couplet, therefore, just a piece of clever word twisting or does its form have a positive relationship to what has gone before? In other words, how is the logic of the

couplet related to the logical development of the first twelve lines? How do the negatives in the last line give a powerful positive ending to the sonnet?

II

1. What are the attributes of friendship that Shakespeare has underscored in the three sonnets: in 29? in 73? in 116? Which one seems to you most compelling as an imaginative experience communicating what true friendship is? In your answer discuss the uniting of imagery and theme.

BREAK, BREAK, BREAK   [*1842*]

Alfred Lord Tennyson

Shakespeare's sonnet 116 speaks of friendship as a "marriage of true minds" that is fixed and permanent. It does not alter "when it alteration finds" and it remains constant "even to the edge of doom." It would be foolish to say that he has forgotten the fact of mortality. In the timeless world of the sonnet the question of mortality simply has no relevance.

In contrast to sonnet 116 is Tennyson's poem "Break, Break, Break," which also, in a sense, deals with the "marriage of true minds." Here the question of mortality is at the heart of the matter, for the poem is an expression of intense grief over the death of a friend. Although there is nothing in the poem itself that indicates whose "voice . . . is still," Tennyson is referring to the untimely death at 22 of Arthur Henry Hallam, his closest friend and his sister's fiancé.

Break, break, break,
  On thy cold gray stones, O sea!
And I would that my tongue could utter
  The thoughts that arise in me.

O well for the fisherman's boy,   5
  That he shouts with his sister at play!
O well for the sailor lad,
  That he sings in his boat on the bay!

And the stately ships go on
  To their haven under the hill;   10
But O for the touch of a vanished hand,
  And the sound of a voice that is still!

Break, break, break,
  At the foot of thy crags, O sea!
But the tender grace of a day that is dead 15
  Will never come back to me.

I

1. Where is the speaker situated? What is his attitude toward the sea? Why does he refer to "thy cold gray stones"? What movement of the sea is suggested by the repeated "Break, break, break"? What symbolic reference is there to the speaker's state of mind?

2. What part do the references in stanzas 2 and 3 play in defining the speaker's sense of loss?

3. What is gained by repeating the phrase *break, break, break* in stanza 4? What further suggestion is there in stanza 4 about the relation of the sea to the speaker's state of mind?

4. Tennyson says nothing directly about the quality of the friendship that is now dead. How does his concentration on his own isolation reveal the depth of the friendship?

Divine Love

The five selections which follow pursue the concept of divine love from various points of view. The first, Herrick's "A Thanksgiving to God for His House," is an unadorned, unabashed expression of thanks for all the good things of daily living. The next, Herbert's "Love," is also directly and simply told. In the form of a poetic dialogue the poet dramatizes the compassionate nature of God's love through the striking metaphor of guest and host at an inn.

In a more elaborate and formal manner, the speaker in Sidney's "Leave Me, O Love" rejects the triviality of earthly love, which "reachest but to dust," and admonishes himself "to aspire to higher things," meaning the "light" of "Eternal Love."

In sharp contrast to the subdued tone of Herrick and Herbert and the sober eloquence of Sidney are the two sonnets which follow those poems, Donne's "Holy Sonnet XIV" and Hopkin's "Carrion Comfort." In blunt, almost brutal language both poems record the anguish and torment of men who feel themselves unworthy of God's love and yet long for it intensely. The squeamish or overly pious may find the daring imagery of the sonnets unsuitable for purposes of worship; but for those who see their God as something more than a puritanical deacon, these tortured and in fact violent expressions of love for God will come with the shock of insight.

A THANKSGIVING TO GOD FOR HIS HOUSE *[1647]*

Robert Herrick

Lord, thou hast given me a cell
  Wherein to dwell,
A little house, whose humble roof
  Is weather-proof,
Under the spars of which I lie   5
  Both soft and dry;
Where thou, my chamber for to ward,
  Hast set a guard
Of harmless thoughts to watch and keep
  Me, while I sleep.   10
Low is my porch, as is my fate,
  Both void of state;

And yet the threshold of my door
  Is worn by th' poor,
Who thither come and freely get   15
  Good words, or meat.
Like as my parlor, so my hall
  And kitchen's small;
A little buttery, and therein
  A little bin,   20
Which keeps my little loaf of bread
  Unchipped, unflead;
Some brittle sticks of thorn or briar
  Make me a fire,
Close by whose living coal I sit,   25

---

7. WARD: watch over.
12. STATE: importance, eminence.

17. LIKE AS: like.
22. UNFLEAD: unflayed, i.e., with the crust uncut.

And glow like it.
Lord, I confess, too, when I dine,
  The pulse is thine,
And all those other bits that be
  There placed by thee;   30
The worts, the purslain, and the mess
  Of water-cress,
Which of thy kindness thou hast sent;
  And my content
Makes those, and my belovèd beet,   35
  To be more sweet.
'Tis thou that crown'st my glittering hearth
  With guiltless mirth,
And giv'st me wassail bowls to drink,
  Spiced to the brink.   40
Lord, 'tis thy plenty-dropping hand

That soils my land,
And giv'st me, for my bushel sown,
  Twice ten for one;
Thou mak'st my teeming hen to lay   45
  Her egg each day;
Besides my healthful ewes to bear
  Me twins each year;
The while the conduits of my kine
  Run cream, for wine.   50
All these, and better thou dost send
  Me, to this end,
That I should render, for my part,
  A thankful heart,
Which, fired with incense, I resign,   55
  As wholly thine;
But the acceptance, that must be,
  My Christ, by thee.

---

28. PULSE: pea-like vegetable.
31. WORTS: cabbage. PURSLAIN: salad green.
   MESS: quantity (no derogatory connotation).

55. INCENSE: devotion. RESIGN: yield.

I

1. Under what general headings can the things for which the speaker is thankful be listed? What do the categories tell us about what the speaker considers important in his life? Characterize him.

2. Why, according to the speaker, does God "send . . . All these" (51) to him? What does he give in return (53-54)? How do lines 55-58 reinforce the sense of humility the rest of the poem creates?

3. How does the rhythmic structure of the poem match the sense of ordered and purposeful simplicity? Consider the shortness of the lines, the closeness of the rhymes to each other, and the fact that most of the couplets are self-contained. Compare the poem with "Love Among the Ruins" in these respects.

LOVE [*1633*]

George Herbert

Love bade me welcome, yet my soul drew back,
   Guilty of dust and sin.
But quick-eyed Love, observing me grow slack
   From my first entrance in,
Drew nearer to me, sweetly questioning   5
   If I lacked anything.

A guest, I answered, worthy to be here.
   Love said, You shall be he.
I, the unkind, the ungrateful? ah, my dear,
   I cannot look on thee.   10
Love took my hand and smiling did reply,
   Who made the eyes but I?

Truth, Lord, but I have marred them; let my shame
   Go where it doth deserve.
And know you not, says Love, who bore the blame?   15
   My dear, then I will serve.
You must sit down, says Love, and taste my meat.
   So I did sit and eat.

6. LACKED: wanted; another meaning might be   16. SERVE: at the table.
that he "lacks" being "worthy" (7).

I

1. What is the dramatic situation of the poem? Who are the two speakers? Indicate clearly throughout the poem where one or the other is speaking. What is the underlying metaphor. Show specifically how it is developed.

2. What is the condition of the "I" in the poem? Why is he ashamed to enter in? Does he *want* to enter in? How do you know? At what point is he most despairing?

3. What is the nature of God's love as revealed in the poem? Consider that Love "bade me welcome" (1), "Drew nearer" (5), "took my hand" (11), said to "sit down" (17)—and then did what? Consider also how Love replies to lines 9-10 and 13-14.

4. What difference would there be in the meaning of the poem if the last two lines were:

You must sit down, says Love, and taste my
   fare.
   So Love did feed me there.

How would the effect of the understatement in the last line of the original be lost?

LEAVE ME, O LOVE   [1598]

Sir Philip Sidney

Leave me, O love which reachest but to dust;
And thou, my mind, aspire to higher things;
Grow rich in that which never taketh rust,
Whatever fades but fading pleasure brings.
Draw in thy beams, and humble all thy might   5
To that sweet yoke where lasting freedoms be;
Which breaks the clouds and opens forth the light,
That doth both shine and give us sight to see.
O take fast hold; let that light be thy guide
In this small course which birth draws out to death,   10
And think how evil becometh him to slide,
Who seeketh heav'n, and comes of heav'nly breath.
　　Then farewell, world; thy uttermost I see;
　　Eternal Love, maintain thy life in me.

Splendidis longum valedico nugis.

---

1. REACHEST: comes (see Genesis 3:19). BUT:
only.
3-9. See Matthew 6:9-23.
10. IN . . . DEATH: i.e., in this short passage from
birth to death.
11-12. AND . . . HEAV'N: i.e., and think how evil
it is for one who seeks heaven to slide into
trivial ways.
12. COMES . . . BREATH: see Genesis 2:7.
13. UTTERMOST: limits.
15. SPLENDIDIS . . . NUGIS: a long farewell to glittering trifles.

I

1. What do the "thy's" in line 5 refer to?
What does "Which" in line 7 refer to? What
double meaning is there in "light" in line 7:
How does it "both shine and give us sight to
see" (8)? What are the "beams" of line 5
and how do they relate to the heavenly "light"
of lines 7-9? Explain the paradox of line 6.

2. What exactly is the "love" in line 1 that
the speaker wants to separate himself from?
In what terms is the "world" of line 13 described throughout the sonnet? For one thing,
it "reachest but to dust" (1). What other conditions is it subject to?

3. In what terms is "Eternal Love" referred
to? For one thing, it is the *yoke* which brings
lasting freedom. What else is it?

4. Explain the closing line. If the *love* is
eternal, it certainly doesn't need to *maintain*
its life in the speaker. Is this an impertinent
request on the speaker's part? What other
meaning may the request have?

HOLY SONNET XIV   [*1633*]

John Donne

Batter my heart, three-personed God; for you
As yet but knock, breathe, shine, and seek to mend.
That I may rise and stand, o'erthrow me and bend
Your force to break, blow, burn, and make me new.
I, like an usurped town, to another due,   5
Labor to admit you, but, oh, to no end;
Reason, your viceroy in me, me should defend,
But is captived and proves weak or untrue.

Yet dearly I love you and would be lovèd fain,
But am betrothed unto your enemy: 10
Divorce me, untie or break that knot again,
Take me to you, imprison me, for I,
Except you enthrall me, never shall be free,
Nor ever chaste, except you ravish me.

---

1. THREE-PERSONED GOD: reference to God as the trinity.
2. AS YET: so far.
3. THAT: in order that.
9. FAIN: with joy.

I

1. To what does the metaphor in lines 1-4 compare the speaker? To what does it compare God? Note the verbs; what kind of activity do they have reference to? How do the verbs of line 4 differ from those of line 2 (notice that the fourth verb in each group sums up the first three)? To see the relationship more clearly, read the four lines aloud, putting strong stress on "Batter" and only light stress on "heart." In what ways is the metaphor of lines 1-4 appropriate to the relation of God with man and man with God?

2. What is the metaphor used in the next four lines? What verbs in lines 1-4 have prepared for it? Why is the speaker like *an usurped town*? Why is *Reason*, God's *viceroy*, unable to help in the speaker's attempts to *admit* God? How is the siege to be lifted?

3. What is the metaphor used in lines 9-14? What words in lines 5-8 have prepared for it? Explain specifically how it is developed. How does it say in a new way what was said by the previous two metaphors?

4. How are the three metaphors related? In other words, what manner of action is common to all of them? Would it make any difference if they were introduced in any other order? Explain.

5. Explain the paradoxes in the last two lines. How is that of line 13 related to the metaphor of lines 5-8? How is that of line 14 related to all three metaphors?

CARRION COMFORT   [*1918*]

Gerard Manley Hopkins

Not, I'll not, carrion comfort, Despair, not feast on thee;
Not untwist—slack they may be—these last strands of man
In me ór, most weary, cry *I can no more*. I can;
Can something, hope, wish day come, not choose not to be.
But ah, but O thou terrible, why wouldst thou rude on me   5
Thy wring-world right foot rock? lay a lionlimb against me? scan
With darksome devouring eyes my bruisèd bones? and fan,
O in turns of tempest, me heaped there; me frantic to avoid thee and flee?

   Why? That my chaff might fly; my grain lie, sheer and clear.
Nay in all that toil, that coil, since (seems) I kissed the rod,   10
Hand rather, my heart lo! lapped strength, stole joy, would laugh, chéer.
Cheer whom though? the hero whose heaven-handling flung me, fóot tród
Me? or me that fought him? O which one? is it each one? That night, that year
Of now done darkness I wretch lay wrestling with (my God!) my God.

---

1. CARRION COMFORT: i.e., a despairing, suicidal apathy or indifference, which would be as destructive of the soul as eating *carrion* would be of the body.
5. THOU TERRIBLE: God. RUDE: (1) adjective modifying *thou* and possibly *foot*: (2) adverb modifying *rock*.

"Carrion Comfort" from *Poems of Gerard Manley Hopkins,* third edition, edited by W. H. Gardner. Copyright 1948 by Oxford University Press, Inc., and reprinted by permission.

5-6. BUT . . . ROCK: *rock* is the verb in the sentence; God in his power can *wring* the world and crush it under his foot.
8. HEAPED: (1) crouched in fear; (2) like grain being threshed, which is first beaten and then blown free of chaff with a fan.
10. TOIL . . . COIL: reference to lines 2, 5-8, and 13-14. KISSED THE ROD: accepted correction submissively; here, accepted God's will.
12. HERO: God.

I

1. What is the situation of the speaker? What is he trying to convince himself of in the first four lines? Why does he call Despair "carrion comfort"? By putting "hope" together with "wish day come" and "not choose not to be" (note how negative that choice is) what light does he put "hope" in? If the speaker is insisting that he will not give in to Despair, how much chance does he have for success judging by lines 1-4? Consider, besides what has already been dealt with, the number of "not's" in these lines. What does "I can" mean in line 3?

2. God is referred to as "O thou terrible" (5). What kinds of torments is the "terrible" subjecting the speaker to in lines 5-8? Why is the speaker "frantic to avoid thee and flee"? What is the effect of the series of questions in lines 5-8?

3. The solitary "Why?" as the first word of

line 9 focuses us on the questions of 5-8 and suggests an answer. Is the rest of line 9 an answer or a further question (despite the lack of a question mark)? What does line 9 mean?

4. Do the last four lines suggest that there is now no reason for succumbing to Despair? Or do they suggest that the speaker lost the fight he refers to in lines 13-14? Or are they purposely ambiguous? God is the *hero* referred to in line 12. What connotations are there in the use of the word? What does the speaker mean by saying, "Cheer whom though?" (12) after he has spoken of the "strength" and "joy" his heart felt after the struggle? What was the experience of the night that seemed a year ("That night, that year")? Does the phrase *now done darkness* suggest that the struggle will not be repeated, or does it mean, in conjunction with line 1, that such spiritual wrestlings have to be repeated continually?

5. How does the rhythm of the first four lines match the sense? Consider the number of pauses within lines, the use of repetitions, the internal rhyme. How does the rhythm of lines 5-8 contrast with that in lines 1-4? Consider the run-on lines, the use of alliteration, the use of "ah" and "O." How is the breathlessness of lines 9-13 achieved? Consider the use of many stressed syllables in a row, the unusual alliteration, and the rapid-fire questions of line 13. How does the phrase *now done darkness* force an emphatic reading of line 14? What is the effect of the parenthetical "my God!"?

II

1. Both this sonnet and the one by Donne which precedes it are powerful expressions of tormented individuals seeking assurance of God's love and their worthiness to receive it. Which seems to you more effectively to dramatize the torment and the desire—and why?

"*Good and evil, we know,
grow up together almost inseparably
in the field of this world.*"

John Milton, *Areopagitica*

Unit Four

EVIL

In your reading thus far you may have felt that many of the selections here are not very cheerful. Even the section on love has its share of bitterness and sorrow. Perhaps you have felt for a long time that the "good" literature you are asked to read tends to deal with the gloomy side of life—with defeat, suffering, mischance, disappointment, despair.

If you feel this way, you are not alone; in fact, that very reaction is why so many movies and television plays and radio serials and popular magazine stories, while they may show much unhappiness along the way, always, as a matter of policy, end happily. Evil in these entertainments is not allowed to triumph; nor can crime possibly pay. The good guys win; the bad guys lose. And why not, some in the audience ask? Isn't life bad enough without our amusements being miserable too?

If "amusement" were all we need to ask of literature (or the other arts), there might be sense in such a complaint. But "amusement" is not all we need to ask, nor, for most of us, is it the only thing we *want* to ask. We seek entertainment, but we also seek insight—into ourselves, our world, and the human condition into which we are all born. In the last analysis, we want to know who we are and what we are and why we are here. Great literature dramatizes these questions for us, carries them, as the poet Wordsworth was to say in a similar connection, "alive"—that is, concretely, feelingly—"into the heart." It does not prettify the truth about either man's world or man. It shows us a being who combines good and evil, a being with an equal potential for heroism and cowardice, for sacrifice and selfishness, for love and hate, and a world that is compounded of pain and joy. If there is more emphasis in literature on the pain than the joy, it is because man has naturally asked more searchingly why evil should be at all if God is just or if most men mean to be. The problem of the existence of evil fascinates and perplexes; it is as central to the thinking man today as it was three thousand years ago.

The author of Ecclesiastes said, "The race is not always to the swift, nor the battle to the strong, nor yet bread to the wise . . . but time and chance happeneth to them all." If this is so—and the available evidence suggests that it is—then what is a man to do about it? He can cry out that it is not fair and thus pity his lot. He can blame God or his neighbor. He can say lamely "So be it" and try to think of pleasanter things. Or he can say that upon this very fact rests the deepest meaning of life—that, in fact, out of suffering and defeat can be made to come wisdom and victory. This does not mean that we are to chop off a finger to see what good we can draw from the pain; it does mean that we must face up frankly to the capacities for evil in ourselves and in our society, and come to some convictions about dealing with it. No matter how much we may wish it were not so, we *are* accountable to ourselves: and we *are* our brother's keeper.

In the selections that follow you will find powerful protests against man's inhumanity to man—through social injustice, through war, through personal greed, or—greatest vice of us all—through neglect and indifference. The reader is called on by these selections, not simply to witness and forget, but to make the protest a part of his own commitment to justice and dignity. Anyone who can read Blake's "London" or Owen's "Dulce et Decorum Est" and remain indifferent is less than fully alive. Anyone who can read Auden's "September 1, 1939" or Lawrence's "The Rocking-Horse Winner" and say, upon reflection, "This situation has nothing to do with me" is ignoring his own humanity.

Central in this section is the idea of tragedy, the form of literature which has probed most deeply into the human condition. Tragedy brings to us an awareness of the immensity of man's involvement with evil, and, more important, an awareness that out of his involvement may come moral and spiritual victory. We have seen this with Oedipus; we shall see it again now with Hamlet.

Tragedy's affirmation of the indestructibility of the human spirit shows how irrelevant it is to judge literature by its happy or unhappy endings. It should be judged by its fidelity to the truth about what man is, so clearly put by Bernard Knox in the closing words of his book *Oedipus at Thebes*: "Man is not equated to the gods, but man at his greatest, as in Oedipus, is capable of something which the gods, by definition, cannot experience; the proud tragic view of Sophocles sees in the fragility and inevitable defeat of human greatness the possibility of a purely human heroism to which the gods can never attain, for the condition of their existence is everlasting victory."*

---

* Bernard Knox, *Oedipus at Thebes* (New Haven: Yale University Press).

The following four poems express, from widely different points of view, an intense awareness of those forces in human affairs that men call evil.

You may decide that the first, William Blake's "The Tiger," is concerned not so much with the problem of evil as with the presence in the world of terrifying power. A great many readers have found this poem an unforgettably imaginative rendering of the awesome potential for brute force that we live with all the time. Compare Blake's insight with that in the next poem, James Stephens's "In Waste Places," which probes the nature of terror and fear. There are surface similarities but also important differences in tone and attitude.

The next two poems offer interesting contrasts in theme and treatment. In "Channel Firing," Thomas Hardy, with a detached, ironic flippancy, puts forward a world which has been, is, and always will be dominated by man's blindness and stupidity. In "Thou Art Indeed Just, Lord," Gerard Manley Hopkins, thoroughly convinced that God is "indeed just," nevertheless cries out in an agonizing plea for some reason why "sinners' ways prosper" and nature thrives, while he does not "breed one work that wakes."

THE TIGER   [*1794*]

William Blake

Tiger, tiger, burning bright
In the forests of the night,
What immortal hand or eye
Could frame thy fearful symmetry?

In what distant deeps or skies   5
Burnt the fire of thine eyes?
On what wings dare he aspire?
What the hand dare seize the fire?

And what shoulder, and what art,
Could twist the sinews of thy heart?   10
And when thy heart began to beat,
What dread hand and what dread feet?

What the hammer? What the chain?
In what furnace was thy brain?
What the anvil? What dread grasp   15
Dare its deadly terrors clasp?

----
12. The line is not grammatically complete; originally line 13 was, "Could fetch it from the furnace deep."

When the stars threw down their spears,
And watered heaven with their tears,
Did He smile His work to see?
Did He who made the lamb make thee?   20

Tiger, tiger, burning bright
In the forests of the night,
What immortal hand or eye
Dare frame thy fearful symmetry?

17-18. The reference here is to the revolt of the rebel angels, led by Satan (see Isaiah 14:12 and Revelation 12:3-9).

I

1. How much of the tiger is actually visualized by the speaker? What three physical features of the tiger are mentioned? How have we been given a terrifying sense of its power without getting a literal description of it in action? What qualities of the tiger are suggested?

2. What is the creator of the tiger compared to? Notice particularly lines 10, 13, and 15. How is the metaphor developed?

3. Stanzas 2, 3, and 4 contain a series of questions that grow shorter and more insistent (compare lines 3-4 with lines 13-14). What is the purpose of this development? What effect

of the imagined tiger on the speaker's consciousness is suggested by the grammatical incompleteness of some of the questions? How do the consonants in lines 15-16 support the sense of the lines and bring to a climax the series of questions?

4. The last stanza is the same as the first except for the change of "Could" to "Dare." What is gained by repeating the stanza? What are the implications of "Dare" that are not present in "Could"?

5. Many commentators have said that the tiger is a symbol of evil and the lamb is a symbol of good. There is justification for this reading, but can you argue that it isn't completely validated by a close examination of the poem? What else might the tiger and the lamb stand for?

II

1. A companion poem to "The Tiger" is Blake's "The Lamb," printed below. In a short essay discuss how "The Lamb" differs in treatment from "The Tiger." What qualities of the lamb does the speaker emphasize? Who is the speaker? How does the rhythm and word choice emphasize the condition of the speaker? Both poems have reference to nature; what different aspects are emphasized? In your discussion include some comment on how each poem throws light on the other.

THE LAMB

Little lamb, who made thee?
  Dost thou know who made thee?
Gave thee life, and bid thee feed,
By the stream and o'er the mead;
Gave thee clothing of delight,   5
Softest clothing, woolly, bright;
Gave thee such a tender voice,
Making all the vales rejoice?
  Little lamb, who made thee?
  Dost thou know who made thee?   10

  Little lamb, I'll tell thee,
  Little lamb, I'll tell thee:
He is callèd by thy name,
For he calls himself a Lamb.
He is meek, and he is mild;   15
He became a little child.
I a child, and thou a lamb,
We are callèd by his name.
  Little lamb, God bless thee!
  Little lamb, God bless thee!   20

IN WASTE PLACES [*1926*]

James Stephens

As a naked man I go
Through the desert, sore afraid;
Holding up my head, although
I'm as frightened as a maid.

The lion crouches there! I saw   5
In barren rocks his amber eye!
He parts the cactus with his paw!
He stares at me, as I go by!

He would pad upon my trace
If he thought I was afraid!   10
If he knew my hardy face
Veils the terrors of a maid.

He rises in the night-time, and
He stretches forth! He snuffs the air!
He roars! He leaps along the sand!   15
He creeps! He watches everywhere!

His burning eyes, his eyes of bale
Through the darkness I can see!
He lashes fiercely with his tail!
He makes again to spring at me!   20

I am the lion, and his lair!
I am the fear that frightens me!
I am the desert of despair!
And the night of agony!

Night or day, whate'er befall,   25
I must walk that desert land,
Until I dare my fear, and call
The lion out to lick my hand!

9. TRACE: track.
17. BALE: doom.

I

1. What kind of person is the speaker? Why does he see himself *as a naked man?* What is signified by the setting—desert, barren rocks, cactus? What does the lion stand for? Why does he rise chiefly at night? What keeps him from springing?

2. What does stanza 6 mean? Suppose it were to drop from the poem; would anything essential be lost? Why or why not?

3. Compare Stephens's lion with Blake's tiger. Notice that Stephens describes the lion in action, while Blake concentrates on the creation of the tiger. Which procedure is more evocative of terror and power in these instances? Why?

4. What is the speaker saying about the nature of fear or evil? How does his commentary differ from that of Blake's poem?

CHANNEL FIRING [*1914*]

Thomas Hardy

That night your great guns, unawares,
Shook all our coffins as we lay.
And broke the chancel window-squares,
We thought it was the Judgment-day

And sat upright. While drearisome   5
Arose the howl of wakened hounds:
The mouse let fall the altar-crumb,
The worms drew back into the mounds,

The glebe cow drooled. Till God called, "No;
It's gunnery practice out at sea   10
Just as before you went below;
The world is as it used to be:

"All nations striving strong to make
Red war yet redder. Mad as hatters
They do no more for Christès sake   15
Than you who are helpless in such matters.

"That this is not the judgment-hour
For some of them's a blessed thing,
For if it were they'd have to scour
Hell's floor for so much threatening . . .   20

"Ha, ha. It will be warmer when
I blow the trumpet (if indeed
I ever do; for you are men,
And rest eternal sorely need)."

So down we lay again. "I wonder,   25
Will the world ever saner be,"
Said one, "than when He sent us under
In our indifferent century!"

And many a skeleton shook his head.
"Instead of preaching forty year,"   30
My neighbor Parson Thirdly said,
"I wish I had stuck to pipes and beer."

Again the guns disturbed the hour,
Roaring their readiness to avenge,
As far inland as Stourton Tower,   35
And Camelot, and starlit Stonehenge.

---

14. MAD AS HATTERS: common expression for brainless behavior. Lewis Carroll particularized the saying in the person of the Mad Hatter in *Alice in Wonderland.*

15. CHRISTÈS: medieval spelling; together with the colloquialisms and the references to British history, such a usage suggests the timeless world of the poem.

35. STOURTON TOWER: tower near Stourton in Wiltshire commemorating King Alfred's victories over the Danish invaders.

36. CAMELOT: legendary city of King Arthur and his Round Table. STONEHENGE: prehistoric ruins on Salisbury Plain of unknown origin but probably religious in purpose.

I

1. What is the situation of the poem? Who is referred to in "your" of line 1? Where are they and what are they doing? Who are the

"we" of line 2? Where are they and what are they doing?

2. What non-human activities are referred to in stanza 2? How do these references anticipate the implications of the poem with respect to the warlike activities of human beings?

3. Can Hardy be charged with irreverence in having God speak directly to the coffin dwellers, particularly in such a matter-of-fact, colloquial way? Why or why not? How do the activities of stanza 2 and the comments of the coffin dwellers support the casual, almost flippant, tone of the poem? How does the fact that stanza 1 runs over into stanza 2 take the emphasis off "Judgment-day" and put it on the skeletons' suddenly sitting upright? How does this switch in emphasis support the tone?

4. What is the theme of the poem? What does line 12 have to do with it? What does Parson Thirdly's complaint have to do with it? What do the allusions to past history in the last stanza have to do with it? Note the shift in tone in the last stanza; there's a soberness and heaviness that's missing in the rest of the poem. How does this shift emphasize the theme? What is the effect of ending the poem on four stressed syllables ("starlit Stonehenge")? Why "starlit"?

THOU ART INDEED JUST, LORD   [*1918*]

Gerard Manley Hopkins

Justus quidem tu es, Domine, si disputem tecum: verum tamen justa loquar
ad te: Quare via impiorum prosperatur? &c

Thou art indeed just, Lord, if I contend
With thee; but, sir, so what I plead is just.
Why do sinners' ways prosper? and why must
Disappointment all I endeavor end?
    Wert thou my enemy, O thou my friend,   5
How wouldst thou worse, I wonder, than thou dost
Defeat, thwart me? Oh, the sots and thralls of lust
Do in spare hours more thrive than I that spend,
Sir, life upon thy cause. See, banks and brakes
Now, leavèd how thick! lacèd they are again   10
With fretty chervil, look, and fresh wind shakes
Them; birds build—but not I build; no, but strain,
Time's eunuch, and not breed one work that wakes.
Mine, O thou lord of life, send my roots rain.

"Thou Art Indeed Just, Lord" from *Poems of Gerard Manley Hopkins*, third edition, edited by W. H. Gardner. Published by Oxford University Press.

Title. Jeremiah 12:1; the first three lines of the poem provide the translation for the Latin.

I

1. Put into your own words the meaning of:
a. "why must/ Disappointment all I endeavor end?"
b. "How wouldst thou worse, I wonder, than thou dost/ Defeat, thwart me?"
c. "Do in spare hours more thrive than I that spend,/ Sir, life upon thy cause."
d. "See, banks and brakes/ Now, leavèd how thick!"
e. "birds build—but not I build;"

2. What is the situation of the poem? What does the speaker see around him among men? in nature? in himself? What does this use of "sir" in addressing the Lord show about the attitude of the speaker?

3. How is the line movement throughout most of the poem related to the sense of urgency the speaker feels: the number of run-on lines, the almost choppy effect caused by the many pauses within lines, the distorted syntax, and the number of times stressed syllables in a row are used ("indeed just, Lord," "not breed one work," "send my roots rain")?

4. There is an intense awareness of personal failure here, but what indications are there that this is not the cry of a complainer or defeatist? What is the speaker's attitude toward his failure to *breed one work that wakes*?

II

1. What are the manifestations of evil as revealed in the four preceding poems? Try to define evil, basing your definition on your agreement or disagreement with the insights of the four poems.

EDWARD and LORD RANDAL

In "Channel Firing" there is a surface humor that plays against and strengthens the seriousness of Hardy's recognition of the permanence of evil in human society. There is no humor in the ballads that follow, unless it is the bitter humor in each poem of two people talking about murder as if it were something far less serious. There is, however, the same recognition of the enormity of evil.

The focus on treachery, indifference to suffering, and violent death seems as characteristic of English folk ballads as the ballad form itself. The fact is instructive, for it shows the consciousness of evil and betrayal in the world of men that perpetuates itself in the folk tradition; the ballads that have survived are those that have been closest to man's deepest awareness of what he is capable of doing.

In both "Edward" and "Lord Randal" we have the terrible theme of murder dramatized sharply in brief dialogues between a mother and her son. The manner is quiet and restrained, but it is like the quiet that comes on a ruined city after a cataclysm.

EDWARD

"Why dois your brand sae drap wi bluid,
    Edward, Edward,
Why dois your brand sae drap wi bluid,
    And why sae sad gang yee O?"
"O I hae killed my hauke sae guid,   5
    Mither, mither,

---

1. BRAND: sword. SAE: so.   4. GANG: go.

O I hae killed my hauke sae guid,
    And I had nae mair bot hee O."

"Your haukis bluid was nevir sae reid,
        Edward, Edward,   10
Your haukis bluid was nevir sae reid,
    My deir son I tell thee O."
"O I hae killed my reid-roan steid,
        Mither, mither,
O I hae killed my reid-roan steid,   15
    That erst was sae fair and frie O."

"Your steid was auld, and ye hae gat mair,
        Edward, Edward,
Your steid was auld, and ye hae gat mair,
    Sum other dule ye drie O."   20
"O I hae killed my fadir deir,
        Mither, mither,
O I hae killed my fadir deir,
    Alas, and wae is mee O!"

"And whatten penance wul ye drie for that,   25
        Edward, Edward,
And whatten penance wul ye drie for that?
    My deir son, now tell me O."
"Ile set my feit in yonder boat,
        Mither, mither,   30
Ile set my feit in yonder boat,
    And Ile fare ovir the sea O."

"And what wul ye doe wi your towirs and your ha,
        Edward, Edward,
And what wul ye doe wi your towirs and your ha,   35
    That were sae fair to see O?"
"Ile let thame stand tul they doun fa,
        Mither, mither,
Ile let thame stand tul they doun fa,
    For here nevir mair maun I bee O."   40

"And what wul ye leive to your bairns and your wife,
        Edward, Edward,
And what wul ye leive to your bairns and your wife,

---

8. BOT: but.
9. REID: red.
16. ERST: once. FRIE: spirited.
20. DULE YE DRIE: sorrow you suffer.

33. HA: hall.
40. MAUN: must.
41. BAIRNS: children.

Whan ye gang ovir the sea O?"
"The warldis room, late them beg thrae life,   45
   Mither, mither,
The warldis room, late them beg thrae life,
   For thame nevir mair wul I see O."

"And what wul ye leive to your ain mither dear,
   Edward, Edward,   50
And what wul ye leive to your ain mither dear?
   My deir son, now tell me O."
"The curse of hell frae me sall ye beir,
   Mither, mither,
The curse of hell frae me sall ye beir,   55
   Sic counseils ye gave to me O."

45. WARLDIS: world's. LATE: let. THRAE: through.
53. SALL: shall.
56. SIC: such.

I

1. What do we learn about the situation in the poem, in stanza 1? in stanza 2? in stanza 3? What is the reason for arranging these stanzas in this order?

2. What kind of person is Edward? Why did he kill his father, and what effect has the killing had on him? Why does he lie at first about what has happened?

3. What kind of person is Edward's mother? What may we infer from the fact that she is not satisfied with her son's first and second answers? What additional information do we receive about her in stanza 6? in stanza 7?

4. Show that the order of stanzas 4-7 is an order of climax. In what sense does stanza 6 represent a climax for *both* the mother and the son? In what sense does this climax consist in a reversal of what was anticipated?

5. Why should the wife and children have to "beg thrae life" for a crime they were not guilty of?

6. Comment on the dramatic structure of the poem: what is gained by the question and answer technique? by the repetitions? by the startling opening question?

7. What part is played by irony in the poem?

II

1. Discuss whether the ballad is simply a story of blood and betrayal or, beyond that, a commentary on the theme of crime and punishment.

LORD RANDAL

"O where hae ye been, Lord Randal, my son?
O where hae ye been, my handsome young man?"
"I hae been to the wild wood; mother, make my bed soon,
For I'm weary wi hunting, and fain wald lie down."

"Where gat ye your dinner, Lord Randal, my son?   5
Where gat ye your dinner, my handsome young man?"
"I dined wi my true-love; mother, make my bed soon,
For I'm weary wi hunting, and fain wald lie down."

4. WALD: would.

"What gat ye to your dinner, Lord Randal, my son?
What gat ye to your dinner, my handsome young man?"   10
"I gat eels boiled in broo; mother, make my bed soon,
For I'm weary wi hunting, and fain wald lie down."

"What became of your bloodhounds, Lord Randal, my son?
What became of your bloodhounds, my handsome young man?"
"O they swelld and they died; mother, make my bed soon,   15
For I'm weary wi hunting, and fain wald lie down."

"O I fear ye are poisond, Lord Randal, my son!
O I fear ye are poisond, my handsome young man!"
"O yes! I am poisond; mother, make my bed soon,
For I'm sick at the heart, and I fain wald lie down."   20

---

11. BROO: broth.

I

1. It is customary in ballads to disclose the full facts about the situation of the speaker or speakers gradually. In this poem, each stanza adds a fact. What do we know by the end of stanza 1? stanza 2? stanza 3? stanza 4? stanza 5?

2. In another version of the ballad there are two stanzas covering the death of the hounds. In the first the mother asks, "And wha gat your leavins?" and her son answers, "My hawks and my hounds." In the second she says, "And what becam of them?" and he answers, "They stretched their legs out and died." In our version, with only a single stanza devoted to the bloodhounds, we are left to infer that they too had "eels boiled in broo." Which version has more drama and excitement? Why?

3. In the version referred to in question 2 there are four more stanzas after the mother says, "I fear ye are poisoned." They parallel the end of "Edward." She asks what he will leave his mother, then his sister, then his brother, and finally his true-love. He leaves his family all he owns and leaves his true-love "a

rope from hell to hang her." Which version do you think is more effective and why?

4. What is ironic about "I dined wi my true-love"? What is ironic about the last line of the ballad: "For I'm sick at the heart"? The last lines of the first four stanzas are exactly the same, but the last line of stanza five is quite different; how does this change add to the irony?

5. Compare the dramatic structure of this ballad with that of "Edward." Compare the mother's function and the question of motivation in the two poems. It has been said by critics that "Edward" has a psychological interest greater than that found in "Lord Randal." Do you agree? Why or why not?

II

1. Try writing a short ballad. Before doing so, you might read a few more well-known ones like "Sir Patrick Spens," "Johnie Armestrong," "Barbara Allan," and "The Twa Corbies," all of which deal with the themes of treachery or callous indifference or sudden and violent death. Try to find some modern situation that illustrates one of these themes.

THE ROCKING-HORSE WINNER   *[1933]*

D. H. Lawrence

The ballads we have just read deal vividly with the results of personal hatred and cold-heartedness. The bloody deed is done and the wreckage is on view, but we have to supply our own "story" about the why and the wherefore; the characters and their motives remain undefined.

There is nothing undefined at all about the characters and their motives in Lawrence's short story, "The Rocking-Horse Winner." A mother's greed for more and more money drives her son into a fantastic partnership with the powers of evil. There's a "once-upon-a-time" quality in the telling of the story that you will recognize from the very first sentence, but you will soon see that the fairy-tale technique is used to heighten the sense of terror the story carries, much as the understatement in the ballads we have read and the humor in "Channel Firing" intensify the sense of violence the poems deal with.

The story has obvious relations with a very well-known German legend about a doctor called Faust or Faustus, who sold his soul to the devil in return for superhuman knowledge and magical powers. The theme has been the subject of many literary works, the best known being Goethe's *Faust* and Christopher Marlowe's *Dr. Faustus*.

There was a woman who was beautiful, who started with all the advantages, yet she had no luck. She married for love, and the love turned to dust. She had bonny children, yet she felt they had been thrust upon her, and she could not love them. They looked at her coldly, as if they were finding fault with her. And hurriedly she felt she must cover up some fault in herself. Yet what it was that she must cover up she never knew. Nevertheless, when her children were present, she always felt the center of her heart go hard. This troubled her, and in her manner she was all the more gentle and anxious for her children, as if she loved them very much. Only she herself knew that at the center of her heart was a hard

little place that could not feel love, no, not for anybody. Everybody else said of her: "She is such a good mother. She adores her children." Only she herself, and her children themselves, knew it was not so. They read it in each other's eyes.

There were a boy and two little girls. They lived in a pleasant house, with a garden, and they had discreet servants, and felt themselves superior to anyone in the neighborhood.

Although they lived in style, they felt always an anxiety in the house. There was never enough money. The mother had a small income, and the father had a small income, but not nearly enough for the social position which they had to keep up. The father went in to town to some office. But though he had good prospects, these prospects never materialized. There was always the grinding sense of the shortage of money, though the style was always kept up.

At last the mother said: "I will see if *I* can't make something." But she did not know where to begin. She racked her brains, and tried this thing and the other, but could not find anything successful. The failure made deep lines come into her face. Her children were growing up, they would have to go to school. There must be more money, there must be more money. The father, who was always very handsome and expensive in his tastes, seemed as if he never *would* be able to do anything worth doing. And the mother, who had a great belief in herself, did not succeed any better, and her tastes were just as expensive.

And so the house came to be haunted by the unspoken phrase: *There must be more money! There must be more money!* The children could hear it all the time, though nobody said it aloud. They heard it at Christmas, when the expensive and splendid toys filled the nursery. Behind the shining modern rocking-horse, behind the smart doll's-house, a voice would start whispering: "There *must* be more money! There *must* be more money!" And the children would stop playing, to listen for a moment. They would look into each other's eyes, to see if they had all heard. And each one saw in the eyes of the other two that they too had heard. "There *must* be more money! There *must* be more money!"

It came whispering from the springs of the still-swaying rocking-horse, and even the horse, bending his wooden, champing head, heard it. The big doll, sitting so pink and smirking in her new pram, could hear it quite plainly, and seemed to be smirking all the more self-consciously because of it. The foolish puppy, too, that took the place of the teddy-bear, he was looking so extraordinarily foolish for no other reason but that he heard the secret whisper all over the house: "There *must* be more money!"

Yet nobody ever said it aloud. The whisper was everywhere, and therefore no one spoke it. Just as no one ever says: "We are breathing!" in spite of the fact that breath is coming and going all the time.

"Mother," said the boy Paul one day,

"Why don't we keep a car of our own? Why do we always use uncle's, or else a taxi?"

"Because we're the poor members of the family," said the mother.

"But why *are* we, mother?"

"Well—I suppose," she said slowly and bitterly, "it's because your father has no luck."

The boy was silent for some time.

"Is luck money, mother?" he asked rather timidly.

"No, Paul. Not quite. It's what causes you to have money."

"Oh!" said Paul vaguely. "I thought when Uncle Oscar said *filthy lucker,* it meant money."

"*Filthy lucre* does mean money," said the mother. "But it's lucre, not luck."

"Oh!" said the boy. "Then what *is* luck, mother?"

"It's what causes you to have money. If you're lucky you have money. That's why it's better to be born lucky than rich. If you're rich, you may lose your money. But if you're lucky, you will always get more money."

"Oh! Will you? And is father not lucky?"

"Very unlucky, I should say," she said bitterly.

The boy watched her with unsure eyes.

"Why?" he asked.

"I don't know. Nobody ever knows why one person is lucky and another unlucky."

"Don't they? Nobody at all? Does *nobody* know?"

"Perhaps God. But He never tells."

"He ought to, then. And aren't you lucky either, mother?"

"I can't be, if I married an unlucky husband."

"But by yourself, aren't you?"

"I used to think I was, before I married. Now I think I am very unlucky indeed."

"Why?"

"Well—never mind! Perhaps I'm not really," she said.

The child looked at her, to see if she meant it. But he saw, by the lines of her mouth, that she was only trying to hide something from him.

"Well, anyhow," he said stoutly, "I'm a lucky person."

"Why?" said his mother, with a sudden laugh.

He stared at her. He didn't even know why he had said it.

"God told me," he asserted, brazening it out.

"I hope He did, dear!" she said, again with a laugh, but rather bitter.

"He did, mother!"

"Excellent!" said the mother, using one of her husband's exclamations.

The boy saw she did not believe him; or, rather, that she paid no attention to his assertion. This angered him somewhat, and made him want to compel her attention.

He went off by himself, vaguely, in a childish way, seeking for the clue to "luck." Absorbed, taking no heed of other people, he went about with a sort of stealth, seeking inwardly for luck. He wanted luck, he wanted it, he wanted it. When the two girls were playing dolls in the nursery, he would sit on his big rocking-horse, charging madly into space, with a frenzy that made the little girls peer at him uneasily. Wildly the horse careered, the waving dark hair of the boy tossed, his eyes had a strange glare in them. The little girls dared not speak to him.

When he had ridden to the end of his mad little journey, he climbed down and stood in front of his rocking-horse, staring fixedly into its lowered face. Its red mouth was slightly open, its big eye was wide and glassy-bright.

"Now!" he would silently command the snorting steed. "Now, take me to where there is luck! Now take me!"

And he would slash the horse on the neck with the little whip he had asked Uncle Oscar for. He *knew* the horse could take him to where there was luck, if only he forced it. So he would mount again, and start on his furious ride, hoping at last to get there. He knew he could get there.

"You'll break your horse, Paul!" said the nurse.

"He's always riding like that! I wish he'd leave off!" said his elder sister[1] Joan.

But he only glared down on them in silence. Nurse gave him up. She could make nothing of him. Anyhow he was growing beyond her.

One day his mother and his Uncle Oscar came in when he was on one of his furious rides. He did not speak to them.

"Hallo, you young jockey! Riding a winner?" said his uncle.

"Aren't you growing too big for a rocking-horse? You're not a very little boy any longer, you know," said his mother.

But Paul only gave a blue glare from his big, rather close-set eyes. He would speak to nobody when he was in full tilt. His mother watched him with an anxious expression on her face.

At last he suddenly stopped forcing his horse into the mechanical gallop, and slid down.

"Well, I got there!" he announced fiercely, his blue eyes still flaring, and his sturdy long legs straddling apart.

"Where did you get to?" asked his mother.

"Where I wanted to go," he flared back at her.

"That's right, son!" said Uncle Oscar. "Don't you stop till you get there. What's the horse's name?"

"He doesn't have a name," said the boy.

"Gets on without all right?" asked the uncle.

"Well, he has different names. He was called Sansovino last week."

"Sansovino, eh? Won the Ascot.[2] How did you know his name?"

"He always talks about horse-races with Bassett," said Joan.

The uncle was delighted to find that his

---

1. ELDER SISTER: i.e., the older of his two sisters; both are younger than Paul.
2. ASCOT: a famous English horse race. The other races mentioned later on are also well-known yearly races.

small nephew was posted with all the racing news. Bassett, the young gardener, who had been wounded in the left foot in the war and had got his present job through Oscar Cresswell, whose batman[3] he had been, was a perfect blade of the "Turf."[4] He lived in the racing events, and the small boy lived with him.

Oscar Cresswell got it all from Bassett.

"Master Paul comes and asks me, so I can't do more than tell him, sir," said Bassett, his face terribly serious, as if he were speaking of religious matters.

"And does he ever put anything on a horse he fancies?"

"Well—I don't want to give him away—he's a young sport,[5] a fine sport, sir. Would you mind asking him himself? He sort of takes a pleasure in it, and perhaps he'd feel I was giving him away, sir, if you don't mind."

Bassett was serious as a church.

The uncle went back to his nephew and took him off for a ride in the car.

"Say, Paul, old man, do you ever put anything on a horse?" the uncle asked.

The boy watched the handsome man closely.

"Why, do you think I oughtn't to?" he parried.

"Not a bit of it! I thought perhaps you might give me a tip for the Lincoln."

The car sped on into the country, going down to Uncle Oscar's place in Hampshire.

"Honor bright?" said the nephew.

"Honor bright, son!" said the uncle.

"Well, then, Daffodil."

"Daffodil! I doubt it, sonny. What about Mirza?"

"I only know the winner," said the boy. "That's Daffodil."

"Daffodil, eh?"

There was a pause. Daffodil was an obscure horse comparatively.

"Uncle!"

"Yes, son?"

"You won't let it go any further, will you? I promised Bassett."

"Bassett be damned, old man! What's he got to do with it?"

"We're partners. We've been partners from the first. Uncle, he lent me my first five shillings, which I lost. I promised him, honor bright, it was only between me and him; only you gave me that ten-shilling note I started winning with, so I thought you were lucky. You won't let it go any further, will you?"

The boy gazed at his uncle from those big, hot, blue eyes, set rather close together. The uncle stirred and laughed uneasily.

"Right you are, son! I'll keep your tip private. Daffodil, eh? How much are you putting on him?"

"All except twenty pounds," said the boy. "I keep that in reserve."

The uncle thought it a good joke.

"You keep twenty pounds in reserve, do you, you young romancer? What are you betting, then?"

"I'm betting three hundred," said the boy, gravely. "But it's between you and me, Uncle Oscar! Honor bright?"

The uncle burst into a roar of laughter.

"It's between you and me all right, you young Nat Gould,"[6] he said, laughing. "But where's your three hundred?"

"Bassett keeps it for me. We're partners."

"You are, are you! And what is Bassett putting on Daffodil?"

"He won't go quite as high as I do, I expect. Perhaps he'll go a hundred and fifty."

"What, pennies?" laughed the uncle.

"Pounds," said the child, with a surprised look at his uncle. "Bassett keeps a bigger reserve than I do."

Between wonder and amusement Uncle

---

3. BATMAN: personal servant to an officer in the British Army.
4. PERFECT . . . "TURF": one thoroughly wrapped up in horse-racing.
5. SPORT: here, a gambler.

---

6. NAT GOULD: British novelist (1857-1919), author of 130 novels, mostly on horse-racing.

Oscar was silent. He pursued the matter no further, but he determined to take his nephew with him to the Lincoln races.

"Now, son," he said, "I'm putting twenty on Mirza, and I'll put five for you on any horse you fancy. What's your pick?"

"Daffodil, uncle."

"No, not the fiver on Daffodil!"

"I should if it was my own fiver," said the child.

"Good! Good! Right you are! A fiver for me and a fiver for you on Daffodil."

The child had never been to a race-meeting before, and his eyes were blue fire. He pursed his mouth tight, and watched. A Frenchman just in front had put his money on Lancelot. Wild with excitement, he flayed his arms up and down, yelling *"Lancelot! Lancelot!"* in his French accent.

Daffodil came in first, Lancelot second, Mirza third. The child, flushed and with eyes blazing, was curiously serene. His uncle brought him four five-pound notes, four to one.

"What am I to do with these?" he cried, waving them before the boy's eyes.

"I suppose we'll talk to Bassett," said the boy. "I expect I have fifteen hundred now; and twenty in reserve; and this twenty."

His uncle studied him for some moments.

"Look here, son!" he said. "You're not serious about Bassett and that fifteen hundred, are you?"

"Yes, I am. But it's between you and me, uncle. Honor bright!"

"Honor bright all right, son! But I must talk to Bassett."

"If you'd like to be a partner, uncle, with Bassett and me, we could all be partners. Only, you'd have to promise, honor bright, uncle, not to let it go beyond us three. Bassett and I are lucky, and you must be lucky, because it was your ten shillings I started winning with. . . ."

Uncle Oscar took both Bassett and Paul into Richmond Park for an afternoon, and there they talked.

"It's like this, you see, sir," Bassett said.

"Master Paul would get me talking about racing events, spinning yarns, you know, sir. And he was always keen on knowing if I'd made or if I'd lost. It's about a year since, now, that I put five shillings on Blush of Dawn for him—and we lost. Then the luck turned, with that ten shillings he had from you, that we put on Singhalese. And since that time, it's been pretty steady, all things considering. What do you say, Master Paul?"

"We're all right when we're sure," said Paul. "It's when we're not quite sure that we go down."

"Oh, but we're careful then," said Bassett.

"But when are you *sure?*" smiled Uncle Oscar.

"It's Master Paul, sir," said Bassett, in a secret, religious voice. "It's as if he had it from heaven. Like Daffodil, now, for the Lincoln. That was as sure as eggs."

"Did you put anything on Daffodil?" asked Oscar Cresswell.

"Yes, sir. I made my bit."

"And my nephew?"

Bassett was obstinately silent, looking at Paul.

"I made twelve hundred, didn't I, Bassett? I told uncle I was putting three hundred on Daffodil."

"That's right," said Bassett, nodding.

"But where's the money?" asked the uncle.

"I keep it safe locked up, sir. Master Paul he can have it any minute he likes to ask for it."

"What, fifteen hundred pounds?"

"And twenty! And *forty,* that is, with the twenty he made on the course."

"It's amazing!" said the uncle.

"If Master Paul offers you to be partners, sir, I would, if I were you; if you'll excuse me," said Bassett.

Oscar Cresswell thought about it.

"I'll see the money," he said.

They drove home again, and sure enough, Bassett came round to the garden-house with fifteen hundred pounds in notes. The twenty pounds reserve was left with Joe Glee, in the Turf Commission deposit.

"You see, it's all right, uncle, when I'm *sure!* Then we go strong, for all we're worth. Don't we, Bassett?"

"We do that, Master Paul."

"And when are you sure?" said the uncle, laughing.

"Oh, well, sometimes I'm *absolutely* sure, like about Daffodil," said the boy; "and sometimes I have an idea; and sometimes I haven't even an idea, have I, Bassett? Then we're careful, because we mostly go down."

"You do, do you! And when you're sure, like about Daffodil, what makes you sure, sonny?"

"Oh, well, I don't know," said the boy uneasily. "I'm sure, you know, uncle; that's all."

"It's as if he had it from heaven, sir," Bassett reiterated.

"I should say so!" said the uncle.

But he became a partner. And when the Leger was coming on, Paul was "sure" about Lively Spark, which was a quite inconsiderable horse. The boy insisted on putting a thousand on the horse, Bassett went for five hundred, and Oscar Cresswell two hundred. Lively Spark came in first, and the betting had been ten to one against him. Paul had made ten thousand.

"You see," he said, "I was absolutely sure of him."

Even Oscar Cresswell had cleared two thousand.

"Look here, son," he said, "this sort of thing makes me nervous."

"It needn't, uncle! Perhaps I shan't be sure again for a long time."

"But what are you going to do with your money?" asked the uncle.

"Of course," said the boy, "I started it for mother. She said she had no luck, because father is unlucky, so I thought if *I* was lucky, it might stop whispering."

"What might stop whispering?"

"Our house. I *hate* our house for whispering."

"What does it whisper?"

"Why—why"—the boy fidgeted—"why, I don't know. But it's always short of money, you know, uncle."

"I know it, son, I know it."

"You know people send mother writs, don't you, uncle?"

"I'm afraid I do," said the uncle.

"And then the house whispers, like people laughing at you behind your back. It's awful, that is! I thought if I was lucky . . ."

"You might stop it," added the uncle.

The boy watched him with big blue eyes, that had an uncanny cold fire in them, and he said never a word.

"Well, then!" said the uncle. "What are we doing?"

"I shouldn't like mother to know I was lucky," said the boy.

"Why not, son?"

"She'd stop me."

"I don't think she would."

"Oh!"—and the boy writhed in an odd way—"I *don't* want her to know, uncle."

"All right, son! We'll manage it without her knowing."

They managed it very easily. Paul, at the other's suggestion, handed over five thousand pounds to his uncle, who deposited it with the family lawyer, who was then to inform Paul's mother that a relative had put five thousand pounds into his hands, which sum was to be paid out a thousand pounds at a time, on the mother's birthday, for the next five years.

"So she'll have a birthday present of a thousand pounds for five successive years," said Uncle Oscar. "I hope it won't make it all the harder for her later."

Paul's mother had her birthday in November. The house had been "whispering" worse than ever lately, and, even in spite of his luck, Paul could not bear up against it. He was very anxious to see the effect of the birthday letter, telling his mother about the thousand pounds.

When there were no visitors, Paul now took his meals with his parents, as he was beyond the nursery control. His mother went into town nearly every day. She had discovered that she had an odd knack of sketching furs and dress materials, so she worked secretly in the studio of a friend who was the chief "artist" for the leading drapers. She drew the figures of ladies in furs and ladies in silk and sequins for the newspaper advertisements. This young woman artist earned several thousand pounds a year, but Paul's mother only made several hundreds, and she was again dissatisfied. She so wanted to be first in something, and she did not succeed, even in making sketches for drapery advertisements.

She was down to breakfast on the morning of her birthday. Paul watched her face as she read her letters. He knew the lawyer's letter. As his mother read it, her face hardened and became more expressionless. Then a cold, determined look came on her mouth. She hid the letter under the pile of others, and said not a word about it.

"Didn't you have anything nice in the post for your birthday, mother?" said Paul.

"Quite moderately nice," she said, her voice cold and absent.

She went away to town without saying more.

But in the afternoon Uncle Oscar appeared. He said Paul's mother had had a long interview with the lawyer, asking if the whole five thousand could not be advanced at once, as she was in debt.

"What do you think, uncle?" said the boy.

"I leave it to you, son."

"Oh, let her have it, then! We can get some more with the other," said the boy.

"A bird in the hand is worth two in the bush, laddie!" said Uncle Oscar.

"But I'm sure to *know* for the Grand National; or the Lincolnshire; or else the Derby.[7] I'm sure to know for *one* of them," said Paul.

---

7. DERBY: the most famous horse race in England, at Epsom Downs. Comparable in importance in the United States is the Kentucky Derby, named after the English race.

So Uncle Oscar signed the agreement, and Paul's mother touched the whole five thousand. Then something very curious happened. The voices in the house suddenly went mad, like a chorus of frogs on a spring evening. There were certain new furnishings, and Paul had a tutor. He was *really* going to Eton, his father's school, in the following autumn. There were flowers in the winter, and a blossoming of the luxury Paul's mother had been used to. And yet the voices in the house, behind the sprays of mimosa and almond blossom, and from under the piles of iridescent cushions, simply trilled and screamed in a sort of ecstasy: "There *must* be more money! Oh-h-h; there *must* be more money. Oh, now, now-w! Now-w-w—there *must* be more money!—more than ever! More than ever!"

It frightened Paul terribly. He studied away at his Latin and Greek with his tutors. But his intense hours were spent with Bassett. The Grand National had gone by: he had not "known," and had lost a hundred pounds. Summer was at hand. He was in agony for the Lincoln. But even for the Lincoln he didn't "know," and he lost fifty pounds. He became wild-eyed and strange, as if something were going to explode in him.

"Let it alone, son! Don't you bother about it!" urged Uncle Oscar. But it was as if the boy couldn't really hear what his uncle was saying.

"I've got to know for the Derby! I've got to know for the Derby!" the child reiterated, his big blue eyes blazing with a sort of madness.

His mother noticed how overwrought he was.

"You'd better go to the seaside. Wouldn't you like to go now to the seaside, instead of waiting? I think you'd better," she said, looking down at him anxiously, her heart curiously heavy because of him.

But the child lifted his uncanny blue eyes.

"I couldn't possibly go before the Derby, mother!" he said. "I couldn't possibly!"

"Why not?" she said, her voice becoming heavy when she was opposed. "Why not? You can still go from the seaside to see the Derby with your Uncle Oscar, if that's what you wish. No need for you to wait here. Besides, I think you care too much about these races. It's a bad sign. My family has been a gambling family, and you won't know till you grow up how much damage it has done. But it has done damage. I shall have to send Bassett away, and ask Uncle Oscar not to talk racing to you, unless you promise to be reasonable about it; go away to the seaside and forget it. You're all nerves!"

"I'll do what you like, mother, so long as you don't send me away till after the Derby," the boy said.

"Send you away from where? Just from this house?"

"Yes," he said, gazing at her.

"Why, you curious child, what makes you care about this house so much, suddenly? I never knew you loved it."

He gazed at her without speaking. He had a secret within a secret, something he had not divulged, even to Bassett or to his Uncle Oscar.

But his mother, after standing undecided and a little bit sullen for some moments, said:

"Very well, then! Don't go to the seaside till after the Derby, if you don't wish it. But promise me you won't let your nerves go to pieces. Promise you won't think so much about horse-racing and events, as you call them!"

"Oh, no," said the boy casually. "I won't think much about them, mother. You needn't worry. I wouldn't worry, mother, if I were you."

"If you were me and I were you," said his mother, "I wonder what we *should* do!"

"But you know you needn't worry, mother, don't you?" the boy repeated.

"I should be awfully glad to know it," she said wearily.

"Oh, well, you *can,* you know. I mean, you *ought* to know you needn't worry," he insisted.

"Ought I? Then I'll see about it," she said.

Paul's secret of secrets was his wooden horse, that which had no name. Since he was emancipated from a nurse and a nursery-governess, he had had his rocking-horse removed to his own bedroom at the top of the house.

"Surely, you're too big for a rocking-horse!" his mother had remonstrated.

"Well, you see, mother, till I can have a *real* horse, I like to have *some* sort of animal about," had been his quaint answer.

"Do you feel he keeps you company?" she laughed.

"Oh, yes! He's very good, he always keeps me company, when I'm there," said Paul.

So the horse, rather shabby, stood in an arrested prance in the boy's bedroom.

The Derby was drawing near, and the boy grew more and more tense. He hardly heard what was spoken to him, he was very frail, and his eyes were really uncanny. His mother had sudden strange seizures of uneasiness about him. Sometimes, for half-an-hour, she would feel a sudden anxiety about him that was almost anguish. She wanted to rush to him at once, and know he was safe.

Two nights before the Derby, she was at a big party in town, when one of her rushes of anxiety about her boy, her first-born, gripped her heart till she could hardly speak. She fought with the feeling, might and main, for she believed in common sense. But it was too strong. She had to leave the dance and go downstairs to telephone to the country. The children's nursery-governess was terribly surprised and startled at being rung up in the night.

"Are the children all right, Miss Wilmot?"

"Oh, yes, they are quite all right."

"Master Paul? Is he all right?"

"He went to bed as right as a trivet. Shall I run up and look at him?"

"No," said Paul's mother reluctantly. "No! Don't trouble. It's all right. Don't sit up. We shall be home fairly soon." She did not want her son's privacy intruded upon.

"Very good," said the governess.

It was about one o'clock when Paul's mother and father drove up to their house. All was still. Paul's mother went to her room and slipped off her white fur cloak. She had told her maid not to wait up for her. She heard her husband downstairs, mixing a whisky-and-soda.

And then, because of the strange anxiety at her heart, she stole upstairs to her son's room. Noiselessly she went along the upper corridor. Was there a faint noise? What was it?

She stood, with arrested muscles, outside his door, listening. There was a strange, heavy, and yet not loud noise. Her heart stood still. It was a soundless noise, yet rushing and powerful. Something huge, in violent, hushed motion. What was it? What in God's name was it? She ought to know. She felt that she knew the noise. She knew what it was.

Yet she could not place it. She couldn't say what it was. And on and on it went, like a madness.

Softly, frozen with anxiety and fear, she turned the door-handle.

The room was dark. Yet in the space near the window, she heard and saw something plunging to and fro. She gazed in fear and amazement.

Then suddenly she switched on the light, and saw her son, in his green pajamas, madly surging on the rocking-horse. The blaze of light suddenly lit him up, as he urged the wooden horse, and lit her up, as she stood, blonde, in her dress of pale green and crystal, in the doorway.

"Paul!" she cried. "Whatever are you doing?"

"It's Malabar!" he screamed, in a powerful, strange voice. "It's Malabar!"

His eyes blazed at her for one strange and senseless second, as he ceased urging his wooden horse. Then he fell with a crash to the ground, and she, all her tormented motherhood flooding upon her, rushed to gather him up.

But he was unconscious, and unconscious he remained, with some brain-fever. He talked and tossed, and his mother sat stonily by his side.

"Malabar! It's Malabar! Bassett, Bassett, I *know!* It's Malabar!"

So the child cried, trying to get up and urge the rocking-horse that gave him his inspiration.

"What does he mean by Malabar?" asked the heart-broken mother.

"I don't know," said the father stonily.

"What does he mean by Malabar?" she asked her brother Oscar.

"It's one of the horses running for the Derby," was the answer.

And, in spite of himself, Oscar Cresswell spoke to Bassett, and himself put a thousand on Malabar: at fourteen to one.

The third day of the illness was critical: they were waiting for a change. The boy, with his rather long, curly hair, was tossing ceaselessly on the pillow. He neither slept nor regained consciousness, and his eyes were like blue stones. His mother sat, feeling her heart had gone, turned actually into a stone.

In the evening, Oscar Cresswell did not come, but Bassett sent a message, saying could he come up for one moment, just one moment? Paul's mother was very angry at the intrusion, but on second thought she agreed. The boy was the same. Perhaps Bassett might bring him to consciousness.

The gardener, a shortish fellow with a little brown moustache, and sharp little brown eyes, tip-toed into the room, touched his imaginary cap to Paul's mother, and stole to the bedside, staring with glittering, smallish eyes, at the tossing, dying child.

"Master Paul!" he whispered. "Master Paul! Malabar came in first all right, a clean win. I did as you told me. You've made over seventy thousand pounds, you have; you've got over eighty thousand. Malabar came in all right, Master Paul."

"Malabar! Malabar! Did I say Malabar, mother? Did I say Malabar? Do you think

I'm lucky, mother? I knew Malabar, didn't I? Over eighty thousand pounds! I call that lucky, don't you, mother? Over eighty thousand pounds! I knew, didn't I know I knew! Malabar came in all right. If I ride my horse till I'm sure, then I tell you, Bassett, you can go as high as you like. Did you go for all you were worth, Bassett?"

"I went a thousand on it, Master Paul."

"I never told you, mother, that if I can ride my horse, and *get there,* then I'm ab-solutely sure—oh, absolutely! Mother, did I ever tell you? I *am* lucky!"

"No, you never did," said the mother.

But the boy died in the night.

And even as he lay dead, his mother heard her brother's voice saying to her: "My God, Hester, you're eighty-odd thousand to the good, and a poor devil of a son to the bad. But, poor devil, poor devil, he's best gone out of a life where he rides his rocking-horse to find a winner."

I

1. How does Lawrence introduce the non-realistic world in which Paul *rides his rocking-horse to find a winner?* Consider the following: the opening sentence of paragraph 5; the first reference to the rocking-horse; the *whispers* that the children hear; the comments about the other toys besides the rocking-horse.

2. Why does Paul want to be *lucky?* How does Lawrence unfold the boy's gradual estrangement from the "real" world? What attitude toward him does the older of his sisters have? the nurse? his mother? We get only occasional glimpses of his father. Why? What is Uncle Oscar's attitude? Finally, what does Bassett's relationship to Paul tell us? Why does Lawrence use religious terms to describe his relationship?

3. In connection with the second question of number 2, note the number of different references to Paul's "blue eyes." How do the phrases underscore what is happening to him? What is the significance of the last reference to his eyes?

4. What kind of person is the mother? Point out details that give insight into her character. Why does she feel *the center of her heart go hard* when she is with her children? Why does she call home from the party to ask about Paul? In what sense is she *lucky* and yet blind to the fact?

5. What are the *whispers* in the house? Why do they increase in intensity as the story pro-gresses? After what occurrence are they loudest? Why? How are the *whispers* related to the increasing *frenzy* of Paul's riding?

6. Dramatic irony plays an important part in the story. Note the nurse's comment, "You'll break your horse, Paul!" and her reply to the mother's phone call, "He went to bed as right as a trivet." Also note the mother's comment, "Aren't you growing too big for a rocking-horse? You're not a little boy any longer, you know." Point out why these are ironic comments. Find other examples of dramatic irony.

7. As Paul puts it, he can *get there* on his rocking-horse. What is meant by the phrase? Is he doomed because he sought *luck* or because he used the power he found to satisfy greed? If the rocking-horse is the means of getting *there,* what can it be said to symbolize?

II

1. In an essay discuss what you think the theme of the story is, considering the following questions: Why does Paul try to satisfy his mother's desire for money when he knows as well as she does about the *hard little place* at *the center of her heart?* Why does she go to his room on returning from the party? Is Uncle Oscar's final comment that Paul is "best gone out of a life where he rides his rocking-horse to find a winner" simply the insensitive reaction of a calloused man? Why does Lawrence take the suggestions of the Faust theme and apply them to a small boy riding a rocking-horse? What does it really mean to be "lucky"?

DULCE ET DECORUM EST [*1920*]

Wilfred Owen

Since the time of the *Iliad* the patriotic fervor that sends men into battle singing of its glory has gone hand in hand with revulsion at the horror war brings. The paradox was strikingly put by Robert E. Lee: "It is well that war is so terrible—we should grow too fond of it."

To Wilfred Owen, a young Englishman killed in action a week before the Armistice of 1918 after two long periods of front line action, there was no paradox. War was of the devil, and any suggestion of glory or honor was a product of blind and inhuman ignorance.

> Bent double, like old beggars under sacks,
> Knock-kneed, coughing like hags, we cursed through sludge,
> Till on the haunting flares we turned our backs,
> And towards our distant rest began to trudge.
> Men marched asleep. Many had lost their boots,   5
> But limped on, blood-shod. All went lame, all blind;
> Drunk with fatigue; deaf even to the hoots
> Of gas shells dropping softly behind.
>
> Gas! Gas! Quick, boys!—An ecstasy of fumbling,
> Fitting the clumsy helmets just in time,   10
> But someone still was yelling out and stumbling
> And flound'ring like a man in fire or lime.
> Dim through the misty panes and thick green light,
> As under a green sea, I saw him drowning.
>
> In all my dreams before my helpless sight   15
> He plunges at me, guttering, choking, drowning.
> If in some smothering dreams, you too could pace
> Behind the wagon that we flung him in,
> And watch the white eyes wilting in his face,
> His hanging face, like a devil's sick of sin,   20
> If you could hear, at every jolt, the blood
> Come gargling from the froth-corrupted lungs
> Bitten as the cud
> Of vile, incurable sores on innocent tongues,—
> My friend, you would not tell with such high zest   25
> To children ardent for some desperate glory,
> The old lie: Dulce et decorum est
> Pro patria mori.

27-28. DULCE . . . MORI: "Sweet and fitting it is to die for one's country"—a famous sentiment from Horace's *Odes* (III, ii, 13).

I

1. Note the painstaking attention to detail and the striking choice of metaphor. Explain the following comparisons in the first stanza: "like old beggars under sacks" (1), "haunting flares" (3), "blood-shod" (6), "Drunk with fatigue" (7), "hoots/Of gas shells dropping softly behind" (7-8). Point out other examples in the rest of the poem that bring the reader close to the scene.

2. What were the soldiers doing when the gas-shells exploded nearby? Why is this significant?

3. From line 19 on, the dying man is described as if he were passing from a human being into an animal-like creature. First the *white eyes* wilt in his face, then he becomes like a non-human devil *sick of sin,* then like what? What is the metaphor in lines 21-24? What is a "cud"? Why does the blood come *gargling* from the lungs, and what are "vile, incurable sores on innocent tongues"?

4. What differences are there in sentence length between stanza 1 and stanza 3? How does sentence structure match sense in each stanza?

5. Why does he use only half of the quotation in the title?

6. It has been said by some that in his own revulsion at the suffering described, Owen allows the speaker of the poem to become melodramatic—too emotional to be effective. Do you think this is true? Give evidence pro or con.

II

1. Owen's response to the quotation from Horace shows how "sweet and fitting" he thought violent death in war was. In an imaginary letter-to-the-editor express his (or your) reaction to the use of the word *humane* in the following headline from the front page of the *New York Herald Tribune* on Sunday, August 28, 1960:
GAS, GERM WAR MORE HUMANE THAN A-WAR, U. S. ARMY WANTS IT KNOWN
Utah Forum Learns of Advances in Field

AN IRISH AIRMAN FORESEES HIS DEATH   [*1919*]

William Butler Yeats

None of the shocking detail through which Owen leads us in the preceding poem appears in Yeats's "An Irish Airman Foresees His Death." And yet in its subdued, indifferent tone it as powerfully rejects "The old lie: Dulce et decorum est/Pro patria mori."

The poem deals with the thoughts of an Irish aviator during World War I. Although a good many Irish volunteers fought in the English armed forces during that war, the centuries of Irish resentment and bitterness over British domination of Ireland left most Irishmen with no love whatsoever for their British oppressors and a kind of smoldering disgust at their own inadequacy to change matters.

I know that I shall meet my fate
Somewhere among the clouds above;
Those that I fight I do not hate,
Those that I guard I do not love;
My country is Kiltartan Cross,   5

My countrymen Kiltartan's poor,
No likely end could bring them loss
Or leave them happier than before.
Nor law, nor duty bade me fight,
Nor public men, nor cheering crowds,   10
A lonely impulse of delight
Drove to this tumult in the clouds;
I balanced all, brought all to mind,
The years to come seemed waste of breath
A waste of breath the years behind   15
In balance with this life, this death.

I

1. What is the situation from which the Irish airman speaks? Who are "those" in line 3? Who are "those" in line 4? What usual reason for fighting is rejected in lines 3-4? in lines 5-8? in lines 9-10? How does the state of affairs described in line 6 account for the state of affairs described in line 4? May it also account for the state of affairs described in line 3? Why?

2. Why is "Drove" (12) a particularly appropriate word? Why is "tumult" (12)? What is "A lonely impulse of delight"? Why is "delight" ironic? What is the meaning of "balanced" in line 13? of "balance" in line 16?

3. What is the speaker's attitude toward life and death? What has war got to do with his attitude? What are the implications of the word *foresees* in the title?

4. What factors was the speaker weighing when he *balanced all?*

5. How is the idea of "balance" as a cancellation or negation supported by the grammatical structure of the poem?

SEPTEMBER 1, 1939   [*1940*]

W. H. Auden

In Hardy's "Channel Firing," which the poet wrote in April, 1914, on the eve of World War I, we saw a consciously detached, somewhat resigned, comment on man's persistent pursuit of evil ways, as exemplified in preparations for war aboard ships in the English Channel.

W. H. Auden chooses the date of the opening of World War II, Hitler's invasion of Poland on September 1, 1939, as the title of his commentary on man's pursuit of the same evil. Like Hardy, he ties the present wrongs to those of the past and gives timelessness to his indictment of a "low, dishonest decade," the 1930's. But his tone is very different from Hardy's. The poem is in a sense a civilian counterpart to Wilfred Owen's searing picture of war on the front lines;

here is war's face on the home front of a nation not yet in actual war, viewed from "one of the dives/On Fifty-Second Street" in New York City. The blind, inhuman ignorance that Owen's poem deplores is evident here too, but it is coupled with an expression of the need for compassion that Owen only suggested.

I sit in one of the dives
On Fifty-Second Street
Uncertain and afraid
As the clever hopes expire
Of a low dishonest decade: 5
Waves of anger and fear
Circulate over the bright
And darkened lands of the earth,
Obsessing our private lives;
The unmentionable odor of death   10
Offends the September night.

Accurate scholarship can
Unearth the whole offense
From Luther until now
That has driven a culture mad,   15
Find what occurred at Linz,
What huge imago made
A psychopathic god:
I and the public know
What all schoolchildren learn,   20

Those to whom evil is done
Do evil in return.

Exiled Thucydides knew
All that a speech can say
About Democracy,   25
And what dictators do,
The elderly rubbish they talk
To an apathetic grave;
Analyzed all in his book,
The enlightenment driven away,   30
The habit-forming pain,
Mismanagement and grief:
We must suffer them all again.

Into this neutral air
Where blind skyscrapers use   35
Their full height to proclaim
The strength of Collective Man,
Each language pours its vain
Competitive excuse:
But who can live for long   40
In an euphoric dream;
Out of the mirror they stare,
Imperialism's face
And the international wrong.

2. FIFTY-SECOND STREET: in New York City, famous for its numerous small night clubs featuring jazz.
5. LOW DISHONEST DECADE: Auden probably refers (among other things) to the expedients by which nations rationalized Hitler's activities and argued themselves into not opposing him.
14. LUTHER: Martin Luther, a sixteenth century German Protestant reformer, whose emphasis on individualism is here regarded as an earlier symptom of the same will to separateness that the poem deplores.
15. CULTURE: i.e., Germany.
16. LINZ: an Austrian town where Hitler spent his youth.
17. IMAGO: i.e., dominant image (see note, line 14).

21-22. THOSE . . . RETURN: i.e., evil was done by Germany to France after the Franco-Prussian War of 1871; and evil was done to Germany by the Allies in revenge after World War I, its economy milked to pay reparations. Now Hitler's Germany is returning the evil.
23. THUCYDIDES: Greek historian of fifth century B.C. Athens. His detailed account of the Athens-Sparta war contained many partially fictitious speeches of various leaders. The reference here is to a famous funeral oration by Pericles, a great Athenian statesman, which played on the patriotic zeal of the Athenians and called for more sacrifices.

Faces along the bar 45
Cling to their average day:
The lights must never go out,
The music must always play,
All the conventions conspire
To make this fort assume 50
The furniture of home;
Lest we should see where we are,
Lost in a haunted wood,
Children afraid of the night
Who have never been happy or good. 55

The windiest militant trash
Important Persons shout
Is not so crude as our wish:
What mad Nijinsky wrote
About Diaghilev 60
Is true of the normal heart;
For the error bred in the bone
Of each woman and each man
Craves what it cannot have,
Not universal love 65
But to be loved alone.

From the conservative dark
Into the ethical life
The dense commuters come,
Repeating their morning vow; 70

"I *will* be true to the wife,
I'll concentrate more on my work,"
And helpless governors wake
To resume their compulsory game:
Who can release them now, 75
Who can reach the deaf,
Who can speak for the dumb?

All I have is a voice
To undo the folded lie,
The romantic lie in the brain 80
Of the sensual man-in-the-street
And the lie of Authority
Whose buildings grope the sky:
There is no such thing as the State
And no one exists alone; 85
Hunger allows no choice
To the citizen or the police;
We must love one another or die.

Defenseless under the night
Our world in stupor lies; 90
Yet, dotted everywhere,
Ironic points of light
Flash out wherever the Just
Exchange their messages:
May I, composed like them 95
Of Eros and of dust,
Beleaguered by the same
Negation and despair,
Show an affirming flame.

59. NIJINSKY: Vaslav Nijinsky, famous Russian ballet dancer, who went insane at the age of 29.
60. DIAGHILEV: Sergei Diaghilev, founder of the world-famous Russian Ballet. Nijinsky was one of his star performers. According to Nijinsky and his wife, Diaghilev was notoriously self-centered and jealous and tried to ruin Nijinsky's career when he found he couldn't dominate the dancer's life.

73. GOVERNORS: leaders.
80. ROMANTIC LIE: i.e., that a man *can* exist alone (cf. 85).
82. LIE OF AUTHORITY: i.e., that there *is* such a thing as *the State* (cf. 84).
96. EROS: the god of sexual and romantic love.

I

1. What is the speaker's situation? What are the connotations of "clever" (4)? What is causing the "Waves of anger and fear" (6)? What are the "bright" lands (7)? the "darkened" lands (8)? Why is the "odor of death" there and why is it "unmentionable" (10)? What are the connotations of "Offends" (11)?

Who are in the bar with the speaker? What bearing does their presence have on the meditations that come to his mind? (If you can't answer this final question, come back to it when you have dealt with all the rest.)
2. Why may the "culture" the speaker is talking about in line 15 be regarded as in fact *mad?* Who or what is the "psychopathic god"?

How does the speaker indicate that the explanation in lines 12-18 calls for book-learning? How does he indicate that the explanation in lines 19-22 calls only for common sense?

3. What is the purpose of going back in stanza 3 to the Greeks? What did they discover that in 1939 the world is about to discover again? Why "elderly rubbish" (27)? And why an "apathetic grave" (28)? What does "enlightenment" (30) refer to? What implications are there in calling pain "habit-forming" (31)?

4. In stanza 4, with its skyscrapers and many tongues, there is a quiet allusion to the story of Babel in Genesis 11:1-9. Read the story and show how the poem gains by alluding to it.

5. Looking into the mirror back of the bar (42 ff.), the speaker naturally sees his own face and those of the others gathered there. Why does he call this view "Imperialism's face"? Why is it significant that he sees the faces in the mirror and not by looking directly up or down the bar? Stanza 5 indicates that the others looking into that mirror do not see what he sees. What do *they* see? What do they fail to see?

6. Stanza 6 indicates *why* they do not see what he sees. State the reason in your own words. Why does the speaker say that "our wish" is more "crude" than the "windiest militant trash" (56-58)?

7. How does stanza 7 form a bridge between the first six stanzas and the last two? What are the implications of "dense" (69)? What is the nature of the "morning vow" the commuters make? Why does the speaker call the governors' work a "compulsory game" (74)?

8. What are the "points of light" (92) and why does the speaker refer to them as "Ironic"? Who are "the Just" (93)? Put in your own words what he means by "an affirming flame" (99).

II

1. In one later edition of the poem Auden eliminated stanza 8; in another he changed line 88 to read "We must love one another *and* die." Comment on the effect of these changes on the meaning of the poem.

2. In a sense, this is a poem about war but far different from either "Dulce et Decorum Est" or "An Irish Airman Foresees His Death," in that the poet chooses to comment on the civilians of a nation not directly involved in fighting. In an essay discuss how this poem differs from the preceding two in what it has to say about man's involvement in war and about the conditions which bring on wars.

THE HOLLOW MEN   *[1925]*

T. S. Eliot

In "September 1, 1939" Auden speaks of modern man as:

> Children afraid of the night
> Lost in a haunted wood,
> Who have never been happy or good.

and calls for "an affirming flame" to light the dark corners of the heart and bring "universal love."

Not many years earlier, T. S. Eliot in "The Hollow Men" took an even darker view of the condition of man in the modern world. If in Auden's poem evil expresses itself as the absence of love, in Eliot's poem it expresses itself as the absence of any profound capacity for action, thought, or feeling—the absence of all positives, including even those positive convictions and passions that can give to some forms of evil an heroic grandeur.

"We are the hollow men," the poem begins, "We are the stuffed men"—and as the reader asks to whom "we" refers, he begins to sense uneasily that the finger is pointing at him.

Mistah Kurtz—he dead.

A penny for the Old Guy

I

We are the hollow men
We are the stuffed men
Leaning together
Headpiece filled with straw. Alas!
Our dried voices, when   5
We whisper together
Are quiet and meaningless
As wind in dry grass
Or rats' feet over broken glass
In our dry cellar   10

Shape without form, shade without color,
Paralyzed force, gesture without motion;

Those who have crossed
With direct eyes, to death's other Kingdom
Remember us—if at all—not as lost   15
Violent souls, but only
As the hollow men
The stuffed men.

II

Eyes I dare not meet in dreams
In death's dream kingdom   20

13-14. THOSE . . . KINGDOM: i.e., those who at least did something, in this case evil, and have crossed into Hell.

19. EYES: In Dante's *Purgatorio*, Beatrice's eyes symbolize the reality that calls into account frailty and cowardice; no such accounting occurs where the hollow men are.

20. DEATH'S DREAM KINGDOM: the "Limbo" of the hollow men, where moral necessities can be ignored.

These do not appear:
There, the eyes are
Sunlight on a broken column
There, is a tree swinging
And voices are   25
In the wind's singing
More distant and more solemn
Than a fading star.

Let me be no nearer
In death's dream kingdom   30
Let me also wear
Such deliberate disguises
Rat's coat, crowskin, crossed staves
In a field
Behaving as the wind behaves   35
No nearer—

Not that final meeting
In the twilight kingdom

III

This is the dead land
This is cactus land   40
Here the stone images
Are raised, here they receive
The supplication of a dead man's hand
Under the twinkle of a fading star.

Is it like this   45
In death's other kingdom
Waking alone
At the hour when we are
Trembling with tenderness
Lips that would kiss   50
Form prayers to broken stone.

33-35. CROSSED . . . BEHAVES: scarecrows.
37-38. NOT . . . KINGDOM: see note, line 19; i.e., with the searching eyes of spiritual reality.

IV

The eyes are not here
There are no eyes here
In this valley of dying stars
In this hollow valley   55
This broken jaw of our lost kingdoms

In this last of meeting places
We grope together
And avoid speech
Gathered on this beach of the tumid river   60

Sightless, unless
The eyes reappear
As the perpetual star
Multifoliate rose
Of death's twilight kingdom   65
The hope only
Of empty men.

V

Here we go round the prickly pear
Prickly pear prickly pear
Here we go round the prickly pear   70
At five o'clock in the morning.

---

60. TUMID RIVER: the river Acheron; see *Inferno,*
     III, at the end of the poem; those "whose lives
     concluded neither blame nor praise" cannot
     cross Acheron into Hell.
64. MULTIFOLIATE ROSE: reference is to Dante's
     Paradiso, XXX, 116—"how vast is the spread
     of this rose in its outermost leaves." The rose
     is traditionally Christ's emblem (and the Vir-
     gin's).
68-71. Reference here and in lines 95-97 is to
     the nursery rhyme "Here we go round the mul-
     berry bush" (see the cactus land, lines 39 ff.).

Between the idea
And the reality
Between the motion
And the act   75
Falls the Shadow
          For Thine is the Kingdom

Between the conception
And the creation
Between the emotion   80
And the response
Falls the Shadow
          Life is very long

Between the desire
And the spasm   85
Between the potency
And the existence
Between the essence
And the descent
Falls the Shadow   90
          For Thine is the Kingdom

For Thine is
Life is
For Thine is the

This is the way the world ends   95
This is the way the world ends
This is the way the world ends
Not with a bang but a whimper.

74-75. See *Julius Caesar,* II, i, 63-65:
     "Between the acting of a dreadful thing
     And the first motion, all the interim is
     Like a phantasma or a hideous dream."
98. BANG: reference to Guy Fawkes's plans to
     blow up the Houses of Parliament, a positive, if
     evil, act.

If we are to understand what Eliot is saying about us (and himself) we must understand first of all the two epigraphs and the allusion to Canto III of Dante's *Inferno.* The first epigraph refers to a character in Joseph Conrad's story, "The Heart of Darkness." Mr. Kurtz, an ivory trader in the Belgian Congo, was an idealist who had turned barbarian in the savage jungles of the "heart of dark- ness." The narrator of the story, Marlow, is the captain of a river steamer that picks up Kurtz just before he dies. He says that Kurtz was "hollow at the core," —lustful, murderous, paranoic—but that he had "pronounced a judgment upon the adventures of his soul on this earth"—his last words had been "The horror!

The horror!" Marlow himself almost dies on the steamer trip out of the "heart of darkness" and has this to say about Kurtz—and about life and death:

> "Droll thing life is—that mysterious arrangement of merciless logic for a futile purpose. . . . I have wrestled with death. It is the most unexciting contest you can imagine. . . . I was within a hair's-breadth of the last opportunity for pronouncement, and I found with humiliation that probably I would have nothing to say. This is the reason why I affirm that Kurtz was a remarkable man. He had something to say. He said it. . . . He had summed up—he had judged. 'The horror!' . . . After all, this was the expression of some sort of belief; it had candor, it had conviction, it had a vibrating note of revolt in its whisper, it had the appalling face of a glimpsed truth—the strange commingling of desire and hate . . . . perhaps all the wisdom, and all truth, and all sincerity, are just compressed into that inappreciable moment of time in which we step over the threshold of the invisible. Perhaps! I like to think my summing-up would not have been a word of careless contempt. Better his cry—much better. It was an affirmation, a moral victory paid for by innumerable defeats, by abominable terrors, by abominable satisfactions. But it was a victory!"

Kurtz's death is announced by the cabin boy "in a tone of scathing contempt": "Mistah Kurtz—he dead." Eliot puts his "hollow men" in opposition to Mr. Kurtz, one of the "lost/ Violent souls" who "have crossed/ With direct eyes to death's other Kingdom." Kurtz was "violent" and "lost," but he was at least once alive and saw himself and his world clearly.

The second epigraph serves somewhat the same purpose. The phrase, "A penny for the Old Guy," is used in England by children on Guy Fawkes Day, November 5, to get money for fireworks. Guy Fawkes was one of a group of English Catholics who plotted to blow up the Houses of Parliament on November 5, 1605, when James I was to be present at the opening proceedings. The plot was discovered and Fawkes and his fellow conspirators were hanged. On November 5 English children make scarecrow-like effigies of Guy Fawkes which they parade through the streets before hanging and burning them. Obviously, Guy Fawkes was, like Kurtz, a *lost violent soul.*

One other major allusion should be explained before we look at the sections of the poem separately. There are a number of allusions to Dante's *Divine Comedy,* but the most important one for our purposes is that to Canto III of the "Inferno." Here, "neither in Hell nor out of it," dwell what John Ciardi calls in his translation, the Opportunists, "those souls who in life were neither for good nor evil but only for themselves." Lines 19-48 give a vivid picture of the Opportunists' fate.

> So saying, he put forth his hand to me,
>   and with a gentle and encouraging smile
>   he led me through the gate of mystery.
>
> Here sighs and cries and wails coiled and recoiled
>   on the starless air, spilling my soul to tears.   5
>   A confusion of tongues and monstrous accents toiled

---

1. HE: the shade of Virgil, the great Roman poet, who conducts Dante on his tour of Hell.

in pain and anger. Voices hoarse and shrill
and sounds of blows, all intermingled, raised
tumult and pandemonium that still

whirls on the air forever dirty with it   10
as if a whirlwind sucked at sand. And I,
holding my head in horror, cried: "Sweet Spirit,

what souls are these who run through this black haze?"
And he to me: "These are the nearly soulless
whose lives concluded neither blame nor praise.   15

They are mixed here with that despicable corps
of angels who were neither for God nor Satan,
but only for themselves. The High Creator

scourged them from Heaven for its perfect beauty,
and Hell will not receive them since the wicked   20
might feel some glory over them." And I:

"Master, what gnaws at them so hideously
their lamentation stuns the very air?"
"They have no hope of death," he answered me,

"and in their blind and unattaining state   25
their miserable lives have sunk so low
that they must envy every other fate.

No word of them survives their living season.
Mercy and Justice deny them even a name.
Let us not speak of them: look, and pass on."*   30

17. WHO . . . SATAN: i.e., who did not take sides   * Copyright 1954 by John Ciardi. Published by
in the rebellion against God led by Satan.   permission of the author.

I

1. What are the *hollow men* doing in the first ten lines? How do lines 11 and 12 help to define the hollow men? Who are the inhabitants of "death's other Kingdom" (14)? Why can't the hollow men get there?

2. Why is the kingdom of death to which the hollow men go called a "dream kingdom" (20) or a "twilight kingdom" (38)? What sort of place is it? Consider Parts II, III, and IV. How does its character reflect the character of the hollow men? What does the speaker seem most to fear? Why? Consider in particular lines 19, 29, 36, 37.

3. In stanza 3 we learn that the hollow men have not only fear but also longing. To what powers do they turn in hope of satisfaction? How effectively is their hope answered? What is the meaning of lines 47-51? What do the lips want to do, and what do they do?

4. Contrast the attitude expressed toward the eyes in Part IV with that in Part II. Contrast the "star" of line 63 with those alluded to earlier. At the end of Part IV the speaker says that the hollow men will remain "Sightless, unless/ The eyes reappear/ As the perpetual star/ Multifoliate rose/ Of death's twilight kingdom." What do lines 66-67 suggest about the possibility of such reappearance? Note the position of "only": what two opposing meanings are possible? which one is applicable here? what is significant about the ambiguity?

5. The hollow men remain in the *cactus*

land in Part V and dance childishly around the "prickly pear/At five o'clock in the morning." In what sense is this simply another way of putting what they do in lines 41-42? How is the children's chant in lines 68-71 changed? Why? What does the line "For Thine is the Kingdom" refer to and how is it contrasted with "Life is very long"? The *shadow* that *falls between* is probably fear or the inability to act: how does "shadow" sum up the entire world of the hollow men as pictured throughout the poem? How do lines 92-94 dramatize, or act out grammatically, the condition of the hollow men? Line 95 echoes another verse of the nursery rhyme, "This is the way we go to church"; how is it changed? Why? Whose world is ending? What contrast is presented in the last line?

6. What is Eliot saying about evil? In what sense can it be better to be *lost violent souls* who perform evil acts and know it, like Kurtz and Guy Fawkes, than to be one of the hollow men? How can evil be preferable to anything? What suggestions are there that hollowness and violence are not the only ways open to men? Note particularly lines 61-65. Why is the emphasis in the poem on either hollowness or violence?

II

1. What makes men *hollow*? What conditions of modern life bring about the *shadow* of fear and inaction? What might be the *stone images* of our time and how may modern society be described as a *cactus land*? Include in your discussion a consideration of how much Eliot's world of hollow men is rooted in the absence of religion in the modern world.

2. *a.* Work out all the ways in which the allusions to Kurtz, Guy Fawkes, and the Opportunists of the *Inferno* enhance the meaning of the poem.

   b. Consider whether and why J. Alfred Prufrock might be listed among the *hollow men.*

   c. To what extent are the people of this poem the people of Auden's "September 1, 1939"? To what extent are the themes the same or different?

A MODEST PROPOSAL [*1729*]

Jonathan Swift

In Voyage II of *Gulliver's Travels* we saw one product of Swift's powerful indignation at man's inhumanity to man, conveyed to us through Gulliver's blind and obstinate defense of the vices and stupidities of his native England. This essay is another product of that indignation. In it an Irish counterpart of Lemuel Gulliver, out of a pretended humanitarian sympathy for the suffering of the Irish poor, puts forward what seems to him an obviously beneficial and profitable scheme for relieving the intolerable situation, but what seems to the reader the working of a diseased mind. Ironically, this shocking proposal is practically as humane as many proposals put forward for Ireland soberly, most of which involved wholesale loss of population.

This is an essay few readers forget. As one of the authors of this book has said elsewhere: "Swift thus lays bare (for our own time as well as his) the unconscious gross brutality of mankind, who commonly regard the standard of living of their own country as more important than whether *human* lives can be lived at all in another."

A Modest Proposal for Preventing the Children of Ireland from Being a Burden to Their Parents or Country

It is a melancholy object to those who walk through this great town[1] or travel in the country, when they see the streets, the roads, and cabin-doors crowded with beggars of the female sex, followed by three, four, or six children, all in rags, and importuning every passenger for an alms. These mothers, instead of being able to work for their honest livelihood, are forced to employ all their time in strolling to beg sustenance for their helpless infants, who, as they grow up, either turn thieves for want of work, or leave their dear native country, to fight for the Pretender in Spain,[2] or sell themselves to the Barbadoes.[3]

I think it is agreed by all parties, that this prodigious number of children in the arms, or on the backs, or at the heels of their mothers, and frequently of their fathers, is in the present deplorable state of the kingdom a very great additional grievance; and therefore whoever could find out a fair, cheap, and easy method of making these children sound and useful members of the commonwealth, would deserve so well of the public as to have his statue set up for a preserver of the nation.

But my intention is very far from being confined to provide only for the children of professed beggars; it is of a much greater extent, and shall take in the whole number of infants at a certain age, who are born of parents in effect as little able to support them, as those who demand our charity in the streets.

As to my own part, having turned my thoughts, for many years, upon this important subject, and maturely weighed the several schemes of other projectors,[4] I have always found them grossly mistaken in their computation. It is true, a child just dropped from its dam may be supported by her milk for a solar year with little other nourishment, at most not above the value of two shillings, which the mother may certainly get, or the value in scraps, by her lawful occupation of begging; and it is exactly at one year old that I propose to provide for them in such a manner, as, instead of being a charge upon their parents, or the parish, or wanting food and raiment for the rest of their lives, they shall, on the contrary, contribute to the feeding and partly to the clothing of many thousands.

There is likewise another great advantage in my scheme, that it will prevent those voluntary abortions, and that horrid practice of women murdering their bastard children, alas! too frequent among us—sacrificing the poor innocent babes, I doubt, more to avoid the expense than the shame—which would move tears and pity in the most savage and inhuman breast.

The number of souls in this kingdom being usually reckoned one million and a half, of these I calculate there may be about two hundred thousand couples whose wives are breeders; from which number I subtract thirty thousand couples, who are able to maintain their own children, although I apprehend there cannot be so many, under the present distresses of the kingdom; but this being granted, there will remain an hundred and seventy thousand breeders. I again subtract fifty thousand, for those women who miscarry, or whose children die by accident or disease within the year. There only remain an hundred and twenty thousand children of poor parents annually born: The question therefore is, How this number shall be reared, and provided for? which, as I

---

1. TOWN: Dublin.
2. PRETENDER IN SPAIN: Throughout much of the eighteenth century, descendants of James II, the Catholic king who had been ousted from the English throne in 1688, lived at the courts of friendly Catholic monarchs on the Continent and kept up their claims to England's throne.
3. SELL . . . BARBADOES: i.e., as slaves on the plantations.

4. PROJECTORS: the standard eighteenth century term for theorists and proposers of schemes.

have already said, under the present situation of affairs, is utterly impossible by all the methods hitherto proposed; for we can neither employ them in handicraft or agriculture; we neither build houses, (I mean in the country) nor cultivate land: They can very seldom pick up a livelihood by stealing till they arrive at six years old, except where they are of towardly parts,[5] although, I confess, they learn the rudiments much earlier; during which time they can however be properly looked upon only as probationers; as I have been informed by a principal gentleman in the county of Cavan, who protested to me, that he never knew above one or two instances under the age of six, even in a part of the kingdom so renowned for the quickest proficiency in that art.

I am assured by our merchants, that a boy or a girl before twelve years old, is no saleable commodity, and even when they come to this age, they will not yield above three pounds, or three pounds and half a crown at most, on the exchange; which cannot turn to account either to the parents or kingdom, the charge of nutriment and rags having been at least four times that value.

I shall now therefore humbly propose my own thoughts, which I hope will not be liable to the least objection.

I have been assured by a very knowing American[6] of my acquaintance in London, that a young healthy child well nursed is at a year old a most delicious, nourishing and wholesome food, whether stewed, roasted, baked, or boiled; and I make no doubt that it will equally serve in a fricasee, or a ragout.

I do therefore humbly offer it to public consideration, that of the hundred and twenty thousand children, already computed, twenty thousand may be reserved for breed, whereof only one fourth part to be males; which is more than we allow to sheep, black cattle, or swine, and my reason is, that these children are seldom the fruits of marriage, a circumstance not much regarded by our savages; therefore, one male will be sufficient to serve four females. That the remaining hundred thousand may at a year old be offered in sale to the persons of quality and fortune, through the kingdom, always advising the mother to let them suck plentifully in the last month, so as to render them plump and fat for a good table. A child will make two dishes at an entertainment for friends, and when the family dines alone, the fore or hind quarter will make a reasonable dish, and seasoned with a little pepper or salt will be very good boiled on the fourth day, especially in winter.

I have reckoned upon a medium, that a child just born will weigh 12 pounds, and in a solar year, if tolerably nursed, increaseth to 28 pounds.

I grant this food will be somewhat dear, and therefore very proper for landlords, who, as they have already devoured most of the parents[7] seem to have the best title to the children.

Infant's flesh will be in season throughout the year, but more plentiful in March, and a little before and after; for we are told by a grave author,[8] an eminent French physician, that fish being a prolific diet, there are more children born in Roman Catholic countries about nine months after Lent, than at any other season; therefore reckoning a year after Lent, the markets will be more glutted than usual, because the number of popish infants, is at least three to one in this kingdom, and therefore it will have one other collateral advantage, by lessening the number of papists[9] among us.

---

5. PARTS: talents.
6. AMERICAN: i.e., an American Indian, which it pleases Swift's *projector* to represent as a cannibal.
7. AS . . . PARENTS: Swift takes a satiric flick at the owners of the great Irish estates, who were often Englishmen or at least lived in England, and took no care to make their lands productive yet exacted unbearable rents from their tenant-farmers.
8. GRAVE AUTHOR: Rabelais.
9. LESSENING . . . PAPISTS: The *projector* writes from a Protestant point of view, which in the eighteenth century was strongly hostile to Roman Catholics.

I have already computed the charge of nursing a beggar's child (in which list I reckon all cottagers, laborers, and four-fifths of the farmers) to be about two shillings per annum, rags included; and I believe no gentleman would repine to give ten shillings for the carcass of a good fat child, which, as I have said will make four dishes of excellent nutritive meat, when he hath only some particular friend, or his own family to dine with him. Thus the squire will learn to be a good landlord, and grow popular among his tenants; the mother will have eight shillings neat profit, and be fit for work till she produces another child.

Those who are more thrifty (as I must confess the times require) may flay the carcass; the skin of which, artificially[10] dressed, will make admirable gloves for ladies, and summer boots for fine gentlemen.

As to our city of Dublin, shambles[11] may be appointed for this purpose, in the most convenient parts of it, and butchers we may be assured will not be wanting; although I rather recommend buying the children alive, and dressing them hot from the knife, as we do roasting pigs.

A very worthy person, a true lover of his country, and whose virtues I highly esteem, was lately pleased, in discoursing on this matter, to offer a refinement upon my scheme. He said, that many gentlemen of this kingdom, having of late destroyed their deer, he conceived that the want of venison might be well supplied by the bodies of young lads and maidens, not exceeding fourteen years of age, nor under twelve; so great a number of both sexes in every country being now ready to starve, for want of work and service: And these to be disposed of by their parents if alive, or otherwise by their nearest relations. But with due deference to so excellent a friend, and so deserving a patriot, I cannot be altogether in his sentiments; for as to the males, my American acquaintance assured me from frequent experience, that their flesh was generally tough and lean, like that of our schoolboys, by continual exercise, and their taste disagreeable, and to fatten them would not answer the charge. Then as to the females, it would, I think with humble submission, be a loss to the public, because they soon would become breeders themselves: And besides it is not improbable that some scrupulous people might be apt to censure such a practice (although indeed very unjustly) as a little bordering upon cruelty, which, I confess, hath always been with me the strongest objection against any project, how well soever intended.

But in order to justify my friend, he confessed, that this expedient was put into his head by the famous Psalmanazar,[12] a native of the island Formosa, who came from thence to London, above twenty years ago, and in conversation told my friend, that in his country when any young person happened to be put to death, the executioner sold the carcass to persons of quality, as a prime dainty, and that, in his time, the body of a plump girl of fifteen, who was crucified for an attempt to poison the Emperor, was sold to his Imperial Majesty's prime minister of state, and other great mandarins of the court, in joints from the gibbet, at four hundred crowns. Neither indeed can I deny, that if the same use were made of several plump young girls in this town, who, without one single groat to their fortunes, cannot stir abroad without a chair,[13] and appear at a playhouse and assemblies in foreign fineries which they never will pay for, the kingdom would not be the worse.

Some persons of a desponding spirit are in great concern about that vast number of poor people, who are aged, diseased, or maimed, and I have been desired to employ

---

10. ARTIFICIALLY: skillfully.
11. SHAMBLES: slaughterhouses.

12. PSALMANAZAR: an eccentric Frenchman, who pretended to be a native of Formosa and published a fanciful account of life on the island (1704).
13. WITHOUT A CHAIR: i.e., without being carried in a sedan chair, a mark of wealth.

my thoughts what course may be taken, to ease the nation of so grievous an encumbrance. But I am not in the least pain upon that matter, because it is very well known, that they are every day dying, and rotting, by cold, and famine, and filth, and vermin, as fast as can be reasonably expected. And as to the younger laborers, they are now in almost as hopeful a condition. They cannot get work, and consequently pine away for want of nourishment, to a degree, that if at any time they are accidentally hired to common labor, they have not strength to perform it, and thus the country and themselves are happily delivered from the evils to come.

I have too long digressed, and therefore shall return to my subject. I think the advantages by the proposal which I have made are obvious and many, as well as of the highest importance.

For *first,* as I have already observed, it would greatly lessen the number of papists, with whom we are yearly overrun, being the principal breeders of the nation, as well as our most dangerous enemies, and who stay at home on purpose with a design to deliver the kingdom to the Pretender, hoping to take their advantage by the absence of so many good Protestants,[14] who have chosen rather to leave their country, than stay at home, and pay tithes against their conscience to an episcopal curate.

Secondly, the poorer tenants will have something valuable of their own which by law may be made liable to distress,[15] and help to pay their landlord's rent, their corn and cattle being already seized, and money a thing unknown.

Thirdly, whereas the maintenance of an hundred thousand children, from two years old, and upwards, cannot be computed at less than ten shillings a piece per annum,

the nation's stock[16] will be thereby increased fifty thousand pounds per annum, besides the profit of a new dish, introduced to the tables of all gentlemen of fortune[17] in the kingdom who have any refinement in taste, and the money will circulate among ourselves, the goods being entirely of our own growth and manufacture.

Fourthly, the constant breeders, besides the gain of eight shillings sterling per annum, by the sale of their children, will be rid of the charge of maintaining them after the first year.

Fifthly, this food would likewise bring great custom to taverns, where the vintners will certainly be so prudent as to procure the best receipts for dressing it to perfection; and consequently have their houses frequented by all the fine gentlemen, who justly value themselves upon their knowledge in good eating; and a skillful cook, who understands how to oblige his guests, will contrive to make it as expensive as they please.

Sixthly, this would be a great inducement to marriage, which all wise nations have either encouraged by rewards, or enforced by laws and penalties. It would increase the care and tenderness of mothers towards their children, when they were sure of a settlement for life to the poor babes, provided in some sort by the public, to their annual profit instead of expense; we should soon see an honest emulation among the married women, which of them could bring the fattest child to the market. Men would become as fond of their wives during the time of their pregnancy, as they are now of their mares in foal, their cows in calf, or sows when they are ready to farrow, nor offer to beat or kick them (as is too frequent a practice) for fear of a miscarriage.

Many other advantages might be enumerated. For instance, the addition of some thousand carcasses in our exportation of barreled beef: the propagation of swine's flesh, and improvement in the art of making

---

14. ABSENCE . . . PROTESTANTS: another satiric flick at the irresponsibility of the absentee landlords.

15. LIABLE TO DISTRESS: i.e., to seizure when they can't pay their rent.

16. STOCK: capital.

17. OF FORTUNE: i.e., rich.

good bacon, so much wanted among us by the great destruction of pigs, too frequent at our tables, which are no way comparable in taste or magnificence to a well grown, fat yearling child, which roasted whole will make a considerable figure at a Lord Mayor's feast, or any other public entertainment. But this, and many others, I omit, being studious of brevity.

Supposing that one thousand families in this city, would be constant customers for infant's flesh, besides others who might have it at merry meetings, particularly at weddings and christenings, I compute that Dublin would take off annually about twenty thousand carcasses, and the rest of the kingdom (where probably they will be sold somewhat cheaper) the remaining eighty thousand.

I can think of no one objection, that will possibly be raised against this proposal, unless it should be urged, that the number of people will be thereby much lessened in the kingdom. This I freely own, and 'twas indeed one principal design in offering it to the world. I desire the reader will observe, that I calculate my remedy for this one individual kingdom of Ireland, and for no other that ever was, is, or, I think, ever can be upon earth. Therefore let no man talk to me of other expedients:[18] of taxing our absentees at five shillings a pound: of using neither clothes, nor household furniture, except what is of our own growth and manufacture: of utterly rejecting the materials and instruments that promote foreign luxury: of curing the expensiveness of pride, vanity, idleness, and gaming in our women: of introducing a vein of parsimony, prudence and temperance: of learning to love our country, wherein we differ even from Laplanders,[19] and the inhabitants of Topinamboo:[20] of

quitting our animosities, and factions, nor act any longer like the Jews, who were murdering one another at the very moment their city was taken:[21] of being a little cautious not to sell our country and consciences for nothing: of teaching landlords to have at least one degree of mercy towards their tenants. Lastly, of putting a spirit of honesty, industry, and skill into our shopkeepers, who, if a resolution could now be taken to buy only our native goods, would immediately unite to cheat and exact upon us in the price, the measure, and the goodness, nor could ever yet be brought to make one fair proposal of just dealing, though often and earnestly invited to it.

Therefore I repeat, let no man talk to me of these and the like expedients, till he hath at least some glimpse of hope, that there will ever be some hearty and sincere attempt to put them in practice.

But as to myself, having been wearied out for many years with offering vain, idle, visionary thoughts, and at length utterly despairing of success, I fortunately fell upon this proposal, which as it is wholly new, so it hath something solid and real, of no expense and little trouble, full in our own power, and whereby we can incur no danger in disobliging England. For this kind of commodity will not bear exportation, the flesh being of too tender a consistence to admit a long continuance in salt, although perhaps I could name a country,[22] which would be glad to eat up our whole nation without it.

After all, I am not so violently bent upon my own opinion, as to reject any offer, proposed by wise men, which shall be found equally innocent, cheap, easy, and effectual. But before something of that kind shall be advanced in contradiction to my scheme, and offering a better, I desire the author or authors, will be pleased maturely to consider

18. OTHER EXPEDIENTS: The *other expedients* for giving Ireland a less unfavorable balance of trade are proposals made—ineffectively—by Swift throughout his lifetime.

19. LAPLANDERS: Arctic nomads.

20. TOPINAMBOO: primitive district in Brazil.

21. JEWS . . . TAKEN: During the siege of Jerusalem, 70 A.D., many citizens were charged with aiding the Romans and were put to death.

22. COUNTRY: i.e., England.

two points. *First,* as things now stand, how they will be able to find food and raiment for a hundred thousand useless mouths and backs. And *secondly,* there being a round million of creatures in human figure throughout this kingdom, whose whole subsistence put into a common stock would leave them in debt two millions of pounds sterling— adding those who are beggars by profession, to the bulk of farmers, cottagers and laborers, with their wives and children, who are beggars in effect; I desire those politicians, who dislike my overture, and may perhaps be so bold to attempt an answer, that they will first ask the parents of these mortals, whether they would not at this day think it a great happiness to have been sold for food at a year old, in the manner I prescribe, and thereby have avoided such a perpetual scene of misfortunes as they have since gone through, by the oppression of landlords, the impossibility of paying rent without money or trade, the want of common sustenance, with neither house nor clothes to cover them from the inclemencies of the weather, and the most inevitable prospect of entailing the like, or greater miseries, upon their breed[23] forever.

I profess in the sincerity of my heart, that I have not the least personal interest in endeavoring to promote this necessary work, having no other motive than the public good of my country, by advancing our trade, providing for infants, relieving the poor, and giving some pleasure to the rich. I have no children by which I can propose to get a single penny; the youngest being nine years old and my wife past child-bearing.

---

23. BREED: posterity.

I

1. What do we learn of the speaker in the paragraphs before he outlines his project? Consider such phrases as "helpless infants," "leave their dear native country," "sacrificing the poor innocent babes." What do these (and others like them) reveal about his attitude toward his own good intentions? In contrast, how does his use of such comments as "fair, cheap and easy," "dropped from its dam," and "wives as breeders" (and other similar examples) qualify the impression given in the previous phrases? What kind of total picture do we get of him? What does Swift gain by having such a man make the proposal?

2. How does the speaker give the impression that this is a carefully thought-through proposal? Cite evidence that indicates that the speaker is thorough in preparation and logical in presentation. How does he give the impression that his proposal is made out of concern for all parties involved in the plight of the Irish poor? Most of the listed *advantages* would appeal strongly to his audience if they did not depend on the proposed scheme. What comment is Swift making about the *advantages* themselves?

3. What audience is he most anxious to reach? How do you know? The other expedients suggested by the speaker are reasonable proposals that his principal audience has long ignored. Are the comments out of character? Why or why not?

4. Characterize the speaker's attitude toward his audience. Is he trying to be consciously neutral and dispassionate? sarcastic? righteously indignant? Support your position with references to specific examples. How does the tone of the essay contrast with the subject matter, and why is the contrast effective?

II

1. What conditions that you might be familiar with, either close to home or elsewhere in the world, warrant the kind of treatment Swift gives to the plight of his native Ireland under British domination? Write your own *modest proposal* for the alleviation of whatever condition you think abhorrent.

ON THE LATE MASSACRE
IN PIEDMONT   [*1655*]

John Milton

Another powerful protest against man's inhumanity to man is Milton's "On the Late Massacre in Piedmont." In April, 1655, some three hundred Waldensian Protestants living in Piedmont, a province in the Italian Alps, were murdered on the orders of a Catholic nobleman, a subject of the Duke of Savoy.

In the name of the English government under Cromwell, Milton sent a strong formal protest to the Duke. He also wrote the following sonnet, a magnificent blend of rhythm, sound, and sense as it hammers home Milton's denunciation of the vicious act.

> Avenge, O Lord, thy slaughtered saints, whose bones
>   Lie scattered on the Alpine mountains cold;
>   Even them who kept thy truth so pure of old,
>   When all our fathers worshiped stocks and stones,
> Forget not: in thy book record their groans   5
>   Who were thy sheep, and in their ancient fold
>   Slain by the bloody Piemontese, that rolled
>   Mother with infant down the rocks. Their moans
> The vales redoubled to the hills, and they
>   To heaven. Their martyred blood and ashes sow   10
>   O'er all the Italian fields, where still doth sway
> The triple Tyrant; that from these may grow
>   A hundredfold, who, having learnt thy way,
>   Early may fly the Babylonian woe.

---

3. THEM . . . OLD: The Waldensians had, despite persecution, practiced the ways of the early Christians for several centuries before the Protestant Reformation.

4. FATHERS: pre-Reformation Englishmen and Europeans. STOCKS AND STONES: wood and stone images.

10. MARTYRED . . . SOW: alluding to the doctrine that "the blood of the martyrs is the seed of the church"; and perhaps also to the sowing of the dragon's teeth (in the stories of Jason and Cadmus) which sprang up into armed men (however, Milton is not calling for armed vengeance, only for more Protestants).

12. TRIPLE TYRANT: the Pope.

13. HUNDREDFOLD: See Matthew 13:3-9, the parable of the sowers.

14. BABYLONIAN WOE: Seventeenth century Protestants identified the Roman Catholic Church with the Babylon of the book of Revelation, 14:8, 17:5, and 18:2.

I

1. The poem starts with the imperative verb *avenge* and three other imperatives sustain the stern demand of the first, all four providing the backbone of the sonnet. What are the other three? What change in emphasis comes with each imperative?

2. Put lines 5-7 into normal English syntax. What does "they" refer to in line 9? What does the sentence, "Their moans/The vales redoubled to the hills, and they/To heaven" mean?

3. In line 2, the normal "cold Alpine mountains" is "Alpine mountains cold." What is gained by forcing the stress on the word *cold*? Why didn't Milton start his third line normally, "Forget not them who kept . . ." (or even "Do not forget them who kept . . .") instead of

putting the phrase *forget not* where it is, in an unnatural grammatical position and all alone as a hangover from the fourth line? What is gained by forcing the reader to hold lines 3-4 in mind waiting for the imperative to come?

4. What is the tone of the sonnet? What do the four imperative verbs suggest? What is the principal vowel sound of the rhyme words? How many times does this particular vowel sound appear in the poem. How does the repetition of this sound help set the tone? Compare the opening line to that of one of Shakespeare's sonnets:

"That time of year thou mayst in me behold"

or another of Milton's sonnets:

"When I consider how my light is spent"

All three are in iambic pentameter, but there is a difference in the way each must be read. How do you account for the difference? How does Milton sustain throughout this sonnet the rhythm and stress he has set in line 1? What does this metrical pattern contribute to the tone?

II

1. What is Milton saying here about the possibilities for evil that lie in the different convictions men have about religious belief? How would you answer the charge that a prayer for vengeance is hardly better than the original crime? What is the "vengeance" asked for in the sonnet, and how does it contrast with what happened to the Waldensians?

LONDON [*1794*]

William Blake

Milton's protest was against a specific act growing out of a brutal misdirection of religious fervor; Swift's was against the cruel indifference of English landlords and lawmakers in dealing with Ireland. The following poem by William Blake offers a scathing indictment of man's enslavement of himself in a dehumanized society. The city through which Blake "wanders" is the London of the 1790's, but it is also Anywhere at Anytime so long as man degrades himself and others.

> I wander through each chartered street,
> Near where the chartered Thames does flow,
> And mark in every face I meet
> Marks of weakness, marks of woe.
>
> In every cry of every Man, 5
> In every Infant's cry of fear,
> In every voice, in every ban,
> The mind-forged manacles I hear.
>
> How the Chimney-sweeper's cry
> Every blackening Church appalls; 10
> And the hapless Soldier's sigh
> Runs in blood down Palace walls.
>
> But most through midnight streets I hear
> How the youthful Harlot's curse
> Blasts the new born Infant's tear, 15
> And blights with plagues the Marriage hearse.

I

1. "Chartered" in line 1 probably means "laid out according to plan" or "mapped out," with the suggestion of confined and rigid patterning. What ironic overtones are there in referring to the Thames also as "chartered"? What does "ban" mean besides "curse" (a meaning connected with line 16)? Explain "mind-forged manacles" (8). How can one *hear* "mind-forged manacles"? What is the effect in this context of repeating "mark," "every," and "cry"?

2. The chimney-sweeps were young boys who earned a pittance by cleaning the soot from chimneys in a time when everyone heated his house with coal. A great many of them contracted tuberculosis or other respiratory diseases and died young. What extra meaning does this fact give to the "blackening Church"? What does "appalls" mean: that the Church is appalled by the Chimney-sweeper's cry? or that the cry makes the Church appalling? or both? If we consider that the word might also mean "to throw a pall over" (as one throws a pall over a coffin), what further implication might

this make about the *blackening Church?* Why is "blackening" better than "blackened" would have been?

3. What image do you see in lines 11-12? How can a *sigh* run *in blood?* If the Church stands for religion, what does the Palace stand for? Why a *hapless* soldier? What other word is suggested? Why a soldier?

4. Why "midnight streets" (13)? Why a *youthful* Harlot? What double meaning is there in "curse" (14)? If plagues are infections or diseases, how does the *Harlot's curse* blight the *Marriage hearse?* What comment on this society is implied in the presence of the harlot and the fact that marriage is connected with a hearse?

II

1. Compare this piece with Milton's "On the Late Massacre in Piedmont" and Swift's "A Modest Proposal." Which to you is the most powerful indictment of man's inhumanity to man, and why? Which conveys the strongest sense of compassion for those who suffer the evil conditions, and why?

---

from # BOOK IX, PARADISE LOST   [*1667*]

John Milton

Milton opens his great epic, *Paradise Lost,* with these lines:

> Of man's first disobedience, and the fruit
> Of that forbidden tree whose mortal taste
> Brought death into the World, and all our woe,
> With loss of Eden, till one greater Man
> Restore us, and regain the blissful seat,
> Sing, Heavenly Muse, . . .
> That, to the highth of this great argument,
> I may assert Eternal Providence,
> And justify the ways of God to men.

From the outset it is clear that the poet intends to interpret the Biblical account of the Fall of Man and his restoration through the atonement of Christ ("one greater Man") in such a way as to "justify the ways of God to men." Thus, within the Christian framework, he sets out to answer the problem of the existence of evil in a world created and governed by an all-knowing, all-powerful, loving God.

The twelve books of *Paradise Lost* range backward and forward in time from the revolt of a group of angels under Satan and their fall from Paradise into Hell, to the foretold eventual redemption of man through Christ; but the time covered in the actual narrative reaches only as far as the Fall of Eve and Adam and their expulsion from the Garden. The subject of the selection which follows is their Fall, which Milton presents in terms that are permanently true of human nature.

The first line of Milton's poem gives us the key to his interpretation of the event. To fall is to be disobedient to God, to value something or someone *more* than God. This is his "original sin," which in all our doings, Milton implies, we perpetually reenact. God gives man freedom to choose, and He does not leave him in the dark about the consequences of wrong choice: ". . . of the tree of the knowledge of good and evil, thou shalt not eat of it: for in the day that thou eatest thereof thou shalt surely die."

The situation seems clear enough. Adam and Eve have their earthly Paradise. They know what they are to do and not to do. They have been thoroughly warned that Satan is planning their downfall, and they know how subtle and crafty he is. Why do they succumb? The answer lies in Milton's searching psychological portrayal of the man and woman we see in Book IX. They are the first man and woman; they are also all men and all women.

The first 191 lines of Book IX recount Satan's successful entry into the Garden of Eden despite the vigilance of the angels whom God had sent to guard against such an eventuality. Once arrived he laments the degraded state into which he has fallen as he views the glories of the "Terrestrial Heaven" God has created for man. Bent on destroying man's happiness—"For only in destroying I find ease/To my relentless thoughts"—he seeks a fit creature through which to work his vengeance and chooses the serpent, "subtlest beast of all the field." "In at his mouth/The Devil entered" and awaited "the approach of morn."

> Now when as sacred light began to dawn
> In Eden on the humid flowers, that breathed
> Their morning incense, when all things that breathe
> From the Earth's great altar send up silent praise
> To the Creator, and his nostrils fill   5
> With grateful smell, forth came the human pair,
> And joined their vocal worship to the choir
> Of creatures wanting voice; that done, partake
> The season, prime for sweetest scents and airs;
> Then commune how that day they best may ply   10
> Their growing work—for much their work outgrew
> The hands' dispatch of two gardening so wide:
> And Eve first to her husband thus began:
>   "Adam, well may we labor still to dress
> This Garden, still to tend plant, herb, and flower, 15
> Our pleasant task enjoined; but, till more hands
> Aid us, the work under our labor grows,
> Luxurious by restraint: what we by day
> Lop overgrown, or prune, or prop, or bind,

---

14. STILL: always.

One night or two with wanton growth derides,   20
Tending to wild. Thou, therefore, now advise,
Or hear what to my mind first thoughts present.
Let us divide our labors—thou where choice
Leads thee, or where most needs, whether to wind
The woodbine round this arbor, or direct   25
The clasping ivy where to climb; while I
In yonder spring of roses intermixed
With myrtle find what to redress till noon.
For, while so near each other thus all day
Our task we choose, what wonder if so near   30
Looks intervene and smiles, or objects new
Casual discourse draw on, which intermits
Our day's work, brought to little, though begun
Early, and the hour of supper comes unearned!"
    To whom mild answer Adam thus returned: 35
"Sole Eve, associate sole, to me beyond
Compare above all living creatures dear!
Well hast thou motioned, well thy thoughts employed
How we might best fulfill the work which here
God hath assigned us, nor of me shalt pass   40
Unpraised; for nothing lovelier can be found
In woman than to study household good,
And good works in her husband to promote.
Yet not so strictly hath our Lord imposed
Labor as to debar us when we need   45
Refreshment, whether food, or talk between,
Food of the mind, or this sweet intercourse
Of looks and smiles; for smiles from reason flow
To brute denied, and are of love the food—
Love, not the lowest end of human life.   50
For not to irksome toil, but to delight,
He made us, and delight to reason joined.
These paths and bowers doubt not but our joint hands
Will keep from wilderness with ease, as wide
As we need walk, till younger hands ere long   55
Assist us. But, if much converse perhaps
Thee satiate, to short absence I could yield;
For solitude sometimes is best society,
And short retirement urges sweet return.
But other doubt possesses me, lest harm   60
Befall thee, severed from me; for thou know'st
What hath been warned us—what malicious foe,
Envying our happiness, and of his own
Despairing, seeks to work us woe and shame

20-21. DERIDES . . . WILD: makes a mock of our   27. SPRING: clump.
   labor, restoring all to wildness.   62. WHAT . . . US: in Books V-VIII.

By sly assault, and somewhere nigh at hand   65
Watches, no doubt, with greedy hope to find
His wish and best advantage, us asunder,
Hopeless to circumvent us joined, where each
To other speedy aid might lend at need.
Whether his first design be to withdraw   70
Our fealty from God, or to disturb
Conjugal love—than which perhaps no bliss
Enjoyed by us excites his envy more—
Or this, or worse, leave not the faithful side
That gave thee being, still shades thee and protects.   75
The wife, where danger or dishonor lurks,
Safest and seemliest by her husband stays,
Who guards her, or with her the worst endures."
     To whom the virgin majesty of Eve,
As one who loves, and some unkindness meets,   80
With sweet austere composure thus replied:
     "Offspring of Heaven and Earth, and all Earth's lord!
That such an enemy we have, who seeks
Our ruin, both by thee informed I learn,
And from the parting Angel overheard,   85
As in a shady nook I stood behind,
Just then returned at shut of evening flowers.
But that thou shouldst my firmness therefore doubt
To God or thee, because we have a foe
May tempt it, I expected not to hear.   90
His violence thou fear'st not, being such
As we, not capable of death or pain,
Can either not receive, or can repel.
His fraud is, then, thy fear; which plain infers
Thy equal fear that my firm faith and love   95
Can by his fraud be shaken or seduced:
Thoughts, which how found they harbor in thy breast,
Adam! misthought of her to thee so dear?"
     To whom, with healing words, Adam replied:
"Daughter of God and Man, immortal Eve!—   100
For such thou art, from sin and blame entire—
Not diffident of thee do I dissuade
Thy absence from my sight, but to avoid
The attempt itself, intended by our foe.

---

67. BEST ADVANTAGE: i.e., Adam and Eve separated.
74. OR . . . WORSE: whether Satan's aim is this or a worse one.
74-75. SIDE . . . BEING: reference to Eve's creation out of one of Adam's ribs.
79. VIRGIN: innocent.

85. FROM . . . ANGEL: At the end of Book VIII the Angel Raphael had warned Adam of Satan's designs.
92. NOT . . . PAIN: Adam and Eve, unfallen, are impervious in substance; Satan, because of his "de-gradation," is no longer so.
101. ENTIRE: untouched by.
102. DIFFIDENT: distrustful.

For he who tempts, though in vain, at least asperses   105
The tempted with dishonor foul, supposed
Not incorruptible of faith, not proof
Against temptation. Thou thyself with scorn
And anger wouldst resent the offered wrong,
Though ineffectual found; misdeem not, then,   110
If such affront I labor to avert
From thee alone, which on us both at once
The enemy, though bold, will hardly dare;
Or, daring, first on me the assault shall light.
Nor thou his malice and false guile contemn—   115
Subtle he needs must be who could seduce
Angels—nor think superfluous others' aid.
I from the influence of thy looks receive
Access in every virtue—in thy sight
More wise, more watchful, stronger, if need were   120
Of outward strength; while shame, thou looking on,
Shame to be overcome or overreached,
Would utmost vigor raise, and raised unite.
Why shouldst not thou like sense within thee feel
When I am present, and thy trial choose   125
With me, best witness of thy virtue tried?"
    So spake domestic Adam in his care
And matrimonial love; but Eve, who thought
Less attributed to her faith sincere,
Thus her reply with accent sweet renewed: 130
    "If this be our condition, thus to dwell
In narrow circuit straitened by a foe,
Subtle or violent, we not endued
Single with like defense wherever met,
How are we happy, still in fear of harm?   135
But harm precedes not sin: only our foe
Tempting affronts us with his foul esteem
Of our integrity: his foul esteem
Sticks no dishonor on our front, but turns
Foul on himself; then wherefore shunned or feared   140
By us? who rather double honor gain
From his surmise proved false, find peace within,
Favor from Heaven, our witness from the event.
And what is faith, love, virtue, unassayed

105-108. i.e., even Satan's attempt would dis-
    honor Eve, since it would imply a suspected
    weakness in her.
108-110. THOU . . . FOUND: Eve, of course, does
    nothing of the sort when the *offered wrong*
    comes.
119. ACCESS: increase.
123. UNITE: i.e., unite the virtues of lines 120-121.

124. LIKE SENSE: i.e., the same kind of feeling.
127. DOMESTIC: devoted.
132. STRAITENED: hemmed in.
133-134. WE . . . MET: i.e., if each of us, singly,
    is not equipped with adequate means of de-
    fense against him wherever we meet him.
139. FRONT: forehead.
143. EVENT: outcome.

Alone, without exterior help sustained? 145
Let us not then suspect our happy state
Left so imperfect by the Maker wise
As not secure to single or combined.
Frail is our happiness, if this be so;
And Eden were no Eden, thus exposed." 150
　　To whom thus Adam fervently replied:
"O Woman, best are all things as the will
Of God ordained them; his creating hand
Nothing imperfect or deficient left
Of all that he created—much less Man, 155
Or aught that might his happy state secure,
Secure from outward force. Within himself
The danger lies, yet lies within his power;
Against his will he can receive no harm.
But God left free the Will; for what obeys 160
Reason is free; and Reason he made right,
But bid her well be ware, and still erect,
Lest, by some fair appearing good surprised,
She dictate false, and misinform the Will
To do what God expressly hath forbid. 165
Not then mistrust, but tender love, enjoins
That I should mind thee oft; and mind thou me.
Firm we subsist, yet possible to swerve,
Since Reason not impossibly may meet
Some specious object by the foe suborned, 170
And fall into deception unaware,
Not keeping strictest watch, as she was warned.
Seek not temptation, then, which to avoid
Were better, and most likely if from me
Thou sever not: trial will come unsought. 175
Wouldst thou approve thy constancy, approve
First thy obedience; the other who can know,
Not seeing thee attempted, who attest?
But, if thou think trial unsought may find
Us both securer than thus warned thou seem'st, 180
Go; for thy stay, not free, absents thee more.
Go in thy native innocence; rely
On what thou hast of virtue; summon all;
For God towards thee hath done his part: do thine."

144-145. UNASSAYED . . . SUSTAINED: i.e., not tested alone, without outside aid.
148. AS . . . COMBINED: i.e., as not safe whether we are alone or together.
162. STILL ERECT: always on guard.
163-165. LEST . . . FORBID: another example of dramatic foreshadowing (see lines 108-110 and note).
167. MIND: be vigilant for.
170. SUBORNED: used for evil ends.
176. APPROVE: prove.
180. SECURER: less watchful.

So spake the Patriarch of Mankind; but Eve   185
Persisted; yet submiss, though last, replied:
    "With thy permission, then, and thus forewarned,
Chiefly by what thy own last reasoning words
Touched only, that our trial, when least sought,
May find us both perhaps far less prepared,   190
The willinger I go, nor much expect
A foe so proud will first the weaker seek;
So bent, the more shall shame him his repulse."
    Thus saying, from her husband's hand her hand
Soft she withdrew, and, like a wood-nymph light,   195
Oread or Dryad, or of Delia's train,
Betook her to the groves, but Delia's self
In gait surpassed and goddess-like deport,
Though not as she with bow and quiver armed,
But with such gardening tools as Art, yet rude,   200
Guiltless of fire had formed, or Angels brought.
To Pales, or Pomona, thus adorned,
Likest she seemed—Pomona when she fled
Vertumnus—or to Ceres in her prime,
Yet virgin of Proserpina from Jove.   205
Her long with ardent look his eye pursued
Delighted, but desiring more her stay.
Oft he to her his charge of quick return
Repeated; she to him as oft engaged
To be returned by noon amid the bower,   210
And all things in best order to invite
Noontide repast, or afternoon's repose.
O much deceived, much failing, hapless Eve,
Of thy presumed return! event perverse!
Thou never from that hour in Paradise   215
Found'st either sweet repast or sound repose;
Such ambush, hid among sweet flowers and shades,
Waited, with hellish rancor imminent,
To intercept thy way, or send thee back
Despoiled of innocence, of faith, of bliss.   220
    For now, and since first break of dawn, the Fiend,
Mere serpent in appearance, forth was come,
And on his quest where likeliest he might find
The only two of mankind, but in them
The whole included race, his purposed prey.   225
In bower and field he sought, where any tuft

---

193. SO BENT: so intending (to attack the weaker   203-205. POMONA . . . JOVE: i.e., Eve is young
    first).   and virginal, like Pomona or Ceres before
196. OREAD . . . TRAIN: Mountain or wood nymph   they accepted lovers.
    or one of Diana's huntress train.   222. MERE: pure.
202. PALES, OR POMONA: the goddesses of flocks
    and fruits.

Of grove or garden-plot more pleasant lay,
Their tendance or plantation for delight,
By fountain or by shady rivulet
He sought them both, but wished his hap might find   230
Eve separate; he wished, but not with hope
Of what so seldom chanced, when to his wish,
Beyond his hope, Eve separate he spies,
Veiled in a cloud of fragrance, where she stood,
Half-spied, so thick the roses bushing round   235
About her glowed, oft stooping to support
Each flower of tender stalk, whose head, though gay
Carnation, purple, azure, or specked with gold,
Hung drooping unsustained. Them she upstays
Gently with myrtle band, mindless the while   240
Herself, though fairest unsupported flower,
From her best prop so far, and storm so nigh.
Nearer he drew, and many a walk traversed
Of stateliest covert, cedar, pine, or palm;
Then voluble and bold, now hid, now seen   245
Among thick-woven arborets, and flowers
Imbordered on each bank, the hand of Eve:
Spot more delicious than those gardens feigned
Or of revived Adonis, or renowned
Alcinous, host of old Laertes' son,   250
Or that, not mystic, where the sapient king
Held dalliance with his fair Egyptian spouse.
Much he the place admired, the person more.
As one who, long in populous city pent,
Where houses thick and sewers annoy the air,   255
Forth issuing on a summer's morn, to breathe
Among the pleasant villages and farms
Adjoined, from each thing met conceives delight—
The smell of grain, or tedded grass, or kine,
Or dairy, each rural sight, each rural sound—   260
If chance with nymph-like step fair virgin pass,
What pleasing seemed, for her now pleases more,
She most, and in her look sums all delight:
Such pleasure took the Serpent to behold
This flowery plat, the sweet recess of Eve   265

228. TENDANCE: i.e., object of cultivation.
240. MINDLESS: heedless.
243. WALK: path.
244. COVERT: cover.
245. VOLUBLE: rotating.
246. ARBORETS: shrubs.
247. IMBORDERED: planted as borders. HAND: handiwork.
248. FEIGNED: not real, "mystic" (251).
248-252. THOSE . . . SPOUSE: The three gardens referred to are: the Garden of Adonis (described in Spenser's *Faerie Queene,* III, vi); the Garden of Alcinous, the Phaecian king who entertained Odysseus (Laertes' son); and the Garden of King Solomon.
255. ANNOY: pollute.
259. TEDDED: cut for gathering.
262. FOR HER: on her account.
265. PLAT: plot.

Thus early, thus alone. Her heavenly form
Angelic, but more soft and feminine,
Her graceful innocence, her every air
Of gesture or least action, overawed
His malice, and with rapine sweet bereaved   270
His fierceness of the fierce intent it brought.
That space the Evil One abstracted stood
From his own evil, and for the time remained
Stupidly good, of enmity disarmed,
Of guile, of hate, of envy, of revenge.   275
But the hot hell that always in him burns,
Though in mid Heaven, soon ended his delight,
And tortures him now more, the more he sees
Of pleasure not for him ordained. Then soon
Fierce hate he recollects, and all his thoughts   280
Of mischief, gratulating, thus excites:
    "Thoughts, whither have ye led me? with what sweet
Compulsion thus transported to forget
What hither brought us? hate, not love, nor hope
Of Paradise for Hell, hope here to taste   285
Of pleasure, but all pleasure to destroy,
Save what is in destroying; other joy
To me is lost. Then let me not let pass
Occasion which now smiles. Behold alone
The Woman, opportune to all attempts—   290
Her husband, for I view far round, not nigh,
Whose higher intellectual more I shun,
And strength, of courage haughty, and of limb
Heroic built, though of terrestrial mold;
Foe not informidable, exempt from wound—   295
I not; so much hath Hell debased, and pain
Enfeebled me, to what I was in Heaven.
She fair, divinely fair, fit love for Gods,
Not terrible, though terror be in love
And beauty, not approached by stronger hate,   300
Hate stronger under show of love well feigned—
The way which to her ruin now I tend."
    So spake the Enemy of Mankind, enclosed
In serpent, inmate bad, and toward Eve
Addressed his way—not with indented wave,   305
Prone on the ground, as since, but on his rear,
Circular base of rising folds, that towered
Fold above fold, a surging maze; his head

---

272. ABSTRACTED: i.e., outside of.
274. STUPIDLY GOOD: i.e., his evil nature is dulled
    for the moment.
281. GRATULATING: gloating.

285. HOPE: nor hope.
288. PASS: pass up.
295-296. EXEMPT . . . DEBASED: See note line 92.
300. NOT: i.e., unless.

Crested aloft, and carbuncle his eyes;
With burnished neck of verdant gold, erect   310
Amidst his circling spires, that on the grass
Floated redundant. Pleasing was his shape
And lovely; never since of serpent kind
Lovelier—not those that in Illyria changed
Hermione and Cadmus, or the god   315
In Epidaurus; nor to which transformed
Ammonian Jove, or Capitoline, was seen,
He with Olympias, this with her who bore
Scipio, the highth of Rome. With tract oblique
At first, as one who sought access but feared   320
To interrupt, sidelong he works his way.
As when a ship, by skillful steersman wrought
Nigh river's mouth or foreland, where the wind
Veers oft, as oft so steers, and shifts her sail,
So varied he, and of his tortuous train   325
Curled many a wanton wreath in sight of Eve,
To lure her eye. She, busied, heard the sound
Of rustling leaves, but minded not, as used
To such disport before her through the field
From every beast, more duteous at her call   330
Than at Circean call the herd disguised.
He, bolder now, uncalled before her stood,
But as in gaze admiring. Oft he bowed
His turret crest and sleek enameled neck,
Fawning, and licked the ground whereon she trod.   335
His gentle dumb expression turned at length
The eye of Eve to mark his play; he, glad
Of her attention gained, with serpent-tongue
Organic, or impulse of vocal air,
His fraudulent temptation thus began: 340
     "Wonder not, sovran mistress (if perhaps
Thou canst who art sole wonder), much less arm
Thy looks, the heaven of mildness, with disdain,
Displeased that I approach thee thus, and gaze
Insatiate, I thus single, nor have feared   345

309. CARBUNCLE: red, like carbuncles.
311. SPIRES: coils.
312. REDUNDANT: wave-like.
314-315. THAT . . . CADMUS: i.e., that Harmonia
(Hermione) and Cadmus were changed into.
315-316. GOD . . . EPIDAURUS: Aesculapius, represented in serpent form in his temple at Epidaurus.
316-319. NOR . . . ROME: nor the serpent's form
in which Jupiter Ammon loved Olympias,
mother of Alexander the Great; and Jupiter

Capitoline loved Sempronia, mother of Scipio
Africanus, the great leader (*highth*) of Rome.
319. TRACT: course.
331. HERD DISGUISED: i.e., the men turned into
beasts by Circe's arts (*Odyssey* X).
334. TURRET: towering.
338-339. WITH . . . AIR: i.e., using the serpent's
actual tongue, or in some way creating sound
waves.
341. SOVRAN: sovereign.

Thy awful brow, more awful thus retired.
Fairest resemblance of thy Maker fair,
Thee all things living gaze on, all things thine
By gift, and thy celestial beauty adore,
With ravishment beheld—there best beheld   350
Where universally admired. But here,
In this enclosure wild, these beasts among,
Beholders rude, and shallow to discern
Half what in thee is fair, one man except,
Who sees thee (and what is one?) who shouldst be seen   355
A Goddess among Gods, adored and served
By Angels numberless, thy daily train?"
    So glozed the Tempter, and his proem tuned.
Into the heart of Eve his words made way,
Though at the voice much marveling; at length,   360
Not unamazed, she thus in answer spake:
    "What may this mean? Language of Man pronounced
By tongue of brute, and human sense expressed!
The first at least of these I thought denied
To beasts, whom God on their creation-day   365
Created mute to all articulate sound;
The latter I demur, for in their looks
Much reason, and in their actions, oft appears.
Thee, Serpent, subtlest beast of all the field
I knew, but not with human voice endued;   370
Redouble, then, this miracle, and say,
How cam'st thou speakable of mute, and how
To me so friendly grown above the rest
Of brutal kind that daily are in sight:
Say, for such wonder claims attention due."   375
    To whom the guileful Tempter thus replied:
"Empress of this fair World, resplendent Eve!
Easy to me it is to tell thee all
What thou command'st, and right thou shouldst be obeyed.
I was at first as other beasts that graze   380
The trodden herb, of abject thoughts and low,
As was my food, nor aught but food discerned
Or sex, and apprehended nothing high:
Till on a day, roving the field, I chanced
A goodly tree far distant to behold,   385
Loaden with fruit of fairest colors mixed,
Ruddy and gold. I nearer drew to gaze;

---

346. AWFUL: awesome. RETIRED: withdrawn
    (through surprise at what she sees and hears).
353-354. BEHOLDERS . . . EXCEPT: i.e., except for
    Adam, Eve's beauty lacks a properly apprecia-
    tive audience.
358. GLOZED: flattered. PROEM: formal introduc-

tion, as in an oration.
367. DEMUR: defer decision (on whether beasts
    have reasoning powers).
372. OF: from being.
379. RIGHT: i.e., it is right.

When from the boughs a savory odor blown,
Grateful to appetite, more pleased my sense
Than smell of sweetest fennel, or the teats   390
Of ewe or goat dropping with milk at even,
Unsucked of lamb or kid, that tend their play.
To satisfy the sharp desire I had
Of tasting those fair apples, I resolved
Not to defer; hunger and thirst at once,   395
Powerful persuaders, quickened at the scent
Of that alluring fruit, urged me so keen.
About the mossy trunk I wound me soon;
For, high from ground, the branches would require
Thy utmost reach, or Adam's: round the tree   400
All other beasts that saw, with like desire
Longing and envying stood, but could not reach.
Amid the tree now got, where plenty hung
Tempting so nigh, to pluck and eat my fill
I spared not; for such pleasure till that hour   405
At feed or fountain never had I found.
Sated at length, ere long I might perceive
Strange alteration in me, to degree
Of Reason in my inward powers, and Speech
Wanted not long, though to this shape retained.   410
Thenceforth to speculations high or deep
I turned my thoughts, and with capacious mind
Considered all things visible in Heaven,
Or Earth, or Middle, all things fair and good.
But all that fair and good in thy divine   415
Semblance, and in thy beauty's heavenly ray,
United I beheld—no fair to thine
Equivalent or second; which compelled
Me thus, though importune perhaps, to come
And gaze, and worship thee of right declared   420
Sovran of creatures, universal Dame!"
    So talked the spirited sly Snake; and Eve,
Yet more amazed, unwary thus replied:
    "Serpent, thy overpraising leaves in doubt
The virtue of that fruit, in thee first proved.   425
But say, where grows the tree? from hence how far?
For many are the trees of God that grow

390-391. SMELL . . . EVEN: Serpents were supposed to be fond of fennel (an aromatic vegetable) and of stealing milk from sheep and
goats.
407. ERE . . . PERCEIVE: before long I noticed.
408. TO: even amounting to.
410. THOUGH . . . RETAINED: though I remained
a serpent in shape.

414. MIDDLE: the region between Heaven and
Earth.
417. FAIR: beauty.
421. DAME: mistress.
422. SPIRITED: Satan has "inspired" the snake.
424. OVERPRAISING: i.e., of me; Eve's awakened
vanity is evidenced in this show of false
modesty.

In Paradise, and various, yet unknown
To us; in such abundance lies our choice
As leaves a greater store of fruit untouched,   430
Still hanging incorruptible, till men
Grow up to their provision, and more hands
Help to disburden Nature of her bearth."
    To whom the wily Adder, blithe and glad:
"Empress, the way is ready, and not long—   435
Beyond a row of myrtles, on a flat,
Fast by a fountain, one small thicket past
Of blowing myrrh and balm. If thou accept
My conduct, I can bring thee thither soon."
    "Lead, then," said Eve. He, leading, swiftly rolled   440
In tangles, and made intricate seem straight,
To mischief swift. Hope elevates, and joy
Brightens his crest. As when a wandering fire,
Compact of unctuous vapor, which the night
Condenses, and the cold environs round,   445
Kindled through agitation to a flame
(Which oft, they say, some evil spirit attends),
Hovering and blazing with delusive light,
Misleads the amazed night-wanderer from his way
To bogs and mires, and oft through pond or pool,   450
There swallowed up and lost, from succor far:
So glistered the dire Snake, and into fraud
Led Eve, our credulous mother, to the Tree
Of Prohibition, root of all our woe;
Which when she saw, thus to her guide she spake: 455
    "Serpent, we might have spared our coming hither,
Fruitless to me, though fruit be here in excess,
The credit of whose virtue rest with thee—
Wondrous indeed, if cause of such effects!
But of this tree we may not taste nor touch;   460
God so commanded, and left that command
Sole daughter of his voice: the rest, we live
Law to ourselves; our Reason is our Law."
    To whom the Tempter guilefully replied:
"Indeed! Hath God then said that of the fruit   465
Of all these garden-trees ye shall not eat,
Yet lords declared of all in Earth or Air?"

---

431. INCORRUPTIBLE: undecayed.
431-432. TILL . . . PROVISION: until there are more people around to eat what Nature provides.
433. BEARTH: i.e., "bear-th"—what Nature bears.
437. FAST: near.
438. BLOWING: blossoming.
439. CONDUCT: guidance.
442. MISCHIEF: evil-doing.

443. WANDERING FIRE: will o' the wisp.
444. COMPACT: made up of. UNCTUOUS: oily.
452. GLISTERED: glittered. FRAUD: evil acts.
458. THE . . . THEE: i.e., it will have to be judged by its effects on *you* (since it is forbidden to *me*).
462. THE REST: as for the rest.

To whom thus Eve, yet sinless: "Of the fruit
Of each tree in the garden we may eat;
But of the fruit of this fair tree, amidst   470
The Garden, God hath said, 'Ye shall not eat
Thereof, nor shall ye touch it, lest ye die.' "
   She scarce had said, though brief, when now more bold
The Tempter, but, with show of zeal and love
To Man, and indignation at his wrong,   475
New part puts on, and, as to passion moved,
Fluctuates disturbed, yet comely, and in act
Raised, as of some great matter to begin.
As when of old some orator renowned
In Athens or free Rome, where eloquence   480
Flourished, since mute, to some great cause addressed,
Stood in himself collected, while each part,
Motion, each act, won audience ere the tongue
Sometimes in highth began, as no delay
Of preface brooking through his zeal of right: 485
So standing, moving, or to highth upgrown,
The Tempter, all impassioned, thus began:
   "O sacred, wise, and wisdom-giving Plant,
Mother of science! now I feel thy power
Within me clear, not only to discern   490
Things in their causes, but to trace the ways
Of highest agents, deemed however wise.
Queen of this Universe! do not believe
Those rigid threats of death. Ye shall not die.
How should ye? By the fruit? it gives you life   495
To knowledge. By the Threatener? look on me,
Me who have touched and tasted, yet both live,
And life more perfect have attained than Fate
Meant me, by venturing higher than my lot.
Shall that be shut to Man which to the Beast   500
Is open? or will God incense his ire
For such a petty trespass, and not praise
Rather your dauntless virtue, whom the pain
Of death denounced, whatever thing Death be,
Deterred not from achieving what might lead   505
To happier life, knowledge of Good and Evil?
Of good, how just! of evil—if what is evil
Be real, why not known, since easier shunned?

---

476. PART: role.
481. SINCE MUTE: i.e., no longer practiced.
482. PART: part of his body.
483. AUDIENCE: attention.
484. HIGHTH: in high feeling.
484-485. AS . . . BROOKING: as if unable to endure the delay of a formal introduction.

489. SCIENCE: knowledge.
492. HIGHEST AGENTS: e.g., God.
496. TO: as well as.
501. INCENSE: kindle.
503. PAIN: penalty.
504. DENOUNCED: proclaimed.

God therefore cannot hurt ye, and be just;
Not just, not God; not feared then, nor obeyed: 510
Your fear itself of death removes the fear.
Why then was this forbid! Why but to awe,
Why but to keep ye low and ignorant,
His worshipers? He knows that in the day
Ye eat thereof, your eyes that seem so clear,   515
Yet are but dim, shall perfectly be then
Opened and cleared, and ye shall be as Gods,
Knowing both good and evil, as they know.
That ye should be as Gods, since I as Man,
Internal Man, is but proportion meet—   520
I, of brute, human; ye, of human, Gods.
So ye shall die perhaps, by putting off
Human, to put on Gods—death to be wished,
Though threatened, which no worse than this can bring!
And what are Gods, that Man may not become   525
As they, participating godlike food?
The Gods are first, and that advantage use
On our belief, that all from them proceeds.
I question it; for this fair Earth I see,
Warmed by the Sun, producing every kind,   530
Them nothing; if they all things, who enclosed
Knowledge of good and evil in this tree,
That whoso eats thereof forthwith attains
Wisdom without their leave? and wherein lies
The offense, that Man should thus attain to know?   535
What can your knowledge hurt him, or this tree
Impart against his will, if all be his?
Or is it envy? and can envy dwell
In heavenly breasts? These, these and many more
Causes import your need of this fair fruit.   540
Goddess humane, reach then, and freely taste!"
      He ended; and his words, replete with guile,
Into her heart too easy entrance won.
Fixed on the fruit she gazed, which to behold
Might tempt alone; and in her ears the sound   545
Yet rung of his persuasive words, impregned
With reason, to her seeming, and with truth.
Meanwhile the hour of noon drew on, and waked

---

510. NOT . . . GOD: If He is not just, He is not
    God.
519-521. THAT . . . GODS: i.e., if your advance is
    proportionate to mine (which was from brute
    to human powers), it will be from human to
    Godlike powers.
522-523. SO . . . WISHED: i.e., perhaps this change
    from human to Godlike being is what death
    is.

527-528. THE . . . PROCEEDS: i.e., because the gods
    come into being before we do, they delude us
    with the belief that they created everything.
531. IF THEY: if they produced.
536. HIM: God.
540. IMPORT: prove.
541. HUMANE: gracious.
546. IMPREGNED: impregnated.
547. TO HER SEEMING: as she thought.

An eager appetite, raised by the smell
So savory of that fruit, which with desire,   550
Inclinable now grown to touch or taste,
Solicited her longing eye; yet first,
Pausing a while, thus to herself she mused:
   "Great are thy virtues, doubtless, best of fruits,
Though kept from Man, and worthy to be admired,   555
Whose taste, too long forborne, at first assay
Gave elocution to the mute, and taught
The tongue not made for speech to speak thy praise.
Thy praise he also who forbids thy use
Conceals not from us, naming thee the Tree   560
Of Knowledge, knowledge both of good and evil;
Forbids us then to taste. But his forbidding
Commends thee more, while it infers the good
By thee communicated, and our want;
For good unknown sure is not had, or, had   565
And yet unknown, is as not had at all.
In plain, then, what forbids he but to know?
Forbids us good, forbids us to be wise!
Such prohibitions bind not. But, if Death
Bind us with after-bands, what profits then   570
Our inward freedom? In the day we eat
Of this fair fruit, our doom is we shall die!
How dies the Serpent? He hath eaten, and lives,
And knows, and speaks, and reasons, and discerns,
Irrational till then. For us alone   575
Was death invented? or to us denied
This intellectual food, for beasts reserved?
For beasts it seems; yet that one beast which first
Hath tasted envies not, but brings with joy
The good befallen him, author unsuspect,   580
Friendly to Man, far from deceit or guile.
What fear I then? rather, what know to fear
Under this ignorance of good and evil,
Of God or Death, of law or penalty?
Here grows the cure of all, this fruit divine,   585
Fair to the eye, inviting to the taste,
Of virtue to make wise. What hinders then
To reach, and feed at once both body and mind?"
   So saying, her rash hand in evil hour
Forth-reaching to the fruit, she plucked, she eat.   590
Earth felt the wound, and Nature from her seat,
Sighing through all her works, gave signs of woe

---

556. ASSAY: attempt.
563. INFERS: suggests.
567. IN PLAIN: in plain terms.

580. AUTHOR UNSUSPECT: i.e., a reliable authority.
587. VIRTUE: power.
590. EAT: past tense, pronounced *et.*

That all was lost. Back to the thicket slunk
The guilty Serpent, and well might, for Eve,
Intent now only on her taste, naught else   595
Regarded; such delight till then, as seemed,
In fruit she never tasted, whether true,
Or fancied so through expectation high
Of knowledge; nor was Godhead from her thought.
Greedily she ingorged without restraint,   600
And knew not eating death. Satiate at length,
And heightened as with wine, jocund and boon,
Thus to herself she pleasingly began:
    "O sovran, virtuous, precious of all trees
In Paradise! of operation blest   605
To sapience, hitherto obscured, infamed,
And thy fair fruit let hang, as to no end
Created! but henceforth my early care,
Not without song, each morning, and due praise,
Shall tend thee, and the fertile burden ease   610
Of thy full branches, offered free to all;
Till, dieted by thee, I grow mature
In knowledge, as the Gods who all things know;
Though others envy what they cannot give—
For, had the gift been theirs, it had not here   615
Thus grown! Experience, next to thee I owe,
Best guide: not following thee, I had remained
In ignorance; thou open'st Wisdom's way,
And giv'st access, though secret she retire.
And I perhaps am secret: Heaven is high—   620
High, and remote to see from thence distinct
Each thing on Earth; and other care perhaps
May have diverted from continual watch
Our great Forbidder, safe with all his spies
About him. But to Adam in what sort   625
Shall I appear? Shall I to him make known
As yet my change, and give him to partake
Full happiness with me, or rather not,
But keep the odds of knowledge in my power
Without copartner? so to add what wants   630
In female sex, the more to draw his love,

---

601. KNEW NOT: knew not she was.
602. BOON: jovial.
605-606. OF . . . SAPIENCE: i.e., whose fruit produces wisdom.
606. INFAMED: defamed.
609. NOT . . . PRAISE: The tree, and not God, is
   now uppermost in Eve's thoughts.
614-616. THOUGH . . . GROWN: i.e., try to keep
   from others what is not theirs to give in the

first place.
616-617. EXPERIENCE . . . GUIDE: i.e., next to the
   tree itself, I am indebted to the experimental
   method (which led me to try the fruit).
624. FORBIDDER: Throughout her musing Eve is
   using the terms and arguments Satan used.
   SAFE: not dangerous.

And render me more equal, and perhaps—
A thing not undesirable—sometime
Superior; for, inferior, who is free?
This may be well; but what if God have seen,   635
And death ensue? Then I shall be no more;
And Adam, wedded to another Eve,
Shall live with her enjoying, I extinct!
A death to think! Confirmed, then, I resolve
Adam shall share with me in bliss or woe.   640
So dear I love him that with him all deaths
I could endure, without him live no life."
    So saying, from the tree her step she turned,
But first low reverence done, as to the Power
That dwelt within, whose presence had infused   645
Into the plant sciential sap, derived
From nectar, drink of Gods. Adam the while,
Waiting desirous her return, had wove
Of choicest flowers a garland, to adorn
Her tresses, and her rural labors crown,   650
As reapers oft are wont their harvest-queen.
Great joy he promised to his thoughts, and new
Solace in her return, so long delayed;
Yet oft his heart, divine of something ill,
Misgave him. He the faltering measure felt,   655
And forth to meet her went, the way she took
That morn when first they parted. By the Tree
Of Knowledge he must pass; there he her met,
Scarce from the tree returning, in her hand
A bough of fairest fruit, that downy smiled,   660
New gathered, and ambrosial smell diffused.
To him she hasted; in her face excuse
Came Prologue, and Apology to prompt,
Which, with bland words at will, she thus addressed:
    "Hast thou not wondered, Adam, at my stay?   665
Thee I have missed, and thought it long, deprived
Thy presence—agony of love till now
Not felt, nor shall be twice; for never more
Mean I to try, what rash untried I sought,
The pain of absence from thy sight. But strange   670
Hath been the cause, and wonderful to hear.
This tree is not, as we are told, a tree

---

634. FOR . . . FREE: This is Satan's view of freedom.
644. LOW . . . POWER: further evidence of Eve's
  attitude in line 609.
646. SCIENTIAL SAP: sap that bestows knowledge.
651. ARE WONT: are in the habit of doing for.

654. DIVINE OF: divining.
655. MEASURE: heartbeat.
660. DOWNY SMILED: i.e., looked enticing.
662-663. IN . . . PROMPT: i.e., like the speaker in
  a prologue in a play, with Apology as promp-
  ter.

Of danger tasted, nor to evil unknown
Opening the way, but of divine effect
To open eyes, and make them Gods who taste;   675
And hath been tasted such. The Serpent wise,
Or not restrained as we, or not obeying,
Hath eaten of the fruit, and is become
Not dead, as we are threatened, but thenceforth
Endued with human voice and human sense,   680
Reasoning to admiration, and with me
Persuasively hath so prevailed that I
Have also tasted, and have also found
The effects to correspond—opener mine eyes,
Dim erst, dilated spirits, ampler heart,   685
And growing up to Godhead; which for thee
Chiefly I sought, without thee can despise.
For bliss, as thou hast part, to me is bliss;
Tedious, unshared with thee, and odious soon.
Thou, therefore, also taste, that equal lot   690
May join us, equal joy, as equal love;
Lest, thou not tasting, different degree
Disjoin us, and I then too late renounce
Deity for thee, when fate will not permit."
    Thus Eve with countenance blithe her story told;   695
But in her cheek distemper flushing glowed.
On the other side, Adam, soon as he heard
The fatal trespass done by Eve, amazed,
Astonied stood and blank, while horror chill
Ran through his veins, and all his joints relaxed.   700
From his slack hand the garland wreathed for Eve
Down dropt, and all the faded roses shed.
Speechless he stood and pale, till thus at length
First to himself he inward silence broke:
    "O fairest of Creation, last and best   705
Of all God's works, creature in whom excelled
Whatever can to sight or thought be formed,
Holy, divine, good, amiable, or sweet!
How art thou lost! how on a sudden lost,
Defaced, deflowered, and now to death devote!   710
Rather, how hast thou yielded to transgress
The strict forbiddance, how to violate

---

673. TASTED: if tasted.
676. TASTED SUCH: proved such by tasting.
681. TO ADMIRATION: admirably.
685. ERST: formerly.
688-689. FOR . . . SOON: i.e., there is no bliss un-
    less it is shared with you; if not shared, it be-
    comes tiresome and then hateful.

692. DEGREE: i.e., rank, in the hierarchy of things.
693. RENOUNCE: try to renounce.
699. ASTONIED: astounded.
710. DEVOTE: doomed.

The sacred fruit forbidden? Some cursèd fraud
Of enemy hath beguiled thee, yet unknown,
And me with thee hath ruined; for with thee   715
Certain my resolution is to die.
How can I live without thee? how forgo
Thy sweet converse, and love so dearly joined,
To live again in these wild woods forlorn?
Should God create another Eve, and I   720
Another rib afford, yet loss of thee
Would never from my heart. No, no! I feel
The link of nature draw me: flesh of flesh,
Bone of my bone thou art, and from thy state
Mine never shall be parted, bliss or woe."   725
  So having said, as one from sad dismay
Recomforted, and, after thoughts disturbed,
Submitting to what seemed remediless,
Thus in calm mood his words to Eve he turned:
  "Bold deed thou hast presumed, adventurous Eve, 730
And peril great provoked, who thus hast dared
Had it been only coveting to eye
That sacred food, sacred to abstinence;
Much more to taste it, under ban to touch.
But past who can recall, or done undo?   735
Not God Omnipotent, nor Fate! Yet so
Perhaps thou shalt not die; perhaps the fact
Is not so heinous now—foretasted fruit,
Profaned first by the Serpent, by him first
Made common and unhallowed ere our taste,   740
Nor yet on him found deadly. He yet lives—
Lives, as thou saidst, and gains to live, as Man,
Higher degree of life: inducement strong
To us, as likely, tasting, to attain
Proportional ascent; which cannot be   745
But to be Gods, or Angels, demi-gods.
Nor can I think that God, Creator wise,
Though threatening, will in earnest so destroy
Us, his prime creatures, dignified so high,
Set over all his works; which, in our fall,   750
For us created, needs with us must fail,
Dependent made. So God shall uncreate,
Be frustrate, do, undo, and labor lose—
Not well conceived of God; who, though his power
Creation could repeat, yet would be loath   755

730-734. BOLD . . . TOUCH: i.e., it was presumptuous of you even to eye that fruit, much less
taste it.
737. FACT: deed.

742. AS MAN: i.e., in his new status, having human powers.
744. AS . . . ATTAIN: since it makes it likely that
if *we* taste, we too shall attain.

Us to abolish, lest the Adversary
Triumph and say: 'Fickle their state whom God
Most favors; who can please him long? Me first
He ruined, now Mankind; whom will he next?'—
Matter of scorn not to be given the Foe.   760
However, I with thee have fixed my lot,
Certain to undergo like doom. If death
Consort with thee, death is to me as life;
So forcible within my heart I feel
The bond of Nature draw me to my own—   765
My own in thee, for what thou art is mine:
Our state cannot be severed; we are one,
One flesh; to lose thee were to lose myself."
   So Adam; and thus Eve to him replied:
"O glorious trial of exceeding love,   770
Illustrious evidence, example high!
Engaging me to emulate; but short
Of thy perfection, how shall I attain,
Adam? from whose dear side I boast me sprung,
And gladly of our union hear thee speak,   775
One heart, one soul in both; whereof good proof
This day affords, declaring thee resolved,
Rather than death, or aught than death more dread,
Shall separate us, linked in love so dear,
To undergo with me one guilt, one crime,   780
If any be, of tasting this fair fruit;
Whose virtue (for of good still good proceeds,
Direct, or by occasion) hath presented
This happy trial of thy love, which else
So eminently never had been known.   785
Were it I thought death menaced would ensue
This my attempt, I would sustain alone
The worst, and not persuade thee—rather die
Deserted than oblige thee with a fact
Pernicious to thy peace, chiefly assured   790
Remarkably so late of thy so true,
So faithful, love unequaled. But I feel
Far otherwise the event—not death, but life
Augmented, opened eyes, new hopes, new joys,
Taste so divine that what of sweet before   795
Hath touched my sense, flat seems to this and harsh.
On my experience, Adam, freely taste,
And fear of death deliver to the winds."

---

762. CERTAIN: resolved.
772. ENGAGING . . . EMULATE: requiring that I
   imitate it.
772-773. SHORT . . . ATTAIN: lacking thy perfection, how shall I equal thy "example high"?

786. WERE . . . THOUGHT: i.e., if I thought.
789. DESERTED: alone. OBLIGE: involve. FACT:
   deed.
793. EVENT: consequence.

    So saying, she embraced him, and for joy
Tenderly wept, much won that he his love 800
Had so ennobled as of choice to incur
Divine displeasure for her sake, or death.
In recompense (for such compliance bad
Such recompense best merits), from the bough
She gave him of that fair enticing fruit 805
With liberal hand. He scrupled not to eat,
Against his better knowledge, not deceived,
But fondly overcome with female charm.
Earth trembled from her entrails, as again
In pangs, and Nature gave a second groan; 810
Sky loured, and, muttering thunder, some sad drops
Wept at completing of the mortal Sin
Original; while Adam took no thought,
Eating his fill, nor Eve to iterate
Her former trespass feared, the more to soothe 815
Him with her loved society; that now,
As with new wine intoxicated both,
They swim in mirth, and fancy that they feel
Divinity within them breeding wings
Wherewith to scorn the Earth. But that false fruit 820
Far other operation first displayed,
Carnal desire inflaming. He on Eve
Began to cast lascivious eyes; she him
As wantonly repaid; in lust they burn,
Till Adam thus 'gan Eve to dalliance move: 825
    "Eve, now I see thou art exact of taste
And elegant—of sapience no small part;
Since to each meaning savor we apply,
And palate call judicious. I the praise
Yield thee; so well this day thou hast purveyed. 830
Much pleasure we have lost, while we abstained
From this delightful fruit, nor known till now
True relish, tasting. If such pleasure be
In things to us forbidden, it might be wished
For this one tree had been forbidden ten. 835
But come; so well refreshed, now let us play,
As meet is, after such delicious fare;
For never did thy beauty, since the day
I saw thee first and wedded thee, adorned

807-808. AGAINST . . . CHARM: Unlike Eve, he was not a victim of inferior reasoning power, but with full knowledge lets his passions rule his reason.
812-813. SIN ORIGINAL: i.e., that which all men inherit.
826. EXACT: refined.
828-829. SINCE . . . JUDICIOUS: i.e., we use the term "taste" to mean both the sense of taste and also judiciousness (as in "a man of taste").
835. FOR: instead of.
837. MEET: fit.

With all perfections, so inflame my sense   840
With ardor to enjoy thee, fairer now
Than ever—bounty of this virtuous tree!"
    So said he, and forbore not glance or toy
Of amorous intent, well understood
Of Eve, whose eye darted contagious fire.   845
Her hand he seized, and to a shady bank,
Thick overhead with verdant roof embowered,
He led her, nothing loath; flowers were the couch,
Pansies, and violets, and asphodel,
And hyacinth—Earth's freshest, softest lap.   850
There they their fill of love and love's disport
Took largely, of their mutual guilt the seal,
The solace of their sin, till dewy sleep
Oppressed them, wearied with their amorous play.
    Soon as the force of that fallacious fruit,   855
That with exhilarating vapor bland
About their spirits had played, and inmost powers
Made err, was now exhaled, and grosser sleep,
Bred of unkindly fumes, with conscious dreams
Encumbered, now had left them, up they rose   860
As from unrest, and, each the other viewing,
Soon found their eyes how opened, and their minds
How darkened. Innocence, that as a veil
Had shadowed them from knowing ill, was gone,
Just confidence, and native righteousness,   865
And honor, from about them, naked left
To guilty Shame: he covered, but his robe
Uncovered more. So rose the Danite strong,
Herculean Samson, from the harlot-lap
Of Philistean Dalilah, and waked   870
Shorn of his strength; they destitute and bare
Of all their virtue. Silent, and in face
Confounded, long they sat, as strucken mute;
Till Adam, though not less than Eve abashed,
At length gave utterance to these words constrained: 875
    "O Eve, in evil hour thou didst give ear
To that false Worm, of whomsoever taught
To counterfeit Man's voice—true in our fall,
False in our promised rising; since our eyes
Opened we find indeed, and find we know   880
Both good and evil, good lost and evil got:

---

843. TOY: caress.
859. UNKINDLY: unnatural.
866. NAKED LEFT: i.e., so that they were left
    naked.
867. HE: shame.

868-871. DANITE . . . STRENGTH: See Judges 16:
    4-20.
871. THEY: i.e., just so Adam and Eve waked.
879. RISING: the Godlike status the serpent had
    predicted for them.

Bad fruit of knowledge, if this be to know,
Which leaves us naked thus, of honor void,
Of innocence, of faith, of purity,
Our wonted ornaments now soiled and stained;   885
And in our faces evident the signs
Of foul concupiscence; whence evil store;
Even shame, the last of evils; of the first
Be sure then. How shall I behold the face
Henceforth of God or Angel, erst with joy   890
And rapture so oft beheld? Those Heavenly Shapes
Will dazzle now this earthly with their blaze
Insufferably bright. Oh, might I here
In solitude live savage, in some glade
Obscured, where highest woods, impenetrable   895
To star or sunlight, spread their umbrage broad,
And brown as evening! Cover me, ye pines!
Ye cedars, with innumerable boughs
Hide me, where I may never see them more!
But let us now, as in bad plight, devise   900
What best may, for the present, serve to hide
The parts of each from other that seem most
To shame obnoxious, and unseemliest seen—
Some tree, whose broad smooth leaves, together sewed,
And girded on our loins, may cover round   905
Those middle parts, that this new comer, Shame,
There sit not, and reproach us as unclean."
   So counseled he, and both together went
Into the thickest wood. There soon they chose
The fig-tree—not that kind for fruit renowned,   910
But such as, at this day, to Indians known,
In Malabar or Decan spreads her arms
Branching so broad and long that in the ground
The bended twigs take root, and daughters grow
About the mother tree, a pillared shade   915
High overarched, and echoing walks between:
There oft the Indian herdsman, shunning heat,
Shelters in cool, and tends his pasturing herds
At loop-holes cut through thickest shade. Those leaves
They gathered, broad as Amazonian targe,   920

---

887. WHENCE EVIL STORE: whence came abundant
  evils.
888. LAST: worst. FIRST: lesser.
891-893. THOSE . . . BRIGHT: Becoming an *earthly*
  substance through his sin, Adam will no longer
  be able to stand the blinding light that surrounds "Heavenly Shapes."
897. BROWN: dark.
903. OBNOXIOUS: liable.

906. THAT: so that.
910. FIG-TREE: i.e., the banyan tree.
912. MALABAR: the southwestern coast of India.
  DECAN: the whole peninsula of India.
916. AND: with.
920. AMAZONIAN TARGE: shield of the Amazons,
  the powerful female warriors of Greek mythology.

And with what skill they had, together sewed,
To gird their waist—vain covering, if to hide
Their guilt and dreaded shame! O how unlike
To that first naked glory! Such of late
Columbus found th' American, so girt   925
With feathered cincture, naked else and wild,
Among the trees on isles and woody shores.
Thus fenced, and, as they thought, their shame in part
Covered, but not at rest or ease of mind,
They sat them down to weep. Nor only tears   930
Rained at their eyes, but high winds worse within
Began to rise, high passions—anger, hate,
Mistrust, suspicion, discord—and shook sore
Their inward state of mind, calm region once
And full of peace, now tost and turbulent: 935
For Understanding ruled not, and the Will
Heard not her lore, both in subjection now
To sensual Appetite, who, from beneath
Usurping over sovran Reason, claimed
Superior sway. From thus distempered breast   940
Adam, estranged in look and altered style,
Speech intermitted thus to Eve renewed:
    "Would thou hadst harkened to my words, and stayed
With me, as I besought thee, when that strange
Desire of wandering, this unhappy morn,   945
I know not whence possessed thee! We had then
Remained still happy—not, as now, despoiled
Of all our good, shamed, naked, miserable!
Let none henceforth seek needless cause to approve
The faith they owe; when earnestly they seek   950
Such proof, conclude they then begin to fail."
    To whom, soon moved with touch of blame, thus Eve:
"What words have passed thy lips, Adam severe?
Imput'st thou that to my default, or will
Of wandering, as thou call'st it, which who knows   955
But might as ill have happened thou being by,
Or to thyself perhaps? Hadst thou been there,
Or here the attempt, thou couldst not have discerned
Fraud in the Serpent, speaking as he spake;
No ground of enmity between us known   960
Why he should mean me ill or seek to harm.
Was I to have never parted from thy side?
As good have grown there still, a lifeless rib.

---

926. CINCTURE: girdle.
935. TOST: tossed.
937. HER LORE: i.e., understanding teachings.
941. STYLE: i.e., of speech.
942. INTERMITTED: i.e., which had been inter-

rupted.
946. WHENCE: from what source.
949. APPROVE: prove.
950. OWE: own.

Being as I am, why didst not thou, the head,
Command me absolutely not to go,   965
Going into such danger as thou saidst?
Too facile then, thou didst not much gainsay,
Nay, didst permit, approve, and fair dismiss.
Hadst thou been firm and fixed in thy dissent,
Neither had I transgressed, nor thou with me."   970
    To whom, then first incensed, Adam replied:
"Is this the love, is this the recompense
Of mine to thee, ingrateful Eve, expressed
Immutable when thou wert lost, not I—
Who might have lived, and joyed immortal bliss,   975
Yet willingly chose rather death with thee?
And am I now upbraided as the cause
Of thy transgressing? not enough severe,
It seems, in thy restraint! What could I more?
I warned thee, I admonished thee, foretold   980
The danger, and the lurking enemy
That lay in wait; beyond this had been force,
And force upon free will hath here no place.
But confidence then bore thee on, secure
Either to meet no danger, or to find   985
Matter of glorious trial; and perhaps
I also erred in overmuch admiring
What seemed in thee so perfect that I thought
No evil durst attempt thee. But I rue
That error now, which is become my crime,   990
And thou the accuser. Thus it shall befall
Him who, to worth in women overtrusting,
Lets her will rule: restraint she will not brook;
And, left to herself, if evil thence ensue,
She first his weak indulgence will accuse."   995
    Thus they in mutual accusation spent
The fruitless hours, but neither self-condemning;
And of their vain contést appeared no end.

---

968. FAIR DISMISS: willingly let me go.
973. MINE: i.e., my love.
973-974. EXPRESSED IMMUTABLE: proved to be
  unchangeable.

984. SECURE: over-confident.
989. DURST: dared.
993. BROOK: endure.

I

1. Outline carefully the argument Eve uses in proposing separation from Adam (14-34). What kind of person does she reveal herself to be? Outline Adam's counter-argument (36-78). What impressions do you get of Adam from this?

2. What is Eve's reaction to Adam's reply (82-98)? Put this reaction into modern everyday terms, imagining Eve to be any housewife with a sense of independence. What change is there between the kind of language she uses in her first speech and that in her answer to Adam's concern? What response is drawn from Adam by Eve's attitude (100-126)? Why are his words called "healing" (99)?

3. What truth does Eve's next comment

(132-150) take into account? What truth does it leave out of account? Adam in replying to her stresses this truth. Where? But he does not act on it. Why not? What qualities in Eve's parting words (187-193) suggest that the tempter will find her an easy mark?

4. Milton goes to great lengths (194-302) to describe the beauty of the garden and the loveliness and innocence of Eve. Even Satan is momentarily "abstracted . . ./From his own evil," and he has to remind himself "What hither brought us." How does this interlude point up the failure of Adam and Eve to realize the enormous importance of what is at stake? How does it heighten the sense of loss that the coming temptation and fall will bring?

5. Why does Satan wish to destroy Eve and her happiness? What makes him sure that he can succeed? Outline his line of attack. How well does he understand his victim? What sort of weakness does she show? How have we been prepared for this? Make a list of the terms Satan applies to Eve, and the terms he applies to God. Why should both sets of terms have put Eve on her guard?

6. Relate the arguments Eve uses in her final meditation (554-588) to those used by Satan throughout the temptation and to those used by Adam in lines 152-184.

7. Comment on the significance of lines 591-625, which come immediately after Eve eats the apple. What specific things occur in order? What change is there in Eve? Where does she adopt Satan's view of God? Where does she adopt Satan's idea of what freedom is? How does this idea differ from Milton's or the Christian idea of freedom?

8. Why does Eve want Adam to eat the forbidden fruit? What lies does she tell him when he arrives? What shows that she has no comprehension of the terribleness of her disobedience? What shows that Adam *does*? Then why does he disobey too? What clue to the reason does Milton put in Adam's mouth in lines 705-707? On what grounds might it be argued that such a speech shows Adam to be, to all

intents and purposes, *already* fallen? What do these words show about Adam's wisdom? What word in Eve's reply (770) has two meanings— one of them ironic? How is the irony related to Adam's words in 705-707?

9. How do the lines following Adam's disobedience (809-825) echo those following Eve's (591-603)?

10. Who was the first to condemn? Why? In what terms? What is Eve's reply? Note particularly lines 960-963. How do we see them now?

11. How do lines 936-940 sum up the nature of evil that has come to them through disobedience? Express the thought of the lines in your own words.

II

1. With the previous answers in mind, try to answer the question raised in the introduction: what causes them to disobey—in Eve's case? in Adam's case? If they are Everyman, what does Milton see in man's nature that leads him to bring evil on himself through willfully making wrong choices? What things does he put first to the exclusion of what he should put first? What faculties ought to rule man? What ones too often actually do? In what *different* ways is the operation of the latter illustrated from line 843 to the end?

2. Though Book IX leaves Adam and Eve spending *fruitless hours* in *mutual accusation,* it would be grossly misleading to leave the impression that they remain in degradation. In Book XII *Paradise Lost* ends on the vision of paradise regained. Man may live out his mortal life, according to the poem, trapped by his shortsightedness, his pride, his *sensual appetite,* but he will be redeemed in the end through God's grace. At the end of the poem, though much has been lost to Adam and Eve, something also has been gained. Read the closing lines of Book XII reproduced below and indicate what it is they have learned and what it is they have gained:

Book XII

. . . and thus Adam last replied:
"How soon hath thy prediction, Seer blest,
Measured this transient World, the race of Time,

---

2. SEER: Archangel Michael, who has been revealing the future.   3. RACE: product.

Till Time stand fixed! Beyond is all abyss—
Eternity, whose end no eye can reach.   5
Greatly instructed I shall hence depart,
Greatly in peace of thought, and have my fill
Of knowledge, what this vessel can contain;
Beyond which was my folly to aspire.
Henceforth I learn that to obey is best,   10
And love with fear the only God, to walk
As in his presence, ever to observe
His providence, and on him sole depend,
Merciful ever all his works, with good
Still overcoming evil, and by small   15
Accomplishing great things, by things deemed weak
Subverting worldly-strong, and worldly-wise
By simply meek; that suffering for Truth's sake
Is fortitude to highest victory,
And to the faithful death the gate of life;   20
Taught this by his example whom I now
Acknowledge my Redeemer blest."
    To whom thus also the Angel last replied:
"This having learned, thou hast attained the sum
Of wisdom; hope no higher, though all the stars   25
Thou knew'st by name, and all the ethereal powers,
All secrets of the Deep, all Nature's works,
Or works of God in heaven, air, earth, or sea,
And all the riches of this world enjoy'dst
And all the rule, one empire. Only add   30
Deeds to thy knowledge answerable; add faith;
Add virtue, patience, temperance; add love,
By name to come called Charity, the soul
Of all the rest: then wilt thou not be loath
To leave this Paradise, but shalt possess   35
A Paradise within thee, happier far.
                *   *   *   *   *
We may no longer stay. Go, waken Eve;
Her also I with gentle dreams have calmed,
Portending good, and all her spirits composed
To meek submission: thou, at season fit,   40
Let her with thee partake what thou hast heard—
Chiefly what may concern her faith to know,
The great deliverance by her seed to come
(For by the Woman's Seed) on all mankind—
That ye may live, which will be many days,   45
Both in one faith unanimous; though sad

---

8. VESSEL: body.
18-20. THAT . . . LIFE: grammatically the object
    of learn in line 10.
36. i.e., as Satan contains a hell within him.

44. FOR . . . SEED: with reference to the Immacu-
    late Conception.
45. MANY DAYS: i.e., a long time. (In Genesis,
    Adam lives 930 years.)

With cause for evils past, yet much more cheered
With meditation on the happy end."
    He ended, and they both descend the hill.
Descended, Adam to the bower where Eve   50
Lay sleeping ran before, but found her waked;
And thus with words not sad she him received:
    "Where thou return'st and whither went'st I know;
For God is also in sleep, and dreams advise,
Which he hath sent propitious, some great good   55
Presaging, since, with sorrow and heart's distress
Wearied, I fell asleep: but now lead on,
In me is no delay; with thee to go
Is to stay here; without thee here to stay
Is to go hence unwilling; thou to me   60
Art all things under Heaven, all places thou,
Who for my willful crime are banished hence.
This further consolation yet secure
I carry hence: though all by me is lost,
Such favor I unworthy am vouchsafed,   65
By me the Promised Seed shall all restore."
    So spake our mother Eve; and Adam heard
Well pleased, but answered not; for now too nigh
The Archangel stood, and from the other hill
To their fixed station, all in bright array,   70
The Cherubim descended, on the ground
Gliding meteorous, as evening mist
Risen from a river o'er the marish glides,
And gathers ground fast at the laborer's heel
Homeward returning. High in front advanced,   75
The brandished sword of God before them blazed,
Fierce as a comet; which with torrid heat,
And vapor as the Libyan air adust,
Began to parch that temperate clime; whereat
In either hand the hastening Angel caught   80
Our lingering parents, and to the eastern gate
Led them direct, and down the cliff as fast
To the subjected plain—then disappeared.
They, looking back, all the eastern side beheld
Of Paradise, so late their happy seat,   85
Waved over by that flaming brand; the gate
With dreadful faces thronged and fiery arms.
Some natural tears they dropped, but wiped them soon;
The world was all before them, where to choose
Their place of rest, and Providence their guide.   90
They, hand in hand, with wandering steps and slow,
Through Eden took their solitary way.

---

53. WHERE: from where.
73. MARISH: marsh.

78. AS . . . ADUST: i.e., scorching like a wind from
    the Libyan desert.
83. SUBJECTED: spread out below.

HAMLET

William Shakespeare

Shakespeare's *Hamlet* is not only the most famous of plays; it is also the most controversial. After three and a half centuries, there is still impassioned argument about its meanings. The books and articles on the subject would fill a good-sized library. All this testifies to the play's vitality. People argue about *Hamlet* because it excites them. And it excites them because it is profoundly alive, because it has something to say that is just as true and moving today as it was when the play was written. What is it, then, that gives *Hamlet* its extraordinary life?

One factor is the story: *Hamlet* is a first-rate yarn. It combines, in fact, three of the world's most tried-and-true kinds of plot-interest. The play begins with a ghost story, from which Shakespeare extracts the last ounce of mystery and suspense before he lets it drop at the end of Act I. Acts II and III greatly resemble a detective story, with Prince Hamlet as the detective seeking to find out whether the King, his uncle, is in fact the murderer of his father, as the Ghost has said; and the King as the criminal, made anxious by the behavior of the detective, trying in turn to find out what lies in the Prince's mind. Acts IV and V present a revenge story. It begins when Hamlet stands behind the praying King with sword drawn (III, iii) and ends only when he drives that sword home in the last scene.

The appeal of *Hamlet* does not lie in the story alone, exciting as this is. It lies also in the play's personalities. These are highly individualized, drawn from an exceptionally wide range of physical, mental, and social types, each sharing to some degree in the psychological fascination of the hero himself, whose complexity is proverbial.

Besides interesting people and a sensational plot, *Hamlet* has variety—variety of every conceivable kind: of personalities; of moods—tragic, heroic, meditative, satirical, comic; of incidents—murder, madness, a ghost, a play within the play, suicide, swordplay, poison; of spectacle—soldiers in a chill midnight on a dark parapet waiting tensely for a ghost, a court blazing with light and resplendent in fine costumes and jewels, a lunatic girl pitifully singing scraps of old off-color songs and distributing imaginary flowers, two quiet men in a graveyard musing over a skull, a great fencing match which turns into a duel to the death and claims four lives; of speech patterns—many different mediums (prose, blank verse, couplet verse, ballad stanza) and many different idioms and vocabularies within these.

What has so far been said, practically everyone agrees to. It is when we approach the question—What does the play mean?—that we move into the area of controversy. What can be said that will help us make sense of the play, while not pretending to be the whole truth, or in any sense the final truth? We can say that the play has a political meaning, to which Shakespeare's original audiences were probably a good deal more sensitive than we are, and that it has a broadly human meaning, which is probably clearer to us after three and a half centuries than it was to them.

On its political side, the play is the story of a kingdom corrupted and destroyed from within. The cause of the corruption is the King's crime, with all the consequences that are to flow from it. When the play opens, the corruption is sensed, but it is not yet identified. The soldiers on watch on the castle platform feel that something is wrong, that something is "rotten in the state of Denmark," as one of them puts it later. Hamlet, too, senses that something is wrong: life is hardly worth the living. For the time being, he thinks it is his mother's indecent haste in remarrying with his uncle, and the lack of real feeling for his dead father that this shows. But the trouble lies deeper, as he soon learns from the Ghost: his mother has been seduced, his father murdered, and his uncle is the seducer and poisoner.

What the play proceeds to show us is how this same poison, the King's crime, runs through the whole body politic, with similarly destructive effects. It has already infected the Queen; in due course, through the King's efforts to keep his crime undetected and unpunished, most of the other members of the court become its victims. Shakespeare stresses this point very plainly by placing three scenes of poisoning in the play, each at the climax of one of the three plot movements which we spoke of before: the poisoning that the Ghost describes (I, v), the poisoning that the traveling actors enact in the old play (III, ii), and the poisoning at the fencing match (V, ii). In all three cases the essential poisoner, though he may corrupt others to assist him, is the King.

On its broadly human side, we may consider *Hamlet* to be the story of a young man growing up. It was only a little while ago that the world seemed an enchanting place to Hamlet, and human beings wonderful almost as angels or gods (II, ii, 297-314). But he no longer feels that way as the play opens (I, ii, 129-159). He has suffered a savage shock. He has been called home from the university for his father's funeral, only to find the funeral speedily succeeded by his mother's remarriage—and to a man for whom he has only contempt: "My father's brother, but no more like my father/Than I to Hercules."

Worse is still to come, however; for the blow of his mother's marriage is capped by the discovery of her adultery and his father's murder. With a sickening impact, he discovers that the world and human nature are capable of containing enormous ugliness and evil, and for a time he can think of little else. If this is what human beings are, how can anyone wish to go on living—is it not better to commit suicide and be done with it? "To be or not to be" becomes for him a real question. Moreover, if this is what human beings are, how can anyone wish to perpetuate the human species? And so he cries out to Ophelia, "Get thee to a nunnery. Why wouldst thou be a breeder of sinners?"

While Hamlet is making this discovery of evil, he is also, inevitably, making another: that people and things are not necessarily what they seem. Puzzling surfaces are all about him. The Ghost itself is one: is it a true ghost, or a devil? The King is one: is he a murderer and seducer, as the Ghost alleges, or not? His mother is one: how guilty is she? how much does she know? Ophelia is one: she seems innocent and beautiful, especially at the moment he stumbles on her at prayers; yet something—some movement or some sound behind him as he talks— makes him suspect she is the King's and Polonius's decoy. And the whole court is equally deceptive: only two months ago everyone was in mourning for the great King, his father, supposedly held dear, but now they have forgotten him as if he had never been; their grief was all appearance.

In his effort to take action against the King in this world of appearances, Hamlet makes a third discovery. He discovers how easy it is in the struggle with an underhanded evil to become contaminated by its methods. Before he himself finishes, he has put on a false front—his disguise of lunacy; has helped by his savage unkindness to drive Ophelia to madness and suicide; has killed Polonius; has sent his two school friends to their deaths in order to avoid being sent to his. To be sure, these are spectacular evils—much more spectacular than most of us are ever likely to become involved with. But the problem of contamination is, nevertheless, a real one. We are capable of envy, slander, greed, cruelty, cowardice, betrayal; and if we are honest with ourselves, we can think of many an occasion when our capability has become fact.

Hamlet's last discovery is death. Death is the grimmest of the realities that Hamlet, or any man, has to face. We are aware of it, of course, from an early age; but we never really know what it means till we have seen it at close quarters. In *Hamlet,* Shakespeare presents it to us as close up as a work of literature possibly can. The whole play reverberates with death. Six of the dramatis personae die in the course of it. The Ghost of the dead King walks at night. The young Prince has been brought home for a funeral. The subject of the first court scene (I, ii) is death and what the attitude of the living should be toward it. In the famous lines beginning "To be or not to be" Hamlet meditates on what lies beyond death. The fragment of an old play that the leader of the traveling actors recites on their entrance concerns the death of King Priam of Troy; and in the play that these actors put on before the court the old King is painfully conscious that he is old and death approaches. Mad Ophelia sings snatches of songs about those who are dead and gone and will not come again. And Hamlet, in the scene in the graveyard with Horatio, finds himself encountering death in more and more painful forms. At first it is the anonymous dead: the politician, the courtier, the lawyer, each with his bustling self-importance, who now lie here. Then, closer home, it is Yorick, the court jester, on whose back Hamlet was carried as a child. And then, closest of all, it is Ophelia, whose drowned body the members of the Court now accompany to the grave.

All these things that Hamlet discovers with such anguish—evil, false appearances, contamination, and death—are part of our situation too. We inherit them simply by virtue of being born. Discovering them, learning how to live with them, is part of the process by which we—and Hamlet—grow up. Thus the man who goes to the duel with Laertes is very plainly a different being from the disillusioned undergraduate we met in the play's second scene. If he has hardened, he has also matured, and it strikes us as somehow right that this time he should achieve his objective, even if it comes about in a way he could not have foretold.

[The text of *Hamlet* presented here follows that of the so-called "good" quarto edition of 1604, now very generally held to have been printed from Shakespeare's manuscript. Lines and passages which appeared for the first time in the folio edition of 1623 (probably printed from the prompt-book of Shakespeare's acting company), have been added in square brackets. Square brackets also designate stage directions, except those which appear in the good quarto. Emendation of the text has been avoided so far as possible, the quarto readings of controversial passages being accepted in this text in preference to all others so long as they are not nonsense; but attention is frequently called to alternative readings in the marginal notes and glosses. The act-scene division follows that of the Globe Edition, to which the concordances of Shakespeare refer. In the good quarto, there are no act-scene divisions, and in the folio, none after II, ii.]

THE TRAGEDY OF HAMLET
Prince of Denmark

NAMES OF THE ACTORS

Claudius, KING OF DENMARK

Hamlet, SON TO THE LATE, AND NEPHEW TO THE PRES-
ENT, KING

Polonius, LORD CHAMBERLAIN

Horatio, FRIEND TO HAMLET

Laertes, SON TO POLONIUS

Voltemand
Cornelius
Rosencrantz
Guildenstern   COURTIERS
Osric
A Gentleman

A Priest
Marcellus
Bernardo   OFFICERS

Francisco, A SOLDIER

Reynaldo, SERVANT TO POLONIUS

Players

Two Clowns, GRAVEDIGGERS

Fortinbras, PRINCE OF NORWAY

A Norwegian Captain

English Ambassadors

Gertrude, QUEEN OF DENMARK, MOTHER TO HAMLET

Ophelia, DAUGHTER TO POLONIUS

Ghost of Hamlet's Father

Lords, Ladies, Officers, Soldiers, Sailors, Messengers,
Attendants

Scene: *Elsinore*

I, 1

Enter BERNARDO *and* FRANCISCO, *two sentinels.*

Bernardo. Who's there?

Francisco. Bernardo?

Bernardo. Long live the king!

Francisco. Bernardo?

5 *Bernardo.* He.

Francisco. You come most carefully upon your hour.

Bernardo. 'Tis now struck twelve. Get thee to bed, Francisco.

Francisco. For this relief much thanks. 'Tis bitter cold,
And I am sick at heart.

Bernardo. Have you had quiet guard?

10 *Francisco.*   Not a mouse stirring.

Bernardo. Well, good night.
If you do meet Horatio and Marcellus,
The rivals of my watch, bid them make haste.

Enter HORATIO *and* MARCELLUS.

Francisco. I think I hear them. Stand, ho! Who is there?

Horatio. Friends to this ground.

15 *Marcellus.*   And liegemen to the Dane.

Francisco. Give you good night.

Marcellus.   O, farewell, honest soldier.
Who hath relieved you?

Francisco.   Bernardo hath my place.
Give you good night.   *Exit* FRANCISCO.

Marcellus.   Holla, Bernardo!

Bernardo.   Say—
What, is Horatio there?

Horatio.   A piece of him.

20 *Bernardo.* Welcome, Horatio. Welcome, good Marcellus.

Horatio. What, has this thing appeared again to-night?

Bernardo. I have seen nothing.

Marcellus. Horatio says 'tis but our fantasy,
And will not let belief take hold of him

25 Touching this dreaded sight twice seen of us.
Therefore I have entreated him along
With us to watch the minutes of this night,
That, if again this apparition come,
He may approve our eyes and speak to it.

Horatio. Tush, tush, 'twill not appear.

3. *Long . . . king:* i.e., Bernardo gives the password.

13. *rivals:* partners.

15. *Dane:* Danish king.

16. *give you:* God give you.

19. *A . . . him:* (spoken jestingly).

23. *fantasy:* imagination.

25. *of:* by.

29. *approve:* confirm.

³⁰ *Bernardo.*   Sit down awhile,
    And let us once again assail your ears,
    That are so fortified against our story,
    What we two nights have seen.

33. *What:* with what.

    Horatio.   Well, sit we down,
    And let us hear Bernardo speak of this.

³⁵ *Bernardo.* Last night of all,
    When yond same star that's westward from the pole
    Had made his course t' illume that part of heaven
    Where now it burns, Marcellus and myself,
    The bell then beating one—

36. *pole:* North star.

                Enter GHOST.

⁴⁰ *Marcellus.* Peace, break thee off. Look where it comes
        again.
    Bernardo. In the same figure like the king that's dead.
    Marcellus. Thou art a scholar; speak to it, Horatio.

42. *scholar:* i.e., one who knows the language of spirits and how to exorcise them.

    Bernardo. Looks 'a not like the king? Mark it, Horatio.
    Horatio. Most like. It harrows me with fear and wonder.
    Bernardo. It would be spoke to.

⁴⁵ *Marcellus.*   Speak to it, Horatio.
    Horatio. What art thou that usurp'st this time of night

46. *usurp'st:* Horatio's first address to the apparition seems to imply it is not the ghost of the dead king (*buried Denmark*) but a usurper of the dead king's likeness. Therefore it is *offended.*

    Together with that fair and warlike form
    In which the majesty of buried Denmark
    Did sometimes march? By heaven I charge thee, speak.

49. *sometimes:* formerly.

    Marcellus. It is offended.

⁵⁰ *Bernardo.*   See, it stalks away.
    Horatio. Stay. Speak, speak. I charge thee, speak.

                  Exit GHOST.

    Marcellus. 'Tis gone and will not answer.
    Bernardo. How now, Horatio? You tremble and look pale.
    Is not this something more than fantasy?

⁵⁵   What think you on't?
    Horatio. Before my God, I might not this believe
    Without the sensible and true avouch
    Of mine own eyes.

57. *sensible . . . avouch:* sensory and (therefore) true assurance.

    Marcellus.   Is it not like the king?
    Horatio. As thou art to thyself.

⁶⁰   Such was the very armor he had on
    When he th' ambitious Norway combated.

61. *Norway:* king of Norway.

    So frowned he once when, in an angry parle,

62. *parle:* dispute.

    He smote the sledded Polacks on the ice.
    'Tis strange.

63. *sledded Polacks:* i.e., sled-using Polish forces.

⁶⁵ *Marcellus.* Thus twice before, and jump at this dead hour,
　　With martial stalk hath he gone by our watch.
　Horatio. In what particular thought to work I know not;
　　But, in the gross and scope of my opinion,
　　This bodes some strange eruption to our state.
⁷⁰ *Marcellus.* Good now, sit down, and tell me he that
　　　　knows,
　　Why this same strict and most observant watch
　　So nightly toils the subject of the land,
　　And why such daily cast of brazen cannon
　　And foreign mart for implements of war,
⁷⁵ Why such impress of shipwrights, whose sore task
　　Does not divide the Sunday from the week.
　　What might be toward that this sweaty haste
　　Doth make the night joint-laborer with the day?
　　Who is't that can inform me?
　Horatio.　　　　　　　　　　That can I.
⁸⁰ At least the whisper goes so. Our last king,
　　Whose image even but now appeared to us,
　　Was as you know by Fortinbras of Norway,
　　Thereto pricked on by a most emulate pride,
　　Dared to the combat; in which our valiant Hamlet
⁸⁵ (For so this side of our known world esteemed him)
　　Did slay this Fortinbras; who, by a sealed compact
　　Well ratified by law and heraldry,
　　Did forfeit, with his life, all those his lands
　　Which he stood seized of to the conqueror;
⁹⁰ Against the which a moiety competent
　　Was gagèd by our king, which had returned
　　To the inheritance of Fortinbras
　　Had he been vanquisher, as, by the same comart
　　And carriage of the article designed,
⁹⁵ His fell to Hamlet. Now, sir, young Fortinbras,
　　Of unimprovèd mettle hot and full,
　　Hath in the skirts of Norway here and there
　　Sharked up a list of lawless resolutes
　　For food and diet to some enterprise
¹⁰⁰ That hath a stomach in't; which is no other,
　　As it doth well appear unto our state,
　　But to recover of us by strong hand
　　And terms compulsatory those foresaid lands
　　So by his father lost; and this, I take it,

65. *jump:* just. *dead:* exact.

67-68. *In . . . opinion:* I'm not sure what to make of it *precisely*, but my *general* opinion is that . . .

72. *So . . . land:* so wearies the Danish people night after night.
73-74. *And why . . . war:* Marcellus wonders how to explain the constant production of tools of war at home, and the trade abroad to obtain more.
75. *impress:* forced draft.
76. *Does . . . week:* allows not even Sunday off.
77. *toward:* in preparation. *that:* to account for the fact that.

83. *Thereto . . . pride:* i.e., Fortinbras was impelled to it by jealous pride.

85. *this . . . world:* i.e., Europe.

87. *law and heraldry:* rules laid down by heralds for regulating combats.

89. *stood . . . of:* owned.

90-91. *Against . . . king:* i.e., King Hamlet had put up equal stakes.
91. *had:* would have.

93. *comart:* contract (i.e., co-mart).
94. *carriage . . . designed:* effect of the article aforesaid.
95. *Young Fortinbras:* i.e., King Fortinbras's son.
96. *unimprovèd mettle:* unused (therefore eager to be used).
98. *Sharked up:* snapped up at random (as a shark does food).
99-100. *For . . . in't:* Horatio is saying not only that the desperadoes will get paid food and diet for participating in an enterprise that requires courage *(hath a stomach)*, but also that they will become food and diet to the enterprise, and be swallowed up in its stomach: See *sharked*, 98.
101. *state:* government.
103. *terms compulsatory:* i.e., force.

105 Is the main motive of our preparations,
The source of this our watch, and the chief head
Of this posthaste and romage in the land.
Bernardo. I think it be no other but e'en so.
Well may it sort that this portentous figure
110 Comes armèd through our watch so like the king
That was and is the question of these wars.
Horatio. A mote it is to trouble the mind's eye.
In the most high and palmy state of Rome,
A little ere the mightiest Julius fell,
115 The graves stood tenantless and the sheeted dead
Did squeak and gibber in the Roman streets;
As stars with trains of fire and dews of blood,
Disasters in the sun; and the moist star
Upon whose influence Neptune's empire stands
120 Was sick almost to doomsday with eclipse.
And even the like precurse of feared events,
As harbingers preceding still the fates
And prologue to the omen coming on,
Have heaven and earth together demonstrated
125 Unto our climatures and countrymen.

Enter GHOST.

But soft, behold, lo where it comes again!
I'll cross it, though it blast me.—Stay, illusion.

[GHOST] *spreads his arms.*

If thou hast any sound or use of voice,
Speak to me.
130 If there be any good thing to be done
That may to thee do ease and grace to me,
Speak to me.
If thou art privy to thy country's fate,
Which happily foreknowing may avoid,
135 O, speak!
Or if thou hast uphoarded in thy life
Extorted treasure in the womb of earth,
For which, they say, you spirits oft walk in death,

The cock crows.

Speak of it. Stay and speak. Stop it, Marcellus.
140 *Marcellus.* Shall I strike at it with my partisan?
Horatio. Do, if it will not stand.
Bernardo.   'Tis here.
Horatio.   'Tis here.
Marcellus. 'Tis gone.   [*Exit* GHOST.]

---

106. *head:* origin.
107. *romage:* uproar.
109. *Well . . . sort:* appropriate it may be.
111. *question:* occasion.
112. *mote:* speck.
113. *palmy:* flourishing.
115. *tenantless:* i.e., emptied. *sheeted:* i.e., wearing burial shrouds.
117-118. *As . . . sun:* Horatio lists the portents seen in Rome before Julius Caesar's death; but the Elizabethan printer has apparently omitted a line, and "As" has nothing to refer to.
118. *disasters:* evil signs.
118-120. *the moist . . . eclipse:* the moon on which the tides of the sea depend was darkened as if it were Judgment Day.
121. *precurse of:* advance warning by means of.
122. *harbingers:* forerunners.
123. *omen:* calamity.
125. *our climatures:* our part of the world.
127. *cross it:* (1) cross its path, (2) (en-)counter it with the sign of the cross (a protection against evil spirits). *[Ghost]:* Words and passages in brackets appeared for the first time in the 1623 edition of the play.
131. *to thee . . . me:* bring you ease without doing me dishonor.
133. *privy to:* secretly informed of.
134. *happily:* perhaps (haply).
140. *partisan:* spear.

We do it wrong, being so majestical,
To offer it the show of violence,
145 For it is as the air invulnerable,
And our vain blows malicious mockery.

Bernardo. It was about to speak when the cock crew.

Horatio. And then it started, like a guilty thing
Upon a fearful summons. I have heard
150 The cock, that is the trumpet to the morn,
Doth with his lofty and shrill-sounding throat
Awake the god of day, and at his warning,
Whether in sea or fire, in earth or air,
Th' extravagant and erring spirit hies
155 To his confine; and of the truth herein
This present object made probation.

Marcellus. It faded on the crowing of the cock.
Some say that ever 'gainst that season comes
Wherein our Saviour's birth is celebrated,
160 This bird of dawning singeth all night long,
And then, they say, no spirit dare stir abroad,
The nights are wholesome, then no planets strike,
No fairy takes, nor witch hath power to charm.
So hallowed and so gracious is that time.

165 *Horatio.* So have I heard and do in part believe it.
But look, the morn in russet mantle clad
Walks o'er the dew of yon high eastward hill.
Break we our watch up, and by my advice
Let us impart what we have seen to-night
170 Unto young Hamlet, for upon my life
This spirit, dumb to us, will speak to him.
Do you consent we shall acquaint him with it,
As needful in our loves, fitting our duty?

Marcellus. Let's do't, I pray, and I this morning know
175 Where we shall find him most conveniently.   *Exeunt.*

I, II

Flourish. Enter CLAUDIUS, KING OF DENMARK, GERTRUDE
THE QUEEN, COUNCILLORS, POLONIUS AND HIS SON
LAERTES, HAMLET, CUM ALIIS [*including* VOLTEMAND
and CORNELIUS].

King. Though yet of Hamlet our dear brother's death
The memory be green, and that it us befitted
To bear our hearts in grief, and our whole kingdom
To be contracted in one brow of woe,

146. *malicious mockery:* a mere imitation of harm (because ineffectual).

150. *trumpet:* trumpeter.

152. *god of day:* sun.

154. *extravagant and erring:* straying beyond bounds.
154-155. *hies . . . confine:* hurries back within his normal limits.
156. *probation:* proof.

158. *'gainst:* just before.

162. *strike:* injure (alluding to astrological beliefs in the influence of the stars).
163. *takes:* bewitches.

166. *russet:* (1) ruddy gray-brown color, (2) a rough cloth of this color worn by rustics—i.e., the morn comes on like a farmer up early for his chores.

170. *young Hamlet:* i.e., son of the king whose ghost they believe they have seen.

173. *needful . . . loves:* i.e., since we are his friends.

1. *our:* the king uses the royal "we."

2. *that:* though.

5 Yet so far hath discretion fought with nature
That we with wisest sorrow think on him
Together with remembrance of ourselves.
Therefore our sometime sister, now our queen,
Th' imperial jointress to this warlike state,
10 Have we, as 'twere with a defeated joy,
With an auspicious and a dropping eye,
With mirth in funeral and with dirge in marriage,
In equal scale weighing delight and dole,
Taken to wife. Nor have we herein barred
15 Your better wisdoms, which have freely gone
With this affair along. For all, our thanks.
Now follows, that you know, young Fortinbras,
Holding a weak supposal of our worth,
Or thinking by our late dear brother's death
20 Our state to be disjoint and out of frame,
Colleaguèd with this dream of his advantage,
He hath not failed to pester us with message
Importing the surrender of those lands
Lost by his father, with all bands of law,
25 To our most valiant brother. So much for him.
Now for ourself and for this time of meeting.
Thus much the business is: we have here writ
To Norway, uncle of young Fortinbras—
Who, impotent and bedrid, scarcely hears
30 Of this his nephew's purpose—to suppress
His further gait herein, in that the levies,
The lists, and full proportions are all made
Out of his subject; and we here dispatch
You, good Cornelius, and you, Voltemand,
35 For bearers of this greeting to old Norway,
Giving to you no further personal power
To business with the king, more than the scope
Of these delated articles allow.
Farewell, and let your haste commend your duty.
40 *Cornelius, Voltemand.* In that, and all things, will we
show our duty.
King. We doubt it nothing. Heartily farewell.
[*Exeunt* VOLTEMAND *and* CORNELIUS.]
And now, Laertes, what's the news with you?
You told us of some suit. What is't, Laertes?
You cannot speak of reason to the Dane

5. *discretion:* reason. *nature:* i.e., natural grief.

8. *sometime:* former.

9. *jointress:* partner.

10. *defeated joy:* joy that is also grief.

11. *an . . . dropping:* one joyful and one tearful.

13. *dole:* pain.

17. *that:* what.

18. *weak supposal:* low opinion.

20. *disjoint . . . frame:* upset and disordered.
21. *Colleagued . . . advantage:* added to this imagination of his superiority.

24. *with . . . law:* legitimately.

31. *gait:* progress.

31-33. *in that . . . subject:* because the supplies and forces used are all taken from his (the King of Norway's) subjects.

38. *delated:* specified.

43. *suit:* request.

44. *speak . . . to:* ask anything reasonable of.

45 And lose your voice. What wouldst thou beg, Laertes,
    That shall not be my offer, not thy asking?
    The head is not more native to the heart,   47. *native:* related by nature.
    The hand more instrumental to the mouth,
    Than is the throne of Denmark to thy father.
    What wouldst thou have, Laertes?

50 *Laertes.*   My dread lord,
    Your leave and favor to return to France,
    From whence though willingly I came to Denmark
    To show my duty in your coronation,
    Yet now I must confess, that duty done,
55 My thoughts and wishes bend again toward France
    And bow them to your gracious leave and pardon.

King. Have you your father's leave? What says Polonius?

Polonius. He hath, my lord, wrung from me my slow leave
    By laborsome petition, and at last
60 Upon his will I sealed my hard consent.   60. *will:* desire. *hard:* hard to be ob-
    I do beseech you give him leave to go.   tained.

King. Take thy fair hour, Laertes. Time be thine,   62-63. *Time . . . it:* Enjoy your youth while
    And thy best graces spend it at thy will.   you have it, and let thy best virtues
    But now, my cousin Hamlet, and my son—   control how it is spent.
                                                                64. *cousin:* term applied to a kinsman
65 *Hamlet.* [*aside*] A little more than kin, and less than kind!   who is not a member of one's im-
                                                                     mediate family.
King. How is it that the clouds still hang on you?   65. *A . . . kind:* Hamlet murmurs that
                                                                     the relationship is something more
Hamlet. Not so, my lord. I am too much in the sun.   than is implied in the king's word
                                                                     cousin but somewhat less than is
Queen. Good Hamlet, cast thy nighted color off,   implied in the king's word *son.*
    And let thine eye look like a friend on Denmark.   66. *clouds:* Hamlet wears mourning
70 Do not for ever with thy vailèd lids   and is still grieving for his father.
    Seek for thy noble father in the dust.   67. *sun.* i.e., the sunshine of your
                                                                     favor, with pun on "son"/"sun"
    Thou know'st 'tis common. All that lives must die,   which expresses his resentment at
    Passing through nature to eternity.   his uncle's calling him "my son."
                                                                68. *nighted color:* i.e., dark mood and
Hamlet. Ay, madam, it is common.   mourning clothing.
                                                                69. *Denmark:* i.e., the king.
Queen.   If it be,   70. *vailèd:* downcast.
75 Why seems it so particular with thee?   72. *'tis common:* i.e., death is universal.

Hamlet. Seems, madam? Nay, it is. I know not 'seems.'   75. *particular:* special.
    'Tis not alone my inky cloak, good mother,
    Nor customary suits of solemn black,
    Nor windy suspiration of forced breath,   79. *suspiration:* sighing.
80 No, nor·the fruitful river in the eye,   80. *fruitful:* overflowing.
    Nor the dejected havior of the visage,   81. *havior:* behavior.
    Together with all forms, moods, shapes of grief,
    That can denote me truly. These indeed seem,   83. *denote:* portray.
    For they are actions that a man might play,

85 But I have that within which passeth show—
These but the trappings and the suits of woe.

King. 'Tis sweet and còmmendable in your nature,
    Hamlet,
To give these mourning duties to your father,
But you must know your father lost a father,
90 That father lost, lost his, and the survivor bound
In filial obligation for some term
To do obsequious sorrow. But to persèver
In obstinate condolement is a course
Of impious stubbornness. 'Tis unmanly grief.
95 It shows a will most incorrect to heaven,
A heart unfortified, a mind impatient,
An understanding simple and unschooled.
For what we know must be and is as common
As any the most vulgar thing to sense,
100 Why should we in our peevish opposition
Take it to heart? Fie, 'tis a fault to heaven,
A fault against the dead, a fault to nature,
To reason most absurd, whose common theme
Is death of fathers, and who still hath cried,
105 From the first corse till he that died to-day,
'This must be so.' We pray you throw to earth
This unprevailing woe, and think of us
As of a father, for let the world take note
You are the most immediate to our throne,
110 And with no less nobility of love
Than that which dearest father bears his son
Do I impart toward you. For your intent
In going back to school in Wittenberg,
It is most retrograde to our desire,
115 And we beseech you, bend you to remain
Here in the cheer and comfort of our eye,
Our chiefest courtier, cousin, and our son.

Queen. Let not thy mother lose her prayers, Hamlet.
I pray thee stay with us, go not to Wittenberg.

120 *Hamlet.* I shall in all my best obey you, madam.

King. Why, 'tis a loving and a fair reply.
Be as ourself in Denmark. Madam, come.
This gentle and unforced accord of Hamlet
Sits smiling to my heart, in grace whereof

---

91. *term:* period.
92. *obsequious:* i.e., suited to obsequies (funerals).
93. *condolement:* sorrow.

95. *incorrect to heaven:* i.e., rebellious against heaven's will (in taking the loved person).
96. *impatient:* i.e., unable to accept suffering.

99. *As . . . sense:* as any everyday experience.

105. *corse:* corpse.

107. *unprevailing:* ineffectual.

109. *most immediate:* i.e., the heir.

112. *impart . . . you:* (1) express my mind to you? (2) desire to share with you?
113. *Wittenberg:* the university in Germany from which Hamlet returned for his father's funeral.
114. *retrograde:* contrary.
115. *bend you to:* do yield to our wish that you.

122. *as ourself:* i.e., as if you were king.

124. *grace:* honor.

125 No jocund health that Denmark drinks to-day
But the great cannon to the clouds shall tell,
And the king's rouse the heaven shall bruit again,
Respeaking earthly thunder. Come away.

Flourish. Exeunt all but HAMLET.

Hamlet. O that this too too solid flesh would melt,
130 Thaw, and resolve itself into a dew,
Or that the Everlasting had not fixed
His canon 'gainst self-slaughter. O God, God,
How weary, stale, flat, and unprofitable
Seem to me all the uses of this world!
135 Fie on't, ah, fie, 'tis an unweeded garden
That grows to seed. Things rank and gross in nature
Possess it merely. That it should come to this,
But two months dead, nay, not so much, not two,
So excellent a king, that was to this
140 Hyperion to a satyr, so loving to my mother
That he might not beteem the winds of heaven
Visit her face too roughly. Heaven and earth,
Must I remember? Why, she would hang on him
As if increase of appetite had grown
145 By what it fed on, and yet within a month—
Let me not think on't; frailty, thy name is woman—
A little month, or ere those shoes were old
With which she followed my poor father's body
Like Niobe, all tears, why she, even she—
150 O God, a beast that wants discourse of reason
Would have mourned longer—married with my uncle,
My father's brother, but no more like my father
Than I to Hercules. Within a month,
Ere yet the salt of most unrighteous tears
155 Had left the flushing in her gallèd eyes,
She married. O, most wicked speed, to post
With such dexterity to incestuous sheets!
It is not, nor it cannot come to good.
But break my heart, for I must hold my tongue.

Enter HORATIO, MARCELLUS, *and* BERNARDO.

Horatio. Hail to your lordship!
160 *Hamlet.*   I am glad to see you well.
Horatio—or I do forget myself.
Horatio. The same, my lord, and your poor servant ever.

125-127. *No . . . again:* i.e., every health the king drinks today shall be announced by cannon, and thus the heavens will echo *(bruit)* the king's toast *(rouse).*

129. *solid:* a disputed word (written "sallied" in the Quarto) which may be our modern "solid," or modern "sullied." If the latter, Hamlet is thinking of himself as soiled by his mother's incest.
130. *resolve:* dissolve.
132. *canon:* law.

137. *merely:* wholly.

139-140. *that . . . satyr:* Hamlet contrasts his father (handsome and noble as the sun god Hyperion) with his uncle (ugly and goatish—a satyr).
141. *beteem:* permit.

147. *or ere:* before.

149. *Niobe:* Niobe, in Greek mythology, was transformed into a weeping stone because of her great grief.
150. *wants . . . reason:* lacks human rationality.

154. *unrighteous:* i.e., insincere.

155. *left . . . eyes:* ceased to inflame her irritated eyes.
156. *post:* hurry.

157. *incestuous:* Contemporary theologions held that marriage between a woman and her dead husband's brother was within the forbidden degrees of relationship, and thus incestuous.

160. *I . . . well:* spoken absently, before Hamlet recognizes Horatio.

Hamlet. Sir, my good friend, I'll change that name with
you.

And what make you from Wittenberg, Horatio?
165   Marcellus?

Marcellus. My good lord!

Hamlet. I am very glad to see you. [*to* BERNARDO] Good
even, sir.

But what, in faith, make you from Wittenberg?

Horatio. A truant disposition, good my lord.

170 *Hamlet.* I would not hear your enemy say so,
Nor shall you do my ear that violence
To make it truster of your own report
Against yourself. I know you are no truant.
But what is your affair in Elsinore?

175   We'll teach you to drink deep ere you depart.

Horatio. My lord, I came to see your father's funeral.

Hamlet. I prithee do not mock me, fellow student.
I think it was to see my mother's wedding.

Horatio. Indeed, my lord, it followed hard upon.

180 *Hamlet.* Thrift, thrift, Horatio. The funeral baked meats
Did coldly furnish forth the marriage tables.
Would I had met my dearest foe in heaven
Or ever I had seen that day, Horatio!
My father—methinks I see my father.

Horatio. Where, my lord?

185 *Hamlet.*   In my mind's eye, Horatio.

Horatio. I saw him once. 'A was a goodly king.

Hamlet. 'A was a man, take him for all in all,
I shall not look upon his like again.

Horatio. My lord, I think I saw him yesternight.

190 *Hamlet.* Saw? who?

Horatio. My lord, the king your father.

Hamlet.   The king my father?

Horatio. Season your admiration for a while
With an attent ear till I may deliver
Upon the witness of these gentlemen
This marvel to you.

195 *Hamlet.*   For God's love let me hear!

Horatio. Two nights together had these gentlemen,
Marcellus and Bernardo, on their watch
In the dead waste and middle of the night
Been thus encountered. A figure like your father,
200   Armèd at point exactly, cap-a-pe,

163. *I'll . . . you:* the name I'll exchange with you is *friend,* not *servant.*

164. *what make you:* what are you doing away.

179. *hard:* close.

180-181. *The . . . tables:* i.e., food for the funeral feast had hardly grown cold when it was used again for the wedding feast (Hamlet speaks bitterly).

182. *dearest:* bitterest.

183. *Or ever:* before.

192. *Season . . . admiration:* Moderate your wonder.

193. *attent:* attentive.

198. *waste:* emptiness.

200. *at . . . cap-a-pe:* completely, from head to toe.

Appears before them and with solemn march
Goes slow and stately by them. Thrice he walked
By their oppressed and fear-surprisèd eyes
Within his truncheon's length, whilst they, distilled
205   Almost to jelly with the act of fear,
Stand dumb and speak not to him. This to me
In dreadful secrecy impart they did,
And I with them the third night kept the watch,
Where, as they had delivered, both in time,
210   Form of the thing, each word made true and good,
The apparition comes. I knew your father.
These hands are not more like.
Hamlet.   But where was this?
Marcellus. My lord, upon the platform where we watched.
Hamlet. Did you not speak to it?
Horatio.   My lord, I did,
215   But answer made it none. Yet once methought
It lifted up it head and did address
Itself to motion like as it would speak.
But even then the morning cock crew loud,
And at the sound it shrunk in haste away
And vanished from our sight.
220 *Hamlet.*   'Tis very strange.
Horatio. As I do live, my honored lord, 'tis true,
And we did think it writ down in our duty
To let you know of it.
Hamlet. Indeed, indeed, sirs, but this troubles me.
Hold you the watch to-night?
225 *All.*   We do, my lord.
Hamlet. Armed, say you?
All. Armed, my lord.
Hamlet. From top to toe?
All.   My lord, from head to foot.
Hamlet. Then saw you not his face?
230 *Horatio.* O, yes, my lord. He wore his beaver up.
Hamlet. What, looked he frowningly?
Horatio. A countenance more in sorrow than in anger.
Hamlet. Pale or red?
Horatio. Nay, very pale.
Hamlet.   And fixed his eyes upon you?
Horatio. Most constantly.
235 *Hamlet.*   I would I had been there.
Horatio. It would have much amazed you.

204. *truncheon:* officer's staff.
205. *act:* effect.
216. *it:* its.
216-217. *did . . . as:* made movements as if.
230. *beaver:* visor.

Hamlet. Very like, very like. Stayed it long?

Horatio. While one with moderate haste might tell a hundred.

Both. Longer, longer.

Horatio. Not when I saw't.

240 *Hamlet.*   His beard was grizzled, no?

Horatio. It was as I have seen it in his life,
A sable silvered.

Hamlet.   I will watch to-night.
Perchance 'twill walk again.

Horatio.   I warr'nt it will.

Hamlet. If it assume my noble father's person,

245 I'll speak to it though hell itself should gape
And bid me hold my peace. I pray you all,
If you have hitherto concealed this sight,
Let it be tenable in your silence still,
And whatsomever else shall hap to-night,

250 Give it an understanding but no tongue.
I will requite your loves. So fare you well.
Upon the platform, 'twixt eleven and twelve
I'll visit you.

All.   Our duty to your honor.

Hamlet. Your loves, as mine to you. Farewell.

Exeunt [all but HAMLET].

255 My father's spirit—in arms? All is not well.
I doubt some foul play. Would the night were come!
Till then sit still, my soul. Foul deeds will rise,
Though all the earth o'erwhelm them, to men's eyes.

Exit.

I, III

Enter LAERTES *and* OPHELIA, *his sister.*

Laertes. My necessaries are embarked. Farewell.
And, sister, as the winds give benefit
And convoy is assistant, do not sleep,
But let me hear from you.

Ophelia.   Do you doubt that?

5 *Laertes.* For Hamlet, and the trifling of his favor,
Hold it a fashion and a toy in blood,
A violet in the youth of primy nature,
Forward, not permanent, sweet, not lasting,

---

237. *like:* likely.

238. *tell:* count.

240. *grizzled:* graying.

245. *though . . . gape:* i.e., even if it is a fiend from hell instead of my father.

248. *be tenable:* remain.

254. *Your . . . you:* i.e., you are my friends offering me *love*, not servants owing *duty*.

256. *doubt:* suspect.

2-4. *as . . . you:* According as winds and means of conveyance permit, do not neglect to write me.

5-7. *For . . . nature:* As for Hamlet and his idle fondness for you, consider it a passing fad of adolescence, a fragile bloom of early spring.

8. *Forward:* premature.

The perfume and suppliance of a minute,
No more.
Ophelia.   No more but so?
10 *Laertes.*   Think it no more.
    For nature crescent does not grow alone
    In thews and bulk, but as this temple waxes
    The inward service of the mind and soul
    Grows wide withal. Perhaps he loves you now,
15 And now no soil nor cautel doth besmirch
    The virtue of his will, but you must fear,
    His greatness weighed, his will is not his own.
    [For he himself is subject to his birth.]
    He may not, as unvalued persons do,
20 Carve for himself, for on his choice depends
    The safety and health of this whole state,
    And therefore must his choice be circumscribed
    Unto the voice and yielding of that body
    Whereof he is the head. Then if he says he loves you,
25 It fits your wisdom so far to believe it
    As he in his particular act and place
    May give his saying deed, which is no further
    Than the main voice of Denmark goes withal.
    Then weigh what loss your honor may sustain
30 If with too credent ear you list his songs,
    Or lose your heart, or your chaste treasure open
    To his unmastered importunity.
    Fear it, Ophelia, fear it, my dear sister,
    And keep you in the rear of your affection,
35 Out of the shot and danger of desire.
    The chariest maid is prodigal enough
    If she unmask her beauty to the moon.
    Virtue itself scapes not calumnious strokes.
    The canker galls the infants of the spring
40 Too oft before their buttons be disclosed,
    And in the morn and liquid dew of youth
    Contagious blastments are most imminent.
    Be wary then; best safety lies in fear.
    Youth to itself rebels, though none else near.
45 *Ophelia.* I shall the effect of this good lesson keep
    As watchman to my heart, but, good my brother,
    Do not as some ungracious pastors do,
    Show me the steep and thorny way to heaven,

9. *suppliance:* pastime.

11-14. *For . . . withal:* For growth in human beings is not merely physical, but as we expand in body, we also enlarge in mind.

15. *soil nor cautel:* blemish or deceit.
16. *will:* desire.
17. *His . . . weighed:* his position as crown prince considered.
19. *unvalued:* untitled.
20. *Carve for himself:* take what he wishes.
21. *Safety:* pronounced here with three syllables: sa-fe-ty.
23. *yielding:* assent. *that body:* i.e., Denmark.

26-27. *As . . . deed:* i.e., as he, in actual fact, and being a prince, may put his words into effect.
28. *goes withal:* i.e., will go along with, allow.

30. *credent:* trustful. *list:* listen to.
31. *chaste treasure:* chastity.
32. *unmastered importunity:* unrestrained insistence.

34. *in the rear:* i.e., safely behind the lines (the metaphor is military, as in *shot,* 35).
36. *chariest:* most careful.

38. *scapes . . . strokes:* does not entirely escape slander.
39-40. *The . . . disclosed:* the cankerworm injures the earliest spring flowers too often before their buds are opened.
42. *blastments:* blights.

44. *to itself:* against its better self.

47. *pastors:* (1) ministers, (2) shepherds.

Whiles like a puffed and reckless libertine

50   Himself the primrose path of dalliance treads

And recks not his own rede.

Enter POLONIUS.

Laertes.   O, fear me not.

I stay too long. But here my father comes.

A double blessing is a double grace;

Occasion smiles upon a second leave.

55 *Polonius.* Yet here, Laertes? Aboard, aboard, for shame!

The wind sits in the shoulder of your sail,

And you are stayed for. There—my blessing with thee,

And these few precepts in thy memory

Look thou character. Give thy thoughts no tongue,

60   Nor any unproportioned thought his act.

Be thou familiar, but by no means vulgar.

Those friends thou hast, and their adoption tried,

Grapple them unto thy soul with hoops of steel,

But do not dull thy palm with entertainment

65   Of each new-hatched, unfledged couràge. Beware

Of entrance to a quarrel; but being in,

Bear't that th' opposèd may beware of thee.

Give every man thine ear, but few thy voice;

Take each man's censure, but reserve thy judgment.

70   Costly thy habit as thy purse can buy,

But not expressed in fancy; rich, not gaudy,

For the apparel oft proclaims the man,

And they in France of the best rank and station

Are of a most select and generous chief in that.

75   Neither a borrower nor a lender be,

For loan oft loses both itself and friend,

And borrowing dulleth edge of husbandry.

This above all, to thine own self be true,

And it must follow as the night the day

80   Thou canst not then be false to any man.

Farewell. My blessing season this in thee!

Laertes. Most humbly do I take my leave, my lord.

Polonius. The time invites you. Go, your servants tend.

Laertes. Farewell, Ophelia, and remember well

What I have said to you.

85 *Ophelia.*   'Tis in my memory locked,

And you yourself shall keep the key of it.

Laertes. Farewell.   *Exit* LAERTES.

---

49. *puffed:* puffed up with pride.

51. *recks . . . rede:* doesn't heed his own advice. *fear me not:* don't worry about me.

53. *double:* Laertes had already taken his leave and received his father's blessing once.
54. *Occasion . . . leave:* Opportunity treats me well in allowing me a second leave-taking.

59. *Look . . . character:* see to it that you inscribe.
60. *unproportioned:* inappropriate.
61. *familiar:* friendly. *vulgar:* i.e., undiscriminating, *too* affable.
62. *Those . . . tried:* the friends you already have, whose loyalty you have tested.
64. *dull thy palm:* i.e., as one does by indiscriminate hand shaking.
65. *unfledged:* untested in friendship (the metaphor is of a young bird whose feathers have not yet grown). *couràge:* i.e., a "brave," a man of spirit.
67. *Bear't:* conduct yourself so.

69. *censure:* opinion.

70. *habit:* clothing.

71. *fancy:* singularity.

74. *chief:* eminence ("chiefness").

76. *For . . . friend:* i.e., the friend fails to repay, and is angry at being asked to.
77. *husbandry:* thrift.

81. *season:* ripen (to fulfillment in action).

Polonius. What is't, Ophelia, he hath said to you?

Ophelia. So please you, something touching the Lord
      Hamlet.

90 *Polonius.* Marry, well bethought.

    'Tis told me he hath very oft of late

    Given private time to you, and you yourself

    Have of your audience been most free and bounteous.

    If it be so—as so 'tis put on me,

95   And that in way of caution—I must tell you

    You do not understand yourself so clearly

    As it behooves my daughter and your honor.

    What is between you? Give me up the truth.

Ophelia. He hath, my lord, of late made many tenders

100   Of his affection to me.

Polonius. Affection? Pooh! You speak like a green girl,

    Unsifted in such perilous circumstance.

    Do you believe his tenders, as you call them?

Ophelia. I do not know, my lord, what I should think.

105 *Polonius.* Marry, I will teach you. Think yourself a baby

    That you have ta'en these tenders for true pay

    Which are not sterling. Tender yourself more dearly,

    Or (not to crack the wind of the poor phrase,

    Running it thus) you'll tender me a fool.

110 *Ophelia.* My lord, he hath impòrtuned me with love

    In honorable fashion.

Polonius. Ay, fashion you may call it. Go to, go to.

Ophelia. And hath given countenance to his speech, my
      lord,

    With almost all the holy vows of heaven.

115 *Polonius.* Ay, springes to catch woodcocks. I do know,

    When the blood burns, how prodigal the soul

    Lends the tongue vows. These blazes, daughter,

    Giving more light than heat, extinct in both

    Even in their promise, as it is a-making,

120   You must not take for fire. From this time

    Be something scanter of your maiden presence.

    Set your entreatments at a higher rate

    Than a command to parley. For Lord Hamlet,

    Believe so much in him that he is young,

125   And with a larger tether may he walk

    Than may be given you. In few, Ophelia,

    Do not believe his vows, for they are brokers,

90. *Marry:* i.e., by the Virgin Mary.

93. *audience:* company.

94-95. *as . . . caution:* as someone has told
me by way of warning.

96-97. *You . . . honor:* You do not understand how to behave as suits a daughter of mine and your own good name.

99. *tenders:* offers.

102. *unsifted:* untested (the metaphor is of testing a substance by passing it through a sieve).

106. *tenders:* promises.

107. *Tender:* value.

108-109. *not . . . thus:* not to wear the phrase out by over-using it (the metaphor is of breaking a horse's wind by riding him too hard).

109. *tender . . . fool:* (1) show yourself a fool, (2) make me appear a fool, (3) present me with a baby.

110. *impòrtuned:* entreated.

112. *fashion:* a passing fad. *Go . . . to:* i.e., go away! nonsense!

113. *countenance:* authority.

115. *springes . . . woodcocks:* snares to catch fools (the woodcock is a bird easily taken).

116. *prodigal:* prodigally.

118-119. *Giving . . . a-making:* i.e., having more the look *(light)* than the reality *(heat)* of fire, and dying out in both respects as fast as made.

121-123. *Be . . . parley:* See him less often, and don't be like a town under siege that consents to negotiations just because the enemy demands them.

126. *In few:* in short.

127. *brokers:* (1) middlemen, (2) panders, i.e., procurers for prostitutes.

Not of that dye which their investments show,

But mere implorators of unholy suits,

130   Breathing like sanctified and pious bonds,

The better to beguile. This is for all:

I would not, in plain terms, from this time forth

Have you so slander any moment leisure

As to give words or talk with the Lord Hamlet.

135   Look to't, I charge you. Come your ways.

Ophelia. I shall obey, my lord.   *Exeunt.*

128. *dye:* i.e., of innocence. *invest-ments:* clothes—but with pun on the commercial sense.
129. *suits:* (1) petitions, (2) lawsuits, (3) lusts (again with pun on the clothing sense).
130. *Breathing . . . bonds:* i.e., his vows make the sound of sacred and holy promises. (But some editors alter "bonds" to "bawds.")
127-131. Polonius interweaves a clothing metaphor *(dye, (in)vestments, suits)* with a business and legal metaphor *(brokers, investments, suits, bonds).*
133. *slander:* misuse.

I, IV

Enter HAMLET, HORATIO, *and* MARCELLUS.

Hamlet. The air bites shrewdly; it is very cold.

Horatio. It is a nipping and an eager air.

Hamlet. What hour now?

Horatio.   I think it lacks of twelve.

Marcellus. No, it is struck.

5 *Horatio.* Indeed? I heard it not. It then draws near the
season

Wherein the spirit held his wont to walk.

A flourish of trumpets, and two pieces go off.

What does this mean, my lord?

Hamlet. The king doth wake to-night and takes his rouse,

Keeps wassail, and the swaggering upspring reels,

10   And as he drains his draughts of Rhenish down

The kettledrum and trumpet thus bray out

The triumph of his pledge.

Horatio.   Is it a custom?

Hamlet. Ay, marry, is't,

But to my mind, though I am native here

15   And to the manner born, it is a custom

More honored in the breach than the observance.

This heavy-headed revel east and west

Makes us traduced and taxed of other nations.

They clepe us drunkards and with swinish phrase

20   Soil our addition, and indeed it takes

From our achievements, though performed at height,

The pith and marrow of our attribute.

So oft it chances in particular men

That, for some vicious mole of nature in them,

25   As in their birth, wherein they are not guilty

1. *shrewdly:* sharply.

2. *eager:* keen.

6. *held his wont:* was accustomed.

8. *rouse:* revel

9. *upspring:* German dance. *reels:* Hamlet may mean either that the drunken dance reels through the hall, or that his drunken uncle reels through the dance.
10. *Rhenish:* Rhine wine.
12. *triumph . . . pledge:* achievement of his toast (i.e., in draining the cup at one draught).

16. *More . . . observance:* more honorable when broken than when kept.

18. *traduced . . . of:* defamed and censured by.
19. *clepe:* call.

20. *Soil . . . addition:* dirty our good name.

22. *attribute:* reputation (what is "attributed" to us).
23. *particular men:* individuals (as distinguished from *nations*).
24. *mole of nature:* natural blemish.
24-30. *That . . . manners:* Hamlet discusses two kinds of fault: (a) that which

(Since nature cannot choose his origin),

By the o'ergrowth of some complexion,

Oft breaking down the pales and forts of reason,

Or by some habit that too much o'erleavens

30 The form of plausive manners—that these men,

Carrying, I say, the stamp of one defect,

Being nature's livery, or fortune's star,

Their virtues else, be they as pure as grace,

As infinite as man may undergo,

35 Shall in the general censure take corruption

From that particular fault. The dram of evil

Doth all the noble substance of a doubt,

To his own scandal.

Enter GHOST.

Horatio.　　　　　Look, my lord, it comes.

Hamlet. Angels and ministers of grace defend us!

40 Be thou a spirit of health or goblin damned,

Bring with thee airs from heaven or blasts from hell,

Be thy intents wicked or charitable,

Thou com'st in such a questionable shape

That I will speak to thee. I'll call thee Hamlet,

45 King, father, royal Dane. O, answer me!

Let me not burst in ignorance, but tell

Why thy canònized bones, hearsèd in death,

Have burst their cerements, why the sepulchre

Wherein we saw thee quietly interred

50 Hath oped his ponderous and marble jaws

To cast thee up again. What may this mean

That thou, dead corse, again in complete steel,

Revisits thus the glimpses of the moon,

Making night hideous, and we fools of nature

55 So horridly to shake our disposition

With thoughts beyond the reaches of our souls?

Say, why is this? wherefore? what should we do?

[GHOST] *beckons.*

Horatio. It beckons you to go away with it,

As if it some impartment did desire

To you alone.

60 *Marcellus.*　　　Look with what courteous action

It waves you to a more removèd ground.

But do not go with it.

Horatio.　　　　　No, by no means.

---

may be lodged in us at birth and bring about such excess of some particular trait *(complexion)* that it breaks all reasonable bounds; *(b)* that which we may acquire through habit and which so thoroughly permeates *(o'erleavens)* us that it obscures our pleasing qualities.

32. *Being . . . star:* being either a costume imposed on us by our nature, or a distinguishing mark made on us by our circumstances—our fortune.
33. *Their . . . else:* their other virtues.
35. *censure:* opinion.
36. *dram:* tiny measure.
37. *Doth . . . doubt:* The wording is puzzling, and "of a doubt" has been variously emended to read "often dout" (i.e., extinguish) or even *oft adulter* (adulterate). But the sense is clear: that the small infusion of evil erupts and brings into disrepute the whole noble substance of the man.
38. *scandal:* discredit.

40. *Be . . . damned:* whether you are a good spirit or a devil.
41. *Bring:* whether you bring.
42. *Be thy intents:* whether your intentions are.

47. *canònized:* buried with full Christian rites and hence presumably at peace. *hearsèd:* coffined.
48. *cerements:* grave clothes.

53. *Revisits:* common Elizabethan form of the 2nd person singular: cf. I,v, 84. *the . . . moon:* (1) the moonlight, (2) the regions below the moon, thought of as the scene of human life.
54. *fools of nature:* natural beings dumbfounded by the supernatural.
55. *to . . . disposition:* to lose composure.

59. *impartment:* communication.

Hamlet. It will not speak. Then will I follow it.

Horatio. Do not, my lord.

Hamlet.   Why, what should be the fear?

65   I do not set my life at a pin's fee,

And for my soul, what can it do to that,

Being a thing immortal as itself?

It waves me forth again. I'll follow it.

65. *set . . . fee:* value my life a pin's worth.

Horatio. What if it tempt you toward the flood, my lord,

70   Or to the dreadful summit of the cliff

That beetles o'er his base into the sea,

And there assume some other horrible form,

Which might deprive your sovereignty of reason

And draw you into madness? Think of it.

69. *flood:* sea

71. *beetles o'er:* overhangs.

72. *form:* i.e., a devil's.

73. *deprive . . . reason:* deprive you of rationality.

75   The very place puts toys of desperation,

Without more motive, into every brain

That looks so many fathoms to the sea

And hears it roar beneath.

75. *toys of desperation:* suicidal fancies.

Hamlet.   It waves me still.

Go on. I'll follow thee.

Marcellus. You shall not go, my lord.

80 *Hamlet.*   Hold off your hands.

Horatio. Be ruled. You shall not go.

Hamlet.   My fate cries out

And makes each petty artere in this body

As hardy as the Nemean lion's nerve.

Still am I called. Unhand me, gentlemen.

82. *artere:* artery.

83. *Nemean lion:* the huge lion of Nemea slain by Hercules as one of his Twelve Labors.

85   By heaven, I'll make a ghost of him that lets me!

I say, away! Go on. I'll follow thee.

85. *lets:* hinders.

Exit GHOST, *and* HAMLET.

Horatio. He waxes desperate with imagination.

Marcellus. Let's follow. 'Tis not fit thus to obey him.

Horatio. Have after. To what issue will this come?

87. *waxes:* grows.

89. *Have after:* let's after him.

90 *Marcellus.* Something is rotten in the state of Denmark.

Horatio. Heaven will direct it.

Marcellus.   Nay, let's follow him.   *Exeunt.*

I, v

Enter GHOST *and* HAMLET.

Hamlet. Whither wilt thou lead me? Speak. I'll go no
        further.

Ghost. Mark me.

Hamlet.   I will.

2. *Mark:* hear.

Ghost.   My hour is almost come,
  When I to sulph'rous and tormenting flames
  Must render up myself.
Hamlet.   Alas, poor ghost!
5 *Ghost.* Pity me not, but lend thy serious hearing
  To what I shall unfold.
Hamlet.   Speak. I am bound to hear.
Ghost. So art thou to revenge, when thou shalt hear.
Hamlet. What?
Ghost. I am thy father's spirit,
10 Doomed for a certain term to walk the night,
  And for the day confined to fast in fires,
  Till the foul crimes done in my days of nature
  Are burnt and purged away. But that I am forbid
  To tell the secrets of my prison house,
15 I could a tale unfold whose lightest word
  Would harrow up thy soul, freeze thy young blood,
  Make thy two eyes like stars start from their spheres,
  Thy knotted and combinèd locks to part,
  And each particular hair to stand an end
20 Like quills upon the fretful porpentine.
  But this eternal blazon must not be
  To ears of flesh and blood. List, list, O, list!
  If thou didst ever thy dear father love—
Hamlet. O God!
25 *Ghost.* Revenge his foul and most unnatural murther.
Hamlet. Murther?
Ghost. Murther most foul, as in the best it is,
  But this most foul, strange, and unnatural.
Hamlet. Haste me to know't, that I, with wings as swift
30 As meditation or the thoughts of love,
  May sweep to my revenge.
Ghost.   I find thee apt,
  And duller shouldst thou be than the fat weed
  That roots itself in ease on Lethe wharf,
  Wouldst thou not stir in this. Now, Hamlet, hear.
35 'Tis given out that, sleeping in my orchard,
  A serpent stung me. So the whole ear of Denmark
  Is by a forgèd process of my death
  Rankly abused. But know, thou noble youth,
  The serpent that did sting thy father's life
  Now wears his crown.

3. *flames:* i.e., of Purgatory.

12. *foul crimes:* The ghost refers to the Christian doctrine that all men are sinners, not to any sensational wickedness of his own.
13. *But . . . am:* if I were not.

16. *harrow:* tear
17. *spheres:* the hollow concentric spheres in which, according to Ptolemaic astronomy, planets and stars were believed to be fastened (like the eyes in their sockets).
19. *particular:* individual. *an:* on.

20. *the . . . porpentine:* the irritated porcupine.
21. *eternal blazon:* revelation of the mysteries of eternity.
22. *List:* listen.

30. *meditation . . . love:* two proverbially swift movements: that of the mind to any object, and especially that of the lover's mind to his loved one.
31. *apt:* responsive.

33. *Lethe:* the river of the underworld which brings complete forgetfulness to all who drink of it.
34. *Wouldst . . . stir:* if you would not take action.

37. *process:* story.

38. *abused:* deceived.

40 *Hamlet.*   O my prophetic soul!
        My uncle?

    Ghost. Ay, that incestuous, that adulterate beast,   42. *adulterate:* adulterous.
        With witchcraft of his wit, with traitorous gifts—
        O wicked wit and gifts, that have the power
45   So to seduce!—won to his shameful lust
        The will of my most seeming-virtuous queen.
        O Hamlet, what a falling-off was there,
        From me, whose love was of that dignity
        That it went hand in hand even with the vow   49. *went . . . with:* lived perfectly up
                                                                                  to.
50   I made to her in marriage, and to decline   50-51. *decline upon:* descend to.
        Upon a wretch whose natural gifts were poor
        To those of mine!
        But virtue, as it never will be moved,
        Though lewdness court it in a shape of heaven,   54. *shape of heaven:* angel's guise or
                                                                                          costume.
55   So lust, though to a radiant angel linked,
        Will sate itself in a celestial bed
        And prey on garbage.
        But soft, methinks I scent the morning air.
        Brief let me be. Sleeping within my orchard,
60   My custom always of the afternoon,
        Upon my sècure hour thy uncle stole   61. *sècure: i.e.,* unsuspecting.
        With juice of cursed hebona in a vial,   62. *hebona:* a poisonous tree or plant,
                                                                          probably yew.
        And in the porches of my ears did pour
        The leperous distilment, whose effect   64. *effect:* operation.
65   Holds such an enmity with blood of man
        That swift as quicksilver it courses through
        The natural gates and alleys of the body,
        And with a sudden vigor it doth posset   68. *posset:* curdle.
        And curd, like eager droppings into milk,   69. *eager:* acid.
70   The thin and wholesome blood. So did it mine,
        And a most instant tetter barked about   71. *tetter:* skin eruption. *barked about:*
                                                                          covered as with bark.
        Most lazar-like with vile and loathsome crust   72. *lazar-like:* as if I were a leper
                                                                          (cf. "leperous," 64).
        All my smooth body.
        Thus was I sleeping by a brother's hand
75   Of life, of crown, of queen at once dispatched,   75. *dispatched:* deprived.
        Cut off even in the blossoms of my sin,   76. *the blossoms: i.e.,* the full flower.
        Unhouseled, disappointed, unaneled,   77. *Unhouseled . . . unaneled:* without
                                                                          benefit of the Eucharist, without
        No reck'ning made, but sent to my account   preparation (e.g., by confession),
        With all my imperfections on my head.   without extreme unction.
80   O, horrible! O, horrible! most horrible!
        If thou hast nature in thee, bear it not.   81. *nature:* natural feeling.

Let not the royal bed of Denmark be
A couch for luxury and damnèd incest.
But howsomever thou pursues this act,

85 Taint not thy mind, nor let thy soul contrive
Against thy mother aught. Leave her to heaven
And to those thorns that in her bosom lodge
To prick and sting her. Fare thee well at once.
The glowworm shows the matin to be near

90 And gins to pale his uneffectual fire.
Adieu, adieu, adieu. Remember me.   [*Exit.*]
    Hamlet. O all you host of heaven! O earth! What else?
And shall I couple hell? O fie! Hold, hold, my heart,
And you, my sinews, grow not instant old,

95 But bear me stiffly up. Remember thee?
Ay, thou poor ghost, while memory holds a seat
In this distracted globe. Remember thee?
Yea, from the table of my memory
I'll wipe away all trivial fond records,

100 All saws of books, all forms, all pressures past
That youth and observation copied there,
And thy commandment all alone shall live
Within the book and volume of my brain,
Unmixed with baser matter. Yes, by heaven!

105 O most pernicious woman!
O villain, villain, smiling, damnèd villain!
My tables—meet it is I set it down
That one may smile, and smile, and be a villain.
At least I am sure it may be so in Denmark. [*Writes.*]

110 So, uncle, there you are. Now to my word:
It is 'Adieu, adieu, remember me.'
I have sworn't.
                    Enter HORATIO *and* MARCELLUS.
    Horatio. My lord, my lord!
    Marcellus.   Lord Hamlet!
    Horatio.   Heavens secure him!
    Hamlet. So be it!

115 *Marcellus.* Illo, ho, ho, my lord!
    Hamlet. Hillo, ho, ho, boy! Come, bird, come.
    Marcellus. How is't, my noble lord?
    Horatio.   What news, my lord?
    Hamlet. O, wonderful!
    Horatio. Good my lord, tell it.

83. *luxury:* lust.

84. *pursues:* see I, iv, 53n.

85-86. *Taint . . . aught:* i.e., don't turn against your mother in mind or deed.

89. *matin:* morning.

90. *gins:* begins.

93. *And . . . fie:* Hamlet considers the possibility that the spirit may be a demon, but then dismisses it as unworthy.
94. *instant:* instantaneously.

97. *globe:* head.

98. *table:* notebook.

99. *fond:* foolish.

100. *saws, forms, pressures:* precepts, mental images, impressions.

107. *my tables:* Here Hamlet pulls out his pocket notebook to record the judgment in 108. *meet:* suitable.

110. *word:* i.e., the watchword of his life henceforth.

114. *so . . . it:* an "Amen" to Horatio's exclamation.
115-116. *Illo . . . come:* Marcellus calls Hamlet in the phrase in which a falconer would call his bird, and Hamlet echoes him jestingly.

Hamlet.   No, you will reveal it.

Horatio. Not I, my lord, by heaven.

120 *Marcellus.*   Nor I, my lord.

Hamlet. How say you then? Would heart of man once
    think it?

But you'll be secret?

Both.   Ay, by heaven, my lord.

Hamlet. There's never a villain dwelling in all Denmark
    But he's an arrant knave.

125 *Horatio.* There needs no ghost, my lord, come from the
    grave
    To tell us this.

Hamlet.   Why, right, you are in the right,
    And so, without more circumstance at all,
    I hold it fit that we shake hands and part:
    You, as your business and desire shall point you,

130   For every man hath business and desire
    Such as it is, and for my own poor part,
    Look you, I'll go pray.

Horatio. These are but wild and whirling words, my lord.

Hamlet. I am sorry they offend you, heartily;
    Yes, faith, heartily.

135 *Horatio.*   There's no offense, my lord.

Hamlet. Yes, by Saint Patrick, but there is, Horatio,
    And much offense too. Touching this vision here,
    It is an honest ghost, that let me tell you.
    For your desire to know what is between us,

140   O'ermaster't as you may. And now, good friends,
    As you are friends, scholars, and soldiers,
    Give me one poor request.

Horatio. What is't, my lord? We will.

Hamlet. Never make known what you have seen to-night.

Both. My lord, we will not.

Hamlet.   Nay, but swear't.

145 *Horatio.*   In faith,
    My lord, not I.

Marcellus.   Nor I, my lord—in faith.

Hamlet. Upon my sword.

Marcellus.   We have sworn, my lord, already.

Hamlet. Indeed, upon my sword, indeed.

                    GHOST *cries under the stage.*

Ghost. Swear.

121. *once:* ever.

123-124. *There's . . . knave:* Hamlet suddenly changes his mind about confiding in his friends and utters this mocking tautology instead.
124. *arrant:* thorough.

127. *circumstance:* formality.

136. *Saint Patrick:* keeper of Purgatory (whence *honest* ghosts come).

138. *honest:* i.e., no demon.

139-140. *For . . . may:* since Hamlet later confides the truth to Horatio, it seems likely that this statement is for Marcellus's benefit.

147. *sword:* i.e., upon the cross (of the sword-hilt).

150 *Hamlet.* Ha, ha, boy, say'st thou so? Art thou there, true-
      penny?
    Come on. You hear this fellow in the cellarage.
    Consent to swear.
Horatio.   Propose the oath, my lord.
Hamlet. Never to speak of this that you have seen,
    Swear by my sword.
155 *Ghost.* [*beneath*] Swear.
Hamlet. Hic et ubique? Then we'll shift our ground.
    Come hither, gentlemen,
    And lay your hands again upon my sword.
    Swear by my sword
160   Never to speak of this that you have heard.
Ghost. [*beneath*] Swear by his sword.
Hamlet. Well said, old mole! Canst work i' th' earth so
      fast?
    A worthy pioner! Once more remove, good friends.
Horatio. O day and night, but this is wondrous strange!
165 *Hamlet.* And therefore as a stranger give it welcome.
    There are more things in heaven and earth, Horatio,
    Than are dreamt of in your philosophy.
    But come:
    Here as before, never, so help you mercy,
170   How strange or odd some'er I bear myself
    (As I perchance hereafter shall think meet
    To put an antic disposition on),
    That you, at such times seeing me, never shall,
    With arms encumb'red thus, or this head-shake,
175   Or by pronouncing of some doubtful phrase,
    As 'Well, well, we know,' or 'We could, an if we
      would,'
    Or 'If we list to speak,' or 'There be, an if they might,'
    Or such ambiguous giving out, to note
    That you know aught of me—this do swear,
180   So grace and mercy at your most need help you.
Ghost. [*beneath*] Swear.   [*They swear.*]
Hamlet. Rest, rest, perturbèd spirit! So, gentlemen,
    With all my love I do commend me to you,
    And what so poor a man as Hamlet is
185   May do t' express his love and friending to you,
    God willing, shall not lack. Let us go in together,
    And still your fingers on your lips, I pray.

150. *truepenny:* "old boy."

156. *Hic et ubique:* here and everywhere.

163. *pioner:* digger.

165. *stranger:* (1) to Denmark? (2) to the supernatural?

167. *your philosophy:* a colloquial way of speaking: it does not mean Horatio's personal philosophy but natural philosophy—i.e., "science" —in general.

170. *some'er:* soever.

171. *meet:* proper.

172. *antic disposition:* absurd behavior.

174. *With . . . headshake:* with your arms folded like this (as if you had something important to tell) or with a knowing headshake.
175. *doubtful:* teasingly mysterious.
176. *an if:* if.

177. *list:* choose.

178. *giving out:* hinting. *note:* indicate.

187. *still:* always.

The time is out of joint. O cursèd spite
That ever I was born to set it right!
¹⁹⁰ Nay, come, let's go together.   *Exeunt.*

190. *together:* Again Hamlet courteously insists on treating them as equals.

II, I

Enter old POLONIUS, *with his man* [REYNALDO].

Polonius. Give him this money and these notes, Reynaldo.
Reynaldo. I will, my lord.
Polonius. You shall do marvellous wisely, good Reynaldo,
    Before you visit him, to make inquire
    Of his behavior.

4. *inquire:* inquiry.

⁵ *Reynaldo.*   My lord, I did intend it.
Polonius. Marry, well said, very well said. Look you, sir,
    Enquire me first what Danskers are in Paris,
    And how, and who, what means, and where they keep,
    What company, at what expense; and finding
¹⁰ By this encompassment and drift of question
    That they do know my son, come you more nearer
    Than your particular demands will touch it.
    Take you as 'twere some distant knowledge of him,
    As thus, 'I know his father and his friends,
¹⁵ And in part him'—do you mark this, Reynaldo?
Reynaldo. Ay, very well, my lord.
Polonius. 'And in part him, but,' you may say, 'not well,
    But if't be he I mean, he's very wild
    Addicted so and so.' And there put on him
²⁰ What forgeries you please; marry, none so rank
    As may dishonor him—take heed of that—
    But, sir, such wanton, wild, and usual slips
    As are companions noted and most known
    To youth and liberty.
Reynaldo.   As gaming, my lord.
²⁵ *Polonius.* Ay, or drinking, fencing, swearing, quarrelling,
    Drabbing. You may go so far.
Reynaldo. My lord, that would dishonor him.
Polonius. Faith, no, as you may season it in the charge.
    You must not put another scandal on him,
³⁰ That he is open to incontinency.
    That's not my meaning. But breathe his faults so
        quaintly
    That they may seem the taints of liberty,

7. *Danskers:* Danes.

8. *what . . . keep:* what their wealth and where they live.

10. *encompassment . . . question:* roundabout manner of inquiry.
11-12 *come . . . it:* you come nearer to the truth than by definite question (about Laertes).

20. *forgeries:* false reports. *rank:* extreme.

24. *gaming:* gambling.

26. *Drabbing:* whoring.

28. *season . . . charge:* moderate it by the way you say it.

30. *incontinency:* uncontrolled indulgence.

31. *quaintly:* cunningly.

32. *taints of:* faults resulting from.

The flash and outbreak of a fiery mind,
35 A savageness in unreclaimèd blood,
Of general assault.

Reynaldo. But, my good lord—

Polonius. Wherefore should you do this?

Reynaldo. Ay, my lord,
I would know that.

Polonius. Marry, sir, here's my drift,
And I believe it is a fetch of warrant.
You laying these slight sullies on my son
40 As 'twere a thing a little soiled i' th' working,
Mark you,
Your party in converse, him you would sound,
Having ever seen in the prenominate crimes
The youth you breathe of guilty, be assured
45 He closes with you in this consequence:
'Good sir,' or so, or 'friend,' or 'gentleman'—
According to the phrase or the addition
Of man and country—

Reynaldo. Very good, my lord.

Polonius. And then, sir, does 'a this—'a does—
50 What was I about to say? By the mass, I was about to
 say something! Where did I leave?

Reynaldo. At 'closes in the consequence,' at 'friend or
 so,' and 'gentleman.'

Polonius. At 'closes in the consequence'—Ay, marry!
55 He closes thus: 'I know the gentleman;
I saw him yesterday, or t'other day,
Or then, or then, with such or such, and, as you say,
There was 'a gaming, there o'ertook in's rouse,
There falling out at tennis'; or perchance,
60 'I saw him enter such a house of sale,'
Videlicet, a brothel, or so forth.
See you now—
Your bait of falsehood takes this carp of truth,
And thus do we of wisdom and of reach,
65 With windlasses and with assays of bias,
By indirections find directions out.
So, by my former lecture and advice,
Shall you my son. You have me, have you not?

Reynaldo. My lord, I have.

Polonius. God bye ye, fare ye well.

34. *unreclaimèd:* untamed.
35. *Of . . . assault:* common to youth in general.

38. *fetch of warrant:* lawful stratagem.

40. *working:* making (the metaphor is of a garment soiled in tailoring).

42. *sound:* i.e., sound out.

43-45. *Having . . . consequence:* If he has ever seen the young man you speak of guilty of any of the aforesaid misdeeds, he will agree with you as follows.

47-48. *According . . . country:* depending on the style of address habitual to that man or country.

49. *'a:* he.

58. *O'ertook . . . rouse:* overcome by drink.
59. *falling out:* quarreling.

60. *sale.* prostitution.

61. *Videlicet:* that is to say.

63. *carp:* a species of fish.

64. *reach:* comprehension.

65. *with . . . bias:* circuitous ways and indirect approaches ("bias" refers to the curved course of the weighted ball in English bowling).
66. *By . . . out:* by indirect methods get straight to the point (as the bowling ball goes straight to the mark while following a curve).
68. *have:* understand.

70 *Reynaldo.* Good my lord.

Polonius. Observe his inclination in yourself.

Reynaldo. I shall, my lord.

Polonius. And let him ply his music.

Reynaldo.   Well, my lord.

Polonius. Farewell.   *Exit* REYNALDO.

                    Enter OPHELIA.

                How now, Ophelia, what's the matter?

75 *Ophelia.* O my lord, my lord, I have been so affrighted!

Polonius. With what, i' th' name of God?

Ophelia. My lord, as I was sewing in my closet,

     Lord Hamlet, with his doublet all unbraced,

     No hat upon his head, his stockings fouled,

80   Ungartered, and down-gyvèd to his ankle,

     Pale as his shirt, his knees knocking each other,

     And with a look so piteous in purport

     As if he had been loosèd out of hell

     To speak of horrors—he comes before me.

85 *Polonius.* Mad for thy love?

Ophelia.   My lord, I do not know,

     But truly I do fear it.

Polonius.   What said he?

Ophelia. He took me by the wrist and held me hard.

     Then goes he to the length of all his arm,

     And with his other hand thus o'er his brow

90   He falls to such perusal of my face

     As 'a would draw it. Long stayed he so.

     At last, a little shaking of mine arm

     And thrice his head thus waving up and down,

     He raised a sigh so piteous and profound

95   As it did seem to shatter all his bulk

     And end his being. That done, he lets me go,

     And with his head over his shoulder turned

     He seemed to find his way without his eyes,

     For out o' doors he went without their helps

100   And to the last bended their light on me.

Polonius. Come, go with me. I will go seek the king.

     This is the very ecstasy of love,

     Whose violent property fordoes itself

     And leads the will to desperate undertakings

105   As oft as any passion under heaven

     That does afflict our natures. I am sorry.

71. *in:* for.

73. *ply:* keep up.

77. *closet:* sitting-room.

78. *doublet:* the close-fitting jacket of Elizabethan male attire, properly worn closed. *unbraced:* unfastened.

79. *stockings:* the long hose of Elizabethan male attire, whose neatness of appearance depended on being tightly gartered. *fouled:* soiled.

80. *down-gyvèd . . . ankle:* hanging about his ankles like a prisoner's leg chains.

85. *love:* Hamlet's disarray somewhat resembles that attributed in Shakespeare's time to despairing lovers —hence Polonius's reaction.

88. *goes he:* He draws away.

92. *shaking of:* shaking.

102. *ecstasy:* madness.

103. *property:* nature. *fordoes:* destroys.

What, have you given him any hard words of late?
Ophelia. No, my good lord; but as you did command
    I did repel his letters and denied
    His access to me.
110 *Polonius.*   That hath made him mad.
    I am sorry that with better heed and judgment
    I had not quoted him. I feared he did but trifle
    And meant to wrack thee; but beshrew my jealousy.
    By heaven, it is as proper to our age
115 To cast beyond ourselves in our opinions
    As it is common for the younger sort
    To lack discretion. Come, go we to the king.
    This must be known, which, being kept close, might move
    More grief to hide than hate to utter love.
120 Come.   *Exeunt.*

112. *quoted:* observed.
113. *wrack:* ruin. *beshrew my jealousy:* curse my mistrust.
114-117. *as . . . discretion:* as characteristic of us old men to see too much in something as it is of youth to see too little.
118-119. *being . . . love.* if kept secret might cause more grief than it will cause displeasure if revealed (to the King and Queen).

II, ii

Flourish. Enter KING *and* QUEEN, ROSENCRANTZ, *and* GUILDENSTERN [*with others*].

King. Welcome, dear Rosencrantz and Guildenstern.
    Moreover that we much did long to see you,
    The need we have to use you did provoke
    Our hasty sending. Something have you heard
5 Of Hamlet's transformation—so call it,
    Sith nor th' exterior nor the inward man
    Resembles that it was. What it should be,
    More than his father's death, that thus hath put him
    So much from th' understanding of himself,
10 I cannot dream of. I entreat you both
    That, being of so young days brought up with him,
    And sith so neighbored to his youth and havior,
    That you vouchsafe your rest here in our court
    Some little time, so by your companies
15 To draw him on to pleasures, and to gather
    So much as from occasion you may glean,
    Whether aught to us unknown afflicts him thus,
    That opened lies within our remedy.
Queen. Good gentlemen, he hath much talked of you,
20 And sure I am two men there are not living
    To whom he more adheres. If it will please you

2. *Moreover that:* besides the fact that.
6. *Sith:* since.
7. *that:* what.
11. *That . . . days:* who were in youth.
12. *And . . . havior:* and who have been ever since so near in age and interests.
13. *vouchsafe your rest:* agree to stay.
18. *opened:* when known.
21. *more adheres:* is more attached.

To show us so much gentry and good will
As to expend your time with us awhile
For the supply and profit of our hope,

25   Your visitation shall receive such thanks
As fits a king's remembrance.

Rosencrantz.   Both your majesties
Might, by the sovereign power you have of us,
Put your dread pleasures more into command
Than to entreaty.

Guildenstern.   But we both obey,

30   And here give up ourselves in the full bent
To lay our service freely at your feet,
To be commanded.

King. Thanks, Rosencrantz and gentle Guildenstern.

Queen. Thanks, Guildenstern and gentle Rosencrantz.

35   And I beseech you instantly to visit
My too much changèd son.—Go, some of you,
And bring these gentlemen where Hamlet is.

Guildenstern. Heavens make our presence and our
          practices
Pleasant and helpful to him!

Queen.   Ay, amen!

          Exeunt ROSENCRANTZ *and* GUILDENSTERN
                    [*with some* ATTENDANTS].

          Enter POLONIUS.

40 *Polonius.* Th' ambassadors from Norway, my good lord,
Are joyfully returned.

King. Thou still hast been the father of good news.

Polonius. Have I, my lord? Assure you, my good liege,
I hold my duty as I hold my soul,

45   Both to my God and to my gracious king,
And I do think—or else this brain of mine
Hunts not the trail of policy so sure
As it hath used to do—that I have found
The very cause of Hamlet's lunacy.

50 *King.* O, speak of that! That do I long to hear.

Polonius. Give first admittance to th' ambassadors.
My news shall be the fruit to that great feast.

King. Thyself do grace to them and bring them in.

                              [*Exit* POLONIUS.]

He tells me, my dear Gertrude, he hath found

55   The head and source of all your son's distemper.

22. *gentry:* courtesy.

24. *supply and profit:* aid and fulfillment.

26. *remembrance:* gratitude.

30. *in . . . bent:* to the utmost (as of a bow bent to the limit).

42. *still:* always.

44. *hold:* value.

47. *policy:* political shrewdness.

52. *fruit:* i.e., last course (of a meal).

55. *head:* mainspring.

Queen. I doubt it is no other but the main,
His father's death and our o'erhasty marriage.
King. Well, we shall sift him.

Enter AMBASSADORS [(VOLTEMAND *and* CORNELIUS),
with POLONIUS].

Welcome, my good friends.
Say, Voltemand, what from our brother Norway?
60 *Voltemand.* Most fair return of greetings and desires.
Upon our first, he sent out to suppress
His nephew's levies, which to him appeared
To be a preparation 'gainst the Polack,
But better looked into, he truly found
65 It was against your highness, whereat grieved,
That so his sickness, age, and impotence
Was falsely borne in hand, sends out arrests
On Fortinbras; which he in brief obeys,
Receives rebuke from Norway, and in fine
70 Makes vow before his uncle never more
To give th' assay of arms against your majesty.
Whereon old Norway, overcome with joy,
Gives him threescore thousand crowns in annual fee
And his commission to employ those soldiers,
75 So levied as before, against the Polack,
With an entreaty, herein further shown,

[*Gives a paper.*]

That it might please you to give quiet pass
Through your dominions for this enterprise,
On such regards of safety and allowance
As therein are set down.
80 *King.*   It likes us well;
And at our more considered time we'll read,
Answer, and think upon this business.
Meantime we thank you for your well-took labor.
Go to your rest; at night we'll feast together.
Most welcome home!   *Exeunt* AMBASSADORS.
85 *Polonius.*   This business is well ended.
My liege and madam, to expostulate
What majesty should be, what duty is,
Why day is day, night night, and time is time,
Were nothing but to waste night, day, and time.
90 Therefore, since brevity is the soul of wit,
And tediousness the limbs and outward flourishes,

56. *doubt:* suspect. *the main:* i.e., the main subject that has occupied him.

58. *sift:* test (see I, iii, 102).

60. *desires:* good wishes.

61. *our first:* our first words (about Fortinbras).
62. *levies:* i.e., of troops.

67. *borne in hand:* deluded.

69. *in fine:* in conclusion.

71. *give . . . arms:* go to war.

79. *regards:* terms.

81. *at . . . time:* when we have time to consider the matter.

86. *expostulate:* discuss.
86-89. In this and his following speech, Polonius shows himself such a master of the roundabout approach (see II, i, 64ff) that he can hardly speak in simple English or come directly to his point.

90. *wit:* wisdom.

I will be brief. Your noble son is mad.
Mad call I it, for, to define true madness,
What is't but to be nothing else but mad?
But let that go.
95 *Queen.*   More matter, with less art.
    Polonius. Madam, I swear I use no art at all.
    That he is mad, 'tis true: 'tis true 'tis pity,
    And pity 'tis 'tis true—a foolish figure.
    But farewell it, for I will use no art.
100   Mad let us grant him then, and now remains
    That we find out the cause of this effect—
    Or rather say, the cause of this defect,
    For this effect defective comes by cause.
    Thus it remains, and the remainder thus.
105   Perpend.
    I have a daughter (have while she is mine),
    Who in her duty and obedience, mark,
    Hath given me this. Now gather, and surmise.

                         [*Reads the*] *letter.*

    'To the celestial, and my soul's idol, the most beautified
110 Ophelia,'—
    That's an ill phrase, a vile phrase; 'beautified' is a vile
    phrase. But you shall hear. Thus: [*Reads.*]
    'In her excellent white bosom, these, &c.'
    Queen. Came this from Hamlet to her?
115 *Polonius.* Good madam, stay awhile. I will be faithful.
                                              [*Reads.*]
            'Doubt thou the stars are fire;
                Doubt that the sun doth move;
            Doubt truth to be a liar;
                But never doubt I love.
120   'O dear Ophelia, I am ill at these numbers. I have
    not art to reckon my groans, but that I love thee best,
    O most best, believe it. Adieu.
            'Thine evermore, most dear lady,
                whilst this machine is to him, HAMLET.'
125   This in obedience hath my daughter shown me,
    And more above hath his solicitings,
    As they fell out by time, by means, and place,
    All given to mine ear.
    King.   But how hath she
    Received his love?
    Polonius.   What do you think of me?

95. *More . . . art:* i.e., pay more attention to making your words mean something and less to playing with them.

97-98. *'tis true . . . 'tis true:* a figure, i.e., configuration of words, which illustrates Polonius's delight in playing with words (see also 101-104).

103. *this . . . defective:* i.e., this madness, which is simultaneously *effect* (being the result of some cause), and also *defect* (being a mental flaw).

105. *Perpend:* i.e., ponder this.

109. *beautified:* endowed with beauty (but Polonius takes this to mean beautified by artifice).

118. *Doubt:* suspect.

120. *ill . . . numbers:* poor at verse making.
121. *reckon:* count up.

124. *this . . . him:* this body is his.

126. *above:* besides. *solicitings:* wooings.
127. *As . . . place:* i.e., when, how, and where they happened.

¹³⁰ *King.* As of a man faithful and honorable.

Polonius. I would fain prove so. But what might you
      think,
  When I had seen this hot love on the wing
  (As I perceived it, I must tell you that,
  Before my daughter told me), what might you
¹³⁵   Or my dear majesty your queen here, think,
  If I had played the desk or table book,
  Or given my heart a winking, mute and dumb,
  Or looked upon this love with idle sight?
  What might you think? No, I went round to work
¹⁴⁰   And my young mistress thus I did bespeak:
  'Lord Hamlet is a prince, out of thy star.
  This must not be.' And then I prescripts gave her,
  That she should lock herself from his resort,
  Admit no messengers, receive no tokens.
¹⁴⁵   Which done, she took the fruits of my advice,
  And he, repellèd, a short tale to make,
  Fell into a sadness, then into a fast,
  Thence to a watch, thence into a weakness,
  Thence to a lightness, and, by this declension,
¹⁵⁰   Into the madness wherein now he raves,
  And all we mourn for.

King.   Do you think 'tis this?

Queen. It may be, very like.

Polonius. Hath there been such a time—I would fain
      know that—
  That I have positively said ''Tis so,'
  When it proved otherwise?

¹⁵⁵ *King.*   Not that I know.

Polonius. [*pointing to his head and shoulder*] Take this
      from this, if this be otherwise.
  If circumstances lead me, I will find
  Where truth is hid, though it were hid indeed
  Within the center.

King.   How may we try it further?

¹⁶⁰ *Polonius.* You know sometimes he walks four hours
      together
  Here in the lobby.

Queen.   So he does indeed.

Polonius. At such a time I'll loose my daughter to him.
  Be you and I behind an arras then.
  Mark the encounter. If he love her not,

136. *If . . . book:* If I had passively received the information (like a notebook).

137. *given . . . dumb:* allowed myself to wink (i.e., connive) at what I had seen, and be silent.

138. *idle:* unresponsive.

139. *round:* actively.

140. *bespeak:* address.

141. *out . . . star:* above thy fortune.

142. *prescripts:* orders.

143. *resort:* visitation.

146. *a . . . make:* to put it briefly.

148. *watch:* wakefulness, i.e., insomnia.

149. *lightness:* light-headedness. *declension:* downward route.

159. *center:* i.e., of the earth.

162. *loose:* To emphasize the cynical unconcern with which Polonius is about to treat his daughter, Shakespeare gives him a word sometimes used by cattle breeders of "loosing"' a heifer to a bull.

163. *arras:* wall hanging.

165   And be not from his reason fallen thereon,

Let me be no assistant for a state

But keep a farm and carters.

King.   We will try it.

Enter HAMLET [*reading on a book*].

Queen. But look where sadly the poor wretch comes

reading.

Polonius. Away, I do beseech you both, away.

Exit KING *and* QUEEN [*with* ATTENDANTS].

170   I'll board him presently. O, give me leave.

How does my good Lord Hamlet?

Hamlet. Well, God-a-mercy.

Polonius. Do you know me, my lord?

Hamlet. Excellent well. You are a fishmonger.

175   *Polonius.* Not I, my lord.

Hamlet. Then I would you were so honest a man.

Polonius. Honest, my lord?

Hamlet. Ay, sir. To be honest, as this world goes, is to be

one man picked out of ten thousand.

180   *Polonius.* That's very true, my lord.

Hamlet. For if the sun breed maggots in a dead dog,

being a good kissing carrion—Have you a daughter?

Polonius. I have, my lord.

Hamlet. Let her not walk i' th' sun. Conception is a

185   blessing, but as your daughter may conceive, friend,

look to't.

Polonius. [*aside*] How say you by that? Still harping on

my daughter. Yet he knew me not at first. 'A said I

was a fishmonger. 'A is far gone, far gone. And truly

190   in my youth I suffered much extremity for love, very

near this. I'll speak to him again.—What do you read,

my lord?

Hamlet. Words, words, words.

Polonius. What is the matter, my lord?

195   *Hamlet.* Between who?

Polonius. I mean the matter that you read, my lord.

Hamlet. Slanders, sir, for the satirical rogue says here

that old men have grey beards, that their faces are

wrinkled, their eyes purging thick amber and plumtree

200   gum, and that they have a plentiful lack of wit,

together with most weak hams. All which, sir, though

I most powerfully and potently believe, yet I hold it

not honesty to have it thus set down, for you yourself,

167. *carters:* wagoners, i.e., peasants.

170. *board:* accost. *presently:* immediately.

172. *God-a-mercy:* thank you (literally, "God have mercy!").

174. *fishmonger:* fish-merchant. Intended by Hamlet to sound like madness to Polonius, this term could mean a pimp, one who prostitutes a woman for his own profit. In a figurative sense, this is what Polonius is doing in proposing to use Ophelia as "bait" while he and the king "fish" for information by spying (cf. 162-164 above). Hamlet is hardly yet conscious of the suitability of this meaning, but Shakespeare's audience. One of the characteristics of an Elizabethan stage "madman" was that he might make telling comments on persons and situations that he had, logically, no reason to know about. Hamlet does precisely that in this and several later passages.

181. *sun . . . maggots:* alluding to the old belief that vermin in dead flesh were caused by spontaneous generation under the heat of the sun.

182. *being . . . carrion:* i.e., a dead dog being a pretty piece of flesh for kissing. This is spoken sardonically. (But some editors alter "good" to "god"–i.e., the sun-god, creating spontaneous generation). But the term carrion could also mean prostitute, and it is possibly significant that our attention is shifted at once to Polonius's daughter, whom he is about to prostitute figuratively.

184. *walk . . . sun:* i.e., lest the sun breed life (a child) in her, as it breeds maggots in the carrion. Hamlet's words possibly include a wry allusion to himself as a "son" –and a "sun" (i.e., a prince)– whose attentions to Ophelia Polonius had thought dishonorable.

194. *matter:* Polonius uses "matter" to mean "the substance" (of what you are reading). Hamlet deliberately takes it in a different sense: "the cause of a dispute."

199-200. *thick . . . gum:* alluding to the discharges from the weak eyes of old men.

200. *lack of wit:* as Polonius has been demonstrating in his misunderstanding of Hamlet's words and condition.

201. *hams:* thighs.

sir, should be old as I am if, like a crab, you could

205 go backward.

Polonius. [*aside*] Though this be madness, yet there is method in't.—Will you walk out of the air, my lord?

Hamlet. Into my grave?

Polonius. Indeed, that's out of the air. [*aside*] How preg-

210 nant sometimes his replies are! a happiness that often madness hits on, which reason and sanity could not so prosperously be delivered of. I will leave him and suddenly contrive the means of meeting between him and my daughter.—My honorable lord, I will most

215 humbly take my leave of you.

Hamlet. You cannot, sir, take from me anything that I will more willingly part withal—except my life, except my life, except my life.

Enter GUILDENSTERN *and* ROSENCRANTZ.

Polonius. Fare you well, my lord.

220 *Hamlet.* These tedious old fools!

Polonius. You go to seek the Lord Hamlet. There he is.

Rosencrantz. [*to* POLONIUS] God save you, sir!

[*Exit* POLONIUS.]

Guildenstern. My honored lord!

Rosencrantz. My most dear lord!

225 *Hamlet.* My excellent good friends! How dost thou, Guildenstern? Ah, Rosencrantz! Good lads, how do ye both?

Rosencrantz. As the indifferent children of the earth.

Guildenstern. Happy in that we are not over-happy.

230 On Fortune's cap we are not the very button.

Hamlet. Nor the soles of her shoe?

Rosencrantz. Neither, my lord.

Hamlet. Then you live about her waist, or in the middle of her favors?

235 *Guildenstern.* Faith, her privates we.

Hamlet. In the secret parts of Fortune? O, most true! she is a strumpet. What news?

Rosencrantz. None, my lord, but that the world's grown honest.

240 *Hamlet.* Then is doomsday near. But your news is not true. [Let me question more in particular. What have you, my good friends, deserved at the hands of Fortune that she sends you to prison hither?

203-205. *for . . . backward:* Hamlet turns upside down the usual argument for respecting the old, namely that everyone will eventually be old.

207. *walk . . . air:* come indoors. Fresh air was believed bad for a sick man.

209. *pregnant:* meaningful.

210. *happiness:* appropriateness.

228. *indifferent:* average.

230. *button:* i.e., top.

235. *privates:* ordinary citizens (with punning reference to "private parts").

237. *strumpet:* prostitute (because so fickle).

Guildenstern. Prison, my lord?

245 *Hamlet.* Denmark's a prison.

Rosencrantz. Then is the world one.

Hamlet. A goodly one; in which there are many confines, wards, and dungeons, Denmark being one o' th' worst.

Rosencrantz. We think not so, my lord.

250 *Hamlet.* Why, then 'tis none to you, for there is nothing either good or bad but thinking makes it so. To me it is a prison.

Rosencrantz. Why, then your ambition makes it one. 'Tis too narrow for your mind.

255 *Hamlet.* O God, I could be bounded in a nutshell and count myself a king of infinite space, were it not that I have bad dreams.

Guildenstern. Which dreams indeed are ambition, for the very substance of the ambitious is merely the shadow of 260 a dream.

Hamlet. A dream itself is but a shadow.

Rosencrantz. Truly, and I hold ambition of so airy and light a quality that it is but a shadow's shadow.

Hamlet. Then are our beggars bodies, and our monarchs 265 and outstretched heroes the beggars' shadows. Shall we to th' court? for, by my fay, I cannot reason.

Both. We'll wait upon you.

Hamlet. No such matter. I will not sort you with the rest of my servants, for, to speak to you like an honest 270 man, I am most dreadfully attended.] But in the beaten way of friendship, what make you at Elsinore?

Rosencrantz. To visit you, my lord; no other occasion.

Hamlet. Beggar that I am, I am even poor in thanks, but I thank you; and sure, dear friends, my thanks are too 275 dear a halfpenny. Were you not sent for? Is it your own inclining? Is it a free visitation? Come, come, deal justly with me. Come, come. Nay, speak.

Guildenstern. What should we say, my lord?

Hamlet. Why, anything—but to th' purpose. You were 280 sent for, and there is a kind of confession in your looks, which your modesties have not craft enough to color. I know the good king and queen have sent for you.

Rosencrantz. To what end, my lord?

285 *Hamlet.* That you must teach me. But let me conjure you by the rights of our fellowship, by the consonancy of

248. *wards:* cells.

255-257. Hamlet retorts that far from desiring larger bounds, he could be happy in much smaller ones—except (he says mockingly) that he has bad dreams.

259. *substance:* i.e., object aimed at (which, until attained, is only a dream).

264-265. *Then . . . shadows:* i.e., if ambition is only a shadow, then beggars, who lack it, must be the solid bodies of this world, while kings and heroes, who are possessed by it, are shadows—shadows, in fact, of those very beggars who, being the only solid bodies, are therefore the only casters of shadows.
265. *outstretched:* (1) ambitiously grasping, (2) enlarged beyond reality as shadows so easily are.
266. *fay:* faith.
267. *wait upon:* attend, accompany—but Hamlet chooses to take it as "serve" (cf. 269-270).
268. *sort:* classify.
270. *dreadfully attended:* (1) served by an inadequate retinue (here and below, 269-270, Hamlet cunningly falls in with the insinuations of Rosencrantz and Guildenstern that his "disturbance" comes from being deprived of the throne by his uncle's marriage with his mother), (2) haunted by horrors (such as the ghost's revelations).
270-271. *in . . . friendship:* i.e., tell me honestly (as friends should).
271. *make you:* are you doing.
274-275. *too . . . halfpenny:* i.e., more than adequate compensation for a visit that was arranged by the king (see Hamlet's immediate question).

282. *color:* color over, conceal.

285. *conjure:* urge.
286. *consonancy:* congeniality.

our youth, by the obligation of our ever-preserved love, and by what more dear a better proposer can charge you withal, be even and direct with me whether
290 you were sent for or no.

Rosencrantz. [*aside to* GUILDENSTERN] What say you?

Hamlet. [*aside*] Nay then, I have an eye of you.—If you love me, hold not off.

Guildenstern. My lord, we were sent for.

295 *Hamlet.* I will tell you why. So shall my anticipation prevent your discovery, and your secrecy to the king and queen molt no feather. I have of late—but wherefore I know not—lost all my mirth, forgone all custom of exercises; and indeed, it goes so heavily with my dis-
300 position that this goodly frame the earth seems to me a sterile promontory; this most excellent canopy, the air, look you, this brave o'erhanging firmament, this majestical roof fretted with golden fire—why, it appeareth nothing to me but a foul and pestilent con-
305 gregation of vapors. What a piece of work is a man, how noble in reason, how infinite in faculties, in form and moving how express and ädmirable, in action how like an angel, in apprehension how like a god: the beauty of the world, the paragon of animals! And
310 yet to me what is this quintessence of dust? Man delights not me—nor woman neither, though by your smiling you seem to say so.

Rosencrantz. My lord, there was no such stuff in my thoughts.

315 *Hamlet.* Why did ye laugh then, when I said 'Man delights not me'?

Rosencrantz. To think, my lord, if you delight not in man, what lenten entertainment the players shall receive from you. We coted them on the way, and hither
320 are they coming to offer you service.

Hamlet. He that plays the king shall be welcome—his majesty shall have tribute of me—, the adventurous knight shall use his foil and target, the lover shall not sigh gratis, the humorous man shall end his part in
325 peace, the clown shall make those laugh whose lungs are tickle o' th' sere, and the lady shall say her mind freely, or the blank verse shall halt for't. What players are they?

288. *dear:* important.
288-289. *by . . . withal:* by whatever of even greater value a better speaker might use in appealing to you.

292. *of:* on.

295-296. *prevent . . . discovery:* precede your telling.

297. *molt no feather:* remain whole (the metaphor compares Rosencrantz and Guildenstern to hawks hunting on the King's and Queen's behalf).

301. *promontory:* Perhaps Hamlet means that the temporal world seems like a rocky headland jutting out into the seas of eternity. *canopy:* any covering, but perhaps used here to mean the covering of a throne. See "majestical roof," 297, with reference to the traditional Renaissance view of man as terrestrial king, 300-304.
303. *fretted:* checkered.

307. *express:* precise.

318. *lenten:* frugal (i.e., suited to Lent).

319. *coted:* passed.

321-328. Hamlet enumerates typical acting roles in Elizabethan plays.
323. *foil and target:* sword and shield.
324. *gratis:* i.e., without a tip (for his acting). *the humorous man:* the actor who impersonates a man dominated by a single foible or "humour," like melancholy, irascibility, etc. *in peace;* i.e., without interruption by catcalls.
326. *tickle . . . sere:* easily triggered into laughing (the "sere" is the catch that holds back the hammer on a gun).
327. *freely . . . for't:* uninhibitedly; otherwise, omission of indelicate words will spoil the meter.

Rosencrantz. Even those you were wont to take such de-
330   light in, the tragedians of the city.

Hamlet. How chances it they travel? Their residence,
both in reputation and profit, was better both ways.

Rosencrantz. I think their inhibition comes by the means
of the late innovation.

335   *Hamlet.* Do they hold the same estimation they did when
I was in the city? Are they so followed?

Rosencrantz. No indeed, are they not.

[*Hamlet.* How comes it? Do they grow rusty?

Rosencrantz. Nay, their endeavor keeps in the wonted
340   pace, but there is, sir, an eyrie of children, little
eyases, that cry out on the top of question and are
most tyrannically clapped for't. These are now the
fashion, and so berattle the common stages (so they
call them) that many wearing rapiers are afraid of
345   goosequills and dare scarce come thither.

Hamlet. What, are they children? Who maintains 'em?
How are they escoted? Will they pursue the quality no
longer than they can sing? Will they not say afterwards, if they should grow themselves to common
350   players (as it is most like, if their means are no better),
their writers do them wrong to make them exclaim
against their own succession?

Rosencrantz. Faith, there has been much to do on both
sides, and the nation holds it no sin to tarre them to
355   controversy. There was, for a while, no money bid for
argument unless the poet and the player went to cuffs
in the question.

Hamlet. Is't possible?

Guildenstern. O, there has been much throwing about of
360   brains.

Hamlet. Do the boys carry it away?

Rosencrantz. Ay, that they do, my lord—Hercules and
his load too.]

Hamlet. It is not very strange, for my uncle is King of
365   Denmark, and those that would make mows at him
while my father lived give twenty, forty, fifty, a hundred ducats apiece for his picture in little. 'Sblood,
there is something in this more than natural, if philosophy could find it out.

A flourish.

331. *residence:* i.e., remaining in the city.
333. *inhibition:* prevention (from continuing in the city).
334. *innovation:* This is taken by some to mean political upheaval; by others, to be the new popularity of companies of child-actors (which occurred in London, 1600-1601).
335. *estimation:* popularity.
339-363. This passage grows out of a "War of the Theaters," which took place in London in 1601-1602, and especially out of an unfriendly rivalry existing between acting companies of schoolboys (the Children of the Queen's Chapel and the Children of Paul's) and the adult acting companies of the public playhouses, who felt their livelihood was threatened.
339. *wonted:* usual.
340. *eyrie:* nest.
341. eyases: unfeathered hawks. *cry . . . question:* (1) comment on whatever happens to be the news or fashionable topic of the moment? (2) speak in a shrill high-flown style?
342. *tyrannically:* noisily.
343. *berattle . . . stages:* berate the public playhouses (for which most of Shakespeare's plays were written).
344-345. *many . . . goosequills:* i.e., many gentlemen playgoers are embarrassed to go to the public playhouses because of what the satirical pens ("goosequills") of authors writing for the child-actors say about those who do.
347. *escoted:* supported. *quality:* profession (of acting).
347-348. *no . . . sing:* i.e., only until their voices change.
349-350. *to . . . players:* to be professional actors in the public playhouses.
352. *succession:* future career.
354. *tarre:* incite.
355-357. *no . . . question:* i.e., no market for plays unless playwrights and actors took sides in the controversy.
361. *it:* i.e., victory.
362-363. *Hercules . . . too:* i.e., all the world; but with a specific reference to Hercules carrying the globe on his back, said to be the sign of Shakespeare's playhouse, the Globe —i.e., the success of the child-actors had affected even Shakespeare's company.
365. *mows:* faces.
367. *picture in little:* i.e., portrait in a "miniature." *'Sblood:* God's blood.
368. *more . . . natural:* possibly a riddling reference to the "unnatural" way in which Claudius supplanted Hamlet's father and the "supernatural" revelations of the ghost (see also I,v, 166-167).

370   *Guildenstern.* There are the players.

     Hamlet. Gentlemen, you are welcome to Elsinore. Your hands, come then. Th' appurtenance of welcome is fashion and ceremony. Let me comply with you in this garb, lest my extent to the players (which I tell you

375   must show fairly outwards) should more appear like entertainment than yours. You are welcome. But my uncle-father and aunt-mother are deceived.

     Guildenstern. In what, my dear lord?

     Hamlet. I am but mad north-north-west. When the wind

380   is southerly I know a hawk from a handsaw.

Enter POLONIUS.

     Polonius. Well be with you, gentlemen.

     Hamlet. Hark you, Guildenstern—and you too—at each ear a hearer. That great baby you see there is not yet out of his swaddling clouts.

385   *Rosencrantz.* Happily he is the second time come to them, for they say an old man is twice a child.

     Hamlet. I will prophesy he comes to tell me of the players. Mark it.—You say right, sir; a Monday morning, 'twas then indeed.

390   *Polonius.* My lord, I have news to tell you.

     Hamlet. My lord, I have news to tell you. When Roscius was an actor in Rome—

     Polonius. The actors are come hither, my lord.

     Hamlet. Buzz, buzz.

395   *Polonius.* Upon my honor—

     Hamlet. Then came each actor on his ass—

     Polonius. The best actors in the world, either for tragedy, comedy, history, pastoral, pastoral-comical, historical-pastoral, tragical-historical, tragical-comical-historical-

400   pastoral; scene individable, or poem unlimited. Seneca cannot be too heavy, nor Plautus too light. For the law of writ and the liberty, these are the only men.

     Hamlet. O Jephthah, judge of Israel, what a treasure hadst thou!

405   *Polonius.* What treasure had he, my lord?

     Hamlet. Why,

'One fair daughter, and no more,
The which he lovèd passing well.'

     Polonius. [*aside*] Still on my daughter.

---

372. *appurtenance:* proper accompaniment.

373. *fashion and ceremony:* i.e., gestures of courtesy.

373-376. *Let . . . yours:* Let me welcome you in this (friendly) manner lest my welcome to the players (which must be warm) seem better than yours.

379. *north-north-west:* i.e., part way (Hamlet hints that his madness is put on).

380. *I . . . handsaw:* i.e., I'm not as mad as I seem. *Hawk* (pickaxe) and *handsaw* are both workmen's tools, and there may be a further pun on "hawk" (the bird) and "hernshaw" (a heron).

382-383. *at . . . hearer:* Let me have your ear, each of you.

384. *clouts:* clothes.

385. *Happily:* haply.

388-389. *You . . . indeed:* Hamlet pretends to be in deep conversation with Rosencrantz and Guildenstern.

391. *Roscius:* a great Roman actor of Cicero's time (possibly a "mad" way of telling Polonius that his news is very old).

394. *Buzz, buzz:* mocking imitation of Polonius's talkiness.

396. *on his ass:* a mischievous play on Polonius's "upon my honor" (possibly the line is from a lost song).

398. *history:* e.g., plays like Shakespeare's own *Richard II*, *Henry IV*, *Henry V*., etc. *pastoral:* plays about shepherds. *pastoral-comical:* plays like Shakespeare's *As You Like It*.

399. *tragical-historical:* plays like Shakespeare's *Julius Caesar*.

400. *scene . . . unlimited:* plays that observe the classical "unities," and plays that do not. *Seneca:* Roman writer of tragedies.

401. *Plautus:* Roman writer of farces.

401-402. *For . . . liberty:* for either the orthodox play (adhering to classical rules) or the unorthodox.

403. *Jephthah:* Having vowed to sacrifice to the Lord as a burnt offering whatever he should first meet on his way home if the Lord gave him victory over the enemies of Israel, Jephthah met his own daughter, who therefore became the (cont. on next page) victim (Judges 11: 34-9). Here, as at 174, Shakespeare allows Hamlet in his "madness" to touch on a resemblance that goes deeper than he knows; for Jephthah is like Polonius not only in having a beloved daughter, but in "sacrificing" her for reasons of state.

407-408. Here and below Hamlet quotes from an old ballad on the theme of Jephthah.

408. *passing:* surpassingly.

410   *Hamlet.* Am I not i' th' right, old Jephthah?

Polonius. If you call me Jephthah, my lord, I have a
daughter that I love passing well.

Hamlet. Nay, that follows not.

Polonius. What follows then, my lord?

415   *Hamlet.* Why,

'As by lot, God wot,'

and then, you know,

'It came to pass, as most like it was.'

The first row of the pious chanson will show you more,

420   for look where my abridgment comes.

Enter the PLAYERS.

You are welcome, masters, welcome, all.—I am glad to
see thee well.—Welcome, good friends.—O, old friend,
why, thy face is valanced since I saw thee last. Com'st
thou to beard me in Denmark?—What, my young lady

425   and mistress? By'r Lady, your ladyship is nearer to
heaven than when I saw you last by the altitude of a
chopine. Pray God your voice, like a piece of uncurrent gold, be not cracked within the ring.—Masters,
you are all welcome. We'll e'en to't like French fal-

430   coners, fly at anything we see. We'll have a speech
straight. Come, give us a taste of your quality. Come,
a passionate speech.

Player. What speech, my good lord?

Hamlet. I heard thee speak me a speech once, but it was

435   never acted, or if it was, not above once, for the play,
I remember, pleased not the million; 'twas caviary to
the general, but it was (as I received it, and others,
whose judgments in such matters cried in the top of
mine) an excellent play, well digested in the scenes,

440   set down with as much modesty as cunning. I remember one said there were no sallets in the lines to make
the matter savory, nor no matter in the phrase that
might indict the author of affection, but called it an
honest method, as wholesome as sweet, and by very

445   much more handsome than fine. One speech in't I
chiefly loved. 'Twas Aeneas' tale to Dido, and there-
about of it especially where he speaks of Priam's
slaughter. If it live in your memory, begin at this line—
let me see, let me see:

450   'The rugged Pyrrhus, like th' Hyrcanian beast—'

412-413. *that . . . not:* i.e., (1) that doesn't come next (in the ballad), (2) it does not necessarily follow that you love your daughter surpassingly well.

419. *row:* stanza. *chanson:* ballad.

420. *abridgement:* i.e., the arrival of the players cuts short my talk.

423. *valanced:* draped (with a beard).

424. *beard:* with a pun on the other sense, "challenge." *lady:* Hamlet jestingly addresses one of the boys who, as in all Elizabethan companies, took the women's parts.

425-426. *nearer to heaven:* taller.

427. *chopine:* woman's elevated shoe.

427-428. *like . . . ring:* Hamlet compares the changing of the boy's voice, which will spoil its *ring*, to the deterioration of a coin inside the *ring* surrounding the monarch's head, which made it *uncurrent*—not passable.

429. *French:* i.e., eager (the French were noted for their skill in falconry, the hunting of game by a trained hawk).

431. *straight:* at once. *quality:* profession.

436-437. *caviary . . . general:* too great a delicacy (like caviar) for the general taste.

438. *cried . . . of:* surpassed.

439. *digested:* arranged.

440. *as much . . . cunning:* as much restraint as skill.

441. *sallets:* salads, i.e., spicy bits.

443. *indict . . . affection:* convict the author of affectation.

445. *handsome . . . fine:* dignified than fancy.

446. *Aeneas' . . . Dido:* Aeneas, hero of Virgil's *Aeneid*, flees from burning Troy at the close of the Trojan War and relates to Queen Dido of Carthage, on whose shores he has been shipwrecked, the sad fate of his city.

450. *Pyrrhus:* At the capture of Troy, the Greek warrior Pyrrhus slew the Trojan King Priam in revenge for the death of his father, Achilles, who had been killed in the war. *Hyrcanian beast:* tiger.

'Tis not so; it begins with Pyrrhus:

    'The rugged Pyrrhus, he whose sable arms,
    Black as his purpose, did the night resemble
    When he lay couchèd in the ominous horse,
455   Hath now this dread and black complexion smeared
    With heraldry more dismal. Head to foot
    Now is he total gules, horridly tricked
    With blood of fathers, mothers, daughters, sons,
    Baked and impasted with the parching streets,
460   That lend a tyrannous and a damnèd light
    To their lord's murther. Roasted in wrath and fire,
    And thus o'ersizèd with coagulate gore,
    With eyes like carbuncles, the hellish Pyrrhus
    Old grandsire Priam seeks.'
465   So, proceed you.

Polonius. Fore God, my lord, well spoken, with good accent and good discretion.

Player.   'Anon he finds him,
    Striking too short at Greeks. His antique sword,
470   Rebellious to his arm, lies where it falls,
    Repugnant to command. Unequal matched,
    Pyrrhus at Priam drives, in rage strikes wide,
    But with the whiff and wind of his fell sword
    Th' unnervèd father falls. Then senseless Ilium,
475   Seeming to feel this blow, with flaming top
    Stoops to his base, and with a hideous crash
    Takes prisoner Pyrrhus' ear. For lo! his sword,
    Which was declining on the milky head
    Of reverend Priam, seemed i' th' air to stick.
480   So as a painted tyrant Pyrrhus stood,
    And like a neutral to his will and matter
    Did nothing.
    But as we often see, against some storm,
    A silence in the heavens, the rack stand still,
485   The bold winds speechless, and the orb below
    As hush as death, anon the dreadful thunder
    Doth rend the region, so after Pyrrhus' pause,
    Arousèd vengeance sets him new awork,
    And never did the Cyclops' hammers fall
490   On Mars's armor, forged for proof eterne,
    With less remorse than Pyrrhus' bleeding sword
    Now falls on Priam.

450-498. Shakespeare writes the speech from the play about Priam in a declamatory and pretentious style so as to distinguish it from his own play about Hamlet, which we are to think of as "real."
452. *sable:* black.
454. *horse:* the wooden horse which the Trojans drew within their city walls, not knowing that many Greek warriors were hidden in it.
457. *gules:* heraldic term for red. *tricked:* heraldic term for spotted.
459. *impasted:* crusted (as with pastry). *parching:* i.e., because on fire.
462. *o'er-sizèd:* coated (as with wall-sizing). *coagulate:* clotted.
463. *carbuncles:* glowing red coals.
467. *discretion:* separation of clauses and sentences so as to be clearly intelligible.
471. *Repugnant:* disobedient.
473. *fell:* cruel.
474. *falls:* possibly transitive—i.e., Pyrrhus causes him to fall, brings him down.
474-475. *senseless . . . feel:* i.e., though actually incapable of sensation, yet Troy (*Ilium*) *seemed* to feel.
476. *his:* its.
478. *milky:* i.e., white-haired.
480-481. *a . . . matter:* one suspended between his purpose and its achievement.
483. *against:* before.
484. *rack:* clouds.
485. *orb:* earth.
486. *anon:* presently.
487. *region:* sky.
489. *Cyclops:* assistants to Vulcan, the blacksmith god.
490. *proof eterne:* eternal protection.

Out, out, thou strumpet Fortune! All you gods,
In general synod take away her power,
495   Break all the spokes and fellies from her wheel,
And bowl the round nave down the hill of heaven,
As low as to the fiends.'

Polonius. This is too long.

Hamlet. It shall to the barber's, with your beard.—
500   Prithee say on. He's for a jig or a tale of bawdry, or he
sleeps. Say on; come to Hecuba.

Player. 'But who (ah woe!) had seen the mobled
queen—'

Hamlet. 'The mobled queen'?

Polonius. That's good. 'Mobled queen' is good.

505   *Player.* 'Run barefoot up and down, threat'ning the
flames
With bisson rheum; a clout upon that head
Where late the diadem stood, and for a robe,
About her lank and all o'erteemèd loins,
A blanket in the alarm of fear caught up—
510   Who this had seen, with tongue in venom steeped
'Gainst Fortune's state would treason have
pronounced.
But if the gods themselves did see her then,
When she saw Pyrrhus make malicious sport
In mincing with his sword her husband's limbs,
515   The instant burst of clamor that she made
(Unless things mortal move them not at all)
Would have made milch the burning eyes of heaven
And passion in the gods.'

Polonius. Look, whe'r he has not turned his color, and
520   has tears in's eyes. Prithee no more.

Hamlet. 'Tis well. I'll have thee speak out the rest of this
soon.—Good my lord, will you see the players well
bestowed? Do you hear? Let them be well used, for
they are the abstract and brief chronicles of the time.
525   After your death you were better have a bad epitaph
than their ill report while you live.

Polonius. My lord, I will use them according to their
desert.

Hamlet. God's bodkin, man, much better! Use every man
530   after his desert, and who shall scape whipping? Use
them after your own honor and dignity. The less they

494. *synod:* assembly.
495. *fellies:* segments forming the rim.
496. *nave:* hub.
497. *to . . . fiends:* i.e., hell.

500. *jig:* the comic singing and dancing act that, on the Elizabethan stage, often followed the performance of the serious play.
501. *Hecuba:* Priam's queen.
502. *mobled:* muffled.

506. *bisson rheum:* blinding tears. *clout:* cloth.

508. *all o'erteemèd:* exhausted from child bearing.

510. *who . . . seen:* i.e., anyone who saw this pitiful sight.
511. *would . . . pronounced:* i.e, would have cursed Fortune's government (and thus have been guilty of *treason* against it).

517. *milch:* tearful (literally, "milk-giving"—like "bisson rheum" and "mobled," part of the deliberate pretentiousness of this speech; see 438–485 n).
519. *whe'r . . . color:* if he hasn't gone pale! (Polonius refers to the player.)

523. *bestowed:* lodged.

524. *abstract . . . chronicles:* concise memorializers.

529. *God's bodkin:* by God's little body.
530. *after:* according to.

deserve, the more merit is in your bounty. Take them in.

Polonius. Come, sirs.

Hamlet. Follow him, friends. We'll hear a play to-
535 morrow. [*aside to* PLAYER] Dost thou hear me, old friend? Can you play 'The Murther of Gonzago'?

Player. Ay, my lord.

Hamlet. We'll ha't to-morrow night. You could for a need study a speech of some dozen or sixteen lines
540 which I would set down and insert in't, could you not?

Player. Ay, my lord.

Hamlet. Very well. Follow that lord, and look you mock him not.—My good friends, I'll leave you till night. You are welcome to Elsinore.

　　　　　　　Exeunt POLONIUS *and* PLAYERS.
545 *Rosencrantz.* Good my lord.

　　　　　　　Exeunt [ROSENCRANTZ *and* GUILDENSTERN].

Hamlet. Ay, so, God bye to you.—Now I am alone.
　　　O, what a rogue and peasant slave am I!
　　　Is it not monstrous that this player here,
550 But in a fiction, in a dream of passion,
　　　Could force his soul so to his own conceit
　　　That from her working all his visage wanned,
　　　Tears in his eyes, distraction in 's aspect,
　　　A broken voice, and his whole function suiting
555 With forms to his conceit? And all for nothing,
　　　For Hecuba!
　　　What's Hecuba to him, or he to Hecuba,
　　　That he should weep for her? What would he do
　　　Had he the motive and the cue for passion
560 That I have? He would drown the stage with tears
　　　And cleave the general ear with horrid speech,
　　　Make mad the guilty and appal the free,
　　　Confound the ignorant, and amaze indeed
　　　The very faculties of eyes and ears.
565　Yet I,
　　　A dull and muddy-mettled rascal, peak
　　　Like John-a-dreams, unpregnant of my cause,
　　　And can say nothing. No, not for a king,
　　　Upon whose property and most dear life
570 A damned defeat was made. Am I a coward?
　　　Who calls me villain? breaks my pate across?
　　　Plucks off my beard and blows it in my face?

548. *peasant:* base.

551. *conceit:* conception of the role.
552. *her working:* i.e., the conception's influence. *wanned:* grew pale.
553. *distraction:* agitation.
554-555. *his . . . conceit:* i.e., accommodating his performance of the role to his conception of it.
556-558. Perhaps Hamlet is unconsciously drawn to dwell on the Troy episode because of its relation to his own situation: his father has been killed, like Priam, but *his* mother is not, like Hecuba, grieving.

562. *Make . . . free:* madden those in the audience with guilty consciences, and terrify even the innocent (as Hamlet does through the play within the play, III, ii).
563. *Confound:* stupefy. *amaze:* stun.
566. *dull and muddy-mettled:* sluggish and dull-spirited. *peak:* mope.
567. *John-a-dreams:* i.e., any dreamer. *unpregnant of:* not quickened to action by.

570. *defeat:* destruction.
571. *pate:* head.
572. *Plucks . . . face:* a supreme insult.

Tweaks me by the nose? gives me the lie i' th' throat
As deep as to the lungs? Who does me this?
575   Ha, 'swounds, I should take it, for it cannot be
But I am pigeon-livered and lack gall
To make oppression bitter, or ere this
I should ha' fatted all the region kites
With this slave's offal. Bloody, bawdy villain!
580   Remorseless, treacherous, lecherous, kindless villain!
O, vengeance!
Why, what an ass am I! This is most brave,
That I, the son of a dear murtherèd,
Prompted to my revenge by heaven and hell,
585   Must like a whore unpack my heart with words
And fall a-cursing like a very drab,
A stallion! Fie upon't, foh! About, my brains.
Hum—
I have heard that guilty creatures sitting at a play
590   Have by the very cunning of the scene
Been struck so to the soul that presently
They have proclaimed their malefactions.
For murther, though it have no tongue, will speak
With most miraculous organ. I'll have these players
595   Play something like the murther of my father
Before mine uncle. I'll observe his looks.
I'll tent him to the quick. If 'a do blench,
I know my course. The spirit that I have seen
May be a devil, and the devil hath power
600   T' assume a pleasing shape, yea, and perhaps
Out of my weakness and my melancholy,
As he is very potent with such spirits,
Abuses me to damn me. I'll have grounds
More relative than this. The play's the thing
605   Wherein I'll catch the conscience of the king.   *Exit.*

575. *'swounds:* by God's wounds.

576. *gall:* Pigeons were supposed to lack gall, a bitter excretion of the liver formerly identified with courage.

577. *oppression:* injustice.

578. *region kites:* vultures of the air.

579. *offal:* guts.

580. *kindless:* unnatural (in killing his brother and seducing his brother's wife).

583. *dear:* dear one.

586. *drab:* prostitute.

587. *stallion:* another term for prostitute. *About:* i.e., turn about and get to work.

590. *cunning:* skill.

591. *presently:* at once.

597. *tent:* probe.

601. *weakness, melancholy:* by which Hamlet has been afflicted since his world crashed around him.
602. *spirits:* moods.
603. *Abuses:* deceives.

604. *relative:* relevant, i.e., reliable.

III, 1

Enter KING, QUEEN, POLONIUS, OPHELIA, ROSEN-
   CRANTZ, GUILDENSTERN, LORDS.

King. And can you by no drift of conference
   Get from him why he puts on this confusion,
   Grating so harshly all his days of quiet
   With turbulent and dangerous lunacy?

1. *drift . . . conference:* turn of conversation.
2. *puts . . . confusion:* acts in this odd way.

⁵ *Rosencrantz.* He does confess he feels himself distracted,
　　But from what cause 'a will by no means speak.
Guildenstern. Nor do we find him forward to be sounded,
　　But with a crafty madness keeps aloof
　　When we would bring him on to some confession
　　Of his true state.
¹⁰ *Queen.*　　　　　　Did he receive you well?
Rosencrantz. Most like a gentleman.
Guildenstern. But with much forcing of his disposition.
Rosencrantz. Niggard of question, but of our demands
　　Most free in his reply.
Queen.　　　　　　Did you assay him
¹⁵ To any pastime?
Rosencrantz. Madam, it so fell out that certain players
　　We o'erraught on the way. Of these we told him,
　　And there did seem in him a kind of joy
　　To hear of it. They are here about the court,
²⁰ And, as I think, they have already order
　　This night to play before him.
Polonius.　　　　　　'Tis most true,
　　And he beseeched me to entreat your majesties
　　To hear and see the matter.
King. With all my heart, and it doth much content me
²⁵ To hear him so inclined.
　　Good gentlemen, give him a further edge
　　And drive his purpose into these delights.
Rosencrantz. We shall, my lord.
　　　　　　Exeunt ROSENCRANTZ *and* GUILDENSTERN.
King.　　　　　　Sweet Gertrude, leave us too,
　　For we have closely sent for Hamlet hither,
³⁰ That he, as 'twere by accident, may here
　　Affront Ophelia.
　　Her father and myself (lawful espials)
　　Will so bestow ourselves that, seeing unseen,
　　We may of their encounter frankly judge
³⁵ And gather by him, as he is behaved,
　　If't be th' affliction of his love or no
　　That thus he suffers for.
Queen.　　　　　　I shall obey you.—
　　And for your part, Ophelia, I do wish
　　That your good beauties be the happy cause
⁴⁰ Of Hamlet's wildness. So shall I hope your virtues

5. *distracted:* agitated (to the point of madness).

7. *forward:* eager.

8. *crafty madness:* This apparently means the craftiness that often goes with madness, rather than a madness craftily put on. The king speaks of Hamlet as putting on *this confusion* in line 2, but "put on" was used to mean "assume genuinely" as well as "assume falsely," and everything else in the scene indicates that Hamlet is believed to be suffering from a genuine spiritual affliction: cf. 3-4, 5-6, 24-25, 36-37, 38-41, 164-165.

12. *forcing . . . disposition:* effort, constraint.

13-14. *Niggard . . . reply:* sparing in talk on his own part but very willing to answer our questions.

14. *assay:* tempt.

17. *o'erraught:* overtook.

26. *edge:* incitement.

29. *closely:* secretly.

31. *affront:* encounter.

32. *espials:* spies.

Will bring him to his wonted way again,
To both your honors.

Ophelia.   Madam, I wish it may. [*Exit* QUEEN.]

Polonius. Ophelia, walk you here.—Gracious, so please
    you,
We will bestow ourselves.—[*to* OPHELIA] Read on this
    book,

45 That show of such an exercise may color
Your loneliness. We are oft to blame in this,
'Tis too much proved, that with devotion's visage
And pious action we do sugar o'er
The devil himself.

King.   [*aside*] O, 'tis too true.

50 How smart a lash that speech doth give my con-
    science!
The harlot's cheek, beautied with plast'ring art,
Is not more ugly to the thing that helps it
Than is my deed to my most painted word.
O heavy burthen!

55 *Polonius.* I hear him coming. Let's withdraw, my lord.

                    [*Exeunt* KING *and* POLONIUS.]

              Enter HAMLET.

Hamlet. To be, or not to be—that is the question:
Whether 'tis nobler in the mind to suffer
The slings and arrows of outrageous fortune
Or to take arms against a sea of troubles

60 And by opposing end them. To die, to sleep—
No more—and by a sleep to say we end
The heartache, and the thousand natural shocks
That flesh is heir to. 'Tis a consummation
Devoutly to be wished. To die, to sleep—

65 To sleep—perchance to dream: ay, there's the rub,
For in that sleep of death what dreams may come
When we have shuffled off this mortal coil,
Must give us pause. There's the respect
That makes calamity of so long life.

70 For who would bear the whips and scorns of time,
Th' oppressor's wrong, the proud man's contumely,
The pangs of déspised love, the law's delay,
The insolence of office, and the spurns
That patient merit of th' unworthy takes,

75 When he himself might his quietus make

43. *Gracious:* i.e., my gracious lord.

44. *book:* a missal or prayer book.

45-46. *color . . . loneliness:* make your being found alone seem natural.

47. *devotion's visage:* the mask of religion.

52. *to . . . it:* compared to the rouge and paint.

56. *To be . . . to be:* i.e., whether it is better to be alive or dead.

59. *a . . . troubles:* i.e., troubles as numerous as the waves of the sea.
59-60. *to . . . them:* i.e., to commit suicide.

63. *consummation:* fulfilment.

65. *rub:* obstacle (in the game of bowling).

67. *coil:* fuss, turmoil—but with punning allusion to life as a coil of rope.
68. *respect:* consideration.
69. *makes . . . life:* makes even those who have suffered calamity cling to life.
70. *whips . . . time:* Time is thought of as a constable whipping a poor creature through the streets to the jeers of a mob.
71. *Th' . . . contumely:* the wrong done us by the oppressor, the humiliation inflicted on us by the proud.
73. *office:* men in office. *spurns:* insults.
75. *quietus:* release from life (literally, from debt).

With a bare bodkin? Who would fardels bear,
To grunt and sweat under a weary life,
But that the dread of something after death,
The undiscovered country, from whose bourn
80 No traveller returns, puzzles the will,
And makes us rather bear those ills we have
Than fly to others that we know not of?
Thus conscience does make cowards of us all,
And thus the native hue of resolution
85 Is sicklied o'er with the pale cast of thought,
And enterprises of great pitch and moment
With this regard their currents turn awry
And lose the name of action.—Soft you now,
The fair Ophelia!—Nymph, in thy orisons
Be all my sins remembered.
90 *Ophelia.*   Good my lord,
How does your honor for this many a day?
Hamlet. I humbly thank you, well, well, well.
Ophelia. My lord, I have remembrances of yours
That I have longèd long to re-deliver.
I pray you, now receive them.
95 *Hamlet.*   No, not I,
I never gave you aught.
Ophelia. My honored lord, you know right well you did,
And with them words of so sweet breath composed
As made the things more rich. Their perfume lost,
100 Take these again, for to the noble mind
Rich gifts wax poor when givers prove unkind.
There, my lord.
Hamlet. Ha, ha! Are you honest?
Ophelia. My lord?
105 *Hamlet.* Are you fair?
Ophelia. What means your lordship?
Hamlet. That if you be honest and fair, your honesty
should admit no discourse to your beauty.
Ophelia. Could beauty, my lord, have better commerce
110 than with honesty?
Hamlet. Ay, truly; for the power of beauty will sooner
transform honesty from what it is to a bawd than the
force of honesty can translate beauty into his likeness.
This was sometime a paradox, but now the time gives
115 it proof. I did love you once.

---

76. *bare:* (1) mere? (2) naked? *bodkin:* dagger. *fardels:* burdens.

79. *bourn:* limit.

80. *returns:* i.e., alive. *puzzles:* paralyzes.

83. *conscience:* This probably means the ability to take thought—consciousness; but it may mean moral scruple (against suicide) as well.
84. *native . . . resolution:* i.e., natural ruddy complexion of a resolute man.
85. *cast:* tinge.
86. *pitch and moment:* height and importance.
87. *regard:* consideration. *awry:* i.e., off the direct course.
88. *Soft you:* hush.
89. *orisons:* prayers (since he sees that she carries a prayer book).

101. *wax:* grow.

103. *honest:* chaste—as in 107; but perhaps with an allusion to the dishonesty of 101: it is not *he* who has been unkind.
105. *fair:* beautiful.

108. *admit . . . beauty:* i.e., not allow your beauty to tempt it (into becoming unchaste).
109. *commerce:* association.

111-113. *power . . . likeness:* i.e., beauty has more power to convert chastity to lust than chastity has to convert beauty to self-control.

114. *sometime:* formerly.
114-115 *time . . . proof:* e.g., in the adultery of his mother.

Ophelia. Indeed, my lord, you made me believe so.

Hamlet. You should not have believed me, for virtue cannot so inoculate our old stock but we shall relish of it. I loved you not.

120 *Ophelia.* I was the more deceived.

Hamlet. Get thee to a nunnery. Why wouldst thou be a breeder of sinners? I am myself indifferent honest, but yet I could accuse me of such things that it were better my mother had not borne me: I am very proud,

125 revengeful, ambitious, with more offenses at my beck than I have thoughts to put them in, imagination to give them shape, or time to act them in. What should such fellows as I do crawling between earth and heaven? We are arrant knaves all; believe none of

130 us. Go thy ways to a nunnery. Where's your father?

Ophelia. At home, my lord.

Hamlet. Let the doors be shut upon him, that he may play the fool nowhere but in's own house. Farewell.

Ophelia. O, help him, you sweet heavens!

135 *Hamlet.* If thou dost marry, I'll give thee this plague for thy dowry: be thou as chaste as ice, as pure as snow, thou shalt not escape calumny. Get thee to a nunnery. Go, farewell. Or if thou wilt needs marry, marry a fool, for wise men know well enough what monsters

140 you make of them. To a nunnery, go, and quickly too. Farewell.

Ophelia. O heavenly powers, restore him!

Hamlet. I have heard of your paintings too, well enough. God hath given you one face, and you make yourselves

145 another. You jig, you amble, and you lisp; you nickname God's creatures and make your wantonness your ignorance. Go to, I'll no more on't; it hath made me mad. I say we will have no more marriage. Those that are married already—all but one—shall live. The rest

150 shall keep as they are. To a nunnery, go.   *Exit.*

Ophelia. O, what a noble mind is here o'erthrown!
The courtier's, soldier's, scholar's, eye, tongue, sword,
Th' expectancy and rose of the fair state,
The glass of fashion and the mold of form,

155 Th' observed of all observers, quite, quite down!
And I, of ladies most deject and wretched,
That sucked the honey of his music vows,

117-119. *for . . . it:* Just as fruit grown by grafting new shoots on an old tree (*stock*) will still taste somewhat of the old tree—so man's acquired virtues will still taste somewhat of original sin.

121. *nunnery:* with reference to Ophelia's devotional pose.

122. *sinners:* i.e., what, in Christian doctrine, all human beings must be, owing to the fall of Eve and Adam. *indifferent:* reasonably.

124-127. *I . . . act them in:* Hamlet refers to the potential crimes of which any man is capable.

128. *crawling:* i.e., like vermin.

129. *arrant:* thorough.

130. *father:* This is the point at which, in performances of the play, it is customary for Hamlet to become aware that he is being spied upon—through some movement or noise behind the hanging where Polonius and the King are hidden. His disillusionment with Ophelia increases correspondingly.

139. *monsters:* alluding to the standard Elizabethan joke that men whose wives were unfaithful grew horns.

143. *paintings:* i.e., that you women use paint.

145. *jig . . . lisp:* indulge in affectations of gait and speech. *nickname:* misname (which may refer (a) to false modesty—not calling a spade a spade; or (b) to lack of modesty in favoring the indecent popular names that many common objects had: see IV, vii, 169).

146-147. *make . . . ignorance:* pretend your affectation of (1) modesty? (2) immodesty? results from your ignorance.

149. *all but one:* an obvious threat to the king, who may, or may not, be supposed to hear it.

150. *nunnery:* It has been suggested that, by this point, Hamlet may also intend a slang meaning of this word—house of prostitution—since he has just been identifying Ophelia with all kinds of female frailties (infidelity, painting, affectation, wantonness) and knows now that she has (figuratively) prostituted herself to become the bait in this trap set for him by his uncle and her father.

153. *expectancy and rose:* hope and ornament.

154. *glass:* mirror. *mold of form:* model of deportment.

155. *of:* by.

156. *deject:* cast down.

Now see that noble and most sovereign reason
Like sweet bells jangled, out of time and harsh,
160 That unmatched form and feature of blown youth
Blasted with ecstasy. O, woe is me
T' have seen what I have seen, see what I see!

Enter KING *and* POLONIUS.

King. Love? his affections do not that way tend,
Nor what he spake, though it lacked form a little,
165 Was not like madness. There's something in his soul
O'er which his melancholy sits on brood,
And I do doubt the hatch and the disclose
Will be some danger; which for to prevent,
I have in quick determination
170 Thus set it down: he shall with speed to England
For the demand of our neglected tribute.
Haply the seas, and countries different,
With variable objects, shall expel
This something-settled matter in his heart,
175 Whereon his brains still beating puts him thus
From fashion of himself. What think you on't?
Polonius. It shall do well. But yet do I believe
The origin and commencement of his grief
Sprung from neglected love.—How now, Ophelia?
180 You need not tell us what Lord Hamlet said.
We heard it all.—My lord, do as you please,
But if you hold it fit, after the play
Let his queen mother all alone entreat him
To show his grief. Let her be round with him,
185 And I'll be placed, so please you, in the ear
Of all their conference. If she find him not,
To England send him, or confine him where
Your wisdom best shall think.
King.   It shall be so.
Madness in great ones must not unwatched go.

Exeunt.

III, II

Enter HAMLET *and three of the* PLAYERS.

Hamlet. Speak the speech, I pray you, as I pronounced
it to you, trippingly on the tongue. But if you mouth it,
as many of our players do, I had as lief the town crier

159. *time:* the folio reading is "tune."
160. *feature:* face. *blown:* in full bloom.
161. *Blasted . . . ecstasy:* ruined by madness.

163. *affections:* passions.

166. *on brood:* i.e., like a bird hatching eggs.
167. *doubt:* suspect. *disclose:* disclosure (of what is being hatched).

171. *tribute:* tribute-money (England having been at one period under the domination of the Danes).

173. *variable objects:* varied interests.

174. *something-settled:* obsessive, fixed.

176. *From . . . himself:* out of his usual behavior.

179-181. *How . . . all:* Polonius is oblivious of what the interview has cost his daughter mentally and emotionally: she is his tool, and, once used, dismissed.

184. *round:* blunt.

186. *find him not:* does not find out his trouble.

2. *trippingly:* naturally (as in normal conversation). *mouth:* declaim it.
3. *town crier:* minor town officer who cried public announcements through the streets.

spoke my lines. Nor do not saw the air too much with
your hand, thus, but use all gently, for in the very
torrent, tempest, and (as I may say) whirlwind of your
passion, you must acquire and beget a temperance
that may give it smoothness. O, it offends me to the
soul to hear a robustious periwig-pated fellow tear a
passion to tatters, to very rags, to split the ears of the
groundlings, who for the most part are capable of
nothing but inexplicable dumb shows and noise. I
would have such a fellow whipped for o'erdoing
Termagant. It out-herods Herod. Pray you avoid it.

Player. I warrant your honor.

Hamlet. Be not too tame neither, but let your own discretion be your tutor. Suit the action to the word, the
word to the action, with this special observance, that
you o'erstep not the modesty of nature. For anything
so overdone is from the purpose of playing, whose end,
both at the first and now, was and is, to hold, as
'twere, the mirror up to nature, to show virtue her
own feature, scorn her own image, and the very age
and body of the time his form and pressure. Now
this overdone, or come tardy off, though it make the
unskillful laugh, cannot but make the judicious grieve,
the censure of the which one must in your allowance
o'erweigh a whole theatre of others. O, there be
players that I have seen play, and heard others praise,
and that highly (not to speak it profanely), that
neither having th' accent of Christians, nor the gait of
Christian, pagan, nor man, have so strutted and bellowed that I have thought some of Nature's journeymen had made men, and not made them well, they
imitated humanity so abominably.

Player. I hope we have reformed that indifferently with
us, sir.

Hamlet. O, reform it altogether! And let those that play
your clowns speak no more than is set down for them,
for there be of them that will themselves laugh, to set
on some quantity of barren spectators to laugh too,
though in the mean time some necessary question of
the play be then to be considered. That's villainous
and shows a most pitiful ambition in the fool that uses
it. Go make you ready.   [*Exeunt* PLAYERS.]

7. *temperance:* moderation.

9. *robustious:* noisy. *periwig-pated:*
wig-wearing.

11. *groundlings:* the lowest class of
spectators, who stood on the
ground to watch the play. *capable:*
appreciative.
12. *dumb shows:* pantomimes (one of
which follows after line 132, below).
14. *Termagant:* a loud-mouthed Mohammedan god in some of the
medieval mystery plays. *Herod:*
another boisterous role in the
early plays—that of the ruler who
sought to kill the infant Jesus.

19. *nature:* i.e., what is natural, unaffected.
20. *from:* alien to. *end:* objective.

23. *scorn:* i.e., what is to be scorned
—vice and folly.
23-24. *very . . . pressure:* i.e., the exact
image (even as to age and bodily
shape) of the present times (which
are here compared to a person
whose image is being taken in wax).
25. *come . . . off:* poorly done.
27. *censure . . . one:* judgment of even
one of whom. *allowance:* estimate.

30. *not . . . profanely:* not intending irreverence (in what follows).

33. *journeymen:* workers who are not
yet masters of their craft.

36. *indifferently:* tolerably well.

39. *set down:* Hamlet condemns the
tendency of some Elizabethan co-
medians to speak lines improvised
by themselves and so interrupt the
play.
40. *of them:* some of them.
41. *barren:* stupid.
42. *question:* subject.

Enter POLONIUS, GUILDENSTERN, *and* ROSENCRANTZ.

How now, my lord? Will the king hear this piece of work?

46-47. *piece of work:* masterpiece.

Polonius. And the queen too, and that presently.

48. *presently:* at once.

Hamlet. Bid the players make haste.   [*Exit* POLONIUS.]
50   Will you two help to hasten them?
Rosencrantz. Ay, my lord.   *Exeunt they two.*
Hamlet. What, ho, Horatio!

Enter HORATIO.

Horatio. Here, sweet lord, at your service.
Hamlet. Horatio, thou art e'en as just a man

54. *just:* well-balanced.

55   As e'er my conversation coped withal.

55. *As . . . withal:* as ever my life among men encountered.

Horatio. O, my dear lord—
Hamlet.   Nay, do not think I flatter.
For what advancement may I hope from thee,
That no revenue hast but thy good spirits
To feed and clothe thee? Why should the poor be flattered?
60   No, let the candied tongue lick absurd pomp,

60. *candied:* (1) sweet with offered flatteries. (2) sugared with sweetmeats given (and fawning for more). *pomp:* wealth, greatness.

And crook the pregnant hinges of the knee

61. *pregnant:* supple.

Where thrift may follow fawning. Dost thou hear?

62. *thrift:* reward.

Since my dear soul was mistress of her choice
And could of men distinguish her election,
65   S' hath sealed thee for herself, for thou hast been

65. *sealed:* designated.

As one in suff'ring all that suffers nothing,

66. *that:* who.

A man that Fortune's buffets and rewards
Hast ta'en with equal thanks; and blest are those
Whose blood and judgment are so well commeddled

69. *blood . . . commeddled:* passions and mind are so well blended.

70   That they are not a pipe for Fortune's finger
To sound what stop she please. Give me that man

71. *stop:* note (as on a wind instrument, where tones are controlled by stops).

That is not passion's slave, and I will wear him
In my heart's core, ay, in my heart of heart,
As I do thee. Something too much of this!—
75   There is a play to-night before the king.
One scene of it comes near the circumstance
Which I have told thee, of my father's death.
I prithee, when thou seest that act afoot,
Even with the very comment of thy soul

79. *very comment:* keenest observation.

80   Observe my uncle. If his occulted guilt

80. *occulted:* hidden.

Do not itself unkennel in one speech,

81. *unkennel:* reveal (like an animal driven from its lair).

It is a damnèd ghost that we have seen,

82. *damnèd ghost:* i.e, devil (not my father).

And my imaginations are as foul
As Vulcan's stithy. Give him heedful note,
85   For I mine eyes will rivet to his face,
And after we will both our judgments join
In censure of his seeming.

Horatio.   Well, my lord.
If 'a steal aught the whilst this play is playing,
And scape detecting, I will pay the theft.

Enter TRUMPETS *and* KETTLEDRUMS, KING, QUEEN,
    POLONIUS, OPHELIA, [ROSENCRANTZ, GUILDENSTERN,
    and other LORDS *attendant*].

90 *Hamlet.* They are coming to the play. I must be idle.
  Get you a place.
King. How fares our cousin Hamlet?
Hamlet. Excellent, i' faith, of the chameleon's dish. I eat
  the air, promise-crammed. You cannot feed capons so.
95 *King.* I have nothing with this answer, Hamlet. These
  words are not mine.
Hamlet. No, nor mine now. [*to* POLONIUS] My lord, you
  played once i' th' university, you say?
Polonius. That did I, my lord, and was accounted a good
100   actor.
Hamlet. What did you enact?
Polonius. I did enact Julius Cæsar. I was killed i' th'
  Capitol; Brutus killed me.
Hamlet. It was a brute part of him to kill so capital a calf
105   there. Be the players ready?
Rosencrantz. Ay, my lord. They stay upon your patience.
Queen. Come hither, my dear Hamlet, sit by me.
Hamlet. No, good mother. Here's metal more attractive.
Polonius. [*to the* KING] O ho! do you mark that?
110 *Hamlet.* Lady, shall I lie in your lap?

                        [*He lies at* OPHELIA'S *feet*.]

Ophelia. No, my lord.
Hamlet. I mean, my head upon your lap?
Ophelia. Ay, my lord.
Hamlet. Do you think I meant country matters?
115 *Ophelia.* I think nothing, my lord.
Hamlet. That's a fair thought to lie between maids' legs.
Ophelia. What is, my lord?
Hamlet. Nothing.
Ophelia. You are merry, my lord.

84. *Vulcan's stithy:* forge of the black-smith god, Vulcan.

87. *In . . . seeming:* in evaluation of his appearance.

90. *idle:* lunatic.

93-94. *of . . . promise-crammed:* Hamlet takes the king's *How fares* in the sense of "how feeds" and says that (as the chameleon was supposed to do) he feeds on air—i.e., the king's empty promises about his succeeding to the throne. *Air* may also contain a pun on "heir."

94. *capons:* possibly a "mad" hint of Hamlet's suspicion that he is kept around the court in idleness, like a fowl being fattened, for the king's own malign purposes. If this is my role, he implies sarcastically, you'll have to feed me on more than air.

95. *have . . . with:* can make nothing of.

96. *not mine:* not an answer to my question.

97. *nor . . . now:* i.e., once spoken, the words no longer belong to me either.

104. *part:* act. *so . . . calf:* so eminent a fool.

106. *stay . . . patience:* await your leisure.

110. *lie . . . lap:* at your feet (but with a sexual undermeaning). Hamlet consciously adopts in this scene the uninhibited speech of the lover gone mad, and embarrasses Ophelia by speaking as if she were literally a prostitute.

114. *country:* i.e., obscene, "barnyard" (with a pun on a sexual term).

116. *a . . . to:* a proper notion of what should.

118. *Nothing:* a further sexual pun.

120   *Hamlet.* Who, I?

  Ophelia. Ay, my lord.

  Hamlet. O God, your only jig-maker! What should a
    man do but be merry? For look you how cheerfully my
    mother looks, and my father died within's two hours.

125   *Ophelia.* Nay, 'tis twice two months, my lord.

  Hamlet. So long? Nay then, let the devil wear black, for
    I'll have a suit of sables. O heavens! die two months
    ago, and not forgotten yet? Then there's hope a great
    man's memory may outlive his life half a year. But,

130   by'r Lady, he must build churches then, or else shall
    'a suffer not thinking on, with the hobby-horse, whose
    epitaph is 'For O, for O, the hobby-horse is forgot!'

        The trumpets sound. Dumb show follows:

  *Enter a King and a Queen [very lovingly], the Queen
  embracing him, and he her. [She kneels; and makes
  show of protestation unto him.] He takes her up, and
  declines his head upon her neck. He lies him down upon
  a bank of flowers. She, seeing him asleep, leaves him.
  Anon come in another man: takes off his crown, kisses it,
  pours poison in the sleeper's ears, and leaves him. The
  Queen returns, finds the King dead, makes passionate
  action. The poisoner, with some three or four, come in
  again, seem to condole with her. The dead body is carried
  away. The poisoner woos the Queen with gifts; she seems
  harsh awhile, but in the end accepts love.*   [*Exeunt.*]

  Ophelia. What means this, my lord?

  Hamlet. Marry, this is miching mallecho; it means mis-
135   chief.

  Ophelia. Belike this show imports the argument of the
    play.

            Enter PROLOGUE.

  Hamlet. We shall know by this fellow. The players can-
    not keep counsel; they'll tell all.

140   *Ophelia.* Will 'a tell us what this show meant?

  Hamlet. Ay, or any show that you'll show him. Be not
    you ashamed to show, he'll not shame to tell you what
    it means.

  Ophelia. You are naught, you are naught. I'll mark the
145   play.

---

122. *your . . . jig-maker:* Hamlet replies with bitter anguish that yes, of course, he's as merry as a *jig-maker* (professional stage clown).

124. *'s:* this.

125. *twice two:* Since his father was two months dead when we first saw Hamlet (II, ii, 138), two months more have now passed.

126-127. *So . . . sables:* Hamlet says, with sarcastic reference to the bright costumes all around him: nay, if it's that long, let's leave mourning black to the devil (whose color it is) and I'll have a new suit with rich furs (like the rest of this ungrieving court). Hamlet also puns on the heraldic sense of *sable,* i.e., "black."

130. *churches:* i.e., where his memory will be kept alive by masses.

131. *suffer . . . on:* be forgotten.

132. *hobby-horse:* a performer in Elizabethan May Day dances who rode an imitation horse and became associated with the refrain Hamlet quotes. There may be a further allusion for the benefit of the Elizabethan audience to Puritan disapproval of the May Day celebrations —as if to say: "All the old usages are forgotten now, even as Hamlet's father is by courtiers and queen in this play."

Stage direction. *Dumb show:* pantomime. *Anon:* at once.

134. *miching mallecho:* cunning mischief.

136. *imports:* implies.

144. *naught:* naughty, i.e., indecent.

Prologue. For us and for our tragedy,
　　　　Here stooping to your clemency,
　　　　We beg your hearing patiently.　　　[*Exit.*]

Hamlet. Is this a prologue, or the posy of a ring?

150　*Ophelia.* 'Tis brief, my lord.

Hamlet. As woman's love.

　　　　Enter [*two* PLAYERS *as*] KING *and* QUEEN.

King. Full thirty times hath Phoebus' cart gone round
　　Neptune's salt wash and Tellus' orbèd ground,
　　And thirty dozen moons with borrowed sheen

155　About the world have times twelve thirties been,
　　Since love our hearts, and Hymen did our hands,
　　Unite commutual in most sacred bands.

Queen. So many journeys may the sun and moon
　　Make us again count o'er ere love be done!

160　But woe is me, you are so sick of late,
　　So far from cheer and from your former state,
　　That I distrust you. Yet, though I distrust,
　　Discomfort you, my lord, it nothing must.
　　For women fear too much, even as they love,

165　And women's fear and love hold quantity,
　　In neither aught, or in extremity.
　　Now what my love is, proof hath made you know,
　　And as my love is sized, my fear is so.
　　Where love is great, the littlest doubts are fear;

170　Where little fears grow great, great love grows there.

King. Faith, I must leave thee, love, and shortly too;
　　My operant powers their functions leave to do.
　　And thou shalt live in this fair world behind,
　　Honored, beloved, and haply one as kind

175　For husband shalt thou—

Queen.　　　　　　　　O, confound the rest!
　　Such love must needs be treason in my breast.
　　In second husband let me be accurst!
　　None wed the second but who killed the first.

Hamlet. [*aside*] That's wormwood.

180　*Queen.* The instances that second marriage move
　　Are base respects of thrift, but none of love.
　　A second time I kill my husband dead
　　When second husband kisses me in bed.

King. I do believe you think what now you speak,

185　But what we do determine oft we break.

147. *stooping to:* bowing in the hope of having.

149. *posy:* i.e., the sort of silly jingle that might be engraved on a ring.

152-258. Shakespeare sets *this* play apart from his own not by pretentious diction (as at II, ii, 450ff), but by continuous rhyme.

152-153. *Full . . . ground:* i.e., thirty years have passed (Phoebus, Neptune, and Tellus are gods of sun, sea, and earth, respectively).

154. *borrowed:* i.e., from the sun.

155. *times . . . thirties:* i.e., twelve times thirty.

156. *Hymen:* god of marriage.

157. *bands:* bonds.

162. *distrust:* am worried about.

165. *quantity:* proportion.

166. *In . . . extremity:* either no fear or love at all, or an excess of both.

167. *proof:* experience.

172. *operant:* vital. *leave to do:* stop performing.

179. *wormwood:* i.e., for his mother (wormwood is a bitter herb).

180. *instances:* motives.

181. *respects of thrift:* considerations of profit.

Purpose is but the slave to memory,

Of violent birth, but poor validity,

Which now like fruit unripe sticks on the tree,

But fall unshaken when they mellow be.

190 Most necessary 'tis that we forget

To pay ourselves what to ourselves is debt.

What to ourselves in passion we propose,

The passion ending, doth the purpose lose.

The violence of either grief or joy

195 Their own enactures with themselves destroy.

Where joy most revels, grief doth most lament;

Grief joys, joy grieves, on slender accident.

This world is not for aye, nor 'tis not strange

That even our loves should with our fortunes change,

200 For 'tis a question left us yet to prove,

Whether love lead fortune, or else fortune love.

The great man down, you mark his favorite flies,

The poor advanced makes friends of enemies;

And hitherto doth love on fortune tend,

205 For who not needs shall never lack a friend,

And who in want a hollow friend doth try,

Directly seasons him his enemy.

But, orderly to end where I begun,

Our wills and fates do so contrary run

210 That our devices still are overthrown;

Our thoughts are ours, their ends none of our own.

So think thou wilt no second husband wed,

But die thy thoughts when thy first lord is dead.

Queen. Nor earth to me give food, nor heaven light,

215 Sport and repose lock from me day and night,

To desperation turn my trust and hope,

An anchor's cheer in prison be my scope,

Each opposite that blanks the face of joy

Meet what I would have well, and it destroy,

220 Both here and hence pursue me lasting strife,

If, once a widow, ever I be wife!

Hamlet. If she should break it now!

King. 'Tis deeply sworn. Sweet, leave me here awhile.

My spirits grow dull, and fain I would beguile

225 The tedious day with sleep.

Queen.　　　　　Sleep rock thy brain, [*He sleeps.*]

And never come mischance between us twain!　*Exit.*

186-189. *Purpose . . . be:* our purpose (to be loyal) only holds while memory (of the beloved) is fresh; violent at first, it is not lasting; like green fruit it sticks on the tree now, but like ripe fruit it will fall away later of its own accord.

190-191. *necessary . . . debt:* inevitable it is that we forget to pay what we have promised no one but ourselves.

194-195. *The . . . destroy:* the very violence of grief or joy—since what is violent *cannot* last—destroys the grief or joy and therefore its expression in action.

196-197. *Where . . . accident:* i.e., no emotion lasts: joy is turned to grief, grief to joy, by any trifle.

201. *Whether . . . love:* whether love is superior to considerations of fortune or determined by them.
202. *flies:* i.e., abandons him.

205. *not needs:* i.e., because he has power and wealth.
206-207. *who . . . enemy:* See I, iii, 76 and note.
207. *seasons:* renders.

210. *devices:* intentions.
211. *their . . . own:* their fulfilments are not in our power.

215. *Sport, repose:* objects of the verb. *Sport:* pleasure.

217. *anchor's cheer:* hermit's diet. *scope:* lot.
218-219. Let every contrary thing that can wipe away joy meet every good thing and destroy it.

220. *hence:* i.e., in the world to come.

222. *If . . . now:* (spoken for his mother's benefit).

Hamlet. Madam, how like you this play?

Queen. The lady doth protest too much, methinks.

Hamlet. O, but she'll keep her word.

230 *King.* Have you heard the argument? Is there no offense in't?

Hamlet. No, no, they do but jest, poison in jest; no offense i' th' world.

King. What do you call the play?

235 *Hamlet.* 'The Mousetrap.' Marry, how? Tropically. This play is the image of a murther done in Vienna. Gonzago is the duke's name; his wife, Baptista. You shall see anon. 'Tis a knavish piece of work, but what o' that? Your majesty, and we that have free souls, it

240 touches us not. Let the galled jade wince; our withers are unwrung.

Enter LUCIANUS.

This is one Lucianus, nephew to the king.

Ophelia. You are as good as a chorus, my lord.

Hamlet. I could interpret between you and your love, if

245 I could see the puppets dallying.

Ophelia. You are keen, my lord, you are keen.

Hamlet. It would cost you a groaning to take off mine edge.

Ophelia. Still better, and worse.

250 *Hamlet.* So you must take your husbands.—Begin, murtherer. Leave thy damnable faces and begin. Come, the croaking raven doth bellow for revenge.

Lucianus. Thoughts black, hands apt, drugs fit, and time agreeing,

Confederate season, else no creature seeing,

255 Thou mixture rank, of midnight weeds collected,

With Hecate's ban thrice blasted, thrice infected,

Thy natural magic and dire property

On wholesome life usurps immediately.

[*Pours the poison in his ears.*]

Hamlet. 'A poisons him i' th' garden for his estate. His

260 name's Gonzago. The story is extant, and written in very choice Italian. You shall see anon how the murtherer gets the love of Gonzago's wife.

Ophelia. The king rises.

Hamlet. What, frighted with false fire?

---

228. *protest:* affirm.

230. *argument:* plot (of a play)

235. *Tropically:* i.e., by a trope, a metaphor.

238. *knavish . . . work:* masterpiece of mischief.
239. *free:* innocent.

240-241. *Let . . . unwrung:* let the horse that is *galled,* i.e., chafed (by the load of a guilty conscience) do the wincing, *our* shoulders are not chafed.

243. *chorus:* an actor who summarized or interpreted the action to come, usually in a prologue.
244-245. *I could . . . dallying:* Hamlet thinks of himself as "interpreter," i.e., hidden narrator (at a puppet show) while Ophelia and some imagined lover are making love (*dallying*).
246. *keen:* cruel.
247-248. *It . . . edge:* Hamlet chooses to take "keen" to mean sexually eager, and replies accordingly.
249. *better:* i.e., wittier. *worse:* i.e., more indecent.
250. *So . . . husbands:* i.e., so you women should take your husbands —"for better or for worse," as in the marriage service—but actually you "mis-take" them and then "mistake" (deceive) them.
252. *the . . . revenge:* Hamlet adapts a line from an old melodrama ("the screeching raven sits croaking for revenge") to parody the melodramatic tone of Lucianus's speech.
254. *Confederate . . . seeing:* the time assisting, no one watching.
255. *midnight:* collected at midnight (hence believed to be especially potent).
256. *Hecate:* queen of witches. *ban:* curse.

264. *false fire:* i.e., firing with powder but not ball.

265 *Queen.* How fares my lord?

Polonius. Give o'er the play.

King. Give me some light. Away!

Polonius Lights, lights, lights!

             Exeunt all but HAMLET *and* HORATIO.

Hamlet. Why, let the strucken deer go weep,

270   The hart ungallèd play.

     For some must watch, while some must sleep;

       Thus runs the world away.

Would not this, sir, and a forest of feathers—if the rest of my fortunes turn Turk with me—with two Pro-

275 vincial roses on my razed shoes, get me a fellowship in a cry of players, sir?

Horatio. Half a share.

Hamlet. A whole one, I.

    For thou dost know, O Damon dear,

280   This realm dismantled was

    Of Jove himself; and now reigns here

       A very, very—peacock.

Horatio. You might have rhymed.

Hamlet. O good Horatio, I'll take the ghost's word for a

285 thousand pound. Didst perceive?

Horatio. Very well, my lord.

Hamlet. Upon the talk of the poisoning?

Horatio. I did very well note him.

Hamlet. Aha! Come, some music! Come, the recorders!

290   For if the king like not the comedy,

     Why then, belike he likes it not, perdy.

Come, some music!

    Enter ROSENCRANTZ *and* GUILDENSTERN.

Guildenstern. Good my lord, vouchsafe me a word with you.

295 *Hamlet.* Sir, a whole history.

Guildenstern. The king, sir—

Hamlet. Ay, sir, what of him?

Guildenstern. Is in his retirement marvellous distempered.

Hamlet. With drink, sir?

300 *Guildenstern.* No, my lord, with choler.

Hamlet. Your wisdom should show itself more richer to signify this to the doctor, for for me to put him to his purgation would perhaps plunge him into more choler.

---

266. *Give o'er:* stop.

270. *hart ungallèd:* stag unwounded.

271. *For . . . sleep:* i.e., for men have different destinies.

273. *this:* this rhyme—or possibly, this play that I have put on. *forest of feathers:* alluding to the heavily plumed costumes worn by actors.

274. *turn Turk:* play false.

274-275. *Provincial roses:* ribbon rosettes in form of the damask rose, called Rosa Provincialis from the French town Provins.

275. *razed:* open-work, i.e., fancy. *fellowship:* share (Elizabethan actors could buy shares in the profits of their acting companies).

279. *Damon:* jestingly applied to Horatio (with reference to the legendary ideal friendship of Damon for Pythias).

281. *Jove:* i.e., Hamlet's father, whom he repeatedly compares to a god (see, I, ii, 140; III, iv, 55 ff.).

282. *peacock:* symbol of lechery and pride.

283. Horatio implies that the *rhyme* (to "was") would have been "ass."

289. *recorders:* flute-like wind instruments.

291. *perdy:* i.e., par dieu, "by God."

295. *history:* i.e., you can have a whole bookful (of words).

298. *distempered:* upset.

299. *drink:* Hamlet gibes again at the king's drinking habits.

300. *choler:* anger (but Hamlet deliberately takes it in its other meaning, excess of bile, i.e., upset stomach).

303. *purgation:* (1) purging by cathartics, (2) purging from his guilt. In the latter case the king would be plunged into *more choler,* in the sense of the hangman's noose (collar).

Guildenstern. Good my lord, put your discourse into
305   some frame, and start not so wildly from my affair.

Hamlet. I am tame, sir; pronounce.

Guildenstern. The queen, your mother, in most great
affliction of spirit hath sent me to you.

Hamlet. You are welcome.

310 *Guildenstern.* Nay, good my lord, this courtesy is not
of the right breed. If it shall please you to make me
a wholesome answer, I will do your mother's commandment. If not, your pardon and my return shall
be the end of my business.

315 *Hamlet.* Sir, I cannot.

Rosencrantz. What, my lord?

Hamlet. Make you a wholesome answer; my wit's
diseased. But, sir, such answer as I can make, you
shall command, or rather, as you say, my mother.
320   Therefore no more, but to the matter. My mother,
you say—

Rosencrantz. Then thus she says: your behavior hath
struck her into amazement and admiration.

Hamlet. O wonderful son, that can so stonish a mother!
325   But is there no sequel at the heels of this mother's
admiration? Impart.

Rosencrantz. She desires to speak with you in her closet
ere you go to bed.

Hamlet. We shall obey, were she ten times our mother.
330   Have you any further trade with us?

Rosencrantz. My lord, you once did love me.

Hamlet. And do still, by these pickers and stealers.

Rosencrantz. Good my lord, what is your cause of distemper? You do surely bar the door upon your own
335   liberty, if you deny your griefs to your friend.

Hamlet. Sir, I lack advancement.

Rosencrantz. How can that be, when you have the voice
of the king himself for your succession in Denmark?

Hamlet. Ay, sir, but 'while the grass grows'—the proverb
340   is something musty.

Enter the PLAYER *with recorders.*

O, the recorders. Let me see one. To withdraw with
you—why do you go about to recover the wind of
me, as if you would drive me into a toil?

305. *frame:* order. *start . . . wildly:* i.e., like a skittish horse.

312. *wholesome:* sane.
313. *pardon:* permission to depart (one does not leave a prince's presence till dismissed).

323. *admiration:* wonder.

327. *closet:* private chamber.

332. *pickers and stealers:* hands ("To keep my hands from picking and stealing" is a phrase from the Church of England catechism).
333. *distemper:* disorder.
334-335. *You . . . liberty:* i.e., you will be locked up for a lunatic.
336. Hamlet's "story" for Rosencrantz and Guildenstern to report back to the king is that his malady comes from frustrated ambition for the throne.
339. *While . . . grows:* "while the grass grows, the horse starves."
340. *musty:* stale.

341. *withdraw:* speak in confidence.
342. *recover . . . wind:* take cunning advantage (as a hunter does of game in driving it toward a trap by letting it scent his coming).
343. *toil:* trap.

Guildenstern. O my lord, if my duty be too bold, my love
345   is too unmannerly.

Hamlet. I do not well understand that. Will you play upon
  this pipe?

Guildenstern. My lord, I cannot.

Hamlet. I pray you.

350 *Guildenstern.* Believe me, I cannot.

Hamlet. I do beseech you.

Guildenstern. I know no touch of it, my lord.

Hamlet. It is as easy as lying. Govern these ventages
  with your fingers and thumb, give it breath with your
355   mouth, and it will discourse most eloquent music. Look
  you, these are the stops.

Guildenstern. But these cannot I command to any utt'-
  rance of harmony. I have not the skill.

Hamlet. Why, look you now, how unworthy a thing you
360   make of me! You would play upon me, you would
  seem to know my stops, you would pluck out the heart
  of my mystery, you would sound me from my lowest
  note to the top of my compass; and there is much
  music, excellent voice, in this little organ, yet cannot
365   you make it speak. 'Sblood, do you think I am easier
  to be played on than a pipe? Call me what instrument
  you will, though you can fret me, you cannot play
  upon me.

Enter POLONIUS.

  God bless you, sir!

370 *Polonius.* My lord, the queen would speak with you, and
  presently.

Hamlet. Do you see yonder cloud that's almost in shape
  of a camel?

Polonius. By th' mass and 'tis, like a camel indeed.

375 *Hamlet.* Methinks it is like a weasel.

Polonius. It is backed like a weasel.

Hamlet. Or like a whale.

Polonius. Very like a whale.

Hamlet. Then I will come to my mother by and by.
380   [*aside*] They fool me to the top of my bent.— I will
  come by and by.

Polonius. I will say so.   [*Exit.*]

344-345. *if . . . unmannerly:* if my sense of duty toward you makes me too bold (in asking these questions), it is because my love for you overcomes manners.

347. *pipe:* i.e., the recorder Hamlet has in his hand.

352. *touch:* a musical term meaning to handle an instrument so as to bring out its tone.
353. *lying:* (i.e., at which you are a master). *ventages:* openings.

356. *stops:* finger-holes.

363. *compass:* range.

365. *'Sblood:* by God's blood.

367. *fret:* annoy (but with a pun on "frets," the ridges that guide the fingering on many instruments).

371. *presently:* at once.

379. *by and by:* at once.

380. *top . . . bent:* i.e., of a bow drawn to the utmost.

Hamlet. 'By and by' is easily said. Leave me, friends.

                    [Exeunt all but HAMLET.*]*

    'Tis now the very witching time of night,

385   When churchyards yawn, and hell itself breathes out

    Contagion to this world. Now could I drink hot blood

    And do such bitter business as the day

    Would quake to look on. Soft, now to my mother.

    O heart, lose not thy nature; let not ever

390   The soul of Nero enter this firm bosom.

    Let me be cruel, not unnatural;

    I will speak daggers to her, but use none.

    My tongue and soul in this be hypocrites:

    How in my words somever she be shent,

395   To give them seals never, my soul, consent!   *Exit.*

385. *yawn:* i.e., open their graves.

389. *nature:* i.e., natural affection (for a mother).
390. *Nero:* Roman emperor, who murdered his mother.

393. *hypocrites:* i.e., in expressing and feeling emotions that will not be carried into action.
394. *shent:* shamed.
395. *seals:* i.e., authentication by action (as in sealing a contract).

III, iii

Enter King, Rosencrantz, and Guildenstern.

King. I like him not, nor stands it safe with us

    To let his madness range. Therefore prepare you.

    I your commission will forthwith dispatch,

    And he to England shall along with you.

5   The terms of our estate may not endure

    Hazard so near's as doth hourly grow

    Out of his brows.

Guildenstern.   We will ourselves provide.

    Most holy and religious fear it is

    To keep those many many bodies safe

10   That live and feed upon your majesty.

Rosencrantz. The single and peculiar life is bound

    With all the strength and armor of the mind

    To keep itself from noyance, but much more

    That spirit upon whose weal depends and rests

15   The lives of many. The cess of majesty

    Dies not alone, but like a gulf doth draw

    What's near it with it; or 'tis a massy wheel

    Fixed on the summit of the highest mount,

    To whose huge spokes ten thousand lesser things

20   Are mortised and adjoined, which when it falls,

    Each small annexment, petty consequence,

    Attends the boist'rous ruin. Never alone

    Did the king sigh, but with a general groan.

1. *like . . . not:* mistrust him.

2. *range:* have free range.

3. *dispatch:* have prepared.

5. *terms . . . estate:* i.e., kingship.

6. *near's:* near us.

7. *brows:* affronts (cf. modern "cheek"). (But some editors amend to "braves"—insolences). *provide:* get ready.
8. *fear:* prudence.

9. *those . . . bodies:* i.e., all the people of Denmark.

11. *The . . . peculiar:* each individual.

13. *noyance:* harm.

14. *weal:* well-being.

15. *cess:* cessation, end.

16. *gulf:* whirlpool.

21. *Each . . . consequence:* i.e., the ten thousand lesser things of line 19.
22. *Attends:* shares.

King. Arm you, I pray you, to this speedy voyage,

25   For we will fetters put upon this fear,

Which now goes too free-footed.

Rosencrantz.   We will haste us.

Exeunt GENTLEMEN.

Enter POLONIUS.

Polonius. My lord, he's going to his mother's closet.

Behind the arras I'll convey myself

To hear the process. I'll warrant she'll tax him home,

30   And, as you said, and wisely was it said,

'Tis meet that some more audience than a mother,

Since nature makes them partial, should o'erhear

The speech, of vantage. Fare you well, my liege.

I'll call upon you ere you go to bed

And tell you what I know.

35   *King.*   Thanks, dear my lord.

Exit [POLONIUS].

O, my offense is rank, it smells to heaven;

It hath the primal eldest curse upon't,

A brother's murther. Pray can I not,

Though inclination be as sharp as will.

40   My stronger guilt defeats my strong intent,

And like a man to double business bound

I stand in pause where I shall first begin,

And both neglect. What if this cursèd hand

Were thicker than itself with brother's blood,

45   Is there not rain enough in the sweet heavens

To wash it white as snow? Whereto serves mercy

But to confront the visage of offense?

And what's in prayer but this twofold force,

To be forstallèd ere we come to fall,

50   Or pardoned being down? Then I'll look up.

My fault is past. But, O, what form of prayer

Can serve my turn? 'Forgive me my foul murther'?

That cannot be, since I am still possessed

Of those effects for which I did the murther,

55   My crown, mine own ambition, and my queen.

May one be pardoned and retain th' offense?

In the corrupted currents of this world

Offense's gilded hand may shove by justice,

And oft 'tis seen the wicked prize itself

24. *Arm you:* equip yourselves.

29. *process:* proceedings. *tax . . . home:* thrust home in rebuking him.

30. *as you said:* Polonius made the suggestion, not Claudius; see III, i, 180 ff. With his characteristic "indirection," he suggests the idea, then attributes it to the king so that he can approve it and carry it out.

31. *meet:* proper.

33. *of vantage:* in addition.

36. *rank:* foul, rancid.

37. *curse:* i.e., that put on Cain for murdering his brother Abel.

39. *Though . . . will:* i.e., though he not only *wills* to pray but *longs* to.

44. *thicker . . . itself:* i.e., so crusted as to be double its normal size.

45. *rain:* (1) water (2) divine mercy.

46-47. *Whereto . . . offense:* what is mercy for, if not to meet (and counteract) the face of sin.

54. *effects:* gains.

56. *offense:* i.e., the profits of the crime.

58. *offense's . . . hand:* crime's bribe-giving hand. *by:* aside.

60   Buys out the law. But 'tis not so above.

There is no shuffling; there the action lies

In his true nature, and we ourselves compelled,

Even to the teeth and forehead of our faults,

To give in evidence. What then? What rests?

65   Try what repentance can. What can it not?

Yet what can it when one cannot repent?

O wretched state! O bosom black as death!

O limèd soul, that struggling to be free

Art more engaged! Help, angels! Make assay.

70   Bow, stubborn knees, and, heart with strings of steel,

Be soft as sinews of the new-born babe.

All may be well.   [*He kneels.*]

Enter HAMLET.

Hamlet. Now might I do it pat, now 'a is a-praying,

And now I'll do't, and so 'a goes to heaven,

75   And so am I revenged!—That would be scanned:

A villain kills my father, and for that

I, his sole son, do this same villain send

To heaven.

Why, this is base and silly, not revenge.

80   'A took my father grossly, full of bread,

With all his crimes broad blown, as flush as May;

And how his audit stands, who knows save Heaven?

But in our circumstance and course of thought,

'Tis heavy with him; and am I then revenged,

85   To take him in the purging of his soul,

When he is fit and seasoned for his passage?

No.

Up, sword, and know thou a more horrid hent.

When he is drunk asleep, or in his rage,

90   Or in th' incestuous pleasure of his bed,

At game a-swearing, or about some act

That has no relish of salvation in't—

Then trip him, that his heels may kick at heaven,

And that his soul may be as damned and black

95   As hell, whereto it goes. My mother stays.

This physic but prolongs thy sickly days.   *Exit.*

King. [*rises*] My words fly up, my thoughts remain below.

Words without thoughts never to heaven go.   *Exit.*

60. *above:* i.e., in heaven.

61. *shuffling:* trickery. *lies:* a legal term roughly equivalent here to "is examined."

63. *to . . . faults:* i.e., in face-to-face acknowledgement of our faults (as witnesses appearing in court against us).

64. *rests:* is left (to do).

68. *limèd:* trapped (as with bird lime, a sticky substance spread on twigs).

69. *engaged:* entangled. *assay:* an attempt.

73. *pat:* opportunely.

75. *would be scanned:* needs to be further examined.

79. *base:* i.e., the kind of limited thoughtless revenge that a man low-born might take. *silly:* feeble (For "base and silly," the Quarto reading, the Folio reads "hire and salary" which many editors adopt).

80. *grossly:* i.e., grossly unprepared for divine judgment. *bread:* the enjoyments of this world.

81. *broad blown:* in full bloom. Here, as in I, v, 12, *crime* does not refer to spectacular misdeeds by Hamlet's father, but to the doctrine that all men are sinners: *flush:* abundant.

82. *audit:* account with heaven.

83. *in . . . thought:* according to our earthly notions.

85. *him:* the king.

86. *passage:* to the other world.

88. *hent:* occasion for use.

91. *game:* gambling.

92. *relish:* flavor.

93. *trip:* i.e., as the hangman trips the gallows.

96. *physic:* (1) your praying, (2) my postponement of revenge.

III, IV

Enter [QUEEN] GERTRUDE *and* POLONIUS.

Polonius. 'A will come straight. Look you lay home to
   him.
   Tell him his pranks have been too broad to bear with,
   And that your grace hath screened and stood between
   Much heat and him. I'll silence me even here.
5   Pray you be round with him.
   [*Hamlet. (within)* Mother, mother, mother!]
Queen. I'll warrant you; fear me not. Withdraw; I hear
   him coming.   [POLONIUS *hides behind the arras.*]

Enter HAMLET.

Hamlet. Now, mother, what's the matter?
10 *Queen.* Hamlet, thou hast thy father much offended.
Hamlet. Mother, you have my father much offended.
Queen. Come, come, you answer with an idle tongue.
Hamlet. Go, go, you question with a wicked tongue.
Queen. Why, how now, Hamlet?
Hamlet.   What's the matter now?
15 *Queen.* Have you forgot me?
Hamlet.   No, by the rood, not so!
   You are the queen, your husband's brother's wife,
   And (would it were not so) you are my mother.
Queen. Nay, then I'll set those to you that can speak.
Hamlet. Come, come, and sit you down. You shall not
   budge.
20   You go not till I set you up a glass
   Where you may see the inmost part of you.
Queen. What wilt thou do? Thou wilt not murther me?
   Help, ho!
Polonius. [*behind*] What, ho! help!
25 *Hamlet.* [*draws*] How now? a rat? Dead for a ducat, dead!
   [*Makes a pass through the arras and kills* POLONIUS.]
Polonius. [*behind*] O, I am slain!
Queen.   O me, what hast thou done?
Hamlet. Nay, I know not. Is it the king?
Queen. O, what a rash and bloody deed is this!
Hamlet. A bloody deed—almost as bad, good mother,
30   As kill a king, and marry with his brother.

1. *straight:* at once. *lay:* thrust.

2. *broad:* free.

4. *heat:* i.e., the king's anger. *silence:* hide (in silence).
5. *round:* blunt.

7. *I'll . . . not:* I guarantee it, don't worry.

10. *father,* i.e., the king.

11. *father:* i.e., the former king.

15. *me:* i.e., who I am. *rood:* cross.

18. *those:* i.e., the king, Polonius, etc.

20. *glass:* mirror.

25. *rat:* Hamlet supposes it to be the king. *for a ducat:* I'll bet a ducat.

Queen. As kill a king?

Hamlet.   Ay, lady, it was my word.

[*Lifts up the arras and sees* POLONIUS.]

Thou wretched, rash, intruding fool, farewell!

I took thee for thy better. Take thy fortune.

Thou find'st to be too busy is some danger.—   34. *busy:* i.e., in other peoples' affairs.

35   Leave wringing of your hands. Peace, sit you down

And let me wring your heart, for so I shall

If it be made of penetrable stuff,

If damnèd custom have not brazed it so   38. *brazed:* hardened (like brass).

That it is proof and bulwark against sense.   39. *sense:* feeling.

40 *Queen.* What have I done that thou dar'st wag thy tongue

In noise so rude against me?

Hamlet.   Such an act

That blurs the grace and blush of modesty,

Calls virtue hypocrite, takes off the rose

From the fair forehead of an innocent love,

45   And sets a blister there, makes marriage vows   45. *blister:* i.e., the mark of whores, who were branded on the forehead.

As false as dicers' oaths. O, such a deed   46. *dicers':* gamblers'.

As from the body of contraction plucks   47. *contraction:* the marriage contract.

The very soul, and sweet religion makes   48. *sweet religion:* i.e., marriage rites and vows.

A rhapsody of words! Heaven's face does glow,   49. *rhapsody:* senseless clutter.

50   And this solidity and compound mass,   50. *this . . . mass:* the solid and composite earth.

With heated visage, as against the doom,   51. *With . . . doom:* on fire, as it will be at the Last Judgment.

Is thought-sick at the act.

Queen.   Ay me, what act,

That roars so loud and thunders in the index?   53. *in the index:* i.e., even in being introduced ("index" here means a table of contents preceding the book).

Hamlet. Look here upon this picture, and on this, 54. *Look . . . this:* Here the actor playing Hamlet traditionally seizes his mother's locket (containing a picture of his uncle) and places it beside his own (containing a picture of his father).

55   The counterfeit presentment of two brothers.

See what a grace was seated on this brow:

Hyperion's curls, the front of Jove himself,   55. *counterfeit:* i.e., painted.

An eye like Mars, to threaten and command,   57. *Hyperion:* Apollo (model of manly beauty). *front of Jove:* brow of Jove (model of kingly dignity).

A station like the herald Mercury   59. *station:* posture. *Mercury:* messenger of the gods (model of grace).

60   New lighted on a heaven-kissing hill—

A combination and a form indeed

Where every god did seem to set his seal   62. *seal:* distinctive mark.

To give the world assurance of a man.

This was your husband. Look you now what follows.

65   Here is your husband, like a mildewed ear   65. *ear:* i.e., of grain.

Blasting his wholesome brother. Have you eyes?   66. *Blasting:* infecting.

Could you on this fair mountain leave to feed,   67. *leave:* cease.

And batten on this moor? Ha! have you eyes?   68. *batten:* feed greedily. *moor:* a barren upland growing only scrub and weeds (contrasted here with the good pasturage found on the mountain slopes).

You cannot call it love, for at your age
70 The heyday in the blood is tame, it's humble,
And waits upon the judgment, and what judgment
Would step from this to this? Sense sure you have,
Else could you not have motion, but sure that sense
Is apoplexed, for madness would not err,
75 Nor sense to ecstasy was ne'er so thralled
But it reserved some quantity of choice
To serve in such a difference. What devil was't
That thus hath cozened you at hoodman-blind?
Eyes without feeling, feeling without sight,
80 Ears without hands or eyes, smelling sans all,
Or but a sickly part of one true sense
Could not so mope.
O shame, where is thy blush? Rebellious hell,
If thou canst mutine in a matron's bones,
85 To flaming youth let virtue be as wax
And melt in her own fire. Proclaim no shame
When the compulsive ardor gives the charge,
Since frost itself as actively doth burn,
And reason panders will.

Queen.   O Hamlet, speak no more.
90 Thou turn'st mine eyes into my very soul,
And there I see such black and grainèd spots
As will not leave their tinct.

Hamlet.   Nay, but to live
In the rank sweat of an enseamèd bed,
Stewed in corruption, honeying and making love
Over the nasty sty—

95 *Queen.*   O, speak to me no more.
These words like daggers enter in mine ears.
No more, sweet Hamlet.

Hamlet.   A murtherer and a villain,
A slave that is not twentieth part the tithe
Of your precedent lord, a vice of kings,
100 A cutpurse of the empire and the rule,
That from a shelf the precious diadem stole
And put it in his pocket—

Queen.   No more.

Enter [the] GHOST *[in his nightgown].*

Hamlet. A king of shreds and patches—

---

70. *heyday:* excitement.

71. *waits upon:* obeys.

72. *Sense:* sensory perception.

74. *apoplexed:* paralyzed.
74-77. *for . . . difference:* for even madness would not err so much, nor could sensory perception ever be so subservient to madness that it would not retain some power of choice to be used in such an obvious judgment of differences as this.
78. *cozened . . . hoodman-blind:* tricked you at blindman's buff, i.e., blindfolded you.
80. *sans:* without.

81-82. *but . . . mope:* even a puny fraction of one live sense could not be so insensitive.

83. *hell:* i.e., instincts of hell.

84. *mutine:* mutiny. *matron's:* married woman's.

87. *ardor:* youthful desire. *gives . . . charge:* attacks.
88-89. *Since . . . will:* since *frost* (i.e., a matron's supposed self-control) burns as actively as *wax* (i.e., the passions of youth) and reason solicits in behalf of passion (as a pander solicits on behalf of a prostitute).

91. *grainèd:* fast-dyed.

92. *leave . . . tinct:* lose their color.

93. *enseamèd:* greasy.

98. *twentieth . . . tithe:* one twentieth of a tenth.
99. *precedent:* former. *vice of kings:* a buffoon, not a king (like the character called the Vice in old plays).
100. *cutpurse . . . empire:* pickpocket who stole the power.
101. *diadem:* crown.

103. *A . . . patches:* an imitation king, patched together out of scraps.

Save me and hover o'er me with your wings,
105 You heavenly guards! What would your gracious figure?

Queen. Alas, he's mad.

Hamlet. Do you not come your tardy son to chide,
That, lapsed in time and passion, lets go by
Th' important acting of your dread command?
110 O, say!

Ghost. Do not forget. This visitation
Is but to whet thy almost blunted purpose.
But look, amazement on thy mother sits.
O, step between her and her fighting soul!
115 Conceit in weakest bodies strongest works.
Speak to her, Hamlet.

Hamlet.   How is it with you, lady?

Queen. Alas, how is't with you,
That you do bend your eye on vacancy,
And with th' incorporal air do hold discourse?
120 Forth at your eyes your spirits wildly peep,
And as the sleeping soldiers in th' alarm
Your bedded hairs like life in excrements
Start up and stand an end. O gentle son,
Upon the heat and flame of thy distemper
125 Sprinkle cool patience. Whereon do you look?

Hamlet. On him, on him! Look you, how pale he glares!
His form and cause conjoined, preaching to stones,
Would make them capable. — Do not look upon me,
Lest with this piteous action you convert
130 My stern effects. Then what I have to do
Will want true color—tears perchance for blood.

Queen. To whom do you speak this?

Hamlet.   Do you see nothing there?

Queen. Nothing at all; yet all that is I see.

Hamlet. Nor did you nothing hear?

Queen.   No, nothing but ourselves.
135 *Hamlet.* Why, look you there! Look how it steals away!
My father, in his habit as he lived!
Look where he goes even now out at the portal!

Exit GHOST.

Queen. This is the very coinage of your brain.
This bodiless creation ecstasy
Is very cunning in.

104. *Save me:* Hamlet now sees the ghost.
105. *guards:* angels.
106. *mad:* The Queen cannot see the ghost.
108. *lapsed . . . passion:* fallen away from his duty in respect to both speed and zeal.
109. *important:* urgent.
113. *amazement:* stupefaction.
115. *Conceit:* imagination.
119. *incorporal:* bodiless.
121. *in . . . alarm:* when the alarm sounds.
122. *bedded:* flattened (as if asleep). *excrements:* outgrowths.
123. *an:* on.
124. *distemper:* disorder.
125. *patience:* composure.
127-128. *His . . . capable:* his reproachful bearing (or possibly, his being a ghost) taken together with the injury done him—*his cause*—could preach to stones and make them capable of feeling.
129. *convert:* alter.
130. *effects:* outward appearance.
131. *Will . . . color:* lack proper (1) justification, (2) color (i.e., the bloody color that properly goes with killing).
136. *habit . . . lived:* usual costume.
139-140. *This . . . in:* in creating phantoms (like this) madness is very skilful.

¹⁴⁰ *Hamlet.* Ecstasy?

My pulse as yours doth temperately keep time
And makes as healthful music. It is not madness
That I have uttered. Bring me to the test,
And I the matter will reword, which madness
¹⁴⁵ Would gambol from. Mother, for love of grace,
Lay not that flattering unction to your soul,
That not your trespass but my madness speaks.
It will but skin and film the ulcerous place
Whiles rank corruption, mining all within,
¹⁵⁰ Infects unseen. Confess yourself to heaven,
Repent what's past, avoid what is to come,
And do not spread the compost on the weeds
To make them ranker. Forgive me this my virtue.
For in the fatness of these pursy times
¹⁵⁵ Virtue itself of vice must pardon beg,
Yea, curb and woo for leave to do him good.
Queen. O Hamlet, thou hast cleft my heart in twain.
Hamlet. O, throw away the worser part of it,
And live the purer with the other half.
¹⁶⁰ Good night — but go not to my uncle's bed.
Assume a virtue, if you have it not.
That monster custom, who all sense doth eat,
Of habits devil, is angel yet in this,
That to the use of actions fair and good
¹⁶⁵ He likewise gives a frock or livery
That aptly is put on. Refrain to-night,
And that shall lend a kind of easiness
To the next abstinence; the next more easy;
For use almost can change the stamp of nature,
¹⁷⁰ And either [. . .] the devil, or throw him out
With wondrous potency. Once more, good night,
And when you are desirous to be blest,
I'll blessing beg of you.—For this same lord,
I do repent; but heaven hath pleased it so,
¹⁷⁵ To punish me with this, and this with me,
That I must be their scourge and minister.
I will bestow him and will answer well
The death I gave him. So again, good night.
I must be cruel only to be kind.
¹⁸⁰ Thus bad begins, and worse remains behind.
One word more, good lady.

144. *reword:* repeat word for word.

145. *gambol:* shy away.

146. *flattering unction:* soothing salve.

147. *That:* so that you think.

148. *It:* i.e., such a salve. *skin:* skin over, cover.

151. *what . . . come:* future sin.

153. *this my virtue:* my virtuous preaching.
154. *fatness:* gross indulgence. *pursy:* corpulent.

156. *curb:* bow.

162-166. *That . . . on:* that monster, habituation, who swallows up all sense (by making our actions automatic instead of consciously considered —"sensed"), and who is thus a devil with respect to *habits* (i.e., (1) settled usages (2) costumes that we usually wear) is nevertheless an angel and not a devil in the fact that he does likewise for actions fair and good: he makes *them* also habitual, easy to put on and wear, like a comfortable frock or livery. (Some editors emend the Quarto *devil* to "evil," in which case the first clause runs: "That monster habituation, who swallows up all our consciousness of having evil habits," etc.).
169. *use:* habit.
170. Some such word as "curb" (= restrain) was omitted from this line.

175. *this:* i.e., the dead Polonius.

176. *scourge and minister:* whip and agent.
177. *answer:* account for.

179. *I . . . kind:* referring to his blunt speech to his mother.
180. *Thus . . . begins:* i.e., thus begins a train of evils (referring to his slaying of Polonius). *behind:* to come.

Queen.   What shall I do?

Hamlet. Not this, by no means, that I bid you do:
Let the bloat king tempt you again to bed,
Pinch wanton on your cheek, call you his mouse,
185 And let him, for a pair of reechy kisses,
Or paddling in your neck with his damned fingers,
Make you to ravel all this matter out,
That I essentially am not in madness,
But mad in craft. 'Twere good you let him know,
190 For who that's but a queen, fair, sober, wise,
Would from a paddock, from a bat, a gib,
Such dear concernings hide? Who would do so?
No, in despite of sense and secrecy,
Unpeg the basket on the house's top,
195 Let the birds fly, and like the famous ape,
To try conclusions, in the basket creep
And break your own neck down.

Queen. Be thou assured, if words be made of breath,
And breath of life, I have no life to breathe
200 What thou hast said to me.

Hamlet. I must to England; you know that?

Queen.   Alack,
I had forgot. 'Tis so concluded on.

Hamlet. There's letters sealed, and my two schoolfellows,
Whom I will trust as I will adders fanged,
205 They bear the mandate; they must sweep my way
And marshal me to knavery. Let it work.
For 'tis the sport to have the enginer
Hoist with his own petar, and 't shall go hard
But I will delve one yard below their mines
210 And blow them at the moon. O, 'tis most sweet
When in one line two crafts directly meet.
This man shall set me packing.
I'll lug the guts into the neighbor room.
Mother, good night. Indeed, this counsellor
215 Is now most still, most secret, and most grave,
Who was in life a foolish prating knave.
Come, sir, to draw toward an end with you.
Good night, mother.

[*Exit the* QUEEN. *Then*] *exit* [HAMLET, *tugging in*
POLONIUS].

183. *bloat:* fat and soft with indulgence.

185. *reechy:* greasy.

186. *paddling:* playing.

189. *'Twere . . . know:* Hamlet is still describing, ironically, what he hopes the queen will *not* do.

191. *paddock:* toad. *gib:* tomcat.

192. *dear concernings:* matters that clearly concern him.

194–197. *Unpeg . . . down:* a now lost story, wherein apparently an ape released some birds from a basket on a roof and, seeing them fly, expected the same capacity would come to him from getting in the basket, but instead broke his neck.
196. *conclusions:* experiments.

205. *mandate:* commission. *sweep:* clear.

206. *marshal:* conduct. *knavery:* i.e., some mischievous fate.
207. *enginer:* enginer (in this case one who mines under a city to destroy it).
208. *Hoist:* hoisted, blown up. *petar:* bomb.

211. *crafts:* cunnings.

212. *packing:* (1) out of Denmark in a hurry, (2) hauling off this body on my back, (3) plotting (i.e., how to outwit the king).

215. *still:* circumspect, close-mouthed (with a pun on *still*="motionless"). *grave:* sober, dignified (with a pun on *grave*="tomb").
217. *to . . . you:* a common phrase for coming to the end of one's business with someone (with a pun on "end" in a deeper sense).

IV, 1

Enter KING *and* QUEEN, *with* ROSENCRANTZ *and*
GUILDENSTERN.

King. There's matter in these sighs. These profound
    heaves
    You must translate; 'tis fit we understand them.
    Where is your son?
Queen. Bestow this place on us a little while.

        [*Exeunt* ROSENCRANTZ *and* GUILDENSTERN.]

5   Ah, mine own lord, what have I seen to-night!
King. What, Gertrude? How does Hamlet?
Queen. Mad as the sea and wind when both contend
    Which is the mightier. In his lawless fit,
    Behind the arras hearing something stir,
10   Whips out his rapier, cries, 'A rat, a rat!'
    And in this brainish apprehension kills   11. *brainish:* (1) headstrong? (2) lunatic?
    The unseen good old man.

King.   O heavy deed!
    It had been so with us, had we been there.
    His liberty is full of threats to all,
15   To you yourself, to us, to every one.
    Alas, how shall this bloody deed be answered?   16. *answered:* accounted for.
    It will be laid to us, whose providence   17. *providence:* foresight.
    Should have kept short, restrained, and out of haunt   18. *short:* i.e., on a short rein. *haunt:*
    This mad young man. But so much was our love   company.
20   We would not understand what was most fit,
    But, like the owner of a foul disease,
    To keep it from divulging, let it feed
    Even on the pith of life. Where is he gone?
Queen. To draw apart the body he hath killed;
25   O'er whom his very madness, like some ore   25. *ore:* precious metal.
    Among a mineral of metals base,   26. *mineral:* mine.
    Shows itself pure. 'A weeps for what is done.
King. O Gertrude, come away!
    The sun no sooner shall the mountains touch
30   But we will ship him hence, and this vile deed
    We must with all our majesty and skill
    Both countenance and excuse. Ho, Guildenstern!

Enter ROSENCRANTZ *and* GUILDENSTERN.

Friends both, go join you with some further aid.
Hamlet in madness hath Polonius slain,
35   And from his mother's closet hath he dragged him.
Go seek him out; speak fair, and bring the body   36. *fair:* courteously.
Into the chapel. I pray you haste in this.
        [*Exeunt* ROSENCRANTZ *and* GUILDENSTERN.]
Come, Gertrude, we'll call up our wisest friends
And let them know both what we mean to do
40   And what's untimely done . . .   40. *done:* There is evidently an omis-
Whose whisper o'er the world's diameter,   sion at this point, which is some-
                                                        times conjecturally filled in with
As level as the cannon to his blank   the words: "So haply, slander,"
                                                        etc.
Transports his poisoned shot, may miss our name   42. *level:* unerring. *blank:* target (white
And hit the woundless air. O, come away!   center of).
45   My soul is full of discord and dismay.   *Exeunt.*

IV, II

Enter HAMLET.

Hamlet. Safely stowed.   1. *stowed:* Hamlet refers to the body
Gentlemen. (*within*) Hamlet! Lord Hamlet!   of Polonius, of which he has just
Hamlet. But soft, what noise? Who calls on Hamlet? O, disburdened himself.
  here they come.
    [*Enter*] ROSENCRANTZ, [GUILDENSTERN,] *and others.*
5 *Rosencrantz.* What have you done, my lord, with the
  dead body?
Hamlet. Compounded it with dust, whereto 'tis kin.   6. *Compounded:* mixed.
Rosencrantz. Tell us where 'tis, that we may take it thence,
  And bear it to the chapel.
10 *Hamlet.* Do not believe it.
Rosencrantz. Believe what?
Hamlet. That I can keep your counsel and not mine own. 12. *counsel:* secret—i.e., Hamlet has
  Besides, to be demanded of a sponge, what replication   not told the king or queen that
  should be made by the son of a king?   he knows Rosencrantz and Guild-
                                                        enstern were sent for.
15 *Rosencrantz.* Take you me for a sponge, my lord?   13. *to be . . . of:* being questioned by.
                                                        replication: reply.
Hamlet. Ay, sir, that soaks up the king's countenance, his 16. *countenance:* favor.
  rewards, his authorities. But such officers do the king
  best service in the end. He keeps them, like an apple,
  in the corner of his jaw, first mouthed, to be last swal-
20   lowed. When he needs what you have gleaned, it is but
  squeezing you and, sponge, you shall be dry again.
Rosencrantz. I understand you not, my lord.

Hamlet. I am glad of it. A knavish speech sleeps in a foolish ear.

25 *Rosencrantz.* My lord, you must tell us where the body is and go with us to the king.

Hamlet. The body is with the king, but the king is not with the body. The king is a thing—

Guildenstern. A thing, my lord?

30 *Hamlet.* Of nothing. Bring me to him. Hide fox, and all after.   *Exeunt.*

IV, III

Enter KING, *and two or three.*

King. I have sent to seek him and to find the body.
How dangerous is it that this man goes loose!
Yet must not we put the strong law on him;
He's loved of the distracted multitude,
5 Who like not in their judgment, but their eyes,
And where 'tis so, th' offender's scourge is weighed,
But never the offense. To bear all smooth and even,
This sudden sending him away must seem
Deliberate pause. Diseases desperate grown
10 By desperate appliance are relieved,
Or not at all.

Enter ROSENCRANTZ, [GUILDENSTERN,] *and all the rest.*

How now? What hath befallen?

Rosencrantz. Where the dead body is bestowed, my lord,
We cannot get from him.

King.   But where is he?

Rosencrantz. Without, my lord; guarded, to know your pleasure.

King. Bring him before us.

15 *Rosencrantz.*   Ho! Bring in the lord.

They enter [*with* HAMLET].

King. Now, Hamlet, where's Polonius?

Hamlet. At supper.

King. At supper? Where?

Hamlet. Not where he eats, but where 'a is eaten. A
20 certain convocation of politic worms are e'en at him.
Your worm is your only emperor for diet. We fat
all creatures else to fat us, and we fat ourselves for

---

23. *knavish:* mischievous. *sleeps:* i.e., is not understood.

27-28. *The . . . body:* a riddling speech, designed to confuse Rosencrantz and Guildenstern, about whose meaning there is no agreement. Possibly it means: the body (Polonius) is with the king (my father) —i.e., Polonius is dead; but the king (my uncle) is not (yet) with the body (Polonius)—i.e., Claudius is still alive.
28. *thing:* spoken contemptuously.
30. *Of nothing:* see Psalm 144:4 (in the Anglican Prayer Book): "Man is like a thing of naught . . ."
30-31. *Hide . . . after:* the catch phrase of a game like hide-and-seek, uttered by Hamlet as he slips from the stage.

4. *distracted:* unstable.
5. *Who . . . eyes:* whose approval comes not from judgment of things as they are, but from what things appear to the eye.
6. *scourge:* penalty.
7. *bear:* carry it off.

9. *Deliberate pause:* a carefully planned action.
10. *appliance:* remedy.

20. *politic:* i.e., crafty and prying, the sort best suited to Polonius.
20-21. *convocation . . . diet:* punning references to the famous *Diet,* i.e., parliament or *convocation,* which the Holy Roman Emperor (Charles V) summoned at *Worms* in Germany, in 1521 (to consider the case of Martin Luther).

maggots. Your fat king and your lean beggar is but variable service—two dishes, but to one table. That's
25   the end.

King. Alas, alas!

Hamlet. A man may fish with the worm that hath eat of a king, and eat of the fish that hath fed of that worm.

King. What dost thou mean by this?

30   *Hamlet.* Nothing but to show you how a king may go a progress through the guts of a beggar.

King. Where is Polonius?

Hamlet. In heaven. Send thither to see. If your messenger find him not there, seek him i' th' other place yourself.
35   But if indeed you find him not within this month, you shall nose him as you go up the stairs into the lobby.

King. [*to* ATTENDANTS] Go seek him there.

Hamlet. 'A will stay till you come. [*Exeunt* ATTENDANTS.]

King. Hamlet, this deed, for thine especial safety,
40   Which we do tender as we dearly grieve
For that which thou hast done, must send thee hence
With fiery quickness. Therefore prepare thyself.
The bark is ready and the wind at help.
Th' associates tend, and everything is bent
45   For England.

Hamlet.   For England?

King.   Ay, Hamlet.

Hamlet.   Good.

King. So is it, if thou knew'st our purposes.

Hamlet. I see a cherub that sees them. But come, for England! Farewell, dear mother.

King. Thy loving father, Hamlet.

50   *Hamlet.* My mother—father and mother is man and wife, man and wife is one flesh, and so, my mother. Come, for England!   *Exit.*

King. Follow him at foot; tempt him with speed aboard.
Delay it not; I'll have him hence to-night.
55   Away! for everything is sealed and done
That else leans on th' affair. Pray you make haste.
                    [*Exeunt all but the* KING.]
And, England, if my love thou hold'st at aught—
As my great power thereof may give thee sense,
Since yet thy cicatrice looks raw and red
60   After the Danish sword, and thy free awe

24. *variable service:* a variety of courses.

31. *progress:* journey of state.

40. *tender:* care for.

43. *bark:* ship.

44. *tend:* await. *bent:* i.e., like a bow (to dispatch an arrow).

47. *cherub:* angel (the cherubim were Heaven's watchmen, hence quick-sighted).

53. *at foot:* close.

56. *leans on:* pertains to.

57. *hold'st at aught:* valuest at all.

58. *As . . . sense:* and my great power may give you a keen sense of it (i.e., of the value of my love).

59. *cicatrice:* scar.

Pays homage to us—thou mayst not coldly set
Our sovereign process, which imports at full
By letters congruing to that effect
The present death of Hamlet. Do it, England,
65 For like the hectic in my blood he rages,
And thou must cure me. Till I know 'tis done,
Howe'er my haps, my joys were ne'er begun.   *Exit.*

60-61. *thy . . . homage:* i.e., you pay tribute to us voluntarily.
61. *set:* rate.
62. *process:* command. *imports . . . full:* calls for.
63. *congruing:* agreeing.

65. *hectic:* fever.

67. *Howe'er my haps:* however things go.

IV, iv

Enter FORTINBRAS *with his* ARMY *over the stage.*

Fortinbras. Go, captain, from me greet the Danish king.
Tell him that by his license Fortinbras
Craves the conveyance of a promised march
Over his kingdom. You know the rendezvous.
5 If that his majesty would aught with us,
We shall express our duty in his eye;
And let him know so.
Captain.   I will do't, my lord.
Fortinbras. Go softly on.   [*Exeunt all but the* CAPTAIN.]

3. *the . . . march:* escorted passage as agreed.

5. *if that:* if. *would aught with:* wants anything of.
6. *eye:* presence.

8. *softly:* slowly.

Enter HAMLET, ROSENCRANTZ, [GUILDENSTERN,]
and others.

Hamlet. Good sir, whose powers are these?
10 *Captain.* They are of Norway, sir.
Hamlet. How purposed, sir, I pray you?
Captain. Against some part of Poland.
Hamlet. Who commands them, sir?
Captain. The nephew to old Norway, Fortinbras.
15 *Hamlet.* Goes it against the main of Poland, sir,
Or for some frontier?
Captain. Truly to speak, and with no addition,
We go to gain a little patch of ground
That hath in it no profit but the name.
20 To pay five ducats, five, I would not farm it,
Nor will it yield to Norway or the Pole
A ranker rate, should it be sold in fee.
Hamlet. Why, then the Polack never will defend it.
Captain. Yes, it is already garrisoned.
25 *Hamlet.* Two thousand souls and twenty thousand ducats
Will not debate the question of this straw.
This is th' imposthume of much wealth and peace,

15. *main:* whole.

17. *addition:* i.e., fine words.

20. *To pay:* if the rent were as low as.

22. *ranker:* richer. *in fee:* outright.

26. *Will . . . straw:* will not suffice to settle this trifling matter (if we go to war about it).
27. *imposthume of:* abscess that comes from.

That inward breaks, and shows no cause without
Why the man dies. I humbly thank you, sir.
Captain. God bye you, sir.   [*Exit.*]
30 *Rosencrantz.*   Will't please you go, my
lord?
Hamlet. I'll be with you straight. Go a little before.

[*Exeunt all but* HAMLET.]

How all occasions do inform against me
And spur my dull revenge! What is a man,
If his chief good and market of his time
35 Be but to sleep and feed? A beast, no more.
Sure he that made us with such large discourse,
Looking before and after, gave us not
That capability and godlike reason
To fust in us unused. Now, whether it be
40 Bestial oblivion, or some craven scruple
Of thinking too precisely on th' event—
A thought which, quartered, hath but one part wisdom
And ever three parts coward—I do not know
Why yet I live to say, 'This thing's to do,'
45 Sith I have cause, and will, and strength, and means
To do't. Examples gross as earth exhort me.
Witness this army of such mass and charge,
Led by a delicate and tender prince,
Whose spirit, with divine ambition puffed,
50 Makes mouths at the invisible event,
Exposing what is mortal and unsure
To all that fortune, death, and danger dare,
Even for an eggshell. Rightly to be great
Is not to stir without great argument.
55 But greatly to find quarrel in a straw
When honor's at the stake. How stand I then,
That have a father killed, a mother stained,
Excitements of my reason and my blood,
And let all sleep, while to my shame I see
60 The imminent death of twenty thousand men
That for a fantasy and trick of fame
Go to their graves like beds, fight for a plot
Whereon the numbers cannot try the cause,
Which is not tomb enough and continent
65 To hide the slain? O, from this time forth,
My thoughts be bloody, or be nothing worth!   *Exit.*

32. *inform against:* (1) denounce? (2) take a form that censures?
33. *dull:* lagging.
34. *market of:* wages or compensation for.
36. *discourse:* power of thought.
37. *Looking . . . after:* a traditional distinction of man from the beast: he has memory and foresight.
39. *fust:* mildew
40. *Bestial oblivion:* beast-like lack of memory. *craven:* cowardly.
41. *Of:* i.e., that comes from. *event:* outcome of an action.
44. *to do:* i.e., still to be done.
46. *gross:* (1) visible, (2) weighty.
47. *mass and charge:* size and cost.
49. *puffed:* swelled (like cheeks by wind: see *mouths*).
50. *mouths:* mocking faces. *event:* outcome.
54. *stir:* act. *argument:* cause.
55. *straw.* trifle.
61. *fantasy . . . fame:* imagined trifle of reputation.
62. *like beds:* as willingly as to bed. *plot:* plot of ground.
63-65. *Whereon . . . slain:* not big enough to hold the numbers that will combat about it, or to serve as tomb and container to bury the slain.

IV, v

Enter HORATIO, [QUEEN] GERTRUDE, *and a* GENTLEMAN.

Queen. I will not speak with her.

Gentleman. She is importunate, indeed distract.
  Her mood will needs be pitied.

Queen.   What would she have?

Gentleman. She speaks much of her father, says she hears

5   There's tricks i' th' world, and hems, and beats
        her heart,
  Spurns enviously at straws, speaks things in doubt
  That carry but half sense. Her speech is nothing,
  Yet the unshapèd use of it doth move
  The hearers to collection; they aim at it,

10 And botch the words up fit to their own thoughts,
  Which, as her winks and nods and gestures yield them,
  Indeed would make one think there might be thought,
  Though nothing sure, yet much unhappily.

Horatio. 'Twere good she were spoken with, for she may
        strew

15 Dangerous conjectures in ill-breeding minds.

Queen. Let her come in.   *[Exit* GENTLEMAN.]

  [Aside] To my sick soul (as sin's true nature is)
  Each toy seems prologue to some great amiss.
  So full of artless jealousy is guilt

20 It spills itself in fearing to be spilt.

Enter OPHELIA [*distracted*].

Ophelia. Where is the beauteous majesty of Denmark?

Queen. How now, Ophelia?

Ophelia. (She Sings.) How should I your true-love know
        From another one?

25   By his cockle hat and staff
        And his sandal shoon.

Queen. Alas, sweet lady, what imports this song?

Ophelia. Say you? Nay, pray you mark.
        He is dead and gone, lady,   *(Song.)*

30   He is dead and gone;
        At his head a grass-green turf,
        At his heels a stone.
    O, ho!

Queen. Nay, but Ophelia—

2. *importunate:* insistent. *distract:* insane.

5. *tricks:* cheats. *hems:* clears her throat (in a knowing way).

6. *Spurns enviously:* kicks contemptuously. *things in doubt:* ambiguous things.
7. *nothing:* nonsense.
8. *the . . . it:* its formlessness.
9. *to collection:* to try to make sense of it.
10. *botch . . . thoughts:* make her words fit their theories about her meaning.
11. *yield:* deliver.
12. *thought:* i.e., sense (in what she says).
13. *much:* very.

17. *as . . . is:* as is always the case with those who have sinned.
18. *toy:* trifle. *amiss:* calamity.
19. *artless jealousy:* unregulated anxiety.

20. *spills:* ruins (by revealing).

23-24. *How . . . one:* Ophelia in her madness (as Hamlet in his) sometimes makes references whose potential meanings for the audience go beyond any meaning that either she or her hearers on the stage are aware of: the *true-love* and *another one* of this song, for instance, could be taken by the theater audience as concealed allusions to the Queen's relations with Hamlet's father and with Claudius: see III, iv, 54ff.
25. *cockle hat:* hat with a cockle shell on it (badge of pilgrims who had visited the shrine of St. James of Compostela in Spain).
26. *shoon:* shoes.
25-26. *cockle . . . shoon:* emblems of the conventional true lover, pilgrim at the shrine of his "saint" (adapted from those of religious pilgrims).
29. *dead:* perhaps a mad reference to Polonius' fate, with a hidden further allusion to the fate of the Queen's true love, Hamlet's father.

35 *Ophelia.* Pray you mark.

    [*Sings*] White his shroud as the mountain snow—

        Enter KING.

Queen. Alas, look here, my lord.

Ophelia.   Larded all with sweet flowers;   *(Song.)*

      Which bewept to the grave did . . . not . . . go

40   With true-love showers.

King. How do you, pretty lady?

Ophelia. Well, God dild you! They say the owl was a

  baker's daughter. Lord, we know what we are, but

  know not what we may be. God be at your table!

45 *King.* Conceit upon her father.

Ophelia. Pray let's have no words of this, but when they

  ask you what it means, say you this:

      To-morrow is Saint Valentine's day.   *(Song.)*

        All in the morning betime,

50   And I a maid at your window,

        To be your Valentine.

      Then up he rose and donned his clo'es

        And dupped the chamber door,

      Let in the maid, that out a maid

55   Never departed more.

King. Pretty Ophelia!

Ophelia. Indeed, la, without an oath, I'll make an end

  on't:

  [*Sings*] By Gis and by Saint Charity,

60   Alack, and fie for shame!

      Young men will do't if they come to't.

        By Cock, they are to blame.

      Quoth she, 'Before you tumbled me,

        You promised me to wed.'

65 He answers:

      'So would I 'a' done, by yonder sun,

        An thou hadst not come to my bed.'

King. How long hath she been thus?

Ophelia. I hope all will be well. We must be patient, but I

70   cannot choose but weep to think they would lay him i'

  th' cold ground. My brother shall know of it; and so I

  thank you for your good counsel. Come, my coach!

  Good night, ladies, good night. Sweet ladies, good

  night, good night.   [*Exit.*]

---

35. *mark:* listen.

38. *Larded:* garnished.
39. *not:* perhaps an allusion t
    Polonius' hushed-up burial withou
    ceremony, with again a hidde
    reference to the Queen's insincer
    grief for the death of Hamlet
    father.
42. *dild:* reward.
42-43. *owl . . . daughter:* according to a
    old legend, a baker's daughter gav
    short weight in bread to Jesus an
    was turned into an owl. Perhap
    the mad "sense" of this remark lie
    in the suggestion that Ophelia to
    has been transformed for a decep
    tion, or at least for a failure c
    great-heartedness.
45. *Conceit upon:* obsession with.

49. *betime:* early.

53. *dupped:* opened.
54. *maid:* i.e., a virgin.

59. *Gis:* Jesus.

62. *Cock:* vulgar corruption of Go
    (with appropriateness to the con
    text).

67. *An:* if.

75 *King.* Follow her close; give her good watch, I pray you.

[*Exit* HORATIO.]

O, this is the poison of deep grief; it springs
All from her father's death—and now behold!
O Gertrude, Gertrude,
When sorrows come, they come not single spies,
80 But in battalions: first, her father slain;
Next, your son gone, and he most violent author
Of his own just remove; the people muddied,

82. *muddied:* stirred up.

Thick and unwholesome in their thoughts and whispers
For good Polonius' death, and we have done but
greenly

84. *greenly:* foolishly.

85 In hugger-mugger to inter him; poor Ophelia

85. *hugger-mugger:* furtive haste.

Divided from herself and her fair judgment,
Without the which we are pictures or mere beasts;
Last, and as much containing as all these,
Her brother is in secret come from France,
90 Feeds on his wonder, keeps himself in clouds,

90. *Feeds . . . clouds:* broods on his suspicions (about his father's death), keeps himself in dark confusion.

And wants not buzzers to infect his ear

91. *buzzers:* tattle-tales.

With pestilent speeches of his father's death,
Wherein necessity, of matter beggared,
Will nothing stick our person to arraign

93-94. *Wherein . . . arraign:* in their need to say *something*—since they have no facts—they will not hesitate to accuse me (of the murder of Polonius).

95 In ear and ear. O my dear Gertrude, this,
Like to a murd'ring piece, in many places

96. *murd'ring piece:* a cannon firing a spreading burst of small missiles.

Gives me superfluous death. *A noise within.*

97. *superfluous:* i.e., more wounds than needed to kill.

Enter a MESSENGER.

Queen. Alack, what noise is this?

King. Attend, where are my Switzers? Let them guard the door.

98. *Switzers:* Swiss soldiers formed the personal bodyguard of many kings.

What is the matter?

Messenger. Save yourself, my lord.

100 The ocean, overpeering of his list,

100. *overpeering . . . list:* rising above his bounds.

Eats not the flats with more impiteous haste

101. *impiteous:* unpitying.

Than young Laertes, in a riotous head,

102. *head:* armed force.

O'erbears your officers. The rabble call him lord,
And, as the world were now but to begin,

104-106. *as . . . word:* as if the world had no history, as if all its traditions were forgotten, all its settled customs unknown, and they themselves (instead of *antiquity* and *custom*) were the proper approvers and supporters of every question.

105 Antiquity forgot, custom not known,
The ratifiers and props of every word,
They cry, 'Choose we! Laertes shall be king!'
Caps, hands, and tongues applaud it to the clouds,
'Laertes shall be king! Laertes king!' *A noise within.*

110 *Queen.* How cheerfully on the false trail they cry!

O, this is counter, you false Danish dogs!

King. The doors are broke.

111. *counter:* i.e., away from the animal truly wanted (the killer of Polonius).

Enter LAERTES *with others.*

Laertes. Where is this king?—Sirs, stand you all without.

All. No, let's come in.

115 *Laertes.*   I pray you give me leave.

All. We will, we will.

Laertes. I thank you. Keep the door.

[*Exeunt his* FOLLOWERS.]

O thou vile king,

Give me my father.

Queen.   Calmly, good Laertes.

Laertes. That drop of blood that's calm proclaims me
bastard.

Cries cuckold to my father, brands the harlot

120 Even here between the chaste unsmirchèd brows

Of my true mother.

King.   What is the cause, Laertes,

That thy rebellion looks so giant-like?

Let him go, Gertrude. Do not fear our person.

There's such divinity doth hedge a king

125 That treason can but peep to what it would,

Acts little of his will. Tell me, Laertes,

Why thou art thus incensed. Let him go, Gertrude.

Speak, man.

Laertes. Where is my father?

King.   Dead.

Queen.   But not by him.

130 *King.* Let him demand his fill.

Laertes. How came he dead? I'll not be juggled with.

To hell allegiance, vows to the blackest devil,

Conscience and grace to the profoundest pit!

I dare damnation. To this point I stand,

135 That both the worlds I give to negligence,

Let come what comes, only I'll be revenged

Most throughly for my father.

King.   Who shall stay you?

Laertes. My will, not all the world's.

And for my means, I'll husband them so well

They shall go far with little.

118-121. *That . . . mother:* if any blood in me is calm, it shows me to be a bastard (because no true son could be calm), my father to have been a cuckold, i.e., a deceived husband, and my mother a harlot.

123. *fear:* fear for.

125. *peep:* i.e., as over a barrier.

131. *juggled:* played.

135. *both . . . worlds:* i.e., he wants revenge, whatever it costs in this world or the next.

137. *throughly:* thoroughly.

138. *My . . . world's:* my own will—not the whole world's (opposed) will.

King.   Good Laertes,
   If you desire to know the certainty
   Of your dear father, is't writ in your revenge
   That swoopstake you will draw both friend and foe,   143. *swoopstake:* sweepstake, i.e., in-
   Winner and loser?   discriminately.
145 *Laertes.* None but his enemies.
King.   Will you know them then?   145. *know . . . then:* be informed who
Laertes. To his good friends thus wide I'll ope my arms   they are.
   And like the kind life-rend'ring pelican   147. *pelican:* formerly reputed to feed
   Repast them with my blood.   its young with its own blood.
King.   Why, now you speak
   Like a good child and a true gentleman.
150   That I am guiltless of your father's death,
   And am most sensibly in grief for it,   151. *sensibly:* feelingly.
   It shall as level to your judgment 'pear   152. *level:* plainly. *'pear:* appear.
   As day does to your eye.
                   A noise within: 'Let her come in.'
Laertes. How now? What noise is that?
                   Enter OPHELIA.
155   O heat, dry up my brains; tears seven times salt
   Burn out the sense and virtue of mine eye!   156. *sense and virtue:* feeling and power.
   By heaven, thy madness shall be paid by weight   157. *paid:* paid for.
   Till our scale turn the beam. O rose of May,   158. *till . . . beam:* till our side of the
   Dear maid, kind sister, sweet Ophelia!   balance weighs down the beam.
160   O heavens, is't possible a young maid's wits
   Should be as mortal as an old man's life?
   [Nature is fine in love, and where 'tis fine,
   It sends some precious instance of itself   163. *instance:* memento (thus Ophelia
   After the thing it loves.]   has sent her sanity after her father).
165 Ophelia. They bore him barefaced on the bier   *(Song.)*
              [Hey non nony, nony, hey nony]
           And in his grave rained many a tear—
   Fare you well, my dove!
Laertes. Hadst thou thy wits, and didst persuade revenge,
170   It could not move thus.   170. *move . . . thus:* i.e., incite me as
Ophelia. You must sing 'A-down a-down, and you call   effectively as your madness does.
   him a-down-a.' O, how the wheel becomes it! It is the   172. *wheel:* (1) refrain? (2) spinning
   false steward, that stole his master's daughter.   wheel (over which such refrains
                                                                were often sung)? *becomes:* fits.
Laertes. This nothing's more than matter.   173. *steward . . . daughter:* a story no
175 *Ophelia.* There's rosemary, that's for remembrance. Pray   longer known, but it may have an
   you, love, remember. And there is pansies, that's for   appositeness to the story in 48-66,
   thoughts.   or, in a mad way, to her father's
                                                                refusal to steal his master's *son*
                                                                (II, ii, 131-139), or to Claudius's
                                                                stealing of his brother's queen.
                                                           174. *This . . . matter:* this nonsense
                                                                speaks more eloquently than sense.

Laertes. A document in madness, thoughts and remembrance fitted.

180 *Ophelia.* There's fennel for you, and columbines. There's rue for you, and here's some for me. We may call it herb of grace o' Sundays. O, you must wear your rue with a difference. There's a daisy. I would give you some violets, but they withered all when my father
185 died. They say 'a made a good end.

[*Sings*] For bonny sweet Robin is all my joy.

Laertes. Thought and affliction, passion, hell itself, She turns to favor and to prettiness.

Ophelia. And will 'a not come again?   (*Song.*)
190   And will 'a not come again?
          No, no, he is dead;
          Go to thy deathbed;
          He never will come again.

          His beard was as white as snow,
195   All flaxen was his poll.
          He is gone, he is gone,
          And we cast away moan.
          God 'a' mercy on his soul!
      And of all Christian souls, I pray God. God bye you.
                                          [*Exit.*]
200 *Laertes.* Do you see this, O God?

King. Laertes, I must commune with your grief,
      Or you deny me right. Go but apart,
      Make choice of whom your wisest friends you will,
      And they shall hear and judge 'twixt you and me.
205   If by direct or by collateral hand
      They find us touched, we will our kingdom give,
      Our crown, our life, and all that we call ours,
      To you in satisfaction; but if not,
      Be you content to lend your patience to us,
210   And we shall jointly labor with your soul
      To give it due content.

Laertes.   Let this be so.
      His means of death, his óbscure funeral—
      No trophy, sword, nor hatchment o'er his bones,
      No noble rite nor formal ostentation—
215   Cry to be heard, as 'twere from heaven to earth,
      That I must call't in question.

178. *document:* lesson.
179. *fitted:* i.e., as one would not expect insanity to be able to do.
181-182. *We . . . Sundays:* i.e., on Sunday, the Lord's Day, we may call the herb of repentance the herb of divine grace and mercy.
176-185. *And . . . died:* Ophelia imagines herself distributing symbolic flowers: rosemary = remembrance; pansies = thoughts (i.e., pensées); fennel=flattery; columbine=ingratitude (?); rue=sorrow and repentance; daisy = dissembling; violets = fidelity. Rosemary and pansies are perhaps offered to Laertes; fennel, columbine, and the daisy to Claudius: rue to herself (for sorrow) and to the queen (for repentance): hence the queen must wear her rue *with a difference.* But it is equally possible that she reserves the pansies and the daisy for herself.
187. *passion:* grief.
188. *favor:* charm.

195. *flaxen:* white—but the term can also imply a blonde head, and may suggest a further conflation in Ophelia's mind of the imagined lover (23-40, 48-66) and her father. *poll:* head.
197. *cast away:* (1) adjective: we who are desolate, left behind? (2) verb: put away (our grief)?
199. *And of:* and mercy on.

202. *right:* fair hearing.
203. *whom your:* whichever.

205. *collateral:* indirect.
206. *touched:* to blame.

213. *trophy:* memorial. *hatchment:* coat of arms.
214. *ostentation:* ceremony.
215. *to be heard:* so loud as to be heard.
216. *That:* so that. *call't . . . question:* demand an explanation.

King. So you shall;
And where th' offense is, let the great axe fall.
I pray you go with me. *Exeunt.*

IV, VI

Enter HORATIO *and others.*

Horatio. What are they that would speak with me?
Gentleman. Seafaring men, sir. They say they have let-
ters for you.
Horatio. Let them come in. [*Exit* ATTENDANT.]
5 I do not know from what part of the world
I should be greeted, if not from Lord Hamlet.

Enter Sailors.

Sailor. God bless you, sir.
Horatio. Let him bless thee too.
Sailor. 'A shall, sir, an't please him. There's a letter for
10 you, sir—it came from th' ambassador that was bound
for England—if your name be Horatio, as I am let to
know it is.

Horatio. [*reads the letter*] 'Horatio, when thou shalt have
overlooked this, give these fellows some means to the
15 king. They have letters for him. Ere we were two days
old at sea, a pirate of very warlike appointment gave us
chase. Finding ourselves too slow of sail, we put on a
compelled valor, and in the grapple I boarded them.
On the instant they got clear of our ship; so I alone
20 became their prisoner. They have dealt with me like
thieves of mercy, but they knew what they did: I am
to do a good turn for them. Let the king have the
letters I have sent, and repair thou to me with as much
speed as thou wouldest fly death. I have words to
25 speak in thine ear will make thee dumb; yet are they
much too light for the bore of the matter. These good
fellows will bring thee where I am. Rosencrantz and
Guildenstern hold their course for England. Of them
I have much to tell thee. Farewell.
30 'He that thou knowest thine, HAMLET.'
Come, I will give you way for these your letters,
And do't the speedier that you may direct me
To him from whom you brought them. *Exeunt.*

14. *overlooked:* read. *means to:* i.e.,
of access.

16. *old:* i.e. on our way. *appointment:*
equipment.
17-18. *we . . . valor:* i.e., we were found
to turn and fight.

21. *of:* having.

23. *repair:* come.

25. *make . . . dumb:* dumbfound. *bore:*
calibre, i.e., size.

31. *way:* admittance (to the king).

IV, VII

Enter KING *and* LAERTES.

King. Now must your conscience my acquittance seal,
    And you must put me in your heart for friend,
    Sith you have heard, and with a knowing ear,
    That he which hath your noble father slain
    Pursued my life.

5 *Laertes.*   It well appears. But tell me
    Why you proceeded not against these feats
    So crimeful and so capital in nature,
    As by your safety, greatness, wisdom, all things else,
    You mainly were stirred up.

King.   O, for two special reasons,
10   Which may to you perhaps seem much unsinewed,
    But yet to me they're strong. The queen his mother
    Lives almost by his looks, and for myself—
    My virtue or my plague, be it either which—
    She is so conjunctive to my life and soul
15   That, as the star moves not but in his sphere,
    I could not but by her. The other motive
    Why to a public count I might not go
    Is the great love the general gender bear him,
    Who, dipping all his faults in their affection,
20   Would, like the spring that turneth wood to stone,
    Convert his gyves to graces; so that my arrows,
    Too slightly timbered for so loud a wind,
    Would have reverted to my bow again,
    And not where I had aimed them.

25 *Laertes.* And so have I a noble father lost,
    A sister driven into desp'rate terms,
    Whose worth, if praises may go back again,
    Stood challenger on mount of all the age
    For her perfections. But my revenge will come.

30 *King.* Break not your sleeps for that. You must not think
    That we are made of stuff so flat and dull
    That we can let our beard be shook with danger,
    And think it pastime. You shortly shall hear more.
    I loved your father, and we love ourself,
35   And that, I hope, will teach you to imagine—

1. *my . . . seal:* confirm my acquittal.

6. *feats:* deeds.

7. *capital:* i.e., punishable by death.
8. *greatness:* position as king (the Folio text reduces the line to pentameter by omitting this word).
9. *mainly:* mightily.

10. *much unsinewed:* weak.

13. *My . . . which:* whether it is to be considered a virtue in me or a weakness.
14. *conjunctive:* conjoined.
15. *sphere:* see 1, v, 17n.
16. *but by her:* move except with her.
17. *count:* reckoning (with Hamlet).
18. *general gender:* common people.

20. *spring . . . stone:* Several British springs will petrify with lime deposits anything put into them.
21. *gyves:* leg-irons, i.e., shames. *arrows:* i.e., attacks on Hamlet.
22. *slightly timbered:* light. *wind:* i.e., the approval of the multitude.

26. *terms:* conditions.
27. *go back:* i.e., to what she was.
28. *challenger on mount:* i.e., like a mounted knight ready to challenge and surpass all rivals.

30. *Break . . . that:* have no anxiety about that.

Enter a MESSENGER *with letters.*

[How now? What news?]

Messenger.   [Letters, my lord, from Hamlet:]
These to your majesty, this to the queen.

King. From Hamlet? Who brought them?

Messenger. Sailors, my lord, they say; I saw them not.
40   They were given me by Claudio; he received them
Of him that brought them.

King.   Laertes, you shall hear them.—
Leave us.   [*Exit* MESSENGER.]
[*Reads*] 'High and mighty, you shall know I am set
naked on your kingdom. To-morrow shall I beg leave
45   to see your kingly eyes; when I shall (first asking your
pardon thereunto) recount the occasion of my sudden
and more strange return.   HAMLET.'
What should this mean? Are all the rest come back?
Or is it some abuse, and no such thing?

Laertes. Know you the hand?

50 *King.*   'Tis Hamlet's character. 'Naked'!
And in a postscript here, he says 'alone.'
Can you devise me?

Laertes. I am lost in it, my lord. But let him come.
It warms the very sickness in my heart
55   That I shall live and tell him to his teeth,
'Thus diddest thou.'

King.   If it be so, Laertes
(As how should it be so? how otherwise?),
Will you be ruled by me?

Laertes.   Ay, my lord,
So you will not o'errule me to a peace.

60 *King.* To thine own peace. If he be now returned,
As checking at his voyage, and that he means
No more to undertake it, I will work him
To an exploit now ripe in my device,
Under the which he shall not choose but fall;
65   And for his death no wind of blame shall breathe,
But even his mother shall uncharge the practice
And call it accident.

Laertes.   My lord, I will be ruled;
The rather if you could devise it so
That I might be the organ.

44. *naked:* i.e., all possessions lost.

49. *abuse . . . thing:* trick, and (1) of no importance? (2) not what it seems?

50. *character:* writing.

52. *devise:* explain to.

53. *lost in:* baffled by .

57. *As . . . otherwise:* i.e., how can it be true (that Hamlet has returned) and yet how can it not be?

61. *As . . . at:* because turning aside from (as a falcon from its quarry to other prey).

63. *ripe . . . device:* ready in my thought.

66. *uncharge:* hold innocent.

69. *organ:* instrument. *falls right:* suits my plan.

King.   It falls right.

70   You have been talked of since your travel much,
And that in Hamlet's hearing, for a quality
Wherein they say you shine. Your sum of parts
Did not together pluck such envy from him
As did that one, and that, in my regard,
Of the unworthiest siege.

75   *Laertes.*   What part is that, my lord?

King. A very riband in the cap of youth,
Yet needful too, for youth no less becomes
The light and careless livery that it wears
Than settled age his sables, and his weeds

80   Importing health and graveness. Two months since
Here was a gentleman of Normandy.
I have seen myself, and served against, the French,
And they can well on horseback, but this gallant
Had witchcraft in't. He grew unto his seat,

85   And to such wondrous doing brought his horse
As had he been incorpsed and demi-natured
With the brave beast. So far he topped my thought
That I, in forgery of shapes and tricks,
Come short of what he did.

Laertes.   A Norman was't?

90   *King.* A Norman.

Laertes. Upon my life, Lamord.

King.   The very same.

Laertes. I know him well. He is the brooch indeed
And gem of all the nation.

King. He made confession of you,

95   And gave you such a masterly report
For art and exercise in your defense,
And for your rapier most especial,
That he cried out, 'twould be a sight indeed
If one could match you. The scrimers of their nation

100   He swore had neither motion, guard, nor eye,
If you opposed them. Sir, this report of his
Did Hamlet so envenom with his envy
That he could nothing do but wish and beg
Your sudden coming o'er to play with you.
Now, out of this—

105   *Laertes.*   What out of this, my lord?

King. Laertes, was your father dear to you?

72. *Your . . . parts:* all your capacities combined.

75. *siege:* seat, i.e., rank (because men sat at table in order of rank).
76. *very riband:* mere ribbon.

77. *becomes:* suits.

78. *livery:* uniform.
79. *sables:* gowns furred with sable. *weeds:* clothes.
80. *health:* prosperity.

83. *can well:* are skilled.

86. *As . . . demi-natured:* as if he were grown into one body and one nature.
87. *topped:* outdid.
88. *in . . . tricks:* in imagining feats of horsemanship.

92. *brooch:* i.e., jewel.

94. *made . . . you:* acknowledged your superiority.
95. *masterly report:* i.e., a report asserting you to be a master.
96. *art and exercise:* theory and practice.
97. *rapier:* i.e., skill with the rapier.

99. *match you:* put you in a match with someone your equal. *scrimers:* fencers.

104. *o'er:* i.e., back to Denmark. *to . . . you:* so that he could fence with you.

Or are you like the painting of a sorrow,
A face without a heart?

Laertes.　　　　　　　　Why ask you this?

King. Not that I think you did not love your father,
110　　But that I know love is begun by time,
And that I see, in passages of proof,
Time qualifies the spark and fire of it.
There lives within the very flame of love
A kind of wick or snuff that will abate it,
115　　And nothing is at a like goodness still,
For goodness, growing to a plurisy,
Dies in his own too-much. That we would do
We should do when we would, for this 'would' changes,
And hath abatements and delays as many
120　　As there are tongues, are hands, are accidents,
And then this 'should' is like a spendthrift's sigh,
That hurts by easing. But to the quick o' th' ulcer—
Hamlet comes back; what would you undertake
To show yourself your father's son in deed
More than in words?

125　*Laertes.*　　　　　To cut his throat i' th' church!

King. No place indeed should murther sanctuarize;
Revenge should have no bounds. But, good Laertes,
Will you do this? Keep close within your chamber.
Hamlet returned shall know you are come home.
130　　We'll put on those shall praise your excellence
And set a double varnish on the fame
The Frenchman gave you, bring you in fine together
And wager on your heads. He, being remiss,
Most generous, and free from all contriving,
135　　Will not peruse the foils, so that with ease,
Or with a little shuffling, you may choose
A sword unbated, and, in a pass of practice,
Requite him for your father.

Laertes.　　　　　　　　I will do't,
And for that purpose I'll anoint my sword.
140　　I bought an unction of a mountebank,
So mortal that, but dip a knife in it,
Where it draws blood no cataplasm so rare,
Collected from all simples that have virtue
Under the moon, can save the thing from death
145　　That is but scratched withal. I'll touch my point

111. *in . . . proof:* from experience.

112. *qualifies:* weakens.

114. *snuff:* burnt end of the wick (which has to be removed to keep the candle burning).
115. *still:* always.

116. *plurisy:* excess.

117. *would:* i.e., intend to.

119-120. *And . . . accidents:* i.e., our intention undergoes diminutions and delays from what others say (*tongues*), or do (*hands*), or unforeseen circumstances (*accidents*).
121-122. *And . . . easing:* And then the consciousness that we *should* have acted is like the sigh of a spendthrift for his lost fortune: the sigh, easing the loss, *hurts* by reminding us of it (with an added allusion to the old belief that sighs injured [*hurt*] one by drawing off blood from the heart).
122. *quick:* core.
126. *murther sanctuarize:* give sanctuary (protection) to a murderer.

128. *close:* i.e., so there will be no chance for a meeting of Laertes and Hamlet, which might turn to the king's discredit.
130. *put . . . shall:* instigate some persons to.
131. *set . . . varnish:* i.e., make it glow (as a painting does when varnished).
132. *in fine:* at last.

133. *remiss:* easy-going.

137. *unbated:* not blunted (in a sporting match Hamlet would take it for granted that only blunted foils were used). *a . . . practice:* (1) a sporting match, (2) a treacherous thrust. (Claudius, feeling Laertes out, insinuates the second meaning under cover of the first).

141. *mortal:* deadly.

142. *cataplasm:* poultice.

143. *simples:* herbs. *virtue:* healing power.
144. *Under . . . moon:* (1) anywhere on earth? (2) having special efficacy when gathered by moonlight?
145. *withal:* with it.

With this contagion, that, if I gall him slightly,   146. *gall:* scratch.
It may be death.
    King.   Let's further think of this,
Weigh what convenience both of time and means
May fit us to our shape. If this should fail,   149. *shape:* (actor's) role.
150   And that our drift look through our bad performance,   150. *And that:* and if. *drift:* intention.
'Twere better not assayed. Therefore this project   151. *assayed:* tried.
Should have a back or second, that might hold
If this did blast in proof. Soft, let me see.   153. *blast in proof:* blow up when tested (like a cannon).
We'll make a solemn wager on your cunnings—
155   I ha't!   155. *ha't:* have it (i.e., the right idea).
When in your motion you are hot and dry—
As make your bouts more violent to that end—   157. *As:* therefore.
And that he calls for drink, I'll have preferred him   158. *that:* when. *preferred:* proffered to.
A chalice for the nonce, whereon but sipping,   159. *nonce:* specific purpose.
160   If he by chance escape your venomed stuck,   160. *stuck:* thrust.
Our purpose may hold there.—But stay, what noise?   161. *hold:* succeed.

Enter QUEEN.

Queen. One woe doth tread upon another's heel,
So fast they follow. Your sister's drowned, Laertes.
Laertes. Drowned! O, where?
165 *Queen.* There is a willow grows askant the brook,   165. *askant:* along.
That shows his hoar leaves in the glassy stream.   166. *hoar:* whitish.
Therewith fantastic garlands did she make
Of crowflowers, nettles, daisies, and long purples,   168. *crowflowers:* buttercups. *long purples:* a species of meadow orchid.
That liberal shepherds give a grosser name,   169. *liberal:* licentious.
170   But our cold maids do dead men's fingers call them.   170. *cold:* chaste.
There on the pendent boughs her crownet weeds   171. *crownet weeds:* coronet woven of weeds.
Clamb'ring to hang, an envious sliver broke,
When down her weedy trophies and herself   172. *sliver:* branch.
Fell in the weeping brook. Her clothes spread wide,
175   And mermaid-like awhile they bore her up,
Which time she chanted snatches of old lauds,   176. *lauds:* hymns.
As one incapable of her own distress,   177. *incapable:* i.e., of understanding.
Or like a creature native and indued   178. *indued:* adapted.
Unto that element. But long it could not be   179. *element:* i.e., water.
180   Till that her garments, heavy with their drink,
Pulled the poor wretch from her melodious lay
To muddy death.
    Laertes.   Alas, then she is drowned?
    Queen. Drowned, drowned.

Laertes. Too much of water hast thou, poor Ophelia,
185 And therefore I forbid my tears; but yet
It is our trick; nature her custom holds,
Let shame say what it will. When these are gone,
The woman will be out. Adieu, my lord.
I have a speech o' fire, that fain would blaze
But that this folly drowns it.   *Exit.*
190 *King.*   Let's follow, Gertrude.
How much I had to do to calm his rage!
Now fear I this will give it start again;
Therefore let's follow.   *Exeunt.*

V, I

Enter two Clowns.

Clown. Is she to be buried in Christian burial when she
willfully seeks her own salvation?
Other. I tell thee she is. Therefore make her grave
straight. The crowner hath sate on her, and finds it
5   Christian burial.
Clown. How can that be, unless she drowned herself in
her own defense?
Other. Why, 'tis found so.
Clown. It must be *se offendendo;* it cannot be else. For
10   here lies the point: if I drown myself wittingly, it
argues an act, and an act hath three branches—it is to
act, to do, and to perform. Argal, she drowned herself
wittingly.
Other. Nay, but hear you, Goodman Delver.
15 *Clown.* Give me leave. Here lies the water—good. Here
stands the man—good. If the man go to this water and
drown himself, it is, will he nill he, he goes, mark you
that. But if the water come to him and drown him,
he drowns not himself. Argal, he that is not guilty of
20   his own death shortens not his own life.
Other. But is this law?
Clown. Ay marry, is't—crowner's quest law.
Other. Will you ha' the truth on't? If this had not been a
gentlewoman, she should have been buried out o'
25   Christian burial.
Clown. Why, there thou say'st. And the more pity that

186. *trick:* instinct (i.e., to weep).
187. *these:* i.e., the tears that have sprung to Laertes's eyes.
188. *The . . . out:* my feminine weakness will be ended.
189. *fain would:* wants to.
190. *folly:* his weeping.
    stage direction. *Clowns:* (1) rustics, (2) low comedians.

1. *Christian burial:* i.e., in consecrated ground with the full participation of the church. Such burial was denied to suicides.
4. *straight:* at once—with pun on "strait"/"narrow" (like the way to heaven). *crowner:* coroner.
6-7. *unless . . . defense:* the clown is applying the analogy of homicide: no man who had killed another—unless in self defense—could receive Christian burial.
9. *se offendendo:* the clown's mistake for *se defendendo,* "while defending oneself."
12. *Argal:* error for ergo, "therefore" (but the clown's logic here and elsewhere is daft).
14. *Delver:* digger.
15. *leave:* i.e. to finish what I was saying.
17. *will he nill he:* willy nilly (whether he will or no).
22. *quest:* inquest.
26. *thou say'st:* you are right.

great folk should have count'nance in this world to
drown or hang themselves more than their even-
Christen. Come, my spade. There is no ancient gentle-
30 men but gard'ners, ditchers, and grave-makers. They
hold up Adam's profession.

Other. Was he a gentleman?

Clown. 'A was the first that ever bore arms.

[*Other.* Why, he had none.

35 *Clown.* What, art a heathen? How dost thou understand
the Scripture? The Scripture says Adam digged. Could
he dig without arms?] I'll put another question to thee.
If thou answerest me not to the purpose, confess thyself—

40 *Other.* Go to.

Clown. What is he that builds stronger than either the
mason, the shipwright, or the carpenter?

Other. The gallows-maker, for that frame outlives a thousand tenants.

45 *Clown.* I like thy wit well, in good faith. The gallows does
well. But how does it well? It does well to those that
do ill. Now thou dost ill to say the gallows is built
stronger than the church. Argal, the gallows may do
well to thee. To't again, come.

50 *Other.* Who builds stronger than a mason, a shipwright,
or a carpenter?

Clown. Ay, tell me that, and unyoke.

Other. Marry, now I can tell.

Clown. To't.

55 *Other.* Mass, I cannot tell.

Clown. Cudgel thy brains no more about it, for your dull
ass will not mend his pace with beating. And when you
are asked this question next, say 'a grave-maker.' The
houses he makes last till doomsday. Go, get thee in,
60 and fetch me a stoup of liquor.   [*Exit* OTHER CLOWN.]

Enter HAMLET *and* HORATIO [*as* CLOWN *digs and sings*].

In youth when I did love, did love,   (*Song.*)
Methought it was very sweet
To contract—O—the time for—a—my behove,
O, methought there—a—was nothing—a—meet.

65 *Hamlet.* Has this fellow no feeling of his business, that 'a
sings at grave-making?

27. *count'nance:* privilege.

28. *even-Christen:* fellow Christian.

32. *gentleman:* with allusion to the old rhyme "When Adam delved [digged] and Eve span [spun], Who was then the gentleman?"

33. *bore arms:* (1) had arms, (2) had a gentleman's coat-of-arms (the assistant clown falls into the trap by taking it in the second sense).

38-39. *confess thyself:* proverbial—"confess thyself and be hanged."

40. *go to:* get on with you.

52. *unyoke:* i.e., you may call it a day.

55. *Mass:* by the Mass.

60. *stoup:* tankard.

63. *To . . . behove:* i.e., to make the time pass for my pleasure (the O and a represent the clown's grunts as he heaves the spade).

64. *meet:* i.e. fitting.

Horatio. Custom hath made it in him a property of easiness.

Hamlet. 'Tis e'en so. The hand of little employment hath
70   the daintier sense.

Clown.   But age with his stealing steps   (*Song.*)
          Hath clawed me in his clutch,
      And hath shipped me intil the land,
          As if I had never been such.

                              [*Throws up a skull.*]
75 *Hamlet.* That skull had a tongue in it, and could sing
once. How the knave jowls it to the ground, as if 'twere
Cain's jawbone, that did the first murther! This might
be the pate of a politician, which this ass now
o'erreaches; one that would circumvent God might it
80   not?

Horatio. It might, my lord.

Hamlet. Or of a courtier, which could say 'Good morrow, sweet lord! How dost thou, sweet lord?' This
might be my Lord Such-a-one, that praised my Lord
85   Such-a-one's horse when 'a meant to beg it, might
it not?

Horatio. Ay, my lord.

Hamlet. Why, e'en so, and now my Lady Worm's, chapless, and knocked about the mazzard with a sexton's
90   spade. Here's fine revolution, an we had the trick to
see't. Did these bones cost no more the breeding but
to play at loggets with 'em? Mine ache to think on't.

Clown.   A pickaxe and a spade, a spade,   (*Song.*)
              For and a shrouding sheet;
95   O, a pit of clay for to be made
              For such a guest is meet.

                         [*Throws up another skull.*]
Hamlet. There's another. Why may not that be the skull
of a lawyer? Where be his quiddities now, his quillities, his cases, his tenures, and his tricks? Why does
100 he suffer this mad knave now to knock him about
the sconce with a dirty shovel, and will not tell him
of his action of battery? Hum! This fellow might be
in's time a great buyer of land, with his statutes, his
recognizances, his fines, his double vouchers, his re-
105 coveries. [Is this the fine of his fines, and the recovery
of his recoveries,] to have his fine pate full of fine dirt?

67-68. *made . . . easiness:* made it come
    easy to him.

69-70. *The . . . sense:* i.e. the hand not
    roughed by toil has keener sensi-
    tivity.

72. *clawed:* seized.

73. *intil . . . land:* ashore (i.e., my voy-
    age is over).

76. *jowls:* knocks.

77. *murther:* i.e., of Abel.

79. *o'erreaches:* (1) paws over (with his
    spade), (2) outwits.
79. *circumvent God:* i.e., try to cheat
    even God.

88. *my:* i.e., he is my.
88-89. *chapless:* without a lower jaw.
89. *mazzard:* head.
90. *revolution:* shift in status. *an:* if.
91-92. *cost . . .'em:* cost so little to pro-
    duce that we should toss them
    about (*loggets* is a game played by
    throwing pieces of wood).

94. *For and:* and also.

96. *meet:* suitable.

98. *quiddities, quillities, tenures:* logi-
    cal subtleties, legal distinctions, of
    holding property.
101. *sconce:* head.
102. *battery:* i.e., assault and battery.
103-105. *statutes . . . recoveries:* samples of
    lawyer's jargon, all suggesting
    crafty ways of getting possession
    of property. *Statutes* and *recogni-
    zances* were analogous to promissory
    notes; *fines, recoveries,* and *vouch-
    ers* were devices for preventing
    estates from descending in perpe-
    tuity within a given family (so as to
    free them for outside acquisition).
105. *fine:* ultimate end.

Will his vouchers vouch him no more of his purchases,
and double ones too, than the length and breadth of a
pair of indentures? The very conveyances of his lands
110 will scarcely lie in this box, and must th' inheritor himself have no more, ha?

Horatio. Not a jot more, my lord.

Hamlet. Is not parchment made of sheepskins?

Horatio. Ay, my lord, and of calveskins too.

115 *Hamlet.* They are sheep and calves which seek out
assurance in that. I will speak to this fellow. Whose
grave's this, sirrah?

Clown. Mine, sir.

[*Sings*]   O, a pit of clay for to be made
120   For such a guest is meet.

Hamlet. I think it be thine indeed, for thou liest in't.

Clown. You lie out on't, sir, and therefore 'tis not yours.
For my part, I do not lie in't, yet it is mine.

Hamlet. Thou dost lie in't, to be in't and say it is thine.
125 'Tis for the dead, not for the quick; therefore thou
liest.

Clown. 'Tis a quick lie, sir; 'twill away again from me
to you.

Hamlet. What man dost thou dig it for?

130 *Clown.* For no man, sir.

Hamlet. What woman then?

Clown. For none neither.

Hamlet. Who is to be buried in't?

Clown. One that was a woman, sir; but, rest her soul,
135 she's dead.

Hamlet. How absolute the knave is! We must speak by
the card, or equivocation will undo us. By the Lord,
Horatio, this three years I have taken note of it, the
age is grown so picked that the toe of the peasant
140 comes so near the heel of the courtier he galls his kibe.
—How long hast thou been a grave-maker?

Clown. Of all the days i' th' year, I came to't that day
that our last king Hamlet overcame Fortinbras.

Hamlet. How long is that since?

145 *Clown.* Cannot you tell that? Every fool can tell that. It
was the very day that young Hamlet was born—he
that is mad, and sent into England.

Hamlet. Ay, marry, why was he sent into England?

107-109. *Will . . . indentures:* i.e., will all his vouchers, and even double vouchers, secure him no more of the real estate he has acquired than the ground he is buried in, which is hardly bigger than a couple of legal documents.
109. *conveyances:* title-deeds.
110. *in . . . box:* Hamlet's thought turns from the skull before him to the coffin in which presumably it was buried.

116. *in that:* i.e., in lands (secured to them by parchment deeds).

121. *thou liest:* you tell lies.

122. *out on't:* outside.

123. *do not lie:* am not buried.

125. *quick:* living.

136. *absolute:* precise.

136-137. *by . . . card:* by the compass, i.e., precisely.
137. *equivocation:* ambiguity, punning.

139. *picked:* fastidious. *the toe . . . courtier:* i.e., the lower classes press so close on the upper that they practically step on their heels —specifically, the peasant has become as affected in his use of language as the courtier.

143. *our . . . Fortinbras:* see I, i, 80-95; ii, 23-5.

Clown. Why, because 'a was mad. 'A shall recover his
wits there; or, if 'a do not, 'tis no great matter there.

Hamlet. Why?

Clown. 'Twill not be seen in him there. There the men
are as mad as he.

Hamlet. How came he mad?

Clown. Very strangely, they say.

Hamlet. How strangely?

Clown. Faith, e'en with losing his wits.

Hamlet. Upon what ground?

Clown. Why, here in Denmark. I have been sexton here,
man and boy, thirty years.

Hamlet. How long will a man lie i' th' earth ere he rot?

Clown. Faith, if 'a be not rotten before 'a die (as we
have many pocky corses now-a-days that will scarce
hold the laying in), 'a will last you some eight year or
nine year. A tanner will last you nine year.

Hamlet. Why he more than another?

Clown. Why, sir, his hide is so tanned with his trade that
'a will keep out water a great while, and your water
is a sore decayer of your whoreson dead body. Here's
a skull now hath lien you i' th' earth three-and-twenty
years.

Hamlet. Whose was it?

Clown. A whoreson mad fellow's it was. Whose do you
think it was?

Hamlet. Nay, I know not.

Clown. A pestilence on him for a mad rogue! 'A poured
a flagon of Rhenish on my head once. This same skull,
sir, was—sir—Yorick's skull, the king's jester.

Hamlet. This?

Clown. E'en that.

Hamlet. Let me see. [*Takes the skull.*] Alas, poor Yorick! I knew him, Horatio, a fellow of infinite jest, of
most excellent fancy. He hath borne me on his back
a thousand times. And now how abhorred in my
imagination it is! My gorge rises at it. Here hung
those lips that I have kissed I know not how oft.
Where be your gibes now? Your gambols, your songs,
your flashes of merriment that were wont to set the
table on a roar? Not one now to mock your own
grinning? Quite chapfall'n? Now get you to my lady's

150

155

160

165

170

175

180

185

190

158. *Upon . . . ground:* Hamlet means "upon what cause"; the grave digger chooses to take him to mean "on what terrain."

163. *pocky:* diseased.

164. *hold . . . in:* hold out till buried.

165. *tanner:* leather-worker.

169. *sore:* grievous. *whoreson:* a term of no precise meaning, half jocular, half abusive (like modern "damn-fool").

170. *lien:* lain.

177. *Rhenish:* Rhine wine.

190. *chapfall'n:* (1) glum, down in the mouth, (2) lacking a lower jaw.

chamber, and tell her, let her paint an inch thick, to
this favor she must come. Make her laugh at that.
Prithee, Horatio, tell me one thing.

Horatio. What's that, my lord?

195 *Hamlet.* Dost thou think Alexander looked o' this
fashion i' th' earth?

Horatio. E'en so.

Hamlet. And smelt so? Pah!   [*Puts down the skull.*]

Horatio. E'en so, my lord.

200 *Hamlet.* To what base uses we may return, Horatio!
Why may not imagination trace the noble dust of
Alexander till 'a find it stopping a bunghole?

Horatio. 'Twere to consider too curiously, to consider so.

Hamlet. No, faith, not a jot, but to follow him thither
205 with modesty enough, and likelihood to lead it; as
thus: Alexander died, Alexander was buried, Alexander returneth to dust; the dust is earth; of earth
we make loam; and why of that loam whereto he was
converted might they not stop a beer barrel?

210 Imperious Caesar, dead and turned to clay,
Might stop a hole to keep the wind away.
O, that that earth which kept the world in awe
Should patch a wall t' expel the winter's flaw!
But soft, but soft awhile! Here comes the king—

Enter KING, QUEEN, LAERTES, *and the* CORSE, [*with*
LORDS *attendant and a* DOCTOR *of* DIVINITY *as*
PRIEST].

215 The queen, the courtiers. Who is this they follow?
And with such maimèd rites? This doth betoken
The corse they follow did with desp'rate hand
Fordo it own life. 'Twas of some estate.
Couch we awhile, and mark.   [*Retires with* HORATIO.]

220 *Laertes.* What ceremony else?

Hamlet.   That is Laertes,
A very noble youth. Mark.

Laertes. What ceremony else?

Doctor. Her obsequies have been as far enlarged
As we have warranty. Her death was doubtful,
225 And, but that great command o'ersways the order,
She should in ground unsanctified been lodged
Till the last trumpet. For charitable prayers,

192. *favor:* face.

203. *curiously:* ingeniously.

205. *with . . . it:* without exaggeration
or improbability.

208. *loam:* clay.

210. *Imperious:* imperial.

213. *flaw:* gust of wind.

216. *maimèd:* scanty.

218. *Fordo:* do away with. *it:* its. *estate:*
rank.

219. *Couch:* hide.

224. *warranty:* authorization. *doubtful*
i.e., of doubtful character.

225. *command:* i.e., the king's.

226. *been:* have been.

Shards, flints, and pebbles should be thrown on her.
Yet here she is allowed her virgin crants,
230   Her maiden strewments, and the bringing home
Of bell and burial.

Laertes. Must there no more be done?

Doctor.   No more be done.
We should profane the service of the dead
To sing a requiem and such rest to her
235   As to peace-parted souls.

Laertes.   Lay her i' th' earth,
And from her fair and unpolluted flesh
May violets spring! I tell thee, churlish priest,
A minist'ring angel shall my sister be
When thou liest howling.

240   *Hamlet.*   What, the fair Ophelia?

Queen. Sweets to the sweet! Farewell. [*Scatters flowers.*]
I hoped thou shouldst have been my Hamlet's wife.
I thought thy bride-bed to have decked, sweet maid,
And not have strewed thy grave.

Laertes.   O, treble woe
Fall ten times on that cursèd head
245   Whose wicked deed thy most ingenious sense
Deprived thee of! Hold off the earth awhile,
Till I have caught her once more in mine arms.

                    [*Leaps in the grave.*]
Now pile your dust upon the quick and dead
Till of this flat a mountain you have made
250   T' o'ertop old Pelion or the skyish head
Of blue Olympus.

Hamlet.   [*coming forward*] What is he whose grief
Bears such an emphasis? whose phrase of sorrow
Conjures the wand'ring stars, and makes them stand
Like wonder-wounded hearers? This is I,
255   Hamlet the Dane.

Laertes.   The devil take thy soul!

                  [*Grapples with him.*]

Hamlet. Thou pray'st not well.
I prithee take thy fingers from my throat,
For, though I am not splenitive and rash,
Yet have I in me something dangerous,
260   Which let thy wisdom fear. Hold off thy hand.

King. Pluck them asunder.

---

228. *Shards:* broken pottery.
229. *crants:* garlands (used in funerals of unmarried girls).
230. *strewments:* flowers strewn on the grave.
230-231. *the . . . burial:* the bringing to her last home, accompanied by church bell and burial in Christian ground.
235. *peace-parted:* i.e., departed in peace.
239. *howling:* i.e., in hell.
244. *head:* i.e., Hamlet's.
245. *ingenious sense:* fine mind.
250. *Pelion:* a mountain which the Titans (in Greek mythology) piled on top of Mt. Ossa in an attempt to attack the gods of Mt. Olympus.
252. *emphasis:* i.e., high-flown language.
253. *Conjures:* bewitches.
254. *wonder-wounded:* i.e., paralyzed with amazement.
255. *the Dane:* Hamlet's title as prince. There is a stage tradition that at this point Hamlet leaps into the grave and grapples with Laertes. It seems more likely from the speeches of the two men (255, 257-260) that Laertes is the aggressor, and that at 255 he leaps out of the grave to attack the prince.
258. *splenitive:* quarrelsome.

Queen.   Hamlet, Hamlet!

All. Gentlemen!

Horatio.   Good my lord, be quiet.

Hamlet. Why, I will fight with him upon this theme

    Until my eyelids will no longer wag.

  264. *wag:* open.

265   *Queen.* O my son, what theme?

Hamlet. I loved Ophelia. Forty thousand brothers

    Could not with all their quantity of love

    Make up my sum. What wilt thou do for her?

King. O, he is mad, Laertes.

270   *Queen.* For love of God, forbear him.

Hamlet. 'Swounds, show me what thou't do.

  271. *thou't do:* thou wilt.

    Woo't weep? woo't fight? woo't fast? woo't tear thy-

      self?

  272. *Woo't:* wilt thou.

  273. *esill:* eisel, i.e., vinegar.

    Woo't drink up esill? eat a crocodile?

    I'll do't. Dost thou come here to whine?

275   To outface me with leaping in her grave?

    Be buried quick with her, and so will I.

  276. *quick:* alive.

    And if thou prate of mountains, let them throw

    Millions of acres on us, till our ground,

    Singeing his pate against the burning zone,

  279. *burning zone:* heavenly region of fire (in the old astronomy).

280   Make Ossa like a wart! Nay, an thou'lt mouth,

  280. *Ossa:* see 240n. *mouth:* boast.

    I'll rant as well as thou.

Queen.   This is mere madness;

    And thus a while the fit will work on him.

    Anon, as patient as the female dove

    When that her golden couplets are disclosed,

  284. *her . . . couplets:* her two young, covered with yellow down. *disclosed:* hatched.

285   His silence will sit drooping.

Hamlet.   Hear you, sir.

    What is the reason that you use me thus?

    I loved you ever. But it is no matter.

    Let Hercules himself do what he may,

  288-289. *Let . . . day:* a "mad" statement whose meaning remains obscure.

    The cat will mew, and dog will have his day.

290   *King.* I pray thee, good Horatio, wait upon him.

             Exit HAMLET *and* HORATIO.

    [*To Laertes*] Strengthen your patience in our last

      night's speech.

  291. *in:* by means of.

    We'll put the matter to the present push.—

  292. *the . . . push:* immediate action.

    This grave shall have a living monument.

  293. *living:* (1) lifelike, (2) by the death of one still living, i.e., Hamlet.

    An hour of quiet shortly shall we see;

    Till then in patience our proceeding be.   *Exeunt.*

V, II

Enter HAMLET *and* HORATIO.

Hamlet. So much for this, sir; now shall you see the other. You do remember all the circumstance?

Horatio. Remember it, my lord!

Hamlet. Sir, in my heart there was a kind of fighting
5 That would not let me sleep. Methought I lay
Worse than the mutines in the bilboes. Rashly,
And praised be rashness for it—let us know,
Our indiscretion sometime serves us well
When our deep plots do pall, and that should learn us
10 There's a divinity that shapes our ends,
Rough-hew them how we will—

Horatio.   That is most certain.

Hamlet. Up from my cabin,
My sea-gown scarfed about me, in the dark
Groped I to find out them, had my desire,
15 Fingered their packet, and in fine withdrew
To mine own room again, making so bold,
My fears forgetting manners, to unseal
Their grand commission; where I found, Horatio—
Ah, royal knavery!—an exact command,
20 Larded with many several sorts of reasons,
Importing Denmark's health, and England's too,
With, ho! such bugs and goblins in my life,
That on the supervise, no leisure bated,
No, not to stay the grinding of the axe,
My head should be struck off.

25 *Horatio.*   Is't possible?

Hamlet. Here's the commission; read it at more leisure.
But wilt thou hear me how I did proceed?

Horatio. I beseech you.

Hamlet. Being thus benetted round with villanies,
30 Or I could make a prologue to my brains,
They had begun the play. I sat down,
Devised a new commission, wrote it fair.
I once did hold it, as our statists do,
A baseness to write fair, and labored much
35 How to forget that learning, but, sir, now
It did me yeoman's service. Wilt thou know
Th' effect of what I wrote?

1. *this:* this part of my story.

2. *other:* remainder.

4. *fighting:* altercation.

6. *mutines . . . bilboes:* mutineers in shackles. *Rashly:* impulsively.

8. *indiscretion:* impulse.

9. *pall:* fail.

10. *ends:* (1) outcome of our plans? (2) destinies?

14. *them:* Rosencrantz and Guildenstern.

15. *fingered:* "pinched," i.e., stole.

20. *Larded:* fattened out.

21. *Importing:* involving.

22-23. *such . . . bated:* such bugaboos and terrors to be expected if I lived that, on the first perusal, with no delay allowed.

30-31. *Or . . . play:* i.e., before I could take conscious thought, my mind had instinctively conceived a plan.
32. *fair:* i.e., handsomely, in the hand of a professional scribe.

33. *statists:* statesmen.
34. *baseness:* i.e., because a nobleman could regard such commercial skills as beneath him.

Horatio.   Ay, good my lord.

Hamlet. An earnest conjuration from the king,

As England was his faithful tributary.

40   As love between them like the palm might flourish,

As peace should still her wheaten garland wear

And stand a comma 'tween their amities,

And many such-like as's of great charge,

That on the view and knowing of these contents,

45   Without debatement further, more or less,

He should the bearers put to sudden death,

Not shriving time allowed.

Horatio.   How was this sealed?

Hamlet. Why, even in that was heaven ordinant.

I had my father's signet in my purse,

50   Which was the model of that Danish seal,

Folded the writ up in the form of th' other,

Subscribed it, gave't th' impression, placed it safely,

The changeling never known. Now, the next day

Was our sea-fight, and what to this was sequent

55   Thou know'st already.

Horatio. So Guildenstern and Rosencrantz go to't.

Hamlet. [Why, man, they did make love to this employ-

ment.]

They are not near my conscience; their defeat

Does by their own insinuation grow.

60   'Tis dangerous when the baser nature comes

Between the pass and fell incensèd points

Of mighty opposites.

Horatio.   Why, what a king is this!

Hamlet. Does it not, think thee, stand me now upon—

He that hath killed my king, and whored my mother,

65   Popped in between th' election and my hopes,

Thrown out his angle for my proper life,

And with such coz'nage—is't not perfect conscience

[To quit him with this arm? And is't not to be·damned

To let this canker of our nature come

70   In further evil?

Horatio. It must be shortly known to him from England

What is the issue of the business there.

Hamlet. It will be short; the interim is mine,

And a man's life's no more than to say 'one.'

75   But I am very sorry, good Horatio,

That to Laertes I forgot myself,

---

38. *conjuration:* appeal.

42. *a comma:* i.e., like a comma con-
necting (not separating, as a period
would do).
43. *as's:* pun on *as* and *ass* (Hamlet has
just mocked in his own as-clause
the high-flown style of such com-
munications). *charge:* weight (alluding to the carrying capacity of
asses).

47. *shriving time:* time for confession
and absolution. *How . . . sealed:*
i.e., what sign did you provide that
this letter was genuine.
48. *ordinant:* operative (ordaining what
should happen).

50. *model:* copy.

51. *writ:* writing.
52. *subscribed:* signed. *impression:* i.e.,
of the seal.

53. *changeling:* exchange.

56. *to't:* i.e., to death.
57. *did . . . to:* courted, wooed (by becoming the king's agents).

59. *insinuation:* intrusion.

60. *the . . . nature:* men of lower rank.
61. *pass:* thrust. *fell incensèd:* savagely
angry. *points:* swords.

62. *opposites:* opponents.

63. *stand . . . upon:* become my duty
(to kill Claudius).

65. *election:* the throne of Denmark
was elective.
66. *angle:* fish hook. *proper:* own.

67. *coz'nage:* trickery.

68. *quit:* (1) repay? (2) remove?

69. *canker:* Claudius is thought of as an
ulcer or cancer eating away at
human nature itself.

72. *issue:* outcome.

For by the image of my cause I see

The portraiture of his. I'll court his favors.

But sure the bravery of his grief did put me

Into a tow'ring passion.

80 *Horatio.*   Peace, who comes here?]

        Enter [OSRIC,] *a courier.*

Osric. Your lordship is right welcome back to Denmark.

Hamlet. I humbly thank you, sir. [*aside to* HORATIO] Dost

know this waterfly?

Horatio. [*aside to* HAMLET] No, my good lord.

85 *Hamlet.* [*aside to* HORATIO] Thy state is the more gra-

cious, for 'tis a vice to know him. He hath much land,

and fertile. Let a beast be lord of beasts, and his crib

shall stand at the king's mess. 'Tis a chough, but, as

I say, spacious in the possession of dirt.

90 *Osric.* Sweet lord, if your lordship were at leisure, I

should impart a thing to you from his majesty.

Hamlet. I will receive it, sir, with all diligence of spirit.

Put your bonnet to his right use. 'Tis for the head.

Osric. I thank your lordship, it is very hot.

95 *Hamlet.* No, believe me, 'tis very cold; the wind is north-

erly.

Osric. It is indifferent cold, my lord, indeed.

Hamlet. But yet methinks it is very sultry and hot for my

complexion.

100 *Osric.* Exceedingly, my lord; it is very sultry, as 'twere—

I cannot tell how. But, my lord, his majesty bade me

signify to you that 'a has laid a great wager on your

head. Sir, this is the matter—

Hamlet. I beseech you remember.

        [HAMLET *moves him to put on his hat.*]

105 *Osric.* Nay, good my lord; for mine ease, in good faith.

Sir, here is newly come to court Laertes—believe me,

an absolute gentleman, full of most excellent differ-

ences, of very soft society and great showing. Indeed,

to speak feelingly of him, he is the card or calendar

110 of gentry; for you shall find in him the continent of

what part a gentleman would see.

Hamlet. Sir, his definement suffers no perdition in you,

though, I know, to divide him inventorially would dozy

th' arithmetic of memory, and yet but yaw neither in

---

77. *my cause:* i.e., a father killed.

79. *bravery:* ostentation.

83. *waterfly:* so-called because (1) gaudy in dress, (2) constantly in motion (e.g. in bowing and snatching off his hat to the prince).

87. *crib:* feed box.
87-88. *Let . . . mess:* if even an ass (e.g., Osric) be rich enough, he'll be welcomed to court.
88. *mess:* table. *chough:* chattering small bird.
89. *dirt:* i.e., land and money.

93. *bonnet . . . use:* see 83n.
94. *hot:* Osric pretends it is the weather, not Hamlet's presence, that inclines him to bare his head.

97. *indifferent:* somewhat.

99. *complexion:* i.e., one of my temperament.

105. *for . . . ease:* I keep my hat off for my comfort (not in deference to you as prince).

108. *differences:* distinctive accomplishments. *soft society:* gentle manners. *great showing:* noble appearance.
109. *feelingly:* with true appreciation.
109-110. *card . . . gentry:* map or model of gentlemanliness.
110-111. *continent . . . see:* one who contains all *parts* (capacities) a gentleman would wish to see—with a pun on "continent" in the geographical sense in "card" (i.e., map).
112-119. *Sir . . . more:* Hamlet dumbfounds Osric by mockingly outdoing him in the use of fancy court talk. The sense is approximately as follows: Sir, his description certainly does

115 respect of his quick sail. But, in the verity of extol-
ment, I take him to be a soul of great article, and his
infusion of such dearth and rareness as, to make true
diction of him, his semblable is his mirror, and who
else would trace him, his umbrage, nothing more.

120 *Osric.* Your lordship speaks most infallibly of him.

Hamlet. The concernancy, sir? Why do we wrap the
gentleman in our more rawer breath?

Osric. Sir?

Horatio. Is't not possible to understand in another
125   tongue? You will to't, sir, really.

Hamlet. What imports the nomination of this gentleman?

Osric. Of Laertes?

Horatio. [*aside to* HAMLET] His purse is empty already.
All's golden words are spent.

130 *Hamlet.* Of him, sir.

Osric. I know you are not ignorant—

Hamlet. I would you did, sir; yet, in faith, if you did, it
would not much approve me. Well, sir?

Osric. You are not ignorant of what excellence Laertes
135   is—

Hamlet. I dare not confess that, lest I should compare
with him in excellence; but to know a man well were
to know himself.

Osric. I mean, sir, for his weapon; but in the imputation
140   laid on him by them, in his meed he's unfellowed.

Hamlet. What's his weapon?

Osric. Rapier and dagger.

Hamlet. That's two of his weapons—but well.

Osric. The king, sir, hath wagered with him six Barbary
145   horses, against the which he has impawned, as I take
it, six French rapiers and poniards, with their assigns,
as girdle, hangers, and so. Three of the carriages, in
faith, are very dear to fancy, very responsive to the
hilts, most delicate carriages, and of very liberal con-
150   ceit.

Hamlet. What call you the carriages?

Horatio. [*aside to* HAMLET] I knew you must be edified
by the margent ere you had done.

Osric. The carriages, sir, are the hangers.

155 *Hamlet.* The phrase would be more germane to the matter if we could carry a cannon by our sides. I would

---

not suffer any at your hands—though
I am well aware that to make a
full enumeration (*inventory*) of his
talents would overtax our capacities
in arithmetic and even then fall
behind (*yaw*), for he adds new ones
so fast. But to tell his merits truly,
I take him to be a soul of great
excellence (*article*), and his inbred
character (*infusion*) to be of such
rarity that, to tell the truth, his only
equal (*semblable*) is his image in a
mirror (i.e., himself), and anyone
who would try to keep up with
(*trace*) him would be simply his
shadow (*umbrage*), nothing more.

121-122. *The . . . breath:* what is the relevance of all this? Why are we wrap-
ping the gentleman in our words,
which are too coarse to do him
justice?

124-125. *another tongue:* i.e. plainer language.

125. *to't:* learn.

126. *What . . . of:* what was your point
in naming.

132-133. *I . . . me:* I would you did know
me to be not ignorant; yet if you
did, it would not be much of a
commendation (coming from a
fool).

136. *compare:* compete (since only excellence may judge of excellence
and even to know another man
well is to know oneself first—which
is the peak of wisdom).

139-140. *imputation . . . unfellowed:* in the
reputation he derives from his
weapons he's unmatched in excellence.

145. *impawned:* staked.

146. *assigns:* accessories.

147. *girdle:* swordbelt. *hangers:* straps
attaching sword to belt. *carriages:*
hangers.

148. *dear to fancy:* ornate. *responsive:*
matched.

149-150. *liberal conceit:* imaginative design.

153. *margent:* marginal annotation (i.e.,
Oswald's language is a text so difficult I knew you'd have to consult
the notes before you were through).

156. *cannon:* i.e., because Oswald's term
carriages was normally applied only
to the wheeled frames of cannon.

it might be hangers till then. But on! Six Barbary horses against six French swords, their assigns, and three liberal-conceited carriages—that's the French bet against the Danish. Why is this all impawned, as you call it?

160

Osric. The king, sir, hath laid, sir, that in a dozen passes between yourself and him he shall not exceed you three hits; he hath laid on twelve for nine, and it would come to immediate trial if your lordship would vouchsafe the answer.

165

Hamlet. How if I answer no?

Osric. I mean, my lord, the opposition of your person in trial.

170

Hamlet. Sir, I will walk here in the hall. If it please his majesty, it is the breathing time of day with me. Let the foils be brought, the gentleman willing, and the king hold his purpose, I will win for him an I can; if not, I will gain nothing but my shame and the odd hits.

175

Osric. Shall I deliver you so?

Hamlet. To this effect, sir, after what flourish your nature will.

Osric. I commend my duty to your lordship.

180

Hamlet. Yours, yours. [*Exit Osric.*] He does well to commend it himself; there are no tongues else for's turn.

Horatio. This lapwing runs away with the shell on his head.

Hamlet. 'A did comply, sir, with his dug before 'a sucked it. Thus has he, and many more of the same bevy that I know the drossy age dotes on, only got the tune of the time and, out of an habit of encounter, a kind of yeasty collection, which carries them through and through the most fanned and winnowed opinions; and do but blow them to their trial, the bubbles are out.

185

190

Enter a LORD.

Lord. My Lord, his majesty commended him to you by young Osric, who brings back to him that you attend him in the hall. He sends to know if your pleasure hold to play with Laertes, or that you will take longer time.

195

163. *him:* Laertes.

164. *twelve for nine:* The exact terms of the wager are not clear. Possibly Dover Wilson is correct in suggesting that *he* is Laertes, who has insisted on a match of twelve rather than nine bouts if he is to be required to win "three up."

165-166. *vouchsafe the answer:* accept the challenge (Hamlet deliberately takes answer in its ordinary sense.

171. *breathing:* exercise.

173. *an:* if.

176. *deliver:* report.

181. *for's turn:* i.e., that would commend it.

182-183. *This...head:* this fidgety bird runs away before he is completely hatched (but the shell may refer to Osric's hat which in retiring he had at last put on).

184. *did...dug:* showed formal courtesies to his nurse's nipple.

185. *bevy:* breed.

186. *drossy:* rubbishy. *tune:* mannerism.

187. *habit of encounter:* (surface) clothing of courtesy.

188. *yeasty:* frothy. *collection:* (1) wardrobe (see habit), (2) "head"—what rises to the top of the vat in brewing: see *yeasty.*

188-189. *carries...opinions:* gains them approval among the most discriminating (grain is *fanned* and *winnowed* when the chaff is blown away).

190. *and:* and if you. *bubbles:* i.e., fools (but with reference to the "yeasty collection" of 182-183).

195. *play:* fence. *that:* if.

Hamlet. I am constant to my purposes; they follow the king's pleasure. If his fitness speaks, mine is ready; now or whensoever, provided I be so able as now.

200 *Lord.* The king and queen and all are coming down.

Hamlet. In happy time.

Lord. The queen desires you to use some gentle entertainment to Laertes before you fall to play.

Hamlet. She well instructs me.   [*Exit* LORD.]

205 *Horatio.* You will lose this wager, my lord.

Hamlet. I do not think so. Since he went into France I have been in continual practice. I shall win at the odds. But thou wouldst not think how ill all's here about my heart. But it is no matter.

210 *Horatio.* Nay, good my lord—

Hamlet. It is but foolery, but it is such a kind of gaingiving as would perhaps trouble a woman.

Horatio. If your mind dislike anything, obey it. I will forestall their repair hither and say you are not fit.

215 *Hamlet.* Not a whit, we defy augury. There is special providence in the fall of a sparrow. If it be now, 'tis not to come; if it be not to come, it will be now; if it it be not now, yet it will come. The readiness is all. Since no man of aught he leaves knows, what is't to

220 leave betimes? Let be.

A table prepared. [*Enter*] TRUMPETS, DRUMS, *and* OFFICERS *with cushions;* KING, QUEEN, [OSRIC,] *and all the* STATE, [*with*] *foils, daggers,* [*and stoups of wine borne in*]; *and* LAERTES.

King. Come, Hamlet, come, and take this hand from me.
     [*The* KING *puts* LAERTES' *hand into* HAMLET'S.]

Hamlet. Give me your pardon, sir. I have done you wrong,
But pardon't, as you are a gentleman.
This presence knows, and you must needs have heard,

225 How I am punished with a sore distraction.
What I have done
That might your nature, honor, and exception
Roughly awake, I here proclaim was madness.
Was't Hamlet wronged Laertes? Never Hamlet.

230 If Hamlet from himself be ta'en away,
And when he's not himself does wrong Laertes,

201. *In . . . time:* i.e., opportunely.

203. *entertainment:* courtesy (in view of the outbreak at Ophelia's grave).

212. *gaingiving:* misgiving.

214. *repair:* coming.

216. *fall . . sparrow:* see Matthew, 10:29: "Are not two sparrows sold for a farthing? and one of them shall not fall to the ground without your Father." *it:* death.
218. *all:* all that matters.
219-220. *Since . . . betimes:* since no man knows what lies ahead if he continues living, what does it matter to die young?

224. *presence:* royal assembly.

227. *exception:* disapproval.

Then Hamlet does it not, Hamlet denies it.
Who does it then? His madness. If't be so,
Hamlet is of the faction that is wronged;
235   His madness is poor Hamlet's enemy.
Sir, in this audience,
Let my disclaiming from a purposed evil
Free me so far in your most generous thoughts
That I have shot my arrow o'er the house
240   And hurt my brother.

Laertes.   I am satisfied in nature,
Whose motive in this case should stir me most
To my revenge. But in my terms of honor
I stand aloof, and will no reconcilement
Till by some elder masters of known honor
245   I have a voice and precedent of peace
To keep my name ungored. But till that time
I do receive your offered love like love,
And will not wrong it.

Hamlet.   I embrace it freely,
And will this brother's wager frankly play.
250   Give us the foils. Come on.

Laertes.   Come, one for me.

Hamlet. I'll be your foil, Laertes. In mine ignorance
Your skill shall, like a star i' th' darkest night,
Stick fiery off indeed.

Laertes.   You mock me, sir.

255 *Hamlet.* No, by this hand.

King. Give them the foils, young Osric. Cousin Hamlet,
You know the wager?

Hamlet.   Very well, my lord.
Your grace has laid the odds o' th' weaker side.

King. I do not fear it, I have seen you both;
But since he is bettered, we have therefore odds.

260 *Laertes.* This is too heavy; let me see another.

Hamlet. This likes me well. These foils have all a length?

                              [*Prepare to play.*]

Osric. Ay, my good lord.

King. Set me the stoups of wine upon that table.
If Hamlet give the first or second hit,
265   Or quit in answer of the third exchange,
Let all the battlements their ordnance fire.
The king shall drink to Hamlet's better breath,

237. *purposed:* premeditated.

239. *That:* that you are willing to concede that.

240-246. *I . . . ungored:* i.e., my personal feelings are satisfied, but my "honor" as a gentleman is not, until I am assured by the experts in these matters that my reputation will not suffer if I make peace with you.

249. *brother's wager:* wager as between two brothers.

251. *foil:* sword—with a pun on "foil": a background that sets off the brilliance of something.

253. *Stick . . . off:* stand out brightly.

259. *bettered:* has improved.
260. *another:* i.e., the unblunted and poisoned one.

263. *stoups:* cups.

265. *quit . . . exchange:* i.e., pay back Laertes (by winning the third bout after losing the first two).

And in the cup an union shall he throw

Richer than that which four successive kings

270   In Denmark's crown have worn. Give me the cups,

And let the kettle to the trumpet speak,

The trumpet to the cannoneer without,

The cannons to the heavens, the heaven to earth,

'Now the king drinks to Hamlet.' Come, begin.

Trumpets the while.

And you, the judges, bear a wary eye.

Hamlet. Come on, sir.

Laertes.   Come, my lord.   [*They play.*]

Hamlet.   One.

275   *Laertes.*   No.

Hamlet.   Judgment?

Osric. A hit, a very palpable hit.

Drum, trumpets, and shot. Flourish; a piece
goes off.

Laertes.   Well, again.

King. Stay, give me drink. Hamlet, this pearl is thine.

Here's to thy health. Give him the cup.

280   *Hamlet.* I'll play this bout first; set it by awhile.

Come. [*They play.*] Another hit. What say you?

Laertes. A touch, a touch; I do confess't.

King. Our son shall win.

Queen.   He's fat, and scant of breath.

Here, Hamlet, take my napkin, rub thy brows.

285   The queen carouses to thy fortune, Hamlet.

Hamlet. Good madam!

King.   Gertrude, do not drink.

Queen. I will, my lord; I pray you pardon me. [*Drinks.*]

King. [*aside*] It is the poisoned cup; it is too late.

290   *Hamlet.* I dare not drink yet, madam—by and by.

Queen. Come, let me wipe thy face.

Laertes. My lord, I'll hit him now.

King.   I do not think't.

Laertes. [*aside*] And yet it is almost against my
    conscience.

Hamlet. Come for the third, Laertes. You but dally.

I pray you pass with your best violence;

295   I am afeard you make a wanton of me.

Laertes. Say you so? Come on.   [*They play.*]

Osric. Nothing neither way.

---

268. *union:* pearl (here, one that will be poisoned).

271. *kettle:* kettle drum.

276. *Judgment:* i.e., since there is disagreement, Hamlet turns to the referee (Osric).

279. *Here's . . .cup:* the king drinks, then drops in the pearl and invites Hamlet to drink.

283. *fat:* (1) soft, out of condition? (2) hot, sweating (cf. 284)?

285. *carouses:* drinks.

294. *pass:* thrust.

295. *make . . . me:* merely toy with me.

Laertes. Have at you now!

[*In scuffling they change rapiers, and both are wounded with the poisoned weapon.*]

King.   Part them. They are incensed.

Hamlet. Nay, come—again!   [*The* QUEEN *falls.*]

Osric.   Look to the queen there, ho!

300 *Horatio.* They bleed on both sides. How is it, my lord?

Osric. How is't, Laertes?

Laertes. Why, as a woodcock to mine own springe, Osric.

    I am justly killed with mine own treachery.

Hamlet. How does the queen?

King.   She sounds to see them bleed.

305 *Queen.* No, no, the drink, the drink! O my dear Hamlet!

    The drink, the drink! I am poisoned.   [*Dies.*]

Hamlet. O villainy! Ho! let the door be locked.

    Treachery! Seek it out.   [LAERTES *falls.*]

Laertes. It is here, Hamlet. Hamlet, thou art slain;

310   No med'cine in the world can do thee good.

    In thee there is not half an hour's life.

    The treacherous instrument is in thy hand,

    Unbated and envenomed. The foul practice

    Hath turned itself on me. Lo, here I lie,

315   Never to rise again. Thy mother's poisoned.

    I can no more. The king, the king's to blame.

Hamlet. The point envenomed too?

    Then, venom, to thy work.   [*Hurts the* KING.]

All. Treason! treason!

320 *King.* O, yet defend me, friends, I am but hurt.

Hamlet. Here, thou incestuous, murd'rous, damnèd Dane,

    Drink off this potion. Is thy union here?

    Follow my mother.   [KING *dies.*]

Laertes.   He is justly served.

    It is a poison tempered by himself.

325   Exchange forgiveness with me, noble Hamlet.

    Mine and my father's death come not upon thee,

    Nor thine on me!   [*Dies.*]

Hamlet. Heaven make thee free of it! I follow thee.

    I am dead, Horatio. Wretched queen, adieu!

330   You that look pale and tremble at this chance,

    That are but mutes or audience to this act,

    Had I but time—as this fell sergeant, Death,

---

298. *Have . . . now:* Alarmed that his best skill has not been able to pierce Hamlet's guard, Laertes treacherously wounds Hamlet as he stands catching his breath after the third bout. Hamlet thus realizes that Laertes is using an unblunted foil, and in his anger forces an exchange of weapons on Laertes and in the fourth bout wounds him with the pointed and poisoned sword. The usual procedure for staging this is either that (1) Hamlet throws down his blunted foil, wrests the sharp foil from Laertes, then allows Laertes to pick up the blunted one, and so they fight; or that (2) Hamlet, in a burst of inspired fencing, strikes the sharp foil from Laertes' hand, puts his foot on it so that Laertes cannot recapture it, politely offers Laertes his blunted foil, picks up the sharp foil himself, and then they fight.
302. *springe:* trap.
304. *sounds:* swounds, i.e., faints.

313. *practice:* treachery.

stage direction; *Hurts:* wounds.

324. *tempered:* mixed.

330. *chance:* turn of events.
331. *mutes:* actors without speaking parts.
332. *fell:* pitiless. *sergeant:* i.e., sheriff's assistant.

Is strict in his arrest—O, I could tell you—
But let it be. Horatio, I am dead;
335   Thou livest; report me and my cause aright
To the unsatisfied.

Horatio.   Never believe it.
I am more an antique Roman than a Dane.
Here's yet some liquor left.

Hamlet.   Ast th' art a man,
Give me the cup. Let go. By heaven, I'll ha't!
340   O God, Horatio, what a wounded name,
Things standing thus unknown, shall live behind me!
If thou didst ever hold me in thy heart,
Absent thee from felicity awhile,
And in this harsh world draw thy breath in pain,
345   To tell my story.   *A march afar off.*
                    What warlike noise is this?

Osric. Young Fortinbras, with conquest come from
          Poland,
To the ambassadors of England gives
This warlike volley.

Hamlet.   O, I die, Horatio!
The potent poison quite o'ercrows my spirit.
350   I cannot live to hear the news from England,
But I do prophesy th' election lights
On Fortinbras. He has my dying voice.
So tell him, with th' occurrents, more and less,
Which have solicited—the rest is silence.   *Dies.*
355   *Horatio.* Now cracks a noble heart. Good night, sweet
          prince,
And flights of angels sing thee to thy rest!
                    [*March within.*]
Why does the drum come hither?

Enter FORTINBRAS, *with the* AMBASSADORS [*and with
     his train of* DRUM, COLORS, *and* ATTENDANTS].

Fortinbras. Where is this sight?
Horatio.   What is it you would see?
If aught of woe or wonder, cease your search.
360   *Fortinbras.* This quarry cries on havoc. O proud Death,
What feast is toward in thine eternal cell
That thou so many princes at a shot
So bloodily hast struck?

333. *arrest:* with a pun on *arrest*=stop-
page.

337. *Roman:* Horatio seeks to follow
Hamlet in death, as Roman servants
often followed their masters.

343. *felicity:* i.e., in death.

349. *o'ercrows:* overcomes (as in a match
of fighting cocks).

351. *election:* i.e, of the new king for
Denmark.
352. *voice:* vote.

353. *occurrents:* occurences.
354. *solicited:* brought about (these
happenings).

360. *This . . . havoc:* this heap of slain
cries out there has been savage
slaughter (as when the cry "Havoc!"
is given an army).
361. *toward:* coming.

Ambassador.   The sight is dismal;
   And our affairs from England come too late.
   The ears are senseless that should give us hearing
   To tell him his commandment is fulfilled,
   That Rosencrantz and Guildenstern are dead.
   Where should we have our thanks?
Horatio.   Not from his mouth,
   Had it th' ability of life to thank you.
   He never gave commandment for their death.
   But since, so jump upon this bloody question,   371. *jump upon:* simultaneously with.
   You from the Polack wars, and you from England,
   Are here arrived, give order that these bodies
   High on a stage be placèd to the view,   374. *stage:* platform.
   And let me speak to th' yet unknowing world
   How these things came about. So shall you hear
   Of carnal, bloody, and unnatural acts,
   Of accidental judgments, casual slaughters,   378. *accidental judgments:* accidental
   Of deaths put on by cunning and forced cause,   deaths (like Ophelia's). *casual:* un-
   And, in this upshot, purposes mistook   premeditated (like Hamlet's killing
   Fall'n on th' inventors' heads. All this can I   Polonius).
   Truly deliver.   379. *put on:* prompted. *forced cause:*
Fortinbras.   Let us haste to hear it,   i.e., the need to meet cunning with
   And call the noblest to the audience.   cunning (as with Rosencrantz and
   For me, with sorrow I embrace my fortune.   Guildenstern).
   I have some rights of memory in this kingdom,   380. *mistook:* deceived, i.e., gone astray
   Which now to claim my vantage doth invite me.   (as in the king's and Laertes's plot).
Horatio. Of that I shall have also cause to speak,
   And from his mouth whose voice will draw on more.   386. *to . . . me:* my opportunity invites
   But let this same be presently performed,   me to claim.
   Even while men's minds are wild, lest more mischance
   On plots and errors happen.   388. *whose . . . more:* whose vote will
Fortinbras.   Let four captains   attract others.
   Bear Hamlet like a soldier to the stage,   389. *presently:* at once.
   For he was likely, had he been put on,
   To have proved most royal; and for his passage   391. *On:* resulting from.
   The soldiers' music and the rites of war
   Speak loudly for him.
   Take up the bodies. Such a sight as this   393. *put on:* i.e., tested (by becoming
   Becomes the field, but here shows much amiss.   king).
   Go, bid the soldiers shoot.
              Exeunt [marching; after the which a peal of   395. *The:* let the.
                    ordinance are shot off].

Act I, Scene I

1. The first seventy-five words of *Hamlet* indicate to the audience time of day, kind of place, weather, and the fact that something is amiss. Pick out the phrases that convey this information. For what purpose does Bernardo enter? What is odd about his challenging Francisco instead of vice-versa? What does this reveal about his feelings? What clue does Francisco give us to *his* feelings?

2. Why has Horatio been invited to watch? What is gained by making him express skepticism about the ghost? What does he conclude is the meaning of the Ghost's visitation after he has seen it? What else is said to be abnormal in Denmark besides the Ghost? How is this abnormal condition accounted for by Horatio? What is gained by having the Ghost appear a second time?

3. What kind of physique should the actor have who plays the Ghost? How should he carry himself? What should he wear? What sort of man, altogether, do we gather that the dead King Hamlet was?

4. The emotional pattern of the first scene is often said to be: tension, partial relaxation, extreme tension, increased (though not complete) relaxation. Try to trace these stages in the scene, indicating the means by which the tension and relaxation are accomplished.

5. Set down in a column every piece of information you have about Denmark and the situation there from reading this scene. Indicate opposite each item the line or lines from which you derived the information.

Act I, Scene II

1. Why does King Claudius find it advisable to send Cornelius and Volteman to Norway? Give several reasons why he might not want Hamlet to go back to Wittenburg. State in one sentence the gist of his argument about Hamlet's prolonged mourning for his father. What do you make of the King's character from the evidence of the scene, prior to Hamlet's soliloquy?

2. Hamlet is set apart by his dress in this scene from the rest of the court. How? What other factors make him appear set apart, isolated, on the edge rather than in the center of this society? Why does he resent the King's calling him *son?* How would you account for the King's haste to adjourn the meeting in lines 121-124? How does the description he gives in these lines of Hamlet's present behavior differ from the true facts? Why does he misrepresent it in this way?

3. What three factors about his mother's marriage are touched on in Hamlet's soliloquy (129-159) with distaste? If the comparisons Hamlet uses here about King Claudius are true, how would you compare him as a physical specimen with Hamlet's father? Judging from the hints in Scene i, how was Hamlet's father accustomed to handling problems like that which Claudius sent Volteman and Cornelius to investigate?

4. What is the effect on Hamlet of the news brought by Horatio and the guards? What is the Prince's theory as to why the ghost has appeared?

5. This scene continues the exposition of the situation in Denmark. Write a paragraph stating what you take to be the three or four most important items of information conveyed to the audience in this scene, and be prepared to defend your opinions.

Act I, Scene III

1. Summarize Laertes's advice to his sister on the subject of Hamlet's love. Why is such advice usually called "worldly"? (if you do not know, consult your dictionary) Is worldly advice necessarily good? necessarily bad? Support your opinion with examples drawn from your own experience.

2. Jot down in order the items of Polonius's advice to Laertes. If you were going off for an extended stay in a foreign country, would you find the advice helpful? Why or why not? Laertes's giving his advice to Ophelia and then encountering his father's advice to him is a comic situation. Why? It could also be called *ironical.* Why?

3. Compare and contrast Polonius's advice to Ophelia with Laertes's. In a paragraph, characterize Ophelia as she is revealed in this scene.

Act I, Scene IV

1. Hamlet here speaks of the disastrous effect on a nation's reputation, and also on an individual's, of a single besetting weakness. What inspires his comment on national reputation? Much of what Hamlet says about individual reputation will later prove to have been true of many in the play, including himself. It is thus an instance of what kind of irony?

2. What reasons does Hamlet give for not fearing to follow the Ghost? What reasons does Horatio give to persuade Hamlet against following it? How does Hamlet get away from his companions?

Act I, Scene V

1. Pick out the words and phrases by which Shakespeare establishes an aura of the supernatural around the armored actor who plays the Ghost.

2. What new fact about his mother's past conduct is here revealed to Hamlet? The Ghost mentions having suffered four different kinds of deprivation at Claudius's hands—what are they? What revenge is Hamlet to take upon his mother?

3. What reason might there be for Hamlet's treating the Ghost jocosely in lines 149 ff, when till now he has treated the Ghost with all reverence? What are his companions sworn not to do? For what new mode of behavior on his part does Hamlet specifically prepare us?

Act I, Scenes I-V

1. Write a paper discussing this first act as an exercise in suspense—as an effort on Shakespeare's part to create in the minds of his audience a consciousness of mystery, of questions raised that are not yet answered, of puzzling events, of actions whose motives have not been clarified, of accusations which may or may not be true, etc.

Act II, Scene I

1. For what purpose does Polonius send Reynaldo to Paris? How do his instructions to Reynaldo illustrate his belief that wise men (like himself) *by indirections find directions out?* Describe in detail his *indirection* in this particular case.

2. According to Ophelia's description of Hamlet's visit to her sitting-room, he first studies her face intently, then moves his head up and down, with a great sigh, as if nodding assent to something that it almost tears him apart to assent to. In the light of the whole play so far, state what you think he may be assenting to.

3. In view of Polonius's pride in his ability to *find directions out* when instructing Reynaldo, what is ironical about his conclusion after listening to Ophelia? Hamlet's appearance, as Ophelia describes it, does resemble superficially the appearance that Elizabethans liked to attribute to persons desperately in love. But Polonius obviously overlooks part of the description in jumping to his conclusion. What part especially would hardly describe a lover?

Act II, Scene II

1. Shakespeare places the scene between the King, Queen, Rosencrantz and Guildenstern in close proximity to that between Polonius and Reynaldo. Why? What analogy is there between them? How does the task of Rosencrantz and Guildenstern resemble or differ from Reynaldo's? He also places the scene of the returning ambassadors in close proximity to this one. In what way has their task resembled that assigned to Reynaldo? and that assigned to Rosencrantz and Guildenstern?

2. Audiences laugh, as they are meant to, when Polonius says in line 92: "I will be brief." Why? What does the Queen refer to when she says to him: "More matter with less art"? Give examples of what she apparently means by "art", from lines 86-104. What additional grounds do we have for laughing at Polonius in lines 153-167?

3. Write a paragraph showing why the interview between Polonius and the Prince is comic. (Consultation of the glosses on this passage may help you.)

4. To Rosencrantz and Guildenstern Hamlet gives his own explanation of the change in him. What is it? How does what he says relate to what he has learned since coming home to his father's funeral?

5. According to Rosencrantz and Guildenstern, why are the traveling players on tour? (The explanation that Rosencranz and Guildenstern give for this would have been recognized by Shakespeare's audience as having immediate reference to contemporary happenings in the London theatres. Thus the "real" world and the play world are not kept separate in Shakespeare's theatre, as they are in ours, but repeatedly meet and mingle: see the "Note on the Elizabethan Theater.") In what respects does the fortune that has overtaken these players echo one that we have seen take place elsewhere in Denmark? A recent critic observes: "When Hamlet meets the London players, it is the third set of 'performers' he has met in this scene." Who are the others and in what sense are they "performers"?

6. List two or three ways in which Shakespeare distinguishes the language of the play about Priam from the language of *Hamlet* itself. What is his purpose in drawing attention to Hamlet's query about the phrase *mobled queen?*

7. In what ways does Hamlet's contact with the players account for his passion in his second soliloquy (553-610)? What makes him see himself as a *rogue and peasant slave?* What does a slave lack that Hamlet begins to feel he too lacks? What doubts about the ghost does Hamlet here confess to? How does he plan to remove these doubts?

Act II, Scenes I-II

By the end of Act I Hamlet has taken a resolution to sweep to his revenge on the King. By the end of Act II, he is in a passion with himself for having done nothing. This suggests that a certain amount of time must have passed. Write a brief essay discussing the evidences in Act II of elapsed time since Act I.

Act III, Scene I

1. What is ironical about the King's instruction to Rosencrantz and Guildenstern to encourage Hamlet in his dramatic and theatrical interests? What proof is the audience now given that the ghost's accusation is true? What do we learn of Claudius's feelings about his crime?

2. Parts of Hamlet's third soliloquy (56-88) are again more applicable to the "real" world that we all know outside the play than to Hamlet's own case. The *oppressor's wrong,* the *proud man's contumely,* the *insolence of office,* and the bearing of *fardels*—all which, as Crown Prince, Hamlet has probably never experienced—are a further instance of the easy movement back and forth between play-world and audience-world which characterizes Elizabethan drama. What elements in the soliloquy can be said to spring directly from Hamlet's own experience? For what reason might he long to die? What reason does he give for opposing suicide?

3. During his encounter with Ophelia, Hamlet moves in a crescendo from quiet courtesy to savage, almost hysterical fury.

a. Trace the stages of this crescendo.

b. Which of Ophelia's remarks seem to contribute to it most? What is her state by the scene's end? What are we bound to think of her father after his comment in lines 182-183?

c. How many of Hamlet's remarks to Ophelia relate to disillusionments that we have already seen him struggling with in his first soliloquy?

Act III, Scene II

1. Hamlet's advice to the players (1-43) reminds us once again of Shakespeare's freedom in moving his audience back and forth between imaginary and real, ancient Denmark and contemporary London: the advice given here is doubtless the advice Shakespeare gave his own acting company as they rehearsed his plays in the Globe. What, according to Hamlet, is the purpose of drama? How does all the rest of the advice grow out of this principle? What *is* the rest of the advice?

2. What does Hamlet value in Horatio's character, as he defines it in lines 62-74? Is this a case of friends being alike, or unlike? Explain.

3. When a man who is known to be ordinarily courteous and loving shows marked harshness and even brutal unkindness, we usually regard it as a sign of inward suffering and turmoil in that man. How far does this

diagnosis fit the case of Hamlet? What evidences do we have that he is by nature courteous and kind? From what causes might he be suffering inwardly? Which of these are hinted at in the lines he speaks to Ophelia (110-132)?

4. While the players act *The Murder of Gonzago,* the center of our interest is naturally King Claudius. If you were playing the King in a production of *Hamlet,* how would you react during the so-called dumb-show? How will the way you react here affect the suspense with which the audience watches you when the murder is re-enacted with speeches (152-258)?

5. What reason does the King in the play give for believing that his Queen will not keep forever to the sentiments she utters at lines 175-178? Do you agree or disagree with his view of human nature? State why. We are not to take too literally Hamlet's comment about inserting a passage of 12 to 16 lines of his own in *The Murder of Gonzago;* but if you had to choose, which 12 lines between 152 and 258 would you suggest were most likely to be his, and why? Mention at least two or three stylistic factors by which Shakespeare distinguishes the speech of those acting in the play about Gonzago from that of those acting in *Hamlet.*

6. How does Hamlet "show up" Rosencrantz and Guildenstern with a recorder? What general point does this illustrate about our assessments of human beings? In what way does his short scene with Polonius (370-382) resemble that with Rosencrantz and Guildenstern?

7. Write a short thoughtful essay indicating how you would stage that part of III, ii which begins with the King's and Queen's arrival and ends with their abrupt departure (lines 90-268). Do not fail to take account of what is said about this scene in the "Note on the Elizabethan Theater."

Act III, Scene III

1. What is admirable about the King's speech (36-72)? Why is it inadequate in itself to win him pardon?

2. In 73-96, Hamlet speaks like a typical Elizabethan revenge-play hero, who delays his revenge only so far as is necessary to ensure damnation of the victim's soul (because he kills him while engaged in some sinful act) as well as destruction of his body. From what you have seen of Hamlet so far, would you say that those grounds are in actual fact the cause of his delay in killing the King? Give reasons.

Act III, Scene IV

1. Considering the purpose for which the Queen has called Hamlet to her chamber, what is ironical about the way the scene develops when he gets there?

2. Several further ironies are created by what happens when Hamlet thrusts his sword through the curtain. Write a paragraph discussing one or two of these in detail.

3. Why does the Ghost appear during this scene? Since the Ghost is certainly real and not a creation of Hamlet's imagination (as Act I has demonstrated beyond doubt), what significance might there be in the fact that the Queen cannot see or hear the Ghost?

Act III, Scenes I-IV

This act deals again and again with the difficulty of breaking through the appearances and surfaces of men and things to their inner reality and truth. Write an essay discussing Act III from this point of view.

Act IV, Scene I

1. How does the killing of Polonius play into Claudius's hands?

2. What words of the Queen's show that the scene in her bedroom has effected a profound change in her?

Act IV, Scene II

What significant alteration in Hamlet's tone toward Rosencrantz and Guildenstern is evident here as compared with III, ii, 341-368? How do you account for this?

Act IV, Scene III

This scene between Claudius and Hamlet is crowded with ironies of many kinds. Discover as many of them as you can.

Act IV, Scene IV

What does Hamlet find to admire in Fortinbras's expedition against the Poles? What deficiency in himself makes him admire Fortinbras? What complimentary deficiency in Fortinbras does the scene stress?

Act IV, Scene V

1. What severe stresses and strains in her recent experience might account for Ophelia's going mad? Show that most of her mad words and songs have some relation to such stresses both here (21-67) and later (165-199).
2. What admirable qualities of the King are seen in IV, v? and of the Queen?

Act IV, Scene VI

Discuss the purpose of this scene. Could it be omitted in performance? Why or why not?

Act IV, Scene VII

Through what means has the King succeeded in calming Laertes before the scene begins? Trace the means by which he works on the young man's mind and feelings during the scene to win him to his will. What are the details of the plot against Hamlet? Might it be argued that the report of Ophelia's death is very appropriate, coming just at this point? Why or why not?

Act V, Scene I

1. The scene between the two grave-diggers, or clowns, has a number of purposes and many interesting relationships to themes and situations elsewhere in the play.
   a. Remembering that Shakespeare's stage had no scenery, what is one of the most obvious purposes served by this scene?
   b. Whose grave is being dug?
   c. One of the oldest of comic pairings (still used constantly on stage, screen, and television) is that of the "straight" man whose questions or mistaken inferences set up the joke, and the "funny" man who gets the joke off. Identify straight

man and funny man in the case of these grave-diggers.
   d. The first question the grave-diggers treat in their befuddled and comic way is the question how far human beings may be called "voluntary"—i.e., wholly responsible for their actions, entirely in charge of what they do. Show in what varying forms this question is raised in I, iv, 13-38; III, ii, 57-74; III, ii, 152-221; IV, vii, 109-122.
   e. Another topic they touch on, comically, is the central place of the grave-digger—i.e., death—in human affairs. How does the tone taken toward this by the grave-diggers, and notably by the elder grave-digger, who talks to the Prince, bring out by contrast the tone taken by Hamlet? How would you account for the difference in their attitudes?
2. It is often said that Laertes is a not very reflective young man who can be counted on to react conventionally in thought, word, and deed. What evidence may one see of this in lines 219-251? In lines 252-295? In II, i? IV, v? IV, vii?

Act V, Scene II

1. How did Hamlet escape the King's plot to have him killed in England?
2. The scene with Osric satirizes court manners and court talk.
   a. What does Hamlet object to in Osric's court manners (cf. especially lines 93-101). Where have we seen behavior exactly like this before?
   b. What are the specific characteristics of Osric's court talk?
3. In what respects does the fencing scene resemble that in which the court watches the traveling players put on *The Murder of Gonzago*? In what respects does it differ?
4. What event in the final scene shows that the King is absolutely self-centered and ruthless, despite certain admirable qualities that we have seen him show elsewhere?
5. What do you take to be Shakespeare's point in ending the play with the victorious return of Fortinbras from Poland? Is there any sense in which Laertes may be regarded as a victor too? and Hamlet also? and Denmark?

Topics for longer papers

A. Discuss Horatio, Laertes, and Fortinbras as dramatic foils to Hamlet, bringing out by contrast his distinctive strengths and weaknesses.

B. Discuss the extent to which Polonius and his children show a family likeness in their character traits.

C. Discuss Hamlet's problem in the play as the universal problem of finding one's way among misleading surfaces of every kind.

D. Discuss his problem as an inner weakness or incapacity, seeking to define precisely what the weakness is and what its causes may be.

E. Discuss the use and meaning of madness in the play.

A Note on the Elizabethan Theater

Shakespeare wrote for a theater very different from ours, and this fact accounts for certain characteristics of his plays that we encounter in especially striking form in Hamlet.

In today's theaters, for the most part, audience and play are emphatically separate. They are separated physically by the architecture of the modern theater, which has a drop-curtain, footlights, often an orchestra pit, and always a proscenium arch (the arch covered by the curtain), on one side of which the audience sits hushed in almost total darkness, while on the other side the persons of the play move and talk in spots, or floods, of blazing light.

This separation of audience from play is expressive of the figurative gulf which also divides them in our theater. For the illusion that the modern theater imposes is that the audience is "not really" present, but is eavesdropping, and that the people it looks in on are "really" men and women going about real business in a real room from which one wall has been removed. What this means for those on the bright side of the footlights is that everything must be made as completely "present" as actors, scene-painters, and stage-carpenters can manage; it is not enough to *suggest* reality, it must

be simulated. The implication for those on the dark side of the footlights is that they must become as "unpresent" as they can—in other words, detached, silent, and passive, like the eavesdroppers they are. Actually, neither of these extremes is ever reached in our theater, or even closely approached; but the tendency of enhanced realism on one side of the curtain to generate passivity on the other has spurred many modern playwrights to search for ways of recapturing the cooperative relation between audience and play that Shakespeare's theater had.

Shakespeare's own theater was the Globe, a round or perhaps polygonal building enclosing a central arena open to the sky. It had no footlights, no lights of any sort, and therefore plays were always given in the afternoon. Likewise, it had no curtain, and no proscenium arch. The stage, altogether bare of the "scenery" that a concealing curtain implies, jutted out into the central arena, and the audience sat or stood around it, *enveloping* (as it were) the players and the action; in some instances, members of the audience—men of rank and other privileged persons—had seats upon the stage. The playwright who writes for such a theater as this cannot shape his play as if the audience were not "there": it is irremoveably there, every member of it visible to every other in the broad light coming from the open roof. So he necessarily acknowledges its presence, engages its imagination. He feels free, for example, to give his characters "asides"—speeches spoken wholly or mainly for the benefit of the audience, and which those on the stage are supposed not to hear. (So Hamlet comments privately, to us, before he makes his public reply to the King his uncle, in the scene in which we first meet him, I, ii, 65.) He also gives his characters "soliloquies"—longer speeches by means of which the leading characters may open heart and mind directly to the audience. (Hamlet has four such soliloquies, bringing us into immediate and sympathetic rapport with those inward scruples and anxieties which make this young Prince what he is.) Also, since his stage is a bare platform without scenery, the Elizabethan playwright calls repeatedly on the imagination of the audience to flesh out the suggestions of hour, place, weather, or mood that he can only communicate to them through the play's own words. (As has been mentioned before, Shakespeare establishes, in the first seventy-five words of *Hamlet,* time of day, kind of place, character of the weather, and the fact that something is very wrong.)

Above all, the dramatist who writes for the theater we have been describing has unparalleled opportunities to make the theater audience do duty as an extension, an overflow, an amplification of the very limited stage-audiences which a small company of actors can muster. When, for instance, Shakespeare's Antony addresses the Roman mob in *Julius Caesar,* in a theater where we of the audience surround him on three sides, the realization comes on us increasingly as he speaks that it is we who fill out that tiny group of listeners onstage into the formidable mob that he *seems* to harangue; and when King Harry in *Henry V* exhorts his soldiers—"You noblest English" —to battle bravely against the French, we realize (as Shakespeare's own audiences must have done, and in their case with a sharp quickening of the pulse) that it is *we* who are being addressed: *we* are those "noblest English" who are being implored never to yield.

Hamlet contains an exceptionally interesting example of this involvement of audience with play, in the scene (III, ii) where the traveling players act out *The Murder of Gonzago.* By this time we know that none of the leading personages before us is what he or she seems; we have seen every one of them putting on an act of some kind; and now Hamlet is making, with this play, his climactic effort to pierce through the "act" of the King his uncle to the truth: did he, or did he not, murder Hamlet's

father? The situation onstage is extremely complex. The players are of course putting on their "act," as they have been instructed to do, watched by the guilty King, who, as always, is continuing to put on his own "act," the pretense of innocence. He in turn is watched narrowly by the Prince, who also continues to put on an "act," the simulated madness, or extreme eccentricity of behavior, that he has used to screen his real feelings ever since the revelation of his father's murder by the Ghost. These in turn— players acting, King acting, Prince acting— are watched by such members of the court as Ophelia and Polonius, who, although they have no clear idea of what is going on at the moment, have been involved in their own kinds of "act" during earlier scenes. Finally, watching all these other audiences who in various ways are "acting," there is the theater audience: ourselves. The play, we sense suddenly, has reached out beyond the stage to encircle us, too, with its searching question: are we not *all* in some measure actors, in some measure spectators, keeping up our poses, watching alertly for others' poses, being watched in turn? This is the point, we now see, of Shakespeare's bringing these traveling actors into his play so prominently and keeping them there so long. They symbolize the pretenses and deceptions that reign in the play's Denmark, and reign among us in the real world; but at the same time they symbolize the way in which "art" —especially Shakespeare's own art, the art of playwright and player—may by its own forms of pretense and deception uncover, and lead the mind to, truth.

Interactions like these between play and audience are not impossible in the modern theater, but they were a good deal easier to effect in Shakespeare's. Partly, as we have noticed, because of the close physical proximity of audience to player. Partly, as we have also noticed, because the audience's imagination was implicated in the play by the very austerity of a stage without scenery. And partly because the Elizabethan theater's inheritance from the medieval theater (where the stories acted out were primarily Bible stories and therefore "true" in one sense while remaining "stories" in another sense) encouraged an easy traffic back and forth between what was "real" and what was "play."

Over part of the stage, in the Elizabethan theater, stretched a ceiling called the "Heavens," bearing astronomical figures. Under the stage, reached by a trap door from which witches and other apparitions might rise, lay an area called "Hell." And on the front of the theater, in the case of Shakespeare's Globe, (if we may believe a plausible tradition) was inscribed the legend: *Totus mundus agit histrionem*—"Everybody is an actor"; or, as Shakespeare himself paraphrased it in *As You Like It,* written two or three years before *Hamlet,* "All the world's a stage, And all the men and women merely players." Thus the individual actor whom the audience saw on the stage playing Julius Caesar or Hamlet or Macbeth was capable of being translated, at any moment, by the very symbolism of that stage, into an image of Every Man working out his human destiny (as the men and women watching him would also have to work out theirs) between the powers of Hell and Heaven.

It is because the characters of Shakespeare were created for a theater like this that they take special hold of us. They have the intensity that comes from believing that the world is a stage, where we are given only our little hour to work out eternal salvation or damnation: and they have the grandeur that comes from believing that the stage is a world, which reaches out past the actors to the theater audience, past them to the audience we call history, past this to the cosmic audience of land, sea, air, moon, sun, and stars (which Elizabethan heroes do not hesitate to address), and so at last to the audience Hamlet himself turns to when the appearance of the Ghost makes it unmistakable that there are more things in heaven and earth than are dreamed of in human philosophies: "Angels and ministers of grace defend us!"

"*There are some defeats more*
triumphant than victories."

Michel Eyquem de Montaigne, *Essays*

Unit Five

SUCCESS

When the word "success" first came into use in English about the middle of the sixteenth century, it meant simply the result or the termination (favorable or otherwise) of affairs. There was no suggestion of good or bad; if you wanted to make such a distinction, you talked of "good success" or "ill success." In time, "success" became equivalent to "good success," and today the phrase "ill success" would strike most of us as a contradiction in terms: how can success be ill or bad? Perhaps a moment's reflection will show that this seeming contradiction

suggests a useful truth. It is always possible that some of the goals of success a society sets for its members may be "ill"; hence the old problem of the good man in the corrupt society that we have seen in *Hamlet*. For this reason, the distinction between good success and ill success is not one we can accept from others, but one we must make ourselves, each of us according to his lights.

On what grounds can the distinction be made? The easiest answer is: Shun the crowd's standards—money, prestige, leadership, and all the rest. But the easy answer is not helpful. It is too likely to encourage a self-righteous aloofness. Besides, since each of us is part of the community, subject to its subtle pressures from the day we are born, the easy answer may be impossible. Perhaps the only way to make a practicable distinction between good success and ill success is to question ourselves insistently as to what we are and what we want to be, to spend more time finding out about "I" and less time complaining about "they." The key lies in the questions: Do I worry more about what others expect, or about what I expect? Do others measure my success, or do I measure my own? Do I evaluate the world on its terms, or my own?

Success, then, is above all a private affirmation. It consists not in absolutes, not even in final achievement, but only in a continuing search for self-knowledge. In this light, it is meaningless to wonder how to attain success: success is a process, not a goal; a way of living, not an aim of life; something you are, not something you might become. In a famous essay called "Success," Ralph Waldo Emerson says rightly that success is to "live in the happy, sufficing present, and find the day and its cheap means contenting, which only ask receptivity in you, and no strained exertion and cankering ambition, overstimulating to be at the head of your class and the head of society, and to have distinction and laurels and consumption. We are not strong by our power to penetrate, but by our relatedness. The world is enlarged for us, not by new objects, but by finding more affinities and potencies in those we have."

The selections in this section are designed to raise questions about what success means and can mean to each of us. Some of the selections, like Chaucer's "Pardoner's Tale," Orwell's "Shooting an Elephant," and Browning's "Andrea del Sarto," hold up to the light the time-honored measures of success—money, power, prestige, perfection—and show how hollow or ridiculous they can be. Others, like "The Spectator, Number 26" and "To an Athlete Dying Young," ask us to pause and reflect on the transience of all human achievement and judge our own pretensions accordingly. Still others, "Old China," for instance, or "A Night among the Pines," reaffirm Emerson's advice to "live in the happy, sufficing present," or follow the lead of Sir Gawain in "Sir Gawain and the Green Knight" or the Captain in "The Secret Sharer," each of whom wondered how far he could, in the words of the Captain, "turn out faithful to that ideal conception of one's own personality every man sets up for himself secretly."

THE PARDONER'S TALE [*circa 1385*]

Geoffrey Chaucer

If you read the "General Prologue" to *The Canterbury Tales* you will encounter the Pardoner with his "hair as yellow as wax," his "voice like a goat's bleat," and his "trumped-up stock" of pardons and relics with which he makes "dupes of the parson and his flock . . . To rake in cash."

The Canterbury Tales as a whole offers a delightful variety of stories: folktales, romantic adventures, beast fables, moral tales, barroom anecdotes. Most deal with human frailty and self-deceit, or with human aspirations to be better than we are. Although there is often a sharp contrast between succeeding tales—in subject matter and in tone—we are never allowed to forget the central fact that the pilgrims are telling tales to each other as they move in a group to Canterbury: they comment on the stories told, they interrupt in the middle of a tale, they interject personal references or even tell a tale in direct response to one already told. We may read the tales separately, but we should be aware that Chaucer conceived *The Canterbury Tales* as a dramatic whole, energized by action and reaction among the tellers; he did not create his band of pilgrims as convenient mouthpieces through which to tell isolated stories.

When it comes the Pardoner's turn to tell a tale, the "proper pilgrims" in the company, perfectly aware of his disreputable character, cry:

> . . . Let him speak no ribaldry!
> Tell us a moral tale. . . .

and he answers, "Just as you wish. . . ." True to his word, he does tell a "moral tale," but the context in which he puts it gives it a flavor the gentle folks on the pilgrimage were certainly not asking for. In the contrast between the perfectly moral tale and the perfectly immoral attitude of the Pardoner we may observe a striking commentary on our theme of "success."

In the lengthy prologue to his tale and in the tale itself the Pardoner gives a demonstration of the way he milks money out of dull-witted villagers as a traveling preacher. Far from trying to defend the disgraceful nature of his money-making, he brazenly brags about it and preaches a sermon on the text, "The root of all evil is greed," making it quite clear as he goes along denouncing drunkenness, gluttony, gambling, swearing, and greed that he is the vilest practitioner of at least one of the vices he denounces. He is the successful unscrupulous money-grubber, and he makes no pretense of being anything else.

"The Pardoner's Tale" from *The Portable Chaucer* selected and translated by Theodore Morrison. Copyright 1949 by Theodore Morrison. Reprinted by permission of The Viking Press, Inc.

Prologue to the Pardoner's Tale

"In churches," said the Pardoner, "when I preach,
I use, milords, a lofty style of speech
And ring it out as roundly as a bell,
Knowing by rote all that I have to tell.
My text is ever the same, and ever was: 5
Radix malorum est cupiditas.
    "First I inform them whence I come; that done,
I then display my papal bulls, each one.
I show my license first, my body's warrant,
Sealed by the bishop, for it would be abhorrent   10
If any man made bold, though priest or clerk,
To interrupt me in Christ's holy work.
And after that I give myself full scope.
Bulls in the name of cardinal and pope,
Of bishops and of patriarchs I show.   15
I say in Latin some few words or so
To spice my sermon; it flavors my appeal
And stirs my listeners to greater zeal.
Then I display my cases made of glass
Crammed to the top with rags and bones. They pass   20
For relics with all the people in the place.
I have a shoulder bone in a metal case,
Part of a sheep owned by a holy Jew.
'Good men,' I say, 'heed what I'm telling you:
Just let this bone be dipped in any well   25
And if cow, calf, or sheep, or ox should swell
From eating a worm, or by a worm be stung,
Take water from this well and wash its tongue
And it is healed at once. And furthermore
Of scab and ulcers and of every sore   30
Shall every sheep be cured, and that straightway,
That drinks from the same well. Heed what I say:
If the good man who owns the beasts will go,
Fasting, each week, and drink before cockcrow
Out of this well, his cattle shall be brought   35
To multiply—that holy Jew so taught
Our elders—and his property increase.
    " 'Moreover, sirs, this bone cures jealousies.
Though into a jealous madness a man fell,
Let him cook his soup in water from this well,   40
He'll never, though for truth he knew her sin,

----

6. RADIX . . . CUPIDITAS: "The root of all evil is greed" (see I Timothy 6:10).
8. PAPAL BULLS: edicts issued by the Pope. EACH ONE: i.e., to each person.
9. WARRANT: safeguard.
21. RELICS: objects associated with saints or other holy people; relics were supposed to have miraculous powers.
23. HOLY JEW: i.e., of Old Testament times.
27. WORM: a poisonous snake.

Suspect his wife again, though she took in
A priest, or even two of them or three.
   " 'Now here's a mitten that you all can see.
Whoever puts his hand in it shall gain,   45
When he sows his land, increasing crops of grain,
Be it wheat or oats, provided that he bring
His penny or so to make his offering.
   " 'There is one word of warning I must say,
Good men and women. If any here today   50
Has done a sin so horrible to name
He daren't be shriven of it for the shame,
Or if any woman, young or old, is here
Who has cuckolded her husband, be it clear
They may not make an offering in that case   55
To these my relics; they have no power nor grace.
But any who is free of such dire blame,
Let him come up and offer in God's name
And I'll absolve him through the authority
That by the pope's bull has been granted me.'   60
   "By such hornswoggling I've won, year by year,
A hundred marks since being a pardoner.
I stand in my pulpit like a true divine,
And when the people sit I preach my line
To ignorant souls, as you have heard before,   65
And tell skullduggeries by the hundred more.
Then I take care to stretch my neck well out
And over the people I nod and peer about
Just like a pigeon perching on a shed.
My hands fly and my tongue wags in my head   70
So busily that to watch me is a joy.
Avarice is the theme that I employ
In all my sermons, to make the people free
In giving pennies—especially to me.
My mind is fixed on what I stand to win   75
And not at all upon correcting sin.
I do not care, when they are in the grave,
If souls go berry-picking that I could save.
Truth is that evil purposes determine,
And many a time, the origin of a sermon: 80
Some to please people and by flattery
To gain advancement through hypocrisy,
Some for vainglory, some again for hate.
For when I daren't fight otherwise, I wait
And give him a tongue-lashing when I preach.   85
No man escapes or gets beyond the reach

41-43. The Pardoner cynically alludes to the charge that priests sometimes engaged in adultery.

62. A HUNDRED MARKS: equivalent in purchasing power today to over five thousand dollars. A mark was worth about two-thirds of a pound.

Of my defaming tongue, supposing he
Has done a wrong to my brethren or to me.
For though I do not tell his proper name,
People will recognize him all the same.   90
By sign and circumstance I let them learn.
Thus I serve those who have done us an ill turn.
Thus I spit out my venom under hue
Of sanctity, and seem devout and true!
   "But to put my purpose briefly, I confess   95
I preach for nothing but for covetousness.
That's why my text is still and ever was
Radix malorum est cupiditas.
For by this text I can denounce, indeed,
The very vice I practice, which is greed.   100
But though that sin is lodged in my own heart,
I am able to make other people part
From avarice, and sorely to repent,
Though that is not my principal intent.
   "Then I bring in examples, many a one,   105
And tell them many a tale of days long done.
Plain folk love tales that come down from of old.
Such things their minds can well report and hold.
Do you think that while I have the power to preach
And take in silver and gold for what I teach   110
I shall ever live in willful poverty?
No, no, that never was my thought, certainly.
I mean to preach and beg in sundry lands.
I won't do any labor with my hands,
Nor live by making baskets. I don't intend   115
To beg for nothing; that is not my end.
I won't ape the apostles; I must eat,
I must have money, wool, and cheese, and wheat.
Though I took it from the meanest wretch's tillage
Or from the poorest widow in a village,   120
Yes, though her children starved for want. In fine,
I mean to drink the liquor of the vine
And have a jolly wench in every town.
But, in conclusion, lords, I will get down
To business: you would have me tell a tale.   125
Now that I've had a drink of corny ale,
By God, I hope the thing I'm going to tell
Is one that you'll have reason to like well.

---

105. EXAMPLES: i.e., examples that illustrate his text; an "exemplum" is a story with a moral told as part of the format of a medieval sermon. The Pardoner follows the format here.
111. WILLFUL POVERTY: another example of the Pardoner's cynicism; one of the vows he has taken is to live in *willful poverty*.
126. CORNY: i.e., with a strong malt taste. Keep in mind that throughout the Pardoner's prologue and tale the group is in a tavern.

For though myself a very sinful man,
I can tell a moral tale, indeed I can,   130
One that I use to bring the profits in
While preaching. Now be still, and I'll begin."

The Pardoner's Tale

There was a company of young folk living
One time in Flanders, who were bent on giving
Their lives to follies and extravagances,   135
Brothels and taverns, where they held their dances
With lutes, harps, and guitars, diced at all hours,
And also ate and drank beyond their powers,
Through which they paid the devil sacrifice
In the devil's temple with their drink and dice,   140
Their abominable excess and dissipation.
They swore oaths that were worthy of damnation;
It was grisly to be listening when they swore.
The blessed body of our Lord they tore—
The Jews, it seemed to them, had failed to rend   145
His body enough—and each laughed at his friend
And fellow in sin. To encourage their pursuits
Came comely dancing girls, peddlers of fruits,
Singers with harps, bawds and confectioners
Who are the very devil's officers   150
To kindle and blow the fire of lechery
That is the follower of gluttony.
    Witness the Bible, if licentiousness
Does not reside in wine and drunkenness!
Recall how drunken Lot, unnaturally,   155
With his two daughters lay unwittingly,
So drunk he had no notion what he did.
    Herod, the stories tell us, God forbid,
When full of liquor at his banquet board
Right at his very table gave the word   160
To kill the Baptist, John, though guiltless he.
    Seneca says a good word, certainly.
He says there is no difference he can find
Between a man who has gone out of his mind
And one who carries drinking to excess,   165
Only that madness outlasts drunkenness.
O gluttony, first cause of mankind's fall,

---

134. FLANDERS: on the mainland, across the English Channel from England.
144. BLESSED . . . TORE: see lines 303-305, 342, 345, 358-359.
155-156. See Genesis 19:30-35.
158. HEROD . . . US: See Matthew 14:1-12.

162. SENECA: Roman moralist, dramatist, philosopher (4 B.C.-65 A.D.).
167. GLUTTONY . . . FALL: See *Paradise Lost* IX, 740-744 (549-553 in Section IV of this book, p. 419).

Of our damnation the cursed original
Until Christ bought us with his blood again!
How dearly paid for by the race of men   170
Was this detestable iniquity!
This whole world was destroyed through gluttony.
  Adam our father and his wife also
From paradise to labor and to woe
Were driven for that selfsame vice, indeed.   175
As long as Adam fasted—so I read—
He was in heaven; but as soon as he
Devoured the fruit of that forbidden tree
Then he was driven out in sorrow and pain.
Of gluttony well ought we to complain!   180
Could a man know how many maladies
Follow indulgences and gluttonies
He would keep his diet under stricter measure
And sit at table with more temperate pleasure.
The throat is short and tender is the mouth,   185
And hence men toil east, west, and north, and south,
In earth, and air, and water—alas to think—
Fetching a glutton dainty meat and drink.
  This is a theme, O Paul, that you well treat:
"Meat unto belly, and belly unto meat,   190
God shall destroy them both," as Paul has said.
When a man drinks the white wine and the red—
This is a foul word, by my soul, to say,
And fouler is the deed in every way—
He makes his throat his privy through excess.   195
  The Apostle says, weeping for piteousness,
"There are many of whom I told you—at a loss
I say it, weeping—enemies of Christ's cross,
Whose belly is their god; their end is death."
O cursed belly! Sack of stinking breath   200
In which corruption lodges, dung abounds!
At either end of you come forth foul sounds.
Great cost it is to fill you, and great pain!
These cooks, how they must grind and pound and strain
And transform substance into accident   205
To please your cravings, though exorbitant!
From the hard bones they knock the marrow out.
They'll find a use for everything, past doubt,
That down the gullet sweet and soft will glide.
The spiceries of leaf and root provide   210
Sauces that are concocted for delight,

---

189. O PAUL: the apostle Paul.
205. TRANSFORM . . . ACCIDENT: i.e., change essential reality into secondary qualities (taste, color,
  etc.).

To give a man a second appetite.
But truly, he whom gluttonies entice
Is dead, while he continues in that vice.
    O drunken man, disfigured is your face, 215
Sour is your breath, foul are you to embrace!
You seem to mutter through your drunken nose
The sound of "Samson, Samson," yet God knows
That Samson never indulged himself in wine.
Your tongue is lost, you fall like a stuck swine, 220
And all the self-respect that you possess
Is gone, for of man's judgment, drunkenness
Is the very sepulcher and annihilation.
A man whom drink has under domination
Can never keep a secret in his head. 225
Now steer away from both the white and red,
And most of all from that white wine keep wide
That comes from Lepe. They sell it in Cheapside
And Fish Street. It's a Spanish wine, and sly
To creep in other wines that grow nearby, 230
And such a vapor it has that with three drinks
It takes a man to Spain; although he thinks
He is home in Cheapside, he is far away
At Lepe. Then "Samson, Samson" will he say!
    By God himself, who is omnipotent, 235
All the great exploits in the Old Testament
Were done in abstinence, I say, and prayer.
Look in the Bible, you may learn it there.
    Attila, conqueror of many a place,
Died in his sleep in shame and in disgrace 240
Bleeding out of his nose in drunkenness.
A captain ought to live in temperateness!
And more than this, I say, remember well
The injunction that was laid on Lemuel—
Not Samuel, but Lemuel, I say! 245
Read in the Bible; in the plainest way
Wine is forbidden to judges and to kings.
This will suffice; no more upon these things.
    Now that I've shown what gluttony will do,
Now I will warn you against gambling, too; 250
Gambling, the very mother of low scheming,
Of lying and forswearing and blaspheming

---

218. "SAMSON, SAMSON": imitation of the hissing sound of a drunken man's breathing.

219. SAMSON . . . WINE: Samson was a Nazarite and therefore drank no wine (Judges 13:1-7).

228. LEPE: Spanish town known for its strong wines.

228-229. CHEAPSIDE AND FISH STREET: parts of London.

229-230. SLY . . . NEARBY: i.e., it was cheaper, and unscrupulous merchants mixed it in with other costlier wines.

239. ATTILA: leader of the Huns, who ravaged Europe in the fifth century A.D.; he supposedly died of dissipation on his wedding night in 453.

244. LEMUEL: see Proverbs 31:4-7.

Against Christ's name, of murder and waste as well
Alike of goods and time; and, truth to tell,
With honor and renown it cannot suit   255
To be held a common gambler by repute.
The higher a gambler stands in power and place,
The more his name is lowered in disgrace.
If a prince gambles, whatever his kingdom be,
In his whole government and policy   260
He is, in all the general estimation,
Considered so much less in reputation.
    Stilbon, who was a wise ambassador,
From Lacedaemon once to Corinth bore
A mission of alliance. When he came   265
It happened that he found there at a game
Of hazard all the great ones of the land,
And so, as quickly as it could be planned,
He stole back, saying, "I will not lose my name
Nor have my reputation put to shame   270
Allying you with gamblers. You may send
Other wise emissaries to gain your end,
For by my honor, rather than ally
My countrymen to gamblers, I will die.
For you that are so gloriously renowned   275
Shall never with this gambling race be bound
By will of mine or treaty I prepare."
Thus did this wise philosopher declare.
    Remember also how the Parthians' lord
Sent King Demetrius, as the books record,   280
A pair of golden dice, by this proclaiming
His scorn, because that king was known for gaming,
And the king of Parthia therefore held his crown
Devoid of glory, value, or renown.
Lords can discover other means of play   285
More suitable to while the time away.
    Now about oaths I'll say a word or two,
Great oaths and false oaths, as the old books do.
Great swearing is a thing abominable,
And false oaths yet more reprehensible.   290
Almighty God forbade swearing at all,
Matthew be witness; but specially I call
The holy Jeremiah on this head.

---

263. STILBON: Chilon is his right name; he was a Spartan statesman, one of the Seven Wise Men of Greece.

264. LACEDAEMON: Sparta.

267. HAZARD: an old dice game.

280. KING DEMETRIUS: Syrian king, first century A.D.; Syria and Parthia were rival kingdoms. Both this story and the previous one about Stilbon were taken from a book by John of Salisbury, *Policraticus* (1159), which exposed court vanities and the follies of diplomacy.

292. MATTHEW: 5:33-37.

293. JEREMIAH: 4:2.

"Swear thine oaths truly, do not lie," he said.
"Swear under judgment, and in righteousness."   295
But idle swearing is a great wickedness.
Consult and see, and he that understands
In the first table of the Lord's commands
Will find the second of his commandments this:
"Take not the Lord's name idly or amiss."   300
If a man's oaths and curses are extreme,
Vengeance shall find his house, both roof and beam.
"By the precious heart of God," and "By his nails"—
"My chance is seven, by Christ's blood at Hailes,
Yours five and three." "Cheat me, and if you do,   305
By God's arms, with this knife I'll run you through!"—
Such fruit comes from the bones, that pair of bitches:
Oaths broken, treachery, murder. For the riches
Of Christ's love, give up curses, without fail,
Both great and small!—Now, sirs, I'll tell my tale.   310
 These three young roisterers of whom I tell
Long before prime had rung from any bell
Were seated in a tavern at their drinking,
And as they sat, they heard a bell go clinking
Before a corpse being carried to his grave.   315
One of these roisterers, when he heard it, gave
An order to his boy: "Go out and try
To learn whose corpse is being carried by.
Get me his name, and get it right. Take heed."
 "Sir," said the boy, "there isn't any need.   320
I learned before you came here, by two hours.
He was, it happens, an old friend of yours,
And all at once, there on his bench upright
As he was sitting drunk, he was killed last night.
A sly thief, Death men call him, who deprives   325
All the people in this country of their lives,
Came with his spear and smiting his heart in two
Went on his business with no more ado.
A thousand have been slaughtered by his hand
During this plague. And, sir, before you stand   330
Within his presence, it should be necessary,
It seems to me, to know your adversary.
Be evermore prepared to meet this foe.
My mother taught me thus; that's all I know."
 "Now by St. Mary," said the innkeeper,   335
"This child speaks truth. Man, woman, laborer,

---

304. BY . . . HAILES: English abbey supposedly
 possessing this relic.
304-305. MY . . . THREE: reference is to a dice
 game: "My point is seven, yours is eight."

307. FROM . . . BITCHES: The original is "bicched
 [cursed] bones two"; the term "bones" is still
 applied to dice.
312. PRIME: 9 a.m.
317. BOY: servant.

Servant, and child the thief has slain this year
In a big village a mile or more from here.
I think it is his place of habitation.
It would be wise to make some preparation   340
Before he brought a man into disgrace."
    "God's arms!" this roisterer said. "So that's the case!
Is it so dangerous with this thief to meet?
I'll look for him by every path and street,
I vow it, by God's holy bones! Hear me,   345
Fellows of mine, we are all one, we three.
Let each of us hold up his hand to the other
And each of us become his fellow's brother.
We'll slay this Death, who slaughters and betrays.
He shall be slain whose hand so many slays,   350
By the dignity of God, before tonight!"
    The three together set about to plight
Their oaths to live and die each for the other
Just as though each had been to each born brother,
And in their drunken frenzy up they get   355
And toward the village off at once they set
Which the innkeeper had spoken of before,
And many were the grisly oaths they swore.
They rent Christ's precious body limb from limb—
Death shall be dead, if they lay hands on him!   360
    When they had hardly gone the first half mile,
Just as they were about to cross a stile,
An old man, poor and humble, met them there.
The old man greeted them with a meek air
And said, "God bless you, lords, and be your guide."   365
    "What's this?" the proudest of the three replied.
"Old beggar, I hope you meet with evil grace!
Why are you all wrapped up except your face?
What are you doing alive so many a year?"
    The old man at these words began to peer   370
Into this gambler's face. "Because I can,
Though I should walk to India, find no man,"
He said, "in any village or any town,
Who for my age is willing to lay down
His youth. So I must keep my old age still   375
For as long a time as it may be God's will.
Nor will Death take my life from me, alas!
Thus like a restless prisoner I pass
And on the ground, which is my mother's gate,
I walk and with my staff both early and late   380
I knock and say, 'Dear mother, let me in!
See how I vanish, flesh, and blood, and skin!
Alas, when shall my bones be laid to rest?
I would exchange with you my clothing chest,

384. CLOTHING CHEST: i.e., all I own.

Mother, that in my chamber long has been   385
For an old haircloth rag to wrap me in.'
And yet she still refuses me that grace.
All white, therefore, and withered is my face.
    "But, sirs, you do yourselves no courtesy
To speak to an old man so churlishly   390
Unless he had wronged you either in word or deed.
As you yourselves in Holy Writ may read,
'Before an aged man whose head is hoar
Men ought to rise.' I counsel you, therefore,
No harm nor wrong here to an old man do,   395
No more than you would have men do to you
In your old age, if you so long abide.
And God be with you, whether you walk or ride!
I must go yonder where I have to go."
    "No, you old beggar, by St. John, not so,"   400
Said another of these gamblers. "As for me,
By God, you won't get off so easily!
You spoke just now of that false traitor, Death,
Who in this land robs all our friends of breath.
Tell where he is, since you must be his spy,   405
Or you will suffer for it, so say I
By God and by the holy sacrament.
You are in league with him, false thief, and bent
On killing us young folk, that's clear to my mind."
    "If you are so impatient, sirs, to find   410
Death," he replied, "turn up this crooked way,
For in that grove I left him, truth to say,
Beneath a tree, and there he will abide.
No boast of yours will make him run and hide.
Do you see that oak tree? Just there you will find   415
This Death, and God, who bought again mankind,
Save and amend you!" So said this old man;
And promptly each of these three gamblers ran
Until he reached the tree, and there they found
Florins of fine gold, minted bright and round,   420
Nearly eight bushels of them, as they thought.
And after Death no longer then they sought.
Each of them was so ravished at the sight,
So fair the florins glittered and so bright,
That down they sat beside the precious hoard.   425
The worst of them, he uttered the first word.
    "Brothers," he told them, "listen to what I say.
My head is sharp, for all I joke and play.
Fortune has given us this pile of treasure
To set us up in lives of ease and pleasure.   430

386. HAIRCLOTH RAG: shroud.
420. FLORINS: A florin was worth about one
    dollar.

Lightly it comes, lightly we'll make it go.
God's precious dignity! Who was to know
We'd ever tumble on such luck today?
If we could only carry this gold away,
Home to my house, or either one of yours—   435
For well you know that all this gold is ours—
We'd touch the summit of felicity.
But still, by daylight that can hardly be.
People would call us thieves, too bold for stealth,
And they would have us hanged for our own wealth.   440
It must be done by night, that's our best plan,
As prudently and slyly as we can.
Hence my proposal is that we should all
Draw lots, and let's see where the lot will fall,
And the one of us who draws the shortest stick   445
Shall run back to the town, and make it quick,
And bring us bread and wine here on the sly,
And two of us will keep a watchful eye
Over this gold; and if he doesn't stay
Too long in town, we'll carry this gold away   450
By night, wherever we all agree it's best."
      One of them held the cut out in his fist
And had them draw to see where it would fall,
And the cut fell on the youngest of them all.
At once he set off on his way to town,   455
And the very moment after he was gone
The one who urged this plan said to the other:
"You know that by sworn oath you are my brother.
I'll tell you something you can profit by.
Our friend has gone, that's clear to any eye,   460
And here is gold, abundant as can be,
That we propose to share alike, we three.
But if I worked it out, as I could do,
So that it could be shared between us two,
Wouldn't that be a favor, a friendly one?"   465
      The other answered, "How that can be done,
I don't quite see. He knows we have the gold.
What shall we do, or what shall he be told?"
      "Will you keep the secret tucked inside your head?
And in a few words," the first scoundrel said,   470
"I'll tell you how to bring this end about."
      "Granted," the other told him. "Never doubt,
I won't betray you, that you can believe."
      "Now," said the first, "we are two, as you perceive,
And two of us must have more strength than one.   475
When he sits down, get up as if in fun
And wrestle with him. While you play this game
I'll run him through the ribs. You do the same

With your dagger there, and then this gold shall be
Divided, dear friend, between you and me.   480
Then all that we desire we can fulfill,
And both of us can roll the dice at will."
Thus in agreement these two scoundrels fell
To slay the third, as you have heard me tell.

   The youngest, who had started off to town,   485
Within his heart kept rolling up and down
The beauty of these florins, new and bright.
"O Lord," he thought, "were there some way I might
Have all this treasure to myself alone,
There isn't a man who dwells beneath God's throne   490
Could live a life as merry as mine should be!"
And so at last the fiend, our enemy,
Put in his head that he could gain his ends
If he bought poison to kill off his friends.
Finding his life in such a sinful state,   495
The devil was allowed to seal his fate.
For it was altogether his intent
To kill his friends, and never to repent.
So off he set, no longer would he tarry,
Into the town, to an apothecary,   500
And begged for poison; he wanted it because
He meant to kill his rats; besides, there was
A polecat living in his hedge, he said,
Who killed his capons; and when he went to bed
He wanted to take vengeance, if he might,   505
On vermin that devoured him by night.

   The apothecary answered, "You shall have
A drug that as I hope the Lord will save
My soul, no living thing in all creation,
Eating or drinking of this preparation   510
A dose no bigger than a grain of wheat,
But promptly with his death-stroke he shall meet.
Die, that he will, and in a briefer while
Than you can walk the distance of a mile,
This poison is so strong and virulent."   515

   Taking the poison, off the scoundrel went,
Holding it in a box, and next he ran
To the neighboring street, and borrowed from a man
Three generous flagons. He emptied out his drug
In two of them, and kept the other jug   520
For his own drink; he let no poison lurk
In that! And so all night he meant to work
Carrying off the gold. Such was his plan,
And when he had filled them, this accursed man
Retraced his path, still following his design,   525
Back to his friends with his three jugs of wine.

But why dilate upon it any more?
For just as they had planned his death before,
Just so they killed him, and with no delay.
When it was finished, one spoke up to say: 530
"Now let's sit down and drink, and we can bury
His body later on. First we'll be merry,"
And as he said the words, he took the jug
That, as it happened, held the poisonous drug,
And drank, and gave his friend a drink as well,   535
And promptly they both died. But truth to tell,
In all that Avicenna ever wrote
He never described in chapter, rule, or note
More marvelous signs of poisoning, I suppose,
Than appeared in these two wretches at the close.   540
Thus they both perished for their homicide,
And thus the traitorous poisoner also died.

   O sin accursed above all cursedness,
O treacherous murder, O foul wickedness,
O gambling, lustfulness, and gluttony,   545
Traducer of Christ's name by blasphemy
And monstrous oaths, through habit and through pride!
Alas, mankind! Ah, how may it betide
That you to your Creator, he that wrought you
And even with his precious heart's blood bought you,   550
So falsely and ungratefully can live?

   And now, good men, your sins may God forgive
And keep you specially from avarice!
My holy pardon will avail in this,
For it can heal each one of you that brings   555
His pennies, silver brooches, spoons, or rings.
Come, bow your head under this holy bull!
You wives, come offer up your cloth or wool!
I write your names here in my roll, just so.
Into the bliss of heaven you shall go!   560
I will absolve you here by my high power,
You that will offer, as clean as in the hour
When you were born.—Sirs, thus I preach. And now
Christ Jesus, our souls' healer, show you how
Within his pardon evermore to rest,   565
For that, I will not lie to you, is best.

   But in my tale, sirs, I forgot one thing.
The relics and the pardons that I bring
Here in my pouch, no man in the whole land
Has finer, given me by the pope's own hand.   570
If any of you devoutly wants to offer

---

537. AVICENNA: Arabian physician (980-1036),   557. HOLY BULL: see line 8.
whose works were much studied in the Middle   562. CLEAN: pure.
Ages.

And have my absolution, come and proffer
Whatever you have to give. Kneel down right here,
Humbly, and take my pardon, full and clear,
Or have a new, fresh pardon if you like   575
At the end of every mile of road we strike,
As long as you keep offering ever newly
Good coins, not counterfeit, but minted truly.
Indeed it is an honor I confer
On each of you, an authentic pardoner   580
Going along to absolve you as you ride.
For in the country mishaps may betide—
One or another of you in due course
May break his neck by falling from his horse.
Think what security it gives you all   585
That in this company I chanced to fall
Who can absolve you each, both low and high,
When the soul, alas, shall from the body fly!
By my advice, our Host here shall begin,
For he's the man enveloped most by sin.   590
Come, offer first, Sir Host, and once that's done,
Then you shall kiss the relics, every one,
Yes, for a penny! Come, undo your purse!
    "No, no," said he. "Then I should have Christ's curse!
I'll do nothing of the sort, for love or riches!"   595

I

1. In the *moral tale* itself, what is significant about the fact that the three roisterers start out seeking Death (swearing to *live and die each for the other*) and yet completely forget the object of their search when they find the gold? How could you argue that they had really not given up their search for Death?

2. What contrasts are there between the old man and the drunken young men? What evidence is there that he has remarkable, perhaps superhuman, status? How does his presence intensify the grimness of the tale? They could just as easily have stumbled over the gold without encountering the old man at all.

3. Before the Pardoner has told more than twenty lines of his tale, he is off for 158 lines on a sermon on drunkenness, gluttony, gambling, and swearing. Does he slip almost unwarily into the sermon, and if he does, what does this fact show about him? What connection has the sermon with the story he started out to tell and which he finally gets around to? How

effective is it as a sermon? Is the reader's attitude toward it qualified by what he knows about the speaker? Why or why not?

4. Why does the Pardoner end the tale so abruptly?

5. In the prologue to the tale what techniques described by the Pardoner reveal that he is a very skillful "operator"? Cite specific examples. How well does he understand his usual audience? Note particularly the psychology he uses in lines 49-60.

6. What does it tell us about him that he is perfectly willing to admit to the pilgrims that he is not only a charlatan but about as heartless a one as can be imagined? Why does he try to sell pardons to the pilgrims after he has revealed himself as a complete fraud? He must know that they will scorn his offers, and yet he speaks to them as he would to the dupes in the villages.

7. How seriously are the pilgrims (and the reader) to take lines 563-566? What he says seems strangely out of place coming from him. If he is serious in saying that Christ's pardon is best, what light does that fact throw on him? If

he is mocking the pilgrims, what light does that fact throw? Which seems to you the most valid reading and why?

8. In the tale itself, what is ironic about the servant's comments on the dead man whose funeral cart was passing the tavern? about the fact that the three young men forget about looking for Death when they come across the gold? about the fact that both the old man and the young men are "searching" for Death? Find other examples of the use of irony in the pro-

logue and tale. In the total framework of prologue, sermon, and tale, what is the central irony?

II

1. In an essay discuss: (1) what Chaucer is saying about opportunists and the values by which they measure success; and (2) what he is saying about human nature that makes it so easy for charlatans to get away with fraud and duplicity.

THE WORLD IS TOO MUCH WITH US [*1807*]

William Wordsworth

In his poem, "I Wandered Lonely as a Cloud," Wordsworth gives evidence of intense response to a "host of golden daffodils" that suddenly met his eyes beside a lake. For him Nature was not something "out there," pleasant to be aware of when the daily routine became tiresome; rather, Nature was in some sense filled with the divine presence itself, and man cut himself off from it at his own risk.

This sonnet is a cry for release from the pressures of a purely materialistic evaluation of success. If Wordsworth's world was too much with him, "getting and spending," much more is our society—urbanized and industrialized beyond what Wordsworth could have imagined—too much with us.

> The world is too much with us; late and soon,
> Getting and spending, we lay waste our powers:
> Little we see in Nature that is ours;
> We have given our hearts away, a sordid boon!
> This Sea that bares her bosom to the moon;   5
> The winds that will be howling at all hours,
> And are up-gathered now like sleeping flowers;
> For this, for everything, we are out of tune;
> It moves us not.—Great God! I'd rather be
> A Pagan suckled in a creed outworn;   10
> So might I, standing on this pleasant lea,
> Have glimpses that would make me less forlorn;
> Have sight of Proteus rising from the sea;
> Or hear old Triton blow his wreathèd horn.

---

13. PROTEUS: Greek sea-god, whose changing shape mirrored the sea's changeableness.

14. TRITON: also a Greek sea-god, whose horn was a conch shell with which he controlled the waves.

I

1. What does the speaker mean by the "world" (1)? Does "us" include the speaker? How do you know? What does he mean by "late and soon" (1)? To what have "We . . . given our hearts away" (4)?

2. To what does the speaker turn in line 5? Where is he standing? What kind of a night is it? Why is the setting important to what he has to say?

3. Why does he say, "It moves us not" (9), after he has said practically the same thing with "we are out of tune" (8)? In other words, what is the force of the repetition? What sudden change comes next and why?

4. Why does the speaker switch to "I" in line 9? Why would he "rather be/A Pagan" and what does he mean by "a creed outworn" (10)?

5. How do lines 13-14 recall and contrast with lines 5-7? Why would *glimpses* of Proteus and Triton make the speaker *less forlorn*? What way of understanding Nature did the pagan inventions of such gods reveal? Why was this better, in Wordsworth's view, than the attitude toward Nature he saw in his own time?

6. What is the significance of the rather clipped phrasing and irregular meter of the first four lines? In other words, how does rhythm reinforce sense here? How does the meter of the next three lines contrast with that of the first four? Note that the basic iambic pentameter pattern is not obvious until lines 5-6. How do lines 11-14 echo the rhythm and sound of 5-7? Note the predominance of "s," "r," and "l" sounds in each group. Show how it can be said that the lines which do not deal directly with Nature are themselves *out of tune*.

II

1. In the sestet the speaker refers to mythological Greece to find his harmony between man and Nature. Is he saying that such harmony is not possible in our *getting and spending* world, and if not, why does he choose the reference? How does the choice of a pagan world make more convincing the sense of forlornness he feels about his modern world?

---

from THE SEA AND THE JUNGLE   [1912]

H. M. Tomlinson

The opening pages of H. M. Tomlinson's *The Sea and the Jungle* render in prose much the same vision of the atrophy and stagnation of human powers that Wordsworth speaks of in "The World Is Too Much with Us." Tomlinson sees in the routine of commuting from his suburban London home (whose garden was a "dark area of soddened relics") to his job in the city (where he was "busily climbing the revolving wheel like the squirrel") a complete negation of what a human life should be.

Now, a half-century later, the "squirrel cage" has become the "rat race." The equation between success and "running fastest" persists, however, and we are compelled to ask if our rapidly urbanizing society is not compounding the equation.

"The Sea and the Jungle" from *The Sea and the Jungle* by H. M. Tomlinson. Reprinted by permission of The Society of Authors as the Literary Representatives of the Estate of the late H. M. Tomlinson.

Though it is easier, and perhaps far better, not to begin at all, yet if a beginning is made it is there that most care is needed. Everything is inherent in the genesis. So I have to record the simple genesis of this affair[1] as a winter morning after rain. There was more rain to come. The sky was waterlogged and the grey ceiling, overstrained, had sagged and dropped to the level of the chimneys. If one of them had pierced it! The danger was imminent.

That day was but a thin solution of night. You know those November mornings with a low, corpse-white east where the sunrise should be, as though the day were still-born. Looking to the dayspring,[2] there is what we have waited for, there the end of our hope, prone and shouded. This morning of mine was such a morning. The world was very quiet, as though it were exhausted after tears. Beneath a broken gutterspout the rain (all the night had I listened to its monody) had discovered a nest of pebbles in the path of my garden in a London suburb. It occurs to you at once that a London garden, especially in winter, should have no place in a narrative which tells of the sea and the jungle. But it has much to do with it. It is part of the heredity of this book. It is the essence of this adventure of mine that it began on the kind of day which so commonly occurs for both of us in the year's assortment of days. My garden, on such a morning, is a necessary feature of the narrative, and much as I should like to skip it and get to sea, yet things must be taken in the proper order, and the garden comes first. There it was: the blackened dahlias, the last to fall, prone in the field where death had got all things under his feet. My pleasance[3] was a dark area of sod-

dened relics; the battalions of June were slain, and their bodies in the mud. That was the prospect in life I had. How was I to know the Skipper had returned from the tropics? Standing in the central mud, which also was black, surveying that forlorn end to devoted human effort, what was there to tell me the Skipper had brought back his tramp steamer from the lands under the sun? I knew nothing to look forward to but December, with January to follow. What should you and I expect after November, but the next month of winter? Should the cultivators of London backs[4] look for adventures, even though they had read old Hakluyt?[5] What are the Americas to us, the Amazon and the Orinoco,[6] Barbadoes[7] and Panama, and Port Royal,[8] but tales that are told? We have never been nearer to them, and now know we shall never be nearer to them, than that hill in our neighborhood which gives us a broad prospect of the sunset. There is as near as we can approach. Thither we go and ascend of an evening, like Moses,[9] except for our pipe. It is all the escape vouchsafed us. Did we ever know the chain to give? The chain has a certain length—we know it to a link—to that ultimate link, the possibilities of which we never strain. The mean range[10] of our chain, the office and the polling booth. What a radius! Yet it cannot prevent us ascending that hill which looks, with uplifted and shining brow, to the far vague country whence comes the last of the light, at dayfall.

It is necessary for you to learn that on my way to catch the 8:35 that morning—it is always the 8:35—there came to me no

1. THIS AFFAIR: Tomlinson refers to his decision to uproot himself from the London jungles and seek a calmer world in those of South America.
2. DAYSPRING: dawn.
3. PLEASANCE: pleasure ground, usually referring to spacious formal gardens on an estate; obviously the term is used ironically here.

4. BACKS: backyards.
5. HAKLUYT: editor and compiler of accounts of Elizabethan voyaging.
6. AMAZON . . . ORINOCO: two major rivers of South America.
7. BARBADOES: island in the West Indies.
8. PORT ROYAL: town on the island of Jamaica in the West Indies.
9. LIKE MOSES: who looked upon the Promised Land from Mount Pisgah, but was forbidden to enter into it (Deuteronomy 3:27).
10. MEAN RANGE: i.e., the long and short of it.

premonition of change. No portent was in the sky but the grey wrack.[11] I saw the hale and dominant gentleman, as usual, who arrives at the station in a brougham drawn by two grey horses. He looked as proud and arrogant as ever, for his face is as a bull's. He had the usual bunch of scarlet geraniums in his coat, and the stationmaster assisted him into an apartment,[12] and his footman handed him a rug; a routine as stable as the hills, this. If only the solemn footman would, one morning, as solemnly as ever, hurl that rug at his master, with the umbrella to crash after it! One could begin to hope then. There was the pale girl in black who never, between our suburb and the city, lifts her shy brown eyes, benedictory as they are at such a time, from the soiled book of the local public library, and whose umbrella has lost half its handle, a china nob. (I think I will write this book for her.) And there were all the others who catch that train, except the young fellow with the cough. Now and then he does miss it, using for the purpose, I have no doubt, that only form of rebellion against its accursed tyranny which we have yet learned, physical inability to catch it. Where that morning train starts from is a mystery; but it never fails to come for us, and it never takes us beyond the city, I well know.

I have a clear memory of the newspapers as they were that morning. I had a sheaf of them, for it is my melancholy business to know what each is saying. I learned there were dark and portentous matters, not actually with us, but looming, each already rather larger than a man's hand. If certain things happened, said one half the papers, ruin stared us in the face. If those things did not happen, said the other half, ruin stared us in the face. No way appeared out of it. You paid your half-penny and were damned either way. If you paid a penny you got more for your money. Boding

gloom, full-orbed,[13] could be had for that. There was your extra value for you. I looked round at my fellow passengers, all reading the same papers, and all, it could be reasonably presumed, with foreknowledge of catastrophe. They were indifferent, every one of them. I suppose we have learned, with some bitterness, that nothing ever happens but private failure and tragedy, unregarded by our fellows except with pity. The blare of the political megaphones, and the sustained panic of the party tom-toms, have a message for us, we may suppose. We may be sure the noise means something. So does the butcher's boy when the sheep want to go up a side turning.[14] He makes a noise. He means something, with his warning cries. The driving uproar has a purpose. But we have found out (not they who would break up side turnings, but the people in the second-class carriages of the morning train) that now, though our first instinct is to start in a panic, when we hear another sudden warning shout, there is no need to do so. And perhaps, having attained to that more callous mind which allows us to stare dully from the carriage window though with that urgent din in our ears, a reasonable explanation of the increasing excitement and flushed anxiety of the great Statesmen and their fuglemen[15] may occur to us, in a generation or two. Give us time! But how they wish they were out of it, they who need no more time, but understand.

I put down the papers[16] with their calls to social righteousness pitched in the upper register of the tea-tray, their bright and instructive interviews with flat earthers,[17] and

---

11. WRACK: thin flying clouds.
12. APARTMENT: train compartment.
13. FULL-ORBED: completely encircled or rounded-out.
14. GO . . . TURNING: instead of straight ahead to be slaughtered.
15. FUGLEMEN: people who set examples; models.
16. PAPERS: In this paragraph, Tomlinson points to the diet of trifles and absurdities on which city populaces feed to relieve the boredom and monotony of their lives.
17. FLAT EARTHERS: i.e., the kind of inane people who think the earth is flat.

with the veteran who is topically interesting because, having served one master fifty years, and reared thirteen children on fifteen shillings a week,[18] he has just begun to draw his old age pension. (There's industry, thrift, and success, my little dears!) One paper had a column account of the youngest child actress in London, her toys and her philosophy, initialed by one of our younger brilliant journalists. All had a society divorce case, with sanitary elisions.[19] Another contained an amusing account of a man working his way round the world with a barrel on his head. Again, the young prince, we were credibly informed in all the papers of that morning, did stop to look in at a toy-shop window in Regent Street[20] the previous afternoon. So like a boy, you know, and yet he is a prince of course. The matter could not be doubted. The report was carefully illustrated. The prince stood on his feet outside the toy shop, and looked in.

To think of the future as a modestly long series of such prone mornings, dawns unlit by heaven's light, new days to which we should be awakened always by these clamant cockcrows bringing to our notice what the busy-ness of our fellows had accomplished in nests of intelligent and fruitful china eggs, was enough to make one stand up in the carriage, horrified, and pull the communication cord.[21] So I put down the papers and turned to the landscape. Had I known the Skipper was back from below the horizon— but I did not know. So I must go on to explain that that morning train did stop, with its unfailing regularity, and not the least hint of reprieve, at the place appointed in the Schedule.[22] Soon I was at work, showing, I hope, the right eager and concentrated eye, dutifully and busily climbing the revolving wheel like the squirrel; except, un-

luckier than that wild thing so far as I know, I was clearly conscious, whatever the speed, the wheel remained forever in the same place. Looking up to sigh through the bars after a long spin there was the Skipper smiling at me.

I saw an open door. I got out. It was as though the world had been suddenly lighted, and I could see a great distance.

We stood in Fleet Street[23] later, interrupting the tide. The noise of the traffic came to me from afar, for the sailor was telling me he was sailing soon, and that he was taking his vessel on an experimental voyage through the tropical forests of the Amazon. He was going to Para, and thence up the main stream as far as Manaos, and would then attempt to reach a point on the Madeira river near Bolivia, 800 miles above its junction with the greater river. It would be a noble journey. They would see Obydos and Santarem,[24] and the foliage would brush their rigging at times, so narrow would be the way, and where they anchored at night the jaguars would come to drink. This to me, and I have read Humboldt, and Bates, and Spruce, and Wallace.[25] As I listened my pipe went out.

It was when we were parting that the sailor, who is used to far horizons and habitually deals with affairs in a large way because his standards in his own business are the skyline and the meridian, put to me the most searching question I have had to answer since the city first caught and caged me. He put it casually when he was striking a match for a cigar, so little did he himself think of it.

"Then why," said he, "don't you chuck it?"

What, escape? I had never thought of

---

18. FIFTEEN . . . WEEK: literally, in 1912, $3.75, even then a starvation wage.
19. SANITARY ELISIONS: i.e., with the more sordid details left out.
20. REGENT STREET: fashionable London street.
21. COMMUNICATION CORD: emergency cord.
22. SCHEDULE: timetable.

23. FLEET STREET: center of London's publishing and newspaper world where Tomlinson was employed.
24. PARA . . . SANTAREM: All of these place names can be found on any map of Brazil.
25. HUMBOLDT . . . WALLACE: All well-known naturalists of the nineteenth century; all had explored parts of the Amazon and had written accounts of their travels.

that. It is the last solution which would have occurred to me concerning the problem of captivity. It is a credit to you and to me that we do not think of our chains so disrespectfully as to regard them as anything but necessary and indispensable, though sometimes, sore and irritated, we may bite at them. As if servitude fell to our portion like squints,[26] parents poor in spirit, green fly,[27] reverence for our social superiors, and the other consignments from the stars. How should we live if not in bonds? I have never tried. I do not remember, in all the even and respectable history of my family, that it has ever been tried. The habit of obedience, like our family habit of noses, is bred in the bone. The most we have ever done is to shake our fists at destiny; and I have done most of that.

"Give it up," said the Skipper, "and come with me."

With a sad smile I lifted my foot heavily and showed him what had me round the ankle. "Poo," he said. "You could berth with the second mate. There's room there. I could sign you on as purser. You come."

I stared at him. The fellow meant it. I laughed at him.

"What," I asked conclusively, "shall I do about all this?" I waved my arm round Fleet Street, source of all the light I know, giver of my gift of income tax, limit of my perspective. How should I live when with-

_____
26. SQUINTS: cross-eyes.
27. GREEN FLY: aphids (a garden pest).

drawn from the smell of its ink, the urge of its machinery?

"That," he said. "Oh, damn that!"

It was his light tone which staggered me and not what he said. The sailor's manner was that of one who would be annoyed if I treated him like a practical man, arranging miles of petty considerations and exceptions before him, arguing for hours along rows of trifles, and hoping the harvest of difficulties of no consequence at the end of the argument would convince him. Indeed I know he is always impatient for the next step in any business, and not, like most of us, for more careful consideration. "Look here," said the sailor, pointing to Ludgate Circus,[28] "see that Putney[29] bus? If it takes up two more passengers before it passes this spot then you've got to come."

That made the difficulty much clearer. I agreed. The bus struggled off, and a man with a bag ran at it and boarded it. One! Then it had a clear run—it almost reached us—in another two seconds!—I began to breathe more easily; the danger of liberty was almost gone. Then the sailor jumped for the bus before it was quite level, and as he mounted the steps, turned, held up two fingers with a grin.

Thus was a voyage of great moment[30] and adventure settled for me.

_____
28. LUDGATE CIRCUS: a well-known London bus-stop close to Fleet Street.
29. PUTNEY: i.e., going to Putney, a London suburb.
30. MOMENT: importance.

I

1. Who is the "us" of Tomlinson's phrase *both of us?* the "you" of *you and I?* What does the author gain by shifting back and forth between "I" and "we"?

2. Why does Tomlinson say that his London garden is "part of the heredity of this book"? What does the description of the November day and the rain-trampled garden stand for? How is the reader prevented from imagining the garden on another kind of day, perhaps during the previous June?

3. Tomlinson's choice of detail and vocabulary quite obviously paint a dreary picture. Point out the phrases that do so in the first few paragraphs. How does the sentence structure itself support the mood he wishes to convey?

4. The Skipper isn't described at all, but Tomlinson conveys a vivid impression of him. How does he do it?

5. What is the tone of these opening pages? Consider such phrases as: "as much as I should like to skip it and get to sea," "There's industry, thrift, and success, my little dears!" and "the habit of obedience, like our family habit of

noses, is bred in the bone." Consider also the references to his fellow passengers on the 8:35, their response to the *dark and portentous matters* in the newspapers, and the kind of material in the newspapers. Would you say he is being flippant? somber? light-hearted? sardonic? some combination of these or something quite different?

6. Analyze thoroughly the following metaphorical comments and indicate how they pinpoint Tomlinson's criticism of the values and standards typified by London living:

  a. "the papers with their calls to righteousness pitched in the upper registers of the tea-tray."

  b. "we should be awakened always by these clamant cockcrows bringing to our notice what the busy-ness of our fellows had accomplished in nests of intelligent and fruitful china eggs."

  c. "The blare of the political megaphones, and the sustained panic of the party tom-toms, have a message for us, we may suppose. We may be sure the noise means something. So does the butcher's boy when the sheep want to go up a side turning. He makes a noise. He means

something, with his warning cries. The driving uproar has a purpose."

  d. "The sailor's manner was that of one who would be annoyed if I treated him like a practical man, arranging miles of petty considerations and exceptions before him, arguing for hours along rows of trifles, and hoping the harvest of difficulties of no consequence at the end of the argument would convince him."

7. On what terms can one be a success in Tomlinson's London world? How desirable does he make success seem on those terms, and what kind of people become successes? What guarantees does he have that things will be any different once he takes off for Brazil?

II

1. Tomlinson makes city living and commercial activity appear decidedly unattractive. Most of us, however, will live out our days in much the same circumstances he derides, seeking success in the world of business—*dutifully and busily climbing the revolving wheel.* What can be said in rebuttal to Tomlinson that would take the gloom and stagnation out of his picture of city life?

AUNT HELEN *and* COUSIN NANCY   [1915]

T. S. Eliot

Toward the close of the selection from *The Sea and the Jungle* Tomlinson says, "How should we live if not in bonds? I have never tried. I do not remember, in the even and respectable history of my family, that it has ever been tried. The habit of obedience, like our family habit of noses, is bred in the bone." The implication clearly is that "doing the right thing" is all that really matters, even if it means leading a sterile and degrading existence in a society crammed with others "doing the right thing" without questioning how deadening their way of life has become.

The following two short poems, "Aunt Helen" and "Cousin Nancy," by T. S. Eliot, pursue the same idea. The two ladies represent for Eliot two aspects of a society that has lost its sense of direction, two diverse ways in which human potentialities can wither and go to seed.

We get few details about Miss Helen Slingsby, but at the moment of her death we catch a glimpse of the fact that she had been dead as a person long before her body ceased to function. Her younger counterpart, Nancy Ellicott, attempts to break out of the stagnation of her world, but in a revolt without purpose, revolt for its own sake, that only makes her life emptier and more absurd. Eliot was dealing with a segment of society few of us are familiar with, but his portraits are convincing proof that living by the wrong values can infect any society with dry rot.

AUNT HELEN

Miss Helen Slingsby was my maiden aunt,
And lived in a small house near a fashionable square
Cared for by servants to the number of four.
Now when she died there was silence in heaven
And silence at her end of the street.   5
The shutters were drawn and the undertaker wiped his feet—
He was aware that this sort of thing had occurred before.
The dogs were handsomely provided for,
But shortly afterwards the parrot died too.
The Dresden clock continued ticking on the mantelpiece,   10
And the footman sat upon the dining-table
Holding the second housemaid on his knees—
Who had always been so careful while her mistress lived.

4. SILENCE IN HEAVEN: see Revelation 5-7, 8:1.   10. DRESDEN: made of Dresden ware, finely decorated porcelain.

COUSIN NANCY

Miss Nancy Ellicott
Strode across the hills and broke them,
Rode across the hills and broke them—
The barren New England hills—
Riding to hounds   5
Over the cow pasture.

Miss Nancy Ellicott smoked
And danced all the modern dances;
And her aunts were not quite sure how they felt about it,
But they knew that it was modern.   10

Upon the glazen shelves kept watch
Matthew and Waldo, guardians of the faith,
The army of unalterable law.

12. MATTHEW AND WALDO: Matthew Arnold and Ralph Waldo Emerson, whose essays on social and ethical responsibility enjoyed great prestige in nineteenth century England and America.

13. The line is the last line of George Meredith's "Lucifer in Starlight" (see page 200).

I

1. Characterize Aunt Helen. How do you know what she was like? What is suggested by the words *cared for*? Why does the undertaker wipe his feet? What does the fact that the *dogs were handsomely provided for* show? Why is it necessary to mention that the Dresden clock continued ticking? What is indicated by the activities of the footman and the second house-maid?

2. What is the irony in lines 4-5? Be sure to read Revelation, chapters 5-7 and 8:1.

3. Syntax clashes with sense in the poem. Syntactically, line 7 explains line 6, as indicated by the dash. What connection is there in so far as sense is concerned? Syntactically, "But" (9) means "on the contrary"; does such a meaning make any sense here? Why or why not? What other clashes of syntax and sense are there? How is the effect of disjointedness enhanced by the eccentric use of rhyme? What purpose is served by these devices?

4. What do the details showing Cousin Nancy in action reveal about her? What does Eliot mean when he says that she "broke the hills"? Why does he refer to them as "the barren New England hills"? How does the phrase *over the cow pasture* qualify the phrase *riding to hounds*? Why does he mention the aunts' reaction, and what does he mean by line 10?

5. What is the word *glazen* meant to suggest? What is *glazen* besides the shelves?

6. In so far as the two poems imply its nature, what is the *faith* that Matthew and Waldo are guardians of? What meanings does Eliot gain by using the last line of Meredith's sonnet (p. 200) as the last line of this poem?

7. In what ways is Cousin Nancy different from Aunt Helen? In what ways is she the same kind of person?

8. Quite obviously Aunt Helen and Cousin Nancy see themselves very differently from the way Eliot sees them. How does this fact contribute to the portraits Eliot paints?

II

1. What criticism is Eliot making in the two poems? Can you see manifestations of this same kind of deadness and sterility in other segments of modern society? Discuss.

SHOOTING AN ELEPHANT   [*1950*]

George Orwell

The Pardoner's greed robs him of any measure of decency and self-respect. The pious face he wears before the world, however, is beguiling enough to deceive his public and assure him profit and influence. This same measure of public acceptance is also the measure of success for many of us. While the Pardoner frankly confesses to the hypocrisies he practices, how rarely it is that we bare to others the "acting" we indulge in to gain approval.

With devastating analysis George Orwell here gives an accounting of his private motives in opposition to his public performance in a ticklish situation far different from anything we will experience. The compulsion to perform as one is expected to, however, can easily be fitted to circumstances closer to home.

In Moulmein, in lower Burma, I was hated by large numbers of people—the only time in my life that I have been important enough for this to happen to me. I was sub-divisional police officer of the town, and in an aimless, petty kind of way anti-European feeling was very bitter. No one had the guts to raise a riot, but if a European woman went through the bazaars[1] alone somebody would probably spit betel juice over her dress. As a police officer I was an obvious target and was baited whenever it seemed safe to do so. When a nimble Burman tripped me up on the football field and the referee (another Burman) looked the other way, the crowd yelled with hideous laughter. This happened more than once. In the end, the sneering yellow faces of young men that met me everywhere, the insults hooted after me when I was at a safe distance, got badly on my nerves. The young Buddhist priests were the worst of all. There were several thousands of them in the town and none of them seemed to have anything to do except stand on street corners and jeer at Europeans.

All this was perplexing and upsetting. For at that time I had already made up my mind that imperialism was an evil thing and the sooner I chucked up my job and got out of it the better. Theoretically—and secretly, of course—I was all for the Burmese and all against their oppressors, the British. As for the job I was doing, I hated it more bitterly than I can perhaps make clear. In a job like that you see the dirty work of Empire at close quarters. The wretched prisoners huddling in the stinking cages of the lock-ups,[2] the gray, cowed faces of the long-term convicts, the scarred buttocks of the men who had been flogged with bamboos—all these oppressed me with an intolerable sense of guilt. But I could get nothing into perspective. I was young and ill-educated and I had had to think out my problems in the utter silence that is imposed on every Englishman in the East. I did not even know

that the British Empire is dying, still less did I know that it is a great deal better than the younger empires that are going to supplant it. All I knew was that I was stuck between my hatred of the empire I served and my rage against the evil-spirited little beasts who tried to make my job impossible. With one part of my mind I thought of the British Raj[3] as an unbreakable tyranny, as something clamped down, *in saecula saeculorum,*[4] upon the will of prostrate peoples; with another part I thought that the greatest joy in the world would be to drive a bayonet into a Buddhist priest's guts. Feelings like these are the normal by-products of imperialism; ask any Anglo-Indian official, if you can catch him off duty.

One day something happened which in a roundabout way was enlightening. It was a tiny incident in itself, but it gave me a better glimpse than I had had before of the real nature of imperialism—the real motives for which despotic governments act. Early one morning the sub-inspector at a police station the other end of the town rang me up on the 'phone and said that an elephant was ravaging the bazaar. Would I please come and do something about it? I did not know what I could do, but I wanted to see what was happening and I got on to a pony and started out. I took my rifle, an old .44 Winchester and much too small to kill an elephant, but I thought the noise might be useful *in terrorem.*[5] Various Burmans stopped me on the way and told me about the elephant's doings. It was not, of course, a wild elephant, but a tame one which had gone "must."[6] It had been chained up, as tame elephants always are when their attack of "must" is due, but on the previous night it had broken its chain and escaped. Its mahout,[7] the only person who could manage it when it was in that state, had set out in

---

1. BAZAARS: market places.
2. LOCK-UPS: jails.
3. RAJ: rule.
4. IN SAECULA SAECULORUM: "into centuries of centuries"—i.e., forever.
5. IN TERROREM: "into terror"—i.e., for scaring.
6. "MUST": into a state of frenzy, said of adult male elephants in periods of sexual excitement.
7. MAHOUT: keeper.

pursuit, but had taken the wrong direction and was now twelve hours' journey away, and in the morning the elephant had suddenly reappeared in the town. The Burmese population had no weapons and were quite helpless against it. It had already destroyed somebody's bamboo hut, killed a cow and raided some fruit-stalls and devoured the stock; also it had met the municipal rubbish van and, when the driver jumped out and took to his heels, had turned the van over and inflicted violences upon it.

The Burmese sub-inspector and some Indian constables were waiting for me in the quarter[8] where the elephant had been seen. It was a very poor quarter, a labyrinth of squalid bamboo huts, thatched with palm-leaf, winding all over a steep hillside. I remember that it was a cloudy, stuffy morning at the beginning of the rains. We began questioning the people as to where the elephant had gone and, as usual, failed to get any definite information. That is invariably the case in the East; a story always sounds clear enough at a distance, but the nearer you get to the scene of events the vaguer it becomes. Some of the people said that the elephant had gone in one direction, some said he had gone in another, some professed to have not even heard of an elephant. I had almost made up my mind that the whole story was a pack of lies, when we heard yells a distance away. There was a loud, scandalized cry of "Go away, child! Go away this instant!" and an old woman with a switch in her hand came round the corner of a hut, violently shooing away a crowd of naked children. Some more women followed, clicking their tongues and exclaiming; evidently there was something that the children ought not to have seen. I rounded the hut and saw a man's dead body sprawling in the mud. He was an Indian, a black Dravidian[9] coolie,[10] almost naked, and he could not have been dead many minutes. The people said that the elephant had come suddenly upon him round the corner of the hut, caught him with its trunk, put its foot on his back and ground him into the earth. This was the rainy season and the ground was soft, and his face had scored a trench a foot deep and a couple of yards long. He was lying on his belly with arms crucified and head sharply twisted to one side. His face was coated with mud, the eyes wide open, the teeth bared and grinning with an expression of unendurable agony. (Never tell me, by the way, that the dead look peaceful. Most of the corpses I have seen looked devilish.) The friction of the great beast's foot had stripped the skin from his back as neatly as one skins a rabbit. As soon as I saw the dead man I sent an orderly to a friend's house nearby to borrow an elephant rifle. I had already sent back the pony, not wanting it to go mad with fright and throw me if it smelt the elephant.

The orderly came back in a few minutes with a rifle and five cartridges, and meanwhile some Burmans had arrived and told us that the elephant was in the paddy fields[11] below, only a few hundred yards away. As I started forward practically the whole population of the quarter flocked out of the houses and followed me. They had seen the rifle and were all shouting excitedly that I was going to shoot the elephant. They had not shown much interest in the elephant when he was merely ravaging their homes, but it was different now that he was going to be shot. It was a bit of fun to them, as it would be to an English crowd; besides they wanted the meat. It made me vaguely uneasy. I had no intention of shooting the elephant—I had merely sent for the rifle to defend myself if necessary—and it is always unnerving to have a crowd following you. I marched down the hill, looking and feeling a fool, with the rifle over my shoulder and an ever-growing army of people jostling at my heels. At the bottom, when you got

8. QUARTER: a section of the town.
9. DRAVIDIAN: member of an ancient Indian race.
10. COOLIE: unskilled laborer.

11. PADDY FIELDS: rice fields.

away from the huts, there was a metaled road[12] and beyond that a miry waste of paddy fields a thousand yards across, not yet ploughed but soggy from the first rains and dotted with coarse grass. The elephant was standing eight yards from the road, his left side toward us. He took not the slightest notice of the crowd's approach. He was tearing up bunches of grass, beating them against his knees to clean them, and stuffing them into his mouth.

I had halted on the road. As soon as I saw the elephant I knew with perfect certainty that I ought not to shoot him. It is a serious matter to shoot a working elephant —it is comparable to destroying a huge costly piece of machinery—and obviously one ought not to do it if it can possibly be avoided. And at that distance, peacefully eating, the elephant looked no more dangerous than a cow. I thought then and I think now that his attack of "must" was already passing off; in which case he would merely wander harmlessly about until the mahout came back and caught him. Moreover, I did not in the least want to shoot him. I decided that I would watch him for a little while to make sure that he did not turn savage again, and then go home.

But at that moment I glanced round at the crowd that had followed me. It was an immense crowd, two thousand at the least and growing every minute. It blocked the road for a long distance on either side. I looked at the sea of yellow faces above the garish clothes—faces all happy and excited over this bit of fun, all certain that the elephant was going to be shot. They were watching me as they would watch a conjurer about to perform a trick. They did not like me, but with the magical rifle in my hands I was momentarily worth watching. And suddenly I realized that I should have to shoot the elephant after all. The people expected it of me and I had got to do it; I could feel their two thousand wills pressing me forward, irresistibly. And it was at this moment, as I stood there with the rifle in my hands, that I first grasped the hollowness, the futility of the white man's dominion in the East. Here was I, the white man with his gun, standing in front of the unarmed native crowd—seemingly the leading actor of the piece; but in reality I was only an absurd puppet pushed to and fro by the will of those yellow faces behind. I perceived in this moment that when the white man turns tyrant it is his own freedom that he destroys. He becomes a sort of hollow, posing dummy, the conventionalized figure of a sahib.[13] For it is the condition of his rule that he shall spend his life in trying to impress the "natives," and so in every crisis he has got to do what the "natives" expect of him. He wears a mask, and his face grows to fit it. I had got to shoot the elephant. I had committed myself to doing it when I sent for the rifle. A sahib has got to act like a sahib; he has got to appear resolute, to know his own mind and do definite things. To come all that way, rifle in hand, with two thousand people marching at my heels, and then to trail feebly away, having done nothing—no, that was impossible. The crowd would laugh at me. And my whole life, every white man's life in the East, was one long struggle not to be laughed at.

But I did not want to shoot the elephant. I watched him beating his bunch of grass against his knees with that preoccupied grandmotherly air that elephants have. It seemed to me that it would be murder to shoot him. At that age I was not squeamish about killing animals, but I had never shot an elephant and never wanted to. (Somehow it always seems worse to kill a *large* animal.) Besides, there was the beast's owner to be considered. Alive, the elephant was worth at least a hundred pounds; dead, he would only be worth the value of his tusks, five pounds, possibly. But I had got

---

12. METALED ROAD: road with a base of crushed stone.

13. SAHIB: master, usually used in reference to European officials.

to act quickly. I turned to some experienced-looking Burmans who had been there when we arrived, and asked them how the elephant had been behaving. They all said the same thing: he took no notice of you if you left him alone, but he might charge if you went too close to him.

It was perfectly clear to me what I ought to do. I ought to walk up to within, say, twenty-five yards of the elephant and test his behavior. If he charged, I could shoot; if he took no notice of me, it would be safe to leave him until the mahout came back. But also I knew that I was going to do no such thing. I was a poor shot with a rifle and the ground was soft mud into which one would sink at every step. If the elephant charged and I missed him, I should have about as much chance as a toad under a steam-roller. But even then I was not thinking particularly of my own skin, only of the watchful yellow faces behind. For at that moment, with the crowd watching me, I was not afraid in the ordinary sense, as I would have been if I had been alone. A white man mustn't be frightened in front of "natives"; and so, in general, he isn't frightened. The sole thought in my mind was that if anything went wrong those two thousand Burmans would see me pursued, caught, trampled on, and reduced to a grinning corpse like that Indian up the hill. And if that happened it was quite probable that some of them would laugh. That would never do. There was only one alternative. I shoved the cartridges into the magazine and lay down on the road to get a better aim.

The crowd grew very still, and a deep, low, happy sigh, as of people who see the theater curtain go up at last, breathed from innumerable throats. They were going to have their bit of fun after all. The rifle was a beautiful German thing with cross-hair sights. I did not then know that in shooting an elephant one would shoot to cut an imaginary bar running from ear-hole to ear-hole. I ought, therefore, as the elephant was sideways on, to have aimed straight at his ear-hole; actually I aimed several inches in front of this, thinking the brain would be further forward.

When I pulled the trigger I did not hear the bang or feel the kick—one never does when a shot goes home—but I heard the devilish roar of glee that went up from the crowd. In that instant, in too short a time, one would have thought, even for the bullet to get there, a mysterious, terrible change had come over the elephant. He neither stirred nor fell, but every line of his body had altered. He looked suddenly stricken, shrunken, immensely old, as though the frightful impact of the bullet had paralyzed him without knocking him down. At last, after what seemed a long time—it might have been five seconds, I dare say—he sagged flabbily to his knees. His mouth slobbered. An enormous senility seemed to have settled upon him. One could have imagined him thousands of years old. I fired again into the same spot. At the second shot he did not collapse but climbed with desperate slowness to his feet and stood weakly upright, with legs sagging and head drooping. I fired a third time. That was the shot that did for him. You could see the agony of it jolt his whole body and knock the last remnant of strength from his legs. But in falling he seemed for a moment to rise, for as his hind legs collapsed beneath him he seemed to tower upward like a huge rock toppling, his trunk reaching skyward like a tree. He trumpeted, for the first and only time. And then down he came, his belly toward me, with a crash that seemed to shake the ground even where I lay.

I got up. The Burmans were already racing past me across the mud. It was obvious that the elephant would never rise again, but he was not dead. He was breathing very rhythmically with long rattling gasps, his great mound of a side painfully rising and falling. His mouth was wide open—I could see far down into caverns of pale pink throat.

I waited a long time for him to die, but his breathing did not weaken. Finally I fired my two remaining shots into the spot where I thought his heart must be. The thick blood welled out of him like red velvet, but still he did not die. His body did not even jerk when the shots hit him, the tortured breathing continued without a pause. He was dying, very slowly and in great agony, but in some world remote from me where not even a bullet could damage him further. I felt that I had got to put an end to that dreadful noise. It seemed dreadful to see the great beast lying there, powerless to move and yet powerless to die, and not even to be able to finish him. I sent back for my small rifle and poured shot after shot into his heart and down his throat. They seemed to make no impression. The tortured gasps continued as steadily as the ticking of a clock.

In the end I could not stand it any longer and went away. I heard later that it took him half an hour to die. Burmans were bringing dahs[14] and baskets even before I left, and I was told they had stripped his body almost to the bones by the afternoon.

Afterward, of course, there were endless discussions about the shooting of the elephant. The owner was furious, but he was only an Indian and could do nothing. Besides, legally I had done the right thing, for a mad elephant has to be killed, like a mad dog, if its owner fails to control it. Among the Europeans opinion was divided. The older men said I was right, the younger men said it was a damn shame to shoot an elephant for killing a coolie, because an elephant was worth more than any damn Coringhee coolie. And afterward I was very glad that the coolie had been killed; it put me legally in the right and it gave me a sufficient pretext for shooting the elephant. I often wondered whether any of the others grasped that I had done it solely to avoid looking a fool.

_____
14. DAHS: large, heavy knives.

I

1. In the opening sentence Orwell says: "In Moulmein, in lower Burma, I was hated by large numbers of people—the only time in my life that I have been important enough for this to happen to me"; and in the first two paragraphs he uses such phrases as "had the guts to raise a riot," "the sooner I chucked up my job," and "the evil-spirited little beasts who tried to make my job impossible." How do these comments set a tone for the whole essay? What is the tone?

2. What is Orwell's attitude toward the Burmese? How is it revealed? He says, "Theoretically—and secretly, of course—I was all for the Burmese and all against their oppressors, the British." Are you convinced? Why or why not?

3. In paragraph 4 what is the effect of the sudden discovery of the dead Dravidian coolie and the detailed description of how he died and how he looked? How does the detached matter-of-factness of the first part of the paragraph heighten the shock of the discovery?

4. Reread the description of the dying elephant. With what other death scene in the episode does it contrast, and how?

5. In his last sentence Orwell says, "I often wondered whether any of the others grasped that I had done it solely to avoid looking a fool." How well do you suppose any of the others had grasped it? What does the last paragraph show about the attitudes of *the others*?

6. What is "the real nature of imperialism—the real motives for which despotic governments act"? How does the episode Orwell describes throw light on these motives?

II

1. What does Orwell mean by ". . . when the white man turns tyrant it is his own freedom he destroys"? To what extent is it true that even the leader of a *democratic* government has only limited freedom, since he must take into account what the people expect of him, what his own party expects of him, what the opposing parties demand of him? Give some instances that throw light on the problem from American history past and present.

2. There is certainly self-understanding here. Orwell knows full well why he should have *chucked the job.* Would you say, however, that he suggests that he would act any differently under similar circumstances another time? In other words, how much do you suppose he sees himself trapped by the realities of power and position? Can one simply *decide* to live differently once he faces the truth about himself and his society?

3. Orwell's experience is not an isolated one. We all feel the necessity to *impress the natives;* none of us likes to be laughed at. Indicate some instance when you have acted the fool in order to avoid looking like a fool. What notions of prestige, or face-saving, or misguided self-respect were you trying to maintain?

ANDREA DEL SARTO   [*1855*]

Robert Browning

This is another of Robert Browning's dramatic monologues, in which, as in "My Last Duchess," the speaker reveals more about himself than he intends to. The subject this time is Andrea del Sarto, an important painter of the sixteenth century, contemporary of Raphael, Michelangelo, and Leonardo da Vinci. The theme, however, is the nature of success.

Andrea is well aware of his supreme technical skill as he talks to his young and beautiful wife, who doesn't "care to understand." But he is also aware that his talent, now put to the service of his wife's petty desires, is mocked by the possibilities for a deeper kind of success in art that had once been his.

But do not let us quarrel any more,
No, my Lucrezia! bear with me for once:
Sit down and all shall happen as you wish.
You turn your face, but does it bring your heart?
I'll work then for your friend's friend, never fear,   5
Treat his own subject after his own way,
Fix his own time, accept too his own price,
And shut the money into this small hand
When next it takes mine. Will it? tenderly?
Oh, I'll content him,—but tomorrow, Love!   10
I often am much wearier than you think,
This evening more than usual: and it seems
As if—forgive now—should you let me sit
Here by the window, with your hand in mine,
And look a half hour forth on Fiesolè,   15
Both of one mind, as married people use,
Quietly, quietly the evening through,
I might get up tomorrow to my work
Cheerful and fresh as ever. Let us try.

---

2. LUCREZIA: his wife.
5. YOUR FRIEND'S: her lover's; see line 220.
15. FIESOLÈ: hill town overlooking Florence.
16. USE: are used to.

Tomorrow, how you shall be glad for this!   20
Your soft hand is a woman of itself,
And mine, the man's bared breast she curls inside.
Don't count the time lost, neither; you must serve
For each of the five pictures we require:
It saves a model. So! keep looking so—   25
My serpentining beauty, rounds on rounds!
—How could you ever prick those perfect ears,
Even to put the pearl there! oh, so sweet—
My face, my moon, my everybody's moon,
Which everybody looks on and calls his,   30
And, I suppose, is looked on by in turn,
While she looks—no one's: very dear, no less.
You smile? why, there's my picture ready made,
There's what we painters call our harmony!
A common grayness silvers everything,—   35
All in a twilight, you and I alike
—You, at the point of your first pride in me
(That's gone you know),—but I, at every point;
My youth, my hope, my art, being all toned down
To yonder sober pleasant Fiesolè.   40
There's the bell clinking from the chapel-top;
That length of convent-wall across the way
Holds the trees safer, huddled more inside;
The last monk leaves the garden; days decrease,
And autumn grows, autumn in everything.   45
Eh? the whole seems to fall into a shape
As if I saw alike my work and self
And all that I was born to be and do,
A twilight-piece. Love, we are in God's hand.
How strange now looks the life he makes us lead;   50
So free we seem, so fettered fast we are!
I feel he laid the fetter: let it lie!
This chamber for example—turn your head—
All that's behind us! You don't understand,
Nor care to understand, about my art,   55
But you can hear at least when people speak:
And that cartoon, the second from the door
—It is the thing, Love! so such thing should be—
Behold Madonna!—I am bold to say.
I can do with my pencil what I know,   60
What I see, what at bottom of my heart
I wish for, if I ever wish so deep—
Do easily, too—when I say, perfectly,

---

24. WE REQUIRE: i.e., for the "friend's friend."
26. SERPENTINING . . . ROUNDS: referring to her
    hair.
57. CARTOON: sketch; preliminary drawing.

I do not boast, perhaps: yourself are judge,
Who listened to the Legate's talk last week,   65
And just as much they used to say in France.
At any rate, 'tis easy, all of it!
No sketches first, no studies, that's long past:
I do what many dream of all their lives,
—Dream? strive to do, and agonize to do,   70
And fail in doing. I could count twenty such
On twice your fingers, and not leave this town,
Who strive—you don't know how the others strive
To paint a little thing like that you smeared
Carelessly passing with your robes afloat,—   75
Yet do much less, so much less, Someone says,
(I know his name, no matter)—so much less!
Well, less is more, Lucrezia: I am judged.
There burns a truer light of God in them,
In their vexed, beating, stuffed, and stopped-up brain,   80
Heart, or whate'er else, than goes on to prompt
This low-pulsed forthright craftsman's hand of mine.
Their works drop groundward, but themselves, I know,
Reach many a time a heaven that's shut to me,
Enter and take their place there sure enough,   85
Though they come back and cannot tell the world.
My works are nearer heaven, but I sit here.
The sudden blood of these men! at a word—
Praise them, it boils, or blame them, it boils too.
I, painting from myself and to myself,   90
Know what I do, am unmoved by men's blame
Or their praise either. Somebody remarks
Morello's outline there is wrongly traced,
His hue mistaken; what of that? or else,
Rightly traced and well ordered; what of that?   95
Speak as they please, what does the mountain care?
Ah, but a man's reach should exceed his grasp,
Or what's a heaven for? All is silver-gray,
Placid and perfect with my art: the worse!
I know both what I want and what might gain;   100
And yet how profitless to know, to sigh
"Had I been two, another and myself,
Our head would have o'erlooked the world!" No doubt.
Yonder's a work now, of that famous youth
The Urbinate who died five years ago.   105
('Tis copied, George Vasari sent it me.)

65. LEGATE: the Papal Legate.
66. IN FRANCE: see lines 149-165.
76. SOMEONE: Michelangelo; see line 199.
93. MORELLO: nearby mountain.
105. THE URBINATE: Raphael.

106. GEORGE VASARI: student of Andrea, who wrote *The Lives of the Most Eminent Painters, Sculptors, and Architects,* from which Browning took material for this poem.

Well, I can fancy how he did it all,
Pouring his soul, with kings and popes to see,
Reaching, that heaven might so replenish him,
Above and through his art—for it gives way;   110
That arm is wrongly put—and there again—
A fault to pardon in the drawing's lines,
Its body, so to speak: its soul is right,
He means right—that, a child may understand.
Still, what an arm! and I could alter it;   115
But all the play, the insight and the stretch—
Out of me, out of me! And wherefore out?
Had you enjoined them on me, given me soul,
We might have risen to Rafael, I and you.
Nay, Love, you did give all I asked, I think—   120
More than I merit, yes, by many times.
But had you—oh, with the same perfect brow,
And perfect eyes, and more than perfect mouth,
And the low voice my soul hears, as a bird
The fowler's pipe, and follows to the snare—   125
Had you, with these the same, but brought a mind!
Some women do so. Had the mouth there urged
"God and the glory! never care for gain.
The present by the future, what is that?
Live for fame, side by side with Agnolo!   130
Rafael is waiting: up to God, all three!"
I might have done it for you. So it seems:
Perhaps not. All is as God overrules.
Beside, incentives come from the soul's self;
The rest avail not. Why do I need you?   135
What wife had Rafael, or has Agnolo?
In this world, who can do a thing, will not;
And who would do it, cannot, I perceive:
Yet the will's somewhat—somewhat, too, the power—
And thus we half-men struggle. At the end,   140
God, I conclude, compensates, punishes.
'Tis safer for me, if the award be strict,
That I am something underrated here,
Poor this long while, despised, to speak the truth.
I dared not, do you know, leave home all day,   145
For fear of chancing on the Paris lords.
The best is when they pass and look aside;
But they speak sometimes; I must bear it all.
Well may they speak! That Francis, that first time,
And that long festal year at Fontainebleau!   150
I surely then could sometimes leave the ground,

130. AGNOLO: Michelangelo.
146. PARIS LORDS: from the court of Francis I.
149. FRANCIS: Francis I of France, great art
patron in whose court at Fontainebleau Andrea
had been employed.

Put on the glory, Rafael's daily wear,
In that humane great monarch's golden look,—
One finger in his beard or twisted curl
Over his mouth's good mark that made the smile,   155
One arm about my shoulder, round my neck,
The jingle of his gold chain in my ear,
I painting proudly with his breath on me,
All his court round him, seeing with his eyes,
Such frank French eyes, and such a fire of souls   160
Profuse, my hand kept plying by those hearts,—
And, best of all, this, this, this face beyond,
This in the background, waiting on my work,
To crown the issue with a last reward!
A good time, was it not, my kingly days?   165
And had you not grown restless . . . but I know—
'Tis done and past; 'twas right, my instinct said;
Too live the life grew, golden and not gray,
And I'm the weak-eyed bat no sun should tempt
Out of his grange whose four walls make his world.   170
How could it end in any other way?
You called me, and I came home to your heart.
The triumph was—to reach and stay there; since
I reached it ere the triumph, what is lost?
Let my hands frame your face in your hair's gold,   175
You beautiful Lucrezia that are mine!
"Rafael did this, Andrea painted that;
The Roman's is the better when you pray,
But still the other's Virgin was his wife—"
Men will excuse me. I am glad to judge   180
Both pictures in your presence; clearer grows
My better fortune, I resolve to think.
For, do you know, Lucrezia, as God lives,
Said one day Agnolo, his very self,
To Rafael . . . I have known it all these years . . .   185
(When the young man was flaming out his thoughts
Upon a palace-wall for Rome to see,
Too lifted up in heart because of it)
"Friend, there's a certain sorry little scrub
Goes up and down our Florence, none cares how,   190
Who, were he set to plan and execute
As you are, pricked on by your popes and kings,
Would bring the sweat into that brow of yours!"
To Rafael's!—And indeed the arm is wrong.
I hardly dare . . . yet, only you to see,   195
Give the chalk here—quick, thus the line should go!
Ay, but the soul! he's Rafael! rub it out!

---

162. THIS FACE: i.e., Lucrezia's.
178. THE ROMAN'S: Raphael's.

179. OTHER'S . . . WIFE: Lucrezia served as model
    for Andrea's Virgin Mary.

Still, all I care for, if he spoke the truth,
(What he? why, who but Michel Agnolo?
Do you forget already words like those?)   200
If really there was such a chance so lost,—
Is, whether you're—not grateful—but more pleased.
Well, let me think so. And you smile indeed!
This hour has been an hour! Another smile?
If you would sit thus by me every night   205
I should work better, do you comprehend?
I mean that I should earn more, give you more.
See, it is settled dusk now; there's a star;
Morello's gone, the watch-lights show the wall,
The cue-owls speak the name we call them by.   210
Come from the window, love,—come in, at last,
Inside the melancholy little house
We built to be so gay with. God is just.
King Francis may forgive me: oft at nights
When I look up from painting, eyes tired out,   215
The walls become illumined, brick from brick
Distinct, instead of mortar, fierce bright gold,
That gold of his I did cement them with!
Let us but love each other. Must you go?
That cousin here again? he waits outside?   220
Must see you—you, and not with me? Those loans?
More gaming debts to pay? you smiled for that?
Well, let smiles buy me! have you more to spend?
While hand and eye and something of a heart
Are left me, work's my ware, and what's it worth?   225
I'll pay my fancy. Only let me sit
The grey remainder of the evening out,
Idle, you call it, and muse perfectly
How I could paint, were I but back in France,
One picture, just one more—the Virgin's face,   230
Not yours this time! I want you at my side
To hear them—that is, Michel Agnolo—
Judge all I do and tell you of its worth.
Will you? Tomorrow, satisfy your friend.
I take the subjects for his corridor,   235
Finish the portrait out of hand—there, there,
And throw him in another thing or two
If he demurs; the whole should prove enough
To pay for this same cousin's freak. Beside,
What's better and what's all I care about,   240

210. CUE-OWLS: little owls, named after the sound   235   CORRIDOR: i.e., a corridor to be hung with
   they make.   Andrea's paintings.
220. COUSIN: lover.   239. COUSIN'S FREAK: see line 222.
226. I'LL . . . FANCY: I'll pay what it costs (i.e.,
   by working doubly hard tomorrow).

Get you the thirteen scudi for the ruff!
Love, does that please you? Ah, but what does he,
The cousin! what does he to please you more?
   I am grown peaceful as old age tonight.
I regret little, I would change still less.   245
Since there my past life lies, why alter it?
The very wrong to Francis!—it is true
I took his coin, was tempted and complied,
And built this house and sinned, and all is said.
My father and my mother died of want.   250
Well, had I riches of my own? you see
How one gets rich! Let each one bear his lot.
They were born poor, lived poor, and poor they died:
And I have labored somewhat in my time
And not been paid profusely. Some good son   255
Paint my two hundred pictures—let him try!
No doubt, there's something strikes a balance. Yes,
You loved me quite enough, it seems tonight.
This must suffice me here. What would one have?
In heaven, perhaps, new chances, one more chance—   260
Four great walls in the New Jerusalem
Meted on each side by the angel's reed,
For Leonard, Rafael, Agnolo and me
To cover—the three first without a wife,
While I have mine! So—still they overcome   265
Because there's still Lucrezia,—as I choose.
Again the cousin's whistle! Go, my Love.

---

241. SCUDI: plural of "scudo," Italian coin worth
    in Browning's time about a dollar. RUFF:
    elaborate collar for a dress.

261. NEW JERUSALEM: see Revelation 21:9-27.
262. METED: measured. REED: measuring rod.
263. LEONARD: Leonardo da Vinci.

I

1. Lucrezia is present from the first ("But do not let us quarrel any more") to the last ("Go, my Love"), but the only things we know of her come through Andrea's comments and his response to whatever she does or says. What is she like? Consider lines 1, 4, 37-38, 54-55, 74-75, 118-132, 166, 200, 205-207, 211-212, 242-243.

2. What kind of person is Andrea? Consider whether he is trying to justify his failure to "Put on the glory, Rafael's daily wear" (152), whether he seriously blames his wife for having beauty but not a mind, whether he *is* "the weak-eyed bat no sun should tempt" (169), and whether he means it when he says, "I regret little, I would change still less" (245).

3. Why does Andrea fear *chancing on the Paris lords*? What feeling of guilt does he have about his treatment of King Francis? What *was* his treatment of the King, so far as you can tell?

4. Explain the following lines:
a. "Well, less is more, Lucrezia: I am judged." (78)
b. lines 79-87.
c. "Ah, but a man's reach should exceed his grasp,
    Or what's a heaven for?" (97-98)
d. "In this world, who can do a thing, will not;
    And who would do it, cannot, I perceive:
    Yet the will's somewhat—somewhat, too, the power—

And thus we half-men struggle." (137-140)

e. ". . . And you smile indeed!
This hour has been an hour! Another smile?" (203-204)

f. "You loved me quite enough, it seems tonight.
This must suffice me here. What would one have?" (258-259)

5. Read the poem aloud, trying to communicate clearly the two-sidedness of the conversation. Comment on the way the rhythm of the poem matches the qualities in Andrea that Browning is stressing.

6. How does Browning's use of detail and imagery support the characterization he is making? Note, for instance, lines 35-36, 45, 98-99, 169-170, 208-212, 227, and 244.

7. Andrea says (69-71), "I do what many dream of all their lives,/—Dream? strive to do, and agonize to do,/And fail in doing." If he has reached such perfection in technique, why is he so conscious of failure? What is Browning saying about perfection and success?

II

1. Compare this poem of self-revelation with another of the same order, "The Love Song of J. Alfred Prufrock." Consider the degree of self-understanding each principal comes to, and the nature of the response each makes to his situation.

TO AN ATHLETE DYING YOUNG [*1896*]

A. E. Housman

In all the selections thus far there has been, either stated or implied, a conviction that there is such a thing as "success" and that we can gain it if we forsake the follies which incapacitate us. For Wordsworth, being "in tune" with Nature would bring a renewal of spirit; for Tomlinson, renouncing Fleet Street's drudgery and dullness opened up a new world.

However, it is perfectly possible to believe that success or glory is a fleeting thing at best—that "you can't win" in the long run no matter what you do. In the following poem, A. E. Housman takes a rather gloomy view of the permanence of fame, specifically athletic fame. Success here ironically comes with the end of all possible concern for "success."

The time you won your town the race
We chaired you through the market-place;
Man and boy stood cheering by,
And home we brought you shoulder-high.

Today, the road all runners come,   5
Shoulder-high we bring you home,
And set you at your threshold down,
Townsman of a stiller town.

Smart lad, to slip betimes away
From fields where glory does not stay   10
And early though the laurel grows
It withers quicker than the rose.

Eyes the shady night has shut
Cannot see the record cut,
And silence sounds no worse than cheers   15
After earth has stopped the ears:

Now you will not swell the rout
Of lads that wore their honors out,
Runners whom renown outran
And the name died before the man.   20

So set, before its echoes fade,
The fleet foot on the sill of shade,
And hold to the low lintel up
The still-defended challenge-cup.

And round that early-laureled head   25
Will flock to gaze the strengthless dead,
And find unwithered on its curls
The garland briefer than a girl's.

I

1. What is the situation of the poem as indicated in stanza 2? What previous event described in stanza 1 is being recalled? What words undergo a change of meaning in the first two stanzas?

2. Who is the speaker and whom is he addressing? Why does he call him "Smart lad"? In what sense do stanzas 3, 4, and 5 say the same thing to the *smart lad*? What specifically is the speaker advising him to do in stanza 6? How does what happens in the last stanza echo what happens in the first?

3. The basic metaphor Housman uses is that of foot-racing. Trace the expansion of this metaphor throughout the poem. What other extended metaphor is used, and how is it developed?

4. Explain fully the underlying paradox of the poem.

5. What is the tone of the poem: bitter? gloomy? casually conversational? mocking? pitying? indifferent? What do such phrases as "Smart lad," "silence sounds no worse than cheers/After earth has stopped the ears," and "lads that wore their honors out" contribute to the setting of the tone? What does the clever word-play in stanzas 1 and 2 contribute? Is the tone appropriate to the theme? Why or why not?

6. What do lines 11 and 12 mean? The *laurel* is a traditional symbol of victory. What is the *rose* a symbol of in the poem? How are both symbols active in the final stanza?

II

1. What assumption is the speaker making about the importance of fame? Go beyond athletics: How important is fame or distinction in any undertaking?

WESTMINSTER ABBEY

The Spectator No. 26: Friday, March 30, 1711

Joseph Addison

Housman's speaker in "To an Athlete Dying Young" might well have taken his theme from Ecclesiastes: "The heart of the wise is in the house of mourning; but the heart of a fool is in the house of mirth." Certainly for him the wise man would say that "all is vanity" and that glory is such a fleeting thing that we might all be better off without it in the first place.

In the issue of *The Spectator* that follows, Joseph Addison approaches the same problem of the meaning of earthly achievement or success with much the same recognition of its transitoriness, but with none of Housman's stoic pessimism. While looking at the digging of a grave in Westminster Abbey, he reflects that "beauty, strength, and youth, with old age, weakness, and deformity, lay undistinguished in the same promiscuous heap of matter," and asks us to view in the light of such a simple truth the significance of our pretensions and petty concerns. He does not say, as Housman seems to, that there is no lasting success in this life; rather, he suggests that perhaps it is wise to give no thought to whether there is or not.

Pallida mors aequo pulsat pede pauperum
    tabernas
  Regumque turres. O beate Sesti,
Vitae summa brevis spem nos vetat incohare
    longam:
  Jam te premet nox, fabulaeque manes,
Et domus exilis Plutonia————.[1]

             Horace, Odes, I, IV, 13

When I am in a serious humor, I very often walk by myself in Westminster Abbey;[2] where the gloominess of the place, and the use to which it is applied, with the solemnity of the building, and the condition of the people who lie in it, are apt to fill the mind with a kind of melancholy, or rather thoughtfulness, that is not disagreeable. I yesterday passed a whole afternoon in the churchyard, the cloisters, and the church, amusing myself with the tombstones and inscriptions that I met with in those several regions of the dead. Most of them recorded nothing else of the buried person, but that he was born upon one day, and died upon another: the whole history of his life being comprehended in those two circumstances that are common to all mankind. I could not but look upon these registers of existence, whether of brass or marble, as a kind of satire upon the departed persons; who had left no other me-

morial of them but that they were born, and that they died. They put me in mind of several persons mentioned in the battles of heroic poems,[3] who have sounding names given them, for no other reason but that they may be killed, and are celebrated for nothing but being knocked on the head. . . . The life of these men is finely described in Holy Writ by "the path of an arrow," which is immediately closed up and lost.

Upon my going into the church, I entertained myself with the digging of a grave; and saw in every shovelful of it that was thrown up the fragment of a bone or skull intermixed with a kind of fresh moldering earth that some time or other had a place in the composition of an human body. Upon this, I began to consider with myself, what innumerable multitudes of people lay confused together under the pavement of that ancient Cathedral; how men and women, friends and enemies, priests and soldiers, monks and prebendaries, were crumbled amongst one another, and blended together in the same common mass; how beauty, strength, and youth, with old age, weakness, and deformity, lay undistinguished in the same promiscuous heap of matter.

After having thus surveyed this great magazine of mortality, as it were, in the lump, I examined it more particularly by the accounts which I found on several of the monuments which are raised in every quarter of that ancient fabric. Some of them were covered with such extravagant epitaphs that, if it were possible for the dead person to be acquainted with them, he would blush at the praises which his friends have bestowed upon him. There are others so excessively

1. Epigraph.
  With equal foot, rich friend, impartial fate
  Knocks at the cottage, and the palace gate;
  Life's span forbids thee to extend thy cares,
  And stretch thy hopes beyond thy years;
  Night soon will seize, and you must quickly go
  To storied ghosts, and Pluto's house below.
             Creech.
2. WESTMINSTER ABBEY: in London, perhaps the most famous of English cathedrals; the burial place of royalty and of many of England's leaders in politics, the military, and the arts, some well-remembered, some not remembered. Addison himself is buried there.

3. HEROIC POEMS: epics, i.e., the *Iliad* by Homer and the *Aeneid* by Virgil.

modest that they deliver the character of the person departed in Greek or Hebrew, and by that means are not understood once in a twelve-month. In the poetical quarter, I found there were poets who had no monuments, and monuments which had no poets. I observed, indeed, that the present war had filled the church with many of these uninhabited monuments, which had been erected to the memory of persons whose bodies were perhaps buried in the plains of Blenheim,[4] or in the bosom of the ocean.

I could not but be very much delighted with several modern epitaphs, which are written with great elegance of expression and justness of thought, and therefore do honor to the living as well as to the dead. As a foreigner is very apt to conceive an idea of the ignorance or politeness[5] of a nation from the turn of their public monuments and inscriptions, they should be submitted to the perusal of men of learning and genius before they are put in execution. Sir Cloudesley Shovel's[6] monument has very often given me great offense. Instead of the brave, rough, English admiral, which was the distinguishing character of that plain, gallant man, he is represented on his tomb by the figure of a beau, dressed in a long periwig, and reposing himself upon velvet cushions under a canopy of state. The inscription is answerable to[7] the monument; for, instead of celebrating the many remarkable actions he had performed in the service of his country, it acquaints us only with the manner of his death,[8] in which it was impossible for him to reap any honor. The Dutch, whom we

are apt to despise for want[9] of genius, show an infinitely greater taste of antiquity and politeness in their buildings and works of this nature, than what we meet with in those of our own country. The monuments of their admirals, which have been erected at the public expense, represent them like themselves, and are adorned with rostral crowns and naval ornaments, with beautiful festoons of seaweed, shells, and coral.

But to return to our subject. I have left the repository of our English kings for the contemplation of another day, when I shall find my mind disposed for so serious an amusement. I know that entertainments of this nature are apt to raise dark and dismal thoughts in timorous minds and gloomy imaginations; but for my own part, though I am always serious, I do not know what it is to be melancholy; and can therefore take a view of nature in her deep and solemn scenes, with the same pleasure as in her most gay and delightful ones. By this means I can improve myself with those objects, which others consider with terror. When I look upon the tombs of the great, every emotion of envy dies in me; when I read the epitaphs of the beautiful, every inordinate desire goes out; when I meet with the grief of parents upon a tombstone, my heart melts with compassion; when I see the tomb of the parents themselves, I consider the vanity of grieving for those whom we must quickly follow. When I see kings lying by those who deposed them, when I consider rival wits[10] placed side by side, or the holy men that divided the world with their contests and disputes, I reflect with sorrow and astonishment on the little competitions, factions, and debates of mankind. When I read the several dates of the tombs, of some that died yesterday, and some six hundred years ago, I consider that great day [11] when we shall all of us be contemporaries, and make our appearance together.

---

4. BLENHEIM: site in Bavaria of a great English victory over France and Bavaria in August, 1704.
5. POLITENESS: refinement.
6. SIR CLOUDESLEY SHOVEL: English admiral (1650-1707); commander-in-chief of the fleet, 1705.
7. IS ANSWERABLE TO: matches.
8. MANNER . . . DEATH: On his return from an unsuccessful attack on Toulon, France, Shovel's ship struck a rock in the fog and he was drowned.

---

9. WANT: lack.
10. WITS: i.e., writers.
11. THAT GREAT DAY: Judgment Day.

I

1. What is the tone of the essay: melancholy? amused? bemused? casual? meditative? somber? detached? a combination of these? Consider particularly such phrases as: "being knocked on the head," "multitudes of people lay confused together," "crumbled amongst one another," "this great magazine of mortality, as it were, in the lump."

2. What is the main point of the last paragraph? How is it prepared for and developed?

3. In what ways does the speaker feel he improves himself by such visitations as this one?

4. What is the speaker saying about fame or achievement: that it doesn't last, so it's foolish to strive for it? that a person should not concern himself with whether his successes are remembered or not? that the truly wise man lives for the moment and ignores the past and the future? what?

The Creation of Contentment: Two Essays

If Emerson is right that "The world is enlarged for us, not by new objects, but by finding more affinities and potencies in those we have," then the following two essays suggest, rather simply, ways in which enlargement can come.

At first glance, neither essay may seem to have much to do with the idea of "success." "A Night Among the Pines" is one of a series of essays by Robert Louis Stevenson, *Travels with a Donkey,* recounting his trip through the Cévennes mountains in southeastern France. In this particular essay he describes a night spent alone out-of-doors far from any village or farmhouse. The attitude Stevenson adopts toward what happens to him during that night among the pines is a striking illustration of the wisdom of Emerson's advice to "find the day and its cheap means contenting, which ask only receptivity in you, and no strained exertion and cankering ambition."

In a different vein, "Old China" also underscores Emerson's advice. Charles Lamb and his sister, Mary (called Bridget in the essay), were Londoners first and last, city-dwellers who loved their city. To a friend in Cambridge Lamb wrote, "Ain't you mightily moped [dreary] on the banks of the Cam? Had you not better come and set up here? You can't think what a difference. All the streets and pavements are pure gold, I warrant you. At least I know an alchemy that turns her mud into that metal—a mind that loves to be at home in crowds." In "Old China" that mind dwells on the delights that can be had for very little. As with Stevenson, it is Lamb's attitude toward what the world has to offer, particularly to the young—"the day and its cheap means . . . which ask only receptivity in you"—that brings him, at least for the time, a full measure of successful living.

A NIGHT AMONG THE PINES   [*1879*]

Robert Louis Stevenson

From Bleymard[1] after dinner, although it was already late, I set out to scale a portion of the Lozère.[2] An ill-marked stony drove-road[3] guided me forward; and I met nearly half a dozen bullock carts descending from the woods, each laden with a whole pine tree for the winter's firing. At the top of the woods, which do not climb very high upon this cold ridge, I struck[4] leftward by a path among the pines, until I hit on a dell of green turf, where a streamlet made a little spout over some stones to serve me for a water-tap. "In a more sacred or sequestered bower—nor nymph nor faunus[5] haunted." The trees were not old, but they grew thickly round the glade: there was no outlook, except northeastward upon distant hilltops, or straight upward to the sky; and the encampment felt secure and private like a room. By the time I had made my arrangements and fed Modestine,[6] the day was already beginning to decline. I buckled myself to the knees into my sack[7] and made a hearty meal; and as soon as the sun went down, I pulled my cap over my eyes and fell asleep.

Night is a dead monotonous period under a roof; but in the open world it passes lightly, with its stars and dews and perfumes, and the hours are marked by changes in the face of Nature. What seems a kind of temporal death to people choked between walls and curtains, is only a light and living slumber to the man who sleeps afield. All night long he can hear Nature breathing deeply and freely; even as she takes her rest she turns and smiles; and there is one stirring hour unknown to those who dwell in houses, when a wakeful influence goes abroad over the sleeping hemisphere, and all the outdoor world are on their feet. It is then that the cock first crows, not this time to announce the dawn, but like a cheerful watchman speeding the course of night. Cattle awake on the meadows; sheep break their fast on dewy hillsides, and change to a new lair among the ferns; and houseless men, who have lain down with the fowls, open their dim eyes and behold the beauty of the night.

At what inaudible summons, at what gentle touch of Nature, are all these sleepers thus recalled in the same hour to life? Do the stars rain down an influence, or do we share some thrill of mother earth below our resting bodies? Even shepherds and old country-folk, who are the deepest read in these arcana, have not a guess as to the means or purpose of this nightly resurrection. Towards two in the morning they declare the thing takes place; and neither know nor inquire further. And at least it is a pleasant incident. We are disturbed in our slumber only, like the luxurious Montaigne,[8] "that we may the better and more sensibly relish it." We have a moment to look upon the stars, and there is a special pleasure for some minds in the reflection that we share the impulse with all outdoor creatures in our neighborhood, that we have escaped out of the Bastille[9] of civilization, and are become, for the time being, a mere kindly animal and a sheep of Nature's flock.

When that hour came to me among the pines, I wakened thirsty. My tin was standing by me half full of water. I emptied it at a draught; and feeling broad awake after this internal cold aspersion, sat upright to make

1. BLEYMARD: a town in the Cévennes mountain region in southern France.
2. THE LOZÈRE: a range in the Cévennes.
3. DROVE-ROAD: road for driving sheep and goats.
4. STRUCK: headed.
5. FAUNUS: a rural deity.
6. MODESTINE: his donkey.
7. SACK: sleeping bag.

8. MONTAIGNE: French author (1533-1595), ideal Renaissance gentleman-scholar.
9. BASTILLE: infamous Paris prison.

a cigarette. The stars were clear, colored, and jewel-like, but not frosty. A faint silvery vapor stood for the Milky Way. All around me the black fir-points stood upright and stockstill. By the whiteness of the pack-saddle, I could see Modestine walking round and round at the length of her tether; I could hear her steadily munching at the sward; but there was not another sound, save the indescribable quiet talk of the runnel over the stones. I lay lazily smoking and studying the color of the sky, as we call the void of space, from where it showed a reddish gray behind the pines to where it showed a glossy blue-black between the stars. As if to be more like a pedlar, I wear a silver ring. This I could see faintly shining as I raised or lowered the cigarette; and at each whiff the inside of my hand was illuminated, and became for a second the highest light in the landscape.

A faint wind, more like a moving coolness than a stream of air, passed down the glade from time to time; so that even in my great chamber the air was being renewed all night long. I thought with horror of the inn at Chaseradès[10] and the congregated nightcaps;[11] with horror of the nocturnal prowesses of clerks and students, of hot theaters and pass-keys and close rooms.[12] I have not often enjoyed a more serene possession of myself, nor felt more independent of material aids. The outer world, from which we cower into our houses, seemed after all a gentle habitable place; and night after night a man's bed, it seemed, was laid and waiting for him in the fields, where God keeps an open house. I thought I had rediscovered one of those truths which are revealed to savages and hid from political economists: at the least, I had discovered a new pleasure for myself. And yet even while I was exulting in my solitude I became aware of a strange lack. I wished a companion to lie near me in the starlight, silent and not moving, but ever within touch. For there is a fellowship more quiet even than solitude, and which, rightly understood, is solitude made perfect. And to live out of doors with the woman a man loves is of all lives the most complete and free.

As I thus lay between content and longing, a faint noise stole towards me through the pines. I thought, at first, it was the crowing of cocks or the barking of dogs at some very distant farm; but steadily and gradually it took articulate shape in my ears, until I became aware that a passenger was going by upon the high-road[13] in the valley, and singing loudly as he went. There was more of goodwill than grace in his performance; but he trolled with ample lungs; and the sound of his voice took hold upon the hillside and set the air shaking in the leafy glens. I have heard people passing by night in sleeping cities; some of them sang; one, I remember, played loudly on the bagpipes. I have heard the rattle of a cart or carriage spring up suddenly after hours of stillness, and pass, for some minutes, within the range of my hearing as I lay abed. There is a romance about all who are abroad in the black hours, and with something of a thrill we try to guess their business. But here the romance was double: first, this glad passenger, lit internally with wine, who sent up his voice in music through the night; and then I, on the other hand, buckled into my sack, and smoking alone in the pine woods between four and five thousand feet towards the stars.

When I awoke again . . . many of the stars had disappeared; only the stronger companions of the night still burned visibly overhead; and away towards the east I saw a faint haze of light upon the horizon such as had been the Milky Way when I was last awake. Day was at hand. I lit my lantern,

10. CHASERADÈS: another town in the Cévennes, where he had spent the previous night.
11. CONGREGATED NIGHTCAPS: i.e., with its inmates sound asleep in their beds, with their nightcaps on; mentioned in the preceding essay in *Travels with a Donkey.*
12. NOCTURNAL . . . ROOMS: referring to those who keep late hours in towns.

13. HIGH-ROAD: highway.

and by its glowworm light put on my boots and gaiters; then I broke up some bread for Modestine, filled my can at the water-tap, and lit my spirit-lamp[14] to boil myself some chocolate. The blue darkness lay long in the glade where I had so sweetly slumbered; but soon there was a broad streak of orange melting into gold along the mountain-tops of Vivarais.[15] A solemn glee possessed my mind at this gradual and lovely coming in of day. I heard the runnel with delight; I looked round me for something beautiful and un-expected; but the still black pine trees, the hollow glade, the munching ass, remained unchanged in figure. Nothing had altered but the light, and that, indeed, shed over all a spirit of life and of breathing peace, and moved me to a strange exhilaration.

I drank my water chocolate, which was hot if it was not rich, and strolled here and there, and up and down about the glade. While I was thus delaying, a gush of steady wind, as long as a heavy sigh, poured direct

---

14. SPIRIT-LAMP: alcohol lamp.
15. VIVARAIS: the district in southern France he is traveling through.

out of the quarter of the morning. It was cold, and set me sneezing. The trees near at hand tossed their black plumes in its passage; and I could see the thin distant spires of pine along the edge of the hill rock slightly to and fro against the golden east. Ten minutes after, the sunlight spread at a gallop along the hillside, scattering shadows and sparkles, and the day had come completely.

I hastened to prepare my pack, and tackle the steep ascent that lay before me; but I had something on my mind. It was only a fancy; yet a fancy will sometimes be importunate. I had been most hospitably received and punctually served in my green caravanserai. The room was airy, the water excellent, and the dawn had called me to a moment.[16] I say nothing of the tapestries or the inimitable ceiling, nor yet of the view which I com-manded from the windows; but I felt I was in someone's debt for all this liberal enter-tainment. And so it pleased me, in a half-laughing way, to leave pieces of money on the turf as I went along, until I had left enough for my night's lodging. I trust they did not fall to some rich and churlish drover.

---

16. CALLED . . . MOMENT: awakened me on time.

I

1. What little-known phenomenon is the speaker describing in paragraphs 2-4? Why did he awaken? Why does he remain awake?

2. In paragraph 5, with what does he com-pare his night among the pines? Point out what details develop the comparison. What does he lack in *God's open house*?

3. How does the first sentence of paragraph 6 provide a transition between what has gone before and what is to follow? What does he mean by, "There is a romance about all who are abroad in the black hours. . . . But here the romance was double"?

4. To convince the reader of the impact that the night's experience had on him, Stevenson tries to strike a responsive note in all the senses: sight, sound, smell, touch. Point out examples

of details directed at each of these senses. Note particularly his stress on color.

5. Point out some places where he describes the glade as if it were a room. What does he gain by so doing? What in the last paragraph completes the comparison in an unusual way?

6. Stevenson says, "I thought I had redis-covered one of those truths which are re-vealed to savages and hid from political econo-mists. . . ." Just what is the *truth* he thought he had *rediscovered*?

II

1. In the same kind of personal essay, try to recreate an experience you have had that brought you, to use Stevenson's phrase, a *new pleasure*. Choose one in which there is the sort of rediscovery Stevenson writes about, one which illustrates that pleasure can be found in the ordinary round of activities.

OLD CHINA

Charles Lamb

I have an almost feminine partiality for old china. When I go to see any great house, I inquire for the china-closet, and next for the picture gallery. I cannot defend the order of preference, but by saying, that we have all some taste or other, of too ancient a date to admit of our remembering distinctly that it was an acquired one. I can call to mind the first play, and the first exhibition, that I was taken to; but I am not conscious of a time when jars and saucers were introduced into my imagination.

I had no repugnance then—why should I now have?—to those little, lawless, azure-tinctured grotesques, that under the notion of men and women, float about, uncircumscribed by any element, in that world before perspective—a china tea-cup.[1]

I like to see my old friends—whom distance cannot diminish—figuring up in the air (so they appear to our optics), yet on *terra firma* still—for so we must in courtesy interpret that speck of deeper blue,—which the decorous artist, to prevent absurdity, had made to spring up beneath their sandals.

I love the men with women's faces, and the women, if possible, with still more womanish expressions.

Here is a young and courtly Mandarin, handing tea to a lady from a salver—two miles off. See how distance seems to set off respect! And here the same lady, or another —for likeness is identity on tea-cups—is stepping into a little fairy boat, moored on the hither side of this calm garden river, with a dainty mincing foot, which in a right angle of incidence (as angles go in our world) must infallibly land her in the midst of a flowery mead—a furlong off on the other side of the same strange stream!

Farther on—if far or near can be predicated of their world—see horses, trees, pagodas, dancing the hays.[2]

Here—a cow and rabbit couchant, and co-extensive—so objects show, seen through the lucid atmosphere of fine Cathay.[3]

I was pointing out to my cousin[4] last evening, over our Hyson[5] (which we are old-fashioned enough to drink unmixed still of an afternoon) some of these *speciosa miracula*[6] upon a set of extraordinary old blue china (a recent purchase) which we were now for the first time using; and could not help remarking, how favorable circumstances had been to us of late years, that we could afford to please the eye sometimes with trifles of this sort—when a passing sentiment seemed to overshade the brows of my companion. I am quick at detecting these summer clouds in Bridget.

"I wish the good old times would come again," she said, "when we were not quite so rich. I do not mean, that I want to be poor; but there was a middle state"—so she was pleased to ramble on,—"in which I am sure we were a great deal happier. A purchase is but a purchase, now that you have money enough and to spare. Formerly it used to be a triumph. When we coveted a cheap luxury (and, O! how much ado I had to get you to consent in those times!)—we

---

1. CHINA TEA-CUP: In this and the following five paragraphs the speaker is describing the scenes pictured on pieces of china. There is an unreal quality about the scenes because all sense of proportion or perspective is missing. The speaker tries to describe the topsy-turvy world which his "old friends" (the figures on the pieces) inhabit.

2. HAYS: a rustic dance in which the dancers weave in and out.
3. CATHAY: china.
4. COUSIN: his sister, Mary Lamb, called Bridget in this essay.
5. HYSON: a green tea.
6. SPECIOSA MIRACULA: "glorious wonders."

were used to have a debate two or three days before, and to weigh the *for* and *against,* and think what we might spare it out of, and what saving we could hit upon, that should be an equivalent. A thing was worth buying then, when we felt the money that we paid for it.

"Do you remember the brown suit, which you made to hang upon you, till all your friends cried shame upon you, it grew so threadbare—and all because of that folio Beaumont and Fletcher,[7] which you dragged home late at night from Barker's[8] in Covent Garden?[9] Do you remember how we eyed it for weeks before we could make up our minds to the purchase, and had not come to a determination till it was near ten o'clock of the Saturday night, when you set off from Islington,[10] fearing you should be too late—and when the old bookseller with some grumbling opened his shop, and by the twinkling taper (for he was setting bedwards) lighted out the relic from his dusty treasures—and when you lugged it home, wishing it were twice as cumbersome—and when you presented it to me—and when we were exploring the perfectness of it (*collating* you called it)—and while I was repairing some of the loose leaves with paste, which your impatience would not suffer to be left till daybreak—was there no pleasure in being a poor man? or can those neat black clothes which you wear now, and are so careful to keep brushed, since we have become rich and finical, give you half the honest vanity, with which you flaunted it about in that overworn suit—your old corbeau[11]—for four or five weeks longer than you should have done, to pacify your conscience for the mighty sum of fifteen—or sixteen shillings was it?—a great affair we thought it then—which you had lavished on the old folio.

Now you can afford to buy any book that pleases you, but I do not see that you ever bring me home any nice old purchases now.

"When you came home with twenty apologies for laying out a less number of shillings upon that print after Lionardo,[12] which we christened the 'Lady Blanch'; when you looked at the purchase, and thought of the money—and thought of the money, and looked again at the picture—was there no pleasure in being a poor man? Now, you have nothing to do but to walk into Colnaghi's,[13] and buy a wilderness of Lionardos. Yet do you?

"Then, do you remember our pleasant walks to Enfield, and Potter's bar, and Waltham,[14] when we had a holiday—holidays, and all other fun, are gone now we are rich—and the little hand-basket in which I used to deposit our day's fare of savory cold lamb and salad—and how you would pry about at noontide for some decent house,[15] where we might go in and produce our store—only paying for the ale that you must call for—and speculate upon the looks of the landlady, and whether she was likely to allow us a table-cloth—and wish for such another honest hostess, as Izaak Walton has described many a one on the pleasant banks of the Lea,[16] when he went a fishing—and sometimes they would prove obliging enough, and sometimes they would look grudgingly upon us—but we had cheerful looks still for one another, and would eat our plain food savorily, scarcely grudging Piscator his Trout Hall?[17] Now—when we go out a day's pleasuring, which is seldom moreover, we *ride* part of the way—and go into a fine inn, and order the best of dinners, never debating the expense—which after all never has

---

7. FOLIO . . . FLETCHER: a large collected edition of the works of two early seventeenth-century English dramatists.
8. BARKER'S: a bookseller.
9. COVENT GARDEN: a section of London.
10. ISLINGTON: a suburb of London.
11. CORBEAU: dark coat.

12. LIONARDO: Leonardo da Vinci.
13. COLNAGHI'S: London picture dealer.
14. ENFIELD . . . WALTHAM: towns about ten miles from London.
15. HOUSE: inn.
16. IZAAK . . . LEA: in his *The Compleat Angler.*
17. PISCATOR . . . HALL: Piscator is the chief character in *The Compleat Angler.* Trout Hall is his favorite inn.

half the relish of those chance country snaps,[18] when we were at the mercy of uncertain usage, and a precarious welcome.

"You are too proud to see a play anywhere now but in the pit.[19] Do you remember where it was we used to sit, when we saw the *Battle of Hexham,* and the *Surrender of Calais,* and Bannister and Mrs. Bland in the *Children in the Wood*[20]—when we squeezed out our shillings apiece to sit three or four times in a season in the one-shilling gallery—where you felt all the time you ought not to have brought me—and more strongly I felt obligation to you for having brought me—and the pleasure was the better for a little shame—and when the curtain drew up, what cared we for our place in the house, or what mattered it where we were sitting, when our thoughts were with Rosalind in Arden,[21] or with Viola at the Court of Illyria?[22] You used to say, that the gallery was the best place of all for enjoying a play socially—that the relish of such exhibitions must be in proportion to the infrequency of going—that the company we met there, not being in general readers of plays, were obliged to attend the more, and did attend, to what was going on, on the stage—because a word lost would have been a chasm, which it was impossible for them to fill up. With such reflections we consoled our pride then—and I appeal to you, whether, as a woman, I met generally with less attention and accommodation, than I have done since in more expensive situations in the house? The getting in indeed, and the crowding up those inconvenient staircases, was bad enough,—but there was still a law of civility to woman recognized to quite as great an extent as we ever found in the other

passages—and how a little difficulty overcome heightened the snug seat and the play, afterwards! Now we can only pay our money and walk in. You cannot see, you say, in the galleries now. I am sure we saw, and heard too, well enough then—but sight, and all I think, is gone with our poverty.

"There was pleasure in eating strawberries, before they became quite common—in the first dish of peas, while they were yet dear—to have them for a nice supper, a treat. What treat can we have now? If we were to treat ourselves now—that is, to have dainties a little above our means, it would be selfish and wicked. It is the very little more that we allow ourselves beyond what the actual poor can get at, that makes what I call a treat—when two people living together, as we have done, now and then indulge themselves in a cheap luxury, which both like; while each apologizes, and is willing to take both halves of the blame to his single share. I see no harm in people making much of themselves, in that sense of the word. It may give them a hint how to make much of others. But now—what I mean by the word —we never do make much of ourselves. None but the poor can do it. I do not mean the veriest poor of all, but persons as we were, just above poverty.

"I know what you were going to say, that it is mighty pleasant at the end of the year to make all meet—and much ado we used to have every Thirty-first Night of December to account for our exceedings— many a long face did you make over your puzzled accounts, and in contriving to make it out how we had spent so much—or that we had not spent so much—or that it was impossible we should spend so much next year —and still we found our slender capital decreasing—but then, betwixt ways, and projects, and compromises of one sort or another, and talk of curtailing this charge, and doing without that for the future—and the hope that youth brings, and laughing

---

18. SNAPS: meals.
19. PIT: orchestra.
20. BATTLE . . . WOOD: popular plays of the time; John Bannister and Mrs. Bland were well-known performers.
21. ROSALIND IN ARDEN: in Shakespeare's *As You Like It.*
22. VIOLA . . . ILLYRIA: in Shakespeare's *Twelfth Night.*

now), we pocketed up our loss, and in conclusion, with 'lusty brimmers'[23] (as you used to quote it out of *hearty cheerful Mr. Cotton,*[24] as you called him), we used to welcome in the 'coming guest.' Now we have no reckoning at all at the end of the old year—no flattering promises about the new year doing better for us."

Bridget is so sparing of her speech on most occasions, that when she gets into a rhetorical vein, I am careful how I interrupt it. I could not help, however, smiling at the phantom of wealth which her dear imagination had conjured up out of a clear income of poor—hundred pounds a year. "It is true we were happier when we were poorer, but we were also younger, my cousin. I am afraid we must put up with the excess, for if we were to shake the superflux into the sea, we should not much mend ourselves. That we had much to struggle with, as we grew up together, we have reason to be most thankful. It strengthened, and knit our compact closer. We could never have been what we have been to each other, if we had always had the sufficiency which you now complain of. The resisting power—those natural dilations of the youthful spirit, which circumstances cannot straiten—with us are long since passed away. Competence to age is supplementary youth, a sorry supplement indeed, but I fear the best that is to be had. We must ride where we formerly walked—

23. 'LUSTY BRIMMERS': big glasses of beer or ale.
24. MR. COTTON: Charles Cotton (1630-1687), English poet, who wrote a second part to the 5th edition of Walton's *The Compleat Angler.*

live better and lie softer—and shall be wise to do so—than we had means to do in those good old days you speak of. Yet could those days return—could you and I once more walk our thirty miles a day—could Bannister and Mrs. Bland again be young, and you and I be young to see them—could the good old one-shilling gallery days return—they are dreams, my cousin, now—but could you and I at this moment, instead of this quiet argument, by our well-carpeted fire-side, sitting on this luxurious sofa—be once more struggling up those inconvenient staircases, pushed about, and squeezed, and elbowed by the poorest rabble of poor gallery scramblers—could I once more hear those anxious shrieks of yours—and the delicious *Thank God, we are safe,* which always followed when the topmost stair, conquered, let in the first light of the cheerful theater down beneath us—I know not the fathom line[25] that ever touched a descent so deep as I would be willing to bury more wealth in than Croesus[26] had, or the great Jew R[27] —is supposed to have, to purchase it. And now do just look at that merry little Chinese waiter holding an umbrella, big enough for a bed-tester,[28] over the head of that pretty insipid half Madonna-ish chit of a lady in that very blue summer-house."

25. FATHOM LINE: sounding line, for measuring ocean depths.
26. CROESUS: ancient king in Asia Minor, legendary for his wealth.
27. THE GREAT JEW R: Nathan Meyer Rothschild (1777-1836), head of a great English banking firm.
28. BED-TESTER: bed canopy.

I

1. Obviously, this is in no sense a normal conversation. What does Lamb gain by using two speakers, both of whom speak at great length without being interrupted? Characterize each of the speakers.

2. What are the advantages, as Bridget sees them, of living *just above poverty?* What advantages does the original speaker indicate there were in having been through poverty? Why does he feel that the comforts they now have are a good thing?

3. Why is the title "Old China"? Why does the speaker go into such detail about the scenes on the china? Characterize the scenes. With what in the essay do they contrast? Why does the speaker return to the china in the last sentence?

II

1. In your own experience, how valid is the point of view that things which are not purchased easily bring the most pleasure?

2. Both "A Night among the Pines" and

"Old China" show how it is possible and fruitful to *find the day and its cheap means contenting, which ask only receptivity in you.* The first essay deals with experiences in a remote mountain region of southern France; the second deals with those in the bustle of the world's most densely populated metropolitan area. The differences between the essays are obvious. What do they have in common? Consider more than is indicated in the first sentence of this question (such concerns, for instance, as tone and the use of contrast).

ODE TO A NIGHTINGALE [*1819*]

John Keats

There is a serenity in both "A Night Among the Pines" and "Old China" that lulls us into the unwarranted conviction that if we would but live in the "happy, sufficing present" and shun the activities that dehumanize us, all would be well. The trouble is that by our very natures the present cannot always be "happy" or "sufficing," and certainly neither Stevenson nor Lamb was suggesting that it can. What the reader might overlook in reading their essays is the complexity of human nature that subjects us to constant changes of what are popularly known as "moods."

It is just this complexity that Keats dramatizes so brilliantly in his "Ode to a Nightingale." Over against an awareness of a real world dominated by "The weariness, the fever, and the fret/Here, where men sit and hear each other groan," he sets the world of the imagination, whose pure delights transport man temporarily out of the sorrows that beset him, and yet, paradoxically, make him more sharply aware of those sorrows. Keats is not deploring the unfairness of man's lot nor bemoaning the fact that the moments of intense pleasure the imagination brings are short-lived; he is simply saying that these moments, short as they are, remake the world.

I

My heart aches, and a drowsy numbness pains
    My sense, as though of hemlock I had drunk,
Or emptied some dull opiate to the drains
    One minute past, and Lethe-wards had sunk:
'Tis not through envy of thy happy lot,   5
    But being too happy in thine happiness,—
        That thou, light-winged Dryad of the trees,
          In some melodious plot
Of beechen green, and shadows numberless,
    Singest of summer in full-throated ease.   10

---

2. HEMLOCK: a poison; the kind Socrates drank (see pp. 682-684).
4. LETHE-WARDS: Lethe was the river of forgetfulness in Hades; hence, into oblivion.
7. DRYAD: wood nymph.

II

O, for a draught of vintage! that hath been
    Cooled a long age in the deep-delvèd earth,
Tasting of Flora and the country green,
    Dance, and Provençal song, and sunburnt mirth!
O for a beaker full of the warm South,   15
    Full of the true, the blushful Hippocrene,
        With beaded bubbles winking at the brim,
            And purple-stainèd mouth;
That I might drink, and leave the world unseen,
    And with thee fade away into the forest dim: 20

III

Fade far away, dissolve, and quite forget
    What thou among the leaves hast never known,
The weariness, the fever, and the fret
    Here, where men sit and hear each other groan;
Where palsy shakes a few, sad, last gray hairs,   25
    Where youth grows pale, and specter-thin, and dies;
        Where but to think is to be full of sorrow
            And leaden-eyed despairs,
    Where Beauty cannot keep her lustrous eyes,
        Or new Love pine at them beyond tomorrow.   30

IV

Away! away! for I will fly to thee,
    Not charioted by Bacchus and his pards,
But on the viewless wings of Poesy,
    Though the dull brain perplexes and retards:
Already with thee! tender is the night,   35
    And haply the Queen-Moon is on her throne,
        Clustered around by all her starry Fays;
            But here there is no light,
    Save what from heaven is with the breezes blown
        Through verdurous glooms and winding mossy ways.   40

V

I cannot see what flowers are at my feet,
    Nor what soft incense hangs upon the boughs,
But, in embalmèd darkness, guess each sweet
    Wherewith the seasonable month endows

---

11. VINTAGE: wine.
13. FLORA: spring; Flora was the goddess of flowers.
14. PROVENÇAL: The troubadours first came from Provence, in southern France.

16. HIPPOCRENE: the Muses' fountain, source of poetic inspiration.
32. BACCHUS: god of wine. PARDS: leopards, who drew Bacchus's chariot.
33. VIEWLESS: invisible.
43. EMBALMÈD: fragrant.

The grass, the thicket, and the fruit-tree wild;   45
　　White hawthorn, and the pastoral eglantine;
　　　Fast fading violets covered up in leaves;
　　　　And mid-May's eldest child,
　　The coming musk-rose, full of dewy wine,
　　　The murmurous haunt of flies on summer eves.   50

VI

Darkling I listen; and, for many a time
　　I have been half in love with easeful Death,
Called him soft names in many a musèd rhyme,
　　To take into the air my quiet breath;
Now more than ever seems it rich to die,   55
　　To cease upon the midnight with no pain,
　　　While thou art pouring forth thy soul abroad
　　　　In such an ecstasy!
　　Still wouldst thou sing, and I have ears in vain—
　　To thy high requiem become a sod.   60

VII

Thou wast not born for death, immortal Bird!
　　No hungry generations tread thee down;
The voice I hear this passing night was heard
　　In ancient days by emperor and clown:
Perhaps the self-same song that found a path   65
　　Through the sad heart of Ruth, when, sick for home,
　　　She stood in tears amid the alien corn;
　　　　The same that oft-times hath
　　Charmed magic casements, opening on the foam
　　Of perilous seas, in faery lands forlorn.   70

VIII

Forlorn! the very word is like a bell
　　To toll me back from thee to my sole self!
Adieu! the fancy cannot cheat so well
　　As she is famed to do, deceiving elf.
Adieu! adieu! thy plaintive anthem fades   75
　　Past the near meadows, over the still stream,
　　　Up the hillside; and now 'tis buried deep
　　　　In the next valley glades:
　　Was it a vision, or a waking dream?
　　Fled is that music:—Do I wake or sleep?   80

---

66. RUTH: the girl of Moab whose loyalty in accompanying her Hebrew mother-in-law into
a wholly alien land and culture is recounted
in the Old Testament Book of Ruth.

67. CORN: grain.

73. FANCY: imagination.

I

1. Trace the chronological movement of the poem; in other words, what actually goes on in the speaker's mind from the beginning to the end? The hearing of the nightingale's song is the situation which initiates his meditations; the passing of the song closes them.

2. Where is the nightingale in stanza 1? Can the speaker see it or only hear it? What is the time of day? Why does he wait until line 10 to reveal what it is he is responding to? What do lines 5 and 6 mean? How can "being too happy in [the nightingale's] happiness" lead to the kind of *numbness* and *ache* the first four lines speak of? How do the vowel sounds and the grouped stresses ("My heart aches," "dull opiate") combine to match sound with sense in the first four lines? How does the rhythm of lines 8-10 underline the sense of joy the speaker finds in the nightingale's song?

3. What is he wishing for in stanza 2? Explain the references in lines 13-18. What is the wine supposed to bring to him? What is it to accomplish for him? How do the objects of longing here contrast with those in stanza 1?

4. In stanza 3 he sets up the world of men as he knows it. Why does he want to fly from it? In what ways does it resemble what Wordsworth deplores in "The World Is Too Much with Us" and what Tomlinson flies from in *The Sea and the Jungle*? In what ways does it differ? Which objects of complaint would it be least possible to eliminate so long as man remains man: Wordsworth's? Tomlinson's? Keats's? Explain.

5. Explain lines 31-33. By "Poesy" Keats means the creative powers of the imagination. Why does he choose it rather than Bacchus or *some dull opiate* for his means of escape? What time of day does his imagination choose? How does the imaginative world of stanzas 4 and 5 contrast with that of stanza 2? Why does he imagine such a landscape as the home of the nightingale? What senses does he utilize in his description of the *embalmèd darkness*?

6. What does he mean by lines 52-55? What does "Now" in line 55 refer to? Why does he say *"half* in love with easeful Death"? How is the wish for *death* here different from that in lines 20-21? In what sense would the *death* wished for here ensure for the speaker a continuation of the kind of world his imagination has created in stanzas 4 and 5? What do the last two lines of stanza 6 mean and how do they qualify the preceding lines? More particularly, how do the denotation and the connotation of the word *sod* (60) recall the speaker to the facts of the real world?

7. How is stanza 7 an outgrowth of stanza 6? In stanza 7 the speaker calls the nightingale "immortal Bird!" In what sense is this so? What is the "voice" referred to in line 63? Is it the nightingale or the nightingale's song that is projected backward in time? Why is the distinction significant? What aspects of the story of Ruth is the speaker concerned about: in other words, how does her situation centuries ago parallel his situation? What relationship *might* the nightingale's song have to her that parallels its relationship to him? Similarly, what purpose is served by the reference to the remote, romantic "faery lands forlorn"?

8. In line 70 "forlorn" means "lost, remote," with suggestions only of removal in time or place. What meaning does the word have in line 71? How does its double use serve dramatically to bring the speaker out of his reverie back to "reality"? Why does he say in lines 73-74 that "the fancy cannot cheat so well/ As she is famed to do" when we have seen her *cheat* remarkably well? How well would the speaker like to have her *cheat*? What is significant about the use of the word *cheat* in this context? Why does he call the song a "plaintive anthem" in line 75? How is the sense of lines 75-78 supported by the rhythm of the lines? What do the questions in lines 79-80 mean? Are there any answers? Consider what has been said about the world of the senses and the world of the imagination: what is "reality"?

THE MAN WHO WOULD BE KING   *[1889]*

Rudyard Kipling

In "A Night Among the Pines" and "Old China" the speaker is obviously quite aware of the conscious choice he makes to live a certain way. Even in "Ode to a Nightingale," despite the very real and perplexing question with which the poem ends, "Do I wake or sleep?" the speaker has consciously manipulated the clash between the world of deadening reality and the world of the imagination that he sees operating in his own life.

The vicious, chaotic world of Kipling's "The Man Who Would Be King" has little in common with the worlds of Stevenson, Lamb, and Keats. And at first glance the two heroes of his tale seem the least likely candidates for kingship in anyone's world. However, they suddenly see as clearly in their own way as do Stevenson, Lamb, and Keats in theirs the necessity of consciously affirming what it is that will give meaning to their lives. As one of them puts it, they will "go away to some . . . place where a man isn't crowded and can come to his own. We are not little men. . . . *Therefore,* we are going away to be Kings." And the other adds, "Kings in our own right."

Ironically, they become real *kings* in a way far different from the one they had planned, but real kings nevertheless.

"Brother to a Prince and fellow to a beggar if he be found worthy."

The law, as quoted, lays down a fair conduct of life, and one not easy to follow. I have been fellow to a beggar again and again under circumstances which prevented either of us finding out whether the other was worthy. I have still to be brother to a Prince, though I once came near to kinship with what might have been a veritable King and was promised the reversion of[1] a Kingdom—army, law courts, revenue and policy all complete. But, today, I greatly fear that my King is dead, and if I want a crown I must go and hunt it for myself.

The beginning of everything was in a railway train upon the road to Mhow from Ajmir.[2] There had been a Deficit in the Budget,[3] which necessitated traveling, not Second-class, which is only half as dear as First-class, but by Intermediate, which is very awful indeed. There are no cushions in the Intermediate class, and the population are either Intermediate, which is Eurasian, or native, which for a long night journey is nasty, or Loafer, which is amusing though intoxicated. Intermediates do not patronize refreshment rooms. They carry their food in bundles and pots, and buy sweets[4] from the native sweetmeat-sellers, and drink the roadside water. That is why in the hot weather Intermediates are taken out of the carriages dead, and in all weathers are most properly looked down upon.

My particular Intermediate happened to be empty till I reached Nasirabad, when a huge gentleman in shirt sleeves entered, and, following the custom of Intermediates, passed the time of day. He was a wanderer

---

1. REVERSION OF: right of succession to.
2. MHOW . . . AJMIR: These towns and those mentioned in the paragraphs immediately following can be located on any map of India, in the Northwest and North Central sections, roughly between Bombay and Delhi.
3. DEFICIT . . . BUDGET: i.e., he's broke; the term is used in government and business offices to indicate a shortage of funds.
4. SWEETS: sweetmeats; candy.

and a vagabond like myself, but with an educated taste for whisky. He told tales of things he had seen and done, of out-of-the-way corners of the Empire[5] into which he had penetrated, and of adventures in which he risked his life for a few days' food. "If India was filled with men like you and me, not knowing more than the crows where they'd get their next day's rations, it isn't seventy millions of revenue the land would be paying—it's seven hundred millions," said he; and as I looked at his mouth and chin I was disposed to agree with him. We talked politics—the politics of Loaferdom that sees things from the underside where the lath and plaster is not smoothed off—and we talked postal arrangements because my friend wanted to send a telegram back from the next station to Ajmir, which is the turning-off place from the Bombay to the Mhow line as you travel westward. My friend had no money beyond eight annas[6] which he wanted for dinner, and I had no money at all, owing to the hitch in the Budget before-mentioned. Further, I was going into a wilderness where, though I should resume touch with the Treasury, there were no telegraph offices. I was, therefore, unable to help him in any way.

"We might threaten a Stationmaster, and make him send a wire on tick,"[7] said my friend, "but that'd mean inquiries for you and for me, and I've got my hands full these days. Did you say you are traveling back along this line within any days?"

"Within ten," I said.

"Can't you make it eight?" said he. "Mine is rather urgent business."

"I can send your telegram within ten days if that will serve you," I said.

"I couldn't trust the wire to fetch him now I think of it. It's this way. He leaves Delhi on the twenty-third for Bombay. That means he'll be running through Ajmir about the night of the twenty-third."

"But I'm going into the Indian Desert," I explained.

"Well *and* good," said he. "You'll be changing at Marwar Junction to get into Jodhpore territory—you must do that—and he'll be coming through Marwar Junction in the early morning of the twenty-fourth by the Bombay Mail.[8] Can you be at Marwar Junction on that time? 'Twon't be inconveniencing you because I know that there's precious few pickings to be got out of these Central India States[9]—even though you pretend to be correspondent of the *Backwoodsman.*"[10]

"Have you ever tried that trick?" I asked.

"Again and again, but the Residents find you out, and then you get escorted to the Border before you've time to get your knife into them. But about my friend here. I *must* give him a word o' mouth to tell him what's come to me or else he won't know where to go. I would take it more than kind of you if you was to come out of Central India in time to catch him at Marwar Junction, and say to him, 'He has gone South for the week.' He'll know what that means. He's a big man with a red beard, and a great swell[11] he is. You'll find him sleeping like a gentleman with all his luggage round him in a Second-class compartment. But don't you be afraid. Slip down the window, and say, 'He has gone South for the week,' and he'll tumble. It's only cutting your time of stay in those parts by two days. I ask you as a stranger—going to the West," he said, with emphasis.

"Where have *you* come from?" said I.

"From the East," said he, "and I am hoping that you will give him the message on the Square—for the sake of my Mother as well as your own."

Englishmen are not usually softened by

---

5. EMPIRE: the British Empire, upon which, at that time, the "sun never set."
6. ANNAS: Indian coins worth about two cents.
7. TICK: credit.

8. BOMBAY MAIL: particular train on regular schedule, like the Twentieth Century Limited.
9. STATES: At this time India was divided into many small principalities "ruled" by local rajahs with British officials in overall control.
10. BACKWOODSMAN: English-language newspaper published in India.
11. SWELL: first-rate fellow.

appeals to the memory of their mothers, but for certain reasons, which will be fully apparent, I saw fit to agree.

"It's more than a little matter," said he, "and that's why I ask you to do it—and now I know that I can depend on you doing it. A Second-class carriage at Marwar Junction, and a red-haired man asleep in it. You'll be sure to remember. I get out at the next station, and I must hold on there till he comes or sends me what I want."

"I'll give the message if I catch him," I said, "and for the sake of your Mother as well as mine I'll give you a word of advice. Don't try to run the Central India States just now as the correspondent of the *Backwoodsman*. There's a real one knocking about here, and it might lead to trouble."[12]

"Thank you," said he, simply, "and when will the swine be gone? I can't starve because he's ruining my work. I wanted to get hold of the Degumber[13] Rajah down here about his father's widow, and give him a jump."[14]

"What did he do to his father's widow, then?"

"Filled her up with red pepper and slippered her to death as she hung from a beam. I found that out myself, and I'm the only man that would dare going into the State to get hush money for it. They'll try to poison me, same as they did in Chortumna when I went on the loot there. But you'll give the man at Marwar Junction my message?"

He got out at a little roadside station, and I reflected. I had heard, more than once, of men personating correspondents of newspapers and bleeding small Native States with threats of exposure, but I had never met any of the caste before. They lead a hard life, and generally die with great suddenness. The Native States have a wholesome horror of English newspapers, which may throw light on their peculiar methods of government, and do their best to choke correspondents with champagne, or drive them out of their mind with four-in-hand barouches. They do not understand that nobody cares a straw for the internal administration of Native States so long as oppression and crime are kept within decent limits, and the ruler is not drugged, drunk, or diseased from one end of the year to the other. Native States were created by Providence in order to supply picturesque scenery, tigers, and tall writing.[15] They are the dark places of the earth, full of unimaginable cruelty, touching the Railway and the Telegraph on one side, and, on the other, the days of Harun-al-Raschid.[16] When I left the train I did business with divers Kings, and in eight days passed through many changes of life. Sometimes I wore dress clothes and consorted with Princes and Politicals, drinking from crystal and eating from silver. Sometimes I lay out upon the ground and devoured what I could get, from a plate made of a flapjack, and drank the running water, and slept under the same rug as my servant. It was all in the day's work.

Then I headed for the Great Indian Desert upon the proper date, as I had promised, and the night Mail set me down at Marwar Junction, where a funny little, happy-go-lucky, native-managed railway runs to Jodhpore. The Bombay Mail from Delhi makes a short halt at Marwar. She arrived as I got in, and I had just time to hurry to her platform and go down the carriages. There was only one Second-class on the train. I slipped the window, and looked down upon a flaming red beard, half covered by a railway rug. That was my man, fast asleep, and I dug him gently in the ribs. He woke with a grunt, and I saw his face in the light of the lamps. It was a great and shining face.

"Tickets again?" said he.

"No," said I. "I am to tell you that he is gone South for the week. He is gone South for the week!"

12. THERE'S . . . TROUBLE: the narrator himself.
13. DEGUMBER: one of the small principalities.
14. GIVE . . . JUMP: scare the wits out of him so that he'll pay "hush" money.
15. TALL WRITING: exaggerated or fanciful accounts.
16. HARUN-AL-RASCHID: caliph of Arabia (785-809); celebrated in the *Arabian Nights*.

The train had begun to move out. The red man rubbed his eyes. "He has gone South for the week," he repeated. "Now that's just like his impidence. Did he say that I was to give you anything?—'Cause I won't."

"He didn't," I said, and dropped away, and watched the red lights die out in the dark. It was horribly cold, because the wind was blowing off the sands. I climbed into my own train—not an Intermediate Carriage this time—and went to sleep.

If the man with the beard had given me a rupee[17] I should have kept it as a memento of a rather curious affair. But the consciousness of having done my duty was my only reward.

Later on I reflected that two gentlemen like my friends could not do any good if they foregathered and personated correspondents of newspapers, and might, if they "stuck up" one of the little rat-trap states of Central India or Southern Rajputana, get themselves into serious difficulties. I therefore took some trouble to describe them as accurately as I could remember to people who would be interested in deporting them; and succeeded, so I was later informed, in having them headed back from Degumber borders.

Then I became respectable, and returned to an Office where there were no Kings and no incidents except the daily manufacture of a newspaper. A newspaper office seems to attract every conceivable sort of person, to the prejudice of discipline. Zenana-mission[18] ladies arrive, and beg that the Editor will instantly abandon all his duties to describe a Christian prize-giving in a back-slum of a perfectly inaccessible village; Colonels who have been over-passed for commands sit down and sketch the outline of a series of ten, twelve, or twenty-four leading articles on Seniority *versus* Selection; missionaries wish to know why they have not been permitted

to escape from their regular vehicles of abuse and swear at a brother missionary under special patronage of the editorial We; stranded theatrical companies troop up to explain that they cannot pay for their advertisements, but on their return from New Zealand or Tahiti will do so with interest; inventors of patent punkah-pulling[19] machines, carriage couplings, and unbreakable swords and axletrees call with specifications in their pockets and hours at their disposal; tea companies enter and elaborate their prospectuses with the office pens; secretaries of ball committees clamor to have the glories of their last dance more fully expounded; strange ladies rustle in and say, "I want a hundred lady's cards printed *at once,* please," which is manifestly part of an Editor's duty; and every dissolute ruffian that ever tramped the Grand Trunk Road makes it his business to ask for employment as a proofreader. And, all the time, the telephone bell is ringing madly, and Kings are being killed on the Continent,[20] and Empires are saying— "You're another," and Mister Gladstone[21] is calling down brimstone upon the British Dominions,[22] and the little black copy boys are whining, *"kaa-pi chay-ha-yeh"* (copy wanted) like tired bees, and most of the paper is as blank as Modred's shield.[23]

But that is the amusing part of the year. There are other six months wherein none ever come to call, and the thermometer walks inch by inch up to the top of the glass, and the office is darkened to just above reading light, and the press machines are red-hot of touch, and nobody writes anything but accounts of amusements in the Hill stations[24]

---

17. RUPEE: Indian silver coin worth sixteen annas.
18. ZENANA-MISSION: a mission exclusively for women.
19. PUNKAH: a large ceiling fan.
20. ON THE CONTINENT: i.e., in Europe.
21. MISTER GLADSTONE: William Gladstone, prime minister of England on four different occasions between 1868-1894.
22. BRITISH DOMINIONS: the self-governing units (Canada, Australia), making up, with Great Britain, the British Commonwealth of Nations.
23. MODRED: King Arthur's nephew, who betrays him.
24. HILL STATIONS: government posts in the hills, where the weather is bearable.

or obituary notices. Then the telephone becomes a tinkling terror, because it tells you
of the sudden deaths of men and women
that you knew intimately, and the prickly
heat covers you as with a garment, and you
sit down and write: "A slight increase of
sickness is reported from the Khuda Janta
Khan District. The outbreak is purely spo-
radic in its nature, and, thanks to the energetic efforts of the District authorities, is
now almost at an end. It is, however, with
deep regret we record the death, etc."

Then the sickness really breaks out, and
the less recording and reporting the better for
the peace of the subscribers. But the Empires and the Kings continue to divert themselves as selfishly as before, and the Fore-
man thinks that a daily paper really ought
to come out once in twenty-four hours, and
all the people at the Hill stations in the
middle of their amusements say, "Good gracious! Why can't the paper be sparkling?
I'm sure there's plenty going on up here."

That is the dark half of the moon, and, as
the advertisements say, "must be experienced
to be appreciated."

It was in that season, and a remarkably
evil season, that the paper began running
the last issue of the week on Saturday night,
which is to say, Sunday morning, after the
custom of a London paper. This was a great
convenience, for immediately after the paper
was put to bed,[25] the dawn would lower the
thermometer from 96° to almost 84° for
half an hour, and in that chill—you have no
idea how cold is 84° on the grass until you
begin to pray for it—a very tired man could
set off to sleep ere the heat roused him.

One Saturday night it was my pleasant
duty to put the paper to bed alone. A King
or courtier or a courtesan or a community
was going to die or get a new Constitution,
or do something that was important on the
other side of the world, and the paper was
to be held open till the latest possible minute
in order to catch the telegram. It was a

25. PUT . . . BED: journalistic phrase for decision
to start the press run.

pitchy black night, as stifling as a June night
can be, and the *loo,* the red-hot wind from
the westward, was booming among the
tinder-dry trees and pretending that the rain
was on its heels. Now and again a spot of
almost boiling water would fall on the dust
with the flop of a frog, but all our weary
world knew that was only pretense. It was
a shade cooler in the press room than the
office, so I sat there, while the type clicked
and clicked and the nightjars hooted at the
windows, and the all but naked compositors
wiped the sweat from their foreheads and
called for water. The thing that was keeping
us back, whatever it was, would not come
off, though the *loo* dropped and the last type
was set, and the whole round earth stood
still in the choking heat, with its finger on
its lip, to wait the event. I drowsed, and
wondered whether the telegraph was a blessing, and whether this dying man, or struggling people, was aware of the inconvenience
the delay was causing. There was no special
reason beyond the heat and worry to make
tension, but, as the clock hands crept up to
three o'clock and the machines spun their
flywheels two or three times to see that all
was in order, before I said the word that
would set them off, I could have shrieked
aloud.

Then the roar and rattle of the wheels
shivered the quiet into little bits. I rose to
go away, but two men in white clothes stood
in front of me. The first one said, "It's him!"
The second said, "So it is!" And they both
laughed almost as loudly as the machinery
roared, and mopped their foreheads. "We see
there was a light burning across the road
and we were sleeping in that ditch there for
coolness, and I said to my friend here, 'The
office is open. Let's come along and speak
to him as turned us back from the Degumber State,' " said the smaller of the two. He
was the man I had met in the Mhow train,
and his fellow was the red-bearded man of
Marwar Junction. There was no mistaking
the eyebrows of the one or the beard of the
other.

I was not pleased, because I wished to go to sleep, not to squabble with loafers. "What do you want?" I asked.

"Half an hour's talk with you cool and comfortable, in the office," said the red-bearded man. "We'd *like* some drink—the Contrack doesn't begin yet, Peachey, so you needn't look—but what we really want is advice. We don't want money. We ask you as a favor, because you did us a bad turn about Degumber."

I led from the press room to the stifling office with the maps on the walls, and the red-haired man rubbed his hands. "That's something like," said he. "This was the proper shop to come to. Now, Sir, let me introduce to you Brother[26] Peachey Carnehan, that's him, and Brother Daniel Dravot, that is *me,* and the less said about our professions the better, for we have been most things in our time. Soldier, sailor, compositor, photographer, proofreader, street preacher, and correspondents of the *Backwoodsman* when we thought the paper wanted one. Carnehan is sober, and so am I. Look at us first and see that's sure. It will save you cutting into my talk. We'll take one of your cigars apiece, and you shall see us light."

I watched the test. The men were absolutely sober, so I gave them each a tepid peg.[27]

"Well *and* good," said Carnehan of the eyebrows, wiping the froth from his mustache. "Let me talk now, Dan. We have been all over India, mostly on foot. We have been boiler-fitters, engine-drivers, petty contractors, and all that, and we have decided that India isn't big enough for such as us."

They certainly were too big for the office. Dravot's beard seemed to fill half the room and Carnehan's shoulders the other half, as they sat on the big table. Carnehan continued: "The country isn't half worked out because they that governs it won't let you touch it. They spend all their blessed time in governing it, and you can't lift a spade, nor chip a rock, nor look for oil, nor any-

thing like that without all the Government saying, 'Leave it alone and let us govern.' Therefore, such as it is, we will let it alone, and go away to some other place where a man isn't crowded and can come to his own. We are not little men, and there is nothing that we are afraid of except Drink, and we have signed a Contrack on that. *Therefore,* we are going away to be Kings."

"Kings in our own right," muttered Dravot.

"Yes, of course," I said. "You've been tramping in the sun, and it's a very warm night, and hadn't you better sleep over the notion? Come tomorrow."

"Neither drunk nor sunstruck," said Dravot. "We have slept over the notion half a year, and require to see Books and Atlases, and we have decided that there is only one place now in the world that two strong men can Sar-a-*whack*.[28] They call it Kafiristan.[29] By my reckoning it's the top right-hand corner of Afghanistan, not more than three hundred miles from Peshawur. They have two and thirty heathen idols there, and we'll be the thirty-third. It's a mountainous country, and the women of those parts are very beautiful."

"But that is provided against in the Contrack," said Carnehan. "Neither Women nor Liqu-or, Daniel."

"And that's all we know, except that no one has gone there, and they fight, and in any place where they fight, a man who knows how to drill men can always be a King. We shall go to those parts and say to any King we find, 'D'you want to vanquish your foes?' and we will show him how to drill men; for that we know better than anything else. Then we will subvert that King and seize his Throne and establish a Dy-nasty."

"You'll be cut to pieces before you're fifty

---

26. BROTHER: designation used among freemasons.
27. TEPID PEG: a small, warm drink of whisky.

28. SAR-A-WHACK: refers to Sarawak, northwest Borneo; see note on Rajah Brooke, p. 618.
29. KAFIRISTAN: mountainous section of east Afghanistan, south of Hindu Kush mountains; the Kafirs are an Afghan people, descendants of early Iranian peoples, who speak an archaic Indo-European dialect; some are red-haired and blue-eyed.

miles across the Border," I said. "You have to travel through Afghanistan to get to that country. It's one mass of mountains and peaks and glaciers, and no Englishman has been through it. The people are utter brutes, and even if you reached them you couldn't do anything."

"That's more like," said Carnehan. "If you could think us a little more mad we would be more pleased. We have come to you to know about this country, to read a book about it, and to be shown maps. We want you to tell us that we are fools and to show us your books." He turned to the bookcases.

"Are you at all in earnest?" I said.

"A little," said Dravot, sweetly. "As big a map as you have got, even if it's all blank where Kafiristan is, and any books you've got. We can read, though we aren't very educated."

I uncased the big thirty-two-miles-to-the-inch map of India, and two smaller Frontier maps, hauled down volume INF-KAN of the *Encyclopaedia Britannica,* and the men consulted them.

"See here!" said Dravot, his thumb on the map. "Up to Jagdallak, Peachey and me know the road. We was there with Roberts's Army.[30] We'll have to turn off to the right at Jagdallak through Laghmann territory. Then we get among the hills—fourteen thousand feet—fifteen thousand—it will be cold work there, but it don't look very far on the map."

I handed him Wood on the *Sources of the Oxus.*[31] Carnehan was deep in the *Encyclopaedia.*

"They're a mixed lot," said Dravot, reflectively; "and it won't help us to know the names of their tribes. The more tribes the more they'll fight, and the better for us. From Jagdallak to Ashang. H'mm!"

"But all the information about the country is as sketchy and inaccurate as can be," I protested. "No one knows anything about it really. Here's the file of the *United Services' Institute.* Read what Bellew says."

"Blow Bellew!" said Carnehan. "Dan, they're an all-fired lot of heathens, but this book here says they think they're related to us English."

I smoked while the men pored over *Raverty, Wood,* the maps, and the *Encyclopaedia.*

"There is no use your waiting," said Dravot, politely. "It's about four o'clock now. We'll go before six o'clock if you want to sleep, and we won't steal any of the papers. Don't you sit up. We're two harmless lunatics and if you come, tomorrow evening, down to the Serai[32] we'll say good-by to you."

"You *are* two fools," I answered. "You'll be turned back at the Frontier or cut up the minute you set foot in Afghanistan. Do you want any money or a recommendation down-country? I can help you to the chance of work next week."

"Next week we shall be hard at work ourselves, thank you," said Dravot. "It isn't so easy being a King as it looks. When we've got our Kingdom in going order we'll let you know, and you can come up and help us to govern it."

"Would two lunatics make a Contrack like that?" said Carnehan, with subdued pride, showing me a greasy half sheet of note paper on which was written the following. I copied it, then and there, as a curiosity:

This Contract between me and you persuing witnesseth in the name of God— Amen and so forth.

(ONE) *That me and you will settle this matter together: i.e., to be Kings of Kafiristan.*

(TWO) *That you and me will not, while this matter is being settled, look at any Liquor, nor any Woman,*

---

30. ROBERT'S ARMY: Frederick Sleigh Roberts was a famous British field marshal, who spent four decades in India.
31. OXUS: the Amu Darya River, border of northern Afghanistan; the places named in these paragraphs are all in Afghanistan.
32. SERAI: a kind of inn where caravans are put up.

*black, white or brown, so as to
get mixed up with one or the
other harmful.*

(THREE) *That we conduct ourselves with
dignity and discretion and if one
of us gets into trouble the other
will stay by him.*

Signed by you and me this day.

  PEACHEY TALIAFERRO CARNEHAN.
  DANIEL DRAVOT.
   Both Gentlemen at Large.

"There was no need for the last article," said Carnehan, blushing modestly; "but it looks regular. Now you know the sort of men that Loafers are—we *are* Loafers, Dan, until we get out of India—and *do* you think that we would sign a Contrack like that unless we was in earnest? We have kept away from the two things that make life worth having."

"You won't enjoy your lives much longer if you are going to try this idiotic adventure. Don't set the office on fire," I said, "and go away before nine o'clock."

I left them still poring over the maps and making notes on the back of the "Contrack." "Be sure to come down to the Serai tomorrow," were their parting words.

The Kumharsen Serai is the great four-square sink of humanity where the strings of camels and horses from the North load and unload. All the nationalities of Central Asia may be found there, and most of the folk of India proper. Balkh and Bokhara there meet Bengal and Bombay,[33] and try to draw eyeteeth. You can buy ponies, turquoises, Persian pussy cats, saddlebags, fat-tailed sheep, and musk in the Kumharsen Serai, and get many strange things for nothing. In the afternoon I went down there to see whether my friends intended to keep their word or were lying about drunk.

A priest attired in fragments of ribbons and rags stalked up to me, gravely twisting

a child's paper whirligig. Behind was his servant bending under the load of a crate of mud toys. The two were loading up two camels, and the inhabitants of the Serai watched them with shrieks of laughter.

"The priest is mad," said a horse-dealer to me. "He is going up to Kabul[34] to sell toys to the Amir.[35] He will either be raised to honor or have his head cut off. He came in here this morning and has been behaving madly ever since."

"The witless are under the protection of God," stammered a flat-cheeked Usbeg[36] in broken Hindi. "They foretell future events."

"Would they could have foretold that my caravan would have been cut up by the Shinwaris[37] almost within shadow of the Pass!"[38] grunted the Eusufzai agent of a Rajputana trading house whose goods had been feloniously diverted into the hands of other robbers just across the Border, and whose misfortunes were the laughingstock of the bazaar. "Ohé, priest, whence come you and whither do you go?"

"From Roum[39] have I come," shouted the priest, waving his whirligig; "from Roum, blown by the breath of a hundred devils across the sea! O thieves, robbers, liars, the blessing of Pir Khan[40] on pigs, dogs, and perjurers! Who will take the Protected of God to the North to sell charms that are never still to the Amir? The camels shall not gall,[41] the sons shall not fall sick, and the wives shall remain faithful while they are away, of the men who give me place in their caravan. Who will assist me to slipper the King of the Roos with a golden slipper

---

33. BALKH . . . BOMBAY: Balkh is in northwest Afghanistan; Bokhara is in what is now Soviet territory, northwest of Balkh; Bombay and Bengal are on opposite sides of India.

34. KABUL: capital of Afghanistan.
35. AMIR: the King of Afghanistan.
36. USBEG: native of a region of Turkestan.
37. SHINWARIS: members of a belligerent Afghan tribe.
38. PASS: the Khyber Pass, between Afghanistan and India.
39. ROUM: Arabic name for the Byzantine Empire.
40. PIR KHAN: "Pir" is the Arabic word for a Mohammedan saint or spiritual guide; "Khan" means lord or prince.
41. GALL: get sores on the skin from rubbing.

with a silver heel? The protection of Pir Khan be upon his labors!" He spread out the skirts of his gaberdine and pirouetted between the lines of tethered horses.

"There starts a caravan from Peshawur to Kabul in twenty days, *Huzrut*," said the Eusufzai trader. "My camels go therewith. Do thou also go and bring us good luck."

"I will go even now!" shouted the priest. "I will depart upon my winged camels, and be at Peshawur in a day! Ho! Hazar Mir Khan," he yelled to his servant, "drive out the camels, but let me first mount my own."

He leaped on the back of his beast as it knelt, and, turning round to me, cried, "Come thou also, Sahib, a little along the road, and I will sell thee a charm—an amulet that shall make thee King of Kafiristan."

Then the light broke upon me, and I followed the two camels out of the Serai till we reached open road and the priest halted.

"What d'you think o' that?" said he in English. "Carnehan can't talk their patter, so I've made him my servant. He makes a handsome servant. 'Tisn't for nothing that I've been knocking about the country for fourteen years. Didn't I do that talk neat? We'll hitch on to a caravan at Peshawur till we get to Jagdallak, and then we'll see if we can get donkeys for our camels, and strike into Kafiristan. Whirligigs for the Amir, O Lor'! Put your hand under the camel bags and tell me what you feel."

I felt the butt of a Martini,[42] and another and another.

"Twenty of 'em," said Dravot, placidly. "Twenty of 'em, and ammunition to correspond, under the whirligigs and the mud dolls."

"Heaven help you if you are caught with those things!" I said. "A Martini is worth her weight in silver among the Pathans."[43]

---

42. MARTINI: Martini-Henry rifle, a single-loading .45 calibre rifle used by the British from 1876-1886.
43. PATHANS: members of the principal race of Afghanistan.

"Fifteen hundred rupees of capital—every rupee we could beg, borrow, or steal—are invested on these two camels," said Dravot. "We won't get caught. We're going through the Khyber with a regular caravan. Who'd touch a poor mad priest?"

"Have you got everything you want?" I asked, overcome with astonishment.

"Not yet, but we shall soon. Give us a memento of your kindness, *Brother*. You did me a service yesterday, and that time in Marwar. Half my Kingdom shall you have, as the saying is." I slipped a small charm compass from my watch chain and handed it up to the priest.

"Good-by," said Dravot, giving me his hand cautiously. "It's the last time we'll shake hands with an Englishman these many days. Shake hands with him, Carnehan," he cried, as the second camel passed me.

Carnehan leaned down and shook hands. Then the camels passed away along the dusty road, and I was left alone to wonder. My eye could detect no failure in the disguises. The scene in the Serai attested that they were complete to the native mind. There was just the chance, therefore, that Carnehan and Dravot would be able to wander through Afghanistan without detection. But, beyond, they would find death, certain and awful death.

Ten days later a native friend of mine, giving me the news of the day from Peshawur, wound up his letter with:—"There has been much laughter here on account of a certain mad priest who is going in his estimation to sell petty gauds and insignificant trinkets which he ascribes as great charms to H. H.[44] the Amir of Bokhara. He passed through Peshawur and associated himself to the Second Summer caravan that goes to Kabul. The merchants are pleased, because through superstition they imagine that such mad fellows bring good fortune."

The two, then, were beyond the Border. I would have prayed for them, but, that

---

44. H.H.: His Highness.

night, a real King died in Europe, and demanded an obituary notice.

The wheel of the world swings through the same phases again and again. Summer passed and winter thereafter, and came and passed again. The daily paper continued and I with it, and upon the third summer there fell a hot night, a night issue, and a strained waiting for something to be telegraphed from the other side of the world, exactly as had happened before. A few great men had died in the past two years, the machines worked with more clatter, and some of the trees in the Office garden were a few feet taller. But that was all the difference.

I passed over to the press room, and went through just such a scene as I have already described. The nervous tension was stronger than it had been two years before, and I felt the heat more acutely. At three o'clock I cried, "Print off," and turned to go, when there crept to my chair what was left of a man. He was bent into a circle, his head was sunk between his shoulders, and he moved his feet one over the other like a bear. I could hardly see whether he walked or crawled—this rag-wrapped, whining cripple who addressed me by name, crying that he was come back. "Can you give me a drink?" he whimpered. "For the Lord's sake, give me a drink!"

I went back to the office, the man following with groans of pain, and I turned up the lamp.

"Don't you know me?" he gasped, dropping into a chair, and he turned his drawn face, surmounted by a shock of gray hair, to the light.

I looked at him intently. Once before had I seen eyebrows that met over the nose in an inch-broad black band, but for the life of me I could not tell where.

"I don't know you," I said, handing him the whisky. "What can I do for you?"

He took a gulp of the spirit raw, and shivered in spite of the suffocating heat.

"I've come back," he repeated; "and I was the King of Kafiristan—me and Dravot—crowned Kings we was! In this office we settled it—you setting there and giving us the books. I am Peachey—Peachey Taliaferro Carnehan, and you've been setting here ever since—O Lord!"

I was more than a little astonished, and expressed my feelings accordingly.

"It's true," said Carnehan, with a dry cackle, nursing his feet, which were wrapped in rags. "True as gospel. Kings we were, with crowns upon our heads—me and Dravot—poor Dan—oh, poor, poor Dan, that would never take advice, not though I begged of him!"

"Take the whisky," I said, "and take your own time. Tell me all you can recollect of everything from beginning to end. You got across the border on your camels, Dravot dressed as a mad priest and you his servant. Do you remember that?"

"I ain't mad—yet, but I shall be that way soon. Of course I remember. Keep looking at me, or maybe my words will go all to pieces. Keep looking at me in my eyes and don't say anything."

I leaned forward and looked into his face as steadily as I could. He dropped one hand upon the table and I grasped it by the wrist. It was twisted like a bird's claw, and upon the back was a ragged, red, diamond-shaped scar.

"No, don't look there. Look at *me*," said Carnehan.

"That comes afterward, but for the Lord's sake don't distrack me. We left with that caravan, me and Dravot playing all sorts of antics to amuse the people we were with. Dravot used to make us laugh in the evenings when all the people was cooking their dinners—cooking their dinners, and . . . what did they do then? They lit little fires with sparks that went into Dravot's beard, and we all laughed—fit to die. Little red fires they was, going into Dravot's big red beard—so funny." His eyes left mine and he smiled foolishly.

"You went as far as Jagdallak with that

caravan," I said, at a venture, "after you had lit those fires. To Jagdallak, where you turned off to try to get into Kafiristan."

"No, we didn't neither. What are you talking about? We turned off before Jagdallak, because we heard the roads was good. But they wasn't good enough for our two camels—mine and Dravot's. When we left the caravan, Dravot took off all his clothes and mine too, and said we would be heathen, because the Kafirs didn't allow Mohammedans to talk to them. So we dressed betwixt and between, and such a sight as Daniel Dravot I never saw yet nor expect to see again. He burned half his beard, and slung a sheepskin over his shoulder, and shaved his head into patterns. He shaved mine, too, and made me wear outrageous things to look like a heathen. That was in a most mountaineous country, and our camels couldn't go along any more because of the mountains. They were tall and black, and coming home I saw them fight like wild goats—there are lots of goats in Kafiristan. And these mountains, they never keep still, no more than goats. Always fighting they are, and don't let you sleep at night."

"Take some more whisky," I said, very slowly. "What did you and Daniel Dravot do when the camels could go no further because of the rough roads that led into Kafiristan?"

"What did which do? There was a party called Peachey Taliaferro Carnehan that was with Dravot. Shall I tell you about him? He died out there in the cold. Slap from the bridge fell old Peachey, turning and twisting in the air like a penny whirligig that you can sell to the Amir— No; they was two for three ha'pence, those whirligigs, or I am much mistaken and woeful sore. And then these camels were no use, and Peachey said to Dravot—'For the Lord's sake, let's get out of this before our heads are chopped off,' and with that they killed the camels all among the mountains, not having anything in particular to eat, but first they took off the boxes with the guns and the ammunition,

till two men came along driving four mules. Dravot up and dances in front of them, singing,—'Sell me four mules.' Says the first man,—'If you are rich enough to buy, you are rich enough to rob'; but before ever he could put his hand to his knife, Dravot breaks his neck over his knee, and the other party runs away. So Carnehan loaded the mules with the rifles that was taken off the camels, and together we starts forward into those bitter cold mountaineous parts, and never a road broader than the back of your hand."

He paused for a moment, while I asked him if he could remember the nature of the country through which he had journeyed.

"I am telling you as straight as I can, but my head isn't as good as it might be. They drove nails through it to make me hear better how Dravot died. The country was mountaineous and the mules were most contrary, and the inhabitants was dispersed and solitary. They went up and up, and down and down, and that other party, Carnehan, was imploring of Dravot not to sing and whistle so loud, for fear of bringing down the tremenjus avalanches. But Dravot says that if a King couldn't sing it wasn't worth being King, and whacked the mules over the rump, and never took no heed for ten cold days. We came to a big level valley all among the mountains, and the mules were near dead, so we killed them, not having anything in special for them or us to eat. We sat upon the boxes, and played odd and even[45] with the cartridges that was jolted out.

"Then ten men with bows and arrows ran down that valley, chasing twenty men with bows and arrows, and the row was tremenjus. They was fair men—fairer than you or me—with yellow hair and remarkable well built. Says Dravot, unpacking the guns— 'This is the beginning of the business. We'll fight for the ten men,' and with that he fires

---

45. ODD AND EVEN: a game of guessing whether a group of objects contains an odd or even number.

two rifles at the twenty men, and drops one of them at two hundred yards from the rock where we was sitting. The other men began to run, but Carnehan and Dravot sits on the boxes picking them off at all ranges, up and down the valley. Then we goes up to the ten men that had run across the snow too, and they fires a footy[46] little arrow at us. Dravot he shoots above their heads and they all falls down flat. Then he walks over and kicks them, and then he lifts them up and shakes hands all around to make them friendly like. He calls them and gives them the boxes to carry, and waves his hand for all the world as though he was King already. They takes the boxes and him across the valley and up the hill into a pine wood on the top, where there was half a dozen big stone idols. Dravot he goes to the biggest— a fellow they call Imbra—and lays a rifle and a cartridge at his feet, rubbing his nose respectful with his own nose, patting him on the head, and saluting in front of it. He turns round to the men and nods his head, and says, 'That's all right. I'm in the know too, and all these old jim-jams are my friends.' Then he opens his mouth and points down it, and when the first man brings him food, he says 'No'; and when the second man brings him food, he says 'No'; but when one of the old priests and the boss of the village brings him food, he says 'Yes'; very haughty, and eats it slow. That was how we came to our first village, without any trouble, just as though we had tumbled from the skies. But we tumbled from one of those damned rope bridges, you see, and you couldn't expect a man to laugh much after that."

"Take some more whisky and go on," I said. "That was the first village you came into. How did you get to be King?"

"I wasn't King," said Carnehan. "Dravot he was the King, and a handsome man he looked with the gold crown on his head and all. Him and the other party stayed in that village, and every morning Dravot sat by the side of old Imbra, and the people came

and worshiped. That was Dravot's order. Then a lot of men came into the valley, and Carnehan and Dravot picks them off with the rifles before they knew where they was, and runs down into the valley and up again the other side, and finds another village, same as the first one, and the people all falls down flat on their faces, and Dravot says, 'Now what is the trouble between you two villages?' and the people points to a woman, as fair as you or me, that was carried off, and Dravot takes her back to the first village and counts up the dead—eight there was. For each dead man Dravot pours a little milk on the ground and waves his arms like a whirligig and 'That's all right,' says he. Then he and Carnehan takes the big boss of each village by the arm and walks them down into the valley, and shows them how to scratch a line with a spear right down the valley, and gives each a sod of turf from both sides o' the line. Then all the people comes down and shouts like the devil and all, and Dravot says, 'Go and dig the land, and be fruitful and multiply,'[47] which they did, though they didn't understand. Then we asks the names of things in their lingo—bread and water and fire and idols and such, and Dravot leads the priest of each village up to the idol, and says he must sit there and judge the people, and if anything goes wrong he is to be shot.

"Next week they was all turning up the land in the valley as quiet as bees and much prettier, and the priests heard all the complaints and told Dravot in dumb show what it was about. 'That's just the beginning,' says Dravot. 'They think we're Gods.' He and Carnehan picks out twenty good men and shows them how to click off a rifle, and form fours, and advance in line, and they was very pleased to do so, and clever to see the hang of it. Then he takes out his pipe and his 'baccy pouch and leaves one at one village and one at the other, and off we two goes to see what was to be done in the next valley. That was all rock, and there was a little village there, and Carnehan says, 'Send 'em

---

46. FOOTY: paltry.

47. 'GO . . . MULTIPLY': Genesis 1:28.

to the old valley to plant,' and takes 'em there and gives 'em some land that wasn't took before. They were a poor lot, and we blooded 'em with a kid before letting 'em into the new Kingdom. That was to impress the people, and then they settled down quiet, and Carnehan went back to Dravot, who had got into another valley, all snow and ice and most mountaineous. There was no people there, and the Army got afraid, so Dravot shoots one of them, and goes on till he finds some people in a village, and the Army explains that unless the people want to be killed they had better not shoot their little matchlocks; for they had matchlocks. We makes friends with the priest and I stays there alone with two of the Army, teaching the men how to drill, and a thundering big Chief comes across the snow with kettle-drums and horns twanging, because he heard there was a new God kicking about. Carnehan sights for the brown of the men half a mile across the snow and wings one of them. Then he sends a message to the Chief that, unless he wished to be killed, he must come and shake hands with me and leave his arms behind. The Chief comes alone first, and Carnehan shakes hands with him and whirls his arms about, same as Dravot used, and very much surprised that Chief was, and strokes my eyebrows. Then Carnehan goes alone to the Chief, and asks him in dumb show if he had an enemy he hated. 'I have,' says the Chief. So Carnehan weeds out the pick of his men, and sets the two of the Army to show them drill, and at the end of two weeks the men can maneuver about as well as Volunteers.[48] So he marches with the Chief to a great big plain on the top of a mountain, and the Chief's men rushes into a village and takes it; we three Martinis firing into the brown of the enemy. So we took that village too, and I gives the Chief a rag from my coat and says, 'Occupy till I come';[49] which was scriptural. By way of a

reminder, when me and the Army was eighteen hundred yards away, I drops a bullet near him standing on the snow, and all the people falls flat on their faces. Then I sends a letter to Dravot, wherever he be by land or by sea."

At the risk of throwing the creature out of train[50] I interrupted, "How could you write a letter up yonder?"

"The letter?—Oh!—The letter! Keep looking at me between the eyes, please. It was a string-talk letter, that we'd learned the way of it from a blind beggar in the Punjab."[51]

I remember that there had once come to the office a blind man with a knotted twig and a piece of string which he wound round the twig according to some cipher of his own. He could, after the lapse of days or hours, repeat the sentence which he had reeled up. He had reduced the alphabet to eleven primitive sounds; and tried to teach me his method, but failed.

"I sent that letter to Dravot," said Carnehan; "and told him to come back because this Kingdom was growing too big for me to handle, and then I struck for the first valley, to see how the priests were working. They called the village we took along with the Chief, Bashkai, and the first village we took, Er-Heb. The priests at Er-Heb was doing all right, but they had a lot of pending cases about land to show me, and some men from another village had been firing arrows at night. I went out and looked for that village and fired four rounds at it from a thousand yards. That used all the cartridges I cared to spend, and I waited for Dravot, who had been away two or three months, and I kept my people quiet.

"One morning I heard the devil's own noise of drums and horns, and Dan Dravot marches down the hill with his Army and a tail of hundreds of men, and, which was the most amazing—a great gold crown on his head. 'My Gord, Carnehan,' says Daniel,

---

48. VOLUNTEERS: regular soldiers (not conscripted).
49. 'OCCUPY TILL I COME': Luke 19:12–13.

50. OUT OF TRAIN: i.e., out of his train of thought.
51. PUNJAB: province, northwest India.

'this is a tremenjus business, and we've got the whole country as far as it's worth having. I am the son of Alexander[52] by Queen Semiramis,[53] and you're my younger brother and a God too! It's the biggest thing we've ever seen. I've been marching and fighting for six weeks with the Army, and every footy little village for fifty miles has come in rejoiceful; and more than that, I've got the key of the whole show, as you'll see, and I've got a crown for you! I told 'em to make two of 'em at a place called Shu, where the gold lies in the rock like suet in mutton. Gold I've seen, and turquoise I've kicked out of the cliffs, and there's garnets in the sands of the river, and here's a chunk of amber that a man brought me. Call up all the priests and, here, take your crown.'

"One of the men opens a black hair bag and I slips the crown on. It was too small and too heavy, but I wore it for the glory. Hammered gold it was—five pounds weight, like a hoop of a barrel.

" 'Peachey,' says Dravot, 'we don't want to fight no more. The Craft's the trick,[54] so help me!' and he brings forward that same Chief that I left at Bashkai—Billy Fish we called him afterward, because he was so like Billy Fish that drove the big tank engine at Mach on the Bolan in the old days. 'Shake hands with him,' says Dravot, and I shook hands and nearly dropped, for Billy Fish gave me the Grip. I said nothing, but tried him with the Fellow Craft Grip. He answers, all right, and I tried the Master's Grip, but that was a slip. 'A Fellow Craft he is!' I says to Dan. 'Does he know the word?'

---

52. ALEXANDER: Alexander the Great.
53. SEMIRAMIS: legendary great queen of ancient Assyria, said to have built the city of Babylon.
54. CRAFT: i.e., the secret order of Freemasonry; had its origins in seventeenth century England; an all-male society patterned somewhat after the medieval guilds of masons. The ritualistic details of the Freemasons are adopted by Dravot as his religion: lodges, handclasps, degrees of importance, aprons, wardens. The emphasis in Freemasonry (or, more popularly, Masonry) is on fraternity, faithfulness, and honor.

'He does,' says Dan, 'and all the priests know. It's a miracle! The Chiefs and the priests can work a Fellow Craft Lodge in a way that's very like ours, and they've cut the marks on the rocks, but they don't know the Third Degree, and they've come to find out. It's Gord's Truth. I've known these long years that the Afghans knew up to the Fellow Craft Degree, but this is a miracle. A God and a Grand Master of the Craft am I, and a Lodge in the Third Degree I will open, and we'll raise the head priests and the Chiefs of the villages.'

" 'It's against all the law,' I says, 'holding a Lodge without warrant from anyone; and we never held office in any lodge.'

" 'It's a master stroke of policy,' says Dravot. 'It means running the country as easy as a four-wheeled bogy[55] on a down grade. We can't stop to inquire now, or they'll turn against us. I've forty Chiefs at my heel, and passed and raised according to their merit they shall be. Billet these men on the villages and see that we run up a Lodge of some kind. The temple of Imbra will do for the Lodge room. The women must make aprons as you show them. I'll hold a levee of Chiefs tonight and Lodge tomorrow.'

"I was fair run off my legs, but I wasn't such a fool as not to see what a pull this Craft business gave us. I showed the priests' families how to make aprons of the degrees, but for Dravot's apron the blue border and marks was made of turquoise lumps on white hide, not cloth. We took a great square stone in the temple for the Master's chair, and little stones for the officers' chairs, and painted the black pavement with white squares, and did what we could to make things regular.

"At the levee which was held that night on the hillside with big bonfires, Dravot gives out that him and me were Gods and sons of Alexander, and Past Grand Masters in the Craft, and was come to make Kafiristan a country where every man should eat

---

55. BOGY: a railroad flatcar.

in peace and drink in quiet, and specially obey us. Then the Chiefs come round to shake hands, and they was so hairy and white and fair it was just shaking hands with old friends. We gave them names according as they was like men we had known in India—Billy Fish, Holly Wilworth, Pikky Kergan that was Bazaar-master when I was at Mhow, and so on and so on.

"*The* most amazing miracle was at Lodge next night. One of the old priests was watching us continuous, and I felt uneasy, for I knew we'd have to fudge[56] the Ritual, and I didn't know what the men knew. The old priest was a stranger come in from beyond the village of Bashkai. The minute Dravot puts on the Master's apron that the girls had made for him, the priest fetches a whoop and a howl, and tried to overturn the stone that Dravot was sitting on. 'It's all up now,' I says. 'That comes of meddling with the Craft without warrant!' Dravot never winked an eye, not when ten priests took and tilted over the Grand Master's chair—which was to say the stone of Imbra. The priest begins rubbing the bottom end of it to clear away the black dirt, and presently he shows all the other priests the Master's Mark, same as was on Dravot's apron, cut into the stone. Not even the priests of the temple of Imbra knew it was there. The old chap falls flat on his face at Dravot's feet and kisses 'em. 'Luck again,' says Dravot, across the Lodge to me, 'they say it's the missing Mark that no one could understand the why of. We're more than safe now.' Then he bangs the butt of his gun for a gavel and says, 'By virtue of the authority vested in me by my own right hand and the help of Peachey, I declare myself Grand Master of all Freemasonry in Kafiristan in this the Mother Lodge o' the country, and King of Kafiristan equally with Peachey!' At that he puts on his crown and I puts on mine—I was doing Senior Warden —and we opens the Lodge in most ample form. It was a amazing miracle! The priests

moved in Lodge through the first two degrees almost without telling, as if the memory was coming back to them. After that, Peachey and Dravot raised such as was worthy—high priests and Chiefs of far-off villages. Billy Fish was the first, and I can tell you we scared the soul out of him. It was not in any way according to Ritual, but it served our turn. We didn't raise more than ten of the biggest men, because we didn't want to make the Degree common. And they was clamoring to be raised.

" 'In another six months,' says Dravot, 'we'll hold another Communication and see how you are working.' Then he asks them about their villages, and learns that they was fighting one against the other and were fair sick and tired of it. And when they wasn't doing that they was fighting with the Mohammedans. 'You can fight those when they come into our country,' says Dravot. 'Tell off[57] every tenth man of your tribes for a Frontier guard, and send two hundred at a time to this valley to be drilled. Nobody is going to be shot or speared any more so long as he does well, and I know that you won't cheat me because you're white people—sons of Alexander—and not like common, black Mohammedans. You are *my* people and by God,' says he, running off into English at the end—'I'll make a damned fine Nation of you, or I'll die in the making!'

"I can't tell all we did for the next six months because Dravot did a lot I couldn't see the hang of, and he learned their lingo in a way I never could. My work was to help the people plow, and now and again go out with some of the Army and see what the other villages were doing, and make 'em throw rope bridges across the ravines which cut up the country horrid. Dravot was very kind to me, but when he walked up and down in the pine wood pulling that bloody red beard of his with both fists I knew he was thinking plans I could not advise him about, and I just waited for orders.

56. FUDGE: fake.

57. TELL OFF: number for purposes of special duty.

"But Dravot never showed me disrespect before the people. They were afraid of me and the Army, but they loved Dan. He was the best of friends with the priests and the Chiefs; but anyone could come across the hills with a complaint and Dravot would hear him out fair, and call four priests together and say what was to be done. He used to call in Billy Fish from Bashkai, and Pikky Kergan from Shu, and an old Chief we called Kafuzelum—it was like enough to his real name—and hold councils with 'em when there was any fighting to be done in small villages. That was his Council of War, and the four priests of Bashkai, Shu, Khawak, and Madora was his Privy Council. Between the lot of 'em they sent me, with forty men and twenty rifles, and sixty men carrying turquoises, into the Ghorband[58] country to buy those hand-made Martini rifles, that come out of the Amir's workshops at Kabul, from one of the Amir's Herati[59] regiments that would have sold the very teeth out of their mouths for turquoises.

"I stayed in Ghorband a month, and gave the Governor there the pick of my baskets for hush money, and bribed the Colonel of the regiment some more, and, between the two and the tribespeople, we got more than a hundred hand-made Martinis, a hundred good Kohat Jezails[60] that'll throw to six hundred yards, and forty manloads of very bad ammunition for the rifles. I came back with what I had, and distributed 'em among the men that the Chiefs sent to me to drill. Dravot was too busy to attend to those things, but the old Army that we first made helped me, and we turned out five hundred men that could drill, and two hundred that knew how to hold arms pretty straight. Even those corkscrewed, hand-made guns was a miracle to them. Dravot talked big about powder shops and factories, walking up and

down in the pine wood when the winter was coming on.

" 'I won't make a Nation,' says he. 'I'll make an Empire! These men aren't niggers; they're English! Look at their eyes—look at their mouths. Look at the way they stand up. They sit on chairs in their own houses. They're the Lost Tribes,[61] or something like it, and they've grown to be English. I'll take a census in the spring if the priests don't get frightened. There must be a fair two million of 'em in these hills. The villages are full o' little children. Two million people— two hundred and fifty thousand fighting men —and all English! They only want the rifles and a little drilling. Two hundred and fifty thousand men, ready to cut in on Russia's right flank when she tries for India! Peachey, man,' he says, chewing his beard in great chunks, 'we shall be Emperors—Emperors of the Earth! Rajah Brooke[62] will be a suckling[63] to us. I'll treat the Viceroy[64] on equal terms. I'll ask him to send me twelve picked English—twelve that I know of—to help us govern a bit. There's Mackray, Sergeant-pensioner at Segowli—many's the good dinner he's given me, and his wife a pair of trousers. There's Donkin, the Warder of Tounghoo Jail; there's hundreds that I could lay my hand on if I was in India. The Viceroy shall do it for me. I'll send a man through in the spring for those men, and I'll write for a dispensation from the Grand Lodge for what I've done as Grand Master. That—and all the Sniders[65] that'll be thrown out when the native troops in India take up the Martini. They'll be

---

58. GHORBAND: in northwest Afghanistan.
59. HERATI: men of Herat, city in northwest Afghanistan.
60. KOHAT JEZAILS: long, heavy rifles from Kohat, near Peshawar.
61. LOST TRIBES: In 722 B.C. Israel was defeated by the Assyrians, and thousands of Jews were sent to various parts of the Assyrian Empire, never to return to Palestine.
62. RAJAH BROOKE: Sir James Brooke (1803-1868), Rajah of Sarawak, born in Bengal, the son of a civil servant; on his own he succeeded in bringing civilized government to parts of Malaya.
63. SUCKLING: an unweaned child.
64. VICEROY: the top British official in India.
65. SNIDERS: rifles, inferior to the Martini-Henry.

worn smooth, but they'll do for fighting in these hills. Twelve English, a hundred thousand Sniders run through the Amir's country in driblets—I'd be content with twenty thousand in one year—and we'd be an Empire. When everything was shipshape, I'd hand over the crown—this crown I'm wearing now—to Queen Victoria on my knees, and she'd say: "Rise up, Sir Daniel Dravot."[66] Oh, it's big! It's big, I tell you! But there's so much to be done in every place—Bashkai, Khawak, Shu, and everywhere else.'

" 'What is it?' I says. 'There are no more men coming in to be drilled this autumn. Look at those fat, black clouds. They're bringing the snow.'

" 'It isn't that,' says Daniel, putting his hand very hard on my shoulder; 'and I don't wish to say anything that's against you, for no other living man would have followed me and made me what I am as you have done. You're a first-class Commander-in-Chief, and the people know you; but—it's a big country, and somehow you can't help me, Peachey, in the way I want to be helped.'

" 'Go to your blasted priests, then!' I said, and I was sorry when I made that remark, but it did hurt me sore to find Daniel talking so superior when I'd drilled all the men, and done all he told me.

" 'Don't let's quarrel, Peachey,' says Daniel, without cursing, 'You're a King, too, and the half of this Kingdom is yours; but can't you see, Peachey, we want cleverer men than us now—three or four of 'em, that we can scatter about for our Deputies. It's a hugeous great State, and I can't always tell the right thing to do, and I haven't time for all I want to do, and here's the winter coming on and all.' He put half his beard into his mouth, and it was as red as the gold of his crown.

" 'I'm sorry, Daniel,' says I. 'I've done all I could. I've drilled the men and shown the people how to stack their oats better; and I've brought in those tinware rifles from Ghorband—but I know what you're driving at. I take it Kings always feel oppressed that way.'

" 'There's another thing too,' says Dravot, walking up and down. 'The winter's coming and these people won't be giving much trouble and if they do we can't move about. I want a wife.'

" 'For Gord's sake leave the women alone!' I says. 'We've both got all the work we can, though I *am* a fool. Remember the Contrack, and keep clear o' women.'

" 'The Contrack only lasted till such time as we was Kings; and Kings we have been these months past,' says Dravot, weighing his crown in his hand. 'You go get a wife too, Peachey—a nice, strappin', plump girl that'll keep you warm in the winter. They're prettier than English girls, and we can take the pick of 'em. Boil 'em once or twice in hot water, and they'll come as fair as chicken and ham.'

" 'Don't tempt me!' I says. 'I will not have any dealings with a woman not till we are a dam' side more settled than we are now. I've been doing the work o' two men, and you've been doing the work o' three. Let's lie off a bit, and see if we can get some better tobacco from Afghan country and run in some good liquor; but no women.'

" 'Who's talking o' *women?*' says Dravot. 'I said *wife*—a Queen to breed a King's son for the King. A Queen out of the strongest tribe, that'll make them your blood brothers, and that'll lie by your side and tell you all the people thinks about you and their own affairs. That's what I want.'

" 'Do you remember that Bengali woman I kept at Mogul Serai when I was a plate[67] layer?' says I. 'A fat lot o' good she was to me. She taught me the lingo and one or two other things; but what happened? She ran away with the Stationmaster's servant and half my month's pay. Then she turned up at Dadur Junction in tow of a half-caste,

---

66. QUEEN VICTORIA . . . DRAVOT: Queen of England at the time; Dravot imagines her knighting him.

67. PLATE: rail.

and had the impidence to say I was her husband—all among the drivers in the running shed!'

" 'We've done with that,' says Dravot. 'These women are whiter than you or me, and a Queen I will have for the winter months.'

" 'For the last time o' asking, Dan, do *not*,' I says. 'It'll only bring us harm. The Bible says that Kings ain't to waste their strength on women,[68] 'specially when they've got a new raw Kingdom to work over.'

" 'For the last time of answering, I will,' said Dravot, and he went away through the pine trees looking like a big red devil. The low sun hit his crown and beard on one side and the two blazed like hot coals.

"But getting a wife was not as easy as Dan thought. He put it before the Council, and there was no answer till Billy Fish said that he'd better ask the girls. Dravot damned them all round. 'What's wrong with me?' he shouts, standing by the idol Imbra. 'Am I a dog or am I not enough of a man for your wenches? Haven't I put the shadow of my hand over this country? Who stopped the last Afghan raid?' It was me really, but Dravot was too angry to remember. 'Who brought your guns? Who repaired the bridges? Who's the Grand Master of the sign cut in the stone?' and he thumped his hand on the block that he used to sit on in Lodge, and at Council, which opened like Lodge always. Billy Fish said nothing, and no more did the others. 'Keep your hair on, Dan,' said I; 'and ask the girls. That's how it's done at Home, and these people are quite English.'

" 'The marriage of the King is a matter of State,' says Dan, in a white-hot rage, for he could feel, I hope, that he was going against his better mind. He walked out of the Council room, and the others sat still, looking at the ground.

" 'Billy Fish,' says I to the Chief of Bashkai, 'what's the difficulty here? A straight

answer to a true friend.' 'You know,' says Billy Fish. 'How should a man tell you who know everything? How can daughters of men marry Gods or Devils? It's not proper.'

"I remembered something like that in the Bible; but if, after seeing us as long as they had, they still believed we were Gods, it wasn't for me to undeceive them.

" 'A God can do anything,' says I. 'If the King is fond of a girl he'll not let her die.' 'She'll have to,' said Billy Fish. 'There are all sorts of Gods and Devils in these mountains, and now and again a girl marries one of them and isn't seen any more. Besides, you two know the Mark cut in the stone. Only the Gods know that. We thought you were men till you showed the sign of the Master.'

"I wished then that we had explained about the loss of the genuine secrets of a Master Mason at the first go-off; but I said nothing. All that night there was a blowing of horns in a little dark temple halfway down the hill, and I heard a girl crying fit to die. One of the priests told us that she was being prepared to marry the King.

" 'I'll have no nonsense of that kind,' says Dan. 'I don't want to interfere with your customs, but I'll take my own wife.' 'The girl's a little bit afraid,' says the priest. 'She thinks she's going to die, and they are a-heartening of her up down in the temple.'

" 'Hearten her very tender, then,' says Dravot, 'or I'll hearten you with the butt of a gun so that you'll never want to be heartened again.' He licked his lips, did Dan, and stayed up walking about more than half the night, thinking of the wife that he was going to get in the morning. I wasn't any means comfortable, for I knew that dealings with a woman in foreign parts, though you was crowned King twenty times over, could not but be risky. I got up very early in the morning while Dravot was asleep, and I saw the priests talking together in whispers, and the Chiefs talking together too, and they looked at me out of the corners of their eyes.

68.   THE BIBLE . . . WOMEN: Proverbs 31:1-3.

" 'What is up, Fish?' I says to the Bashkai man, who was wrapped up in his furs and looking splendid to behold.

" 'I can't rightly say,' says he; 'but if you can induce the King to drop all this nonsense about marriage, you'll be doing him and me and yourself a great service.'

" 'That I do believe,' says I. 'But sure, you know, Billy, as well as me, having fought against and for us, that the King and me are nothing more than two of the finest men that God Almighty ever made. Nothing more, I do assure you.'

" 'That may be,' says Billy Fish, 'and yet I should be sorry if it was.' He sinks his head upon his great fur cloak for a minute and thinks. 'King,' says he, 'be you man or God or Devil, I'll stick by you today. I have twenty of my men with me, and they will follow me. We'll go to Bashkai until the storm blows over.'

"A little snow had fallen in the night, and everything was white except the greasy fat clouds that blew down and down from the north. Dravot came out with his crown on his head, swinging his arms and stamping his feet, and looking more pleased than Punch.

" 'For the last time, drop it, Dan,' says I, in a whisper. 'Billy Fish here says that there will be a row.'

" 'A row among my people!' says Dravot. 'Not much. Peachey, you're a fool not to get a wife too. Where's the girl?' says he, with a voice as loud as the braying of a jackass. 'Call up all the Chiefs and priests, and let the Emperor see if his wife suits him.'

"There was no need to call anyone. They were all there leaning on their guns and spears round the clearing in the center of the pine wood. A deputation of priests went down to the little temple to bring up the girl, and the horns blew up fit to wake the dead. Billy Fish saunters round and gets as close to Daniel as he could, and behind him stood his twenty men with matchlocks. Not a man of them under six feet. I was next to Dravot, and behind me was twenty men of the regular Army. Up comes the girl, and a strapping wench she was, covered with silver and turquoises, but white as death, and looking back every minute at the priests.

" 'She'll do,' said Dan, looking her over. 'What's to be afraid of, lass? Come and kiss me.' He puts his arm round her. She shuts her eyes, gives a bit of a squeak, and down goes her face in the side of Dan's flaming red beard.

" 'The slut's bitten me!' says he, clapping his hand to his neck, and, sure enough, his hand was red with blood. Billy Fish and two of his matchlock men catches hold of Dan by the shoulders and drags him into the Bashkai lot, while the priests howl in their lingo, 'Neither God nor Devil, but a man!' I was all taken aback, for a priest cut at me in front, and the Army behind began firing into the Bashkai men.

" 'God A-mighty!' says Dan. 'What is the meaning o' this?'

" 'Come back! Come away!' says Billy Fish. 'Ruin and Mutiny is the matter. We'll break for Bashkai if we can.'

"I tried to give some sort of orders to my men—the men o' the regular Army—but it was no use, so I fired into the brown of 'em with an English Martini and drilled three beggars in a line. The valley was full of shouting, howling creatures, and every soul was shrieking, 'Not a God nor a Devil, but only a man!' The Bashkai troops stuck to Billy Fish all they were worth, but their matchlocks wasn't half as good as the Kabul breech-loaders, and four of them dropped. Dan was bellowing like a bull, for he was very wrathy; and Billy Fish had a hard job to prevent him running out at the crowd.

" 'We can't stand,' says Billy Fish. 'Make a run for it down the valley! The whole place is against us.' The matchlock men ran, and we went down the valley in spite of Dravot's protestations. He was swearing horribly and crying out that he was a King. The priests rolled great stones on us, and the regular Army fired hard, and there wasn't more than six men, not counting Dan, Billy

Fish, and Me, that came down to the bottom of the valley alive.

"Then they stopped firing and the horns in the temple blew again. 'Come away—for Gord's sake come away!' says Billy Fish. 'They'll send runners out to all the villages before ever we get to Bashkai. I can protect you there, but I can't do anything now.'

"My own notion is that Dan began to go mad in his head from that hour. He stared up and down like a stuck pig. Then he was all for walking back alone and killing the priests with his bare hands; which he could have done. 'An Emperor am I,' says Daniel, 'and next year I shall be a Knight of the Queen.'

" 'All right, Dan,' says I; 'but come along now while there's time.'

" 'It's your fault,' says he, 'for not looking after your Army better. There was mutiny in the midst and you didn't know—you damned engine-driving, plate-laying, missionary's-pass-hunting hound!' He sat upon a rock and called me every foul name he could lay tongue to. I was too heartsick to care, though it was all his foolishness that brought the smash.[69]

" 'I'm sorry, Dan,' says I, 'but there's no accounting for natives. This business is our Fifty-Seven.[70] Maybe we'll make something out of it yet, when we've got to Bashkai.'

" 'Let's get to Bashkai, then,' says Dan, 'and, by God, when I come back here again I'll sweep the valley so there isn't a bug in a blanket left!'

"We walked all that day, and all that night Dan was stumping up and down on the snow, chewing his beard and muttering to himself.

" 'There's no hope o' getting clear,' said Billy Fish. 'The priests will have sent runners to the villages to say that you are only

---

men. Why didn't you stick on as Gods till things was more settled? I'm a dead man,' says Billy Fish, and he throws himself down on the snow and begins to pray to his Gods.

"Next morning we was in a cruel bad country—all up and down, no level ground at all, and no food either. The six Bashkai men looked at Billy Fish hungrywise as if they wanted to ask something, but they said never a word. At noon we came to the top of a flat mountain all covered with snow, and when we climbed up into it, behold, there was an Army in position waiting in the middle!

" 'The runners have been very quick,' says Billy Fish, with a little bit of a laugh. 'They are waiting for us.'

"Three or four men began to fire from the enemy's side, and a chance shot took Daniel in the calf of the leg. That brought him to his senses. He looks across the snow at the Army, and sees the rifles that we had brought into the country.

" 'We're done for,' says he. 'They are Englishmen, these people—and it's my blasted nonsense that has brought you to this. Get back, Billy Fish, and take your men away; you've done what you could, and now cut for it. Carnehan,' says he, 'shake hands with me and go along with Billy. Maybe they won't kill you. I'll go and meet 'em alone. It's me that did it. Me, the King!'

" 'Go!' says I. 'Go to Hell, Dan. I'm with you here. Billy Fish, you clear out, and we two will meet those folk.'

" 'I'm a Chief,' says Billy Fish, quite quiet. 'I stay with you. My men can go.'

"The Bashkai fellows didn't wait for a second word, but ran off, and Dan and Me and Billy Fish walked across to where the drums were drumming and the horns were horning. It was cold— awful cold. I've got that cold in the back of my head now. There's a lump of it there."

The punkah coolies had gone to sleep. Two kerosene lamps were blazing in the office, and the perspiration poured down my face and splashed on the blotter as I leaned

---

69. SMASH: utter collapse; ruin.
70. FIFTY-SEVEN: reference is to the Indian Mutiny of 1857, led by the Bengal native army. The Mutiny marked the end of private rule in India by the East India Company, and the assumption of full control by the British government.

forward. Carnehan was shivering, and I feared that his mind might go. I wiped my face, took a fresh grip of the piteously mangled hands, and said, "What happened after that?"

The momentary shift of my eyes had broken the clear current.

"What was you pleased to say?" whined Carnehan. "They took them without any sound. Not a little whisper all along the snow, not though the King knocked down the first man that set hand on him—not though old Peachey fired his last cartridge into the brown of 'em. Not a single solitary sound did those swines make. They just closed up tight, and I tell you their furs stunk. There was a man called Billy Fish, a good friend of us all, and they cut his throat, Sir, then and there, like a pig; and the King kicks up the bloody snow and says, 'We've had a dashed fine run for our money. What's coming next?' But Peachey, Peachey Taliaferro, I tell you, Sir, in confidence as betwixt two friends, he lost his head, Sir. No, he didn't neither. The King lost his head, so he did, all along o' one of those cunning rope bridges. Kindly let me have the paper cutter, Sir. It tilted this way. They marched him a mile across that snow to a rope bridge over a ravine with a river at the bottom. You may have seen such. They prodded him like an ox. 'Damn your eyes!' says the King. 'D'you suppose I can't die like a gentleman?' He turns to Peachey—Peachey that was crying like a child. 'I've brought you to this, Peachey,' says he. 'Brought you out of your happy life to be killed in Kafiristan, where you was late Commander-in-Chief of the Emperor's forces. Say you forgive me, Peachey.' 'I do,' says Peachey. 'Fully and freely do I forgive you, Dan.' 'Shake hands, Peachey,' says he. 'I'm going now.' Out he goes, looking neither right nor left, and when he was plumb in the middle of those dizzy dancing ropes, 'Cut, you beggars,' he shouts; and they cut, and old Dan fell, turning round and round and round twenty thousand miles, for he took

half an hour to fall till he struck the water, and I could see his body caught on a rock with the gold crown close beside.

"But do you know what they did to Peachey between two pine trees? They crucified him, Sir, as Peachey's hand will show. They used wooden pegs for his hands and his feet; and he didn't die. He hung there and screamed, and they took him down next day, and said it was a miracle that he wasn't dead. They took him down—poor old Peachey that hadn't done them any harm—that hadn't done them any . . ."

He rocked to and fro and wept bitterly, wiping his eyes with the back of his scarred hands and moaning like a child for some ten minutes.

"They was cruel enough to feed him up in the temple, because they said he was more of a God than old Daniel that was a man. Then they turned him out on the snow, and told him to go home, and Peachey came home in about a year, begging along the roads quite safe; for Daniel Dravot he walked before and said, 'Come along, Peachey. It's a big thing we're doing.' The mountains they danced at night, and the mountains they tried to fall on Peachey's head, but Dan he held up his hand, and Peachey came along bent double. He never let go of Dan's hand, and he never let go of Dan's head. They gave it to him as a present in the temple, to remind him not to come again, and though the crown was pure gold, and Peachey was starving, never would Peachey sell the same. You knew Dravot, Sir! You knew Right Worshipful Brother Dravot! Look at him now!"

He fumbled in the mass of rags round his bent waist; brought out a black horse-hair bag embroidered with silver thread; and shook therefrom on to my table—the dried, withered head of Daniel Dravot! The morning sun that had long been paling the lamps struck the red beard and blind sunken eyes; struck, too, a heavy circlet of gold studded with raw turquoises, that Carnehan placed tenderly on the battered temples.

"You behold now," said Carnehan, "the Emperor in his habit as he lived—the King of Kafiristan with his crown upon his head. Poor old Daniel that was a monarch once!"

I shuddered, for, in spite of defacements manifold, I recognized the head of the man of Marwar Junction. Carnehan rose to go. I attempted to stop him. He was not fit to walk abroad. "Let me take away the whisky, and give me a little money," he gasped. "I was a King once. I'll go to the Deputy Commissioner and ask to set in the Poorhouse till I get my health. No, thank you, I can't wait till you get a carriage for me. I've urgent private affairs—in the South—at Marwar."

He shambled out of the office and departed in the direction of the Deputy Commissioner's house. That day at noon I had occasion to go down the blinding hot Mall, and I saw a crooked man crawling along the white dust of the roadside, his hat in his hand, quavering dolorously after the fashion of street-singers at Home. There was not a soul in sight, and he was out of all possible earshot of the houses. And he sang through his nose, turning his head from right to left:

> *The Son of Man goes forth to war,*
> *A golden crown to gain;*
> *His blood-red banner streams afar—*
> *Who follows in his train?*[71]

I waited to hear no more, but put the poor wretch into my carriage and drove him off to the nearest missionary for eventual transfer to the Asylum.[72] He repeated the hymn twice while he was with me, whom he did not in the least recognize, and I left him singing it to the missionary.

Two days later I inquired after his welfare of the Superintendent of the Asylum.

"He was admitted suffering from sunstroke. He died early yesterday morning," said the Superintendent. "Is it true that he was half an hour bareheaded in the sun at midday?"

"Yes," said I, "but do you happen to know if he had anything upon him by any chance when he died?"

"Not to my knowledge," said the Superintendent.

And there the matter rests.

---

71. THE SON . . . TRAIN?: first stanza of a popular hymn by Reginald Heber (1783-1826).
72. ASYLUM: for the insane.

I

1. What is the purpose of the first part of the story that deals with the narrator's rather strange encounters with the two *loafers*? What is the necessity of having the narrator at all? How does his presence in the story help define the characters of Peachey and Dravot?

2. What kind of person is the narrator? Does he have anything in common with Peachey and Dravot? What? How is he different? Why does he cut short his own trip to deliver Peachey's message? Why does he get the two men thrown out of Degumber State? Does his attitude toward them change during the story? How? What is significant about his holding fast to Peachey's hand while the latter unfolds his story?

3. Peachey and Dravot seem to be making out all right in India: why, then, do they go away "to be Kings . . . Kings in our own right"? Why don't they want to use their cleverness to subvert some Rajah's principality instead of going to an isolated and uncivilized corner of Afghanistan? What kind of kings do they want to be? What light does their reference to Sar-a-*whack* and Rajah Brooke throw on their motivations?

4. Comment on whether their "Contrack" is ludicrous or childish or admirable. What does it reveal about the two men and their motives for going to Kafiristan? Would you expect such a contract from what you learned of the two men up to this point in the story? Explain.

5. Do they change at all once they reach Kafiristan? Consider whether they ever develop qualms about killing people; whether Dravot's aim to bring peace to the villages is genuine; why he wants to bring in more capable administrators; how seriously Dravot sees himself annexing Kafiristan to Her Majesty's Empire; why he wants a wife and a public marriage ceremony; and how they both react to the collapse of their Kingdom.

6. Why did the natives react to Peachey and Dravot as gods? Why did they turn on the two when they found out the truth? What is significant about the fact that Billy Fish sticks with them until the end when he knew perfectly well that they were not gods? Why is Dravot's stumbling on the gimmick of Freemasonry as his religion ironically appropriate? Refer again to the note on Freemasonry on p. 616.

7. How are the terms of the contract fulfilled? Under what circumstances does Dravot seek to break item two? What are Peachey's misgivings? How is at least part of item three faithfully carried out? In what sense is there more "dignity" in Dravot's death than in his life? In what sense does Peachey act with even more dignity than Dravot does? What is significant about the fact that the natives crucify him, and that he sings the particular hymn he sings just before his death? Why is he so intent on telling his story to the narrator, and why does he starve himself to keep Dravot's head and crown? What is significant about the fact that he had nothing "on him" when he died?

II

1. In the first paragraph the narrator says, "But, today, I greatly fear that my King is dead, and if I want a crown I must go and hunt it for myself." In the light of the whole story, how might it be argued that this sentence embodies the theme of the story? Consider, for instance, the contrast between the desires and achievements of Peachey and Dravot and the newspaper office routine the narrator is involved in. Consider also the number of different times, and in what different contexts, "Kings" are referred to in the story. What does it mean to be a "King"? How have Peachey and Dravot become "Kings" only when they have ceased being "Kings"? Consider also just what the title means.

Success As Self-knowledge

The three selections that follow center on three very different individuals living in worlds far apart from each other in time and space. And yet there is a common bond among them that throws the differences into shadow: each individual exemplifies in the way he meets the test set for him the truth that success is a continuing search for self-knowledge in the light of that "ideal conception of one's own personality every man sets up for himself secretly."

The words are those of the first individual we meet, a young sea captain of the early twentieth century, on board his first command, in Joseph Conrad's story, "The Secret Sharer." The second individual is also a young man, this time from the legendary world of King Arthur's England—Sir Gawain, Arthur's nephew and the embodiment of chivalrous knighthood, as seen in the Middle English poem "Sir Gawain and the Green Knight." The third individual, Socrates, lived almost twenty-five hundred years ago in fifth century B. C. Athens. In Plato's *Apology* and *Phaedo* we see him, a vigorous man of seventy, defending his way of life against those who would silence him, and accepting death rather than silence.

THE SECRET SHARER   [*1912*]

Joseph Conrad

"The Secret Sharer" is one of many Conrad works dealing with the problem of a man's reaction to the conflicting drives within him, those that negate the virtues that give life dignity—loyalty, honor, courage, self-respect—and those that sustain these virtues. Success or failure is wholly a personal concern. In this story the contest involves man and ship "measuring our fitness for a long and arduous enterprise, the appointed task of both our existences to be carried out, far from all human eyes, with only sky and sea for spectators and for judges."

On my right hand there were lines of fishing stakes resembling a mysterious system of half-submerged bamboo fences, incomprehensible in its division of the domain of tropical fishes, and crazy of aspect as if abandoned forever by some nomad tribe of fishermen now gone to the other end of the ocean; for there was no sign of human habitation as far as the eye could reach. To the left a group of barren islets, suggesting ruins of stone walls, towers, and blockhouses, had its foundations set in a blue sea that itself looked solid, so still and stable did it lie below my feet; even the track of light from the westering sun shone smoothly, without that animated glitter which tells of an imperceptible ripple. And when I turned my head to take a parting glance at the tug which had just left us anchored outside the bar, I saw the straight line of the flat shore joined to the stable sea, edge to edge, with a perfect and unmarked closeness, in one leveled floor half brown, half blue under the enormous dome of the sky. Corresponding in their insignificance to the islets of the sea, two small clumps of trees, one on each side of the only fault in the impeccable joint, marked the mouth of the river Meinam[1] we had just left on the first preparatory stage of our homeward journey; and, far back on the inland level, a larger and loftier mass, the grove surrounding the great Paknam pagoda, was the only thing on which the eye could rest from the vain task of exploring the monotonous sweep of the horizon. Here and there gleams as of a few scattered pieces of silver marked the windings of the great river; and on the nearest of them, just within the bar,[2] the tug steaming right into the land became lost to my sight, hull and funnel and masts, as though the impassive earth had swallowed her up without an effort, without a tremor. My eye followed the light cloud of her smoke, now here, now there, above the plain, according to the devious curves of the stream, but always fainter and farther away, till I lost it at last behind the miter-shaped hill of the great pagoda. And then I was left alone with my ship, anchored at the head of the Gulf of Siam.

She floated at the starting point of a long journey, very still in an immense stillness, the shadows of her spars flung far to the eastward by the setting sun. At that moment I was alone on her decks. There was not a sound in her—and around us nothing moved, nothing lived, not a canoe on the water, not a bird in the air, not a cloud in the sky. In this breathless pause at the threshold of a long passage we seemed to be measuring our fitness for a long and

---

1. RIVER MEINAM: The ship is anchored in the Gulf of Siam; the Meinam empties into the Gulf below Paknam.

"The Secret Sharer" from *Twixt Land and Sea* by Joseph Conrad. Reprinted by permission of J. M. Dent & Sons Ltd.

---

2. BAR: sand bar.

arduous enterprise, the appointed task of both our existences to be carried out, far from all human eyes, with only sky and sea for spectators and for judges.

There must have been some glare in the air to interfere with one's sight, because it was only just before the sun left us that my roaming eyes made out beyond the highest ridge of the principal islet of the group something which did away with the solemnity of perfect solitude. The tide of darkness flowed on swiftly; and with tropical suddenness a swarm of stars came out above the shadowy earth, while I lingered yet, my hand resting lightly on my ship's rail as if on the shoulder of a trusted friend. But, with all that multitude of celestial bodies staring down at one, the comfort of quiet communion with her was gone for good. And there were also disturbing sounds by this time—voices, footsteps forward; the steward flitted along the main deck, a busily ministering spirit; a hand bell tinkled urgently under the poop deck. . . .

I found my two officers waiting for me near the supper table, in the lighted cuddy. We sat down at once, and as I helped the chief mate, I said:

"Are you aware that there is a ship anchored inside the islands? I saw her mastheads above the ridge as the sun went down."

He raised sharply his simple face, overcharged by a terrible growth of whisker, and emitted his usual ejaculations: "Bless my soul, sir! You don't say so!"

My second mate was a round-cheeked, silent young man, grave beyond his years, I thought; but as our eyes happened to meet I detected a slight quiver on his lips. I looked down at once. It was not my part to encourage sneering on board my ship. It must be said, too, that I knew very little of my officers. In consequence of certain events of no particular significance, except to myself, I had been appointed to the command only a fortnight before. Neither did I know much of the hands forward. All these people had been together for eighteen months or so, and my position was that of

the only stranger on board. I mention this because it has some bearing on what is to follow. But what I felt most was my being a stranger to the ship; and if all the truth must be told, I was somewhat of a stranger to myself. The youngest man on board (barring the second mate), and untried as yet by a position of the fullest responsibility, I was willing to take the adequacy of the others for granted. They had simply to be equal to their tasks; but I wondered how far I should turn out faithful to that ideal conception of one's own personality every man sets up for himself secretly.

Meantime the chief mate, with an almost visible effect of collaboration on the part of his round eyes and frightful whiskers, was trying to evolve a theory of the anchored ship. His dominant trait was to take all things into earnest consideration. He was of a painstaking turn of mind. As he used to say, he "liked to account to himself" for practically everything that came in his way, down to a miserable scorpion he had found in his cabin a week before. The why and the wherefore of that scorpion—how it got on board and came to select his room rather than the pantry (which was a dark place and more what a scorpion would be partial to), and how on earth it managed to drown itself in the inkwell of his writing desk—had exercised him infinitely. The ship within the islands was much more easily accounted for; and just as we were about to rise from table he made his pronouncement. She was, he doubted not, a ship from home lately arrived. Probably she drew too much water to cross the bar except at the top of spring tides. Therefore she went into that natural harbor to wait for a few days in preference to remaining in an open roadstead.[3]

"That's so," confirmed the second mate, suddenly, in his slightly hoarse voice. "She draws over twenty feet.[4] She's the Liverpool

---

3. ROADSTEAD: a protected area where ships can anchor.
4. DRAWS . . . FEET: needs more than twenty feet of water to float.

ship *Sephora* with a cargo of coal. Hundred and twenty-three days from Cardiff."[5]

We looked at him in surprise.

"The tugboat skipper told me when he came on board for your letters, sir," explained the young man. "He expects to take her up the river the day after tomorrow."

After thus overwhelming us with the extent of his information he slipped out of the cabin. The mate observed regretfully that he "could not account for that young fellow's whims." What prevented him telling us all about it at once, he wanted to know.

I detained him as he was making a move. For the last two days the crew had had plenty of hard work, and the night before they had very little sleep. I felt painfully that I—a stranger—was doing something unusual when I directed him to let all hands turn in without setting an anchor watch. I proposed to keep on deck myself till one o'clock or thereabouts. I would get the second mate to relieve me at that hour.

"He will turn out[6] the cook and the steward at four," I concluded, "and then give you a call. Of course at the slightest sign of any sort of wind we'll have the hands up and make a start at once."

He concealed his astonishment. "Very well, sir." Outside the cuddy he put his head in the second mate's door to inform him of my unheard-of caprice to take a five hours' anchor watch on myself. I heard the other raise his voice incredulously—"What? The Captain himself?" Then a few more murmurs, a door closed, then another. A few moments later I went on deck.

My strangeness, which had made me sleepless, had prompted that unconventional arrangement, as if I had expected in those solitary hours of the night to get on terms with the ship of which I knew nothing, manned by men of whom I knew very little more. Fast alongside a wharf, littered like any ship in port with a tangle of unrelated things, invaded by unrelated shore people,

I had hardly seen her yet properly. Now, as she lay cleared for sea, the stretch of her main deck seemed to me very fine under the stars. Very fine, very roomy for her size, and very inviting. I descended the poop and paced the waist,[7] my mind picturing to myself the coming passage through the Malay Archipelago, down the Indian Ocean, and up the Atlantic. All its phases were familiar enough to me, every characteristic, all the alternatives which were likely to face me on the high seas—everything! . . . except the novel responsibility of command. But I took heart from the reasonable thought that the ship was like other ships, the men like other men, and that the sea was not likely to keep any special surprises expressly for my discomfiture.

Arrived at that comforting conclusion, I bethought myself of a cigar and went below to get it. All was still down there. Everybody at the after end of the ship was sleeping profoundly. I came out again on the quarter-deck,[8] agreeably at ease in my sleeping suit on that warm breathless night, barefooted, a glowing cigar in my teeth, and, going forward, I was met by the profound silence of the fore end of the ship. Only as I passed the door of the forecastle[9] I heard a deep, quiet, trustful sigh of some sleeper inside. And suddenly I rejoiced in the great security of the sea as compared with the unrest of the land, in my choice of that untempted life presenting no disquieting problems, invested with an elementary moral beauty by the absolute straightforwardness of its appeal and by the singleness of its purpose.

The riding light in the forerigging[10] burned with a clear, untroubled, as if symbolic, flame, confident and bright in the mysterious

---

5. CARDIFF: seaport in Wales.
6. TURN OUT: wake up.

7. DESCENDED . . . WAIST: climbed down from the poop deck and walked around the main deck.
8. QUARTER-DECK: that part of the upper deck used by officers and passengers.
9. FORECASTLE: in merchant ships, the sailors' quarters in the front part of the ship.
10. RIDING . . . FORERIGGING: warning light in the front rigging.

shades of the night. Passing on my way aft[11] along the other side of the ship, I observed that the rope side-ladder, put over, no doubt, for the master of the tug when he came to fetch away our letters, had not been hauled in as it should have been. I became annoyed at this, for exactitude in small matters is the very soul of discipline. Then I reflected that I had myself peremptorily dismissed my officers from duty, and by my own act had prevented the anchor watch being formally set and things properly attended to. I asked myself whether it was wise ever to interfere with the established routine of duties even from the kindest of motives. My action might have made me appear eccentric. Goodness only knew how that absurdly whiskered mate would "account" for my conduct, and what the whole ship thought of that informality of their new captain. I was vexed with myself.

Not from compunction certainly, but, as it were mechanically, I proceeded to get the ladder in myself. Now a side-ladder of that sort is a light affair and comes in easily, yet my vigorous tug, which should have brought it flying on board, merely recoiled upon my body in a totally unexpected jerk. What the devil! . . . I was so astounded by the immovableness of that ladder that I remained stockstill, trying to account for it to myself like that imbecile mate of mine. In the end, of course, I put my head over the rail.

The side of the ship made an opaque belt of shadow on the darkling glassy shimmer of the sea. But I saw at once something elongated and pale floating very close to the ladder. Before I could form a guess a faint flash of phosphorescent light, which seemed to issue suddenly from the naked body of a man, flickered in the sleeping water with the elusive, silent play of summer lightning in a night sky. With a gasp I saw revealed to my stare a pair of feet, the long legs, a broad livid back immersed right up to the neck in a greenish cadaverous glow. One hand, awash, clutched the bot-

---

11. AFT: toward the rear.

tom rung of the ladder. He was complete but for the head. A headless corpse! The cigar dropped out of my gaping mouth with a tiny plop and a short hiss quite audible in the absolute stillness of all things under heaven. At that I suppose he raised up his face, a dimly pale oval in the shadow of the ship's side. But even then I could only barely make out down there the shape of his black-haired head. However, it was enough for the horrid, frost-bound sensation which had gripped me about the chest to pass off. The moment of vain exclamations was past, too. I only climbed on the spare spar and leaned over the rail as far as I could, to bring my eyes nearer to that mystery floating alongside.

As he hung by the ladder, like a resting swimmer, the sea-lightning played about his limbs at every stir; and he appeared in it ghastly, silvery, fishlike. He remained as mute as a fish, too. He made no motion to get out of the water, either. It was inconceivable that he should not attempt to come on board, and strangely troubling to suspect that perhaps he did not want to. And my first words were prompted by just that troubled incertitude.

"What's the matter?" I asked in my ordinary tone, speaking down to the face upturned exactly under mine.

"Cramp," it answered, no louder. Then slightly anxious, "I say, no need to call anyone."

"I was not going to," I said.

"Are you alone on deck?"

"Yes."

I had somehow the impression that he was on the point of letting go the ladder to swim away beyond my ken—mysterious as he came. But, for the moment, this being appearing as if he had risen from the bottom of the sea (it was certainly the nearest land to the ship) wanted only to know the time. I told him. And he, down there, tentatively:

"I suppose your captain's turned in?"

"I am sure he isn't," I said.

He seemed to struggle with himself, for

I heard something like the low, bitter murmur of doubt. "What's the good?" his next words came out with a hesitating effort.

"Look here, my man. Could you call him out quietly?"

I thought the time had come to declare myself.

"*I* am the captain."

I heard a "By Jove!" whispered at the level of the water. The phosphorescence flashed in the swirl of the water all about his limbs, his other hand seized the ladder.

"My name's Leggatt."

The voice was calm and resolute. A good voice. The self-possession of that man had somehow induced a corresponding state in myself. It was very quietly that I remarked:

"You must be a good swimmer."

"Yes. I've been in the water practically since nine o'clock. The question for me now is whether I am to let go this ladder and go on swimming till I sink from exhaustion, or—to come on board here."

I felt this was no mere formula of desperate speech, but a real alternative in the view of a strong soul. I should have gathered from this that he was young; indeed it is only the young who are ever confronted by such clear issues. But at the time it was pure intuition on my part. A mysterious communication was established already between us two—in the face of that silent darkened tropical sea. I was young, too; young enough to make no comment. The man in the water began suddenly to climb up the ladder, and I hastened away from the rail to fetch some clothes.

Before entering the cabin I stood still, listening in the lobby at the foot of the stairs. A faint snore came through the closed door of the chief mate's room. The second mate's door was on the hook, but the darkness in there was absolutely soundless. He, too, was young and could sleep like a stone. Remained the steward, but he was not likely to wake up before he was called. I got a sleeping suit out of my room and, coming back on deck, saw the naked man from the sea sitting on the main hatch, glimmering white in the darkness, his elbows on his knees and his head in his hands. In a moment he had concealed his damp body in a sleeping suit of the same gray-stripe pattern as the one I was wearing and followed me like my double on the poop. Together we moved right aft, barefoot, silent.

"What is it?" I asked in a deadened voice, taking the lighted lamp out of the binnacle,[12] and raising it to his face.

"An ugly business."

He had rather regular features; a good mouth; light eyes under somewhat heavy, dark eyebrows; a smooth, square forehead; no growth on his cheeks; a small, brown mustache, and a well-shaped round chin. His expression was concentrated, meditative, under the inspecting light of the lamp I held up to his face; such as a man thinking hard in solitude might wear. My sleeping suit was just right for his size. A well-knit fellow of twenty-five at most. He caught his lower lip with the edge of white, even teeth.

"Yes," I said, replacing the lamp in the binnacle. The warm, heavy tropical night closed upon his head again.

"There's a ship over there," he murmured.

"Yes, I know. The *Sephora.* Did you know of us?"

"Hadn't the slightest idea. I am the mate of her——" He paused and corrected himself. "I should say I *was.*"

"Aha! Something wrong?"

"Yes. Very wrong indeed. I've killed a man."

"What do you mean? Just now?"

"No, on the passage. Weeks ago. Thirty-nine south.[13] When I say a man——"

---

12. BINNACLE: a stand holding the ship's compass; a light is kept on it at night.
13. THIRTY-NINE SOUTH: i.e., somewhere along the thirty-ninth south latitude line, a good distance from the head of the Gulf of Siam, which is approximately at the thirteenth north. The *Sephora* had sailed from Cardiff around the tip of Africa, then up through the Indian Ocean to the Sunda Straits between Sumatra and Java; you can determine on a map approximately where the storm took place.

"Fit of temper," I suggested, confidently.

The shadowy, dark head, like mine, seemed to nod imperceptibly above the ghostly gray of my sleeping suit. It was, in the night, as though I had been faced by my own reflection in the depths of a somber and immense mirror.

"A pretty thing to have to own up to for a Conway[14] boy," murmured my double, distinctly.

"You're a Conway boy?"

"I am," he said, as if startled. Then slowly . . . "Perhaps you too——"

It was so; but being a couple of years older I had left before he joined. After a quick interchange of dates a silence fell; and I thought suddenly of my absurd mate with his terrific whiskers and the "Bless my soul—you don't say so" type of intellect. My double gave me an inkling of his thoughts by saying: "My father's a parson in Norfolk. Do you see me before a judge and jury on that charge? For myself I can't see the necessity. There are fellows that an angel from heaven——And I am not that. He was one of those creatures that are just simmering all the time with a silly sort of wickedness. Miserable devils that have no business to live at all. He wouldn't do his duty and wouldn't let anybody else do theirs. But what's the good of talking! You know well enough the sort of ill-conditioned snarling cur——"

He appealed to me as if our experiences had been identical as our clothes. And I knew well enough the pestiferous danger of such a character where there are no means of legal repression. And I knew well enough also that my double there was no homicidal ruffian. I did not think of asking him for details, and he told me the story roughly in brusque, disconnected sentences. I needed no more. I saw it all going on as though I were myself inside that other sleeping suit.

"It happened while we were setting a reefed foresail,[15] at dusk. Reefed foresail! You understand the sort of weather. The only sail we had left to keep the ship running; so you may guess what it had been like for days. Anxious sort of job, that. He gave me some of his cursed insolence at the sheet.[16] I tell you I was overdone with this terrific weather that seemed to have no end to it. Terrific, I tell you—and a deep ship. I believe the fellow himself was half-crazed with funk.[17] It was no time for gentlemanly reproof, so I turned round and felled him like an ox. He up and at me. We closed just as an awful sea made for the ship. All hands saw it coming and took to the rigging, but I had him by the throat, and went on shaking him like a rat, the men above us yelling, 'Look out! Look out!' Then a crash as if the sky had fallen on my head. They say that for over ten minutes hardly anything was to be seen of the ship—just the three masts and a bit of the forecastle head and of the poop all awash driving along in a smother of foam. It was a miracle that they found us, jammed together behind the forebits.[18] It's clear that I meant business, because I was holding him by the throat still when they picked us up. He was black in the face. It was too much for them. It seems they rushed us aft together, gripped as we were, screaming 'Murder!' like a lot of lunatics, and broke into the cuddy. And the ship running for her life, touch and go all the time, any minute her last in a sea fit to turn your hair gray only a-looking at it. I understand that the skipper, too, started raving like the rest of them. The man had been deprived of sleep for more than a week, and to have this sprung on him at the height of a furious gale nearly drove him out of his

---

14. CONWAY: English naval school; the "Conway" is a cadet ship anchored in the Mersey River at Liverpool and used for training young men for the merchant marine.

15. REEFED FORESAIL: "reefed" means folded or rolled up to reduce sail area; the foresail is at the front of the ship.

16. SHEET: a rope or chain which controls the sail angle in relation to the wind.

17. FUNK: fright, fear.

18. FOREBITS: a "bit" (or "bitt") is a fixed timber or metal piece used on deck for securing cables or lines; they usually come in pairs.

mind. I wonder they didn't fling me over-board after getting the carcass of their precious shipmate out of my fingers. They had rather a job to separate us, I've been told. A sufficiently fierce story to make an old judge and a respectable jury sit up a bit. The first thing I heard when I came to my-self was the maddening howling of that endless gale, and on that the voice of the old man. He was hanging on to my bunk, staring into my face out of his sou-wester.[19]

" 'Mr. Leggatt, you have killed a man. You can act no longer as chief mate of this ship.' "

His care to subdue his voice made it sound monotonous. He rested a hand on the end of the skylight to steady himself with, and all that time did not stir a limb, so far as I could see. "Nice little tale for a quiet tea party," he concluded in the same tone.

One of my hands, too, rested on the end of the skylight; neither did I stir a limb, so far as I knew. We stood less than a foot from each other. It occurred to me that if old "Bless my soul—you don't say so" were to put his head up the companion and catch sight of us, he would think he was see-ing double, or imagine himself come upon a scene of weird witchcraft; the strange cap-tain having a quiet confabulation by the wheel with his own gray ghost. I became very much concerned to prevent anything of the sort. I heard the other's soothing undertone.

"My father's a parson in Norfolk," it said. Evidently he had forgotten he had told me this important fact before. Truly a nice little tale.

"You had better slip down into my state-room now," I said, moving off stealthily. My double followed my movements; our bare feet made no sound; I let him in, closed the door with care, and, after giving a call to the second mate, returned on deck for my relief.

19. SOU'WESTER: a kind of canvas or oiled-cloth hat with a flap in the back, worn during stormy weather.

"Not much sign of any wind yet," I re-marked when he approached.

"No sir. Not much," he assented, sleepily, in his hoarse voice, with just enough defer-ence, no more, and barely suppressing a yawn.

"Well, that's all you have to look out for. You have got your orders."

"Yes, sir."

I paced a turn or two on the poop and saw him take up his position face forward with his elbow in the ratlines of the mizzen-rigging before I went below. The mate's faint snoring was still going on peacefully. The cuddy lamp was burning over the table on which stood a vase with flowers, a polite attention from the ship's provision mer-chant—the last flowers we should see for the next three months at the very least. Two bunches of bananas hung from the beam symmetrically, one on each side of the rudder-casing. Everything was as before in the ship—except that two of her captain's sleeping suits were simultaneously in use, one motionless in the cuddy, the other keep-ing very still in the captain's stateroom.

It must be explained here that my cabin had the form of the capital letter L, the door being within the angle and opening into the short part of the letter. A couch was to the left, the bed-place to the right; my writing desk and the chronometers' table faced the door. But anyone opening it, unless he stepped right inside, had no view of what I call the long (or vertical) part of the let-ter. It contained some lockers surmounted by a bookcase; and a few clothes, a thick jacket or two, caps, oilskin coat, and such-like, hung on hooks. There was at the bot-tom of that part a door opening into my bathroom, which could be entered also di-rectly from the saloon. But that way was never used.

The mysterious arrival had discovered the advantage of this particular shape. Entering my room, lighted strongly by a big bulkhead lamp swung on gimbals above my writing desk, I did not see him anywhere till he stepped out quietly from behind the coats hung in the recessed part.

"I heard somebody moving about, and went in there at once," he whispered.

I, too, spoke under my breath.

"Nobody is likely to come in here without knocking and getting permission."

He nodded. His face was thin and the sunburn faded, as though he had been ill. And no wonder. He had been, I heard presently, kept under arrest in his cabin for nearly seven weeks. But there was nothing sickly in his eyes or in his expression. He was not a bit like me, really; yet, as we stood leaning over my bed-place, whispering side by side, with our dark heads together and our backs to the door, anybody bold enough to open it stealthily would have been treated to the uncanny sight of a double captain busy talking in whispers with his other self.

"But all this doesn't tell me how you came to hang on to our side-ladder," I inquired, in the hardly audible murmurs we used, after he had told me something more of the proceedings on board the *Sephora* once the bad weather was over.

"When we sighted Java Head I had had time to think all those matters out several times over. I had six weeks of doing nothing else, and with only an hour or so every evening for a tramp on the quarter-deck."

He whispered, his arms folded on the side of my bed-place, staring through the open port. And I could imagine perfectly the manner of this thinking out—a stubborn if not a steadfast operation; something of which I should have been perfectly incapable.

"I reckoned it would be dark before we closed with the land," he continued, so low that I had to strain my hearing, near as we were to each other, shoulder touching shoulder almost. "So I asked to speak to the old man. He always seemed very sick when he came to see me—as if he could not look me in the face. You know, that foresail saved the ship. She was too deep to have run long under bare poles. And it was I

that managed to set it for him. Anyway, he came. When I had him in my cabin—he stood by the door looking at me as if I had the halter around my neck already—I asked him right away to leave my cabin door unlocked at night while the ship was going through Sunda Straits. There would be the Java coast within two or three miles, off Angier Point. I wanted nothing more. I've had a prize for swimming my second year in the Conway."

"I can believe it," I breathed out.

"God only knows why they locked me in every night. To see some of their faces you'd have thought they were afraid I'd go about at night strangling people. Am I a murdering brute? Do I look it? By Jove! If I had been, he wouldn't have trusted himself like that into my room. You'll say I might have chucked him aside and bolted out, there and then—it was dark already. Well, no. And for the same reason I wouldn't think of trying to smash the door. There would have been a rush to stop me at the noise, and I did not mean to get into a confounded scrimmage. Somebody else might have got killed—for I would not have broken out only to get chucked back, and I did not want any more of that work. He refused, looking more sick than ever. He was afraid of the men, and also of that old second mate of his who had been sailing with him for years—a gray-headed old humbug; and his steward, too, had been with him devil knows how long—seventeen years or more —a dogmatic sort of loafer who hated me like poison, just because I was the chief mate. No chief mate ever made more than one voyage in the *Sephora,* you know. Those two old chaps ran the ship. Devil only knows what the skipper wasn't afraid of (all his nerve went to pieces altogether in that hellish spell of bad weather we had) —of what the law would do to him—of his wife, perhaps. Oh, yes! she's on board. Though I don't think she would have meddled. She would have been only too glad to have me out of the ship in any way. The 'brand of Cain'[20] business, don't you see. That's all right. I was ready enough to go off wandering on the face of the earth— and that was price enough to pay for an Abel of that sort. Anyhow, he wouldn't listen to me. 'This thing must take its course. I represent the law here.' He was shaking like a leaf. 'So you won't?' 'No!' 'Then I hope you will be able to sleep on that,' I said, and turned my back on him. 'I wonder that *you* can,' cries he, and locks the door.

"Well, after that, I couldn't. Not very well. That was three weeks ago. We have had a slow passage through the Java Sea; drifted about Carimata[21] for ten days. When we anchored here they thought, I suppose, it was all right. The nearest land (and that's five miles) is the ship's destination; the consul would soon set about catching me; and there would have been no object in bolting to these islets there. I don't suppose there's a drop of water on them. I don't know how it was, but tonight that steward, after bringing me my supper, went out to let me eat it, and left the door unlocked. And I ate it—all there was, too. After I had finished I strolled out on the quarter-deck. I don't know that I meant to do anything. A breath of fresh air was all I wanted, I believe. Then a sudden temptation came over me. I kicked off my slippers and was in the water before I had made up my mind fairly. Somebody heard the splash and they raised an awful hullaballoo. 'He's gone! Lower the boats! He's committed suicide! No, he's swimming.' Certainly I was swimming. It's not so easy for a swimmer like me to commit suicide by drowning. I landed on the nearest islet before the boat left the ship's side. I heard them pulling about in the dark, hailing, and so on, but after a bit they gave up. Everything quieted down and the anchorage became as still as death. I sat down on a stone and began to think. I felt certain they would start searching for me at daylight.

There was no place to hide on those stony things—and if there had been, what would have been the good? But now I was clear of that ship, I was not going back. So after a while I took off my clothes, tied them up in a bundle with a stone inside, and dropped them in the deep water on the outer side of that islet. That was suicide enough for me. Let them think what they liked, but I didn't mean to drown myself. I meant to swim till I sank—but that's not the same thing. I struck out for another of these little islands, and it was from that one that I first saw your riding light. Something to swim for. I went on easily, and on the way I came upon a flat rock a foot or two above water. In the daytime, I dare say, you might make it out with a glass from your poop. I scrambled up on it and rested myself for a bit. Then I made another start. That last spell must have been over a mile."

His whisper was getting fainter and fainter, and all the time he stared straight out through the porthole, in which there was not even a star to be seen. I had not interrupted him. There was something that made comment impossible in his narrative, or perhaps in himself; a sort of feeling, a quality, which I can't find a name for. And when he ceased, all I found was a futile whisper: "So you swam for our light?"

"Yes—straight for it. It was something to swim for. I couldn't see any stars low down because the coast was in the way, and I couldn't see the land, either. The water was like glass. One might have been swimming in a confounded thousand-feet deep cistern with no place for scrambling out anywhere, but what I didn't like was the notion of swimming round and round like a crazed bullock before I gave out; and as I didn't mean to go back . . . No. Do you see me being hauled back, stark naked, off one of these little islands by the scruff of the neck and fighting like a wild beast? Somebody would have got killed for certain, and I did not want any of that. So I went on. Then your ladder——"

20. BRAND OF CAIN: see Genesis 4:16.
21. CARIMATA: strait between Sumatra and Borneo.

"Why didn't you hail the ship?" I asked, a little louder.

He touched my shoulder lightly. Lazy footsteps came right over our heads and stopped. The second mate had crossed from the other side of the poop and might have been hanging over the rail, for all we knew.

"He couldn't hear us talking—could he?" My double breathed into my very ear, anxiously.

His anxiety was an answer, a sufficient answer, to the question I had put to him. An answer containing all the difficulty of that situation. I closed the porthole quietly, to make sure. A louder word might have been overheard.

"Who's that?" he whispered then.

"My second mate. But I don't know much more of the fellow than you do."

And I told him a little about myself. I had been appointed to take charge while I least expected anything of the sort, not quite a fortnight ago. I didn't know either the ship or the people. Hadn't had the time in port to look about me or size anybody up. And as to the crew, all they knew was that I was appointed to take the ship home. For the rest, I was almost as much of a stranger on board as himself, I said. And at the moment I felt it most acutely. I felt that it would take very little to make me a suspect person in the eyes of the ship's company.

He had turned about meantime; and we, the two strangers in the ship, faced each other in identical attitudes.

"Your ladder——" he murmured, after a silence. "Who'd have thought of finding a ladder hanging over at night in a ship anchored out here! I felt just then a very unpleasant faintness. After the life I've been leading for nine weeks, anybody would have got out of condition. I wasn't capable of swimming round as far as your rudder chains. And, lo and behold! there was a ladder to get hold of. After I gripped it I said to myself, 'What's the good?' When I saw a man's head looking over I thought I would swim away presently and leave him

shouting—in whatever language it was. I didn't mind being looked at. I—I liked it. And then you speaking to me so quietly— as if you had expected me—made me hold on a little longer. It had been a confounded lonely time—I don't mean while swimming. I was glad to talk a little to somebody that didn't belong to the *Sephora*. As to asking for the captain, that was a mere impulse. It could have been no use, with all the ship knowing about me and the other people pretty certain to be round here in the morning. I don't know—I wanted to be seen, to talk to somebody, before I went on. I don't know what I would have said. . . . 'Fine night, isn't it?' or something of the sort."

"Do you think they will be round here presently?" I asked with some incredulity.

"Quite likely," he said, faintly.

He looked extremely haggard all of a sudden. His head rolled on his shoulders.

"H'm. We shall see then. Meantime get into that bed," I whispered. "Want help? There."

It was a rather high bed-place with a set of drawers underneath. This amazing swimmer really needed the lift I gave him by seizing his leg. He tumbled in, rolled over on his back, and flung one arm across his eyes. And then, with his face nearly hidden, he must have looked exactly as I used to look in that bed. I gazed upon my other self for a while before drawing across carefully the two green serge curtains, which ran on a brass rod. I thought for a moment of pinning them together for greater safety, but I sat down on the couch, and once there I felt unwilling to rise and hunt for a pin. I would do it in a moment. I was extremely tired, in a peculiarly intimate way, by the strain of stealthiness, by the effort of whispering and the general secrecy of this excitement. It was three o'clock by now and I had been on my feet since nine, but I was not sleepy; I could not have gone to sleep. I sat there, fagged out, looking at the curtains, trying to clear my mind of the confused sensation of being in two places at once, and greatly bothered by an exasperating knocking in my head. It was a relief to discover suddenly that it was not in my head at all, but on the outside of the door. Before I could collect myself, the words "Come in" were out of my mouth, and the steward entered with a tray, bringing in my morning coffee. I had slept, after all, and I was so frightened that I shouted, "This way! I am here, Steward," as though he had been miles away. He put down the tray on the table next the couch and only then said, very quietly, "I can see you here, sir." I felt him give me a keen look, but I dared not meet his eyes just then. He must have wondered why I had drawn the curtains of my bed before going to sleep on the couch. He went out, hooking the door open as usual.

I heard the crew washing decks above me. I knew I would have been told at once if there had been any wind. Calm, I thought, and I was doubly vexed. Indeed, I felt dual more than ever. The steward reappeared suddenly in the doorway. I jumped up from the couch so quickly that he gave a start.

"What do you want here?"

"Close your port, sir—they are washing decks."

"It is closed," I said, reddening.

"Very well, sir." But he did not move from the doorway and returned my stare in an extraordinary, equivocal manner for a time. Then his eyes wavered, all his expression changed, and in a voice unusually gentle, almost coaxingly:

"May I come in to take the empty cup away, sir?"

"Of course!" I turned my back on him while he popped in and out. Then I unhooked and closed the door and even pushed the bolt. This sort of thing could not go on very long. The cabin was as hot as an oven, too. I took a peep at my double, and discovered that he had not moved, his arm was still over his eyes; but his chest heaved; his hair was wet; his chin glistened with perspiration. I reached over him and opened the port.

"I must show myself on deck," I reflected.

Of course, theoretically, I could do what I liked, with no one to say nay to me within the whole circle of the horizon; but to lock my cabin door and take the key away I did not dare. Directly I put my head out of the companion I saw the group of my two officers, the second mate barefooted, the chief mate in long India-rubber boots, near the break of the poop, and the steward halfway down the poop ladder talking to them eagerly. He happened to catch sight of me and dived, the second ran down on the main deck shouting some order or other, and the chief mate came to meet me, touching his cap.

There was a sort of curiosity in his eye that I did not like. I don't know whether the steward had told them that I was "queer" only, or downright drunk, but I know the man meant to have a good look at me. I watched him coming with a smile which, as he got into point-blank range, took effect and froze his very whiskers. I did not give him time to open his lips.

"Square the yards by lifts and braces before the hands go to breakfast."

It was the first particular order I had given on board that ship; and I stayed on deck to see it executed, too. I had felt the need of asserting myself without loss of time. That sneering young cub got taken down a peg or two on that occasion, and I also seized the opportunity of having a good look at the face of every foremast man as they filed past me to go to the after braces. At breakfast time, eating nothing myself, I presided with such frigid dignity that the two mates were only too glad to escape from the cabin as soon as decency permitted; and all the time the dual working of my mind distracted me almost to the point of insanity. I was constantly watching myself, my secret self, as dependent on my actions as my own personality, sleeping in that bed, behind that door which faced me as I sat at the head of the table. It was very much like being mad, only it was worse because one was aware of it.

I had to shake him for a solid minute, but when at last he opened his eyes it was in the full possession of his senses, with an inquiring look.

"All's well so far," I whispered. "Now you must vanish into the bathroom."

He did so, as noiseless as a ghost, and then I rang for the steward, and facing him boldly, directed him to tidy up my stateroom while I was having my bath—"and be quick about it." As my tone admitted of no excuses, he said, "Yes, sir," and ran off to fetch his dustpan and brushes. I took a bath and did most of my dressing, splashing, and whistling softly for the steward's edification, while the secret sharer of my life stood drawn up bolt upright in that little space, his face looking very sunken in daylight, his eyelids lowered under the stern, dark line of his eyebrows drawn together by a slight frown.

When I left him there to go back to my room the steward was finishing dusting. I sent for the mate and engaged him in some insignificant conversation. It was, as it were, trifling with the terrific character of his whiskers; but my object was to give him an opportunity for a good look at my cabin. And then I could at last shut, with a clear conscience, the door of my stateroom and get my double back into the recessed part. There was nothing else for it. He had to sit on a small folding stool, half smothered by the heavy coats hanging there. We listened to the steward going into the bathroom out of the saloon, filling the water bottles there, scrubbing the bath, setting things to rights, whisk, bang, clatter—out again into the saloon—turn the key—click. Such was my scheme for keeping my second self invisible. Nothing better could be contrived under the circumstances. And there we sat; I at my writing desk ready to appear busy with some papers, he behind me out of

sight of the door. It would not have been prudent to talk in daytime; and I could not have stood the excitement of that queer sense of whispering to myself. Now and then, glancing over my shoulder, I saw him far back there, sitting rigidly on the low stool, his bare feet close together, his arms folded, his head hanging on his breast—and perfectly still. Anybody would have taken him for me.

I was fascinated by it myself. Every moment I had to glance over my shoulder. I was looking at him when a voice outside the door said:

"Beg pardon, sir."

"Well!" . . . I kept my eyes on him, and so, when the voice outside the door announced, "There's a ship's boat coming our way, sir," I saw him give a start—the first movement he had made for hours. But he did not raise his bowed head.

"All right. Get the ladder over."

I hesitated. Should I whisper something to him? But what? His immobility seemed to have been never disturbed. What could I tell him he did not know already? . . . Finally I went on deck.

II

The skipper of the *Sephora* had a thin red whisker all round his face, and the sort of complexion that goes with hair of that color; also the particular, rather smeary shade of blue in the eyes. He was not exactly a showy figure; his shoulders were high, his stature but middling—one leg slightly more bandy than the other. He shook hands, looking vaguely around. A spiritless tenacity was his main characteristic, I judged. I behaved with a politeness which seemed to disconcert him. Perhaps he was shy. He mumbled to me as if he were ashamed of what he was saying; gave his name (it was something like Archbold— but at this distance of years I hardly am sure), his ship's name, and a few other particulars of that sort, in the manner of a criminal making a reluctant and doleful confession. He had had terrible weather on the passage out—terrible—terrible—wife aboard, too.

By this time we were seated in the cabin and the steward brought in a tray with a bottle and glasses. "Thanks! No." Never took liquor. Would have some water, though. He drank two tumblerfuls. Terrible thirsty work. Ever since daylight had been exploring the islands round his ship.

"What was that for—fun?" I asked, with an appearance of polite interest.

"No!" He sighed. "Painful duty."

As he persisted in his mumbling and I wanted my double to hear every word, I hit upon the notion of informing him that I regretted to say I was hard of hearing.

"Such a young man, too!" he nodded, keeping his smeary blue, unintelligent eyes fastened upon me. "What was the cause of it—some disease?" he inquired, without the least sympathy and as if he thought that, if so, I'd got no more than I deserved.

"Yes; disease," I admitted in a cheerful tone which seemed to shock him. But my point was gained, because he had to raise his voice to give me his tale. It is not worthwhile to record that version. It was just over two months since all this had happened, and he had thought so much about it that he seemed completely muddled as to its bearings, but still immensely impressed.

"What would you think of such a thing happening on board your own ship? I've had the *Sephora* for these fifteen years. I am a well-known shipmaster."

He was densely distressed—and perhaps I should have sympathized with him if I had been able to detach my mental vision from the unsuspected sharer of my cabin as though he were my second self. There he was on the other side of the bulkhead, four or five feet from us, no more, as we sat in the saloon. I looked politely at Captain Archbold (if that was his name), but it was the other I saw, in a gray sleeping suit, seated on a low stool, his bare feet close together, his arms folded, and every word said between us falling into the ears of his dark head bowed on his chest.

"I have been at sea now, man and boy, for seven-and-thirty years, and I've never heard of such a thing happening in an English ship. And that it should be my ship. Wife on board, too."

I was hardly listening to him.

"Don't you think," I said, "that the heavy sea which, you told me, came aboard just then might have killed the man? I have seen the sheer weight of a sea kill a man very neatly, by simply breaking his neck."

"Good God!" he uttered, impressively, fixing his smeary blue eyes on me. "The sea! No man killed by the sea ever looked like that." He seemed positively scandalized at my suggestion. And as I gazed at him, certainly not prepared for anything original on his part, he advanced his head close to mine and thrust his tongue out at me so suddenly that I couldn't help starting back.

After scoring over my calmness in this graphic way he nodded wisely. If I had seen the sight, he assured me, I would never forget it as long as I lived. The weather was too bad to give the corpse a proper sea burial. So next day at dawn they took it up on the poop, covering its face with a bit of bunting; he read a short prayer, and then, just as it was, in its oilskins and long boots, they launched it amongst those mountainous seas that seemed ready every moment to swallow up the ship herself and the terrified lives on board of her.

"That reefed foresail saved you," I threw in.

"Under God—it did," he exclaimed fervently. "It was by a special mercy, I firmly believe, that it stood some of those hurricane squalls."

"It was the setting of that sail which——" I began.

"God's own hand in it," he interrupted me. "Nothing less could have done it. I don't mind telling you that I hardly dared give max

the order. It seemed impossible that we could touch anything without losing it, and then our last hope would have been gone."

The terror of that gale was on him yet. I let him go on for a bit, then said, casually—as if returning to a minor subject:

"You were very anxious to give up your mate to the shore people, I believe?"

He was. To the law. His obscure tenacity on that point had in it something incomprehensible and a little awful; something, as it were, mystical, quite apart from his anxiety that he should not be suspected of "countenancing any doings of that sort." Seven-and-thirty virtuous years at sea, of which over twenty of immaculate command, and the last fifteen in the *Sephora,* seemed to have laid him under some pitiless obligation.

"And you know," he went on, groping shamefacedly amongst his feelings, "I did not engage that young fellow. His people had some interest with my owners. I was in a way forced to take him on. He looked very smart, very gentlemanly, and all that. But do you know—I never liked him, somehow. I am a plain man. You see, he wasn't exactly the sort for the chief mate of a ship like the *Sephora.*"

I had become so connected in thoughts and impressions with the secret sharer of my cabin that I felt as if I, personally, were being given to understand that I, too, was not the sort that would have done for the chief mate of a ship like the *Sephora.* I had no doubt of it in my mind.

"Not at all the style of man. You understand," he insisted, superfluously, looking hard at me.

I smiled urbanely. He seemed at a loss for a while.

"I suppose I must report a suicide."

"Beg pardon?"

"Sui-cide! That's what I'll have to write to my owners directly I get in."

"Unless you manage to recover before tomorrow," I assented, dispassionately. . . . "I mean, alive."

He mumbled something which I really did not catch, and I turned my ear to him in a puzzled manner. He fairly bawled:

"The land—I say, the mainland is at least seven miles off my anchorage."

"About that."

My lack of excitement, of curiosity, of surprise, of any sort of pronounced interest, began to arouse his distrust. But except for the felicitous pretense of deafness I had not tried to pretend anything. I had felt utterly incapable of playing the part of ignorance properly, and therefore was afraid to try. It is also certain that he had brought some ready-made suspicions with him, and that he viewed my politeness as a strange and unnatural phenomenon. And yet how else could I have received him? Not heartily! That was impossible for psychological reasons, which I need not state here. My only object was to keep off his inquiries. Surlily? Yes, but surliness might have provoked a point-blank question. From its novelty to him and from its nature, punctilious courtesy was the manner best calculated to restrain the man. But there was the danger of his breaking through my defense bluntly. I could not, I think, have met him by a direct lie, also for psychological (not moral) reasons. If he had only known how afraid I was of putting my feeling of identity with the other to the test! But, strangely enough—(I thought of it only afterward)—I believe that he was not a little disconcerted by the reverse side of that weird situation, by something in me that reminded him of the man he was seeking—suggested a mysterious similitude to the young fellow he had distrusted and disliked from the first.

However that might have been, the silence was not very prolonged. He took another oblique step.

"I reckon I had no more than a two-mile pull to your ship. Not a bit more."

"And quite enough, too, in this awful heat," I said.

Another pause full of mistrust followed. Necessity, they say, is mother of invention, but fear, too, is not barren of ingenious suggestions. And I was afraid he would ask me point-blank for news of my other self.

"Nice little saloon, isn't it?" I remarked, as if noticing for the first time the way his eyes roamed from one closed door to the other. "And very well fitted out, too. Here, for instance," I continued, reaching over the back of my seat negligently and flinging the door open, "is my bathroom."

He made an eager movement, but hardly gave it a glance. I got up, shut the door of the bathroom, and invited him to have a look round, as if I were very proud of my accommodation. He had to rise and be shown round, but he went through the business without any raptures whatever.

"And now we'll have a look at my stateroom," I declared, in a voice as loud as I dared to make it, crossing the cabin to the starboard side with purposely heavy steps.

He followed me in and gazed around. My intelligent double had vanished. I played my part.

"Very convenient—isn't it?"

"Very nice. Very comf . . ." He didn't finish, and went out brusquely as if to escape from some unrighteous wiles of mine. But it was not to be. I had been too frightened not to feel vengeful; I felt I had him on the run, and I meant to keep him on the run. My polite insistence must have had something menacing in it, because he gave in suddenly. And I did not let him off a single item; mate's room, pantry, storerooms, the very sail locker which was also under the poop—he had to look into them all. When at last I showed him out on the quarterdeck he drew a long, spiritless sigh, and mumbled dismally that he must really be going back to his ship now. I desired my mate, who had joined us, to see to the captain's boat.

The man of whiskers gave a blast on the whistle which he used to wear hanging round his neck, and yelled, *"Sephora's* away!" My double down there in my cabin must have heard, and certainly could not feel more relieved than I. Four fellows came running

out from somewhere forward and went over the side, while my own men, appearing on deck too, lined the rail. I escorted my visitor to the gangway ceremoniously, and nearly overdid it. He was a tenacious beast. On the very ladder he lingered, and in that unique, guiltily conscientious manner of sticking to the point:

"I say . . . you . . . you don't think that——"

I covered his voice loudly:

"Certainly not. . . . I am delighted. Good-by."

I had an idea of what he meant to say, and just saved myself by the privilege of defective hearing. He was too shaken generally to insist, but my mate, close witness of that parting, looked mystified and his face took on a thoughtful cast. As I did not want to appear as if I wished to avoid all communication with my officers, he had the opportunity to address me.

"Seems a very nice man. His boat's crew told our chaps a very extraordinary story, if what I am told by the steward is true. I suppose you had it from the captain, sir?"

"Yes. I had a story from the captain."

"A very horrible affair—isn't it, sir?"

"It is."

"Beats all these tales we hear about murders in Yankee ships."

"I don't think it beats them. I don't think it resembles them in the least."

"Bless my soul—you don't say so! But of course I've no acquaintance whatever with American ships, not I, so I couldn't go against your knowledge. It's horrible enough for me. . . . But the queerest part is that those fellows seemed to have some idea the man was hidden aboard here. They had really. Did you ever hear of such a thing?"

"Preposterous—isn't it?"

We were walking to and fro athwart the quarter-deck. No one of the crew forward could be seen (the day was Sunday), and the mate pursued:

"There was some little dispute about it. Our chaps took offense. 'As if we would harbor a thing like that,' they said. 'Wouldn't you like to look for him in our coalhole?' Quite a tiff. But they made it up in the end. I suppose he did drown himself. Don't you, sir?"

"I don't suppose anything."

"You have no doubt in the matter, sir?"

"None whatever."

I left him suddenly. I felt I was producing a bad impression, but with my double down there it was most trying to be on deck. And it was almost as trying to be below. Altogether a nerve-trying situation. But on the whole I felt less torn in two when I was with him. There was no one in the whole ship whom I dared to take into my confidence. Since the hands had got to know his story, it would have been impossible to pass him off for anyone else, and an accidental discovery was to be dreaded now more than ever. . . .

The steward being engaged in laying the table for dinner, we could talk only with our eyes when I first went down. Later in the afternoon we had a cautious try at whispering. The Sunday quietness of the ship was against us; the stillness of air and water around her was against us; the elements, the men were against us—everything was against us in our secret partnership; time itself— for this could not go on forever. The very trust in Providence was, I suppose, denied to his guilt. Shall I confess that this thought cast me down very much? And as to the chapter of accidents which counts for so much in the book of success, I could only hope that it was closed. For what favorable accident could be expected?

"Did you hear everything?" were my first words as soon as we took up our position side by side, leaning over my bed-place.

He had. And the proof of it was his earnest whisper, "The man told you he hardly dared to give the order."

I understood the reference to be to that saving foresail.

"Yes. He was afraid of it being lost in the setting."

"I assure you he never gave the order. He may think he did, but he never gave it.

He stood there with me on the break of the poop after the main-topsail blew away, and whimpered about our last hope—positively whimpered about it and nothing else—and the night coming on! To hear one's skipper go on like that in such weather was enough to drive any fellow out of his mind. It worked me up into a sort of desperation. I just took it into my own hands and went away from him, boiling, and—— But what's the use telling you? *You* know! . . . Do you think that if I had not been pretty fierce with them I should have got the men to do anything? Not it! The bo's'n perhaps? Perhaps! It wasn't a heavy sea—it was a sea gone mad! I suppose the end of the world will be something like that; and a man may have the heart to see it coming once and be done with it—but to have to face it day after day—— I don't blame anybody. I was precious little better than the rest. Only—I was an officer of that old coal wagon, anyhow——"

"I quite understand," I conveyed that sincere assurance into his ear. He was out of breath with whispering; I could hear him pant slightly. It was all very simple. The same strung-up force which had given twenty-four men a chance, at least, for their lives, had, in a sort of recoil, crushed an unworthy mutinous existence.

But I had no leisure to weigh the merits of the matter—footsteps in the saloon, a heavy knock. "There's enough wind to get under way with, sir." Here was the call of a new claim upon my thoughts and even upon my feelings.

"Turn the hands up," I cried through the door. "I'll be on deck directly."

I was going out to make the acquaintance of my ship. Before I left the cabin our eyes met—the eyes of the only two strangers on board. I pointed to the recessed part where the little camp-stool awaited him and laid my finger on my lips He made a gesture— somewhat vague—a little mysterious, accompanied by a faint smile, as if of regret.

This is not the place to enlarge upon the sensations of a man who feels for the first time a ship move under his feet to his own independent word. In my case they were not unalloyed. I was not wholly alone with my command; for there was that stranger in my cabin. Or rather, I was not completely and wholly with her. Part of me was absent. That mental feeling of being in two places at once affected me physically as if the mood of secrecy had penetrated my very soul. Before an hour had elapsed since the ship had begun to move, having occasion to ask the mate (he stood by my side) to take a compass bearing of the pagoda, I caught myself reaching up to his ear in whispers. I say I caught myself, but enough had escaped to startle the man. I can't describe it otherwise than by saying that he shied. A grave, preoccupied manner, as though he were in possession of some perplexing intelligence, did not leave him henceforth. A little later I moved away from the rail to look at the compass with such a stealthy gait that the helmsman noticed it—and I could not help noticing the unusual roundness of his eyes. These are trifling instances, though it's to no commander's advantage to be suspected of ludicrous eccentricities. But I was also more seriously affected. There are to a seaman certain words, gestures, that should in given conditions come as naturally, as instinctively as the winking of a menaced eye. A certain order should spring on to his lips without thinking; a certain sign should get itself made, so to speak, without reflection. But all unconscious alertness had abandoned me. I had to make an effort of will to recall myself back (from the cabin) to the conditions of the moment. I felt that I was appearing an irresolute commander to those people who were watching me more or less critically.

And, besides, there were the scares. On the second day out, for instance, coming off the deck in the afternoon (I had straw slippers on my bare feet) I stopped at the open pantry door and spoke to the steward. He was doing something there with his back to me. At the sound of my voice he nearly jumped out of his skin, as the saying is, and incidentally broke a cup.

"What on earth's the matter with you?" I asked, astonished.

He was extremely confused. "Beg your pardon, sir. I made sure you were in your cabin."

"You see I wasn't."

"No, sir. I could have sworn I had heard you moving in there not a moment ago. It's most extraordinary . . . very sorry, sir."

I passed on with an inward shudder. I was so identified with my secret double that I did not even mention the fact in those scanty, fearful whispers we exchanged. I suppose he had made some slight noise of some kind or other. It would have been miraculous if he hadn't at one time or another. And yet, haggard as he appeared, he looked always perfectly self-controlled, more than calm—almost invulnerable. On my suggestion he remained almost entirely in the bathroom, which, upon the whole, was the safest place. There could be really no shadow of an excuse for anyone ever wanting to go in there, once the steward had done with it. It was a very tiny place. Sometimes he reclined on the floor, his legs bent, his head sustained on one elbow. At others I would find him on the camp-stool, sitting in his gray sleeping suit and with his cropped dark hair like a patient, unmoved convict. At night I would smuggle him into my bed-place, and we would whisper together, with the regular footfalls of the officer of the watch passing and repassing over our heads. It was an infinitely miserable time. It was lucky that some tins of fine preserves were stowed in a locker in my stateroom; hard bread I could always get hold of; and so he lived on stewed chicken, *pâté de foie gras*, asparagus, cooked oysters, sardines—on all sorts of abominable sham delicacies out of tins. My early morning coffee he always drank; and it was all I dared do for him in that respect.

Every day there was the horrible maneuvering to go through so that my room and then the bathroom should be done in the usual way. I came to hate the sight of the steward, to abhor the voice of that harmless man. I felt that it was he who would bring on the disaster of discovery. It hung like a sword over our heads.

The fourth day out, I think (we were then working down the east side of the Gulf of Siam, tack for tack, in light winds and smooth water)—the fourth day, I say, of this miserable juggling with the unavoidable, as we sat at our evening meal, that man, whose slightest movement I dreaded, after putting down the dishes ran up on deck busily. This could not be dangerous. Presently he came down again; and then it appeared that he had remembered a coat of mine which I had thrown over a rail to dry after having been wetted in a shower which had passed over the ship in the afternoon. Sitting stolidly at the head of the table I became terrified at the sight of the garment on his arm. Of course he made for my door. There was no time to lose.

"Steward," I thundered. My nerves were so shaken that I could not govern my voice and conceal my agitation. This was the sort of thing that made my terrifically whiskered mate tap his forehead with his forefinger. I had detected him using that gesture while talking on deck with a confidential air to the carpenter. It was too far to hear a word, but I had no doubt that this pantomime could only refer to the strange new captain.

"Yes, sir," the pale-faced steward turned resignedly to me. It was this maddening course of being shouted at, checked without rhyme or reason, arbitrarily chased out of my cabin, suddenly called into it, sent flying out of his pantry on incomprehensible errands, that accounted for the growing wretchedness of his expression.

"Where are you going with that coat?"

"To your room, sir."

"Is there another shower coming?"

"I'm sure I don't know, sir. Shall I go up again and see, sir?"

"No! never mind."

My object was attained, as of course my other self in there would have heard everything that passed. During this interlude my two officers never raised their eyes off their respective plates; but the lip of that confounded cub, the second mate, quivered visibly.

I expected the steward to hook my coat on and come out at once. He was very slow about it; but I dominated my nervousness sufficiently not to shout after him. Suddenly I became aware (it could be heard plainly enough) that the fellow for some reason or other was opening the door of the bathroom. It was the end. The place was literally not big enough to swing a cat in. My voice died in my throat and I went stony all over. I expected to hear a yell of surprise and terror, and made a movement, but had not the strength to get on my legs. Everything remained still. Had my second self taken the poor wretch by the throat? I don't know what I could have done next moment if I had not seen the steward come out of my room, close the door, and then stand quietly by the sideboard.

"Saved," I thought. "But, no! Lost! Gone! He was gone!"

I laid my knife and fork down and leaned back in my chair. My head swam. After a while, when sufficiently recovered to speak in a steady voice, I instructed my mate to put the ship round at eight o'clock himself.

"I won't come on deck," I went on. "I think I'll turn in, and unless the wind shifts I don't want to be disturbed before midnight. I feel a bit seedy."

"You did look middling bad a little while ago," the chief mate remarked without showing any great concern.

They both went out, and I stared at the steward clearing the table. There was nothing to be read on that wretched man's face. But why did he avoid my eyes I asked myself. Then I thought I should like to hear the sound of his voice.

"Steward!"

"Sir!" Startled as usual.

"Where did you hang up that coat?"

"In the bathroom, sir." The usual anxious tone. "It's not quite dry yet, sir."

For some time longer I sat in the cuddy. Had my double vanished as he had come? But for his coming there was an explanation, whereas his disappearance would be inexplicable. . . . I went slowly into my dark room, shut the door, lighted the lamp, and for a time dared not turn round. When at last I did I saw him standing bolt upright in the narrow recessed part. It would not be true to say I had a shock, but an irresistible doubt of his bodily existence flitted through my mind. Can it be, I asked myself, that he is not visible to other eyes than mine? It was like being haunted. Motionless, with a grave face, he raised his hands slightly at me in a gesture which meant clearly, "Heavens! What a narrow escape!" Narrow indeed. I think I had come creeping quietly as near insanity as any man who has not actually gone over the border. That gesture restrained me, so to speak.

The mate with the terrific whiskers was now putting the ship on the other tack. In the moment of profound silence which follows upon the hands going to their stations I heard on the poop his raised voice: "Hard alee!" and the distant shout of the order repeated on the main deck. The sails, in that light breeze, made but a faint fluttering noise. It ceased. The ship was coming round slowly; I held my breath in the renewed stillness of expectation; one wouldn't have thought that there was a single living soul on her decks. A sudden brisk shout, "Mainsail haul!" broke the spell, and in the noisy cries and rush overhead of the men running away with the main brace we two, down in my cabin, came together in our usual position by the bed-place.

He did not wait for my question. "I heard him fumbling here and just managed to squat myself down in the bath," he whispered to me. "The fellow only opened the door and put his arm in to hang the coat up. All the same——"

"I never thought of that," I whispered

back, even more appalled than before at the closeness of the shave, and marveling at that something unyielding in his character which was carrying him through so finely. There was no agitation in his whisper. Whoever was being driven distracted, it was not he. He was sane. And the proof of his sanity was continued when he took up the whispering again.

"It would never do for me to come to life again."

It was something that a ghost might have said. But what he was alluding to was his old captain's reluctant admission of the theory of suicide. It would obviously serve his turn—if I had understood at all the view which seemed to govern the unalterable purpose of his action.

"You must maroon me as soon as ever you can get amongst these islands off the Cambodge[22] shore," he went on.

"Maroon you! We are not living in a boy's adventure tale," I protested. His scornful whispering took me up.

"We aren't indeed! There's nothing of a boy's tale in this. But there's nothing else for it. I want no more. You don't suppose I am afraid of what can be done to me? Prison or gallows or whatever they may please. But you don't see me coming back to explain such things to an old fellow in a wig and twelve respectable tradesmen, do you? What can they know whether I am guilty or not—or of *what* I am guilty, either? That's my affair. What does the Bible say? 'Driven off the face of the earth.'[23] Very well. I am off the face of the earth now. As I came at night so I shall go."

"Impossible!" I murmured. "You can't."

"Can't? . . . Not naked like a soul on the Day of Judgment. I shall freeze on to this sleeping suit. The Last Day is not yet—and . . . you have understood thoroughly. Didn't you?"

I felt suddenly ashamed of myself. I may say truly that I understood—and my hesitation in letting that man swim away from my

22. CAMBODGE: Cambodia.
23. 'DRIVEN . . . EARTH': see Genesis 4:14.

ship's side had been a mere sham sentiment, a sort of cowardice.

"It can't be done now till next night," I breathed out. "The ship is on the off-shore tack and the wind may fail us."

"As long as I know that you understand," he whispered. "But of course you do. It's a great satisfaction to have got somebody to understand. You seem to have been there on purpose." And in the same whisper, as if we two whenever we talked had to say things to each other which were not fit for the world to hear, he added, "It's very wonderful."

We remained side by side talking in our secret way—but sometimes silent or just exchanging a whispered word or two at long intervals. And as usual he stared through the port. A breath of wind came now and again into our faces. The ship might have been moored in dock, so gently and on an even keel she slipped through the water, that did not murmur even at our passage, shadowy and silent like a phantom sea.

At midnight I went on deck, and to my mate's great surprise put the ship round on the other tack. His terrible whiskers flitted round me in silent criticism. I certainly should not have done it if it had been only a question of getting out of that sleepy gulf as quickly as possible. I believe he told the second mate, who relieved him, that it was a great want of judgment. The other only yawned. That intolerable cub shuffled about so sleepily and lolled against the rails in such a slack, improper fashion that I came down on him sharply.

"Aren't you properly awake yet?"

"Yes, sir! I am awake."

"Well, then, be good enough to hold yourself as if you were. And keep a lookout. If there's any current we'll be closing with some islands before daylight."

The east side of the gulf is fringed with islands, some solitary, others in groups. On the blue background of the high coast they seem to float on silvery patches of calm water, arid and gray, or dark green and rounded like clumps of evergreen bushes, with the larger ones, a mile or two long, showing the outlines of ridges, ribs of gray rock under the dank mantle of matted leafage. Unknown to trade, to travel, almost to geography, the manner of life they harbor is an unsolved secret. There must be villages —settlements of fishermen at least—on the largest of them, and some communication with the world is probably kept up by native craft. But all that forenoon, as we headed for them, fanned along by the faintest of breezes, I saw no sign of man or canoe in the field of the telescope I kept on pointing at the scattered group.

At noon I gave no orders for a change of course, and the mate's whiskers became much concerned and seemed to be offering themselves unduly to my notice. At last I said:

"I am going to stand right in. Quite in— as far as I can take her."

The stare of extreme surprise imparted an air of ferocity also to his eyes, and he looked truly terrific for a moment.

"We're not doing well in the middle of the gulf," I continued, casually. "I am going to look for the land breezes tonight."

"Bless my soul! Do you mean, sir, in the dark amongst the lot of all them islands and reefs and shoals?"

"Well—if there are any regular land breezes at all on this coast one must get close inshore to find them, mustn't one?"

"Bless my soul!" he exclaimed again under his breath. All that afternoon he wore a dreamy, contemplative appearance which in him was a mark of perplexity. After dinner I went into my stateroom as if I meant to take some rest. There we two bent our dark heads over a half-unrolled chart lying on my bed.

"There," I said. "It's got to be Koh-ring.[24] I've been looking at it ever since sunrise. It has got two hills and a low point. It must be inhabited. And on the coast opposite there is what looks like the mouth of a biggish river—with some town, no doubt,

---

24. KOH-RING: island off of Cochin China.

not far up. It's the best chance for you that I can see."

"Anything. Koh-ring let it be."

He looked thoughtfully at the chart as if surveying chances and distances from a lofty height—and following with his eyes his own figure wandering on the blank land of Cochin China,[25] and then passing off that piece of paper clean out of sight into uncharted regions. And it was as if the ship had two captains to plan her course for her. I had been so worried and restless running up and down that I had not had the patience to dress that day. I had remained in my sleeping suit, with straw slippers and a soft floppy hat. The closeness of the heat in the gulf had been most oppressive, and the crew were used to see me wandering in that airy attire.

"She will clear the south point as she heads now," I whispered into his ear. "Goodness only knows when, though, but certainly after dark. I'll edge her in to half a mile, as far as I may be able to judge in the dark——"

"Be careful," he murmured, warningly—and I realized suddenly that all my future, the only future for which I was fit, would perhaps go irretrievably to pieces in any mishap to my first command.

I could not stop a moment longer in the room. I motioned him to get out of sight and made my way on the poop. That unplayful cub had the watch. I walked up and down for a while thinking things out, then beckoned him over.

"Send a couple of hands to open the two quarter-deck ports," I said, mildly.

He actually had the impudence, or else so forgot himself in his wonder at such an incomprehensible order, as to repeat:

"Open the quarter-deck ports! What for, sir?"

"The only reason you need concern yourself about is because I tell you to do so. Have them open wide and fastened properly."

He reddened and went off, but I believe

made some jeering remark to the carpenter as to the sensible practice of ventilating a ship's quarter-deck. I know he popped into the mate's cabin to impart the fact to him because the whiskers came on deck, as it were by chance, and stole glances at me from below—for signs of lunacy or drunkenness, I suppose.

A little before supper, feeling more restless than ever, I rejoined, for a moment, my second self. And to find him sitting so quietly was surprising, like something against nature, inhuman.

I developed my plan in a hurried whisper.

"I shall stand in as close as I dare and then put her round.[26] I will presently find means to smuggle you out of here into the sail locker, which communicates with the lobby. But there is an opening, a sort of square for hauling the sails out, which gives straight on the quarter-deck and which is never closed in fine weather, so as to give air to the sails. When the ship's way is deadened in stays[27] and all the hands are aft at the main-braces you will have a clear road to slip out and get overboard through the open quarter-deck port. I've had them both fastened up. Use a rope's end to lower yourself into the water so as to avoid a splash—you know. It could be heard and cause some beastly complication."

He kept silent for a while, then whispered, "I understand."

"I won't be there to see you go," I began with an effort. "The rest . . . I only hope I have understood, too."

"You have. From first to last"—and for the first time there seemed to be a faltering, something strained in his whisper. He caught hold of my arm, but the ringing of the supper bell made me start. He didn't, though; he only released his grip.

After supper I didn't come below again till well past eight o'clock. The faint, steady breeze was loaded with dew; and the wet,

25. COCHIN CHINA: on the Gulf of Siam, south of Cambodia; now part of South Vietnam.

26. STAND . . . ROUND: sail as close as I dare to the island and then head seaward again.

27. WHEN . . . STAYS: when the ship is turning, moving slowly while the sails are changed.

darkened sails held all there was of propelling power in it. The night, clear and starry, sparkled darkly, and the opaque, lightless patches shifting slowly against the low stars were the drifting islets. On the port bow there was a big one more distant and shadowily imposing by the great space of sky it eclipsed.

On opening the door I had a back view of my very own self looking at a chart. He had come out of the recess and was standing near the table.

"Quite dark enough," I whispered.

He stepped back and leaned against my bed with a level, quiet glance. I sat on the couch. We had nothing to say to each other. Over our heads the officer of the watch moved here and there. Then I heard him move quickly. I knew what that meant. He was making for the companion; and presently his voice was outside my door.

"We are drawing in pretty fast, sir. Land looks rather close."

"Very well," I answered. "I am coming on deck directly."

I waited till he was gone out of the cuddy, then rose. My double moved too. The time had come to exchange our last whispers, for neither of us was ever to hear each other's natural voice.

"Look here!" I opened a drawer and took out three sovereigns. "Take this anyhow. I've got six and I'd give you the lot, only I must keep a little money to buy some fruit and vegetables for the crew from native boats as we go through Sunda Straits."

He shook his head.

"Take it," I urged him, whispering desperately. "No one can tell what——"

He smiled and slapped meaningly the only pocket of the sleeping jacket. It was not safe, certainly. But I produced a large old silk handkerchief of mine, and tying the three pieces of gold in a corner, pressed it on him. He was touched, I suppose, because he took it at last and tied it quickly round his waist under the jacket, on his bare skin.

Our eyes met; several seconds elapsed, till, our glances still mingled, I extended my hand and turned the lamp out. Then I passed through the cuddy, leaving the door of my room wide open. . . . "Steward!"

He was still lingering in the pantry in the greatness of his zeal, giving a rub-up to a plated cruet stand the last thing before going to bed. Being careful not to wake up the mate, whose room was opposite, I spoke in an undertone.

He looked round anxiously. "Sir!"

"Can you get me a little hot water from the galley?"

"I am afraid, sir, the galley fire's been out for some time now."

"Go and see."

He fled up the stairs.

"Now," I whispered, loudly, into the saloon—too loudly, perhaps, but I was afraid I couldn't make a sound. He was by my side in an instant—the double captain slipped past the stairs—through the tiny dark passage . . . a sliding door. We were in the sail locker, scrambling on our knees over the sails. A sudden thought struck me. I saw myself wandering barefooted, bareheaded, the sun beating on my dark poll. I snatched off my floppy hat and tried hurriedly in the dark to ram it on my other self. He dodged and fended off silently. I wonder what he thought had come to me before he understood and suddenly desisted. Our hands met gropingly, lingered united in a steady, motionless clasp for a second. . . . No word was breathed by either of us when they separated.

I was standing quietly by the pantry door when the steward returned.

"Sorry, sir. Kettle barely warm. Shall I light the spirit lamp?"

"Never mind."

I came out on deck slowly. It was now a matter of conscience to shave the land as close as possible—for now he must go overboard whenever the ship was put in stays. Must! There could be no going back for him. After a moment I walked over to leeward and my heart flew into my mouth at the nearness of the land on the bow. Under any other circumstances I would not have held on a minute longer. The second mate had followed me anxiously.

I looked on till I felt I could command my voice.

"She will weather," I said then in a quiet tone.

"Are you going to try that, sir?" he stammered out incredulously.

I took no notice of him and raised my tone just enough to be heard by the helmsman.

"Keep her good full."

"Good full, sir."

The wind fanned my cheek, the sails slept, the world was silent. The strain of watching the dark loom of the land grow bigger and denser was too much for me. I had shut my eyes—because the ship must go closer. She must! The stillness was intolerable. Were we standing still?

When I opened my eyes the second view started my heart with a thump. The black southern hill of Koh-ring semed to hang right over the ship like a towering fragment of the everlasting night. On that enormous mass of blackness there was not a gleam to be seen, not a sound to be heard. It was gliding irresistibly toward us, and yet seemed already within reach of the hand. I saw the vague figures of the watch grouped in the waist, gazing in awed silence.

"Are you going on, sir?" inquired an unsteady voice at my elbow.

I ignored it. I had to go on.

"Keep her full. Don't check her way. That won't do now," I said warningly.

"I can't see the sails very well," the helmsman answered me, in strange, quavering tones.

Was she close enough? Already she was, I won't say in the shadow of the land, but in the very blackness of it, already swallowed up, as it were, gone too close to be recalled, gone from me altogether.

"Give the mate a call," I said to the young man who stood at my elbow as still as death. "And turn all hands up."

My tone had a borrowed loudness reverberated from the height of the land. Several voices cried out together: "We are all on deck, sir."

Then stillness again, with the great shadow gliding closer, towering higher, without a light, without a sound. Such a hush had fallen on the ship that she might have been a bark of the dead floating in slowly under the very gate of Erebus.[28]

"My God! Where are we?"

It was the mate moaning at my elbow. He was thunderstruck, and as it were deprived of the moral support of his whiskers. He clapped his hands and absolutely cried out, "Lost!"

"Be quiet," I said, sternly.

He lowered his tone, but I saw the shadowy gesture of his despair. "What are we doing here?"

"Looking for the land wind."

He made as if to tear his hair, and addressed me recklessly.

"She will never get out. You have done it, sir. I knew it'd end in something like this. She will never weather, and you are too close now to stay. She'll drift ashore before she's round. O my God!"

I caught his arm as he was raising it to batter his poor devoted head, and shook it violently.

"She's ashore already," he wailed, trying to tear himself away.

"Is she? . . . Keep good full there!"

"Good full, sir," cried the helmsman in a frightened, thin, childlike voice.

I hadn't let go the mate's arm and went on shaking it. "Ready about, do you hear? You go forward"—shake—"and stop there"——shake—"and hold your noise"—shake—"and see these headsheets properly overhauled"—shake, shake—shake.

And all the time I dared not look toward the land lest my heart should fail me. I released my grip at last and he ran forward as if fleeing for dear life.

I wondered what my double there in the

---

28. EREBUS: In Greek mythology the underground cavern one must pass through on the way to Hades.

sail locker thought of this commotion. He was able to hear everything—and perhaps he was able to understand why, on my conscience, it had to be thus close—no less. My first order "Hard alee!" re-echoed ominously under the towering shadow of Koh-ring as if I had shouted in a mountain gorge. And then I watched the land intently. In that smooth water and light wind it was impossible to feel the ship coming-to. No! I could not feel her. And my second self was making now ready to slip out and lower himself overboard. Perhaps he was gone already . . . ?

The great black mass brooding over our mastheads began to pivot away from the ship's side silently. And now I forgot the secret stranger ready to depart, and remembered only that I was a total stranger to the ship. I did not know her. Would she do it? How was she to be handled?

I swung the main yard and waited helplessly. She was perhaps stopped, and her very fate hung in the balance, with the black mass of Koh-ring like the gate of the everlasting night towering over her taffrail. What would she do now? Had she way on her yet? I stepped to the side swiftly, and on the shadowy water I could see nothing except a faint phosphorescent flash revealing the glassy smoothness of the sleeping surface. It was impossible to tell—and I had not learned yet the feel of my ship. Was she moving? What I needed was something easily seen, a piece of paper, which I could throw overboard and watch. I had nothing on me. To run down for it I didn't dare. There was no time. All at once my strained, yearning stare distinguished a white object floating within a yard of the ship's side. White on the black water. A phosphorescent flash passed under it. What was that thing? . . . I recognized my own floppy hat. It must have fallen off his head . . . and he didn't bother. Now I had what I wanted—the saving mark for my eyes. But I hardly thought of my other self, now gone from the ship, to be hidden forever from all friendly faces, to be a fugitive and a vagabond on the earth, with no brand of the curse on his sane forehead to stay a slaying hand . . . too proud to explain.

And I watched the hat—the expression of my sudden pity for his mere flesh. It had been meant to save his homeless head from the dangers of the sun. And now—behold—it was saving the ship, by serving me for a mark to help out the ignorance of my strangeness. Ha! It was drifting forward, warning me just in time that the ship had gathered sternway.

"Shift the helm," I said in a low voice to the seaman standing still like a statue.

The man's eyes glistened wildly in the binnacle light as he jumped round to the other side and spun round the wheel.

I walked to the break of the poop. On the overshadowed deck all hands stood by the forebraces waiting for my order. The stars ahead seemed to be gliding from right to left. And all was so still in the world that I heard the quiet remark "She's round," passed in a tone of intense relief between two seamen.

"Let go and haul."

The foreyards ran round with a great noise, amidst cheery cries. And now the frightful whiskers made themselves heard giving various orders. Already the ship was drawing ahead. And I was alone with her. Nothing! no one in the world should stand now between us, throwing a shadow on the way of silent knowledge and mute affection, the perfect communion of a seaman with his first command.

Walking to the taffrail, I was in time to make out, on the very edge of a darkness thrown by a towering black mass like the very gateway of Erebus—yes, I was in time to catch an evanescent glimpse of my white hat left behind to mark the spot where the secret sharer of my cabin and of my thoughts, as though he were my second self, had lowered himself into the water to take his punishment: a free man, a proud swimmer striking out for a new destiny.

I

1. How does Conrad create a setting of great loneliness, of motionless anticipation, and of overwhelming perfectness in nature in the opening three paragraphs? Why does he create such a setting? How does it set up a contrast with the story of the Captain and his double?

2. The Captain refers to Leggatt as his *double* almost from the first moment of meeting. In what sense is Leggatt his double? What specifically do they have in common? In what ways is the physical bond between them intensified as the story progresses?

3. There are two plots running concurrently. One is the adventure story of the escaped murderer: will he make it? The other is the Captain's adventure within himself: will he win full command of the ship and of himself? Where does the climax come in each plot, and why do you think so?

4. Why doesn't the Captain turn Leggatt over to the captain of the *Sephora*? Isn't he legally and morally wrong for harboring a criminal? Isn't he taking the law into his own hands? Why shouldn't Leggatt take his chances with the courts? If his punishment is that he must walk the earth a fugitive, why does the Captain call him "a free man, a proud swimmer striking out for a new destiny"? How does the phrase also apply to the Captain?

5. The Captain takes the ship dangerously close to Koh-ring ostensibly to pick up an offshore wind and to give Leggatt a chance to swim ashore. How necessary is the maneuver for either purpose? What is his real reason for taking such a risk? In connection with this part of the story, how has Conrad used descriptions of nature to underscore dramatic human action? Consider particularly the descriptions of Koh-ring.

6. The Captain's hat is used as a symbol. Of what? Why had the Captain given it to Leggatt? Why is it returned?

7. What does the Captain learn through Leggatt? Does he see in himself the possibility of doing what Leggatt had done under similar circumstances? Or does Leggatt's plight in some sense parallel his own? Or both? Discuss.

8. What part do the minor characters play?

Consider specifically the chief mate and the captain of the *Sephora*:

   a. The Captain says of the chief mate: "His dominant trait was to take all things into earnest consideration. He was of a painstaking turn of mind. As he used to say, he 'liked to account to himself' for everything that came in his way down to a miserable scorpion he found in the cabin a week before." Contrast this with what the Captain says about himself a few lines before. What is different about their attitudes? How does the chief mate's character as revealed here and in the rest of the story throw light by contrast on the Captain's character?

   b. What is the captain of the *Sephora* like? What responsibility does he have in the murder committed by Leggatt? What is his chief concern as captain of a ship? How does he contrast with the narrator?

9. To what extent does the Captain worry about what other men think of him? Is he indifferent to their opinions, spoken and unspoken? In the moment of crisis, how concerned is he about their reactions?

II

1. Most of us will go through life without meeting crises approaching the seriousness of those the Captain and Leggatt had to face. But is Conrad talking about crisis situations only or about a way of living? What makes the chief mate and the captain of the *Sephora* seem so spineless? What makes a man *a free man, a proud swimmer striking out for a new destiny*? What is "success" to men like the Captain and Leggatt?

2. Compare the two main characters in "The Secret Sharer" with the two in "The Man Who Would Be King." What do the four of them have in common? How are they quite different? What in the training of Leggatt and the Captain would lead you to expect the kind of honor and faithfulness and courage they show? What in the background of the other two would suggest that they might or might not react the way they did to the collapse of their dreams? Define "character" as illustrated by the way these men meet moments of crisis.

FROM SIR GAWAIN
AND THE GREEN KNIGHT   [*circa 1400*]

In "The Secret Sharer" the young Captain puts to the test his fitness to command, his "ideal conception of [his] own personality," and meets successfully the demands of that test. In much the same way the hero of "Sir Gawain and the Green Knight" faces a test of the personal values by which he lives. The fact that his values are those of the community of knights only serves to heighten the importance of the individual commitment each knight must make.

As one of the greatest of King Arthur's knights, Gawain accepts a strange challenge brought by the Green Knight to Arthur's Round Table at Christmas time, and proves his worthiness anew in meeting the demands and temptations the challenge brings. His courage and fidelity prove less perfect than he thought them to be, but they are as near perfect as they can be in mortal man.

The poet of "Sir Gawain and the Green Knight" remains unknown, but he was undoubtedly Chaucer's contemporary, living in the Northwest Midlands far from the center of intellectual life in London. The rich detail of the poem tells us he was a man of learning and good breeding. The poem has been praised as second only in scope and achievement to *The Canterbury Tales* in the literature of the Middle English period.

Mr. Banks's translation of the poem tries to keep the original movement of the alliterative and stressed verse. Below are four lines of the original together with Mr. Banks's rendering. In essence the line is dominated by four heavy stresses (three of which alliterate), two on each side of a pause, or caesura, in the middle of the line; the stresses may fall anywhere, and there is no set pattern or number for unstressed syllables. You can easily notice the difference between the movement of these lines and Chaucer's—and most English poetry of the last five hundred years:

> Mist muged on the mor, /   malt on the mountes,
> Ech hille hade a hatte, /   a mist-hakel huge.
> Brokes byled and breke /   bi bonkkes aboute,
> Shyre shaterande on shores, /   ther thay doun shoved.

> On the moor dripped the mist, on the mountains melted;
> Each hill had a hat, a mist-cloak right huge.
> The brooks foamed and bubbled on hillsides about them,
> And brightly broke on their banks as they rushed down.

In Camelot Arthur the King lay at Christmas,
With many a peerless lord princely companioned,
The whole noble number of knights of the Round Table;
Here right royally held his high revels,
Carefree and mirthful. Now much of the company,   5
Knightly born gentlemen, joyously jousted,
Now came to the court to make caroles; so kept they
For full fifteen days this fashion of feasting,
All meat and all mirth that a man might devise.

    •   •   •

Moreover, the King was moved by a custom   10
He once had assumed in a spirit of splendor:
Never to fall to his feast on a festival
Till a strange story of something eventful
Was told him, some marvel that merited credence   15
Of kings, or of arms, or all kinds of adventures;
Or someone besought him to send a true knight
To join him in proving the perils of jousting,
Life against life, each leaving the other
To have, as fortune would help him, the fairer lot.

    •   •   •

And scarcely the music had ceased for a moment,   20
The first course been suitably served in the court,
When a being most dreadful burst through the hall-door,
Among the most mighty of men in his measure.
From his throat to his thighs so thick were his sinews,   25
His loins and his limbs so large and so long,
That I hold him half-giant, the hugest of men,
And the handsomest, too, in his height, upon horseback.
Though stalwart in breast and in back was his body,
His waist and his belly were worthily small;   30
Fashioned fairly he was in his form, and in features
                         Cut clean.

    •   •   •

All green was the man, and green were his garments:
A coat, straight and close, that clung to his sides,
A bright mantle on top of this, trimmed on the inside   35
With closely-cut fur, right fair, that showed clearly,
The lining with white fur most lovely, and hood too,
Caught back from his locks, and laid on his shoulders,
Neat stockings that clung to his calves, tightly stretched,
Of the same green, and under them spurs of gold shining   40
Brightly on bands of fine silk, richly barred;

---

1. CAMELOT: Arthur's capital in southern England.
LAY: sojourned. AT CHRISTMAS: i.e., at Christmas time.
7. CAROLES: dances accompanied by singing.

23. MEASURE: height.
39. UNDER: below.
40. BARRED: striped.

. . .

And everything metal enameled in emerald.
The stirrups he stood on the same way were colored,
His saddle-bows too, and the studded nails splendid,
That all with green gems ever glimmered and glinted.
The horse he bestrode was in hue still the same,   45

. . .

   This hero in green was habited gaily,
And likewise the hair on the head of his good horse;
Fair, flowing tresses enfolded his shoulders,
And big as a bush a beard hung on his breast.

. . .

   Yet the hero carried nor helmet nor hauberk,   50
But bare was of armor, breastplate or gorget,
Spear-shaft or shield, to thrust or to smite.
But in one hand he bore a bough of bright holly,
That grows most greenly when bare are the groves,
In the other an axe, gigantic, awful,   55
A terrible weapon, wondrous to tell of.
Large was the head, in length a whole ell-yard,
The blade of green steel and beaten gold both;
The bit had a broad edge, and brightly was burnished,
As suitably shaped as sharp razors for shearing.   60

. . .

Thus into the hall came the hero, and hastened
Direct to the dais, fearing no danger.
He gave no one greeting, but haughtily gazed,
And his first words were, "Where can I find him who governs
This goodly assemblage? for gladly that man   65
I would see and have speech with." . . .

. . . the King, ever keen and courageous,
Saw from on high, and saluted the stranger
Suitably, saying, "Sir, you are welcome.
I, the head of this household, am Arthur;   70
In courtesy light, and linger, I pray you,
And later, my lord, we shall learn your desire."
"Nay, so help me He seated on high," quoth the hero,
"My mission was not to remain here a moment;

. . .

Since here, I have heard, is the highest of courtesy—   75
Truly, all these things have brought me at this time.

---

53. HOLLY: to indicate that he came in peace
(see lines 77-78).
55. AWFUL: awesome.
57. ELL-YARD: forty-five inches.
62. DAIS: the raised platform on which the most
important members of the court sat. The rest
occupied two long tables along the walls that
ran the length of the room. The Green Knight
rode between the tables to the dais.
71. LIGHT: alight.

Sure ye may be by this branch that I bear
That I pass as in peace, proposing no fight.

•   •   •

"Nay, I ask for no fight; in faith, now I tell thee
But beardless babes are about on this bench.   80
Were I hasped in my armor, and high on a horse,
Here is no man to match me, your might is so feeble.
So I crave but a Christmas game in this court;
Yule and New Year are come, and here men have courage;
If one in this house himself holds so hardy,   85
So bold in his blood, in his brain so unbalanced
To dare stiffly strike one stroke for another,
I give this gisarme, this rich axe, as a gift to him,
Heavy enough, to handle as pleases him;
Bare as I sit, I shall bide the first blow.   90
If a knight be so tough as to try what I tell,
Let him leap to me lightly; I leave him this weapon,
Quitclaim it forever, to keep as his own;
And his stroke here, firm on this floor, I shall suffer,
This boon if thou grant'st me, the blow with another   95
                              To pay;
                    Yet let his respite be
                    A twelvemonth and a day.
                    Come, let us quickly see
                    If one here aught dare say."   100

If at first he had startled them, stiller then sat there
The whole of the court, low and high, in the hall.
The knight on his steed turned himself in his saddle,
And fiercely his red eyes he rolled all around,
Bent his bristling brows, with green gleaming brightly,   105
And waved his beard, waiting for one there to rise.
And when none of the knights spoke, he coughed right noisily,
Straightened up proudly, and started to speak:
"What!" quoth the hero. "Is this Arthur's household,
The fame of whose fellowship fills many kingdoms?   110
Now where is your vainglory? Where are your victories?
Where is your grimness, your great words, your anger?
For now the Round Table's renown and its revel
Is worsted by one word of one person's speech,
For all shiver with fear before a stroke's shown."   115
Then so loudly he laughed that the lord was grieved greatly,
And into his fair face his blood shot up fiercely
                              For shame.

---

80. BUT BEARDLESS BABES: i.e., only striplings (see
    line 49 for comparison).
100. AUGHT: anything.
116. LORD: Arthur.

•   •   •

And said, "Sir, by heaven, strange thy request is;
As folly thou soughtest, so shouldest thou find it.   120
I know that not one of the knights is aghast
Of thy great words. Give me thy weapon, for God's sake,
And gladly the boon thou hast begged I shall grant thee."

•   •   •

Gawain by Guinevere
Did to the King incline: 125
"I pray in accents clear
To let this fray be mine.

"If you now, honored lord," said this knight to King Arthur,
"Would bid me to step from this bench, and to stand there
Beside you—so could I with courtesy quit then   130
The table, unless my liege lady disliked it—
I'd come to your aid before all your great court."

•   •   •

The King then commanded his kinsman to rise,
And quickly he rose up and came to him courteously,
Kneeled by the King, and caught the weapon,   135
He left it graciously, lifted his hand,
And gave him God's blessing, and gladly bade him
Be sure that his heart and his hand both were hardy.
"Take care," quoth the King, "how you start, coz, your cutting,
And truly, I think, if rightly you treat him,   140
That blow you'll endure that he deals you after."

•   •   •

"By God," said the Green Knight, "Sir Gawain, it pleases me—
Here, at thy hand, I shall have what I sought."

•   •   •

With speed then the Green Knight took up his stand,
Inclined his head forward, uncovering the flesh,   145
And laid o'er his crown his locks long and lovely,
And bare left the nape of his neck for the business.
His axe Gawain seized, and swung it on high;
On the floor his left foot he planted before him,
And swiftly the naked flesh smote with his weapon.   150
The sharp edge severed the bones of the stranger,
Cut through the clear flesh and cleft it in twain,
So the blade of the brown steel bit the ground deeply.
The fair head fell from the neck to the floor,
So that where it rolled forth with their feet many spurned it.   155
The blood on the green glistened, burst from the body;
And yet neither fell nor faltered the hero,
But stoutly he started forth, strong in his stride;

---

139. coz: short for cousin, kinsman; Gawain is
Arthur's nephew.

Fiercely he rushed 'mid the ranks of the Round Table,
Seized and uplifted his lovely head straightway;   160
Then back to his horse went, laid hold of the bridle,
Stepped into the stirrup and strode up aloft,
His head holding fast in his hand by the hair.
And the man as soberly sat in his saddle
As if he unharmed were, although now headless,   165
         Instead.

      • • •

 For upright he holds the head in his hand,
And confronts with the face the fine folk on the dais.
It lifted its lids, and looked forth directly,
Speaking this much with its mouth, as ye hear: 170
"Gawain, look that to go as agreed you are ready,
And seek for me faithfully, sir, till you find me,
As, heard by these heroes, you vowed in this hall.
To the Green Chapel go you, I charge you, to get
Such a stroke as you struck. You are surely deserving,   175
Sir knight, to be promptly repaid at the New Year.
As Knight of the Green Chapel many men know me;
If therefore to find me you try, you will fail not;
Then come, or be recreant called as befits thee."
With furious wrench of the reins he turned round,   180
And rushed from the hall-door, his head in his hands,
So the fire of the flint flew out from the foal's hoofs.

      • • •

    Now take heed Gawain lest,
    Fearing the Green Knight's brand,
    Thou shrinkest from the quest   185
    That thou hast ta'en in hand.

II

      • • •

Full swift flies a year, never yielding the same
The start and the close very seldom according.
So past went this Yule, and the year followed after,
Each season in turn succeeding the other.   190

      • • •

 Till the tide of Allhallows with Arthur he tarried;
The King made ado on that day for his sake
With rich and rare revel of all of the Round Table,
Knights most courteous, comely ladies,
All of them heavy at heart for the hero.   195

---

162. STRODE: bestrode.
191. TIDE: time. ALLHALLOWS: All Saints' Day;
  November 1.

Yet nothing but mirth was uttered, though many
Joyless made jests for that gentleman's sake.
After meat, with sorrow he speaks to his uncle,
And openly talks of his travel, saying:
"Liege lord of my life, now I ask of you leave.   200
You know my case and condition, nor care I
To tell of its troubles even a trifle.
I must, for the blow I am bound to, tomorrow
Go seek as God guides me the man in the green."

> • • •

When in arms he was clasped, his costume was costly;   205
The least of the lacings or loops gleamed with gold.
And armed in this manner, the man heard mass,
At the altar adored and made offering, and afterward
Came to the King and all of his courtiers,
Gently took leave of the ladies and lords;   210
Him they kissed and escorted, to Christ him commending.

> • • •

He set spurs to his steed, and sprang on his way
So swiftly that sparks from the stone flew behind him.
All who saw him, so seemly, sighed, sad at heart;
The same thing, in sooth, each said to the other,   215
Concerned for that comely man: "Christ, 't is a shame
Thou, sir knight, must be lost whose life is so noble!
To find, faith! his equal on earth is not easy."

> • • •

Over many cliffs climbed he in foreign countries;
From friends far sundered, he fared as a stranger;   220
And wondrous it were, at each water or shore
That he passed, if he found not before him a foe,
So foul too and fell that to fight he could fail not.
The marvels he met with amount to so many
Too tedious were it to tell of the tenth part.   225
For sometimes with serpents he struggled and wolves too,
With wood-trolls sometimes in stony steeps dwelling,
And sometimes with bulls and with bears and with boars;
And giants from high fells hunted and harassed him.
If he'd been not enduring and doughty, and served God,   230
These doubtless would often have done him to death.
Though warfare was grievous, worse was the winter,
When cold, clear water was shed from the clouds
That froze ere it fell to the earth, all faded.

---

219. FOREIGN COUNTRIES: parts of England new
and strange to him. The details of his travels
are not clear, but he goes from Camelot in
the south of England, up through Wales, and
probably as far north as Cumberland.
228. BULLS: i.e., wild bulls.

With sleet nearly slain, he slept in his armor   235
More nights than enough on the naked rocks,
Where splashing the cold stream sprang from the summit,
And hung in hard icicles high o'er his head.
Thus in peril and pain and desperate plights,
Till Christmas Eve wanders this wight through the country   240
                                   Alone.

                •   •   •

Through many a marsh and many a mire,
Unfriended, fearing to fail in devotion,
And see not His service, that Sire's, on that very night
Born of a Virgin to vanquish our pain.   245
And so sighing he said: "Lord, I beseech Thee,
And Mary, the mildest mother so dear,
For some lodging wherein to hear mass full lowly,
And matins, meekly I ask it, tomorrow;
So promptly I pray my pater and ave   250
                          And creed."

                •   •   •

  He scarcely had signed himself thrice, ere he saw
In the wood on a mound a moated mansion,
Above a fair field, enfolded in branches
Of many a huge tree hard by the ditches: 255
The comeliest castle that knight ever kept.

                •   •   •

  Gawain gazed at the man who so graciously greeted him;
Doughty he looked, the lord of that dwelling,
A hero indeed huge, hale, in his prime;
His beard broad and bright, its hue all of beaver;   260
Stern, and on stalwart shanks steadily standing;
Fell faced as the fire, in speech fair and free.
In sooth, well suited he seemed, thought Gawain,
To govern as prince of a goodly people.

                •   •   •   265

  Much mirth was that day and the day after made,
And the third followed fast, as full of delight.

                •   •   •

  Then the man with courteous questions inquired
What dark deed that feast time had driven him forth,
From the King's court to journey alone with such courage,
Ere fully in homes was the festival finished.   270
"In sooth," said the knight, "sir, ye say but the truth;
From these hearths a high and a hasty task took me.
Myself, I am summoned to seek such a place
As to find it I know not whither to fare.

---

250. PATER: i.e., the Lord's Prayer, which in Latin
begins: *Pater noster,* etc. AVE: i.e., the prayers
beginning: *Ave Maria*—"Hail, Mary."

252. SIGNED HIMSELF: made the sign of the cross.
260. BEAVER: reddish-brown.
262. FELL: fierce.

• • •

Tell me, in truth, if you ever heard tale   275
Of the Chapel of Green, of the ground where it stands,
And the knight, green colored, who keeps it. By solemn
Agreement a tryst was established between us,
That man at that landmark to meet if I lived."

• • •

Then laughing the lord said: "You longer must stay,   280
For I'll point out the way to that place ere the time's end,
The ground of the Green Chapel. Grieve no further;
For, sir, you shall be in your bed at your ease
Until late, and fare forth the first of the year,
To your meeting place come by mid-morning, to do there   285
                              Your pleasure.
                Tarry till New Year's day,
                Then rise and go at leisure.
                I'll set you on your way;
                Not two miles is the measure."   290

    Then was Gawain right glad, and gleefully laughed.
"Now for this more than anything else, sir, I thank you.
I have come to the end of my quest; at your will
I shall bide, and in all things act as you bid me."

• • •

"You have toiled," said the lord; "from afar have traveled,   295
And here have caroused, nor are wholly recovered
In sleep or in nourishment, know I for certain.
In your room you shall linger, and lie at your ease
Tomorrow till mass-time, and go to your meat
When you will, and with you my wife to amuse you   300
With company, till to the court I return.
                              You stay
                And I shall early rise,
                And hunting go my way."
                Bowing in courteous wise,   305
                Gawain grants all this play.

    "And more," said the man, "let us make an agreement:
Whatever I win in the wood shall be yours;
And what chance you shall meet shall be mine in exchange.
Sir, let's so strike our bargain and swear to tell truly   310
Whate'er fortune brings, whether bad, sir, or better."
Quoth Gawain the good: "By God, I do grant it.
What pastime you please appears to me pleasant."
"On the beverage brought us the bargain is made,"
So the lord of the land said. All of them laughed,   315
And drank, and light-heartedly reveled and dallied,
Those ladies and lords, as long as they liked.

---

308. IN THE WOOD: i.e., out hunting.   309. CHANCE: fortune.

•   •   •

Gawain had arrived at the castle on Christmas Eve, and he prepared to leave with the rest of the guests on December 28th. But his host indicated that the Green Chapel was not far off and that he could easily stay on until New Year's Day and still keep his appointment. The following three days (29th through 31st) are strange ones for Gawain. As we see at the end of Section II, his host has proposed an agreement whereby he will give Gawain whatever he kills while hunting, and Gawain will give him in exchange "whate'er fortune brings" back at the castle.

Early in the morning of the 29th the host leaves the castle and spends the whole day hunting deer. "Gawain the good in his gay bed reposed" until late morning. Much to his surprise he awakes to find that his host's wife has stolen into his chamber. She chides him for not being more alert and then proceeds to make quite open suggestions that he make love to her. Torn between fear of insulting his hostess or being disloyal to his host, he fends off her advances as politely as he can. She agrees to withdraw, but asks for a kiss, which he willingly gives. When the host returns and gives Gawain the slain deer, Gawain gives him a kiss in exchange.

That evening his host suggests a repetition of the agreement the following day and Gawain assents. Again his host rises early and Gawain sleeps late, but not so soundly. He expects the lady and is ready to resist her advances, politely but firmly. In the most courteous of verbal exchanges he parries her suggestions, and does nothing more than give her the two kisses she asks for. "Thus the fair lady tempted and tested him often/To make the man sin," but she is not successful. When her husband returns, he gives Gawain the boar he has killed and gets two kisses in exchange.

Before we turn again to the poem for the events of the third day, it might be well to point out that the brief summary of action we have given necessarily leaves out much that is important in the poem. The hunting scenes are described in vigorous and brutal detail. In contrast the temptation scenes are couched in the niceties of polite conversation even though there is no doubt about the lady's intentions. Quite obviously, the poet is making a direct contrast between what is going on in the forest and what is going on in the castle. The first day's hunt is for deer, a noble animal whose defense lies in its elusiveness; the second day's hunt is for boar, also a noble animal but one which willingly turns to face its tormentors. Now follow what happens on the third day; the quarry this time is the fox, an animal noted for its cunning and deceit.

III

•   •   •

The men there make merry and drink, and once more
The same pact for New Year's Eve is proposed;
But the knight craved permission to mount on the morrow: 320
The appointment approached where he had to appear.
But the lord him persuaded to stay and linger,
And said, "On my word as a knight I assure you
You'll get to the Green Chapel, Gawain, on New Year's,

And far before prime, to finish your business.   325
Remain in your room then, and take your rest.
I shall hunt in the wood and exchange with you winnings,
As bound by our bargain, when back I return,
For twice I've found you were faithful when tried:
In the morning 'best be the third time,' remember.   330
Let's be mindful of mirth while we may, and make merry,
For care when one wants it is quickly encountered."
At once this was granted, and Gawain is stayed;

•   •   •

The host was early dressed.

   After mass a morsel he took with his men.   335
The morning was merry; his mount he demanded.
The knights who'd ride in his train were in readiness,
Dressed and horsed at the door of the hall.
Wondrous fair were the fields, for the frost was clinging;
Fire-red in the cloud-rack rises the sun,   340
And brightens the skirts of the clouds in the sky.
The hunters unleashed all the hounds by a woodside:
The rocks with the blast of their bugles were ringing.
Some dogs there fall on the scent where the fox is,
And trail oft a traitoress using her tricks.   345

•   •   •

So he led all astray the lord and his men,
In this manner along through the hills until mid-day.
At home, the noble knight wholesomely slept
In the cold of the morn within comely curtains.
But the lady, for love, did not let herself sleep,   350
Or fail in the purpose fixed in her heart;
But quickly she roused herself, came there quickly,
Arrayed in a gay robe that reached to the ground,
The skins of the splendid fur skillfully trimmed close.
On her head no colors save jewels, well-cut,   355
That were twined in her hair-fret in clusters of twenty.
Her fair face was completely exposed, and her throat;
In front her breast too was bare, and her back.
She comes through the chamber-door, closes it after her,
Swings wide a window, speaks to the wight,   360
And rallies him soon in speech full of sport

And good cheer.

•   •   •

The lovely lady came near, sweetly laughing,
Bent down o'er his fair face and daintily kissed him.

---

325. PRIME: early morning.
340. CLOUD-RACK: cloud-drift.
345. TRAITORESS: i.e., a vixen who confused the
dogs by crossing the trail of the male fox.

346. HE: the fox.
356. HAIR-FRET: wire headdress for containing
her hair.

And well, in a worthy manner, he welcomed her.   365
Seeing her glorious, gaily attired,
Without fault in her features, most fine in her color,
Deep joy came welling up, warming his heart.
With sweet, gentle smiling they straightway grew merry;
So passed naught between them but pleasure, joy,   370

And delight.
Goodly was their debate,
Nor was their gladness slight.
Their peril had been great
Had Mary quit her knight.   375

For that noble princess pressed him so closely,
Brought him so near the last bound, that her love
He was forced to accept, or, offending, refuse her:
Concerned for his courtesy not to prove caitiff,
And more for his ruin if wrong he committed,   380
Betraying the hero, the head of that house.
"God forbid," said the knight; "that never shall be";
And lovingly laughing a little, he parried
The words of fondness that fell from her mouth.

• • •

His parrying is successful. The lady asks if there is another he is pledged to, and Gawain assures her that there is not. She asks him for some gift so that she will remember him, but he says he has nothing worthy of her. She then offers him a "rich ring," which he politely refuses to accept. Finally, she offers him her green silk belt:

"Refuse ye this silk," the lady then said,   385
"As slight in itself? Truly it seems so.
Lo! it is little, and less is its worth;
But one knowing the nature knit up within it,
Would give it a value more great, peradventure;
For no man girt with this girdle of green,   390
And bearing it fairly made fast about him,
Might ever be cut down by any on earth,
For his life in no way in the world could be taken."
Then mused the man, and it came to his mind
In the peril appointed him precious 't would prove,   395
When he'd found the chapel, to face there his fortune.
The device, might he slaying evade, would be splendid.
Her suit then he suffered, and let her speak;
And the belt she offered him, earnestly urging it

---

375. MARY: the Virgin Mary.   384. FONDNESS: love.
379. CAITIFF: cowardly.   392. CUT DOWN: i.e., killed.

(And Gawain consented), and gave it with good will,   400
And prayed him for her sake ne'er to display it,
But, true, from her husband to hide it. The hero
Agreed that no one should know of it ever.

•   •   •

The lord's in the meadow still, leading his men.
He has slain this fox that he followed so long;   405
As he vaulted a hedge to get view of the villain,
Hearing the hounds that hastened hard after him,
Reynard from out a rough thicket came running,
And right at his heels in a rush all the rabble.
He seeing that wild thing, wary, awaits him,   410
Unsheathes his bright brand and strikes at the beast.
And he swerved from its sharpness and back would have started;
A hound, ere he could, came hurrying up to him;
All of them fell on him fast by the horse's feet,
Worried that sly one with wrathful sound.   415
And quickly the lord alights, and catches him,
Takes him in haste from the teeth of the hounds,
And over his head holds him high, loudly shouting,
Where brachets, many and fierce, at him barked.

•   •   •

And now, since near was the night, they turned homeward,   420
Strongly and sturdily sounding their horns.
At last at his loved home the lord alighted,
A fire on the hearth found, the hero beside it,
Sir Gawain the good, who glad was withal,
For he had 'mong the ladies in love much delight.   425

•   •   •

He, mid-most, met the good man in the hall,
And greeted him gladly, graciously saying:
"Now shall I first fulfill our agreement
We struck to good purpose, when drink was not spared."
Then Gawain embraced him, gave him three kisses,   430
The sweetest and soundest a man could bestow.
"By Christ, you'd great happiness," quoth then the host,
"In getting these wares, if good were your bargains."
"Take no care for the cost," the other said quickly,
"Since plainly the debt that is due I have paid."   435
Said the other, "By Mary, mine's of less worth.
The whole of the day I have hunted, and gotten
The skin of this fox—the fiend take its foulness!—
Right poor to pay for things of such price
As you've pressed on me here so heartily, kisses   440
So good."

---

409. RABBLE: hounds.
411. BRAND: sword.
419. BRACHETS: small female hounds.

• • •

"May God you reward for the welcome you gave me
This high feast, the splendid sojourn I've had here.
I give you myself, if you'd like it, to serve you.
I must, as you know, on the morrow move on;   445
Give me someone to show me the path, as you said,
To the Green Chapel, there, as God will allow me,
On New Year the fate that is fixed to perform."
"With a good will, indeed," said the good man; "whatever
I promised to do I deem myself ready."   450
He a servant assigns on his way to set him,
To take him by hills that no trouble he'd have,
And through grove and wood by the way most direct
                                   Might repair.

• • •

IV

   The New Year draws near, and the nighttime now passes;   455
The day, as the Lord bids, drives on to darkness.
Outside, there sprang up wild storms in the world;
The clouds cast keenly the cold to the earth
With enough of the north sting to trouble the naked;
Down shivered the snow, nipping sharply the wild beasts;   460
The wind from the heights, shrilly howling, came rushing,
And heaped up each dale full of drifts right huge.
Full well the man listened who lay in his bed.
Though he shut tight his lids, he slept but a little;
He knew by each cock that crowed 't was the tryst time,   465
And swiftly ere dawn of the day he arose,
For there shone then the light of a lamp in his room;
To his chamberlain called, who answered him quickly,
And bade him his saddle to bring and his mailshirt.

• • •

Yet he left not the lace, the gift of the lady: 470
That, Gawain did not, for his own sake, forget.
When the brand on his rounded thighs he had belted,
He twisted his love-token two times about him.
That lord round his waist with delight quickly wound
The girdle of green silk, that seemed very gay   475
Upon royal red cloth that was rich to behold.
But Gawain the girdle wore not for its great price,
Or pride in its pendants although they were polished,
Though glittering gold there gleamed on the ends,
But himself to save when he needs must suffer   480
The death, nor could stroke then of sword or of knife
                                   Him defend.

● ● ●

On the moor dripped the mist, on the mountains melted;
Each hill had a hat, a mist-cloak right huge.
The brooks foamed and bubbled on hillsides about them,   485
And brightly broke on their banks as they rushed down.
Full wandering the way was they went through the wood,
Until soon it was time for the sun to be springing.

● ● ●

"I have led you hither, my lord, at this time,
And not far are you now from that famous place   490
You have sought for, and asked so especially after.
Yet, sir, to you surely I'll say, since I know you,
A man in this world whom I love right well,
If you'd follow my judgment, the better you'd fare.
You make haste to a place that is held full of peril;   495
One dwells, the worst in the world, in that waste,
For he's strong and stern, and takes pleasure in striking.

● ● ●

"So let him alone, good Sir Gawain, and leave
By a different road, for God's sake, and ride
To some other country where Christ may reward you.   500
And homeward again I will hie me, and promise
To swear by the Lord and all his good saints
(So help me the oaths on God's halidom sworn)
That I'll guard well your secret, and give out no story
You hastened to flee any hero I've heard of."   505
"Thank you," said Gawain, and grudgingly added,
"Good fortune go with you for wishing me well.
And truly I think you'd not tell; yet though never
So surely you hid it, if hence I should hasten,
Fearful, to fly in the fashion you tell of,   510
A coward I'd prove, and could not be pardoned.
The chapel I'll find whatsoever befalls,
And talk with that wight the way that I want to,
Let weal or woe follow as fate may wish.

● ● ●

"Of a truth," said Gawain, "the glade here is gloomy;   515
The Green Chapel's ugly, with herbs overgrown.
It greatly becomes here that hero, green-clad,
To perform in the devil's own fashion his worship.
I feel in my five senses this is the fiend
Who has made me come to this meeting to kill me.   520
Destruction fall on this church of ill-fortune!
The cursedest chapel that ever I came to!"
With helm on his head and lance in his hand
He went right to the rock of that rugged abode.

---

503. HALIDOM: holiness.
517. BECOMES: befits.

From that high hill he heard, from a hard rock over   525
The stream, on the hillside, a sound wondrous loud.
Lo! it ground and it grated, grievous to hear.
"By God, this thing, as I think," then said Gawain,
"Is done now for me, since my due turn to meet it
                          Is near,   530
          God's will be done! 'Ah woe!'
          No whit doth aid me here.
          Though I my life forego
          No sound shall make me fear."

    And then the man there commenced to call loudly,   535
"Who here is the master, with me to hold tryst?
For Gawain the good now is going right near.
He who craves aught of me let him come hither quickly;
'T is now or never; he needs to make haste."
Said somebody, "Stop," from the slope up above him,   540
"And promptly you'll get what I promised to give you."
Yet he kept up the whirring noise quickly a while,
Turned to finish his sharpening before he'd descend.
Then he came by a crag, from a cavern emerging,
Whirled out of a den with a dreadful weapon,   545
A new Danish axe to answer the blow with:
Its blade right heavy, curved back to the handle,
Sharp filed with the filing tool, four feet in length,
'T was no less, by the reach of that lace gleaming brightly.
The fellow in green was garbed as at first,   550
Both his face and his legs, his locks and his beard,
Save that fast o'er the earth on his feet he went fairly,
The shaft on the stone set, and stalked on beside it.
On reaching the water, he would not wade it;
On his axe he hopped over, and hastily strode,   555
Very fierce, through the broad field filled all about him
                        With snow.

                  •   •   •

    Said the green man, "Gawain, may God you guard!
You are welcome indeed, sir knight, at my dwelling.
Your travel you've timed as a true man should,   560
And you know the compact we came to between us;
A twelvemonth ago you took what chance gave,
And I promptly at New Year was pledged to repay you.
In truth, we are down in this dale all alone;
Though we fight as we please, here there's no one to part us.   565
Put your helm from your head, and have here your payment;
Debate no further than I did before,
When you slashed off my head with a single stroke."

---

532. NO WHIT: nothing.

"Nay," quoth Gawain, "by God who gave me my spirit,
I'll harbor no grudge whatever harm happens.   570
Exceed not one stroke and still I shall stand;
You may do as you please, I'll in no way oppose
                              The blow."
                         •   •   •

    Then the man in green raiment quickly made ready,
Uplifted his grim tool Sir Gawain to smite;   575
With the whole of his strength he heaved it on high,
As threateningly swung it as though he would slay him.
Had it fallen again with the force he intended
That lord, ever-brave, from the blow had been lifeless.
But Gawain a side glance gave at the weapon   580
As down it came gliding to do him to death;
With his shoulders shrank from the sharp iron a little.
The other with sudden jerk stayed the bright axe,
And reproved then that prince with proud words in plenty:
"Not Gawain thou art who so good is considered,   585
Ne'er daunted by host in hill or in dale;
Now in fear, ere thou feelest a hurt, thou art flinching;
Such cowardice never I knew of that knight.
When you swung at me, sir, I fled not nor started;
No cavil I offered in King Arthur's castle.   590
My head at my feet fell, yet never I flinched,
And thy heart is afraid ere a hurt thou feelest,
And therefore thy better I'm bound to be thought
                              On that score."
                    "I shrank once," Gawain said,   595
                    "And I will shrink no more;
                    Yet cannot I my head,
                    If it fall down, restore."
                         •   •   •

He mightily swung but struck not the man,
Withheld on a sudden his hand ere it hurt him.   600
And firmly he waited and flinched in no member,
But stood there as still as a stone or a stump
In rocky ground held by a hundred roots.
                         •   •   •

    "Come! lay on, thou dread man; too long thou art threatening.
I think that afraid of your own self you feel."   605
"In sooth," said the other, "thy speech is so savage
No more will I hinder thy mission nor have it
                              Delayed."
                         •   •   •

    He lifts his axe lightly, and lets it down deftly,
The blade's edge next to the naked neck.   610

---

583. STAYED . . . AXE: stopped the blow.   599. HE: the Green Knight.
586. HOST: large numbers.   601. HE: Gawain. MEMBER: i.e., part of his body.

Though he mightily hammered he hurt him no more
Than to give him a slight nick that severed the skin there.
Through fair skin the keen axe so cut to the flesh
That shining blood shot to the earth o'er his shoulders.
As soon as he saw his blood gleam on the snow   615
He sprang forth in one leap, for more than a spear length;
His helm fiercely caught up and clapped on his head;
With his shoulders his fair shield shot round in front of him,
Pulled out his bright sword, and said in a passion   620
(And since he was mortal man born of his mother
The hero was never so happy by half),
"Cease thy violence, man; no more to me offer,
For here I've received, unresisting, a stroke.
If a second thou strikest I soon will requite thee,   625
And swiftly and fiercely, be certain of that,

                                  Will repay."

                          •   •   •

Then gaily the Green Knight spoke in a great voice,
And said to the man in speech that resounded,
"Now be not so savage, bold sir, for towards you   630
None here has acted unhandsomely, save
In accord with the compact arranged in the King's court.
I promised the stroke you've received, so hold you
Well paid. I free you from all duties further.
If brisk I had been, peradventure a buffet   635
I'd harshly have dealt that harm would have done you.
In mirth, with a feint I menaced you first,
With no direful wound rent you; right was my deed,
By the bargain that bound us both on the first night,
When, faithful and true, you fulfilled our agreement,   640
And gave me your gain as a good man ought to.
The second I struck at you, sir, for the morning
You kissed my fair wife and the kisses accorded me.
Two mere feints for both times I made at you, man,

                              Without woe.
                   True men restore by right,   645
                   One fears no danger so;
                   You failed the third time, knight,
                   And therefore took that blow.

"'T is my garment you're wearing, that woven girdle,
Bestowed by my wife, as in truth I know well.   650
I know also your kisses and all of your acts
And my wife's advances; myself, I devised them.
I sent her to try you, and truly you seem

---

615. HE: Gawain.   634. BUFFET: blow.
618. WITH . . . HIM: Gawain's shield was strapped
  on his back; with a quick flip of his shoulders
  he brings it around to the front.

The most faultless of men that e'er fared on his feet.
As a pearl compared to white peas is more precious, 655
So next to the other gay knights is Sir Gawain.
But a little you lacked, and loyalty wanted,
Yet truly 't was not for intrigue or for wooing,
But love of your life; the less do I blame you."
Sir Gawain stood in a study a great while, 660
So sunk in disgrace that in spirit he groaned;
To his face all the blood in his body was flowing;
For shame, as the other was talking, he shrank.
And these were the first words that fell from his lips:
"Be cowardice cursed, and coveting! In you 665
Are vice and villainy, virtue destroying."
The lace he then seized, and loosened the strands,
And fiercely the girdle flung at the Green Knight.
"Lo! there is faith-breaking! evil befall it.
To coveting came I, for cowardice caused me 670
From fear of your stroke to forsake in myself
What belongs to a knight: munificence, loyalty.
I'm faulty and false, who've been ever afraid
Of untruth and treachery; sorrow betide both

And care! 675
Here I confess my sin;
All faulty did I fare.
Your good will let me win,
And then I will beware."

Then the Green Knight laughed, and right graciously said, 680
"I am sure that the harm is healed that I suffered.
So clean you're confessed, so cleared of your faults,
Having had the point of my weapon's plain penance,
I hold you now purged of offense, and as perfectly
Spotless as though you'd ne'er sinned in your life. 685
And I give to you, sir, the golden-hemmed girdle,
As green as my gown. Sir Gawain, when going
Forth on your way among famous princes,
Think still of our strife and this token right splendid,
'Mid chivalrous knights, of the chapel's adventure." 690

• • •

"But your girdle," said Gawain, "may God you reward!
With a good will I'll use it, yet not for the gold,
The sash or the silk, or the sweeping pendants,
Or fame, or its workmanship wondrous, or cost,
But in sign of my sin I shall see it oft. 695
When in glory I move, with remorse I'll remember
The frailty and fault of the stubborn flesh,

---

660. STUDY: deep thought on what he had done.
665. IN YOU: i.e., in cowardice and coveting.

How soon 't is infected with stains of defilement;
And thus when I'm proud of my prowess in arms,
The sight of this sash shall humble my spirit.   700
But one thing I pray, if it prove not displeasing;
Because you are lord of the land where I stayed
In your house with great worship (may He now reward you
Who sitteth on high and upholdeth the heavens),
What name do you bear? No more would I know."   705
And then "That truly I'll tell," said the other;
"Bercilak de Hautdesert here am I called.

                            •   •   •

    "I was sent in this way to your splendid hall
To make trial of your pride, and to see if the people's
Tales were true of the Table's great glory.   710

                            •   •   •

And I, sir, wish thee as well, on my word,
As any on earth for thy high sense of honor."

                            •   •   •

The men kiss, embrace, and each other commend
To the Prince of Paradise; there they part
                                        In the cold.   715

                            •   •   •

    Through the wood now goes Sir Gawain by wild ways
On Gringolet, given by God's grace his life.
Oft in houses, and oft in the open he lodged,
Met many adventures, won many a victory:
These I intend not to tell in this tale.   720
Now whole was the hurt he had in his neck,
And about it the glimmering belt he was bearing,
Bound to his side like a baldric obliquely,
Tied under his left arm, that lace, with a knot
As a sign that with stain of sin he'd been found.   725
And thus to the court he comes all securely.

                            •   •   •

The King kissed the lord, and the Queen did likewise,
And next many knights drew near him to greet him
And ask how he'd fared; and he wondrously answered,
Confessed all the hardships that him had befallen,   730
The happenings at chapel, the hero's behavior,
The lady's love, and lastly the lace.
He showed them the nick in his neck all naked
The blow that the Green Knight gave for deceit
                                        Him to blame.   735
                    In torment this he owned;
                    Blood in his face did flame;
                    With wrath and grief he groaned,
                    When showing it with shame.

_____

717. GRINGOLET: Gawain's horse.   736. OWNED: admitted.

Laying hold of the lace, quoth the hero, "Lo! lord!   740
The band of this fault I bear on my neck;
And this is the scathe and damage I've suffered,
For cowardice caught there, and coveting also,
The badge of untruth in which I was taken.
And this for as long as I live I must wear,   745
For his fault none may hide without meeting misfortune,
For once it is fixed, it can ne'er be unfastened."
To the knight then the King gave comfort; the court too
Laughed greatly, and made this gracious agreement:
That ladies and lords to the Table belonging,   750
All of the brotherhood, baldrics should bear
Obliquely about them, bands of bright green,
Thus following suit for the sake of the hero.
For the Round Table's glory was granted that lace,
And he held himself honored who had it thereafter,   755
As told in the book, the best of romances.
In the days of King Arthur this deed was done. . . .

I

1. What is Arthur's custom before feasting on a festival day? How is his desire fulfilled in good measure in this instance? Why does Arthur offer to take up the challenge? What do lines 128-132 show about the code of behavior Gawain lives by? What is ironic about Arthur's comment in lines 139-141 besides the fact that severing the Green Knight's head won't end the matter, as Arthur naturally supposed it would?

2. How do such details as "On the floor his left foot he planted before him" (149), "where it rolled forth with their feet many spurned it" (155), and "he rushed 'mid the ranks of the Round Table" (159) give the scene of the beheading a plausibility our common sense tells us it shouldn't have?

3. Gawain leaves on All Saints' Day and does not arrive at the Green Knight's castle until Christmas Eve. What kinds of dangers and handicaps does he encounter in his quest? How do they contrast with life at Camelot and at the Green Knight's castle? In so far as the *Christmas game* is concerned, all Gawain has to do is present his neck for the Green Knight's blow. Why must he undergo miseries and temptations before reaching the chapel?

4. Indicate specifically what happens on each day of Gawain's sojourn at the Green Knight's castle in connection with the temptation. What knightly duties is he forced to choose between? Who is in more danger, Gawain in the comfort of the castle, or the Green Knight and the hunters pursuing wild animals? Explain. Why does Gawain accept the green sash and fail to give it to the Green Knight as his part of the bargain?

5. Outline the events of the meeting at the Green Knight's chapel. Why are there three blows, the last of which actually draws blood? Why does Gawain have to submit to the last two? Why is he ashamed of his behavior? What explanation does the Green Knight have for the *Christmas game*? What larger meaning does it have for Gawain and for the reader? Why does Gawain continue to wear the green lace in full view? Why do the members of Arthur's court follow suit?

6. There is a good deal of light-hearted pleasantry in the poem; it almost seems as if the characters are unconcerned about the terror that surrounds them. What does the poet gain by emphasizing the youthful gaiety of Arthur's court and the excessive politeness and good humor at the Green Knight's castle?

7. The poem is certainly not realistic in the usual sense of the term, and yet we easily accept the characters as very real people. Why is this so? How important is the supernatural to the poem?

8. At the end of the poem the Green Knight calls Gawain, "The most faultless of men." What characteristics of the true knight does Gawain embody? What does the Green Knight's test teach him? Do you suppose the poet's purpose was simply to dramatize a Christian moral lesson? Why or why not?

II

1. The original is over three times as long as the version we have here. Obviously, much of the rich detail has been left out as a result. Using the version here or the full text, write a paper dealing with the following two questions: *1/*What part do the time of year and the references to the change of seasons play in the poem? *2/*What significance do the many references to color have, particularly the extensive use of green and gold?

2. A critic has said that at the heart of the poem is the "technique of juxtaposing—or combining—opposite and contrary moods, characters, settings, and actions." Show how this comment is valid.

THE TRIAL AND DEATH OF SOCRATES

Plato

Unlike the Captain and Gawain, Socrates in the following selection is no longer young, but there is in him the same kind of intense necessity to live up to his "ideal conception" of himself. Perhaps nowhere else in literature is there a more striking example of a man who understands himself completely and has no misgivings about what right action is, no misgivings about what constitutes "success."

Most of what we know of Socrates we find in the writings of his pupil and friend, Plato. The so-called Socratic dialogues of Plato give, in the words of the *Phaedo,* the essentials of Socrates's insight into "temperance, and justice, and courage, and nobility, and truth."

What we have excerpted here are parts of the *Apology* and *Phaedo,** which deal with the trial, imprisonment, and death of Socrates in his seventieth year. For half his lifetime he had devoted himself to lengthy and probing conversations with anyone who would talk with him, particularly the young men of Athens. He felt he had a mission to expose ignorance and encourage self-knowledge. He called himself "a sort of gadfly, given to the state by God," whose duty it was to fasten himself upon men, "arousing, persuading, and reproaching" them. This is certainly no way to endear yourself to your fellow citizens, and although Socrates found many devoted followers, he also found many confirmed enemies. Finally, in 399 B. C., he was accused of certain crimes against the state and was brought to trial.

This was not a trial as we know one. Some five hundred Athenian citizens sat as a jury, with a simple majority vote deciding guilt or innocence. A man's accuser stated his side of the case, and the defendant stated his. If the jury found a man guilty, both the accuser and the accused proposed penalties; the jury could decide on one or the other, but could make no third, or compromise, proposal. In Plato's *Apology* ("Defense" would be a more accurate translation of the Greek word for modern readers) we get only Socrates's three speeches to

* Translated by Benjamin Jowett.

the court: the first in answer to the charges against him, the second after his conviction, and the third after the death penalty has been voted. The quality of the man and the life he chose to live come through clearly in the account Plato gives us of what he said. And, perhaps more compelling than anything in the *Apology,* we see, in the *Phaedo,* the way he chose to die.

from THE APOLOGY

How you, O Athenians, have been affected by my accusers, I cannot tell; but I know that they almost made me forget who I was —so persuasively did they speak; and yet they have hardly uttered a word of truth. But of the many falsehoods told by them, there was one which quite amazed me;—I mean when they said that you should be upon your guard and not allow yourselves to be deceived by the force of my eloquence. To say this, when they were certain to be detected as soon as I opened my lips and proved myself to be anything but a great speaker, did indeed appear to me most shameless—unless by the force of eloquence they mean the force of truth; for if such is their meaning, I admit that I am eloquent. But in how different a way from theirs! Well, as I was saying, they have scarcely spoken the truth at all; but from me you shall hear the whole truth: not, however, delivered after their manner in a set oration duly ornamented with words and phrases. No, by heaven! but I shall use the words and arguments which occur to me at the moment; for I am confident in the justice of my cause: at my time of life I ought not to be appearing before you, O men of Athens, in the character of a juvenile orator—let no one expect it of me. And I must beg of you to grant me a favor:—If I defend myself in my accustomed manner, and you hear me using the words which I have been in the habit of using in the agora,[1] at the tables of the money-changers, or anywhere else, I would ask you not to be surprised, and not to interrupt me on this account. For I am more than seventy years of age, and appear-

ing now for the first time in a court of law, I am quite a stranger to the language of the place; and therefore I would have you regard me as if I were really a stranger, whom you would excuse if he spoke in his native tongue, and after the fashion of his country: —Am I making an unfair request of you? Never mind the manner, which may or may not be good; but think only of the truth of my words, and give heed to that: let the speaker speak truly and the judge decide justly. . . .

I will begin at the beginning, and ask what is the accusation which has given rise to the slander of me, and in fact has encouraged Meletus[2] to prefer this charge against me. Well, what do the slanderers say? They shall be my prosecutors, and I will sum up their words in an affidavit: "Socrates is an evildoer, and a curious person, who searches into things under the earth and in heaven, and he makes the worse appear the better cause; and he teaches the aforesaid doctrines to others." Such is the nature of the accusation: it is just what you have yourselves seen in the comedy of Aristophanes,[3] who has introduced a man whom he calls Socrates, going about and saying that he walks in air, and talking a deal of nonsense concerning matters of which I do not pretend to know either much or little—not that I mean to speak disparagingly of anyone who is a student of natural philosophy.[4] I should be very sorry if Meletus

---

1. AGORA: market place.

2. MELETUS: one of his three accusers.
3. ARISTOPHANES: greatest of the Greek comic dramatists; he had satirized Socrates in *The Clouds.*
4. NATURAL PHILOSOPHY: study of the physical universe.

could bring so grave a charge against me. But the simple truth is, O Athenians, that I have nothing to do with physical speculations. Very many of those here present are witnesses to the truth of this, and to them I appeal. Speak then, you who have heard me, and tell your neighbors whether any of you have ever known me hold forth in few words or in many upon such matters. . . . You hear their answer. And from what they say of this part of the charge you will be able to judge of the truth of the rest.

As little foundation is there for the report that I am a teacher, and take money; this accusation has no more truth in it than the other. Although, if a man were really able to instruct mankind, to receive money for giving instruction would, in my opinion, be an honor to him. . . .

I dare say, Athenians, that someone among you will reply, "Yes, Socrates, but what is the origin of these accusations which are brought against you; there must have been something strange which you have been doing? All these rumors and this talk about you would never have arisen if you had been like other men: tell us, then, what is the cause of them, for we should be sorry to judge hastily of you." Now, I regard this as a fair challenge, and I will endeavor to explain to you the reason why I am called wise and have such an evil fame. Please to attend then. And although some of you may think that I am joking, I declare that I will tell you the entire truth. Men of Athens, this reputation of mine has come of a certain sort of wisdom which I possess. If you ask me what kind of wisdom, I reply, wisdom such as may perhaps be attained by man, for to that extent I am inclined to believe that I am wise; whereas the persons of whom I was speaking have a superhuman wisdom, which I may fail to describe, because I have it not myself; and he who says that I have, speaks falsely, and is taking away my character. And here, O men of Athens, I must beg you not to interrupt me, even if I seem to say something

extravagant. For the word which I will speak is not mine. I will refer you to a witness who is worthy of credit; that witness shall be the God of Delphi[5]—he will tell you about my wisdom, if I have any, and of what sort it is. You must have known Chaerephon;[6] he was early a friend of mine, and also a friend of yours, for he shared in the recent exile of the people,[7] and returned with you. Well, Chaerephon, as you know, was very impetuous in all his doings, and he went to Delphi and boldly asked the oracle to tell him whether—as I was saying, I must beg you not to interrupt—he asked the oracle to tell him whether anyone was wiser than I was, and the Pythian prophetess[8] answered, that there was no man wiser. Chaerephon is dead himself; but his brother, who is in court, will confirm the truth of what I am saying.

Why do I mention this? Because I am going to explain to you why I have such an evil name. When I heard the answer, I said to myself, What can the God mean? and what is the interpretation of his riddle? for I know that I have no wisdom, small or great. What then can he mean when he says that I am the wisest of men? And yet he is a god, and cannot lie; that would be against his nature. After long consideration, I thought of a method of trying the question. I reflected that if I could only find a man wiser than myself, then I might go to the god with a refutation in my hand. I should say to him, "Here is a man who is wiser than I am; but you said that I was the wisest." Accordingly I went to one who had the reputation of wisdom, and observed him —his name I need not mention; he was a

5. GOD OF DELPHI: Apollo, whose temple was at Delphi. Mortals wanting answers about the future consulted the priestess of Apollo, whose responses were usually ambiguous or obscure.
6. CHAEREPHON: a close friend of Socrates.
7. RECENT . . . PEOPLE: In 404 B.C. those who strongly favored democratic rule in Athens were forced into exile by the anti-democratic Thirty Tyrants, who were in control.
8. PYTHIAN PROPHETESS: the priestess of Apollo.

politician whom I selected for examination —and the result was as follows: When I began to talk with him, I could not help thinking that he was not really wise, although he was thought wise by many, and still wiser by himself; and thereupon I tried to explain to him that he thought himself wise, but was not really wise; and the consequence was that he hated me, and his enmity was shared by several who were present and heard me. So I left him, saying to myself, as I went away: Well, although I do not suppose that either of us knows anything really beautiful and good, I am better off than he is,—for he knows nothing, and thinks that he knows; I neither know nor think that I know. . . .

Then I went to one man after another, being not unconscious of the enmity which I provoked, and I lamented and feared this: but necessity was laid upon me,—the word of God, I thought, ought to be considered first. And I said to myself, Go I must to all who appear to know, and find out the meaning of the oracle. And I swear to you, Athenians, by the dog I swear![9]—for I must tell you the truth—the result of my mission was just this: I found that the men most in repute were all but the most foolish; and that others less esteemed were really wiser and better. I will tell you the tale of my wanderings and of the "Herculean" labors,[10] as I may call them, which I endured only to find at last the oracle irrefutable. After the politicians, I went to the poets; tragic, dithyrambic,[11] and all sorts. And there, I said to myself, you will be instantly detected; now you will find out that you are more ignorant than they are. Accordingly I took them some of the most elaborate passages in their own writings, asked what was the meaning of them—thinking that they

would teach me something. Will you believe me? I am almost ashamed to confess the truth, but I must say that there is hardly a person present who would not have talked better about their poetry than they did themselves. Then I knew that not by wisdom do poets write poetry, but by a sort of genius and inspiration; they are like diviners or soothsayers who also say many fine things, but do not understand the meaning of them. The poets appeared to me to be much in the same case; and I further observed that upon the strength of their poetry they believed themselves to be the wisest of men in other things in which they were not wise. So I departed, conceiving myself to be superior to them for the same reason that I was superior to the politicians.

At last I went to the artisans. I was conscious that I knew nothing at all, as I may say, and I was sure that they knew many fine things; and here I was not mistaken, for they did know many things of which I was ignorant, and in this they certainly were wiser than I was. But I observed that even the good artisans fell into the same error as the poets;—because they were good workmen they thought that they also knew all sorts of high matters, and this defect in them overshadowed their wisdom; and therefore I asked myself on behalf of the oracle, whether I would like to be as I was, neither having their knowledge nor their ignorance, or like them in both; and I made answer to myself and to the oracle that I was better off as I was.

This inquisition has led to my having many enemies of the worst and most dangerous kind, and has given occasion also to many calumnies. And I am called wise, for my hearers always imagine that I myself possess the wisdom which I find wanting in others: but the truth is, O men of Athens, that God only is wise; and by his answer he intends to show that the wisdom of men is worth little or nothing; he is not speaking of Socrates, he is only using my name by way of illustration, as if he said, He, O men,

---

9. BY . . . SWEAR: a mild oath.
10. "HERCULEAN" LABORS: to gain immortality Hercules had to perform twelve difficult and dangerous tasks.
11. DITHYRAMBIC: a dithyramb was a short poem in honor of Dionysus, the god of wine.

is the wisest, who, like Socrates, knows that his wisdom is in truth worth nothing. And so I go about the world obedient to the god, and search and make enquiry into the wisdom of anyone, whether citizen or stranger, who appears to be wise; and if he is not wise, then in vindication of the oracle I show him that he is not wise; and my occupation quite absorbs me, and I have no time to give either to any public matter of interest or to any concern of my own, but I am in utter poverty by reason of my devotion to the god.

There is another thing:—young men of the richer classes, who have not much to do, come about me of their own accord; they like to hear the pretenders examined, and they often imitate me, and proceed to examine others; there are plenty of persons, as they quickly discover, who think that they know something, but really know little or nothing; and then those who are examined by them instead of being angry with themselves are angry with me: This confounded Socrates, they say; this villainous misleader of youth!—and then if somebody asks them, Why, what evil does he practice or teach? they do not know, and cannot tell; but in order that they may not appear to be at a loss, they repeat the ready-made charges which are used against all philosophers about teaching things up in the clouds and under the earth, and having no gods, and making the worse appear the better cause; for they do not like to confess that their pretense of knowledge has been detected—which is the truth; and as they are numerous and ambitious and energetic, and are drawn up in battle array and have persuasive tongues, they have filled your ears with their loud and inveterate calumnies. And this is the reason why my three accusers, Meletus and Anytus and Lycon,[12] have set upon me; Meletus, who has a quarrel with me on behalf of the poets; Anytus, on behalf of the craftsmen and politicians; Lycon, on behalf of the rhetoricians: and, as I said at the beginning, I cannot expect to get rid of such a mass of calumny all in a moment. And this, O men of Athens, is the truth and the whole truth; I have concealed nothing, I have dissembled nothing. And yet, I know that my plainness of speech makes them hate me, and what is their hatred but a proof that I am speaking the truth? Hence has arisen the prejudice against me; and this is the reason of it, as you will find out either in this or in any future inquiry.

. . . I know only too well how many are the enmities which I have incurred, and this is what will be my destruction if I am destroyed;—not Meletus, nor yet Anytus, but the envy and detraction of the world, which has been the death of many good men, and will probably be the death of many more; there is no danger of my being the last of them.

Some one will say: And are you not ashamed, Socrates, of a course of life which is likely to bring you to an untimely end? To him I may fairly answer: There you are mistaken: a man who is good for anything ought not to calculate the chance of living or dying; he ought only to consider whether in doing anything he is doing right or wrong—acting the part of a good man or of a bad. Whereas, upon your view, the heroes who fell at Troy were not good for much, and the son of Thetis[13] above all, who altogether despised danger in comparison with disgrace; and when he was so eager to slay Hector, his goddess mother said to him, that if he avenged his companion Patroclus, and slew Hector, he would die himself—"Fate," she said, in these or the like words, "waits for you next after Hector"; he, receiving this warning, utterly despised danger and death, and instead of fearing them, feared rather to live in dishonor, and not to avenge his friend. "Let me die forthwith," he replies, "and be avenged of my enemy, rather than abide here by the beaked ships,

---

12. MELETUS . . . LYCON: Meletus was a poet, Anytus a prominent politician and tanner, and Lycon an orator.

13. SON OF THETIS: Achilles.

a laughing-stock and a burden of the earth." Had Achilles any thought of death and danger? For wherever a man's place is, whether the place which he has chosen or that in which he has been placed by a commander, there he ought to remain in the hour of danger; he should not think of death or of anything but of disgrace. And this, O men of Athens, is a true saying.

Strange, indeed, would be my conduct, O men of Athens, if I, who, when I was ordered by the generals whom you chose to command me at Potidaea and Amphipolis and Delium,[14] remained where they placed me, like any other man, facing death—if now, when, as I conceive and imagine, God orders me to fulfill the philosopher's mission of searching into myself and other men, I were to desert my post through fear of death, or any other fear; that would indeed be strange, and I might justly be arraigned in court for denying the existence of the gods, if I disobeyed the oracle because I was afraid of death, fancying that I was wise when I was not wise. For the fear of death is indeed the pretense of wisdom, and not real wisdom, being a pretense of knowing the unknown; and no one knows whether death, which men in their fear apprehend to be the greatest evil, may not be the greatest good. Is not this ignorance of a disgraceful sort, the ignorance which is the conceit that a man knows what he does not know? And in this respect only I believe myself to differ from men in general, and may perhaps claim to be wiser than they are:—that whereas I know but little of the world below, I do not suppose that I know: but I do know that injustice and disobedience to a better, whether God or man, is evil and dishonorable, and I will never fear or avoid a possible good rather than a certain evil. And therefore if you let me go now, and are not convinced by Anytus, who said that since I had been prosecuted I must be put to death;

(or if not that I ought never to have been prosecuted at all); and that if I escape now, your sons will all be utterly ruined by listening to my words—if you say to me, Socrates, this time we will not mind Anytus, and you shall be let off, but upon one condition, that you are not to inquire and speculate in this way any more, and that if you are caught doing so again you shall die;—if this was the condition on which you let me go, I should reply: Men of Athens, I honor and love you; but I shall obey God rather than you, and while I have life and strength I shall never cease from the practice and teaching of philosophy, exhorting anyone whom I meet and saying to him after my manner: You, my friend,—a citizen of the great and mighty and wise city of Athens, are you not ashamed of heaping up the greatest amount of money and honor and reputation, and caring so little about wisdom and truth and the greatest improvement of the soul, which you never regard or heed at all? . . . For know that this is the command of God; and I believe that no greater good has ever happened in the State than my service to the god. For I do nothing but go about persuading you all, old and young alike, not to take thought for your persons or your properties, but first and chiefly to care about the greatest improvement of the soul. I tell you that virtue is not given by money, but that from virtue comes money and every other good of man, public as well as private. This is my teaching, and if this is the doctrine which corrupts the youth, I am a mischievous person. But if anyone says that this is not my teaching, he is speaking an untruth. Wherefore, O men of Athens, I say to you, do as Anytus bids or not as Anytus bids, and either acquit me or not; but whichever you do, understand that I shall never alter my ways, not even if I have to die many times.

* * * * *

And now, Athenians, I am not going to argue for my own sake, as you may think,

14. POTIDAEA . . . DELIUM: battles during the Peloponnesian War in which Socrates had fought.

but for yours, that you may not sin against the God by condemning me, who am his gift to you. For if you kill me you will not easily find a successor to me, who, if I may use such a ludicrous figure of speech, am a sort of gadfly, given to the State by God; and the State is a great and noble steed who is tardy in his motions owing to his very size, and requires to be stirred into life. I am that gadfly which God has attached to the State, and all day long and in all places am always fastening upon you, arousing and persuading and reproaching you. You will not easily find another like me, and therefore I would advise you to spare me. . . . When I say that I am given to you by God, the proof of my mission is this:—if I had been like other men, I should not have neglected all my own concerns or patiently seen the neglect of them during all these years, and have been doing yours, coming to you individually like a father or elder brother, exhorting you to regard virtue. . . .

Some one may wonder why I go about in private giving advice and busying myself with the concerns of others, but do not venture to come forward in public and advise the State. I will tell you why. You have heard me speak at sundry times and in divers places of an oracle or sign which comes to me, and is the divinity which Meletus ridicules in the indictment. This sign, which is a kind of voice, first began to come to me when I was a child; it always forbids but never commands me to do anything which I am going to do. This is what deters me from being a politician. And rightly, as I think. For I am certain, O men of Athens, that if I had engaged in politics, I should have perished long ago, and done no good either to you or to myself. And do not be offended at my telling you the truth: for the truth is, that no man who goes to war with you or any other multitude, honestly striving against the many lawless and unrighteous deeds which are done in a state, will save his life; he who will fight for the right, if he would live even for a brief space, must have a private station and not a public one.

* * * * *

Now, do you really imagine that I could have survived all these years, if I had led a public life, supposing that like a good man I had always maintained the right and had made justice, as I ought, the first thing? No, indeed, men of Athens, neither I nor any other man. But I have been always the same in all my actions, public as well as private, and never have I yielded any base compliance to those who are slanderously termed my disciples, or to any other. . . . And if any one says that he has ever learned or heard anything from me in private which all the world has not heard, let me tell you that he is lying.

* * * * *

Well, Athenians, this and the like of this is all the defense which I have to offer. Yet a word more. Perhaps there may be someone who is offended at me, when he calls to mind how he himself on a similar, or even a less serious occasion, prayed and entreated the judges with many tears, and how he produced his children in court, which was a moving spectacle, together with a host of relations and friends; whereas I, who am probably in danger of my life, will do none of these things. The contrast may occur to his mind, and he may be set against me, and vote in anger because he is displeased at me on this account. Now, if there be such a person among you,—mind, I do not say that there is,—to him I may fairly reply: My friend, I am a man, and like other men, a creature of flesh and blood, and not "of wood or stone," as Homer says; and I have a family, yes, and sons, O Athenians, three in number, one almost a man, and two others who are still young; and yet I will not bring any of them hither in order to petition you for an acquittal. And why not? Not from any self-assertion or want of respect for you. Whether I am or am not afraid of death is another question, of which

I will not now speak. But, having regard to public opinion, I feel that such conduct would be discreditable to myself, and to you, and to the whole State. One who has reached my years, and who has a name for wisdom, ought not to demean himself. Whether this opinion of me be deserved or not, at any rate the world has decided that Socrates is in some way superior to other men. . . . And I say that these things ought not to be done by those of us who have a reputation; and if they are done, you ought not to permit them; you ought rather to show that you are far more disposed to condemn the man who gets up a doleful scene and makes the city ridiculous, than him who holds his peace.

But, setting aside the question of public opinion, there seems to be something wrong in asking a favor of a judge, and thus procuring an acquittal, instead of informing and convincing him. . . . For if, O men of Athens, by force of persuasion and entreaty I could overpower your oaths, then I should be teaching you to believe that there are no gods, and in defending should simply convict myself of the charge of not believing in them. But that is not so—far otherwise. For I do believe that there are gods, and in a sense higher than that in which any of my accusers believe in them. And to you and to God I commit my cause, to be determined by you as is best for you and me.

There are many reasons why I am not grieved, O men of Athens, at the vote of condemnation. I expected it, and am only surprised that the votes are so nearly equal; for I had thought that the majority against me would have been far larger; but now, had thirty votes gone over to the other side, I should have been acquitted. . . .

And so [Meletus] proposes death as the penalty. And what shall I propose on my part, O men of Athens? Clearly that which is my due. And what is my due? What returns shall be made to the man who has never had the wit to be idle during his whole life; but has been careless of what the many care for—wealth, and family interests, and military offices, and speaking in the assembly, and magistracies, and plots. and parties. Reflecting that I was really too honest a man to be a politician and live, I did not go where I could do no good to you or to myself; but where I could do the greatest good privately to every one of you, thither I went, and sought to persuade every man among you that he must look to himself, and seek virtue and wisdom before he looks to his private interests, and look to the State before he looks to the interests of the State; and that this should be the order which he observes in all his actions. What shall be done to such an one? Doubtless some good thing, O men of Athens, if he has his reward; and the good should be of a kind suitable to him. What would be a reward suitable to a poor man who is your benefactor, and who desires leisure that he may instruct you? There can be no reward so fitting as maintenance in the Prytaneum,[15] O men of Athens, a reward which he deserves far more than the citizen who has won the prize at Olympia in the horse or chariot race, whether the chariots were drawn by two horses or by many. For I am in want, and he has enough; and he only gives you the appearance of happiness, and I give you the reality. And if I am to estimate the penalty fairly, I should say that maintenance in the Prytaneum is the just return.

Perhaps you think that I am braving[16] you in what I am saying now, as in what I said before about the tears and prayers. But this is not so. I speak rather because I am convinced that I never intentionally wronged anyone, although I cannot convince you— the time has been too short; if there were a law at Athens, as there is in other cities, that a capital cause should not be decided in one day, then I believe that I should have convinced you. But I cannot in a moment

---

15. PRYTANEUM: the place where the Prytanes, a body representing the city, honored distinguished individuals.

16. BRAVING: mocking.

refute great slanders; and, as I am convinced that I never wronged another, I will assuredly not wrong myself. I will not say to myself that I deserve any evil, or propose any penalty. Why should I? Because I am afraid of the penalty of death which Meletus proposes? When I do not know whether death is a good or an evil, why should I propose a penalty which would certainly be an evil? Shall I say imprisonment? And why should I live in prison, and be the slave of the magistrate of the year—of the Eleven?[17] Or shall the penalty be a fine, and imprisonment until the fine is paid? There is the same objection. I should have to lie in prison, for money I have none, and cannot pay. And if I say exile (and this may possibly be the penalty which you will affix), I must indeed be blinded by the love of life, if I am so irrational as to expect that when you, who are my own citizens, cannot endure my discourses and words, and have found them so grievous and odious that you will have no more of them, others are likely to endure me. . . .

* * * * *

Someone will say: Yes, Socrates, but cannot you hold your tongue, and then you may go into a foreign city, and no one will interfere with you? Now, I have great difficulty in making you understand my answer to this. For if I tell you that to do as you say would be a disobedience to the God, and therefore that I cannot hold my tongue, you will not believe that I am serious; and if I say again that daily to discourse about virtue, and of those other things about which you hear me examining myself and others, is the greatest good of man, and that the unexamined life is not worth living, you are still less likely to believe me. Yet I say what is true, although a thing of which it is hard for me to persuade you. Also, I have never been accustomed to think that I deserve to suffer any harm. Had I money I might have estimated the offense at what I was able to pay, and not have been much the worse. But I have none, and therefore I must ask you to proportion the fine to my means. Well, perhaps I could afford a mina,[18] and therefore I propose that penalty: Plato, Crito, Critobulus, and Apollodorus, my friends here, bid me say thirty minae, and they will be the sureties. Let thirty minae be the penalty; for which sum they will be ample security to you.

* * * * *

Not much time will be gained, O Athenians, in return for the evil name which you will get from the detractors of the city, who will say that you killed Socrates, a wise man; for they will call me wise, even although I am not wise, when they want to reproach you. If you had waited a little while, your desire would have been fulfilled in the course of nature. For I am far advanced in years, as you may perceive, and not far from death. I am speaking now not to all of you, but only to those who have condemned me to death. And I have another thing to say to them: You think that I was convicted because I had no words of the sort which would have procured my acquittal—I mean, if I had thought fit to leave nothing undone or unsaid. Not so; the deficiency which led to my conviction was not of words—certainly not. But I had not the boldness or impudence or inclination to address you as you would have liked me to do, weeping and wailing and lamenting, and saying and doing many things which you have been accustomed to hear from others, and which, as I maintain, are unworthy of me. I thought at the time that I ought not to do anything common or mean when in danger: nor do I now repent of the style of my defense; I would rather die having spoken after my manner, than speak in your manner and live. For neither in war nor yet at law ought I or any man use every way of escaping death. Often in battle there can be no doubt that

---

17. THE ELEVEN: the group of citizens in charge of imprisonments and executions.

18. MINA: a mina was worth a considerable sum of money and was regarded as a reasonable ransom for a war prisoner.

if a man will throw away his arms, and fall on his knees before his pursuers, he may escape death; and in other dangers there are other ways of escaping death, if a man is willing to say and do anything. The difficulty, my friends, is not to avoid death, but to avoid unrighteousness; for that runs faster than death. I am old and move slowly, and the slower runner has overtaken me, and my accusers are keen and quick, and the faster runner, who is unrighteousness, has overtaken them. And now I depart hence condemned by you to suffer the penalty of death,—they too go their ways condemned by the truth to suffer the penalty of villainy and wrong; and I must abide by my award —let them abide by theirs. I suppose that these things may be regarded as fated,— and I think that they are well.

And now, O men who have condemned me, I would fain prophesy to you. . . . I say that there will be more accusers of you than there are now; accusers whom hitherto I have restrained: and as they are younger they will be more inconsiderate with you, and you will be more offended at them. If you think that by killing men you can prevent someone from censuring your evil lives, you are mistaken; that is not a way of escape which is either possible or honorable; the easiest and the noblest way is not to be disabling others, but to be improving yourselves. This is the prophecy which I utter before my departure to the judges who have condemned me.

Friends, who would have acquitted me, I would like also to talk with you about the thing which has come to pass, while the magistrates are busy, and before I go to the place at which I must die. . . . I should like to tell you of a wonderful circumstance. Hitherto the divine faculty of which the internal oracle is the source has constantly been in the habit of opposing me even about trifles, if I was going to make a slip or error in any matter; and now as you see there

has come upon me that which may be thought, and is generally believed to be, the last and worst evil. But the oracle made no sign of opposition, either when I was leaving my house in the morning, or when I was on my way to the court, or while I was speaking, at anything which I was going to say. . . . What do I take to be the explanation of this silence? I will tell you. It is an intimation that what has happened to me is a good, and that those of us who think that death is an evil are in error. For the customary sign would surely have opposed me had I been going to evil and not to good.

* * * * *

Wherefore, O judges, be of good cheer about death, and know of a certainty, that no evil can happen to a good man, either in life or after death. He and his are not neglected by the gods; nor has my own approaching end happened by mere chance. But I see clearly that the time had arrived when it was better for me to die and be released from trouble; wherefore the oracle gave no sign. For which reason, also, I am not angry with my condemners, or with my accusers; they have done me no harm, although they did not mean to do me any good; and for this I may gently blame them.

Still, I have a favor to ask of them. When my sons are grown up, I would ask you, O my friends, to punish them; and I would have you trouble them, as I have troubled you, if they seem to care about riches, or anything, more than about virtue; or if they pretend to be something when they are really nothing,—then reprove them, as I have reproved you, for not caring about that for which they ought to care, and thinking that they are something when they are really nothing. And if you do this, both I and my sons will have received justice at your hands.

The hour of departure has arrived, and we go our ways—I to die, and you to live. Which is better God only knows.

from THE PHAEDO

A man of sense ought not to say, nor will I be very confident, that the description which I have given of the soul and her mansions is exactly true. But I do say that, inasmuch as the soul is shown to be immortal, he may venture to think, not improperly or unworthily, that something of the kind is true. The venture is a glorious one, and he ought to comfort himself with words like these, which is the reason why I lengthen out the tale. Wherefore, I say, let a man be of good cheer about his soul, who having cast away the pleasures and ornaments of the body as alien to him and working harm rather than good, has sought after the pleasures of knowledge; and has arrayed the soul, not in some foreign attire, but in her own proper jewels, temperance, and justice, and courage, and nobility, and truth—in these adorned she is ready to go on her journey to the world below, when her hour comes. . . . Soon I must drink the poison;[1] and I think that I had better repair to the bath first, in order that the women may not have the trouble of washing my body after I am dead.

When he had done speaking, Crito[2] said: And have you any commands for us, Socrates—anything to say about your children, or any other matter in which we can serve you?

Nothing particular, Crito, he replied: only, as I have always told you, take care of yourselves; that is a service which you may be ever rendering to me and mine and to all of us, whether you promise to do so or not. But if you have no thought for yourselves, and care not to walk according to the rule which I have prescribed for you, not now for the first time, however much you

may profess or promise at the moment, it will be of no avail.

We will do our best, said Crito: And in what way shall we bury you?

In any way that you like; but you must get hold of me, and take care that I do not run away from you. Then he turned to us, and added with a smile:—I cannot make Crito believe that I am the same Socrates who has been talking and conducting the argument; he fancies that I am the other Socrates whom he will soon see, a dead body—and he asks, How shall he bury me? And though I have spoken many words in the endeavor to show that when I have drunk the poison I shall leave you and go to the joys of the blessed,—these words of mine, with which I was comforting you and myself, have had, as I perceive, no effect upon Crito. And therefore I want you to be surety for me to him now, as at the trial he was surety to the judges for me: but let the promise be of another sort; for he was surety for me to the judges that I would remain, and you must be my surety to him that I shall not remain, but go away and depart; and then he will suffer less at my death, and not be grieved when he sees my body being burned or buried. I would not have him sorrow at my hard lot, or say at the burial, Thus we lay out Socrates, or, Thus we follow him to the grave or bury him; for false words are not only evil in themselves, but they inflict the soul with evil. Be of good cheer then, my dear Crito, and say that you are burying my body only, and do with that whatever is usual, and what you think best.

When he had spoken these words, he arose and went into a chamber to bathe; Crito followed him and told us to wait. So we remained behind, talking and thinking of the subject of discourse, and also of the greatness of our sorrow; he was like a father of whom we were being bereaved, and we were about to pass the rest of our

---

1. POISON: hemlock, usually used for executions at the time.
2. CRITO: one of Socrates's friends who offered to pay his proposed fine at his trial; one of Plato's dialogues is named after him.

lives as orphans. When he had taken the bath his children were brought to him (he had two young sons and an elder one); and the women of his family also came, and he talked to them and gave them a few directions in the presence of Crito; then he dismissed them and returned to us.

Now the hour of sunset was near, for a good deal of time had passed while he was within. When he came out, he sat down with us again after his bath, but not much was said. Soon the jailer, who was the servant of the Eleven, entered and stood by him, saying:—To you, Socrates, whom I know to be the noblest and gentlest and best of all who ever came to this place, I will not impute the angry feeling of other men, who rage and swear at me, when, in obedience to the authorities, I bid them drink the poison—indeed, I am sure that you will not be angry with me; for others, as you are aware, and not I, are to blame. And so fare you well, and try to bear lightly what must needs be—you know my errand. Then bursting into tears he turned away and went out.

Socrates looked at him and said: I return your good wishes, and will do as you bid. Then turning to us, he said, How charming the man is: since I have been in prison he has always been coming to see me, and at times he would talk to me, and was as good to me as could be, and now see how generously he sorrows on my account. We must do as he says, Crito; and therefore let the cup be brought, if the poison is prepared: if not, let the attendant prepare some.

Yet, said Crito, the sun is still upon the hill-tops, and I know that many a one has taken the draught late, and after the announcement has been made to him, he has eaten and drunk, and enjoyed the society of his beloved: do not hurry—there is time enough.

Socrates said: Yes, Crito, and they of whom you speak are right in so acting, for they think that they will be gainers by the delay; but I am right in not following their example, for I do not think that I should

gain anything by drinking the poison a little later; I should only be ridiculous in my own eyes for sparing and saving a life which is already forfeit. Please then to do as I say, and not to refuse me.

Crito made a sign to the servant, who was standing by; and he went out, and having been absent for some time, returned with the jailer carrying the cup of poison. Socrates said: You, my good friend, who are experienced in these matters, shall give me directions how I am to proceed. The man answered: You have only to walk about until your legs are heavy, and then to lie down, and the poison will act. At the same time he handed the cup to Socrates, who in the easiest and gentlest manner, without the least fear or change of color or feature, looking at the man with all his eyes . . . as his manner was, took the cup and said: What do you say about making a libation out of this cup to any god? May I, or not? The man answered: We only prepare, Socrates, just so much as we deem enough. I understand, he said: but I may and must ask the gods to prosper my journey from this to the other world—even so—and so be it according to my prayer. Then raising the cup to his lips, quite readily and cheerfully he drank off the poison. And hitherto most of us had been able to control our sorrow; but now when we saw him drinking, and saw too that he had finished the draught, we could no longer forbear, and in spite of myself my own tears were flowing fast; so that I covered my face and wept, not for him, but at the thought of my own calamity in having to part from such a friend. Nor was I the first; for Crito, when he found himself unable to restrain his tears, had got up, and I followed; and at that moment, Apollodorus, who had been weeping all the time, broke out in a loud and passionate cry which made cowards of us all. Socrates alone retained his calmness: What is this strange outcry? he said. I sent away the women mainly in order that they might not misbehave in this way, for I have been told that a man should die in peace. Be quiet then, and have patience. When we heard his words we were ashamed, and refrained our tears; and he walked about until, as he said, his legs began to fail, and then he lay on his back, according to directions, and the man who gave him the poison now and then looked at his feet and legs; and after a while he pressed his foot hard, and asked him if he could feel; and he said, No; and then his leg, and so upwards and upwards, and showed us that he was cold and stiff. And he felt them himself, and said: When the poison reaches the heart, that will be the end. He was beginning to grow cold about the groin, when he uncovered his face, for he had covered himself up, and said—they were his last words—he said: Crito, I owe a cock to Asclepius;[3] will you remember to pay the debt? The debt shall be paid, said Crito; is there anything else? There was no answer to this question; but in a minute or two a movement was heard, and the attendants uncovered him; his eyes were set, and Crito closed his eyes and mouth.

Such was the end . . . of our friend; concerning whom I may truly say, that of all men of his time whom I have known, he was the wisest and justest and best.

3. A COCK TO ASCLEPIUS: Asclepius was the god of healing; the sacrifice of the cock would probably be in thanks for a painless death.

I

1. What are the charges brought against Socrates? How specific do they seem to be, judging by what we have here? What is probably the real reason for the accusations? How seriously does he take the charges? How much consideration should be given to the fact that we get only Socrates's view of the case here?

2. What is the *wisdom* Socrates says he has? What makes the politicians, poets, and artisans less wise than Socrates? How does his statement, "for my hearers always imagine that I myself possess the wisdom which I find wanting in others," show clearly in what sense he interprets the oracle's answer "that there was no man wiser" than Socrates?

3. Why is he not "ashamed . . . of a course of life which is likely to bring [him] to an untimely end"? What does he think is the greatest evil which can befall a man?

4. What is Socrates's attitude toward death?

5. In what sense is he arguing for the Athenians' sake and not his own?

6. Try to characterize Socrates as he appears in the *Apology*. Is he arrogant? conceited? judicious? blunt? reasonable? unreasonable? none of these, or a combination? Do we get different insights in the *Phaedo*? Explain.

7. His accusers wanted only to silence him, not kill him. How and why does he force the court to vote the death penalty? How "right" were they in their decision?

II

1. In what sense was he a corrupter of youth? What is meant by "corrupt" here? How responsible is a teacher for what he teaches, particularly if his students misinterpret what he says or put his ideas into practice in ways he would consider distortions of his beliefs? (Two of Socrates's pupils had acted in just such a manner, with evil consequences to Athens.)

2. Use any of the following statements as a basis for an essay.

a. ". . . a man who is good for anything ought not to calculate the chance of living or dying; he ought only to consider whether in doing anything he is doing right or wrong."

b. ". . . he who will fight for the right, if he would live even for a brief space, must have a private station and not a public one."

c. ". . . the unexamined life is not worth living."

d. "I am better off than he is—for he knows nothing, and thinks that he knows; I neither know nor think that I know."

e. ". . . be of good cheer about death, and know of a certainty, that no evil can happen to a good man, either in life or after death."

ARMS AND THE MAN   [*1898*]

George Bernard Shaw

Satire is man's master weapon against the folly and inhumanity of his own species. We have seen with what skill Pope in "Atticus," Dryden in "Zimri," Addison in "A Lady's Diary," Chaucer in "The Pardoner's Tale," and Swift in *Gulliver's Travels* and "A Modest Proposal" delivered (in Dryden's words) "the fineness of a stroke that separates the head from the body, and leaves it standing in its place."

No modern writer has managed the satiric weapon with more "fineness" in this respect than George Bernard Shaw. From the closing years of the nineteenth century until the middle of the present one he never let Englishmen—or men in general—forget that their foibles were showing. His plays brought new life to the British theater for four decades and renewed common sense to anyone willing to see the truth in his wit.

One of his earliest comedies was *Arms and the Man.* He took the title from the opening words of Virgil's *Aeneid,* but instead of extolling the glories of heroic combat, he shows what an absurdity war really is. In the course of doing so, he effectively deflates our ideas of romantic love, prestige, position, and success.

CHARACTERS

in the order of their appearance

RAINA PETKOFF, *a young Bulgarian lady*

CATHERINE PETKOFF, *her mother*

LOUKA, *Raina's maid*

CAPTAIN BLUNTSCHLI, *a Swiss in the Servian army*

A RUSSIAN OFFICER *in the Bulgarian army*

NICOLA, *the Petkoffs' manservant*

MAJOR PETKOFF, *Raina's father*

MAJOR SERGIUS SARANOFF, *Raina's fiancé*

The action takes place at the home of Major Petkoff, in a small town in Bulgaria, in the years 1885 and 1886.

ACT ONE

Night. A lady's bedchamber in Bulgaria, in a small town near the Dragoman Pass. It is late in November in the year 1885, and through an open window with a little bal-

Arms and the Man. Used by permission of the Society of Authors, The Public Trustee and Dodd, Mead & Company.

cony on the left can be seen a peak of the Balkans, wonderfully white and beautiful in the starlit snow. The interior of the room is not like anything to be seen in the east of Europe. It is half rich Bulgarian, half cheap Viennese. The counterpane and hangings of the bed, the window curtains, the little carpet, and all the ornamental textile fabrics in the room are oriental and gorgeous: the paper on the walls is occidental and paltry. Above the head of the bed, which stands against a little wall cutting off the right hand corner of the room diagonally, is a painted wooden shrine, blue and gold, with an ivory image of Christ, and a light hanging before it in a pierced metal ball suspended by three chains. On the left, further forward, is an ottoman. The washstand, against the wall on the left, consists of an enameled iron basin with a pail beneath it in a painted metal frame, and a single towel on the rail at the side. A chair near it is Austrian bent wood, with cane seat. The dressing table, between the bed and the window, is an ordinary pine table, covered with a cloth of many colors, but with an expensive toilet mirror on it. The door is on the right; and there is a chest of drawers between the door and the bed. This chest of drawers is also covered by a variegated native cloth, and on it there is a pile of paper-backed novels, a box of chocolate creams, and a miniature easel, on which is a large photograph of an extremely handsome officer, whose lofty bearing and magnetic glance can be felt even from the portrait. The room is lighted by a candle on the chest of drawers, and another on the dressing table, with a box of matches beside it.

The window is hinged doorwise and stands wide open, folding back to the left. Outside, a pair of wooden shutters, opening outwards, also stand open. On the balcony, a young lady, intensely conscious of the romantic beauty of the night, and of the fact that her own youth and beauty is a part of it, is gazing at the snowy Balkans. She is covered by a long mantle of furs, worth, on a moderate estimate, about three times the furniture of her room.

Her reverie is interrupted by her mother, Catherine Petkoff, a woman over forty, imperiously energetic, with magnificent black hair and eyes, who might be a very splendid specimen of the wife of a mountain farmer, but is determined to be a Viennese lady, and to that end wears a fashionable tea gown on all occasions.

CATHERINE (*entering hastily, full of good news*). Raina—(*She pronounces it Raheena, with the stress on the ee.*) Raina—(*She goes to the bed, expecting to find Raina there.*) Why, where—(*Raina looks into the room.*) Heavens! child, are you out in the night air instead of in your bed? You'll catch your death. Louka told me you were asleep.

RAINA (*coming in*). I sent her away. I wanted to be alone. The stars are so beautiful! What is the matter?

CATHERINE. Such news. There has been a battle!

RAINA (*her eyes dilating*). Ah! (*She throws the cloak on the ottoman, and comes eagerly to Catherine in her nightgown, a pretty garment, but evidently the only one she has on.*)

CATHERINE. A great battle at Slivnitza! A victory! And it was won by Sergius.

RAINA (*with a cry of delight*). Ah! (*rapturously*) Oh, mother! (*then, with sudden anxiety*) Is father safe?

CATHERINE. Of course: he sent me the news. Sergius is the hero of the hour, the idol of the regiment.

RAINA. Tell me, tell me. How was it! (*ecstatically*) Oh, mother, mother, mother! (*Raina pulls her mother down on the ottoman; and they kiss one another frantically.*)

CATHERINE (*with surging enthusiasm*). You can't guess how splendid it is. A cavalry charge—think of that! He defied our Russian commanders—acted without orders—led a charge on his own responsibility—headed it himself—was the first man to sweep through their guns. Can't you see it, Raina; our gallant splendid Bulgarians with their swords and eyes flashing, thundering down like an avalanche and scattering the wretched Servian dandies like chaff. And you—you kept Sergius waiting a year before you would be betrothed to him. Oh, if you have a drop of Bulgarian blood in your veins, you will worship him when he comes back.

RAINA. What will he care for my poor little worship after the acclamations of a whole army of heroes? But no matter: I am so happy—so proud! (*She rises and walks about excitedly.*) It proves that all our ideas were real after all.

CATHERINE (*indignantly*). Our ideas real! What do you mean?

RAINA. Our ideas of what Sergius would do—our patriotism—our heroic ideals. Oh, what faithless little creatures girls are!—I sometimes used to doubt whether they were anything but dreams. When I buckled on Sergius's sword he looked so noble: it was treason to think of disillusion or humiliation or failure. And yet—and yet—. (*quickly*) Promise me you'll never tell him.

CATHERINE. Don't ask me for promises until I know what I am promising.

RAINA. Well, it came into my head just as he was holding me in his arms and looking into my eyes, that perhaps we only had our heroic ideas because we are so fond of reading Byron[1] and Pushkin,[2] and because we were so delighted with the opera that season at Bucharest. Real life is so seldom like that—indeed never, as far as I knew it then. (*remorsefully*) Only think, mother, I doubted him: I wondered whether all his heroic qualities and his soldiership might not prove mere imagination when he went into a real battle. I had an uneasy fear that he might cut a poor figure there beside all those clever Russian officers.

CATHERINE. A poor figure! Shame on you! The Servians have Austrian officers who are just as clever as our Russians; but we have beaten them in every battle for all that.

RAINA (*laughing and sitting down again*). Yes, I was only a prosaic little coward. Oh, to think that it was all true—that Sergius is just as splendid and noble as he looks—that the world is really a glorious world for women who can see its glory and men who can act its romance! What happiness! what unspeakable fulfillment! Ah! (*She throws herself on her knees beside her mother and flings her arms passionately round her. They are interrupted by the entry of Louka, a handsome, proud girl in a pretty Bulgarian peasant dress with double apron, so defiant that her servility to Raina is almost insolent. She is afraid of Catherine, but even with her goes as far as she dares. She is just now excited like the others; but she has no sympathy for Raina's raptures and looks contemptuously at the ecstasies of the two before she addresses them.*)

LOUKA. If you please, madam, all the windows are to be closed and the shutters made fast. They say there may be shooting in the streets. (*Raina and Catherine rise together, alarmed.*) The Servians are being chased right back through the pass; and they

say they may run into the town. Our cavalry will be after them; and our people will be ready for them you may be sure, now that they are running away. (*She goes out on the balcony and pulls the outside shutters to; then steps back into the room.*)

RAINA. I wish our people were not so cruel. What glory is there in killing wretched fugitives?

CATHERINE (*business-like, her housekeeping instincts aroused*). I must see that everything is made safe downstairs.

RAINA (*to Louka*). Leave the shutters so that I can just close them if I hear any noise.

CATHERINE (*authoritatively, turning on her way to the door*). Oh, no, dear, you must keep them fastened. You would be sure to drop off to sleep and leave them open. Make them fast, Louka.

LOUKA. Yes, madam. (*She fastens them.*)

RAINA. Don't be anxious about me. The moment I hear a shot, I shall blow out the candles and roll myself up in bed with my ears well covered.

CATHERINE. Quite the wisest thing you can do, my love. Good-night.

RAINA. Good-night. (*They kiss one another, and Raina's emotion comes back for a moment.*) Wish me joy of the happiest night of my life—if only there are no fugitives.

CATHERINE. Go to bed, dear, and don't think of them. (*She goes out.*)

LOUKA (*secretly, to Raina*). If you would like the shutters open, just give them a push like this. (*She pushes them: they open: she pulls them to again.*) One of them ought to be bolted at the bottom; but the bolt's gone.

RAINA (*with dignity, reproving her*). Thanks, Louka; but we must do what we are told. (*Louka makes a grimace.*) Goodnight.

LOUKA (*carelessly*). Good-night. (*She goes out, swaggering.*)

(*Raina, left alone, goes to the chest of drawers, and adores the portrait there with feelings that are beyond all expression. She*

---

1. BYRON: Byron was the best known of the English romantic poets outside of England; the "Byronic hero," melancholy, noble, supremely brave, was a popular image throughout the nineteenth century.

2. PUSHKIN: Alexander Pushkin (1799-1837), Russian poet, greatly influenced by Byron.

does not kiss it or press it to her breast, or show it any mark of bodily affection; but she takes it in her hands and elevates it like a priestess.)

RAINA (*looking up at the picture with worship*). Oh, I shall never be unworthy of you any more, my hero—never, never, never. (*She replaces it reverently, and selects a novel from the little pile of books. She turns over the leaves dreamily; finds her page; turns the book inside out at it; and then, with a happy sigh, gets into bed and prepares to read herself to sleep. But before abandoning herself to fiction, she raises her eyes once more, thinking of the blessed reality and murmurs*) My hero! my hero! (*A distant shot breaks the quiet of the night outside. She starts, listening; and two more shots, much nearer, follow, startling her so that she scrambles out of bed, and hastily blows out the candle on the chest of drawers. Then, putting her fingers in her ears, she runs to the dressing table and blows out the light there, and hurries back to bed. The room is now in darkness: nothing is visible but the glimmer of the light in the pierced ball before the image, and the starlight seen through the slits at the top of the shutters. The firing breaks out again: there is a startling fusillade quite close at hand. Whilst it is still echoing, the shutters disappear, pulled open from without, and for an instant the rectangle of snowy starlight flashes out with the figure of a man in black upon it. The shutters close immediately and the room is dark again. But the silence is now broken by the sound of panting. Then there is a scrape; and the flame of a match is seen in the middle of the room.*)

RAINA (*crouching on the bed*). Who's there? (*The match is out instantly.*) Who's there? Who is that?

A MAN'S VOICE (*in the darkness, subduedly, but threateningly*). Sh—sh! Don't call out or you'll be shot. Be good; and no harm will happen to you. (*She is heard leaving her bed, and making for the door.*) Take care, there's no use in trying to run

away. Remember, if you raise your voice my pistol will go off. (*commandingly*) Strike a light and let me see you. Do you hear? (*Another moment of silence and darkness. Then she is heard retreating to the dressing-table. She lights a candle, and the mystery is at an end. A man of about 35, in a deplorable plight, bespattered with mud and blood and snow, his belt and the strap of his revolver case keeping together the torn ruins of the blue coat of a Servian artillery officer. As far as the candlelight and his unwashed, unkempt condition make it possible to judge, he is a man of middling stature and undistinguished appearance, with strong neck and shoulders, a roundish, obstinate looking head covered with short crisp bronze curls, clear quick blue eyes and good brows and mouth, a hopelessly prosaic nose like that of a strong-minded baby, trim soldierlike carriage and energetic manner, and with all his wits about him in spite of his desperate predicament—even with a sense of humor of it, without, however, the least intention of trifling with it or throwing away a chance. He reckons up what he can guess about Raina—her age, her social position, her character, the extent to which she is frightened—at a glance, and continues, more politely but still most determinedly*) Excuse my disturbing you; but you recognize my uniform—Servian. If I'm caught I shall be killed. (*determinedly*) Do you understand that?

RAINA. Yes.

MAN. Well, I don't intend to get killed if I can help it. (*still more determinedly*) Do you understand that? (*He locks the door with a snap.*)

RAINA (*disdainfully*). I suppose not. (*She draws herself up superbly, and looks him straight in the face, saying with emphasis*) Some soldiers, I know, are afraid of death.

MAN (*with grim good humor*). All of them, dear lady, all of them, believe me. It is our duty to live as long as we can, and kill as many of the enemy as we can. Now if you raise an alarm—

RAINA (*cutting him short*). You will shoot me. How do you know that I am afraid to die?

MAN (*cunningly*). Ah; but suppose I don't shoot you, what will happen then? Why, a lot of your cavalry—the greatest blackguards in your army—will burst into this pretty room of yours and slaughter me here like a pig; for I'll fight like a demon: they shan't get me into the street to amuse themselves with: I know what they are. Are you prepared to receive that sort of company in your present undress? (*Raina, suddenly conscious of her nightgown, instinctively shrinks and gathers it more closely about her. He watches her, and adds, pitilessly*) It's rather scanty, eh? (*She turns to the ottoman. He raises his pistol instantly, and cries*) Stop! (*She stops.*) Where are you going?

RAINA (*with dignified patience*). Only to get my cloak.

MAN (*darting to the ottoman and snatching the cloak*). A good idea. No: I'll keep the cloak: and you will take care that nobody comes in and sees you without it. This is a better weapon than the pistol. (*He throws the pistol down on the ottoman.*)

RAINA (*revolted*). It is not the weapon of a gentleman!

MAN. It's good enough for a man with only you to stand between him and death. (*As they look at one another for a moment, Raina hardly able to believe that even a Servian officer can be so cynically and selfishly unchivalrous, they are startled by a sharp fusillade in the street. The chill of imminent death hushes the man's voice as he adds*) Do you hear? If you are going to bring those scoundrels in on me you shall receive them as you are. (*Raina meets his eye with unflinching scorn. Suddenly he starts, listening. There is a step outside. Someone tries the door, and then knocks hurriedly and urgently at it. Raina looks at the man, breathless. He throws up his head with the gesture of a man who sees that*

it is all over with him, and, dropping the manner which he has been assuming to intimidate her, flings the cloak to her, exclaiming, sincerely and kindly) No use: I'm done for. Quick! wrap yourself up: they're coming!

RAINA (*catching the cloak eagerly*). Oh, thank you. (*She wraps herself up with great relief. He draws his saber and turns to the door, waiting.*)

LOUKA (*outside, knocking*). My lady, my lady! Get up, quick, and open the door.

RAINA (*anxiously*). What will you do?

MAN (*grimly*). Never mind. Keep out of the way. It will not last long.

RAINA (*impulsively*). I'll help you. Hide yourself, oh, hide yourself, quick, behind the curtain. (*She seizes him by a torn strip of his sleeve, and pulls him towards the window.*)

MAN (*yielding to her*). There is just half a chance, if you keep your head. Remember: nine soldiers out of ten are born fools. (*He hides behind the curtain, looking out for a moment to say, finally*) If they find me, I promise you a fight—a devil of a fight! (*He disappears. Raina takes off the cloak and throws it across the foot of the bed. Then with a sleepy, disturbed air, she opens the door. Louka enters excitedly.*)

LOUKA. A man has been seen climbing up the waterpipe to your balcony—a Servian. The soldiers want to search for him; and they are so wild and drunk and furious. My lady says you are to dress at once.

RAINA (*as if annoyed at being disturbed*). They shall not search here. Why have they been let in?

CATHERINE (*coming in hastily*). Raina, darling, are you safe? Have you seen anyone or heard anything?

RAINA. I heard the shooting. Surely the soldiers will not dare come in here?

CATHERINE. I have found a Russian officer, thank Heaven: he knows Sergius. (*speaking through the door to someone outside*) Sir, will you come in now! My daughter is ready.

(A young Russian officer, in Bulgarian uniform, enters, sword in hand.)

THE OFFICER (*with soft, feline politeness and stiff military carriage*). Good evening, gracious lady; I am sorry to intrude, but there is a fugitive hiding on the balcony. Will you and the gracious lady your mother please to withdraw whilst we search?

RAINA (*petulantly*). Nonsense, sir, you can see that there is no one on the balcony. (*She throws the shutters wide open and stands with her back to the curtain where the man is hidden, pointing to the moonlit balcony. A couple of shots are fired right under the window, and a bullet shatters the glass opposite Raina, who winks and gasps, but stands her ground, whilst Catherine screams, and the officer rushes to the balcony.*)

THE OFFICER (*on the balcony, shouting savagely down to the street*). Cease firing there, you fools: do you hear? Cease firing, damn you. (*He glares down for a moment; then turns to Raina, trying to resume his polite manner.*) Could anyone have got in without your knowledge? Were you asleep?

RAINA. No, I have not been to bed.

THE OFFICER (*impatiently, coming back into the room*). Your neighbors have their heads so full of runaway Servians that they see them everywhere. (*politely*) Gracious lady, a thousand pardons. Good-night. (*Military bow, which Raina returns coldly. Another to Catherine, who follows him out. Raina closes the shutters. She turns and sees Louka, who has been watching the scene curiously.*)

RAINA. Don't leave my mother, Louka, whilst the soldiers are here. (*Louka glances at Raina, at the ottoman, at the curtain; then purses her lips secretively, laughs to herself, and goes out. Raina follows her to the door, shuts it behind her with a slam, and locks it violently. The man immediately steps out from behind the curtain, sheathing his saber, and dismissing the danger from his mind in a businesslike way.*)

MAN. A narrow shave; but a miss is as good as a mile. Dear young lady, your servant until death. I wish for your sake I had joined the Bulgarian army instead of the Servian. I am not a native Servian.

RAINA (*haughtily*). No, you are one of the Austrians who set the Servians on to rob us of our national liberty, and who officer their army for them. We hate them!

MAN. Austrian! not I. Don't hate me, dear young lady. I am only a Swiss, fighting merely as a professional soldier. I joined Servia because it was nearest to me. Be generous: you've beaten us hollow.

RAINA. Have I not been generous?

MAN. Noble!—heroic! But I'm not saved yet. This particular rush will soon pass through; but the pursuit will go on all night by fits and starts. I must take my chance to get off during a quiet interval. You don't mind my waiting just a minute or two, do you?

RAINA. Oh, no: I am sorry you will have to go into danger again. (*motioning towards ottoman*) Won't you sit—(*She breaks off with an irrepressible cry of alarm as she catches sight of the pistol. The man, all nerves, shies like a frightened horse.*)

MAN (*irritably*). Don't frighten me like that. What is it?

RAINA. Your pistol! It was staring that officer in the face all the time. What an escape!

MAN (*vexed at being unnecessarily terrified*). Oh, is that all?

RAINA (*staring at him rather superciliously, conceiving a poorer and poorer opinion of him, and feeling proportionately more and more at her ease with him*). I am sorry I frightened you. (*She takes up the pistol and hands it to him.*) Pray take it to protect yourself against me.

MAN (*grinning wearily at the sarcasm as he takes the pistol*). No use, dear young lady: there's nothing in it. It's not loaded. (*He makes a grimace at it, and drops it disparagingly into his revolver case.*)

RAINA. Load it by all means.

MAN. I've no ammunition. What use are

cartridges in battle? I always carry chocolate instead; and I finished the last cake of that yesterday.

RAINA (*outraged in her most cherished ideals of manhood*). Chocolate! Do you stuff your pockets with sweets—like a schoolboy—even in the field?

MAN. Yes. Isn't it contemptible?

(*Raina stares at him, unable to utter her feelings. Then she sails away scornfully to the chest of drawers, and returns with the box of confectionery in her hand.*)

RAINA. Allow me. I am sorry I have eaten them all except these. (*She offers him the box.*)

MAN (*ravenously*). You're an angel! (*He gobbles the comfits.*) Creams! Delicious! (*He looks anxiously to see whether there are any more. There are none. He accepts the inevitable with pathetic good humor, and says, with grateful emotion*) Bless you, dear lady. You can always tell an old soldier by the inside of his holsters and cartridge boxes. The young ones carry pistols and cartridges; the old ones, grub. Thank you. (*He hands back the box. She snatches it contemptuously from him and throws it away. This impatient action is so sudden that he shies again.*) Ugh! Don't do things so suddenly, gracious lady. Don't revenge yourself because I frightened you just now.

RAINA (*superbly*). Frighten me! Do you know, sir, that though I am only a woman, I think I am at heart as brave as you.

MAN. I should think so. You haven't been under fire for three days as I have. I can stand two days without showing it much; but no man can stand three days: I'm as nervous as a mouse. (*He sits down on the ottoman, and takes his head in his hands.*) Would you like to see me cry?

RAINA (*quickly*). No.

MAN. If you would, all you have to do is to scold me just as if I were a little boy and you my nurse. If I were in camp now they'd play all sorts of tricks on me.

RAINA (*a little moved*). I'm sorry. I won't scold you. (*Touched by the sympathy in her tone, he raises his head and looks gratefully at her: she immediately draws back and says stiffly*) You must excuse me: our soldiers are not like that. (*She moves away from the ottoman*).

MAN. Oh, yes, they are. There are only two sorts of soldiers: old ones and young ones. I've served fourteen years: half of your fellows never smelt powder before. Why, how is it that you've just beaten us? Sheer ignorance of the art of war, nothing else. (*indignantly*) I never saw anything so unprofessional.

RAINA (*ironically*). Oh, was it unprofessional to beat you?

MAN. Well, come, is it professional to throw a regiment of cavalry on a battery of machine guns, with the dead certainty that if the guns go off not a horse or man will ever get within fifty yards of the fire? I couldn't believe my eyes when I saw it.

RAINA (*eagerly turning to him, as all her enthusiasm and her dream of glory rush back on her*). Did you see the great cavalry charge? Oh, tell me about it. Describe it to me.

MAN. You never saw a cavalry charge, did you?

RAINA. How could I?

MAN. Ah, perhaps not—of course. Well, it's a funny sight. It's like slinging a handful of peas against a window pane: first one comes; then two or three close behind him; and then all the rest in a lump.

RAINA (*her eyes dilating as she raises her clasped hands ecstatically*). Yes, first One! —the bravest of the brave!

MAN (*prosaically*). Hm! you should see the poor devil pulling at his horse.

RAINA. Why should he pull at his horse?

MAN (*impatient of so stupid a question*). It's running away with him, of course: do you suppose the fellow wants to get there before the others and be killed? Then they all come. You can tell the young ones by their wildness and their slashing. The old ones come bunched up under the number one guard: they know that they are mere projectiles, and that it's no use trying to fight. The wounds are mostly broken knees, from the horses cannoning together.

RAINA. Ugh! But I don't believe the first man is a coward. I believe he is a hero!

MAN (*goodhumoredly*). That's what you'd have said if you'd seen the first man in the charge today.

RAINA (*breathless*). Ah, I knew it! Tell me—tell me about him.

MAN. He did it like an operatic tenor— a regular handsome fellow, with flashing eyes and lovely moustache, shouting a war-cry and charging like Don Quixote at the windmills.[3] We nearly burst with laughter at him; but when the sergeant ran up as white as a sheet, and told us they'd sent us the wrong cartridges, and that we couldn't fire a shot for the next ten minutes, we laughed at the other side of our mouths. I never felt so sick in my life, though I've been in one or two very tight places. And I hadn't even a revolver cartridge—nothing but chocolate. We'd no bayonets—nothing. Of course, they just cut us to bits. And there was Don Quixote flourishing like a drum major, thinking he'd done the cleverest thing ever known, whereas he ought to be court-martialed for it. Of all the fools ever let loose on a field of battle, that man must be the very maddest. He and his regiment simply committed suicide—only the pistol missed fire, that's all.

RAINA (*deeply wounded, but steadfastly loyal to her ideals*). Indeed! Would you know him again if you saw him?

MAN. Shall I ever forget him. (*She again goes to the chest of drawers. He watches her with a vague hope that she may have something else for him to eat. She takes the portrait from its stand and brings it to him.*)

RAINA. That is a photograph of the gentleman—the patriot and hero—to whom I am betrothed.

MAN (*looking at it*). I'm really very sorry. (*looking at her*) Was it fair to lead me on? (*He looks at the portrait again.*) Yes: that's him: not a doubt of it. (*He stifles a laugh.*)

RAINA (*quickly*). Why do you laugh?

MAN (*shamefacedly, but still greatly tickled*). I didn't laugh, I assure you. At least I didn't mean to. But when I think of him charging the windmills and thinking he was doing the finest thing—(*chokes with suppressed laughter*).

RAINA (*sternly*). Give me back the portrait, sir.

MAN (*with sincere remorse*). Of course. Certainly. I'm really very sorry. (*She deliberately kisses it, and looks him straight in the face, before returning to the chest of drawers to replace it. He follows her, apologizing.*) Perhaps I'm quite wrong, you know: no doubt I am. Most likely he had got wind of the cartridge business somehow, and knew it was a safe job.

RAINA. That is to say, he was a pretender and a coward! You did not dare say that before.

MAN (*with a comic gesture of despair*). It's no use, dear lady: I can't make you see it from the professional point of view. (*As he turns away to get back to the ottoman, the firing begins again in the distance.*)

RAINA (*sternly, as she sees him listening to the shots*). So much the better for you.

MAN (*turning*). How?

RAINA. You are my enemy; and you are at my mercy. What would I do if I were a professional soldier?

MAN. Ah, true, dear young lady: you're always right. I know how good you have been to me: to my last hour I shall remember those three chocolate creams. It was unsoldierly; but it was angelic.

RAINA (*coldly*). Thank you. And now I will do a soldierly thing. You cannot stay here after what you have just said about my future husband; but I will go out on the balcony and see whether it is safe for you to climb down into the street. (*She turns to the window.*)

---

3. DON QUIXOTE . . . WINDMILLS: In Cervantes's *Don Quixote* the simple-minded hero thinks a group of windmills are giants, and recklessly attacks them.

MAN (*changing countenance*). Down that waterpipe! Stop! Wait! I can't! I daren't! The very thought of it makes me giddy. I came up it fast enough with death behind me. But to face it now in cold blood!— (*He sinks on the ottoman.*) It's no use: I give up: I'm beaten. Give the alarm. (*He drops his head in his hands in the deepest dejection.*)

RAINA (*disarmed by pity*). Come, don't be disheartened. (*She stoops over him almost maternally: he shakes his head.*) Oh, you are a very poor soldier—a chocolate cream soldier. Come, cheer up: it takes less courage to climb down than to face capture—remember that.

MAN (*dreamily, lulled by her voice*). No, capture only means death; and death is sleep—oh, sleep, sleep, sleep, undisturbed sleep! Climbing down the pipe means doing something—exerting myself—thinking! Death ten times over first.

RAINA (*softly and wonderingly, catching the rhythm of his weariness*). Are you so sleepy as that?

MAN. I've not had two hours undisturbed sleep since the war began. I'm on the staff: you don't know what that means. I haven't closed my eyes for thirty-six hours.

RAINA (*desperately*). But what am I to do with you.

MAN (*staggering up*). Of course I must do something. (*He shakes himself; pulls himself together; and speaks with rallied vigor and courage.*) You see, sleep or no sleep, hunger or no hunger, tired or not tired, you can always do a thing when you know it must be done. Well, that pipe must be got down—(*He hits himself on the chest, and adds*)—Do you hear that, you chocolate cream soldier? (*He turns to the window.*)

RAINA (*anxiously*). But if you fall?

MAN. I shall sleep as if the stones were a feather bed. Good-bye. (*He makes boldly for the window, and his hand is on the shutter when there is a terrible burst of firing in the street beneath.*)

RAINA (*rushing to him*). Stop! (*She catches him by the shoulder, and turns him quite round.*) They'll kill you.

MAN (*coolly, but attentively*). Never mind: this sort of thing is all in my day's work. I'm bound to take my chance. (*decisively*) Now do what I tell you. Put out the candles, so that they shan't see the light when I open the shutters. And keep away from the window, whatever you do. If they see me, they're sure to have a shot at me.

RAINA (*clinging to him*). They're sure to see you: it's bright moonlight. I'll save you —oh, how can you be so indifferent? You want me to save you, don't you?

MAN. I really don't want to be troublesome. (*She shakes him in her impatience.*) I am not indifferent, dear young lady, I assure you. But how is it to be done?

RAINA. Come away from the window— please. (*She coaxes him back to the middle of the room. He submits humbly. She releases him, and addresses him patronizingly.*) Now listen. You must trust to our hospitality. You do not yet know in whose house you are. I am a Petkoff.

MAN. What's that?

RAINA (*rather indignantly*). I mean that I belong to the family of the Petkoffs, the richest and best known in our country.

MAN. Oh, yes, of course. I beg your pardon. The Petkoffs, to be sure. How stupid of me!

RAINA. You know you never heard of them until this minute. How can you stoop to pretend?

MAN. Forgive me: I'm too tired to think; and the change of subject was too much for me. Don't scold me.

RAINA. I forgot. It might make you cry. (*He nods, quite seriously. She pouts and then resumes her patronizing tone.*) I must tell you that my father holds the highest command of any Bulgarian in our army. He is (*proudly*) a Major.

MAN (*pretending to be deeply impressed*). A Major! Bless me! Think of that!

RAINA. You showed great ignorance in thinking that it was necessary to climb up to the balcony, because ours is the only private house that has two rows of windows. There is a flight of stairs inside to get up and down by.

MAN. Stairs! How grand! You live in great luxury indeed, dear young lady.

RAINA. Do you know what a library is?

MAN. A library? A roomful of books.

RAINA. Yes, we have one, the only one in Bulgaria.

MAN. Actually a real library! I should like to see that.

RAINA (*affectedly*). I tell you these things to show you that you are not in the house of ignorant country folk who would kill you the moment they saw your Servian uniform, but among civilized people. We go to Bucharest every year for the opera season; and I have spent a whole month in Vienna.

MAN. I saw that, dear young lady. I saw at once that you knew the world.

RAINA. Have you ever seen the opera of Ernani?[4]

MAN. Is that the one with the devil in it in red velvet, and a soldiers' chorus?

RAINA (*contemptuously*). No!

MAN (*stifling a heavy sigh of weariness*). Then I don't know it.

RAINA. I thought you might have remembered the great scene where Ernani, flying from his foes just as you are tonight, takes refuge in the castle of his bitterest enemy, an old Castilian noble. The noble refuses to give him up. His guest is sacred to him.

MAN (*quickly waking up a little*). Have your people got that notion?

RAINA (*with dignity*). My mother and I can understand that notion, as you call it. And if instead of threatening me with your pistol as you did, you had simply thrown yourself as a fugitive on our hospitality, you would have been as safe as in your father's house.

MAN. Quite sure?

RAINA (*turning her back on him in dis-*

gust). Oh, it is useless to try and make you understand.

MAN. Don't be angry: you see how awkward it would be for me if there was any mistake. My father is a very hospitable man: he keeps six hotels; but I couldn't trust him as far as that. What about your father?

RAINA. He is away at Slivnitza fighting for his country. I answer for your safety. There is my hand in pledge of it. Will that reassure you? (*She offers him her hand.*)

MAN (*looking dubiously at his own hand*). Better not touch my hand, dear young lady. I must have a wash first.

RAINA (*touched*). That is very nice of you. I see that you are a gentleman.

MAN (*puzzled*). Eh?

RAINA. You must not think I am surprised. Bulgarians of really good standing— people in our position—wash their hands nearly every day. But I appreciate your delicacy. You may take my hand. (*She offers it again.*)

MAN (*kissing it with his hands behind his back*). Thanks, gracious young lady: I feel safe at last. And now would you mind breaking the news to your mother? I had better not stay here secretly longer than is necessary.

RAINA. If you will be so good as to keep perfectly still whilst I am away.

MAN. Certainly. (*He sits down on the ottoman.*)

(*Raina goes to the bed and wraps herself in the fur cloak. His eyes close. She goes to the door, but on turning for a last look at him, sees that he is dropping off to sleep.*)

RAINA (*at the door*). You are not going asleep, are you? (*He murmurs inarticulately: she runs to him and shakes him.*) Do you hear? Wake up: you are falling asleep.

MAN. Eh? Falling aslee—? Oh, no, not the least in the world: I was only thinking. It's all right: I'm wide awake.

RAINA (*severely*). Will you please stand

---

4. ERNANI: an opera by Verdi.

up while I am away. (*He rises reluctantly.*) All the time, mind.

MAN (*standing unsteadily*). Certainly— certainly: you may depend on me.

(*Raina looks doubtfully at him. He smiles foolishly. She goes reluctantly, turning again at the door, and almost catching him in the act of yawning. She goes out.*)

MAN (*drowsily*). Sleep, sleep, sleep, sleep, slee—(*The words trail off into a murmur. He wakes again with a shock on the point of falling.*) Where am I? That's what I want to know: where am I? Must keep awake. Nothing keeps me awake except danger—remember that—(*intently*) danger, danger, danger, dan— Where's danger? Must find it. (*He starts off vaguely around the room in search of it.*) What am I looking for? Sleep—danger—don't know. (*He stumbles against the bed.*) Ah, yes: now I know. All right now. I'm to go to bed, but not to sleep—be sure not to sleep—because of danger. Not to lie down, either, only sit down. (*He sits on the bed. A blissful expression comes into his face.*) Ah! (*With a happy sigh he sinks back at full length; lifts his boots into the bed with a final effort; and falls fast asleep instantly.*)

(*Catherine comes in, followed by Raina.*)

RAINA (*looking at the ottoman*). He's gone! I left him here.

CATHERINE. Here! Then he must have climbed down from the—

RAINA (*seeing him*). Oh! (*She points.*)

CATHERINE (*scandalized*). Well! (*She strides to the left side of the bed, Raina following and standing opposite her on the right.*) He's fast asleep. The brute!

RAINA (*anxiously*). Sh!

CATHERINE (*shaking him*). Sir! (*Shaking him again, harder.*) Sir!! (*vehemently shaking very hard*) Sir!!!

RAINA (*catching her arm*). Don't, mama: the poor dear is worn out. Let him sleep.

CATHERINE (*letting him go and turning amazed to Raina*). The poor dear! Raina!!! (*She looks sternly at her daughter. The man sleeps profoundly.*)

ACT TWO

The sixth of March, 1886. In the garden of Major Petkoff's house. It is a fine spring morning; and the garden looks fresh and pretty. Beyond the paling the tops of a couple of minarets can be seen, showing that there is a valley there, with the little town in it. A few miles further the Balkan mountains rise and shut in the view. Within the garden the side of the house is seen on the right, with a garden door reached by a little flight of steps. On the left the stable yard, with its gateway, encroaches on the garden. There are fruit bushes along the paling and house, covered with washing hung out to dry. A path runs by the house, and rises by two steps at the corner where it turns out of the sight along the front. In the middle a small table, with two bent wood chairs at it, is laid for breakfast with Turkish coffee pot, cups, rolls, etc.; but the cups have been used and the bread broken. There is a wooden garden seat against the wall on the left.

Louka, smoking a cigarette, is standing between the table and the house, turning her back with angry disdain on a manservant who is lecturing her. He is a middle-aged man of cool temperament and low but clear and keen intelligence, with the complacency of the servant who values himself on his rank in servility, and the imperturbability of the accurate calculator who has no illusions. He wears a white Bulgarian costume jacket with decorated border, sash, wide knickerbockers, and decorated gaiters. His head is shaved up to the crown, giving him a high Japanese forehead. His name is Nicola.

NICOLA. Be warned in time, Louka: mend your manners. I know the mistress. She is so grand that she never dreams that any servant could dare to be disrespectful to her; but if she once suspects that you are defying her, out you go.

LOUKA. I do defy her. I will defy her. What do I care for her?

NICOLA. If you quarrel with the family,

I never can marry you. It's the same as if you quarreled with me!

LOUKA. You take her part against me, do you?

NICOLA (*sedately*). I shall always be dependent on the good will of the family. When I leave their service and start a shop in Sofia, their custom will be half my capital: their bad word would ruin me.

LOUKA. You have no spirit. I should like to see them dare say a word against me!

NICOLA (*pityingly*). I should have expected more sense from you, Louka. But you're young, you're young!

LOUKA. Yes; and you like me the better for it, don't you? But I know some family secrets they wouldn't care to have told, young as I am. Let them quarrel with me if they dare!

NICOLA (*with compassionate superiority*). Do you know what they would do if they heard you talk like that?

LOUKA. What could they do?

NICOLA. Discharge you for untruthfulness. Who would believe any stories you told after that? Who would give you another situation? Who in this house would dare be seen speaking to you ever again? How long would your father be left on his little farm? (*She impatiently throws away the end of her cigarette and stamps on it.*) Child, you don't know the power such high people have over the like of you and me when we try to rise out of our poverty against them. (*He goes close to her and lowers his voice.*) Look at me, ten years in their service. Do you think I know no secrets? I know things about the mistress that she wouldn't have the master know for a thousand levas.[5] I know things about him that she wouldn't let him hear the last of for six months if I blabbed them to her. I know things about Raina that would break off her match with Sergius if—

LOUKA (*turning on him quickly*). How do you know? I never told you!

NICOLA (*opening his eyes cunningly*). So

that's your little secret, is it? I thought it might be something like that. Well, you take my advice, and be respectful; and make the mistress feel that no matter what you know or don't know, they can depend on you to hold your tongue and serve the family faithfully. That's what they like; and that's how you'll make most out of them.

LOUKA (*with searching scorn*). You have the soul of a servant, Nicola.

NICOLA (*complacently*). Yes: that's the secret of success in service.

(*A loud knocking with a whip handle on a wooden door, outside on the left, is heard.*)

MALE VOICE OUTSIDE. Hollo! Hollo there! Nicola!

LOUKA. Master! back from the war!

NICOLA (*quickly*). My word for it, Louka, the war's over. Off with you and get some fresh coffee. (*He runs out into the stable yard.*)

LOUKA (*as she puts the coffee pot and the cups upon the tray, and carries it into the house*). You'll never put the soul of a servant into me.

(*Major Petkoff comes from the stable yard, followed by Nicola. He is a cheerful, excitable, insignificant, unpolished man of about 50, naturally unambitious except as to his income and his importance in local society, but just now greatly pleased with the military rank which the war has thrust on him as a man of consequence in his town. The fever of plucky patriotism which the Servian attack roused in all the Bulgarians has pulled him through the war; but he is obviously glad to be home again.*)

PETKOFF (*pointing to the table with his whip*). Breakfast out here, eh?

NICOLA. Yes, sir. The mistress and Miss Raina have just gone in.

PETKOFF (*sitting down and taking a roll*). Go in and say I've come; and get me some fresh coffee.

NICOLA. It's coming, sir. (*He goes to the house door. Louka, with fresh coffee, a clean cup, and a brandy bottle on her tray meets him.*) Have you told the mistress?

---

5. LEVAS: plural of lev, a Bulgarian coin worth about twenty cents at the time.

LOUKA. Yes: she's coming.

(*Nicola goes into the house. Louka brings the coffee to the table.*)

PETKOFF. Well, the Servians haven't run away with you, have they?

LOUKA. No, sir.

PETKOFF. That's right. Have you brought me some cognac?

LOUKA (*putting the bottle on the table*). Here, sir.

PETKOFF. That's right. (*He pours some into his coffee.*)

(*Catherine who has at this early hour made only a very perfunctory toilet, and wears a Bulgarian apron over a once brilliant, but now half worn out red dressing gown, and a colored handkerchief tied over her thick black hair, with Turkish slippers on her bare feet, comes from the house, looking astonishingly handsome and stately under all the circumstances. Louka goes into the house.*)

CATHERINE. My dear Paul, what a surprise for us. (*She stoops over the back of his chair to kiss him.*) Have they brought you fresh coffee?

PETKOFF. Yes, Louka's been looking after me. The war's over. The treaty was signed three days ago at Bucharest; and the decree for our army to demobolize was issued yesterday.

CATHERINE (*springing erect, with flashing eyes*). The war over! Paul: have you let the Austrians force you to make peace?

PETKOFF (*submissively*). My dear: they didn't consult me. What could *I* do? (*She sits down and turns away from him.*) But of course we saw to it that the treaty was an honorable one. It declares peace—

CATHERINE (*outraged*). Peace!

PETKOFF (*appeasing her*). —but not friendly relations: remember that. They wanted to put that in; but I insisted on its being struck out. What more could I do?

CATHERINE. You could have annexed Servia and made Prince Alexander Emperor of the Balkans. That's what I would have done.

PETKOFF. I don't doubt it in the least, my dear. But I should have had to subdue the whole Austrian Empire first; and that would have kept me too long away from you. I missed you greatly.

CATHERINE (*relenting*). Ah! (*Stretches her hand affectionately across the table to squeeze his.*)

PETKOFF. And how have you been, my dear?

CATHERINE. Oh, my usual sore throats, that's all.

PETKOFF (*with conviction*). That comes from washing your neck every day. I've often told you so.

CATHERINE. Nonsense, Paul!

PETKOFF (*over his coffee and cigarette*). I don't believe in going too far with these modern customs. All this washing can't be good for the health: it's not natural. There was an Englishman at Phillipopolis who used to wet himself all over with cold water every morning when he got up. Disgusting! It all comes from the English: their climate makes them so dirty that they have to be perpetually washing themselves. Look at my father: he never had a bath in his life; and he lived to be ninety-eight, the healthiest man in Bulgaria. I don't mind a good wash once a week to keep up my position; but once a day is carrying the thing to a ridiculous extreme.

CATHERINE. You are a barbarian at heart still, Paul. I hope you behaved yourself before all those Russian officers.

PETKOFF. I did my best. I took care to let them know that we had a library.

CATHERINE. Ah; but you didn't tell them that we have an electric bell in it? I have had one put up.

PETKOFF. What's an electric bell?

CATHERINE. You touch a button; something tinkles in the kitchen; and then Nicola comes up.

PETKOFF. Why not shout for him?

CATHERINE. Civilized people never shout for their servants. I've learned that while you were away.

PETKOFF. Well, I'll tell you something I've learned, too. Civilized people don't hang out their washing to dry where visitors can see it; so you'd better have all that (*indicating the clothes on the bushes*) put somewhere else.

CATHERINE. Oh, that's absurd, Paul: I don't believe really refined people notice such things.

(*Someone is heard knocking at the stable gates.*)

PETKOFF. There's Sergius. (*shouting*) Hollo, Nicola!

CATHERINE. Oh, don't shout, Paul: it really isn't nice.

PETKOFF. Bosh! (*He shouts louder than before.*) Nicola!

NICOLA (*appearing at the house door*). Yes, sir.

PETKOFF. If that is Major Saranoff, bring him round this way. (*He pronounces the name with the stress on the second syllable —Sarah noff.*)

NICOLA. Yes, sir. (*He goes into the stable yard.*)

PETKOFF. You must talk to him, my dear, until Raina takes him off our hands. He bores my life out about our not promoting him—over my head, mind you.

CATHERINE. He certainly ought to be promoted when he marries Raina. Besides, the country should insist on having at least one native general.

PETKOFF. Yes, so that he could throw away whole brigades instead of regiments. It's no use, my dear: he has not the slightest chance of promotion until we are quite sure that the peace will be a lasting one.

NICOLA (*at the gate, announcing*). Major Sergius Saranoff! (*He goes into the house and returns presently with a third chair, which he places at the table. He then withdraws.*)

(*Major Sergius Saranoff, the original of the portrait in Raina's room, is a tall, romantically handsome man, with the physical hardihood, the high spirit, and the suscep-* tible imagination of an untamed mountaineer chieftain. But his remarkable personal distinction is of a characteristically civilized type. The ridges of his eyebrows, curving with a ram's-horn twist round the marked projections at the outer corners, his jealously observant eye, his nose, thin, keen, and apprehensive in spite of the pugnacious high bridge and large nostril, his assertive chin, would not be out of place in a Paris salon. In short, the clever, imaginative barbarian has an acute critical faculty which has been thrown into intense activity by the arrival of western civilization in the Balkans; and the result is precisely what the advent of nineteenth century thought first produced in England: to wit, Byronism. By his brooding on the perpetual failure, not only of others, but of himself, to live up to his imaginative ideals, his consequent cynical scorn for humanity, the jejune credulity as to the absolute validity of his ideals and the unworthiness of the world in disregarding them, his wincings and mockeries under the sting of the petty disillusions which every hour spent among men brings to his infallibly quick observation, he has acquired the half tragic, half ironic air, the mysterious moodiness, the suggestion of a strange and terrible history that has left him nothing but undying remorse, by which Childe Harold[6] fascinated the grandmothers of his English contemporaries. Altogether it is clear that here or nowhere is Raina's ideal hero. Catherine is hardly less enthusiastic, and much less reserved in showing her enthusiasm. As he enters from the stable gate, she rises effusively to greet him. Petkoff is distinctly less disposed to make a fuss about him.*)

PETKOFF. Here already, Sergius. Glad to see you!

CATHERINE. My dear Sergius! (*She holds out both her hands.*)

SERGIUS (*kissing them with scrupulous gallantry*). My dear mother, if I may call you so.

_____

6. CHILDE HAROLD: hero of Byron's poem of the same name.

PETKOFF (*drily*). Mother-in-law, Sergius; mother-in-law! Sit down, and have some coffee.

SERGIUS. Thank you, none for me. (*He gets away from the table with a certain distaste for Petkoff's enjoyment of it, and posts himself with conscious grace against the rail of the steps leading to the house.*)

CATHERINE. You look superb—splendid. The campaign has improved you. Everybody here is mad about you. We were all wild with enthusiasm about that magnificent cavalry charge.

SERGIUS (*with grave irony*). Madam: it was the cradle and the grave of my military reputation.

CATHERINE. How so?

SERGIUS. I won the battle the wrong way when our worthy Russian generals were losing it the right way. That upset their plans, and wounded their self-esteem. Two of their colonels got their regiments driven back on the correct principles of scientific warfare. Two major-generals got killed strictly according to military etiquette. Those two colonels are now major-generals; and I am still a simple major.

CATHERINE. You shall not remain so, Sergius. The women are on your side; and they will see that justice is done you.

SERGIUS. It is too late. I have only waited for the peace to send in my resignation.

PETKOFF (*dropping his cup in his amazement*). Your resignation!

CATHERINE. Oh, you must withdraw it!

SERGIUS (*with resolute, measured emphasis, folding his arms*). I never withdraw!

PETKOFF (*vexed*). Now who could have supposed you were going to do such a thing?

SERGIUS (*with fire*). Everyone that knew me. But enough of myself and my affairs. How is Raina; and where is Raina?

RAINA (*suddenly coming round the corner of the house and standing at the top of the steps in the path*). Raina is here. (*She makes a charming picture as they all turn to look at her. She wears an underdress of pale green silk, draped with an overdress of thin ecru canvas embroidered with gold. On her head she wears a pretty Phrygian cap of gold tinsel. Sergius, with an exclamation of pleasure, goes impulsively to meet her. She stretches out her hand: he drops chivalrously on one knee and kisses it.*)

PETKOFF (*aside to Catherine, beaming with parental pride*). Pretty, isn't it? She always appears at the right moment.

CATHERINE (*impatiently*). Yes: she listens for it. It is an abominable habit.

(*Sergius leads Raina forward with splendid gallantry, as if she were a queen. When they come to the table, she turns to him with a bend of the head; he bows; and thus they separate, he coming to his place, and she going behind her father's chair.*)

RAINA (*stooping and kissing her father*). Dear father! Welcome home!

PETKOFF (*patting her cheek*). My little pet girl. (*He kisses her; she goes to the chair left by Nicola for Sergius, and sits down.*)

CATHERINE. And so you're no longer a soldier, Sergius.

SERGIUS. I am no longer a soldier. Soldiering, my dear madam, is the coward's art of attacking mercilessly when you are strong, and keeping out of harm's way when you are weak. That is the whole secret of successful fighting. Get your enemy at a disadvantage; and never, on any account, fight him on equal terms. Eh, Major!

PETKOFF. They wouldn't let us make a fair stand-up fight of it. However, I suppose soldiering has to be a trade like any other trade.

SERGIUS. Precisely. But I have no ambition to succeed as a tradesman; so I have taken the advice of that bagman of a captain that settled the exchange of prisoners with us, at Peerot, and given it up.

PETKOFF. What, that Swiss fellow? Sergius: I've often thought of that exchange since. He over-reached[7] us about those horses.

SERGIUS. Of course he over-reached us. His father was a hotel and livery stable

-----
7. OVER-REACHED: cheated.

keeper; and he owed his first step to his knowledge of horse-dealing. (*with mock enthusiasm*) Ah, he was a soldier—every inch a soldier! If only I had bought the horses for my regiment instead of foolishly leading it into danger, I should have been a field-marshal now!

CATHERINE. A Swiss? What was he doing in the Servian army?

PETKOFF. A volunteer of course—keen on picking up his profession. (*chuckling*) We shouldn't have been able to begin fighting if these foreigners hadn't shown us how to do it: we knew nothing about it; and neither did the Servians. Egad, there'd have been no war without them.

RAINA. Are there many Swiss officers in the Servian army?

PETKOFF. No—all Austrians, just as our officers were all Russians. This was the only Swiss I came across. I'll never trust a Swiss again. He cheated us—humbugged us into giving him fifty able-bodied men for two hundred confounded worn-out chargers. They weren't even eatable!

SERGIUS. We were two children in the hands of that consummate soldier, Major: simply two innocent little children.

RAINA. What was he like?

CATHERINE. Oh, Raina, what a silly question!

SERGIUS. He was like a commercial traveler[8] in uniform. Bourgeois to his boots.

PETKOFF (*grinning*). Sergius: tell Catherine that queer story his friend told us about him—how he escaped after Slivnitza. You remember?—about his being hid by two women.

SERGIUS (*with bitter irony*). Oh, yes, quite a romance. He was serving in the very battery I so unprofessionally charged. Being a thorough soldier, he ran away like the rest of them, with our cavalry at his heels. To escape their attentions, he had the good taste to take refuge in the chamber of some patriotic young Bulgarian lady. The young lady was enchanted by his persuasive commercial

traveler's manners. She very modestly entertained him for an hour or so and then called in her mother lest her conduct should appear unmaidenly. The old lady was equally fascinated; and the fugitive was sent on his way in the morning, disguised in an old coat belonging to the master of the house, who was away at the war.

RAINA (*rising with marked stateliness*). Your life in the camp has made you coarse, Sergius. I did not think you would have repeated such a story before me. (*She turns away coldly.*)

CATHERINE (*also rising*). She is right, Sergius. If such women exist, we should be spared the knowledge of them.

PETKOFF. Pooh! nonsense! what does it matter?

SERGIUS (*ashamed*). No, Petkoff: I was wrong. (*to Raina, with earnest humility*) I beg your pardon. I have behaved abominably. Forgive me, Raina. (*She bows reservedly.*) And you, too, madam. (*Catherine bows graciously and sits down. He proceeds solemnly, again addressing Raina.*) The glimpses I have had of the seamy side of life during the last few months have made me cynical; but I should not have brought my cynicism here—least of all into your presence, Raina. I—(*Here, turning to the others, he is evidently about to begin a long speech when the Major interrupts him.*)

PETKOFF. Stuff and nonsense, Sergius. That's quite enough fuss about nothing: a soldier's daughter should be able to stand up without flinching to a little strong conversation. (*He rises.*) Come: it's time for us to get to business. We have to make up our minds how those three regiments are to get back to Phillipopolis:—there's no forage for them on the Sofia route. (*He goes towards the house.*) Come along. (*Sergius is about to follow him when Catherine rises and intervenes.*)

CATHERINE. Oh, Paul, can't you spare Sergius for a few moments? Raina has hardly seen him yet. Perhaps I can help you to settle about the regiments.

---

8. COMMERCIAL TRAVELER: traveling salesman.

SERGIUS (*protesting*). My dear madam, impossible: you—

CATHERINE (*stopping him playfully*). You stay here, my dear Sergius: there's no hurry. I have a word or two to say to Paul. (*Sergius instantly bows and steps back.*) Now, dear (*taking Petkoff's arm*), come and see the electric bell.

PETKOFF. Oh, very well, very well. (*They go into the house together affectionately. Sergius, left alone with Raina, looks anxiously at her, fearing that she may be still offended. She smiles, and stretches out her arms to him.*)

SERGIUS (*hastening to her, but refraining from touching her without express permission*). Am I forgiven?

RAINA (*placing her hands on his shoulder as she looks up at him with admiration and worship*). My hero! My king.

SERGIUS. My queen! (*He kisses her on the forehead with holy awe.*)

RAINA. How I have envied you, Sergius! You have been out in the world, on the field of battle, able to prove yourself there worthy of any woman in the world; whilst I have had to sit at home inactive—dreaming—useless—doing nothing that could give me the right to call myself worthy of any man.

SERGIUS. Dearest, all my deeds have been yours. You inspired me. I have gone through the war like a knight in a tournament with his lady looking on at him!

RAINA. And you have never been absent from my thoughts for a moment. (*very solemnly*) Sergius: I think we two have found the higher love. When I think of you, I feel that I could never do a base deed, or think an ignoble thought.

SERGIUS. My lady, and my saint! (*clasping her reverently*)

RAINA (*returning his embrace*). My lord and my g—

SERGIUS. Sh—sh! Let me be the worshipper, dear. You little know how unworthy even the best man is of a girl's pure passion!

RAINA. I trust you. I love you. You will never disappoint me, Sergius. (*Louka is heard singing within the house. They quickly release each other.*) Hush! I can't pretend to talk indifferently before her: my heart is too full. (*Louka comes from the house with her tray. She goes to the table, and begins to clear it, with her back turned to them.*) I will go and get my hat; and then we can go out until lunch time. Wouldn't you like that?

SERGIUS. Be quick. If you are away five minutes, it will seem five hours. (*Raina runs to the top of the steps and turns there to exchange a look with him and wave him a kiss with both hands. He looks after her with emotion for a moment, then turns slowly away, his face radiant with the exultation of the scene which has just passed. The movement shifts his field of vision, into the corner of which there now comes the tail of Louka's double apron. His eye gleams at once. He takes a stealthy look at her, and begins to twirl his moustache nervously, with his left hand akimbo on his hip. Finally, striking the ground with his heels in something of a cavalry swagger, he strolls over to the left of the table, opposite her, and says*) Louka: do you know what the higher love is?

LOUKA (*astonished*). No, sir.

SERGIUS. Very fatiguing thing to keep up for any length of time, Louka. One feels the need of some relief after it.

LOUKA (*innocently*). Perhaps you would like some coffee, sir? (*She stretches her hand across the table for the coffee pot.*)

SERGIUS (*taking her hand*). Thank you, Louka.

LOUKA (*pretending to pull*). Oh, sir, you know I didn't mean that. I'm surprised at you!

SERGIUS (*coming clear of the table and drawing her with him*). I am surprised at myself, Louka. What would Sergius, the hero of Slivnitza, say if he saw me now? What would Sergius, the apostle of the higher love, say if he saw me now? What would the half dozen Sergiuses who keep popping in and out of this handsome figure of mine say if they caught us here? (*letting go her hand and slipping his arm dexterously round her waist*) Do you consider my figure handsome, Louka?

LOUKA. Let me go, sir. I shall be disgraced. (*She struggles: he holds her inexorably.*) Oh, will you let go?

SERGIUS (*looking straight into her eyes*). No.

LOUKA. Then stand back where we can't be seen. Have you no common sense?

SERGIUS. Ah, that's reasonable. (*He takes her into the stableyard gateway, where they are hidden from the house.*)

LOUKA (*complaining*). I may have been seen from the windows: Miss Raina is sure to be spying about after you.

SERGIUS (*stung—letting her go*). Take care, Louka. I may be worthless enough to betray the higher love; but do not you insult it.

LOUKA (*demurely*). Not for the world, sir, I'm sure. May I go on with my work please, now?

SERGIUS (*again putting his arm round her*). You are a provoking little witch, Louka. If you were in love with me, would you spy out of windows on me?

LOUKA. Well, you see, sir, since you say you are half a dozen different gentlemen all at once, I should have a great deal to look after.

SERGIUS (*charmed*). Witty as well as pretty. (*He tries to kiss her.*)

LOUKA (*avoiding him*). No, I don't want your kisses. Gentlefolk are all alike—you making love to me behind Miss Raina's back, and she doing the same behind yours.

SERGIUS (*recoiling a step*). Louka!

LOUKA. It shows how little you really care!

SERGIUS (*dropping his familiarity and speaking with freezing politeness*). If our conversation is to continue, Louka, you will please remember that a gentleman does not discuss the conduct of the lady he is engaged to with her maid.

LOUKA. It's so hard to know what a gentleman considers right. I thought from your

trying to kiss me that you had given up being so particular.

SERGIUS (*turning from her and striking his forehead as he comes back into the garden from the gateway*). Devil! devil!

LOUKA. Ha! ha! I expect one of the six of you is very like me, sir, though I am only Miss Raina's maid. (*She goes back to her work at the table, taking no further notice of him.*)

SERGIUS (*speaking to himself*). Which of the six is the real man?—that's the question that torments me. One of them is a hero, another a buffoon, another a humbug, another perhaps a bit of a blackguard. (*He pauses and looks furtively at Louka, as he adds with deep bitterness*) And one, at least, is a coward—jealous, like all cowards. (*He goes to the table.*) Louka.

LOUKA. Yes?

SERGIUS. Who is my rival?

LOUKA. You shall never get that out of me, for love or money.

SERGIUS. Why?

LOUKA. Never mind why. Besides, you would tell that I told you; and I should lose my place.

SERGIUS (*holding out his right hand in affirmation*). No; on the honor of a—(*He checks himself, and his hand drops nerveless as he concludes, sardonically*)—of a man capable of behaving as I have been behaving for the last five minutes. Who is he?

LOUKA. I don't know. I never saw him. I only heard his voice through the door of her room.

SERGIUS. Damnation! How dare you?

LOUKA (*retreating*). Oh, I mean no harm: you've no right to take up my words like that. The mistress knows all about it. And I tell you that if that gentleman ever comes here again, Miss Raina will marry him, whether he likes it or not. I know the difference between the sort of manner you and she put on before one another and the real manner. (*Sergius shivers as if she had stabbed him. Then, setting his face like iron, he strides grimly to her, and grips her above the elbows with both hands.*)

SERGIUS. Now listen you to me!

LOUKA (*wincing*). Not so tight: you're hurting me!

SERGIUS. That doesn't matter. You have stained my honor by making me a party to your eavesdropping. And you have betrayed your mistress—

LOUKA (*writhing*). Please—

SERGIUS. That shows that you are an abominable little clod of common clay, with the soul of a servant. (*He lets her go as if she were an unclean thing, and turns away, dusting his hands of her, to the bench by the wall, where he sits down with averted head, meditating gloomily.*)

LOUKA (*whimpering angrily with her hands up her sleeves, feeling her bruised arms*). You know how to hurt with your tongue as well as with your hands. But I don't care, now I've found out that whatever clay I'm made of, you're made of the same. As for her, she's a liar; and her fine airs are a cheat; and I'm worth six of her. (*She shakes the pain off hardily; tosses her head; and sets to work to put the things on the tray. He looks doubtfully at her once or twice. She finishes packing the tray, and laps the cloth over the edges, so as to carry all out together. As she stoops to lift it, he rises.*)

SERGIUS. Louka! (*She stops and looks defiantly at him with the tray in her hands.*) A gentleman has no right to hurt a woman under any circumstances. (*with profound humility, uncovering his head*) I beg your pardon.

LOUKA. That sort of apology may satisfy a lady. Of what use is it to a servant?

SERGIUS (*thus rudely crossed in his chivalry, throws it off with a bitter laugh and says slightingly*). Oh, you wish to be paid for the hurt? (*He puts on his shako, and takes some money from his pocket.*)

LOUKA (*her eyes filling with tears in spite of herself*). No, I want my hurt made well.

SERGIUS (*sobered by her tone*). How?

(*She rolls up her left sleeve; clasps her arm with the thumb and fingers of her right hand; and looks down at the bruise. Then she raises her head and looks straight at him. Finally, with a superb gesture she presents her arm to be kissed. Amazed, he looks at her; at the arm; at her again; hesitates; and then, with shuddering intensity, exclaims*) Never! (*and gets away as far as possible from her.*)

(*Her arm drops. Without a word, and with unaffected dignity, she takes her tray, and is approaching the house when Raina returns wearing a hat and jacket in the height of the Vienna fashion of the previous year, 1885. Louka makes way proudly for her, and then goes into the house.*)

RAINA. I'm ready! What's the matter? (*gaily*) Have you been flirting with Louka?

SERGIUS (*hastily*). No, no. How can you think such a thing?

RAINA (*ashamed of herself*). Forgive me, dear: it was only a jest. I am so happy today.

(*He goes quickly to her, and kisses her hand remorsefully. Catherine comes out and calls to them from the top of the steps.*)

CATHERINE (*coming down to them*). I am sorry to disturb you, children; but Paul is distracted over those three regiments. He does not know how to get them to Phillipopolis; and he objects to every suggestion of mine. You must go and help him, Sergius. He is in the library.

RAINA (*disappointed*). But we are just going out for a walk.

SERGIUS. I shall not be long. Wait for me just five minutes. (*He runs up the steps to the door.*)

RAINA (*following him to the foot of the steps and looking up at him with timid coquetry*). I shall go round and wait in full view of the library windows. Be sure you draw father's attention to me. If you are a moment longer than five minutes, I shall go in and fetch you, regiments or no regiments.

SERGIUS (*laughing*). Very well. (*He goes in. Raina watches him until he is out of her sight. Then, with a perceptible relaxation of manner, she begins to pace up and down about the garden in a brown study.*)

CATHERINE. Imagine their meeting that Swiss and hearing the whole story! The very first thing your father asked for was the old coat we sent him off in. A nice mess you have got us into!

RAINA (*gazing thoughtfully at the gravel as she walks*). The little beast!

CATHERINE. Little beast! What little beast?

RAINA. To go and tell! Oh, if I had him here, I'd stuff him with chocolate creams till he couldn't ever speak again!

CATHERINE. Don't talk nonsense. Tell me the truth, Raina. How long was he in your room before you came to me?

RAINA (*whisking round and recommencing her march in the opposite direction*). Oh, I forget.

CATHERINE. You cannot forget! Did he really climb up after the soldiers were gone, or was he there when that officer searched the room?

RAINA. No. Yes, I think he must have been there then.

CATHERINE. You think! Oh, Raina, Raina! Will anything ever make you straightforward? If Sergius finds out, it is all over between you.

RAINA (*with cool impertinence*). Oh, I know Sergius is your pet. I sometimes wish you could marry him instead of me. You would just suit him. You would pet him, and spoil him, and mother him to perfection.

CATHERINE (*opening her eyes very widely indeed*). Well, upon my word!

RAINA (*capriciously—half to herself*). I always feel a longing to do or say something dreadful to him—to shock his propriety—to scandalize the five senses out of him! (*to Catherine perversely*) I don't care whether he finds out about the chocolate cream soldier or not. I half hope he may. (*She again turns flippantly away and strolls up the path to the corner of the house.*)

CATHERINE. And what should I be able to say to your father, pray?

RAINA (*over her shoulder, from the top of the two steps*). Oh, poor father! As if he could help himself! (*She turns the corner and passes out of sight.*)

CATHERINE (*looking after her, her fingers itching*). Oh, if you were only ten years younger! (*Louka comes from the house with a salver, which she carries hanging down by her side.*) Well?

LOUKA. There's a gentleman just called, madam—a Servian officer—

CATHERINE (*flaming*). A Servian! How dare he—(*Checking herself bitterly.*) Oh, I forgot. We are at peace now. I suppose we shall have them calling every day to pay their compliments. Well, if he is an officer why don't you tell your master? He is in the library with Major Saranoff. Why do you come to me?

LOUKA. But he asks for you, madam. And I don't think he knows who you are: he said the lady of the house. He gave me this little ticket for you. (*She takes a card out of her bosom; puts it on the salver and offers it to Catherine.*)

CATHERINE (*reading*). "Captain Bluntschli!" That's a German name.

LOUKA. Swiss, madam, I think.

CATHERINE (*with a bound that makes Louka jump back*). Swiss! What is he like?

LOUKA (*timidly*). He has a big carpet bag, madam.

CATHERINE. Oh, Heavens, he's come to return the coat! Send him away—say we're not at home—ask him to leave his address and I'll write to him—Oh, stop: that will never do. Wait! (*She throws herself into a chair to think it out. Louka waits.*) The master and Major Saranoff are busy in the library, aren't they?

LOUKA. Yes, madam.

CATHERINE (*decisively*). Bring the gentleman out here at once. (*imperatively*) And be very polite to him. Don't delay. Here (*impatiently snatching the salver from her*): leave that here; and go straight back to him.

LOUKA. Yes, madam. (*going*)

CATHERINE. Louka!

LOUKA (*stopping*). Yes, madam.

CATHERINE. Is the library door shut?

LOUKA. I think so, madam.

CATHERINE. If not, shut it as you pass through.

LOUKA. Yes, madam. (*going*)

CATHERINE. Stop! (*Louka stops.*) He will have to go out that way (*indicating the gate of the stable yard.*) Tell Nicola to bring his bag here after him. Don't forget.

LOUKA (*surprised*). His bag?

CATHERINE. Yes, here, as soon as possible. (*vehemently*) Be quick! (*Louka runs into the house. Catherine snatches her apron off and throws it behind a bush. She then takes up the salver and uses it as a mirror, with the result that the handkerchief tied round her head follows the apron. A touch to her hair and a shake to her dressing gown makes her presentable.*) Oh, how—how—how can a man be such a fool! Such a moment to select! (*Louka appears at the door of the house, announcing "Captain Bluntschli"; and standing aside at the top of the steps to let him pass before she goes in again. He is the man of the adventure in Raina's room. He is now clean, well brushed, smartly uniformed, and out of trouble, but still unmistakably the same man. The moment Louka's back is turned, Catherine swoops on him with hurried, urgent, coaxing appeal.*) Captain Bluntschli, I am very glad to see you; but you must leave this house at once. (*He raises his eyebrows.*) My husband has just returned, with my future son-in-law; and they know nothing. If they did, the consequences would be terrible. You are a foreigner: you do not feel our national animosities as we do. We still hate the Servians: the only effect of the peace on my husband is to make him feel like a lion balked of his prey. If he discovered our secret, he would never forgive me; and my daughter's life would hardly be safe. Will you, like the chivalrous gentleman and soldier you are, leave at once before he finds you here?

BLUNTSCHLI (*disappointed, but philosophical*). At once, gracious lady. I only came to thank you and return the coat you lent me. If you will allow me to take it out of my bag and leave it with your servant as I pass out, I need detain you no further. (*He turns to go into the house.*)

CATHERINE (*catching him by the sleeve*). Oh, you must not think of going back that way. (*coaxing him across to the stable gates*) This is the shortest way out. Many thanks. So glad to have been of service to you. Good-bye.

BLUNTSCHLI. But my bag?

CATHERINE. It will be sent on. You will leave me your address.

BLUNTSCHLI. True. Allow me. (*He takes out his cardcase, and stops to write his address, keeping Catherine in an agony of impatience. As he hands her the card, Petkoff, hatless, rushes from the house in a fluster of hospitality, followed by Sergius.*)

PETKOFF (*as he hurries down the steps*). My dear Captain Bluntschli—

CATHERINE. Oh Heavens! (*She sinks on the seat against the wall.*)

PETKOFF (*too preoccupied to notice her as he shakes Bluntschli's hand heartily*). Those stupid people of mine thought I was out here, instead of in the—haw!—library. (*He cannot mention the library without betraying how proud he is of it.*) I saw you through the window. I was wondering why you didn't come in. Saranoff is with me: you remember him, don't you?

SERGIUS (*saluting humorously, and then offering his hand with great charm of manner*). Welcome, our friend the enemy!

PETKOFF. No longer the enemy, happily. (*rather anxiously*) I hope you've come as a friend, and not on business.

CATHERINE. Oh, quite as a friend, Paul. I was just asking Captain Bluntschli to stay to lunch; but he declares he must go at once.

SERGIUS (*sardonically*). Impossible, Bluntschli. We want you here badly. We have to send on three cavalry regiments to Phillipopolis; and we don't in the least know how to do it.

BLUNTSCHLI (*suddenly attentive and businesslike*). Phillipopolis! The forage is the trouble, eh?

PETKOFF (*eagerly*). Yes, that's it. (*to Sergius*) He sees the whole thing at once.

BLUNTSCHLI. I think I can show you how to manage that.

SERGIUS. Invaluable man! Come along! (*Towering over Bluntschli, he puts his hand on his shoulder and takes him to the steps, Petkoff following. As Bluntschli puts his foot on the first step, Raina comes out of the house.*)

RAINA (*completely losing her presence of mind*). Oh, the chocolate cream soldier!

(*Bluntschli stands rigid. Sergius, amazed, looks at Raina, then at Petkoff, who looks back at him and then at his wife.*)

CATHERINE (*with commanding presence of mind.*) My dear Raina, don't you see that we have a guest here—Captain Bluntschli, one of our new Servian friends?

(*Raina bows; Bluntschli bows.*)

RAINA. How silly of me! (*She comes down into the center of the group, between Bluntschli and Petkoff.*) I made a beautiful ornament this morning for the ice pudding; and that stupid Nicola has just put down a pile of plates on it and spoiled it. (*to Bluntschli, winningly*) I hope you didn't think that you were the chocolate cream soldier, Captain Bluntschli.

BLUNTSCHLI (*laughing*). I assure you I did. (*stealing a whimsical glance at her*) Your explanation was a relief.

PETKOFF (*suspiciously, to Raina*). And since when, pray, have you taken to cooking?

CATHERINE. Oh, whilst you were away. It is her latest fancy.

PETKOFF (*testily*). And has Nicola taken to drinking? He used to be careful enough. First he shows Captain Bluntschli out here when he knew quite well I was in the—hum!—library; and then he goes downstairs

and breaks Raina's chocolate soldier. He must—(*At this moment Nicola appears at the top of the steps R., with a carpet bag. He descends; places it respectfully before Bluntschli; and waits for further orders. General amazement. Nicola, unconscious of the effect he is producing, looks perfectly satisfied with himself. When Petkoff recovers his power of speech, he breaks out at him with*) Are you mad, Nicola?

NICOLA (*taken aback*). Sir?

PETKOFF. What have you brought that for?

NICOLA. My lady's orders, sir. Louka told me that—

CATHERINE (*interrupting him*). My orders! Why should I order you to bring Captain Bluntschli's luggage out here? What are you thinking of, Nicola?

NICOLA (*after a moment's bewilderment, picking up the bag as he addresses Bluntschli with the very perfection of servile discretion*). I beg your pardon, sir, I am sure. (*to Catherine*) My fault, madam! I hope you'll overlook it! (*He bows, and is going to the steps with the bag, when Petkoff addresses him angrily.*)

PETKOFF. You'd better go and slam that bag, too, down on Miss Raina's ice pudding! (*This is too much for Nicola. The bag drops from his hands on Petkoff's corns, eliciting a roar of anguish from him.*) Begone, you butter-fingered donkey.

NICOLA (*snatching up the bag, and escaping into the house*). Yes, sir.

CATHERINE. Oh, never mind, Paul, don't be angry!

PETKOFF (*muttering*). Scoundrel. He's got out of hand while I was away. I'll teach him. (*recollecting his guest*) Oh, well, never mind. Come, Bluntschli, let's have no more nonsense about you having to go away. You know very well you're not going back to Switzerland yet. Until you do go back you'll stay with us.

RAINA. Oh, do, Captain Bluntschli.

PETKOFF (*to Catherine*). Now, Catherine,

it's of you that he's afraid. Press him and he'll stay.

CATHERINE. Of course I shall be only too delighted if (*appealingly*) Captain Bluntschli really wishes to stay. He knows my wishes.

BLUNTSCHLI (*in his driest military manner*). I am at madame's orders.

SERGIUS (*cordially*). That settles it!

PETKOFF (*heartily*). Of course!

RAINA. You see, you must stay!

BLUNTSCHLI (*smiling*). Well, if I must, I must!

(*gesture of despair from Catherine*)

ACT THREE

In the library after lunch. It is not much of a library, its literary equipment consisting of a single fixed shelf stocked with old paper covered novels, broken backed, coffee stained, torn and thumbed, and a couple of little hanging shelves with a few gift books on them, the rest of the wall space being occupied by trophies of war and the chase. But it is a most comfortable sitting-room. A row of three large windows in the front of the house show a mountain panorama, which is just now seen in one of its softest aspects in the mellowing afternoon light. In the left hand corner, a square earthenware stove, a perfect tower of colored pottery, rises nearly to the ceiling and guarantees plenty of warmth. The ottoman in the middle is a circular bank of decorated cushions, and the window seats are well upholstered divans. Little Turkish tables, one of them with an elaborate hookah on it, and a screen to match them, complete the handsome effect of the furnishing. There is one object, however, which is hopelessly out of keeping with its surroundings. This is a small kitchen table, much the worse for wear, fitted as a writing table with an old canister full of pens, an eggcup filled with ink, and a deplorable scrap of severely used pink blotting paper.

At the side of this table, which stands on the right, Bluntschli is hard at work, with a couple of maps before him, writing orders. At the head of it sits Sergius, who is also supposed to be at work, but who is actually gnawing the feather of a pen, and contemplating Bluntschli's quick, sure, business-like progress with a mixture of envious irritation at his own incapacity, and awestruck wonder at an ability which seems to him almost miraculous, though its prosaic character forbids him to esteem it. The major is comfortably established on the ottoman, with a newspaper in his hand and the tube of the hookah within his reach. Catherine sits at the stove, with her back to them, embroidering. Raina, reclining on the divan under the left hand window, is gazing in a daydream out at the Balkan landscape, with a neglected novel in her lap.

The door is on the left. The button of the electric bell is between the door and the fireplace.

PETKOFF (*looking up from his paper to watch how they are getting on at the table*). Are you sure I can't help you in any way, Bluntschli?

BLUNTSCHLI (*without interrupting his writing or looking up*). Quite sure, thank you. Saranoff and I will manage it.

SERGIUS (*grimly*). Yes: we'll manage it. He finds out what to do; draws up the orders; and I sign 'em. Division of labor, Major. (*Bluntschli passes him a paper.*) Another one? Thank you. (*He plants the papers squarely before him; sets his chair carefully parallel to them; and signs with the air of a man resolutely performing a difficult and dangerous feat.*) This hand is more accustomed to the sword than to the pen.

PETKOFF. It's very good of you, Bluntschli, it is indeed, to let yourself be put upon in this way. Now are you quite sure I can do nothing?

CATHERINE (*in a low, warning tone*). You can stop interrupting, Paul.

PETKOFF (*starting and looking round at*

her). Eh? Oh! Quite right, my love, quite right. (*He takes his newspaper up, but lets it drop again.*) Ah, you haven't been campaigning, Catherine: you don't know how pleasant it is for us to sit here, after a good lunch, with nothing to do but enjoy ourselves. There's only one thing I want to make me thoroughly comfortable.

CATHERINE. What is that?

PETKOFF. My old coat. I'm not at home in this one: I feel as if I were on parade.

CATHERINE. My dear Paul, how absurd you are about that old coat! It must be hanging in the blue closet where you left it.

PETKOFF. My dear Catherine, I tell you I've looked there. Am I to believe my own eyes or not? (*Catherine quietly rises and presses the button of the electric bell by the fireplace*). What are you showing off that bell for? (*She looks at him majestically, and silently resumes her chair and her needlework.*) My dear: if you think the obstinacy of your sex can make a coat out of two old dressing gowns of Raina's, your waterproof, and my mackintosh, you're mistaken. That's exactly what the blue closet contains at present. (*Nicola presents himself.*)

CATHERINE (*unmoved by Petkoff's sally*). Nicola: go to the blue closet and bring your master's old coat here—the braided one he usually wears in the house.

NICOLA. Yes, madam. (*Nicola goes out.*)

PETKOFF. Catherine.

CATHERINE. Yes, Paul?

PETKOFF. I bet you any piece of jewelry you like to order from Sofia against a week's housekeeping money, that the coat isn't there.

CATHERINE. Done, Paul.

PETKOFF (*excited by the prospect of a gamble*). Come: here's an opportunity for some sport. Who'll bet on it? Bluntschli: I'll give you six to one.

BLUNTSCHLI (*imperturbably*). It would be robbing you, Major. Madame is sure to be right. (*Without looking up, he passes another batch of papers to Sergius.*)

SERGIUS (*also excited*). Bravo, Switzerland! Major: I bet my best charger against an Arab mare for Raina that Nicola finds the coat in the blue closet.

PETKOFF (*eagerly*). Your best char—

CATHERINE (*hastily interrupting him*). Don't be foolish, Paul. An Arabian mare will cost you 50,000 levas.

RAINA (*suddenly coming out of her picturesque revery*). Really, mother, if you are going to take the jewelry, I don't see why you should grudge me my Arab.

(*Nicola comes back with the coat and brings it to Petkoff, who can hardly believe his eyes.*)

CATHERINE. Where was it, Nicola?

NICOLA. Hanging in the blue closet, madam.

PETKOFF. Well, I am d—

CATHERINE (*stopping him*). Paul!

PETKOFF. I could have sworn it wasn't there. Age is beginning to tell on me. I'm getting hallucinations. (*to Nicola*) Here: help me to change. Excuse me, Bluntschli. (*He begins changing coats, Nicola acting as valet.*) Remember: I didn't take that bet of yours, Sergius. You'd better give Raina that Arab steed yourself, since you've roused her expectations. Eh, Raina? (*He looks round at her; but she is again rapt in the landscape. With a little gush of paternal affection and pride, he points her out to them and says*) She's dreaming, as usual.

SERGIUS. Assuredly she shall not be the loser.

PETKOFF. So much the better for her. *I* shan't come off so cheap, I expect. (*The change is now complete. Nicola goes out with the discarded coat.*) Ah, now I feel at home at last. (*He sits down and takes his newspaper with a grunt of relief.*)

BLUNTSCHLI (*to Sergius, handing a paper*). That's the last order.

PETKOFF (*jumping up*). What! finished?

BLUNTSCHLI. Finished. (*Petkoff goes beside Sergius; looks curiously over his left shoulder as he signs; and says with childlike envy*) Haven't you anything for me to sign?

BLUNTSCHLI. Not necessary. His signature will do.

PETKOFF. Ah, well, I think we've done a thundering good day's work. (*He goes away from the table.*) Can I do anything more?

BLUNTSCHLI. You had better both see the fellows that are to take these. (*to Sergius*) Pack them off at once; and show them that I've marked on the orders the time they should hand them in by. Tell them that if they stop to drink or tell stories—if they're five minutes late, they'll have the skin taken off their backs.

SERGIUS (*rising indignantly*). I'll say so. And if one of them is man enough to spit in my face for insulting him, I'll buy his discharge and give him a pension. (*He strides out, his humanity deeply outraged.*)

BLUNTSCHLI (*confidentially*). Just see that that he talks to them properly, Major, will you?

PETKOFF (*officiously*). Quite right, Bluntschli, quite right. I'll see to it. (*He goes to the door importantly, but hesitates on the threshold.*) By the bye, Catherine, you may as well come, too. They'll be far more frightened of you than of me.

CATHERINE (*putting down her embroidery*). I daresay I had better. You will only splutter at them. (*She goes out, Petkoff holding the door for her and following her.*)

BLUNTSCHLI. What a country! They make cannons out of cherry trees; and the officers send for their wives to keep discipline! (*He begins to fold and docket the papers. Raina, who has risen from the divan, strolls down the room with her hands clasped behind her, and looks mischievously at him.*)

RAINA. You look ever so much nicer than when we last met. (*He looks up, surprised.*) What have you done to yourself?

BLUNTSCHLI. Washed; brushed; good night's sleep and breakfast. That's all.

RAINA. Did you get back safely that morning?

BLUNTSCHLI. Quite, thanks.

RAINA. Were they angry with you for running away from Sergius's charge?

BLUNTSCHLI. No, they were glad; because they'd all just run away themselves.

RAINA (*going to the table, and leaning over it towards him*). It must have made a lovely story for them—all that about me and my room.

BLUNTSCHLI. Capital story. But I only told it to one of them—a particular friend.

RAINA. On whose discretion you could absolutely rely?

BLUNTSCHLI. Absolutely.

RAINA. Hm! He told it all to my father and Sergius the day you exchanged the prisoners. (*She turns away and strolls carelessly across to the other side of the room.*)

BLUNTSCHLI (*deeply concerned and half incredulous*). No! you don't mean that, do you?

RAINA (*turning, with sudden earnestness*). I do indeed. But they don't know that it was in this house that you hid. If Sergius knew, he would challenge you and kill you in a duel.

BLUNTSCHLI. Bless me! then don't tell him.

RAINA (*full of reproach for his levity*). Can you realize what it is to me to deceive him? I want to be quite perfect with Sergius —no meanness, no smallness, no deceit. My relation to him is the one really beautiful and noble part of my life. I hope you can understand that.

BLUNTSCHLI (*skeptically*). You mean that you wouldn't like him to find out that the story about the ice pudding was a—a—a— You know.

RAINA (*wincing*). Ah, don't talk of it in that flippant way. I lied: I know it. But I did it to save your life. He would have killed you. That was the second time I ever uttered a falsehood. (*Bluntschli rises quickly and looks doubtfully and somewhat severely at her.*) Do you remember the first time?

BLUNTSCHLI. I! No. Was I present?

RAINA. Yes; and I told the officer who was searching for you that you were not present.

BLUNTSCHLI. True. I should have remembered it.

RAINA (*greatly encouraged*). Ah, it is natural that you should forget it first. It cost you nothing: it cost me a lie!—a lie! ! (*She sits down on the ottoman, looking straight before her with her hands clasped on her knee. Bluntschli, quite touched, goes to the ottoman with a particularly reassuring and considerate air, and sits down beside her.*)

BLUNTSCHLI. My dear young lady, don't let this worry you. Remember: I'm a soldier. Now what are the two things that happen to a soldier so often that he comes to think nothing of them? One is hearing people tell lies (*Raina recoils*): the other is getting his life saved in all sorts of ways by all sorts of people.

RAINA (*rising in indignant protest*). And so he becomes a creature incapable of faith and of gratitude.

BLUNTSCHLI (*making a wry face*). Do you like gratitude? I don't. If pity is akin to love, gratitude is akin to the other thing.

RAINA. Gratitude! (*turning on him*) If you are incapable of gratitude you are incapable of any noble sentiment. Even animals are grateful. Oh, I see now exactly what you think of me! You were not surprised to hear me lie. To you it was something I probably did every day—every hour. That is how men think of women. (*She walks up the room melodramatically.*)

BLUNTSCHLI (*dubiously*). There's reason in everything. You said you'd told only two lies in your whole life. Dear young lady: isn't that rather a short allowance? I'm quite a straightforward man myself; but it wouldn't last me a whole morning.

RAINA (*staring haughtily at him*). Do you know, sir, that you are insulting me?

BLUNTSCHLI. I can't help it. When you get into that noble attitude and speak in that thrilling voice, I admire you; but I find it impossible to believe a single word you say.

RAINA (*superbly*). Captain Bluntschli!

BLUNTSCHLI (*unmoved*). Yes?

RAINA (*coming a little towards him, as if she could not believe her senses*). Do you mean what you said just now? Do you know what you said just now?

BLUNTSCHLI. I do.

RAINA (*gasping*). I! I!!! (*She points to herself incredulously, meaning "I, Raina Petkoff, tell lies!" He meets her gaze unflinchingly. She suddenly sits down beside him, and adds, with a complete change of manner from the heroic to the familiar*) How did you find me out?

BLUNTSCHLI (*promptly*). Instinct, dear young lady. Instinct, and experience of the world.

RAINA (*wonderingly*). Do you know, you are the first man I ever met who did not take me seriously?

BLUNTSCHLI. You mean, don't you, that I am the first man that has ever taken you quite seriously?

RAINA. Yes, I suppose I do mean that. (*cosily, quite at her ease with him*) How strange it is to be talked to in such a way! You know, I've always gone on like that— I mean the noble attitude and the thrilling voice. I did it when I was a tiny child to my nurse. She believed in it. I do it before my parents. They believe in it. I do it before Sergius. He believes in it.

BLUNTSCHLI. Yes: he's a little in that line himself, isn't he?

RAINA (*startled*). Do you think so?

BLUNTSCHLI. You know him better than I do.

RAINA. I wonder—I wonder is he? If I thought that—! (*discouraged*) Ah, well, what does it matter? I suppose, now that you've found me out, you despise me.

BLUNTSCHLI (*warmly, rising*). No, my dear young lady, no, no, no a thousand times. It's part of your youth—part of your charm. I'm like all the rest of them—the nurse—your parents—Sergius: I'm your infatuated admirer.

RAINA (*pleased*). Really?

BLUNTSCHLI (*slapping his breast smartly with his hand, German fashion*). Hand aufs Herz! Really and truly.

RAINA (*very happy*). But what did you

think of me for giving you my portrait?

BLUNTSCHLI (*astonished*). Your portrait! You never gave me your portrait.

RAINA (*quickly*). Do you mean to say you never got it?

BLUNTSCHLI. No. (*He sits down beside her, with renewed interest, and says, with some complacency*) When did you send it to me?

RAINA (*indignantly*). I did not send it to you. (*She turns her head away, and adds, reluctantly*) It was in the pocket of that coat.

BLUNTSCHLI (*pursing his lips and rounding his eyes*). Oh-o-oh! I never found it. It must be there still.

RAINA (*springing up*). There still!—for my father to find the first time he puts his hand in his pocket! Oh, how could you be so stupid?

BLUNTSCHLI (*rising also*). It doesn't matter: it's only a photograph: how can he tell who it was intended for? Tell him he put it there himself.

RAINA (*impatiently*). Yes, that is so clever —so clever! What shall I do?

BLUNTSCHLI. Ah, I see. You wrote something on it. That was rash!

RAINA (*annoyed almost to tears*). Oh, to have done such a thing for you, who care no more—except to laugh at me—oh! Are you sure nobody has touched it?

BLUNTSCHLI. Well, I can't be quite sure. You see I couldn't carry it about with me all the time: one can't take much luggage on active service.

RAINA. What did you do with it?

BLUNTSCHLI. When I got through to Peerot I had to put it in safe keeping somehow. I thought of the railway cloak room; but that's the surest place to get looted in modern warfare. So I pawned it.

RAINA. Pawned it! ! !

BLUNTSCHLI. I know it doesn't sound nice; but it was much the safest plan. I redeemed it the day before yesterday. Heaven only knows whether the pawnbroker cleared out the pockets or not.

RAINA (*furious—throwing the words right into his face*). You have a low, shopkeeping mind. You think of things that would never come into a gentleman's head.

BLUNTSCHLI (*phlegmatically*). That's the Swiss national character, dear lady.

RAINA. Oh, I wish I had never met you. (*She flounces away and sits at the window fuming.*)

(*Louka comes in with a heap of letters and telegrams on her salver, and crosses, with her bold, free gait, to the table. Her left sleeve is looped up to the shoulder with a brooch, showing her naked arm, with a broad gilt bracelet covering the bruise.*)

LOUKA (*to Bluntschli*). For you. (*She empties the salver recklessly on the table.*) The messenger is waiting. (*She is determined not to be civil to a Servian, even if she must bring him his letters.*)

BLUNTSCHLI (*to Raina*). Will you excuse me: the last postal delivery that reached me was three weeks ago. These are the subsequent accumulations. Four telegrams—a week old. (*He opens one.*) Oho! Bad news!

RAINA (*rising and advancing a little remorsefully*). Bad news?

BLUNTSCHLI. My father's dead. (*He looks at the telegram with his lips pursed, musing on the unexpected change in his arrangements.*)

RAINA. Oh, how very sad!

BLUNTSCHLI. Yes: I shall have to start for home in an hour. He has left a lot of big hotels behind him to be looked after. (*Takes up a heavy letter in a long blue envelope.*) Here's a whacking letter from the family solicitor. (*He pulls out the enclosures and glances over them.*) Great Heavens! Seventy! Two hundred! (*In a crescendo of dismay.*) Four hundred! Four thousand! Nine thousand six hundred! ! ! What on earth shall I do with them all?

RAINA (*timidly*). Nine thousand hotels?

BLUNTSCHLI. Hotels! Nonsense. If you only knew!—oh, it's too ridiculous! Excuse me: I must give my fellow orders about starting. (*He leaves the room hastily, with the documents in his hand.*)

LOUKA (*tauntingly*). He has not much heart, that Swiss, though he is so fond of the Servians. He has not a word of grief for his poor father.

RAINA (*bitterly*). Grief!—a man who has been doing nothing but killing people for years! What does he care? What does any soldier care? (*She goes to the door, evidently restraining her tears with difficulty.*)

LOUKA. Major Saranoff has been fighting, too; and he has plenty of heart left. (*Raina, at the door, looks haughtily at her and goes out.*) Aha! I thought you wouldn't get much feeling out of your soldier. (*She is following Raina when Nicola enters with an armful of logs for the fire.*)

NICOLA (*grinning amorously at her*). I've been trying all the afternoon to get a minute alone with you, my girl. (*His countenance changes as he notices her arm.*) Why, what fashion is that of wearing your sleeve, child?

LOUKA (*proudly*). My own fashion.

NICOLA. Indeed! If the mistress catches you, she'll talk to you. (*He throws the logs down on the ottoman, and sits comfortably beside them.*)

LOUKA. Is that any reason why you should take it on yourself to talk to me?

NICOLA. Come: don't be so contrary with me. I've some good news for you. (*He takes out some paper money. Louka, with an eager gleam in her eyes, comes close to look at it.*) See, a twenty leva bill! Sergius gave me that out of pure swagger. A fool and his money are soon parted. There's ten levas more. The Swiss gave me that for backing up the mistress's and Raina's lies about him. He's no fool, he isn't. You should have heard old Catherine downstairs as polite as you please to me, telling me not to mind the Major being a little impatient; for they knew what a good servant I was—after making a fool and a liar of me before them all! The twenty will go to our savings; and you shall have the ten to spend if you'll only talk to me so as to remind me I'm a human being. I get tired of being a servant occasionally.

LOUKA (*scornfully*). Yes: sell your manhood for thirty levas, and buy me for ten! Keep your money. You were born to be a servant. I was not. When you set up your shop you will only be everybody's servant instead of somebody's servant.

NICOLA (*picking up his logs, and going to the stove*). Ah, wait till you see. We shall have our evenings to ourselves; and I shall be master in my own house, I promise you. (*He throws the logs down and kneels at the stove.*)

LOUKA. You shall never be master in mine. (*She sits down on Sergius's chair.*)

NICOLA (*turning, still on his knees, and squatting down rather forlornly, on his calves, daunted by her implacable disdain*). You have a great ambition in you, Louka. Remember: if any luck comes to you, it was I that made a woman of you.

LOUKA. You!

NICOLA (*with dogged self-assertion*). Yes, me. Who was it made you give up wearing a couple of pounds of false black hair on your head and reddening your lips and cheeks like any other Bulgarian girl? I did. Who taught you to trim your nails, and keep your hands clean, and be dainty about yourself, like a fine Russian lady? Me! do you hear that? me! (*She tosses her head defiantly; and he rises, ill-humoredly, adding more coolly*) I've often thought that if Raina were out of the way, and you just a little less of a fool and Sergius just a little more of one, you might come to be one of my grandest customers, instead of only being my wife and costing me money.

LOUKA. I believe you would rather be my servant than my husband. You would make more out of me. Oh, I know that soul of yours.

NICOLA (*going up close to her for greater emphasis*). Never you mind my soul; but just listen to my advice. If you want to be a lady, your present behavior to me won't do at all, unless when we're alone. It's too sharp and impudent; and impudence is a sort of familiarity: it shows affection for me. And don't you try being high and mighty with me either. You're like all country girls: you think it's genteel to treat a servant the way I treat a stable-boy. That's only your ignorance; and don't you forget it. And don't be so ready to defy everybody. Act as if you expected to have your own way, not as if you expected to be ordered about. The way to get on as a lady is the same as the way to get on as a servant: you've got to know your place; that's the secret of it. And you may depend on me to know my place if you get promoted. Think over it, my girl. I'll stand by you: one servant should always stand by another.

LOUKA (*rising impatiently*). Oh, I must behave in my own way. You take all the courage out of me with your cold-blooded wisdom. Go and put those logs on the fire: that's the sort of thing you understand. (*Before Nicola can retort, Sergius comes in. He checks himself a moment on seeing Louka; then goes to the stove.*)

SERGIUS (*to Nicola*). I am not in the way of your work, I hope.

NICOLA (*in a smooth, elderly manner*). Oh, no, sir, thank you kindly. I was only speaking to this foolish girl about her habit of running up here to the library whenever she gets a chance, to look at the books. That's the worst of her education, sir: it gives her habits above her station. (*to Louka*) Make that table tidy, Louka, for the Major. (*He goes out sedately.*)

(*Louka, without looking at Sergius, begins to arrange the papers on the table. He crosses slowly to her, and studies the arrangement of her sleeve reflectively.*)

SERGIUS. Let me see: is there a mark there? (*He turns up the bracelet and sees the bruise made by his grasp. She stands motionless, not looking at him: fascinated, but on her guard.*) Ffff! Does it hurt?

LOUKA. Yes.

SERGIUS. Shall I cure it?

LOUKA (*instantly withdrawing herself proudly, but still not looking at him*). No. You cannot cure it now.

SERGIUS (*masterfully*). Quite sure? (*He makes a movement as if to take her in his arms.*)

LOUKA. Don't trifle with me, please. An officer should not trifle with a servant.

SERGIUS (*touching the arm with a merciless stroke of his forefinger*). That was no trifle, Louka.

LOUKA. No. (*looking at him for the first time.*) Are you sorry?

SERGIUS (*with measured emphasis, folding his arms*). I am never sorry.

LOUKA (*wistfully*). I wish I could believe a man could be so unlike a woman as that. I wonder are you really a brave man?

SERGIUS (*unaffectedly, relaxing his attitude*). Yes: I am a brave man. My heart jumped like a woman's at the first shot; but in the charge I found that I was brave. Yes: that at least is real about me.

LOUKA. Did you find in the charge that the men whose fathers are poor like mine were any less brave than the men who are rich like you?

SERGIUS (*with bitter levity*). Not a bit. They all slashed and cursed and yelled like heroes. Psha! the courage to rage and kill is cheap. I have an English bull terrier who has as much of that sort of courage as the whole Bulgarian nation, and the whole Russian nation at its back. But he lets my groom thrash him, all the same. That's your soldier all over! No, Louka, your poor men can cut throats; but they are afraid of their officers; they put up with insults and blows; they stand by and see one another punished like children—aye, and help to do it when they are ordered. And the officers!—well (*with a short, bitter laugh*) *I* am an officer. Oh (*fervently*) give me the man who will defy to the death any power on earth or in heaven that sets itself up against his own will and conscience: he alone is the brave man.

LOUKA. How easy it is to talk! Men never seem to me to grow up: they all have schoolboy's ideas. You don't know what true courage is.

SERGIUS (*ironically*). Indeed! I am willing to be instructed.

LOUKA. Look at me! how much am I allowed to have my own will? I have to get your room ready for you—to sweep and dust, to fetch and carry. How could that degrade me if it did not degrade you to have it done for you? But (*with subdued passion*) if I were Empress of Russia, above everyone in the world, then—ah, then, though according to you I could show no courage at all; you should see, you should see.

SERGIUS. What would you do, most noble Empress?

LOUKA. I would marry the man I loved, which no other queen in Europe has the courage to do. If I loved you, though you would be as far beneath me as I am beneath you, I would dare to be the equal of my inferior. Would you dare as much if you loved me? No: if you felt the beginnings of love for me you would not let it grow. You dare not: you would marry a rich man's daughter because you would be afraid of what other people would say of you.

SERGIUS (*carried away*). You lie: it is not so, by all the stars! If I loved you, and I were the Czar himself, I would set you on the throne by my side. You know that I love another woman, a woman as high above you as heaven is above earth. And you are jealous of her.

LOUKA. I have no reason to be. She will never marry you now. The man I told you of has come back. She will marry the Swiss.

SERGIUS (*recoiling*). The Swiss!

LOUKA. A man worth ten of you. Then you can come to me; and I will refuse you. You are not good enough for me. (*She turns to the door.*)

SERGIUS (*springing after her and catching her fiercely in his arms*). I will kill the Swiss; and afterwards I will do as I please with you.

LOUKA (*in his arms, passive and steadfast*). The Swiss will kill you, perhaps. He has beaten you in love. He may beat you in war.

SERGIUS (*tormentedly*). Do you think I believe that she—she! whose worst thoughts are higher than your best ones, is capable of trifling with another man behind my back?

LOUKA. Do you think she would believe the Swiss if he told her now that I am in your arms?

SERGIUS (*releasing her in despair*). Damnation! Oh, damnation! Mockery, mockery everywhere: everything I think is mocked by everything I do. (*He strikes himself frantically on the breast.*) Coward, liar, fool! Shall I kill myself like a man, or live and pretend to laugh at myself? (*She again turns to go.*) Louka! (*She stops near the door.*) Remember: you belong to me.

LOUKA (*quietly*). What does that mean—an insult?

SERGIUS (*commandingly*). It means that you love me, and that I have had you here in my arms, and will perhaps have you there again. Whether that is an insult I neither know nor care: take it as you please. But (*vehemently*) I will not be a coward and a trifler. If I choose to love you, I dare marry you, in spite of all Bulgaria. If these hands ever touch you again, they shall touch my affianced bride.

LOUKA. We shall see whether you dare keep your word. But take care. I will not wait long.

SERGIUS (*again folding his arms and standing motionless in the middle of the room*). Yes, we shall see. And you shall wait my pleasure.

(*Bluntschli, much preoccupied, with his papers still in his hand, enters, leaving the door open for Louka to go out. He goes across to the table, glancing at her as he passes. Sergius, without altering his resolute attitude, watches him steadily. Louka goes out, leaving the door open.*)

BLUNTSCHLI (*absently, sitting at the table as before, and putting down his papers*). That's a remarkable looking young woman.

SERGIUS (*gravely, without moving*). Captain Bluntschli.

BLUNTSCHLI. Eh?

SERGIUS. You have deceived me. You are my rival. I brook no rivals. At six o'clock

I shall be in the drilling-ground on the Klissoura road, alone, on horseback, with my saber. Do you understand?

BLUNTSCHLI (*staring, but sitting quite at his ease*). Oh, thank you: that's a cavalry man's proposal. I'm in the artillery; and I have the choice of weapons. If I go, I shall take a machine gun. And there shall be no mistake about the cartridges this time.

SERGIUS (*flushing, but with deadly coldness*). Take care, sir. It is not our custom in Bulgaria to allow invitations of that kind to be trifled with.

BLUNTSCHLI (*warmly*). Pooh! don't talk to me about Bulgaria. You don't know what fighting is. But have it your own way. Bring your saber along. I'll meet you.

SERGIUS (*fiercely delighted to find his opponent a man of spirit*). Well said, Switzer. Shall I lend you my best horse?

BLUNTSCHLI. No: damn your horse!— thank you all the same, my dear fellow. (*Raina comes in, and hears the next sentence.*) I shall fight you on foot. Horseback's too dangerous: I don't want to kill you if I can help it.

RAINA (*hurrying forward anxiously*). I have heard what Captain Bluntschli said, Sergius. You are going to fight. Why? (*Sergius turns away in silence, and goes to the stove, where he stands watching her as she continues, to Bluntschli*) What about?

BLUNTSCHLI. I don't know: he hasn't told me. Better not interfere, dear young lady. No harm will be done: I've often acted as sword instructor. He won't be able to touch me; and I'll not hurt him. It will save explanations. In the morning I shall be off home; and you'll never see me or hear of me again. You and he will then make it up and live happily ever after.

RAINA (*turning away deeply hurt, almost with a sob in her voice*). I never said I wanted to see you again.

SERGIUS (*striding forward*). Ha! That is a confession.

RAINA (*haughtily*). What do you mean?
SERGIUS. You love that man!

RAINA (*scandalized*). Sergius!

SERGIUS. You allow him to make love to you behind my back, just as you accept me as your affianced husband behind his. Bluntschli: you knew our relations; and you deceived me. It is for that that I call you to account, not for having received favors that I never enjoyed.

BLUNTSCHLI (*jumping up indignantly*). Stuff! Rubbish! I have received no favors. Why, the young lady doesn't even know whether I'm married or not.

RAINA (*forgetting herself*). Oh! (*collapsing on the ottoman*) Are you?

SERGIUS. You see the young lady's concern, Captain Bluntschli. Denial is useless. You have enjoyed the privilege of being received in her own room, late at night—

BLUNTSCHLI (*interrupting him pepperily*). Yes; you blockhead! She received me with a pistol at her head. Your cavalry were at my heels. I'd have blown out her brains if she'd uttered a cry.

SERGIUS (*taken aback*). Bluntschli! Raina: is this true?

RAINA (*rising in wrathful majesty*). Oh, how dare you, how dare you?

BLUNTSCHLI. Apologize, man, apologize! (*He resumes his seat at the table.*)

SERGIUS (*with the old measured emphasis, folding his arms*). I never apologize.

RAINA (*passionately*). This is the doing of that friend of yours, Captain Bluntschli. It is he who is spreading this horrible story about me. (*She walks about excitedly.*)

BLUNTSCHLI. No: he's dead—burnt alive.

RAINA (*stopping, shocked*). Burnt alive!

BLUNTSCHLI. Shot in the hip in a woodyard. Couldn't drag himself out. Your fellows' shells set the timber on fire and burnt him, with half a dozen other poor devils in the same predicament.

RAINA. How horrible!

SERGIUS. And how ridiculous! Oh, war! war! the dream of patriots and heroes! A fraud, Bluntschli, a hollow sham, like love.

RAINA (*outraged*). Like love! You say that before me.

BLUNTSCHLI. Come, Saranoff: that matter is explained.

SERGIUS. A hollow sham, I say. Would you have come back here if nothing had passed between you, except at the muzzle of your pistol? Raina is mistaken about our friend who was burnt. He was not my informant.

RAINA. Who then? (*suddenly guessing the truth*) Ah, Louka! my maid, my servant! You were with her this morning all that time after—after— Oh, what sort of god is this I have been worshiping! (*He meets her gaze with sardonic enjoyment of her disenchantment. Angered all the more, she goes closer to him, and says, in a lower, intenser tone*) Do you know that I looked out of the window as I went upstairs, to have another sight of my hero; and I saw something that I did not understand then. I know now that you were making love to her.

SERGIUS (*with grim humor*). You saw that?

RAINA. Only too well. (*She turns away, and throws herself on the divan under the center window, quite overcome.*)

SERGIUS (*cynically*). Raina: our romance is shattered. Life's a farce.

BLUNTSCHLI (*to Raina, good humoredly*). You see: he's found himself out now.

SERGIUS. Bluntschli: I have allowed you to call me a blockhead. You may now call me a coward as well. I refuse to fight you. Do you know why?

BLUNTSCHLI. No; but it doesn't matter. I didn't ask the reason when you cried on; and I don't ask the reason now that you cry off. I'm a professional soldier. I fight when I have to, and am very glad to get out of it when I haven't to. You're only an amateur: you think fighting's an amusement.

SERGIUS. You shall hear the reason all the same, my professional. The reason is that it takes two men—real men—men of heart, blood and honor—to make a genuine combat. I could no more fight with you than I could make love to an ugly woman. You've no magnetism: you're not a man, you're a machine.

BLUNTSCHLI (*apologetically*). Quite true, quite true. I always was that sort of chap. I'm very sorry. But now that you've found that life isn't a farce, but something quite sensible and serious, what further obstacle is there to your happiness?

RAINA (*rising*). You are very solicitous about my happiness and his. Do you forget his new love—Louka? It is not you that he must fight now, but his rival, Nicola.

SERGIUS. Rival!! (*striking his forehead*)

RAINA. Did you not know that they are engaged?

SERGIUS. Nicola! Are fresh abysses opening! Nicola! !

RAINA (*sarcastically*). A shocking sacrifice, isn't it? Such beauty, such intellect, such modesty, wasted on a middle-aged servant man! Really, Sergius, you cannot stand by and allow such a thing. It would be unworthy of your chivalry.

SERGIUS (*losing all self-control*). Viper! Viper! (*He rushes to and fro, raging.*)

BLUNTSCHLI. Look here, Saranoff; you're getting the worst of this.

RAINA (*getting angrier*). Do you realize what he has done, Captain Bluntschli? He has set this girl as a spy on us; and her reward is that he makes love to her.

SERGIUS. False! Monstrous!

RAINA. Monstrous! (*confronting him*) Do you deny that she told you about Captain Bluntschli being in my room?

SERGIUS. No; but—

RAINA. (*interrupting*). Do you deny that you were making love to her when she told you?

SERGIUS. No; but I tell you—

RAINA (*cutting him short contemptuously*). It is unnecessary to tell us anything more. That is quite enough for us. (*She turns her back on him and sweeps majestically back to the window.*)

BLUNTSCHLI (*quietly, as Sergius, in an agony of mortification, sinks on the ottoman, clutching his averted head between his fists*).

I told you you were getting the worst of it, Saranoff.

SERGIUS. Tiger cat!

RAINA (*running excitedly to Bluntschli*). You hear this man calling me names, Captain Bluntschli?

BLUNTSCHLI. What else can he do, dear lady? He must defend himself somehow. Come (*very persuasively*), don't quarrel. What good does it do? (*Raina, with a gasp, sits down on the ottoman, and after a vain effort to look vexedly at Bluntschli, she falls a victim to her sense of humor, and is attacked with a disposition to laugh.*)

SERGIUS. Engaged to Nicola! (*He rises.*) Ha! ha! (*going to the stove and standing with his back to it*) Ah, well, Bluntschli, you are right to take this huge imposture of a world coolly.

RAINA (*to Bluntschli with an intuitive guess of his state of mind*). I daresay you think us a couple of grown up babies, don't you?

SERGIUS (*grinning a little*). He does, he does. Swiss civilization nursetending Bulgarian barbarism, eh?

BLUNTSCHLI (*blushing*). Not at all, I assure you. I'm only very glad to get you two quieted. There now, let's be pleasant and talk it over in a friendly way. Where is this other young lady?

RAINA. Listening at the door, probably.

SERGIUS (*shivering as if a bullet had struck him, and speaking with quiet but deep indignation*). I will prove that that, at least, is a calumny. (*He goes with dignity to the door and opens it. A yell of fury bursts from him as he looks out. He darts into the passage, and returns dragging in Louka, whom he flings against the table, R., as he cries*) Judge her, Bluntschli—you, the moderate, cautious man: judge the eavesdropper.

(*Louka stands her ground, proud and silent.*)

BLUNTSCHLI (*shaking his head*). I mustn't judge her. I once listened myself outside a tent when there was a mutiny brewing. It's

all a question of the degree of provocation. My life was at stake.

LOUKA. My love was at stake. (*Sergius flinches, ashamed of her in spite of himself.*) I am not ashamed.

RAINA (*contemptuously*). Your love! Your curiosity, you mean.

LOUKA (*facing her and retorting her contempt with interest*). My love, stronger than anything you can feel, even for your chocolate cream soldier.

SERGIUS (*with quick suspicion—to Louka*). What does that mean?

LOUKA (*fiercely*). It means—

SERGIUS (*interrupting her slightingly*). Oh, I remember, the ice pudding. A paltry taunt, girl.

(*Major Petkoff enters, in his shirtsleeves.*)

PETKOFF. Excuse my shirtsleeves, gentlemen. Raina: somebody has been wearing that coat of mine: I'll swear it—somebody with bigger shoulders than mine. It's all burst open at the back. Your mother is mending it. I wish she'd make haste. I shall catch cold. (*He looks more attentively at them.*) Is anything the matter?

RAINA. No. (*She sits down at the stove with a tranquil air.*)

SERGIUS. Oh, no! (*He sits down at the end of the table, as at first.*)

BLUNTSCHLI (*who is already seated*). Nothing, nothing.

PETKOFF (*sitting down on the ottoman in his old place*). That's all right. (*He notices Louka.*) Anything the matter, Louka?

LOUKA. No, sir.

PETKOFF (*genially*). That's all right. (*He sneezes.*) Go and ask your mistress for my coat, like a good girl, will you? (*She turns to obey; but Nicola enters with the coat; and she makes a pretense of having business in the room by taking the little table with the hookah away to the wall near the windows.*)

RAINA (*rising quickly, as she sees the coat on Nicola's arm*). Here it is, papa. Give it to me, Nicola; and do you put some more wood on the fire. (*She takes the coat, and brings it to the Major, who stands up to put it on. Nicola attends to the fire.*)

PETKOFF (*to Raina, teasing her affectionately*). Aha! Going to be very good to poor old papa just for one day after his return from the wars, eh?

RAINA (*with solemn reproach*). Ah, how can you say that to me, father?

PETKOFF. Well, well, only a joke, little one. Come, give me a kiss. (*She kisses him.*) Now give me the coat.

RAINA. Now, I am going to put it on for you. Turn your back. (*He turns his back and feels behind him with his arms for the sleeves. She dexterously takes the photograph from the pocket and throws it on the table before Bluntschli, who covers it with a sheet of paper under the very nose of Sergius, who looks on amazed, with his suspicions roused in the highest degree. She then helps Petkoff on with his coat.*) There, dear! Now are you comfortable?

PETKOFF. Quite, little love. Thanks. (*He sits down; and Raina returns to her seat near the stove.*) Oh, by the bye, I've found something funny. What's the meaning of this? (*He puts his hand into the picked pocket.*) Eh? Hallo! (*He tries the other pocket.*) Well, I could have sworn—(*Much puzzled, he tries the breast pocket.*) I wonder —(*Tries the original pocket.*) Where can it—(*A light flashes on him; he rises, exclaiming*) Your mother's taken it.

RAINA (*very red*). Taken what?

PETKOFF. Your photograph, with the inscription: "Raina, to her Chocolate Cream Soldier—a souvenir." Now you know there's something more in this than meets the eye; and I'm going to find it out. (*shouting*) Nicola!

NICOLA (*dropping a log, and turning*). Sir!

PETKOFF. Did you spoil any pastry of Miss Raina's this morning?

NICOLA. You heard Miss Raina say that I did, sir.

PETKOFF. I know that, you idiot. Was it true?

NICOLA. I am sure Miss Raina is incapable of saying anything that is not true, sir.

PETKOFF. Are you? Then I'm not. (*turning to the others*) Come: do you think I don't see it all? (*Goes to Sergius, and slaps him on the shoulder.*) Sergius: you're the chocolate cream soldier, aren't you?

SERGIUS (*starting up*). I! a chocolate cream soldier! Certainly not.

PETKOFF. Not! (*He looks at them. They are all very serious and very conscious.*) Do you mean to tell me that Raina sends photographic souvenirs to other men?

SERGIUS (*enigmatically*). The world is not such an innocent place as we used to think, Petkoff.

BLUNTSCHLI (*rising*). It's all right, Major. I'm the chocolate cream soldier. (*Petkoff and Sergius are equally astonished.*) The gracious young lady saved my life by giving me chocolate creams when I was starving— shall I ever forget their flavor! My late friend Stolz told you the story at Peerot. I was the fugitive.

PETKOFF. You! (*He gasps.*) Sergius: do you remember how those two women went on this morning when we mentioned it? (*Sergius smiles cynically. Petkoff confronts Raina severely.*) You're a nice young woman, aren't you?

RAINA (*bitterly*). Major Saranoff has changed his mind. And when I wrote that on the photograph, I did not know that Captain Bluntschli was married.

BLUNTSCHLI (*much startled—protesting vehemently*). I'm not married.

RAINA (*with deep reproach*). You said you were.

BLUNTSCHLI. I did not. I positively did not. I never was married in my life.

PETKOFF (*exasperated*). Raina: will you kindly inform me, if I am not asking too much, which gentleman you are engaged to?

RAINA. To neither of them. This young lady (*introducing Louka, who faces them all *proudly*) is the object of Major Saranoff's affections at present.

PETKOFF. Louka! Are you mad, Sergius? Why, this girl's engaged to Nicola.

NICOLA (*coming forward*). I beg your pardon sir. There is a mistake. Louka is not engaged to me.

PETKOFF. Not engaged to you, you scoundrel! Why, you had twenty-five levas from me on the day of your betrothal; and she had that gilt bracelet from Miss Raina.

NICOLA (*with cool unction*). We gave it out so, sir. But it was only to give Louka protection. She had a soul above her station; and I have been no more than her confidential servant. I intend, as you know, sir, to set up a shop later on in Sofia; and I look forward to her custom and recommendation should she marry into the nobility. (*He goes out with impressive discretion, leaving them all staring after him.*)

PETKOFF (*breaking the silence*). Well, I am—hm!

SERGIUS. This is either the finest heroism or the most crawling baseness. Which is it, Bluntschli?

BLUNTSCHLI. Never mind whether it's heroism or baseness. Nicola's the ablest man I've met in Bulgaria. I'll make him manager of a hotel if he can speak French and German.

LOUKA (*suddenly breaking out at Sergius*). I have been insulted by everyone here. You set them the example. You owe me an apology. (*Sergius immediately, like a repeating clock of which the spring has been touched, begins to fold his arms.*)

BLUNTSCHLI (*before he can speak*). It's no use. He never apologizes.

LOUKA. Not to you, his equal and his enemy. To me, his poor servant, he will not refuse to apologize.

SERGIUS (*approvingly*). You are right. (*He bends his knee in his grandest manner.*) Forgive me!

LOUKA. I forgive you. (*She timidly gives him her hand, which he kisses.*) That touch makes me your affianced wife.

SERGIUS (*springing up*). Ah, I forgot that!

LOUKA (*coldly*). You can withdraw if you like.

SERGIUS. Withdraw! Never! You belong to me! (*He puts his arm about her and draws her to him.*)

(*Catherine comes in and finds Louka in Sergius's arms, and all the rest gazing at them in bewildered astonishment.*)

CATHERINE. What does this mean? (*Sergius releases Louka.*)

PETKOFF. Well, my dear, it appears that Sergius is going to marry Louka instead of Raina. (*She is about to break out indignantly at him: he stops her by exclaiming testily*) Don't blame me: I've nothing to do with it. (*He retreats to the stove.*)

CATHERINE. Marry Louka! Sergius: you are bound by your word to us!

SERGIUS (*folding his arms*). Nothing binds me.

BLUNTSCHLI (*much pleased by this piece of common sense*). Saranoff: your hand. My congratulations. These heroics of yours have their practical side after all. (*To Louka.*) Gracious young lady: the best wishes of a good Republican! (*He kisses her hand, to Raina's great disgust.*)

CATHERINE (*threateningly*). Louka: you have been telling stories.

LOUKA. I have done Raina no harm.

CATHERINE (*haughtily*). Raina! (*Raina is equally indignant at the liberty.*)

LOUKA. I have a right to call her Raina: she calls me Louka. I told Major Saranoff she would never marry him if the Swiss gentleman came back.

BLUNTSCHLI (*surprised*). Hallo!

LOUKA (*turning to Raina*). I thought you were fonder of him than of Sergius. You know best whether I was right.

BLUNTSCHLI. What nonsense! I assure you, my dear Major, my dear Madame, the gracious young lady simply saved my life, nothing else. She never cared two straws for me. Why, bless my heart and soul, look at the young lady and look at me. She, rich, young, beautiful, with her imagination full of fairy princes and noble natures and cavalry charges and goodness knows what! And I, a commonplace Swiss soldier who hardly knows what a decent life is after fifteen years of barracks and battles—a vagabond—a man who has spoiled all his chances in life through an incurably romantic disposition—a man—

SERGIUS (*starting as if a needle had pricked him and interrupting Bluntschli in incredulous amazement*). Excuse me, Bluntschli: what did you say had spoiled your chances in life?

BLUNTSCHLI (*promptly*). An incurably romantic disposition. I ran away from home twice when I was a boy. I went into the army instead of into my father's business. I climbed the balcony of this house when a man of sense would have dived into the nearest cellar. I came sneaking back here to have another look at the young lady when any other man of my age would have sent the coat back—

PETKOFF. My coat!

BLUNTSCHLI.—Yes: that's the coat I mean—would have sent it back and gone quietly home. Do you suppose I am the sort of fellow a young girl falls in love with? Why, look at our ages! I'm thirty-four: I don't suppose the young lady is much over seventeen. (*This estimate produces a marked sensation, all the rest turning and staring at one another. He proceeds innocently.*) All that adventure which was life or death to me, was only a schoolgirl's game to her—chocolate creams and hide and seek. Here's the proof! (*He takes the photograph from the table.*) Now, I ask you, would a woman who took the affair seriously have sent me this and written on it: "Raina, to her chocolate cream soldier—a souvenir"? (*He exhibits the photograph triumphantly, as if it settled the matter beyond all possibility of refutation.*)

PETKOFF. That's what I was looking for. How the deuce did it get there?

BLUNTSCHLI (*to Raina complacently*). I have put everything right, I hope, gracious young lady!

RAINA (*in uncontrollable vexation*). I quite agree with your account of yourself. You are a romantic idiot. (*Bluntschli is unspeakably taken aback.*) Next time I hope you will know the difference between a schoolgirl of seventeen and a woman of twenty-three.

BLUNTSCHLI (*stupefied*). Twenty-three! (*She snaps the photograph contemptuously from his hand; tears it across; and throws the pieces at his feet.*)

SERGIUS (*with grim enjoyment of Bluntschli's discomfiture*). Bluntschli: my one last belief is gone. Your sagacity is a fraud, like all the other things. You have less sense than even I have.

BLUNTSCHLI (*overwhelmed*). Twenty-three! Twenty-three!! (*He considers.*) Hm! (*Swiftly making up his mind*) In that case, Major Petkoff, I beg to propose formally to become a suitor for your daughter's hand, in place of Major Saranoff retired.

RAINA. You dare!

BLUNTSCHLI. If you were twenty-three when you said those things to me this afternoon, I shall take them seriously.

CATHERINE (*loftily polite*). I doubt, sir, whether you quite realize either my daughter's position or that of Major Sergius Saranoff, whose place you propose to take. The Petkoffs and the Saranoffs are known as the richest and most important families in the country. Our position is almost historical: we can go back for nearly twenty years.

PETKOFF. Oh, never mind that, Catherine. (*to Bluntschli*) We should be most happy, Bluntschli, if it were only a question of your position; but hang it, you know, Raina is accustomed to a very comfortable establishment. Sergius keeps twenty horses.

BLUNTSCHLI. But what on earth is the use of twenty horses? Why, it's a circus.

CATHERINE (*severely*). My daughter, sir, is accustomed to a first-rate stable.

RAINA. Hush, mother, you're making me ridiculous.

BLUNTSCHLI. Oh, well, if it comes to a question of an establishment, here goes! (*He goes impetuously to the table and seizes the papers in the blue envelope.*) How many horses did you say?

SERGIUS. Twenty, noble Switzer!

BLUNTSCHLI. I have two hundred horses. (*They are amazed.*) How many carriages?

SERGIUS. Three.

BLUNTSCHLI. I have seventy. Twenty-four of them will hold twelve inside, besides two on the box, without counting the driver and conductor. How many tablecloths have you?

SERGIUS. How the deuce do I know?

BLUNTSCHLI. Have you four thousand?

SERGIUS. No.

BLUNTSCHLI. I have. I have nine thousand six hundred pairs of sheets and blankets, with two thousand four hundred eider-down quilts. I have ten thousand knives and forks, and the same quantity of dessert spoons. I have six hundred servants. I have six palatial establishments, besides two livery stables, a tea garden and a private house. I have four medals for distinguished services; I have the rank of an officer and the standing of a gentleman; and I have three native languages. Show me any man in Bulgaria that can offer as much.

PETKOFF (*with childish awe*). Are you Emperor of Switzerland?

BLUNTSCHLI. My rank is the highest known in Switzerland: I'm a free citizen.

CATHERINE. Then Captain Bluntschli, since you are my daughter's choice, I shall not stand in the way of her happiness. (*Petkoff is about to speak.*) That is Major Petkoff's feeling also.

PETKOFF. Oh, I shall be only too glad. Two hundred horses! Whew!

SERGIUS. What says the lady?

RAINA (*pretending to sulk*). The lady says that he can keep his tablecloths and his omnibuses. I am not here to be sold to the highest bidder.

BLUNTSCHLI. I won't take that answer. I appealed to you as a fugitive, a beggar, and a starving man. You accepted me. You gave me your hand to kiss, your bed to sleep in, and your roof to shelter me—

RAINA (*interrupting him*). I did not give them to the Emperor of Switzerland!

BLUNTSCHLI. That's just what I say. (*He catches her hand quickly and looks her straight in the face as he adds, with confident mastery*) Now tell us who you did give them to.

RAINA (*succumbing with a shy smile*). To my chocolate cream soldier!

BLUNTSCHLI (*with a boyish laugh of delight*). That'll do. Thank you. (*Looks at his watch and suddenly becomes business-like.*) Time's up, Major. You've managed those regiments so well that you are sure to be asked to get rid of some of the Infantry of the Teemok division. Send them home by way of Lom Palanka. Saranoff: don't get married until I come back: I shall be here punctually at five in the evening on Tuesday fortnight. Gracious ladies—good evening. (*He makes them a military bow, and goes.*)

SERGIUS. What a man! What a man!

I

Act One

1. What impression do we get of the Petkoffs from the description of Raina's room and from the comment, "She is in her nightgown, well covered by a long mantle of furs, worth, on a moderate estimate, about three times the furniture of the room"? By what details is this impression reinforced throughout the first act: in Raina's comments about the Petkoffs' social position? in Louka's attitude toward her employers? in Bluntschli's comments?

2. What background information do we get in the dialogue between Raina and her mother? between Raina and Louka? between Raina and Bluntschli?

3. Characterize Raina. Her imagination is full of foolish romantic notions, but how do her words and actions show that she is not just a brainless dreamer? What is Bluntschli like?

What details show him to be anything but a storybook soldier?

4. Why does Raina protect Bluntschli? Does her attitude toward him change during Act I? How? How does it contrast with her attitude toward Sergius? Why did she take so long to become betrothed? What do her actions after her mother has left the room show about her relationship with Sergius? How does her treatment of Bluntschli differ from her treatment of Sergius?

Act Two

1. What is the purpose of the by-play between Nicola and Louka?

2. Why the elaborate description of Sergius? Why doesn't Petkoff react to him the way Catherine does? What misgivings does Sergius have about his own behavior? What details show that the act he puts on with Raina is enjoyable and yet discomforting to him?

3. What is Louka like? How does her behavior give hints of the kind of person Raina is if she could get rid of the romantic notions she has? What details of Raina's behavior parallel Louka's?

4. How does Nicola's attitude toward service throw light on the attitudes of Catherine, Raina, and Sergius toward idealized chivalrous behavior?

5. What further evidences are there of Bluntschli's good sense?

6. What comments are there in Act II that put war in a ludicrous light? Consider, for one, Petkoff's statement, "We shouldn't have been able to begin fighting if those foreigners hadn't shown us how to do it." What comments put aristocracy in a ludicrous light? Consider, for instance, Louka's comment, "It's so hard to know what a gentleman considers right. I thought from your trying to kiss me that you had given up being so particular." How applicable are the comments to other societies not so obviously comic as this particular one?

Act Three

1. What is significant about the fact that as Act III opens Raina is sitting on the divan *with a neglected novel in her lap*? In what way and for what purpose does another piece of property from Act I, the "chocolate creams," reappear in Act III?

2. What does Bluntschli mean when he says

to Raina, "You mean, don't you, that I am the first man that has ever taken you quite seriously"? In what sense have her parents and Sergius taken her *seriously*? In what sense does Bluntschli take her *seriously*?

3. The romantic nonsense that Raina, Sergius, and Catherine keep up for a time in Act III is quite obvious. Not so obvious is what Bluntschli means when he says he has "an incurably romantic disposition." What does he mean? And why does Raina call him a *romantic idiot* a few lines later?

4. Petkoff's *old overcoat* with Raina's picture in it is of great importance in Act III. Show how Shaw has centered the plot development around it. Consider, among other things, Bluntschli's return to the Petkoffs' house, Petkoff's fondness for the coat, and Raina's attempts to get the picture back.

General questions on the entire play

I

1. How does the Louka-Sergius romance parallel the Raina-Bluntschli one? In other words, if the play dramatizes the conflict between illusion and reality, how does Louka's attitude play off against Raina's? and how does Bluntschli's play off against Sergius's?

2. Much of the humor in the play comes through Shaw's skillful use of anticlimax, in which a sudden switch of emphasis robs a speech or scene of its importance or intensity and makes the pretentious seem ludicrous. One very simple example is Catherine's, "I doubt, sir, whether you quite realize either my daughter's position or that of Major Sergius Saranoff, whose place you propose to take. The Petkoffs and the Saranoffs are known as the richest and most important families in the country. Our position is almost historical; we can go back for twenty years." Another is the delightful scene where Bluntschli tells Raina, "When you strike that noble attitude and speak in that thrilling voice, I admire you; but I find it impossible to believe a single word you say." Raina, shocked, responds imperiously to the insult and then says meekly, "How did you find me out?" Point out other examples of the use of anticlimax in the play.

3. The social satire here is built around affairs in a small Balkan country, but quite

obviously, Shaw isn't the least concerned about what people do in his make-believe Bulgaria. If he wishes to deflate English and Irish notions about war and love and aristocracy, what does he gain by setting his play in Bulgaria?

II

1. Specifically, what attitudes toward war, romantic love, prestige, position—success in general—is Shaw satirizing? Don't assume he is only satirizing romantic foolishness. How does he make the attitudes he is satirizing look ridiculous? Consider what makes Bluntschli a successful soldier, Raina a successful coquette, Sergius a successful hero, Louka a successful social climber, Petkoff a successful minor aristocrat, Catherine a successful mother, and Nicola a successful servant. Consider also what kind of behavior Shaw has respect for, over against which he sets inanity and self-delusion.

"... persuasion and belief
Had ripened into faith, and faith become
A passionate intuition."

William Wordsworth, *The Excursion*

Unit Six

FAITH

The word "faith" is usually applied to man's belief that some sort of power outside himself is operating for his good. But to let the definition rest here is to fail to account for either the vital place of faith in human affairs or its undeniable influence in shaping art and literature. Early in his book, *Five Stages of Greek Religion,* Gilbert Murray places faith at the center of human existence: ". . . the fact remains that man must have some relationship towards the uncharted, the mysterious, tracts of life which surround him on every side. And for my own part I am content to say that his method must be to a large extent very much what St. Paul calls . . . faith: that is, some attitude not of the conscious intellect but of the whole being, using all its powers of sensitiveness, all its feeblest and most articulate feelers and tentacles, in the effort somehow to touch by these that which cannot be grasped by the definite senses or analyzed by the conscious reason. What we gain thus is an insecure but precious possession. We gain no dogma, at least no safe dogma, but we gain much more. We gain something hard to define, which lies at the heart not only of religion, but of art and poetry and all the higher strivings of human emotion. I believe at times we actually gain practical guidance in some questions where experience and argument fail."*

The selections in this section express a variety of attitudes toward faith; all, even the negative ones, are expressions of men and women who have come to terms, if only for the moment, with the world in which they live. There is the strong apprehension, expressed by Arnold and Hardy, that simply putting up with it all is a kind of victory. There is the resolute personal conviction that man can shape his own ends, expressed by Forster,

---

* Gilbert Murray, *Five Stages of Greek Religion* (Boston: Beacon Press). Reprinted by permission of the Beacon Press.

Browning, and Tennyson. There is the clear call to work for the emancipation of man from all bondages that enslave, frustrate, or pervert in Shelley's "Ode to the West Wind" or Blake's "And Did Those Feet . . ." And there is, finally, the total commitment to a God-centered life expressed in varied manners by the concluding selections in this book.

The great writers have shown the sensitiveness of which Gilbert Murray speaks. They have simply put into words a lifetime of puzzling over what it means to become an adult man or woman. We—and they—may, in the words of St. Paul, "see through a glass darkly," but the willingness to try to see is what counts. To the extent that any man's vision helps our vision, to that extent are we wiser in the ways of man and of God.

DOVER BEACH

[*1867*]

Matthew Arnold

One of the best-known poems in English literature, Matthew Arnold's "Dover Beach," deals with the decline of faith in the modern world. To Arnold and his contemporaries in the mid-nineteenth century it seemed clear that the old securities about religion were being chipped away under the impact of new sciences like geology, zoology, paleontology, and the new close linguistic and historical examination of the Bible.

We have seen in Arnold's "To Marguerite" the conviction that "in the sea of life enisled . . . We mortal millions live alone" separated symbolically by the "unplumbed, salt, estranging sea." The sea reappears as symbol in "Dover Beach," but this time the estrangement is from religious faith, which, the speaker says, was "once . . . at the full, and round earth's shore/Lay like the folds of a bright girdle furled," but which is now withdrawing like the tide at ebb. In the last stanza a call for human love and faithfulness emerges as the only hope possible in a chaotic world, but even this seems swallowed in darkness before the poem's close.

> The sea is calm tonight,
> The tide is full, the moon lies fair
> Upon the Straits;—on the French coast, the light
> Gleams, and is gone; the cliffs of England stand,
> Glimmering and vast, out in the tranquil bay.   5
> Come to the window, sweet is the night air!
> Only, from the long line of spray
> Where the sea meets the moon-blanched sand,
> Listen! you hear the grating roar
> Of pebbles which the waves suck back, and fling,   10
> At their return, up the high strand,
> Begin, and cease, and then again begin,
> With tremulous cadence slow, and bring
> The eternal note of sadness in.
>
> Sophocles long ago   15
> Heard it on the Aegean, and it brought
> Into his mind the turbid ebb and flow
> Of human misery; we
> Find also in the sound a thought,
> Hearing it by this distant northern sea.   20

3. STRAITS: of Dover; strait between Dover, England, and Calais, France; the English Channel is only twenty miles wide at this point.

4. CLIFFS OF ENGLAND: the white chalk cliffs of Dover.

15. SOPHOCLES: the reference in lines 15-18 is probably to Sophocle's *Antigone* (Ode II, Strophe I, p. 794).

16. AEGEAN: the sea between Greece and Asia Minor.

The sea of faith
Was once, too, at the full, and round earth's shore
Lay like the folds of a bright girdle furled;
But now I only hear
Its melancholy, long, withdrawing roar,   25
Retreating to the breath
Of the night-wind down the vast edges drear
And naked shingles of the world.

　　Ah, love, let us be true
To one another! for the world, which seems   30
To lie before us like a land of dreams,
So various, so beautiful, so new,
Hath really neither joy, nor love, nor light,
Nor certitude, nor peace, nor help for pain;
And we are here as on a darkling plain   35
Swept with confused alarms of struggle and flight,
Where ignorant armies clash by night.

---

23. GIRDLE: sash.　　　　　　　　　　28. SHINGLES: gravel-covered beaches.

I

1. What is the situation in stanza 1? What kind of night is it? What is the speaker describing and to whom?

2. What is the condition of the tide at the beginning of stanza 1? What change is there as the stanza progresses? How does this lead into stanza 2? into stanza 3? Is the image of the sea still implied in any way in stanza 4? Explain.

3. How does stanza 2 expand upon the specific seascape of stanza 1? What word in line 14 prepares for this expansion? What is the purpose of the reference to Sophocles? To whom does "we" refer in line 18: the two people of stanza 1?

4. How is the "thought" (19) that the speaker *finds* related in stanza 3 to his observation in stanza 1 and his allusion in stanza 2?

5. How is stanza 4 a further development of the seascape idea and also a conclusion? To whom does the "us" in line 29 refer?

6. Trace the use of terms referring to "light" and "darkness." What has happened to the *moon-blanched* scene by stanza 4? What meanings besides the usual ones are there in "darkling" (35) and "ignorant" (37)? How has the meaning of "night" changed from the first stanza to the last, and why is it significant that the very last word of the poem is "night"?

7. Rhythm and sound echo sense very effectively in stanza 1. How is the stillness of the scene emphasized rhythmically in the first six lines? Consider particularly the use of pauses. How is the rhythm of wave motion echoed in lines 9-15? What effect is achieved by the use of long vowel sounds in lines 13-14? Substitute "finicky" for "tremulous" (both have the same stress pattern) to see what a difference sound patterns can make. For contrast, note lines 36-37; how does sound pattern match sense in this instance?

8. What is the theme of the poem: that just so long as we are *true to one another* we can surmount the loss of religious faith in the world? that faith, like the tide, is sure to return if we hold on until it does? that the old certitude won't return until human relationships improve? none of these? Explain your interpretation.

THE DARKLING THRUSH   [*1900*]

Thomas Hardy

Matthew Arnold finds faith passing from the world and calls for a reaffirmation of the personal ties—love and faithfulness—that alone remain to sustain hope. However, the sense of anxious melancholy that pervades "Dover Beach" seems to drown out the call for love, and we are left with the powerful image of "ignorant armies [that] clash by night."

Thomas Hardy sees life in much the same way. In his novels, his short stories, and his poems, he pictures an undirected and often chaotic world, totally indifferent to the nightmares visited upon individuals. What counts with Hardy is the way the suffering individual responds to the unmerited misery of his lot. His faith lies in uncomplaining dignity, acceptance, endurance. "The Darkling Thrush," written almost as a closing commentary on the nineteenth century's naive conviction that everything was good and getting better, is an excellent example of Hardy's point of view.

I leaned upon a coppice gate
  When Frost was specter-gray,
And Winter's dregs made desolate
  The weakening eye of day.
The tangled bine-stems scored the sky   5
  Like strings from broken lyres,
And all mankind that haunted nigh
  Had sought their household fires.

The land's sharp features seemed to be
  The Century's corpse outleant;   10
His crypt the cloudy canopy,
  The wind his death-lament.
The ancient pulse of germ and birth
  Was shrunken hard and dry,
And every spirit upon earth   15
  Seemed fervorless as I.

At once a voice burst forth among
  The bleak twigs overhead
In a full-hearted evensong
  Of joy illimited;   20
An agèd thrush, frail, gaunt and small,
  In blast-beruffled plume,
Had chosen thus to fling his soul
  Upon the growing gloom.

So little cause for carolings   25
  Of such ecstatic sound
Was written on terrestrial things
  Afar or nigh around,
That I could think there trembled through
  His happy good-night air   30
Some blessed hope, whereof he knew
  And I was unaware.

Title. DARKLING: i.e., being in darkness; not clearly seen or understood.
7. HAUNTED: lived.
10. OUTLEANT: leaned out, i.e., both thinned down and, perhaps, outstretched (into the twentieth century).

19. EVENSONG: "evening song," but probably with allusion to the vesper service that in the Anglican Church is called "evensong."
20. ILLIMITED: unlimited.

I

1. How does Hardy create a sense of lifelessness and decay throughout the first two stanzas? State exactly what is being compared to what in "Frost was specter-gray" (2), "Winter's dregs" (3), "weakening eye of day" (4), "scored the sky/Like strings from broken lyres" (5-6), "mankind that haunted" (7), lines 9-10, line 11, line 12, lines 13-14?

2. What contrasts in word choice are there between the first two stanzas and the last two? What is suggested by "evensong," "carolings," "ecstatic," "blessed"? What is the force of "trembled through"?

3. Notice that the meter of the first two stanzas is almost perfectly regular, with each pair of lines coming to a definite close and each line being a self-contained unit. What happens to the meter in stanzas three and four? What is significant about the change? How and why does Hardy force an emphasis on "hope" in the middle of line 31? Consider where the pauses have come in the stanza.

4. Why does the speaker pick a particular bird, the thrush, as his subject, and why one "aged . . . frail, gaunt and small"? Why "darkling"?

5. The speaker says that the thrush knew of "Some blessed hope," of which "I was unaware." Just what does he mean by this as the final comment in the poem? Discuss whether the speaker's attitude has changed from what it was in the first two stanzas.

II

1. Compare "Dover Beach" and "The Darkling Thrush." Both describe a *darkling, fervorless* world. Does each seem to be saying that there is no hope for any change? What is the attitude of each speaker toward the situation he observes: resigned? indifferent? frustrated? bitter? none of these? Do their attitudes differ? How?

"WHAT I BELIEVE"
from Two Cheers for Democracy   [*1939*]

E. M. Forster

With just as much conviction that we live in "a world full of violence and cruelty" but without the anxiety and even gloom that pervade the Arnold and Hardy poems, E. M. Forster, in his essay "What I Believe," published on the eve of World War II, spells out his faith in personal relationships of a kind tougher and deeper than the romantic love Arnold vaguely hopes for in "Dover Beach."

He says, in a startling first sentence, "I do not believe in Belief," and goes on to say further on in the paragraph, "I dislike the stuff. I do not believe in it, for its own sake, at all." But he concedes that since "Faith . . . is a stiffening process, a sort of mental starch," and since "there are so many militant creeds that, in self-defense, one has to formulate a creed of one's own," he will try to define what convictions, what beliefs, sustain him.

There is nothing religious or mystical in Forster's "creed." He does not think that "Christianity [or any present-day religion, for that matter] will ever cope with the present world-wide mess." He asks for a regeneration that begins at home with the individual. "The people I respect most," he says, "behave as if they were immortal and as if society was eternal. Both assumptions are false: both of them must be accepted as true if we are to go on eating and working and loving, and are to keep open a few breathing holes for the human spirit." There's no formula for a better world here, and not much conviction that there ever will be a better world, but there is a powerful faith that those "breathing holes" will never be closed, that there will always be "an aristocracy of the sensitive, the considerate and the plucky" to "represent the true human tradition, the one permanent victory of our queer race over cruelty and chaos."

I do not believe in Belief. But this is an age of faith, and there are so many militant creeds that, in self-defense, one has to formulate a creed of one's own. Tolerance, good temper and sympathy are no longer enough in a world which is rent by religious and racial persecution, in a world where ignorance rules, and science, who ought to have ruled, plays the subservient pimp. Tolerance, good temper, and sympathy—they are what matter really, and if the human race is not to collapse, they must come to the front before long. But for the moment they are not enough; their action is no stronger than a flower, battered beneath a military jack boot. They want stiffening, even if the process coarsens them. Faith, to my mind, is a stiffening process, a sort of mental starch, which ought to be applied as sparingly as possible. I dislike the stuff. I do not believe in it, for its own sake, at all. Herein I probably differ from most people, who believe in Belief, and are only sorry they cannot swallow even more than they do. My law-givers are Erasmus and Montaigne,[1] not Moses and St. Paul. My temple stands not upon Mount Moriah[2] but in that Elysian Field[3] where even the immoral are admitted. My motto is: "Lord, I disbelieve—help thou my unbelief."

1. ERASMUS AND MONTAIGNE: the former a Dutch scholar (1466?-1536), the latter a French scholar and writer (1533-1595), both leading humanists of the Renaissance and thus concerned primarily with secular, not religious, matters.
2. MOUNT MORIAH: hill in Jerusalem on which Solomon built the Temple (II Chronicles 3:1).
3. ELYSIAN FIELD: The Elysian Fields represented paradise in Greek mythology.

I have, however, to live in an Age of Faith—the sort of epoch I used to hear praised when I was a boy. It is extremely unpleasant really. It is bloody in every sense of the word. And I have to keep my end up in it. Where do I start?

With personal relationships. Here is something comparatively solid in a world full of violence and cruelty. Not absolutely solid, for Psychology has split and shattered the idea of a "Person," and has shown that there is something incalculable in each of us, which may at any moment rise to the surface and destroy our normal balance. We don't know what we are like. We can't know what other people are like. How, then, can we put any trust in personal relationships, or cling to them in the gathering political storm? In theory we cannot. But in practice we can and do. Though A is not unchangeably A or B unchangeably B, there can still be love and loyalty between the two. For the purpose of living one has to assume that the personality is solid, and the "self" is an entity, and to ignore all contrary evidence. And since to ignore evidence is one of the characteristics of faith, I certainly can proclaim that I believe in personal relationships.

Starting from them, I get a little order into the contemporary chaos. One must be fond of people and trust them if one is not to make a mess of life, and it is therefore essential that they should not let one down. They often do. The moral of which is that I must, myself, be as reliable as possible, and this I try to be. But reliability is not a matter of contract—that is the main difference between the world of personal relationships and the world of business relationships.

It is a matter for the heart, which signs no documents. In other words, reliability is impossible unless there is a natural warmth. Most men possess this warmth, though they often have bad luck and get chilled. Most of them, even when they are politicians, *want* to keep faith. And one can, at all events, show one's own little light here, one's own poor little trembling flame, with the knowledge that it is not the only light that is shining in the darkness, and not the only one which the darkness does not comprehend. Personal relations are despised today. They are regarded as bourgeois luxuries, as products of a time of fair weather which is now past, and we are urged to get rid of them, and to dedicate ourselves to some movement or cause instead. I hate the idea of causes, and if I had to choose between betraying my country and betraying my friend, I hope I should have the guts to betray my country. Such a choice may scandalize the modern reader, and he may stretch out his patriotic hand to the telephone at once and ring up the police. It would not have shocked Dante, though. Dante places Brutus and Cassius in the lowest circle of Hell because they had chosen to betray their friend Julius Caesar rather than their country Rome.[4] Probably one will not be asked to make such an agonizing choice. Still, there lies at the back of every creed something terrible and hard for which the worshipper may one day be required to suffer, and there is even a terror and a hardness in this creed of personal relationships, urbane and mild though it sounds. Love and loyalty to an individual can run counter to the claims of the State. When they do—down with the State, say I, which means that the State would down me.

This brings me along to Democracy, "even Love, the Beloved Republic, which feeds upon Freedom and lives."[5] Democracy is not a Beloved Republic really, and never will be. But it is less hateful than other contemporary forms of government, and to that extent it deserves our support. It does start from the assumption that the individual is important, and that all types are needed to make a civilization. It does not divide its citizens into the bossers and the bossed —as an efficiency-regime[6] tends to do. The people I admire most are those who are sensitive and want to create something or discover something, and do not see life in terms of power, and such people get more of a chance under a democracy than elsewhere. They found religions, great or small, or they produce literature and art, or they do disinterested scientific research, or they may be what is called "ordinary people," who are creative in their private lives, bring up their children decently, for instance, or help their neighbors. All these people need to express themselves; they cannot do so unless society allows them liberty to do so, and the society which allows them most liberty is a democracy.

Democracy has another merit. It allows criticism, and if there is not public criticism there are bound to be hushed-up scandals. That is why I believe in the Press, despite all its lies and vulgarity, and why I believe in Parliament. Parliament is often sneered at because it is a Talking Shop. I believe in it *because* it is a talking shop. I believe in the Private Member who makes himself a nuisance. He gets snubbed and is told that he is cranky or ill-informed, but he does expose abuses which would otherwise never have been mentioned, and very often an abuse gets put right just by being mentioned. Occasionally, too, a well-meaning public official starts losing his head in the cause of efficiency, and thinks himself God Almighty. Such officials are particularly frequent in the Home Office.[7] Well, there will

---

4. BETRAY . . . ROME: but even more because Julius Caesar had founded the Roman Empire, for Dante the forerunner of Rome's eternal spiritual empire.

5. "EVEN . . . LIVES": see last sentence, p. 733.

---

6. EFFICIENCY-REGIME: dictatorship.

7. HOME OFFICE: the department of the British government that deals with the internal affairs of the country.

be questions about them in Parliament sooner or later, and then they will have to mind their steps. Whether Parliament is either a representative body or an efficient one is questionable, but I value it because it criticizes and talks, and because its chatter gets widely reported.

So Two Cheers for Democracy: one because it admits variety, and two because it permits criticism. Two cheers are quite enough; there is no occasion to give three. Only Love the Beloved Republic deserves that.

What about Force, though? While we are trying to be sensitive and advanced and affectionate and tolerant, an unpleasant question pops up: does not all society rest upon force? If a government cannot count upon the police and the army, how can it hope to rule? And if an individual gets knocked on the head or sent to a labor camp,[8] of what significance are his opinions?

This dilemma does not worry me as much as it does some. I realize that all society rests upon force. But all the great creative actions, all the decent human relations, occur during the intervals when force has not managed to come to the front. These intervals are what matter. I want them to be as frequent and as lengthy as possible, and I call them "civilization." Some people idealize force and pull it into the foreground and worship it, instead of keeping it in the background as long as possible. I think they make a mistake, and I think that their opposites, the mystics, err even more when they declare that force does not exist. I believe that it exists, and that one of our jobs is to prevent it from getting out of its box.[9] It gets out sooner or later, and then it destroys us and all the lovely things which we have made. But it is not out all the time, for the fortunate reason that the strong are so stupid. Consider their conduct for a moment in the Niebelung's Ring.[10] The giants there have the guns, or in other words the gold; but they do nothing with it, they do not realize that they are all-powerful, with the result that the catastrophe is delayed and the castle of Walhalla, insecure but glorious, fronts the storms. Fafnir, coiled round his hoard, grumbles and grunts; we can hear him under Europe today; the leaves of the wood already tremble, and the Bird calls its warnings uselessly. Fafnir will destroy us, but by a blessed dispensation he is stupid and slow, and creation goes on just outside the poisonous blast of his breath. The Nietzschean[11] would hurry the monster up, the mystic would say he did not exist, but Wotan, wiser than either, hastens to create warriors before doom declares itself. The Valkyries[12] are symbols not only of courage but of intelligence; they represent the human spirit snatching its opportunity while the going is good, and one of them even finds time to love. Brünnhilde's[13] last song hymns the recurrence of love, and since it is the privilege of art to exaggerate, she goes even further, and proclaims the love which is eternally triumphant and feeds upon freedom, and lives.

---

8. LABOR CAMP: slave labor camp.

9. BOX: Pandora, in Greek mythology, was given a box as a wedding present by Zeus, king of the gods, to present to her husband. When she opened it, all the evils that can befall man flew out of it and have afflicted us ever since.

10. NIEBELUNG'S RING: The references from here to the end of the paragraph are to Scandinavian mythology. Briefly, the giants build the gods a magnificent castle, Walhalla; in payment, Wotan, chief of the gods, steals the hoard of Rhine gold, which confers unbounded power on the possessor, and gives it to them. The giant, Fafnir, kills his brother, turns himself into a dragon, and wraps himself around the hoard. The reference to "the Bird" is to a later development in the legend. Siegfried, grandson of Wotan, kills Fafnir, and a drop of the dragon's blood on his tongue gives him power to understand the language of the birds.

11. NIETZSCHEAN: i.e., follower of the philosopher Nietzsche (see note, p. 340).

12. VALKYRIES: the twelve nymphs who served the heroes of Walhalla.

13. BRÜNNHILDE: the favorite Valkyrie.

So that is what I feel about force and violence. It is, alas! the ultimate reality on this earth, but it does not always get to the front. Some people call its absences "decadence"; I call them "civilization" and find in such interludes the chief justification for the human experiment. I look the other way until fate strikes me. Whether this is due to courage or to cowardice in my own case I cannot be sure. But I know that if men had not looked the other way in the past, nothing of any value would survive. The people I respect most behave as if they were immortal and as if society was eternal. Both assumptions are false: both of them must be accepted as true if we are to go on eating and working and loving, and are to keep open a few breathing holes for the human spirit. No millennium seems likely to descend upon humanity; no better and stronger League of Nations will be instituted; no form of Christianity and no alternative to Christianity will bring peace to the world or integrity to the individual; no "change of heart" will occur. And yet we need not despair, indeed, we cannot despair; the evidence of history shows us that men have always insisted on behaving creatively under the shadow of the sword; that they have done their artistic and scientific and domestic stuff for the sake of doing it, and that we had better follow their example under the shadow of the airplanes. Others, with more vision or courage than myself, see the salvation of humanity ahead, and will dismiss my conception of civilization as paltry, a sort of tip-and-run[14] game. Certainly it is presumptuous to say that we *cannot* improve, and that Man, who has only been in power for a few thousand years, will never learn to make use of his power. All I mean is that, if people continue to kill one another as they do, the world cannot get better than it is, and that since there are more people than formerly, and their means for destroying one

another superior, the world may well get worse. What is good in people—and consequently in the world—is their insistence on creation, their belief in friendship and loyalty for their own sakes; and though violence remains and is, indeed, the major partner in this muddled establishment, I believe that creativeness remains too, and will always assume direction when violence sleeps. So, though I am not an optimist, I cannot agree with Sophocles that it were better never to have been born.[15] And although, like Horace,[16] I see no evidence that each batch of births is superior to the last, I leave the field open for the more complacent view. This is such a difficult moment to live in, one cannot help getting gloomy and also a bit rattled, and perhaps short-sighted.

In search of a refuge, we may perhaps turn to hero-worship. But here we shall get no help, in my opinion. Hero-worship is a dangerous vice, and one of the minor merits of a democracy is that it does not encourage it, or produce that unmanageable type of citizen known as the Great Man. It produces instead different kinds of small men—a much finer achievement. But people who cannot get interested in the variety of life, and cannot make up their own minds, get discontented over this, and they long for a hero to bow down before and follow blindly. It is significant that a hero is an integral part of the authoritarian stock-in-trade today. An efficiency-regime cannot be run without a few heroes stuck about it to carry off the dullness—much as plums have to be put into a bad pudding to make it palatable. One hero at the top and a smaller one each side of him is a favorite arrangement, and the timid and the bored are comforted by the trinity, and, bowing down, feel exalted and strengthened.

No, I distrust Great Men. They produce a desert of uniformity around them and

14. TIP-AND-RUN: a kind of cricket in which the batter must run every time his bat touches a bowled ball.

15. SOPHOCLES . . . BORN: see final chorus of *King Oedipus* (p. 362).
16. HORACE: Roman poet and satirist (65-8 B.C.).

often a pool of blood too, and I always feel a little man's pleasure when they come a cropper. Every now and then one reads in the newspapers some such statement as: "The coup d'état appears to have failed, and Admiral Toma's[17] whereabouts is at present unknown." Admiral Toma had probably every qualification for being a Great Man—an iron will, personal magnetism, dash, flair, sexlessness—but fate was against him, so he retires to unknown whereabouts instead of parading history with his peers. He fails with a completeness which no artist and no lover can experience, because with them the process of creation is itself an achievement, whereas with him the only possible achievement is success.

I believe in aristocracy, though—if that is the right word, and if a democrat may use it. Not an aristocracy of power, based upon rank and influence, but an aristocracy of the sensitive, the considerate and the plucky. Its members are to be found in all nations and classes, and all through the ages, and there is a secret understanding between them when they meet. They represent the true human tradition, the one permanent victory of our queer race over cruelty and chaos. Thousands of them perish in obscurity, a few are great names. They are sensitive for others as well as for themselves, they are considerate without being fussy, their pluck is not swankiness but the power to endure, and they can take a joke. I give no examples —it is risky to do that—but the reader may as well consider whether this is the type of person he would like to meet and to be, and whether (going farther with me) he would prefer that this type should *not* be an ascetic one. I am against asceticism myself. I am with the old Scotsman who wanted less chastity and more delicacy. I do not feel that my aristocrats are a real aristocracy if they thwart their bodies, since bodies are the instruments through which we register and enjoy the world. Still, I do not insist. This is not a major point. It is clearly possible to

be sensitive, considerate and plucky and yet be an ascetic too; if anyone possesses the first three qualities, I will let him in! On they go—an invincible army, yet not a victorious one. The aristocrats, the elect, the chosen, the Best People—all the words that describe them are false, and all attempts to organize them fail. Again and again Authority, seeing their value, has tried to net them and to utilize them as the Egyptian Priesthood or the Christian Church or the Chinese Civil Service or the Group Movement,[18] or some other worthy stunt. But they slip through the net and are gone; when the door is shut, they are no longer in the room; their temple, as one of them remarked, is the Holiness of the Heart's Affection,[19] and their kingdom, though they never possess it, is the wide-open world.

With this type of person knocking about, and constantly crossing one's path if one has eyes to see or hands to feel, the experiment of earthly life cannot be dismissed as a failure. But it may well be hailed as a tragedy, the tragedy being that no device has been found by which these private decencies can be transmitted to public affairs. As soon as people have power they go crooked and sometimes dotty as well, because the possession of power lifts them into a region where normal honesty never pays. For instance, the man who is selling newspapers outside the Houses of Parliament can safely leave his papers to go for a drink and his cap beside them: anyone who takes a paper is sure to drop a copper[20] into the cap. But the men who are inside the Houses of Parliament—they cannot

17. ADMIRAL TOMA: a fictitious name.

18. GROUP MOVEMENT: a twentieth century effort to arouse men to "moral rearmament," to which Forster compares earlier efforts to organize and systematize men of intelligence and good will.

19. HOLINESS . . . AFFECTION: from a letter by John Keats to Benjamin Bailey, November 22, 1817: "I am certain of nothing but of the holiness of the heart's affections, and the truth of imagination."

20. COPPER: penny.

trust one another like that, still less can the Government they compose trust other governments. No caps upon the pavement here, but suspicion, treachery and armaments. The more highly public life is organized the lower does its morality sink; the nations of today behave to each other worse than they ever did in the past, they cheat, rob, bully and bluff, make war without notice, and kill as many women and children as possible; whereas primitive tribes were at all events restrained by taboos. It is a humiliating outlook—though the greater the darkness, the brighter shine the little lights, reassuring one another, signalling: "Well, at all events, I'm still here. I don't like it very much, but how are you?" Unquenchable lights of my aristocracy! Signals of the invincible army! "Come along—anyway, let's have a good time while we can." I think they signal that too.

The Savior of the future—if ever he comes—will not preach a new Gospel. He will merely utilize my aristocracy, he will make effective the good will and the good temper which are already existing. In other words, he will introduce a new technique. In economics, we are told that if there was a new technique of distribution, there need be no poverty, and people would not starve in one place while crops were being ploughed under in another. A similar change is needed in the sphere of morals and politics. The desire for it is by no means new; it was expressed, for example, in theological terms by Jacopone da Todi[21] over six hundred years ago. "Ordina questo amore, O tu che m'ami," he said; "O thou who lovest me—set this love in order." His prayer was not granted, and I do not myself believe that it ever will be, but here, and not through a change of heart, is our probable route. Not by becoming better, but by ordering and distributing his native goodness, will Man shut up Force into its box, and so gain time

21. JACOPONE DA TODI: Italian Franciscan monk (1230?-1306); supposed author of *Stabat Mater*, famous Latin hymn.

to explore the universe and to set his mark upon it worthily. At present he only explores it at odd moments, when Force is looking the other way, and his divine creativeness appears as a trivial by-product, to be scrapped as soon as the drums beat and the bombers hum.

Such a change, claim the orthodox, can only be made by Christianity, and will be made by it in God's good time: man always has failed and always will fail to organize his own goodness, and it is presumptuous of him to try. This claim—solemn as it is—leaves me cold. I cannot believe that Christianity will ever cope with the present worldwide mess, and I think that such influence as it retains in modern society is due to the money behind it, rather than to its spiritual appeal. It was a spiritual force once, but the indwelling spirit will have to be restated if it is to calm the waters again, and probably restated in a non-Christian form. Naturally a lot of people, and people who are not only good but able and intelligent, will disagree here; they will vehemently deny that Christianity has failed, or they will argue that its failure proceeds from the wickedness of men, and really proves its ultimate success. They have Faith, with a large F. My faith has a very small one, and I only intrude it because these are strenuous and serious days, and one likes to say what one thinks while speech is comparatively free: it may not be free much longer.

The above are the reflections of an individualist and a liberal who has found liberalism crumbling beneath him and at first felt ashamed. Then, looking around, he decided there was no special reason for shame, since other people, whatever they felt, were equally insecure. And as for individualism—there seems no way of getting off this, even if one wanted to. The dictator-hero can grind down his citizens till they are all alike, but he cannot melt them into a single man. That is beyond his power. He can order them to merge, he can incite them to mass-antics, but they are obliged to be born separately, and to die separately, and, owing to these unavoidable termini, will always be running off the totalitarian rails. The memory of birth and the expectation of death always lurk within the human being, making him separate from his fellows and consequently capable of intercourse with them. Naked I came into the world, naked I shall go out of it![22] And a very good thing too, for it reminds me that I am naked under my shirt, whatever its color.[23]

---

22. NAKED . . . IT: see Job 1:21.
23. NAKED . . . COLOR: reference to the practice of Fascist groups being known by the color of their uniform shirts: e.g., Hitler's Brown Shirts, Mussolini's Black Shirts, Sir Oswald Mosley's (British Fascist leader) Black Shirts. The point is that all men, including the mass man of the *dictator-hero,* are *naked under [their] shirt[s]*.

does he add to *tolerance, good temper, and sympathy* to make *enough?*

6. Forster depends a great deal on allusions in getting his point across. Explain specifically the following allusions:
   a. "My temple stands not upon Mount Moriah but in that Elysian Field where even the immoral are admitted".
   b. the references to Scandinavian mythology.
   c. "Naked I came into the world, naked I shall go out of it! And a very good thing too, for it reminds me that I am naked under my shirt, whatever its color."

Point out other effective uses of allusions.

7. Why does Forster deliberately choose to be colloquial in the language he uses? Note, for example, "I dislike the stuff", "have the guts to betray my country", "come a cropper", "knocking about", "dotty". Find others. Why might the weightiness of a more formal style be undesirable in such an essay?

I

1. What does Forster like about democracy? Why is he willing to give it only *two cheers?*

2. Define "civilization" as Forster uses the term in the essay. What relationship does he see between *force and violence* and *civilization?* What keeps force in check?

3. What does he mean when he says: "[The Great Man] fails with a completeness which no artist and no lover can experience, because with them the process of creation is itself an achievement, whereas with him the only possible achievement is success"?

4. Why does he think that the "experiment of earthly life cannot be dismissed as a failure. But it may well be hailed as a tragedy . . ."? What chances are there that the ultimate *tragedy* can be averted?

5. In the first paragraph Forster says, "Tolerance, good temper, and sympathy are no longer enough," although "they are what matters really." In his statement of faith what

II

1. Take any one of the following controversial statements (or any other in the essay) and discuss the pro's and con's of it, particularly as it applies to present situations and your own convictions about *belief:*
   a. "I hate the idea of causes, and if I had to choose between betraying my country and betraying my friend, I hope I should have the guts to betray my country." In this connection refer to Auden's line in "September 1, 1939": "There is no such thing as the State."
   b. "No millennium seems likely to descend upon humanity; no better and stronger League of Nations will be instituted; no form of Christianity and no alternative to Christianity will bring peace to the world or integrity to the individual; no 'change of heart' will occur."
   c. "Hero-worship is a dangerous vice, and one of the minor merits of democracy is that it does not encourage it, or produce that unmanageable type of citizen known as the Great Man."

PROSPICE

[*1864*]

Robert Browning

Forster, asserting the capacity of the individual to survive with dignity even in a world in which power and force seem to rule, associates himself with "the aristocracy of the sensitive, the considerate, and the plucky." Browning, in "Prospice," asserts the capacity of the individual to die with dignity and associates himself with the "strong men," the "fighters," and the "heroes" who have met death as simply an unavoidable hazard on the way to new goals.

The poem was written shortly after the death of Browning's wife, Elizabeth Barrett Browning, following some fifteen years of an exceptionally happy marriage.

> Fear death?—to feel the fog in my throat,
>   The mist in my face,
> When the snows begin, and the blasts denote
>   I am nearing the place,
> The power of the night, the press of the storm,   5
>   The post of the foe;
> Where he stands, the Arch Fear in a visible form,
>   Yet the strong man must go:
> For the journey is done and the summit attained,
>   And the barriers fall,   10
> Though a battle's to fight ere the guerdon be gained,
>   The reward of it all.
> I was ever a fighter, so—one fight more,
>   The best and the last!
> I would hate that death bandaged my eyes, and forebore,   15
>   And bade me creep past.
> No! let me taste the whole of it, fare like my peers
>   The heroes of old,
> Bear the brunt, in a minute pay glad life's arrears
>   Of pain, darkness and cold.   20
> For sudden the worst turns the best to the brave,
>   The black minute's at end,
> And the elements' rage, the fiend-voices that rave,
>   Shall dwindle, shall blend,
> Shall change, shall become first a peace out of pain,   25
>   Then a light, then thy breast,
> O thou soul of my soul! I shall clasp thee again,
>   And with God be the rest!

Title. PROSPICE: "Look forward."
7. ARCH FEAR: death.
19. GLAD: gladly.
26. THY: Mrs. Browning's.

I

1. What metaphor for death does Browning develop beginning at line 6? By what details does he develop it? How appropriate is it to the theme? What other metaphor for death does he develop in lines 1-5? Where does it reappear?

2. Who are the *heroes of old*? By what right does the speaker feel he may call them his *peers?* What kind of person is the speaker?

3. How and why is the rhythm quickened beginning with line 23?

4. What is the tone of the poem: boastful? self-important? unsure but assertive? self-possessed? optimistic? a combination of these? none of these? Be specific in referring to words and phrases that support your answer.

5. State clearly what the speaker is saying about death and about himself. What does the last line mean?

HOLY SONNET X   [*1633*]

John Donne

A different attitude toward death, but one which also clearly reveals the poet's faith that he is equal to the test, is expressed in John Donne's "Holy Sonnet X."

Browning acknowledges death as the "Arch Fear," a terrible foe against whom he must make "one fight more,/The best and the last!" Donne wittily denies Death any such eminence and argues rather convincingly that Death has no power whatsoever. He is not being flippant—far from it; he is simply writing from the Christian conviction that the soul is immortal through Christ.

> Death, be not proud, though some have callèd thee
> Mighty and dreadful, for thou art not so;
> For those whom thou think'st thou dost overthrow
> Die not, poor Death, nor yet canst thou kill me.
> From rest and sleep, which but thy pictures be,   5
> Much pleasure, then from thee much more must flow;
> And soonest our best men with thee do go,
> Rest of their bones and soul's delivery.
> Thou'rt slave to fate, chance, kings, and desperate men,
> And dost with poison, war, and sickness dwell;   10
> And poppy or charms can make us sleep as well,
> And better than thy stroke. Why swell'st thou then?
> One short sleep passed, we wake eternally,
> And death shall be no more. Death, thou shalt die.

---

7. SOONEST: most readily.
11. POPPY: i.e., opium, made from the poppy.
12. SWELL'ST: i.e., with pride.

I

1. What is the argument in lines 1-4? 5-8? 9-12? 13-14? Show that each argument takes more away from death than the one before.

2. Explain lines 5-6, 8, and 9. What does "die" mean in line 4? in line 14?

3. Point out specifically how the poet has prepared for the final paradox of the sonnet— "Death, thou shalt die!"—with earlier paradoxes and surprises.

4. What tone does the speaker take toward death in the poem—formal or informal, sober or light-hearted? How do you know?

5. The regular meter is that of line 5—and what others? Yet there are many variations. How do the two halves of line 2 play against each other and why? Point out places where there are several stressed syllables in a row; what purpose is served in each instance? What contrast, for instance, is there between the rhythm of lines 5-8 and that of line 9? What is gained by ending the poem with four stressed syllables—"Death, thou shalt die!"?

6. How essential is an acceptance of the conviction of line 13—"One short sleep passed, we wake eternally"—to our acceptance of the speaker's argument?

II

1. Compare the poems on death by Browning and Donne. In what terms does each speaker see death as an adversary? How do the tones of the poems differ? What assumptions are made about an after-life in each? Which seems to you the most effective commentary on death as a fact to be faced—and why?

ULYSSES   [*1842*]

Alfred Lord Tennyson

Browning's metaphor in "Prospice" of the fighter facing his last and greatest battle does not picture him as the brave defender awaiting attack but rather as the willing warrior on the offensive.

Tennyson's "Ulysses" expresses the same approval of "sallying forth" to meet one's fate, though it is not a poem about facing death but rather about living life. The poet introduces Ulysses to us after his participation in the Trojan War and his successful ten-year struggle to reach his home in Ithaca, where he is now faced with the prospect of being an "idle king" awaiting old age and death. Tennyson speaks through Ulysses, using him as a symbol of man's romantic individualism, forever eager "to strive, to seek, to find, and not to yield," even if this means sweeping a good many community duties under the rug. The poem is a superb expression of one aspect of human greatness, but we must not forget that there are other aspects. Dante, as we shall see, puts Ulysses in his Hell.

> It little profits that an idle king,
> By this still hearth, among these barren crags,
> Matched with an agèd wife, I mete and dole
> Unequal laws unto a savage race,
> That hoard, and sleep, and feed, and know not me.   5
> I cannot rest from travel. I will drink

---

1. IDLE KING: Ulysses himself.

Life to the lees. All times I have enjoyed
Greatly, have suffered greatly, both with those
That loved me, and alone; on shore, and when
Through scudding drifts the rainy Hyades　　　　　　　10
Vexed the dim sea. I am become a name;
For always roaming with a hungry heart
Much have I seen and known,—cities of men
And manners, climates, councils, governments,
Myself not least, but honored of them all,—　　　　15
And drunk delight of battle with my peers,
Far on the ringing plains of windy Troy.
I am a part of all that I have met;
Yet all experience is an arch where-through
Gleams that untraveled world whose margin fades　20
Forever and forever when I move.
How dull it is to pause, to make an end,
To rust unburnished, not to shine in use!
As though to breathe were life! Life piled on life
Were all too little, and of one to me　　　　　　　25
Little remains; but every hour is saved
From that eternal silence, something more.
A bringer of new things; and vile it were
For some three suns to store and hoard myself,
And this gray spirit yearning in desire　　　　　30
To follow knowledge like a sinking star,
Beyond the utmost bound of human thought.
　　This is my son, mine own Telemachus,
To whom I leave the scepter and the isle—
Well-loved of me, discerning to fulfill　　　　　35
This labor, by slow prudence to make mild
A rugged people, and through soft degrees
Subdue them to the useful and the good.
Most blameless is he, centered in the sphere
Of common duties, decent not to fail　　　　　40
In offices of tenderness, and pay
Meet adoration to my household gods,
When I am gone. He works his work, I mine.
　　There lies the port; the vessel puffs her sail;
There gloom the dark, broad seas. My mariners,　45
Souls that have toiled, and wrought, and thought with me,—
That ever with a frolic welcome took
The thunder and the sunshine, and opposed
Free hearts, free foreheads,—you and I are old;
Old age hath yet his honor and his toil.　　　　50
Death closes all; but something ere the end,

---

10. HYADES: group of stars whose influence was
supposed to bring rain.

Some work of noble note, may yet be done,
Not unbecoming men that strove with gods.
The lights begin to twinkle from the rocks;
The long day wanes; the slow moon climbs; the deep   55
Moans round with many voices. Come, my friends.
'Tis not too late to seek a newer world.
Push off, and sitting well in order smite
The sounding furrows; for my purpose holds
To sail beyond the sunset, and the baths   60
Of all the western stars, until I die.
It may be that the gulfs will wash us down;
It may be we shall touch the Happy Isles,
And see the great Achilles, whom we knew.
Though much is taken, much abides; and though   65
We are not now that strength which in old days
Moved earth and heaven, that which we are, we are,—
One equal temper of heroic hearts,
Made weak by time and fate, but strong in will
To strive, to seek, to find, and not to yield.   70

---

55. DEEP: sea.
58. SITTING . . . ORDER: Ulysses's ship is a galley propelled by many oarsmen sitting in rows.
60. BATHS: i.e., distant waters into which stars seem to descend.

62. GULFS: whirlpools.
63. HAPPY ISLES: the Islands of the Blessed, where heroes dwell after death.
64. ACHILLES: one of the Greek leaders, along with Ulysses, in the Trojan War.

I

1. Why does Ulysses want to leave Ithaca again? What does he want *to seek, to find*? What impression does he give of his wife and son? Why does he mention them at all? How would you read line 43 ("He works his work, I mine") and what does it mean? What kind of person does Ulysses reveal himself to be? Don't be satisfied with listing the obvious personality traits he shows.

2. What do the following phrases mean in context?
    a. ". . . and not know me" (5).
    b. "a hungry heart" (12).
    c. "Myself not least, but honored of them all" (15).
    d. "To rust unburnished, not to shine in use" (23).
    e. "Life piled on life/Were all too little" (24-25).
    f. "That ever with a frolic welcome took
        The thunder and the sunshine, and opposed
        Free hearts, free foreheads,—" (47-49).
    g. "It may be that the gulfs will wash us down" (62).

3. This is obviously a dramatic monologue, like "My Last Duchess" and "Andrea del Sarto." How does it compare in "drama" with those poems? To whom does Ulysses speak? How effectively does Tennyson give the reader a sense of the real presence of listeners? Do lines 1-32 strike you as the kind of talk a man would be likely to give to such an audience? Why or why not?

4. Tennyson himself stated that " 'Ulysses' . . . was written soon after Arthur Hallam's death [Hallam was Tennyson's closest friend and was engaged to his sister; he died at the age of 22, in 1833, when Tennyson was 24] and gave my feeling about the need of going forward and braving the struggle of life." Comment on Tennyson's choice of the old Ulysses to express this feeling, and discuss his conviction that to be up and doing is the way to be "braving the struggle of life."

II

1. There is nothing in Homer about Ulysses's later years, but Dante mentions the old warrior in *The Inferno*, from which Tennyson probably got the suggestions he expands upon here. The

lines from *The Inferno* (Canto XXVI, 90-142) are reproduced below. Here, in the eighth circle of Hell, "the Evil Counselors move about endlessly, hidden from view inside great flames. Their sin was to abuse the gifts of the Almighty, to steal his virtues for low purposes. And as they stole from God in their lives and worked by hidden ways, so are they stolen from sight and hidden in the great flames which are their own guilty consciences."

> "I stood on the bridge, and leaned out from the edge;
>   so far, that but for a jut of rock I held to
>   I should have been sent hurtling from the ledge
>
> without being pushed. And seeing me so intent,
>   my Guide said: 'There are souls within those flames;   5
>   each sinner swathes himself in his own torment.'
>
> 'Master,' I said, 'your words make me more sure,
>   but I had seen already that it was so
>   and meant to ask what spirit must endure
>
> the pains of that great flame which splits away   10
>   in two great horns, as if it rose from the pyre
>   where Eteocles and Polynices lay?'
>
> He answered me: 'Forever round this path
>   Ulysses and Diomede move in such dress,
>   united in pain as once they were in wrath;   15
>
> there they lament the ambush of the Horse
>   which was the door through which the noble seed
>   of the Romans issued from its holy source;
>
> there they mourn that for Achilles slain
>   sweet Deidamia weeps even in death;   20
>   there they recall the Palladium in their pain.'
>
> 'Master,' I cried, 'I pray you and repray
>   till my prayer becomes a thousand—if these souls
>   can still speak from the fire, oh let me stay
>
> until the flame draws near! Do not deny me;   25
>   You see how fervently I long for it!'
>   And he to me: 'Since what you ask is worthy,

---

5. GUIDE: Virgil (representing pagan insight) guides Dante through the Inferno, but must stop short of Purgatory and Paradise.

12. ETEOCLES AND POLYNICES: Oedipus's two sons, who died by each other's hands, one attacking and one defending Thebes.

14. DIOMEDE: another of the Greek heroes of the siege of Troy. Dante felt strongly that the Greeks were in the wrong at Troy and therefore sees as evil the activities of Ulysses and Diomede in bringing about Trojan defeat.

16. THE HORSE: i.e., the stratagem of the Wooden Horse, through which Troy fell.

18. ROMANS: Aeneas, founder of Rome, fought against the Greeks at Troy.

20. DEIDAMIA: a loved one of Achilles; when Ulysses talked him into going to Troy, she died of grief.

21. PALLADIUM: Ulysses stole the statue of Pallas from Troy. It was believed that so long as the statue remained in Troy, the city would be safe.

it shall be. But be still and let me speak;
  for I know your mind already, and they perhaps
  might scorn your manner of speaking, since they were Greek.'   30

And when the flame had come where time and place
  seemed fitting to my Guide, I heard him say
  these words to it: 'O you two souls who pace

together in one flame!—if my days above   35
  won favor in your eyes, if I have earned
  however much or little of your love

in writing my High Verses, do not pass by,
  but let one of you be pleased to tell where he,
  having disappeared from the known world, went to die.'

As if it fought the wind, the greater prong   40
  of the ancient flame began to quiver and hum;
  then moving its tip as if it were the tongue

that spoke, gave out a voice above the roar.
  'When I left Circe,' it said, 'who more than a year   45
  detained me near Gaëta long before

Aeneas came and gave the place that name,
  not fondness for my son, nor reverence
  for my aged father, nor Penelope's claim

to the joys of love, could drive out of my mind   50
  the lust to experience the far-flung world
  and the failings and felicities of mankind.

I put out on the high and open sea
  with a single ship and only those few souls
  who stayed true when the rest deserted me.

As far as Morocco and as far as Spain   55
  I saw both shores; and I saw Sardinia
  and the other islands of the open main.

I and my men were stiff and slow with age
  when we sailed at last into the narrow pass
  where, warning all men back from further voyage,   60

33-37. TWO . . . VERSES: Virgil had celebrated both Ulysses and Diomede in his poetry.
44. CIRCE: who had changed Ulysses's men to swine and had prevented him from leaving her island for a time.
45. GAËTA: town on southwest coast of Italy.
46. AENEAS: hero of Virgil's *Aeneid* (see lines 17-18 and note).
48. PENELOPE: Ulysses's wife.

Hercules' Pillars rose upon our sight.
  Already I had left Ceuta on the left;
  Seville now sank behind me on the right.

'Shipmates,' I said, 'who through a hundred thousand
  perils have reached the West, do not deny   65
  to the brief remaining watch our senses stand

experience of the world beyond the sun.
  Greeks! You were not born to live like brutes,
  but to press on toward manhood and recognition!'

With this brief exhortation I made my crew   70
  so eager for the voyage I could hardly
  have held them back from it when I was through;

and turning our stern toward morning, our bow toward night,
  we bore southwest out of the world of man;
  we made wings of our oars for our fool's flight.   75

That night we raised the other pole ahead
  with all its stars, and ours had so declined
  it did not rise out of its ocean bed.

Five times since we had dipped our bending oars
  beyond the world, the light beneath the moon   80
  had waxed and waned, when dead upon our course

we sighted, dark in space, a peak so tall
  I doubted any man had seen the like.
  Our cheers were hardly sounded, when a squall

broke hard upon our bow from the new land: 85
  three times it sucked the ship and the sea about
  as it pleased Another to order and command.

At the fourth, the poop rose and the bow went down
  till the sea closed over us and the light was gone.' "*

----

61. HERCULES' PILLARS: the eastern end of the narrow Strait of Gibraltar. Hercules was supposed to have parted the land at this point.
62. CEUTA: in Africa, opposite Gibraltar.
63. SEVILLE: name given to Spain in general; Ulysses is now in the Atlantic.
65-67. DO . . . SUN: i.e., let's not deny ourselves this last great experience of sailing into the unknown.

73. MORNING . . . NIGHT: East and West.
77. STARS: the Southern stars. OURS: North Star.
79-81. FIVE . . . WANED: i.e., five months passed.
82. PEAK: Purgatory.
87. ANOTHER: God.

What details has Tennyson taken from Dante's *Inferno* on which to build his poem? What has he left out or changed? How is his Ulysses the same kind of man as Dante's? how different?

Notice that line 75 in Ciardi's translation refers to the voyage as "our fool's flight." In what sense is this so? Does Tennyson see the voyage in this light? Explain.

ODE TO THE WEST WIND   [*1819*]

Percy Bysshe Shelley

The intensity with which Ulysses communicates his longing to do "Some work of noble note . . ./To sail beyond the sunset, and the baths/Of all the western stars" gives Tennyson's poem a power that for the moment wipes away our second thoughts to the effect that it may not be so noble to abandon an "agèd wife" and ask your son to handle your obligations to your subjects and your gods. We applaud his commitment "To follow knowledge like a sinking star/ Beyond the utmost bound of human thought," not because we have any idea of just what "knowledge" he will follow or where "beyond the sunset" is, but because we know that the attitude which drives the adventurous, questing mind is one of the attitudes which can give most dignity and heroism to the human spirit.

In just this same way Shelley's "Ode to the West Wind" has been felt by readers for nearly one hundred and fifty years to be a compelling summons to the regeneration of mankind. One does not find in the poem the slightest sug- gestion of just what Shelley means by "quicken a new birth" or what practical measures he would undertake to bring it about, but one does find in his impassioned invocation a statement of expectation and unconquerable desire that, like the wind, sweeps all before it.

I

O wild West Wind, thou breath of Autumn's being,
Thou, from whose unseen presence the leaves dead
Are driven, like ghosts from an enchanter fleeing,

Yellow, and black, and pale, and hectic red,
Pestilence-stricken multitudes: O thou,   5
Who chariotest to their dark wintry bed

The wingèd seeds, where they lie cold and low,
Each like a corpse within its grave, until
Thine azure sister of the Spring shall blow

Her clarion o'er the dreaming earth, and fill   10
(Driving sweet buds like flocks to feed in air)
With living hues and odors plain and hill:

Wild Spirit, which art moving everywhere;
Destroyer and preserver; hear, oh, hear!

II

Thou on whose stream, mid the steep sky's commotion,   15
Loose clouds like earth's decaying leaves are shed,
Shook from the tangled boughs of Heaven and Ocean,

Angels of rain and lightning: there are spread
On the blue surface of thine airy surge,
Like the bright hair uplifted from the head   20

Of some fierce Maenad, even from the dim verge
Of the horizon to the zenith's height,
The locks of the approaching storm. Thou dirge

Of the dying year, to which this closing night
Will be the dome of a vast sepulchre,   25
Vaulted with all thy congregated might

Of vapors, from whose solid atmosphere
Black rain, and fire, and hail will burst: oh, hear!

III

Thou who didst waken from his summer dreams
The blue Mediterranean, where he lay,   30
Lulled by the coil of his crystàlline streams,

Beside a pumice isle in Baiae's bay,
And saw in sleep old palaces and towers
Quivering within the wave's intenser day,

All overgrown with azure moss and flowers   35
So sweet, the sense faints picturing them! Thou
For whose path the Atlantic's level powers

Cleave themselves into chasms, while far below
The sea-blooms and the oozy woods which wear
The sapless foliage of the ocean, know   40

Thy voice, and suddenly grow gray with fear,
And tremble and despoil themselves: oh, hear!

IV

If I were a dead leaf thou mightest bear;
If I were a swift cloud to fly with thee;
A wave to pant beneath thy power, and share   45

The impulse of thy strength, only less free
Than thou, O uncontrollable! If even
I were as in my boyhood, and could be

---

21. MAENAD: female attendant of Dionysus, the
    god of wine; hence a frenzied woman.
24. THIS CLOSING NIGHT: i.e., this night closing in.

32. BAIAE: fashionable Roman sea-resort near
    Naples, much of which was later covered by
    the sea (33-34).

The comrade of thy wanderings over Heaven,
As then, when to outstrip thy skiey speed   50
Scarce seemed a vision; I would ne'er have striven

As thus with thee in prayer in my sore need.
Oh, lift me as a wave, a leaf, a cloud!
I fall upon the thorns of life! I bleed!

A heavy weight of hours has chained and bowed   55
One too like thee: tameless, and swift, and proud.

V

Make me thy lyre, even as the forest is:
What if my leaves are falling like its own!
The tumult of thy mighty harmonies

Will take from both a deep, autumnal tone,   60
Sweet though in sadness. Be thou, Spirit fierce,
My spirit! Be thou me, impetuous one!

Drive my dead thoughts over the universe
Like withered leaves to quicken a new birth!
And, by the incantation of this verse,   65

Scatter, as from an unextinguished hearth
Ashes and sparks, my words among mankind!
Be through my lips to unawakened earth

The trumpet of a prophecy! O, Wind,
If Winter comes, can Spring be far behind?   70

50-51. AS . . . VISION: i.e., in childhood it seemed
perfectly possible to outrun the wind.

I

1. The theme of the poem emerges from the two-fold conception of the wind established in the first stanza: *destroyer and preserver*. Which of these aspects of the wind is covered in lines 1-5? Which in lines 6-12? How does the simile in line 11 extend our consciousness of the aspect covered in these lines? What word in line 11 also stresses this aspect? In lines 8-10 there is an allusion to another occasion when death leads to life. What is it?

    2. *a.* In stanza 2 what corresponds to the leaves of stanza 1? What are the "tangled boughs of Heaven and Ocean"? Consider the appearance of sea and sky before an "approaching storm" (23), and also where the water comes from that falls as rain. What justification is there for calling the clouds "Angels of rain and lightning"? What similarities of appearance might they have with our usual conception of angels? What similarities of function?

    b. Lines 18-23 may at first sight seem confusing syntactically: "there" in line 18 refers to "On the blue surface"; "locks" in line 23 is the subject of the verb phrase "are spread" in line 18. In more conventional word order the lines might read: "There, on the blue surface of thine airy surge, the locks of the approaching storm are spread, from the dim verge of the horizon to the zenith's height, like the bright hair uplifted from the head of some fierce Maenad." What is lost by this paraphrase in addition to rhyme and rhythm?

c. The comparison of the gathering storm clouds to the hair of "some fierce Maenad" can also be confusing at first sight. Evidently the face of the Maenad is below the level of the horizon so all that can be seen are her wild locks— *uplifted*—streaking the sky. How does the allusion to "some fierce Maenad" add to our consciousness of what is happening?

d. Is the West Wind still a *destroyer* in stanza 2? In what way? Is there any hint that there may be a creative purpose behind it? Consider the comparison of the clouds to "angels," of the storm to a "Maenad," of the wind to a dirge for the "dying year," etc.

3. a. What in stanza 3 corresponds to the leaves of stanza 1 and the clouds of stanza 2? What kind of scene do lines 29-36 depict? Why the reference to the ancient Roman sea-resort whose *old palaces and towers* lie beneath the waves? How do lines 37-42 extend the activities described in lines 29-36?

b. In stanza 1 the Wind is an outside agent: it drives the leaves and seeds. In stanza 2 it is described not as an outside agent but as an inseparable part of the whole storm pattern: the clouds move *with* the Wind. What further change in point of view is there in stanza 3? How can "the Atlantic's level powers/Cleave themselves" to make a "path" for the Wind? Why does

the speaker see the West Wind here as a *presence* (see line 2) that infects the things it moves with its own power to act?

c. Is the West Wind still a *destroyer* in stanza 3? In what way? What indications are there that it is also a *preserver* here?

4. In stanza 4 the speaker turns to his own condition. How does he see himself? How does he relate himself to what he has dealt with in the first three stanzas? What has happened to him since boyhood? Are the experiences obscurely referred to in lines 54-56 peculiar to him, or are they pretty generally the experiences common to every man in growing up? What meaning will they have if we read them in the light of Wordsworth's sonnet "The World Is Too Much with Us"? in the light of the selection from Tomlinson's *The Sea and the Jungle*? in the light of Browning's "Andrea del Sarto"? in the light of *Oedipus*? or *Hamlet*?

5. In stanza 5 the speaker tries to absorb into himself the strengths of the West Wind. How are the varying attitudes toward the Wind as discussed in question 3b carried through in this stanza? How is the two-fold *destroyer and preserver* conception maintained? What is the *new birth*, the *prophecy*? What does the last line mean and how does it sum up the theme and action of the poem? The allusion referred to in question 2 reappears in this stanza. In what word? How does the presence of the allusion enrich the meaning of the last line? What is the process that Shelley sees to be inherent and necessary in all life at all times?

6. Note that the stanzas are fourteen lines long, the regular sonnet length. How does the verse form differ from that of the sonnet? What is the rhyme scheme? Characterize the rhythm of the poem. Note particularly the number of run-on lines. Comment on the relationship between the rhyme and rhythm and the subject matter of the poem.

AND DID THOSE FEET . . .   [*circa 1806*]

William Blake

Shelley's impassioned prayer for the power, through his verse, to "Scatter . . . my words among mankind" in order to "quicken a new birth" is clearly a reference to some kind of spiritual rebirth, not in terms of historical Christianity but in terms of an intense faith in man's capacity to improve the institutions that, depending on their character and vitality, may either liberate or degrade him, and to set up on earth a good society. Poets have always acted, sometimes without conscious intention, as the consciences of men. Occasionally, as in Blake's "London," the poet's vision spotlights the depths to which men can sink so that our deadened sense of decency and compassion may come again to life. Or, as in the following poem, we are recalled to our own deepest awareness of what we might be if we would. This, too, is an expression of faith in spiritual rebirth, an expression quite different from Shelley's but no less animated by prophetic force.

And did those feet in ancient time
Walk upon England's mountains green?
And was the holy Lamb of God
On England's pleasant pastures seen?

And did the Countenance Divine   5
Shine forth upon our clouded hills?
And was Jerusalem builded here
Among these dark Satanic Mills?

Bring me my Bow of burning gold:
Bring me my Arrows of desire: 10
Bring me my Spear: O clouds unfold!
Bring me my Chariot of fire.

I will not cease from Mental Fight,
Nor shall my Sword sleep in my hand
Till we have built Jerusalem   15
In England's green and pleasant Land.

1-2. AND . . . GREEN: see Isaiah 52:7.
8. SATANIC MILLS: Blake probably refers to the grim, man-devouring factories of the first decade of the Industrial Revolution.

15. JERUSALEM: i.e., the "New Jerusalem" of Biblical prophetic writing: the City of God on earth.

I

1. What is the effect of the series of questions in the first two stanzas, and why does Blake begin each with "And"? Leave out the "And's" and see what change in tone occurs. What do "those feet" and "ancient time" refer to? Is there any answer to the questions asked in the first two stanzas? Does it make any difference? Why or why not?

2. Notice how regular the metrical pattern is in the first two stanzas. The only variations are in lines 2, 6, and 7. You can see the value of the variations by substituting regular lines, such as:

And did those feet in ancient time
   Oft walk on England's mountains green
And was the holy Lamb of God
   On England's pleasant pastures seen?

And did the countenance divine
   E'er shine upon our clouded hills?
And was *Beersheba* builded here
   Among these dark Satanic mills?

How is the pattern changed in stanza 3? What is gained by the new pattern? What is the force of repeating "Bring" four times? How does Blake heighten intensity within the stanza? Locate and account for other changes in pattern in stanza 4. What is the effect of the return to regular meter in the poem's last line?

3. What makes the weapons of stanza 3 effective instruments of attack? In other words, why do we respond to these unreal weapons as having the power to do the work necessary to build "Jerusalem/In England's green and pleasant Land"?

II

1. Compare Blake's poem and Shelley's in the power of each to move the imagination.

I THINK CONTINUALLY OF THOSE
WHO WERE TRULY GREAT   [*1933*]

Stephen Spender

A modern British poet, Stephen Spender, has summed up in the idiom of our own times the inextinguishable human longing, in all of us at our best, "to strive, to seek, to find," to be to unawakened earth "the trumpet of a prophecy," to build "Jerusalem" in every "green and pleasant land."

Spender's "those who were truly great" are all those "Whose lovely ambition/ Was that their lips, still touched with fire,/Should tell of the Spirit clothed from head to foot in song." In other words, they are the poets or "singers"—but also the creators, prophets, self-givers of every kind—and their "lovely ambition" is a faith like Blake's and Tennyson's and Shelley's in the eternal "flowering of the spirit."

I think continually of those who were truly great.
Who, from the womb, remembered the soul's history
Through corridors of light where the hours are suns,
Endless and singing. Whose lovely ambition
Was that their lips, still touched with fire,   5
Should tell of the spirit clothed from head to foot in song.
And who hoarded from the spring branches
The desires falling across their bodies like blossoms.

What is precious is never to forget
The delight of the blood drawn from ageless springs   10
Breaking through rocks in worlds before our earth;
Never to deny its pleasure in the simple morning light,
Nor its grave evening demand for love;
Never to allow gradually the traffic to smother
With noise and fog the flowering of the spirit.   15

Near the snow, near the sun, in the highest fields
See how these names are fêted by the waving grass,
And by the streamers of white cloud,
And whispers of wind in the listening sky;
The names of those who in their lives fought for life,   20
Who wore at their hearts the fire's center.
Born of the sun they traveled a short while towards the sun,
And left the vivid air signed with their honor.

I

1. What are the usual connotations of "great"? Spender's "those who were truly great" scarcely fit into the usual categories of "greatness"; why then does he use the term?

2. What are the characteristics of the *truly great*? What is the "soul's history . . . Endless and singing" (2-4) that they remembered? Why did they hoard the desires from the "spring branches" (7-8)? What is the "delight of the blood" (10)? What is "the fire's center" that they "wore at their hearts" (21)? What prevents most men from being *truly great?*

3. How does the speaker develop the idea of timelessness in the poem besides using such terms as "Endless" and "ageless"? Why does he want such an idea?

4. There is no regular metrical pattern here, but even if the poem were printed in conventional prose form, you could not miss the rhythm of it. How is it achieved? What metrical regularities can you find (consider lines 5-6)? What key words are repeated? What vowel sounds are repeated (consider particularly lines 2, 11, 17, and 19)?

THE OTHER SIDE OF THE HEDGE   [*1911*]

E. M. Forster

The four preceding selections variously praise the active, creative, dedicated life that finds fulfillment in being used, in seeking goals beyond self-contentment. For anyone who takes seriously the consequences of his humanity each selection is an affirmation and a challenge. At the same time the attitudes expressed in each selection have often been distorted by misguided zeal and self-righteous smugness.

It is the zealot and the hypocrite whom E. M. Forster dissects in the following short story, "The Other Side of the Hedge." With the same attitude of irreverence that marked "What I Believe," he asks us to take a close look at striving and seeking, at progress, at getting ahead, at what he calls "science and the spirit of emulation"—and to ask loudly "Wherefore?"

My pedometer told me that I was twenty-five;[1] and, though it is a shocking thing to stop walking, I was so tired that I sat down on a milestone to rest. People outstripped me, jeering as they did so, but I was too apathetic to feel resentful, and even when Miss Eliza Dimbleby, the great educationist,[2] swept past, exhorting me to persevere, I only smiled and raised my hat.

At first I thought I was going to be like my brother, whom I had had to leave by the roadside a year or two round the corner. He had wasted his breath on singing, and his strength on helping others. But I had traveled more wisely, and now it was only the monotony of the highway that oppressed me —dust under foot and brown crackling hedges on either side, ever since I could remember.

And I had already dropped several things —indeed, the road behind was strewn with the things we all had dropped; and the white dust was settling down on them, so that already they looked no better than stones. My muscles were so weary that I could not even bear the weight of those things I still carried. I slid off the milestone into the road, and lay there prostrate, with my face to the great parched hedge, praying that I might give up.

A little puff of air revived me. It seemed to come from the hedge; and, when I opened my eyes, there was a glint of light through the tangle of boughs and dead leaves. The hedge could not be as thick as usual. In my weak, morbid state, I longed to force my way in, and see what was on the other side. No one was in sight, or I should not have dared to try. For we of the road do not admit in conversation that there is another side at all.

I yielded to the temptation, saying to myself that I would come back in a minute.

The thorns scratched my face, and I had to use my arms as a shield, depending on my feet alone to push me forward. Halfway through I would have gone back, for in the passage all the things I was carrying were scraped off me, and my clothes were torn. But I was so wedged that return was impossible, and I had to wriggle blindly forward, expecting every moment that my strength would fail me, and that I should perish in the undergrowth.

Suddenly cold water closed round my head, and I seemed sinking down for ever. I had fallen out of the hedge into a deep pool. I rose to the surface at last, crying for help, and I heard someone on the opposite bank laugh and say: "Another!" And then I was twitched out and laid panting on the dry ground.

Even when the water was out of my eyes, I was still dazed, for I had never been in so large a space, nor seen such grass and sunshine. The blue sky was no longer a strip, and beneath it the earth had risen grandly into hills—clean, bare buttresses, with beech trees in their folds, and meadows and clear pools at their feet. But the hills were not high, and there was in the landscape a sense of human occupation—so that one might have called it a park or garden, if the words did not imply a certain triviality and constraint.

As soon as I got my breath, I turned to my rescuer and said:

"Where does this place lead to?"

"Nowhere, thank the Lord!" said he, and laughed. He was a man of fifty or sixty— just the kind of age we mistrust on the road —but there was no anxiety in his manner, and his voice was that of a boy of eighteen.

"But it must lead somewhere!" I cried, too much surprised at his answer to thank him for saving my life.

"He wants to know where it leads!" he shouted to some men on the hillside, and they laughed back, and waved their caps.

I noticed then that the pool into which I had fallen was really a moat which bent

---

1. PEDOMETER . . . TWENTY-FIVE: A pedometer measures walking distances; here it ironically measures time (years), since what is important on *the road* is getting ahead as one grows older.
2. EDUCATIONIST: derogatory term for teacher.

round to the left and to the right, and that the hedge followed it continually. The hedge was green on this side—its roots showed through the clear water, and fish swam about in them—and it was wreathed over with dog-roses and Traveler's Joy. But it was a barrier, and in a moment I lost all pleasure in the grass, the sky, the trees, the happy men and women, and realized that the place was but a prison, for all its beauty and extent.

We moved away from the boundary, and then followed a path almost parallel to it, across the meadows. I found it difficult walking, for I was always trying to out-distance my companion, and there was no advantage in doing this if the place led nowhere. I had never kept step with anyone since I left my brother.

I amused him by stopping suddenly and saying disconsolately, "This is perfectly terrible. One cannot advance: one cannot progress. Now we of the road—"

"Yes. I know."

"I was going to say, we advance continually."

"I know."

"We are always learning, expanding, developing. Why, even in my short life I have seen a great deal of advance—the Transvaal War,[3] the Fiscal Question,[4] Christian Science,[5] Radium. Here for example—"

I took out my pedometer, but it still marked twenty-five, not a degree more.

"Oh, it's stopped! I meant to show you. It should have registered all the time I was walking with you. But it makes me only twenty-five."

"Many things don't work in here," he

3. TRANSVAAL WAR: usually known as the Boer War, between the British and the Dutch settlers of South Africa, 1899-1902.
4. FISCAL QUESTION: Fiscal usually refers to governmental financial affairs; hence, there is always a "Fiscal Question."
5. CHRISTIAN SCIENCE: a religious movement founded by Mary Baker Eddy in 1866. One of its principal beliefs is that healing comes by spiritual means rather than by surgery or medicine.

said. "One day a man brought in a Lee-Metford,[6] and that wouldn't work."

"The laws of science are universal in their application. It must be the water in the moat that has injured the machinery. In normal conditions everything works. Science and the spirit of emulation—those are the forces that have made us what we are."

I had to break off and acknowledge the pleasant greetings of people whom we passed. Some of them were singing, some talking, some engaged in gardening, hay-making, or other rudimentary industries. They all seemed happy; and I might have been happy too, if I could have forgotten that the place led nowhere.

I was startled by a young man who came sprinting across our path, took a little fence in fine style, and went tearing over a plowed field till he plunged into a lake, across which he began to swim. Here was true energy, and I exclaimed: "A cross-country race! Where are the others?"

"There are no others," my companion replied; and, later on, when we passed some long grass from which came the voice of a girl singing exquisitely to herself, he said again: "There are no others." I was bewildered at the waste in production, and murmured to myself, "What does it all mean?"

He said: "It means nothing but itself"— and he repeated the words slowly, as if I were a child.

"I understand," I said quietly, "but I do not agree. Every achievement is worthless unless it is a link in the chain of development. And I must not trespass on your kindness any longer. I must get back somehow to the road, and have my pedometer mended."

"First, you must see the gates," he replied, "for we have gates, though we never use them."

I yielded politely, and before long we reached the moat again, at a point where it was spanned by a bridge. Over the bridge

6. LEE-METFORD: a British military rifle, adopted in 1888.

was a big gate, as white as ivory,[7] which was fitted into a gap in the boundary hedge. The gate opened outwards, and I exclaimed in amazement, for from it ran a road—just such a road as I had left—dusty under foot, with brown crackling hedges on either side as far as the eye could reach.

"That's my road!" I cried.

He shut the gate and said: "But not your part of the road. It is through this gate that humanity went out countless ages ago, when it was first seized with the desire to walk."

I denied this, observing that the part of the road I myself had left was not more than two miles off. But with the obstinacy of his years he repeated: "It is the same road. This is the beginning, and though it seems to run straight away from us, it doubles so often, that it is never far from our boundary and sometimes touches it." He stooped down by the moat, and traced on its moist margin an absurd figure like a maze. As we walked back through the meadows, I tried to convince him of his mistake.

"The road sometimes doubles, to be sure, but that is part of our discipline. Who can doubt that its general tendency is onward? To what goal we know not—it may be to some mountain where we shall touch the sky, it may be over precipices into the sea. But that it goes forward—who can doubt that? It is the thought of that that makes us strive to excel, each in his own way, and gives us an impetus which is lacking with you. Now that man who passed us—it's true that he ran well, and jumped well, and

swam well; but we have men who can run better, and men who can jump better, and who can swim better. Specialization has produced results which would surprise you. Similarly, that girl—"

Here I interrupted myself to exclaim: "Good gracious me! I could have sworn it was Miss Eliza Dimbleby over there, with her feet in the fountain!"

He believed that it was.

"Impossible! I left her on the road, and she is due to lecture this evening at Tunbridge Wells. Why, her train leaves Cannon Street in—of course my watch has stopped like everything else. She is the last person to be here."

"People always are astonished at meeting each other. All kinds come through the hedge, and come at all times—when they are drawing ahead in the race, when they are lagging behind, when they are left for dead. I often stand near the boundary listening to the sounds of the road—you know what they are—and wonder if anyone will turn aside. It is my great happiness to help someone out of the moat, as I helped you. For our country fills up slowly, though it was meant for all mankind."

"Mankind have other aims," I said gently, for I thought him well-meaning; "and I must join them." I bade him good evening, for the sun was declining, and I wished to be on the road by nightfall. To my alarm, he caught hold of me, crying: "You are not to go yet!" I tried to shake him off, for we had no interests in common, and his civility was becoming irksome to me. But for all my struggles the tiresome old man would not let go; and, as wrestling is not my specialty, I was obliged to follow him.

It was true that I could have never found alone the place where I came in, and I hoped that, when I had seen the other sights about which he was worrying, he would take me back to it. But I was determined not to sleep in the country, for I mistrusted it, and the people too, for all their friendliness. Hungry though I was, I would not join them

---

7. GATE . . . IVORY: In Book XIX of the *Odyssey* Penelope says to her husband, Odysseus, who has finally returned to his home but has not yet revealed himself: "The truth is, we don't know how to deal with dreams; what they tell us is uncertain, and they do not all come true. For there are two different gates which let out the shadowy dreams; one is made of horn, one of polished elephant's tooth. The elephant's tooth is full of untruth, so that any dreams which there come through never come true. But carven horn is ne'er forsworn, and if any one has a dream which came by that gate, it tells him the truth."

in their evening meals of milk and fruit, and, when they gave me flowers, I flung them away as soon as I could do so unobserved. Already they were lying down for the night like cattle—some out on the bare hillside, others in groups under the beeches. In the light of an orange sunset I hurried on with my unwelcome guide, dead tired, faint for want of food, but murmuring indomitably: "Give me life, with its struggles and victories, with its failures and hatreds, with its deep moral meaning and its unknown goal!"

At last we came to a place where the encircling moat was spanned by another bridge, and where another gate interrupted the line of the boundary hedge. It was different from the first gate; for it was half transparent like horn,[8] and opened inwards. But through it, in the waning light, I saw again just such a road as I had left—monotonous, dusty, with brown crackling hedges on either side, as far as the eye could reach.

8. GATE . . . HORN: see quotation from Book XIX of the *Odyssey;* note on page 755.

I was strangely disquieted at the sight, which seemed to deprive me of all self-control. A man was passing us, returning for the night to the hills, with a scythe over his shoulder and a can of some liquid in his hand. I forgot the destiny of our race. I forgot the road that lay before my eyes, and I sprang at him, wrenched the can out of his hand, and began to drink.

It was nothing stronger than beer, but in my exhausted state it overcame me in a moment. As in a dream, I saw the old man shut the gate, and heard him say: "This is where your road ends, and through this gate humanity—all that is left of it—will come in to us."

Though my senses were sinking into oblivion, they seemed to expand ere they reached it. They perceived the magic song of nightingales, and the odor of invisible hay, and stars piercing the fading sky. The man whose beer I had stolen lowered me down gently to sleep off its effects, and, as he did so, I saw that he was my brother.

I

1. What are the characteristics of *the road?* What kind of people move along it? What suggestions are there in the first three paragraphs that there is something unreal and warped about life on *the road?*

2. How is life on *the other side of the hedge* different from life on *the road?* What is significant about the fact that the speaker does the describing and yet is not in the least affected by the contrast? What kind of person is the speaker?

3. The force of the story depends in good part upon the unintentional humor of the narrator, a humorless man. Notice the art of the first paragraph: why a milestone? What picture does "jeering" suggest? What do you see in Miss Eliza Dimpleby, *a great educationist who swept past, exhorting me to persevere?* What picture do you get from "I only smiled and raised my hat"? Point out other examples of

humor throughout the story. Indicate how much of it comes through irony.

4. Explain the allusion to the one-way ivory gate "that humanity went out countless ages ago, when it was first seized with the desire to walk." Explain the allusion to the second gate, the one "half transparent like horn," this time one-way inward.

5. What other meaning is suggested in the last line besides the fact that the speaker had found the brother he had left behind on the road? What connection is there with the second paragraph?

II

1. What constitutes the good life on *the other side of the hedge?* Is the way of life in Forster's paradise in conflict with the aspirations expressed in any of the four preceding selections? Is it an image of their fulfillment? Discuss.

GOD'S GRANDEUR *and* THE WINDHOVER   [*1877*]

Gerard Manley Hopkins

The "faith" expressed in most of the preceding selections has been primarily man-centered, even though in at least three of the pieces—Donne's "Holy Sonnet X," Browning's "Prospice," and Blake's "And Did Those Feet . . ."—the presence of a controlling deity is implicit throughout.

The following two sonnets by Gerard Manley Hopkins are more clearly religious in the usual sense of the word than are any of the selections in this section thus far. Both glorify the world of nature as one perfect expression of "God's grandeur." We have already seen in "Thou Art Indeed Just, Lord" and "Carrion Comfort" that Hopkins's faith was not something he wore lightly. Like Milton, he tried to justify to himself and to mankind the visible disorder and chaos in a world created just and ordered.

Hopkins was converted to Catholicism while a young man studying at Oxford. Upon joining the Jesuit order he destroyed the poems he had written and did not write any more for a period of seven years, because he felt that poetry would detract from the strict vows he had taken to serve God. However, the need to write was great, and he became convinced that there was no necessary contradiction between writing poetry and serving God. Both of the sonnets reproduced here show the intensity of Hopkins's response to the glories of the natural world and the even greater intensity of his religious convictions.

GOD'S GRANDEUR

The world is charged with the grandeur of God.
   It will flame out, like shining from shook foil;
   It gathers to a greatness, like the ooze of oil
Crushed. Why do men then now not reck his rod?
Generations have trod, have trod, have trod;   5
   And all is seared with trade; bleared, smeared with toil;
   And wears man's smudge and shares man's smell: the soil
Is bare now, nor can foot feel, being shod.

And for all this, nature is never spent;
   There lives the dearest freshness deep down things;   10
And though the last lights off the black West went
   Oh, morning, at the brown brink eastward, springs—
Because the Holy Ghost over the bent
   World broods with warm breast and with ah! bright wings.

"God's Grandeur" from *Poems of Gerard Manley Hopkins,* third edition, edited by W. H. Gardner. Published by Oxford University Press, Inc.

3. OOZE OF OIL: from olives.
9. FOR: in spite of.

I

1. Explain the comparisons in lines 2, 3-4, 6, and 13-14.

2. The poem is full of surprising structural effects, but they are not just verbal tricks. Why do you suppose Hopkins included "then now" in line 4? He could have had an acceptable metrical line with just "Why do men not reck his rod." In other words, what advantage to meaning comes from including the words side by side in juxtaposition? What two senses does "then" bear in this line?

3. What does the repetition of "have trod" in line 5 and of the vowel sounds in line 6 accomplish? How would line 11 be written normally? What is gained by rearranging the normal word order and putting no punctuation mark after "went"? How does the inclusion of the simple "ah!" in line 14 help to account for the drama and power of the conclusion?

Find, and discuss the effectiveness of, other examples of unusual word order.

4. Find at least two different internal rhymes in addition to those in line 6. What relationship of meaning between the words that rhyme do they ask us to see? Can you see such relationships between any of the words that alliterate?

5. Discuss Hopkins's use of light-dark contrasts throughout the sonnet.

6. The opening line has a majesty about it reminiscent of the opening line of the nineteenth psalm: "The heavens declare the glory of God." How does the rhythm reinforce this majestic effect? Discuss other lines in which rhythm matches sense, such as 11 and 14.

II

1. How does Hopkins's praise of nature's religious effect on man differ from Wordsworth's, as reflected in "The World Is Too Much with Us" and "Tintern Abbey"?

THE WINDHOVER:
To Christ Our Lord

I caught this morning morning's minion, king-
   dom of daylight's dauphin, dapple-dawn-drawn Falcon, in his riding
Of the rolling level underneath him steady air, and striding
High there, how he rung upon the rein of a wimpling wing
In his ecstasy! then off, off forth on swing,   5
   As a skate's heel sweeps smooth on a bow-bend: the hurl and gliding
Rebuffed the big wind. My heart in hiding
Stirred for a bird,—the achieve of, the mastery of the thing!

Brute beauty and valor and act, oh, air, pride, plume, here
   Buckle! AND the fire that breaks from thee then, a billion   10
Times told lovelier, more dangerous, O my chevalier!

No wonder of it: shéer plód makes plow down sillion
Shine, and blue-bleak embers, ah my dear,
   Fall, gall themselves, and gash gold-vermilion.

Title. WINDHOVER: kestrel or small falcon (see line 2); it has a habit of riding the wind, matching its speed to the wind's.
1. CAUGHT: saw. MINION: favorite.
2. DAUPHIN: originally the title of the eldest son

of the King of France, the heir to the throne; the meaning here is obvious.
4. RUNG . . . REIN: "To ring" in falconry means to rise in the air spirally; this image is combined with that of a horse circling at the end of a long rein.
6. SWEEPS . . . BOW-BEND: makes a bow-shaped sweep.
9. PRIDE: the peak of the climb.
12. SILLION: furrow.

I

1. Several readings aloud will solve most of the syntax problems. It may help to put the phrase *this morning* before *I caught* in line 1, to recognize that the Falcon is the *dauphin of the kingdom of daylight* and is *drawn* on by the "dapple[d] dawn" (2), and to read line 3 as if it said "Of the rolling, level, underneath-him-steady air." What is gained by each of these shifts from normal syntax?

2. This poem is even more intricate musically than "God's Grandeur." How do the rhyme words of the first six lines emphasize the majesty and movement of the bird? Why does Hopkins split "kingdom"? How does leaving out normal punctuation in "rolling level steady underneath him air" help to dramatize the sense of the line? How does Hopkins force emphasis on the word *high* in "and striding/ High there" and why does he do so? How does the rest of line 4 link sound with sense? How is the link made in line 6? In general, how does the rhythm reinforce the visual imagery of the octave?

3. There have been many critical commentaries on "The Windhover," with a number of different interpretations of what it means. Partly because of the subtitle ("To Christ Our Lord") and partly because of an awareness of Hopkins's religious convictions, most critics say that the "thee" of line 10 and the "Oh, my chevalier" of line 11 refer directly to Christ. With this position assumed, let us look at the dramatic structure of the sonnet:

a. What is there about the windhover that *stirred* the heart of the speaker? How does line 9 sum up the awesome qualities of the bird? Why "Brute beauty" (notice that the bird *rebuffed the big wind*)?

b. In what sense has the speaker's heart been *in hiding*? *Hiding* from what? Where is the "here" of line 9? "Buckle" has several possible meanings, but with our assumptions, "collapse" is probably the most useful one. Why does the speaker want the things listed in line 9 to *buckle*? How can the *fire that breaks* from Christ (after the speaker has called for the buckling of "Brute beauty and valor and act, . . . air, pride, plume") be *lovelier, more dangerous?*

c. The last three lines might need some explanation. The first part of line 12 means that there's *no wonder* in the truth that what Christ can mean to man is "a billion/ Times . . . lovelier, more dangerous" than even nature at her grandest can offer. The last two images are set in contrast to the picture of the windhover in action. Plowing is laborious, "plodding" work, but the very act of cutting through the soil ("down sillion" or "down the furrow") makes the plow shine. A log that is not flaming—seemingly black and lifeless ("blue-bleak embers")—will reveal the burning inside when it falls and splits open in places ("fall, gall themselves, and gash gold-vermilion"). What suggested meanings going far beyond these rather flat explanations are there in the way Hopkins has phrased the two images? What contrasts are there between the two images and the description of the windhover? How do the contrasts support the speaker's contention about the power of the *fire that breaks* from Christ?

II

1. What is the relationship between nature and God that Hopkins creates and dramatizes here—or between man and nature and God? Is he saying that the attributes applicable to the falcon are incompatible with the life Christ taught man to lead? Or is he saying that as the falcon flies successfully into the teeth of the big wind and rebuffs it, so Christ through His sacrifice ("gash gold-vermilion") shows man how to face successfully the buffetings of life? Discuss. Remember that it isn't necessarily a question of one or the other.

THE COLLAR *and* VIRTUE   [*1633*]

George Herbert

We have seen in Gerard Manley Hopkins the coupling of an intense desire to believe and a frank recognition of the struggle and anguish involved in believing. In "The Windhover" the poet refers to the "fire that breaks" from Christ as being "a billion/Times . . . lovelier" than the beauty and courage of the falcon in flight, but also adds, "more dangerous." What makes belief "more dangerous" is the awareness of how difficult it is to follow Christ, or to live any religion.

George Herbert, who lived at the beginning of the seventeenth century, wrote poetry of a kind very different from that of Hopkins, but it has in it a kinship with Hopkins in its frank delight in the everyday world as a reflection of God's glory, in its use of striking images, and in its effort to communicate the difficult yet rewarding struggle to keep God's will at the center of his life. Herbert had been born into a family of position and power and felt keenly, despite one's early commitment to the church, the attractions of a worldly life of influence at court.

He reflects this struggle in "The Collar," in which a call for freedom from the restraint of religious demands becomes a recognition that the only true freedom rests, paradoxically, in the controlling force of God's love. In the second poem, "Virtue," he contrasts the impermanence of the world of nature with the permanence of a "sweet and virtuous soul."

THE COLLAR

I struck the board and cried, No more!
        I will abroad.
What? Shall I ever sigh and pine?
My lines and life are free, free as the road,
        Loose as the wind, as large as store.   5
                Shall I be still in suit?
        Have I no harvest but a thorn
        To let me blood, and not restore
What I have lost with cordial fruit?
                Sure there was wine   10
        Before my sighs did dry it; there was corn
        Before my tears did drown it.
        Is the year only lost to me?
        Have I no bays to crown it?
No flowers, no garlands gay? All blasted?   15
                All wasted?
        Not so, my heart! But there is fruit,
                And thou hast hands.
        Recover all thy sigh-blown age

---

1. BOARD: table.
5. STORE: abundance.
6. IN SUIT: pleading (as in a court or law-court).

9. CORDIAL: reviving.
14. BAYS: laurel wreaths (see line 15).
19. SIGH-BLOWN: wasted in sighs.

On double pleasures. Leave thy cold dispute   20
Of what is fit and not. Forsake thy cage,
    Thy rope of sands,
Which petty thoughts have made, and made to thee
  Good cable, to enforce and draw,
    And be thy law,   25
While thou didst wink and wouldst not see.
    Away! Take heed!
    I will abroad.
Call in thy death's head there. Tie up thy fears.
    He that forbears   30
    To suit and serve his need
    Deserves his load.
But as I raved and grew more fierce and wild
    At every word,
Methoughts I heard one calling, Child!   35
    And I replied, My Lord.

21-22. FORSAKE . . . SANDS: i.e., the teachings of the church.
26. WINK: avoid seeing by shutting one's eyes.

29. DEATH'S HEAD: skull; i.e., don't try to frighten me with thoughts of death.

I

1. From line 1 through line 31 (almost the entire poem) the speaker quotes himself. To whom is he speaking? Why isn't there any answering voice? What is he protesting against? What does he want as replacement? What do "wine" (10) and "corn" (11) stand for? Why is the poem in the past tense?

2. What do lines 4-5 mean? line 12? What does "only" modify in line 13? What do lines 20-26 mean? What double meaning is there in lines 30-32; in other words, what is ironic about "Deserves"?

3. What double meaning is there in "Child" (35)? In what sense can the word be applied to what has gone before? How has Herbert communicated the sense of "raving"? What makes the last two lines particularly effective and how have they been prepared for?

4. What is the significance of the title? What is a *collar* for? The word "choler" (-anger) is pronounced the same way but spelled differently. How appropriate is the pun?

VIRTUE

Sweet day, so cool, so calm, so bright,
The bridal of the earth and sky;
The dew shall weep thy fall tonight,
    For thou must die.

Sweet rose, whose hue angry and brave   5
Bids the rash gazer wipe his eye;
Thy root is ever in its grave,
    And thou must die.

Sweet spring, full of sweet days and roses,
A box where sweets compacted lie;   10
My music shows ye have your closes,
    And all must die.

Only a sweet and virtuous soul,
Like seasoned timber, never gives;
But though the whole world turn to coal,   15
    Then chiefly lives.

5. HUE . . . BRAVE: i.e., the color of choler (anger) and courage, which was red.
11. CLOSES: ends of musical phrases; hence, endings, terminations.

15. COAL: ashes (at Judgment Day); see II Peter 3:10-13.

I

1. In stanza 1 how do the very conditions of the "cool . . . calm . . . bright" day bring about the dew which will *weep* its fall? What is meant by the comparison in line 2? Why is "weep" effective and appropriate?

2. How is the idea and imagery of stanza 1 carried over into stanza 2? Why does *the rash gazer wipe his eye?* Relate lines 3-4 and 7-8 to the themes of Shelley's "Ode to the West Wind."

3. How does stanza 3 build on the first two? What is playfully witty about the comparison in line 10? How is the wittiness consistent with the tone of the comparisons in the first two stanzas? How do you account for the sudden shift of subject in line 11? What word in line 10 can have a second meaning that would explain the shift? What pun in line 11 supports the playful idea that music shows all must die?

4. The image of lines 13-14 is based on the making of charcoal from *seasoned timber*. How is a *virtuous soul* like *seasoned timber*? If line 15 refers to Judgment Day, what is Herbert saying about *a sweet and virtuous soul?*

5. What is the effect of the short last lines and the repeating of the first three with slight changes? What is the effect of the change from "die" as the last word in the first three stanzas to "lives" as the last one of the fourth? What changes in the basic metrical pattern are there and what purpose do they serve? Comment on the effectivenes of the stress pattern and vowel structure of line 15.

THE KINGDOM OF GOD
"In No Strange Land"   [*1913*]

Francis Thompson

A third English poet whose poetry concerns itself with the indwelling spirit of God in man is Francis Thompson, who wrote during the latter half of the nineteenth century.

Thompson's life, particularly the first thirty years of it, was about as dreary and unrewarding as can be imagined. He was a total failure at everything he did. Estranged from his family, he lived a drifter's existence in London, almost ruining his health in the process. Fortunately, some of his poetry came to the attention of a sympathetic editor, Wilfred Meynell, who provided Thompson with a home and friendship for the last nineteen years of his life.

It is not surprising that out of misery and degradation has often come the most convincing and intense religious poetry. *De profundis clamavi* ("From the depths I have cried out") say the writers of the Old Testament psalms, and they know whereof they speak. The poem which follows asks us to look no further than the lives we lead to find God's glory; for Thompson, that life was found, not in Wordsworth's idealized nature, but in the grimy streets of London, which had for years been his only home.

O world invisible, we view thee,
O world intangible, we touch thee,
O world unknowable, we know thee,
Inapprehensible, we clutch thee!

Does the fish soar to find the ocean,   5
The eagle plunge to find the air—
That we ask of the stars in motion
If they have rumor of thee there?

Title. See Luke 17:20-21.

Sub-title. See Psalm 137:4.

Not where the wheeling systems darken,
And our benumbed conceiving soars!— 10
The drift of pinions, would we hearken,
Beats at our own clay-shuttered doors.

The angels keep their ancient places;
Turn but a stone, and start a wing!
'Tis ye, 'tis your estrangèd faces, 15
That miss the many-splendored thing.

But, when so sad thou canst not sadder,
Cry;—and upon thy so sore loss
Shall shine the traffic of Jacob's ladder
Pitched betwixt Heaven and Charing Cross. 20

Yea, in the night, my Soul, my daughter,
Cry,—clinging Heaven by the hems;
And lo, Christ walking on the water
Not of Gennesareth, but Thames!

---

19. TRAFFIC . . . LADDER: see Genesis 28:10-17.
20. CHARING CROSS: one of the busiest sections of modern London.
22. CLINGING . . . HEMS: see Matthew 9:20-22 and 14:33-36.
24. GENNESARETH: Sea of Galilee; see Matthew 14:22-33.

I

1. To whom or what does "thee" refer in stanza 1? Explain the paradoxes. Suppose the poem had started with stanza 2: what would have been lost?

2. What do lines 5-6 mean? How do they answer the question of lines 7-8?

3. What do the "wheeling systems" of stanza 3 refer to in stanza 2? What are "our own clay-shuttered doors"? What contrast is intended between the two? What does the "drift of pinions" refer to and how is the image developed in the next two stanzas in lines 13 and 19?

4. What do lines 15-16 mean? To whom do "ye" and "your" refer? How do lines 15-16 answer the question of lines 7-8?

5. What contrasts between colloquial, even racy, statement and exalted idea stated are to be found in the last two stanzas? How do these colloquialisms further contrast with the language of stanza 1? What is gained by the use of lofty phrasing and blunt colloquialisms?

6. Show specifically what each Biblical allusion adds to the total meaning of the poem.

HYMN TO GOD THE FATHER [*circa 1622*]

John Donne

We have already looked at two of John Donne's "Holy Sonnets," but they were very different in tone from the following "Hymn to God the Father." In this poem we see an expression of quiet submission to God's judgment coupled with a recognition of the poet's continuing susceptibility to error and a hope for final forgiveness and peace.

Donne said of the poem: "The words of this hymn have restored me to the same thoughts of joy that possessed my soul in my sickness when I composed it, [and have left me] with an unexpressible tranquillity of mind, and a willingness to leave the world."

You may find it hard to associate "joy" and "tranquillity" with death, but the statement and the poem clearly reveal the secure faith of one who has made his peace with his world and with his God. In the security of his faith Donne can even delight in a pun on his own name.

> Wilt Thou forgive that sin where I begun,
> Which is my sin, though it were done before?
> Wilt Thou forgive that sin through which I run,
> And do run still, though still I do deplore?
> When Thou hast done, Thou hast not done,   5
> For I have more.
>
> Wilt Thou forgive that sin by which I have won
> Others to sin? and made my sin their door?
> Wilt Thou forgive that sin which I did shun
> A year, or two, but wallowed in a score?   10
> When Thou hast done, Thou hast not done,
> For I have more.
>
> I have a sin of fear, that when I have spun
> My last thread, I shall perish on the shore;
> Swear by Thyself, that at my death Thy Son   15
> Shall shine as He shines now, and heretofore;
> And, having done that, Thou hast done,
> I fear no more.

I

1. What sin do the first two lines refer to? What kind of sin is referred to in lines 3-4? What meanings are there in the pun on the poet's name in line 5?

2. What further ways of sinning are brought out in lines 7-10? Is any answer suggested to the four questions asked in stanzas 1 and 2? Explain. What is the effect of repeating lines 5-6 as lines 11-12?

3. In the last stanza what is the fear that the speaker has? Why is this fear a sin? How can the fear be removed? What other pun is there in line 15?

4. Does the use of the two puns and of such a phrase as "Swear by Thyself" constitute irreverence on the speaker's part? Why or why not?

II

1. Looking back at the last six poems by Hopkins, Herbert, Thompson, and Donne, which one or ones seem to you most successfully to communicate, in the words of Elizabeth Drew, "what it feels like to believe a religion"?

PROLOGUE *to* IN MEMORIAM   [*1850*]

Alfred Lord Tennyson

The inner peace found in a God-centered life has been shown in the six preceding selections to have come from moments or periods of turmoil, doubt or conflict, and most of the selections have dramatized the struggle involved.

The following "Prologue" to Tennyson's long poetic record of spiritual striving, "In Memoriam," is a powerful statement of unwavering faith, with only a suggestion of the agony of doubt and despair that Tennyson experienced during the seventeen years the poem was in the making. Although the "Prologue" comes first in the poem, it was one of the last sections to be written and represents the firm conviction he had come to that, in his own words, "fear, doubts, and suffering will find answer and relief only through Faith in a God of Love."

Tennyson began writing "In Memoriam" soon after the untimely death of his friend, Arthur Henry Hallam, in 1833 at the age of 22. The shock of his young friend's death was to haunt Tennyson for years, and many of his poems have direct reference to it. We have already noted the connection in the introduction to "Break, Break, Break," and Tennyson himself said that "Ulysses" has direct reference to the tragic event in its statement of the necessity to face unflinchingly "the struggle of life." "In Memoriam" was written intermittently for seventeen years following Hallam's death and is a closely personal, if not autobiographical, account of Tennyson's emancipation from grief and doubt into the kind of "Faith in a God of Love" and belief in immortality that we find in the "Prologue."

Strong Son of God, immortal love,
  Whom we, that have not seen thy face,
  By faith, and faith alone, embrace,
Believing where we cannot prove;

Thine are these orbs of light and shade;   5
  Thou madest life in man and brute;
  Thou madest death; and lo, thy foot
Is on the skull which thou hast made.

Thou wilt not leave us in the dust:
  Thou madest man, he knows not why,[10]
  He thinks he was not made to die;
And thou hast made him; thou art just.

Thou seemest human and divine,
  The highest, holiest manhood, thou.

Our wills are ours, we know not how;   15
Our wills are ours, to make them thine.

Our little systems have their day;
  They have their day and cease to be;
  They are but broken lights of thee,
And thou, O Lord, art more than they.   20

We have but faith; we cannot know,
  For knowledge is of things we see;
  And yet we trust it comes from thee,
A beam in darkness; let it grow.

Let knowledge grow from more to more,   25
  But more of reverence in us dwell;
  That mind and soul, according well,
May make one music as before,

1-4. STRONG SON . . . CANNOT PROVE: Cf. John 20:24-31.

5. ORBS: planets.

7-8. LO . . . MADE: *the skull* refers to Death; God has made Death and therefore controls Death.

25-26. LET . . . DWELL: By *knowledge* Tennyson means scientific advances; he is calling for more knowledge and more religion, seeing no opposition between the two, as many saw in his day.

27. ACCORDING: agreeing.

But vaster. We are fools and slight;
  We mock thee when we do not fear.   30
  But help thy foolish ones to bear;
Help thy vain worlds to bear thy light.

Forgive what seemed my sin in me,
  What seemed my worth since I began;
  For merit lives from man to man,   35
And not from man, O Lord, to thee.

Forgive my grief for one removed,
  Thy creature, whom I found so fair.
  I trust he lives in thee, and there
I find him worthier to be loved.   40

Forgive these wild and wandering cries,
  Confusions of a wasted youth;
  Forgive them where they fail in truth,
And in thy wisdom make me wise.

---

28. AS BEFORE: i.e., before the great scientific advances of his time called religious certainties into doubt; see note, lines 25-26.

33-36. FORGIVE . . . TO THEE: i.e., the things in myself that I thought bad or good are thought so from the limited point of view of man, and not from the point of view of God; therefore, O Lord, forgive the limitations of my understanding.

37. ONE REMOVED: Arthur Henry Hallam.

41. THESE . . . CRIES: The reference is to the series of loosely connected lyrics which follow and which make up "In Memoriam."

42. WASTED: made desolate.

I

1. How does line 9 reinforce what the speaker is saying in lines 7-8? What is "the dust" referred to in line 9? How do lines 10-12 further reinforce the meaning of 7-9?

2. What is meant by lines 13-14? What connection is there between 13-14 and 15-16? What does the speaker mean by "wills" and what does line 16 mean?

3. How do stanzas 5-7 make more specific the demand upon man stated in line 16? In other words, what is it that men must do to make their *wills* the Lord's will?

4. What does line 30 mean? Why is it that men *mock* the Son of God when they *do not*
fear? In what sense should men *fear?* How does line 32 carry out the idea of line 30? What is "thy light"?

5. What shift in emphasis is there in the last three stanzas, signaled most obviously in the shift from "we" to "I"? What specifically is the speaker asking the Son of God to forgive? How are these three stanzas related to the preceding ones?

6. "In Memoriam," in a sense, is the record of the speaker's struggle with doubt and despair and his eventual reassertion of faith in the *Son of God, immortal love.* Why do you suppose Tennyson used this selection as a Prologue rather than an Epilogue?

Foundations of Faith

The last three selections in this book span the world of Western literature; each presents an image of man that is a distillation of the insights Western man at his best has had into those conditions of mind, heart, and spirit that give human life its deepest meaning.

The first selection is from "Faith and Freedom," a contemporary essay by Barbara Ward, which asks us to look at ourselves in the light of the Greek and Hebrew visions of man's ability to create a "rational order" and man's destiny to become a co-worker with God "in the coming reign of righteousness." Next is Milton's "Areopagitica," written in 1644, a powerful expression of man's inviolable right to do his own thinking and have the means of exchange of thought open to him; the essay is rooted in one of the most exalted views in any literature of the potentialities of human character. The last selection is from the fifth century B. C., Sophocles's *Antigone,* whose theme is faith not in the city of man, but in the everlasting and unchangeable laws of Zeus.

from FAITH AND FREEDOM   *[1954]*

Barbara Ward

Barbara Ward is a contemporary British economist and writer whose sane and penetrating comments on current affairs have appeared for a number of years in *The New York Times Magazine* and other periodicals in England and the United States. "Faith and Freedom" is the last essay in a book of the same title.

In the book as a whole Miss Ward traces the growth of freedom in Western society. She sees the achievements of Western man as an outgrowth of the "tremendous acts of faith in man and in his destiny" that our Greek and Jewish forebears made. The faith is in man, but it is rooted in God as the "higher loyalty" to whom man must turn if he is not to be trapped by the "appetites and despairs which rational codes alone are unable to control." She argues that faith in God made possible the conditions for human freedom as we know it in the West, and she points out that when that faith weakens—as she feels it is doing today—man becomes a victim of the all-powerful state and loses his freedom.

Miss Ward offers no easy way back to faith; she simply says it must come if our freedoms are to survive. "It is a question of conviction and dedication and both spring from one source only—from the belief in God as a fact, as the supreme Fact of existence. Faith will not be restored in the West because people believe it to be useful. It will return only when they find that it is true." In her essay she suggests a way in which each of us can "find that it is true."

However rational, however compelling, however logical the arguments for Western unity may be, however obvious the benefits of economic co-operation, however hopeful the promise of amity between the nations, one may still question whether reason or logic, of themselves, are enough to change the direction of Western development. The vitalities that must be mastered are the fiercest in the world. They appeal to the ultimate instincts in mankind—the protection of the tribe and the struggle for physical survival. Reason may be outmatched in its struggle with such giants. Has Western man other forces to summon to his aid?

There is, of course, the fact of fear. It is not to be despised. Many things have been accomplished in recent years—including the groundwork of the Atlantic alliance[1]—which would never have been achieved without Soviet pressure. Moreover, even if the Soviets were outwardly unaggressive, they could still—like their totalitarian brethren the Nazis—inspire in the West a salutary fear by demonstrating, in its ultimate stages, the rake's progress[2] in which all Western civilization is to some extent involved. Both these systems of absolute dictatorship have sprung from the Western world. Both have carried to an extreme degree principles and policies which have already made their appearance in the West. The nationalism which Hitler turned to a horror of blood and butchery presides in a sedate form over all Western democracies. The confidence in state action, the glorification of technology, the unlimited faith in science, the centralization of decision, and the subordination of law to so-called mass interests—all these, which in an extreme form have gone to set an inhuman stamp upon Soviet society, have helped in the West to create communities in which the

individual citizen feels overwhelmed, isolated, and helpless before the anonymities of public and private bureaucracy. We are right to fear these vast distortions of tendencies already at work in our own society. Both the Soviet and the Nazi systems must stand as dread reminders that in the twentieth century, the line of least resistance in politics tends toward the full apparatus of totalitarian rule. It is not wrong to fear such warnings. It is the beginning of wisdom.

But fear alone is a poor counselor because it is essentially negative. The Western world cannot combat Communism on such a basis. A people guided only by fear leaves all the initiative and all the advantage with the other side and is reduced to a blind defensive maneuvering in order to counter the other's positive actions, to inferiority, to loss of control, and in all probability to ultimate defeat. Throughout history, the men with a positive goal and a persistent aim have had their way. Like artists at work on the raw material of stone or wood or canvas, they have imposed their vision and drawn the rough vitalities of human existence together into new patterns of society. True, the materials have often proved recalcitrant and the vision has been distorted. Yet such ideals as the Greek *polis,* the "chosen people" of Jewry, the unity of Christendom, the American Republic—or indeed the Dictatorship of the Proletariat—have proved instruments in the hands of men by virtue of which the forces of hunger and power and fear, which are the inchoate stuff of existence, have been molded into something nearer the visionaries' desire. If, in the second half of the twentieth century, the Western peoples have lost all their visions and dreamed all their dreams, then the world is open to the powerful myths of the totalitarians. The society which they picture may be in many respects a nightmare, but nightmares are potent in a world without good dreams.

The West will prove more vulnerable than any other society if it abandons the pursuit of visions and ideals for, more than any other

1. ATLANTIC ALLIANCE: NATO, the North Atlantic Treaty Organization.
2. RAKE'S PROGRESS: referring to a famous series of engravings by William Hogarth (1735) showing the downward "progress" of a "rake," a lewd, dissolute fellow.

community, it is the product not of geographical and racial forces but of the molding power of the human spirit. Geographically, Europe is no more than the small Western promontory of the land mass of Asia. It is "Europe" solely because its frontiers mark the frontiers of Christendom. Racially, the United States is a melting pot of every nation under the sun. Only by force of an idea—the "proposition" that men are created equal and possess inalienable rights—has it risen to be the most powerful community in the history of man. Both European society and its extension into the New World have been sustained by a unique faith in man—in his freedom, in his responsibility, in the laws which should safeguard him, in the rights that are his and in the duties by which he earns those rights. So accustomed are we to this view of man that we do not realize the audacity which was needed to bring it into being. At a time when humanity was subject to every physical calamity, when perpetual labor was needed to wring a livelihood from the soil, when the fatalities of tempest and sickness and the general recalcitrance of matter lay heavily upon man's spirit, and when the world, unpenetrated by rational discovery, was a vast unknown—in such a time, the Greek and Jewish forebears of our own civilization made their tremendous acts of faith in man and in his destiny. They declared him to be the crown of the universe. They saw nature as a field open to his reason and his dominion. The Greeks affirmed his power to build a rational order, the Jews proclaimed him a co-worker in the coming reign of righteousness.

It was because this picture of man was so high and so untrammeled and its ambition so vast that it led to the discovery of material instruments of mastery, to science and industry and all the material means of our own day. Man is not master of the universe because he can split the atom. He has split the atom because he first believed in his own unique mastery. Faith led to the material achievement, not the achievement

to the faith. In fact, now that the means of mastering the environment, of building—physically—a better world, are more complete than ever before, it is a paradox that the faith is slackening. The men of the West believed in man's high destiny and in his power to remold society in a divine pattern more entirely when their physical means were inadequate and their control marginal than they do today when science and industry offer unlimited opportunities of creation. The reason is that the old audacious view of man and of his destiny was sustained only by faith. Reduce man to a creature of his environment, projected from the fatality of birth by anonymous forces on to the fatality of death—then he is ready to surrender his freedom, his rights, his greatness. He is ready for dictatorship and the slave state.

The human heart has both appetites and despairs which rational codes alone are unable to control. Man is lonely. He is not self-sufficient. He rebels against meaninglessness in life. He is haunted by death. He is afraid. He needs to feel himself part of a wider whole and he has unassuageable powers of dedication and devotion which must find expression in worship and service. If, therefore, there is no other outlet for these powers, then the community in which he lives, the tribe, the state, Caesar,[3] the dictator, become the natural and inevitable objects of his religious zeal. Religion is not abolished by the "abolition" of God; the religion of Caesar takes its place. And since, for a few men, the need to worship is satisfied in *hubris*,[4] in the worship of the self, the multitudes who look for a god can nearly always be certain of finding a willing candidate. In times of crisis, when insecurity, anxiety, loneliness, and the meaninglessness of life become well-nigh insupportable—how can a man tolerate years

---

3. CAESAR: see Matthew 22:21; Caesar stands for civil power as opposed to God's power.
4. HUBRIS: Greek term meaning wanton indifference to any restraint.

without work in modern industrial society? —the hunger for godlike leadership, for religious reassurance, for a merging of the self in the security of the whole becomes irresistible. Even when faith in God survives, the desire wells up for strong government. Where religious faith has vanished, all the energies of the soul are poured into the one channel of political faith. In our own day, Communism and National Socialism[5] have proved to be powerful religions and have brought back into the world the identification of state and church, city and temple, king and god which made up the monolithic unity of archaic society and the universal servitude of archaic man.

Few deny the historical role of Christianity in creating a double order of reality and a division of power out of which the possibility of freedom has grown. Even the most doubtful must confront the fact that totalitarian government in its extremest form has returned when the waning of religion left the altars of the soul empty and turned men back to the oldest gods of all—the idols of the tribe. Nor is it easy to conceive of any means other than religious faith for preserving a genuine division of power in society; for if man is no more than the creature of his environment, and a product of his social order, on what foundations can he base claims and loyalties which go beyond the social order? From what source can he draw the strength to resist the claims of society? To what justice can he appeal beyond the dictates of the state? The state is by nature so powerful and compelling and voracious an institution that the citizen, standing alone against it, is all but powerless. He needs counter-institutions, above all the counter-institution of the Church, which of all organized bodies alone can look Caesar in the face and claim a higher loyalty.

It is, however, one thing to argue that a recovery of faith in God is necessary as a safeguard of Western freedom. It is quite

another to put forward sociological and political and historical facts as the basis for a revival of faith. Such a procedure runs the risk of resembling the hypocrisy of eighteenth-century cynics who argued that religion was good for the poor because it kept them contented. Faith is not a matter of convenience nor even—save indirectly—a matter of sociology. It is a question of conviction and dedication and both spring from one source only—from the belief in God as a fact, as the supreme Fact of existence. Faith will not be restored in the West because people believe it to be useful. It will return only when they find that it is true.

The firmest proofs of religion are rooted in the nature of reality—in the necessities of reason, in the underivative character of such concepts as truth and goodness. Since, however, the Western mind has in the last century become more and more accustomed to think of proof in the pragmatic terms of modern science—a thing being "true" if it can be shown to work—it is perhaps worth remembering that even here in the sphere of pragmatic proof faith and science conform to a similar pattern and claim a comparable validity. The world which science lays bare, in its capacity as weigher and measurer, is one of soundless, colorless impulses of energy which under given conditions appear to behave in certain ways. This clearly is not reality as such for, at the very least, reality must be allowed to be colored, scented, and noisy—qualities which do not appear in the scientific picture. Yet science can predict up to a point how, under given conditions, this queer universe of energy will behave. Proceed in a given way to set up your experiment and the experiment will work; and, on the theory of probability, repeat the same conditions and the experiment will work again. Thus, even if science cannot say what reality is, still less say whether its abstracted picture is "true," it can say that certain methods of handling reality work.

---

5. NATIONAL SOCIALISM: the Nazi movement in Germany in the 1930's and early 1940's.

What is perhaps not very generally realized is that if this is the full extent of science's claim to lay bare reality, religion can proceed with much the same degree of certitude. The saint can say: "This universe I tell you of, in which God's being and energy and love fill all reality and in which the base of your own soul is anchored in the Source of Being, may seem to you very far removed from the colorful material reality which you meet every day. But is it stranger than the colorless, soundless energies of science? Stranger than the notion that you are sitting this moment upon an intersection of physical impulses? Than that reality is a dance of electrons? The energy of God and the energy of nuclear power are equally remote from daily experience."

But, some will say, we can prove the existence of nuclear power by setting up immensely complicated experiments, processing matter through them, and at the other end receiving a predictable explosion. "Then," the saint continues, "I say that the experiments of the religious life work in exactly the same way. We, the scientists of goodness, tell you that if you will take the raw materials of your all too human mind and body and process them through the laboratory of detachment, humility, prayer, and neighborly love, the result will be the explosion into your life of the overwhelming love and knowledge of God. Do not think you can know God except by hearsay unless you submit yourself to this experimental process, any more than you can produce nuclear fission without an Oak Ridge[6] or a Harwell.[7] But we promise that if the experiment is carried out under clinically pure conditions—as it has been in the life of the best and purest of mankind—then the result is scientifically certain. The pure of heart shall see God. That statement of fact is as experimentally certain as that H_2O is the constitution of water, and it is proved by the same experimental means."

If science is known by results—and this is in fact where its certitude rests—so, too, are the truths of religion. The experimental tests of religion are more delicate and unstable than those of science, for the raw material—the heart of man—has not that implicit obedience to the law of its own nature which is observable in metals or minerals or even living tissues. Inconveniently but gloriously, it has a free and unconditioned element. Again and again, in the laboratory itself, the experiment is botched. Yet where it is triumphantly concluded—in a Buddha, in a Laotse, in a St. Francis of Assisi, in a St. Peter Claver or a John Woolman[8]—the experimental proof of religion shines forth with a light no less clear than that of science.

*   *   *   *   *

The physical universe, in its stupendous richness and variety, is without doubt a profound mystery. The questions which the Almighty leveled at Job to illustrate the gap between the Mind that made the world and human intelligence still hold good for modern man:

"Where wast thou when I laid the foundations of the world? Who hath laid the measure thereof, if thou knowest? Or hath stretched the line upon it? Upon what are its bases grounded? Or who laid the cornerstone thereof?

"Shalt thou be able to join together the shining stars, the Pleiades, or canst thou stop the turning about of Arcturus?

"Canst thou bring forth the day star in its time and make the evening star to rise upon the children of earth?"

Yet if this bewildering panorama is studied,

---

6. OAK RIDGE: Oak Ridge, Tennessee; American atomic power research center.
7. HARWELL: British counterpart to Oak Ridge.

8. BUDDHA . . . WOOLMAN: all famous religious leaders: Buddha, founder of Buddhism in India, sixth century B.C.; Laotse (ca. 604-523 B.C.), Chinese philosopher; St. Francis of Assisi, founder of the Franciscan order, thirteenth century; St. Peter Claver, seventeenth century Spanish Jesuit priest in Latin America (called the "Apostle of the Negroes"); John Woolman, eighteenth century American Quaker.

as natural science has made it possible for us to study it in the last hundred years, some hint of pattern seems nonetheless to emerge. Even if the possibility of purposive creation is dismissed and the processes of blind determinism are accepted, the direction of those processes is at least significant. A type of life on earth has evolved over the millennia which, with all the false starts, tragedies, holocausts, and blind alleys, has moved from the conditioned and limited to the increasingly free and undetermined. Indeed, one of the preconditions of advance appears to have been the avoidance of perfect adaptation to environment. When life becomes fixed in too complete and rigid a physical form, the least unbalance condemns it to destruction. The evolution is from matter to powers which are increasingly difficult to express in terms of matter. Choice, curiosity, questioning, inquiry, deduction, the powers of the questing mind—in a word, a certain freedom —appear to crown the present stage of evolutionary advance; and even those who do not accept the idea of a spiritual order would not deny that if advance is to continue, it is unlikely to take the direction of purely material mutations. Reason, however evolved, holds the key to the future.

To a Christian, this sense of a shadowy pattern underlying the immensities of nature is in no way remarkable. Although no human mind could have invented such a plot to the history of humanity, the plot, once unveiled, is consistent with what a man might gropingly know of his Creator. The highest good of which reason has any experience is disinterested love. Faced with the vast conundrum of why a self-subsistent, perfect, timeless First Cause should will anything to exist beyond Itself, our human reason can dimly grasp that the aim might be the creation of beings capable of conceiving disinterested love and giving it freely back to the primal Giver. The kind of universe in which such beings could be drawn from nothing—from the dust of the Scriptures, from the microscopic cells floating in warm shallow primeval seas of evolutionary theory

—is as inconceivable to us as it was to Job. No one faintly knows what kind of a universe he or she would find credible. But some aspects of this particular universe which are as puzzling to us as to Job himself seem to divulge a part of their meaning if the purpose of creation is indeed the exchange of disinterested love.

A condition of such love is that it should not be balanced against some system of exact rewards or punishments. Love which knows that every demonstration will open the cupboard door would quickly degenerate into self-interest. The fact that the wicked flourish like the green bay tree has always been a scandal to the would-be just. No poet has expressed the agony more keenly than Gerard Manley Hopkins:

"Wert thou my enemy, O thou my friend,
  How wouldst thou worse, I wonder, than
    thou dost
  Defeat, thwart me? Oh the sots and
    thralls of lust
  Do in spare hours more thrive than I
    that spend
  Sir, life upon thy cause."

Yet consider the opposite—a universe in which every virtuous act were followed by earthly success and every aspiration toward the good—which is the essence of the love of God—were instantly rewarded with mental ease and physical comfort. Under such conditions how soon would a selfish calculus of advantage stifle that pure disinterested search for the good which is the crown of every moral being, that spendthrift love which repays neglect and indifference with devotion and fills up with its own full measure the inadequacy of another's response, the love, one should remark, most prized by the world's greatest creator, Shakespeare, the love of Imogen,[9] the love of Cordelia,[10] the love of the dying Desdemona?[11] It seems as though the very disharmonies and injustices of the universe are a condition of

9. IMOGEN: heroine of Shakespeare's *Cymbeline*.
10. CORDELIA: faithful daughter in Shakespeare's *King Lear*.
11. DESDEMONA: heroine of Shakespeare's *Othello*.

producing its supremest good. As the great nineteenth-century liberal Walter Bagehot wrote: "We could not be what we ought to be, if we lived in the sort of universe we should expect . . . a latent Providence, a confused life, an odd material world, our existence broken short in the midst are not real difficulties but real helps. . . . They, or something like them, are essential conditions of a moral life in a subordinate being."

This "confused life" and "odd material world" seem essential to man's full stature in another sense. An energy of the mind akin to love is that of creation. Man cannot create from nothing. Equally in a completed, regulated universe he would have nothing to create. But in this earthly arena of growth and change in which in fact he finds himself, he possesses within and without the raw materials for his creativity. Both in his own physical organism and in the social organism to which he belongs, the physical vitalities of growth, survival, and reproduction are the given materials out of which, by the higher powers of reason and moral choice, he labors to produce the whole personality and the balanced social order. The vitalities themselves are almost neutral. They can be used to build or to destroy. Like an artist, man has to learn both to work along the grain of his material and to subordinate it to the ideal form at which he aims. In a perfect universe, man the creator would have no place.

And this, perhaps, is another way of saying that the basis of both disinterested love and of creativity is freedom. Constraint destroys both the lover and the artist. Yet if a man is to be left a measure of unconditioned living, he is left with the power of choosing well or ill. His power to create is inevitably balanced by his power to destroy. It is almost as though, at the unimaginable origins of life, the Creator had faced the choice which all forms of authority must face—parents, guardians, school teachers, governments: Is the system to be a benevolent despotism in which the power of choice is reduced to a minimum and with it

the power to disrupt? Or shall the risk of freedom be run? Shall it be love or the rod? It seems that in our universe the risk, in spite of all its appalling consequences, has been run. The love is not to be compelled; the good is to be chosen, not imposed. Freedom is to be a reality. It will not be limited by preserving men from the power of choosing wrong. They are to be left the full range of self-determination.

*   *   *   *   *

It cannot be too often repeated that one of the chief reasons why Communism exercises such power in the modern world is because it has unashamedly made a religion of its political objectives. Some of the jargon may be scientific. The aims may seem, in many ways, highly prosaic—fifty new power stations, a hundred per cent rise in coal production, canals across the desert, irrigation to make the wastelands fertile. But behind these material aims lurks a lyrical passion for physical expansion, an impassioned belief that men will be brothers and society a classless paradise once the problems of production are mastered and every man works, not for "monopolists and exploiters," but for the single master, the state. There is no fear of enthusiasm, no deprecation of faith and vision in Soviet propaganda, and the appeal it has often made in the West has been above all to those who feel intensely the need in life for an explanation of reality, for an ideal and for a path to follow. Adolescents asking their first questions of life, young men and women at college grappling for the first time with philosophy and sociology, educated workingmen who look for a status and a role in life denied them in industrial society— these are the natural converts to the faith of Communism. The more irrational and indifferent Western society appears—as it must appear in the throes of depression or war—the more entire their conversion to a visionary materialist religion which offers them the disciplines and the guidance that will make them co-workers in the coming of an earthly kingdom. And in the world of Asia, these attractions are doubled by the old deep-rooted suspicion of the West, the belief that its way of life is imperialist and exploitative, and the desire to assert a newfound independence even if it involves imminent risk from the Soviet side.

In this contest with the attractions of Communism the Western world cannot rely on the momentum of past achievements and relationships. It has to reassert its vision of a free and just society, of a humanity united as brothers under the Fatherhood of God. The reason for bringing the great vitalities of nationhood and of material possessions under rational control is not only that survival demands a reordering of Western institutions. It is, above all, because new experiments in international and social relations will show to the world at large—to the young, to the students, to the new voters in Asia and Africa, to the natural leaders of the world's masses—that the traditional faith of the West is strong enough to remold society, strong enough to fulfill the promise of brotherhood which, whatever the blindness of nationalism or the selfishness of property, remains imbedded in our society as a judgment and a challenge.

Nor can we doubt, as the Western world shows signs of recovering the faith which lies at its foundation, that Communism will begin to give ground even in the territories it has already conquered. Whatever the material achievements of the Communist system— and they are likely to be immense—a society which is imprisoned within the limits of time and which systematically debars its citizens from any sense of a more than human destiny will, when the first excitement of material creation has worn away, become a closed order of deadening monotony. At best, it will achieve the mummified survival of the great planned experiment of Egyptian society. But the Egyptian experiment took place before the cycle of Western history had opened to mankind the vistas of freedom and growth and creation inherent in the vision of man as son and coworker of the external and omnipotent Godhead. This phase of history cannot be canceled. The "immortal longings" implanted in the human soul, of which Communism in this its first untried phase of activity takes advantage, will not be satisfied by bread and metallurgy and atomic power alone. Indeed, even now, the fact of freedom in the West is so explosive that the Soviet regime does not permit its citizens to travel at will abroad and encounter freedom at first hand. How much more certain would be the infiltration and reconversion of Soviet society if the Western world were not only free but patently generous and brotherly and unafraid. It is useless to suppose that a reversal of pressure can come about solely through material competition. Today, the vast material superiority of the United States is not felt, in the rest of the world, as a moral as well as a physical challenge. The West will reassert its powers of attraction only if its material achievements are seen to express a vision of spiritual order.

No one can forecast the possibility of such a renewal of the springs of faith in the West. Freedom is the essence of any spiritual movement and freedom implies that unpredictability which belongs to the really creative activities of mankind. We cannot stand and prophesy "that these dry bones shall live."[12] Nor can we expect to hear, above the braying of secular propaganda, the still, small voice[13] with which the greatest inspirations of humanity—of saint and philosopher, of poet and scientist—have been breathed. Yet at least we can say that in human history it is often the days of greatest tribulation and deepest despair that are the preludes to a time of enlightenment. The world religions grew up in the collapse of archaic civilization. Christianity renewed a Mediterranean world disintegrating beneath the material load of the Roman empire. In the most arid decades of eighteenth-century rationalism, Wesley[14] carried the gospel of

12. "THAT . . . LIVE": see Ezekiel 37:1-6.
13. STILL, SMALL VOICE: see I Kings 19:4-14.
14. WESLEY: John Wesley, famous eighteenth century British preacher.

salvation to the people. After the catastrophe of the French Revolution, the French
Church recovered its soul of sanctity and
learning. Today, the scale of our distress is
certainly sufficient to prompt the question
whether we have not, in the presumption of
nationalism and the pride of material
achievement, brought our society to the verge
of annihilation. The roads we have followed
in blind confidence have proved false roads.
To realize this is the first step in the search
for another route. And of that search, it
can be said in the light of man's spiritual
history that those who seek shall find, to
those who ask shall be given, and those who
knock shall have reopened to them the doors
of creation, freedom, and spiritual life.[15]

15. THOSE WHO SEEK . . . LIFE: see Matthew
    7:7-8.

I

1. How are the Soviet and Nazi systems *vast
distortions of tendencies already at work in our
own society?*
2. Why is the West particularly vulnerable to
the positive program of the modern totalitarians?
3. What is the *faith* Miss Ward is talking

about? Upon what does it rest? What are the
forces in man that work against his faith in his
own mastery of himself and his world?
4. In the opening paragraph of her essay
Miss Ward says: ". . . one may . . . question
whether reason or logic, of themselves, are
enough to change the direction of Western development." Later on she says: "Reason, however evolved, holds the key to the future." Discuss whether there is a contradiction here or
whether she is using "reason" in different senses.
5. What does she mean by "disinterested
love"? Paradoxically, what does it thrive on?
What does she mean by "creativity"? What has
"freedom" got to do with "disinterested love"
and "creativity"?

II

1. What is Miss Ward's "scientific proof" of
the existence of God? From your understanding
of the methods of science would you say that
her analogy is simply ingenious or that it is a
usable test? What are the difficulties in following her advice? Compare her essay with "What
I Believe." Forster says, ". . . no device has
been found by which . . . private decencies can
be transmitted to public affairs." Are his "private decencies" equivalent to Miss Ward's "detachment, humility, prayer, and neighborly
love"? Wherein are their positions the same
and wherein different?

from AREOPAGITICA [1]   [*1644*]

John Milton

John Milton is England's foremost example of the man of letters who expended
a great deal of his time and energy in the arena of social and political affairs.
As a supporter of Puritanism and Cromwell against the Anglican church and the
crown, he used the power of his pen in defense of liberty wherever he saw it
threatened. His "Areopagitica," written in 1644 in protest to the Puritan-controlled
Parliament for its reintroduction of prior licensing of books and pamphlets, had

1. The title is from a famous address delivered
   to the Athenian Areopagus, or court, by Isoc-
   rates (436-338 B.C.).

little effect on the Parliament, but it has lived through the years as the most powerful argument in the English language for freedom of publication.

What has given "Areopagitica" its appeal to men's minds is not so much the admitted strength of its reasoning, but rather the fundamental assumption about man on which it rests: the belief that he is capable, in large numbers, of self-discipline, of a dedicated search for truth, and of a rigorous sense of personal morality.

Milton came to hold little hope for the kind of England he envisioned in "Areopagitica," but his argument loses none of its force for all man's inability to live up to the heroic potentialities Milton saw in him.

. . . This is not the liberty which we can hope, that no grievance ever should arise in the Commonwealth—that let no man in this world expect; but when complaints are freely heard, deeply considered, and speedily reformed, then is the utmost bound of civil liberty attained that wise men look for. . . .

If ye be thus resolved,[2] as it were injury to think ye were not, I know not what should withhold me from presenting ye with a fit instance wherein to show both that love of truth which ye eminently profess, and that uprightness of your judgment which is not wont to be partial to yourselves; by judging over again that Order which ye have ordained *to regulate Printing: that no book, pamphlet, or paper shall be henceforth printed, unless the same be first approved and licensed by such,* or at least one of such as shall be thereto appointed. . . .

I deny not but that it is of greatest concernment in the Church and Commonwealth to have a vigilant eye how books demean[3] themselves as well as men; and thereafter[4] to confine, imprison, and do sharpest justice on them as malefactors. For books are not absolutely dead things, but do contain a potency of life in them to be as active as that soul was whose progeny they are; nay, they do preserve as in a vial the purest efficacy and extraction of that living intellect that bred them. I know they are as lively, and as vigorously productive, as those fabulous dragon's teeth;[5] and being sown up and down, may chance to spring up armed men. And yet, on the other hand, unless wariness be used, as good almost kill a man as kill a good book: who kills a man kills a reasonable creature, God's image; but he who destroys a good book, kills reason itself, kills the image of God, as it were, in the eye. Many a man lives a burden to the earth; but a good book is the precious life-blood of a master spirit, embalmed and treasured up on purpose to a life beyond life. 'Tis true, no age can restore a life, whereof perhaps there is no great loss; and revolutions[6] of ages do not oft recover the loss of a rejected truth, for the want of which whole nations fare the worse. We should be wary, therefore, what persecution we raise against the living labors of public men, how we spill that seasoned life of man, preserved and stored up in books; since we see a kind of homicide may be thus committed, sometimes a martyrdom; and if it extend to the whole impression,[7] a kind of massacre, whereof the execution ends not in the slaying of an elemental life, but strikes at that ethereal and fifth essence,[8] the breath of reason itself, slays an immortality rather than a life. . . .

---

5. DRAGON'S TEETH: Cadmus sowed the teeth of a dragon he had killed and they sprung up armed men.

6. REVOLUTIONS: cycles.

7. IF . . . IMPRESSION: i.e., if we suppress the whole edition.

8. ELEMENTAL . . . ESSENCE: An "elemental" life is a material life, made up of the four elements; the *fifth essence* is not material, but spiritual.

---

2. IF . . . RESOLVED: i.e., to hear complaints and make reforms.

3. DEMEAN: behave.

4. THEREAFTER: i.e., after publication.

Good and evil we know in the field of this world grow up together almost inseparably; and the knowledge of good is so involved and interwoven with the knowledge of evil, and in so many cunning resemblances hardly to be discerned, that those confused seeds which were imposed upon Psyche as an incessant labor to cull out, and sort asunder, were not more intermixed.[9] It was from out the rind of one apple tasted, that the knowledge of good and evil, as two twins cleaving together, leaped forth into the world. And perhaps this is that doom which Adam fell into of knowing good and evil, that is to say, of knowing good by evil.

As therefore the state of man now is, what wisdom can there be to choose, what continence to forbear without the knowledge of evil? He that can apprehend and consider vice with all her baits and seeming pleasures, and yet abstain, and yet distinguish, and yet prefer that which is truly better, he is the true wayfaring Christian. I cannot praise a fugitive[10] and cloistered virtue, unexercised and unbreathed, that never sallies out and sees her adversary, but slinks out of the race where that immortal garland[11] is to be run for, not without dust and heat. Assuredly we bring not innocence into the world, we bring impurity much rather: that which purifies us is trial, and trial is by what is contrary. That virtue therefore which is but a youngling in the contemplation of evil, and knows not the utmost that vice promises to her followers, and rejects it, is but a blank virtue, not a pure; her whiteness is but an excremental[12] whiteness. . . .

Since therefore, the knowledge and survey of vice is in this world so necessary to the constituting of human virtue, and the scanning of error to the confirmation of truth, how can we more safely, and with less danger, scout into the regions of sin and falsity, than by reading all manner of tractates[13] and hearing all manner of reason? And this is the benefit which may be had of books promiscuously read. . . .

Seeing, therefore, that those books, and those in great abundance, which are likeliest to taint both life and doctrine, cannot be suppressed without the fall of learning, and of all ability in disputation; and that these books of either sort are most and soonest catching to the learned, from whom to the common people whatever is heretical or dissolute may quickly be conveyed; and that evil manners are as perfectly learned without books a thousand other ways which cannot be stopped; and evil doctrine not with books can propagate, except[14] a teacher guide, which he might also do without writing, and so[15] beyond prohibiting: I am not able to unfold how this cautelous[16] enterprise of licensing can be exempted from the number of vain and impossible attempts. And he who were pleasantly disposed, could not well avoid to liken it to the exploit of that gallant man who thought to pound up the crows by shutting his park gate.

Besides another inconvenience, if learned men be the first receivers out of books and dispreaders both of vice and error, how shall the licensers themselves be confided in, unless we can confer upon them, or they assume to themselves above all others in the land, the grace of infallibility and uncorruptedness? And again, if it be true that a wise man, like a good refiner, can gather gold out of the drossiest volume, and that a fool will be a fool with the best book, yea or without book, here is no reason that we should deprive a wise man of any advantage to his wisdom, while we seek to restrain from a fool that which being restrained will be no hindrance to his folly. For if there should be so much exactness always used to keep that from him which is unfit for his

9. CONFUSED . . . INTERMIXED: Irritated by Cupid's love for Psyche, Venus set her a task of sorting out the different kinds of grain in a huge mixed heap.
10. FUGITIVE: i.e., which flees life.
11. THAT IMMORTAL GARLAND: immortality.
12. EXCREMENTAL: surface.
13. TRACTATES: treatises.
14. EXCEPT: unless.
15. SO: so be.
16. CAUTELOUS: ticklish.

reading, we should, in the judgment of Aristotle not only, but of Solomon and of our Saviour,[17] not vouchsafe him good precepts, and by consequence not willingly admit him to good books; as being certain that a wise man will make better use of an idle pamphlet than a fool will do of sacred Scripture.

'Tis next alleged we must not expose ourselves to temptations without necessity, and, next to that, not employ our time in vain things. To both these objections one answer will serve, out of the grounds already laid; that to all men such books are not temptations nor vanities, but useful drugs and materials wherewith to temper and compose effective and strong medicines which man's life cannot want.[18] The rest, as children and childish men, who have not the art to qualify[19] and prepare these working minerals, well may be exhorted to forbear, but hindered forcibly they cannot be by all the licensing that sainted Inquisition could ever yet contrive. Which is what I promised to deliver next: that this order of licensing conduces nothing to the end for which it was framed. . . .

If we think to regulate printing, thereby to rectify manners, we must regulate all recreations and pastimes, all that is delightful to man. No music must be heard, no song be set or sung, but what is grave and Doric.[20] There must be licensing dancers, that no gesture, motion, or deportment be taught our youth, but what by their[21] allowance shall be thought honest;[22] . . . It will ask more than the work of twenty licensers to examine all the lutes, violins, and the guitars in every house; they must not be suffered to prattle as they do, but must be licensed what they may say. And who shall silence all the airs and madrigals that whisper softness in chambers? The windows also, and the balconies must be thought on; there are shrewd[23] books, with dangerous frontispieces,[24] set to sale; who shall prohibit them? Shall twenty licensers? The villages also must have their visitors[25] to inquire what lectures the bagpipe and the rebeck[26] reads even to the ballatry,[27] and the gamut[28] of every municipal fiddler, for these are the countryman's Arcadias, and his Monte Mayors.[29]

Next, what more national corruption, for which England hears ill abroad, than household gluttony? Who shall be the rectors[30] of our daily rioting? And what shall be done to inhibit the multitudes that frequent those houses where drunkenness is sold and harbored? Our garments also should be referred to the licensing of some more sober workmasters, to see them cut into a less wanton garb. Who shall regulate all the mixed conversation of our youth, male and female together, as is the fashion of this country? Who shall still appoint what shall be discoursed, what presumed, and no further? Lastly, who shall forbid and separate all

17. ARISTOTLE . . . SAVIOUR: Aristotle notes in his *Nicomachean Ethics* (X, viii, 3) that the ordinary man is unaffected by ethical study; Proverbs, attributed to Solomon, states (17:24) that the eyes of the fool are always elsewhere than on wisdom; and Christ's advice in Matthew (7:6) is "Neither cast ye your pearls before swine."
18. WANT: do without.
19. QUALIFY: compound.
20. DORIC: Doric music was held by Plato and Aristotle to have a tonic moral effect.
21. THEIR: the licensers'.
22. HONEST: decent.
23. SHREWD: wicked.
24. FRONTISPIECES: used in its architectural sense (the façade of a building) as well as its bookmaking sense.
25. VISITORS: inspectors.
26. REBECK: a kind of violin.
27. EVEN . . . BALLATRY: as accompaniment to ballads.
28. AND THE GAMUT: i.e., the inspectors must inquire about the gamut (range).
29. FOR . . . MONTE MAYORS: i.e., these are the countryman's substitutes for the pastoral romances that appeal to the courtier. The reference is to works like Sir Philip Sidney's *Arcadia* (1590) and Jorge de Montemayor's *Diana Enamorada* (English translation, 1598).
30. RECTORS: regulators.

idle resort,[31] all evil company? These things will be, and must be; but how they shall be least hurtful, how least enticing, herein consists the grave and governing wisdom of a state. . . .

Impunity and remissness, for certain, are the bane of a commonwealth; but here the great art lies, to discern in what the law is to bid restraint and punishment, and in what things persuasion only is to work. If every action which is good or evil in man at ripe years, were to be under pittance[32] and prescription and compulsion, what were virtue but a name, what praise could be then due to well-doing, what gramercy[33] to be sober, just, or continent?

Many there be that complain of divine Providence for suffering Adam to transgress. Foolish tongues! when God gave him reason, he gave him freedom to choose, for reason is but choosing; he had been else a mere artificial[34] Adam, such an Adam as he is in the motions.[35] We ourselves esteem not of that obedience, or love, or gift, which is of force. God, therefore, left him free, set before him a provoking[36] object, ever almost in his eyes; herein consisted his merit, herein the right of his reward, the praise of his abstinence. Wherefore did he create passions within us, pleasures round about us, but that these rightly tempered are the very ingredients of virtue? They are not skillful considerers of human things, who imagine to remove sin by removing the matter of sin. For, besides that it is a huge heap increasing under the very act of diminishing, though some part of it may for a time be withdrawn from some persons, it cannot from all, in such a universal thing as books are; and when this is done, yet the sin remains entire. Though ye take from a covetous man all his treasure, he has yet one jewel left— ye cannot bereave him of his covetousness. Banish all objects of lust, shut up all youth into the severest discipline that can be exercised in any hermitage, ye cannot make them chaste, that came not thither so: such great care and wisdom is required to the right managing of this point.

Suppose we could expel sin by this means; look how much we thus expel of sin, so much we expel of virtue: for the matter of them both is the same; remove that, and ye remove them both alike. This justifies the high providence of God, who, though he command us temperance, justice, continence, yet pours out before us, even to a profuseness, all desirable things, and gives us minds that can wander beyond all limit and satiety. Why should we then affect[37] a rigor contrary to the manner of God and of nature, by abridging or scanting those means which books freely permitted are, both to the trial of virtue, and the exercise of truth?

I lastly proceed from the no good it can do, to the manifest hurt it causes in being first the greatest discouragement and affront that can be offered to learning and to learned men. . . .

What advantage is it to be a man over it is to be[38] a boy at school, if we have only scaped[39] the ferula[40] to come under the fescue[41] of an Imprimatur;[42] if serious and elaborate writings, as if they were no more than the theme of a grammar-lad under his pedagogue, must not be uttered[43] without the cursory[44] eyes of a temporizing and extemporizing[45] licenser? He who is not trusted

31. RESORT: i.e., gathering together.
32. PITTANCE: ration.
33. GRAMERCY: thanks.
34. ARTIFICIAL: i.e., made by "art," not created by God.
35. MOTIONS: puppet shows.
36. PROVOKING: enticing.

37. AFFECT: adopt.
38. IT . . . BE: being.
39. SCAPED: escaped.
40. FERULA: rod.
41. FESCUE: a schoolmaster's pointer.
42. IMPRIMATUR: the Latin for "Let it be printed" affixed by the censor; hence, it means the whole system of censorship.
43. UTTERED: published.
44. CURSORY: hasty.
45. TEMPORIZING AND EXTEMPORIZING: compliant and offhand.

with his own actions, his drift not being known to be evil, and standing to the hazard of[46] law and penalty, has no great argument to think himself reputed, in the commonwealth wherein he was born, for other than a fool or a foreigner.

When a man writes to the world, he summons up all his reason and deliberation to assist him; he searches, meditates, is industrious, and likely consults and confers with his judicious friends, after all which done he takes himself to be informed in what he writes, as well as any that writ before him. If in this the most consummate act of his fidelity and ripeness, no years, no industry, no former proof of his abilities can bring him to that state of maturity as not to be still mistrusted and suspected (unless he carry all his considerate diligence, all his midnight watchings, and expense of Palladian oil,[47] to the hasty view of an unleisured licenser, perhaps much his younger, perhaps far his inferior in judgment, perhaps one who never knew the labor of book-writing), and if he be not repulsed, or slighted, must appear in print like a puny[48] with his guardian, and his censor's hand on the back of his title to be his bail and surety that he is in no idiot, or seducer; it cannot be but a dishonor and derogation to the author, to the book, to the privilege and dignity of learning.

*   *   *   *   *

And how can a man teach with authority, which is the life of teaching, how can he be a doctor in his book as he ought to be, or else had better be silent, whenas all he teaches, all he delivers, is but under the tuition, under the correction of his patriarchal[49] licenser to blot or alter what precisely accords not with the hide-bound humor which he calls his judgment? When every acute reader upon the first sight of a pedantic license, will be ready with these like words to ding the book a quoit's distance[50] from him: "I hate a pupil teacher, I endure not an instructor that comes to me under the wardship of an overseeing fist. I know nothing of the licenser, but that I have his own hand here for his arrogance; who shall warrant me his judgment?" . . .

Nay, which is more lamentable, if the work of any deceased author, though never so famous in his lifetime, and even to this day, come to their hands for license to be printed, or reprinted; if there be found in his book one sentence of a venturous edge, uttered in the height of zeal, and who knows whether it might not be the dictate of a divine spirit, yet not suiting with every low, decrepit humor of their own, though it were Knox[51] himself, the reformer of a kingdom, that spake it, they will not pardon him their dash;[52] the sense of that great man shall to all posterity be lost, for the fearfulness, or the presumptuous rashness, of a perfunctory licenser. . . .

Yet if these things be not resented seriously and timely by them who have the remedy in their power, but that such ironmolds[53] as these shall have authority to gnaw out the choicest periods of exquisitest books, and to commit such a treacherous fraud against the orphan remainders[54] of worthiest men after death, the more sorrow will belong to that hapless race of men whose misfortune it is to have understanding. Henceforth, let no man care to learn, or care to be more than wordly wise; for certainly in higher matters to be ignorant and slothful, to be a common steadfast dunce, will be the only pleasant life, and only in request.

---

46. STANDING . . . OF: liable to.
47. PALLADIAN OIL: oil of Pallas Athene, i.e., of wisdom.
48. PUNY: minor.
49. PATRIARCHAL: belonging to a patriarchate, i.e., an archbishopric.
50. DING . . . DISTANCE: toss as far as one tosses a quoit (in a game of quoits).
51. KNOX: John Knox (1505-1572), leader of the Scottish Presbyterians.
52. DASH: i.e., with the censoring pen.
53. IRON-MOLDS: stains, i.e., expungers
54. REMAINDERS: i.e., books.

* * * * *

. . . to include the whole nation, and those that never yet thus offended, under such a diffident[55] and suspectful prohibition, may plainly be understood what a disparagement it is. So much the more, whenas debtors and delinquents may walk abroad without a keeper, but unoffensive books must not stir forth without a visible jailor in their title. Nor is it to the common people less than a reproach; for if we be so jealous over them as that we dare not trust them with an English pamphlet, what do we but censure them for a giddy, vicious, and ungrounded people; in such a sick and weak state of faith and discretion, as to be able to take nothing down but through the pipe[56] of a licenser. . . .

* * * * *

And lest some should persuade ye, Lords and Commons,[57] that these arguments of learned men's discouragement at this your Order are mere flourishes, and not real, I could recount what I have seen and heard in other countries where this kind of inquisition tyrannizes; when I have sat among their learned men, for that honor I had, and been counted happy to be born in such a place of philosophic freedom as they supposed England was, while themselves did nothing but bemoan the servile condition into which learning amongst them was brought; that this was it which had damped the glory of Italian wits; that nothing had been there written now these many years but flattery and fustian.[58] There it was that I found and visited the famous Galileo,[59] grown old, a prisoner to the Inquisition for thinking in astronomy otherwise than the Franciscan and Dominican licensers thought. . . .

That this is not, therefore, the disburdening of a particular fancy, but the common grievance of all those who had prepared their minds and studies above the vulgar pitch[60] to advance truth in others, and from others to entertain it, thus much may satisfy. And in their name I shall for neither friend nor foe conceal what the general murmur is; that if it come to inquisitioning again and licensing, and that we are so timorous of ourselves and so suspicious of all men as to fear each book and the shaking of every leaf, before we know what the contents are; if some[61] who but of late were little better than silenced from preaching, shall come now to silence us from reading, except what they please, it cannot be guessed what is intended by some but a second tyranny over learning;[62] and will soon put it out of controversy that bishops and presbyters are the same to us both name and thing. . . .

* * * * *

Lords and Commons of England, consider what nation it is whereof ye are, and whereof ye are the governors; a nation not slow and dull, but of a quick, ingenious, and piercing spirit, acute to invent, subtle and sinewy to discourse, not beneath the reach of any point the highest that human capacity can soar to. . . .

* * * * *

Now once again by all concurrence of signs, and by the general instinct of holy and devout men, as they daily and solemnly express their thoughts, God is decreeing to begin some new and great period in his Church, even to the reforming of reformation itself. What does he then but reveal himself to his servants, and, as his manner is, first to his Englishmen; I say as his manner is, first to us, though we mark[63] not the method of his counsels, and are unworthy. Behold

---

55. DIFFIDENT: untrusting.
56. PIPE: feeding-tube.
57. LORDS AND COMMONS: those in the House of Lords and the House of Commons.
58. FUSTIAN: exaggerated nonsense.
59. GALILEO: Italian astronomer and physicist;

Milton had visited him in Florence during his Italian journey, 1638-1639.
60. THE VULGAR PITCH: the ordinary.
61. SOME: the Puritans, who had been restrained by the Anglican bishops when Charles I was still in power.
62. SECOND . . . LEARNING: the Puritan Parliament is doing what the Anglicans had done.
63. MARK: understand.

now this vast city, a city of refuge, the mansion house of Liberty, encompassed and surrounded with his protection. The shop of war hath not there more anvils and hammers waking, to fashion out the plates[64] and instruments of armed justice in defense of beleaguered truth, than there be pens and heads there, sitting by their studious lamps, musing, searching, revolving new notions and ideas wherewith to present, as with their homage and their fealty, the approaching reformation; others as fast reading, trying all things, assenting to the force of reason and convincement.

What could a man require more from a nation so pliant and so prone to seek after knowledge? What wants there to such a towardly[65] and pregnant soil, but wise and faithful laborers, to make a knowing people, a nation of prophets, of sages, and of worthies? We reckon more than five months yet to harvest; there need not be five weeks, had we but eyes to lift up; the fields are white already.[66] Where there is much desire to learn, there of necessity will be much arguing, much writing, many opinions; for opinion in good men is but knowledge in the making. Under these fantastic terrors of sect and schism, we wrong the earnest and zealous thirst after knowledge and understanding which God hath stirred up in this city.

What some lament of, we rather should rejoice at, should rather praise this pious forwardness among men, to reassume the ill-deputed care of their religion into their own hands again. A little generous prudence, a little forbearance of one another, and some grain of charity might win all these diligences to join and unite into one general and brotherly search after truth. . . .

Yet these are the men cried out against for schismatics and sectaries; as if, while the temple of the Lord was building, some cutting, some squaring the marble, others hewing the cedars, there should be a sort of irrational man who could not consider there

must be many schisms[67] and many dissections made in the quarry and in the timber, ere the house of God can be built. And when every stone is laid artfully together, it cannot be united into a continuity, it can but be contiguous in this world; neither can every piece of the building be of one form; nay rather the perfection consists in this, that out of many moderate varieties and brotherly dissimilitudes that are not vastly disproportional, arises the goodly and the graceful symmetry that commends the whole pile and structure.

Let us, therefore, be more considerate builders, more wise in spiritual architecture, when great reformation is expected. . . .

* * * * *

Methinks I see in my mind a noble and puissant nation rousing herself like a strong man after sleep, and shaking her invincible locks. Methinks I see her as an eagle mewing[68] her mighty youth, and kindling her undazzled[69] eyes at the full midday beam; purging and unscaling her long-abused sight at the fountain itself of heavenly radiance; while the whole noise of timorous and flocking birds,[70] with those also that love the twilight, flutter about, amazed at what she means, and in their envious gabble would prognosticate a year of sects and schisms.

What should ye do then, should ye suppress all this flowery crop of knowledge and new light sprung up and yet springing daily in this city? Should ye set an oligarchy of twenty engrossers[71] over it, to bring a famine upon our minds again, when we shall know nothing but what is measured to us by their bushel? Believe it, Lords and Commons, they who counsel ye to such a suppressing, do as good as bid ye suppress yourselves. . . .

* * * * *

---

64. PLATES: armor.
65. TOWARDLY: favorable.
66. FIELDS . . . ALREADY: see John 4:35.

67. SCHISMS: a pun on the literal sense, cutting.
68. MEWING: renewing by molting.
69. UNDAZZLED: The eagle was reputed to be able to behold the sun without going blind.
70. TIMOROUS . . . BIRDS: for instance, the Presbyterians, who are, Milton implies, afraid of uncensored publishing.
71. ENGROSSERS: monopolists.

And now the time in special is, by privilege to write and speak what may help to the further discussing of matters in agitation. The temple of Janus with his two controversial faces might now not unsignificantly be set open.[72] And though all the winds of doctrine were let loose to play upon the earth, so Truth be in the field, we do injuriously by licensing and prohibiting to misdoubt her strength. Let her and Falsehood grapple; who ever knew Truth put to the worse, in a free and open encounter. . . .

For who knows not that Truth is strong, next to the Almighty. She needs no policies, nor stratagems, nor licensings to make her victorious—those are the shifts and the defenses that error uses against her power. . . .

*   *   *   *   *

This I know, that errors in a good government and in a bad are equally almost incident; for what magistrate may not be misinformed and much the sooner, if liberty of printing be reduced into the power of a few; but to redress willingly and speedily what hath been erred,[73] and in highest authority to esteem a plain advertisement[74] more than others have done a sumptuous bribe, is a virtue, honored Lords and Commons, answerable to your highest actions, and whereof none can participate but greatest and wisest men.

---

72. TEMPLE . . . OPEN: i.e., as in Rome in time of war; this, too, is a time of war, between falsehood and truth.

73. ERRED: done wrong.
74. ADVERTISEMENT: notice, like this treatise.

I

1. What is the gist of the argument against censorship in paragraph 3? State what the metaphor is around which Milton builds this argument and show specifically how it is developed.

2. Put the reasoning of paragraphs 4, 5, and 6 into your own words. What assumption is made about the existence of good and evil in the world? How does the allusion to Psyche and the seeds illustrate that assumption? How does the argument about *knowing good by evil* differ from the argument Eve uses in Book IX of *Paradise Lost* (131-150, pp. 408-409)? Consider the fact that there was no evil in the Garden until Eve ate the apple. Why does Milton say that Adam fell into the *doom* of "knowing good and evil"?

3. What is the basis of the metaphor beginning "I cannot praise a fugitive and cloistered virtue"? Show how "unexercised," "unbreathed," "sallies," "adversary," "immortal garland," and "dust and heat" expand the metaphor? Why is it appropriate to the argument here? What distinction is made in the phrase "is but a blank virtue, not a pure"?

4. How does the reference to the "gallant man who thought to pound up the crows by shutting his park gate" sum up the observations made in paragraph 7?

5. What is the reasoning in paragraphs 8-9? What two metaphors are used to drive home the meaning? How do the allusions to Aristotle, Solomon, and Jesus support the argument here?

6. How does the argument in paragraphs 10, 11, and 12 make the whole process of censorship appear impossible and even foolish? Why are a series of rhetorical questions used instead of statements?

7. How is the argument in paragraphs 13-14 related to the argument in paragraphs 4, 5, and 6?

8. What general point is made in paragraphs 15-23 and what specific applications are discussed? What is the tone of this section: indignant? scornful? bitter? supercilious? Consider the contrast between the language used in referring to the censor and that used referring to the writer.

9. What vision of the English nation is presented in the last paragraphs of the essay? How essential to the total argument is this praise? How are metaphors based on war, farming, and building introduced and later expanded? Explain the metaphor built around the contrast between the eagle and the *timorous and flocking birds*. Show the appropriateness of each metaphor in underscoring the elevated view of English character Milton presents.

II

1. This is a plea for the elimination of censorship *before* publication. Milton was not advocating the elimination of all control over printed matter. In the final analysis he rested his case on the good judgment and strong moral character of the individual Englishman. How applicable is his argument today? Is there anything about the times we live in that makes it too dangerous to trust the individual with the freedom to publish and read anything he wants to, subject of course to laws against libel and obscenity?

ANTIGONE*   [*441* B.C.]

Sophocles

The third selection that illustrates the nature of faith, not so much in man as in man's recognition of where his ultimate loyalties lie, is Sophocles's *Antigone,* whose theme is the supremacy of individual conscience over the demands of political authority and community conformity.

Antigone comes last in the chronology of Sophocles's three plays on the Oedipus myth, but it was the first to be written, some fourteen years before *King Oedipus* and some thirty-seven before *Oedipus at Colonus.* There are differences of fact between the interpretations, as you will see in comparing *Antigone* with *King Oedipus,* but they are unimportant for our purposes; an author is free within obvious limits to use the materials of myth in the way which best suits what he has to say at a particular time; he is not dealing with history. What is important is his focus of attention, which here is on Antigone, upholding the inviolability of the demands of religious conviction—her slain brother must be buried—and not on Creon, the earlier counterpart of Oedipus, insisting for reasons of order and stability on the obedience of all men to the decrees of lawful authority.

The play's focus is on Antigone despite the fact that she remains a relatively static figure throughout and goes to her death almost willfully, while Creon changes as he comes to understand how wrong he has been. And the focus is on her despite the fact that almost everything about her behavior is irrational and headstrong. We are drawn to her and to her stand for the simple reason that she is right and no degree of fanaticism or obstinacy or faulty reasoning can change that fact. The clarity with which she sees what she must do shines through her muddled reasoning about why she acts as she does. Furthermore, we respond to her, not because we feel pity or sympathy for a young girl trampled by political power and not because our sense of justice or even reasonableness is outraged, but simply because she adamantly refuses to compromise on a matter of conscience. The circumstances which call forth Antigone's stand may seem distant to us today, but her recognition that there are inviolable truths is the most significant understanding man can have.

* Some of the names in *King Oedipus* reappear in *Antigone* but with different spellings. For example, Jocasta, Tiresias, Menoeceus, and Laius are now Iocaste, Teiresias, Menoikeus, and Laios.

The Story

King Oedipus of Thebes unknowingly slew his father, King Laios, and married his mother, Iocaste. When the truth came to light, he was exiled from Thebes by his own edict, and the government of the city was assumed by Iocaste's brother, Creon. Subsequently, Oedipus's sons, Polyneices and Eteocles, rebelled against Creon and against each other. When Eteocles received the support of most of the Thebans, Polyneices went to Argos for aid and returned with seven great captains to lay siege to his native city. Thebes withstood the assault, but the two brothers killed each other. Thereupon Creon, again master of the city, issued an edict refusing burial to Polyneices. Ismene and Antigone, the two remaining children of Oedipus, are discussing this as the play opens.

CHARACTERS

in the order of their appearance

ANTIGONE

ISMENE, *her sister*

CHORUS *and* CHORAGOS, *old men of Thebes*

CREON, *King of Thebes*

A SENTRY

HAIMON, *Creon's son*

TEIRESIAS, *a prophet*

A MESSENGER

EURYDICE, *Queen of Thebes*

GUARDS

SERVANTS

Scene: *Before the palace of* CREON. *A central double door and two lateral doors. A platform extends the length of the façade, and from this platform three steps lead down into the "orchestra," or chorus-ground.*

Time: *dawn of the day after the repulse of the Argive army from the assault on Thebes.*

PROLOGUE

ANTIGONE *and* ISMENE *enter from the central door of the palace.*

ANTIGONE. Ismene, dear sister,
You would think that we had already suffered enough
For the curse on Oedipus:
I cannot imagine any grief
That you and I have not gone through. And now—
Have they told you of the new decree of our King Creon?
ISMENE. I have heard nothing: I know
That two sisters lost two brothers, a double death
In a single hour; and I know that the Argive army
Fled in the night; but beyond this, nothing. 10
ANTIGONE. I thought so. And that is why I wanted you
To come out here with me. There is something we must do.
ISMENE. Why do you speak so strangely?
ANTIGONE. Listen, Ismene:
Creon buried our brother Eteocles
With military honors, gave him a soldier's funeral,
And it was right that he should; but Polyneices,
Who fought as bravely and died as miserably—
They say that Creon has sworn
No one shall bury him, no one mourn for him, 20
But his body must lie in the fields, a sweet treasure
For carrion birds to find as they search for food.
That is what they say, and our good Creon is coming here
To announce it publicly; and the penalty—
Stoning to death in the public square!
There it is,
And now you can prove what you are:

19-22. CREON . . . FOOD: Not to carry out proper burial was considered a dishonor to the dead and to the gods.

A true sister, or a traitor to your family.

ISMENE. Antigone, you are mad! What
could I possibly do?

ANTIGONE. You must decide whether you
will help me or not.   30

ISMENE. I do not understand you. Help
you in what?

ANTIGONE. Ismene, I am going to bury
him. Will you come?

ISMENE. Bury him! You have just said
the new law forbids it.

ANTIGONE. He is my brother. And he is
your brother, too.

ISMENE. But think of the danger! Think
what Creon will do!

ANTIGONE. Creon is not strong enough to
stand in my way.

ISMENE. Ah sister!

Oedipus died, everyone hating him

For what his own search brought to light,
his eyes

Ripped out by his own hand; and Iocaste
died,   40

His mother and wife at once: she twisted the
cords

That strangled her life; and our two brothers
died,

Each killed by the other's sword. And we
are left:

But oh, Antigone,

Think how much more terrible than these

Our own death would be if we should go
against Creon

And do what he has forbidden! We are only
women,

We cannot fight with men, Antigone!

The law is strong, we must give in to the
law

In this thing, and in worse. I beg the dead   50

To forgive me, but I am helpless: I must
yield

To those in authority. And I think it is
dangerous business

To be always meddling.

ANTIGONE.   If that is what you
think,

I should not want you, even if you asked to
come.

You have made your choice, you can be
what you want to be.

But I will bury him; and if I must die,

I say that this crime is holy: I shall lie
down

With him in death, and I shall be as dear

To him as he to me.

It is the dead,

Not the living, who make the longest demands: 60

We die forever. . . .

You may do as you like,

Since apparently the laws of the gods mean
nothing to you.

ISMENE. They mean a great deal to me;
but I have no strength

To break laws that were made for the public
good.

ANTIGONE. That must be your excuse, I
suppose. But as for me,

I will bury the brother I love.

ISMENE.   Antigone,

I am so afraid for you!

ANTIGONE.   You need not be:

You have yourself to consider, after all.

ISMENE. But no one must hear of this,
you must tell no one!

I will keep it a secret, I promise!

ANTIGONE. Oh tell it! Tell everyone! 70

Think how they'll hate you when it all comes
out

If they learn that you knew about it all the
time!

ISMENE. So fiery! You should be cold
with fear.

ANTIGONE. Perhaps. But I am doing only
what I must.

ISMENE. But can you do it? I say that
you cannot.

ANTIGONE. Very well: when my strength
gives out, I shall do no more.

ISMENE. Impossible things should not be
tried at all.

38-40. OEDIPUS . . . HAND: One version of the
Oedipus myth is that he died in Thebes soon
after the events recounted in *King Oedipus*;
another, which Sophocles used for the later
Oedipus at Colonus, has him dying much later
at Colonus, honored by the gods.

ANTIGONE. Go away, Ismene:
I shall be hating you soon, and the dead will
    too,
For your words are hateful. Leave me my
    foolish plan: 80
I am not afraid of the danger; if it means
    death,
It will not be the worst of deaths—death
    without honor.
    ISMENE. Go then, if you feel that you
    must.
You are unwise,
But a loyal friend indeed to those who love
    you.
(ISMENE *goes into the palace.* ANTIGONE
                            goes off left.)

CHORUS *and* CHORAGOS *enter.*

PARODOS

(Strophe 1)

CHORUS. Now the long blade of the sun,
    lying
Level east to west, touches with glory
Thebes of the Seven Gates. Open, unlidded
Eye of golden day! O marching light
Across the eddy and rush of Dirce's stream,
Striking the white shields of the enemy
Thrown headlong backward from the blaze
    of morning!

CHORAGOS. Polyneices their commander
Roused them with windy phrases,
He the wild eagle screaming   10
Insults above our land,
His wings their shields of snow,
His crest their marshaled helms.

1-43. PARODOS: entrance-song of the Chorus.
1-13. STROPHE: literally "a turning"; the move-
    ment of the Chorus from one side of the or-
    chestra (see opening scene description) to the
    other; here it refers to the part of the choral
    ode sung during the strophe.
5. DIRCE'S STREAM: river west of Thebes.
8. CHORAGOS: leader of the Chorus.

(Antistrophe 1)

CHORUS. Against our seven gates in a
    yawning ring
The famished spears came onward in the
    night;
But before his jaws were sated with our
    blood,
Or pinefire took the garland of our towers,
He was thrown back; and as he turned, great
    Thebes—
No tender victim for his noisy power—
Rose like a dragon behind him, shouting
    war.   20

CHORAGOS. For God hates utterly
The bray of bragging tongues;
And when he beheld their smiling,
Their swagger of golden helms,
The frown of his thunder blasted
Their first man from our walls.

(Strophe 2)

CHORUS. We heard his shout of triumph
    high in the air
Turn to a scream; far out in a flaming arc
He fell with his windy torch, and the earth
    struck him.
And others storming in fury no less than
    his   30
Found shock of death in the dusty joy of
    battle.

CHORAGOS. Seven captains at seven gates
Yielded their clanging arms to the god
That bends the battle-line and breaks it.
These two only, brothers in blood,
Face to face in matchless rage,
Mirroring each the other's death,
Clashed in long combat.

14-26. ANTISTROPHE: the part of the choral ode
    answering the strophe.
21-29. The reference is to one of the seven Argive
    leaders, Capaneus, who boasted he would scale
    the walls of Thebes in spite of Zeus himself.
    When he mounted his scaling ladder, he was
    struck down by a thunderbolt.

(Antistrophe 2)

CHORUS. But now in the beautiful morning of victory
Let Thebes of the many chariots sing for joy!   40
With hearts for dancing we'll take leave of war:
Our temples shall be sweet with hymns of praise,
And the long night shall echo with our chorus.

SCENE I

CHORAGOS. But now at last our new King is coming:
Creon of Thebes, Menoikeus' son.
In this auspicious dawn of his reign
What are the new complexities
That shifting Fate has woven for him?
What is his counsel? Why has he summoned
The old men to hear him?

CREON *enters from the palace and addresses the* CHORUS *from the top step.*

CREON. Gentlemen: I have the honor to inform you that our ship of state, which recent storms have threatened to destroy,   10
has come safely to harbor at last, guided by the merciful wisdom of heaven. I have summoned you here this morning because I know that I can depend upon you: your devotion to King Laios was absolute; you never hesitated in your duty to our late ruler Oedipus; and when Oedipus died, your loyalty was transferred to his children. Unfortunately, as you know, his two sons, the princes Eteocles and Polyneices, have   20
killed each other in battle; and I, as the next in blood, have succeeded to the full power of the throne.

I am aware, of course, that no ruler can expect complete loyalty from his subjects until he has been tested in office. Nevertheless, I say to you at the very outset that I have nothing but contempt for the kind of governor who is afraid, for whatever reason, to follow the course that he knows is best   30
for the state; and as for the man who sets private friendship above the public welfare —I have no use for him, either. I call God to witness that if I saw my country headed for ruin, I should not be afraid to speak out plainly; and I need hardly remind you that I would never have any dealings with an enemy of the people. No one values friendship more highly than I; but we must remember that friends made at the risk of   40
wrecking our ship are not real friends at all.

These are my principles, at any rate, and that is why I have made the following decision concerning the sons of Oedipus: Eteocles, who died as a man should die, fighting for his country, is to be buried with full military honors, with all the ceremony that is usual when the greatest heroes die; but his brother Polyneices, who broke his exile to come back with fire and sword   50
against his native city and the shrines of his fathers' gods, whose one idea was to spill the blood of his blood and sell his own people into slavery—Polyneices, I say, is to have no burial: no man is to touch him or say the least prayer for him; he shall lie on the plain, unburied; and the birds and the scavenging dogs can do with him whatever they like.

This is my command, and you can see   60
the wisdom behind it. As long as I am King, no traitor is going to be honored with the loyal man. But whoever shows by word and deed that he is on the side of the state—he shall have my respect while he is living, and my reverence when he is dead.

CHORAGOS. If that is your will, Creon son of Menoikeus,
You have the right to enforce it: we are yours.

CREON. That is my will. Take care that you do your part.

CHORAGOS. We are old men: let the younger ones carry it out.   70

CREON. I do not mean that: the sentries have been appointed.

CHORAGOS. Then what is it that you would have us do?

CREON. You will give no support to whoever breaks this law.

CHORAGOS. Only a crazy man is in love with death!

CREON. And death it is; yet money talks, and the wisest

Have sometimes been known to count a few coins too many.

A SENTRY *enters.*

SENTRY. I'll not say that I'm out of breath from running, King, because every time I stopped to think about what I have to tell you, I felt like going back. And all the   80 time a voice kept saying, "You fool, don't you know you're walking straight into trouble?"; and then another voice: "Yes, but if you let somebody else get the news to Creon first, it will be even worse than that for you!" But good sense won out, at least I hope it was good sense, and here I am with a story that makes no sense at all; but I'll tell it anyhow, because, as they say, what's going to happen's going to hap-   90 pen, and—

CREON. Come to the point. What have you to say?

SENTRY. I did not do it. I did not see who did it. You must not punish me for what someone else has done.

CREON. A comprehensive defense! More effective, perhaps,

If I knew its purpose. Come: what is it?

SENTRY. A dreadful thing . . . I don't know how to put it—

CREON. Out with it!

SENTRY.   Well, then;   100
The dead man—
        Polyneices—
(*Pause. The* SENTRY *is overcome, fumbles for words.* CREON *waits impassively.*)
            out there—
                 someone—
New dust on the slimy flesh!
(*Pause. No sign from* CREON.)

Someone has given it burial that way, and
Gone. . . .
(*Long pause.* CREON *finally speaks with deadly control.*)

CREON. And the man who dared do this?

SENTRY.   I swear I
Do not know! You must believe me!
                       Listen:
The ground was dry, not a sign of digging, no,
Not a wheeltrack in the dust, no trace of anyone.
It was when they relieved us this morning: and one of them,
The corporal, pointed to it.   110
                There it was,
The strangest—
      Look:
The body, just mounded over with light dust: you see?
Not buried really, but as if they'd covered it
Just enough for the ghost's peace. And no sign
Of dogs or any wild animal that had been there.
And then what a scene there was! Every man of us
Accusing the other: we all proved the other man did it,
We all had proof that we could not have done it.
We were ready to take hot iron in our hands,
Walk through fire, swear by all the gods,   120
It was not I!
I do not know who it was, but it was not I!
(CREON's *rage has been mounting steadily, but the* SENTRY *is too intent upon his story to notice it.*)
And then, when this came to nothing, someone said
A thing that silenced us and made us stare
Down at the ground: you had to be told the news,
And one of us had to do it! We threw the dice,
And the bad luck fell to me. So here I am,
No happier to be here than you are to have me:

Nobody likes the man who brings bad news.

CHORAGOS. I have been wondering, King:
can it be that the gods have done
this?   130

CREON (*furiously*). Stop!

Must you doddering wrecks
Go out of your heads entirely? "The gods!"
Intolerable!

The gods favor this corpse? Why? How had
he served them?

Tried to loot their temples, burn their images,
Yes, and the whole state, and its laws with
it!

Is it your senile opinion that the gods love to
honor bad men?

A pious thought!—

No, from the very beginning

There have been those who have whispered
together,   140

Stiff-necked anarchists, putting their heads
together,

Scheming against me in alleys. These are the
men,

And they have bribed my own guard to do
this thing.

(*sententiously*) Money!

There's nothing in the world so demoralizing
as money.

Down go your cities,

Homes gone, men gone, honest hearts corrupted,

Crookedness of all kinds, and all for money!

(*to* SENTRY) But you—!

I swear by God and by the throne of God,

The man who has done this thing shall pay
for it!   150

Find that man, bring him here to me, or your
death

Will be the least of your problems: I'll
string you up

Alive, and there will be certain ways to make
you

Discover your employer before you die;

And the process may teach you a lesson you
seem to have missed:

The dearest profit is sometimes all too dear:

That depends on the source. Do you understand me?

A fortune won is often misfortune.

SENTRY. King, may I speak?

CREON. Your very voice distresses me.   160

SENTRY. Are you sure that it is my voice,
and not your conscience?

CREON. By God, he wants to analyze me
now!

SENTRY. It is not what I say, but what has
been done, that hurts you.

CREON. You talk too much.

SENTRY.   Maybe; but I've done nothing.

CREON. Sold your soul for some silver:
that's all you've done.

SENTRY. How dreadful it is when the right
judge judges wrong!

CREON. Your figures of speech

May entertain you now; but unless you bring
me the man,

You will get little profit from them in the
end.   170

(CREON *goes into the palace.*)

SENTRY. "Bring me the man"—!

I'd like nothing better than bringing him the
man!

But bring him or not, you have seen the last
of me here.

At any rate, I am safe!

(*The* SENTRY *goes out.*)

ODE I

(Strophe 1)

CHORUS. Numberless are the world's wonders, but none

More wonderful than man; the stormgray
sea

Yields to his prows, the huge crests bear him
high;

Earth, holy and inexhaustible, is graven

With shining furrows where his plows have
gone

Year after year, the timeless labor of
stallions.

(Antistrophe 1)

The lightboned birds and beasts that cling to
cover,

The lithe fish lighting their reaches of dim
water,

All are taken, tamed in the net of his mind;
The lion on the hill, the wild horse windy-
maned,   10
Resign to him; and his blunt yoke has broken
The sultry shoulders of the mountain bull.

(Strophe 2)

Words also, and thought as rapid as air,
He fashions to his good use; statecraft is his,
And his the skill that deflects the arrows of
snow,
The spears of winter rain: from every wind
He has made himself secure—from all but
one:
In the late wind of death he cannot stand.

(Antistrophe 2)

O clear intelligence, force beyond all
measure!
O fate of man, working both good and
evil!   20
When the laws are kept, how proudly his
city stands!
When the laws are broken, what of his city
then?
Never may the anarchic man find rest at my
hearth,
Never be it said that my thoughts are his
thoughts.

SCENE II

The SENTRY *returns, leading* ANTIGONE.

CHORAGOS. What does this mean? Surely
this captive woman
Is the Princess, Antigone. Why should she
be taken?
SENTRY. Here is the one who did it! We
caught her
In the very act of burying him.—Where is
Creon?
CREON *enters from the palace.*
CHORAGOS. Just coming from the house.
CREON.   What has happened?
Why have you come back so soon?
SENTRY (*expansively*).   O King,
A man should never be too sure of anything:
I would have sworn
That you'd not see me here again: your anger

Frightened me so, and the things you threat-
ened me with;   10
But how could I tell then
That I'd be able to solve the case so soon?
No dice-throwing this time: I was only too
glad to come!
Here is this woman. She is the guilty one:
We found her trying to bury him.

Take her, then; question her; judge her as
you will.
I am through with the whole thing now, and
glad of it.
CREON. But this is Antigone! Why have
you brought her here?
SENTRY. She was burying him, I tell you!
CREON (*severely*).   Is this the truth?
SENTRY. I saw her with my own eyes. Can
I say more?   20
CREON. The details: come, tell me quickly!
SENTRY.   It was like this:
After those terrible threats of yours, King,
We went back and brushed the dust away
from the body.
The flesh was soft by now, and stinking,
So we sat on a hill to windward and kept
guard.
No napping this time! We kept each other
awake.
But nothing happened until the white round
sun
Whirled in the center of the round sky over
us:
Then, suddenly,
A storm of dust roared up from the earth,
and the sky   30
Went out, the plain vanished with all its trees
In the stinging dark. We closed our eyes and
endured it.
The whirlwind lasted a long time, but it
passed;
And then we looked, and there was
Antigone!

I have seen
A mother bird come back to a stripped nest,
heard
Her crying bitterly a broken note or two

For the young ones stolen. Just so, when this girl
Found the bare corpse, and all her love's work wasted,
She wept, and cried on heaven to damn the hands   40
That had done this thing.
                    And then she brought more dust
And sprinkled wine three times for her brother's ghost.

We ran and took her at once. She was not afraid,
Not even when we charged her with what she had done.
She denied nothing.
                    And this was a comfort to me,
And some uneasiness: for it is a good thing
To escape from death, but it is no great pleasure
To bring death to a friend.
                    Yet I always say
There is nothing so comfortable as your own safe skin!
    CREON *(slowly, dangerously)*. And you, Antigone,   50
You with your head hanging, do you confess this thing?
    ANTIGONE. I do. I deny nothing.
    CREON *(to* SENTRY*)*.   You may go.
                    (The SENTRY *goes.)*
(to ANTIGONE*)* Tell me, tell me briefly:
Had you heard my proclamation touching this matter?
    ANTIGONE. It was public. Could I help hearing it?
    CREON. And yet you dared defy the law.
    ANTIGONE.   I dared.
It was not God's proclamation. That final Justice
That rules the world below makes no such laws.

Your edict, King, was strong,
But all your strength is weakness itself against   60
The immortal unrecorded laws of God.

They are not merely now: they were, and shall be,
Operative forever, beyond man utterly.

I knew I must die, even without your decree:
I am only mortal. And if I must die
Now, before it is my time to die,
Surely this is no hardship: can anyone
Living, as I live, with evil all about me,
Think death less than a friend? This death of mine
Is of no importance; but if I had left my brother   70
Lying in death unburied, I should have suffered.
Now I do not.
                    You smile at me. Ah Creon,
Think me a fool, if you like; but it may well be
That a fool convicts me of folly.
    CHORAGOS. Like father, like daughter: both headstrong, deaf to reason!
She has never learned to yield.
    CREON.   She has much to learn.
The inflexible heart breaks first, the toughest iron
Cracks first, and the wildest horses bend their necks
At the pull of the smallest curb.
                    Pride? In a slave?
This girl is guilty of a double insolence,   80
Breaking the given laws and boasting of it.
Who is the man here,
She or I, if this crime goes unpunished?
Sister's child, or more than sister's child,
Or closer yet in blood—she and her sister
Win bitter death for this!
(to servants)   Go, some of you,
Arrest Ismene. I accuse her equally.
Bring her: you will find her sniffling in the house there.

Her mind's a traitor: crimes kept in the dark
Cry for light, and the guardian brain shudders;   90
But how much worse than this

Is brazen boasting of barefaced anarchy!

ANTIGONE. Creon, what more do you want than my death?

CREON.   Nothing.
That gives me everything.

ANTIGONE.   Then I beg you: kill me.
This talking is a great weariness: your words
Are distasteful to me, and I am sure that mine
Seem so to you. And yet they should not seem so:
I should have praise and honor for what I have done.
All these men here would praise me
Were their lips not frozen with fear of you.   100

(bitterly) Ah the good fortune of kings,
Licensed to say and do whatever they please!

CREON. You are alone here in that opinion.

ANTIGONE. No, they are with me. But they keep their tongues in leash.

CREON. Maybe. But you are guilty, and they are not.

ANTIGONE. There is no guilt in reverence for the dead.

CREON. But Eteocles—was he not your brother too?

ANTIGONE. My brother too.

CREON.   And you insult his memory?

ANTIGONE (softly). The dead man would not say that I insult it.

CREON. He would: for you honor a traitor as much as him.   110

ANTIGONE. His own brother, traitor or not, and equal in blood.

CREON. He made war on his country. Eteocles defended it.

ANTIGONE. Nevertheless, there are honors due all the dead.

CREON. But not the same for the wicked as for the just.

ANTIGONE. Ah Creon, Creon,
Which of us can say what the gods hold wicked?

CREON. An enemy is an enemy, even dead.

ANTIGONE. It is my nature to join in love, not hate.

CREON (finally losing patience). Go join them, then; if you must have your love,
Find it in hell!   120

CHORAGOS. But see, Ismene comes:

ISMENE *enters, guarded.*

Those tears are sisterly, the cloud
That shadows her eyes rains down gentle sorrow.

CREON. You too, Ismene,
Snake in my ordered house, sucking my blood
Stealthily—and all the time I never knew
That these two sisters were aiming at my throne!
                              Ismene,
Do you confess your share in this crime, or deny it?
Answer me.

ISMENE. Yes, if she will let me say so. I am guilty.   130

ANTIGONE (coldly). No, Ismene. You have no right to say so.
You would not help me, and I will not have you help me.

ISMENE. But now I know what you meant; and I am here
To join you, to take my share of punishment.

ANTIGONE. The dead man and the gods who rule the dead
Know whose act this was. Words are not friends.

ISMENE. Do you refuse me, Antigone? I want to die with you:
I too have a duty that I must discharge to the dead.

ANTIGONE. You shall not lessen my death by sharing it.

ISMENE. What do I care for life when you are dead?   140

ANTIGONE. Ask Creon. You're always hanging on his opinions.

ISMENE. You are laughing at me. Why, Antigone?

ANTIGONE. It's a joyless laughter, Ismene.

ISMENE.   But can I do nothing?

ANTIGONE. Yes. Save yourself. I shall not envy you.
There are those who will praise you; I shall have honor, too.
ISMENE. But we are equally guilty!
ANTIGONE.   No more, Ismene.
You are alive, but I belong to death.
CREON (*to the* CHORUS). Gentlemen, I beg you to observe these girls:
One has just now lost her mind; the other,
It seems, has never had a mind at all.   150
ISMENE. Grief teaches the steadiest minds to waver, King.
CREON. Yours certainly did, when you assumed guilt with the guilty!
ISMENE. But how could I go on living without her?
CREON. You are.
She is already dead.
ISMENE.   But your own son's bride!
CREON. There are places enough for him to push his plow.
I want no wicked women for my sons!
ISMENE. O dearest Haimon, how your father wrongs you!
CREON. I've had enough of your childish talk of marriage!
CHORAGOS. Do you really intend to steal this girl from your son?
CREON. No; death will do that for me.
CHORAGOS.   Then she must die?   160
CREON (*ironically*). You dazzle me.
                    —But enough of this talk!
(*to* GUARDS) You, there, take them away and guard them well:
For they are but women, and even brave men run
When they see death coming.
(ISMENE, ANTIGONE, *and* GUARDS *go out*.)

ODE II

(Strophe 1)

CHORUS. Fortunate is the man who has never tasted God's vengeance!
Where once the anger of heaven has struck, that house is shaken
Forever: damnation rises behind each child
Like a wave cresting out of the black northeast,
When the long darkness under sea roars up
And bursts drumming death upon the wind-whipped sand.

(Antistrophe 1)

I have seen this gathering sorrow from time long past
Loom upon Oedipus' children: generation from generation
Takes the compulsive rage of the enemy god.
So lately this last flower of Oedipus' line   10
Drank the sunlight! but now a passionate word
And a handful of dust have closed up all its beauty.

(Strophe 2)

What mortal arrogance
Transcends the wrath of Zeus?
Sleep cannot lull him, nor the effortless long months
Of the timeless gods: but he is young forever,
And his house is the shining day of high Olympos.
All that is and shall be,
And all the past, is his.
No pride on earth is free of the curse of heaven.   20

(Antistrophe 2)

The straying dreams of men
May bring them ghosts of joy:
But as they drowse, the waking embers burn them;
Or they walk with fixed eyes, as blind men walk.
But the ancient wisdom speaks for our own time:
Fate works most for woe
With Folly's fairest show.
Man's little pleasure is the spring of sorrow.

SCENE III

HAIMON *enters.*

CHORAGOS. But here is Haimon, King, the
last of all your sons.
Is it grief for Antigone that brings him here,
And bitterness at being robbed of his bride?
CREON. We shall soon see, and no need of
diviners.
—Son,
You have heard my final judgment on that
girl:
Have you come here hating me, or have you
come
With deference and with love, whatever I do?
HAIMON. I am your son, father. You are
my guide.
You make things clear for me, and I obey
you.
No marriage means more to me than your
continuing wisdom.   10
CREON. Good. That is the way to behave:
subordinate
Everything else, my son, to your father's
will.
This is what a man prays for, that he may
get
Sons attentive and dutiful in his house,
Each one hating his father's enemies,
Honoring his father's friends. But if his sons
Fail him, if they turn out unprofitably,
What has he fathered but trouble for himself
And amusement for the malicious?
So you are
right
Not to lose your head over this woman.   20
Your pleasure with her would soon grow
cold, Haimon,
And then you'd have a hellcat in bed and
elsewhere.
Let her find her husband in hell!
Of all the people in this city, only she
Has had contempt for my law and broken it.

Do you want me to show myself weak before
the people?
Or to break my sworn word? No, and I
will not.

The woman dies.
I suppose she'll plead "family ties." Well,
let her.
If I permit my own family to rebel,   30
How shall I earn the world's obedience?
Show me the man who keeps his house in
hand,
He's fit for public authority.
I'll have no deal-
ings
With law-breakers, critics of the government:
Whoever is chosen to govern should be
obeyed—
Must be obeyed, in all things, great and
small,
Just and unjust! O Haimon,
The man who knows how to obey, and that
man only,
Knows how to give commands when the
time comes.
You can depend on him, no matter how
fast   40
The spears come: he's a good soldier, he'll
stick it out.

Anarchy, anarchy! Show me a greater evil!
This is why cities tumble and the great
houses rain down,
This is what scatters armies!

No, no: good lives are made so by discipline.
We keep the laws then, and the lawmakers,
And no woman shall seduce us. If we must
lose,
Let's lose to a man, at least! Is a woman
stronger than we?
CHORAGOS. Unless time has rusted my wits,
What you say, King, is said with point and
dignity.   50
HAIMON (*boyishly earnest*). Father:
Reason is God's crowning gift to man, and
you are right
To warn me against losing mine. I cannot
say—
I hope that I shall never want to say!—that
you
Have reasoned badly. Yet there are other
men

Who can reason, too; and their opinions
    might be helpful.
You are not in a position to know everything
That people say or do, or what they feel:
Your temper terrifies them—everyone
Will tell you only what you like to hear.   60
But I, at any rate, can listen; and I have
    heard them
Muttering and whispering in the dark about
    this girl.
They say no woman has ever, so unreason-
    ably,
Died so shameful a death for a generous act:
"She covered her brother's body. Is this in-
    decent?
She kept him from dogs and vultures. Is
    this a crime?
Death?—She should have all the honor that
    we can give her!"

This is the way they talk out there in the
    city.

You must believe me:
Nothing is closer to me than your happi-
    ness.   70
What could be closer? Must not any son
Value his father's fortune as his father does
    his?
I beg you, do not be unchangeable:
Do not believe that you alone can be right.
The man who thinks that,
The man who maintains that only he has the
    power
To reason correctly, the gift to speak, the
    soul—
A man like that, when you know him, turns
    out empty.

It is not reason never to yield to reason!

In flood time you can see how some trees
    bend,   80
And because they bend, even their twigs are
    safe,
While stubborn trees are torn up, roots and
    all.
And the same thing happens in sailing:

Make your sheet fast, never slacken—and
    over you go,
Head over heels and under: and there's your
    voyage.
Forget you are angry! Let yourself be moved!
I know I am young; but please let me say
    this:
The ideal condition
Would be, I admit, that men should be right
    by instinct;
But since we are all too likely to go astray, 90
The reasonable thing is to learn from those
    who can teach.
    CHORAGOS. You will do well to listen to
        him, King,
If what he says is sensible. And you, Hai-
    mon,
Must listen to your father.—Both speak well.
    CREON. You consider it right for a man of
        my years and experience
To go to school to a boy?
    HAIMON.   It is not right
If I am wrong. But if I am young, and right,
What does my age matter?
    CREON. You think it right to stand up for
        an anarchist?
    HAIMON. Not at all. I pay no respect to
        criminals.   100
    CREON. Then she is not a criminal?
    HAIMON. The city would deny it, to a man.
    CREON. And the city proposes to teach me
        how to rule?
    HAIMON. Ah. Who is it that's talking like
        a boy now?
    CREON. My voice is the one voice giving
        orders in this city!
    HAIMON. It is no city if it takes orders
        from one voice.
    CREON. The state is the king!
    HAIMON.   Yes, if the state
        is a desert.
                              (*Pause.*)
    CREON. This boy, it seems, has sold out
        to a woman.
    HAIMON. If you are a woman: my con-
        cern is only for you.
    CREON. So? Your "concern"! In a public
        brawl with your father!   110

HAIMON. How about you, in a public brawl with justice?

CREON. With justice, when all that I do is within my rights?

HAIMON. You have no right to trample on God's right.

CREON. (*completely out of control*). Fool, adolescent fool! Taken in by a woman!

HAIMON. You'll never see me taken in by anything vile.

CREON. Every word you say is for her!

HAIMON (*quietly, darkly*). And for you.
And for me. And for the gods under the earth.

CREON. You'll never marry her while she lives.

HAIMON. Then she must die.—But her death will cause another.

CREON. Another?   120
Have you lost your senses? Is this an open threat?

HAIMON. There is no threat in speaking to emptiness.

CREON. I swear you'll regret this superior tone of yours!
You are the empty one!

HAIMON.   If you were not my father,
I'd say you were perverse.

CREON. You girlstruck fool, don't play at words with me!

HAIMON. I am sorry. You prefer silence.

CREON.   Now, by God—!
I swear, by all the gods in heaven above us,
You'll watch it, I swear you shall!
            (*to the* SERVANTS) Bring her out!
Bring the woman out! Let her die before his eyes!   130
Here, this instant, with her bridegroom beside her!

HAIMON. Not here, no; she will not die here, King.
And you will never see my face again.
Go on raving as long as you've a friend to endure you.   (HAIMON *goes out.*)

CHORAGOS. Gone, gone.
Creon, a young man in a rage is dangerous!

CREON. Let him do, or dream to do, more than a man can.
He shall not save these girls from death.

CHORAGOS.   These girls?
You have sentenced them both?

CREON.   No, you are right.
I will not kill the one whose hands are clean.   140

CHORAGOS. But Antigone?

CREON (*somberly*). I will carry her far away
Out there in the wilderness and lock her
Living in a vault of stone. She shall have food,
As the custom is, to absolve the state of her death.
And there let her pray to the gods of hell:
They are her only gods:
Perhaps they will show her an escape from death,
Or she may learn,
            though late,
That piety shown the dead is pity in vain.
            (CREON *goes out.*)

ODE III

(Strophe)

CHORUS. Love, unconquerable
Waster of rich men, keeper
Of warm lights and all-night vigil
In the soft face of a girl:
Sea-wanderer, forest-visitor!
Even the pure immortals cannot escape you,
And mortal man, in his one day's dusk,
Trembles before your glory.

(Antistrophe)

Surely you swerve upon ruin
The just man's consenting heart,   10
As here you have made bright anger
Strike between father and son—
And none has conquered but love!

---

144. CUSTOM: It was believed that if food were placed with a criminal who was being buried alive, his death might be considered due to natural causes.

A girl's glance working the will of heaven:
Pleasure to her alone who mocks us,
Merciless Aphrodite.

SCENE IV

ANTIGONE *enters, guarded.*

CHORAGOS. But I can no longer stand in
    awe of this,
Nor, seeing what I see, keep back my tears.
Here is Antigone, passing to that chamber
Where all find sleep at last.

(Strophe 1)

ANTIGONE. Look upon me, friends, and
    pity me
Turning back at the night's edge to say
Goodby to the sun that shines for me no
    longer;
Now sleepy death
Summons me down to Acheron, that cold
    shore:
There is no bridesong there, nor any music. 10

CHORUS. Yet not unpraised, not without a
    kind of honor,
You walk at last into the underworld;
Untouched by sickness, broken by no sword.
What woman has ever found your way to
    death?

(Antistrophe 1)

ANTIGONE. How often I have heard the
    story of Niobe,
Tantalos' wretched daughter, how the stone
Clung fast about her, ivy-close: and they
    say
The rain falls endlessly

And sifting soft snow; her tears are never
    done.
I feel the loneliness of her death in mine. 20

CHORUS. But she was born of heaven, and
    you
Are woman, woman-born. If her death is
    yours,
A mortal woman's, is this not for you
Glory in our world and in the world beyond?

(Strophe 2)

ANTIGONE. You laugh at me. Ah, friends,
    friends,
Can you not wait until I am dead? O Thebes,
O men many-charioted, in love with Fortune,
Dear springs of Dirce, sacred Theban grove,
Be witnesses for me, denied all pity,
Unjustly judged! and think a word of love 30
For her whose path turns
Under dark earth, where there are no more
    tears.

CHORUS. You have passed beyond human
    daring and come at last
Into a place of stone where justice sits.
I cannot tell
What shape of your father's guilt appears in
    this.

(Antistrophe 2)

ANTIGONE. You have touched it at last:
    that bridal bed
Unspeakable, horror of son and mother min-
    gling:
Their crime, infection of all our family!
O Oedipus, father and brother!   40
Your marriage strikes from the grave to
    murder mine.
I have been a stranger here in my own land:
All my life
The blasphemy of my birth has followed me.

CHORUS. Reverence is a virtue, but
    strength
Lives in established law: that must prevail.

---

16. APHRODITE: goddess of love.
9. ACHERON: river of the underworld.
15. NIOBE: wife of Amphion, king of Thebes, who boasted that she had borne more children than Leto, mother of Apollo and Artemis. In revenge, Apollo and Artemis destroyed all of Niobe's children and turned her to stone upon Mt. Sipylus.

21. BORN OF HEAVEN: Niobe's father, Tantalos, was a son of Zeus.

You have made your choice,
Your death is the doing of your conscious hand.

(Epode)

ANTIGONE. Then let me go, since all your words are bitter,
And the very light of the sun is cold to me. ⁵⁰
Lead me to my vigil, where I must have
Neither love nor lamentation; no song, but silence.
CREON (*interrupting impatiently*). If dirges and planned lamentations could put off death,
Men would be singing forever.
(*to the* SERVANTS) Take her, go!
You know your orders: take her to the vault
And leave her alone there. And if she lives or dies,
That's her affair, not ours: our hands are clean.
ANTIGONE. O tomb, vaulted bride-bed in eternal rock,
Soon I shall be with my own again
Where Persephone welcomes the thin ghosts underground: ⁶⁰
And I shall see my father again, and you, mother,
And dearest Polyneices—
dearest indeed
To me, since it was my hand
That washed him clean and poured the ritual wine:
And my reward is death before my time!

And yet, as men's hearts know, I have done no wrong,
I have not sinned before God. Or if I have,
I shall know the truth in death. But if the guilt
Lies upon Creon who judged me, then, I pray,
May his punishment equal my own.
CHORAGOS. O passionate heart, ⁷⁰
Unyielding, tormented still by the same winds!
CREON. Her guards shall have good cause to regret their delaying.
ANTIGONE. Ah! That voice is like the voice of death!
CREON. I can give you no reason to think you are mistaken.
ANTIGONE. Thebes, and you my father's gods,
And rulers of Thebes, you see me now, the last
Unhappy daughter of a line of kings,
Your kings, led away to death. You will remember
What things I suffer, and at what men's hands,
Because I would not transgress the laws of heaven. ⁸⁰
(*to the* GUARDS, *simply*) Come: let us wait no longer.

(ANTIGONE *goes out, guarded.*)

48-82. EPODE: the third part of the choral ode.
60. PERSEPHONE: queen of the underworld.
65. AND MY REWARD: The translators have omitted a passage of sixteen lines. The passage has been questioned by some editors, but the consensus of modern scholarship is against excluding it and against the simplification of Antigone's character which results from excluding it. A free prose translation of the omitted lines follows: "Yet those who think rightly, Polyneices, know that I have honored you rightly. Not even for children or husband would I have done this deed against the will of the city. On what principle do I say

so? On the ground that if a husband had died, I could have married another, and if a child had died, I could have had another by another man; but I could never have another brother, now that my father and mother are in the grave. On this principle, my brother, putting you above all other considerations, I seemed in Creon's eyes to commit a crime and to be fearless where I should have been afraid. So now, taking me by force, he leads me away, without my ever having known the marriage bed or marriage hymn, or the life of marriage or the rearing of children: a wretched woman, deserted by my friends, I go alive to the cave of the dead."

ODE IV

(Strophe 1)

CHORUS. All Danaë's beauty was locked
   away
In a brazen cell where the sunlight could not
   come:
A small room, still as any grave, enclosed
   her.
Yet she was a princess too,
And Zeus in a rain of gold poured love upon
   her.
O child, child,
No power in wealth or war
Or tough sea-blackened ships
Can prevail against untiring destiny!

(Antistrophe 1)

And Dryas' son also, that furious king,   10
Bore the god's prisoning anger for his pride:
Sealed up by Dionysos in deaf stone,
His madness died among echoes.
So at the last he learned what dreadful
   power
His tongue had mocked:
For he had profaned the revels,
And fired the wrath of the nine
Implacable sisters that love the sound of the
   flute.

(Strophe 2)

And old men tell a half-remembered tale
Of horror done where a dark ledge splits the
   sea   20

And a double surf beats on the gray shores:
How a king's new woman, sick
With hatred for the queen he had imprisoned,
Ripped out his two sons' eyes with her
   bloody hands
While grinning Ares watched the shuttle
   plunge
Four times: four blind wounds crying for
   revenge,

(Antistrophe 2)

Crying, tears and blood mingled.—Piteously
   born,
Those sons whose mother was of heavenly
   birth!
Her father was the god of the north wind
And she was cradled by gales,   30
She raced with young colts on the glittering
   hills
And walked untrammeled in the open light:
But in her marriage deathless fate found
   means
To build a tomb like yours for all her joy.

SCENE V

The blind TEIRESIAS *enters, led by a boy.*

(*The opening speeches of* TEIRESIAS *should
be in singsong contrast to the realistic lines
of* CREON.)

TEIRESIAS. This is the way the blind man
   comes, Princes, Princes,
Lock-step, two heads lit by the eyes of one.
CREON. What new thing have you to tell
   us, old Teiresias?
TEIRESIAS. I have much to tell you: listen
   to the prophet, Creon.
CREON. I am not aware that I have ever
   failed to listen.
TEIRESIAS. Then you have done wisely,
   King, and ruled well.
CREON. I admit my debt to you. But what
   have you to say?

1-34. ODE IV: The Chorus recalls in this ode three other persons whose sufferings included imprisonment: Danaë, Lycurgus, and Cleopatra of Thrace. Danaë was imprisoned by her father because he had been told by an oracle that if she ever bore a child, the child would kill him; but Zeus penetrated the prison in a shower of gold and begot Perseus. Lycurgus (*Dryas' son*, line 10) opposed the wild rites of the god Dionysos and so was driven mad by the god and imprisoned. Cleopatra of Thrace, daughter of the wind-god Boreas, married King Phineus of Salmydessos and bore him two sons. Phineus later imprisoned her and married a second wife, who put out the eyes of Cleopatra's sons.

25. ARES: The god of war was worshipped in Salmydessos.

TEIRESIAS. This, Creon: you stand once more on the edge of fate.

CREON. What do you mean? Your words are a kind of dread.

TEIRESIAS. Listen, Creon:　　　　　10
I was sitting in my chair of augury, at the place
Where the birds gather about me. They were all a-chatter,
As is their habit, when suddenly I heard
A strange note in their jangling, a scream, a
Whirring fury; I knew that they were fighting,
Tearing each other, dying
In a whirlwind of wings clashing. And I was afraid.
I began the rites of burnt-offering at the altar,
But Hephaistos failed me: instead of bright flame,
There was only the sputtering slime of the fat thigh-flesh　　　20
Melting: the entrails dissolved in gray smoke,
The bare bone burst from the welter. And no blaze!
This was a sign from heaven. My boy described it,
Seeing for me as I see for others.

I tell you, Creon, you yourself have brought
This new calamity upon us. Our hearths and altars
Are stained with the corruption of dogs and carrion birds
That glut themselves on the corpse of Oedipus' son.
The gods are deaf when we pray to them, their fire
Recoils from our offering, their birds of omen　　　30
Have no cry of comfort, for they are gorged
With the thick blood of the dead.
　　　　　　　　　　　O my son,
These are no trifles! Think: all men make mistakes,
But a good man yields when he knows his course is wrong,
And repairs the evil. The only crime is pride.

Give in to the dead man, then: do not fight with a corpse—
What glory is it to kill a man who is dead?
Think, I beg you:
It is for your own good that I speak as I do.
You should be able to yield for your own good.　　　40
CREON. It seems that prophets have made me their especial province.
All my life long
I have been a kind of butt for the dull arrows
Of doddering fortune-tellers!
　　　　　　　　　　　No, Teiresias:
If your birds—if the great eagles of God himself
Should carry him stinking bit by bit to heaven,
I would not yield. I am not afraid of pollution:
No man can defile the gods.
　　　　　　　　　　　Do what you will,
Go into business, make money, speculate
In India gold or that synthetic gold from Sardis,　　　50
Get rich otherwise than by my consent to bury him.
Teiresias, it is a sorry thing when a wise man
Sells his wisdom, lets out his words for hire!
TEIRESIAS. Ah, Creon! Is there no man left in the world—
CREON. To do what?—Come, let's have the aphorism!
TEIRESIAS. No man who knows that wisdom outweighs any wealth?
CREON. As surely as bribes are baser than any baseness.
TEIRESIAS. You are sick, Creon! You are deathly sick!
CREON. As you say: it is not my place to challenge a prophet.

---

19. HEPHAISTOS: god of fire.

50. GOLD FROM SARDIS: electrum, an ore containing silver as well as gold, was mined at Tmolus, south of Sardis, the capital of Lydia.

TEIRESIAS. Yet you have said my prophecy
is for sale.   60
CREON. The generation of prophets has
always loved gold.
TEIRESIAS. The generation of kings has
always loved brass.
CREON. You forget yourself! You are
speaking to your King.
TEIRESIAS. I know it. You are a king be-
cause of me.
CREON. You have a certain skill; but you
have sold out.
TEIRESIAS. King, you will drive me to
words that—
CREON. Say them, say them!
Only remember: I will not pay you for them.
TEIRESIAS. No, you will find them too
costly.
CREON.   No doubt. Speak:
Whatever you say, you will not change my
will.
TEIRESIAS. Then take this, and take it to
heart!   70
The time is not far off when you shall pay
back
Corpse for corpse, flesh of your own flesh.
You have thrust the child of this world into
living night,
You have kept from the gods below the
child that is theirs:
The one in a grave before her death, the
other,
Dead, denied the grave. This is your crime:
And the Furies and the dark gods of hell
Are swift with terrible punishment for you.

Do you want to buy me now, Creon?
                                  Not many
        days
And your house will be full of men and
women weeping,   80
And curses will be hurled at you from far
Cities grieving for sons unburied, left to rot
Before the walls of Thebes.
These are my arrows, Creon: they are all

---

for you.
(*to* BOY) But come, child: lead me home.
Let him waste his fine anger upon younger
men.
Maybe he will learn at last
To control a wiser tongue in a better head.
            (TEIRESIAS *and* BOY *go out.*)
CHORAGOS. The old man has gone, King,
but his words
Remain to plague us. I am old, too,   90
But I cannot remember that he was ever
false.
CREON. That is true. . . . It troubles me.
Oh it is hard to give in! but it is worse
To risk everything for stubborn pride.
CHORAGOS. Creon: take my advice.
CREON.   What shall I do?
CHORAGOS. Go quickly: free Antigone
from her vault
And build a tomb for the body of Poly-
neices.
CREON. You would have me do this?
CHORAGOS.   Creon, yes!
And it must be done at once: God moves
Swiftly to cancel the folly of stubborn men.[100]
CREON. It is hard to deny the heart! But I
Will do it: I will not fight with destiny.
CHORAGOS. You must go yourself, you
cannot leave it to others.
CREON. I will go.
                —Bring axes, servants:
Come with me to the tomb. I buried her, I
Will set her free.
                Oh quickly! My mind misgives—
The laws of the gods are mighty, and a man
must serve them
To the last day of his life!
                    (CREON *goes out.*)

PÆAN

                            (Strophe 1)

CHORAGOS. God of many names—
CHORUS.   O Iacchos
                                son
of Cadmeian Semele
            O born of the Thunder!

---

77. FURIES: The three avenging spirits who bring
retribution on evil-doers who are not subject
to human justice.

1-20. PÆAN: The Chorus now sings to Dionysos,

Guardian of the West

                 regent

of Eleusis' plain

           O Prince of maenad Thebes

and the Dragon Field by rippling Ismenos:

(Antistrophe 1)

CHORAGOS. God of many names

CHORUS.

                    the flame of

  torches

flares on our hills

             the nymphs of Iacchos

dance at the spring of Castalia:

from the vine-close mountain

                come ah come in

  ivy:

Evohé evohé! sings through the streets of

  Thebes   10

(Strophe 2)

CHORAGOS. God of many names

CHORUS.

                   Iacchos of

  Thebes

heavenly Child

         of Semele bride of the Thun-

derer!

The shadow of plague is upon us:

                   come

with clement feet

         oh come from Parnasos

down the long slopes

         across the lamenting water

(Antistrophe 2)

CHORAGOS. Io Fire! Chorister of the throbbing stars!

O purest among the voices of the night!
Thou son of God, blaze for us!

CHORUS. Come with choric rapture of
  circling maenads
Who cry *Io Iacche!*
           God of many names! 20

EXODOS

A MESSENGER *enters.*

MESSENGER. Men of the line of Cadmos,
  you who live
Near Amphion's citadel:
             I cannot say
Of any condition of human life, "This is
  fixed,
This is clearly good, or bad." Fate raises up,
And fate casts down the happy and unhappy
  alike:
No man can foretell his fate.
           Take the case of Creon:
Creon was happy once, as I count happi-
  ness:
Victorious in battle, sole governor of the
  land,
Fortunate father of children nobly born.
And now it has all gone from him! Who
  can say   10
That a man is still alive when his life's joy
  fails?

---

near Lysa in Euboea; on Mt. Parnasos in
Phocis), but keeps returning to the thought
that the center of his cult is Thebes, on the
river Ismenos, home of his worshipping
maenads, line 4, land where Cadmus, Thebes's
founder, sowed the dragon's teeth from which
his people sprang.
9. IVY: sacred to Dionysos.
10. EVOHÉ EVOHÉ: cry of Dionysos's worshipers,
like *Io* in line 16.
16. FIRE: The climax of the Pæan associates the
god with the elemental fire of the stars, and
perhaps also with the torches of his worshipers.
1-142. EXODOS: conclusion.
2. AMPHION'S CITADEL: so called because Amphion
was said to have built the walls of Thebes by
the music of his lyre.

---

also known as *Iacchos,* line 7, son of Theban
(*Cadmeian,* line 2) Semele by Zeus, who visited
her in thunder. The Chorus addresses him by
the names of places where his cult is honored
(in the West; at Eleusis in Attica; at the Cas-
talian spring near Delphi; on the vined slopes

He is a walking dead man. Grant him rich,
Let him live like a king in his great house:
If his pleasure is gone, I would not give
So much as the shadow of smoke for all he
    owns.
    CHORAGOS. Your words hint at sorrow:
    what is your news for us?
    MESSENGER. They are dead. The living
    are guilty of their death.
    CHORAGOS. Who is guilty? Who is dead?
    Speak!
    MESSENGER. Haimon.
Haimon is dead; and the hand that killed
    him
Is his own hand.
    CHORAGOS.   His father's? or his own? 20
    MESSENGER. His own, driven mad by the
    murder his father had done.
    CHORAGOS. Teiresias, Teiresias, how
    clearly you saw it all!
    MESSENGER. This is my news: you must
    draw what conclusions you can from it.
    CHORAGOS. But look: Eurydice, our
    Queen: Has she overheard us?

EURYDICE *enters from the palace door.*

    EURYDICE. I have heard something,
    friends:
As I was unlocking the gate of Pallas' shrine,
For I needed her help today, I heard a voice
Telling of some new sorrow. And I fainted
There at the temple with all my maidens
    about me.   30
But speak again: whatever it is, I can bear
    it:
Grief and I are no strangers.
    MESSENGER.   Dearest lady,
I will tell you plainly all that I have seen.
I shall not try to comfort you: what is the
    use,
Since comfort could lie only in what is not
    true?
The truth is always best.
                        I went with Creon
To the outer plain where Polyneices was ly-
    ing,

No friend to pity him, his body shredded by
    dogs.
We made our prayers in that place to Hecate
And Pluto, that they would be merciful. And
    we bathed   40
The corpse with holy water, and we brought
Fresh-broken branches to burn what was left
    of it,
And upon the urn we heaped up a towering
    barrow
Of the earth of his own land.
                    When we were done, we ran
To the vault where Antigone lay on her
    couch of stone.
One of the servants had gone ahead,
And while he was yet far off he heard a
    voice
Grieving within the chamber, and he came
    back
And told Creon. And as the King went
    closer,
The air was full of wailing, the words lost, 50
And he begged us to make all haste. "Am
    I a prophet?"
He said, weeping, "And must I walk this
    road,
The saddest of all that I have gone before?
My son's voice calls me on. Oh quickly,
    quickly!
Look through the crevice there, and tell me
If it is Haimon, or some deception of the
    gods!"

We obeyed; and in the cavern's farthest
    corner
We saw her lying:
She had made a noose of her fine linen veil
And hanged herself. Haimon lay beside
    her,   60
His arms about her waist, lamenting her,
His love lost underground, crying out
That his father had stolen her away from
    him.

When Creon saw him the tears rushed to his
    eyes

---

39. HECATE; PLUTO: a goddess of the underworld
    and its king.

And he called to him: "What have you done, child? Speak to me.

What are you thinking that makes your eyes so strange?

O my son, my son, I come to you on my knees!"

But Haimon spat in his face. He said not a word,

Staring—

And suddenly drew his sword

And lunged. Creon shrank back, the blade missed; and the boy,   70

Desperate against himself, drove it half its length

Into his own side, and fell. And as he died

He gathered Antigone close in his arms again,

Choking, his blood bright red on her white cheek.

And now he lies dead with the dead, and she is his

At last, his bride in the houses of the dead.

          (EURYDICE *goes into the palace.*)

    CHORAGOS. She has left us without a word. What can this mean?

    MESSENGER. It troubles me, too; yet she knows what is best;

Her grief is too great for public lamentation,

And doubtless she has gone to her chamber to weep   80

For her dead son, leading her maidens in his dirge.

    CHORAGOS. It may be so: but I fear this deep silence.

                    (*Pause.*)

    MESSENGER. I will see what she is doing. I will go in.

    (MESSENGER *goes into the palace.*)

    CREON, *bearing* HAIMON'S *body, enters with attendants.*

    CHORAGOS. But here is the King himself: oh look at him,

Bearing his own damnation in his arms.

    CREON. Nothing you say can touch me any more.

My own blind heart has brought me

From darkness to final darkness. Here you see

The father murdering, the murdered son—

And all my civic wisdom!   90

Haimon my son, so young, so young to die,

I was the fool, not you; and you died for me.

    CHORAGOS. That is the truth; but you were late in learning it.

    CREON. This truth is hard to bear. Surely a god

Has crushed me beneath the hugest weight of heaven,

And driven me headlong a barbaric way

To trample out the thing I held most dear.

The pains that men will take to come to pain!

    MESSENGER *enters from the palace.*

    MESSENGER. The burden you carry in your hands is heavy,

But it is not all: you will find more in your house.   100

    CREON. What burden worse than this shall I find there?

    MESSENGER. The Queen is dead.

    CREON. O port of death, deaf world,

Is there no pity for me? And you, angel of evil,

I was dead, and your words are death again.

Is it true, boy? Can it be true?

Is my wife dead? Has death bred death?

    MESSENGER. You can see for yourself.

The doors are opened, and the body of EURYDICE *is disclosed within.*

    CREON. Oh pity!

All true, all true, and more than I can bear!   110

O my wife, my son!

    MESSENGER. She stood before the altar, and her heart

Welcomed the knife her own hand guided,

And a great cry burst from her lips for Megareus dead,

And for Haimon dead, her sons; and her last breath

---

114. MEGAREUS: killed in the recent battle.

Was a curse for their father, the murderer
of her sons.
And she fell, and the dark flowed in through
her closing eyes.
  CREON. O God, I am sick with fear.
Are there no swords here? Has no one a
blow for me?
  MESSENGER. Her curse is upon you for
the deaths of both.   120
  CREON. It is right that it should be. I
alone am guilty.
I know it, and I say it. Lead me in
Quickly, friends.
I have neither life nor substance. Lead me
in.
  CHORAGOS. You are right, if there can be
right in so much wrong.
The briefest way is best in a world of sorrow.
  CREON. Let it come,
Let death come quickly, and be kind to me.
I would not ever see the sun again.
  CHORAGOS. All that will come when it
will; but we, meanwhile,   130
Have much to do. Leave the future to itself.
  CREON. All my heart was in that prayer!
  CHORAGOS. Then do not pray any more:
the sky is deaf.
  CREON. Lead me away. I have been rash
and foolish.
I have killed my son and my wife.
I look for comfort; my comfort lies here
dead.
Whatever my hands have touched has come
to nothing.
Fate has brought all my pride to a thought
of dust.
(*As* CREON *is being led into the house,
the* CHORAGOS *advances and speaks directly
to the audience.*)
  CHORAGOS. There is no happiness where
there is no wisdom;
No wisdom but in submission to the gods.140
Big words are always punished,
And proud men in old age learn to be wise.

I

1. *a.* Characterize Antigone in the first scene with Ismene. What are her reasons for deciding that she must go against Creon's edict? Is her decision that of a headstrong, rebellious person eager to assert her independence or simply that of a strong-willed woman who bluntly announces what must be done regardless of the consequences? Or is there something of both in her character? Explain, with specific reference to what she says and how she says it. What does her attitude toward Ismene's fear reveal about her?

   b. What further insights do we get into her character in her first meeting with Creon in Scene I? What do lines 64-67 show about her attitude toward death? Is there any indication that in a sense she is courting death? Why or why not? Why doesn't she immediately deny Ismene's participation in the deed when Creon jumps to the conclusion that both sisters are involved? What do her three separate comments in lines 98-100, 115-116, and 118 reveal? Why is she so cold to Ismene when the latter tries to join her in responsibility? Consider her replies to Ismene in lines 131-148. What is further revealed about her?

   c. What is the final picture we get of her? Why does she say lines 25-32 in Scene IV to the Chorus? How have they "laugh[ed]" at her? Indicate specifically what Antigone says in the omitted lines added in the footnote on page 799. What is gained or lost with the inclusion or exclusion of these lines? Comment also on whether what is said in them is inconsistent with Antigone's character as it has been previously revealed.

   d. In line 48, Scene IV, the Chorus says, "Your death is the doing of your conscious hand." In one sense this is true, but how could you argue that Antigone is simply the embodiment for Creon, the Chorus, and the audience of the truth she has stated earlier (Scene II, 59-63):

Your edict, King, was strong,
But all your strength is weakness itself against
The immortal unrecorded laws of God.

They are not merely now: they were and shall
be,
Operative forever, beyond men utterly.

Is the impact of the clash between
Antigone and Creon lessened if this
latter view of her plight is taken?
Explain.

2. *a.* What kind of man do Creon's opening
speeches and actions show him to be?
Consider the irony of his comment
about his devotion to the welfare of *the
State* and the inviolability of *law;* his
reaction to the sentry's news; his scornful treatment of the Chorus; his obsession with bribery; his temper; and
the sentry's willingness to talk back to
him even though he greatly fears the
man's power. Compare him here with
the kind of ruler we see in the opening
scenes of *King Oedipus.*

b. What further insights do we get into
his character in his first encounter with
Antigone?

c. What further is revealed in his meeting
with Haimon? What ironies are there
in the fatherly advice to Haimon and
the subsequent quarrel? What does his
decision about the manner of Antigone's death reveal about him? Note
particularly lines 129-131 and 141-149
in Scene III.

d. What is his initial reaction to Teiresias's revelations? How is it consistent
with his earlier reactions to the sentry
and to Haimon? How does the scene
between Teiresias and Creon parallel
the one between Haimon and Creon?
What significant difference is there in
Creon's reaction at the close of each
scene? What does the difference reveal?

e. What is significant about the fact that
Creon went first to bury Polyneices?

f. Is there anything in Creon's position
up until Teiresias's intervention that
can be defended as reasonable and
valid? Explain.

3. What is Haimon's role in the play? Consider the good sense of his argument with his
father. How does it contrast with Antigone's
defiance? Is Creon's reaction to it any different
from his reaction to Antigone's position? Why
or why not? How does Haimon's joining with
Antigone in opposition to Creon's edict differ
from Ismene's attempt?

4. Show how the following serve as foils to
Antigone in their attitudes toward death, reason,
and obedience to authority: Ismene, the sentry,
the Chorus.

5. *a.* Put into your own words the substance
of each of the choral episodes. Try to
determine what part each plays as a
commentary on man and his relationship to the gods. Is there any pattern
of development in the choruses? Explain.

b. How does the Chorus function as actor
as well as commentator in the play?
Consider specifically whether the final
comment spoken by the leader is consistent with other attitudes expressed
previously.

II

1. Write a paper on one or more of the following:

a. Another translator, E. F. Watling, has
commented that the center of the tragedy
is not "the 'martyrdom' of Antigone" but
the "retribution brought upon Creon for
his defiance of sacred obligations." Comment on the extent to which this is so.

b. Compare *King Oedipus* and *Antigone* as
commentaries on human strength and
weakness, human wisdom and ignorance,
human possibilities and limitations.

c. Compare Oedipus and Antigone. The
Chorus leader says of her: "Like father,
like daughter: both headstrong, deaf to
reason!/She has never learned to yield."
How is she like her father and yet not like
him?

d. Compare the Creon of this play with the
Creon of *King Oedipus* as examples of
"practical" rulers.

e. The concern with the burial of the dead
is not as important for us as it was for
those in *Antigone* or even for the
Athenian audience. What present-day issues could carry the same intense concern
for "conscience" as this issue carried for
Antigone? Jean Anouilh, a leading
modern French playwright, found Sophocles's play a striking commentary on the
German occupation of France in World
War II and translated it for production
during that occupation as a statement of
human resistance to tyranny. What other
situations relevant to our own times might
also be used?

APPENDIX

Glossary of Critical Terms

Biographies

Available Recordings

GLOSSARY OF CRITICAL TERMS

(Those marked with an asterisk are from *A Glossary of Literary Terms,* revised by M. H. Abrams (Rinehart English Pamphlets). Copyright 1957, Holt, Rinehart and Winston, Inc.)

Act The principal divisions of a play are commonly called acts. Following the lead of Latin tragedy writers, the Elizabethans divided their plays into five acts, roughly corresponding to major changes in the dramatic action. There is no set pattern today, but most modern plays are divided into three acts. Within any act there may be one or more scenes, again roughly corresponding to specific changes in place or time.

* Allegory An allegory undertakes to make a doctrine or thesis interesting and persuasive by converting it into a narrative in which the agents, and sometimes the setting as well, represent general concepts, moral qualities, or other abstractions. In *The Pilgrim's Progress* Bunyan allegorizes his doctrine of Christian salvation by telling how Christian, warned by Evangelist, flees from the City of Destruction and makes his way toilsomely to the Celestial City; en route he encounters such characters as Faithful, Hopeful, and the Giant Despair, and wins through places like the Slough of Despond, the Valley of the Shadow of Death, and Vanity Fair. A paragraph from this work will give a glimpse of the allegorical process:

> Now as Christian was walking solitary by himself, he espied one afar off come crossing over the field to meet him; and their hap was to meet just as they were crossing the way of each other. The Gentleman's name was Mr. Worldly-Wiseman; he dwelt in the Town of Carnal-Policy, a very great Town, and also hard by from whence Christian came.

A great variety of literary forms have been used for allegory. The medieval *Everyman* is an allegorical drama Spenser's *Faerie Queene* an allegorical romance, *The Pilgrim's Progress* an allegorical prose narrative. . . .

Alliteration refers usually to the recurrence of the initial consonant sounds at the beginning of words or syllables:

> "The *f*air *b*reeze *b*lew, the white *f*oam *f*lew,
> The *f*urrow *f*ollowed *f*ree:
> *W*e *w*ere the *f*irst that e*v*er *b*urst
> Into that *s*ilent *s*ea.

Allusion   is a reference for purposes of comparison to any significant literary or historical person, place, event, tradition, idea, etc. For instance, when Romeo says of Juliet, "It seems she hangs upon the cheek of night,/As a rich jewel in an Ethiop's ear," Shakespeare is comparing the night lit up by Juliet's shining youth and beauty to the cheek of an Ethiopian prince or tribal chieftain lit up by the fire of a great diamond (or ruby). Recognizing what is being alluded to sometimes presents problems. When there is a reference to an historical or literary or legendary event, place, or person, the necessary information, if we lack it, can usually be found in some kind of encyclopedia or dictionary. The allusions to Lazarus, Michelangelo, Hamlet, and Dante's "Inferno," for instance, in "The Love Song of J. Alfred Prufrock" can easily be traced. But often allusions refer to a tradition the knowledge of which can only be obtained from one's previous exposure to the tradition. The style of Coleridge's "Ancient Mariner" *alludes* to the English ballad tradition; Suckling's "Constancy" (p. 276) alludes mockingly to a long tradition of love poetry in which the lover claims his love will last forever—the tradition to which Burns's lines (p. 242) belong.

* Ambiguity   Since William Empson published *Seven Types of Ambiguity* (1930), this term has been widely used to signify that often, in poetry, two or more meanings of a word or phrase are relevant. "Multiple meaning" and "plurisignation" are alternate terms for the same phenomenon; they have the advantage of avoiding the implication, in the ordinary use of "ambiguity," that the quality is a stylistic fault rather than a valuable poetic device.

When Shakespeare's Cleopatra, exciting the asp to a frenzy, says,

> Come, thou mortal wretch,
> With thy sharp teeth this knot intrinsicate
> Of life at once untie; poor venemous fool,
> Be angry, and despatch—,

her speech is richly multiple in significance. For example, "mortal" means "fatal" or "death-dealing," and at the same time serves as a reminder that the asp is itself mortal, or subject to death. "Wretch" is a contemptuous epithet, yet also expresses pity (Cleopatra goes on to refer to the asp as "my baby at my breast, That sucks the nurse asleep"). And the two meanings of "despatch"—"make haste" and "kill"—are equally relevant. Compare CONNOTATION AND DENOTATION and PUN.

"Intrinsicate" in the same passage exemplifies a special type of multiple meaning, the portmanteau word. The term was introduced into literary criticism by Humpty Dumpty, in explicating to Alice the meaning of the opening lines of "Jabberwocky":

> 'Twas brillig, and the slithy toves
> Did gyre and gimble in the wabe.

"Slithy," Humpty Dumpty explained, "means 'lithe and slimy' . . . You see it's like a portmanteau—there are two meanings packed up into one word." A portmanteau word, then, is a word coined by fusing two other words; thus Shakespeare's "intrinsicate" is a blend of "intrinsic" and "intricate." James Joyce exploited this device to the full in order to sustain the multiple levels of meaning in his dream narrative, *Finnegans Wake.*

Antagonist (see PROTAGONIST)

Anticlimax refers to an intentional lessening of importance, usually for sharp contrast, of two or more items listed together. The desired effect is almost always a humorous one. In Pope's "The Rape of the Lock" one of the most effective satiric devices is anticlimax:

> "This day, black Omens threat the brightest Fair
> That e'er deserved a watchful spirit's care;
> Some dire disaster, or by force, or slight;
> But what, or where, the fates have wrapt in night:
> Whether the nymph shall break Diana's law,
> Or some frail China jar receive a flaw;
> Or stain her honor or her new brocade;
> Forget her prayers, or miss a masquerade;

Antithesis (see COUPLET)

Aside A remark made by an actor that only the audience is supposed to hear. In a sense the audience is being let in on something the other characters don't know. The device is now considered a rather crude way of revealing inner thoughts, although it has in the past been used very successfully.

Assonance usually refers to the recurrence of vowel sounds in accented syllables in the presence of changing consonant sounds ("ch*air*," "s*a*me," "w*eigh*t").

Ballad Traditionally a ballad is a story in verse form meant to be sung. *Folk ballads* are usually associated with no particular author but have been passed on from generation to generation by word of mouth so that there are many versions of the same story-song. Ballads are still sung today, but more often they are simply read, aloud or silently. The stories are usually built around common human experiences: love, physical bravery, treachery, revenge. The story is directly and simply told, dramatic and unembellished. Also characteristic of the folk ballad is the use of repetitious phrasing and dialogue. In the *literary ballad* (such as Coleridge's "Ancient Mariner") a writer adopts the forms and techniques of the folk ballad. The common ballad stanza is four lines rhyming a b c b, with four stresses to lines 1 and 3 and three stresses to lines 2 and 4.

* **Blank Verse**   is unrhymed iambic pentameter verse (see METER). Of all the regular English verse forms it is the most fluid and comes closest to the natural rhythms of English speech, yet it is readily heightened for passages of passion and grandeur. Soon after blank verse was introduced by Surrey in the sixteenth century, it was adopted as the standard meter for Elizabethan drama; a free form of blank verse is still found in modern poetic dramas such as those by Maxwell Anderson and T. S. Eliot. Milton used blank verse for the epic, *Paradise Lost,* James Thomson for his descriptive and philosophical *Seasons,* Wordsworth for his autobiographical *Prelude,* Tennyson for the narrative *Idylls of the King,* and Browning for many of his dramatic monologues. A number of long meditative lyrics have also been written in blank verse, among which are Coleridge's "Frost at Midnight" and Wordsworth's "Tintern Abbey." Blank verse lacks the rhyme which usually sets the pattern for stanza divisions (see STANZA), but some poets write blank verse so that it falls into rhetorical units called *verse paragraphs;* these units can readily be detected in Milton's *Paradise Lost* and Wordsworth's *Prelude.* The beginning and end of the opening verse paragraph from Wordsworth's "Tintern Abbey" will show the music and flexibility of which blank verse is capable in the hands of a master. Notice the shifts in stress, managed so that they give the effect of a living voice without violating the basic iambic pulse; the way the end of a syntactical unit sometimes coincides with the end of a line and sometimes runs on beyond it; the variation of the caesural pauses within the lines; and the ever-renewing run of the lyric voice up to the cadence that concludes the paragraph:

> Five years have past; five summers, with the length
> Of five long winters! And again I hear
> These waters, rolling from their mountain-springs
> With a soft inland murmur.—Once again
> Do I behold these steep and lofty cliffs,
> That on a wild secluded scene impress
> Thoughts of more deep seclusion; and connect
> The landscape with the quiet of the sky.
> 　　　　　. . . Once again I see
> These hedge-rows, hardly hedge-rows, little lines
> Of sportive wood run wild: these pastoral farms,
> Green to the very door; and wreaths of smoke
> Sent up, in silence, from among the trees!
> With some uncertain notice, as might seem,
> Of vagrant dwellers in the houseless woods,
> Or of some Hermit's cave, where by his fire
> The Hermit sits alone.

Caesura   refers to any pause or break within a line, usually at the mid-point.

Caricature   refers to the description of an individual through the distortion of some prominent personal characteristic for purposes of good-natured ribbing or ridicule. The term usually applies to drawings or cartoons, but verbal caricatures are also possible.

Character   (see PLOT)

Characters   The term applies specifically to a popular literary form of the seventeenth century in which brief sketches of certain types of individuals exemplified certain desirable or undesirable human characteristics: the busybody, the happy milkmaid, a mere young gentleman of the university.

Chorus   Originally, in pre-5th century B.C. Greece, the chorus was simply a group of male dancers and singers who performed religious rites. From this quasi-dramatic form grew the Greek drama we know. The Chorus first were given speaking parts, then individual actors were introduced with the Chorus still playing an important role, and finally the Chorus lost its central position and acted more or less as commentators on the action taking place. There have been attempts to use Chorus-like devices in non-Greek drama, but the use has not been particularly important or successful.

Cliché   In French the word means "stereotype plate," used in printing. Metaphorically, therefore, it refers to a word or phrase produced over and over until any suggestion of freshness or originality is gone. Clichés are the stock in trade of the boneheads who are as dull as dishwater. Examples are: "stock in trade," "bonehead," "dull as dishwater," "happy-go-lucky," "greased lightning," "sad but true."

Climax   refers to the point of highest interest in a piece of fiction, a narrative poem, or a play, usually the point at which all the various threads of plot meet and some sort of resolution is clearly foretold. The concept of "turning point" is often useful in trying to determine where the climax occurs.

Comedy   In broad terms comedy refers to literary works (usually plays) in which the approach is light-hearted and relatively detached. Characters get involved in exaggerated and complicated incidents in which human frailties and follies are exposed, but in such a way that everything turns out for the best. Comedy is often serious but never fateful, often sober-sided but not for long. *High comedy* refers to works whose appeal is largely to the intellect through wit and a sort of Olympian detachment from human stupidity; *low comedy* refers to works whose appeal is to anything but the intellect, through such standard devices as thrown pies. FARCE is a respectable form of low comedy in which unbelievable characters get involved in improbable situations; the language is witty, and the situations are imaginatively contrived.

*** Connotation
and Denotation**   The denotation of a word, in the usage of critics, is the thing or situation the word specifically refers to; its connotation consists of the associated meanings it implies or suggests. "Home" denotes the place where one lives, but connotes intimacy, privacy, and coziness. "Horse" and "steed" both denote the same quadruped, but "steed" has a different connotation, deriving from the romantic literary contexts in which we commonly find that word used. An expert writer is no less sensitive to the nuances of connotation than to denotative meaning in selecting his words. George Herbert wrote,

> Sweet day, so cool, so calm, so bright,
> The *bridal* of the earth and sky. . . .

The word "marriage," although metrically and denotatively equivalent to "bridal," would have been less apt in this context, because more commonplace in its connotation. Keats, in the passage,

> Charmed magic casements, opening on the foam
> Of perilous seas, in *faery* lands forlorn,

altered his original spelling of "fairy" in order to evoke the connotations of antiquity and of the magic world of Spenser's *Faerie Queene* in the older form, "faery." Compare AMBIGUITY.

A related distinction frequently made since the 1920's is that between EMOTIVE AND REFERENTIAL LANGUAGE. Referential—language—the language of science and of unemotional exposition —makes neutral assertions about matters of fact. Emotive language— including the language of poetry—may make reference to facts, or represent an object or state of affairs, but it expresses also feelings and attitudes toward the matters referred to. The difference is that between a weather report—"the day is fair and cool, with little wind" —and the passage from Herbert cited above. . . .

Consonance   usually refers to the recurrence of consonant sounds, especially final consonant sounds in the presence of differing vowel sounds ("wi*tch*," "wa*tch*").

* Couplet   Couplets are lines of poetry rhyming in pairs. Couplets have been composed in all meters, but . . . the most widely used couplet form is the iambic pentameter, known as the *heroic couplet*.

The heroic couplet was introduced into English poetry by Geoffrey Chaucer and has been in constant use ever since. It was employed most persistently in the neoclassic period, by some poets almost to the exclusion of other meters. Neoclassic practice imposed various limitations on the form, of which the most important are (1) The inclusion in each line of exactly ten syllables, with limited departure from a strict iambic rhythm. (2) The use of end-stopped lines; a pause often occurs at the end of the first line, and the end of the second line usually marks the end of the sentence, or of an independent unit of syntax. Such a couplet, in which the second line concludes the sense, is called a *closed couplet*. (3) The frequent use of a decided CAESURA, or pause, placed somewhere near the middle of the line, but varied in position to avoid monotony.

The sustained employment of the closed couplet meant that two lines had to serve something of the function of a stanza in neoclassic verse, and one purpose of the caesura was to break the two lines into subunits, in order to maximize the possible interrelations of the parts within a single couplet. Frequently the relationship between the first and second line, or between the two halves of a single line, is one of ANTITHESIS. That is, there is a balance, or parallelism, of grammatical pattern, but a strong contrast or opposition in the meaning. . . . The following passage from John Denham's *Cooper's Hill* (1642) is an early example of the artful management of the closed couplet which fascinated neoclassic poets, and served Dryden, Pope, and other writers as a model. A close reading will show the subtle ways in which Denham has achieved diversity and emphasis within the straitness of the closed couplet by the variable positioning of nouns and adjectives, the manipulation of vowel and consonant sounds, the shifts in caesura, and the use of balance and antithesis in the last two lines. The poet is addressing the river Thames:

> O could I flow like thee, and make thy stream
> My great example, as it is my theme!
> Though deep, yet clear; though gentle, yet not dull;
> Strong without rage, without o'erflowing full.

And here is one of the many instances of antithetic structure around a caesura in Pope's "The Rape of the Lock":

> Here Britain's statesmen oft the fall foredoom
> Of foreign tyrants, and of nymphs at home.

Diction   refers to the word choice in any given context, oral or written.

* Dramatic Monologue   The dramatic monologue was a poetic form perfected and exploited by Robert Browning, although poems as early as Donne's "Canonization" and "The Flea" exhibit many of its characteristics. Insofar as a dramatic monologue presents a single character speaking, it resembles the SOLILOQUY, in which a character in a play utters his thoughts aloud. But in a stage soliloquy, unlike a dramatic monologue, the speaker does not address other characters, or even the audience; the convention is that the audience overhears him talking to himself. . . . In its most complete form as employed by Robert Browning (although even some of Browning's monologues lack one or another of these attributes), the dramatic monologue has the following characteristics: (1) A single person, not the poet himself, is presented speaking at a critical moment: the Bishop is dying, Andrea del Sarto once more attempts wistfully to believe his wife's lies, Fra Lippo Lippi has been caught by the watchmen and must explain that to paint angels is not to be one. (2) This person is addressing one or more other people; but, it has been said, a dramatic monologue is like overhearing one end of a telephone conversation—we know of the auditors' presence, who they are, and what they say or do only by the clues in the discourse of the single speaker. (3) The monologue is contrived so that the main focus is on the interesting temperament or character revealed by the dramatic speaker. For example, although Wordsworth's "Tintern Abbey" is spoken by one person to a silent auditor at a significant moment in his life, it is not, like Browning's "My Last Duchess," a dramatic monologue, both because the speaker seems to be the poet himself, and because what he says is presented for the inherent interest of the evolving thought and feeling, instead of being subordinated to the revelation of the speaker's distinctive character. . . .

Tennyson wrote "Ulysses" and other dramatic monologues; the form has also been used by Robert Frost and E. A. Robinson, as well as by T. S. Eliot in "The Love Song of J. Alfred Prufrock." . . .

Elegy   Today the term refers quite specifically to a poem of meditation on the death of some particular person. More loosely the term refers to any highly personal expression of grief.

Emotive and Referential Language   (see CONNOTATION AND DENOTATION)

Epic   An epic is a long narrative poem in exalted language celebrating heroic men and heroic actions. The subject matter must be of great magnitude and the treatment of it must be elevated. Obviously, the number of epics is small. The most famous are Homer's *Iliad* and *Odyssey,* Virgil's *Aeneid,* and Milton's *Paradise Lost.* The *mock epic* or *mock heroic* poem adopts the conventions of the epic for purposes of satire, such as Pope's "The Rape of the Lock."

Essay   The term applies to a wide variety of prose pieces, and the only general considerations applicable are that the piece must be relatively short, non-technical, and restricted in scope. The terms *formal* and *informal* offer useful distinctions. The formal essay is impersonal, carefully and logically organized, serious, and dignified in its use of language. The informal essay is highly personal, often rambling, serious (perhaps) but never somber, intimate, often unconventional, and gracefully colloquial.

Fable   A brief story in which animals are the chief characters and through which some moral is illustrated. The most famous are those of

Aesop and La Fontaine. The late James Thurber wrote a good many delightful fables.

Falling Action The section of a play following the climax, during which the foretold resolution is carried out.

Farce (see COMEDY)

Figurative Language The term refers to language used in a non-literal sense. *Figures of speech* are various kinds of stated or implied comparisons that ask the reader or listener to suspend his literal response to words and constructions for the moment. When Burns said that his love was "like a red, red rose" he hardly expected to be taken literally. He expected his listener to suspend his literal response for the moment and concentrate on certain characteristics of a rose "newly sprung in June" and ignore other characteristics of the same rose. The non-literal sense thus achieved is not simply something fanciful added; figurative language is as basic to meaning as is literal language. The most commonly used figures of speech are SIMILE, METAPHOR and PERSONIFICATION. A SIMILE is a comparison between two essentially dissimilar things in which the comparison is overtly made by the use of "as" or "like." A METAPHOR is the comparison without the "as" or "like." Romeo's lines about Juliet ("It seems she hangs upon the cheek of night,/As a rich jewel in an Ethiop's ear") illustrates both figures of speech. In the first eight words of the sentence, Romeo establishes a metaphor that compares Juliet to something, possibly a jewel, hanging upon the cheek of night; in the remainder of the sentence he establishes a simile, introduced by "as" ("like" would do as well), which clarifies and expands the metaphor: night now becomes an Ethiop, and Juliet definitely a jewel. PERSONIFICATION is a comparison in which inanimate objects or ideas or abstractions are given human form or characteristics. In Romeo's lines above, "night" is spoken of as having a "cheek." The words "metaphor" and "metaphorical" are often used today in the more general sense of applying to any comparison in which certain similarities are noted between essentially dissimilar things. Figurative language, particularly in the form of metaphor, is so integral a part of meaning that we are often unable to determine which is the literal meaning and which the metaphorical or figurative meaning: consider how many different meanings there are for simple words like "run" or "train."

Free Verse refers to verse which has definite cadences and repeated phrasal patterns, making it more rhythmic than prose, but no regular meter and generally no use of rhyme. The Psalms in the King James version of the Bible are in free verse form; Stephen Spender's "I Think Continually of Those Who Were Truly Great" is a good modern example.

* **Imagery**   This term is one of the most common in modern criticism, and one of the most ambiguous. Its applications range all the way from "mental pictures" to the total meaning presented by a poem; C. Day Lewis, for example, has said that a poem is "an image composed from a multiplicity of images." Two particular senses of the word, however, are of frequent occurrence:

    1. The word "imagery" (i.e., images taken collectively) is used to signify descriptive passages in poetry, especially if the descriptions are vivid and particularized, as in Coleridge's

> The rock shone bright, the kirk no less,
> That stands above the rock:
> The moonlight steeped in silentness
> The steady weathercock.

The term "image" should not be taken to imply a visual reproduction of the scene described; some readers of the passage have visual images, some do not. Also, the description may be of any sensations, not only visual ones. Tennyson, for example, appeals to the senses of smell and hearing, as well as sight, in the lines:

> And many a rose-carnation feeds
> With summer spice the humming air.

    2. Still more commonly, "imagery" is now used to signify figurative language, especially metaphors and similes. . . . Recent criticism has gone far beyond older criticism in the emphasis on imagery, in this sense, as the clue to poetic meaning, structure, and effect. . . . Caroline Spurgeon, in *Shakespeare's Imagery and What It Tells Us* (1935), pointed out the frequent presence in Shakespeare's plays of "image-clusters," or recurrent groups of metaphors, such as the combination of dog-fawning—melting candy; she also presented evidence that a number of the individual plays of Shakespeare have characteristic image motifs—one instance is the frequency of the figures of sickness, disease, and corruption in *Hamlet*. . . . Since then many critics have joined the hunt for "image patterns" and "thematic imagery" in literature. Some critical extremists even maintain that the implications of the imagery, rather than the literal speech and actions of the characters, constitute the basic plot, or underlying "theme," of many plays, novels, and narrative poems. . . .

* **Irony**   "Rhetorical" or "verbal irony" is a mode of speech in which the implied attitudes or evaluation are opposed to those literally expressed. Ostensible praise or approval that implies dispraise or disapproval is more frequent than the converse form. Thus in Pope's "The Rape of the Lock," after Sir Plume, egged on by the ladies, has stammered out his incoherent request for the return of the stolen lock,

> "It grieves me much," replied the Peer again,
> "Who speaks so well should ever speak in vain."

This is a simple bit of irony, because it is obvious in the circumstances that the Peer is far from grieved, and that poor Sir Plume has not spoken at all well. Sometimes, however, the use of irony by Pope and other practitioners is very complex indeed, and the clues to the ironic reversals (especially since the writer lacks a speaker's resort to such ironic indicators as facial expression and vocal intonation) are subtle and difficult. That is why the use of irony by a writer carries an implicit compliment to the intelligence of the reader, who is associated with the knowing minority not taken in by the literal meaning. That is also why so many ironists are misinterpreted and sometimes (like Defoe and Swift) get into serious trouble with the obtuse authorities. Following the intricate maneuvers of a great ironist like Swift or Henry James is an ultimate test of a student's skill in reading.

To keep up a sustainedly ironic document, the writer is apt to utilize the device of a naive hero, or of a naive narrator or expositor, whose invincible obtuseness leads him to persist in putting an interpretation on affairs which the smiling reader just as persistently alters or reverses. Examples are Swift's well-meaning but stupid economist who makes the *Modest Proposal* to convert the children of the poverty-stricken Irish into a financial and gastronomic asset, or Swift's stubbornly credulous Gulliver. . . . SARCASM is a caustic and heavy use of apparent praise for actual dispraise: "Oh, you're just a great guy, a prince—I don't think"; it is the common man's usual form of irony. UNDERSTATEMENT . . . is the kind of irony which derives from deliberately representing something as much less than it really is. Swift wrote, "Last week I saw a woman flayed, and you will hardly believe how much it altered her appearance for the worse." The effect . . . is often comic: "The reports of my death," Mark Twain commented, "are greatly exaggerated." . . .

The word "irony" is also used in a number of extended and nonrhetorical ways. "Socratic irony" takes its name and meaning from Socrates's characteristic assumption, in his philosophical discussions, of an attitude of modesty, ignorance, and readiness to entertain points of view which differ from his own, but invariably turn out to be absurd. "Dramatic irony," or "tragic irony," is applied to the words and actions of characters in a play who confidently expect the opposite of what fate holds in store, or who say something that anticipates the tragic outcome, but in a sense very different from the one they intended. . . . The Greek dramatists, especially Sophocles, who based their plots on legends whose outcome was already known to their audience, made frequent use of this device. A concentrated instance of dramatic irony is to be found in the Oriental story of the frightened servant who obtains permission from his master to flee to Samarrah in order to escape Death, who had looked at him strangely in the market place. The master himself encounters Death in the market place and asks him why he had looked so strangely at his servant. "Because," said Death, "I was surprised to see him here. I have an appointment with him this afternoon, in Samarrah." "Cosmic irony," or the "irony of fate" is attributed to literary works in which God or Destiny is represented to be manipulating events as though deliberately to frustrate and mock the protagonist. This is a favorite structural device of Thomas Hardy. In his *Tess of the D'Urbervilles* the heroine, having lost her virtue because of her innocence, then loses her happiness because of her honesty, finds it again only through murder, and having been briefly happy, is hanged. Hardy concludes: "The President of the Immortals, in Aeschylean phrase, had ended his sport with Tess." "Romantic irony" is a term used by German writers of the late eighteenth and early nineteenth centuries to designate a mode of dramatic or narrative writing in which the author builds up and then deliberately breaks down the illusion, by revealing himself to be the willful creator and manipulator of his characters and their actions. . . . Byron's great narrative poem, *Don Juan*, constantly employs this device for comic or satiric effect.

In some recent critics we find "irony" used in a greatly extended sense, as a general criterion of literary value. It is claimed that only in poems of an inferior order does the poet commit himself unreservedly to any one attitude or outlook, such as love or admiration or idealism, and that superior poems always include an "ironic" awareness of the opposite and complementary attitudes as well. . . .

Lyric   Originally the term referred to a song accompanied by a lyre. The melodic aspect is still essential, but the term no longer refers to something sung. Broadly speaking, a lyric is any poem relatively short, highly subjective, concerned with emotions or feelings or even complicated developments of an idea but not with any narrative content. Obviously, therefore, most poetry falls under this heading. The most notable exceptions are the epic and the ballad.

Metaphor   (see FIGURATIVE LANGUAGE)

Meter   Rhythmic recurrence in poetry—when it is fairly regular—is called *meter*. Everything we say in daily speech has a rhythm—regular, irregular, light, heavy, swift, slow. "Don't leave all books here" is a sentence in which each word normally receives a fairly heavy stress, and any native speaker of English would be hard put not to read the sentence slowly and distinctly. A similar example can be found in the last four words of Hopkins's sonnet (p. 370) "send my roots rain." If we lengthen the first sentence to, "Don't, if you please, leave all of the books lying out here" "Don't," "all," "lying," and "here" receive heaviest stress, and the words "leave" and "books" receive a stress not quite so heavy but certainly heavier than the remaining words in the sentence, which are barely audible in contrast with the others. The point is that the stream of speech is made up of stressed and unstressed syllables which we all handle in about the same way: there is *word accent* (we say *ly* ing, not ly *ing*), and there is *syntactic accent* (we know by the sentence environment which words receive stress and which don't), as witness the fact that any native speaker will automatically put the stresses in the right places in "Don't, if you please, leave all of the books lying out here"). Usually the stress pattern of daily speech is very irregular; when it is regular—either by accident, as often occurs, or by plan—we get what is called *metrical accent* or *meter*.

The poet is simply a man who pays attention to this basic fact about speech, and makes it his business to arrange the words so that their rhythms will accomplish something. The two things normally accomplished are (1) the heightening of pleasure—because we all enjoy rhythm; and (2) the heightening or clarification of meaning. Let us look at an instance of the latter first:

> The old dog barks backward without getting up.
> I can remember when he was a pup.

In this short poem by Robert Frost, entitled "The Span of Life," the *old dog* is contrasted with the *pup* he once was. The words of the first line describe his behavior now; the words of the second line, notably the word *pup,* refer to the dog as he was then. This contrast in what the lines say is paralleled in the respective rhythms. The first line contains heavy stresses bunched together. Speaking playfully, we might say that the line, like the dog, refuses to get up off its haunches and move. Speaking more exactly, we can at least say that the rhythm of the line is heavy and halting in a way that suits the idea of an old dog not wanting to get up. The second line, on the other hand, has a swift, light, and fairly regular movement. Its movement is lively—like the pup's. And here there is a further point to notice. Though some sort of contrasting relation is established between the old dog and the young by what the words say, we do not know *precisely* what the contrast is until we listen to the rhythm. So far as what the words say is concerned, the point might be that the old dog is no longer so good a watch dog as he was. It is the contrast in the rhythm which helps direct our attention specifically to the differing movements of the two ages of dog, and so helps us to understand that the young one is all curiosity, barking at everything it sees, and rushing to see everything it barks at, while the old one, having been through all this and having no longer this kind of curiosity, or energy, simply turns his head and *barks backward.**

The heightening of pleasure comes from the combining of regularity with irregularity, as music does. The factor of regularity is supplied chiefly by meter—i.e., a specific type of continuously recurring measure or "foot." The five main types of *feet* distinguished in English poetry are: *iambic*—unstressed followed by stressed (re-*cur*); *anapestic*—two unstressed followed by a stressed (in-dis-*tinct*);

*Analysis of Frost's poem reprinted by permission of Dr. Maynard Mack.

trochaic—stressed followed by unstressed (*foll*-ow); *dactylic*—stressed followed by two unstressed (*eas*-i-ly); *spondaic*—two successive stressed (*star-lit*). The factor of irregularity is supplied chiefly by speech rhythms—i.e., the way we normally say something. We might say that we have polar opposites operating. At one end is pure speech rhythm, uncontrolled by any specific system of recurrence. This is prose. At the other end is pure metrical recurrence, the monotonous tick-tock of the metronome. Between these two extremes falls the spectrum of rhythms that can be called poetic.

It will be noticed in the foregoing paragraph that the factor of regularity is said to be supplied *chiefly* by meter, and the factor of irregularity *chiefly* by speech rhythms. The reason for the qualification is that there may be other elements in a poem contributing to regularity and irregularity—e.g., *line-length* and *stanza-pattern*. *Line-length* is determined by the number of feet making up the line. English verse lines rarely contain less than two feet or more than six, and most of them contain three (called trimeter), four (called tetrameter), or five (called pentameter). *Stanza-pattern* is determined both by line-length and rhyme-scheme.

Scansion is the process of describing the meter of a line of poetry in terms of the kind of foot and the number of feet it contains. Quite obviously, this is a useful but very rough and often inadequate description of the rich variation of rhythmical structure possible in English verse. More important than any mechanical scansion is the constant recognition that the emphases our speech rhythms require and should always get are balanced against the emphases that the underlying meter requires and should always get, producing a sort of tug-of-war, or tension, which brings pleasure and a sense of vitality.

Mock Epic   (see EPIC)

* Myth   In its primary significance a myth is one story in a "mythology," or system of narratives, which were once widely believed to be true, and which served to explain, in terms of the intentions and actions of supernatural beings, why the world is what it is and why things happen as they do. One way of putting it is to say that a mythology is a religion in which we no longer believe. Poets, however, long after they ceased to believe in the historical truth of these tales, have persisted in using the myths of Jove, Hercules, Prometheus, and Wotan for allusions, episodes, or plots; as Coleridge said, "still doth the old instinct bring back the old names." The term "myth" has also been extended in various ways. Plato used "myth," or accounts of supernatural beings and actions that he invented himself, in order to project philosophical speculation beyond the point at which it is possible to have certain knowledge; see, e.g., the "Myth of Er" in Book X of *The Republic*. Some German romantic critics proposed that to write great poetry, modern poets must deliberately invent for themselves a central and unifying "mythology," analogous to the genuine, or hereditary, mythologies of the past. In the same period in England, William Blake, who felt "I must create a system or be enslaved by another man's," presented in his poems a mythology constructed by fusing his own intuitions and visions with fragments from traditional legends. A number of modern critics, like the Germans earlier, have affirmed that myth, whether inherited or invented, is essential to poetry. Yeats is the chief modern example of a poet who undertook to construct a mythology of his own, which he expounded in *A Vision* (1926) and employed as the basis for a number of great lyric poems.

Myth is a very prominent word in modern criticism where, in addition to the meanings already described, it exhibits a variety of other meanings ranging all the way from a widely held fallacy (we speak, e.g., of "the myth of progress" and "the American success myth") to a solidly imagined, though fictitious, milieu in which the action of a literary work is represented as taking place ("Faulkner's myth of Yoknapatawpha County," "the mythical world of *Moby Dick*"). . . .

Ode A lyric poem, usually of some length, devoted to a serious theme and marked by a complex stanza form.

Parable A brief narrative that illustrates indirectly a moral or lesson. The parable was used extensively by Jesus as a teaching device.

Paradox A statement which seems to contradict itself, but which, on close inspection, proves to be quite true.

Parody An imitation, usually for debunking purposes, of a literary form or style.

Personification (see FIGURATIVE LANGUAGE)

Plot In simple (and misleading) terms a plot is the series of events that are interconnected in more or less complicated ways in any dramatic or narrative structure. It is helpful to distinguish between the unplanned, often disconnected, much too confusingly varied, uninterpreted events of daily life from what is called plot. Any plot must be planned out as a reasonably logical series of happenings; there must be a careful selection that ignores the trivial and random; there must be an interplay of events in which some resolution is demanded and carried through; and there must be an explicit or implicit interpretation of the "why" of the events. All of this presupposes human involvement—CHARACTER. Even if the "characters" are animals, or strange creatures, or forces (as in George Stewart's *Storm*), there can be no plot without the presence of strictly human motivations, human conflicts, human concerns. Plot and character are, therefore, inseparable.

* Point of View   refers to the outlook from which the events in a novel or short story are related. There are many variations and combinations of points of view, but the principal modes are (1) The author tells the story omnisciently, moving from character to character and event to event, having free access to the motivation, thoughts, and feelings of his characters, and introducing information to the reader when and where he chooses. In a number of novels so constructed, such as Fielding's *Tom Jones* and Thackeray's *Vanity Fair,* the novelist does not tell the tale impersonally but acts as a commentator on the characters and their actions. (2) The author narrates the story in the third person, but chooses one character as his "sentient center" whom he follows throughout the action, restricting the reader to the field of vision and range of knowledge of that character alone (Henry James's *The Ambassadors*). (3) The story is told in the first person by one of the characters himself, who may be the protagonist (Dickens's *David Copperfield*) or only a minor observer of the action (Emily Brontë's *Wuthering Heights*). John Dos Passos's *USA,* Virginia Woolf's *Mrs. Dalloway,* and James Joyce's *Ulysses* and *Finnegans Wake* give some notion of the directions and vigor of the experimentation with point of view in modern fiction. . . .

Protagonist   The main character, often called loosely the "hero," of any dramatic or narrative work. His opposite, or his opponent, is the ANTAGONIST (although there doesn't have to be one in any given work).

Pun   A play on words that sound alike but have quite different meanings, one of which is amusingly (usually) inappropriate: Gladly the cross I'd bear/Gladly, the cross-eyed bear. Puns are not always used humorously, and they are not necessarily the lowest form of humor even when used humorously.

Rhetorical Question   A question that answers itself by its very nature. The close of Shelley's "Ode to the West Wind" is an often-quoted example: "If Winter comes, can Spring be far behind?"

Rhyme   refers to the repetition of vowel sounds and following consonant sounds (if any) in the final accented syllables of words (words-birds; lighten-heighten; enjoy-employ). When there is an unaccented syllable after the accented one, the rhyme is called a *feminine rhyme;* when there isn't, it is called a *masculine rhyme.* The most familiar use of rhyme is at the end of lines (*end-rhymes*). The following stanza from Byron's *Don Juan* illustrates both masculine and feminine end-rhymes (and shows to what lengths a poet can go for humorous effects):

> But now at thirty years my hair is gray—
> (I wonder what it will be like at forty?
> I thought of a peruke the other day)—
> My heart is not much greener; and in short, I

> Have squandered my whole summer while 'twas May,
>   And feel no more the spirit to retort; I
> Have spent my life, both interest and principal,
>   And deem not, what I deemed, my soul invincible.

The "forty"—"short, I"—"retort; I" feminine rhyme is often called a *double rhyme,* and the "principal-invincible" rhyme is called a *triple rhyme.* A less familiar use of rhyme is *internal rhyme,* as in the following stanza from the "Ancient Mariner":

> "The fair breeze *blew,* the white foam *flew,*
>   The furrow followed free;
> We were the *first* that ever *burst*
>   Into that silent sea.

If the sound repetition is exact, a *perfect rhyme* results. Often, however, the repetition is not exact, and what is known as *imperfect rhyme* or *slant rhyme* results. It may be a case of eye-rhyme (ever-fever) or of only identical vowels (home-tone) or of only identical end consonants (body-shady). Poets usually employ perfect rhyme, but may very well choose to use slant rhyme to achieve certain effects; the imperfect underlines in some way what is being said.

   Quite obviously, rhyme is an important aspect of the sound patterning of a stanza; it serves to reinforce the musical quality of the lines and also acts syntactically as a unifying or linking element.

Rising Action   That part of the dramatic action that sets and keeps the complication in motion, leading up to the climax.

Sarcasm   (see IRONY)

* Satire   is the literary art of diminishing a subject by making it ridiculous and evoking towards it attitudes of amusement, contempt, or scorn. It differs from comedy in that comedy evokes laughter as an end in itself, while satire "derides"; that is, it uses laughter as a weapon, and against a butt existing outside the work itself. That butt may be an individual (in "personal satire"), or a type of person, a class, a nation, or even (as in Rochester's "A Satyr against Mankind" and Swift's *Gulliver's Travels*) the whole race of man. . . . The distinction between the comic and the satiric, however, is a sharp one only at its extremes. Shakespeare's Falstaff is a purely comic creation; his puritanical Malvolio is for the most part comic but has aspects of satire directed against a human type; Jonson's Volpone clearly satirizes the type of man whose cleverness is put at the service of his cupidity; and Dryden's MacFlecknoe, while representing a permanent type of the pretentious poetaster, ridicules specifically the living individual, Shadwell.

   Satire has usually been justified by those who practice it as a corrective of human vice and folly. As such, its claim has been to ridicule the failing rather than the individual, and to limit its ridicule to corrigible faults, excluding those for which a man is not responsible. As Swift said, speaking of himself in his "Verses on the Death of Dr. Swift":

> Yet malice never was his aim;
> He lashed the vice, but spared the name. . . .
> His satire points at no defect,
> But what all mortals may correct. . . .
> He spared a hump, or crooked nose,
> Whose owners set not up for beaux.

Satire is frequently found as an incidental element in many works whose over-all form is not satiric, in a certain character, or situation, or passing reference. But in many great literary achievements satire —the attempt to diminish a subject by ridicule—is the organizing principle of the whole. . . .

Setting refers to the background against which a play or story takes place; it may include place or location, time, environment, manner of living.

Short Story A great many different kinds of fiction are listed under the heading "Short Story," but essentially they are all stories that are short. The question of length is a relative matter which is best left to common sense. The question of what constitutes a story in this connection is best handled by reference to the following considerations: (1) there must be some sort of conflict that is resolved; (2) this involves an interpretation of human activity of some kind (physical, mental, spiritual); (3) the situation must be reasonably limited to a single series of closely connected events or activities; (4) character development must be present to some extent but any complexity of development is impossible in the space involved.

Simile (see FIGURATIVE LANGUAGE)

Soliloquy (see DRAMATIC MONOLOGUE)

* Sonnet is the name for a lyric stanza form consisting of fourteen lines and written in an elaborate rhyme scheme which, in English, usually follows one of two patterns. The "Petrarchan sonnet," named after the Italian writer, Petrarch (1304-1374), is divided into octave (8 lines) and sestet (6 lines) by the rhyme scheme: *a b b a a b b a   c d e c d e.* The sestet is variable, sometimes containing only two instead of three rhymes, and with the rhymes in differing arrangements. Petrarch's sonnets were first imitated in England by Sir Thomas Wyatt in the early sixteenth century . . . ; the form was later used by Milton, Wordsworth, D. G. Rossetti, and other sonneteers. English experimenters in the sixteenth century also developed a new form of the sonnet, called the "English" or

"Shakespearean sonnet," in which the rhyme scheme falls into three quatrains (4-line units) and a concluding couplet: a b a b c d c d e f e f g g.

The sonnet has been a popular form because it is just long enough to permit a fairly complex lyric development, yet so short, and so exigent in its rhymes, as to pose a standing challenge to the artistry of the poet. The rhyme pattern of the Petrarchan sonnet has on the whole favored a statement of problem, situation, or incident in the octave, with a resolution in the sestet. The English form sometimes falls into a similar division of material, and sometimes presents a repetition-with-variation of the statement in the three quatrains; the final couplet, however, usually imposes an epigrammatic turn at the end. In Drayton's fine English sonnet, "Since there's no help, come let us kiss and part," the lover brusquely declares in the first two quatrains that he is glad the affair is cleanly broken off, pauses in the third quatrain as though at the threshold, and in the last two rhymed lines suddenly drops his swagger to make one last plea. Here are the concluding quatrain and couplet:

> Now at the last gasp of love's latest breath,
> When, his pulse failing, passion speechless lies,
> When faith is kneeling by his bed of death,
> And innocence is closing up his eyes,
>> Now if thou wouldst, when all have given him over,
>> From death to life thou mightst him yet recover.

A number of sixteenth-century English poets, including Sidney, Spenser, and Shakespeare, followed Petrarch's example and wrote a "sonnet sequence," in which a series of sonnets are linked together by exploring various aspects of a relationship between lovers, or by indicating a development in that relationship which constitutes a kind of implicit plot. . . .

Speaker   Any piece of literature is quite obviously told by someone, but that someone is not necessarily the writer himself speaking in his own person, though it certainly may be. Often the writer adopts a voice, or a *speaker,* an assumed personality through whom he says what he has to say. It is important not to equate the assumed personality automatically with the author. For instance, neither the speaker of "A Modest Proposal" nor Lemuel Gulliver, the "I" of *Gulliver's Travels,* is Jonathan Swift; rather they are personalities Swift has assumed for specific reasons.

Stanza   A stanza is the main large unit in a poem. Usually it is a uniformly repeated pattern of a certain number of lines with a given rhyme scheme (such as the four-line ballad stanza), but this is not always the case; there can be stanzas of varying length with varying rhyme schemes or no rhyme scheme at all.

* **Symbol**   A symbol, in the broadest use of the term, is anything which signifies something else; in this sense, all words are symbols. As commonly used in criticism, however, "symbol" is applied only to a word or phrase signifying an object which itself has significance; that is, the object referred to has a range of meaning beyond itself. Some symbols are "conventional," or "public"; thus "the Cross," "the Red, White, and Blue," "the Good Shepherd" are terms that signify objects of which the symbolic meanings are widely known. Poets, like all of us, use these conventional symbols; but some poets also use "private symbols," which are not widely known, or which they develop for themselves (usually by expanding and elaborating pre-existing associations of an object), and these set a more difficult problem in interpretation.

Take as an example the word "rose," which in its literal meaning is a kind of flower. In Burns's line, "O my luve's like a red, red rose," the word is used as a simile, and in the version "O my love is a red, red rose," it is used as a metaphor. William Blake wrote:

> O Rose, thou art sick!
> The invisible worm
> That flies in the night,
> In the howling storm,
>
> Has found out thy bed
> Of crimson joy,
> And his dark secret love
> Does thy life destroy.

This rose is not the vehicle for a simile or a metaphor, because it lacks the paired subject—"my love," in the examples just cited—which is characteristic of these figures. . . . Blake's rose *is* a rose—yet it is also something more; words like "bed," "joy," "love," indicate that the described object has a further range of significance which makes it a symbol. But Blake's rose is not, like the symbolic rose of Dante's *Paradiso* and other medieval poems, an element in a complex set of traditional religious symbols which were widely known to contemporary readers. Only from the clues in Blake's poem itself, supplemented by a knowledge of parallel elements in his other poems, do we come to see that Blake's worm-eaten rose symbolizes such matters as the destruction wrought by furtiveness, deceit, and hypocrisy in what should be a frank and joyous relationship of physical love.

Other romantic poets, particularly Shelley, employed a number of symbols in their poetry, but Blake's persistent and sustained symbolic mode of writing had no close parallel until the Symbolist movement of the followers of the French poet, Baudelaire, during the later nineteenth century. The period since the first World War has been a notable era of "symbolism" in literature. Many important writers of this period use symbol systems in part drawn from largely forgotten religious and esoteric traditions and in part developed by themselves. Some of the most notable works of the age are symbolic in every element: in their settings, their agents, their actions, and their language. Instances of a persistently symbolist procedure can be found in short lyrics (Yeats's "Byzantium" poems), longer poems (Eliot's "The Waste Land"), dramas (Elmer Rice's *The Adding Machine*), and novels (Kafka's *The Trial,* Joyce's *Ulysses*). . . .

* Tone   In recent criticism "tone" is often employed, after the example of I. A. Richards, for the attitudes to the subject matter and to the audience implied in a discourse or literary piece. The tone of a passage might be characterized, for example, as formal or intimate, solemn or playful, serious or ironic, condescending or obsequious. . . .

Tragedy   In everyday use the word refers to events as widely different as a catastrophic earthquake, a head-on collision, or the breakup of a marriage: almost any event involving death or suffering—or even unhappiness—is labeled a "tragedy." As applied to literature, particularly drama, the meaning of "tragedy" has an obvious (if not very illuminating) connection with everyday uses—the fact that "tragedy" is a form of drama (most often) that deals with serious actions that involve suffering and usually death.

Aristotle, a Greek philosopher and critic who lived in the fourth century B.C., outlined in his *Poetics* the nature of tragic drama as revealed in the work of the great Greek tragic dramatists of the preceding century, particularly Aeschylus, Sophocles, and Euripides. He was not laying down rules for future writers; he was simply analyzing what had already been done as he saw it.

Briefly, Aristotle makes the following observations, all of which have been discussed at great length by many commentators:

1. Tragedy is "an imitation of an action that is serious, complete, and of a certain magnitude." By "imitation" he meant a faithful representation of life as it is or might be. By "complete" he meant a unified whole; the beginning, middle and end—the cause or causes of the action, the action itself, and the outcome or catastrophe— must all be presented to the audience. Also, generally speaking, the action must occur within a twenty-four hour period and must center around one location. "Of a certain magnitude" means that the events must happen to a person of some importance and must make a real difference to the person and to the audience.

2. The hero must be an essentially good person who, through some weakness of character or error of judgment, unknowingly brings doom on himself. At some point during the action he must discover the truth of his wrong choice or decision and accept responsibility for the catastrophe he has unwittingly brought about. Important also is the fact that his choice was intended by him to produce results opposite to what actually happens. This reversal of fortune and

recognition of the truth must bring about a change in him—most characteristically an understanding of his limitations as a man.

3. The hero must be a more admirable man in defeat than he was before. He must gain in stature through the way in which he meets catastrophe. Tragedy, therefore, "paints men as finer than they ordinarily are."

4. The audience is moved to "pity and fear" by tragedy—"pity" for the way the hero is overwhelmed by seemingly unavoidable circumstances, and "fear" over the fact that he is the author of his own undoing. Furthermore, "through pity and fear . . . the proper purgation of such emotions" is brought about. By "purgation" (or "catharsis") Aristotle does not mean that the viewer is cleansed of such passions, but simply that the passions are given a healthy airing for two or three hours and are put into the balancing perspective of eternal human conduct. There is emotional relief for the audience in the workout.

Much of what Aristotle had to say about the Greek tragedy he was familiar with has application to works written since his time that have been subsumed under the heading of tragedy, but Aristotle's observations do not limit the possibilities of the term. There have been so many distinctions made that it is impossible to say that such-and-such must be present to have "tragedy." In general, Aristotle's insistence on (1) "an action that is serious," (2) a hero who is essentially a good person with an obviously strong character, but in whom the possibilities for error reside, (3) a recognition that some sort of self-understanding must evolve, and (4) a dramatic situation in which the audience sees human behavior in the throes of decision-making that exposes both human failure and potentiality, must be present to some degree. The heroes we identify with today are not necessarily "great men," but they must have aspirations that go beyond the humdrum or the ordinary, and they must have some measure of control over their own destinies. What happens to them must move us to more than sympathy for the underdog or anger at blind injustice. At the heart of all ideas of "tragedy" lies the concept of self-directed and responsible human beings who fail themselves in the moment of trial and yet somehow come through defeat wiser and stronger—even, in a sense, nobler.

Understatement   (see IRONY)

Verse   There are two main uses of the term: (1) a line of poetry; (2) any composition in meter and rhyme. A third use, as a synonym for stanza, is common today.

BIOGRAPHIES

JOSEPH ADDISON (*1672-1719*)

Life. Son of Lancelot Addison, Dean of Litchfield. He distinguished himself at Oxford and was granted a pension for travel on the continent (1699-1703) in preparation for the diplomatic service. As a successful Whig politician he held a number of government posts and retired from office with a large pension in 1718.

Addison is now best known for his contributions to Richard Steele's periodical *The Tatler* (1709-1711) and, more important, to *The Spectator* (1711-1712), produced by Steele and himself. The latter is probably the most famous English literary periodical despite its short life. Stylistically graceful and urbane, it published literary criticism and directed gentle satire at a rapidly growing middle class whose follies were showing. Addison was a tactful social commentator, not a social reformer, and Pope's portrait of him as Atticus is probably quite accurate, severe as it may be.

Important Works. PROSE: contributions to *The Tatler* (1709-1711), *The Spectator* (1711-1712), and *The Guardian* (1713), all periodicals; PLAYS: *Cato* (1713), *The Drummer* (1715).

MATTHEW ARNOLD (*1822-1888*)

Life. Son of Thomas Arnold, famous headmaster of Rugby, one of the great English public schools. He attended Rugby and later Oxford. By his early thirties he had published three volumes of poetry and in 1857 was appointed Professor of Poetry at Oxford, a post he held for ten years. In his late thirties he turned from poetry to literary criticism and still later to social criticism.

Arnold is best known for his searching attacks on the materialism of his times, for his attempts to bring together religious certainty and freedom of inquiry, and for his powerful expression of the sense of personal isolation still characteristic of modern man.

Important Works. POETRY: *The Strayed Reveller* (1849), *Empedocles on Etna* (1852), *Poems* (1853-55), *Merope* (1858); PROSE: *Culture and Anarchy* (1869), *Literature and Dogma* (1869).

WYSTAN HUGH AUDEN (*1907-   *)

Life. Born in York, England. He was educated at Christ Church, Oxford, and was a schoolmaster for five years. In 1935 he married Erika Mann, daughter of Thomas Mann. During the Spanish Civil War (1936-1939) he drove an ambulance for the Loyalists. He has lived in the United States since 1939, has become an American citizen, and has taught at a number of colleges and universities.

Auden is one of the most versatile of modern poets and has experimented widely in verse forms. Born to well-to-do parents, he early rebelled against his class and was for a time an ardent Marxist Socialist. He became disillusioned with Socialism in the late 1930's, but has remained one of the most searching satirists of modern life, committed to no particular dogma, skeptical of all systems and panaceas, and convinced of the rudderless drifting of modern man.

Important Works. POETRY: *Poems* (1930), *Selected Poems* (1940), *New Year Letter* (1941), *For the Time Being* (1944), *Collected Poems* (1945), *The Age of Anxiety* (1947); VERSE PLAYS: (with Christopher Isherwood) *The Dog Beneath the Skin* (1935), *The Ascent of F6* (1936), *On the Frontier* (1938).

FRANCIS BACON (*1561-1626*)

Life. Younger son of Sir Nicholas Bacon, a prominent nobleman. He was educated at Trinity College, Cambridge, and prepared for the law. He entered Parliament in 1584, and with the coming of James I to the throne in 1603 he rose rapidly in the government, becoming Lord Chancellor in 1618. Three years later he was convicted of bribery and was dismissed from the government. Even though he was later pardoned, he never went back to government service, but spent his remaining years writing.

Bacon was the true Renaissance scholar, a man of broad learning and great intellect who was at the same time a practical man of affairs. As a philosopher-scientist he is perhaps best remembered for his championing of the inductive or experimental method of scientific inquiry, the cornerstone of modern scientific achievement. As a literary man, he is best re-membered for his *Essays,* a series of shrewd and cynical observations on how to get along successfully in a none-too-moral world.

Important Works. PROSE: *Essays* (1597, 1621), *The Advancement of Learning* (1605), *Novum Organum* (1620), *De Augmentis Scientarium* (1623), *New Atlantis* (1624).

WILLIAM BLAKE (*1757-1827*)

Life. Born in London, the son of a hosier, a kind and loving man who was not able to give the boy any formal education but saw to it that his obvious talent for drawing and his delight in the world of the imagination were given free rein. At an early age Blake studied art and was apprenticed to an engraver. Later he opened his own print shop, from which he made only a modest living. His illustrations of Dante, Milton, Bunyan, the Book of Job, and other works, however, earned him a limited though richly deserved fame.

Blake was a remarkable blend of artist, poet, religious mystic, and implacable foe of almost any form of religious or social organization. His illustrations of his own works and those mentioned above are unexcelled examples of the engraver's art at the service of an intense imagination and an overpowering spiritual vision. He is undoubtedly England's foremost poet-artist.

Important Works. POETRY: *Poetical Sketches* (1783), *Songs of Innocence* (1789), *The Book of Thel* (1789), *The Marriage of Heaven and Hell* (1790), *The Vision of the Daughters of Albion* (1793), *Songs of Experience* (1794), *Milton* (1804).

JAMES BOSWELL (*1740-1795*)

Life. Born in Edinburgh, the son of Alexander Boswell, Lord Auchinleck, a prominent Scottish judge and landed proprietor. In line with his father's wishes he studied for the law in Scotland and on the Continent, but his heart was in the literary, political, and social world of London. He devoted his life partly to the management of his inherited estate, partly to the cultivation of the friendship of famous men (such as Rousseau, Voltaire, Hume, and the members of the Literary Club: Johnson, Reynolds, Burke, Goldsmith, Garrick, and Charles James Fox), and partly to the writing of essays, poems, travel-diaries, sketches, letters, and his remarkable biography of Samuel Johnson.

Few men have done a more conscientious and thorough job of keeping records of their daily activities. In straightforward, painstaking, and refreshing prose he faithfully recorded a multitude of details about himself, his contemporaries, and the world he lived in. His recently discovered journals have revealed him as one of the great stylists of the eighteenth century, and as a personality as fascinating in his own way as is the subject of his great biography.

Important Works. PROSE: *The London Journal* (1762-1763), *Boswell in Holland* (1763-1764), *An Account of Corsica* (1768), *The Journal of a Tour to the Hebrides* (1785), *The Life of Samuel Johnson* (1791).

ROBERT BROWNING (*1812-1889*)

Life. Son of a successful banker and a talented, deeply religious mother. His schooling, under the guidance of his sensitive and cultured parents, was informal but thorough. He was successful early as a writer, and he had an established reputation when he married Elizabeth Barrett, a semi-invalid who was herself a well-known poet. Their fifteen years together in Italy were happy and productive, and her death in 1861 came as a severe shock to him. In his later years he became a prominent social figure in England and in Venice, and his reputation as a writer grew steadily.

Browning's poetry reveals a steady note of optimism, a conviction that a loving God is constantly at work, that this earthly life is not the end-product of existence, that "man's reach should exceed his grasp" regardless of the fact that perfection of any kind is unattainable. His psychological studies, particularly as revealed through his dramatic monologues, are unusually penetrating and often disturbing in their insight into what man is.

Important Works. POETRY: *Pauline* (1833), *Paracelsus* (1835), *Sordello* (1840), *Men and Women* (1855), *Dramatis Personae* (1864), *The Ring and the Book* (1868-1869), *Dramatic Idylls* (1878-1879).

JOHN BUNYAN (*1628-1688*)

Life. Born in November, 1628, near Bedford, the son of a tinsmith, and early trained in his father's trade. When only sixteen he fought in the Parliamentary army in the English Civil War. In 1653 he joined a Baptist group in Bedford and became a lay preacher. With the restoration of Stuart monarchy under Charles II in 1660 he was imprisoned for refusing to comply with laws against unlicensed preaching and spent twelve years in the Bedford prison, during which time he wrote his spiritual autobiography. He was imprisoned again in 1675 for a brief time.

Bunyan's early years were almost unbearable. He saw himself as the most wicked of sinners, and his over-active imagination, regularly stimulated by Biblical accounts of punishment for wrong-doing, left him in a perpetual state of self-condemnation and fear. The sense of his own great sinfulness subsided as he reached manhood, but he never lost his intense powers of imagination. Simply and directly, with a style greatly influenced by the King James Bible, he tried to illuminate the path to salvation for erring man.

Important Works. PROSE: *Grace Abounding to the Chief of Sinners* (1666), *Pilgrim's Progress* (1678, 1684), *The Life and Death of Mr. Badman* (1680), *The Holy War* (1682).

ROBERT BURNS (*1759-1796*)

Life. Born in Ayrshire, Scotland, son of an impoverished farmer. Although he had little formal schooling, Burns evidently read a great deal of poetry, particularly that of medieval Scottish poets. After his father's death, he tried farming with his brother, but the critical success of his first published volume of poetry took him off his farm for good. He spent several winters in Edinburgh enjoying his popularity and then settled down in Dumfries as a tax official, where he died of rheumatic heart disease at the age of thirty-seven.

The delight his Scottish audiences first found in Burns's poetry is repeated with each new generation of listeners or readers. There is an exuberance, a reviving lilt in everything he wrote. His subject matter was the everyday world; and whether he is singing of the joys of home, or of the love of country or of women, or of the indifference and coldness that separate men from their fellows, he convinces us by the intensity of his feelings that he is a singer who knows whereof he sings.

Important Works. POETRY: *Poems, Chiefly in the Scottish Dialect* (1786): later enlarged editions 1787, 1793.

GEORGE GORDON, LORD BYRON
(*1788-1824*)

Life. Born in London, son of "Mad Jack" and Catherine Gordon Byron (his father's second wife). Byron inherited his title and estate at the age of ten from his great-uncle. He was educated at Harrow, where he excelled in athletics, and at Trinity College, Cambridge, where he literally did as he pleased. Upon graduation he entered the House of Lords but almost immediately took off on a tour of Portugal, Spain, Albania, and the Near East (1809-1811). Back in England his unconventional, licentious, and often arrogant behavior turned an adoring public against him, and he left in disgust in 1816 to live in self-exile in Italy, Switzerland, and Greece. In the 1820's he became deeply involved in the Greek struggle for independence and died of a fever at Missolonghi on April 19, 1824, at the age of thirty-six.

From an early age Byron was in revolt against the conventions of the society into which he was born. Handsome, proud, sensitive, restless, he was unsparingly critical of himself and of the hypocrisy and muddle-mindedness of his English contemporaries. His personal morals and his intensely independent spirit both shocked and fascinated the English and European public, and he skillfully exploited the image that public opinion responded to and partially created. His poetry reveals an unusual blend of the romantic and sentimental, tempered by the wit and irreverence of a satirical turn of mind.

Important Works. POETRY: *English Bards and Scotch Reviewers* (1809), *Childe Harold's Pilgrimage* (1812-1818), *Manfred* (1817), *Don Juan* (1818-1824), *Cain* (1821), *Beppo* (1822), *The Vision of Judgment* (1822).

GEOFFREY CHAUCER (*1340?-1400*)

Life. The exact date of his birth is unknown, but he was born into the family of well-to-do wine merchants and all his life had important court connections. As a youth still in his teens he fought in Europe and served in the household of relatives of Edward III. Later he married the sister of the wife of John of Gaunt.

He studied law and was sent on several diplomatic missions to the Continent. In succeeding years he was Controller of Customs in the port of London, administrator of several of the King's enterprises, and a member of Parliament for one session. Despite the busy life of a man of affairs, he found time to compose the works that established him as the foremost writer of his age.

Chaucer's audience was the influential and educated world of London. With none of the reformer's zeal or the cynic's indifference, he paraded before his sophisticated contemporaries the whole panorama of fourteenth century England seen through the eyes of a compassionate but scrupulously accurate observer. His humor is never malicious, even when most biting, and if his satiric insights spare few aspects of the society he knew, he convinces us that he does not exclude himself from involvement in human folly and short-sightedness. A point of great significance is the fact that he wrote most of his works in the English vernacular at a time when few educated people had any respect for their native English as a medium for literature.

Important Works. POETRY: *Canterbury Tales, Troilus and Criseyde, The Book of the Duchess, The House of Fame, The Parliament of Fowls, The Legend of Good Women* (none of Chaucer's work can be accurately dated).

GILBERT KEITH CHESTERTON
(1874-1936)

Life. Born in London, the son of a real estate dealer. He was educated at St. Paul's and the Slade School of Art. For most of his adult life he was a reviewer, journalist, and magazine editor. In 1922 he joined the Roman Catholic Church. He received honorary degrees from Edinburgh, Dublin, and Notre Dame, and lectured at Notre Dame in 1930.

Chesterton was a prolific writer, publishing in his lifetime upwards of 100 volumes: essays, biographies, novels, short stories, plays, verse, and books on history and travel. His witty and provocative comments on twentieth-century life reveal a mind rooted in an ordered and stable past that was probably never what Chesterton liked to think it was. He delighted in argument and saw almost any subject—and there are few subjects he failed to look at—in surprisingly uncommon ways. He was at home in the turmoil of political controversy, in the heat of religious debate, in the elusiveness of art criticism, and in the twists and surprises of the detective story and fantasy. Few writers have matched his energy, wide-ranging interests, and extravagant delight in language.

Important Works. NOVELS: *The Man Who Was Thursday* (1912), *The Flying Inn* (1914); DETECTIVE STORIES: *The Innocence of Father Brown* (1911), *The Scandal of Father Brown* (1935); ESSAYS: *Heretics* (1905), *Orthodoxy* (1908), *Tremendous Trifles* (1909); CRITICISM: *Charles Dickens* (1906), *George Bernard Shaw* (1909)—and many others.

JOSEPH CONRAD *(1857-1924)*

Life. Born Teodor Josef Konrad Korzeniowski in the Ukraine, the son of a scholarly Polish aristocrat. In opposition to his family's wishes he left home at sixteen to become a sailor and spent twenty-one years on the sea, mostly as an officer on British ships. In 1894 he left the sea for good and turned to full-time writing in English. In the next thirty years he produced a great many short stories and novels, most of them rooted in his knowledge of the sea or of the many mysterious corners of the world he knew so well.

For Conrad the recesses of the human heart and soul were more strange and forbidding than any faraway spot on the globe. Although he uses the isolation of the sea and the "lands beyond the sun" as a backdrop, what he is chiefly concerned with is how a man lives up to his ideal image of himself, how he reasserts the durability of courage and dignity and loyalty against the forces of nature and the evil in man that would negate those virtues.

Important Works. NOVELS: *Almayer's Folly* (1895), *An Outcast of the Islands* (1896), *The Nigger of the "Narcissus"* (1898), *Lord Jim* (1900), *Nostromo* (1904), *Under Western Eyes* (1911), *Chance* (1914), *Victory* (1915); SHORTER TALES: *Typhoon* (1902), *Youth* (1902), *Heart of Darkness* (1902), *Within the Tides* (1915); CRITICAL WORKS: *Notes on Life and Letters* (1921), *Notes on My Books* (1921).

ANTHONY ASHLEY COOPER, FIRST EARL OF SHAFTESBURY (*1621-1683*)

Life. Born in Dorsetshire into an important landed family. For most of his adult life Shaftesbury was deeply involved in English politics. At the age of nineteen he was a member of Parliament, and from then on until his self-imposed exile from England shortly before his death, he was one of the leading figures in Parliament and has been called "the first real Parliamentary leader in English history." He was the leader of the anti-royalist group during the Restoration and was also active in the colonization of Carolina.

Important Works. Shaftesbury's genius was in politics, not in literature, but his collected papers include diaries, autobiographical sketches (from which the *Portrait of Henry Hastings* comes), letters, and documents dealing with the Carolina settlement.

CHARLES DICKENS (*1812-1870*)

Life. Born in Portsmouth, the second of eight children of an impoverished clerk who was constantly on the move through whim or necessity. His boyhood was spent in poverty, and he learned early to shift for himself; at twelve he was putting in a full day at a blacking warehouse. As a youth he worked for a time as a clerk in a law office and as a newspaper reporter. With the appearance of magazine articles and of the *Pickwick Papers* in 1836 his popularity was established, and his reputation grew steadily on both sides of the Atlantic through a steady succession of serialized novels. He made two lecture tours to the United States, one in 1842 and one in 1867-1868.

Dickens's novels are filled with an amazing assortment of characters, many of whom live on outside the novels as prototypes of one or another distortion of human nature. His indignation against degrading social conditions marks almost every novel, but the social satirist seldom gains the upper hand over the story-teller, and his novels are rich in unforgettable people crowding through the world of mid-nineteenth century England.

Important Works. NOVELS: *Pickwick Papers* (1836), *Oliver Twist* (1838), *Martin Chuzzlewit* (1844), *David Copperfield* (1850), *Bleak House* (1853), *Hard Times* (1854), *A Tale of Two Cities* (1859), *Great Expectations* (1861).

JOHN DONNE (*1572-1631*)

Life. Born in London, the son of a London shopkeeper and a very devout Catholic mother. Donne attended both Oxford and Cambridge and studied law for several years. In the middle 1590's he engaged in some minor diplomatic activities and, in 1598, became secretary to the Lord Keeper, Sir Thomas Egerton. Three years later he fell in love with and secretly married Egerton's young niece, Anne More, against Egerton's wishes, and was bluntly dismissed from service and imprisoned. For fourteen years the Donnes lived in poverty and relative obscurity. He was eager for court preferment, but James I wanted him to join the Anglican priesthood, which he did in 1615. By 1621 he was Dean of St. Paul's in London and was in line for a bishopric when he died in 1631.

Chiefly for his own amusement Donne wrote in his pre-Anglican years a number of wise and witty love poems, some cynical, some richly sensual, some unashamedly worshipful. He was a master of technique, particularly of the close-packed metaphor and unusual image. He was the most skillful member of what has come to be known as the "metaphysical" school of poetry. Poets of this school frequently based their metaphors or images on similarities revealed through the logical connection of ideas rather than through the senses. Strangely enough, the poet who had so successfully probed the complexities of physical love became the most celebrated preacher of his time, and there is in his religious prose and poetry the same intensity of commitment and the same brilliant use of imagery as there is in his earlier love poetry.

Important Works. POETRY: *Songs and Sonnets* (1598), *Divine Poems* (1607), *Holy Sonnets* (1618); PROSE: *Essays in Divinity* (1614), *Devotions on Emergent Occasions* (1624), *Sermons* (1640).

JOHN DRYDEN (*1631?-1700*)

Life. Born in 1631 or 1632 in Northamptonshire. He was brought up in a strongly Puritan household and was educated at Westminster

School and Trinity College, Cambridge. After the Restoration of Charles II in 1660 his political and religious allegiances shifted toward the Tory party and the Roman Catholic Church. In 1670 he was appointed Poet Laureate. In 1686 he became a Catholic and subsequently lost all preferment when he refused to renounce his Catholicism with the coming of William and Mary to the throne after the Revolution of 1688.

Dryden was the outstanding literary figure of the Restoration as a successful poet, dramatist, translator, and literary critic. He earned his living by writing for the theater, but he was more interested in the political and religious turmoil of his times and used his pen to further a cause or wither an opponent through brilliant satire. He made the heroic couplet the servant of closely reasoned argument and neatly packaged invectives, and launched it as the dominant mode of poetry for over a century.

Important Works. POETRY: *Absalom and Achitophel* (1681), *The Medal* (1682), *MacFlecknoe* (1682), *The Hind and the Panther* (1685); TRANSLATIONS: Parts of Homer, Lucretius, Ovid, Juvenal, and Virgil's *Aeneid;* DRAMA: *Aurengzebe* (1676), *All for Love* (1678); CRITICISM: *An Essay of Dramatic Poesy* (1668).

THOMAS STEARNS ELIOT (*1888-   *)

Life. Born in St. Louis, Missouri, and educated at Milton Academy and Harvard. He did graduate study at the Sorbonne, Harvard, and Oxford, then settled in England, and taught school in London. Later he founded a magazine, *The Criterion* (1922), and joined the publishing house of Faber and Faber. In 1927 he became a British citizen, and in 1948 he was awarded the Nobel Prize for literature.

Though Eliot is best known as one of the outstanding poets in English of this century, he is also a highly successful dramatist and literary critic. Through his poetry and criticism he has exerted tremendous influence on modern poetry, both in subject matter and in form. Eliot is concerned with the conservation of time-tested values in the chaotic "waste land" of modern life. In his poetry, drama, and criticism he has exposed the vapidness and tawdriness

of twentieth century life and has reasserted the need for order and discipline.

Important Works. POETRY: *Prufrock and Other Observations* (1917), *The Waste Land* (1922), *Collected Poems, 1909-1935* (1936), *Four Quartets* (1944); VERSE PLAYS: *The Rock* (1934), *Murder in the Cathedral* (1935), *The Family Reunion* (1939), *The Cocktail Party* (1950), *The Confidential Clerk* (1954); CRITICISM: *The Sacred Wood* (1920), *Selected Essays* (1932), *The Use of Poetry and the Use of Criticism* (1933), *Essays Ancient and Modern* (1936).

EDWARD MORGAN FORSTER
(*1879-   *)

Life. Born in London. His early schooling was an unhappy experience, but he found life quite different in his years at Cambridge. On leaving Cambridge, he traveled extensively in Greece, Italy, India, and Egypt. Up until 1924 he produced a number of short stories and essays and a handful of very successful novels. Since 1924 he has written no fiction, but has instead been writing critical essays and reviews and has lectured extensively.

For over half a century Forster has been an unsparing critic of the self-deceivers and pious frauds, the smug "better people" whose conventional world is built on narrow-mindedness and exclusion. He doesn't have much faith that people in general will improve, but he does have faith that decency and mutual respect are desirable commodities.

Important Works. FICTION: *A Room With a View* (1908), *Howards End* (1910), *The Celestial Omnibus* (1911 - short stories), *A Passage to India* (1924), *The Eternal Moment* (1928 - short stories); CRITICISM: *Aspects of the Novel* (1927); ESSAYS: *Abinger Harvest* (1936), *Two Cheers for Democracy* (1951); BIOGRAPHIES: *G. Lowes Dickinson* (1934), *Virginia Woolf* (1941).

JOHN GALSWORTHY (*1867-1933*)

Life. Born of well-to-do parents at Kingston, Surrey. He attended Harrow and New College, Oxford, and spent most of his time enjoying himself. He was trained as a lawyer, but never settled down to practice; instead he made a number of long trips throughout the world.

He did not start to write until he was 30; a decade later he had gained great popularity as a novelist and dramatist and was awarded the Nobel Prize for literature in 1932.

Almost all of Galsworthy's novels and plays show his intense distaste for the money-grubbing commercialism, the indifference to poverty and suffering, and the vulgar tastes of the wealthy middle class into which he was born.

Important Works. FICTION: *The Man of Property* (1906), *The Dark Flower* (1913), *The Freelands* (1915), *Saint's Progress* (1919), *In Chancery* (1920), *To Let* (1921), *The Forsyte Saga* (1922), *A Modern Comedy* (1928); PLAYS: *The Silver Box* (1909), *Strife* (1909), *Justice* (1910), *Loyalties* (1922); ESSAYS: *The Inn of Tranquillity* (1912), *Addresses in America* (1919), *Glimpses and Reflections* (1937); POETRY: *Verses, New and Old* (1926), *Collected Poems* (1934).

OLIVER GOLDSMITH (*1728-1774*)

Life. Born in the small village of Lissoy in Ireland. He struggled through Trinity College, Dublin, and lived a rather aimless existence for the half dozen subsequent years, studying medicine briefly at Edinburgh and Leyden and wandering through France, Germany, Switzerland, and Italy on foot. In 1756 he settled down in London and three years later turned to full-time writing. His skill in almost every literary form won him the admiration of the public and the friendship and respect of the important literary figures of his day.

Not much of Goldsmith's voluminous output is read today, but there is no denying him a place of great importance in English letters. There is no form—poetry, novel, drama, essay—that he did not attempt, and he was successful in them all, an unusual and seldom attained achievement. He was a good-natured, kind-hearted, uncomplicated man who brought these qualities to everything he wrote.

Important Works. ESSAYS: *The Citizen of the World* (1762), *Retaliation* (1774); NOVEL: *The Vicar of Wakefield* (1766); POETRY: *The Traveler* (1764), *The Deserted Village* (1770); PLAYS: *The Good-Natured Man* (1768), *She Stoops to Conquer* (1773).

THOMAS GRAY (*1716-1771*)

Life. Born in London, one of twelve children and the only one to grow to maturity. After an unhappy early childhood, he went on to Eton and to Peterhouse College, Cambridge. After a brief tour of the continent with his friend, Horace Walpole, he settled down to the quiet, scholarly life at Cambridge. He was offered the poet laureateship of England in 1757, but refused it. In 1767 he was appointed Regius Professor of Modern History.

Gray's poetic output was small, but he has long been recognized as the most important forerunner of the Romantic period, which flourished in the first part of the nineteenth century. In addition, his letters have stamped him as a man of warmth and great learning, and as perhaps the most discerning literary writer of his day.

Important Works. POETRY: *Elegy Written in a Country Churchyard* (1751), *Six Poems* (1753), *The Progress of Poesy* (1757), *The Bard* (1757).

JOSEPH HALL (*1574-1656*)

Life. Born near Ashby de la Zouch, Leichestershire, England. He was educated at the Ashby School and at Emanuel College, Cambridge, where he was an outstanding scholar. He joined the active ministry and became, eventually, Bishop of Exeter and, later, of Norwich. At the time of the Civil Wars, Hall engaged in pamphleteering on the side of the Anglicans against the Puritans (specifically, in one important instance, against Milton); his goal was not a narrow partisanship victory but an honest attempt to find paths of reconciliation. Hall was widely known throughout the Continent as a moral philosopher, and in England his reputation was also established as a literary man of unusual versatility.

Best known in literature today as the first writer of "characters," Hall also wrote several volumes of satire on English literature, social life, and general moral conditions. In later life he produced a series of meditations.

Important Works. PROSE: *Virgidemiarum: Six Books* (1597-1598), *Characters of Virtues and Vices* (1608), *Meditations and Vows Divine and Moral* (1605), *Heaven Upon Earth* (1606), *Contemplations* (1612-1626).

THOMAS HARDY (*1840-1928*)

Life. Born in Dorsetshire (the Wessex region of Anglo-Saxon times), the son of a stone mason. At sixteen he was apprenticed to an architect, after which he continued his architectural studies in London. He practiced his profession for only a short time and spent the rest of his life writing. His first efforts were in poetry, but in 1870 he turned to prose and wrote novels and short stories for twenty-five years. Generally hostile criticism of his last novel, *Jude the Obscure,* turned him back permanently to his first love, poetry.

Hardy's work is marked by a deep pessimism, a conviction that man is inevitably doomed to tragedy and suffering. His novels are powerful studies of human defeat and despair; his most characteristic poetry ironically underscores in the plainest terms the daily thwarting of human hope and desire.

Important Works. NOVELS: *Far From the Madding Crowd* (1874), *The Return of the Native* (1878), *The Mayor of Casterbridge* (1886), *Tess of the D'Urbervilles* (1891), *Jude the Obscure* (1896); POETRY: *Wessex Poems* (1898), *Poems of the Past and Present* (1902), *The Dynasts* (1903-1908), *Satires of Circumstance* (1914), *Human Shows* (1925).

GEORGE HERBERT (*1593-1633*)

Life. Born in Wales into a wealthy and influential family. He had a very successful academic career at Cambridge where he was Reader in Rhetoric and Public Orator from 1620 to 1627. He seemed headed for a brilliant career at court, but his mother's influence led him into the church, and he reluctantly abandoned any thought of worldly success. He became vicar of the country parish at Bemerton and lived quietly there until his death at the age of forty.

Much of the struggle between the lure of an influential life at court and the even stronger desire to live humbly and quietly in God's service is evident in Herbert's poetry. He found his subjects for poetry in the everyday world, and he gloried in the daily proof of God's love with much conviction. There is in Herbert some of the same delight in intellectually complex and unadorned imagery that marks many of his contemporaries. The simplicity he sought was not a simplicity of thinking but a simplicity of living.

Important Works. POETRY: *The Temple* (1633).

ROBERT HERRICK (*1591-1674*)

Life. Born in London, the son of a goldsmith. After a long apprenticeship with his uncle, also a goldsmith, he entered St. John's College, Cambridge, and then transferred to Trinity Hall to study law. He received his degree in 1617. He spent the next ten years in London enjoying the bright and witty tavern company of Ben Jonson and his circle. In 1627 he entered the Anglican Church and was made Vicar of Dean Prior in Devonshire, a country parish. During the period of Puritan rule he was ousted from his parish and spent his time in London, but in 1660 Charles II restored him to his post.

Herrick's poetic output was unbelievably large; some thirteen hundred lyrics came from his pen. Though his lifetime spanned one of the most turbulent periods in English history, he seems to have been little affected by it all, if one can judge by his poetry. His interest is in the commonplaces of life, or as he puts it in the "Argument" (i.e. summary) to his *Hesperides:* "I sing of brooks, of blossoms, birds, and bowers: /of April, May, of June, and July flowers/ . . . I sing of times trans-shifting; and I write /How roses first came red, and lilies white."

Important Works. POETRY: *Hesperides* (1648), *Noble Numbers* (1648).

GERARD MANLEY HOPKINS
(*1844-1889*)

Life. Born at Stratford in Essex. He was an exceptional student at Balliol College, Oxford, and had an intensely religious turn of mind. He embraced Roman Catholicism in his early twenties and later became a Jesuit priest. He was convinced at the time that his literary inclinations were incompatible with his priestly vows, and he burned all that he had written. A half dozen or so years later he reconciled the two and began writing poetry again, but none of it was published until 1918.

Hopkins's poetry is rooted in the verse forms

of the Anglo-Saxon and early Middle-English periods. Strongly alliterative and irregularly stressed with no definite pattern of unstressed syllables, it has little in common with the much more regular rhythm of most English verse of the last six hundred years. And yet it is strikingly modern in its compactness and complexity of imagery. Certainly no one has caught more convincingly the intensity of religious experience.

Important Works. POETRY: *Poems* (1918); PROSE: *Notebooks and Papers* (1937).

ALFRED EDWARD HOUSMAN
(1859-1936)

Life. Born in the Shropshire country, in the village of Bromsgrove. He was educated at Oxford, and after a brief career in the British Patent Office, he turned to teaching, and became one of the great scholars of his day, first as Professor of Latin at University College, London, and then at Cambridge.

In a handful of carefully wrought lyrics whose lilting beauty contrasts strangely with their gloomy content, Housman repeated the proposition that the world has little to offer except sorrow and defeat and disappointment, relieved only by occasional delights in a simple country scene or an act of simple defiance of the fate which dooms us all.

Important Works. POETRY: *A Shropshire Lad* (1896), *Last Poems* (1922), *More Poems* (1936); ESSAY: *The Name and Nature of Poetry* (1933).

SAMUEL JOHNSON *(1709-1784)*

Life. Born in Lichfield, the son of a bookseller. He entered Oxford but was unable, for financial reasons, to get a degree. For a while he taught school and then went to London to earn his living through writing. He soon established a reputation as a scholar (particularly with his monumental dictionary in 1755) and writer of rare abilities, as an uncommonly able and willing conversationalist, and as an essentially kind and generous man of odd personal habits and ill-concealed prejudices.

To his good fortune and ours, the faithful note-taking of his young friend, Boswell, has preserved Johnson's image in vivid outline,

and the qualities of common sense, personal integrity, and critical judgment that brought such respect for the man from his contemporaries become clear to each new generation of readers.

Important Works. PROSE: *Dictionary of the English Language* (1755), *The Lives of the English Poets* (1779-1781); PERIODICAL ESSAYS: *The Rambler* (1750-1752), *The Idler* (1758-1760); FICTION: *Rasselas* (1759); POETRY: *London* (1738), *The Vanity of Human Wishes* (1749); PLAY: *Irene* (1749).

BEN JONSON *(1572-1637)*

Life. Born in London and educated at Westminster School. At an early age, he took up his stepfather's trade, bricklaying, but soon ran away to fight on the continent. Back in London in his middle twenties he joined an acting company and thus began a lifelong association with the theater. He was a brusque and boisterous man who took all of London as fair game for his barbs. While his bluntness brought him many quarrels, his obvious talents and high-spirited manner brought him many friends and admirers among the brilliant circle of writers who lived in London in the days of James I and were proud to call themselves "Sons of Ben."

Overshadowed only by Shakespeare as a dramatist, Jonson was also highly influential as a critic and lyric poet. His satirical comedies of London life, built largely around exaggerations of certain deplorable characteristics of the Londoners he knew, have few equals in the language. As a poet and critic he brought charm, taste, and an unfailing sense of craftsmanship to everything he wrote.

Important Works. PLAYS: *Every Man in His Humor* (1598), *Every Man Out of His Humor* (1599), *Volpone* (1605?), *The Silent Woman* (1609-1610), *The Alchemist* (1610); CRITICISM: *Timber, or Discoveries Made Upon Men and Matters* (1641); POETRY: *Oberon* (1610-1611), *Works* (1616).

JAMES JOYCE *(1882-1941)*

Life. Born in Dublin and educated in Jesuit schools. In great disgust with everything Irish he left his native country in 1902, never to return except for a few brief visits on family matters. His life on the continent was anything but serene. He tried his hand at medicine and language teaching (he spoke a dozen languages), went through a series of painful eye operations, and ran repeatedly into official censorship of his works while unscrupulous publishers put out pirated editions with no thought of paying him royalties.

There is no denying Joyce's place among the first rank of twentieth century writers. His first group of short stories, entitled "Dubliners," written when he was in his early twenties, proved him the master of the modern short story form. From then on his fiction increased in complexity as he sought to break the bands that the language itself imposed on him. His great works, *Ulysses* and *Finnegans Wake,* make demands on any reader that few are willing to meet, yet the books are not quixotically obscure; they simply ask of the reader the willingness to make the same kind of intense effort to re-create that Joyce put into the original creation.

Important Works. FICTION: *Dubliners* (1914), *A Portrait of the Artist as a Young Man* (1916), *Ulysses* (1922), *Finnegans Wake* (1939); POETRY: *Chamber Music* (1907), *Pomes Penyeach* (1927); PLAY: *Exiles* (1915).

JOHN KEATS (*1795-1821*)

Life. Born in London, the son of a hostler. The accidental death of his father and his mother's death from tuberculosis ended his schooling at fifteen, and he was apprenticed to an apothecary-surgeon. He later continued his medical studies and was licensed to practice, but turned to poetry instead. Almost from the beginning his great talent was recognized by such established poets as Leigh Hunt, Wordsworth, and Shelley, if not by the reviewers. Almost at the same time his health failed him; he contracted tuberculosis (from which his mother and younger brother had died), went to Italy in a desperate attempt to find relief, and died in Rome in 1821 at the tragically early age of twenty-five.

In a brief span of five years Keats had shown himself one of the handful of truly great talents in English poetry. The mark of his mind and personality—tough, sensitive, high-spirited—is on everything he wrote, coupled with a command of sensuous imagery

and a painstaking attention to form. He handled the full range of the language as few writers have before or since.

Important Works. POETRY: *Poems* (1817), *Endymion* (1818), *Lamia, Isabella, The Eve of St. Agnes and Other Poems* (1820).

RUDYARD KIPLING (*1865-1936*)

Life. Born at Bombay, India, and spent his first six years in that country. He returned to England for schooling, but elected not to attend any university and went home to India. Through his father's good offices he got a newspaper job and threw himself eagerly into journalism for a number of years, all the while writing short stories and poems with India as the setting. His newspaper sent him to London in 1889; three years later he married an American and moved to Brattleboro, Vermont, for four years. After his return to England he was repeatedly and outspokenly involved in the great issues of his day.

Despite a great deal of controversy over his public opinions, there was general public agreement that his talents as a storyteller and master of language were unassailable. And even those who most disliked his strongly imperialistic leanings and complacent belief in the natural superiority of white man (especially English white men) have honored his commitment to the strenuous life in the cause of courage and fidelity.

Important Works. FICTION: (short stories) *Plain Tales from the Hills* (1887), *Soldiers Three* (ca. 1887); (juveniles) *The Jungle Books* (1894, 1895), *Captains Courageous* (1897), *Stalky and Co.* (1899), *Just So Stories* (1902), *Puck of Pook's Hill* (1906); (novels) *The Light That Failed* (1890), *Kim* (1901); POETRY: *Departmental Ditties* (1886), *Barrack-Room Ballads* (1892), *The Five Nations* (1903).

CHARLES LAMB (*1775-1834*)

Life. Born in London, the son of a law clerk. He was educated at Christ's Hospital School (where he knew Coleridge) but did not go on to a university. To support himself and his sister, Mary, who was subject to fits of insanity, he had a full-time job as a bookkeeper in the East India Company, but this necessity did not prevent him from pursuing his real interest, literary study and writing. Despite the burdens his responsibilities placed on him, he remained a remarkably cheerful and generous man to the rich circle of literary friends he had in London.

Lamb is undoubtedly the best-known writer of familiar essays in English. His interests were many, his freshness of vision prevented him from ever being dull, and his usually unerring taste gives an unpretentious dignity and charm to everything he wrote.

Important Works. PROSE: *Tales from Shakespeare* (with Mary Lamb, 1807), *Specimens of English Dramatic Poets* (1808), *Essays of Elia* (1823), *Last Essays of Elia* (1833).

DAVID HERBERT LAWRENCE
(1885-1930)

Life. Born in a Nottinghamshire mining town, Lawrence was the son of a coal-miner and a school teacher. He took his university education at University College, Nottingham, and afterwards taught school. He soon achieved fame by his poems and novels, notoriety by running away (in 1912) with Frieda von Richtofen Weekly, wife of a university professor and mother of three, whom he married in 1914. They lived much abroad thereafter, including a stay at Taos in New Mexico, and he died in France in 1930.

Revolting against the tawdry world of the working class he was born into, and against the smugness and flabbiness of classes he was not born into, Lawrence embodied a point of view which (stripped of the excesses to which he occasionally carried it) aimed at restoring wonder, reverence, freedom, dignity, and joy to the central experiences of human life: the relations of man with nature, of men with women, of the individual with his work.

Important Works. POETRY: *Collected Poems* (1928), *Last Poems* (1932); FICTION: *Sons and Lovers* (1913), *The Prussian Officer and Other Stories* (1914), *The Rainbow* (1915), *Women in Love* (1920).

CLIVE STAPLES LEWIS *(1898-   )*

Life. Born in Belfast, Northern Ireland. He is one of the most honored of contemporary British scholars and critics, has taught at Oxford,

and now teaches at Cambridge. Besides his critical and historical studies of English literature, he has written some fascinating novels combining allegory with fantasy and science fiction, together with a large number of wise and witty commentaries on topics moral and religious.

Lewis has a particular gift for simplifying (without falsifying) subjects that are very complex, well illustrated in his *The Four Loves*.

Important Works. LITERARY HISTORY AND CRITICISM: *The Allegory of Love* (1936), *A Preface to Paradise Lost* (1942), *English Literature in the Sixteenth Century* (1954); GENERAL PROSE: *The Problem of Pain* (1940), *The Case for Christianity* (1943), *The Abolition of Man* (1943), *Surprised by Joy* (an autobiography, 1955), *The Four Loves* (1961); FICTION: *The Screwtape Letters* (1942), *Out of the Silent Planet* (1943), *Perlandra* (1943), *That Hideous Strength* (1946).

RICHARD LOVELACE *(1618-1658)*

Life. Born into wealth and position. He was educated at Charterhouse School and Oxford and was one of the most courtly of the courtly gentlemen of Charles I's England. A strong supporter of the king, he took part in military expeditions of both Charles and his French ally; in 1642 he courageously petitioned Parliament on Charles's behalf and got himself thrown in prison for so doing. With the execution of the King in 1649 he lost the last of his fortune, and while little is specifically known of his last years, the story is that he died a rag-covered beggar in a London alley.

Lovelace's poetic output was small, but in his best poems, of which there are only a few, he wrote of the ideal courtly attitude toward life with a simple gracefulness of rhythm and diction.

Important Works. POETRY: *Lucasta* (1649), *Lucasta: Posthume Poems* (1659).

LOUIS MACNEICE *(1907-   )*

Life. Born in Belfast, Northern Ireland, son of an Anglican clergyman. MacNeice was educated in England, taking his undergraduate degree with highest honors (in Classics) at Merton College, Oxford, where he overlapped several other now well-known English poets—among them Stephen Spender, C. Day Lewis, and W. H. Auden. For many years a teacher of Classics, he now devotes his time to writing.

Jaunty and often breathless in pace, Mac-Neice's poems have a way of uncovering the moment of pathos or insight in the commonplace incidents of commonplace life.

Important Works. POETRY: *Collected Poems, 1925-1948* (1949), *Eighty-five Poems* (1959).

KATHERINE MANSFIELD (*1888-1923*)

Life. Pen name of Kathleen Beauchamp, who was born in Wellington, New Zealand. After a not altogether happy childhood, she was sent for a musical education and further study of the cello to Queen's College and the Royal Academy of Music, in London. She turned to writing, suffered a number of scarring experiences including an unhappy love affair and the death of her only brother (in World War I), contracted tuberculosis, and from about 1917 traveled restlessly but vainly in search of improved health. She was married to the critic, J. Middleton Murry.

An innovator in the short story, Katherine Mansfield turned from narrative and characterization in the ordinary sense toward evocation of inner mood in scene and person, often employing stream-of-consciousness techniques.

Important Works. FICTION: *Bliss and Other Stories* (1920), *The Garden Party and Other Stories* (1922), *The Dove's Nest and Other Stories* (1923).

GEORGE MEREDITH (*1828-1909*)

Life. Born in Portsmouth, England, son of a naval outfitter, and educated as a boy in Germany. He studied law on his return to England, but soon abandoned it for writing—as journalist, publisher's reader, novelist, and poet—and became by the latter years of his life a venerated sage.

Meredith's work is likely to deal in one way or other with the permanent need of human beings and their institutions to maintain vitality without becoming anarchic, and discipline without becoming fossilized.

Important Works. POETRY: *Modern Love* (1862), *Poems and Lyrics of the Joy of Earth*

(1883), *Ballads and Poems of Tragic Life* (1887). FICTION: *The Ordeal of Richard Feverel* (1859), *The Egoist* (1879), *Diana of the Crossways* (1885).

JOHN MILTON (*1608-1674*)

Life. Born into a well-to-do London Puritan family, Milton took his formal education at St. Paul's School and at Christ's College, Cambridge. A further six years of reading and study at his father's country house, followed by fifteen months in Italy, gave him the foundation of learning, modern as well as ancient, broad as well as deep, which later qualified him to speak with authority in his great tracts on divorce, freedom of the press, education, and church-government (1643-1645), to serve Oliver Cromwell as Latin Secretary of State in the Commonwealth and Protectorate, which followed the fall of the monarchy and the execution of Charles I, and eventually to write the greatest long poem in English: *Paradise Lost.* When the monarchy was restored in 1660, Milton, who had defended before all Europe the execution of Charles I, was in considerable danger, but was happily spared by Charles II, and allowed to live on in retirement, dictating to his daughters and other copyists (for he had gone completely blind in the 1650's) the three poems for which he is now known the world over: *Paradise Lost, Paradise Regained, Samson Agonistes.*

Important Works. POETRY: *Poems* (1645), *Paradise Lost* (1667, 1674), *Paradise Regained* (1671), *Samson Agonistes* (1671); PROSE: *Areopagitica* (1644), *Of Education* (1644).

FRANK O'CONNOR (*1903-   *)

Life. Pen name of Michael O'Donovan, who was born in Cork, Ireland, of a drunken but well-meaning father and a small, strong, serene mother of whom he has written lovingly in *An Only Child* (1961). He became involved while a youth in all the troubles springing from the struggle for Irish independence, but escaped with his life and eventually made his way to the United States, where he has lived for a number of years.

One of the most capable short-story writers of our time, O'Connor sees familiar things freshly and warmly, as in *First Confession,* by adopting an unexpected or unconventional point of view.

Important Works. FICTION: *The Stories of Frank O'Connor* (1952), *More Stories by Frank O'Connor* (1954), *Domestic Relations* (1957); PROSE: *The Mirror in the Roadway* (a study of the modern novel, 1956), *An Only Child* (autobiographical, 1961).

GEORGE ORWELL (*1903-1950*)

Life. Pen name of Eric Hugh Blair, who was born in Bengal, India, son of a British Customs official. He was educated at Eton, and then spent five years with the Indian Imperial Police in Burma, where he was torn between shame at the workings of Colonialism and embarrassed contempt for its victims, who were usually still less admirable than the system. Taking his terminal pay, he spent eighteen months in Paris in abject poverty, writing stories and sketches that no one consented to publish, and four or five more years in London in the same circumstances. In 1937 he went to Spain to fight on the Loyalist side against the Fascists, was wounded, barely escaped with his life, and as an after-effect contracted tuberculosis, which plagued him off and on during the rest of his days and ultimately caused his death.

A Laborite and Socialist by conviction, Orwell writes tellingly against all forces in the modern world, whether socialist or capitalist, which threaten to impose conformity on the individual.

Important Works. PROSE: *Homage to Catalonia* (1938), *Critical Essays* (1946), *Shooting an Elephant* (1950), *"Such, Such Were the Joys"* (1953); FICTION: *Keep the Aspidistra Flying* (1936), *Coming Up for Air* (1939), *Animal Farm* (1945), *Nineteen Eighty-Four* (1949).

WILFRED OWEN (*1893-1918*)

Life. Born in Shropshire and educated at the Birkenhead Institute, Liverpool. He was killed in France at the age of 25, just one week before the signing of the Armistice at the end of World War I (November, 1918), having a month earlier been awarded the Military Cross for gallantry under fire.

Owen's poetry is the moving record of a young man's revulsion at the barbarities and futilities of war; his governing emotion, an angry pity.

Important Works. POETRY: *Poems* (1920), *Poems* (1931).

SAMUEL PEPYS (*1633-1703*)

Life. Born into the family of a London tailor, educated at St. Paul's School in London and Magdalene College, Cambridge. In 1658 he married Elizabeth St. Michel—"my wife, poor wretch" of his *Diary*—who was then 15, and whose youthful tastes and ways exasperated and delighted him by turns. He held important posts in the British Admiralty, including the Secretaryship (like our former Secretaryship of the Navy), and was largely responsible for naval organization and building that made England for two centuries mistress of the seas.

Pepys's *Diary,* begun in 1660 and closed in 1669 because of his failing eyesight, is one of the great human documents because it sets down with such zest, intimacy, and style the public and personal news of a remarkable decade, which saw both the Great Plague and the Great Fire of London. The *Diary* is Pepys's only literary work.

PLATO (*428 B.C.-347 B.C.*)

Life. Born in Athens toward the beginning of the war with Sparta that was to destroy Athens as a powerful city and center of Greek Culture. He attached himself early to the circle of pupils taught by Socrates, and was present at his trial and death in 399 B.C. Later he traveled widely, and returned to Athens to found the Academy, his own philosophical school, and to write the dialogues (wherein Socrates is chief speaker) that have spread his influence through the centuries and across the world.

Plato presents a vision of the unity of all life and thought: a vision that later ages have not been entirely able to accept and yet have never been able to forget.

Important Works. PROSE: *The Dialogues of Plato.*

ALEXANDER POPE (*1688-1744*)

Life. Born into the family of a retired Roman Catholic linen-merchant and educated mostly at home, owing to the then-existing restrictions on the education and movement of Roman Catholics in England. (Among other things, they could not hold public office, attend the universities, or live within ten miles of London.) Pope grew up in the country along the Thames near Windsor and settled later at Twickenham (then a small village outside London), where he spent his time in building, gardening, writing, and caring for his mother, who lived to the age of 91. Early famous for his ability to pack much meaning into little space, he became a brilliant satirist of the vices and follies of human nature and the first English poet to make his living by his pen.

In Pope's hands, the English closed couplet became an instrument of simultaneous beauty, delicacy, and strength.

Important Works. POETRY: *An Essay on Criticism* (1711), translations of Homer's *Iliad* (1715-1720) and *Odyssey* (1725-1726), *An Essay on Man* (1733-1734), *Moral Essays* (1731-1735), *An Epistle to Dr. Arbuthnot* (1734), *An Epistle to Augustus* (1737), *The Dunciad* (1728-1729, 1743-1744).

WILLIAM SHAKESPEARE (*1564-1616*)

Life. Born in Stratford-upon-Avon, the son of John Shakespeare, a thriving tanner and town official, and his Roman Catholic wife, Mary Arden. He probably had a grammar-school education (narrow, but intense in those days, involving the constant construing of Latin), but not more. At 18 he married Ann Hathaway, two years his elder, who presented him in 1583 with a daughter, Susanna, and in 1585 with twins, Hamnet and Judith. By 1592 he had migrated to London and become an actor and successful playwright. Shortly after he was received as a shareholder into the acting company known as the Lord Chamberlain's Men, which in 1598 built the Globe Theater, where all of his greatest plays were first performed, and which on the death of Queen Elizabeth and the accession of James I became the King's Men, continuing to prosper for many years. Shakespeare seems to have retired increasingly to Stratford from about 1610, where he lived as a prominent citizen in a large house called New Place.

Plays and Poems. (The dates given are generally accepted, but remain tentative.)

1589 *Comedy of Errors*
1590 *I Henry VI*
1591 *II and III Henry VI*
     Titus Andronicus
     Taming of the Shrew
1592 *Two Gentlemen of Verona*
1593 *Venus and Adonis*
     Richard III
1594 *Rape of Lucrece*
     Love's Labours Lost
     King John
1595 *Richard II*
     Midsummer Night's Dream
     Romeo and Juliet
1596 *Merchant of Venice*
1597 *I Henry IV*
     Merry Wives of Windsor
1598 *II Henry IV*
     Much Ado About Nothing
1599 *Henry V*
     Julius Caesar
1600 *As You Like It*
     Twelfth Night
1601 *Hamlet*
     Troilus and Cressida
1602 *All's Well That Ends Well*
1604 *Othello*
     Measure for Measure
1605 *King Lear*
1606 *Macbeth*
1607 *Timon of Athens*
     Antony and Cleopatra
1608 *Coriolanus*
     Pericles
1609 *Sonnets* (in process of composition for many years)
1610 *Cymbeline*
1611 *Winter's Tale*
     Tempest

GEORGE BERNARD SHAW (*1856-1950*)

Life. Born in Dublin of Irish Protestant parents, who separated early, his mother going to London to teach music, where in due course Shaw followed her. There he supported himself by lecturing and writing on music and drama, and eventually began to write plays in illustration of his dramatic theories. He became one of the most important of modern playwrights, and won the Nobel Prize for literature in 1925. An ardent Socialist, a convinced vegetarian, a crusader for simplified spelling, and always a teacher at heart, Shaw often prefaces his plays with discourses as long as the plays themselves in which he airs his theories and pokes the audience unmercifully with his wit—simply (as he would probably have said) to stir the animals up.

Shaw's plays usually deal with men and women who undergo some kind of conversion from a dead but still confining system of morality and belief to new and more creative outlooks.

Important Works. PLAYS: *Arms and the Man* (1898), *Caesar and Cleopatra* (1901), *Man and Superman* (1903), *Major Barbara* (1913), *Androcles and the Lion* (1916), *Heartbreak House* (1918), *Saint Joan* (1924), *The Apple Cart* (1930); PROSE: *The Intelligent Woman's Guide to Socialism and Capitalism* (1928), *The Adventures of the Black Girl in Her Search for God* (1932).

PERCY BYSSHE SHELLEY (*1792-1822*)

Life. Shelley was born into an upper-class Sussex family, schooled at Eton, and sent to Oxford, from which he was expelled for publishing an atheistical pamphlet. He married Harriet Westbrook at 19, had two children, and then left her to elope with Mary Godwin, who became his wife on Harriet's death. He spent the last four years of his life in Italy, where he met death by drowning when the boat he was sailing capsized in a storm.

Of a tempestuous nature, revolutionary both in his personal life and his political and social thought, Shelley belongs with the great celebrators of free, untrammeled energy, and his poetry catches powerfully the rhythm of things and ideas in restless and exultant movement.

Important Works. POETRY: *Alastor* (1816), *Epipsychidion* (1821), *Adonais* (1821), *Hellas* (1822), *Posthumous Poems* (1824), *Poetical Works* (1839); PLAYS: *Prometheus Unbound* (1820), *The Cenci* (1820).

SIR PHILIP SIDNEY (*1554-1586*)

Life. A nobleman by birth, Sidney achieved great fame even in his own short lifetime as an exemplar of the complete or universal man (a Renaissance ideal, exhibited at length in Prince Hamlet) who is scholar, soldier, courtier, lover, musician, athlete, and poet all in one and at once. He was knighted in 1583, made governor of Flushing (in Holland) in 1585, and received his death wound during a skirmish connected with the siege of nearby Zutphen.

The special quality of Sidney's poetry is an elevation of subject-matter and feeling which can only be called noble, and a speech that, like the ideal courtier's, is sufficiently versatile to handle all sorts of occasions: intimate and humble, lofty and ceremonial.

Important Works. POETRY: *Astrophel and Stella* (a sequence of love sonnets, 1591); PROSE: *Arcadia* (an epic romance, 1590), *The Defence of Poesie* (1594).

SOPHOCLES (*495 B.C.-406 B.C.*)

Life. Born at Colonus, near Athens. He was victorious over his great predecessor, the dramatist Aeschylus, in the dramatic contest of 468 B.C., with a play that has not survived. (These contests were open to all Athenians, and by their means three tragedies and a comedy were selected to be played at the annual festival in honor of the god Dionysus, which all citizens attended as a religious observance.) In 440 B.C. he was appointed one of the ten generals to serve with Pericles in the expedition against Samos, and is reputed to have served his city in other high official capacities such as foreign embassies.

Sophocles is one of those very great artists, like Homer, Dante, and Shakespeare, who both show us our condition and give us courage to bear it.

Important Works. PLAYS: Seven of Sophocles's plays survive: *Antigone* (441? B.C.), *Ajax*, *King Oedipus*, *Electra*, *Trachiniae*, *Philoctetes* (409 B.C.), and *Oedipus at Colonus* (performed posthumously in 401 B.C.).

STEPHEN SPENDER (*1909-   *)

Life. Born in London, son of a journalist and novelist. He was educated at University College, Oxford, has spent much of his life as editor and journalist, and now edits the English periodical *Encounter*.

At their best, Spender's poems illustrate the way in which an unpretentious, almost prose-like speech may be pruned and tightened into poetry without bizarre metaphor, insistent rhythm, or departure from normal syntax and word order.

Important Works. POETRY: *Poems* (1933), *The Burning Cactus* (1936), *The Edge of Being* (1949), *Collected Poems, 1928-53* (1955); PROSE: *The Destructive Element* (1935).

EDMUND SPENSER (*1552?-1599*)

Life. Educated at Merchant Taylors' School, London, and Pembroke Hall, Cambridge. Served as secretary to various Elizabethan noblemen (including the Earl of Leicester, Queen Elizabeth's favorite), and for many years in Ireland, where by 1590 he had finished the first three of twelve books planned for his verse romance *The Faerie Queene,* and by 1596 three more. The poem remained unfinished at his death.

Spenser is a master at bringing before the mind's eye all sorts and conditions of things and persons that do not actually exist, or if they do, do not exist in precisely this way. He thus achieves effects of great beauty and also of great eeriness.

Important Works. POETRY: *The Faerie Queene* (I-III, 1590; IV-VI, and a few cantos of VII, 1596), *Epithalamion* (1595), *Prothalamion* (1596).

JAMES STEPHENS (*1882-1950*)

Life. Born in great poverty to Irish parents in Dublin. Stephens received no formal schooling to speak of, and set out to make his own way very early. For a number of years he supported himself, his wife, and children as typist in an attorney's office. His poems came eventually to the attention of George William Russell, Dublin's most respected man of letters, through whom he was helped to a publisher and a salaried post in Ireland's National Gallery. Later, he was able to live by his writing and lecturing.

Important Works. POETRY: *Insurrections* (1909), *The Hill of Vision* (1912), *Songs from the Clay* (1915), *Street Joy* (1931), *Kings and the Moon* (1938).

ROBERT LOUIS BALFOUR STEVENSON (*1850-1894*)

Life. Born in Edinburgh, Scotland, and schooled there. He entered his father's profession, civil engineering, found the life too taxing for his always fragile health, transferred to the law profession, but made his reputation with essays, novels, and poems. Prolonged periods of ill health persuaded him in 1887 to leave England, after which he spent nearly a year at Saranac Lake in the Adirondacks, then set out for the tropical climates of Tahiti, Honolulu, and particularly Samoa, where he remained until his death.

Stevenson was one of the most attractive personalities of his age, combining masculinity with grace, selflessness with self-awareness—qualities that still draw readers to his works.

Important Works. PROSE: *An Inland Voyage* (1878), *Travels with a Donkey* (1879), *Pulvis et Umbra* (1888); FICTION: *Treasure Island* (1883), *Dr. Jekyll and Mr. Hyde* (1886), *Kidnapped* (1886), *The Master of Ballantrae* (1889); POETRY: *A Child's Garden of Verses* (1885), *Underwoods* (1887).

SIR JOHN SUCKLING (*1609-1642*)

Life. Son of a wealthy father, who held important posts under James I and had been knighted by him. Suckling ran through a considerable fortune and is said at last to have taken his own life for fear of poverty. He received his undergraduate education at Trinity College, Cambridge, later studied law, then traveled, bowled, gambled (he was reputed the greatest bowler and card-player of his time), soldiered, made love, wrote poems, masques, and plays (which he produced at his own expense), and made himself generally useful as a courtier and poet to the court of Charles I—whence the title, "Cavalier Poets," often applied to him and to fellow courtly poets like Richard Lovelace.

As might be expected in the poems of a courtier, witty and graceful compliment is Suckling's forte, often combined with a festive country exuberance.

Important Works. POETRY: *Fragments Aurea* (1646).

JONATHAN SWIFT (*1667-1745*)

Life. Born in Dublin of English parents and educated at Trinity College, Dublin. He took holy orders and held various posts in the Irish Anglican church, including, for some thirty years, the deanship of St. Patrick's Cathedral in

Dublin. He spent several interludes in England, especially the years 1708-1714, when he served the Tory government as its chief political writer and formed a number of lifelong friendships with English writers, among them Alexander Pope. In Ireland, Swift did much, both as clergyman and writer, to alleviate and force attention to the misery of the country and its people, the economy of Ireland being regularly milked at this period for the advantage of England. At his death, he left the bulk of his fortune to establish a fund for the maintenance of the feeble-minded and the poor. He is buried in the cathedral he served, beneath an epitaph he wrote for himself: *Ubi saeva indignatio ulterius cor lacerare nequit* ("Where savage indignation can tear the heart no more.")

Swift's greatest gift is his ability to uncover, and make us see, taste, and smell the horror and brutality that often lie just under the polite and prosperous surfaces over which we so unthinkingly glide.

Important Works. PROSE: *The Battle of The Books* (1704), *A Tale of a Tub* (1704), *An Argument Against Abolishing Christianity* (1708), *A Modest Proposal* (1729); FICTION: *Gulliver's Travels* (1726): POETRY: *Stella's Birthday, March 13, 1718-1719; On the Death of Dr. Swift* (1731).

FRANK ARTHUR SWINNERTON
(1884-   )

Life. Born in London. He entered a journalistic career as office-boy for a newspaper at the age of 14, and has remained in journalistic and related activities ever since: as reporter, reviewer, commentator, and as publisher's assistant and editor. He is the author of a great number of novels and books of essays.

Swinnerton's one assured masterpiece is *Nocturne,* in which he creates with loving humor the world and language of the "cockney," i.e., the native lower-class Londoner.

Important Works. FICTION: *Nocturne* (1917), *Harvest Comedy* (1938), *Death of a Highbrow* (1962).

ALFRED LORD TENNYSON *(1809-1892)*

Life. Son of an Anglican clergyman, educated at Trinity College, Cambridge. Plagued by extreme poverty during the first forty years of his life, he was finally able to acquire enough

money by 1850 to marry the girl to whom he had been betrothed in 1836. He was helped by the government with a small pension in 1845, created poet laureate in 1850, enjoyed over the next thirty years an enormous popularity, and was created Baron Tennyson in 1884.

Tennyson is especially the poet of moments of recollection and anticipation, of hopes, fears, premonitions, regrets, nostalgias, voiced with a grave eloquence (not entirely free of momentary hysterias) that shows a mind striving to be reconciled to a world where everything comes or goes, and nothing stays.

Important Works. POETRY: *Poems Chiefly Lyrical* (1830), *Poems* (1833), *Poems* (1842), *In Memoriam* (1850), *Maud* (1855).

WILLIAM MAKEPEACE THACKERAY
(1811-1863)

Life. Born at Calcutta, India, into the family of a British civil servant. He was educated in England at the Charterhouse School and at Trinity College, Cambridge. Later he studied law in London and painting in Paris, but after 1837 gave himself to journalism and the writing of fiction. His papers on snobs were first published in *Punch,* the English humor-magazine.

Thackeray is the great chronicler of nineteenth-century English social life, seeing his world always in terms of the metaphor he borrowed from John Bunyan and used as title to his greatest novel, as a carnival or Fair where every sort of foolishness and emptiness is exhibited and can be acquired.

Important Works. PROSE: *The Book of Snobs* (1846), *The English Humorists of the Eighteenth Century* (1851); FICTION: *Vanity Fair* (1846-8), *Pendennis* (1850), *Henry Esmond* (1852).

DYLAN THOMAS *(1914-1953)*

Life. Born in Wales, son of an English teacher; educated at Swansea Grammar School. Thereafter he was a newspaper reporter, odd-job man, writer of film and radio scripts, and public reader of poems "with a voice like the chiming of great bells."

Thomas is likely to be long known for his sketches of a Welsh childhood, and for poems which recreate the green and golden world of dream and wonder that all men inwardly know is hidden somewhere in their individual and racial past.

Important Works. POETRY: *18 Poems* (1934), *The Map of Love* (1939), *New Poems* (1943), *Collected Poems* (1953); PROSE: *Portrait of the Artist as a Young Dog* (1940), *Quite Early One Morning* (1954); PLAYS: *The Doctor and the Devils* (1953), *Under Milk Wood* (1954).

FRANCIS THOMPSON (*1860-1907*)

Life. Son of a Roman Catholic doctor in Lancashire. He sought to follow his father's profession, but found he had no interest in it and turned to writing. A long period of misery and near-starvation followed, from which he was rescued by Alice and Wilfred Meynell (fellow Roman Catholics and fellow writers), who obtained publication of his first book of poems.

Sometimes eccentric and even pretentious, Thompson's poetry at its best (as in "The Kingdom of God") attains to energetic eloquence and nobility.

Important Works. POETRY: *Poems* (1893), *Sister Songs* (1895), *New Poems* (1897).

HENRY MAJOR TOMLINSON (*1873-1958*)

Life. Born in the East End, or dock area, of London, where by the age of 12 he was employed as a shipping clerk. He transferred to newspaper work in 1904, which he carried on until 1923, when he became a free-lance writer. He wrote novels, essays, and a great number of travel books.

Most of Tomlinson's best work has to do with faraway places (a heritage no doubt from the ships he saw come and go as a boy), in the evoking of which for the stay-at-home reader he reveals a descriptive imagination of high order.

Important Works. PROSE: *The Sea and the Jungle* (1912), *Waiting for Daylight* (1922), *South to Cadiz* (1934); FICTION: *Gallion's Reach* (1927), *All Our Yesterdays* (1930).

EDMUND WALLER (*1606-1687*)

Life. Born into a wealthy country gentleman's family and educated at Eton and at King's College, Cambridge, he served in Parliament most of his life, where he stood for a temperate balance in government policy that is very much the character of his poetry also.

In poetry, Waller combines two worlds, preserving in his songs the old spirit of the courtly lover, but helping to found also the idiom of political and social comment which Dryden and Pope would later bring to perfection.

Important Works. POETRY: *Poems* (1645), *A Panegyric to My Lord Protector* (i.e. Oliver Cromwell, 1655), *St. James's Park* (1661).

BARBARA WARD (*1914-   *)

Life. Educated at European schools and Somerville College, Oxford. She has held a variety of influential posts, as teacher, editor, trustee of the Old Vic (London repertory theater), governor of Sadler's Wells (London ballet theater), governor of the B.B.C. (British Broadcasting Corporation); and has written much on international affairs. She is now the wife of Sir Robert Jackson, British civil servant in the highest echelons.

As a writer who refuses to let the human world split into easy compartments, but insists instead on keeping religion united to morals, morals to politics, politics to social ideals; Barbara Ward upholds the tradition which has given the Western world whatever grandeur it has.

Important Works. PROSE: *Policy for the West* (1951), *Faith and Freedom* (1954), *Five Ideas That Change the World* (1959).

GEORGE WITHER (*1588-1667*)

Life. Received his undergraduate education at Magdalen College, Oxford. Later he studied law and frequented the court circles of James I and Charles I, but owing to his deepening attachment to the Puritans he went over to the Parliamentary side during the Civil War and fought against the King. Much of his later poetry is religious, but his "Shall I Wasting in Despair" belongs to the love poetry of his young manhood and was first printed in 1615.

In much of his poetry, Wither cultivates the manner of a wide-eyed child who knows no subtleties of rhetoric but only truth. "Shall I Wasting" gives us this same no-nonsense doctrine in a playful mood.

Important Works. POETRY: *The Shepherd's Pipe* (1614), *Fidelia* (1615), *Fair Virtue* (1622).

WILLIAM WORDSWORTH (*1770-1850*)

Life. Born in Cumberland, England, and orphaned in early youth. He was educated at St. John's College, Cambridge, and spent a year in France (in 1792) during the middle phases of the French Revolution, where he met Annette Villon. He returned to England just before the lengthy war between England and France, effectively separating himself from Annette, who bore him a daughter. He settled with his sister Dorothy in the Lake Country of Northwest England and eventually married (1802) Mary Hutchinson, by whom he had five children. Unlike most poets he was repeatedly dogged by financial *good* fortune in the shape of legacies, and appointments, and was therefore able to devote the whole of a long life to poetry. Though his work was ridiculed at first, it had made its way with a wide public by 1830, and in 1843 won him the laureateship.

Whereas commonplace objects and experiences brought to Swift's mind glimpses of the horror of human pettiness, brutality, and self-deception, they came to Wordsworth as evidences of the glory of God, the beneficence of nature, the infinitude of man's mind and heart.

Important Works. POETRY: *Lyrical Ballads* (in collaboration with Coleridge, 1798, 1800), *Poems in Two Volumes* (1807), *The Excursion* (1814), *The Prelude* (written by 1805, published 1850).

WILLIAM BUTLER YEATS (*1865-1939*)

Life. Born in Dublin, son of an Irish artist. Yeats turned first to painting, then to writing. He lived much in London, where he founded The Rhymers' Club (a group of late Victorian aspirants to poetry), but also became associated with playwrights John Synge and Lady Gregory in founding the Abbey Theatre in Dublin, for which he wrote many plays. Yeats was appointed to the Irish Free State Senate in 1922, and was awarded the Nobel Prize for literature in 1923.

Beginning as a belated Victorian and Romantic, for whom the poetic subject was usually a long way removed from the fume and fuss of daily life, Yeats changed the whole nature of his poetry at about the middle of his career, schooled his language to the abrupt rhythms and racy informalities of ordinary speech, and became, along with Ezra Pound, T. S. Eliot, and a very few others, one of the prime creators of a "modern" poetry—modern in his case more in idiom than in subject.

Important Works. POETRY: *The Wind Among the Reeds* (1899), *The Green Helmet* (1910), *Responsibilities* (1914), *The Wild Swans at Coole* (1919), *The Tower* (1928), *The Winding Stair* (1933), *Last Poems and Plays* (1940); PROSE: *Ideas of Good and Evil* (1903), *Autobiographies* (1926), *A Vision* (1925, 1937); PLAYS: *Collected Plays* (1952).

AVAILABLE RECORDINGS
(all 33⅓ r.p.m.)

UNIT I

Holiday Memory, DYLAN THOMAS, VOLUME 5 (read by the author)—Caedmon 1132.

My Last Duchess, HEARING POETRY, VOLUME II (read by Hurd Hatfield, Jo Van Fleet, and Frank Silvera)—Caedmon 1022.

From London Journal, BOSWELL'S LONDON JOURNAL (read by Anthony Quayle)—Caedmon 1093.

Portrait of Zimri from *Absalom and Achitophel*, THE POETRY OF DRYDEN (read by Paul Scofield)—Caedmon 1125.

Hotspur on a Certain Lord from *Henry IV, Part I*, HENRY IV, PART I (Marlowe Society, Cambridge: 4 records)—London A4421.

From *The General Prologue* to *The Canterbury Tales*, BEOWULF - CHAUCER (read by Helge Kökeritz and John C. Pope)—Lexington 5505. THE CANTERBURY TALES (read by Nevil Coghill: 4 records, in Modern English)—Spoken Word 101.

UNIT II

From *Gulliver's Travels*, GULLIVER'S TRAVELS, SELECTIONS (read by Alec Guinness)—MGM 3620. GULLIVER'S TRAVELS, SELECTIONS (read by Michael Redgrave)—Caedmon 1099.

Meditation XVII, SERMONS AND MEDITATIONS OF JOHN DONNE (read by Herbert Marshall)—Caedmon 1051. NO MAN IS AN ISLAND (read by Orson Wells)—Decca DL 9060. NO SINGLE THING ABIDES (read by David Allen)—Poetry 202.

Elegy Written in a Country Churchyard, NO SINGLE THING ABIDES (read by David Allen)—Poetry 202. POET'S GOLD, II

(read by Helen Hayes, Raymond Massey, Thomas Mitchell)—RCA Victor LM 1813.

I Wandered Lonely as a Cloud, THE POETRY OF WORDSWORTH (read by Sir Cedric Hardwicke)—Caedmon 1026. WORDSWORTH AND DONNE (read by Christopher Hassall)—Argo RG 24. HEARING POETRY, VOLUME II—Caedmon 1022. PALGRAVE'S GOLDEN TREASURY (Claire Bloom, Eric Portman, John Neville: 2 records)—Caedmon 2011.

The Solitary Reaper, WORDSWORTH AND DONNE—Argo RG 24.

Lines: Composed a Few Miles Above Tintern Abbey, THE POETRY OF WORDSWORTH —Caedmon 1026.

On First Looking into Chapman's Homer, THE POETRY OF KEATS (read by Sir Ralph Richardson)—Caedmon 1087. PALGRAVE'S GOLDEN TREASURY—Caedmon 2011. POET'S GOLD, II—RCA Victor LM 1813. GOLDEN TREASURY OF MILTON, KEATS AND SHELLEY (read by Hilton Edwards)—Spoken Arts 768.

Fern Hill, DYLAN THOMAS, VOLUME I— Caedmon 1002. CAEDMON TREASURY OF MODERN POETS—Caedmon 2006.

The Wild Swans at Coole, THE POETRY OF YEATS (read by Siobhan McKenna and Cyril Cusack)—Caedmon 1081. READING IRISH POETRY (Siobhan McKenna)— Spoken Arts 707.

The Love Song of J. Alfred Prufrock, THE WASTE LAND AND OTHER POEMS (read by Robert Speaight)—Spoken Arts 734. T. S. ELIOT (read by the poet)— Caedmon 1045.

King Oedipus, OEDIPUS REX (Amherst College)—Folkways 9862. OEDIPUS REX (Stratford, Ontario, Players, 2 records: Yeats translation)—Caedmon 2012.

UNIT III

A Red, Red Rose, PALGRAVE'S GOLDEN TREASURY—Caedmon 2011.

She Was a Phantom of Delight, PALGRAVE'S GOLDEN TREASURY—Caedmon 2011.

She Walks in Beauty, PALGRAVE'S GOLDEN TREASURY—Caedmon 2011. THE POETRY OF BYRON (read by Tyrone Power)—Caedmon 1042.

Constancy, PALGRAVE'S GOLDEN TREASURY—Caedmon 2011.

Go, Lovely Rose, PALGRAVE'S GOLDEN TREASURY—Caedmon 2011.

After Long Silence, THE POEMS OF WILLIAM BUTLER YEATS (Yeats, Siobhan McKenna, Michael MacLiammoir)—Spoken Arts 753.

The Rape of the Lock (selection) A THOUSAND YEARS OF ENGLISH PRONUNCIATION (read by Helge Kökeritz)—Lexington 7650/55.

Go and Catch a Falling Star, PALGRAVE'S GOLDEN TREASURY—Caedmon 2011. ELIZABETHAN SONNETS AND LYRICS (read by Anthony Quayle)—Spoken Arts 729.

The Clod and the Pebble, THE POETRY OF BLAKE (read by Sir Ralph Richardson)—Caedmon 1101.

A Prayer for My Daughter, THE IRISH LITERARY TRADITION (read by Frank O'Connor)—Folkways 9825.

Shakespeare's *Sonnets 29, 73, 116,* ELIZABETHAN SONNETS AND LYRICS—Spoken Arts 729. PALGRAVE'S GOLDEN TREASURY (29, 73)—Caedmon 2011. SONNETS (complete: 3 records)—London A4341.

Break, Break, Break, ANTHOLOGY OF ENGLISH AND AMERICAN POETRY, VOLUME IV—Lexington 7525.

Love, METAPHYSICAL AND LOVE LYRICS OF THE SEVENTEENTH CENTURY (read by Sir Cedric Hardwicke and Robert Newton)—Caedmon 1049.

Carrion Comfort, THE POETRY OF GERARD MANLEY HOPKINS (read by Cyril Cusack)—Caedmon 1111. WILLIAM BLAKE AND GERARD MANLEY HOPKINS (read by Robert Speaight)—Spoken Arts 814.

UNIT IV

The Tiger, THE POETRY OF BLAKE—Caedmon 1101. WILLIAM BLAKE AND GERARD MANLEY HOPKINS—Spoken Arts 814.

Channel Firing, THE POETRY OF HARDY (read by Richard Burton)—Caedmon 1140.

Thou Art Indeed Just, Lord, THE POETRY OF GERARD MANLEY HOPKINS—Caedmon 1111. WILLIAM BLAKE AND GERARD MANLEY HOPKINS—Spoken Arts 814.

Edward, THE POETRY OF ROBERT BURNS AND SCOTTISH BORDER BALLADS (read by Frederick Worlock and C. R. M. Brooks)—Caedmon 1103.

Lord Randal, EARLY ENGLISH BALLADS (read by Kathleen Danson Read)—Folkways 9881.

An Irish Airman Foresees His Death, LENNOX ROBINSON PRESENTS WILLIAM BUTLER YEATS—Spoken Arts 751.

The Hollow Men, T. S. ELIOT: THE WASTE LAND AND OTHER POEMS (read by Robert Speaight)—Spoken Arts 734.

A Modest Proposal, GULLIVER'S TRAVELS (includes other selections; read by Alec Guinness)—MGM 3620.

On the Late Massacre in Piedmont, GOLDEN TREASURY OF MILTON, KEATS AND SHELLEY (read by Hilton Edwards)—Spoken Arts 768.

London, THE POETRY OF BLAKE—Caedmon 1101.

Hamlet, HAMLET (John Gielgud and the Old Vic: 4 records)—RCA Victor LM 6404. HAMLET (Marlowe Society, Cambridge: 5 records)—London A4507.

UNIT V

The Pardoner's Tale, TWO CANTERBURY

TALES (read in Middle English by Robert Ross)—Caedmon 1008.

The World Is Too Much with Us, THE POETRY OF WORDSWORTH—Caedmon 1026. PALGRAVE'S GOLDEN TREASURY—Caedmon 2011.

Andrea del Sarto, THE POETRY OF BROWNING (read by James Mason)—Caedmon 1048.

Ode to a Nightingale, THE POETRY OF KEATS—Caedmon 1087. PALGRAVE'S GOLDEN TREASURY—Caedmon 2011. GOLDEN TREASURY OF MILTON, KEATS, AND SHELLEY—Spoken Arts 768. KEATS AND SHELLEY (read by Theodore Marcuse)—Lexington 7505.

Sir Gawain and the Green Knight, EARLY ENGLISH POETRY (read in Middle English by Charles W. Dunn)—Folkways 9851. A THOUSAND YEARS OF ENGLISH PRONUNCIATION (selection)—Lexington 7650/55.

The Trial and Death of Socrates, ON THE DEATH OF SOCRATES (read in Greek and English by Moses Hadas)—Folkways 9979. THE TRIAL OF SOCRATES (the *Apology* and *Crito* complete, read by Thomas Mitchell)—Audio-Books GL 604.

UNIT VI

Dover Beach, PALGRAVE'S GOLDEN TREASURY—Caedmon 2011.

What I Believe, WHAT I BELIEVE (read by the author)—Argo RG 153.

Holy Sonnet X, HEARING POETRY, VOLUME I—Caedmon 1021. WORDSWORTH AND DONNE—Argo RG 24.

Ulysses, THE POETRY OF TENNYSON (read by Dame Sybil Thorndike and Sir Lewis Casson)—Caedmon 1080.

Ode to the West Wind, THE POETRY OF SHELLEY (read by Vincent Price)—Caedmon 1059. GOLDEN TREASURY OF MILTON, KEATS AND SHELLEY—Spoken Arts 768. KEATS AND SHELLEY—Lexington 7505.

And Did Those Feet . . ., THE POETRY OF BLAKE—Caedmon 1101. WILLIAM BLAKE AND GERARD MANLEY HOPKINS—Spoken Arts 814.

I Think Continually of Those Who Were Truly Great, CAEDMON TREASURY OF MODERN POETS—Caedmon 2006. STEPHEN SPENDER (read by the poet)—Caedmon 1084.

God's Grandeur, THE POETRY OF GERARD MANLEY HOPKINS—Caedmon 1111. WILLIAM BLAKE AND GERARD MANLEY HOPKINS—Spoken Arts 814.

The Windhover, THE POETRY OF GERARD MANLEY HOPKINS—Caedmon 1111. WILLIAM BLAKE AND GERARD MANLEY HOPKINS—Spoken Arts 814.

The Collar, HEARING POETRY, VOLUME I—Caedmon 1021.

Hymn to God the Father, WORDSWORTH AND DONNE—Argo RG 24.

Prologue to *In Memoriam*, THE POETRY OF TENNYSON—Caedmon 1080.

Areopagitica, CAMBRIDGE TREASURY OF ENGLISH PROSE, VOLUME 2—Caedmon 1054.

Antigone, ANTIGONE (McGill University students)—Folkways 9861.

INDEX OF AUTHORS AND TITLES

INDEX OF FIRST LINES OF POETRY